English
Novel
Explication

Supplement VII

Compiled by
Christian J. W. Kloesel

ARCHON BOOKS
North Haven, Connecticut   2002

Library of Congress Cataloging-in-Publication Data
(Revised for volume 7)

English novel explication. Supplement.
Supplements: English novel explication/
compiled by Helen H. Palmer & Anne Jane Dyson.
Supplement I / compiled by Peter L. Abernethy,
Christian J. W. Kloesel, Jeffrey R. Smitten;
supplement II / compiled by Christian J. W. Kloesel,
Jeffery R. Smitten; supplements III–VII / compiled
by Christian J. W. Kloesel.
Includes bibliographical references and indexes.
1. English fiction — Explication — Bibliography
I. Abernethy, Peter L.   II. Kloesel, Christian J. W.
III. Smitten, Jeffrey R. IV. Title: English novel explication

Z2014.F5P26 Suppl. [PR821]   016.823'009   84-137107
ISBN 0-208-01464-0 (v. 1)
ISBN 0-208-02488-3 (v. 7 alk. paper)

The paper in this publication meets the minimum
requirements of American National Standard
for Information Sciences — Permanence of Paper
for Printed Library Materials,
ANSI Z39.48–1984 ∞

Printed in the United States of America

For Alicia and Kelly

diction, and structure are included here (including those of the poststructuralist, deconstructionist, and semiotic kind), whereas those wholly or exclusively devoted to sources and influence, critical reception, biography, or bibliography are ordinarily excluded.

The format of the present supplement is similar to that of the six earlier ones. I have abbreviated book titles to conserve space; full titles, together with complete bibliographical information, may be found in the *List of Books Indexed* at the end of the volume. In addition, I have used the generally accepted abbreviations of the journals of the American and Australian Modern Language Associations (*PMLA* and *AUMLA*), and have abbreviated several frequently repeated words in journal and serial titles. These words include, without periods, Academy (Acad), American (Am), Association (Assoc), British (Brit), Bulletin (Bull), Century (Cent), Chronicle (Chron), College (Coll), Comparative (Compar), Conference (Conf), Contemporary (Contemp), Critical (Crit), Department (Dept), Education (Educ), English (Engl), History (Hist), Humanities (Hum), Institute (Inst), International (Intl), Journal (J), Language (Lang), Library (Lib), Linguistics (Ling), Literary (Liter), Literature (Lit), Magazine (Mag), Modern (Mod), National (Natl), Newsletter (Newsl), Philological (Philol), Philosophy (Philos), Proceedings (Proc), Psychology (Psych), Publications (Publs), Quarterly (Q), Religion (Rel), Research (Res), Review (R), Society (Soc), Studies (Stud), Supplement (Suppl), Transactions (Trans), University (Univ), and Yearbook (Yrbk). A few abbreviations, like *ANQ, ELH, GRAAT, LIT,* or *SPAN,* are themselves journal titles. In another matter—the same article treating two or more of a single author's novels—I have continued the practice of the preceding two (and the first three) supplements, with full citations in all instances; for though the practice of abbreviating subsequent citations may be useful for such rarely cited or moderately productive novelists as Elaine Feinstein, Ronald Firbank, Penelope Fitzgerald, Val McDermid, Naomi Mitchison, and Piers Paul Read, it unnecessarily complicates the reader's task in such productive and much-discussed authors as Jane Austen, Charles Dickens, George Eliot, James Joyce, D. H. Lawrence, Salman Rushdie, and Virginia Woolf.

Readers should remember that, as in the six previous supplements, page numbers in a citation correspond, in most instances, to the passage of explication for a given novel and not necessarily to the entire article or book. When an entire book is devoted to explication of the novel under which it appears, it is sometimes listed

PREFACE

This seventh supplement extends the *English Novel Explication* series from the early months of 1997 through the first half of 2001. Accordingly, it has been my primary responsibility to gather materials published in those four years, although I have added a number of earlier items not included in the sixth supplement, as well as everything published in 2001 that had arrived in nearby libraries. But readers should be reminded that it has not been possible to include all items published during those four years, especially those appearing toward the very end of the period. Because *English Novel Explication* is a continuing series, it must have a fixed date of publication, and that date cannot be affected by printing and library binding schedules or by the inevitable delays in acquisitions, cataloguing, interlibrary loans, and the return of charged or overdue books. Consequently, readers not finding an item they expect to be here must consult the next supplement.

The scope of the present supplement is the same as that of the six previous ones. The very broad definition of the term "novel" is again based on Ernest A. Baker's *History of the English Novel,* and that is why such works as Malory's *Le Morte Darthur,* Bunyan's *The Pilgrim's Progress,* Swift's *Gulliver's Travels,* Johnson's *Rasselas,* and Orwell's *Down and Out in Paris and London* are included. An "English" novelist is a writer born in England, Scotland, Wales, Ireland, or the British Commonwealth who has lived in Great Britain during some significant portion of her/his creative years. This definition excludes writers like Brian Moore and Henry James, and it includes others like Buchi Emecheta, George Lamming, Doris Lessing, Malcolm Lowry, Timothy Mo, V. S. Naipaul, Salman Rushdie, and Olive Schreiner. By "explication" is meant the interpretation of the significance and meaning of a novel. Consequently, discussions of theme, imagery, symbolism,

CONTENTS

Preface   vii
English Novel Explication   1
Anonymous Novels   511
List of Books Indexed   513
Index   559

without page numbers. (As in previous supplements, I have not included World Wide Web resources.)

As always, I am grateful to the library staffs at Indiana University Purdue University at Indianapolis and Indiana University at Bloomington—as well as to English novelists and the critics who explicate them.

Indianapolis, Indiana C.J.W.K.
October 2001

EDWIN ABBOTT

Flatland, 1884

McGurl, Mark. "Social Geographies: Taking Place in Henry James." *Representations* 68 (1999), 59–83.

Smith, Jonathan, Lawrence I. Barkove, and Gerald A. Baker. "A Grammar of Dissent: *Flatland*, Newman, and the Theology of Probability." *Victorian Stud* 39:2 (1996), 129–50.

PETER ACKROYD

Chatterton, 1987

Clingham, Greg. "Chatterton, Ackroyd, and the Fiction of Eighteenth-Century Historiography." *Bucknell R* 42:1 (1998), 40–53.

Hotho, Sabine. "'The Rescue of Some Stranded Ghost': The Rewriting of Literary History in Contemporary British and German Novels," in Susanne Stark, ed., *The Novel in Anglo-German Context*, 388–98.

Jukic, Tatjana. "From Worlds to Worlds and the Other Way Around: The Victorian Inheritance in the Postmodern British Novel," in Richard Todd and Luisa Flora, eds., *Theme Parks*, 80–82.

Nünning, Ansgar. "An Intertextual Quest for Thomas Chatterton: The Deconstruction of the Romantic Cult of Originality and the Paradoxes of Life-Writing in Peter Ackroyd's Fictional Metabiography *Chatterton*," in Martin Middeke and Werner Huber, eds., *Biofictions*, 27–45.

Onega, Susana. *Metafiction and Myth*, 58–73.

Shiller, Dana. "The Redemptive Past in the Neo-Victorian Novel." *Stud in the Novel* 29 (1997), 552–58.

Zwierlein, Anne-Julia. "'Bless the Thief for he Lightens your Burden': Fälschung und Subjektkonstitution in Peter Ackroyds *Chatterton* (1987) und Alan Walls *Bless the Thief* (1997)." *Poetica* (Munich) 32 (2000), 499–526.

Dan Leno and the Limehouse Golem, 1994

Onega, Susana. *Metafiction and Myth*, 133–47.

English Music, 1992

Brînzeu, Pia. *Corridors of Mirrors*, 140–43.

Freiburg, Rudolf. "Imagination in Contemporary British Fiction," in Barbara Korte and Klaus Peter Müller, eds., *Unity in Diversity Revisited?*, 236–39.

Gallix, François. "*English Music* de Peter Ackroyd: de l'autre côté du tableau." *Etudes Anglaises* 50 (1997), 218–30.

Onega, Susana. *Metafiction and Myth*, 103–12.

Roessner, Jeffrey. "God Save the Canon: Tradition and the British Subject in Peter Ackroyd's *English Music*." *Post-Identity* 1:2 (1998), 104–24.

First Light, 1989

Onega, Susana. *Metafiction and Myth*, 74–90, 187–89.

The Great Fire of London, 1982

Onega, Susana. *Metafiction and Myth*, 19–32.

Hawksmoor, 1985

> Ahearn, Edward J. "The Modern English Visionary: Peter Ackroyd's *Hawksmoor* and Angela Carter's *The Passion of New Eve.*" *Twentieth Cent Lit* 46 (2000), 453–60.
>
> Byatt, A. S. *On Histories and Stories,* 43–44.
>
> Onega, Susana. *Metafiction and Myth,* 43–58, 186–87.
>
> Spekat, Susanne. "Postmoderne Gattungshybriden: Peter Ackroyds *Hawksmoor* als generische Kombination aus *historical novel, gothic novel* und *detective novel.*" *Literatur in Wissenschaft und Unterricht* 30 (1997), 183–99.

The House of Doctor Dee, 1993

> Hickman, Alan Forrest. "It's a Wise Child: Teaching the Lessons of History in the Contemporary British Novel." *Publs of the Arkansas Philol Assoc* 24:1 (1998), 41–45.
>
> Onega, Susana. *Metafiction and Myth,* 112–30.
>
> Schenkel, Elmar. "Exploring Unity in Contradiction: The Return of Alchemy in Contemporary British Fiction," in Barbara Korte and Klaus Peter Müller, eds., *Unity in Diversity Revisited?,* 219–20.

The Last Testament of Oscar Wilde, 1983

> Moran, Joe. "'Simple Words': Peter Ackroyd's Autobiography of Oscar Wilde." *Biography* 22 (1999), 356–69.
>
> Onega, Susana. *Metafiction and Myth,* 32–40.

Milton in America, 1996

> Canavesi, Angelo. "*Milton in America* e il vate tradotto, o la necessità del tradurre." *Confronto Letterario* 16 (1999), 17–34.
>
> Onega, Susana. *Metafiction and Myth,* 147–77, 183–84.
>
> Onega, Susana. "Postmodernist Re-writings of the Puritan Commonwealth: Winterson, Ackroyd, Mukherjee," in Heinz Antor and Kevin L. Cope, eds., *Intercultural Encounters,* 453–58.

DOUGLAS ADAMS

Dirk Gently's Holistic Detective Agency, 1987

> Owen, Kathleen Belin. "'The Game's Afoot': Predecessors and Pursuits of a Postmodern Detective Novel," in Jerome H. Delamater and Ruth Prigozy, eds., *Theory and Practice,* 80–84.

RICHARD ADAMS

Watership Down, 1972

> Perrin, Noel. *A Child's Delight,* 122–26.

WILLIAM HARRISON AINSWORTH

Jack Sheppard, 1839

> Liggins, Emma. "'Such fine young chaps as them': Representations of the Male Criminal in the Newgate Novel," in Antony Rowland et al., eds., *Signs of Masculinity,* 71–74, 77–79.

RICHARD ALDINGTON

Death of a Hero, 1929

    Ayers, David. *English Literature of the 1920s,* 19–29.
    Ayers, David. "Richard Aldington's *Death of a Hero*: A Proto-Fascist
    Novel." *English* 47 (1998), 89–97.
    Bergonzi, Bernard. *War Poets,* 15–19.
    McCormick, John. *Catastrophe and Imagination,* 214–17.
    Tate, Trudi. *Modernism, History and the First World War,* 81–83.
    Willis, J. H., Jr. "The Censored Language of War: Richard Aldington's
    Death of a Hero and Three Other War Novels of 1929." *Twentieth
    Cent Lit* 45 (1999), 473–84.

BRIAN ALDISS

Barefoot in the Head: A European Fantasia, 1969
    Henighan, Tom. *Brian W. Aldiss,* 68–73.
The Brightfount Diaries, 1955
    Henighan, Tom. *Brian W. Aldiss,* 90–92.
Cryptozoic, 1967
    Henighan, Tom. *Brian W. Aldiss,* 68–70.
The Dark Light Years, 1964
    Henighan, Tom. *Brian W. Aldiss,* 23–24.
Dracula Unbound, 1991
    Henighan, Tom. *Brian W. Aldiss,* 88–89.
The Eighty-Minute Hour, 1974
    Henighan, Tom. *Brian W. Aldiss,* 76–81.
Enemies of the System: A Tale of Homo Uniformis, 1978
    Henighan, Tom. *Brian W. Aldiss,* 29–32.
Forgotten Life, 1988
    Henighan, Tom. *Brian W. Aldiss,* 100–103.
Frankenstein Unbound, 1973
    Henighan, Tom. *Brian W. Aldiss,* 73–76.
Greybeard, 1964
    Henighan, Tom. *Brian W. Aldiss,* 20–23.
The Hand-Reared Boy, 1970
    Henighan, Tom. *Brian W. Aldiss,* 94–95.
Hellonica Spring, 1982
    Henighan, Tom. *Brian W. Aldiss,* 33–47.
Hellonica Summer, 1983
    Henighan, Tom. *Brian W. Aldiss,* 47–54.
Hellonica Winter, 1985
    Henighan, Tom. *Brian W. Aldiss,* 54–62.
An Island Called Moreau, 1980
    Henighan, Tom. *Brian W. Aldiss,* 83–88.

Life in the West, 1980
   Henighan, Tom. *Brian W. Aldiss,* 97–100.
The Long Afternoon of Earth, 1962
   Henighan, Tom. *Brian W. Aldiss,* 16–20.
The Malacia Tapestry, 1976
   Henighan, Tom. *Brian W. Aldiss,* 25–27.
Remembrance Day, 1993
   Henighan, Tom. *Brian W. Aldiss,* 103–6.
Report on Probability A, 1968
   Henighan, Tom. *Brian W. Aldiss,* 66–68.
A Rude Awakening, 1978
   Henighan, Tom. *Brian W. Aldiss,* 96–97.
The Saliva Tree and Other Strange Growths, 1988
   Henighan, Tom. *Brian W. Aldiss,* 63–66.
A Soldier Erect; or, Further Adventures of the Hand-Reared Boy, 1971
   Henighan, Tom. *Brian W. Aldiss,* 95–96.
Somewhere East of Life, 1994
   Henighan, Tom. *Brian W. Aldiss,* 106–7.
Starship, 1958
   Henighan, Tom. *Brian W. Aldiss,* 11–15.

RUPERT ALEXANDER

Maureen Moore: A Romance of '98, 1899
   Reilly, Eileen. "Rebel, Muse, and Spouse: The Female in '98 Fiction."
   Eire-Ireland 34:2 (1999), 148–51.

DOT ALLAN

Makeshift, 1928
   McCulloch, Margery Palmer. "Fictions of Development, 1920–1970,"
   in Douglas Gifford and Dorothy McMillan, eds., *A History,* 364–65.

GRANT ALLEN

The Type-writer Girl, 1897
   Keep, Christopher. "The Cultural Work of the Type-Writer Girl."
   Victorian Stud 40:3 (1997), 415–18.
   Willis, Chris. "'Heaven defend me from political or highly-educated
   women!': Packaging the New Woman for Mass Consumption," in
   Angelique Richardson and Chris Willis, eds., *The New Woman in
   Fiction and in Fact,* 57–58.
The Woman Who Did, 1895
   Ledger, Sally. *The New Woman,* 14–16.
   Young, Arlene. *Culture, Class and Gender,* 142–45.

MARGERY ALLINGHAM

Death of a Ghost, 1935
Rowland, Susan. *From Agatha Christie to Ruth Rendell*, 30–32.
The Fashion in Shrouds, 1938
Rowland, Susan. *From Agatha Christie to Ruth Rendell*, 173–74.
Flowers for the Judge, 1936
Rowland, Susan. *From Agatha Christie to Ruth Rendell*, 102–4.
Look to the Lady, 1931
Rowland, Susan. *From Agatha Christie to Ruth Rendell*, 127–28.
Police at the Funeral, 1931
Rowland, Susan. *From Agatha Christie to Ruth Rendell*, 54–55.
Sweet Danger, 1933
Rowland, Susan. *From Agatha Christie to Ruth Rendell*, 148–50.
Traitor's Purse, 1941
Rowland, Susan. *From Agatha Christie to Ruth Rendell*, 77–79.

ERIC AMBLER

Cause for Alarm, 1938
Frigerio, Vittorio. "The Foreign Solution: The Role and Representation of the Foreigner in the Popular Novel." *Paradoxa 5* (1999–2000), 303–23.

KINGSLEY AMIS

The Alteration, 1976
Dose, Gerd. "Alternate Worlds: Kingsley Amis' *The Alteration* and Keith Roberts' *Pavane*," in Rüdiger Ahrens and Fritz-Wilhelm Neumann, eds., *Fiktion und Geschichte*, 327–36.
Laskowski, William. *Kingsley Amis*, 53–58.
The Anti-Death League, 1966
Laskowski, William. *Kingsley Amis*, 79–82.
The Biographer's Moustache, 1995
Laskowski, William. *Kingsley Amis*, 136–39.
Colonel Sun, 1968
Laskowski, William. *Kingsley Amis*, 77–79.
The Crime of the Century, 1988
Laskowski, William. *Kingsley Amis*, 67–68.
Difficulties With Girls, 1988
Laskowski, William. *Kingsley Amis*, 124–26.
Ending Up, 1974
Laskowski, William. *Kingsley Amis*, 111–14.
The Folks That Live on the Hill, 1990
Laskowski, William. *Kingsley Amis*, 126–29.

Girl, 20, 1971

    Laskowski, William. *Kingsley Amis,* 107–11.

The Green Man, 1969

    Laskowski, William. *Kingsley Amis,* 69–73.

I Like It Here, 1958

    Laskowski, William. *Kingsley Amis,* 89–92.

I Want It Now, 1969

    Graver, Lawrence. "Ending Up with Amis," in Robert H. Bell, ed., *Critical Essays on Kingsley Amis,* 135–36.

    Laskowski, William. *Kingsley Amis,* 104–7.

Jake's Thing, 1978

    Laskowski, William. *Kingsley Amis,* 114–17.

Lucky Jim, 1954

    Bell, Robert H. "Seriocomic Amis and True Comic Edge: *Lucky Jim* and *You Can't Do Both,*" in Bell, ed., *Critical Essays on Kingsley Amis,* 141–49.

    Benstock, Shari. "Can a Feminist (Still) Read Kingsley Amis?," in Robert H. Bell, ed., *Critical Essays on Kingsley Amis,* 332–38.

    Laskowski, William. *Kingsley Amis,* 83–86.

    Rossen, Janice. "Philip Larkin and *Lucky Jim.*" *J of Mod Lit* 22 (1998), 147–64.

The Old Devils, 1986

    Graver, Lawrence. "Ending Up with Amis," in Robert H. Bell, ed., *Critical Essays on Kingsley Amis,* 136–38.

    Laskowski, William. *Kingsley Amis,* 121–24.

One Fat Englishman, 1963

    Laskowski, William. *Kingsley Amis,* 97–101.

The Riverside Villas Murder, 1973

    Laskowski, William. *Kingsley Amis,* 64–67.

The Russian Girl, 1994

    Laskowski, William. *Kingsley Amis,* 131–33.

Russian Hide-and-Seek, 1980

    Laskowski, William. *Kingsley Amis,* 58–62.

Stanley and the Women, 1984

    Laskowski, William. *Kingsley Amis,* 117–21.

Take A Girl Like You, 1960

    Graver, Lawrence. "Ending Up with Amis," in Robert H. Bell, ed., *Critical Essays on Kingsley Amis,* 132–35.

    Laskowski, William. *Kingsley Amis,* 92–97.

That Uncertain Feeling, 1955

    Graver, Lawrence. "Ending Up with Amis," in Robert H. Bell, ed., *Critical Essays on Kingsley Amis,* 131–32.

    Laskowski, William. *Kingsley Amis,* 86–89.

You Can't Do Both, 1994

    Bell, Robert H. "Seriocomic Amis and True Comic Edge: *Lucky Jim* and *You Can't Do Both*," in Bell, ed., *Critical Essays on Kingsley Amis*, 149–57.

Laskowski, William. *Kingsley Amis*, 133–36.

KINGSLEY AMIS and ROBERT CONQUEST

The Egyptologists, 1965

Laskowski, William. *Kingsley Amis*, 101–4.

MARTIN AMIS

Dead Babies, 1975

Mecklenburg, Susanne. *Martin Amis und Graham Swift*, 38–41.

The Information, 1995

Mecklenburg, Susanne. *Martin Amis und Graham Swift*, 84–95.

Moran, Joe. "Artists and Verbal Mechanics: Martin Amis's *The Information*." *Critique* (Washington, DC) 41 (2000), 307–16.

London Fields, 1989

Bernard, Catherine. "A Certain Hermeneutic Slant: Sublime Allegories in Contemporary English Fiction." *Contemp Lit* 38 (1997), 170–76.

Mecklenburg, Susanne. *Martin Amis und Graham Swift*, 56–69.

Stokes, Peter. "Martin Amis and the Postmodern Suicide: Tracing the Postnuclear Narrative at the Fin de Millennium." *Critique* (Washington, DC) 38 (1997), 305–11.

Money: A Suicide Note, 1984

Edmondson, Elie A. "Martin Amis Writes Postmodern Man." *Critique* (Washington, DC) 42 (2001), 147–54.

Mecklenburg, Susanne. *Martin Amis und Graham Swift*, 49–56.

Paccaud-Huguet, Josiane. "De la fiction pornographique à l'errance littéraire: *Money* de Martin Amis." *Etudes Anglaises* 50 (1997), 244–55.

Stokes, Peter. "Martin Amis and the Postmodern Suicide: Tracing the Postnuclear Narrative at the Fin de Millennium." *Critique* (Washington, DC) 38 (1997), 302–5.

Other People: A Mystery Story, 1981

Caputo, Nicoletta. "L'etica della forma: Strategie di straniamento in *Other People: A Mystery Story* (1981) e *Time's Arrow* (1991) di Martin Amis." *Confronto Letterario* 12 (1995), 73–104.

François, Pierre. *Inlets of the Soul*, 175–208.

Mecklenburg, Susanne. *Martin Amis und Graham Swift*, 45–49.

The Rachel Papers, 1973

Edmondson, Elie A. "Martin Amis Writes Postmodern Man." *Critique* (Washington, DC) 42 (2001), 145–47.

Mecklenburg, Susanne. *Martin Amis und Graham Swift*, 34–38.

Success, 1978

Mecklenburg, Susanne. *Martin Amis und Graham Swift*, 41–45.

Time's Arrow, 1991
> Byatt, A. S. *On Histories and Stories*, 34–35.
> Caputo, Nicoletta. "L'etica della forma: Strategie di straniamento in *Other People: A Mystery Story* (1981) e *Time's Arrow* (1991) di Martin Amis." *Confronto Letterario* 12 (1995), 73–104.
> Harris, Greg. "Men Giving Birth to New World Orders: Martin Amis's *Time's Arrow*." *Stud in the Novel* 31 (1999), 489–504.
> Joffe, Phil. "Language Damage: Nazis and Naming in Martin Amis's *Time's Arrow*." *Nomina Africana* 9:2 (1995), 1–10.
> McCarthy, Dermot. "The Limits of Irony: The Chronillogical World of Martin Amis' *Time's Arrow*." *War, Lit, and the Arts* 11:1 (1999), 294–320.
> Marta, Jan. "Postmodernizing the Literature-and-Medicine Canon: Self-Conscious Narration, Unruly Texts, and the Viae Ruptae of Narrative Medicine." *Lit and Medicine* 16:1 (1997), 43–69.
> Mecklenburg, Susanne. *Martin Amis und Graham Swift*, 69–83.
> Menke, Richard. "Narrative Reversals and the Thermodynamics of History in Martin Amis's *Time's Arrow*." *Mod Fiction Stud* 44 (1998), 959–77.
> Parry, Ann. "The Caesura of the Holocaust in Martin Amis's *Time's Arrow* and Bernhard Schlink's *The Reader*." *J of European Stud* 29 (1999), 249–59.
> Vice, Sue. *Holocaust Fiction*, 11–37.

THOMAS AMORY

The Life of John Buncle, Esq., 1756–1766
> Trumpener, Katie. *Bardic Nationalism*, 105–7.

Memoirs: containing the Lives of Several Ladies of Great Britain, 1755
> Trumpener, Katie. *Bardic Nationalism*, 105–7.

LINDA ANDERSON

To Stay Alive, 1985
> St. Peter, Christine. *Changing Ireland*, 112–14.

JAMES ANNESLEY

The Lady's Drawing Room, 1744
> Wheeler, Roxann. "The Complexion of Desire: Racial Ideology and Mid-Eighteenth-Century British Novels." *Eighteenth-Cent Stud* 32 (1999), 319–23.

JEFFREY ARCHER

First Among Equals, 1984
> York, R. A. *The Rules of Time*, 185–91.

MICHAEL ARLEN

The Green Hat, 1924
  Ayers, David. *English Literature of the 1920s*, 158–62.

ELIZABETH VON ARNIM

Father, 1931
  Hennegan, Alison. "In a Class of Her Own: Elizabeth von Arnim," in Maroula Joannou, ed., *Women Writers of the 1930s*, 103–6.
The Jasmine Farm, 1934
  Hennegan, Alison. "In a Class of Her Own: Elizabeth von Arnim," in Maroula Joannou, ed., *Women Writers of the 1930s*, 106–9.
Mr. Skeffington, 1940
  Hennegan, Alison. "In a Class of Her Own: Elizabeth von Arnim," in Maroula Joannou, ed., *Women Writers of the 1930s*, 110–12.

W. D. ARNOLD

Oakfield, or Fellowship in the East, 1853
  Peck, John. *War, the Army and Victorian Literature*, 73–79.

HELEN ASHTON

The Half-Crown House, 1956
  Philips, Deborah, and Ian Haywood. *Brave New Causes*, 48–50.

KATE ATKINSON

Behind the Scenes at the Museum, 1995
  Reckwitz, Erhard. "Intertextuality: Between Continuity and Innovation," in Barbara Korte and Klaus Peter Müller, eds., *Unity in Diversity Revisited?*, 190–91.

PENELOPE AUBIN

Adventures of the Lady Lucy, 1726
  Prescott, Sarah. "The Debt to Pleasure: Eliza Haywood's *Love in Excess* and Women's Fiction of the 1720s." *Women's Writing* 7 (2000), 432–33.
  Swan, Beth. *Fictions of Law*, 103–4.
Count de Vinevil, 1721
  Prescott, Sarah. "The Debt to Pleasure: Eliza Haywood's *Love in Excess* and Women's Fiction of the 1720s." *Women's Writing* 7 (2000), 434–35.
  Swan, Beth. *Fictions of Law*, 101–3.

The Life and Amorous Adventures of Lucinda, 1722

Snader, Joe. *Caught Between Worlds*, 157–58.

The Life of Charlotta du Pont, 1723

Prescott, Sarah. "The Debt to Pleasure: Eliza Haywood's *Love in Excess* and Women's Fiction of the 1720s." *Women's Writing* 7 (2000), 433–34.

The Life of Madam de Beaumont, 1721

Fendler, Susanne. "Intertwining Literary Histories: Women's Contribution to the Rise of the Novel," in Fendler, ed., *Feminist Contributions*, 49–53.

The Noble Slaves, 1722

Prescott, Sarah. "The Debt to Pleasure: Eliza Haywood's *Love in Excess* and Women's Fiction of the 1720s." *Women's Writing* 7 (2000), 435–36.

Snader, Joe. *Caught Between Worlds*, 149–52.

JANE AUSTEN

Emma, 1816

Bander, Elaine. "*Emma*: The Pique of Perfection." *Persuasions* 21 (1999), 155–62.

Benedict, Barbara M. "Jane Austen and the Culture of Circulating Libraries: The Construction of Female Literacy," in Paula R. Backscheider, ed., *Revising Women*, 155–57, 190–92.

Bilger, Audrey. *Laughing Feminism*, 136–37.

Bray, Joe. "The Source of 'Dramatized Consciousness': Richardson, Austen, and Stylistic Influence." *Style* 35:1 (2001), 18–28.

Brink, André. *The Novel*, 104–25.

Brooke, Christopher. *Jane Austen*, 97–109, 151–53, 160–64, 170–71.

Brownstein, Rachel M. "England's *Emma*." *Persuasions* 21 (1999), 224–40.

Cavaliero, Glen. *The Alchemy of Laughter*, 150–55.

Copeland, Edward. "Money," in Edward Copeland and Juliet McMaster, eds., *The Cambridge Companion to Jane Austen*, 141–43.

Copeland, Edward. *Women Writing about Money*, 106–9.

Cousineau, Diane. *Letters and Labyrinths*, 32–50.

Currie, Mark. *Postmodern Narrative Theory*, 20–23.

Dabbs, Thomas. "Lampoon and Lampoonability: *Emma* and the Riddle of Popularity," in Laura Cooner Lambdin and Robert Thomas Lambdin, eds., *A Companion to Jane Austen Studies*, 87–95.

Dabundo, Laura. "Jane Austen's Opacities," in Dabundo, ed., *Jane Austen and Mary Shelley*, 55–58.

Dames, Nicholas. *Amnesiac Selves*, 40–43.

Dames, Nicholas. "Austen's Nostalgics." *Representations* 73 (2001), 132–34.

Delany, Paul. "'A Sort of Notch in the Donwell Estate': Intersections of Status and Class in *Emma*." *Eighteenth-Cent Fiction* 12 (2000), 533–48.

Doody, Terrence. *Among Other Things*, 73–77.

Duckworth, Alistair M. "Jane Austen and George Stubbs: Two Speculations." *Eighteenth-Cent Fiction* 13:1 (2000), 60–66.

Ellis, Lorna. *Appearing to Diminish*, 114–29.

Ferguson, Frances. "Jane Austen, *Emma*, and the Impact of Form." *Mod Lang Q* 61 (2000), 157–80.

Ferriss, Suzanne. "*Emma* Becomes Clueless," in Linda Troost and Sayre Greenfield, eds., *Jane Austen in Hollywood*, 122–29.

Fletcher, Loraine. *Charlotte Smith*, 313–16.

Ford, Susan Allen. "Romance, Pedagogy and Power: Jane Austen Rewrites Madame de Genlis." *Persuasions* 21 (1999), 172–86.

Gallop, David. "Jane Austen and the Aristotelean Ethic." *Philos and Lit* 23 (1999), 103–4.

Galperin, William. "Austen's Earliest Readers and the Rise of the Janeites," in Deidre Lynch, ed., *Janeites*, 96–102.

Galperin, William. "The Picturesque, the Real, and the Consumption of Jane Austen." *Wordsworth Circle* 28 (1997), 19–26.

Garson, Marjorie. "Associationism and the Dialogue in *Emma*." *Eighteenth-Cent Fiction* 10 (1997), 79–100.

Gilson, David. "Jane Austen and *Rhoda*." *Persuasions* 20 (1998), 21–29.

Gohrisch, Jana. "'Indifferent Differences': Everyday Life in Jane Austen's *Emma*." *J for the Study of Brit Cultures* 6:2 (1999), 153–66.

Gooneratne, Yasmine. "Making Sense: Jane Austen on the Screen," in Heinz Antor and Kevin L. Cope, eds., *Intercultural Encounters*, 259–66.

Graves, David Andrew. "Computer Analysis of Word Usage in *Emma*." *Persuasions* 21 (1999), 203–11.

Grossman, Jonathan H. "The Labor of the Leisured in *Emma*: Class, Manners, and Austen." *Nineteenth-Cent Lit* 54 (1999), 143–64.

Grove, Robin. "*Emma*: Love in Place." *Crit R* (Melbourne) 39 (1999), 61–76.

Harding, D. W. *Regulated Hatred*, 171–89.

Hawkridge, Audrey. *Jane and Her Gentlemen*, 69–73, 112–15, 131–34.

Heydt-Stevenson, Jill. "'Slipping into the Ha-Ha': Bawdy Humor and Body Politics in Jane Austen's Novels." *Nineteenth-Cent Lit* 55 (2000), 316–23.

Hopkins, Lisa. "Food and Growth in *Emma*." *Women's Writing* 5 (1998), 61–69.

Kaplan, Deborah. "Mass Marketing Jane Austen: Men, Women, and Courtship in Two Film Adaptations," in Linda Troost and Sayre Greenfield, eds., *Jane Austen in Hollywood*, 182–84.

Korba, Susan M. "'Improper and Dangerous Distinctions': Female Relationships and Erotic Domination in *Emma*." *Stud in the Novel* 29 (1997), 139–60.

LeClair, Annette M. "Owning Her Work: Austen, the Artist, and the Audience in *Emma*." *Persuasions* 21 (1999), 115–26.

Lloyd, Tom. *Crises of Realism*, 38–55.

Loncar, Kathleen. *Legal Fiction*, 184–86.

Lynch, Deidre. "Homes and Haunts: Austen's and Mitford's English Idylls." *PMLA* 115 (2000), 1103–7.

McDonald, Richard. "'And Very Good Lists They Were': Select Critical Readings of Jane Austen's *Emma*," in Laura Cooner Lambdin and Robert Thomas Lambdin, eds., *A Companion to Jane Austen Studies*, 97–112.

McKee, Patricia. *Public and Private*, 53–67.

McMaster, Juliet. "Class," in Edward Copeland and Juliet McMaster, eds., *The Cambridge Companion to Jane Austen*, 122–28.

Marsh, Nicholas. *Jane Austen*, 10–15, 29–32, 40–49, 74–78, 86–89, 106–13, 137–44, 166–68, 177–78, 201–4.

Martin, Maureen M. "What Does Emma Want? Sovereignty and Sexuality in Austen's *Emma*." *Nineteenth-Cent Feminisms* 3 (2000), 10–23.

Meyer, Rosalind S. "Mr Knightley's Education: Parallels in *Emma*." *Engl Stud* (Amsterdam) 79 (1998), 212–23.

Moore, Lisa L. *Dangerous Intimacies*, 19–21, 109–43.

Morris, Ivor. *Jane Austen and the Interplay of Character*, 46–51, 57–59, 88–90, 98–102, 155–58.

Morse, David. *The Age of Virtue*, 172–75.

Nachumi, Nora. "'As If!': Translating Austen's Ironic Narrator to Film," in Linda Troost and Sayre Greenfield, eds., *Jane Austen in Hollywood*, 130–37.

Neill, Edward. *The Politics of Jane Austen*, 95–111.

Nord, Deborah Epstein. "'Marks of Race': Gypsy Figures and Eccentric Femininity in Nineteenth-Century Women's Writing." *Victorian Stud* 41:2 (1998), 193–94.

O'Farrell, Mary Ann. "Jane Austen's Friendship," in Deidre Lynch, ed., *Janeites*, 47–51.

O'Farrell, Mary Ann. *Telling Complexions*, 3–5.

Parker, Jo Alyson. *The Author's Inheritance*, 184–86.

Piper, William Bowman. *Reconcilable Differences*, 195–99.

Rogers, John E., Jr. "Emma Woodhouse: Betrayed by Place." *Persuasions* 21 (1999), 163–71.

Ruderman, Anne Crippen. *The Pleasures of Virtue*, 24–54, 103–5, 154–65.

Seeber, Barbara K. *General Consent in Jane Austen*, 38–46.

Simons, Judy. "Classics and Trash: Reading Austen in the 1990s." *Women's Writing* 5 (1998), 27–37.

Smith, Peter. "Politics and Religion in Jane Austen's *Emma*." *Cambridge Q* 26 (1997), 219–41.

Sorensen, Janet. *The Grammar of Empire*, 199–221.

Stroup, William. "'I Live Out of the World': The Problem of Nature in *Emma*." *Wordsworth Circle* 28 (1997), 155–61.

Sutherland, John. *Who Betrays Elizabeth Bennet?*, 28–33.

Teachman, Debra. *Student Companion to Jane Austen*, 89–108.

Tomalin, Claire. *Jane Austen*, 248–51.

Toohey, Elizabeth. "*Emma* and the Countryside: Weather and a Place for a Walk." *Persuasions* 21 (1999), 44–52.

Tsomondo, Thorell Porter. "Temporal, Spatial, and Linguistic Configurations and the Geopolitics of *Emma*." *Persuasions* 21 (1999), 188–201.

Vorachek, Laura. "'The Instrument of the Century': The Piano as an Icon of Female Sexuality in the Nineteenth Century." *George Eliot-George Henry Lewes Stud* 38–39 (2000), 26–43.

Waldron, Mary. *Jane Austen and the Fiction of Her Time*, 112–34.

Warren, Victoria. "'Experience Means Nothing Till It Repeats Itself': Elizabeth Bowen's *The Death of the Heart* and Jane Austen's *Emma*." *Mod Lang Stud* 29:1 (1999), 131–52.

Watson, Nicola J. *Revolution and the Form of the British Novel*, 93–104.

Wenner, Barbara Britton. "'Enclaves of Civility amidst Clamorous Impertinence': Will as Reflected in the Landscape of *Emma*." *European Romantic R* 8:1 (1997), 95–115.

Wheeler, David. "The British Postal Service, Privacy, and Jane Austen's *Emma*." *South Atlantic R* 63:4 (1998), 34–46.

White, Laura Mooneyham. "*Emma* and New Comedy." *Persuasions* 21 (1999), 128–40.

Wiltshire, John. "*Mansfield Park, Emma, Persuasion*," in Edward Copeland and Juliet McMaster, eds., *The Cambridge Companion to Jane Austen*, 66–75.

Wolfe, Jesse. "Jane Austen and the Sin of Pride." *Renascence* 51 (1999), 113–17, 127–29.

Wye, Margaret Enright. "Re-viewing Mr. Elton and Frank Churchill Through the Circle Metaphors in *Emma*." *Persuasions* 21 (1999), 142–54.

Lady Susan, 1871

Buck, Paula. "Tender Toes, Bow-wows, Meow-meows and the Devil: Jane Austen and the Nature of Evil," in Laura Cooner Lambdin and Robert Thomas Lambdin, eds., *A Companion to Jane Austen Studies*, 199–213.

Knuth, Deborah. "*Lady Susan*: A Bibliographical Essay," in Laura Cooner Lambdin and Robert Thomas Lambdin, eds., *A Companion to Jane Austen Studies*, 215–22.

Nelson, Bonnie. "*Emily Herbert*: Forerunner of Jane Austen's *Lady Susan*." *Women's Writing* 1 (1994), 317–22.

Nokes, David. *Jane Austen*, 151–53, 281–83.

Scholz, Anne-Marie. "'Facts are such horrid things!': The Austen Canon and *Lady Susan*." *Zeitschrift für Anglistik und Amerikanistik* 45 (1997), 33–42.

Seeber, Barbara K. *General Consent in Jane Austen*, 127–31.

Simpkins, Scott. "The Agon for the Male Signifier: Austen's *Lady Susan*," in C. W. Spinks and John Deely, eds., *Semiotics 1997*, 375–86.

Love and Freindship, 1922

Brodey, Inger Sigrun. "Adventures of a Female Werther: Jane Austen's Revision of Sensibility." *Philos and Lit* 23 (1999), 113–14.

Butler, Marilyn. "The Juvenilia and *Northanger Abbey*," in Richard Kroll, ed., *The English Novel, Volume II*, 271–73.

McMaster, Juliet. "From *Laura and Augustus* to *Love and Freindship*." *Thalia* 16:1–2 (1996), 16–25.

McMaster, Juliet. "Young Jane Austen and the First Canadian Novel:

From *Emily Montague* to 'Amelia Webster' and *Love and Freindship*." *Eighteenth-Cent Fiction* 11 (1999), 342–46.

Wiesenthal, Chris. *Figuring Madness in Nineteenth-Century Fiction*, 41–62, 128–34.

Mansfield Park, 1814

Ang, Susan. *The Widening World of Children's Literature*, 59–61.

Bilger, Audrey. *Laughing Feminism*, 182–85.

Boyd, Brian. "Jane, Meet Charles: Literature, Evolution, and Human Nature." *Philos and Lit* 22 (1998), 16–23.

Brooke, Christopher. *Jane Austen*, 85–96, 160–64, 178–83, 189–91.

Byrne, Paula. "'We must descend a little': *Mansfield Park* and the Comic Theatre." *Women's Writing* 5 (1998), 91–101.

Cavaliero, Glen. *The Alchemy of Laughter*, 88–92.

Clarke, Stephen. "What Smith did at Compton: Landscape Gardening, Humphrey Repton, and *Mansfield Park*." *Persuasions* 21 (1999), 59–66.

Copeland, Edward. "Money," in Edward Copeland and Juliet McMaster, eds., *The Cambridge Companion to Jane Austen*, 139–41.

Copeland, Edward. *Women Writing about Money*, 102–6.

Crick, Brian. "Jane Austen on the 'Relative Situation': What Became of Mrs. Norris's 'Morally Impossible' in *Mansfield Park*." *Crit R* (Melbourne) 39 (1999), 77–105.

Dabundo, Laura. "Jane Austen's Opacities," in Dabundo, ed., *Jane Austen and Mary Shelley*, 55–58.

Dadlez, E. M. *What's Hecuba to Him?*, 119–21.

Dames, Nicholas. *Amnesiac Selves*, 35–39, 53–64.

Dames, Nicholas. "Austen's Nostalgics." *Representations* 73 (2001), 127–28, 135–36.

Day, Aidan. *Romanticism*, 139–40.

Derry, Stephen. "*Mansfield Park*, Sterne's Starling, and Bunyan's Man of Despair." *Notes and Queries* 44 (1997), 322–23.

Dingley, R. J. "Henry Crawford between Tragedy and Comedy in Jane Austen's *Mansfield Park*." *Stud in Iconography* 14 (1995), 306–8.

Dole, Carol M. "Austen, Class, and the American Market," in Linda Troost and Sayre Greenfield, eds., *Jane Austen in Hollywood*, 64–66.

Easton, Fraser. "The Political Economy of *Mansfield Park*: Fanny Price and the Atlantic Working Class." *Textual Practice* 12 (1998), 459–82.

Flynn, Christopher. "'No Other Island in the World': *Mansfield Park*, North America and Post-Imperial Malaise." *Symbiosis* 4:2 (2000), 173–86.

Fraiman, Susan. "Jane Austen and Edward Said: Gender, Culture, and Imperialism," in Deidre Lynch, ed., *Janeites*, 206–21.

Gardiner, Ellen. *Regulating Readers*, 134–51.

Giffin, Michael. "Jane Austen and the Economy of Salvation: Renewing the Drifting Church in *Mansfield Park*." *Lit and Theology* 14 (2000), 17–33.

Gillooly, Eileen. *Smile of Discontent*, 81–110.

Giotta, Peter C. "Characterization in *Mansfield Park*: Tom Bertram and Colman's *The Heir at Law*." *R of Engl Stud* 49 (1998), 466–71.

Harding, D. W. *Regulated Hatred*, 106–26, 190–210.

Hawkridge, Audrey. *Jane and Her Gentlemen*, 72–74, 129–31.

Heydt-Stevenson, Jill. "'Slipping into the Ha-Ha': Bawdy Humor and Body Politics in Jane Austen's Novels." *Nineteenth-Cent Lit* 55 (2000), 323–32.

Hipchen, Emily. "'My house ... turned topsy-turvy': Order and Acting in *The Loiterer* and *Mansfield Park*." *Persuasions* 19 (1997), 31–35.

Jacobus, Mary. *Psychoanalysis and the Scene of Reading*, 67–80.

Johnston, Freya. "Public and Private Space in Jane Austen." *English* 46 (1997), 199–204.

Kane, Penny. *Victorian Families in Fact and Fiction*, 40–42.

McGrail, Anne B. "Fanny Price's 'Customary' Subjectivity: Rereading the Individual in *Mansfield Park*," in Laura Cooner Lambdin and Robert Thomas Lambdin, eds., *A Companion to Jane Austen Studies*, 57–69.

Marsh, Nicholas. *Jane Austen*, 16–21, 50–55, 66–68, 79–83, 113–22, 144–52, 168–70, 178–82, 190–94, 199–201.

Mathur, Piyush. "The Archigenderic Territories: *Mansfield Park* and *A Handful of Dust*." *Women's Writing* 5 (1998), 71–79.

Menon, Patricia. "The Mentor-Lover in *Mansfield Park*: 'At Once Both Tragedy and Comedy.'" *Cambridge Q* 29 (2000), 145–64.

Morris, Ivor. *Jane Austen and the Interplay of Character*, 26–28, 36–38, 44–47, 75–78, 86–89, 93–97, 111–19.

Morse, David. *The Age of Virtue*, 167–72.

Murray, Douglas. "Spectatorship in *Mansfield Park*: Looking and Overlooking." *Nineteenth-Cent Lit* 52 (1997), 1–26.

Nardin, Jane. "Jane Austen, Hannah More, and the Novel of Education." *Persuasions* 20 (1998), 15–20.

Neill, Edward. *The Politics of Jane Austen*, 70–94.

Neill, Edward. "'Une Affaire de Cœur': Jane Austen and Kierkegaard." *Cambridge Q* 27:2 (1998), 148–58.

Nokes, David. *Jane Austen*, 412–15.

Nunn, Roger Charles. "Empire and Jane Austen: A Contrapuntal Reading." *Stud in Engl Lit* (Tokyo) 75 (1999), 1–17.

O'Farrell, Mary Ann. "Jane Austen's Friendship," in Deidre Lynch, ed., *Janeites*, 57–59.

O'Toole, Tess. "Adoption and the 'Improvement of the Estate' in Trollope and Craik." *Nineteenth-Cent Lit* 52 (1997), 72–74.

Palmer, Sally B. "Austen's *Mansfield Park*." *Explicator* 56:4 (1998), 181–83.

Parker, Jo Alyson. *The Author's Inheritance*, 155–80.

Parker, Jo Alyson. "Complicating *A Simple Story*: Inchbald's Two Versions of Female Power." *Eighteenth-Cent Stud* 30 (1997), 265–67.

Peck, John. *Maritime Fiction*, 30–32, 36–42.

Piper, William Bowman. *Reconcilable Differences*, 189–93.

Plasa, Carl. *Textual Politics from Slavery to Postcolonialism*, 32–59.

Posner, Richard A. *Law and Literature*, 325–26.

Price, Leah. *The Anthology and the Rise of the Novel*, 79–80.

Quaintance, Richard. "Humphry Repton, 'any Mr. Repton,' and the 'Improvement' Metonym in *Mansfield Park*." *Stud in Eighteenth-Cent Culture* 27 (1998), 365–81.

Rogers, J. Pat. "The Critical History of *Mansfield Park*," in Laura
    Cooner Lambdin and Robert Thomas Lambdin, eds., *A Companion
    to Jane Austen Studies*, 71–84.
Ruderman, Anne Crippen. *The Pleasures of Virtue*, 81–93, 124–28,
    144–49, 175–79.
Schöneich, Christoph. "Bewegung und Konfiguration in *Mansfield
    Park*." *Anglia* 117 (1999), 32–52.
Seeber, Barbara K. *General Consent in Jane Austen*, 47–54, 59–65,
    95–115.
Sendbuehler, Fran. "The Art of Doing Nothing." *Angelaki* 2:1 (1995),
    169–78.
Simons, Judy. "Classics and Trash: Reading Austen in the 1990s."
    Women's Writing 5 (1998), 27–37.
Sutherland, John. *Who Betrays Elizabeth Bennet?*, 23–27.
Teachman, Debra. *Student Companion to Jane Austen*, 71–88.
Tomalin, Claire. *Jane Austen*, 224–33.
Trumpener, Katie. *Bardic Nationalism*, 174–85.
Trumpener, Katie. "The Virago Jane Austen," in Deidre Lynch, ed.,
    Janeites, 154–56.
Waldron, Mary. *Jane Austen and the Fiction of Her Time*, 85–111.
Watson, Nicola J. *Revolution and the Form of the British Novel*, 90–93.
Wiltshire, John. "*Mansfield Park, Emma, Persuasion*," in Edward
    Copeland and Juliet McMaster, eds., *The Cambridge Companion to
    Jane Austen*, 59–66.
Wolfe, Jesse. "Jane Austen and the Sin of Pride." *Renascence* 51
    (1999), 118–20.
Wood, Michael. *Children of Silence*, 162–65.

Northanger Abbey, 1818

Alexander, Christine. "The Prospect of Blaise: Landscape and
    Perception in *Northanger Abbey*." *Persuasions* 21 (1999), 17–31.
Armstrong, Nancy. "Captivity and Cultural Capital in the English
    Novel." *Novel* 31 (1998), 381–86.
Arnold-de Simine, Silke. "'Are you sure they are all horrid?': Jane
    Austens *Northanger Abbey* als Parodie auf die Gattung der 'gothic
    novels,'" in Andreas Böhn, ed., *Formzitate, Gattungsparodien, iro-
    nische Formverwendung*, 109–32.
Axelrod, Mark. *The Poetics of Novels*, 28–54.
Bander, Elaine. "*Sanditon, Northanger Abbey*, and *Camilla*: Back to
    the Future?" *Persuasions* 19 (1997), 195–204.
Becker, Susanne. *Gothic Forms of Feminine Fictions*, 68–70.
Benedict, Barbara M. "Jane Austen and the Culture of Circulating
    Libraries: The Construction of Female Literacy," in Paula R.
    Backscheider, ed., *Revising Women*, 179–81.
Bilger, Audrey. *Laughing Feminism*, 92–94, 174–76.
Bilger, Audrey. "Mocking the 'Lords of Creation': Comic Male
    Characters in Frances Burney, Maria Edgeworth and Jane Austen."
    Women's Writing 1 (1994), 91–92.
Brantlinger, Patrick. *The Reading Lesson*, 32–34.
Brooke, Christopher. *Jane Austen*, 58–64, 158–59.

Brownstein, Rachel M. "*Northanger Abbey, Sense and Sensibility, Pride and Prejudice*," in Edward Copeland and Juliet McMaster, eds., *The Cambridge Companion to Jane Austen*, 36–42.

Burgess, Miranda J. *British Fiction and the Production of Social Order*, 150–57, 162–64, 169–75.

Butler, Marilyn. "The Juvenilia and *Northanger Abbey*," in Richard Kroll, ed., *The English Novel, Volume II*, 275–81.

Butler, Marilyn. "The Purple Turban and the Flowering Aloe Tree: Signs of Distinction in the Early-Nineteenth-Century Novel." *Mod Lang Q* 58 (1997), 482–88.

Casal, Elvira. "Motherhood and Reality in *Northanger Abbey*." *Persuasions* 20 (1998), 146–53.

Clarke, Stephen. "Abbeys Real and Imagined: Northanger, Fonthill, and Aspects of the Gothic Revival." *Persuasions* 20 (1998), 93–104.

Collins, Irene. "The Rev. Henry Tilney, Rector of Woodston." *Persuasions* 20 (1998), 154–64.

Dabundo, Laura. "Jane Austen's Opacities," in Dabundo, ed., *Jane Austen and Mary Shelley*, 55–57.

Dawson, Brett. "Giraudoux, Jane Austen et l'art de l'anti-pastiche." *Cahiers Jean Giraudoux* 27 (1999), 167–80.

Derry, Stephen. "John Thorpe's 'Old Song' in *Northanger Abbey*." *Notes and Queries* 46 (1999), 28.

Dussinger, John A. "Parents Against Children: General Tilney as Gothic Monster." *Persuasions* 20 (1998), 165–74.

Fay, Elizabeth A. *A Feminist Introduction to Romanticism*, 108–10, 137–39.

Gerster, Carole. "Rereading Jane Austen: Dialogic Feminism in *Northanger Abbey*," in Laura Cooner Lambdin and Robert Thomas Lambdin, eds., *A Companion to Jane Austen Studies*, 115–29.

Graham, Kenneth W. "The Case of the Petulant Patriarch." *Persuasions* 20 (1998), 119–33.

Harding, D. W. *Regulated Hatred*, 127–46.

Hermansson, Casie. "Neither Northanger Abbey: The Reader Presupposes." *Papers on Lang and Lit* 36 (2000), 337–54.

Hoeveler, Diane Long. *Gothic Feminism*, 127–43.

Johnson, Claudia L. "The Juvenilia and *Northanger Abbey*: The Authority of Men and Books," in Richard Kroll, ed., *The English Novel, Volume II*, 289–305.

Justice, George. "*Northanger Abbey* as Anti-Courtship Novel." *Persuasions* 20 (1998), 185–94.

Keller, James R. "Austen's *Northanger Abbey*: A Bibliographic Study," in Laura Cooner Lambdin and Robert Thomas Lambdin, eds., *A Companion to Jane Austen Studies*, 131–41.

Kindred, Sheila J. "From Puppet to Person: The Development of Catherine's Character in the Bath Chapters of *Northanger Abbey*." *Persuasions* 20 (1998), 196–206.

Knox-Shaw, Peter. "*Northanger Abbey* and the Liberal Historians." *Essays in Criticism* 49 (1999), 319–40.

Lane, Maggie. "The French Bread at Northanger." *Persuasions* 20 (1998), 135–45.

Le Fay, Deirdre. "*Northanger Abbey* and Mrs Allen's Maxims." *Notes and Queries* 46 (1999), 449–50.

Levy, Anita. *Reproductive Urges*, 54–60.

Levy, Anita. "Reproductive Urges: Literacy, Sexuality, and Eighteenth-Century Englishness," in Susan C. Greenfield and Carol Barash, eds., *Inventing Maternity*, 205–9.

Litvak, Joseph. "Charming Men, Charming History," in Ann Kibbey et al., eds., *On Your Left*, 248–70.

Litvak, Joseph. *Strange Gourmets*, 33–54.

McMaster, Juliet. "Clothing the Thought in the Word: The Speakers of *Northanger Abbey.*" *Persuasions* 20 (1998), 207–20.

Merrett, Robert. "Consuming Modes in *Northanger Abbey*: Jane Austen's Economic View of Literary Nationalism." *Persuasions* 20 (1998), 222–34.

Morris, Ivor. *Jane Austen and the Interplay of Character*, 13–17, 22–26, 35–40, 90–93, 108–10, 126–28.

Neill, Edward. *The Politics of Jane Austen*, 15–30.

Neill, Edward. "The Secret of *Northanger Abbey.*" *Essays in Criticism* 47 (1997), 13–29.

Parker, Jo Alyson. *The Author's Inheritance*, 39–41, 47–60.

Pearson, Jacqueline. *Women's Reading in Britain*, 209–13.

Pici, Nick. "A Heroine's Vision Undermined: Expectation, Disillusionment, and Initiation in *Northanger Abbey.*" *Persuasions* 20 (1998), 38–43.

Piper, William Bowman. *Reconcilable Differences*, 183–89.

Price, Leah. *The Anthology and the Rise of the Novel*, 91–93.

Ruderman, Anne Crippen. *The Pleasures of Virtue*, 35–42.

Sato, Megumi. "Women's Reading and Creation in *Northanger Abbey.*" *Shiron* 38 (1999), 55–68.

Sears, Albert C. "Male Novel Reading of the 1790s, Gothic Literature, and *Northanger Abbey.*" *Persuasions* 21 (1999), 106–11.

Seeber, Barbara K. *General Consent in Jane Austen*, 116–26.

Séllei, Nóra. "Self-Reflexive Literariness in Jane Austen's *Northanger Abbey*: Or, How a Book Reveals Itself as a Book." *B.A.S.: Brit and Am Stud* 1 (1996), 17–23.

Shaw, Harry E. *Narrating Reality*, 147–61.

Sorensen, Janet. *The Grammar of Empire*, 199–221.

Stovel, Bruce. "*Northanger Abbey* at the Movies." *Persuasions* 20 (1998), 236–46.

Teachman, Debra. *Student Companion to Jane Austen*, 109–28.

Ty, Eleanor. "Catherine's Real and Imagined Fears: What Happens to Female Bodies in Gothic Castles." *Persuasions* 20 (1998), 248–59.

Waldron, Mary. *Jane Austen and the Fiction of Her Time*, 26–36.

Williams, Carolyn D. "General Tilney and the Maidens all Forlorn: Typecasting in *Northanger Abbey.*" *Women's Writing* 5 (1998), 41–57.

Wordsworth, Jonathan. *The Bright Work Grows*, 224–28.

Persuasion, 1818

Bilger, Audrey. *Laughing Feminism*, 137–39.

Brooke, Christopher. *Jane Austen*, 110–18, 164–66, 186–89.

Burgess, Miranda J. *British Fiction and the Production of Social Order*, 175–85.

Cantor, Paul A. "A Class Act: *Persuasion* and the Lingering Death of the Aristocracy." *Philos and Lit* 23 (1999), 127–36.

Clausen, Christopher. "Jane Austen Changes Her Mind." *Am Scholar* 68:2 (1999), 89–99.

Cohen, Monica F. *Professional Domesticity*, 13–37.

Copeland, Edward. *Women Writing about Money*, 109–13.

Dalton, Elizabeth. "Mourning and Melancholia in *Persuasion*." *Partisan R* 62:1 (1995), 49–59.

Dames, Nicholas. *Amnesiac Selves*, 65–73.

Dames, Nicholas. "Austen's Nostalgics." *Representations* 73 (2001), 136–38.

Dole, Carol M. "Austen, Class, and the American Market," in Linda Troost and Sayre Greenfield, eds., *Jane Austen in Hollywood*, 61–64.

Favret, Mary A. "Being True to Jane Austen," in John Kucich and Dianne F. Sadoff, eds., *Victorian Afterlife*, 72–80.

Fletcher, Loraine. "Time and Mourning in *Persuasion*." *Women's Writing* 5 (1998), 81–88.

Fott, David. "Prudence and *Persuasion*: Jane Austen on Virtue in Democratizing Eras." *Lamar J of the Hum* 24:1 (1999), 17–32.

Fulford, Tim. "Romanticizing the Empire: The Naval Heroes of Southey, Coleridge, Austen, and Marryat." *Mod Lang Q* 60 (1999), 161–96.

Gillooly, Eileen. *Smile of Discontent*, 110–23.

Gores, Steven J. *Psychosocial Spaces*, 81–83, 89–93.

Groenendyk, Kathi L. "The Importance of Vision: *Persuasion* and the Picturesque." *Rhetoric Soc Q* 30:1 (2000), 9–28.

Harding, D. W. *Regulated Hatred*, 147–70.

Hawkridge, Audrey. *Jane and Her Gentlemen*, 115–18.

Heydt-Stevenson, Jill. "'Slipping into the Ha-Ha': Bawdy Humor and Body Politics in Jane Austen's Novels." *Nineteenth-Cent Lit* 55 (2000), 332–39.

Ireland, Ken. *The Sequential Dynamics of Narrative*, 125–37.

Johnston, Freya. "Public and Private Space in Jane Austen." *English* 46 (1997), 207–10.

Lambdin, Laura Cooner, and Robert Thomas Lambdin. "Degrees of Maturity: The Bibliographic History of Jane Austen's *Persuasion*," in Lambdin and Lambdin, eds., *A Companion to Jane Austen Studies*, 159–68.

Lynch, Deidre Shauna. *The Economy of Character*, 210–20, 239–49.

Marsh, Nicholas. *Jane Austen*, 21–24, 55–62, 83–85, 122–28, 152–59, 170–75, 182–89, 204–6.

Medalie, David. "'Only as the Event Decides': Contingency in *Persuasion*." *Essays in Criticism* 49 (1999), 152–68.

Mellor, Anne K. *Mothers of the Nation*, 121–39.

Michie, Helena. "Under Victorian Skins: The Bodies Beneath," in Herbert F. Tucker, ed., *A Companion to Victorian Literature and Culture*, 413–14.

Morris, Ivor. *Jane Austen and the Interplay of Character*, 34–36, 62–65, 78–81, 130–32, 145–47.

Neill, Edward. *The Politics of Jane Austen*, 112–35.

Nokes, David. *Jane Austen*, 487–94.

Nunn, Roger Charles. "Empire and Jane Austen: A Contrapuntal Reading." *Stud in Engl Lit* (Tokyo) 75 (1999), 2–17.

O'Farrell, Mary Ann. *Telling Complexions*, 30–57.

Peck, John. *Maritime Fiction*, 42–49.

Rawson, Claude. *Satire and Sentiment*, 267–98.

Ruderman, Anne Crippen. *The Pleasures of Virtue*, 59–74, 77–81, 107–9, 122–24, 131–34, 142–54, 172–74, 176–78.

Sales, Roger. "In Face of All the Servants: Spectators and Spies in Austen (with special reference to the 1995 adaptation of *Persuasion*)," in Deidre Lynch, ed., *Janeites*, 188–203.

Seeber, Barbara K. *General Consent in Jane Austen*, 55–58, 67–69, 76–84.

Shaw, Harry E. *Narrating Reality*, 160–66.

Spacks, Patricia Meyer. "Ideology and Form: Novels at Work," in David H. Richter, ed., *Ideology and Form*, 21–25.

Stabler, Jane. "'Perswasion' in *Persuasion*," in Richard Gravil, ed., *Master Narratives*, 55–67.

Stein, Claudia. "*Persuasion*'s Box of Contradictions," in Laura Cooner Lambdin and Robert Thomas Lambdin, eds., *A Companion to Jane Austen Studies*, 145–57.

Teachman, Debra. *Student Companion to Jane Austen*, 129–48.

Tomalin, Claire. *Jane Austen*, 255–58.

Trumpener, Katie. "The Virago Jane Austen," in Deidre Lynch, ed., *Janeites*, 158–60.

Vorachek, Laura. "Crossing Boundaries: Land and Sea in Jane Austen's *Persuasion*." *Persuasions* 19 (1997), 36–40.

Waldron, Mary. *Jane Austen and the Fiction of Her Time*, 135–56.

Watson, Nicola J. *Revolution and the Form of the British Novel*, 105–8.

Wiltshire, John. "*Mansfield Park, Emma, Persuasion*," in Edward Copeland and Juliet McMaster, eds., *The Cambridge Companion to Jane Austen*, 76–83.

Wordsworth, Jonathan. *The Bright Work Grows*, 228–32.

Pride and Prejudice, 1813

Alsop, Derek, and Chris Walsh. *The Practice of Reading*, 51–75.

Benedict, Barbara M. "Jane Austen and the Culture of Circulating Libraries: The Construction of Female Literacy," in Paula R. Backscheider, ed., *Revising Women*, 171–73, 185–87.

Bilger, Audrey. *Laughing Feminism*, 71–75, 122–25, 161–65.

Bilger, Audrey. "Mocking the 'Lords of Creation': Comic Male Characters in Frances Burney, Maria Edgeworth and Jane Austen." *Women's Writing* 1 (1994), 84–86.

Braden, Wilbur S. "Education, Pride, and Prejudice." *Willamette J of the Liberal Arts* 6 (1991), 35–46.

Brooke, Christopher. *Jane Austen*, 74–84, 158–60, 172–77.

Brownstein, Rachel M. "*Northanger Abbey, Sense and Sensibility,*

Pride and Prejudice," in Edward Copeland and Juliet McMaster, eds., *The Cambridge Companion to Jane Austen,* 49–57.

Cavaliero, Glen. *The Alchemy of Laughter,* 45–48.

Clay, George R. "In Defense of Flat Characters: A Discussion of Their Value to Charles Dickens, Jane Austen, and Leo Tolstoy." *Intl Fiction R* 27:1–2 (2000), 20–24.

Copeland, Edward. "Money," in Edward Copeland and Juliet McMaster, eds., *The Cambridge Companion to Jane Austen,* 134–36.

Copeland, Edward. *Women Writing about Money,* 96–99.

Crowe, Marian E. "G. K. Chesterton and the Orthodox Romance of *Pride and Prejudice.*" *Renascence* 49 (1997), 209–21.

Dabundo, Laura. "The Devil and Jane Austen: Elizabeth Bennet's Temptations in the Wilderness." *Persuasions* 21 (1999), 53–57.

Dames, Nicholas. *Amnesiac Selves,* 37–39, 72–74.

Dames, Nicholas. "Austen's Nostalgics." *Representations* 73 (2001), 119–21, 128–31.

Damstra, K. St. John. "The Case against Charlotte Lucas." *Women's Writing* 7 (2000), 165–74.

Deresiewicz, William. "Community and Cognition in *Pride and Prejudice.*" *ELH* 64 (1997), 503–31.

Doody, Terrence. *Among Other Things,* 108–10, 245–47.

Duckworth, Alistair M. "Jane Austen and George Stubbs: Two Speculations." *Eighteenth-Cent Fiction* 13:1 (2000), 55–60.

Ellington, H. Elisabeth. "'A Correct Taste in Landscape': Pemberley as Fetish and Commodity," in Linda Troost and Sayre Greenfield, eds., *Jane Austen in Hollywood,* 99–109.

Ellis, Lorna. *Appearing to Diminish,* 114–18, 129–37.

Fay, Elizabeth A. *A Feminist Introduction to Romanticism,* 40–47.

Fletcher, Loraine. *Charlotte Smith,* 310–12.

Gallop, David. "Jane Austen and the Aristotelean Ethic." *Philos and Lit* 23 (1999), 99–101, 104–6.

Gaskell, Philip. *Landmarks in English Literature,* 50–52.

Hale, John K. "'In Vain Have I Struggled': *Pride and Prejudice,* Chapter 34." *Persuasions* 21 (1999), 79–82.

Harding, D. W. *Regulated Hatred,* 217.

Hawkridge, Audrey. *Jane and Her Gentlemen,* 121–25, 139–42.

Heinrich, Hans. *Zur Geschichte des 'Libertin,'* 150–52.

Hopkins, Lisa. "Mr. Darcy's Body: Privileging the Female Gaze," in Linda Troost and Sayre Greenfield, eds., *Jane Austen in Hollywood,* 111–20.

Joseph, Gerhard. "Prejudice in Jane Austen, Emma Tennant, Charles Dickens—and Us." *Stud in Engl Lit, 1500–1900* 40 (2000), 680–84.

Langland, Elizabeth. "*Pride and Prejudice*: Jane Austen and Her Readers," in Laura Cooner Lambdin and Robert Thomas Lambdin, eds., *A Companion to Jane Austen Studies,* 41–54.

Lau, Beth. "Jane Austen, *Pride and Prejudice,*" in Duncan Wu, ed., *A Companion to Romanticism,* 219–24.

Litvak, Joseph. *Strange Gourmets,* 21–30.

Lynch, Deidre Shauna. *The Economy of Character,* 130–32, 211–13.

McMaster, Juliet. "Class," in Edward Copeland and Juliet McMaster, eds., *The Cambridge Companion to Jane Austen*, 116–18.

Marsh, Nicholas. *Jane Austen*, 3–10, 32–40, 68–74, 96–106, 130–37, 162–66, 175–77, 206–10.

Morris, Ivor. *Jane Austen and the Interplay of Character*, 1–3, 6–12, 19–24, 31–37, 47–56, 59–70, 81–90, 94–98, 100–108, 110–13, 121–27, 134–42, 147–52, 157–62.

Morse, David. *The Age of Virtue*, 165–67.

Mulvihill, James. "A Burke Source for the Opening of Austen's *Pride and Prejudice*." *Engl Lang Notes* 38:3 (2001), 68–70.

Neill, Edward. *The Politics of Jane Austen*, 51–69, 136–42.

Nixon, Cheryl L. "Balancing the Courtship Hero: Masculine Emotional Display in Film Adaptations of Austen's Novels," in Linda Troost and Sayre Greenfield, eds., *Jane Austen in Hollywood*, 33–35.

Nokes, David. *Jane Austen*, 401–3, 477–82.

O'Farrell, Mary Ann. "Jane Austen's Friendship," in Deidre Lynch, ed., *Janeites*, 51–54.

O'Farrell, Mary Ann. *Telling Complexions*, 15–27.

Parker, Jo Alyson. *The Author's Inheritance*, 93–116.

Parrill, A. Sue. "*Pride and Prejudice* on A&E: Visions and Revisions." *Lit/Film Q* 27 (1999), 142–47.

Parrill, Sue. "What Meets the Eye: Landscape in the Films *Pride and Prejudice* and *Sense and Sensibility*." *Persuasions* 21 (1999), 32–42.

Peña Cervel, Ma. Sandra. "*Pride and Prejudice*: A Cognitive Analysis." *Cuadernos de Investigación Filológica* 23–24 (1997–1998), 233–58.

Reilly, Susan. "'A Nobler Fall of Ground': Nation and Narration in *Pride and Prejudice*." *Symbiosis* 4:1 (2000), 19–34.

Ruderman, Anne Crippen. *The Pleasures of Virtue*, 74–79, 99–115, 145–47, 176–79.

Seeber, Barbara K. *General Consent in Jane Austen*, 85–92.

Smith, Johanna M. "The Oppositional Reader and *Pride and Prejudice*," in Laura Cooner Lambdin and Robert Thomas Lambdin, eds., *A Companion to Jane Austen Studies*, 27–38.

Sorensen, Janet. *The Grammar of Empire*, 199–221.

Sutherland, John. *Who Betrays Elizabeth Bennet?*, 17–22.

Teachman, Debra. *Student Companion to Jane Austen*, 53–69.

Teachman, Debra. *Understanding "Pride and Prejudice,"* 1–23.

Tomalin, Claire. *Jane Austen*, 159–65.

Waldron, Mary. *Jane Austen and the Fiction of Her Time*, 41–61.

Sanditon, 1925

Bander, Elaine. "*Sanditon, Northanger Abbey*, and *Camilla*: Back to the Future?" *Persuasions* 19 (1997), 195–202.

Bell, David. "'Here & There & Every Where': Is Sidney Parker the Intended Hero of *Sanditon*?" *Persuasions* 19 (1997), 160–66.

Benedict, Barbara M. "Jane Austen and the Culture of Circulating Libraries: The Construction of Female Literacy," in Paula R. Backscheider, ed., *Revising Women*, 194–98.

Benson, Robert. "Jane Goes to Sanditon: An Eighteenth Century Lady in a Nineteenth Century Landscape." *Persuasions* 19 (1997), 211–18.

Brodey, Inger Sigrun. "Resorting and Consorting with Strangers: Jane Austen's 'Multiculturalism.'" *Persuasions* 19 (1997), 130–42.

Copeland, Edward. "*Sanditon* and 'my Aunt': Jane Austen and the National Debt." *Persuasions* 19 (1997), 117–28.

Curry, Mary Jane. "A New Kind of Pastoral: Anti-Development Satire in *Sanditon*." *Persuasions* 19 (1997), 167–75.

Ford, Susan Allen. "The Romance of Business and the Business of Romance: The Circulating Library and Novel-Reading in *Sanditon*." *Persuasions* 19 (1997), 177–84.

Huey, Peggy. "Jane Austen's *Sanditon*," in Laura Cooner Lambdin and Robert Thomas Lambdin, eds., *A Companion to Jane Austen Studies*, 253–57.

Kuwahara, Kuldip Kaur. "*Sanditon*, Empire, and the Sea: Circles of Influence, Wheels of Power." *Persuasions* 19 (1997), 144–48.

Lynch, Deidre Shauna. *The Economy of Character*, 222–26.

McMaster, Juliet. "The Watchers of *Sanditon*." *Persuasions* 19 (1997), 149–58.

Quaintance, Richard. "Salutes and Satire in Jane Austen's Characters' Sense of 'Nature.'" *Persuasions* 19 (1997), 219–24.

Tuite, Clara. "Decadent Austen Entails: Forster, James, Firbank, and the 'Queer Taste' of *Sanditon* (comp. 1817, publ. 1925)," in Deidre Lynch, ed., *Janeites*, 126–36.

Waldron, Mary. *Jane Austen and the Fiction of Her Time*, 157–65.

Wiltshire, John. "Sickness and Silliness in *Sanditon*." *Persuasions* 19 (1997), 93–102.

Sense and Sensibility, 1811

Bate, Jonathan. "Culture and Environment: From Austen to Hardy." *New Liter Hist* 30 (1999), 546–50.

Benedict, Barbara M. "Jane Austen and the Culture of Circulating Libraries: The Construction of Female Literacy," in Paula R. Backscheider, ed., *Revising Women*, 181–85.

Bilger, Audrey. *Laughing Feminism*, 169–73.

Bristow, Catherine. "Unlocking the Rape: An Analysis of Austen's Use of Pope's Symbolism in *Sense and Sensibility*." *Persuasions* 20 (1998), 31–36.

Brodey, Inger Sigrun. "Adventures of a Female Werther: Jane Austen's Revision of Sensibility." *Philos and Lit* 23 (1999), 114–24.

Brooke, Christopher. *Jane Austen*, 65–73, 158–59, 171–74.

Brownstein, Rachel M. "*Northanger Abbey, Sense and Sensibility, Pride and Prejudice*," in Edward Copeland and Juliet McMaster, eds., *The Cambridge Companion to Jane Austen*, 42–49.

Collins, Amanda. "Jane Austen, Film, and the Pitfalls of Postmodern Nostalgia," in Linda Troost and Sayre Greenfield, eds., *Jane Austen in Hollywood*, 84–87.

Copeland, Edward. *Women Writing about Money*, 93–96.

Dames, Nicholas. *Amnesiac Selves*, 44–53.

Dames, Nicholas. "Austen's Nostalgics." *Representations* 73 (2001), 119, 134–35.

Diana, M. Casey. "Emma Thompson's *Sense and Sensibility* as Gateway to Austen's Novel," in Linda Troost and Sayre Greenfield, eds., *Jane Austen in Hollywood*, 140–47.

Dickson, Rebecca. "Misrepresenting Jane Austen's Ladies: Revising Texts (and History) to Sell Films," in Linda Troost and Sayre Greenfield, eds., *Jane Austen in Hollywood*, 51–56.

Duncan, Rebecca Stephens. "A Critical History of *Sense and Sensibility*," in Laura Cooner Lambdin and Robert Thomas Lambdin, eds., *A Companion to Jane Austen Studies*, 17–25.

Duncan, Rebecca Stephens. "*Sense and Sensibility*: A Convergence of Readers/Viewers/ Browsers," in Laura Cooner Lambdin and Robert Thomas Lambdin, eds., *A Companion to Jane Austen Studies*, 1–16.

Favret, Mary A. "Being True to Jane Austen," in John Kucich and Dianne F. Sadoff, eds., *Victorian Afterlife*, 66–72.

Fletcher, Loraine. *Charlotte Smith*, 308–10.

Goodlad, Lauren M. E. "England's 'Glorious "Middle Way"': Self-Disciplinary Self-Making and Jane Austen's *Sense and Sensibility*." *Genre* 33 (2000), 51–78.

Haggerty, George E. *Unnatural Affections*, 73–87.

Harding, D. W. *Regulated Hatred*, 211–16.

Hawkridge, Audrey. *Jane and Her Gentlemen*, 118–20, 127–29, 147–49.

Heinrich, Hans. *Zur Geschichte des 'Libertin,'* 148–50.

Kaplan, Deborah. "Mass Marketing Jane Austen: Men, Women, and Courtship in Two Film Adaptations," in Linda Troost and Sayre Greenfield, eds., *Jane Austen in Hollywood*, 180–82, 184–85.

Loncar, Kathleen. *Legal Fiction*, 147–49.

Looser, Devoney. "Feminist Implications of the Silver Screen Austen," in Linda Troost and Sayre Greenfield, eds., *Jane Austen in Hollywood*, 171–73.

Lynch, Deidre Shauna. *The Economy of Character*, 210–20, 228–40.

Moody, Ellen. "A Calendar for *Sense and Sensibility*." *Philol Q* 78 (1999), 301–32.

Morris, Ivor. *Jane Austen and the Interplay of Character*, 37–43, 53–55, 91–94, 143–46.

Morse, David. *The Age of Virtue*, 159–65.

Nachumi, Nora. "'As If!': Translating Austen's Ironic Narrator to Film," in Linda Troost and Sayre Greenfield, eds., *Jane Austen in Hollywood*, 131–33.

Neill, Edward. *The Politics of Jane Austen*, 31–50.

Nixon, Cheryl L. "Balancing the Courtship Hero: Masculine Emotional Display in Film Adaptations of Austen's Novels," in Linda Troost and Sayre Greenfield, eds., *Jane Austen in Hollywood*, 39–43.

Parrill, Sue. "What Meets the Eye: Landscape in the Films *Pride and Prejudice* and *Sense and Sensibility*." *Persuasions* 21 (1999), 32–42.

Perkins, Moreland. *Reshaping the Sexes in "Sense and Sensibility."*

Piper, William Bowman. *Reconcilable Differences*, 200–205.

Rehder, Robert. "The Moment as a Form: Jane Austen and Chateaubriand." *Colloquium Helveticum* 25 (1997), 195–223.

Ruderman, Anne Crippen. *The Pleasures of Virtue*, 59–81, 115–21, 128–31, 165–69.

Samuelian, Kristin Flieger. "'Piracy Is Our Only Option': Postfeminist Intervention in *Sense and Sensibility*," in Linda Troost and Sayre Greenfield, eds., *Jane Austen in Hollywood*, 148–56.

Seeber, Barbara K. *General Consent in Jane Austen*, 27–37, 70–75.

Seeber, Barbara K. "'I See Every Thing As You Desire Me to Do': The Scolding and Schooling of Marianne Dashwood." *Eighteenth-Cent Fiction* 11 (1999), 223–33.

Shaw, Peter Knox. "*Sense and Sensibility*, Godwin and the Empiricists." *Cambridge Q* 27 (1998), 183–208.

Sorensen, Janet. *The Grammar of Empire*, 199–221.

Spacks, Patricia Meyer. "Privacy, Dissimulation, and Propriety: Frances Burney and Jane Austen." *Eighteenth-Cent Fiction* 12 (2000), 526–31.

Teachman, Debra. *Student Companion to Jane Austen*, 37–52.

Tomalin, Claire. *Jane Austen*, 155–59.

Waldron, Mary. *Jane Austen and the Fiction of Her Time*, 62–83.

Watson, Nicola J. *Revolution and the Form of the British Novel*, 87–90.

The Watsons, 1871

Copeland, Edward. *Women Writing about Money*, 99–102.

Hamblin, Laura. "On the Virtues of Stout Half-Boots, *Speculation* and a Little Fresh Hair Powder: A Political, Yet Jovial, Reading of Jane Austen's *The Watsons*," in Laura Cooner Lambdin and Robert Thomas Lambdin, eds., *A Companion to Jane Austen Studies*, 225–40.

Hourigan, Maureen. "*The Watsons*: Critical Interpretations," in Laura Cooner Lambdin and Robert Thomas Lambdin, eds., *A Companion to Jane Austen Studies*, 241–50.

James-Cavan, Kathleen. "Closure and Disclosure: The Significance of Conversation in Jane Austen's *The Watsons*." *Stud in the Novel* 29 (1997), 437–50.

Johnston, Freya. "Public and Private Space in Jane Austen." *English* 46 (1997), 194–99.

Simpkins, Scott. "White Semiotics: Austen's *The Watsons* and the Performance of Caucasianality," in C. W. Spinks and John Deely, eds., *Semiotics 1998*, 299–305.

Tomalin, Claire. *Jane Austen*, 182–84.

Waldron, Mary. *Jane Austen and the Fiction of Her Time*, 38–44.

ROBERT BAGE

Barham Downs, 1784

Skinner, Gillian. *Sensibility and Economics in the Novel*, 117–53.

Hermsprong, or Man as He Is Not, 1796

London, April. *Women and Property*, 149–53.

Man As He Is, 1792

Bellamy, Liz. *Commerce, Morality and the Eighteenth-Century Novel,* 160–62.

Sahni, Chaman L. "India in the Novels of Robert Bage." *South Asian R* 20:17 (1996), 21–29.

Mt. Henneth, 1781

London, April. *Women and Property,* 145–48.

Sahni, Chaman L. "India in the Novels of Robert Bage." *South Asian R* 20:17 (1996), 21–29.

ENID BAGNOLD

The Happy Foreigner, 1920

Deen, Stella. "Enid Bagnold's *The Happy Foreigner:* The Wider World Beyond Love." *Engl Lit in Transition* 44 (2001), 131–44.

National Velvet, 1935

Stoneley, Peter. "Feminism, Fascism and the Racialized Body: *National Velvet.*" *Women: A Cultural R* 9:3 (1998), 252–65.

Tyler, Lisa. "Food, Femininity, and Achievement: The Mother-Daughter Relationship in *National Velvet.*" *Children's Lit Assoc Q* 18:4 (1993–1994), 154–58.

PAUL BAILEY

Kitty and Virgil, 1998

Brînzeu, Pia. *Corridors of Mirrors,* 104–8.

BERYL BAINBRIDGE

Harriet Said . . ., 1972

Smith, Patricia Juliana. *Lesbian Panic,* 157–63.

ELIZABETH BAINES

The Birth Machine, 1983

Armitt, Lucie. *Contemporary Women's Fiction,* 151–59.

WILLIAM BALDWIN

Beware the Cat, 1570

Bonahue, Edward T., Jr. "'I Know the Place and the Persons': The Play of Textual Frames in Baldwin's *Beware the Cat.*" *Stud in Philology* 91 (1994), 283–300.

Bowers, Terence N. "The Production and Communication of Knowledge in William Baldwin's *Beware the Cat:* Toward a Typographic Culture." *Criticism* 33:1 (1991), 1–29.

Hadfield, Andrew. *Literature, Travel, and Colonial Writing,* 141–47.

Maslen, Robert. "'The Cat Got Your Tongue': Pseudo-Translation, Conversion, and Control in William Baldwin's *Beware the Cat*." *Translation and Lit* 8:1 (1999), 3–27.

ROBERT MICHAEL BALLANTYNE

Black Ivory, 1873

Logan, Mawuena Kossi. *Narrating Africa*, 53–60.
Petzold, Jochen. "Zwischen 'Nigger' und 'Noble Savage': Das Afrikabild in R. M. Ballantynes *Black Ivory*," in Titus Heydenreich and Eberhard Späth, eds., *Afrika in den europäischen Literaturen*, 171–88.

The Coral Island, 1858

Dutheil, Martine Hennard. "The Representation of the Cannibal in Ballantyne's *The Coral Island*: Colonial Anxieties in Victorian Popular Fiction." *Coll Lit* 28:1 (2001), 105–22.
Harrex, Syd. "Personal Islands." *Overland* 136 (1994), 51–56.
Kutzer, M. Daphne. *Empire's Children*, 2–10.
Phillips, Richard. *Mapping Men and Empire*, 36–41.
Singh, Minnie. "The Government of Boys: Golding's *Lord of the Flies* and Ballantyne's *Coral Island*." *Children's Lit* 25 (1997), 205–12.

The Gorilla Hunters, 1861

Gohrbrandt, Detlev. "Mapping or Constructing Africa? Notes on R. M. Ballantyne's Juvenile Fiction," in Peter O. Stummer and Christopher Balme, eds., *Fusion of Cultures?*, 132–38.

Martin Rattler, 1859

Forman, Ross G. "When Britons Brave Brazil: British Imperialism and the Adventure Tale in Latin America." *Victorian Stud* 42:3 (1999/2000), 462–67.

The Young Fur Traders, 1856

Phillips, Richard. *Mapping Men and Empire*, 56–67.

J. G. BALLARD

The Atrocity Exhibition, 1969

Luckhurst, Roger. *"The Angle Between Two Walls,"* 73–117.

Concrete Island, 1974

Engélibert, Jean-Paul. *La postérité de Robinson Crusoé*, 96, 145–70, 267–73.
Legault, Christine. "Vitesse et inertie: Les Deux Univers de *L'Ile de béton*." *Tangence* 55 (1997), 8–17.
Luckhurst, Roger. *"The Angle Between Two Walls,"* 134–37.
Orr, Leonard. "The Utopian Disasters of J. G. Ballard." *Coll Lang Assoc J* 43 (2000), 488–90.

Crash, 1972

Baker, Brian. "The Resurrection of Desire: J. G. Ballard's *Crash* as a Transgressive Text." *Foundation* 80 (2000), 84–95.

Botting, Fred, and Scott Wilson. "Automatic Lover." *Screen* 39 (1998), 186–92.

Bozzetto, Roger. *Territoires des fantastiques*, 197–201.

Bruce, Donald. "L'inscription corporelle de la vitesse: La 'Nouvelle Décadence' dans *Crash* de J. G. Ballard." *Tangence* 55 (1997), 118–37.

Davis, Nick. "'An Unrehearsed Theatre of Technology': Oedipalization and Vision in Ballard's *Crash*," in David Seed, ed., *Imagining Apocalypse*, 136–49.

Day, Aidan. "Ballard and Baudrillard: Close Reading *Crash*." *English* 49 (2000), 277–93.

Grant, Michael. "Crimes of the Future." *Screen* 39 (1998), 180–85.

Gundman, Roy. "Plight of the Crash Fest Mummies: David Cronenberg's *Crash*." *Cineaste* 22:4 (1997), 24–27.

Luckhurst, Roger. *"The Angle Between Two Walls,"* 123–29.

Pordzik, Ralph. "James G. Ballard's *Crash* and the Postmodernization of the Dystopian Novel." *Arbeiten aus Anglistik und Amerikanistik* 24:1 (1999), 77–94.

Rodley, Chris. "Crash." *Sight and Sound* 6:6 (1996), 7–11.

Sey, James. "Psychoanalysis, Science Fiction and Cyborgianism." *Literator* 17:2 (1996), 105–16.

Sobchack, Vivian. "Beating the Meat/Surviving the Text, or How to Get Out of This Century Alive," in Paula A. Treichler et al., eds., *The Visible Woman*, 310–12.

Ziegler, Robert. "Reader-Text Collisions in J. G. Ballard's *Crash*." *Notes on Contemp Lit* 29:2 (1999), 10–12.

The Crystal World, 1966

Luckhurst, Roger. *"The Angle Between Two Walls,"* 58–61.

Orr, Leonard. "The Utopian Disasters of J. G. Ballard." *Coll Lang Assoc J* 43 (2000), 487–88.

The Drought, 1964

Luckhurst, Roger. *"The Angle Between Two Walls,"* 62–68.

Orr, Leonard. "The Utopian Disasters of J. G. Ballard." *Coll Lang Assoc J* 43 (2000), 486–87.

The Drowned World, 1962

Luckhurst, Roger. *"The Angle Between Two Walls,"* 53–58.

McCarthy, Patrick A. "Allusions in Ballard's *The Drowned World*." *Science-Fiction Stud* 24 (1997), 302–8.

Orr, Leonard. "The Utopian Disasters of J. G. Ballard." *Coll Lang Assoc J* 43 (2000), 484–86.

Empire of the Sun, 1984

Bényei, Tamás. "White Light: J. G. Ballard's *Empire of the Sun* as a War Story." *AnaChronist* 2000: 249–77.

Luckhurst, Roger. *"The Angle Between Two Walls,"* 153–68.

Hello America, 1981

Luckhurst, Roger. *"The Angle Between Two Walls,"* 140–50.

High-Rise, 1975

Orr, Leonard. "The Utopian Disasters of J. G. Ballard." *Coll Lang Assoc J* 43 (2000), 490–93.

The Kindness of Women, 1991
Luckhurst, Roger. *"The Angle Between Two Walls,"* 153–68.
Running Wild, 1969
Ziegler, Robert. "Mediation as Violence in J. G. Ballard's *Running Wild.*" *Notes on Contemp Lit* 30:1 (2000), 2–4.
Vermilion Sands, 1985
Luckhurst, Roger. *"The Angle Between Two Walls,"* 169–80.

RAMSDEN BALMFORTH

Landon Deecroft, 1886
Schäffner, Raimund. *Anarchismus und Literatur in England,* 249–51.

EDWARD BANCROFT

The History of Charles Wentworth, 1770
London, April. "Novel and Natural History: Edward Bancroft in Guiana." *Genre* 31:2 (1998), 101–16.
London, April. *Women and Property,* 91–96.

IAIN BANKS

Against a Dark Background, 1993
Middleton, Tim. "The Works of Iain M. Banks: A Critical Introduction." *Foundation* 76 (1999), 11–12.
Palmer, Christopher. "Galactic Empires and the Contemporary Extravaganza: Dan Simmons and Iain M. Banks." *Science-Fiction Stud* 26 (1999), 86–88.
Complicity, 1993
Walker, Marshall. *Scottish Literature since 1707,* 344–45.
Consider Phlebas, 1987
Guerrier, Simon. "Culture Theory: Iain M. Banks's 'Culture' as Utopia." *Foundation* 76 (1999), 28–37.
Middleton, Tim. "The Works of Iain M. Banks: A Critical Introduction." *Foundation* 76 (1999), 7–8.
Palmer, Christopher. "Galactic Empires and the Contemporary Extravaganza: Dan Simmons and Iain M. Banks." *Science-Fiction Stud* 26 (1999), 79–81.
The Crow Road, 1992
McMillan, Dorothy. "Constructed Out of Bewilderment: Stories of Scotland," in Ian A. Bell, ed., *Peripheral Visions,* 88–91.
Middleton, Tim. "The Works of Iain M. Banks: A Critical Introduction." *Foundation* 76 (1999), 5–7.
Excession, 1997
Guerrier, Simon. "Culture Theory: Iain M. Banks's 'Culture' as Utopia." *Foundation* 76 (1999), 28–37.

Middleton, Tim. "The Works of Iain M. Banks: A Critical Introduction." *Foundation* 76 (1999), 12–13.

Inversions, 1998

Middleton, Tim. "The Works of Iain M. Banks: A Critical Introduction." *Foundation* 76 (1999), 13–14.

The Player of Games, 1988

Guerrier, Simon. "Culture Theory: Iain M. Banks's 'Culture' as Utopia." *Foundation* 76 (1999), 28–37.

Use of Weapons, 1990

Guerrier, Simon. "Culture Theory: Iain M. Banks's 'Culture' as Utopia." *Foundation* 76 (1999), 28–37.

Hardesty, William H. "Mercenaries and Special Circumstances: Iain M. Banks's Counter-Narrative of Utopia, *Use of Weapons.*" *Foundation* 76 (1999), 39–47.

Middleton, Tim. "The Works of Iain M. Banks: A Critical Introduction." *Foundation* 76 (1999), 8–10.

Palmer, Christopher. "Galactic Empires and the Contemporary Extravaganza: Dan Simmons and Iain M. Banks." *Science-Fiction Stud* 26 (1999), 85–86.

Walking on Glass, 1985

Walker, Marshall. *Scottish Literature since 1707*, 345–47.

The Wasp Factory, 1984

Butler, Andrew M. "Strange Case of Mr Banks: Doubles and *The Wasp Factory.*" *Foundation* 76 (1999), 17–25.

Schoene-Harwood, Berthold. "Dams Burst: Devolving Gender in Iain Banks's *The Wasp Factory.*" *Ariel* 30:1 (1999), 131–47.

Walker, Marshall. *Scottish Literature since 1707*, 343–44.

LYNN REID BANKS

The L-Shaped Room, 1959

Dervin, Dan. *Matricentric Narratives*, 30–32.

JOHN BANVILLE

Athena, 1995

Izarra, Laura P. Zuntini de. *Mirrors and Holographic Labyrinths*, 143–56.

McMinn, Joseph. *The Supreme Fictions*, 129–40.

Birchwood, 1973

Corcoran, Neil. *After Yeats and Joyce*, 52–54.

Diez Fabre, Silvia. "The Conversational Approach to the Big House Novel Called into Question in the Work of John Banville." *Cuadernos de Literatura Inglesa y Norteamericana* 3:1–2 (1998), 63–75.

Izarra, Laura P. Zuntini de. *Mirrors and Holographic Labyrinths*, 29–48.

Kelleher, Margaret. *The Feminization of Famine*, 150–51.
Kreilkamp, Vera. *The Anglo-Irish Novel*, 247–56.
McMinn, Joseph. *The Supreme Fictions*, 32–45.
Skinner, John. *The Stepmother Tongue*, 283–84.

The Book of Evidence, 1989

Canon-Roger, Françoise. "John Banville's Imagines in *The Book of Evidence*." *European J of Engl Stud* 4:1 (2000), 25–38.
Izarra, Laura P. Zuntini de. *Mirrors and Holographic Labyrinths*, 129–35.
Jackson, Tony E. "Science, Art, and the Shipwreck of Knowledge: The Novels of John Banville." *Contemp Lit* 38 (1997), 515–32.
McMinn, Joseph. *The Supreme Fictions*, 101–15.

Doctor Copernicus, 1976

Booker, M. Keith. "Cultural Crisis Then and Now: Science, Literature, and Religion in John Banville's *Doctor Copernicus* and *Kepler*." *Critique* (Washington, DC) 39 (1998), 176–84.
Izarra, Laura P. Zuntini de. *Mirrors and Holographic Labyrinths*, 61–80.
Jackson, Tony E. "Science, Art, and the Shipwreck of Knowledge: The Novels of John Banville." *Contemp Lit* 38 (1997), 512–13.
McMinn, Joseph. *The Supreme Fictions*, 46–63.

Ghosts, 1993

Fiérobe, Claude. "Spectres et fin de siècle: *The Woman's Daughter* de Dermot Bolger et *Ghosts* de John Banville." *Etudes Irlandaises* 24:2 (1999), 99–112.
Ireland, Ken. "Rococo Paradise: Watteau's Cythera in Nayantara Sahgal and John Banville." *New Comparison* 21 (1996), 139–45.
Izarra, Laura P. Zuntini de. *Mirrors and Holographic Labyrinths*, 135–43, 147–49.
Jackson, Tony E. "Science, Art, and the Shipwreck of Knowledge: The Novels of John Banville." *Contemp Lit* 38 (1997), 515–32.
Louvel, Liliane. "Et quasi tristes sous leur déguisements fantasques.'" *Imaginaires* 3 (1998), 123–44.
Louvel, Liliane. "John Banville: *Ghosts*—'l'étoffe des rêves.'" *Etudes Irlandaises* 22:1 (1997), 35–51.
McMinn, Joseph. *The Supreme Fictions*, 116–28.
Reckwitz, Erhard. "Intertextuality: Between Continuity and Innovation," in Barbara Korte and Klaus Peter Müller, eds., *Unity in Diversity Revisited?*, 188–90.
Schwall, Hedwig. "Banville's Caliban as a Prestidigitator," in Nadia Lie and Theo D'haen, eds., *Constellation Caliban*, 291–311.
Schwenger, Peter. *Fantasm and Fiction*, 20–25.

Kepler, 1981

Booker, M. Keith. "Cultural Crisis Then and Now: Science, Literature, and Religion in John Banville's *Doctor Copernicus* and *Kepler*." *Critique* (Washington, DC) 39 (1998), 184–90.
Izarra, Laura P. Zuntini de. *Mirrors and Holographic Labyrinths*, 74–76, 80–96.

Jackson, Tony E. "Science, Art, and the Shipwreck of Knowledge: The Novels of John Banville." *Contemp Lit* 38 (1997), 512–13.

McMinn, Joseph. *The Supreme Fictions*, 64–80.

Mefisto, 1986

Izarra, Laura P. Zuntini de. *Mirrors and Holographic Labyrinths,* 113–23.

Jackson, Tony E. "Science, Art, and the Shipwreck of Knowledge: The Novels of John Banville." *Contemp Lit* 38 (1997), 514–15.

McMinn, Joseph. *The Supreme Fictions*, 91–100.

The Newton Letter, 1982

Frehner, Ruth. *The Colonizers' Daughters,* 137–48.

Izarra, Laura P. Zuntini de. *Mirrors and Holographic Labyrinths,* 97–107.

Jackson, Tony E. "Science, Art, and the Shipwreck of Knowledge: The Novels of John Banville." *Contemp Lit* 38 (1997), 513–14.

Kreilkamp, Vera. *The Anglo-Irish Novel,* 256–60.

McMinn, Joseph. *The Supreme Fictions*, 81–90.

Sharman, Gundula. "Elective Affinities with Ireland: John Banville's *The Newton Letter* and Goethe's *Die Wahlverwandtschaften,*" in Susanne Stark, ed., *The Novel in Anglo-German Context,* 369–83.

Nightspawn, 1971

Izarra, Laura P. Zuntini de. *Mirrors and Holographic Labyrinths,* 18–28.

McMinn, Joseph. *The Supreme Fictions*, 24–31.

The Untouchable, 1997

McMinn, Joseph. *The Supreme Fictions*, 141–56.

Mikowski, Sylvie. "*The Untouchable* de John Banville: portrait de l'artiste en menteur." *Etudes Irlandaises* 25:2 (2000), 141–54.

LELAND BARDWELL

Girl on a Bicycle, 1977

St. Peter, Christine. *Changing Ireland,* 53–56.

SABINE BARING-GOULD

Grettir the Outlaw, 1890

Wawn, Andrew. *The Vikings and the Victorians,* 296–99.

Winefred: A Story of the Chalk Cliffs, 1900

Trezise, Simon. *The West Country as a Literary Invention,* 180–90.

JAMES BARKE

The End of the High Bridge, 1935

Klaus, H. Gustav. "Writing Scotland in the 1930s: The Fiction of James Barke." *Recherches Anglaises et Nord-Américaines* 30 (1997), 69–70, 72.

The Land of the Leal, 1939

Klaus, H. Gustav. "Writing Scotland in the 1930s: The Fiction of James Barke." *Recherches Anglaises et Nord-Américaines* 30 (1997), 69–70, 72–75, 84–85.

Major Operation, 1941

Cunningham, Valentine. "The Age of Anxiety and Influence; or, Tradition and the Thirties Talents," in Keith Williams and Steven Matthews, eds., *Rewriting the Thirties,* 5–22.

Klaus, H. Gustav. "Writing Scotland in the 1930s: The Fiction of James Barke." *Recherches Anglaises et Nord-Américaines* 30 (1997), 75–81.

The Wild MacRaes, 1934

Klaus, H. Gustav. "Writing Scotland in the 1930s: The Fiction of James Barke." *Recherches Anglaises et Nord-Américaines* 30 (1997), 67–69.

The World His Pillow, 1933

Klaus, H. Gustav. "Writing Scotland in the 1930s: The Fiction of James Barke." *Recherches Anglaises et Nord-Américaines* 30 (1997), 63–67, 70–72, 81–82.

ELSPETH BARKER

O Caledonia, 1991

McMillan, Dorothy. "Constructed Out of Bewilderment: Stories of Scotland," in Ian A. Bell, ed., *Peripheral Visions,* 93–95.

JANE BARKER

Exilius, or, The Banished Roman, 1715

King, Kathryn R. *Jane Barker, Exile,* 150–54.

The Lining of the Patch-Work Screen, 1726

Donovan, Josephine. "Women and the Framed-Novelle: A Tradition of Their Own." *Signs* 22 (1997), 972–75.

King, Kathryn R. *Jane Barker, Exile,* 164–69, 213–17.

Spencer, Jane. *Aphra Behn's Afterlife,* 167–73.

Love's Intrigues, 1713

Backscheider, Paula R. "The Novel's Gendered Space," in Backscheider, ed., *Revising Women,* 10–13.

Doody, Margaret Anne. "Deserts, Ruins and Troubled Waters: Female Dreams in Fiction and the Development of the Gothic Novel," in Richard Kroll, ed., *The English Novel, Volume II,* 58–60.

King, Kathryn R. *Jane Barker, Exile,* 182–92.

A Patch-Work Screen for the Ladies, 1723

Anderson, Misty G. "Tactile Places: Materializing Desire in Margaret Cavendish and Jane Barker." *Textual Practice* 13 (1999), 329–49.

Donovan, Josephine. "Women and the Framed-Novelle: A Tradition of Their Own." *Signs* 22 (1997), 972–75.

King, Kathryn R. *Jane Barker, Exile,* 72–75, 162–64, 193–213, 221–32.

King, Kathryn R. "Of Needles and Pens and Women's Work." *Tulsa Stud in Women's Lit* 14:1 (1995), 77–93.
Spencer, Jane. *Aphra Behn's Afterlife*, 167–73.

PAT BARKER

Blow Your House Down, 1984

Armitt, Lucie. *Contemporary Women's Fiction*, 195–98.
Kirk, John. "Recovered Perspectives: Gender, Class, and Memory in Pat Barker's Writing." *Contemp Lit* 40 (1999), 603–24.

The Century's Daughter, 1986

Kirk, John. "Recovered Perspectives: Gender, Class, and Memory in Pat Barker's Writing." *Contemp Lit* 40 (1999), 603–24.

The Eye in the Door, 1993

Bergonzi, Bernard. *War Poets,* 3–14.
Lanone, Catherine. "'No man's land': les fantômes asexués de Pat Barker," in Sophie Marret, ed., *Féminin/Masculin,* 110–15.
Löschnigg, Martin. "'. . . the novelist's responsibility to the past': History, Myth, and the Narratives of Crisis in Pat Barker's Regeneration Trilogy (1991–1995)." *Zeitschrift für Anglistik und Amerikanistik* 47 (1999), 214–28.
Waterman, David F. *Disordered Bodies and Disrupted Borders,* 112–20.

The Ghost Road, 1995

Bergonzi, Bernard. *War Poets,* 3–14.
Harris, Greg. "Compulsory Masculinity, Britain, and the Great War: The Literary-Historical Work of Pat Barker." *Critique* (Washington, DC) 39 (1998), 296–97.
Lanone, Catherine. "'No man's land': les fantômes asexués de Pat Barker," in Sophie Marret, ed., *Féminin/Masculin,* 115–21.
Lanone, Catherine. "Scattering the Seed of Abraham: The Motif of Sacrifice in Pat Barker's *Regeneration* and *The Ghost Road*." *Lit and Theology* 13 (1999), 259–67.
Löschnigg, Martin. "'. . . the novelist's responsibility to the past': History, Myth, and the Narratives of Crisis in Pat Barker's Regeneration Trilogy (1991–1995)." *Zeitschrift für Anglistik und Amerikanistik* 47 (1999), 214–28.
Waterman, David F. *Disordered Bodies and Disrupted Borders,* 112–20.

The Man Who Wasn't There, 1989

Byatt, A. S. *On Histories and Stories,* 29–30.

Regeneration, 1991

Bergonzi, Bernard. *War Poets,* 3–14.
Byatt, A. S. *On Histories and Stories,* 30–31.
Harris, Greg. "Compulsory Masculinity, Britain, and the Great War: The Literary-Historical Work of Pat Barker." *Critique* (Washington, DC) 39 (1998), 292–303.

Hickman, Alan F. "Looking Before and After: The Search for the 'Inner Warrior' in Today's British Novel." *Publs of the Arkansas Philol Assoc* 25:1 (1999), 46–50.

Lanone, Catherine. "'No man's land': les fantômes asexués de Pat Barker," in Sophie Marret, ed., *Féminin/Masculin*, 109–10.

Lanone, Catherine. "Scattering the Seed of Abraham: The Motif of Sacrifice in Pat Barker's *Regeneration* and *The Ghost Road*." *Lit and Theology* 13 (1999), 259–67.

Löschnigg, Martin. "'. . . the novelist's responsibility to the past': History, Myth, and the Narratives of Crisis in Pat Barker's Regeneration Trilogy (1991–1995)." *Zeitschrift für Anglistik und Amerikanistik* 47 (1999), 214–28.

Middleton, Peter, and Tim Woods. *Literatures of Memory*, 86–92.

Sinker, Mark. "Temporary Gentlemen." *Sight and Sound* 7:12 (1997), 22–24.

Waterman, David F. *Disordered Bodies and Disrupted Borders*, 112–20.

Whitehead, Anne. "Open to Suggestion: Hypnosis and History in Pat Barker's *Regeneration*." *Mod Fiction Stud* 44 (1998), 674–92.

Union Street, 1982

Haywood, Ian. *Working-Class Fiction*, 145–47.

Kirk, John. "Recovered Perspectives: Gender, Class, and Memory in Pat Barker's Writing." *Contemp Lit* 40 (1999), 603–24.

Malm, Monica. "*Union Street*: Thoughts on Mothering." *Moderna Sprak* 92:2 (1998), 143–46.

Wotton, George. "Writing from the Margins," in Ian A. Bell, ed., *Peripheral Visions*, 206–14.

JULIAN BARNES

Before She Met Me, 1982

Moseley, Merritt. *Understanding Julian Barnes*, 54–68.

Cross Channel, 1996

Freiburg, Rudolf. "Imagination in Contemporary British Fiction," in Barbara Korte and Klaus Peter Müller, eds., *Unity in Diversity Revisited?*, 239–44.

Duffy, 1980

Moseley, Merritt. *Understanding Julian Barnes*, 33–42.

Fiddle City, 1981

Moseley, Merritt. *Understanding Julian Barnes*, 42–45.

Flaubert's Parrot, 1984

Antor, Heinz. "(Post-)Moderne Historiographie und Biographie im englischen Roman des 20. Jahrhunderts: Virginia Woolf und Julian Barnes," in Rüdiger Ahrens and Fritz-Wilhelm Neumann, eds., *Fiktion und Geschichte*, 420–28.

Brooks, Neil. "Interred Textuality: *The Good Soldier* and *Flaubert's Parrot*." *Critique* (Washington, DC) 41 (1999), 45–51.

Doody, Terrence. *Among Other Things*, 188–90, 193–202.
Freiburg, Rudolf. *"'Just Voices Echoing in the Dark'*: Geschichte als literarisches Genre bei Julian Barnes," in Rüdiger Ahrens and Fritz-Wilhelm Neumann, eds., *Fiktion und Geschichte*, 434–37.
Johnston, Georgia. "Textualizing Ellen: The Patriarchal 'I' of *Flaubert's Parrot*." *West Virginia Univ Philol Papers* 46 (2000), 64–69.
Moseley, Merritt. *Understanding Julian Barnes*, 69–90.
Nünning, Ansgar. "'How do we seize the past?': Julian Barnes' fiktionale Metabiographie *Flaubert's Parrot* als Paradigma historiographischer und biographischer Metafiktion." *Literatur in Wissenschaft und Unterricht* 31 (1998), 145–67.
Raykowski, Harald. "Gegenwartsromane im Englischunterricht? Julian Barnes und der neue historische Roman." *Neusprachliche Mitteilungen aus Wissenschaft und Praxis* 50:2 (1997), 93–97.
Shepherd, Tania. "Towards a Description of Atypical Narratives: A Study of the Underlying Organisation of *Flaubert's Parrot*." *Lang and Discourse* 5 (1997), 71–95.

Going to the Dogs, 1987

Moseley, Merritt. *Understanding Julian Barnes*, 49–53.

A History of the World in 10 1/2 Chapters, 1989

Bernard, Catherine. "A Certain Hermeneutic Slant: Sublime Allegories in Contemporary English Fiction." *Contemp Lit* 38 (1997), 166–69.
Buxton, Jackie. "Julian Barnes's Theses on History (in 10 1/2 Chapters)." *Contemp Lit* 41 (2000), 56–85.
Byatt, A. S. *On Histories and Stories*, 48–51.
Candel, Daniel. "Julian Barnes's *A History of Science in 10 1/2 Chapters*." *Engl Stud* (Amsterdam) 82 (2001), 253–60.
Freiburg, Rudolf. *"'Just Voices Echoing in the Dark'*: Geschichte als literarisches Genre bei Julian Barnes," in Rüdiger Ahrens and Fritz-Wilhelm Neumann, eds., *Fiktion und Geschichte*, 438–45.
Hallet, Wolfgang. *"A History of the World in 10 1/2 Chapters*: Ein Hinweis auf Julian Barnes' postmoderne Weltgeschichte." *Anglistik und Englischunterricht* 49 (1993), 137–48.
Kotte, Claudia. "Random Patterns? Orderly Disorder in Julian Barnes's *A History of the World in 10 and 1/2 Chapters*." *Arbeiten aus Anglistik und Amerikanistik* 22:1 (1997), 107–28.
Moseley, Merritt. *Understanding Julian Barnes*, 108–24.
Raykowski, Harald. "Gegenwartsromane im Englischunterricht? Julian Barnes und der neue historische Roman." *Neusprachliche Mitteilungen aus Wissenschaft und Praxis* 50:2 (1997), 93–97.
Samb, Bathie. "Histoire, fiction et remaniement de soi dans *A History of the World in 10 1/2 Chapters* de Julian Barnes." *Bridges* (Dakar) 7 (1996), 107–27.

Metroland, 1980

Moseley, Merritt. *Understanding Julian Barnes*, 18–32.

The Porcupine, 1992

Brînzeu, Pia. *Corridors of Mirrors*, 108–10.

Freiburg, Rudolf. "*'Just Voices Echoing in the Dark'*: Geschichte als literarisches Genre bei Julian Barnes," in Rüdiger Ahrens and Fritz-Wilhelm Neumann, eds., *Fiktion und Geschichte*, 445–51.

Moseley, Merritt. *Understanding Julian Barnes*, 145–57.

Noll, Marcus, and Christoph Reinfandt. "Das Stachelschwein im Klassenraum: Gegenwartsliteratur im Englischunterricht der Oberstufe—Ein Vorschlag zur Behandlung von Julian Barnes' Roman *The Porcupine.*" *Literatur in Wissenschaft und Unterricht* 33 (2000), 159–78.

Reinfandt, Christoph. *Der Sinn der fiktionalen Wirklichkeiten*, 255–81.

Putting the Boot In, 1985

Moseley, Merritt. *Understanding Julian Barnes*, 45–49.

Staring at the Sun, 1986

Moseley, Merritt. *Understanding Julian Barnes*, 91–107.

Talking It Over, 1991

Moseley, Merritt. *Understanding Julian Barnes*, 125–44.

EATON STANNARD BARRETT

The Heroine; or Adventures of a Fair Romance Reader, 1813

Pearson, Jacqueline. *Women's Reading in Britain*, 206–9.

JAMES MATTHEW BARRIE

The Little Minister, 1891

Nash, Andrew. "From Realism to Romance: Gender and Narrative Technique in J. M. Barrie's *The Little Minister.*" *Scottish Liter J* 26:1 (1999), 77–91.

Peter Pan in Kensington Gardens, 1906

Hunt, Peter. *Children's Literature*, 202–4.

McGavran, James Holt. "Wordsworth, Lost Boys, and Romantic Hom(e)ophobia," in McGavran, ed., *Literature and the Child*, 138–40.

Morris, Tim. *You're Only Young Twice*, 87–92, 107–18.

Sentimental Tommy, 1896

Nash, Andrew. "'A Phenomenally Slow Producer': J. M. Barrie, Scribner's, and the Publication of *Sentimental Tommy.*" *Yale Univ Lib Gazette* 74:1–2 (1999), 41–53.

Nash, Andrew. "'Trying to Be a Man': J. M. Barrie and Sentimental Masculinity." *Forum for Mod Lang Stud* 35 (1999), 116–24.

Tommy and Grizel, 1900

Nash, Andrew. "'Trying to Be a Man': J. M. Barrie and Sentimental Masculinity." *Forum for Mod Lang Stud* 35 (1999), 116–24.

STAN BARSTOW

A Kind of Loving, 1960

Haywood, Ian. *Working-Class Fiction*, 107–9.

COLIN BATEMAN

Divorcing Jack, 1995
Smyth, Gerry. *The Novel and the Nation*, 123–26.

AUBREY BEARDSLEY

Venus and Tannhäuser, 1907
Doroholschi, Claudia Ioana. "The Story of *Venus and Tannhäuser*:
The Challenges of the Surface." *B.A.S.: Brit and Am Stud* 6 (2000),
73–77.

MARY BECKETT

Give Them Stones, 1987
St. Peter, Christine. *Changing Ireland*, 114–16.
Smyth, Gerry. *The Novel and the Nation*, 135–38.
Sullivan, Megan. "'Instead I Said I Am a Home Baker': Nationalist
Ideology and Materialist Politics in Mary Beckett's *Give Them
Stones*," in Kathryn Kirkpatrick, ed., *Border Crossings*, 227–45.
Sullivan, Megan. *Women in Northern Ireland*, 40–65.

SAMUEL BECKETT

Company, 1980
Axelrod, Mark. *The Poetics of Novels*, 205–13.
Brown, Llewellyn. "La voix, signe de l'impossible chez Samuel Beckett,"
in Marius Buning et al., eds., *Beckett versus Beckett*, 173–74.
Butler, Lance St. John. *Registering the Difference*, 133–35.
Cohn, Ruby. *A Beckett Canon*, 349–55.
Federman, Raymond. "*Company*: The Voice of Language," in Henry
Sussman and Christopher Devenney, eds., *Engagement and
Indifference*, 11–18.
Fraser, Graham. "'No More Than Ghosts Make': The Hauntology and
Gothic Minimalism of Beckett's Late Work." *Mod Fiction Stud* 46
(2000), 780–83.
Ghose, Zulfikar. "Beckett's *Company*." *Raritan* 14:3 (1995), 141–50.
Gibson, Andrew. *Postmodernity, Ethics and the Novel*, 141–43.
Houppermans, Sjef. "Proust and Beckett: Visions of Mourning," in
Wim Tigges, ed., *Moments of Moment*, 347–49.
Jopling, Michael. "'Es gibt ja nur Gescheitertes': Bernhard as
Company for Beckett." *J of European Stud* 27 (1997), 52–60.
Katz, Daniel. *Saying I No More*, 160–74.
Krance, Charles. "French for *Company*," in Bruce Stewart, ed.,
Beckett and Beyond, 187–92.
Lawley, Paul. "'The Scene of My Disgrace': 'Enough' and 'Memory,'"
in Marius Buning et al., eds., *Beckett versus Beckett*, 262–74.
Long, Joseph. "The Reading of *Company*: Beckett and the Bi-Textual
Work." *Forum for Mod Lang Stud* 32 (1996), 314–27.

McCrudden, Ian C. "The Phenomenon of the Voice in *Company*: Listening to the 'I.'" *Constructions* 9 (1994), 47–60.

Milne, Drew. "The Dissident Imagination: Beckett's Late Prose Fiction," in Rod Mengham, ed., *An Introduction to Contemporary Fiction*, 103–4.

Roesler, L. M. "Beckett lecteur de Descartes: vers une métaphysique parodique," in Michèle Touret, ed., *Lectures de Beckett*, 183–200. (Also in *Romanic R* 87 [1996], 557–74.)

Schlüter, Gisela. "Beckett on Page and Stage: *Company/Compagnie*." *Romanistische Zeitschrift für Literaturgeschichte* 19:1–2 (1995), 132–52.

Toonder, Jeanette den. "*Compagnie*: Chimère autobiographique et métatexte," in Sjef Houppermans, ed., *Beckett & La Psychanalyse*, 143–51.

Wilson, Ian W. "'Confusion too is company up to a point': Irony, Self-Translation and the Text of Samuel Beckett's *Company/Compagnie*." *Canadian R of Compar Lit* 26 (1999), 94–104.

Wood, Michael. *Children of Silence*, 37–40.

Wulf, Catharina. *The Imperative of Narration*, 148–56.

How It Is, 1964

Boulter, Jonathan. "'A word from me and I am again': Repetition and Suffering in Samuel Beckett's *How It Is*." *LIT* 9 (1998), 85–99.

Bryden, Mary. *Samuel Beckett and the Idea of God*, 117–18, 136–37, 150–52.

Cohn, Ruby. *A Beckett Canon*, 254–62.

Cousineau, Tom. "The Lost Father in Beckett's Novels," in Sjef Houppermans, ed., *Beckett & La Psychanalyse*, 81–83.

Devenney, Christopher. "What Remains?," in Henry Sussman and Christopher Devenney, eds., *Engagement and Indifference*, 148–50.

Gowd, Garin. "Mud as Plane of Immanence in *How It Is*." *J of Beckett Stud* 8:2 (1999), 1–23.

Hardy, Barbara. "Samuel Beckett: Adapting Objects and Adapting to Objects," in Bruce Stewart, ed., *Beckett and Beyond*, 151–52.

Haughton, Hugh. "Purgatory Regained? Dante and Late Beckett," in Nick Havely, ed., *Dante's Modern Afterlife*, 147–54.

Heise, Ursula K. *Chronoschisms*, 147–75.

Locatelli, Carla. "Beckett's 'Obligation to Express': From a Mythology of Demystification to the Utterance of Better Failures," in Bruce Stewart, ed., *Beckett and Beyond*, 199–202.

Moore, Patrick J. "*Ars Poetica*: A Study of Samuel Beckett's *How It Is* (*Comment c'est*)." *J of Evolutionary Psych* 17:1–2 (1996), 82–89.

Olsen, Lance. "Narrative Overdrive: Postmodern Fantasy, Deconstruction, and Cultural Critique in Beckett and Barthelme," in Brett Cooke et al., eds., *The Fantastic Other*, 78–80.

O'Reilly, Magessa. "Ni prose ni vers: *Comment c'est* de Samuel Beckett." *Dalhousie French Stud* 35 (1996), 45–53.

Pien, Nicolas. "Le Rôle de *Comment c'est* dans l'évolution de la forme littéraire chez S. Beckett." *Littératures* 42 (2000), 143–60.

Smith, Frederik N. "Beckett and Berkeley: A Reconsideration," in Marius Buning et al., eds., *Beckett versus Beckett*, 341–44.

Terry, Philip. "Waiting for God to Go: *How It Is* and *Inferno* VII–VIII," in Marius Buning et al., eds., *Beckett versus Beckett*, 349–60.

Ill Seen Ill Said, 1982

Baker, Phil. *Beckett and the Mythology of Psychoanalysis*, 153–65.

Catanzaro, Mary F. "Deleuze, Guattari, and the Shadowy Other: Samuel Beckett's *Ill Seen Ill Said.*" *Notes on Mod Irish Lit* 10 (1998), 40–45.

Cohn, Ruby. *A Beckett Canon*, 363–69.

Fraser, Graham. "'No More Than Ghosts Make': The Hauntology and Gothic Minimalism of Beckett's Late Work." *Mod Fiction Stud* 46 (2000), 777–83.

Hansen, Joel. "Seeing without a Subject: Reading *Ill Seen Ill Said.*" *J of Beckett Stud* 6:2 (1997), 63–84.

Houppermans, Sjef. "Proust and Beckett: Visions of Mourning," in Wim Tigges, ed., *Moments of Moment*, 349–50.

Milne, Drew. "The Dissident Imagination: Beckett's Late Prose Fiction," in Rod Mengham, ed., *An Introduction to Contemporary Fiction*, 104–6.

Smock, Ann. "Patchwork Beckett." *L'Esprit Créateur* 40:1 (2000), 61–67.

Tagliaferri, Aldo. "*Ill Seen Ill Said*: A Sacrificial Workshop," in Bruce Stewart, ed., *Beckett and Beyond*, 246–53.

Wood, Michael. *Children of Silence*, 40–42.

Wulf, Catharina. *The Imperative of Narration*, 148–50, 156–59.

The Lost Ones, 1971

Baker, Phil. *Beckett and the Mythology of Psychoanalysis*, 90–92, 124–27.

Casanova, Pascal. "Beckett chez les philosophes," in Marius Buning et al., eds., *Beckett versus Beckett*, 370–73.

Casanova, Pascal. *Beckett l'abstracteur*, 108–16.

Cohn, Ruby. *A Beckett Canon*, 308–14.

Devenney, Christopher. "What Remains?," in Henry Sussman and Christopher Devenney, eds., *Engagement and Indifference*, 148–49.

Dowd, Garin. "The Abstract Literary Machine: Guattari, Deleuze and Beckett's *The Lost Ones.*" *Forum for Mod Lang Stud* 37 (2001), 204–15.

Haughton, Hugh. "Purgatory Regained? Dante and Late Beckett," in Nick Havely, ed., *Dante's Modern Afterlife*, 154–55.

McHale, Brian. "Lost in the Mall: Beckett, Federman, Space," in Henry Sussman and Christopher Devenney, eds., *Engagement and Indifference*, 112–22.

Milne, Drew. "The Dissident Imagination: Beckett's Late Prose Fiction," in Rod Mengham, ed., *An Introduction to Contemporary Fiction*, 101–3.

Oppenheim, Lois. *The Painted Word*, 168–71.

Schwab, Gabriele. "Cosmographical Meditations on the In/Human:

Beckett's *The Lost Ones* and Lyotard's 'Scapeland.'" *Parallax* 6:4 (2000), 58–75.

Watson, David. "The Fictional Body: *Le Dépeupleur, Bing, Imagination morte imaginez*," in Jennifer Birkett and Kate Ince, eds., *Samuel Beckett*, 165–68.

Malone Dies, 1956

Alsop, Derek, and Chris Walsh. *The Practice of Reading*, 140–62.

Athanasopoulou-Kypriou, Spyridoula. "Samuel Beckett Beyond the Problem of Good." *Lit and Theology* 14 (2000), 40–48.

Begam, Richard. "Samuel Beckett and Antihumanism." *REAL: Yrbk of Res in Engl and Am Lit* 13 (1997), 301–10.

Begam, Richard. *Samuel Beckett and the End of Modernity*, 120–48.

Billy, Ted. "'Nothing to Be Done': Conrad, Beckett, and the Poetics of Immobility." *Conradiana* 32 (2000), 66–71.

Boxall, Peter. "'The Existence I Ascribe': Memory, Invention, and Autobiography in Beckett's Fiction." *Yrbk of Engl Stud* 30 (2000), 138–43.

Brush, AnJanette. "The Same Old Hag: Gender and (In)Difference in Samuel Beckett's *Trilogy*," in Henry Sussman and Christopher Devenney, eds., *Engagement and Indifference*, 126–37.

Butler, Lance St. John. *Registering the Difference*, 159–65.

Cohn, Ruby. *A Beckett Canon*, 168–76.

Collinge, Linda. "Auto-Traduction et Auto-Censure dans *Malone meurt/Malone Dies*: Beckett traduit devant le tribunal de sa langue maternelle," in Marius Buning et al., eds., *Beckett versus Beckett*, 57–71.

Collinge, Linda. *Beckett traduit Beckett*, 29–187.

Cousineau, Thomas. "Anti-Oedipal Tendencies in the Trilogy," in Bruce Stewart, ed., *Beckett and Beyond*, 70–77.

Cousineau, Tom. "The Lost Father in Beckett's Novels," in Sjef Houppermans, ed., *Beckett & La Psychanalyse*, 77–78.

Critchley, Simon. "Who Speaks in the Work of Samuel Beckett?" *Yale French Stud* 93 (1998), 114–30.

Dowd, Garin V. "Nomadology: Reading the Beckettian Baroque." *J of Beckett Stud* 8:1 (1998), 24–28.

Duffy, Brian. "*Malone meurt*: The Comfort of Narrative." *J of Beckett Stud* 6:1 (1996), 25–47.

Gleason, Paul. "Dante, Joyce, Beckett, and the Use of Memory in the Process of Literary Creation." *Joyce Stud Annual* 10 (1999), 104–40.

Grossman, Evelyne. *L'Esthétique de Beckett*, 41–74.

Hill, Leslie. "The Trilogy Translated," in Jennifer Birkett and Kate Ince, eds., *Samuel Beckett*, 99–114.

Hill, Leslie. "'Up the Republic!': Beckett, Writing, Politics." *Mod Lang Notes* 112 (1997), 911–17.

Josipovici, Gabriel. *On Trust*, 246–49.

Katz, Daniel. *Saying I No More*, 95–100.

Lawley, Paul. "'The Rapture of Vertigo': Beckett's Turning-Point." *Mod Lang R* 95 (2000), 29–32.

Lawley, Paul. "'The Scene of My Disgrace': 'Enough' and 'Memory,'" in Marius Buning et al., eds., *Beckett versus Beckett*, 266–71.

Mihály, Arpád. "'I Too Have the Right to Be Shown Impossible': Re-Reading the *Beckett Trilogy*." *AnaChronist* 1997: 93–112.

Pultar, Gönül. *Technique and Tradition*, 31–70, 93–129, 131–61.

Ross, Ciaran. "La 'pensée de la mère': Fonction et structure d'un fantasme," in Sjef Houppermans, ed., *Beckett & La Psychanalyse*, 14–15.

Schwalm, Helga. "Beckett's Trilogy and the Limits of Self-Deconstruction." *Samuel Beckett Today* 6 (1997), 181–91.

Uhlmann, Anthony. *Beckett and Poststructuralism*, 91–106, 120–31.

Uhlmann, Anthony. "To Have Done with Judgment: Beckett and Deleuze." *SubStance* 25:3 (1996), 110–31.

Wulf, Catharina. *The Imperative of Narration*, 67–71, 84–88.

Mercier and Camier, 1970

Cohn, Ruby. *A Beckett Canon*, 133–40.

Gaffney, Phyllis. "Neither Here Nor There: Ireland, Saint-Lô, and Beckett's First Novel in French." *J of Beckett Stud* 9:1 (1999), 1–18.

Pilling, John. *Beckett before Godot*, 202–12.

Shidlo, Anna. "'The Horror of Existence': A Labyrinth of Evasions in *Mercier et Camier*," in Marius Buning et al., eds., *Beckett versus Beckett*, 231–39.

Molloy, 1955

Ackerley, Chris. "Forest Murmurs: Beckett, Molloy and Siegfried." *J of Beckett Stud* 8:2 (1999), 73–74.

Alsop, Derek, and Chris Walsh. *The Practice of Reading*, 140–62.

Athanasopoulou-Kypriou. Spyridoula. "Samuel Beckett Beyond the Problem of Good." *Lit and Theology* 14 (2000), 38–48.

Baker, Phil. *Beckett and the Mythology of Psychoanalysis*, 37–47.

Bataille, Georges. "Molloy's Silence," in Jennifer Birkett and Kate Ince, eds., *Samuel Beckett*, 85–92.

Begam, Richard. "Samuel Beckett and Antihumanism." *REAL: Yrbk of Res in Engl and Am Lit* 13 (1997), 301–10.

Begam, Richard. *Samuel Beckett and the End of Modernity*, 98–119.

Bernard, Michel. "Stratégies du désir: Parole contre langage," in Marius Buning et al., eds., *Beckett versus Beckett*, 207–14.

Billy, Ted. "'Nothing to Be Done': Conrad, Beckett, and the Poetics of Immobility." *Conradiana* 32 (2000), 66–71.

Boxall, Peter. "'The Existence I Ascribe': Memory, Invention, and Autobiography in Beckett's Fiction." *Yrbk of Engl Stud* 30 (2000), 138–43.

Brush, AnJanette. "The Same Old Hag: Gender and (In)Difference in Samuel Beckett's *Trilogy*," in Henry Sussman and Christopher Devenney, eds., *Engagement and Indifference*, 126–37.

Bryden, Mary. *Samuel Beckett and the Idea of God*, 52–54, 56–57, 72–77.

Butler, Lance St. John. *Registering the Difference*, 159–65.

Cohn, Ruby. *A Beckett Canon*, 161–68.

Cousineau, Thomas. "Anti-Oedipal Tendencies in the Trilogy," in Bruce Stewart, ed., *Beckett and Beyond*, 70–77.

Cousineau, Tom. "The Lost Father in Beckett's Novels," in Sjef Houppermans, ed., *Beckett & La Psychanalyse*, 76–77.

Critchley, Simon. "Who Speaks in the Work of Samuel Beckett?" *Yale French Stud* 93 (1998), 114–30.

Duerfahrd, Lance. "Beckett's Circulation: Molloy's Dereliction," in C. W. Spinks and John Deely, eds., *Semiotics 1996*, 144–50.

Duffy, Brian. "*Molloy*: As the Story Was Told. Or Not," in Marius Buning et al., eds., *Beckett versus Beckett*, 177–92.

Furlani, André. "Samuel Beckett's *Molloy*: Spartan Maieutics," in Sjef Houppermans, ed., *Beckett & La Psychanalyse*, 105–19.

Grossman, Evelyne. *L'Esthétique de Beckett*, 41–74.

Hardy, Barbara. "Samuel Beckett: Adapting Objects and Adapting to Objects," in Bruce Stewart, ed., *Beckett and Beyond*, 149–51.

Hill, Leslie. "The Trilogy Translated," in Jennifer Birkett and Kate Ince, eds., *Samuel Beckett*, 99–114.

Hill, Leslie. "'Up the Republic!': Beckett, Writing, Politics." *Mod Lang Notes* 112 (1997), 921–25.

Josipovici, Gabriel. *On Trust*, 239–43.

Katz, Daniel. *Saying I No More*, 31–33, 71–94, 157–60.

King, Adele. "Camus and Beckett: *L'étranger*, *Molloy* and *En attendant Godot*," in Bruce Stewart, ed., *Beckett and Beyond*, 168–74.

Lawley, Paul. "'The Rapture of Vertigo': Beckett's Turning-Point." *Mod Lang R* 95 (2000), 28–29.

Levy, Eric P. "The Beckettian Mimesis of Seeing Nothing." *Univ of Toronto Q* 70 (2001), 623–24.

Levy, Eric P. "Living Without a Life: The Disintegration of the Christian-Humanist Synthesis in *Molloy*." *Stud in the Novel* 33:1 (2001), 80–91.

McGinnis, Reginald. "The Turdy Madonna: Religion and the Novel in George Sand and Samuel Beckett." *Cincinnati Romance R* 18 (1999), 54–60.

Meche, Jude R. "'A Country that Called Itself His': *Molloy* and Beckett's Estranged Relationship with Ireland." *Colby Q* 36 (2000), 226–40.

Mihály, Arpád. "'I Too Have the Right to Be Shown Impossible': Re-Reading the *Beckett Trilogy*." *AnaChronist* 1997: 93–112.

Prigent, Christian. "A Descent from Clowns," in Henry Sussman and Christopher Devenney, eds., *Engagement and Indifference*, 58–78.

Pultar, Gönül. *Technique and Tradition*, 1–30, 93–129, 131–61.

Richardson, Brian. *Unlikely Stories*, 128–38.

Ross, Ciaran. "La 'pensée de la mère': Fonction et structure d'un fantasme," in Sjef Houppermans, ed., *Beckett & La Psychanalyse*, 10–14.

Schwalm, Helga. "Beckett's Trilogy and the Limits of Self-Deconstruction." *Samuel Beckett Today* 6 (1997), 181–91.

Trezise, Thomas. "Dispossession," in Jennifer Birkett and Kate Ince, eds., *Samuel Beckett*, 138–51.

Uhlmann, Anthony. *Beckett and Poststructuralism*, 40–59, 67–87.

Weisberg, David. *Chronicles of Disorder*, 83–97, 102–16.

Wulf, Catharina. *The Imperative of Narration*, 61–67, 84–88.

Murphy, 1938

Ackerley, C. J. "The Annotated *Murphy*." *J of Beckett Stud* 7:1–2 (1998), ix–xxvi, 1–215.

Ackerley, Chris. "'Do Not Despair': Samuel Beckett and Robert Greene." *J of Beckett Stud* 6:1 (1996), 119–24.

Ackerley, Chris. "Samuel Beckett's Sibilants; or, Why Does Murphy Hiss?" *J of Beckett Stud* 8:1 (1998), 119–20.

Ackerley, Chris J. "Beckett's *Murphy*." *Explicator* 55:4 (1997), 226–27.

Begam, Richard. *Samuel Beckett and the End of Modernity*, 38–65.

Bisschops, Ralph. "Entropie et *élan vital* chez Beckett," in Sjef Houppermans, ed., *Beckett & La Psychanalyse*, 126–28.

Brockmeier, Peter. "Komisches Unglück: Erzähler und Erzählfiguren Samuel Becketts," in Peter Brockmeier and Carola Veit, eds., *Komik und Solipsismus*, 239–54.

Butler, Lance St. John. *Registering the Difference*, 155–58.

Casanova, Pascal. *Beckett l'abstracteur*, 52–56, 95–100.

Cavaliero, Glen. *The Alchemy of Laughter*, 204–6.

Cohn, Ruby. *A Beckett Canon*, 73–85.

Cousineau, Tom. "The Lost Father in Beckett's Novels," in Sjef Houppermans, ed., *Beckett & La Psychanalyse*, 74–75.

Elam, Keir. "World's End: West Brompton, Turdy and Other Godforsaken Holes." *Samuel Beckett Today* 6 (1997), 165–75.

Gray, Katherine Martin. "Beckettian Interiority," in Sjef Houppermans, ed., *Beckett & La Psychanalyse*, 97–100.

Grossman, Evelyne. *L'Esthétique de Beckett*, 26–28.

Katz, Daniel. *Saying I No More*, 28–42.

Kiely, Declan D. "'The Termination of This Solitaire': A Textual Error in *Murphy*." *J of Beckett Stud* 6:1 (1996), 135–36.

Korte, Barbara. *Body Language in Literature*, 160–62.

Miller, Tyrus. *Late Modernism*, 186–200.

Pilling, John. *Beckett before Godot*, 125–48.

Rabaté, Jean-Michel. "Beckett's Ghosts and Fluxions," in Sjef Houppermans, ed., *Beckett & La Psychanalyse*, 25–31.

Weisberg, David. *Chronicles of Disorder*, 30–41.

The Unnamable, 1958

Alsop, Derek, and Chris Walsh. *The Practice of Reading*, 140–62.

Athanasopoulou-Kypriou. Spyridoula. "Samuel Beckett Beyond the Problem of Good." *Lit and Theology* 14 (2000), 36–48.

Begam, Richard. "Samuel Beckett and Antihumanism." *REAL: Yrbk of Res in Engl and Am Lit* 13 (1997), 301–10.

Begam, Richard. *Samuel Beckett and the End of Modernity*, 149–83.

Billy, Ted. "'Nothing to Be Done': Conrad, Beckett, and the Poetics of Immobility." *Conradiana* 32 (2000), 66–71.

Blau, Herbert. *Sails of the Herring Fleet*, 89–93, 103–6.

Boxall, Peter. "'The Existence I Ascribe': Memory, Invention, and Autobiography in Beckett's Fiction." *Yrbk of Engl Stud* 30 (2000), 138–43.

Brown, Llewellyn. "La voix, signe de l'impossible chez Samuel Beckett," in Marius Buning et al., eds., *Beckett versus Beckett*, 165–73.

Brush, AnJanette. "The Same Old Hag: Gender and (In)Difference in Samuel Beckett's *Trilogy*," in Henry Sussman and Christopher Devenney, eds., *Engagement and Indifference*, 126–37.

Bryden, Mary. "Rats in and around Beckett," in Marius Buning et al., eds., *Beckett versus Beckett*, 323–24.

Bryden, Mary. *Samuel Beckett and the Idea of God*, 42–43, 73–76, 139–40, 160–61, 173–75.

Butler, Lance St. John. *Registering the Difference*, 165–68.

Casanova, Pascal. *Beckett l'abstracteur*, 139–43.

Cohn, Ruby. *A Beckett Canon*, 184–94.

Cousineau, Thomas. "Anti-Oedipal Tendencies in the Trilogy," in Bruce Stewart, ed., *Beckett and Beyond*, 70–77.

Cousineau, Tom. "The Lost Father in Beckett's Novels," in Sjef Houppermans, ed., *Beckett & La Psychanalyse*, 78–81.

Critchley, Simon. "Who Speaks in the Work of Samuel Beckett?" *Yale French Stud* 93 (1998), 114–30.

Davies, Paul. *Beckett and Eros*, 119–22.

Devenney, Christopher. "What Remains?," in Henry Sussman and Christopher Devenney, eds., *Engagement and Indifference*, 142–46.

Dowd, Garin V. "Nomadology: Reading the Beckettian Baroque." *J of Beckett Stud* 8:1 (1998), 28–43.

Duffy, Brian. "Narrative and Identity in Samuel Beckett's *L'innommable*." *Etudes Irlandaises* 24:1 (1999), 63–76.

Duffy, Brian. "The Prisoners in the Cave and Worm in the Pit: Plato and Beckett on Authority and Truth." *J of Beckett Stud* 8:1 (1998), 51–71.

Grossman, Evelyne. *L'Esthétique de Beckett*, 41–74.

Hill, Leslie. "The Trilogy Translated," in Jennifer Birkett and Kate Ince, eds., *Samuel Beckett*, 99–114.

Hill, Leslie. "'Up the Republic!': Beckett, Writing, Politics." *Mod Lang Notes* 112 (1997), 917–25.

Katz, Daniel. *Saying I No More*, 78–84, 95–124.

Levy, Eric P. "The Beckettian Mimesis of Seeing Nothing." *Univ of Toronto Q* 70 (2001), 624–31.

Mihály, Arpád. "'I Too Have the Right to Be Shown Impossible': Re-Reading the *Beckett Trilogy*." *AnaChronist* 1997: 93–112.

Pultar, Gönül. *Technique and Tradition*, 71–129, 131–61.

Schwab, Gabriele. "The Politics of Small Differences: Beckett's *The Unnamable*," in Henry Sussman and Christopher Devenney, eds., *Engagement and Indifference*, 42–56.

Schwalm, Helga. "Beckett's Trilogy and the Limits of Self-Deconstruction." *Samuel Beckett Today* 6 (1997), 181–91.

Uhlmann, Anthony. *Beckett and Poststructuralism*, 137–77, 180–86.

Vogel, Christina. "Raum-Körper-Konstellationen in der modernen Literatur." *Kodikas/Code/Ars semeiotica* 23 (1998), 182–95.

Weisberg, David. *Chronicles of Disorder*, 124–37, 153–55.

Wulf, Catharina. *The Imperative of Narration*, 71–74, 84–88.

Watt, 1953

Baker, Phil. *Beckett and the Mythology of Psychoanalysis*, 21–23, 74–76.

Begam, Richard. *Samuel Beckett and the End of Modernity*, 66–97.

Benjamin, Shoshana. "What's *Watt*." *Poetics Today* 18 (1997), 375–95.

Bisschops, Ralph. "Entropie et *élan vital* chez Beckett," in Sjef Houppermans, ed., *Beckett & La Psychanalyse*, 129–31.

Boulter, Jonathan Stuart. "'Delicate Questions': Hermeneutics and Beckett's *Watt*." *Samuel Beckett Today* 6 (1997), 149–63.

Bryden, Mary. "Rats in and around Beckett," in Marius Buning et al., eds., *Beckett versus Beckett*, 320–21.

Bryden, Mary. *Samuel Beckett and the Idea of God*, 37–39, 43–44, 54–56, 61–63, 80–82, 137–39.

Cavaliero, Glen. *The Alchemy of Laughter*, 206–8.

Cohn, Ruby. *A Beckett Canon*, 109–23.

Cousineau, Tom. "The Lost Father in Beckett's Novels," in Sjef Houppermans, ed., *Beckett & La Psychanalyse*, 75–76.

Dragoman, György. "The Narrative Paradox: The Virus of Nothingness in Samuel Beckett's *Watt*." *AnaChronist* 2000: 278–91.

Hawthorne, Mark D. "Beckett's *Watt* and 'Darwin's Caterpillar.'" *Notes on Contemp Lit* 28:2 (1998), 4–6.

Hayman, David. "Beckett's *Watt*—the Graphic Accompaniment: Marginalia in the Manuscripts." *Word and Image* 13:2 (1997), 172–82.

Katz, Daniel. *Saying I No More*, 43–70.

Kennedy, Sighle. "'Astride of a Grave and a Difficult Birth': Samuel Beckett's *Watt* Struggles to Life (1940–42)." *Dalhousie French Stud* 42 (1998), 45–53.

Parrott, Jeremy. "When Is a Pot Not a Pot . . . ?: A Study of Samuel Beckett's *Watt* in the Light of Thai and Zen Buddhism." *B.A.S.: Brit and Am Stud* 1998: 9–17.

Pilling, John. *Beckett before Godot*, 168–86.

Topia, André. "La prolifération du potentiel: séries joyciennes, séries beckettiennes." *Etudes Anglaises* 53 (2000), 29–35.

Weisberg, David. *Chronicles of Disorder*, 42–54.

Wulf, Catharina. *The Imperative of Narration*, 32–56.

Wulf, Catharina. "La Quête de l'inexplicable: *Watt* de Samuel Beckett et *Marcher* de Thomas Bernhard." *Samuel Beckett Today* 6 (1997), 73–85.

WILLIAM BECKFORD

Vathek, 1786

Benedict, Barbara M. *Curiosity*, 175–77.

Conger, Syndy M. "Maternal Negotiations with the Underworld: Origins and Ends in William Beckford's *Vathek* and Mary Shelley's *Proserpine*." *Stud on Voltaire and the Eighteenth Cent* 346 (1996), 448–51.

Dellamora, Richard. "Benjamin Disraeli, Judaism, and the Legacy of William Beckford," in Jay Losey and William D. Brewer, eds., *Mapping Male Sexuality*, 148–51.

Elfenbein, Andrew. *Romantic Genius*, 39–43, 48–60.

Garrett, John. "Beckford's Amorality: Deconstructing the House of Faith." *Stud on Voltaire and the Eighteenth Cent* 346 (1996), 455–58.

Haggerty, George E. *Men in Love*, 140–51.

Heinrich, Hans. *Zur Geschichte des 'Libertin,'* 158–63.

Jack, Malcolm. "William Beckford: The Poor Arabian Story-Teller." *Stud on Voltaire and the Eighteenth Cent* 346 (1996), 451–54.

Montandon, Alain. *Le roman au XVIIIe siècle*, 456–57.

Oueijan, Naji B. *The Progress of an Image*, 52–58.

Rajan, Balachandra. *Under Western Eyes*, 84–85.

Shaffer, Elinor. "William Beckford in Venice, Liminal City: The Pavilion and the Interminable Staircase," in Manfred Pfister and Barbara Schaff, eds., *Venetian Views*, 73–88.

MAX BEERBOHM

Zuleika Dobson, 1911

Bonaparte, Felicia. "Reading the Deadly Text of Modernism: Vico's Philosophy of History and Max Beerbohm's *Zuleika Dobson*." *Clio* 27 (1998), 335–61.

Dougill, John. *Oxford in English Literature*, 166–72.

Engel, Arthur. "A Note on Max Beerbohm's *Zuleika Dobson*." *Notes and Queries* 46 (1999), 491–92.

Goldman, Jonathan. "The Parrotic Voice of the Frivolous: Fiction by Ronald Firbank, I. Compton-Burnett, and Max Beerbohm." *Narrative* 7 (1999), 299–304.

BRENDAN BEHAN

Borstal Boy, 1959

Hogan, Patrick Colm. "Brendan Behan on the Politics of Identity: Nation, Culture, Class, and Human Empathy in *Borstal Boy*." *Colby Q* 35 (1999), 154–71.

Schrank, Bernice. "Brendan Behan's *Borstal Boy* as Ironic Pastoral." *Canadian J of Irish Stud* 18:2 (1992), 68–74.

APHRA BEHN

The Dumb Virgin; or, The Force of Imagination, 1700

Ellis, Lorna. *Appearing to Diminish*, 43–44, 51–53.

Robitaille, Marilyn. "Patterns of Iconicity in Aphra Behn's *The Dumb Virgin, Or the Force of the Imagination*." *Conf of Coll Teachers of Engl Stud* 62 (1997), 1–10.

The Fair Jilt, 1688

Dhuicq, Bernard. "Violence physique, violence morale dans *The Fair Jilt* d'Aphra Behn." *Bull de la Société d'Etudes Anglo-Américaines des XVIIe et XVIIIe Siècles* 44 (1997), 7–16.

Fendler, Susanne. "Intertwining Literary Histories: Women's Contribution to the Rise of the Novel," in Fendler, ed., *Feminist Contributions*, 37–42.

Flint, Christopher. *Family Fictions*, 84–90, 92–116.

Hammond, Brean S. *Professional Imaginative Writing*, 110–11.

The History of the Nun; or, The Fair Vow-Breaker, 1689

Altaba-Artal, Dolors. *Aphra Behn's English Feminism*, 151–58.

Spencer, Jane. *Aphra Behn's Afterlife*, 125–29.

Love Letters Between a Nobleman and His Sister, 1683–1687

Altaba-Artal, Dolors. *Aphra Behn's English Feminism,* 127–45.

Carnell, Rachel K. "Subverting Tragic Conventions: Aphra Behn's Turn to the Novel." *Stud in the Novel* 31 (1999), 139–40.

Chernaik, Warren. "Unguarded Hearts: Transgression and Epistolary Form in Aphra Behn's *Love-Letters* and the *Portuguese Letters.*" *JEGP* 97 (1998), 13–33.

Ireland, Ken. *The Sequential Dynamics of Narrative,* 171–72.

Mudge, Bradford K. *The Whore's Story,* 126–36.

Richetti, John. *The English Novel in History,* 22–29.

Richetti, John. "*Love Letters Between a Nobleman and His Sister:* Aphra Behn and Amatory Fiction," in Albert J. Rivero, ed., *Augustan Subjects,* 13–27.

Rivero, Albert J. "'Hieroglifick'd' History in Aphra Behn's *Love-Letters between a Nobleman and his Sister.*" *Stud in the Novel* 30 (1998), 126–36.

Spencer, Jane. *Aphra Behn's Afterlife,* 139–41.

Starr, G. Gabrielle. "Rereading Prose Fiction: Lyric Convention in Aphra Behn and Eliza Haywood." *Eighteenth-Cent Fiction* 12 (1999), 4–13.

Todd, Janet. *The Critical Fortunes of Aphra Behn,* 58–60, 97–101.

Todd, Janet. "Fatal Fluency: Behn's Fiction and the Restoration Letter." *Eighteenth-Cent Fiction* 12 (2000), 417–34.

Todd, Janet. "'The hot brute drudges on': Ambiguities of Desire in Aphra Behn's *Love-Letters between a Nobleman and his Sister.*" *Women's Writing* 1 (1994), 277–89.

Todd, Janet. "*Love-Letters* and Critical History," in Mary Ann O'Donnell et al., eds., *Aphra Behn,* 197–201.

Todd, Janet. "Who is Silvia? What is she?: Feminine Identity in Aphra Behn's *Love-Letters between a Nobleman and his Sister,*" in Todd, ed., *Aphra Behn Studies,* 199–217.

Warner, William B. "The Elevation of the Novel in England: Hegemony and Literary History," in Richard Kroll, ed., *The English Novel, Volume I,* 60–64.

The Lucky Mistake: A New Novel, 1689

Altaba-Artal, Dolors. *Aphra Behn's English Feminism,* 176–81.

The Nun; or, The Perjur'd Beauty: A True Novel, 1696

Altaba-Artal, Dolors. *Aphra Behn's English Feminism,* 159–63.

Oroonoko, 1688

Benedict, Barbara M. "The Curious Genre: Female Inquiry in Amatory Fiction." *Stud in the Novel* 30 (1998), 196–97.

Biondi, Carminella. "Aphra Behn: La Première narratrice anti-esclavagiste de la littérature moderne?," in Mary Ann O'Donnell et al., eds., *Aphra Behn,* 125–30.

Bratach, Anne. "Following the Intrigue: Aphra Behn, Genre, and Restoration Science." *J of Narrative Technique* 26 (1996), 209–24.

Brown, Laura. "The Romance of Empire: *Oroonoko* and the Trade in Slaves," in Anita Pacheco, ed., *Early Women Writers,* 197–218.

Carnell, Rachel K. "Subverting Tragic Conventions: Aphra Behn's Turn to the Novel." *Stud in the Novel* 31 (1999), 144–47.

Corman, Brian. "Restoration Studies and the New Historicism: The Case of Aphra Behn," in W. Gerald Marshall, ed., *The Restoration Mind*, 260–66.

Erickson, Robert A. *The Language of the Heart*, 162–72.

Fogarty, Anne. "Looks That Kill: Violence and Representation in Aphra Behn's *Oroonoko*," in Carl Plasa and Betty J. Ring, eds., *The Discourse of Slavery*, 1–15.

Gallagher, Catherine. "*Oroonoko*'s Blackness," in Janet Todd, ed., *Aphra Behn Studies*, 235–54.

Goldberg, Jonathan. *Desiring Women Writing*, 44–70.

Holmesland, Oddvar. "Aphra Behn's *Oroonoko*: Cultural Dialectics and the Novel." *ELH* 68 (2001), 57–76.

Iwanisziw, Susan B. "Behn's Novel Investment in *Oroonoko*: Kingship, Slavery and Tobacco in English Colonialism." *South Atlantic R* 63:2 (1998), 75–95.

Kraft, Elizabeth. "Aphra Behn's *Oroonoko* in the Classroom: A Review of Texts." *Restoration* 22 (1998), 79–95.

Lipking, Joanna. "Confusing Matters: Searching the Backgrounds of *Oroonoko*," in Janet Todd, ed., *Aphra Behn Studies*, 259–79.

Lobsien, Verena Olejniczak. "Caliban erzählen: Strukturelle Skepsis und die Erfindung des anderen in der englischen Literatur der Frühen Neuzeit." *LiLi* 110 (1998), 98–101, 113–26.

Lobsien, Verena Olejniczak. "Oroonokos 'Great Mistress': Fremdheit und Macht bei Montaigne, Shakespeare und Aphra Behn," in Roland Galle and Rudolf Behrens, eds., *Konfigurationen der Macht*, 145–65.

MacDonald, Joyce Green. "The Disappearing African Woman: Imoinda in *Oroonoko* after Behn." *ELH* 66 (1999), 71–82.

McLeod, Bruce. *The Geography of Empire*, 121–32, 146–48, 153–59.

Mayer, Robert. *History and the Early English Novel*, 149–51.

Medoff, Jeslyn. "'Very Like a Fiction': Some Early Biographies of Aphra Behn," in Barbara Smith and Ursula Appelt, eds., *Write or Be Written*, 250–52, 254–57.

Nussbaum, Felicity A. "Women and Race: 'A Difference of Complexion,'" in Vivien Jones, ed., *Women and Literature in Britain*, 74–76.

Pearson, Jacqueline. "Slave Princes and Lady Monsters: Gender and Ethnic Difference in the Work of Aphra Behn," in Janet Todd, ed., *Aphra Behn Studies*, 219–20, 230–32.

Pigg, Daniel. "Trying to Frame the Unframable: Oroonoko as Discourse in Aphra Behn's *Oroonoko*." *Stud in Short Fiction* 34 (1997), 105–10.

Rivero, Albert J. "Aphra Behn's *Oroonoko* and the 'Blank Spaces' of Colonial Fictions." *Stud in Engl Lit, 1500–1900* 39 (1999), 443–58.

Rubik, Margarete. "Estranging the Familiar, Familiarizing the Strange: Self and Other in *Oroonoko* and *The Widdow Ranter*," in Mary Ann O'Donnell et al., eds., *Aphra Behn*, 197–201.

Schille, Candy B. K. "Harems and Master Narratives: Imoinda's Story in *Oroonoko*." *J of African Travel Writing* 5 (1998), 15–24.

Spencer, Jane. *Aphra Behn's Afterlife*, 223–64.

Spencer, Jane. "Aphra Behn's *Oroonoko* and Women's Literary Authority," in Anita Pacheco, ed., *Early Women Writers*, 183–94.

Tatum, Shirley. "Aphra Behn's *Oroonoko* and the Anxiety of Decay," in Mary Ann O'Donnell et al., eds., *Aphra Behn*, 131–38.

Todd, Janet. *The Critical Fortunes of Aphra Behn*, 49–61, 114–29.

Williams, Andrew P. "The African as Text: Ownership and Authority in Aphra Behn's *Oroonoko*." *J of African Travel Writing* 5 (1998), 5–14.

Wyrick, Laura. "Facing Up to the Other: Race and Ethics in Levinas and Behn." *Eighteenth Cent* 40 (1999), 206–16.

The Unfortunate Bride; or, The Blind Lady a Beauty, 1696

Altaba-Artal, Dolors. *Aphra Behn's English Feminism*, 195–98.

Gallagher, Catherine. "*Oroonoko*'s Blackness," in Janet Todd, ed., *Aphra Behn Studies*, 236–38.

The Unfortunate Happy Lady: A True History, 1696

Altaba-Artal, Dolors. *Aphra Behn's English Feminism*, 189–92.

The Unhappy Mistake; or, The Impious Vow Punish'd, 1696

Altaba-Artal, Dolors. *Aphra Behn's English Feminism*, 170–76.

ANNA MARIA BENNETT

Anna: or Memoirs of a Welch Heiress, 1785

Rhydderch, Francesca. "Dual Nationality, Divided Identity: Ambivalent Narratives of Britishness in the Welsh Novels of Anna Maria Bennett." *Welsh Writing in Engl* 3 (1997), 1–17.

Skinner, Gillian. *Sensibility and Economics in the Novel*, 117–53.

Ellen, Countess of Castle Howel, 1805

Rhydderch, Francesca. "Dual Nationality, Divided Identity: Ambivalent Narratives of Britishness in the Welsh Novels of Anna Maria Bennett." *Welsh Writing in Engl* 3 (1997), 1–17.

ARNOLD BENNETT

Anna of the Five Towns, 1902

Gillies, Mary Ann. "The Literary Agent and the Sequel," in Paul Budra and Betty A. Schellenberg, eds., *Part Two*, 136–41.

Ormerod, David. "Doorway and Windowframe: Aestheticism and the Iconography of Bennett's *Anna of the Five Towns*." *Engl Stud* (Amsterdam) 78 (1997), 127–38.

Squillace, Robert. *Modernism, Modernity, and Arnold Bennett*, 117–19, 137–41.

The Card, 1911

Young, Arlene. *Culture, Class and Gender*, 115–18.

Clayhanger, 1910

Hertel, Kirsten. *London zwischen Naturalismus und Moderne*, 54–104.

Squillace, Robert. *Modernism, Modernity, and Arnold Bennett*, 84–113.

A Great Man, 1904

Keep, Christopher. "The Cultural Work of the Type-Writer Girl." *Victorian Stud* 40:3 (1997), 408–9.

Hilda Lessways, 1911

Hertel, Kirsten. *London zwischen Naturalismus und Moderne*, 54–104.
Squillace, Robert. *Modernism, Modernity, and Arnold Bennett*, 101–7.

Lord Raingo, 1926

Squillace, Robert. *Modernism, Modernity, and Arnold Bennett*, 162–64, 166–81.

A Man from the North, 1898

Hertel, Kirsten. *London zwischen Naturalismus und Moderne*, 349–86.
McDonald, Peter D. *British Literary Culture*, 101–17.
Squillace, Robert. *Modernism, Modernity, and Arnold Bennett*, 163–65.
Young, Arlene. *Culture, Class and Gender*, 112–15.

The Old Wives' Tale, 1908

Hertel, Kirsten. *London zwischen Naturalismus und Moderne*, 54–104.
Ireland, Ken. *The Sequential Dynamics of Narrative*, 252–54.
Nyman, Jopi. *Under English Eyes*, 117–38.
Squillace, Robert. *Modernism, Modernity, and Arnold Bennett*, 31–33, 35–84, 165–68.

The Pretty Lady, 1918

Squillace, Robert. *Modernism, Modernity, and Arnold Bennett*, 120–36.

Riceyman Steps, 1923

Squillace, Robert. *Modernism, Modernity, and Arnold Bennett*, 25–27, 142–60.

Whom God Hath Joined, 1906

Harris, Janice Hubbard. *Edwardian Stories of Divorce*, 120–25.

RONAN BENNETT

The Second Prison, 1991

Corcoran, Neil. *After Yeats and Joyce*, 162–64.

E. F. BENSON

Dodo, 1893

Weatherhead, A. K. *Upstairs*, 46–48.

GODFREY R. BENSON

Tracks in the Snow, 1906

Kestner, Joseph A. *The Edwardian Detective*, 136–48.

E. C. BENTLEY

Trent's Last Case, 1913
    Kestner, Joseph A. *The Edwardian Detective*, 281–94.

JOHN BENTLEY

Pattern for Perfidy, 1946
    Turnbull, Malcolm J. *Victims or Villains*, 123–25.

PHYLLIS BENTLEY

Freedom, Farewell!, 1936
    Hoberman, Ruth. *Gendering Classicism*, 157–62.
Sleep in Peace, 1938
    Hoberman, Ruth. *Gendering Classicism*, 156–58.

J. D. BERESFORD

The Camberwell Miracle, 1933
    Johnson, George M. *J. D. Beresford*, 112–14.
Cleo, 1937
    Johnson, George M. *J. D. Beresford*, 118–20.
A Common Enemy, 1942
    Hooley, Tristram. "Blow It Up and Start All Over Again: Second World War Apocalypse Fiction and the Decadence of Modernity," in Michael St. John, ed., *Romancing Decay*, 193–94, 195–96.
    Johnson, George M. *J. D. Beresford*, 148–50.
The Early History of Jacob Stahl, 1911
    Johnson, George M. *J. D. Beresford*, 77–80.
The Faithful Lovers, 1936
    Johnson, George M. *J. D. Beresford*, 116–18.
God's Counterpoint, 1918
    Johnson, George M. *J. D. Beresford*, 88–92.
The House in Demetrius Road, 1914
    Johnson, George M. *J. D. Beresford*, 82–83.
Housemates, 1917
    Johnson, George M. *J. D. Beresford*, 84–87.
An Imperfect Mother, 1920
    Johnson, George M. *J. D. Beresford*, 92–95.
The Long View, 1943
    Johnson, George M. *J. D. Beresford*, 125–26.
Love's Pilgrim, 1923
    Johnson, George M. *J. D. Beresford*, 95–96.

The Monkey Puzzle, 1925
    Johnson, George M. *J. D. Beresford*, 99–101.
On a Huge Hill, 1935
    Johnson, George M. *J. D. Beresford*, 115–16.
Peckover, 1934
    Johnson, George M. *J. D. Beresford*, 114–15.
The Prisoner, 1946
    Johnson, George M. *J. D. Beresford*, 126–28.
The Prisoners of Hartling, 1922
    Johnson, George M. *J. D. Beresford*, 96–97.
Quiet Corner, 1940
    Johnson, George M. *J. D. Beresford*, 145–46.
Revolution: A Story of the Near Future in England, 1921
    Johnson, George M. *J. D. Beresford*, 141–44.
The Riddle of the Tower, 1944
    Johnson, George M. *J. D. Beresford*, 152–55.
Seven, Bobsworth, 1930
    Johnson, George M. *J. D. Beresford*, 108–11.
Snell's Folly, 1939
    Johnson, George M. *J. D. Beresford*, 122–24.
The Tapestry, 1927
    Johnson, George M. *J. D. Beresford*, 102–3.
These Lynnekers, 1916
    Johnson, George M. *J. D. Beresford*, 83–84.
The Unfinished Road, 1937
    Johnson, George M. *J. D. Beresford*, 120–21.
Unity, 1924
    Johnson, George M. *J. D. Beresford*, 98–99.
What Dreams May Come, 1941
    Johnson, George M. *J. D. Beresford*, 146–48.
The Wonder, 1911
    Johnson, George M. *J. D. Beresford*, 134–38.
A World of Women, 1913
    Johnson, George M. *J. D. Beresford*, 138–41.

JOHN BERGER

Lilac and Flag: An Old Wives' Tale of a City, 1990
    Hitchcock, Peter. "They Must Be Represented? Problems in
    Theories of Working-Class Representation." *PMLA* 115 (2000),
    20–32.
    Hitchcock, Peter. "'Work Has the Smell of Vinegar': Sensing Class in
    John Berger's Trilogy." *Mod Fiction Stud* 47 (2000), 14–39.

Once in Europa, 1987

    Hitchcock, Peter. "They Must Be Represented? Problems in Theories of Working-Class Representation." *PMLA* 115 (2000), 20–32.

    Hitchcock, Peter. "'Work Has the Smell of Vinegar': Sensing Class in John Berger's Trilogy." *Mod Fiction Stud* 47 (2000), 14–39.

Pig Earth, 1979

    Hitchcock, Peter. "They Must Be Represented? Problems in Theories of Working-Class Representation." *PMLA* 115 (2000), 20–32.

    Hitchcock, Peter. "'Work Has the Smell of Vinegar': Sensing Class in John Berger's Trilogy." *Mod Fiction Stud* 47 (2000), 14–39.

WALTER BESANT

All Sorts and Conditions of Man, 1882

    Joyce, Simon. "Castles in the Air: The People's Palace, Cultural Reformism, and the East End Working Class." *Victorian Stud* 39:4 (1996), 515–36.

    Swafford, Kevin R. "Walter Besant's *All Sorts and Conditions of Men* and the Project of Paternalism in the East End of London." *European Stud J* 14:2 (1997), 57–80.

The Inner House, 1888

    Machann, Clinton. Violence and the Construction of Masculinity in Walter Besant's *The Inner House.*" *J of Men's Stud* 4:2 (1995), 131–40.

HERBERT BEST

The Twenty-Fifth Hour, 1940

    Hooley, Tristram. "Blow It Up and Start All Over Again: Second World War Apocalypse Fiction and the Decadence of Modernity," in Michael St. John, ed., *Romancing Decay,* 194–95.

DAN BILLANY

The Trap, 1950

    Rawlinson, Mark. *British Writing of the Second World War,* 161–64.

RICHARD D. BLACKMORE

Lorna Doone, 1869

    Case, Alison A. *Plotting Women,* 1–6.

    Trezise, Simon. *The West Country as a Literary Invention,* 118–38.

ROBERT BLATCHFORD

The Sorcery Shop, 1907

    Schäffner, Raimund. *Anarchismus und Literatur in England,* 251–53.

ENID BLYTON

The *Famous Five* Series
  Rudd, David. *Enid Blyton and the Mystery*, 88–121.
The *Malory Towers* Series
  Rudd, David. *Enid Blyton and the Mystery*, 121–31.
The Mountain of Adventure, 1949
  Watson, Victor. *Reading Series Fiction*, 88–91.
The *Noddy* Series
  Rudd, David. *Enid Blyton and the Mystery*, 63–87.

M. MCDONNELL BODKIN

The Capture of Paul Beck, 1909
  Klein, Kathleen Gregory. *The Woman Detective*, 58–62.
Dora Myrl, the Lady Detective, 1900
  Klein, Kathleen Gregory. *The Woman Detective*, 58–62.

DERMOT BOLGER

The Journey Home, 1990
  MacCarthy, Conor. "Ideology and Geography in Dermot Bolger's
    The Journey Home." *Irish Univ R* 27:1 (1997), 98–110.
  Smyth, Gerry. *The Novel and the Nation*, 76–79.
The Woman's Daughter, 1987
  Fiérobe, Claude. "Spectres et fin de siècle: *The Woman's Daughter* de
    Dermot Bolger et *Ghosts* de John Banville." *Etudes Irlandaises* 24:2
    (1999), 99–112.

GEORGE BORROW

Lavengro, 1851
  Duncan, Ian. "Wild England: George Borrow's Nomadology."
    Victorian Stud 41:3 (1998), 383–401.
  Jackson-Houlston, C. M. *Ballads, Songs and Snatches*, 68–72.
  Mencher, M. B. "George Borrow." *Engl Stud* (Amsterdam) 79 (1998),
    540–47.
The Romany Rye, 1857
  Jackson-Houlston, C. M. *Ballads, Songs and Snatches*, 68–74.

LUCY BOSTON

The Children of Green Knowe, 1954
  Perrin, Noel. *A Child's Delight*, 55–59.
  Watson, Victor. *Reading Series Fiction*, 135–40.

The River at Green Knowe, 1959
  Watson, Victor. *Reading Series Fiction*, 141–45.
The Stones of Green Knowe, 1976
  Watson, Victor. *Reading Series Fiction*, 150–52.
A Stranger at Green Knowe, 1961
  Watson, Victor. *Reading Series Fiction*, 145–49.

ELIZABETH BOWEN

The Death of the Heart, 1938
  Coates, John. *Social Discontinuity*, 133–54.
  Coughlan, Patricia. "Women and Desire in the Work of Elizabeth Bowen," in Éibhear Walshe, ed., *Sex, Nation and Dissent*, 126–27.
  Giobbi, Giuliana. "A Blurred Picture: Adolescent Girls Growing Up in Fanny Burney, George Eliot, Rosamond Lehmann, Elizabeth Bowen and Dacia Maraini." *J of European Stud* 25 (1995), 141–61.
  Hanson, Clare. *Hysterical Fictions*, 59–64.
  Hopkins, Chris. "Elizabeth Bowen: Realism, Modernism and Gendered Identity in Her Novels of the 1930s." *J of Gender Stud* 4 (1995), 271–78.
  Kitagawa, Yoriko. "Anticipating the Postmodern Self: Elizabeth Bowen's *The Death of the Heart*." *Engl Stud* (Amsterdam) 81 (2000), 484–96.
  Korte, Barbara. *Body Language in Literature*, 167–71.
  MacCarthy, Robert. "Bowen Religion," in Éibhear Walshe, ed., *Elizabeth Bowen Remembered*, 37–39.
  Warren, Victoria. "'Experience Means Nothing Till It Repeats Itself': Elizabeth Bowen's *The Death of the Heart* and Jane Austen's *Emma*." *Mod Lang Stud* 29:1 (1999), 131–52.
Eva Trout, 1969
  Coates, John. "The Misfortunes of Eva Trout." *Essays in Criticism* 48 (1998), 59–78.
  Coates, John. *Social Discontinuity*, 232–38.
  Connolly, Claire. "(Be)Longing: The Strange Place of Elizabeth Bowen's *Eva Trout*," in Monika Reif-Hulser, ed., *Borderlands*, 135–43.
  Smith, Patricia Juliana. *Lesbian Panic*, 113–24.
Friends and Relations, 1931
  Coates, John. *Social Discontinuity*, 47–70.
  Coughlan, Patricia. "Women and Desire in the Work of Elizabeth Bowen," in Éibhear Walshe, ed., *Sex, Nation and Dissent*, 118–21.
  Weatherhead, A. K. *Upstairs*, 126–28.
The Heat of the Day, 1949
  Byatt, A. S. *On Histories and Stories*, 14–16.
  Coates, John. *Social Discontinuity*, 155–77.
  Coughlan, Patricia. "Women and Desire in the Work of Elizabeth Bowen," in Éibhear Walshe, ed., *Sex, Nation and Dissent*, 121–23.

Glendinning, Victoria. "Gardens and Gardening in the Writings of Elizabeth Bowen," in Éibhear Walshe, ed., *Elizabeth Bowen Remembered*, 30–32.

Hanson, Clare. *Hysterical Fictions*, 64–69.

Kreilkamp, Vera. *The Anglo-Irish Novel*, 158–67.

Leray, Josette. "'War's Awful Illumination': Elizabeth Bowen's *The Heat of the Day*," in Kathleen Devine, ed., *Modern Irish Writers and the Wars*, 190–204.

MacCarthy, Robert. "Bowen Religion," in Éibhear Walshe, ed., *Elizabeth Bowen Remembered*, 37–39.

Miller, Kristine A. "'Even a Shelter's Not Safe': The Blitz on Homes in Elizabeth Bowen's Wartime Writing." *Twentieth Cent Lit* 45 (1999), 138–55.

Rawlinson, Mark. *British Writing of the Second World War*, 99–103.

Tracy, Robert. *The Unappeasable Host*, 237–41.

Weatherhead, A. K. *Upstairs*, 124–25.

York, R. A. *The Rules of Time*, 94–109.

The Hotel, 1927

Coughlan, Patricia. "Women and Desire in the Work of Elizabeth Bowen," in Éibhear Walshe, ed., *Sex, Nation and Dissent*, 116–18.

Gray, Rosemary. "Heeding the Nostalgic Imperative in Elizabeth Bowen's *The Hotel*," in Thomas Wagenbaur, ed., *The Poetics of Memory*, 159–70.

Smith, Patricia Juliana. *Lesbian Panic*, 75–78.

Tracy, Robert. *The Unappeasable Host*, 232–34, 236–37.

The House in Paris, 1935

Coates, John. *Social Discontinuity*, 107–31.

Hanson, Clare. *Hysterical Fictions*, 55–59.

Radford, Jean. "Late Modernism and the Politics of History," in Maroula Joannou, ed., *Women Writers of the 1930s*, 39–43.

Trodd, Anthea. *Women's Writing in English*, 201–3.

The Last September, 1929

Backus, Margot Gayle. *The Gothic Family Romance*, 179–94.

Coates, John. *Social Discontinuity*, 9–45.

Concilio, Carmen. "Things that do Speak in Elizabeth Bowen's *The Last September*," in Wim Tigges, ed., *Moments of Moment*, 279–92.

Corcoran, Neil. *After Yeats and Joyce*, 45–47.

Coughlan, Patricia. "Women and Desire in the Work of Elizabeth Bowen," in Éibhear Walshe, ed., *Sex, Nation and Dissent*, 123–25.

Frehner, Ruth. *The Colonizers' Daughters*, 42–55.

Glendinning, Victoria. "Gardens and Gardening in the Writings of Elizabeth Bowen," in Éibhear Walshe, ed., *Elizabeth Bowen Remembered*, 33–34.

Kiberd, Declan. "Elizabeth Bowen: The Dandy in Revolt," in Éibhear Walshe, ed., *Sex, Nation and Dissent*, 135–49.

Kiberd, Declan. *Inventing Ireland*, 365–79.

Kreilkamp, Vera. *The Anglo-Irish Novel*, 150–58.

Tracy, Robert. *The Unappeasable Host*, 202–21.

Weatherhead, A. K. *Upstairs*, 125–26.

Weekes, Ann Owens. "A Trackless Road: Irish Nationalisms and Lesbian Writing," in Kathryn Kirkpatrick, ed., *Border Crossings*, 131–32.

Weihman, Lisa Golmitz. "The Problem of National Culture: Virginia Woolf's *Between the Acts* and Elizabeth Bowen's *The Last September*," in Ann Ardis and Bonnie Kime Scott, eds., *Virginia Woolf*, 69–77.

The Little Girls, 1964

Coates, John. *Social Discontinuity*, 209–33.

Smith, Patricia Juliana. *Lesbian Panic*, 102–13.

To the North, 1932

Coates, John. *Social Discontinuity*, 71–105.

Glendinning, Victoria. "Gardens and Gardening in the Writings of Elizabeth Bowen," in Éibhear Walshe, ed., *Elizabeth Bowen Remembered*, 29–32.

Hanson, Clare. *Hysterical Fictions*, 50–55.

Hopkins, Chris. "Elizabeth Bowen: Realism, Modernism and Gendered Identity in Her Novels of the 1930s." *J of Gender Stud* 4 (1995), 271–78.

A World of Love, 1955

Coates, John. *Social Discontinuity*, 179–206.

Frehner, Ruth. *The Colonizers' Daughters*, 60–68.

Hanson, Clare. *Hysterical Fictions*, 69–73.

Kreilkamp, Vera. *The Anglo-Irish Novel*, 167–73.

Tracy, Robert. *The Unappeasable Host*, 242–55.

ELIZABETH BOYD

The Happy Unfortunate; or, The Female Page, 1732

Richetti, John. "Popular Narrative in the Early Eighteenth Century: Formats and Formulas," in Richard Kroll, ed., *The English Novel, Volume I*, 92–95.

WILLIAM BOYD

The Blue Afternoon, 1995

Hickman, Alan Forrest. "It's a Wise Child: Teaching the Lessons of History in the Contemporary British Novel." *Publs of the Arkansas Philol Assoc* 24:1 (1998), 37–41.

A Good Man in Africa, 1981

Hickman, Alan F. "Looking Before and After: The Search for the 'Inner Warrior' in Today's British Novel." *Publs of the Arkansas Philol Assoc* 25:1 (1999), 43–46.

MALCOLM BRADBURY

Doctor Criminale, 1992

Brînzeu, Pia. *Corridors of Mirrors*, 163–65.

Rates of Exchange, 1983
Brînzeu, Pia. *Corridors of Mirrors*, 28–31.

MARY ELIZABETH BRADDON

Aurora Floyd, 1863

Chase, Karen, and Michael Levenson. *The Spectacle of Intimacy*, 204–6, 208–10.

Curtis, Jeni. "The 'Espaliered' Girl: Pruning the Docile Body in *Aurora Floyd*," in Marlene Tromp et al., eds., *Beyond Sensation*, 77–91.

Dingley, Robert. "Mrs. Conyers's Secret: Decoding Sexuality in *Aurora Floyd*." *Victorian Newsl* 95 (1999), 16–17.

Liggins, Emma. "The 'Evil Days' of the Female Murderer: Subverted Marriage Plots and the Avoidance of Scandal in the Victorian Sensation Novel." *J of Victorian Culture* 2 (1997), 34–39.

Tromp, Marlene. "The Dangerous Woman: M. E. Braddon's Sensational (En)gendering of Domestic Law," in Marlene Tromp et al., eds., *Beyond Sensation*, 93–106.

Tromp, Marlene. *The Private Rod*, 103–52.

Tyler, Shirley. "Power and Patriarchal Hegemony in the Fiction of Mary Elizabeth Braddon." *Nineteenth-Cent Feminisms* 3 (2000), 64–69.

Tyler, Shirley. "Women, Romantic Love and the Companionate Marriage in the Fiction of Mrs Gaskell and M. E. Braddon." *Australasian Victorian Stud J* 3:1 (1997), 113–16.

The Black Band, 1861–62

Carnell, Jennifer. *The Literary Lives of Mary Elizabeth Braddon*, 204–8.

The Doctor's Wife, 1864

Carnell, Jennifer. *The Literary Lives of Mary Elizabeth Braddon*, 215–18.

Gilbert, Pamela K. "Braddon and Victorian Realism: *Joshua Haggard's Daughter*," in Marlene Tromp et al., eds., *Beyond Sensation*, 183–85.

Gilbert, Pamela K. *Disease, Desire, and the Body*, 106–12.

Gilbert, Pamela K. "Ingestion, Contagion, Seduction: Victorian Metaphors of Reading." *LIT* 8 (1997), 96–103.

Leckie, Barbara. *Culture and Adultery*, 139–51.

Sparks, Tabitha. "Fiction Becomes Her: Representations of Female Character in Mary Braddon's *The Doctor's Wife*," in Marlene Tromp et al., eds., *Beyond Sensation*, 197–208.

Eleanor's Victory, 1863

Carnell, Jennifer. *The Literary Lives of Mary Elizabeth Braddon*, 195–97, 261–66.

Johnson, Heidi H. "Electra-fying the Female Sleuth: Detecting the Father in *Eleanor's Victory* and *Thou Art the Man*," in Marlene Tromp et al., eds., *Beyond Sensation*, 255–64.

Fenton's Quest, 1871

Tyler, Shirley. "Women, Illness and Sexuality in the Fiction of Mary Braddon." *Australasian Victorian Stud Annual* 1 (1995), 94–96.

Henry Dunbar, 1864

Carnell, Jennifer. *The Literary Lives of Mary Elizabeth Braddon*, 266–69.

John Marchmont's Legacy, 1863

Marcus, Laura. "Oedipus Express: Trains, Trauma and Detective Fiction," in Warren Chernaik et al., eds., *The Art of Detective Fiction*, 210–11.

Joshua Haggard's Daughter, 1877

Gilbert, Pamela K. "Braddon and Victorian Realism: *Joshua Haggard's Daughter*," in Marlene Tromp et al., eds., *Beyond Sensation*, 183–94.

Lady Audley's Secret, 1862

Blodgett, Harriet. "The Greying of *Lady Audley's Secret*." *Papers on Lang and Lit* 37 (2001), 132–45.

Brantlinger, Patrick. *The Reading Lesson*, 149–54.

Carnell, Jennifer. *The Literary Lives of Mary Elizabeth Braddon*, 142–47, 154–56, 196–200, 251–56.

Chase, Karen, and Michael Levenson. *The Spectacle of Intimacy*, 202–9.

Cropp, Mary Seraly. "A Detective for Us Ordinary Folk?: The Reinscription of the Dupin-esque Detective in Mary Braddon's *Lady Audley's Secret*." *Clues* 19:2 (1998), 87–94.

Daly, Nicholas. "Railway Novels: Sensation Fiction and the Modernization of the Senses." *ELH* 66 (1999), 472–75.

Denisoff, Dennis. "Lady in Green with Novel: The Gendered Economics of the Visual Arts and Mid-Victorian Women's Writing," in Nicola Diane Thompson, ed., *Victorian Women Writers*, 160–64.

Gilbert, Pamela K. *Disease, Desire, and the Body*, 92–105.

Hall, R. Mark. "A Victorian Sensation Novel in the 'Contact Zone': Reading *Lady Audley's Secret* through *Imperial Eyes*." *Victorian Newsl* 98 (2000), 22–26.

Haynie, Aeron. "'An idle hand that was never turned, and a lazy rope so rotten': The Decay of the Country Estate in *Lady Audley's Secret*," in Marlene Tromp et al., eds., *Beyond Sensation*, 63–73.

Houston, Gail Turley. "Mary Braddon's Commentaries on the Trials and Legal Secrets of Audley Court," in Marlene Tromp et al., eds., *Beyond Sensation*, 17–30.

Howard, Greg. "Masculinity and Economics in *Lady Audley's Secret*." *Victorians Inst J* 27 (1999), 33–49.

Jones, Susan. *Conrad and Women*, 192–99.

Kane, Mary Patricia. "Structure and Ideology in *Lady Audley's Secret*: Demystifying the Sensational." *Rivista di Studi Vittoriani* 7:4 (1999), 89–102.

Langland, Elizabeth. "Enclosure Acts: Framing Women's Bodies in

Braddon's *Lady Audley's Secret*," in Marlene Tromp et al., eds., *Beyond Sensation*, 3–14.

Liggins, Emma. "The 'Evil Days' of the Female Murderer: Subverted Marriage Plots and the Avoidance of Scandal in the Victorian Sensation Novel." *J of Victorian Culture* 2 (1997), 34–39.

McCuskey, Brian W. "The Kitchen Police: Servant Surveillance and Middle-Class Transgression." *Victorian Lit and Culture* 28 (2000), 359–63.

Mighall, Robert. *A Geography of Victorian Gothic Fiction*, 119–24.

Montwieler, Katherine. "Marketing Sensation: *Lady Audley's Secret* and Consumer Culture," in Marlene Tromp et al., eds., *Beyond Sensation*, 43–59.

Nayder, Lillian. "Rebellious Sepoys and Bigamous Wives: The Indian Mutiny and Marriage Law Reform in *Lady Audley's Secret*," in Marlene Tromp et al., eds., *Beyond Sensation*, 31–40.

O'Farrell, Mary Ann. *Telling Complexions*, 113–15.

Petch, Simon. "Robert Audley's Profession." *Stud in the Novel* 32 (2000), 1–11.

Rignall, John. "From City Streets to Country Houses: The Detective as Flâneur," in H. Gustav Klaus and Stephen Knight, eds., *The Art of Murder*, 71–75.

Stern, Rebecca. "'Personation' and 'Good Marking-Ink': Sanity, Performativity, and Biology in Victorian Sensation Fiction." *Nineteenth Cent Stud* 14 (2000), 46–49.

Tyler, Shirley. "Power and Patriarchal Hegemony in the Fiction of Mary Elizabeth Braddon." *Nineteenth-Cent Feminisms* 3 (2000), 62–64.

Weliver, Phyllis. "Music and Female Power in Sensation Fiction." *Wilkie Collins Soc J* 2 (1999), 40–55.

Wynne, Deborah. "Two Audley Courts: Tennyson and M. E. Braddon." *Notes and Queries* 44 (1997), 344–45.

The Lady's Mile, 1866

Schroeder, Natalie, and Ronald A. Schroeder. "Miserable Bondage: Marital Companionship and Neglect in Mary Elizabeth Braddon's *The Lady's Mile*." *Nineteenth-Cent Feminisms* 2 (2000), 81–101.

Tyler, Shirley. "Women, Illness and Sexuality in the Fiction of Mary Braddon." *Australasian Victorian Stud Annual* 1 (1995), 89–93.

Tyler, Shirley. "Women, Romantic Love and the Companionate Marriage in the Fiction of Mrs Gaskell and M. E. Braddon." *Australasian Victorian Stud J* 3:1 (1997), 112–13.

The Story of Barbara, 1880

Tyler, Shirley. "Women, Illness and Sexuality in the Fiction of Mary Braddon." *Australasian Victorian Stud Annual* 1 (1995), 93–94.

Thou Art the Man, 1894

Johnson, Heidi H. "Electra-fying the Female Sleuth: Detecting the Father in *Eleanor's Victory* and *Thou Art the Man*," in Marlene Tromp et al., eds., *Beyond Sensation*, 264–72.

The Trail of the Serpent, 1861

Carnell, Jennifer. *The Literary Lives of Mary Elizabeth Braddon*, 103–6, 239–41.

The Venetians, 1892

Schaff, Barbara. "Venetian Views and Voices in Radcliffe's *The Mysteries of Udolpho* and Braddon's *The Venetians*," in Manfred Pfister and Barbara Schaff, eds., *Venetian Views*, 89–98.

EDWARD BRADLEY

The Adventures of Mr. Verdant Green, an Oxford Undergraduate, 1853–1857

Dougill, John. *Oxford in English Literature*, 115–22.

JOHN BRAINE

Room at the Top, 1957

Fjågesund, Peter. "John Braine's *Room at the Top*: The Stendhal Connection." *Engl Stud* (Amsterdam) 80 (1999), 247–64.

Haywood, Ian. *Working-Class Fiction*, 95–100.

Heinrich, Hans. *Zur Geschichte des 'Libertin,'* 226–29.

Philips, Deborah, and Ian Haywood. *Brave New Causes*, 70–71.

NICHOLAS BRETON

The Miseries of Mavillia, 1597

Davis, Walter R. "Silenced Women," in Constance C. Relihan, ed., *Framing Elizabethan Fictions*, 204–9.

MARGARET BREW

The Chronicles of Cloyne, 1884

Kelleher, Margaret. *The Feminization of Famine*, 66–70.

WALTER BRIERLY

Means-Test Man, 1935

Haywood, Ian. *Working-Class Fiction*, 66–68.

Sandwichman, 1937

Haywood, Ian. *Working-Class Fiction*, 68–71.

VERA BRITTAIN

The Dark Tide, 1923

Wallace, Diana. *Sisters and Rivals in British Women's Fiction*, 126–32.

Honourable Estate, 1936

Wallace, Diana. "Revising the Marriage Plot in Women's Fiction of the 1930s," in Maroula Joannou, ed., *Women Writers of the 1930s*, 69–71.

Wallace, Diana. *Sisters and Rivals in British Women's Fiction*, 150–56.
Testament of Friendship, 1940
Wallace, Diana. *Sisters and Rivals in British Women's Fiction*, 156–59.
Testament of Youth, 1933
Albrinck, Meg. "Borderline Women: Gender Confusion in Vera
Brittain's and Evadne Price's War Narratives." *Narrative* 6 (1998),
271–88.

JOHN BRODERICK

The Waking of Willie Ryan, 1965
Emprin, Jacques. "Esquisse d'une typologie du prêtre dans le roman
irlandais (1900–1970)." *Etudes Irlandaises* 25:1 (2000), 45–46.

ANNE BRONTË

Agnes Grey, 1847
Camus, Marianne. "L'exil des gouvernantes dans la fiction des
Brontë." *Cahiers Victoriens et Edouardiens* 51 (2000), 147–59.
Duffy, Daniel. "'Fiends instead of men': Sarah Ellis, Anne Brontë, and
the Eclipse of the Early-Victorian Masculine Ideal," in Antony
Rowland et al., eds., *Signs of Masculinity*, 98–114.
Freeman, Janet H. "Discord in the Parsonage, or, How to Speak (or
Not Speak) for Yourself: *Agnes Grey* and *Jane Eyre*." *Brontë Soc
Trans* 22 (1997), 65–71.
Newman, Hilary. "Animals in *Agnes Grey*." *Brontë Soc Trans* 21:6
(1996), 237–42.
Shaw, Marion. "Anne Brontë: A Quiet Feminist." *Brontë Soc Trans*
21:4 (1994), 126–29.
Thormählen, Marianne. *The Brontës and Religion*, 54–57, 185–91.
Whittome, Timothy. "The Impressive Lessons of *Agnes Grey*." *Brontë
Soc Trans* 21:1–2 (1993), 33–41.
The Tenant of Wildfell Hall, 1848
Berry, Laura C. *The Child, the State, and the Victorian Novel*, 93–126.
Carnell, Rachel K. "Feminism and the Public Sphere in Anne
Brontë's *The Tenant of Wildfell Hall*." *Nineteenth-Cent Lit* 53
(1998), 113–22.
Chitham, Edward. "Religion, Nature and Art in the Work of Anne
Brontë." *Brontë Soc Trans* 24 (1999), 136–42.
Clapp. Alisa Marie. "The Tenant of Patriarchal Culture: Anne
Brontë's Problematic Female Artist." *Michigan Academician* 28
(1996), 241–58.
Duffy, Daniel. "'Fiends instead of men': Sarah Ellis, Anne Brontë, and
the Eclipse of the Early-Victorian Masculine Ideal," in Antony
Rowland et al., eds., *Signs of Masculinity*, 101–14.
Gay, Penny. "Anne Brontë and the Forms of Romantic Comedy."
Brontë Soc Trans 23 (1998), 54–61.
Gruner, Elisabeth Rose. "Plotting the Mother: Caroline Norton,

Helen Huntingdon, and Isabel Vane." *Tulsa Stud in Women's Lit* 16 (1997), 303–19.

Jackson, Rebecca L. "Women as Wares: Reading the Rhetoric of Economy in Anne Brontë's *The Tenant of Wildfell Hall.*" *Conf of Coll Teachers of Engl Stud* 60 (1996), 57–64.

Loncar, Kathleen. *Legal Fiction*, 192–98.

Maunsell, Melinda. "The Hand-Made Tale: Hand Codes and Power Transactions in Anne Brontë's *The Tenant of Wildfell Hall.*" *Victorian R* 23 (1997), 43–60.

Nunokawa, Jeff. "Sexuality in the Victorian Novel," in Deirdre David, ed., *The Cambridge Companion to the Victorian Novel*, 127–31.

O'Toole, Tess. "Siblings and Suitors in the Narrative Architecture of *The Tenant of Wildfell Hall.*" *Stud in Engl Lit, 1500–1900* 39 (1999), 715–29.

Shaw, Marion. "Anne Brontë: A Quiet Feminist." *Brontë Soc Trans* 21:4 (1994), 130–35.

Terrien, Nicole. "Portrait of a Lady as an Artist in *The Tenant of Wildfell Hall* by Anne Brontë." *Imaginaires* 3 (1998), 57–72.

Thormählen, Marianne. *The Brontës and Religion*, 74–76, 82–85, 90–95, 123–26.

Villacañas Palomo, Beatriz. "*The Tenant of Wildfell Hall*: The Revolt of the 'Gentlest' Brontë." *Revista Canaria de Estudios Ingleses* 29 (1994), 187–96.

Woelfel, James. "The Christian Humanism of Anne Brontë." *1650–1850: Ideas, Aesthetics, and Inquiries in the Early Mod Era* 2 (1996), 305–17.

CHARLOTTE BRONTË

Jane Eyre, 1847

Alton, Anne Hiebert. "Books in the Novels of Charlotte Brontë." *Brontë Soc Trans* 21:7 (1996), 266–68.

Ang, Susan. *The Widening World of Children's Literature*, 39–48.

Ardholm, Helena M. *The Emblem and the Emblematic Habit*, 71–106.

Auerbach, Nina. *Daphne du Maurier*, 117–20.

Avery, Simon. "'Some strange and spectral dream': The Brontës' Manipulation of the Gothic Mode." *Brontë Soc Trans* 23 (1998), 123–26.

Bachleitner, Norbert. "Die deutsche Rezeption englischer Romanautorinnen des neunzehnten Jahrhunderts, insbesondere Charlotte Brontës," in Susanne Stark, ed., *The Novel in Anglo-German Context*, 184–94.

Barney, Richard A. *Plots of Enlightenment*, 316–20.

Battisti, Chiara. "*Jane Eyre* da *Jane Eyre*: Analisi di un remake." *Rivista di Studi Vittoriani* 8:4 (1999), 111–29.

Baumlin, Tita French, and James S. Baumlin. "'Reader, I Married Him': Archetypes of the Feminine in *Jane Eyre*." *CEA Critic* 60:1 (1997), 14–31.

Becker, Susanne. *Gothic Forms of Feminine Fictions*, 34–38, 51–53.

Beer, John. *Providence and Love*, 10–15.

Bell, Millicent. "*Jane Eyre*: The Tale of the Governess." *Am Scholar* 65:2 (1996), 263–69.

Bender, Todd K. *Literary Impressionism*, 96–102.

Berman, Carolyn Vellenga. "Undomesticating the Domestic Novel: Creole Madness in *Jane Eyre*." *Genre* 32 (1999), 267–92.

Brantlinger, Patrick. *The Reading Lesson*, 115–18.

Byerly, Alison. *Realism, Representation, and the Arts*, 93–100.

Camus, Marianne. "L'exil des gouvernantes dans la fiction des Brontë." *Cahiers Victoriens et Edouardiens* 51 (2000), 147–59.

Carter, Keryn. "The Consuming Fruit: Oranges, Demons, and Daughters." *Critique* (Washington, DC) 40:1 (1998), 15–22.

Case, Alison A. *Plotting Women*, 90–106.

Cheadle, Brian. "The Pressure of the 'Low' in *Jane Eyre*." *Engl Stud in Africa* 40:1 (1997), 1–12.

Chi, Hsin Ying. *Artist and Attic*, 91–115.

Clarke, Micael M. "Brontë's *Jane Eyre* and the Grimms' Cinderella." *Stud in Engl Lit, 1500–1900* 40 (2000), 695–708.

Connor, Margaret. "*Jane Eyre*: The Moravian Connection." *Brontë Soc Trans* 22 (1997), 37–43.

Constable, Kathleen. *A Stranger Within the Gates*, 91–107, 126–34.

Cosslett, Tess. "Intertextuality in *Oranges Are Not The Only Fruit*: The Bible, Malory, and *Jane Eyre*," in Helena Grice and Tim Woods, eds., "*I'm telling you stories*," 23–26.

Craig, Sheryl. "'My Inward Cravings': Anorexia Nervosa in *Jane Eyre*." *Publs of the Missouri Philol Assoc* 22 (1997), 40–46.

Craig, Randall. *Promising Language*, 121–51.

Csengei, Ildiko. "The Unreadability of the Bildungsroman: Reading Jane Eyre Reading." *AnaChronist* 2000: 102–38.

Dames, Nicholas. *Amnesiac Selves*, 95–97.

Deiter, Kristen. "Cultural Expressions of the Victorian Age: The New Woman, *Jane Eyre*, and Interior Design." *Lamar J of the Hum* 25...2 (2000), 27–42.

Dessart, Jamie Thomas. "'Surrounded by a Gilt Frame': Mirrors and Reflection of Self in *Jane Eyre*, *Mill on the Floss*, and *Wide Saragasso Sea*." *Jean Rhys R* 8:1–2 (1997), 16–24.

Dupras, Joseph A. "Tying the Knot in the Economic Warp of *Jane Eyre*." *Victorian Lit and Culture* 26 (1998), 395–406.

Ellis, Lorna. *Appearing to Diminish*, 138–61.

Farkas, Carol-Ann. "Beauty is as Beauty Does: Action and Appearance in Brontë and Eliot." *Dickens Stud Annual* 29 (2000), 323–46.

Fermi, Sarah, and Judith Smith. "The Real Miss Andrews: Teacher, Mother, Abolitionist." *Brontë Soc Trans* 25 (2000), 136–44.

Fermi, Sarah, and Robin Greenwood. "*Jane Eyre* and the Greenwood Family." *Brontë Soc Trans* 22 (1997), 44–52.

Fjågesund, Peter. "Samson and Delilah: Chapter 37 of Charlotte Brontë's *Jane Eyre*." *Engl Stud* (Amsterdam) 80 (1999), 449–53.

Freeman, Janet H. "Discord in the Parsonage, or, How to Speak (or Not Speak) for Yourself: *Agnes Grey* and *Jane Eyre*." *Brontë Soc Trans* 22 (1997), 65–71.

Garson, Marjorie. "Alice Munro and Charlotte Brontë." *Univ of Toronto Q* 69 (2000), 783–89, 791–823.

Gaskell, Philip. *Landmarks in English Literature*, 32–41.

Gibson, Mary Ellis. "Henry Martyn and England's Christian Empire: Rereading *Jane Eyre* through Missionary Biography." *Victorian Lit and Culture* 27 (1999), 419–37.

Gilbert, Sandra M. "*Jane Eyre* and the Secrets of Furious Lovemaking." *Novel* 31 (1998), 351–70.

Gordon, Jan B. "Charlotte Brontë's Alternative 'European Community,'" in Susanne Fendler and Ruth Wittlinger, eds., *The Idea of Europe in Literature*, 6–8.

Harvey, John. *Men in Black*, 36–39.

Hendershot, Cyndy. *The Animal Within*, 166–87.

Hoddinott, Alison. "The Endings of Charlotte Brontë's Novels." *Brontë Soc Trans* 25 (2000), 35–36.

Hoeveler, Diane Long. "'A Draught of Sweet Poison': Food, Love, and Wounds in *Jane Eyre* and *Villette*." *Prism(s)* 7 (1999), 149–73.

Hoeveler, Diane Long. *Gothic Feminism*, 203–22.

Hoeveler, Diane Long, and Lisa Jadwin. *Charlotte Brontë*, 57–85.

Hughes, John. "Charlotte Brontë's Art of Sensation." *Brontë Soc Trans* 26 (2001), 19–25.

Ireland, Ken. *The Sequential Dynamics of Narrative*, 204.

James, Susan E. "Is Thurland Castle 'Thornfield Hall'?" *Brontë Soc Trans* 25 (2000), 147–52.

Judd, Catherine. *Bedside Seductions*, 55–79.

Keen, Suzanne. *Victorian Renovations of the Novel*, 78–88.

Kincaid, James. "Pip and Jane and Recovered Memories." *Dickens Stud Annual* 25 (1996), 211–24.

Knight, Charmian. "Reader, What Next?: The Final Chapter of *Jane Eyre*." *Brontë Soc Trans* 23 (1998), 27–29.

Kreilkamp, Ivan. "Unuttered: Withheld Speech and Female Authorship in *Jane Eyre* and *Villette*." *Novel* 32 (1999), 331–38.

Kromm, Jane. "Visual Culture and Scopic Custom in *Jane Eyre* and *Villette*." *Victorian Lit and Culture* 26 (1998), 369–91.

Kunkel, Deonne. "Patriarchy Revisited: Lessing's Reinvention of *Jane Eyre*." *Doris Lessing Newsl* 21:1 (2000), 3–5, 14–15.

Levine, Caroline. "'Harmless Pleasure': Gender, Suspense, and *Jane Eyre*." *Victorian Lit and Culture* 28 (2000), 275–84.

Lloyd, Tom. *Crises of Realism*, 72–87.

Logan, Deborah Anna. *Fallenness in Victorian Women's Writing*, 145–58.

Lonac, Susan. "The Doll and the Double: Charlotte Brontë and the Representation of the Female Self." *Brontë Soc Trans* 21:7 (1996), 285–91.

Lykiard, Alexis. *Jean Rhys Revisited*, 86–92.

Marchetti, Leo. "Stoicismo e sublimazione in *Jane Eyre*." *Rivista di Studi Vittoriani* 7:4 (1999), 59–69.

Mucci, Clara. "*Jane Eyre* or Figurations of Femininity in the Victorian Novel." *Rivista di Studi Vittoriani* 3:5 (1998), 39–76.

Murphy, Sharon. "Charlotte Brontë and the Appearance of Jane Eyre." *Brontë Soc Trans* 23 (1998), 17–25.

Nelson, Barbara. "The Exorcism of Madness." *B.A.S.: Brit and Am Stud* 1997: 89–97.

Nelson, Barbara A. "The Graying of *Jane Eyre*: Margaret Drabble's *The Waterfall* as Revision." *Michigan Academician* 29 (1997), 99–107.

Nord, Deborah Epstein. "'Marks of Race': Gypsy Figures and Eccentric Femininity in Nineteenth-Century Women's Writing." *Victorian Stud* 41:2 (1998), 194–97.

Nunokawa, Jeff. "Sexuality in the Victorian Novel," in Deirdre David, ed., *The Cambridge Companion to the Victorian Novel*, 133–38.

Penner, Louise. "Domesticity and Self-Possession in *The Morgensons* and *Jane Eyre*." *Stud in Am Fiction* 27:2 (1999), 131–47.

Plasa, Carl. "'Silent Revolt': Slavery and the Politics of Metaphor in *Jane Eyre*," in Carl Plasa and Betty J. Ring, eds., *The Discourse of Slavery*, 64–87.

Plasa, Carl. *Textual Politics from Slavery to Postcolonialism*, 60–81.

Plotz, John. *The Crowd*, 182–86.

Pollock, Lori. "(An)Other Politics of Reading *Jane Eyre*." *J of Narrative Technique* 26 (1996), 249–70.

Pool, Daniel. *Dickens' Fur Coat*, 65–73, 86–91.

Sadrin, Anny. "The Trappings of Romance in *Jane Eyre* and *Great Expectations*." *Dickens Q* 14 (1997), 69–89.

Starzyk, Lawrence J. "'The Gallery of Memory': The Pictorial in *Jane Eyre*." *Papers on Lang and Lit* 33 (1997), 288–307.

Sternlieb, Lisa. "*Jane Eyre*: 'Hazarding Confidences.'" *Nineteenth-Cent Lit* 53 (1999), 452–79.

Stoneman, Patsy. "The Brontë Legacy: *Jane Eyre* and *Wuthering Heights* as Romance Archetypes." *Rivista di Studi Vittoriani* 3:5 (1998), 5–24.

Swann, Charles. "*Jane Eyre* and *Clara Hopgood*." *Notes and Queries* 46 (1999), 64–65.

Thaden, Barbara Z. *The Maternal Voice in Victorian Fiction*, 24–28.

Thomas, Sue. "The Tropical Extravagance of Bertha Mason." *Victorian Lit and Culture* 27 (1999), 1–17.

Thompson, Nicola Diane. *Reviewing Sex*, 49–52.

Thormählen, Marianne. *The Brontës and Religion*, 66–70, 78–81, 95–98, 183–85, 204–19.

Thum, Angela M. "*Wide Saragasso Sea*: A Rereading of Colonialism." *Michigan Academician* 30 (1998), 147–61.

Walker, Joseph S. "When Texts Collide: The Re-Visioning Power of the Margin." *Colby Q* 35:1 (1999), 35–48.

Warhol, Robyn R. "Double Gender, Double Genre in *Jane Eyre* and *Villette*." *Stud in Engl Lit, 1500–1900* 36 (1996), 857–71.

Watson, Reginald. "Images of Blackness in the Works of Charlotte and Emily Brontë." *Coll Lang Assoc J* 44 (2001), 462–68.

Wylie, Judith. "Incarnate Crimes: Masculine Gendering and the Double in *Jane Eyre*." *Victorians Inst J* 27 (1999), 55–68.

Zlotnick, Susan. "Jane Eyre, Anna Leonowens, and the White Woman's Burden: Governesses, Missionaries, and Maternal Imperialists in Mid-Victorian Britain." *Victorians Inst J* 24 (1996), 27–50.

The Professor, 1857

Alton, Anne Hiebert. "Books in the Novels of Charlotte Brontë." *Brontë Soc Trans* 21:7 (1996), 266.

Brown, Kate E. "Beloved Objects: Mourning, Materiality, and Charlotte Brontë's 'Never-Ending Story.'" *ELH* 65 (1998), 396–401.

Case, Alison A. *Plotting Women,* 85–90.

Dames, Nicholas. *Amnesiac Selves,* 97–114.

Elfenbein, Andrew. *Byron and the Victorians,* 144–49.

Gordon, Jan B. "Charlotte Brontë's Alternative 'European Community,'" in Susanne Fendler and Ruth Wittlinger, eds., *The Idea of Europe in Literature,* 9–12, 20–22.

Hoddinott, Alison. "The Endings of Charlotte Brontë's Novels." *Brontë Soc Trans* 25 (2000), 31–35.

Hoeveler, Diane Long, and Lisa Jadwin. *Charlotte Brontë,* 34–56.

Hughes, John. "Charlotte Brontë's Art of Sensation." *Brontë Soc Trans* 26 (2001), 19–25.

Jedrzejewski, Jan. "Charlotte Brontë and Roman Catholicism." *Brontë Soc Trans* 25 (2000), 121–30.

Myers, William. *The Presence of Persons,* 180–86.

Newman, Neville F. "Workers, Gentlemen and Landowners: Identifying Social Class in *The Professor* and *Wuthering Heights.*" *Brontë Soc Trans* 26 (2001), 10–18.

Plasa, Carl. "Charlotte Brontë's Foreign Bodies: Slavery and Sexuality in *The Professor.*" *J of Narrative Theory* 30 (2000), 1–25.

Rauch, Alan. *Useful Knowledge,* 129–63.

Thormählen, Marianne. *The Brontës and Religion,* 36–37.

Watson, Reginald. "Images of Blackness in the Works of Charlotte and Emily Brontë." *Coll Lang Assoc J* 44 (2001), 468–70.

Shirley, 1849

Alton, Anne Hiebert. "Books in the Novels of Charlotte Brontë." *Brontë Soc Trans* 21:7 (1996), 268–69.

Baumann, Uwe. "'Brotherhood in Error': William Shakespeares *Coriolanus* als Exemplum in Charlotte Brontës *Shirley,*" in Bernd Engler and Kurt Müller, eds., *Exempla,* 315–32.

Brantlinger, Patrick. *The Reading Lesson,* 112–17.

Collier, Patrick. "'The lawless by force ... the peaceable by kindness': Strategies of Social Control in Charlotte Brontë's *Shirley* and the *Leeds Mercury.*" *Victorian Periodicals R* 32 (1999), 279–95.

Cornut-Gentille D'Arcy, Chantal. "Fictive and Compositional Time in Charlotte Brontë's Novel *Shirley.*" *Studium: Filología* 8 (1992), 181–96.

D'Agata d'Ottavi, Stefania. "Il narratore invadente: *Shirley* di Charlotte Brontë." *Rivista di Letterature Moderne e Comparate* 47 (1994), 241–58.

DeCuir, André L. "The Portrayal of Nature in Her Tribute to Emily: Charlotte Brontë's *Shirley.*" *Brontë Soc Trans* 24 (1999), 50–54.

Figart, Linda B. "Charlotte on the Plain of Shinar: Biblical Connections in *Shirley.*" *Brontë Soc Trans* 22 (1997), 54–58.

Franklin, J. Jeffrey. *Serious Play,* 81–86, 93–98, 103–8.

Gardner, Julia. "'Neither Monsters nor Temptresses nor Terrors': Representing Desire in Charlotte Brontë's *Shirley*." *Victorian Lit and Culture* 26 (1998), 409–19.

Gordon, Jan B. "Charlotte Brontë's Alternative 'European Community,'" in Susanne Fendler and Ruth Wittlinger, eds., *The Idea of Europe in Literature*, 13–14, 16–25.

Hesketh, Sally. "Needlework in the Lives and Novels of the Brontë Sisters." *Brontë Soc Trans* 22 (1997), 76–83.

Hoddinott, Alison. "The Endings of Charlotte Brontë's Novels." *Brontë Soc Trans* 25 (2000), 36–38.

Hoeveler, Diane Long, and Lisa Jadwin. *Charlotte Brontë*, 86–107.

Hughes, John. "Charlotte Brontë's Art of Sensation." *Brontë Soc Trans* 26 (2001), 19–25.

Keen, Suzanne. *Victorian Renovations of the Novel*, 88–95.

Langer, Nancy Quick. "'There is no such ladies now-a-days': Capsizing 'the patriarch bull' in Charlotte Brontë's *Shirley*." *J of Narrative Technique* 27 (1997), 276–91.

Loncar, Kathleen. *Legal Fiction*, 91–99, 177–80.

Morris, Pam. "Heroes and Hero-Worship in Charlotte Brontë's *Shirley*." *Nineteenth-Cent Lit* 54 (1999), 285–307.

Myers, William. *The Presence of Persons*, 151–54, 190–92.

Padilla, Yolanda. "Dreaming of Eve, Prometheus, and the Titans: The Romantic Vision of Shirley Keeldar." *Brontë Soc Trans* 21:1–2 (1993), 9–14.

Peck, John. *War, the Army and Victorian Literature*, 102–5.

Plasa, Carl. "Reading 'The Geography of Hunger' in Tsitsi Dangarembga's *Nervous Conditions*: From Frantz Fanon to Charlotte Brontë." *J of Commonwealth Lit* 33:1 (1998), 37–44.

Plotz, John. *The Crowd*, 154–93.

Thormählen, Marianne. *The Brontës and Religion*, 76–78, 146–50, 152–53, 193–203.

Tuman, Myron. "Desire and Slow Time: Reading Charlotte Brontë in the Information Age." *Works and Days* 17–18 (1999–2000), 233–38.

Watson, Reginald. "Images of Blackness in the Works of Charlotte and Emily Brontë." *Coll Lang Assoc J* 44 (2001), 468–70.

Young, Arlene. *Culture, Class and Gender*, 124–26.

Zlotnick, Susan. *Women, Writing, and the Industrial Revolution*, 66–75, 87–99.

Villette, 1853

D'Albertis, Deirdre. "Make-believes in Bayswater and Belgravia: Brontë, Linton, and the Victorian 'Flirt.'" *Victorians Inst J* 24 (1996), 12–18.

Alton, Anne Hiebert. "Books in the Novels of Charlotte Brontë." *Brontë Soc Trans* 21:7 (1996), 269–72.

Ardholm, Helena M. *The Emblem and the Emblematic Habit*, 65–70.

Avery, Simon. "'Some strange and spectral dream': The Brontës' Manipulation of the Gothic Mode." *Brontë Soc Trans* 23 (1998), 132–34.

Berns, Ute. "Modi der Fremdkonstruktion: Orientalismus in

Charlotte Brontës Roman *Villette*." *Poetica* (Munich) 32 (2000), 99–123.

Byerly, Alison. *Realism, Representation, and the Arts*, 91–93, 100–104.

Camus, Marianne. "L'exil des gouvernantes dans la fiction des Brontë." *Cahiers Victoriens et Edouardiens* 51 (2000), 147–59.

Chi, Hsin Ying. *Artist and Attic*, 19–41.

Cohen, Monica F. *Professional Domesticity*, 44–69.

Dames, Nicholas. *Amnesiac Selves*, 82–87, 99–102, 113–24.

Farkas, Carol-Ann. "Beauty is as Beauty Does: Action and Appearance in Brontë and Eliot." *Dickens Stud Annual* 29 (2000), 323–46.

Forsyth, Beverly. "The Two Faces of Lucy Snowe: A Study in Deviant Behavior." *Stud in the Novel* 29 (1997), 17–24.

Franklin, J. Jeffrey. *Serious Play*, 112–17.

Garson, Marjorie. "Alice Munro and Charlotte Brontë." *Univ of Toronto Q* 69 (2000), 789–91.

Gordon, Jan B. "Charlotte Brontë's Alternative 'European Community,'" in Susanne Fendler and Ruth Wittlinger, eds., *The Idea of Europe in Literature*, 3–5, 15–16, 20–21.

Hall, Kate. "Maternal Influence on Charlotte Brontë." *Brontë Soc Trans* 21:1–2 (1993), 4–7.

Helfield, Randa. "Confession as Cover-Up in Brontë's *Villette*." *Engl Stud in Canada* 23 (1997), 155–80.

Hennelly, Mark M., Jr. "The 'Surveillance of Désirée': Freud, Foucault, and *Villette*." *Victorian Lit and Culture* 26 (1998), 421–37.

Herrera, Andrea O'Reilly. "'Herself Beheld': Marriage, Motherhood, and Oppression in Brontë's *Villette* and Jacobs's *Incidents in the Life of a Slave Girl*," in Herrera et al., eds., *Family Matters*, 55–66.

Herrera, Andrea O'Reilly. "Imagining a Self between a Husband or a Wall: Charlotte Brontë's *Villette*," in Marilyn Demarest Button and Toni Reed, eds., *The Foreign Woman in British Literature*, 67–76.

Hoddinott, Alison. "The Endings of Charlotte Brontë's Novels." *Brontë Soc Trans* 25 (2000), 38–41.

Hoeveler, Diane Long. "'A Draught of Sweet Poison': Food, Love, and Wounds in *Jane Eyre* and *Villette*." *Prism(s)* 7 (1999), 149–73.

Hoeveler, Diane Long. *Gothic Feminism*, 222–41.

Hoeveler, Diane Long, and Lisa Jadwin. *Charlotte Brontë*, 108–33.

Hughes, John. "The Affective World of Charlotte Brontë's *Villette*." *Stud in Engl Lit, 1500–1900* 40 (2000), 711–25.

Hughes, John. "Charlotte Brontë's Art of Sensation." *Brontë Soc Trans* 26 (2001), 19–25.

Jedrzejewski, Jan. "Charlotte Brontë and Roman Catholicism." *Brontë Soc Trans* 25 (2000), 130–34.

Keen, Suzanne. *Victorian Renovations of the Novel*, 95–110.

Kreilkamp, Ivan. "Unuttered: Withheld Speech and Female Authorship in *Jane Eyre* and *Villette*." *Novel* 32 (1999), 339–52.

Kromm, Jane. "Visual Culture and Scopic Custom in *Jane Eyre* and *Villette*." *Victorian Lit and Culture* 26 (1998), 369–91.

Kushen, Betty. "Volition and the Repetition Compulsion in Charlotte Brontë's *Villette*." *J of Evolutionary Psych* 17:1–2 (1996), 64–73.

Levy, Anita. "Public Spaces, Private Eyes: Gender and the Social Work of Aesthetics in Charlotte Brontë's *Villette*." *Nineteenth-Cent Contexts* 22 (2000), 391–411.

Levy, Anita. *Reproductive Urges*, 63–92.

Lonac, Susan. "The Doll and the Double: Charlotte Brontë and the Representation of the Female Self." *Brontë Soc Trans* 21:7 (1996), 285–91.

Melfi, Mary Ann. "Consumption as Metaphor: On the Verge of Life in *Villette*." *J of Evolutionary Psych* 20:3–4 (1999), 110–18.

Murray, Piper. "Brontë's Lunatic Ball: Constituting 'A Very Safe Asylum' in *Villette*." *Victorian R* 26:2 (2000), 24–43.

Myers, William. *The Presence of Persons*, 187–89.

Preston, Elizabeth. "Relational Reconsiderations: Reliability, Heterosexuality, and Narrative Authority in *Villette*." *Style* 30 (1996), 386–403.

Sandner, David. "The Little Puzzle: The Two Shipwrecks in Charlotte Brontë's *Villette*." *Engl Lang Notes* 36:3 (1999), 67–74.

Schmitt, Cannon. *Alien Nation*, 76–106, 108–10.

Sutherland, John. *Who Betrays Elizabeth Bennet?*, 87–89.

Thormählen, Marianne. *The Brontës and Religion*, 30–36, 99–100.

Towheed, Shafquat. "The Chronology of Charlotte Brontë's *Villette*." *Notes and Queries* 45 (1998), 217–18.

Tuman, Myron. "Desire and Slow Time: Reading Charlotte Brontë in the Information Age." *Works and Days* 17–18 (1999–2000), 212–25.

Vlock, Deborah. *Dickens, Novel Reading*, 62–65.

Warhol, Robyn R. "Double Gender, Double Genre in *Jane Eyre* and *Villette*." *Stud in Engl Lit, 1500–1900* 36 (1996), 857–71.

Wein, Toni. "Gothic Desire in Charlotte Brontë's *Villette*." *Stud in Engl Lit, 1500–1900* 39 (1999), 733–43.

EMILY BRONTË

Wuthering Heights, 1847

Al-Madani, Yusur. "Male, Female Expressions of Heathen Love: Brontë's Heathcliff and Hawthorne's Hester." *Intl J of Arabic Engl Stud* 1:2 (2000), 313–30.

Ardholm, Helena M. *The Emblem and the Emblematic Habit*, 107–39.

Armstrong, Nancy. *Fiction in the Age of Photography*, 169–71, 177–81, 185–87, 197–99.

Auerbach, Nina. *Daphne du Maurier*, 112–17.

Avery, Simon. "'Some strange and spectral dream': The Brontës' Manipulation of the Gothic Mode." *Brontë Soc Trans* 23 (1998), 126–32.

Axelrod, Mark. *The Poetics of Novels*, 55–76.

Banerjee, Jacqueline. "Sources and Outcomes of Adolescent Crises in *Wuthering Heights.*" *Victorian Newsl* 94 (1998), 17–25.

Barnard, Robert. "What Does *Wuthering Heights* Mean?" *Brontë Soc Trans* 23 (1998), 112–19.

Berry, Laura C. *The Child, the State, and the Victorian Novel*, 93–126.

Brantlinger, Patrick. *The Reading Lesson*, 118–20.

Brennan, Matthew C. *The Gothic Psyche*, 77–95.

Broadhead, Helen. "'Crumbling Griffins and Shameless Little Boys': The Social and Moral Background of *Wuthering Heights*." *Brontë Soc Trans* 25 (2000), 53–64.

Burns, Bonnie. "Nostalgia, Apostrophe, *Wuthering Heights*: The Queer Destiny of Heterosexuality." *Nineteenth-Cent Feminisms* 1 (1999), 81–92.

Burwick, Frederick. "*Wuthering Heights* as Bifurcated Novel," in Richard Gravil, ed., *Master Narratives*, 69–85.

Camus, Marianne. "L'exil des gouvernantes dans la fiction des Brontë." *Cahiers Victoriens et Edouardiens* 51 (2000), 147–59.

Cole, David W. "'The Fate of Milo' and the Moral Vision of *Wuthering Heights*." *ANQ* 11:2 (1998), 23–29.

Coste, Bénédicte. "Science et conscience: Les Brontë et le discours psychologique victorien." *Cahiers Victoriens et Edouardiens* 46 (1997), 105–21.

Cottom, Daniel. *Ravishing Tradition*, 68–82.

Curtu, Maria Filippa. "Proust lettore di Emily Brontë: Una ipotesi sulla genesi dei due 'côtés.'" *Rivista di Letterature Moderne e Comparate* 49 (1996), 203–13.

Daly, A. Stuart. "A Revised Chronology of *Wuthering Heights*." *Brontë Soc Trans* 21:5 (1995), 169–73.

Davies, Stevie. "Reflections on the Poetry of *Wuthering Heights*." *Brontë Soc Trans* 23 (1998), 103–11.

De Andrado, Pabha Nidhani. "The Identity of Heathcliff in Emily Brontë's *Wuthering Heights*: Wolf or Waif?" *Sri Lanka J of the Hum* 24–25:1–2 (1998–1999), 195–206.

DeRosa, Robin. "'To Save the Life of the Novel': Sadomasochism and Representation in *Wuthering Heights*." *Rocky Mountain R of Lang and Lit* 52:1 (1998), 27–42.

Donnelly, Peter J. "Lockwood and Mrs Dean as Observers." *Brontë Soc Trans* 23 (1998), 142–47.

Doody, Terrence. *Among Other Things*, 85–87.

Downing, Crystal. "Unheimliche Heights: The (En)Gendering of Brontë Sources." *Texas Stud in Lit and Lang* 40 (1998), 347–64.

Efron, Arthur. "Reichian Criticism: The Human Body in *Wuthering Heights*." *Paunch* 67–68 (1997), 93–130.

Elfenbein, Andrew. *Byron and the Victorians*, 148–68.

Ewbank, Inga-Stina. "Emily Brontë and Immortality." *Brontë Soc Trans* 24 (1999), 46–48.

Ferguson, Susan L. "Drawing Fictional Lines: Dialect and Narrative in the Victorian Novel." *Style* 32:1 (1998), 1–17.

Gill, Linda. "The Unpardonable Sin: Lockwood's Dream in Emily Brontë's *Wuthering Heights*." *Victorians Inst J* 28 (2000), 97–106.

Giobbi, Giuliana. "'No Bread Will Feed My Hungry Soul': Anorexic Heroines in Female Fiction—From the Example of Emily Brontë as Mirrored by Anita Brookner, Gianna Schelotto and Alessandra Arachi." *J of European Stud* 27:1 (1997), 73–92.

Gorsky, Susan Rubinow. "'I'll Cry Myself Sick': Illness in *Wuthering Heights*." *Lit and Medicine* 18 (1999), 173–89.

Graziano, Alba. "Note su *Wuthering Heights*: Tra mito e romanzo di formazione." *Rivista di Studi Vittoriani* 1:1 (1996), 93–110.

Gruner, Elisabeth Rose. "Born and Made: Sisters, Brothers, and the Deceased Wife's Sister Bill." *Signs* 24 (1999), 427–29.

Heywood, Christopher. "Yorkshire Landscapes in *Wuthering Heights*." *Essays in Criticism* 48 (1998), 13–32.

Hinton, Laura. *The Perverse Gaze of Sympathy*, 147–70.

Hoeveler, Diane Long. *Gothic Feminism*, 190–203.

Holbrook, David. "*Wuthering Heights*," 24–181.

Ireland, Ken. *The Sequential Dynamics of Narrative*, 205.

Kelly, Lionel. "*Wuthering Heights*, Writing, and Representation." *Rivista di Studi Vittoriani* 3:5 (1998), 25–37.

Kennard, Jean E. "Lesbianism and the Censoring of *Wuthering Heights*." *NWSA J* 8:2 (1996), 17–31.

Knoepflmacher, U. C. *Ventures into Childhood*, 26–28.

Krebs, Paula M. "Folklore, Fear, and the Feminine: Ghosts and Old Wives' Tales in *Wuthering Heights*." *Victorian Lit and Culture* 26 (1998), 41–50.

Lamonica, Drew. "Confounded Commas: Confusion in an Interpretation of Heathcliff." *Notes and Queries* 44 (1997), 336.

Liao, Ping-hui. "Disrupting the Single Voice Narrative: Sexuality vs. Textual Economy in *Wuthering Heights*." *Stud in Lang and Lit* (Taipei) 3 (1988), 37–55.

Lovell-Smith, Rose. "Qu'a donc pu lire Emily Brontë? Arrivals in the Waverley Novels and *Wuthering Heights*." *Brontë Soc Trans* 21:3 (1994), 79–85.

McCormick, John. *Catastrophe and Imagination*, 161–64.

Marsh, Nicholas. *Emily Brontë: "Wuthering Heights*," 3–207.

May, Leila Silvana. *Disorderly Sisters*, 177–94.

Mills, Pamela. "Wyler's Version of Brontë's Storms in *Wuthering Heights*." *Lit/Film Q* 24 (1996), 414–21.

Myer, Michael Grosvenor. "An Inconsistency in *Wuthering Heights*." *Notes and Queries* 44 (1997), 335–36.

Myers, William. *The Presence of Persons*, 134–38, 145–47.

Nemesvari, Richard. "Strange Attractors on the Yorkshire Moors: Chaos Theory and *Wuthering Heights*." *Victorian Newsl* 92 (1997), 15–20.

Newman, Neville F. "Workers, Gentlemen and Landowners: Identifying Social Class in *The Professor* and *Wuthering Heights*." *Brontë Soc Trans* 26 (2001), 10–18.

Ngom, Abdou. "Tellurism and the Apotheosis of Nature in Emily Brontë's *Wuthering Heights*." *Bridges* (Dakar) 8 (1997–1998), 144–59.

Nord, Deborah Epstein. "'Marks of Race': Gypsy Figures and Eccentric Femininity in Nineteenth-Century Women's Writing." *Victorian Stud* 41:2 (1998), 197–99.

Pinion, F. B. "Byron and *Wuthering Heights*." *Brontë Soc Trans* 21:5 (1995), 195–200.

Pinion, F. B. "Scott and *Wuthering Heights*." *Brontë Soc Trans* 21:7 (1996), 313–22.

Scheltens, Maartje. "Hareton Earnshaw; Parentage in *Wuthering Heights*." *Brontë Soc Trans* 23 (1998), 136–41.

Shires, Linda M. "The Aesthetics of the Victorian Novel: Form, Subjectivity, Ideology," in Deirdre David, ed., *The Cambridge Companion to the Victorian Novel*, 64–67.

Spencer, Luke. "The Voices of *Wuthering Heights*." *Brontë Soc Trans* 24 (1999), 82–93.

Spencer, Luke. "*Wuthering Heights* as a Version of Pastoral." *Brontë Soc Trans* 23 (1998), 46–53.

Steinitz, Rebecca. "Diaries and Displacement in *Wuthering Heights*." *Stud in the Novel* 32 (2000), 407–18.

Stoneman, Patsy. "The Brontë Legacy: *Jane Eyre* and *Wuthering Heights* as Romance Archetypes." *Rivista di Studi Vittoriani* 3:5 (1998), 5–24.

Stoneman, Patsy. *Emily Brontë: "Wuthering Heights,"* 11–183.

Stoneman, Patsy. "From Classic Text to Intertext: *Wuthering Heights* in a Post-Kristevan World." *Versus* 77–78 (1997), 75–96.

Surridge, Lisa. "Animals and Violence in *Wuthering Heights*." *Brontë Soc Trans* 24 (1999), 161–71.

Sutherland, John. *Who Betrays Elizabeth Bennet?*, 67–77.

Thompson, Nicola Diane. "The Many Faces of *Wuthering Heights*: 1847–1997." *Brontë Soc Trans* 23 (1998), 31–44.

Thompson, Nicola Diane. *Reviewing Sex*, 42–69.

Thormählen, Marianne. *The Brontës and Religion*, 81–82, 100–109, 134–42.

Thormählen, Marianne. "The Lunatic and the Devil's Disciple: The 'Lovers' in *Wuthering Heights*." *R of Engl Stud* 48 (1997), 183–97.

Tytler, Graeme. "Physiognomy in *Wuthering Heights*." *Brontë Soc Trans* 21:4 (1994), 137–46.

Van Der Meer, Carolyne A. "Branwell's Role in the Creation of Heathcliff." *Brontë Soc Trans* 25 (2000), 42–51.

Vine, Steve. "Crypts of Identity: The Refusal of Mourning in *Wuthering Heights*." *English* 48 (1999), 169–85.

Vine, Steve. *Emily Brontë*, 80–111, 128–45.

Wang, Lisa. "The Holy Spirit in Emily Brontë's *Wuthering Heights* and Poetry." *Lit and Theology* 14 (2000), 160–70.

Watson, Reginald. "Images of Blackness in the Works of Charlotte and Emily Brontë." *Coll Lang Assoc J* 44 (2001), 452–62.

EMMA BROOKE

A Superfluous Woman, 1894

Heilmann, Ann. *New Woman Fiction*, 82–84, 89–90.

Liggins, Emma. "Writing against the 'Husband-Fiend': Syphilis and Male Sexual Vice in the New Woman Novel." *Women's Writing* 7 (2000), 187–90.

Transition, 1895

Schäffner, Raimund. *Anarchismus und Literatur in England*, 247–49.

FRANCES BROOKE

The History of Emily Montague, 1769

Antor, Heinz. "The International Contexts of Frances Brooke's *The History of Emily Montague,*" in Heinz Antor and Klaus Stierstorfer, eds., *English Literatures in International Contexts,* 245–77.

Cuder Dominguez, Pilar. "Negotiations of Gender and Nationhood in Early Canadian Literature." *Intl J of Canadian Stud* 18 (1998), 115–31.

McMaster, Juliet. "Young Jane Austen and the First Canadian Novel: From *Emily Montague* to 'Amelia Webster' and *Love and Freindship.*" *Eighteenth-Cent Fiction* 11 (1999), 339–46.

Lady Julia Mandeville, 1763

Bannet, Eve Tavor. *The Domestic Revolution,* 68–73.

Skinner, Gillian. *Sensibility and Economics in the Novel,* 61–81.

HENRY BROOKE

The Fool of Quality, 1764–1770

Bellamy, Liz. *Commerce, Morality and the Eighteenth-Century Novel,* 144–50.

Ellis, Markman. *The Politics of Sensibility,* 130–59.

Richetti, John. *The English Novel in History,* 259–65.

Skinner, Gillian. *Sensibility and Economics in the Novel,* 119–21.

CHRISTINE BROOKE-ROSE

Amalgamemnon, 1984

Little, Judy. *The Experimental Self,* 143–52.

Between, 1968

Little, Judy. *The Experimental Self,* 137–42.

Simon, Sherry. "*Entre* les langues: *Between* de Christine Brooke-Rose." *TTR: Traduction, Terminologie, Rédaction* 9:1 (1996), 55–70.

Out, 1964

Little, Judy. *The Experimental Self,* 133–36.

Textermination, 1991

Lawrence, Karen R. "Saving the Text: Cultural Crisis in Textermination and Masterpiece Theatre." *Narrative* 5:1 (1997), 108–16.

Little, Judy. *The Experimental Self,* 155–57.

Thru, 1975

Lawrence, Karen R. "Dialogizing Theory in Brooke-Rose's *Thru.*" *Western Hum R* 50–51 (1997), 352–58.

Verbivore, 1990

Little, Judy. *The Experimental Self,* 153–55.

ANITA BROOKNER

Brief Lives, 1990

Hanson, Clare. *Hysterical Fictions*, 162–67.

A Closed Eye, 1991

Usandizaga, Aránzazu. "The Female Bildungsroman at the Fin de Siècle: The 'Utopian Imperative' in Anita Brookner's *A Closed Eye* and *Fraud*." *Critique* (Washington, DC) 39 (1998), 328–34.

The Debut, 1981

Button, Marilyn Demarest. "A Losing Tradition: The Exotic Female of Anita Brookner's Early Fiction," in Marilyn Demarest Button and Toni Reed, eds., *The Foreign Woman in British Literature*, 171–75.

Family and Friends, 1985

Ceserani, Remo. "Ekphrasis and Photography: A Story by Mario Praz and a Novel by Anita Brookner." *Arcadia* 35 (2000), 218–23.

A Family Romance, 1993

Hanson, Clare. *Hysterical Fictions*, 167–71.

Fraud, 1992

Giobbi, Giuliana. "'No Bread Will Feed My Hungry Soul': Anorexic Heroines in Female Fiction—From the Example of Emily Brontë as Mirrored by Anita Brookner, Gianna Schelotto and Alessandra Arachi." *J of European Stud* 27:1 (1997), 73–92.

Usandizaga, Aránzazu. "The Female Bildungsroman at the Fin de Siècle: The 'Utopian Imperative' in Anita Brookner's *A Closed Eye* and *Fraud*." *Critique* (Washington, DC) 39 (1998), 334–39.

Hotel du Lac, 1984

Fullbrook, Kate. "Anita Brookner: On Reaching for the Sun," in Abby H. P. Werlock, ed., *British Women Writing Fiction*, 97–99.

Hanson, Clare. *Hysterical Fictions*, 157–62.

Hanson, Clare. "Marketing the 'Woman Writer,'" in Judy Simons and Kate Fullbrook, eds., *Writing: A Woman's Business*, 76–79.

A Private View, 1994

Fullbrook, Kate. "Anita Brookner: On Reaching for the Sun," in Abby H. P. Werlock, ed., *British Women Writing Fiction*, 101–2.

Providence, 1982

Button, Marilyn Demarest. "A Losing Tradition: The Exotic Female of Anita Brookner's Early Fiction," in Marilyn Demarest Button and Toni Reed, eds., *The Foreign Woman in British Literature*, 175–80.

Hanson, Clare. *Hysterical Fictions*, 153–57.

Malcolm, Cheryl Alexander. "Compromise and Cultural Identity: British and American Perspectives in Anita Brookner's *Providence* and Cynthia Ozick's 'Virility.'" *Engl Stud* (Amsterdam) 78 (1997), 459–71.

Specht, Henrik. "Self-Deception and Moral Growth in Anita Brookner's *Providence*." *Engl Stud* (Amsterdam) 82:1 (2001), 44–51.

A Start in Life, 1981

Hanson, Clare. *Hysterical Fictions*, 149–53.

BRIGID BROPHY

The King of a Rainy Country, 1956
   Smith, Patricia Juliana. *Lesbian Panic,* 133–43.

RHODA BROUGHTON

A Beginner, 1894
   Gilbert, Pamela K. *Disease, Desire, and the Body,* 127–39.
Dear Faustina, 1897
   Murphy, Patricia. "Disdained and Disempowered: The 'Inverted' New Woman in Rhoda Broughton's *Dear Faustina." Tulsa Stud in Women's Lit* 19 (2000), 57–76.
Not Wisely But Too Well, 1867
   Debenham, Helen. "Rhoda Broughton's *Not Wisely But Too Well* and the Art of Sensation," in Ruth Robbins and Julian Wolfreys, eds., *Victorian Identities,* 9–22.
   Gilbert, Pamela K. *Disease, Desire, and the Body,* 63–65, 114–27.

GEORGE DOUGLAS BROWN

The House with the Green Shutters, 1901
   Radford, Andrew. "A Note on Hardy's *The Mayor of Casterbridge* and Brown's *The House with the Green Shutters." Thomas Hardy J* 15:3 (1999), 107–8.
   Walker, Marshall. *Scottish Literature since 1707,* 219–23.

GEORGE MACKAY BROWN

Beside the Ocean of Time, 1994
   Spear, Hilda D. "The Novels," in Spear, ed., *George Mackay Brown,* 86–88.
Greenvoe, 1972
   Spear, Hilda D. "The Novels," in Spear, ed., *George Mackay Brown,* 82–86.
Magnus, 1973
   Spear, Hilda D. "The Novels," in Spear, ed., *George Mackay Brown,* 76–82.
Time in a Red Coat, 1984
   Spear, Hilda D. "The Novels," in Spear, ed., *George Mackay Brown,* 88–94.
Vinland, 1992
   Spear, Hilda D. "The Novels," in Spear, ed., *George Mackay Brown,* 76–82.

ALAN BROWNJOHN

The Long Shadows, 1996
   Brînzeu, Pia. *Corridors of Mirrors,* 49–53.

JOHN BRUNNER

The Crucible of Time, 1995

Westfahl, Gary. "The Quintessence of Science Fiction, Forged in Brunner's *The Crucible of Time*." *Foundation* 69 (1997), 5–16.

MARY BRUNTON

Discipline, 1814

Anderson, Carol, and Aileen M. Riddell. "The Other Great Unknowns: Women Fiction Writers of the Early Nineteenth Century," in Douglas Gifford and Dorothy McMillan, eds., *A History*, 186–87.

Bour, Isabelle. "Mary Brunton's Novels, or, The Twilight of Sensibility." *Scottish Liter J* 24:2 (1997), 29–31.

Walker, Marshall. *Scottish Literature since 1707*, 52–53.

Emmeline, 1819

Bour, Isabelle. "Mary Brunton's Novels, or, The Twilight of Sensibility." *Scottish Liter J* 24:2 (1997), 31–34.

Self-Control, 1811

Anderson, Carol, and Aileen M. Riddell. "The Other Great Unknowns: Women Fiction Writers of the Early Nineteenth Century," in Douglas Gifford and Dorothy McMillan, eds., *A History*, 185–86.

Bour, Isabelle. "Mary Brunton's Novels, or, The Twilight of Sensibility." *Scottish Liter J* 24:2 (1997), 25–29.

Copeland, Edward. *Women Writing about Money*, 163–65.

Evans, Jennifer. "Physiognomy, Judgment and Art in Mary Brunton's *Self-Control*." *Lit and Aesthetics* 7 (1997), 67–77.

Walker, Marshall. *Scottish Literature since 1707*, 52–53.

WINIFRED BRYHER

The Coin of Carthage, 1963

Hoberman, Ruth. *Gendering Classicism*, 167–71.

Gate to the Sea, 1958

Hoberman, Ruth. *Gendering Classicism*, 91–101.

Roman Wall, 1954

Hoberman, Ruth. *Gendering Classicism*, 171–73.

JOHN BUCHAN

Greenmantle, 1916

Späth, Eberhard. "Religion und Politik in den Hannay-Romanen Buchans," in Rüdiger Ahrens and Fritz-Wilhelm Neumann, eds., *Fiktion und Geschichte*, 292–96.

Weatherhead, A. K. *Upstairs*, 35–36.

The Island of Sheep, 1936

Gornall, John. "John Buchan's *The Island of Sheep* and *Færeyinga Saga.*" *Saga-Book* 24 (1997), 351–54.

Mr. Standfast, 1918

Idle, Jeremy. "The Pilgrim's Plane-Crash: Buchan, Bunyan and Canonicity." *Lit and Theology* 13 (1999), 249–57.

Späth, Eberhard. "Religion und Politik in den Hannay-Romanen Buchans," in Rüdiger Ahrens and Fritz-Wilhelm Neumann, eds., *Fiktion und Geschichte,* 296–303.

The Power House, 1913

Kestner, Joseph A. *The Edwardian Detective,* 307–15.

Prester John, 1910

Zander, Horst. "'The Church of Empire' and 'The Church of Africa': John Buchan's *Prester John,*" in Titus Heydenreich and Eberhard Späth, eds., *Afrika in den europäischen Literaturen,* 229–44.

The Thirty-Nine Steps, 1915

Kestner, Joseph A. *The Edwardian Detective,* 354–64.

Späth, Eberhard. "Religion und Politik in den Hannay-Romanen Buchans," in Rüdiger Ahrens and Fritz-Wilhelm Neumann, eds., *Fiktion und Geschichte,* 288–92.

The Three Hostages, 1924

Späth, Eberhard. "Religion und Politik in den Hannay-Romanen Buchans," in Rüdiger Ahrens and Fritz-Wilhelm Neumann, eds., *Fiktion und Geschichte,* 303–10.

Witch Wood, 1927

Milbank, Alison. *Dante and the Victorians,* 218–19.

EDWARD BULWER-LYTTON

The Caxtons, 1849

Sinnema, Peter W. "Domesticating Bulwer-Lytton's 'Colonial' Fiction: Mentorship and Masculinity in the *Caxtons* Trilogy." *Engl Stud in Canada* 26 (2000), 155–80.

The Coming Race, 1871

Brantlinger, Patrick. "Race and the Victorian Novel," in Deirdre David, ed., *The Cambridge Companion to the Victorian Novel,* 165–66.

Simmons, Clare A. *Eyes Across the Channel,* 182–87.

Eugene Aram, 1832

Liggins, Emma. "'Such fine young chaps as them': Representations of the Male Criminal in the Newgate Novel," in Antony Rowland et al., eds., *Signs of Masculinity,* 75–77.

Harold, Last of the Saxon Kings, 1837

Wawn, Andrew. *The Vikings and the Victorians,* 315–18.

Lucretia; or, The Children of the Night, 1846

Simmons, Clare A. *Eyes Across the Channel,* 102–11.

My Novel, 1853

Sinnema, Peter W. "Domesticating Bulwer-Lytton's 'Colonial'" Fiction: Mentorship and Masculinity in the *Caxtons* Trilogy." *Engl Stud in Canada* 26 (2000), 155–80.

Night and Morning, 1841

Roberts, Adam. "Dickens's Jarndyce and Lytton's Gawtrey." *Notes and Queries* 43 (1996), 45–46.

Paul Clifford, 1830

Liggins, Emma. "'Such fine young chaps as them': Representations of the Male Criminal in the Newgate Novel," in Antony Rowland et al., eds., *Signs of Masculinity*, 71–74.

Pelham, 1828

Elfenbein, Andrew. *Byron and the Victorians*, 101–4, 219–29.

Harvey, John. *Men in Black*, 28–31.

Lane, Christopher. *The Burdens of Intimacy*, 45–72.

A Strange Story, 1862

Brown, Andrew. "The 'Supplementary Chapter' to Bulwer Lytton's *A Strange Story*." *Victorian Lit and Culture* 26 (1998), 157–75.

What Will He Do with It?, 1859

Sinnema, Peter W. "Domesticating Bulwer-Lytton's 'Colonial'" Fiction: Mentorship and Masculinity in the *Caxtons* Trilogy." *Engl Stud in Canada* 26 (2000), 155–80.

Zanoni, 1842

Poston, Lawrence. "Beyond the Occult: The Godwinian Nexus of Bulwer's *Zanoni*." *Stud in Romanticism* 37 (1998), 131–61.

Simmons, Clare A. *Eyes Across the Channel*, 139–42.

JOHN BUNYAN

The Life and Death of Mr. Badman, 1680

Davies, Michael. "'Bawdy in Thoughts, precise in Words': Decadence, Divinity and Dissent in the Restoration," in Michael St. John, ed., *Romancing Decay*, 50–52.

Hawkes, David. "Commodification and Subjectivity in John Bunyan's Fiction." *Eighteenth Cent* 41 (2000), 41–52.

Randall, James Gregory. "'The Primrose Way': John Bunyan's *The Life and Death of Mr. Badman* and the Picaresque." *1650–1850: Ideas, Aesthetics, and Inquiries in the Early Mod Era* 2 (1996), 167–84.

The Pilgrim's Progress, 1678

Aaron, Melissa D. "'Christiana and her train': Bunyan and the Alternative Society in the Second Part of *The Pilgrim's Progress*," in David Gay et al., eds., *Awakening Words*, 169–84.

Ardholm, Helena M. *The Emblem and the Emblematic Habit*, 34–39.

Breen, Margaret Soenser. "Christiana's Rudeness: Spiritual Authority in *The Pilgrim's Progress*." *Bunyan Stud* 7 (1997), 96–111.

Daigle, Marsha. "Pilgrim's Regress: Bunyan or Dante?," in Ulrich Müller and Kathleen Verduin, eds., *Mittelalter Rezeption*, 165–71.

Davies, Michael. "'Bawdy in Thoughts, precise in Words': Decadence, Divinity and Dissent in the Restoration," in Michael St. John, ed., *Romancing Decay*, 45–63.

Davies, Michael. "Bunyan's Exceeding Maze: *Grace Abounding* and the Labyrinth of Predestination," in David Gay et al., eds., *Awakening Words*, 106–10.

Davis, Paul. "John Bunyan and Heavenly Conversation." *Essays in Criticism* 50 (2000), 215–36.

Derry, Stephen. "*Mansfield Park*, Sterne's Starling, and Bunyan's Man of Despair." *Notes and Queries* 44 (1997), 322–23.

Gladfelder, Hal. "Criminal Trials and the Dilemmas of Narrative Realism, 1650–1750." *Prose Stud* 20:3 (1997), 21–24.

Hawkes, David. "Commodification and Subjectivity in John Bunyan's Fiction." *Eighteenth Cent* 41 (2000), 38–41.

Idle, Jeremy. "The Pilgrim's Plane-Crash: Buchan, Bunyan and Canonicity." *Lit and Theology* 13 (1999), 249–57.

Ireland, Ken. *The Sequential Dynamics of Narrative*, 170–71.

Johnson, Galen. "'Be Not Extream': The Limits of Theory in Reading John Bunyan." *Christianity and Lit* 49 (2000), 447–61.

Knott, John R. "Bunyan and the Cry of Blood," in David Gay et al., eds., *Awakening Words*, 51–54, 61–66.

Lewis, Robert P. "'Full Consciousness': Passion and Conversion in *Adam Bede*." *Rel and the Arts* 2 (1998), 423–42.

Lewis, Robert P. "The Pilgrim Maggie: Natural Glory and Natural History in *The Mill on the Floss*." *Lit and Theology* 12 (1998), 121–33.

Michie, Allen. "Between Calvin and Calvino: Postmodernism and Bunyan's *The Pilgrim's Progress*." *Bucknell R* 41:2 (1998), 37–54.

Morel, Michel. "Du texte comme intériorité emblématique." *La Licorne* 28 (1994), 151–62.

Mullett, Michael. *John Bunyan in Context*, 191–206, 243–59.

Ross, Aileen. "'Baffled, and Befooled': Misogyny in the Works of John Bunyan," in David Gay et al., eds., *Awakening Words*, 153–67.

Schellenberg, Betty A. "'To Renew Their Former Acquaintance': Print, Gender, and Some Eighteenth-Century Sequels," in Paul Budra and Betty A. Schellenberg, eds., *Part Two*, 86–97.

Sim, Stuart, and David Walker. *Bunyan and Authority*, 131–53, 155–72.

Simpson, Ken. "'For the Best Improvement of Time': *Pilgrim's Progress* and the Liturgies of Nonconformity," in David Gay et al., eds., *Awakening Words*, 113–25.

Spargo, Tamsin. *The Writing of John Bunyan*, 99–121.

Zimmerman, Everett. *The Boundaries of Fiction*, 81–89.

Zinck, Arlette M. "'Doctrine by Ensample': Sanctification through Literature in Milton and Bunyan." *Bunyan Stud* 6 (1995–1996), 44–55.

KATHARINE BURDEKIN

Proud Man, 1934

Williams, Keith. "Back from the Future: Katharine Burdekin and Science Fiction in the 1930s," in Maroula Joannou, ed., *Women Writers of the 1930s*, 151–63.

Swastika Night, 1937

Holden, Kate. "Formations of Discipline and Manliness: Culture, Politics and 1930's Women's Writing." *J of Gender Stud* 8:2 (1999), 141–57.

Shaw, Debra Benita. *Women, Science and Fiction,* 42–64.

ANTHONY BURGESS

A Clockwork Orange, 1962

Goh, Robbie B. H. "'Clockwork' Language Reconsidered: Iconicity and Narrative in Anthony Burgess's *A Clockwork Orange.*" *J of Narrative Theory* 30 (2000), 263–77.

Lobdell, Jared C. "Stone Pastorals: Three Men on the Side of the Horses." *Extrapolation* 37 (1996), 351–56.

O'Keefe, Vincent A. "The 'Truth' about Reading: Interpretive Instability in the Evolution of Anthony Burgess's *A Clockwork Orange.*" *Reader* 41 (1999), 31–53.

Sisk, David W. *Transformations of Language,* 57–79.

Earthly Powers, 1980

Schlüter, Kurt. "Zeichen und Wunder: Eine postmoderne Beispielgeschichte in Anthony Burgess' *Earthly Powers,*" in Bernd Engler and Kurt Müller, eds., *Exempla,* 473–82.

The Long Day Wanes, 1965

Amirthanayagam, Guy. *The Marriage of Continents,* 161–71.

Nothing Like the Sun, 1964

Franssen, Paul. "The Bard, the Bible, and the Desert Island," in Paul Franssen and Ton Hoenselaars, eds., *The Author as Character,* 113–15.

The Wanting Seed, 1962

Kone, Boubacar. "Sex, Good, Evil in *The Wanting Seed.*" *Bridges* (Dakar) 6 (1995), 115–28.

FRANCES HODGSON BURNETT

Little Lord Fauntleroy, 1889

Wilson, Anna. "*Little Lord Fauntleroy*: The Darling of Mothers and the Abomination of a Generation." *Am Liter Hist* 8 (1996), 232–58.

A Little Princess, 1905

Ang, Susan. *The Widening World of Children's Literature,* 112–13.

Emery, Mary Lou. "Refiguring the Postcolonial Imagination: Tropes of Visuality in Writing by Rhys, Kincaid, and Cliff." *Tulsa Stud in Women's Lit* 16 (1997), 260–62.

Gruner, Elisabeth Rose. "Cinderella, Marie Antoinette, and Sara: Roles and Role Models in *A Little Princess.*" *Lion and the Unicorn* 22 (1998), 163–80.

Kutzer, M. Daphne. *Empire's Children,* 49–56.

The Secret Garden, 1911

Ang, Susan. *The Widening World of Children's Literature,* 119–23.

Cadden, Mike. "Home is a Matter of Blood, Time, and Genre: Existentialism in Burnett and McKinley." *Ariel* 28:1 (1997), 53–66.

Eckford-Prossor, Melanie. "Colonizing Children: Dramas of Transformation." *J of Narrative Theory* 30 (2000), 237–62.

Hunt, Peter. *Children's Literature*, 211–13.

Kutzer, M. Daphne. *Empire's Children*, 56–63.

Morris, Tim. *You're Only Young Twice*, 89–107.

Silver, Anna Krugovoy. "Domesticating Brontë's Moors: Motherhood in *The Secret Garden*." *Lion and the Unicorn* 21 (1997), 193–200.

Stephens, John, and Robyn McCallum. "Ideological Re-Shapings: Pruning *The Secret Garden* in 1990s Film." *Paradoxa* 2 (1996), 357–68.

FANNY BURNEY

Camilla, 1796

Austin, Sara K. "'All Wove into One': *Camilla*, the Prose Epic, and Family Values." *Stud in Eighteenth-Cent Culture* 29 (2000), 273–93.

Bander, Elaine. "*Sanditon, Northanger Abbey*, and *Camilla*: Back to the Future?" *Persuasions* 19 (1997), 195–204.

Bilger, Audrey. *Laughing Feminism*, 149–55.

Bilger, Audrey. "Mocking the 'Lords of Creation': Comic Male Characters in Frances Burney, Maria Edgeworth and Jane Austen." *Women's Writing* 1 (1994), 88–91.

Burgess, Miranda J. *British Fiction and the Production of Social Order*, 93–96.

Chisholm, Kate. *Fanny Burney*, 173–90.

Decker, Catherine H. "Women and Public Space in the Novel of the 1790s," in Linda Lang-Peralta, ed., *Women, Revolution, and the Novels of the 1790s*, 10–12.

Doody, Margaret Anne. "Deserts, Ruins and Troubled Waters: Female Dreams in Fiction and the Development of the Gothic Novel," in Richard Kroll, ed., *The English Novel, Volume II*, 71–73.

Doody, Margaret Anne. "Missing *Les Muses*: Madame De Staël and Frances Burney." *Colloquium Helveticum* 25 (1997), 81–117.

Epstein, Julia. "Marginality in Frances Burney's Novels," in John Richetti, ed., *The Cambridge Companion*, 200–201, 205–6.

Haggerty, George E. *Unnatural Affections*, 137–57.

Henderson, Andrea. "Commerce and Masochistic Desire in the 1790s: Frances Burney's *Camilla*." *Eighteenth-Cent Stud* 31 (1997), 69–84.

Lynch, Deidre Shauna. *The Economy of Character*, 167–99.

Rizzo, Betty. "Renegotiating the Gothic," in Paula R. Backscheider, ed., *Revising Women*, 90–93.

Shaffer, Julie. "Romance, Finance, and the Marketable Woman: The Economics of Femininity in Late Eighteenth- and Early Nineteenth-Century English Novels," in Deborah S. Wilson and Christine Moneera Laennec, eds., *Bodily Discursions*, 48–53.

Swan, Beth. *Fictions of Law*, 51–53.

Thaddeus, Janice Farrar. *Frances Burney*, 109–35.

Thompson, James. *Models of Value*, 162–67.

Zonitch, Barbara. *Familiar Violence*, 85–112.

Cecilia, 1782

Bannet, Eve Tavor. *The Domestic Revolution*, 77–78, 81–82.

Bilger, Audrey. *Laughing Feminism*, 104–7.

Chisholm, Kate. *Fanny Burney*, 100–110.

Epstein, Julia. "*Cecilia*: Money and Anarchy," in Richard Kroll, ed., *The English Novel, Volume II*, 209–27.

Epstein, Julia. "Marginality in Frances Burney's Novels," in John Richetti, ed., *The Cambridge Companion*, 203–5.

Frank, Judith. *Common Ground*, 127–64.

Macey, J. David, Jr. "'Where the World May Ne'er Invade'?: Green Retreats and Garden Theatre in *La Princesse de Clèves, The History of Miss Betsy Thoughtless*, and *Cecilia*." *Eighteenth-Cent Fiction* 12 (1999), 87–100.

Richetti, John. *The English Novel in History*, 229–40.

Rizzo, Betty. "Renegotiating the Gothic," in Paula R. Backscheider, ed., *Revising Women*, 83–87.

Thaddeus, Janice Farrar. *Frances Burney*, 67–90.

Thompson, James. *Models of Value*, 160–63.

Waldron, Mary. *Jane Austen and the Fiction of Her Time*, 37–38.

Zonitch, Barbara. *Familiar Violence*, 59–84.

Evelina, 1778

Allen, Emily. "Staging Identity: Frances Burney's Allegory of Genre." *Eighteenth-Cent Stud* 31 (1998), 433–46.

Bannet, Eve Tavor. *The Domestic Revolution*, 75–76.

Bilger, Audrey. *Laughing Feminism*, 101–3, 215–16.

Burgess, Miranda J. *British Fiction and the Production of Social Order*, 83–87.

Chisholm, Kate. *Fanny Burney*, 44–64.

Choi, Samuel. "Signing Evelina: Female Self-Inscription in the Discourse of Letters." *Stud in the Novel* 31 (1999), 259–76.

Damoff, Sharon Long. "The Unaverted Eye: Dangerous Charity in Burney's *Evelina* and *The Wanderer*." *Stud in Eighteenth-Cent Culture* 26 (1998), 231–38.

DeRitter, Jones. "Blaming the Audience, Blaming the Gods: Unwitting Incest in Three Eighteenth-Century English Novels," in Thomas DiPiero and Pat Gill, eds., *Illicit Sex*, 221–38.

Ellis, Lorna. *Appearing to Diminish*, 88–113.

Epstein, Julia. "Marginality in Frances Burney's Novels," in John Richetti, ed., *The Cambridge Companion*, 200–203.

Gillooly, Eileen. *Smile of Discontent*, 43–51.

Giobbi, Giuliana. "A Blurred Picture: Adolescent Girls Growing Up in Fanny Burney, George Eliot, Rosamond Lehmann, Elizabeth Bowen and Dacia Maraini." *J of European Stud* 25 (1995), 141–61.

Gores, Steven J. *Psychosocial Spaces*, 49–51.

Hunter, J. Paul. "The Novel and Social/Cultural History," in John Richetti, ed., *The Cambridge Companion*, 33–34.

Lynch, Deidre Shauna. *The Economy of Character*, 164–67.

Parrinder, Patrick. "Highway Robbery and Property Circulation in Eighteenth-Century English Narratives." *Eighteenth-Cent Fiction* 13 (2001), 519–21.

Pitofsky, Alex. "'Detested for Being a Scotchman': English Nationalism in Frances Burney's *Evelina*." *Engl Lang Notes* 36:4 (1999), 56–62.

Quawas, Rula. "Evelina: A New Womanly Woman." *Studia Anglica Posnaniensia* 32 (1997), 219–27.

Richetti, John. *The English Novel in History*, 216–29.

Shaffer, Julie. "Familial Love, Incest, and Female Desire in Late Eighteenth- and Early Nineteenth-Century British Women's Novels." *Criticism* 41 (1999), 68–69.

Starr, George. "'Only a Boy': Notes on Sentimental Novels," in Richard Kroll, ed., *The English Novel, Volume I*, 49–51.

Swan, Beth. *Fictions of Law*, 189–91.

Thaddeus, Janice Farrar. *Frances Burney*, 26–51.

Thompson, Helen. "*Evelina*'s Two Publics." *Eighteenth Cent* 39 (1998), 147–65.

Thompson, James. *Models of Value*, 178–80.

Zomchick, John. "Satire and the Bourgeois Subject in Frances Burney's *Evelina*," in James E. Gill, ed., *Cutting Edges*, 347–64.

Zonitch, Barbara. *Familiar Violence*, 35–58.

The Wanderer, 1814

Anderson, Kathleen. "Frances Burney's *The Wanderer*: Actress as Virtuous Deceiver." *European Romantic R* 10 (1999), 424–51.

Barrell, John. "Afterword: Moving Stories, Still Lives," in Gerald MacLean et al., eds., *The Country and the City Revisited*, 245–48.

Bilger, Audrey. *Laughing Feminism*, 78–81, 155–57, 177–82.

Burgess, Miranda J. *British Fiction and the Production of Social Order*, 106–12.

Chisholm, Kate. *Fanny Burney*, 218–39.

Cook, Elizabeth Heckendorn. "Crown Forests and Female Georgic: Frances Burney and the Reconstruction of Britishness," in Gerald MacLean et al., eds., *The Country and the City Revisited*, 197–98, 204–10.

Crump, Justine. "'Turning the World Upside Down': Madness, Moral Management, and Frances Burney's *The Wanderer*." *Eighteenth-Cent Fiction* 10 (1998), 325–40.

Damoff, Sharon Long. "The Unaverted Eye: Dangerous Charity in Burney's *Evelina* and *The Wanderer*." *Stud in Eighteenth-Cent Culture* 26 (1998), 238–44.

Doody, Margaret Anne. "Missing *Les Muses*: Madame De Staël and Frances Burney." *Colloquium Helveticum* 25 (1997), 81–117.

Epstein, Julia. "Marginality in Frances Burney's Novels," in John Richetti, ed., *The Cambridge Companion*, 206–9.

Fay, Elizabeth A. *A Feminist Introduction to Romanticism*, 227–33.

Frank, Judith. *Common Ground*, 165–83.

Kennedy, Deborah. "Responding to the French Revolution: Williams's *Julia* and Burney's *The Wanderer*," in Laura Dabundo, ed., *Jane Austen and Mary Shelley*, 9–16.

Lynch, Deidre Shauna. *The Economy of Character*, 200–206.
Salih, Sarah. "'Her Blacks, Her Whites and Her Double Face!':
    Altering Alterity in *The Wanderer*." *Eighteenth-Cent Fiction* 11
    (1999), 301–15.
Spacks, Patricia Meyer. "Privacy, Dissimulation, and Propriety:
    Frances Burney and Jane Austen." *Eighteenth-Cent Fiction* 12
    (2000), 520–26.
Thaddeus, Janice Farrar. *Frances Burney*, 151–79.
Thompson, James. *Models of Value*, 167–71, 177–79.
Wordsworth, Jonathan. *The Bright Work Grows*, 180–89.
Zonitch, Barbara. *Familiar Violence*, 113–38.

LADY CHARLOTTE BURY

The Divorced, 1837

Humpherys, Anne. "Breaking Apart: The Early Victorian Divorce
    Novel," in Nicola Diane Thompson, ed., *Victorian Women Writers*,
    47–49.

SAMUEL BUTLER

Erewhon, 1872

Ketabgian, Tamara. "The Human Prosthesis: Workers and Machines
    in the Victorian Industrial Scene." *Crit Matrix* 11 (1997), 4–32.
Lamb, Jonathan. *Preserving the Self in the South Seas*, 294–96.
Simmons, Clare A. *Eyes Across the Channel*, 181–83.

The Way of All Flesh, 1903

Cavaliero, Glen. *The Alchemy of Laughter*, 115–18.
Klein, Alfons. "Die Familie als Gefängnis: Varianten des Vater-Sohn-
    Konflikts in Samuel Butlers *The Way of All Flesh*," in Theodor
    Wolpers, ed., *Familienbildung als Schicksal*, 223–42.
Marsh, Joss. *Word Crimes*, 182–86.
Peltason, Timothy. "Life Writing," in Herbert F. Tucker, ed., *A
    Companion to Victorian Literature and Culture*, 366–67.

MARY BUTTS

Armed with Madness, 1928

Blaser, Robin. "'Here Lies the Woodpecker Who was Zeus,'" in
    Christopher Wagstaff, ed., *A Sacred Quest*, 159–220.
Foy, Roslyn Reso. *Ritual, Myth, and Mysticism*, 51–71.
Foy, Roslyn Reso. "Sanity and Madness; Art and Life: A Study of
    Community in Virginia Woolf's *To the Lighthouse* and Mary Butts's
    Armed with Madness." *Atenea* 20:2 (2000), 95–102.
Kroll, Jennifer. "Mary Butts's 'Unrest Cure' for *The Waste Land*."
    Twentieth Cent Lit 45 (1999), 159–71.

Ashe of Rings, 1925

Foy, Roslyn Reso. *Ritual, Myth, and Mysticism*, 31–49.

Hamer, Mary. "Mary Butts, Mothers, and War," in Suzanne Raitt and Trudi Tate, eds., *Women's Fiction and the Great War*, 234–38.

Death of Felicity Taverner, 1932

Foy, Roslyn Reso. *Ritual, Myth, and Mysticism*, 81–94.

Hoberman, Ruth. *Gendering Classicism*, 48–51.

Patterson, Ian. "'The Plan Behind the Plan': Russians, Jews and Mythologies of Change—The Case of Mary Butts," in Bryan Cheyette and Laura Marcus, eds., *Modernity, Culture and 'the Jew,'*" 133–38.

Wagstaff, Barbara O'Brien. "The Effectual Angel in *Death of Felicity Taverner*," in Christopher Wagstaff, ed., *A Sacred Quest*, 224–42.

Imaginary Letters, 1928

Foy, Roslyn Reso. *Ritual, Myth, and Mysticism*, 73–77.

Hamer, Mary. "Mary Butts, Mothers, and War," in Suzanne Raitt and Trudi Tate, eds., *Women's Fiction and the Great War*, 229–33.

The Macedonian, 1933

Foy, Roslyn Reso. *Ritual, Myth, and Mysticism*, 118–21.

Hoberman, Ruth. *Gendering Classicism*, 51–55.

Scenes from the Life of Cleopatra, 1935

Hoberman, Ruth. *Gendering Classicism*, 137–49.

A. S. BYATT

Babel Tower, 1996

Brosch, Renate. "Inszenierung, Visualisierung und Fiktionalisierung als Strategien der Herstellung von individueller und kultureller Identität: Vom historischen zum historiographischen Text in A. S. Byatts Romantetralogie." *Anglistik* 10:2 (1999), 49–65.

Noble, Michael J. "Presence of Mind: A. S. Byatt, George Eliot, and the Ontology of Ideas." *CEA Critic* 62:3 (2000), 48–56.

The Game, 1967

Hanson, Clare. *Hysterical Fictions*, 127–31.

Possession, 1990

Alsop, Derek, and Chris Walsh. *The Practice of Reading*, 163–83.

Becker, Susanne. *Gothic Forms of Feminine Fictions*, 260–69.

Brink, André. *The Novel*, 288–308.

Broich, Ulrich. "A. S. Byatts *Possession* (1990): ein Pastiche postmoderner Fiktion?," in Stefan Horlacher and Marion Islinger, eds., *Expedition nach der Wahrheit*, 617–33.

Brosch, Renate. "Inszenierung, Visualisierung und Fiktionalisierung als Strategien der Herstellung von individueller und kultureller Identität: Vom historischen zum historiographischen Text in A. S. Byatts Romantetralogie." *Anglistik* 10:2 (1999), 49–65.

Chinn, Nancy. "'I Am My Own Riddle'—A. S. Byatt's Christabel LaMotte: Emily Dickinson and Melusina." *Papers on Lang and Lit* 37 (2001), 179–203.

Desblache, Lucile. "Penning Secrets: Presence and Essence of the

Epistolary Genre in A. S. Byatt's *Possession.*" *L'Esprit Créateur* 40:4 (2000), 89–95.

Djordjevic, Ivana. "In the Footsteps of Giambattista Vico: Patterns of Signification in A. S. Byatt's *Possession.*" *Anglia* 115 (1997), 44–82.

Flegel, Monica. "Enchanted Readings and Fairy-Tale Endings in A. S. Byatt's *Possession.*" *Engl Stud in Canada* 24 (1988), 413–30.

Fountain, J. Stephen. "'A Tree, of Mary, One': The Child on the Margins of Byatt's Gardens," in Kiyoshi Tsuchiya, ed., *Dissent and Marginality*, 154–62.

Freiburg, Rudolf. "Imagination in Contemporary British Fiction," in Barbara Korte and Klaus Peter Müller, eds., *Unity in Diversity Revisited?*, 233–36.

Gilmour, Robin. "Using the Victorians: The Victorian Age in Contemporary Fiction," in Alice Jenkins and Juliet John, eds., *Rereading Victorian Fiction*, 193–94.

Giobbi, Giuliana. "Know the Past, Know Thyself: Literary Pursuits and Quest for Identity in A. S. Byatt's *Possession* and in F. Duranti's *Effetti Personali.*" *J of European Stud* 24 (1994), 41–53.

Gremm, Trude. "'I read, writ in the ancient chronicle . . .': Eine unbekannte Quelle für die Melusinengestalt in A. S. Byatts *Possession.*" *Anglistik* 12:1 (2001), 73–86.

Gutleben, Christian. "La tradition victorienne à l'heure du postmodernisme: John Fowles, David Lodge, A. S. Byatt." *Etudes Anglaises* 51 (1998), 168–79.

Hanson, Clare. *Hysterical Fictions*, 141–46.

Hantiu, Ecaterina Lia. "On Solitude and the Interplay of Human Relationships in A. S. Byatt's *Possession.*" *B.A.S.: Brit and Am Stud* 1998: 118–24.

Horatschek, Annegreth. "'A Witness of Difference': Individualität als Moral im Dialog zwischen Viktorianismus und Postmoderne in dem Roman *Possession* von A. S. Byatt." *Anglia* 117 (1999), 49–70.

Hotho, Sabine. "'The Rescue of Some Stranded Ghost': The Rewriting of Literary History in Contemporary British and German Novels," in Susanne Stark, ed., *The Novel in Anglo-German Context*, 388–98.

Jukic, Tatjana. "From Worlds to Worlds and the Other Way Around: The Victorian Inheritance in the Postmodern British Novel," in Richard Todd and Luisa Flora, eds., *Theme Parks*, 82–86.

Lund, Mark F. "Lindsay Clarke and A. S. Byatt: The Novel on the Threshold of Romance." *Deus Loci* 2 (1993), 151–59.

Morse, Deborah Denenholz. "Crossing Boundaries: The Female Artist and the Sacred Word in A. S. Byatt's *Possession*," in Abby H. P. Werlock, ed., *British Women Writing Fiction*, 148–64.

Sabine, Maureen. "'Thou Art the Best of Mee': A. S. Byatt's *Possession* and the Literary Possession of Donne." *John Donne J* 14 (1995), 127–48.

Sanders, Katrina. "Polemical Plot-Coils: Thematising the Postmodern in *Possession.*" *Sydney Stud in Engl* 26 (2000), 92–111.

Shiffman, Adrienne. "'Burn what they should not see': The Private Journal as Public Text in A. S. Byatt's *Possession.*" *Tulsa Stud in Women's Lit* 20:1 (2001), 93–103.

Shiller, Dana. "The Redemptive Past in the Neo-Victorian Novel."
    Stud in the Novel 29 (1997), 546–52.
Tosi, Laura. "Riscrittura, rievocazione, riproduzione della storia let-
    teraria in *Possession* di A. S. Byatt e *Arcadia* di T. Stoppard." *Annali
    di Ca' Foscari* 37 (1998), 519–38.
Walsh, Chris. "Postmodernist Reflections: A. S. Byatt's *Possession*," in
    Richard Todd and Luisa Flora, eds., *Theme Parks*, 185–94.
Shadow of a Sun, 1964
    Hanson, Clare. *Hysterical Fictions*, 124–27.
Still Life, 1985
    Brosch, Renate. "Inszenierung, Visualisierung und Fiktionalisierung
    als Strategien der Herstellung von individueller und kultureller
    Identität: Vom historischen zum historiographischen Text in A. S.
    Byatts Romantetralogie." *Anglistik* 10:2 (1999), 49–65.
    Fountain, J. Stephen. "'A Tree, of Mary, One': The Child on the
    Margins of Byatt's Gardens," in Kiyoshi Tsuchiya, ed., *Dissent and
    Marginality*, 151–54.
    Hanson, Clare. *Hysterical Fictions*, 137–41.
The Virgin in the Garden, 1978
    Brosch, Renate. "Inszenierung, Visualisierung und Fiktionalisierung
    als Strategien der Herstellung von individueller und kultureller
    Identität: Vom historischen zum historiographischen Text in A. S.
    Byatts Romantetralogie." *Anglistik* 10:2 (1999), 49–65.
    Hanson, Clare. *Hysterical Fictions*, 131–37.
    Leonard, Elisabeth Anne. "'The Burden of Intolerable Strangeness':
    Using C. S. Lewis to See Beyond Realism in the Fiction of A. S.
    Byatt." *Extrapolation* 39 (1998), 236–47.

HALL CAINE

The Woman of Knockaloe, 1923
    Skrine, Peter. "Hall Caine's *The Woman of Knockaloe*: An Anglo-
    German War Novel from the Isle of Man," in Susanne Stark, ed.,
    The Novel in Anglo-German Context, 263–76.

MONA CAIRD

The Daughters of Danaus, 1894
    Heilmann, Ann. *New Woman Fiction*, 146–48.
    Ledger, Sally. *The New Woman*, 24–31.
    Richardson, Angelique. "'People Talk a Lot of Nonsense about
    Heredity': Mona Caird and Anti-Eugenic Feminism," in Angelique
    Richardson and Chris Willis, eds., *The New Woman in Fiction and in
    Fact*, 188–90, 199–200, 202–4.
The Great Wave, 1931
    Richardson, Angelique. "'People Talk a Lot of Nonsense about
    Heredity': Mona Caird and Anti-Eugenic Feminism," in Angelique

Richardson and Chris Willis, eds., *The New Woman in Fiction and in Fact*, 198–99, 206–7.

Pathway of the Gods, 1898
Pykett, Lyn. *Engendering Fictions*, 58–60.

The Wing of Azrael, 1889
Heilmann, Ann. *New Woman Fiction*, 175–77.
Richardson, Angelique. "'People Talk a Lot of Nonsense about Heredity': Mona Caird and Anti-Eugenic Feminism," in Angelique Richardson and Chris Willis, eds., *The New Woman in Fiction and in Fact*, 196–98.

MARY ROSE CALLAGHAN

The Awkward Girl, 1990
St. Peter, Christine. *Changing Ireland*, 159–60.

HAZEL CAMPBELL

Olga Knaresbrook, Detective, 1933
Klein, Kathleen Gregory. *The Woman Detective*, 104–7.

WILLIAM CARLETON

The Black Prophet, 1846
Kelleher, Margaret. *The Feminization of Famine*, 29–39.

LEWIS CARROLL

Alice's Adventures in Wonderland, 1865
Addecott, Grahame. "*Alice* Examined." *The Use of Engl* 47 (1996), 245–49.
Ang, Susan. *The Widening World of Children's Literature*, 107–10, 116–18.
Armstrong, Nancy. *Fiction in the Age of Photography*, 220–34, 236–38.
Austin, Guy. "Gangsters in Wonderland: René Clément's *And Hope To Die* as a Reading of Lewis Carroll's *Alice* Stories." *Lit/Film Q* 26 (1998), 263–66.
Carol, Luiza. "Alice and the Transactional Analysis." *Jabberwocky* 24 (1997), 91–98.
Ciolkowski, Laura E. "Visions of Life on the Border: Wonderland Women, Imperial Travelers, and Bourgeois Womanhood in the Nineteenth Century." *Genders* 27 (1998).
Dougill, John. *Oxford in English Literature*, 127–33.
Feldmann, Doris. "Victorian (Dis)Enchantments: Fantasy and Realism in the Visions and Revisions of Scrooge and Alice." *Anglistik und Englischunterricht* 59 (1996), 101–25.
Harrison, Stephen. "Falling Alice." *Jabberwocky* 24 (1997), 32–37.

Hayashi, Toyomi. "A Reading of the Alice Books as Seen from a Feministic Viewpoint." *Jabberwocky* 24 (1997), 63–73.

Irwin, Michael. "*Alice*: Reflections and Relativities," in Alice Jenkins and Juliet John, eds., *Rereading Victorian Fiction*, 115–28.

Israel, Kali. "Asking Alice: Victorian and Other Alices in Contemporary Culture," in John Kucich and Dianne F. Sadoff, eds., *Victorian Afterlife*, 252–80.

Jones, Jo Elwyn, and J. Francis Gladstone. *The "Alice" Companion*, 5–295.

Kasai, Katsuko. "The Hatter's Watch." *Jabberwocky* 23 (1994), 69–70.

Knoepflmacher, U. C. *Ventures into Childhood*, 168–90.

Leach, Karoline. *In the Shadow of the Dreamchild*, 35–41, 173–76.

Lecercle, Jean-Jacques. "Alice and the Sphinx." *REAL: Yrbk of Res in Engl and Am Lit* 13 (1997), 27–34.

Leclerq, Guy. "Les Mondes sonores d'Alice: Lire les 'Livres d'Alice' avec l'Oreille." *Q/W/E/R/T/Y* 4 (1994), 161–65.

Lucas, Ann Lawson. "Enquiring Mind, Rebellious Spirit: Alice and Pinocchio as Nonmodel Children." *Children's Lit in Educ* 30 (1999), 157–69.

Martin, Molly. "The Truth about the Hatter's Madness." *Jabberwocky* 24 (1997), 55–58.

Melrose, Robin, and Diana Gardner. "The Language of Control in Victorian Children's Literature," in Ruth Robbins and Julian Wolfreys, eds., *Victorian Identities*, 159–62.

Morgentaler, Goldie. "The Long and the Short of Oliver and Alice: The Changing Size of the Victorian Child." *Dickens Stud Annual* 29 (2000), 83–94.

Mucci, Clara. "Alice's *jouissance*: The Predominance of the Letter and/as Wonderland." *Rivista di Studi Vittoriani* 1:2 (1996), 109–24.

Muscardin, Roberta. "Fantastico e narrazione in *Alice's Adventures in Wonderland* e *Through the Looking-Glass* di Lewis Carroll." *Annali di Ca' Foscari* 30:1–2 (1991), 203–14.

Natov, Roni, and Wendy W. Fairey. "Dickens's David and Carroll's Alice: Representations of Victorian Liminality." *Australasian Victorian Stud J* 5 (1999), 149–55.

Reichertz, Ronald. *The Making of the Alice Books*, 33–51, 61–78.

Robson, Catherine. *Men in Wonderland*, 146–48.

Sandner, David. *The Fantastic Sublime*, 137–39.

Scrittori, Anna Rosa. "*Alice* di Lewis Carroll." *Annali di Ca' Foscari* 30:1–2 (1991), 285–96.

Shelston, Alan. "Nell, Alice and Lizzie: Three Sisters amidst the Grotesque," in Richard Gravil, ed., *Master Narratives*, 109–14.

Sigler, Carolyn. "Authorizing Alice: Professional Authority, the Literary Marketplace, and Victorian Women's Re-Visions of the Alice Books." *Lion and the Unicorn* 22 (1998), 351–61.

Sundmark, Björn. *Alice's Adventures in the Oral-Literary Continuum*, 37–198.

Sutherland, John. *Who Betrays Elizabeth Bennet?*, 182–84.

Sweeney, Kevin W. "Alice's Discriminating Palate." *Philos and Lit* 23:1 (1999), 17–31.

Warren, Austin. *In Continuity*, 15–33.

Sylvie and Bruno, 1889

Leach, Karoline. *In the Shadow of the Dreamchild,* 185–88, 190–92, 250–52.

Purdy, Strother B. "Is There a Multiverse in *Finnegans Wake,* and Does That Make It a Religious Book?" *James Joyce Q* 36:3 (1999), 593–97.

Robson, Catherine. *Men in Wonderland,* 129–31, 150–52.

Through the Looking-Glass, 1871

Dougill, John. *Oxford in English Literature,* 127–33.

Feldmann, Doris. "Victorian (Dis)Enchantments: Fantasy and Realism in the Visions and Revisions of Scrooge and Alice." *Anglistik und Englischunterricht* 59 (1996), 101–25.

Hayashi, Toyomi. "A Reading of the Alice Books as Seen from a Feministic Viewpoint." *Jabberwocky* 24 (1997), 73–88.

Irwin, Michael. "*Alice*: Reflections and Relativities," in Alice Jenkins and Juliet John, eds., *Rereading Victorian Fiction,* 115–28.

Jones, Jo Elwyn, and J. Francis Gladstone. *The "Alice" Companion,* 5–295.

Knoepflmacher, U. C. *Ventures into Childhood,* 193–227.

Leach, Karoline. *In the Shadow of the Dreamchild,* 174–79.

Lecercle, Jean-Jacques. "Alice and the Sphinx." *REAL: Yrbk of Res in Engl and Am Lit* 13 (1997), 27–34.

Leclerq, Guy. "Les Mondes sonores d'Alice: Lire les 'Livres d'Alice' avec l'Oreille." *Q/W/E/R/T/Y* 4 (1994), 161–65.

Muscardin, Roberta. "Fantastico e narrazione in *Alice's Adventures in Wonderland* e *Through the Looking-Glass* di Lewis Carroll." *Annali di Ca' Foscari* 30:1–2 (1991), 203–14.

Newby, M. J. N. "Dyslexia *Through the Looking-Glass.*" *Jabberwocky* 24 (1997), 49–53.

Reichertz, Ronald. *The Making of the Alice Books,* 33–51, 61–78.

Robson, Catherine. *Men in Wonderland,* 148–50.

Sigler, Carolyn. "Authorizing Alice: Professional Authority, the Literary Marketplace, and Victorian Women's Re-Visions of the *Alice* Books." *Lion and the Unicorn* 22 (1998), 351–61.

Sundmark, Björn. *Alice's Adventures in the Oral-Literary Continuum,* 37–198.

Warren, Austin. *In Continuity,* 15–33.

CATHERINE CARSWELL

Open the Door!, 1920

Anderson, Carol. "'Behold I make all things new': Catherine Carswell and the Visual Arts," in Carol Anderson and Aileen Christianson, eds., *Scottish Women's Fiction,* 21–30.

Laplace, Philippe. "Emotion and Motion in Catherine Carswell's *Open the Door!*: Towards a Female *Bildungsroman,*" in Sophie Marret, ed., *Féminin/Masculin,* 233–47.

McCulloch, Margery Palmer. "Fictions of Development, 1920–1970," in Douglas Gifford and Dorothy McMillan, eds., *A History,* 361–62.

Norquay, Glenda. "Catherine Carswell: *Open the Door!*," in Douglas Gifford and Dorothy McMillan, eds., *A History*, 389–98.

Pilditch, Jan. "Opening the Door on Catherine Carswell." *Scotlands* 2 (1994), 53–65.

Walker, Marshall. *Scottish Literature since 1707*, 225–29.

ANGELA CARTER

Heroes and Villains, 1969

Day, Aidan. *Angela Carter*, 41–55.

Gamble, Sarah. *Angela Carter*, 73–82.

Karpinski, Eva C. "Signifying Passion: Angela Carter's *Heroes and Villains* as a Dystopian Romance." *Utopian Stud* 11 (2000), 137–51.

Koenen, Anne. "Vampire of the Senses: The Feminist Fantastic of Angela Carter." *Anglistik und Englischunterricht* 59 (1996), 143–61.

Lee, Alison. *Angela Carter*, 52–60.

Lesinska, Sophie. "Sixty Years After the Surrealist Revolt: Epistemology and Politics in Angela Carter's *Heroes and Villains* and *The Sadeian Woman*." *CEA Critic* 61:2–3 (1999), 102–6.

Mahoney, Elisabeth. "'But elsewhere?': The Future of Fantasy in *Heroes and Villains*," in Joseph Bristow and Trev Lynn Broughton, eds., *The Infernal Desires*, 73–85.

Parker, Emma. "The Consumption of Angela Carter: Women, Food, and Power." *Ariel* 31:3 (2000), 147–48.

Sceats, Sarah. *Food, Consumption and the Body*, 44–46.

The Infernal Desire Machines of Doctor Hoffmann, 1972

Armitt, Lucie. *Contemporary Women's Fiction*, 175–80.

Buschini, Marie Pascale. "Les Maisons closes chez Angela Carter." *Imaginaires* 2 (1997), 151–67.

Day, Aidan. *Angela Carter*, 65–91.

Gamble, Sarah. *Angela Carter*, 109–15.

Lee, Alison. *Angela Carter*, 61–76.

Mikkonen, Kai. "The Hoffman(n) Effect and the Sleeping Prince: Fairy Tales in Angela Carter's *The Infernal Desire Machines of Doctor Hoffman*." *Marvels and Tales* 12:1 (1998), 155–74.

Parker, Emma. "The Consumption of Angela Carter: Women, Food, and Power." *Ariel* 31:3 (2000), 144–45.

Robinson, Sally. "The Anti-Hero as Oedipus: Gender and the Postmodern Narrative in *The Infernal Desire Machines of Doctor Hoffman*," in Alison Easton, ed., *Angela Carter*, 107–26.

Sceats, Sarah. "The Infernal Appetites of Angela Carter," in Joseph Bristow and Trev Lynn Broughton, eds., *The Infernal Desires*, 108–10.

Love, 1987

Day, Aidan. *Angela Carter*, 55–64.

Gamble, Sarah. *Angela Carter*, 82–87.

Lee, Alison. *Angela Carter*, 35–41.

Parker, Emma. "The Consumption of Angela Carter: Women, Food, and Power." *Ariel* 31:3 (2000), 149–52.

The Magic Toyshop, 1967

Armitt, Lucie. *Contemporary Women's Fiction,* 190–93.

Dapprich-Barrett, Ute. "Magical Realism: Sources and Affinities in Contemporary German and English Writing," in Susanne Stark, ed., *The Novel in Anglo-German Context,* 338–43.

Day, Aidan. *Angela Carter,* 22–32.

Gamble, Sarah. *Angela Carter,* 68–73.

Goertz, Dee. "To Pose or Not to Pose: The Interplay of Object and Subject in the Works of Angela Carter," in Abby H. P. Werlock, ed., *British Women Writing Fiction,* 214–17.

Lee, Alison. *Angela Carter,* 43–52.

Mahoney, Elisabeth. "'But elsewhere?': The Future of Fantasy in *Heroes and Villains,*" in Joseph Bristow and Trev Lynn Broughton, eds., *The Infernal Desires,* 75–82.

Parker, Emma. "The Consumption of Angela Carter: Women, Food, and Power." *Ariel* 31:3 (2000), 144–45.

Rudaityte, Regina. "The Transformation of the Bildungsroman in Angela Carter's Novel *The Magic Toyshop.*" *Literatura* (Vilnius) 41:3 (1999), 69–76.

Sceats, Sarah. *Food, Consumption and the Body,* 35–38.

Wyatt, Jean. "The Violence of Gendering: Castration Images in Angela Carter's *The Magic Toyshop, The Passion of New Eve,* and 'Peter and the Wolf.'" *Women's Stud* 25 (1996), 555–66.

Nights at the Circus, 1984

Armitt, Lucie. *Contemporary Women's Fiction,* 21–23, 164–66, 180–84.

Bannock, Sarah. "Auto/biographical Souvenirs in *Nights at the Circus,*" in Joseph Bristow and Trev Lynn Broughton, eds., *The Infernal Desires,* 198–213.

Buschini, Marie Pascale. "Les Maisons closes chez Angela Carter." *Imaginaires* 2 (1997), 151–67.

Carroll, Rachel. "Return of the Century: Time, Modernity, and the End of History in Angela Carter's *Nights at the Circus.*" *Yrbk of Engl Stud* 30 (2000), 187–201.

Dapprich-Barrett, Ute. "Magical Realism: Sources and Affinities in Contemporary German and English Writing," in Susanne Stark, ed., *The Novel in Anglo-German Context,* 337–43.

Day, Aidan. *Angela Carter,* 167–94.

Finney, Brian H. "Tall Tales and Brief Lives: Angela Carter's *Nights at the Circus.*" *J of Narrative Technique* 28 (1998), 161–83.

Gamble, Sarah. *Angela Carter,* 156–66.

Goertz, Dee. "To Pose or Not to Pose: The Interplay of Object and Subject in the Works of Angela Carter," in Abby H. P. Werlock, ed., *British Women Writing Fiction,* 220–24.

Hanson, Clare. "'The red dawn breaking over Clapham': Carter and the Limits of Artifice," in Joseph Bristow and Trev Lynn Broughton, eds., *The Infernal Desires,* 62–67.

Lee, Alison. *Angela Carter,* 93–111.

Martin, Sara. "The Power of Monstrous Women: Fay Weldon's *The Life and Loves of a She-Devil* (1983), Angela Carter's *Nights at the*

Circus (1984) and Jeanette Winterson's *Sexing the Cherry* (1989)." *J of Gender Stud* 8 (1999), 193–209.

Parker, Emma. "The Consumption of Angela Carter: Women, Food, and Power." *Ariel* 31:3 (2000), 157–66.

Roberts, Nancy. *Schools of Sympathy*, 135–41.

Russo, Mary. "Revamping Spectacle: Angela Carter's *Nights at the Circus*," in Alison Easton, ed., *Angela Carter*, 136–60.

Sceats, Sarah. *Food, Consumption and the Body*, 57–60.

Surányi, Agnes. "A Comparison of Angela Carter's *Nights at the Circus* and Christina Stead's *Little Hotel*," in Richard Todd and Luisa Flora, eds., *Theme Parks*, 167–72.

Watkins, Susan. *Twentieth-Century Women Novelists*, 130–45.

Wood, Michael. *Children of Silence*, 138–43.

The Passion of New Eve, 1977

Ahearn, Edward J. "The Modern English Visionary: Peter Ackroyd's *Hawksmoor* and Angela Carter's *The Passion of New Eve*." *Twentieth Cent Lit* 46 (2000), 460–67.

Bellina, Elena. "Il clarinetto postmoderno de Thea Musgrave e il movimento narrativo in *The Passion of New Eve*." *Confronto Letterario* 16 (1999), 231–50.

Chang, Hui-chuan. "Feminist Utopias as an Alternative Canon: Strategies and Dilemmas." *Stud in Lang and Lit* (Taipei) 6 (1994), 50–52.

Costantini, Mariaconcetta. "'On the Beach of Elsewhere': Angela Carter e il modello utopico di *The Passion of New Eve*." *Lettore di Provincia* 29 (1998), 95–110.

Day, Aidan. *Angela Carter*, 107–31.

Ferreira, Maria Aline Seabra. "Myth and Anti-Myth in Angela Carter's *The Passion of New Eve*." *J of the Fantastic in the Arts* 9 (1998), 284–302.

Ferreira, Maria Aline Seabra. "The Uncanny (M)Other: Angela Carter's *The Passion of New Eve*." *Paradoxa* 3 (1997), 471–88.

Gamble, Sarah. *Angela Carter*, 119–29.

Ivory, James Maurice. *Identity and Narrative Metamorphoses*, 75–103.

Johnson, Heather L. "Unexpected Geometries: Transgressive Symbolism and the Transsexual Subject in Angela Carter's *The Passion of New Eve*," in Joseph Bristow and Trev Lynn Broughton, eds., *The Infernal Desires*, 166–80.

Jouve, Nicole Ward. *Female Genesis*, 143–46, 153–55.

King, Jeannette. *Women and the Word*, 135–51.

Koenen, Anne. "Vampire of the Senses: The Feminist Fantastic of Angela Carter." *Anglistik und Englischunterricht* 59 (1996), 143–61.

Lee, Alison. *Angela Carter*, 77–92.

Leusmann, Harald. "Angela Carter's *The Passion of New Eve*: A Modern Initiation Story." *Notes on Contemp Lit* 27:3 (1997), 2–4.

Makinen, Marja. "Sexual and Textual Aggression in *The Sadeian Woman* and *The Passion of New Eve*," in Joseph Bristow and Trev Lynn Broughton, eds., *The Infernal Desires*, 149–63.

Sceats, Sarah. *Food, Consumption and the Body*, 54–56.

Wyatt, Jean. "The Violence of Gendering: Castration Images in Angela Carter's *The Magic Toyshop*, *The Passion of New Eve*, and 'Peter and the Wolf.'" *Women's Stud* 25 (1996), 551–55.

Several Perceptions, 1968

Day, Aidan. *Angela Carter*, 32–41.
Gamble, Sarah. *Angela Carter*, 57–63.
Lee, Alison. *Angela Carter*, 29–35.
Sceats, Sarah. *Food, Consumption and the Body*, 43–45.

Shadow Dance, 1966

Day, Aidan. *Angela Carter*, 14–22.
Gamble, Sarah. *Angela Carter*, 48–57.
Lee, Alison. *Angela Carter*, 23–29.
Sceats, Sarah. "Oral Sex: Vampiric Transgression and the Writing of Angela Carter." *Tulsa Stud in Women's Lit* 20:1 (2001), 110–14.
Wood, Michael. *Children of Silence*, 129–32.

Wise Children, 1991

Armitt, Lucie. *Contemporary Women's Fiction*, 184–90.
Day, Aidan. *Angela Carter*, 195–215.
Gamble, Sarah. *Angela Carter*, 169–85.
Goertz, Dee. "To Pose or Not to Pose: The Interplay of Object and Subject in the Works of Angela Carter," in Abby H. P. Werlock, ed., *British Women Writing Fiction*, 224–25.
Hanson, Clare. "'The red dawn breaking over Clapham': Carter and the Limits of Artifice," in Joseph Bristow and Trev Lynn Broughton, eds., *The Infernal Desires*, 67–71.
Lee, Alison. *Angela Carter*, 112–28.
Macedo, Ana Gabriela. "From the Amazon to the *Flâneuse*: Women at the Turn of the Century." *BELLS: Barcelona Engl Lang and Lit Stud* 7 (1996), 63–71.
Mohr, Hans Ulrich. "Drei Konstrukte weiblicher Verhaltensräume: Charlotte Smith, Olive Schreiner, Angela Carter." *Arbeiten aus Anglistik und Amerikanistik* 20 (1995), 317–33.
Parker, Emma. "The Consumption of Angela Carter: Women, Food, and Power." *Ariel* 31:3 (2000), 157–66.
Richardson, Brian. *Unlikely Stories*, 175–77.
Sceats, Sarah. *Food, Consumption and the Body*, 30–32, 179–83.
Webb, Kate. "Seriously Funny: *Wise Children*," in Alison Easton, ed., *Angela Carter*, 192–215.

JOYCE CARY

A Fearful Joy, 1949

McCormick, John. *Catastrophe and Imagination*, 151–54.

The Horse's Mouth, 1944

Cavaliero, Glen. *The Alchemy of Laughter*, 142–45.

Mister Johnson, 1939

Bivona, Daniel. *British Imperial Literature*, 165–80.

Criswell, Stephen. "Colonialism, Corruption, and Culture: A Fanonian Reading of *Mister Johnson* and *No Longer at Ease*." *Liter Griot* 10:1 (1998), 43–64.

Davis, Richard S. "In Search of Agency among Colonized Africans: Chinua Achebe's *No Longer at Ease* and Joyce Cary's *Mister Johnson*." *J of Commonwealth and Postcolonial Stud* 2:1 (1994), 12–26.

DAVID CAUTE

The Decline of the West, 1966

Booker, M. Keith. "The Historical Novel in Ayi Kwei Armah and David Caute: African Literature, Socialist Literature, and the Bourgeois Cultural Tradition." *Critique* (Washington, DC) 38 (1997), 237–47.

MARGARET CAVENDISH

The Description of a New Blazing-World, 1666

Battigelli, Anna. "Between the Glass and the Hand: The Eye in Margaret Cavendish's *Blazing World*." *1650–1850: Ideas, Aesthetics, and Inquiries in the Early Mod Era* 2 (1996), 25–38.

Battigelli, Anna. *Margaret Cavendish and the Exiles of the Mind*, 103–13.

Hintz, Carrie. "'But One Opinion': Fear of Dissent in Cavendish's *New Blazing World*." *Utopian Stud* 7:1 (1996), 25–37.

Holmesland, Oddvar. "Margaret Cavendish's *The Blazing World*: Natural Art and the Body Politic." *Stud in Philology* 96 (1999), 457–79.

Hutton, Sarah. "In Dialogue with Thomas Hobbes: Margaret Cavendish's Natural Philosophy." *Women's Writing* 4 (1997), 425–30.

Jowitt, Claire. "Imperial Dreams? Margaret Cavendish and the Cult of Elizabeth." *Women's Writing* 4 (1997), 391–96.

Kegl, Rosemary. "'The world I have made': Margaret Cavendish, Feminism, and the *Blazing-World*," in Valerie Traub et al., eds., *Feminist Readings*, 119–37.

Leslie, Marina. "Antipodal Anxieties: Joseph Hall, Richard Brome, Margaret Cavendish and the Cartographies of Gender." *Genre* 30 (1997), 67–76.

Leslie, Marina. "Gender, Genre and the Utopian Body in Margaret Cavendish's *Blazing World*." *Utopian Stud* 7:1 (1996), 6–24.

Pordzik, Ralph. "'No Other Mystery but Reckoning or Counting': Margaret Cavendishs *Blazing-World* und die Konstruktion des wissenschaftlichen Weltbildes im 17. Jahrhundert." *Germanisch-Romanische Monatsschrift* 49 (1999), 275–90.

Shaver, Anne. "Agency and Marriage in the Fictions of Lady Mary Wroth and Margaret Cavendish, Duchess of Newcastle," in Sigrid King, ed., *Pilgrimage for Love*, 177–90.

Sutherland, Christine Mason. "Aspiring to the Rhetorical Tradition: A Study of Margaret Cavendish," in Molly Meijer Wertheimer, ed., *Listening to Their Voices*, 266–70.

Sociable Letters, 1664

Battigelli, Anna. *Margaret Cavendish and the Exiles of the Mind*, 86–88.
Fitzmaurice, Susan. "Tentativeness and Insistence in the Expression of Politeness in Margaret Cavendish's *Sociable Letters.*" *Lang and Lit* (Harlow) 9:1 (2000), 7–24.

AIDAN CHAMBERS

The Toll Bridge, 1992

Klinker, Joanna J. "The Pedagogy of the Post-Modern Text: Aidan Chambers's *The Toll Bridge.*" *Lion and the Unicorn* 23 (1999), 257–70.

SID CHAPLIN

The Day of the Sardine, 1961

Smith, Penny. "Remembered Poverty: The North-East of England," in Ian A. Bell, ed., *Peripheral Visions*, 108–10.

The Thin Seam, 1950

Colls, Robert. "Cookson, Chaplin and Common: Three Northern Writers in 1951," in K. D. M. Snell, ed., *The Regional Novel*, 175–79.

The Watchers and the Watched, 1962

Smith, Penny. "Remembered Poverty: The North-East of England," in Ian A. Bell, ed., *Peripheral Visions*, 110–12.

MOIE CHARLES

Eve at the Driving Wheel, 1957

Philips, Deborah, and Ian Haywood. *Brave New Causes*, 69–70.

BRUCE CHATWIN

On the Black Hill, 1982

Meanor, Patrick. *Bruce Chatwin*, 61–86.

The Songlines, 1987

Blanton, Casey. *Travel Writing*, 95–97, 103–5.
Jacobs, J. U. "Names for Nomads in *The Songlines* by Bruce Chatwin." *Nomina Africana* 9:2 (1995), 11–22.
Johnson, Brian. "In a Savage Hand: Allegories of Writing in Chatwin and Levi-Strauss." *Henry Street* 6:2 (1997), 16–52.
Meanor, Patrick. *Bruce Chatwin*, 87–125.
Porter, Eleanor. "Mother Earth and the Wandering Hero: Mapping Gender in Bruce Chatwin's *The Songlines* and Robyn Davidson's *Tracks.*" *J of Commonwealth Lit* 32:1 (1997), 35–46.

Wegner, Hart L. "The Travel Writer as Missionary in Reverse: Bruce Chatwin's *Songlines.*" *West Virginia Univ Philol Papers* 40 (1994–1995), 77–81.

Youngs, Tim. "Punctuating Travel: Paul Theroux and Bruce Chatwin." *Lit and Hist* 6:2 (1997), 82–86.

Utz, 1988

Meanor, Patrick. *Bruce Chatwin*, 126–46.

The Viceroy of Ouidah, 1980

Bernard, Catherine. "Bruce Chatwin: Fiction on the Frontier," in Richard Todd and Luisa Flora, eds., *Theme Parks*, 67–68, 71–73.

Meanor, Patrick. *Bruce Chatwin*, 37–60.

GEORGE CHESNEY

The Battle of Dorking, 1871

Clarke, I. F. "Before and After *The Battle of Dorking.*" *Science-Fiction Stud* 24:1 (1997), 33–46.

G. K. CHESTERTON

The Ball and the Cross, 1910

Knight, Mark. "G. K. Chesterton and the Cross." *Christianity and Lit* 49 (2000), 485–87.

Schwartz, Adam. "G. K. C.'s Methodical Madness: Sanity and Social Control in Chesterton." *Renascence* 49 (1996), 24–36.

The Flying Inn, 1914

Schenkel, Elmar. "Paradoxical Affinities: Chesterton and Nietzsche," in Susanne Stark, ed., *The Novel in Anglo-German Context*, 245–47.

The Man Who Knew Too Much, 1922

Glover, David. "The Writers Who Knew Too Much: Populism and Paradox in Detective Fiction's Golden Age," in Warren Chernaik et al., eds., *The Art of Detective Fiction*, 38–41.

The Man Who Was Thursday, 1908

Calanchi, Alessandra. "The Spies that Were Used Up: Vulnerability and Disguise in *The Secret Agent* and *The Man Who Was Thursday.*" *Merope* 9 (1997), 105–21.

Caserio, Robert L. "G. K. Chesterton and the Terrorist God outside Modernism," in Lynne Hapgood and Nancy L. Paxton, eds., *Outside Modernism*, 63–81.

Hein, Rolland. "G. K. Chesterton: Myth, Paradox, and the Commonplace." *Seven* 13 (1996), 18–23.

Kestner, Joseph A. *The Edwardian Detective*, 171–84.

Knight, Mark. "Chesterton and the Problem of Evil." *Lit and Theology* 14 (2000), 380–82.

Knight, Mark. "G. K. Chesterton and the Cross." *Christianity and Lit* 49 (2000), 490–94.

Schäffner, Raimund. *Anarchismus und Literatur in England*, 177–87.

Schenkel, Elmar. "Paradoxical Affinities: Chesterton and Nietzsche," in Susanne Stark, ed., *The Novel in Anglo-German Context*, 247–51.

Manalive, 1912

Hein, Rolland. "G. K. Chesterton: Myth, Paradox, and the Commonplace." *Seven* 13 (1996), 15–18.

The Napoleon of Notting Hill, 1904

Bergonzi, Bernard. *War Poets,* 166–81.

Colebatch, Hal G. P. "The Meanings of *The Napoleon of Notting Hill*." *Chesterton R* 25 (1999), 437–48.

Fleming, Tom. "*The Napoleon of Notting Hill.*" *Chesterton R* 26 (2000), 509–11.

Knight, Mark. "G. K. Chesterton and the Cross." *Christianity and Lit* 49 (2000), 487–90.

Lobdell, Jared C. "Stone Pastorals: Three Men on the Side of the Horses." *Extrapolation* 37 (1996), 341–46.

HENRY CHETTLE

Piers Plainness: Seven Years' Prenticeship, 1595

Burnett, Mark Thornton. "Henry Chettle's *Piers Plainness: Seven Years' Prenticeship*: Contexts and Consumers," in Constance C. Relihan, ed., *Framing Elizabethan Fictions*, 169–86.

WILLIAM RUFUS CHETWOOD

The Voyages and Adventures of Captain Robert Boyle, 1726

Snader, Joe. *Caught Between Worlds,* 142–49.

The Voyages, Dangerous Adventures, and Imminent Escapes of Captain Richard Falconer, 1720

Snader, Joe. *Caught Between Worlds,* 184–91.

The Voyages, Travels, and Adventures of William Owen Gwin Vaughan, 1736

Wheeler, Roxann. "The Complexion of Desire: Racial Ideology and Mid-Eighteenth-Century British Novels." *Eighteenth-Cent Stud* 32 (1999), 316–19.

ERSKINE CHILDERS

The Riddle of the Sands, 1903

Kestner, Joseph A. *The Edwardian Detective,* 68–79.

Nyman, Jopi. *Under English Eyes,* 83–97.

MARY CHOLMONDELEY

Red Pottage, 1899

Heilmann, Ann. *New Woman Fiction,* 157–59.

Parkins, Wendy. "Home and Away: The New Woman and Domesticity in Mary Cholmondeley's *Red Pottage.*" *Women: A Cultural R* 10:1 (1999), 47–55.

AGATHA CHRISTIE

The ABC Murders, 1935

    Schmid, David. "The Locus of Disruption: Serial Murder and Generic Conventions in Detective Fiction," in Warren Chernaik et al., eds., *The Art of Detective Fiction,* 75–83.

Appointment with Death, 1938

    Rowland, Susan. *From Agatha Christie to Ruth Rendell,* 144–46.

The Body in the Library, 1942

    Klein, Kathleen Gregory. "Truth, Authority, and Detective Fiction: The Case of Agatha Christie's *The Body in the Library,*" in Jerilyn Fisher and Ellen S. Silber, eds., *Analyzing the Different Voice,* 103–15.

Crooked House, 1949

    Philips, Deborah, and Ian Haywood. *Brave New Causes,* 149–51.

Curtain: Poirot's Last Case, 1975

    Hühn, Peter. "The Politics of Secrecy and Publicity: The Functions of Hidden Stories in Some Recent British Mystery Fiction," in Jerome H. Delamater and Ruth Prigozy, eds., *Theory and Practice,* 44–45.

    Woods, Robin. "'It Was the Mark of Cain': Agatha Christie and the Murder of the Mystery," in Jerome H. Delamater and Ruth Prigozy, eds., *Theory and Practice,* 103–10.

Death on the Nile, 1937

    Merrill, Robert. "Christie's Narrative Games," in Jerome H. Delamater and Ruth Prigozy, eds., *Theory and Practice,* 88–93.

    Rowland, Susan. *From Agatha Christie to Ruth Rendell,* 73–74.

Evil under the Sun, 1941

    Merrill, Robert. "Christie's Narrative Games," in Jerome H. Delamater and Ruth Prigozy, eds., *Theory and Practice,* 88–93.

    Pyrhönen, Heta. *Mayhem and Murder,* 197–206.

The Hollow, 1946

    Rowland, Susan. *From Agatha Christie to Ruth Rendell,* 98–99.

The Murder at the Vicarage, 1930

    Rowland, Susan. *From Agatha Christie to Ruth Rendell,* 49–51.

The Murder of Roger Ackroyd, 1926

    Bayard, Pierre. *Who Killed Roger Ackroyd?,* 3–145.

    Cohen, Michael. *Murder Most Fair,* 74–75.

    Rowland, Susan. *From Agatha Christie to Ruth Rendell,* 27–28.

    Ungerer, Friedrich. "The Conversational Game: A Discourse-Linguistic Approach to Agatha Christie's Detective Stories," in H. Gustav Klaus and Stephen Knight, eds., *The Art of Murder,* 95–97.

Murder on the Orient Express, 1934

    Thomas, Ronald R. *Detective Fiction,* 258–60, 269–75.

Ungerer, Friedrich. "The Conversational Game: A Discourse-Linguistic Approach to Agatha Christie's Detective Stories," in H. Gustav Klaus and Stephen Knight, eds., *The Art of Murder*, 98–105.

The Mysterious Affair at Styles, 1920

Turnbull, Malcolm J. *Victims or Villains*, 78–79.

Sleeping Murder, 1976

Ungerer, Friedrich. "The Conversational Game: A Discourse-Linguistic Approach to Agatha Christie's Detective Stories," in H. Gustav Klaus and Stephen Knight, eds., *The Art of Murder*, 97–98.

They Do It with Mirrors, 1952

Rowland, Susan. *From Agatha Christie to Ruth Rendell*, 123–24.

ARTHUR C. CLARKE

Childhood's End, 1953

Hull, Elizabeth Anne. "On His Shoulders: Shaw's Influence on Clarke's *Childhood's End*," in Milton T. Wolf, ed., *Shaw and Science Fiction*, 107–17.

The Fountains of Paradise, 1978

Reid, Robin Anne. *Arthur C. Clarke*, 75–94.

The Ghost from the Grand Banks, 1990

Reid, Robin Anne. *Arthur C. Clarke*, 145–60.

The Hammer of God, 1993

Reid, Robin Anne. *Arthur C. Clarke*, 161–72.

Imperial Earth, 1976

Reid, Robin Anne. *Arthur C. Clarke*, 59–74.

Rendezvous with Rama, 1973

Miller, Timothy C. "Arthur C. Clarke's *Rendezvous with Rama*: Agent of Evolution." *J of the Fantastic in the Arts* 9 (1998), 336–44.
Reid, Robin Anne. *Arthur C. Clarke*, 37–57.

The Songs of Distant Earth, 1986

Reid, Robin Anne. *Arthur C. Clarke*, 113–28.

3001: The Final Odyssey, 1997

Hollinger, Veronica. "Future/Present: The End of Science Fiction," in David Seed, ed., *Imagining Apocalypse*, 216–17.
Reid, Robin Anne. *Arthur C. Clarke*, 173–90.

2001: A Space Odyssey, 1968

Freedman, Carl. "Kubrick's *2001* and the Possibility of a Science-Fiction Cinema." *Science-Fiction Stud* 25 (1998), 300–315.

2061: Odyssey Three, 1987

Reid, Robin Anne. *Arthur C. Clarke*, 129–43.

2010: Odyssey Two, 1982

Reid, Robin Anne. *Arthur C. Clarke*, 95–112.

AUSTIN CLARKE

The Bright Temptation, 1932

Lanters, José. *Unauthorized Versions,* 109–28.

The Singing-Men at Cashel, 1936

Lanters, José. "'To Keep Body and Soul Together': Austin Clarke's *The Singing-Men at Cashel,* 1936." *New Hibernia R* 1 (1997), 134–51.

Lanters, José. *Unauthorized Versions,* 129–52.

The Sun Dances at Easter, 1952

Lanters, José. *Unauthorized Versions,* 153–71.

LINDSAY CLARKE

The Chymical Wedding, 1990

Lund, Mark F. "Lindsay Clarke and A. S. Byatt: The Novel on the Threshold of Romance." *Deus Loci* 2 (1993), 151–59.

Schenkel, Elmar. "Exploring Unity in Contradiction: The Return of Alchemy in Contemporary British Fiction," in Barbara Korte and Klaus Peter Müller, eds., *Unity in Diversity Revisited?,* 220–32.

JOHN CLELAND

Fanny Hill, 1748

Bernier, Marc André. "Des mouvements de la nature à la mise en scène du corps libertin: La Savante Eloquence d'une *Fille de joye.*" *Tangence* 60 (1999), 84–94.

Graham, Rosemary. "The Prostitute in the Garden: Walt Whitman, *Fanny Hill,* and the Fantasy of Female Pleasure." *ELH* 64 (1997), 569–92.

Gwilliam, Tassie. "Female Fraud: Counterfeit Maidenheads in the Eighteenth Century." *J of the Hist of Sexuality* 6 (1996), 518–48.

Levin, Kate. "The Meanness of Writing for a Bookseller: John Cleland's Fanny on the Market." *J of Narrative Technique* 28 (1998), 329–49.

McFarlane, Cameron. *The Sodomite in Fiction and Satire,* 161–73.

Montandon, Alain. *Le roman au XVIIIe siècle,* 338–41.

Moore, Lisa L. *Dangerous Intimacies,* 53–75.

Mudge, Bradford K. *The Whore's Story,* 199–214.

Parker, Todd C. *Sexing the Text,* 135–75.

Paulson, Ronald. *The Beautiful, Novel, and Strange,* 136–42.

Sabor, Peter. "From Sexual Liberation to Gender Trouble: Reading *Memoirs of a Woman of Pleasure* from the 1960s to the 1990s." *Eighteenth-Cent Stud* 33 (2000), 561–78.

Skinner, Gillian. *Sensibility and Economics in the Novel,* 40–41.

Wahl, Elizabeth Susan. *Invisible Relations,* 238–43.

Weed, David. "Fitting Fanny: Cleland's *Memoirs* and the Politics of Male Pleasure." *Novel* 31 (1997), 7–19.

Werner, Florian. "Kindred Spirits? John Cleland's *Fanny Hill* and Laurence Sterne's *A Sentimental Journey*." *Zeitschrift für Anglistik und Amerikanistik* 48 (2000), 17–25.

Memoirs of a Coxcomb, 1751

Mudge, Bradford K. *The Whore's Story*, 223–30.
Parker, Todd C. *Sexing the Text*, 142–47, 152–55, 164–67.

MARY CLELAND

The Sure Traveller, 1923

McCulloch, Margery Palmer. "Fictions of Development, 1920–1970," in Douglas Gifford and Dorothy McMillan, eds., *A History*, 363–64.

LUCY CLIFFORD

Mrs Keith's Crime, 1885

Demoor, Marysa. "Self-Fashioning at the Turn of the Century: The Discursive Life of Lucy Clifford (1846–1929)." *J of Victorian Culture* 4 (1999), 285–89.

LIZA CODY

Monkey Wrench, 1994

Maassen, Irmgard. "An Unsuitable Job for a Woman?: Gender, Genre and the New Detective Heroine," in H. Gustav Klaus and Stephen Knight, eds., *The Art of Murder*, 161–63.

JOHN COLLIER

His Monkey Wife, 1930

Brann, Eva. "A Portrait of a Lady: *His Monkey Wife*." *New England R* 21:2 (2000), 83–89.
Warren, Alan. "John Collier: Fantastic Miniaturist," in Darrell Schweitzer, ed., *Discovering Classic Fantasy Fiction*, 68–70.

WILKIE COLLINS

Antonina, 1850

Nayder, Lillian. *Wilkie Collins*, 21–29.

Armadale, 1866

Brantlinger, Patrick. *The Reading Lesson*, 154–56.
Case, Alison A. *Plotting Women*, 137–46.
Daly, Nicholas. "Railway Novels: Sensation Fiction and the Modernization of the Senses." *ELH* 66 (1999), 475–77.
Mighall, Robert. *A Geography of Victorian Gothic Fiction*, 124–29.
Nayder, Lillian. *Wilkie Collins*, 102–15.

Peck, John. *Maritime Fiction*, 141–42.

Reitz, Caroline. "Colonial 'Gwilt': In and Around Wilkie Collins's *Armadale.*" *Victorian Periodicals R* 33 (2000), 92–101.

Taylor, Jenny Bourne. "*Armadale*: The Sensitive Subject as Palimpsest," in Lyn Pykett, ed., *Wilkie Collins*, 149–74.

Basil, 1852

Bisla, Sundeep. "The Manuscript as Writer's Estate: Wilkie Collins's *Basil*, Sensation Fiction, and the Early-Victorian Copyright Act." *Genre* 31 (1998), 269–301.

Nayder, Lillian. *Wilkie Collins*, 29–37.

The Dead Secret, 1857

Nayder, Lillian. *Wilkie Collins*, 52–59.

Heart and Science, 1883

Wiesenthal, Chris. *Figuring Madness in Nineteenth-Century Fiction*, 97–107.

Hide and Seek, 1854

Nayder, Lillian. *Wilkie Collins*, 42–52.

The Law and the Lady, 1875

Mangum, Teresa. "Wilkie Collins, Detection, and Deformity." *Dickens Stud Annual* 26 (1998), 285–303.

Maynard, Jessica. "Telling the Whole Truth: Wilkie Collins and the Lady Detective," in Ruth Robbins and Julian Wolfreys, eds., *Victorian Identities*, 190–97.

Nayder, Lillian. *Wilkie Collins*, 59–70.

Man and Wife, 1870

Nayder, Lillian. *Wilkie Collins*, 92–99.

The Moonstone, 1868

Arata, Stephen. *Fictions of Loss*, 133–36.

Coad, David. "Other in *The Moonstone* and *Dracula.*" *Annales du Monde Anglophone* 4 (1996), 33–53.

Cohen, Michael. *Murder Most Fair*, 108–9.

Dames, Nicholas. *Amnesiac Selves*, 178–82, 198–204.

GoGwilt, Christopher. *The Fiction of Geopolitics*, 60–85.

Gruner, Elisabeth Rose. "Family Secrets and the Mysteries of *The Moonstone*," in Lyn Pykett, ed., *Wilkie Collins*, 221–43.

Heller, Tamar. "Blank Spaces: Ideological Tensions and the Detective Work of *The Moonstone*," in Lyn Pykett, ed., *Wilkie Collins*, 244–70.

Ireland, Ken. *The Sequential Dynamics of Narrative*, 227–28.

Lepaludier, Laurent. "Apports et limites des modèles du savoir à l'âge scientifique dans *The Moonstone* de Wilkie Collins." *Cahiers Victoriens et Edouardiens* 47 (1998), 173–85.

McCuskey, Brian W. "The Kitchen Police: Servant Surveillance and Middle-Class Transgression." *Victorian Lit and Culture* 28 (2000), 363–67.

MacDonald, Janice. "Parody and Detective Fiction," in Jerome H. Delamater and Ruth Prigozy, eds., *Theory and Practice*, 66–68.

Marsh, Joss. *Word Crimes*, 181–82.

Miller, D. A. "From Roman Policier to Roman Police: Wilkie Collins's *The Moonstone*," in Lyn Pykett, ed., *Wilkie Collins*, 197–220.

Nayder, Lillian. *Wilkie Collins*, 115–25.

Peck, John. *War, the Army and Victorian Literature*, 91–93.

Pionke, Albert D. "Secreting Rebellion: From the Mutiny to the Moonstone." *Victorians Inst J* 28 (2000), 122–32.

Reitz, Caroline. "Making an English Virtue of Necessity: Detective Fiction and Imperialism." *Genre* 31 (1998), 321–31.

Rignall, John. "From City Streets to Country Houses: The Detective as Flâneur," in H. Gustav Klaus and Stephen Knight, eds., *The Art of Murder*, 71–72.

Roberts, Lewis. "The 'Shivering Sands' of Reality: Narration and Knowledge in Wilkie Collins' *The Moonstone*." *Victorian R* 23 (1997), 168–81.

Sutherland, John. *Who Betrays Elizabeth Bennet?*, 191–96.

Thomas, Ronald R. "Detection in the Victorian Novel," in Deirdre David, ed., *The Cambridge Companion to the Victorian Novel*, 183–84.

Thoms, Peter. *Detection and Its Designs*, 93–120.

Wills, Adele. "Witnesses and Truth: Juridical Narratives and Dialogism in Wilkie Collins' *The Moonstone* and *The Woman in White*." *New Formations* 32 (1997), 91–98.

The New Magdalen, 1873

Nayder, Lillian. *Wilkie Collins*, 125–32.

No Name, 1862

David, Deirdre. "Rewriting the Male Plot in Wilkie Collins's *No Name*," in Lyn Pykett, ed., *Wilkie Collins*, 136–48.

GoGwilt, Christopher. *The Fiction of Geopolitics*, 60–66.

Jones, Anna. "A Victim in Search of a Torturer: Reading Masochism in Wilkie Collins's *No Name*." *Novel* 33 (2000), 196–210.

May, Leila Silvana. *Disorderly Sisters*, 145–60.

Morris, Debra. "Maternal Roles and the Production of Name in Wilkie Collins's *No Name*." *Dickens Stud Annual* 27 (1998), 271–85.

Nayder, Lillian. *Wilkie Collins*, 85–92.

Taylor, Jenny Bourne. "Representing Illegitimacy in Victorian Culture," in Ruth Robbins and Julian Wolfreys, eds., *Victorian Identities*, 139–40.

Wicke, Jennifer. "Commercial," in Herbert F. Tucker, ed., *A Companion to Victorian Literature and Culture*, 267–69.

The Woman in White, 1860

Bisla, Sundeep. "Copy-Book Morals: *The Woman in White* and Publishing History." *Dickens Stud Annual* 28 (1999), 103–38.

Case, Alison A. *Plotting Women*, 147–61.

Cvetkovich, Ann. "Ghostlier Determinations: The Economy of Sensation and *The Woman in White*," in Lyn Pykett, ed., *Wilkie Collins*, 109–35.

Daly, Nicholas. "Railway Novels: Sensation Fiction and the Modernization of the Senses." *ELH* 66 (1999), 462–64, 466–68.

Dames, Nicholas. *Amnesiac Selves*, 176–83, 190–93, 195–204.

Dever, Carolyn. *Death and the Mother*, 107–39.

Erickson, Laurel. "'In Short, She Is an Angel; and I Am —': Odd Women and Same-Sex Desire in Wilkie Collins's *Woman in White*," in Marilyn Demarest Button and Toni Reed, eds., *The Foreign Woman in British Literature*, 95–113.

Fu, Yu-hsiang Bennett. "Re-imag(in)ing (Fe)male Subjectivities in *The Woman in White*." *Stud in Lang and Lit* (Taipei) 9 (2000), 183–200.

Gindele, Karen C. "Wonders Taken for Signs: Marian and Fosco in *The Woman in White*." *Lit and Psych* 46:3 (2000), 65–75.

GoGwilt, Christopher. *The Fiction of Geopolitics*, 60–64.

Gomel, Elana, and Stephen Weninger. "The Tell-Tale Surface: Fashion and Gender in *The Woman in White*." *Victorians Inst J* 25 (1997), 29–53.

Harvey, John. *Men in Black*, 205–8.

Hennelly, Mark M., Jr. "Reading Detection in *The Woman in White*," in Lyn Pykett, ed., *Wilkie Collins*, 88–108.

Ireland, Ken. *The Sequential Dynamics of Narrative*, 225–27.

Kendrick, Walter M. "The Sensationalism of *The Woman in White*" in Lyn Pykett, ed., *Wilkie Collins*, 70–87.

Knoepflmacher, U. C. "The Counterworld of Victorian Fiction and *The Woman in White*," in Lyn Pykett, ed., *Wilkie Collins*, 58–69.

Losseff, Nicky. "Absent Melody and *The Woman in White*." *Music and Letters* 81 (2000), 532–50.

MacDonagh, Gwendolyn, and Jonathan Smith. "'Fill Up All the Gaps': Narrative and Illegitimacy in *The Woman in White*." *J of Narrative Technique* 26 (1996), 274–88.

McEathron, Scott. "Romantic Portraiture: *The Memoirs of William Collins* and *The Woman in White*." *Victorians Inst J* 25 (1997), 7–23.

May, Leila Silvana. *Disorderly Sisters*, 124–45.

Nayder, Lillian. *Wilkie Collins*, 74–85.

Oulton, Carolyn. "'The Good Angel of Our Lives': Subversive Religion and *The Woman in White*." *Dickens Stud Annual* 30 (2001), 309–19.

Pedlar, Valerie. "Drawing a Blank: The Construction of Identity in *The Woman in White*," in Dennis Walder, ed., *The Nineteenth-Century Novel*, 69–94.

Pedlar, Valerie. "*The Woman in White*: Sensationalism, Secrets and Spying," in Dennis Walder, ed., *The Nineteenth-Century Novel*, 48–68.

Schmitt, Cannon. *Alien Nation*, 124–35.

Schramm, Jan-Melissa. *Testimony and Advocacy*, 11–13.

Smajic, Srdjan. "Rationalism and Science: Aides to Crime in Wilkie Collins' Novel *The Woman in White*." *B.A.S.: Brit and Am Stud* 2 (1997), 80–88.

Stave, Shirley A. "The Perfect Murder: Patterns of Repetition and Doubling in Wilkie Collins's *The Woman in White*." *Dickens Stud Annual* 25 (1996), 287–302.

Stern, Rebecca. "'Personation' and 'Good Marking-Ink': Sanity, Performativity, and Biology in Victorian Sensation Fiction." *Nineteenth Cent Stud* 14 (2000), 35–36, 39–46.

Sutherland, John. *Who Betrays Elizabeth Bennet?*, 161–67.

Taylor, Jenny Bourne. "Representing Illegitimacy in Victorian Culture," in Ruth Robbins and Julian Wolfreys, eds., *Victorian Identities*, 139–40.

Thomas, Ronald R. *Detective Fiction*, 57–74.

Tromp, Marlene. *The Private Rod*, 69–102.

Weliver, Phyllis. "Music and Female Power in Sensation Fiction." *Wilkie Collins Soc J* 2 (1999), 40–55.

Williams, M. Kellen. "'Traced and Captured By the Men in the Chaise': Pursuing Sexual Difference in Wilkie Collins's *The Woman in White*." *J of Narrative Technique* 28 (1998), 91–106.

Wills, Adele. "Witnesses and Truth: Juridical Narratives and Dialogism in Wilkie Collins' *The Moonstone* and *The Woman in White*." *New Formations* 32 (1997), 91–98.

Wynne, Deborah. "Vidocq, the Spy: A Possible Source for Count Fosco in Wilkie Collins's *The Woman in White*." *Notes and Queries* 44 (1997), 341–42.

JACK COMMON

The Ampersand, 1954

Smith, Penny. "Remembered Poverty: The North-East of England," in Ian A. Bell, ed., *Peripheral Visions*, 105–8.

Kiddar's Luck, 1951

Colls, Robert. "Cookson, Chaplin and Common: Three Northern Writers in 1951," in K. D. M. Snell, ed., *The Regional Novel*, 190–97.

Smith, Penny. "Remembered Poverty: The North-East of England," in Ian A. Bell, ed., *Peripheral Visions*, 105–8.

Wotton, George. "Writing from the Margins," in Ian A. Bell, ed., *Peripheral Visions*, 200–206.

IVY COMPTON-BURNETT

Pastors and Masters, 1925

Goldman, Jonathan. "The Parrotic Voice of the Frivolous: Fiction by Ronald Firbank, I. Compton-Burnett, and Max Beerbohm." *Narrative* 7 (1999), 296–99.

The Present and the Past, 1953

Cavaliero, Glen. *The Alchemy of Laughter*, 168–70.

JOSEPH CONRAD

Almayer's Folly, 1895

Bross, Addison. "*Almayer's Folly* and the Polish Debate about Materialism," in Laura L. Davis, ed., *Conrad's Century*, 29–44.

Dryden, Linda. *Joseph Conrad and the Imperial Romance*, 51–76.

Dryden, Linda. "Joseph Conrad and the Novel of Adventure and

Romance: *Almayer's Folly*," in Laura L. Davis, ed., *Conrad's Century*, 93–111.

Epstein, Hugh. "*Bleak House* and Conrad: The Presence of Dickens in Conrad's Writing," in Gene M. Moore et al., eds., *Conrad: Intertexts and Appropriations*, 120–21.

Ford, Jane M. "Father/Suitor Conflict in the Conrad Canon." *Conradiana* 32 (2000), 73–80.

Ford, Jane M. *Patriarchy and Incest*, 103–5.

Goodman, Robin Truth. "Conrad's Closet." *Conradiana* 30 (1998), 96–102.

Hampson, Robert. *Cross-Cultural Encounters*, 14–17, 99–107, 110–16.

Hampson, Robert. "Verdi in Berau," in Laura L. Davis, ed., *Conrad's Century*, 81–91.

Ireland, Ken. *The Sequential Dynamics of Narrative*, 257–58.

Jones, Susan. *Conrad and Women*, 86–89.

Lane, Christopher. "Almayer's Defeat: The Trauma of Colonialism in Conrad's Early Work." *Novel* 32 (1999), 401–10.

Ribeiro de Oliveira, Solange. "The Woman in White and the Man in Motley: Aspects of Hybridism in Conrad's *Almayer's Folly* and 'Heart of Darkness,'" in Wieslaw Krajka, ed., *Joseph Conrad*, 257–71.

Roberts, Andrew Michael. *Conrad and Masculinity*, 32–39.

Schwarz, Daniel R. *Rereading Conrad*, 123–25.

Simmons, Allan H. "'Conflicting Impulses': Focalization and the Presentation of Culture in *Almayer's Folly*." *Conradiana* 29 (1997), 163–72.

Szczypien, Jean M. "Echoes from *Konrad Wallenrod* in *Almayer's Folly* and *A Personal Record*." *Nineteenth-Cent Lit* 53 (1998), 91–110.

Vallorani, Nicoletta. "Falso movimento: La dialettica evoluzione/ ereditarietà in *Almayer's Folly*, di Joseph Conrad." *Acme* (Milano) 47:1 (1994), 5–37.

Visser, Ron. "An Out-of-the-Way Placed Called Berau." *Conradian* 18:1 (1993), 37–47.

West, Russell. "Travel and the Failure(s) of Masculinity in *Almayer's Folly* and *An Outcast of the Islands*." *L'Epoque Conradienne* 23 (1997), 11–28.

The Arrow of Gold, 1919

Brodsky, G. W. Stephen. "Joseph Conrad and the Art of Unlove: Art, Love, and the Deadly Paradox of Service." *Conradiana* 31 (1999), 131–41.

Ford, Jane M. "Father/Suitor Conflict in the Conrad Canon." *Conradiana* 32 (2000), 73–80.

Hausmann, Vincent. "Joseph Conrad and the Arts of Letters." *Conradiana* 31 (1999), 148–69.

Jones, Susan. *Conrad and Women*, 171–76, 185–87.

Roberts, Andrew Michael. *Conrad and Masculinity*, 176–85.

Schwarz, Daniel R. *Rereading Conrad*, 166–78.

Chance, 1913

Berthoud, Jacques. "Conrad the Englishman: The Case of *Chance*," in Laura L. Davis, ed., *Conrad's Century*, 133–47.

Davies, Laurence. "Conrad, *Chance*, and Women Readers." *Conradian* 17:2 (1993), 75–88.

Ford, Jane M. *Patriarchy and Incest*, 105–10.

Goodman, Robin Truth. "Conrad's Closet." *Conradiana* 30 (1998), 83–96, 107–20.

Hampson, Robert. "*Chance* and the Secret Life: Conrad, Thackeray, Stevenson." *Conradian* 17:2 (1993), 105–22.

Hayes, Peter. "Conrad, Male Tyranny, and the Idealization of Women." *Ariel* 28:3 (1997), 102–4.

Jones, Susan. *Conrad and Women*, 99–160.

Jones, Susan. "Representing Women: Conrad, Marguerite Poradowska, and *Chance*." *Conradian* 17:2 (1993), 59–74.

Jones, Susan. "The Three Texts of *Chance*." *Conradian* 21:1 (1996), 57–78.

Mroczkowski, Przemyslaw. *Chaucer to Chesterton*, 299300, 304–5.

Roberts, Andrew Michael. *Conrad and Masculinity*, 154–62.

Roberts, Andrew Michael. "Secret Agents and Secret Objects: Action, Passivity, and Gender in *Chance*." *Conradian* 17:2 (1993), 89–104.

Schwarz, Daniel R. *Rereading Conrad*, 31–33, 166–78.

Watt, Ian. "The Politics of Sex in Conrad's *Chance*." *Stanford Hum R* 8:1 (2000), 121–24.

Lord Jim, 1900

Ash, Beth Sharon. *Writing In Between*, 105–13, 153–76.

Barrett, Gerard. "The Ghost of Doubt: Writing, Speech and Language in *Lord Jim*," in Richard Gravil, ed., *Master Narratives*, 159–68.

Bender, Todd K. *Literary Impressionism*, 107–18.

Bivona, Daniel. *British Imperial Literature*, 111–21.

Brudney, Daniel. "*Lord Jim* and Moral Judgment: Literature and Moral Philosophy." *J of Aesthetics and Art Criticism* 56 (1998), 265–81.

Condon, Matthew G. "The Cost of Redemption in Conrad's *Lord Jim*." *Lit and Theology* 12 (1998), 135–44.

Delmas, Catherine. "Paysages d'orient dans les romans malais de Joseph Conrad." *Imaginaires* 5 (2000), 93–106.

Deresiewicz, William. "*Lord Jim* and the Transformation of Community." *Raritan* 20:2 (2000), 71–105.

Dolin, Kieran. *Fiction and the Law*, 148–68.

Dryden, Linda. *Joseph Conrad and the Imperial Romance*, 137–94.

Ferraro, Julian. "Jim, Marlow, and the Reader: Persuasion as Theme in *Lord Jim*." *Conradian* 20:1–2 (1995), 1–18.

Fincham, Gail. "The Dialogism of *Lord Jim*," in Andrew Gibson and Robert Hampson, eds., *Conrad and Theory*, 58–74. (Also in *Conradian* 22:1–2 [1997], 58–74.)

Gasiorek, Andrzej. "'To Season with a Pinch of Romance': Ethics and Politics in *Lord Jim*," in Andrew Gibson and Robert Hampson, eds., *Conrad and Theory*, 75–112. (Also in *Conradian* 22:1–2 [1997], 75–112.)

Gaskell, Philip. *Landmarks in English Literature*, 60–63.

Gill, David. "The Fascination of the Abomination: Conrad and Cannibalism." *Conradian* 24:2 (1999), 1–30.

Gill, David. "Joseph Conrad, William Paramor, and the Guano Island: Links to *A Personal Record* and *Lord Jim*." *Conradian* 23:2 (1998), 17–26.

Gordon, Paul. "*Lord Jim*, Paul de Man, and the Debate between Deconstructive and Humanistic Criticism." *LIT* 9 (1998), 65–80.

Gottschall, Jonathan A. "Subversive Commentary Upon Prominent Christian Themes in Conrad's *Lord Jim*." *Arkansas R* 5:1–2 (1996), 88–100.

Hampson, Robert. *Cross-Cultural Encounters*, 129–45.

Henthorne, Tom. "An End to Imperialism: *Lord Jim* and the Postcolonial Conrad." *Conradiana* 32 (2000), 203–23.

Houston, Amy. "Conrad and Alfred Russel Wallace," in Gene M. Moore et al., eds., *Conrad: Intertexts and Appropriations*, 33–45.

Içöz, Nursel. "Commitment to the Ego-Ideal and Betrayal," in Wieslaw Krajka, ed., *Joseph Conrad*, 12–24.

Ireland, Ken. *The Sequential Dynamics of Narrative*, 259–60.

Israel, Nico. *Outlandish*, 58–74.

Kang, Sukjin. "Joseph Conrad's Polyphonism." *Crit R* (Melbourne) 39 (1999), 107–12.

Katz, Tamar. *Impressionist Subjects*, 88–107.

Kermode, Frank. "*Under Western Eyes* Revisited," in Shlomith Rimmon-Kenan et al., eds., *Rereading Texts*, 270–72.

Lepaludier, Laurent. "'Understand the pauses between the words': A l'Ecoute des silences de *Lord Jim*." *Cahiers Victoriens et Edouardiens* 45 (1977), 115–31.

McCracken, Scott. "'A Hard and Absolute Condition of Existence': Reading Masculinity in *Lord Jim*." *Conradian* 17:2 (1993), 17–38.

Madden, Fred. "The Ethical Dimensions of *Heart of Darkness* and *Lord Jim*: Conrad's Debt to Schopenhauer." *Conradiana* 31 (1999), 42–58.

Martinière, Nathalie. "La Figure du saut comme dynamique d'écriture dans *Lord Jim*." *L'Epoque Conradienne* 24 (1998), 75–90.

Melas, Natalie. "Brides of Opportunity: Figurations of Women and Colonial Territory in *Lord Jim*." *Qui Parle* 3:2 (1989), 54–75.

Middleton, Tim. "Re-reading Conrad's 'Complete Man': Constructions of Masculine Subjectivity in 'Heart of Darkness' and *Lord Jim*," in Keith Carabine and Owen Knowles, eds., *Conrad, James and Other Relations*, 261–65, 269–73.

Moniga, Padmini. "'Ghosts of the Gothic': Spectral Women and Colonized Spaces in *Lord Jim*." *Conradian* 17:2 (1993), 1–16.

Moutet, Muriel. "Jim's Trial: Sympathy, or the New Voice of Conviction." *L'Epoque Conradienne* 25 (1999), 67–87.

Mroczkowski, Przemyslaw. *Chaucer to Chesterton*, 295–99, 301–7.

Najder, Zdzislaw. *Conrad in Perspective*, 81–94.

Nettels, Elsa. "Unread Words: The Power of Letters in the Fiction of Henry James and Joseph Conrad," in Keith Carabine and Owen Knowles, eds., *Conrad, James and Other Relations*, 66–69.

Panagopoulos, Nic. *The Fiction of Joseph Conrad*, 23–72.

Pauly, Véronique. "Responsibility and Otherness in Conrad's *Lord Jim*." *L'Epoque Conradienne* 25 (1999), 89–104.

Peck, John. *Maritime Fiction*, 170–72.

Perkins, Wendy. "Joseph Conrad's *Lord Jim*: Narratives from Within and Beyond the Sheltering Pale," in Laura L. Davis, ed., *Conrad's Century*, 167–87.

Peters, John G. *Conrad and Impressionism*, 61–74, 77–84, 110–13, 130–37, 155–58.

Peters, John G. "Joseph Conrad's 'Sudden Holes' in Time: The Epistemology of Temporality." *Stud in the Novel* 32 (2000), 423–25, 427–31.

Ray, Martin. "Conrad's *Lord Jim*: The Source of the *Sephora* Incident." *Notes and Queries* 45 (1998), 230–31.

Roberts, Andrew Michael. *Conrad and Masculinity*, 58–64.

Roberts, Andrew Michael. "Conrad, Theory and Value," in Andrew Gibson and Robert Hampson, eds., *Conrad and Theory*, 183–202.

Ruppel, Richard. "'They always leave us': *Lord Jim*, Colonialist Discourse, and Conrad's Magic Naturalism." *Stud in the Novel* 30 (1998), 50–60.

Schneider, Lissa. "Torches, Blindfolds, and the Light of the Feminine in Conrad," in Laura L. Davis, ed., *Conrad's Century*, 210–21.

Schwarz, Daniel R. *Rereading Conrad*, 11–13, 15–17, 79–96.

Shires, Linda M. "The Aesthetics of the Victorian Novel: Form, Subjectivity, Ideology," in Deirdre David, ed., *The Cambridge Companion to the Victorian Novel*, 61–64.

Sokolowska, Katarzyna. "Artistic Aspects of Character Creation in *Lord Jim* by Conrad and *Rudin* by Turgenev," in Wieslaw Krajka, ed., *Joseph Conrad*, 113–29.

Stape, J. H. "'Gaining Conviction': Conradian Borrowing and the *Patna* Episode in *Lord Jim*," in Gene M. Moore et al., eds., *Conrad: Intertexts and Appropriations*, 59–80.

Sullivan, Ernest W., II. "Eight New Holograph Leaves of *Lord Jim*." *Conradiana* 31 (1999), 109–13.

Tanner, Tony. "Paper-Boats and Casual Cradles," in Shlomith Rimmon-Kenan et al., eds., *Rereading Texts*, 323–31.

Toth, Tibor. "Joseph Conrad: *Lord Jim*." *AnaChronist* 1996: 210–30.

Trout, Steven. "The Imperial Editor: Language, Race, and Conrad's *Lord Jim*," in Wieslaw Krajka, ed., *Joseph Conrad*, 277–92.

The Nigger of the "Narcissus," 1897

Ash, Beth Sharon. *Writing In Between*, 19–73.

Brodsky, G. W. Stephen. "Joseph Conrad and the Art of Unlove: Art, Love, and the Deadly Paradox of Service." *Conradiana* 31 (1999), 131–41.

Clark, Lorrie. "Rousseau and Political Compassion in *The Nigger of the 'Narcissus.'*" *Conradiana* 31 (1999), 120–29.

Delmas, Catherine. "Paysages d'orient dans les romans malais de Joseph Conrad." *Imaginaires* 5 (2000), 93–106.

Kane, Michael. *Modern Men*, 121–74.

Kang, Sukjin. "Joseph Conrad's Polyphonism." *Crit R* (Melbourne) 39 (1999), 114–17.

McDonald, Peter. "Men of Letters and Children of the Sea: Conrad and the Henley Circle Revisited." *Conradian* 21:1 (1996), 45–56.

McDonald, Peter D. *British Literary Culture*, 27–32, 53–67.

Marcus, Miriam. "Writing, Race, and Illness in *The Nigger of the 'Narcissus.'*" *Conradian* 23:1 (1998), 37–50.

Martinière, Nathalie. "Effets de rupture: Le Paratexte dans *The Nigger of the Narcissus, Nostromo* et *Victory.*" *L'Epoque Conradienne* 22 (1996), 29–39.

Peck, John. *Maritime Fiction*, 165–70.

Peters, John G. *Conrad and Impressionism*, 150–53.

Polloczek, Dieter Paul. "Case and Curse: Confinement, Legal Fiction, and Solidarity in Conrad's *The Nigger of the 'Narcissus.'*" *Conradiana* 30 (1998), 183–201.

Polloczek, Dieter Paul. *Literature and Legal Discourse*, 203–42.

Roberts, Andrew Michael. *Conrad and Masculinity*, 56–58.

Schwarz, Daniel R. *Rereading Conrad*, 20–22.

Woryma, Piotr. "A Sample Contrastive Analysis of 'The Blue Hotel' by Stephen Crane and *The Nigger of the 'Narcissus'* by Joseph Conrad." *Studia Anglica Posnaniensia* 30 (1996), 159–68.

Nostromo, 1904

Bartlett, Andrew. "Señor Hirsch as Sacrificial Victim and the Modernism of Conrad's *Nostromo.*" *Contagion* 4 (1997), 47–66.

Bivona, Daniel. *British Imperial Literature*, 121–30.

Brodsky, G. W. Stephen. "Joseph Conrad and the Art of Unlove: Art, Love, and the Deadly Paradox of Service." *Conradiana* 31 (1999), 131–41.

Carpenter, Rebecca. "From Naiveté to Knowledge: Emilia Gould and the 'Kinder, Gentler' Imperialism." *Conradiana* 29 (1997), 83–99.

Caterson, Simon. "Literary Influence and the Superfluous Man: J. G. Farrell, Richard Hughes, Joseph Conrad," in Ralph J. Crane, ed., *J. G. Farrell*, 36–47.

Chou, Sooyoung. "Nostromo: A Postmodern Conrad?" *Conradian* 20:1–2 (1995), 57–76.

Curreli, Mario. "Genuine Genoese Names in *Nostromo.*" *Conradiana* 31 (1999), 99–106.

Dodson, Sandra. "Conrad and the Politics of the Sublime," in Andrew Gibson and Robert Hampson, eds., *Conrad and Theory*, 29–38.

Epstein, Hugh. "*Bleak House* and Conrad: The Presence of Dickens in Conrad's Writing," in Gene M. Moore et al., eds., *Conrad: Intertexts and Appropriations*, 132–36.

Epstein, Hugh. "Reading *Nostromo* 'With Conditions Attached.'" *Conradian* 24:2 (1999), 75–94.

Fincham, Gail. "Orality, Literacy and Community: Conrad's *Nostromo* and Ngugi's *Petals of Blood.*" *Conradian* 17:1 (1992), 45–71.

Ford, Jane M. "Father/Suitor Conflict in the Conrad Canon." *Conradiana* 32 (2000), 73–80.

Hawthorn, Jeremy. *Cunning Passages*, 181–90.

Hawthorn, Jeremy. "Repetitions and Revolutions: Conrad's Use of the Pseudo-Iterative in *Nostromo*," in Josiane Paccaud-Huguet, ed., *Joseph Conrad 1*, 125–47. (Also in *Revue des Lettres Modernes* 1342–48 [1998], 125–49.)

Hayes, Peter. "Conrad, Male Tyranny, and the Idealization of Women." *Ariel* 28:3 (1997), 109–11.

Huerta, Teresa. "Modelos colectivos circulares en *Nostromo* de Conrad, *The Plumed Serpent* de Lawrence, y *Tirano Banderas* de Valle-Inclán." *RLA: Romance Languages Annual* 7 (1995), 509–14.

Ireland, Ken. *The Sequential Dynamics of Narrative*, 260–61.

Knowles, Owen. "Conrad, Anatole France, and the Early French Romantic Tradition: Some Influences," in Gene M. Moore et al., eds., *Conrad: Intertexts and Appropriations*, 82–90.

Le Boulicaut, Yannick. "L'Eden perdu dans *Tomorrow and Victory*." *L'Epoque Conradienne* 24 (1998), 65–73.

Maisonnat, Claude. "*Nostromo*'s Scriptive Fate: From Romance to Modernity." *L'Epoque Conradienne* 23 (1997), 69–99.

Martinière, Nathalie. "Effets de rupture: Le Paratexte dans *The Nigger of the Narcissus, Nostromo* et *Victory*." *L'Epoque Conradienne* 22 (1996), 29–39.

Mroczkowski, Przemyslaw. *Chaucer to Chesterton*, 281–83, 285–87.

Nettels, Elsa. "Unread Words: The Power of Letters in the Fiction of Henry James and Joseph Conrad," in Keith Carabine and Owen Knowles, eds., *Conrad, James and Other Relations*, 66–69.

Parry, Benita. "Narrating Imperialism: *Nostromo*'s Dystopia," in Keith Ansell-Pearson et al., eds., *Cultural Readings of Imperialism*, 227–44.

Peters, John G. *Conrad and Impressionism*, 43–45, 50–53.

Phillips, Gene D, S.J. "Exiled in Eden: Screen Versions of Conrad's *Nostromo*." *Lit/Film Q* 26 (1998), 288–94.

Ramirez, Luz Elena. "The Rhetoric of Development in Joseph Conrad's *Nostromo*." *Texas Stud in Lit and Lang* 42 (2000), 93–114.

Rasula, Jed. "*Nostromo* as Fairy Tale Epic." *Genre* 33 (2000), 83–112.

Richardson, Brian. *Unlikely Stories*, 112–19.

Roberts, Andrew Michael. *Conrad and Masculinity*, 94–117.

Schwarz, Daniel R. *Rereading Conrad*, 97–120.

Wager, Timothy J. "'There is Meaning in Endeavour': Conrad's Artistic Labor." *Conradiana* 30 (1998), 213–25.

Watts, Cedric. "Drake's Trumpets in Conrad's *Nostromo*." *Conradiana* 31 (1999), 213–15.

Watts, Cedric. "*Nostromo* and *Wild Scenes* Again." *R of Engl Stud* 48 (1997), 211–17.

Wilson, Reuel K. "The Devil in Three Political Novels: Dostoevsky's *The Devils*, Conrad's *Nostromo* and Kazimierz Orlos' *The Drunk Tank*." *Polish R* 43:1 (1998), 69–78.

The Rescue, 1920

Hampson, Robert. *Cross-Cultural Encounters*, 161–81.

Jones, Susan. *Conrad and Women*, 186–91.

Schneider, Lissa. "Torches, Blindfolds, and the Light of the Feminine in Conrad," in Laura L. Davis, ed., *Conrad's Century*, 210–21.

Schwarz, Daniel R. *Rereading Conrad*, 166–78.

Tagge, Anne. "'A Glimpse of Paradise': Feminine Impulse and Ego in Conrad's Malay World." *Conradiana* 29 (1997), 101–11.

The Rover, 1923

> Eggert, Paul. "Conrad's Last Novels: Surveillance and Action." *Conradian* 24:2 (1999), 61–73.
>
> Ford, Jane M. *Patriarchy and Incest,* 110–18.
>
> Hampson, Robert. *Cross-Cultural Encounters,* 186–87.
>
> Jones, Susan. *Conrad and Women,* 165–69.
>
> Schwarz, Daniel R. *Rereading Conrad,* 166–78.

The Secret Agent, 1907

> Ash, Beth Sharon. *Writing In Between,* 179–226.
>
> Bender, Todd K. *Literary Impressionism,* 54–56.
>
> Biskupski, M. B. "Conrad and the International Politics of the Polish Question, 1914–1918: Diplomacy, *Under Western Eyes,* Or Almost *The Secret Agent.*" *Conradiana* 31 (1999), 84–93.
>
> Calanchi, Alessandra. "The Spies that Were Used Up: Vulnerability and Disguise in *The Secret Agent* and *The Man Who Was Thursday.*" *Merope* 9 (1997), 105–21.
>
> Epstein, Hugh. "*Bleak House* and Conrad: The Presence of Dickens in Conrad's Writing," in Gene M. Moore et al., eds., *Conrad: Intertexts and Appropriations,* 125–32, 136–40.
>
> Gill, David. "The Fascination of the Abomination: Conrad and Cannibalism." *Conradian* 24:2 (1999), 1–30.
>
> Glover, David. "Aliens, Anarchists and Detectives: Legislating the Immigrant Body." *New Formations* 32 (1997), 22–33.
>
> GoGwilt, Christopher. *The Fiction of Geopolitics,* 171–90.
>
> Gorak, Jan. "Popular/Canonical: The Case of *The Secret Agent.*" *Denver Q* 34:1 (1999), 75–100.
>
> Gordon, Jan. "The 'Talking Cure' (Again): Gossip and the Paralyzed Patriarchy," in David T. Mitchell and Sharon L. Snyder, eds., *The Body and Physical Difference,* 218–19.
>
> Guimond, James, and Katherine Kearney Maynard. "Kaczynski, Conrad, and Terrorism." *Conradiana* 31 (1999), 3–21.
>
> Hama, Mark. "Time as Power: The Politics of Social Time in Conrad's *The Secret Agent.*" *Conradiana* 32 (2000), 123–40.
>
> Hand, Richard J. "Christopher Hampton's Adaptation of Joseph Conrad's *The Secret Agent.*" *Conradiana* 32 (2000), 195–201.
>
> Hand, Richard James. "'The Stage is a Terribly Searching Thing': Joseph Conrad's Dramatization of *The Secret Agent.*" *Conradiana* 32 (2000), 57–64.
>
> Harrington, Ellen Burton. "That 'Blood-Stained Inanity': Detection, Repression, and Conrad's *The Secret Agent.*" *Conradiana* 31 (1999), 114–19.
>
> Hertel, Kirsten. *London zwischen Naturalismus und Moderne,* 303–48.
>
> Hooper, Myrtle. "Exploding Privacy in *The Secret Agent.*" *L'Epoque Conradienne* 25 (1999), 59–66.
>
> Houen, Alex. "*The Secret Agent*: Anarchism and the Thermodynamics of Law." *ELH* 65 (1998), 995–1010.
>
> Houston, Amy. "Joseph Conrad Takes the Stage: Dramatic Irony in *The Secret Agent.*" *Conradian* 23:2 (1998), 55–69.

Humphires, Reynold. "Tarrying with History: *The Secret Agent* as Agency of Contradiction." *L'Epoque Conradienne* 22 (1996), 57–68.

Ingersoll, Earl G. "Conrad and Film: *The Secret Agent* and Hitchcock's *Sabotage*." *Conradiana* 29 (1997), 134–48.

Ingersoll, Earl G. "Tragic Jokes: Narration in *The Secret Agent*." *Conradian* 16:1 (1991), 37–47.

Ireland, Ken. *The Sequential Dynamics of Narrative*, 261–63.

Jones, Susan. *Conrad and Women*, 200–3.

Juhasz, Tamas. "The Voice and the Facts: Ideological Transactions in Conrad's *Secret Agent*." *AnaChronist* 2000: 202–28.

Kaplan, Carola M. "No Refuge: The Duplicity of Domestic Safety in Conrad's Fiction," in Andrew Gibson and Robert Hampson, eds., *Conrad and Theory*, 138–46.

Kaye, Peter. *Dostoevsky and English Modernism*, 140–42.

Kestner, Joseph A. *The Edwardian Detective*, 157–71.

Kolani, Ruth. "Secret Agent, Absent Agent?: Ethical-Stylistic Aspects of Anarchy in Conrad's *The Secret Agent*," in Andrew Hadfield et al., eds., *The Ethics in Literature*, 86–98.

McLaughlin, Joseph. *Writing the Urban Jungle*, 23–26, 133–67.

Majewska, Monika. "Stevie: Conrad's Christ?," in Wieslaw Krajka, ed., *Joseph Conrad*, 87–109.

Matin, A. Michael. "'We Aren't German Slaves Here, Thank God': Conrad's Transposed Nationalism and British Literature of Espionage and Invasion." *J of Mod Lit* 21 (1997), 260–80.

Mulry, David. "Popular Accounts of the Greenwich Bombing and Conrad's *The Secret Agent*." *Rocky Mountain R of Lang and Lit* 54:2 (2000), 43–61.

Najder, Zdzislaw. *Conrad in Perspective*, 110–17.

Panagopoulos, Nic. *The Fiction of Joseph Conrad*, 107–28.

Panichas, George A. "Joseph Conrad's *The Secret Agent* as a Moral Tale." *Mod Age* 39 (1997), 143–52.

Pauly, Véronique. "Le Chaos et la totalité dans *The Secret Agent*," in Josiane Paccaud-Huguet, ed., *Joseph Conrad 1*, 43–61. (Also in *Revue des Lettres Modernes* 1342–48 [1998], 43–63.)

Peters, John G. *Conrad and Impressionism*, 86–94, 111–22.

Peters, John G. "Joseph Conrad's 'Sudden Holes' in Time: The Epistemology of Temporality." *Stud in the Novel* 32 (2000), 421–23.

Phillips, Gene D., S.J. "To Sup on Horrors: Christopher Hampton's Film Version of Joseph Conrad's *Secret Agent*." *Lit/Film Q* 27 (1999), 173–77.

Pike, David. "Streetwalking, Underground London, and the Urban Vision of *The Secret Agent*," in Laura L. Davis, ed., *Conrad's Century*, 113–29.

Purdy, Dwight R. "*The Secret Agent* under Edwardian Eyes." *Conradian* 16:2 (1992), 1–17.

Roberts, Andrew Michael. *Conrad and Masculinity*, 82–93, 137–41.

Ross, Stephen. "A Note on Geometrical Symbols and the Address Label in Conrad's *The Secret Agent*." *Conradiana* 32 (2000), 119–21.

Schäffner, Raimund. *Anarchismus und Literatur in England*, 163–77.

Stevenson, Randall. "Greenwich Meanings: Clocks and Things in

Modernist and Postmodernist Fiction." *Yrbk of Engl Stud* 30 (2000), 130–32.

Stott, Rebecca. "The Woman in Black: Race and Gender in *The Secret Agent*." *Conradian* 17:2 (1993), 39–58.

Sudbury, Rodie. "Anarchism and Suicide in *The Princess Casamassima* and *The Secret Agent*," in Keith Carabine and Owen Knowles, eds., *Conrad, James and Other Relations*, 25–36.

Surgal, Jon. "*The Secret Agent*: A Simple Tale of the XIX Century?" *Conradiana* 29 (1997), 123–32.

Thomas, Ronald R. *Detective Fiction*, 276–85.

Watson, Garry. "Fundamental Information: *The Secret Agent, Billy Budd, Sailor* and the Sacrifial Crisis," in Keith Carabine and Owen Knowles, eds., *Conrad, James and Other Relations*, 217–41.

Whitworth, Michael. "Inspector Heat Inspected: *The Secret Agent* and the Meanings of Entropy." *R of Engl Stud* 49 (1998), 40–59.

Wollaeger, Mark A. "Killing Stevie: Modernity, Modernism, and Mastery in Conrad and Hitchcock." *Mod Lang Q* 58 (1997), 323–50.

Zimring, Rishona. "Conrad's Pornography Shop." *Mod Fiction Stud* 43 (1997), 320–41.

Suspense, 1925

Eggert, Paul. "Conrad's Last Novels: Surveillance and Action." *Conradian* 24:2 (1999), 61–73.

Ford, Jane M. *Patriarchy and Incest*, 156–59.

Jones, Susan. *Conrad and Women*, 192–220.

Jones, Susan. "'Stepping Out of the Narrow Frame': Conrad's *Suspense* and the Novel of Sensation." *R of Engl Stud* 49 (1998), 306–21.

Marle, Hans van, and Gene M. Moore. "The Crying of Lot 16: The Drafts and Typescripts of Joseph Conrad's *Suspense*." *Papers of the Bibliographical Soc of America* 88 (1994), 217–26.

Marle, Hans van, and Gene M. Moore. "The Sources of Conrad's *Suspense*," in Gene M. Moore et al., eds., *Conrad: Intertexts and Appropriations*, 141–63.

Under Western Eyes, 1911

Andersen, Mildred C. "Conrad's Perspectives on Dostoyevsky's *Crime and Punishment*: An Examination of *Under Western Eyes*," in Wieslaw Krajka, ed., *Joseph Conrad*, 61–81.

Armstrong, Paul B. "Cultural Differences in Conrad and James: *Under Western Eyes* and *The Ambassadors*," in Keith Carabine and Owen Knowles, eds., *Conrad, James and Other Relations*, 43–51.

Ash, Beth Sharon. *Writing In Between*, 253–305.

Baldwin, Debra Romanick. "Politics, Martyrdom and the Legend of Saint Thekla in *Under Western Eyes*." *Conradiana* 32 (2000), 144–56.

Bernstein, Stephen. "Conrad and Postmodernism: *Under Western Eyes*." *Conradian* 20:1–2 (1995), 31–56.

Berthoud, Jacques. "Anxiety in *Under Western Eyes*." *Conradian* 18:1 (1993), 1–13.

Biskupski, M. B. "Conrad and the International Politics of the Polish

Question, 1914–1918: Diplomacy, *Under Western Eyes*, Or Almost *The Secret Agent.*" *Conradiana* 31 (1999), 84–93.

Carabine, Keith. *The Life and the Art*, 1–251.

Casertano, Angelo. "*Under Western Eyes* di Joseph Conrad: Un'analisi dei motivi ricorrenti." *Acme* (Milano) 49:2 (1996), 203–15.

Eggert, Paul. "Conrad's Last Novels: Surveillance and Action." *Conradian* 24:2 (1999), 61–73.

Fothergill, Anthony. "Signs, Interpolations, Meanings: Conrad and the Politics of Utterance," in Andrew Gibson and Robert Hampson, eds., *Conrad and Theory*, 39–57. (Also in *Conradian* 22:1–2 [1997], 39–57.)

Hamilton, Alissa. "The Construction and Deconstruction of National Identities through Language in the Narratives of Ngũgî wa Thiong'o's *A Grain of Wheat* and Joseph Conrad's *Under Western Eyes.*" *African Languages and Cultures* 8:2 (1995), 137–51.

Hayes, Peter. "Conrad, Male Tyranny, and the Idealization of Women." *Ariel* 28:3 (1997), 111–15.

Içöz, Nursel. "Commitment to the Ego-Ideal and Betrayal," in Wieslaw Krajka, ed., *Joseph Conrad*, 12–24.

Jones, Susan. *Conrad and Women*, 58–69.

Kang, Sukjin. "Joseph Conrad's Polyphonism." *Crit R* (Melbourne) 39 (1999), 110–14.

Kaye, Peter. *Dostoevsky and English Modernism*, 128–34, 143–55.

Kermode, Frank. "*Under Western Eyes* Revisited," in Shlomith Rimmon-Kenan et al., eds., *Rereading Texts*, 263–72.

Kirschner, Paul. "The French Face of Dostoyevsky in Conrad's *Under Western Eyes*: Some Consequences for Criticism." *Conradiana* 30 (1998), 24–39, 163–78.

Kristal, Efrain. "A Reading of the Real Life of Alejandro Mayta's Story in the Light of Joseph Conrad's *Under Western Eyes.*" *Antípodas* 8–9 (1996–1997), 205–15.

Larson, Jil. *Ethics and Narrative in the English Novel*, 114–36.

Leavis, L. R. "Guilt, Love and Extinction: *Born in Exile* and *Under Western Eyes.*" *Neophilologus* 85 (2001), 155–60.

Mathew, Anita. "An Eastern Appreciation of Joseph Conrad: His Treatment of Evil in 'Heart of Darkness' and *Under Western Eyes*," in Wieslaw Krajka, ed., *Joseph Conrad*, 311–25.

Mozina, Andrew. "An Outcast Twice Removed: Conrad, Razumov, and the Martyr as Model in *Under Western Eyes.*" *Conradiana* 30 (1998), 125–37.

Najder, Zdzislaw. *Conrad in Perspective*, 119–21, 128–38.

Nettels, Elsa. "Unread Words: The Power of Letters in the Fiction of Henry James and Joseph Conrad," in Keith Carabine and Owen Knowles, eds., *Conrad, James and Other Relations*, 70–72.

Nyman, Jopi. *Under English Eyes*, 165–91.

Okuda, Yoko. "*Under Western Eyes*: Words and the Living Body." *Conradian* 16:1 (1991), 19–36.

Panagopoulos, Nic. *The Fiction of Joseph Conrad*, 129–63.

Panichas, George A. "Joseph Conrad's *Under Western Eyes*: In Sight of Moral Discovery." *Mod Age* 40 (1998), 359–73.

Perera, S. W. "Confession and Assertion in Conrad's *Under Western Eyes*." *Sri Lanka J of the Hum* 21:1–2 (1995), 42–56.

Peters, John G. "Joseph Conrad's 'Sudden Holes' in Time: The Epistemology of Temporality." *Stud in the Novel* 32 (2000), 423–26.

Roberts, Andrew Michael. *Conrad and Masculinity*, 141–54.

Romanick, Debra. "Victorious Wretch?: The Puzzle of Haldin's Name in *Under Western Eyes*." *Conradiana* 30 (1998), 44–50.

Schäffner, Raimund. *Anarchismus und Literatur in England*, 163–77.

Schwarz, Daniel R. *Rereading Conrad*, 129–31.

Simmons, Allan H. "*Under Western Eyes*: The Ludic Text." *Conradian* 16:2 (1992), 18–37.

Spence, Gordon. "The Feminism of Peter Ivanovitch." *Conradiana* 29 (1997), 113–20.

Toy, Phyllis. "Joseph Conrad's *Under Western Eyes*: The Language of Politics and the Politics of Language," in Wieslaw Krajka, ed., *Joseph Conrad*, 41–57.

Wheatley, Alison E. "An Experiment in Understanding: Narrative Strategies of Association and Accumulation in Conrad's *Under Western Eyes*." *J of Narrative Theory* 30 (2000), 206–32.

Victory, 1915

Alexander, Ian. "The Twitching of an Amputated God: Grotesque Doubling in Conrad's *Victory*," in Alice Mills, ed., *Seriously Weird*, 63–76.

Billy, Ted. "'Nothing to Be Done': Conrad, Beckett, and the Poetics of Immobility." *Conradiana* 32 (2000), 66–71.

Delmas, Catherine. "Paysages d'orient dans les romans malais de Joseph Conrad." *Imaginaires* 5 (2000), 93–106.

Epstein, Hugh. "*Victory*'s Marionettes: Conrad's Revisitation of Stevenson," in Keith Carabine and Owen Knowles, eds., *Conrad, James and Other Relations*, 189–215.

Hampson, Robert. *Cross-Cultural Encounters*, 146–60.

Knowles, Owen. "Conrad, Anatole France, and the Early French Romantic Tradition: Some Influences," in Gene M. Moore et al., eds., *Conrad: Intertexts and Appropriations*, 90–102.

Lippe, Hans. "The Geographic Position of Samburan Island in *Victory*." *Conradian* 16:1 (1991), 51–54.

Martinière, Nathalie. "Effets de rupture: Le Paratexte dans *The Nigger of the Narcissus, Nostromo* et *Victory*." *L'Epoque Conradienne* 22 (1996), 29–39.

Mroczkowski, Przemyslaw. *Chaucer to Chesterton*, 295–99.

Panagopoulos, Nic. *The Fiction of Joseph Conrad*, 165–97.

Panichas, George A. "Moral Warfare in Joseph Conrad's *Victory*." *Mod Age* 41 (1999), 240–51.

Roberts, Andrew Michael. *Conrad and Masculinity*, 186–210.

Romanick, Debra. "'The Worker in Prose': Conrad's Anti-Theoretical Theory of Art," in Laura L. Davis, ed., *Conrad's Century*, 190–201.

Schwarz, Daniel R. *Rereading Conrad*, 31–33.

JOSEPH CONRAD AND FORD MADOX FORD

The Inheritors, 1901

Bender, Todd K. *Literary Impressionism,* 56–60.

Glover, David. "The 'Spectrality Effect' in Early Modernism," in Andrew Smith and Jeff Wallace, eds., *Gothic Modernisms,* 35–42.

Kleiner, Elaine L. "H. G. Wells, Joseph Conrad and the Scientific Romance." *Cahiers Victoriens et Edouardiens* 46 (1997), 159–66.

Romance, 1903

Mroczkowski, Przemyslaw. *Chaucer to Chesterton,* 284–85.

STORM CONSTANTINE

The Bewitchments of Love and Hate, 1988

Gough, Val. "Stylish Apocalypse: Storm Constantine's *Wraeththu* Trilogy," in David Seed, ed., *Imagining Apocalypse,* 181–97.

The Enchantments of Flesh and Spirit, 1987

Gough, Val. "Stylish Apocalypse: Storm Constantine's *Wraeththu* Trilogy," in David Seed, ed., *Imagining Apocalypse,* 181–97.

The Fulfilments of Fate and Desire, 1988

Gough, Val. "Stylish Apocalypse: Storm Constantine's *Wraeththu* Trilogy," in David Seed, ed., *Imagining Apocalypse,* 181–97.

CATHERINE COOKSON

The House of Women, 1992

Cosslett, Tess. "Feminism, Matrilinealism, and the 'House of Women' in Contemporary Women's Fiction." *J of Gender Stud* 5 (1996), 11–14.

Kate Hannigan, 1950

Colls, Robert. "Cookson, Chaplin and Common: Three Northern Writers in 1951," in K. D. M. Snell, ed., *The Regional Novel,* 179–90.

SUSAN MARY COOPER

The Dark Is Rising, 1965

Drout, Michael D. C. "Reading the Signs of Light: Anglo Saxonism, Education, and Obedience in Susan Cooper's *The Dark is Rising.*" *Lion and the Unicorn* 21 (1997), 230–45.

Filmer-Davies, Cath. "Presence and Absence: God in Fantasy Literature." *Christianity and Lit* 47 (1997), 61–64.

Hunt, Peter. *Children's Literature,* 157–60.

Kutzer, M. Daphne. "Thatchers and Thatcherites: Lost and Found Empires in Three British Fantasies." *Lion and the Unicorn* 22 (1998), 196–210.

Watson, Victor. *Reading Series Fiction,* 153–69.

ELIZABETH BURGOYNE CORBETT

New Amazonia: A Foretaste of the Future, 1889

Beaumont, Matthew. "The New Woman in Nowhere: Feminism and Utopianism at the *Fin de Siècle*," in Angelique Richardson and Chris Willis, eds., *The New Woman in Fiction and in Fact*, 216–22.

Rose, Anita. "Elizabeth Burgoyne Corbett's *New Amazonia*: Gender Equity, Science, Utopia." *Engl Lit in Transition* 40 (1997), 6–18.

MARIE CORELLI

The Murder of Delicia, 1896

Federico, Annette R. *Idol of Suburbia*, 87–88.

Federico, Annette R. "Marie Corelli: Aestheticism in Suburbia," in Talia Schaffer and Kathy Alexis Psomiades, eds., *Women and British Aestheticism*, 93–95.

The Sorrows of Satan, 1896

Federico, Annette R. *Idol of Suburbia*, 75–85.

Federico, Annette R. "Marie Corelli: Aestheticism in Suburbia," in Talia Schaffer and Kathy Alexis Psomiades, eds., *Women and British Aestheticism*, 90–93.

Federico, Annette R. "'An "Old-Fashioned" Young Woman': Marie Corelli and the New Woman," in Nicola Diane Thompson, ed., *Victorian Women Writers*, 248–56.

MacLeod, Kirsten. "Marie Corelli and *Fin-de-Siècle* Francophobia: The Absinthe Trail of French Art." *Engl Lit in Transition* 43 (2000), 66–79.

The Soul of Lilith, 1892

Federico, Annette R. *Idol of Suburbia*, 118–20.

Wormwood: A Drama of Paris, 1890

Federico, Annette R. *Idol of Suburbia*, 72–75.

Federico, Annette R. "Marie Corelli: Aestheticism in Suburbia," in Talia Schaffer and Kathy Alexis Psomiades, eds., *Women and British Aestheticism*, 87–90.

MacLeod, Kirsten. "Marie Corelli and *Fin-de-Siècle* Francophobia: The Absinthe Trail of French Art." *Engl Lit in Transition* 43 (2000), 66–79.

The Young Diana: An Experiment of the Future, 1918

Federico, Annette R. *Idol of Suburbia*, 121–26.

MARY COSTELLO

Titanic Town, 1998

St. Peter, Christine. *Changing Ireland*, 105–7.

FRANCIS COVENTRY

The History of Pompey the Little; or, The Life and Adventures of a Lap-Dog, 1751

Barchas, Janine. "Prefiguring Genre: Frontispiece Portraits from *Gulliver's Travels* to *Millenium Hall*." *Stud in the Novel* 30 (1998), 275–79.

Bellamy, Liz. *Commerce, Morality and the Eighteenth-Century Novel*, 121–24, 126–28.

Graeber, Wilhelm. *Der englische Roman in Frankreich*, 198–210.

ANTHONY BERKELEY COX

As for the Woman, 1939
  Turnbull, Malcolm J. *Elusion Aforethought*, 89–92.
Before the Fact, 1931
  Turnbull, Malcolm J. *Elusion Aforethought*, 85–89.
Death in the House, 1939
  Turnbull, Malcolm J. *Elusion Aforethought*, 68–70.
Malice Aforethought, 1931
  Turnbull, Malcolm J. *Elusion Aforethought*, 81–85.
The Piccadilly Murder, 1929
  Turnbull, Malcolm J. *Elusion Aforethought*, 64–66.
The Poisoned Chocolates Case, 1929
  Cohen, Michael. *Murder Most Fair*, 30–31.
The Silk Stocking Murders, 1928
  Turnbull, Malcolm J. *Victims or Villains*, 94–96.
Trial and Error, 1937
  Turnbull, Malcolm J. *Elusion Aforethought*, 62–67.

CHARLOTTE DACRE

Confessions of the Nun of St. Omer, 1805
  Dunn, James E. "Charlotte Dacre and the Feminization of Violence." *Nineteenth-Cent Lit* 53 (1998), 315–17.
The Libertine, 1807
  Dunn, James E. "Charlotte Dacre and the Feminization of Violence." *Nineteenth-Cent Lit* 53 (1998), 314–15.
The Passions, 1811
  Dunn, James E. "Charlotte Dacre and the Feminization of Violence." *Nineteenth-Cent Lit* 53 (1998), 319–27.
Zofloya, 1806
  Dunn, James E. "Charlotte Dacre and the Feminization of Violence." *Nineteenth-Cent Lit* 53 (1998), 313–14.
  Haggerty, George E. *Unnatural Affections*, 173–77.
  Hoeveler, Diane Long. "Charlotte Dacre's Zofloya: A Case Study in Miscegenation as Sexual and Racial Nausea." *European Romantic R* 8:2 (1997), 185–99.
  Hoeveler, Diane Long. *Gothic Feminism*, 143–58.

MARY DAMANT

Peggy: A Tale of the Irish Rebellion, 1887
> Reilly, Eileen. "Rebel, Muse, and Spouse: The Female in '98 Fiction."
> *Eire-Ireland* 34:2 (1999), 142–43.

THOMAS DANGERFIELD

Don Tomazo, or The Juvenile Rambles of Thomas Dangerfield, 1680
> Colahan, Clark. "Dangerfield's Picaresque *Don Tomazo*: English
> Novelists as Spanish (Anti-)Heroes." *Neohelicon* 25:2 (1998),
> 311–28.

MARY DAVYS

Familiar Letters Betwixt a Gentleman and a Lady, 1725
> Riley, Lindy. "Mary Davys's Satiric Novel *Familiar Letters*: Refusing
> Patriarchal Inscription of Women," in James E. Gill, ed., *Cutting
> Edges,* 206–20.

The Reform'd Coquet, 1724
> Ballaster, Ros. "Women and the Rise of the Novel: Sexual Prescripts,"
> in Vivien Jones, ed., *Women and Literature in Britain,* 204–5.
> Fendler, Susanne. "Intertwining Literary Histories: Women's
> Contribution to the Rise of the Novel," in Fendler, ed., *Feminist
> Contributions,* 53–57.
> Richetti, John. "Popular Narrative in the Early Eighteenth Century:
> Formats and Formulas," in Richard Kroll, ed., *The English Novel,
> Volume I,* 98–100.
> Swan, Beth. *Fictions of Law,* 35–38.

SEAMUS DEANE

Reading in the Dark, 1996
> Kelly, Dermot. "Joycean Epiphany in Seamus Deane's *Reading in the
> Dark,*" in Wim Tigges, ed., *Moments of Moment,* 435–43.
> Mikowski, Sylvie. "Contemporary War Fiction." *Etudes Irlandaises*
> 24:2 (1999), 67–80.
> Schwall, Hedwig. "Ruse, Rite and Riot: A Psychoanalytic Approach
> to Seamus Deane's *Reading in the Dark,*" in Geert Lernout and
> Marc Maufort, eds., *Interpreting Minority,* 66–95.

DANIEL DEFOE

Captain Singleton, 1720
> Armstrong, Katherine A. *Defoe: Writer as Agent,* 51–68.
> Berry, David W. "The Influence of Defoe's 'Moderate' Position on
> American Views of Race." *Pennsylvania Engl* 22:1–2 (2000), 17–21.
> De Michelis, Lidia. "'A Tale-Gathering in Those Idle Desarts':

Movement as Improvement in Defoe's *Captain Singleton*."
Quaderni di Acme 30 (1997), 45–90.

Detis, Elisabeth. *Daniel Defoe démasqué*, 77–89, 114–21.

Novak, Max. "Defoe as an Innovator of Fictional Form," in John
Richetti, ed., *The Cambridge Companion*, 53–56.

Peck, John. *Maritime Fiction*, 20–22.

Thompson, James. *Models of Value*, 100–104.

Turley, Hans. "Piracy, Identity, and Desire in *Captain Singleton*."
Eighteenth-Cent Stud 31 (1997–98), 199–211.

Colonel Jacque, 1722

Armstrong, Katherine A. *Defoe: Writer as Agent*, 90–112.

Armstrong, Katherine A. "'I was a kind of an Historian': The
Productions of History in Defoe's *Colonel Jack*," in Alvaro Ribeiro
and James G. Basker, eds., *Tradition in Transition*, 97–110.

Backscheider, Paula R. "The Novel's Gendered Space," in
Backscheider, ed., *Revising Women*, 20–22.

Berry, David W. "The Influence of Defoe's 'Moderate' Position on
American Views of Race." *Pennsylvania Engl* 22:1–2 (2000), 17–21.

Detis, Elisabeth. *Daniel Defoe démasqué*, 12, 31–33, 184–92.

Gladfelder, Hal. *Criminality and Narrative*, 102–12.

Montandon, Alain. *Le roman au XVIIIe siècle*, 163–64.

Novak, Max. "Defoe as an Innovator of Fictional Form," in John
Richetti, ed., *The Cambridge Companion*, 61–63.

O'Brien, John. "Union Jack: Amnesia and the Law in Daniel Defoe's
Colonel Jack." *Eighteenth-Cent Stud* 32 (1998), 65–79.

Richetti, John. *The English Novel in History*, 57–59.

Starr, George. "'Only a Boy': Notes on Sentimental Novels," in
Richard Kroll, ed., *The English Novel, Volume I*, 36–38.

Thompson, James. *Models of Value*, 104–12.

A Journal of the Plague Year, 1722

Benedict, Barbara M. *Curiosity*, 104–5.

Benedict, Barbara M. "The Curious Genre: Female Inquiry in
Amatory Fiction." *Stud in the Novel* 30 (1998), 201–3.

Bogel, Fredric V. *The Difference Satire Makes*, 248–49.

Campe, Rüdiger. "Was heisst: Eine Statistik lesen?: Beobachtungen
zu Daniel Defoes *A Journal of the Plague Year*." *Mod Lang Notes*
116 (2001), 521–35.

Gregg, Stephen. "Godly Manliness: Defoe's Good Men in Bad
Times," in Andrew P. Williams, ed., *The Image of Manhood*, 141–57.

Irwin, Michael. "Readings of Realism," in Philip Davis, ed., *Real
Voices*, 213–14.

Lowczanin, Agnieszka. "Intimations of Mortality in the Fiction of
Daniel Defoe: A Description of the Marginal." *Folia Litteraria
Anglica* (Lodz) 2 (1998), 43–52.

McLeod, Bruce. *The Geography of Empire*, 172–74.

Mayer, Robert. *History and the Early English Novel*, 199–201, 207–26.

Sherman, Sandra. *Finance and Fictionality*, 144–55.

Wall, Cynthia. "Novel Streets: The Rebuilding of London and Defoe's
A Journal of the Plague Year." *Stud in the Novel* 30 (1998), 164–75.

Zimmerman, Everett. *The Boundaries of Fiction*, 89–98.

The Memoirs of a Cavalier, 1720

Armstrong, Katherine A. *Defoe: Writer as Agent*, 29–50.

Bignami, Marialuisa. "Daniel Defoe's Military Autobiographies: History and Fictional Character." *Quaderni di Acme* 30 (1997), 91–108.

Detis, Elisabeth. *Daniel Defoe démasqué*, 114–21.

Logaldo, Mara. "*Memoirs of a Cavalier* and *Memoirs of an English Officer*: New Narrative Forms and the Legacy of Literary Genres." *Quaderni di Acme* 30 (1997), 109–29.

Moll Flanders, 1722

Ardholm, Helena M. *The Emblem and the Emblematic Habit*, 45–47.

Armstrong, Katherine A. *Defoe: Writer as Agent*, 69–89.

Backscheider, Paula R. "The Novel's Gendered Space," in Backscheider, ed., *Revising Women*, 23–27.

Bandry, Anne, and Françoise Deconinck-Brossard. "On peut compter sur Moll." *Bull de la Société d'Etudes Anglo-Américaines des XVIIe et XVIIIe Siècles* 45 (1997), 171–90.

Bender, John. "The Novel and the Rise of the Penitentiary: Narrative and Ideology in Defoe, Gay, Hogarth and Fielding," in Richard Kroll, ed., *The English Novel, Volume I*, 115–18.

Bhat, K. Sripad. "The Politics of Reading and the Birth of a Classic: Juxtaposing *Moll Flanders* with *If Tomorrow Comes*." *Indian J of Am Stud* 23:1 (1993), 93–95.

Bony, Alain. "'. . . And Takes It As He Pleases': L'Etrange Contrat de lecture de *Moll Flanders*." *Bull de la Société d'Etudes Anglo-Américaines des XVIIe et XVIIIe Siècles* 45 (1997), 91–115.

Brink, André. *The Novel*, 65–85.

Caldwell, Tanya. "Sure Instinct: Incest, Politics, and Genre in Dryden and Defoe." *Genre* 33 (2000), 45–49.

Case, Alison A. *Plotting Women*, 19–22.

Caton, Lou. "Doing the Right Thing with *Moll Flanders*: A 'Reasonable' Difference between the Picara and the Penitent." *Coll Lang Assoc J* 40 (1997), 508–16.

Connor, Rebecca E. "'Can you apply Arithmetick to Every Thing?': *Moll Flanders*, William Petty, and Social Accounting." *Stud in Eighteenth-Cent Culture* 27 (1998), 169–86.

Copeland, Edward. "Defoe and the London Wall: Mapped Perspectives." *Eighteenth-Cent Fiction* 10 (1998), 407–28.

Denizot, Paul. "De Moll Flanders à Moll Hackabout: Tolérance et/ou rigeur." *Bull de la Société d'Etudes Anglo-Américaines des XVIIe et XVIIIe Siècles* 45 (1997), 191–206.

DeRitter, Jones. "Blaming the Audience, Blaming the Gods: Unwitting Incest in Three Eighteenth-Century English Novels," in Thomas DiPiero and Pat Gill, eds., *Illicit Sex*, 221–38.

Detis, Elisabeth. *Daniel Defoe démasqué*, 13–15, 22–26, 29–31, 35–47, 54–58, 143–49, 184–92.

Di Giuseppe, Rita. "The Ghost in the Machine: *Moll Flanders* and the Body Politic." *Quaderni di Lingue e Letterature* 18 (1993), 311–26.

Downie, J. A. *To Settle the Succession of the State*, 102–5.

Dromart, Anne. "Moll Flanders l'héroïque." *Q/W/E/R/T/Y* 7 (1997), 51–57.

Dunn, Tony. "Moll Flanders: Body and Capital." *Q/W/E/R/T/Y* 7 (1997), 59–67.

Dupas, Jean-Claude. "Le Coq d'Orbaneja: *Moll Flanders*, entre *exemplum* et *fabula*." *Bull de la Société d'Etudes Anglo-Américaines des XVIIe et XVIIIe Siècles* 45 (1997), 117–35.

Flynn, Christopher. "Nationalism, Commerce, and Imperial Anxiety in Defoe's Later Works." *Rocky Mountain R of Lang and Lit* 54:2 (2000), 20–23.

Gladfelder, Hal. *Criminality and Narrative*, 113–17, 123–30.

Huguet, Christine. "*Moll Flanders* et la tradition picaresque." *Bull de la Société d'Etudes Anglo-Américaines des XVIIe et XVIIIe Siècles* 45 (1997), 67–90.

Hunter, J. Paul. "The Novel and Social/Cultural History," in John Richetti, ed., *The Cambridge Companion*, 31–33.

Iannàccaro, Giuliana. "Predestinarian Doctrine in *Moll Flanders*: A Controversial Presence." *Quaderni di Acme* 30 (1997), 145–68.

Kietzman, Mary Jo. "Defoe Masters the Serial Subject." *ELH* 66 (1999), 677–701.

Lowczanin, Agnieszka. "Intimations of Mortality in the Fiction of Daniel Defoe: A Description of the Marginal." *Folia Litteraria Anglica* (Lodz) 2 (1998), 43–52.

McCormick, John. *Catastrophe and Imagination*, 136–39.

McIntosh, Carey. *The Evolution of English Prose*, 81–84.

Mayer, Robert. *History and the Early English Novel*, 201–5.

Miller, Louise M. "Moll Flanders: The Fortunate Female Houdini." *Q/W/E/R/T/Y* 7 (1997), 69–77.

Moglen, Helene. *The Trauma of Gender*, 35–44.

Montandon, Alain. *Le roman au XVIIIe siècle*, 159–63.

Morse, David. *The Age of Virtue*, 76–79, 110–12.

Mudge, Bradford K. *The Whore's Story*, 174–78.

Novak, Max. "Defoe as an Innovator of Fictional Form," in John Richetti, ed., *The Cambridge Companion*, 56–59.

Richetti, John. *The English Novel in History*, 59–64.

Sherman, Sandra. *Finance and Fictionality*, 71–74, 81–85, 175–78.

Simms, Norman. "A Plain Conviction to the Contrary: Moll Flanders' Name and Other Lies." *Q/W/E/R/T/Y* 7 (1997), 79–88.

Soupel, Serge. "*Moll Flanders*: Conditions et labyrinthe." *Bull de la Société d'Etudes Anglo-Américaines des XVIIe et XVIIIe Siècles* 45 (1997), 137–50.

Soupel, Serge. "*Moll Flanders*: duplicité, mensonges, prudence." *Etudes Anglaises* 51 (1998), 17–25.

Suarez, Michael F., S.J. "The Shortest Way to Heaven?: Moll Flanders' Repentance Reconsidered." *1650–1850: Ideas, Aesthetics, and Inquiries in the Early Mod Era* 3 (1997), 3–28.

Sutherland, John. *Who Betrays Elizabeth Bennet?*, 1–8.

Swan, Beth. *Fictions of Law*, 26–31, 67–71, 150–57.

Swan, Beth. "Moll Flanders: The Felon as Lawyer." *Eighteenth-Cent Fiction* 11 (1998), 33–48.

Tadié, Alexis. "Sex, Lies and No Videotapes: Les Fictions du secret dans *Moll Flanders*." *Bull de la Société d'Etudes Anglo-Américaines des XVIIe et XVIIIe Siècles* 45 (1997), 151–70.

Vescovi, Alessandro. "*Moll Flanders*: The Cohesion of the Picaresque." *Quaderni di Acme* 30 (1997), 131–43.

Wall, Cynthia. *The Literary and Cultural Spaces*, 143–47.

A New Voyage Round the World, 1724

Furbank, P. N., and W. R. Owens. "Defoe's 'South-Sea' and 'North-Sea' Schemes: A Footnote to *A New Voyage Round the World*." *Eighteenth-Cent Fiction* 13 (2001), 501–8.

Rummell, Kathryn. "Defoe and the Black Legend: The Spanish Stereotype in *A New Voyage Round the World*." *Rocky Mountain R of Lang and Lit* 52:2 (1998), 13–25.

Robinson Crusoe, 1719

Andries, Lise. "Les Images et les choses dans *Robinson* et les robinsonnades." *Etudes Françaises* 35:1 (1999), 95–122.

Armstrong, Katherine A. *Defoe: Writer as Agent*, 113–26.

Attar, Samar. "Serving God or Mammon? Echoes from *Hayy Ibn Yaqzan* and *Sinbad the Sailor* in *Robinson Crusoe*," in Lieve Spaas and Brian Stimpson, eds., *Robinson Crusoe*, 78–92.

Audigier, Jean-Pierre. "Le Roman de l'origine." *Corps Ecrit* 32 (1989), 125–33.

Barney, Richard A. *Plots of Enlightenment*, 223–54, 267–70, 301–4, 307–9.

Bartra, Roger. *The Artificial Savage*, 157–74.

Bell, Ian A. "Crusoe's Women: Or, the Curious Incident of the Dog in the Night-Time," in Lieve Spaas and Brian Stimpson, eds., *Robinson Crusoe*, 28–44.

Bellamy, Liz. *Commerce, Morality and the Eighteenth-Century Novel*, 57–59, 69–72.

Bellman, Patrizia Nerozzi. "La conversazione nel romanzo inglese del Settecento." *Confronto Letterario* 12 (1995), 5–21.

Bender, John. "The Novel and the Rise of the Penitentiary: Narrative and Ideology in Defoe, Gay, Hogarth and Fielding," in Richard Kroll, ed., *The English Novel, Volume I*, 121–24.

Benedict, Barbara M. *Curiosity*, 108–10.

Berry, David W. "The Influence of Defoe's 'Moderate' Position on American Views of Race." *Pennsylvania Engl* 22:1–2 (2000), 17–21.

Bouillaguet, Annick. "De Defoe à Tournier: Le Destin ou le désordre des choses—Sur trois incipit." *Etudes Françaises* 35:1 (1999), 55–64.

Bozzetto, Roger. "*L'Invention de Morel*: Robinson, les choses et les simulacres." *Etudes Françaises* 35:1 (1999), 65–77.

Brown, Homer O. "The Displaced Self in the Novels of Daniel Defoe," in Richard Kroll, ed., *The English Novel, Volume I*, 162–66, 179–86.

Chan, Stephen C. K. "Tactics of Space in Defoe and Foucault." *Stud in Lang and Lit* (Taipei) 4 (1990), 43–57.

Compère, Daniel. "Les Déclinaisons de Robinson Crusoé dans *L'Ile mystérieuse* de Jules Verne." *Etudes Françaises* 35:1 (1999), 43–53.

Cope, Kevin L. "All Aboard the Ark of Possibility; or, Robinson Crusoe Returns from Mars as a Small-Footprint, Multi-Channel Indeterminacy Machine." *Stud in the Novel* 30 (1998), 150–61.

Cruise, James. *Governing Consumption*, 93–122.

Detis, Elisabeth. *Daniel Defoe démasqué*, 27–29, 69–76, 78–86, 90–99, 101–12, 126–28, 150–53.

Dharwadker, Aparna. "Nation, Race, and the Ideology of Commerce in Defoe." *Eighteenth Cent* 39 (1998), 69–82.

Dolezel, Lubomir. *Heterocosmica*, 37–42.

Downie, Alan. "*Robinson Crusoe*'s Eighteenth-Century Contexts," in Lieve Spaas and Brian Stimpson, eds., *Robinson Crusoe*, 13–26.

Dubois, Jacques. "Du roman au mythe: Un Robinson hédoniste et helvète." *Études Françaises* 35:1 (1999), 25–42.

Durand, Pascal. "La Leçon des choses: Robinson ou la répétition." *Études Françaises* 35:1 (1999), 7–23.

Dutheil de la Rochère, Martine Hennard. *Origin and Originality*, 35–53.

Ellis, Markman. "Crusoe, Cannibalism and Empire," in Lieve Spaas and Brian Stimpson, eds., *Robinson Crusoe*, 45–58.

Engélibert, Jean-Paul. *La postérité de Robinson Crusoé*, 51–84, 93–94.

Ferreira, Fernanda Durão. *As fontes portuguesas*, 11–57.

Figuerola, Carmen. "The Robinson Myth in Jean-Richard Bloch's *Le Robinson juif*," in Lieve Spaas and Brian Stimpson, eds., *Robinson Crusoe*, 157–63.

Fisch, Harold. *New Stories for Old*, 27–40.

Flanders, Todd R. "Rousseau's Adventure with Robinson Crusoe." *Interpretation* (Flushing, NY) 24:3 (1997), 319–34.

Fleck, Andrew. "Crusoe's Shadow: Christianity, Colonization and the Other," in John C. Hawley, ed., *Christian Encounters with the Other*, 74–85.

Flint, Christopher. *Family Fictions*, 117–60.

Flynn, Christopher. "Nationalism, Commerce, and Imperial Anxiety in Defoe's Later Works." *Rocky Mountain R of Lang and Lit* 54:2 (2000), 14–20.

Gauvin, Lise. "La Bibliothèque des Robinsons." *Études Françaises* 35:1 (1999), 79–93.

Gregg, Stephen. "'Strange Longing' and 'Horror' in *Robinson Crusoe*," in Antony Rowland et al., eds., *Signs of Masculinity*, 37–59.

Hamm, Jean-Jacques. "Caliban, Friday and their Masters," in Lieve Spaas and Brian Stimpson, eds., *Robinson Crusoe*, 110–22.

Hammond, Brean S. *Professional Imaginative Writing*, 271–74.

James, Louis. "Unwrapping Crusoe: Retrospective and Prospective Views," in Lieve Spaas and Brian Stimpson, eds., *Robinson Crusoe*, 1–8.

Jenkins, Hugh. "Crusoe's Country House(s)." *Eighteenth Cent* 38 (1997), 118–31.

Jooma, Minaz. "Robinson Crusoe Inc(corporates): Domestic Economy, Incest and the Trope of Cannibalism." *LIT* 8 (1997), 61–77.

Kumamoto, Tetsyya. "Le 'Topos' de l'île chez Rousseau et le roman *Robinson Crusoé*." *Études de Langue et Littérature Françaises* 70 (1997), 42–54.

Lamb, Jonathan. *Preserving the Self in the South Seas*, 183–89.

Liu, Lydia H. "Robinson Crusoe's Earthenware Pot." *Crit Inquiry* 25 (1999), 728–57.

Logan, Mawuena Kossi. *Narrating Africa*, 30–36.

Lowczanin, Agnieszka. "Intimations of Mortality in the Fiction of Daniel Defoe: A Description of the Marginal." *Folia Litteraria Anglica* (Lodz) 2 (1998), 43–52.

McCarron, Kevin. "'In Contemplation of my Deliverance': *Robinson Crusoe* and *Pincher Martin*," in Lieve Spaas and Brian Stimpson, eds., *Robinson Crusoe*, 285–93.

McLeod, Bruce. *The Geography of Empire*, 193–201.

Mayer, Robert. *History and the Early English Novel*, 183–97.

Meagher, Sharon. "Resisting Robinson Crusoe in Dechanel's Film," in Lieve Spaas and Brian Stimpson, eds., *Robinson Crusoe*, 148–55.

Moglen, Helene. *The Trauma of Gender*, 22–35.

Montandon, Alain. *Le roman au XVIIIe siècle*, 62–69.

Morse, David. *The Age of Virtue*, 74–76.

Moyes, Craig. "La Politique ironique de *Robinson Crusoe*." *Littératures Classiques* 40 (2000), 365–83.

Mudge, Bradford K. *The Whore's Story*, 172–78.

Neill, Anna. "Crusoe's Farther Adventures: Discovery, Trade, and the Law of Nations." *Eighteenth Cent* 38 (1997), 213–29.

Novak, Max. "Defoe as an Innovator of Fictional Form," in John Richetti, ed., *The Cambridge Companion*, 48–52.

Novak, Maximillian E. "Friday: or, the Power of Naming," in Albert J. Rivero, ed., *Augustan Subjects*, 110–20.

Paschetto, Anna. "Robinson Crusoe e l'isola che non c'era: Nota sul realismo di Defoe." *Confronto Letterario* 13 (1996), 609–15.

Peck, John. *Maritime Fiction*, 17–20.

Phillips, Richard. *Mapping Men and Empire*, 22–35.

Racault, Jean-Michel. "Insularité et origine." *Corps Ecrit* 32 (1989), 111–23.

Richetti, John. *The English Novel in History*, 65–72.

Richetti, John. "Ideas and Voices: The New Novel in Eighteenth-Century England." *Eighteenth-Cent Fiction* 12 (2000), 327–30 and 341–44.

Ritchie, Daniel E. "Robinson Crusoe as Narrative Theologian." *Renascence* 49 (1997), 95–109.

Schellenberg, Betty A. "'To Renew Their Former Acquaintance': Print, Gender, and Some Eighteenth-Century Sequels," in Paul Budra and Betty A. Schellenberg, eds., *Part Two*, 86–97.

Seidel, Michael. "Crusoe's Island Exile," in Richard Kroll, ed., *The English Novel, Volume I*, 188–208.

Sherman, Sandra. *Finance and Fictionality*, 70–81.

Sill, Geoffrey. "The Source of Robinson Crusoe's 'Sudden Joys.'" *Notes and Queries* 45 (1998), 67–68.

Sill, Geoffrey M. "Neurology and the Novel: Alexander Monro *primus* and *secundus*, *Robinson Crusoe*, and the Problem of Sensibility." *Lit and Medicine* 16 (1997), 250–62.

Smith, Christopher. "Charles Guilbert de Pixérécourt's *Robinson*

Crusoé (1805)," in Lieve Spaas and Brian Stimpson, eds., *Robinson Crusoe*, 127–38.

Smith, Vanessa. "Crusoe in the South Seas: Beachcombers, Missionaries and the Myth of the Castaway," in Lieve Spaas and Brian Stimpson, eds., *Robinson Crusoe*, 62–75.

Snader, Joe. *Caught Between Worlds*, 138–41.

Soncini, Sara. "The Island as Social Experiment: A Reappraisal of Daniel Defoe's Political Discourse(s) in *Robinson Crusoe* and *The Farther Adventures.*" *Quaderni di Acme* 30 (1997), 11–43.

Soupel, Serge. "D'un archtype à l'autre: *The Mysteries of Udolpho* et *Robinson Crusoe.*" *Bull de la Société d'Etudes Anglo-Américaines des XVIIe et XVIIIe Siècles* 43 (1996), 51–61.

Spaas, Lieve. "Narcissus and Friday: From Classical to Anthropological Myth," in Lieve Spaas and Brian Stimpson, eds., *Robinson Crusoe*, 98–108.

Stotesbury, John A. "Constructions of Heroic Resistance: Crusoe, Mandela, and Their Desert Island," in Jopi Nyman and John A. Stotesbury, eds., *Postcolonialism and Cultural Resistance*, 244–52.

Thompson, James. *Models of Value*, 90–93.

Varney, Andrew. *Eighteenth-Century Writers in their World*, 4–6, 11–23.

Wall, Cynthia. *The Literary and Cultural Spaces*, 194–204.

Zimmerman, Everett. *The Boundaries of Fiction*, 66–70.

Roxana, 1724

Backscheider, Paula R. "The Novel's Gendered Space," in Backscheider, ed., *Revising Women*, 23–25.

Brown, Laura. "The Feminization of Ideology: Form and the Female in the Long Eighteenth Century," in David H. Richter, ed., *Ideology and Form*, 230–32.

Canavesi, Angelo. "*Roxana, the Fortunate Mistress*: Orchestration of Contexts and Escape of Words from Their Literal Meaning." *Quaderni di Acme* 30 (1997), 179–89.

Detis, Elisabeth. *Daniel Defoe démasqué*, 15–17, 47–49, 51–58, 113–21, 128–33, 143–53, 173–80, 184–205.

Flint, Christopher. *Family Fictions*, 155–60.

Gladfelder, Hal. *Criminality and Narrative*, 117–19, 131–47.

Hammond, Brean S. *Professional Imaginative Writing*, 227–30.

Joseph, Betty. "Mutations of the Imperial Contract," in Ann Kibbey et al., eds., *On Your Left*, 38–61.

Lowczanin, Agnieszka. "Intimations of Mortality in the Fiction of Daniel Defoe: A Description of the Marginal." *Folia Litteraria Anglica* (Lodz) 2 (1998), 43–52.

Lynch, Deidre Shauna. *The Economy of Character*, 36–38.

Moglen, Helene. *The Trauma of Gender*, 44–52.

Mudge, Bradford K. *The Whore's Story*, 178–82.

Novak, Max. "Defoe as an Innovator of Fictional Form," in John Richetti, ed., *The Cambridge Companion*, 63–66.

Novak, Maximillian E. "Defoe's *Roxana* and the New World of Luxury." *Stud on Voltaire and the Eighteenth Cent* 348 (1996), 1174–75.

Pagetti, Carlo. "Deceiving Roxana." *Quaderni di Acme* 30 (1997), 169–78.

Richetti, John. *The English Novel in History*, 73–81.

Sherman, Sandra. *Finance and Fictionality*, 84–92, 156–78.

Sill, Geoffrey. "*Roxana*'s Susan: Whose Daughter Is She Anyway?" *Stud in Eighteenth-Cent Culture* 29 (2000), 261–71.

Skinner, Gillian. *Sensibility and Economics in the Novel*, 39–40.

Swan, Beth. *Fictions of Law*, 31–35, 67–75, 157–62.

Terrien, Nicole. "Roxana: Une Femme perdue pour les hommes?" *Imaginaires* 2 (1997), 75–90.

Thompson, James. *Models of Value*, 113–22.

Varney, Andrew. *Eighteenth-Century Writers in their World*, 70–77.

Wall, Cynthia. *The Literary and Cultural Spaces*, 204–12.

E. M. DELAFIELD

The Optimist, 1922

Trumpener, Katie. "The Virago Jane Austen," in Deidre Lynch, ed., *Janeites*, 154–59.

THOMAS DELONEY

Jack of Newbury, 1597

Cheney, Donald. "Narrative, Romance, and Epic," in Arthur F. Kinney, ed., *The Cambridge Companion*, 212–13.

Culpepper, Jonathan, and Merja Kyto. "Investigating Nonstandard Language in a Corpus of Early Modern English Dialogues: Methodological Considerations and Problems," in Irma Taavitsainen et al., eds., *Writing in Nonstandard English*, 181–83.

Kinney, Jane M. "Rewriting History: Thomas Deloney's *Jack of Newbury* and Elizabethan Politics." *West Virginia Univ Philol Papers* 44 (1998–1999), 50–57.

THOMAS DE QUINCEY

Klosterheim, 1832

Morrison, Robert. "The Opium-Eater on Stage: Eleanora Louisa Montagu's Dramatization of De Quincey's *Klosterheim*." *Charles Lamb Bull* 110 (2000), 78–83.

Wordsworth, Jonathan. *Visionary Gleam*, 229–35.

MICHAEL DIBDIN

Dead Lagoon, 1994

Ghose, Indira. "Venice Confidential," in Manfred Pfister and Barbara Schaff, eds., *Venetian Views*, 213–24.

CHARLES DICKENS

Barnaby Rudge, 1841

Ayres, Brenda. *Dissenting Women in Dickens' Novels,* 33–63.

Bowen, John. *Other Dickens,* 157–82.

Brantlinger, Patrick. "Did Dickens Have a Philosophy of History? The Case of *Barnaby Rudge.*" *Dickens Stud Annual* 30 (2001), 59–71.

Chase, Karen, and Michael Levenson. *The Spectacle of Intimacy,* 89–91.

Crawford, Iain. "Dickens, Classical Myth, and the Representation of Social Order in *Barnaby Rudge.*" *Dickensian* 93 (1997), 185–95.

Dransfield, Scott. "Reading the Gordon Riots in 1841: Social Violence and Moral Management in *Barnaby Rudge.*" *Dickens Stud Annual* 27 (1998), 69–90.

Glancy, Ruth. *Student Companion to Charles Dickens,* 35–38.

Glavin, John. "Politics and *Barnaby Rudge*: Surrogation, Restoration and Revival." *Dickens Stud Annual* 30 (2001), 95–111.

Morgentaler, Goldie. *Dickens and Heredity,* 111–22.

Morgentaler, Goldie. "Executing Beauty: Dickens and the Aesthetics of Death." *Dickens Stud Annual* 30 (2001), 45–55.

Newsom, Robert. *Charles Dickens Revisited,* 96–100.

Palmer, William J. *Dickens and New Historicism,* 63–67.

Pionke, Albert D. "Combining the Two Nations: Trade Unions as Secret Societies, 1837–1845." *Victorian Newsl* 97 (2000), 7–10.

Sanders, Andrew. *Dickens and the Spirit of the Age,* 167–70.

Slater, Michael. *An Intelligent Person's Guide,* 24–25.

Tracy, Robert. "Clock Work: *The Old Curiosity Shop* and *Barnaby Rudge.*" *Dickens Stud Annual* 30 (2001), 34–42.

Wilt, Judith. "Masques of the English in *Barnaby Rudge.*" *Dickens Stud Annual* 30 (2001), 75–91.

Bleak House, 1853

Armstrong, Nancy. *Fiction in the Age of Photography,* 135–40, 144–46, 148–59, 164–66.

Ayres, Brenda. *Dissenting Women in Dickens' Novels,* 141–55.

Bigelow, Gordon. "Market Indicators: Banking and Domesticity in Dickens's *Bleak House.*" *ELH* 67 (2000), 589–611.

Birden, Lorene. "Trois analyses du sel: le personnage du faux charitable dans les œuvres de George Eliot, Charles Dickens et Rebecca West." *Cahiers Victoriens et Edouardiens* 45 (1977), 53–67.

Blake, Kathleen. "*Bleak House,* Political Economy, Victorian Studies." *Victorian Lit and Culture* 25 (1997), 1–17.

Buzard, James. "'Anywhere's Nowhere': *Bleak House* as Autoethnography." *Yale J of Criticism* 12:1 (1999), 7–39.

Carens, Timothy L. "The Civilizing Mission at Home: Empire, Gender, and National Reform in *Bleak House.*" *Dickens Stud Annual* 26 (1998), 121–40.

Case, Alison A. *Plotting Women,* 125–33.

Cheadale, Brian. "Mystification and the Mystery of Origins in *Bleak House.*" *Dickens Stud Annual* 25 (1996), 29–44.

Currie, Richard A. "Against the Feminine Stereotype: Dickens's

Esther Summerson and Conduct Book Heroines." *Dickens Q* 16 (1999), 13–20.

Davis, Philip. "Victorian Realist Prose and Sentimentality," in Alice Jenkins and Juliet John, eds., *Rereading Victorian Fiction*, 20–22.

Derbyshire, A. J. "Guppy's Treat." *Dickensian* 95 (1999), 229.

Dever, Carolyn. *Death and the Mother*, 81–103.

Dolin, Kieran. *Fiction and the Law*, 77–96.

Doody, Terrence. *Among Other Things*, 163–67.

Dunstan, William. "The Real Jarndyce and Jarndyce." *Dickensian* 93 (1997), 27–33.

Edgecombe, Rodney Stenning. "Personification in the Late Novels of Dickens." *Dickensian* 95 (1999), 232–33.

Edgecombe, Rodney Stenning. "Prophetic Moments in Dickens and Carlyle." *Victorian Newsl* 95 (1999), 18–19.

Ferguson, Susan L. "Drawing Fictional Lines: Dialect and Narrative in the Victorian Novel." *Style* 32:1 (1998), 1–17.

Fisher, Benjamin Franklin, IV. "Dickens' *Bleak House*: A Twilight Story." *Worcester R* 7 (1984), 44–49.

Fletcher, LuAnn McCracken. "A Recipe for Perversion: The Feminine Narrative Challenge in *Bleak House*." *Dickens Stud Annual* 25 (1996), 67–83.

Ford, Jane M. *Patriarchy and Incest*, 64–75.

Glancy, Ruth. *Student Companion to Charles Dickens*, 146–48.

Glavin, John. *After Dickens*, 39–46.

Good, James. "Dickens's *Bleak House* and Norris's *McTeague*." *Explicator* 55:3 (1997), 135–36.

Gordon, Jan. "The 'Talking Cure' (Again): Gossip and the Paralyzed Patriarchy," in David T. Mitchell and Sharon L. Snyder, eds., *The Body and Physical Difference*, 215–16.

Gravil, Richard. "The Androgyny of *Bleak House*," in Gravil, ed., *Master Narratives*, 123–37.

Hack, Daniel. "'Sublimation Strange': Allegory and Authority in *Bleak House*." *ELH* 66 (1999), 129–51.

Harvey, John. *Men in Black*, 34–36, 170–72.

Hennelly, Mark M., Jr. "'Betwixt 'Em Somewheres': From Liminal to Liminoid in *David Copperfield, Bleak House,* and *Great Expectations*." *Dickens Q* 17 (2000), 199–212; 18 (2001), 37–45.

Hennelly, Mark M., Jr. "The 'Mysterious Portal': Liminal Play in *David Copperfield, Bleak House* and *Great Expectations*." *Dickens Q* 15 (1998), 155–64 and 195–204.

Henson, Louise. "'Phantoms Arising from the Scenes of Our Too-Long Neglect': Charles Dickens, Victorian Chemistry, and the Folklore of the Ghost." *Victorian R* 26:1 (2000), 15–21.

Higbie, Robert. *Dickens and Imagination*, 112–22.

Hill, James. "Authority and the *Bildungsroman*: The Double Narrative of *Bleak House*." *Dickens Stud Annual* 29 (2000), 163–90.

Hochman, Baruch. "On the Bleakness of *Bleak House*," in Shlomith Rimmon-Kenan et al., eds., *Rereading Texts*, 71–82.

Hochman, Baruch, and Ilja Wachs. *Dickens: The Orphan Condition*, 86–126.

Hornback, Bert G. "The Narrator of *Bleak House*." *Dickens Q* 16 (1999), 3–11.

Kran, Paul A. "Signification and Rhetoric in *Bleak House*." *Dickens Stud Annual* 26 (1998), 147–64.

Lenard, Mary. "'Mr. Popular Sentiment': Dickens and the Gender Politics of Sentimentalism and Social Reform Literature." *Dickens Stud Annual* 27 (1998), 58–61.

Lloyd, Tom. *Crises of Realism*, 99–103, 117–21.

Loesberg, Jonathan. "Dickensian Deformed Children and the Hegelian Sublime." *Victorian Stud* 40:4 (1997), 633–43.

Marlow, James E. "Towards a Dickens Poetic: Iconic and Indexical Elements in *Bleak House*." *Dickens Stud Annual* 30 (2001), 173–90.

Mighall, Robert. *A Geography of Victorian Gothic Fiction*, 69–77.

Miller, J. Hillis. "Moments of Decision in *Bleak House*," in John O. Jordan, ed., *The Cambridge Companion*, 49–62.

Morgentaler, Goldie. *Dickens and Heredity*, 88–96.

Nelson, Harland S. "Dickens, Religion, and Nubile Girls." *Dickens Q* 14 (1997), 34–38.

Newsom, Robert. *Charles Dickens Revisited*, 113–30.

Oost, Regina B. "'More Like Than Life': Painting, Photography, and Dickens's *Bleak House*." *Dickens Stud Annual* 30 (2001), 141–55.

Peck, John. *War, the Army and Victorian Literature*, 106–9.

Plotkin, David. "Home-Made Savages: Cultivating English Children in *Bleak House*." *Pacific Coast Philology* 32:1 (1997), 17–31.

Polloczek, Dieter Paul. *Literature and Legal Discourse*, 124–202.

Polloczek, Dieter Paul. "The Marginal, the Equitable and the Unparalleled: Lady Dedlock's Case in Dickens's *Bleak House*." *New Liter Hist* 30 (1999), 453–76.

Posner, Richard A. *Law and Literature*, 140–43.

Roberts, Adam. "Dickens's Jarndyce and Lytton's Gawtrey." *Notes and Queries* 43 (1996), 45–46.

Sadrin, Anny. "Time, Tense, Weather in Three 'Flood Novels': *Bleak House*, *The Mill on the Floss*, *To the Lighthouse*." *Yrbk of Engl Stud* 30 (2000), 100–102.

Salotto, Eleanor. "Detecting Esther Summerson's Secrets: Dickens's Bleak House of Representation." *Victorian Lit and Culture* 25 (1997), 333–47.

Samet, Elizabeth Dale. "'When Constabulary Duty's To Be Done': Dickens and the Metropolitan Police." *Dickens Stud Annual* 27 (1998), 131–40.

Schiffman, Robyn L. "Wax-Work, Clock-Work, and Puppet-Shews: *Bleak House* and the Uncanny." *Dickens Stud Annual* 30 (2001), 159–68.

Schor, Hilary M. *Dickens and the Daughter of the House*, 101–23.

Schramm, Jan-Melissa. *Testimony and Advocacy*, 134–36.

Sen, Sambudha. "*Bleak House* and *Little Dorrit*: The Radical Heritage." *ELH* 65 (1998), 959–66.

Sen, Sambudha. "*Bleak House*, *Vanity Fair*, and the Making of an Urban Aesthetic." *Nineteenth-Cent Lit* 54 (2000), 480–502.

Storor, David. "Grotesque Storytelling: Dickens's Articulation of the

'Crisis of the Knowable Community' in *Bleak House* and *Little Dorrit.*" *Dickensian* 94 (1998), 25–40.

Sung, Enuai. "Double Narrative and Double Vision in *Bleak House.*" *J of Engl Lang and Lit* 42 (1996), 611–27.

Sutherland, John. *Who Betrays Elizabeth Bennet?*, 115–27.

Thomas, Ronald R. "Detection in the Victorian Novel," in Deirdre David, ed., *The Cambridge Companion to the Victorian Novel*, 176–78.

Thomas, Ronald R. *Detective Fiction*, 131–49.

Thomas, Ronald R. "Double Exposure: Arresting Images in *Bleak House* and *The House of the Seven Gables.*" *Novel* 31:1 (1997), 87–113.

Thoms, Peter. *Detection and Its Designs*, 71–92.

Tick, Stanley. "In the Case of *Bleak House*: A Brief Brief in Defense of Mr. Tulkinghorn." *Dickens Q* 15 (1998), 210–15.

Valenti, Teresa. "The Forgotten Father in Charles Dickens's *Bleak House.*" *Dickens Q* 17 (2000), 88–92.

Ward, David A. "Distorted Religion: Dickens, Dissent, and *Bleak House.*" *Dickens Stud Annual* 29 (2000), 195–225.

Waters, Catherine. "Gender, Family, and Domestic Ideology," in John O. Jordan, ed., *The Cambridge Companion*, 128–30.

Welsh, Alexander. *Dickens Redressed*, 1–146.

West, Gilian. "The Macabre Use of the Pastoral in *Bleak House.*" *Dickensian* 93 (1997), 133–35.

The Chimes, 1844

Daleski, H. M. "Seasonal Offerings: Some Recurrent Features in Dickens's Christmas Books." *Dickens Stud Annual* 27 (1998), 97–110.

Glancy, Ruth. *Student Companion to Charles Dickens*, 61–63.

Pollin, Burton R. "Dickens' *Chimes* and Its Pathway into Poe's 'Bells.'" *Mississippi Q* 51 (1998), 217–31.

A Christmas Carol, 1843

Bowen, John. *Other Dickens*, 5–7.

Cerny, Lothar. "Dickens' *A Christmas Carol*: Revisiting and Reformation." *Connotations* 7 (1997–1998), 255–72.

Chase, Karen, and Michael Levenson. *The Spectacle of Intimacy*, 86–88.

Daleski, H. M. "Seasonal Offerings: Some Recurrent Features in Dickens's Christmas Books." *Dickens Stud Annual* 27 (1998), 97–110.

Davis, Philip. "Victorian Realist Prose and Sentimentality," in Alice Jenkins and Juliet John, eds., *Rereading Victorian Fiction*, 25–27.

Erickson, Lee. "The Primitive Keynesianism of Dickens's *A Christmas Carol.*" *Stud in the Liter Imagination* 30:1 (1997), 51–61.

Feldmann, Doris. "Victorian (Dis)Enchantments: Fantasy and Realism in the Visions and Revisions of Scrooge and Alice." *Anglistik und Englischunterricht* 59 (1996), 101–25.

Glancy, Ruth. *Student Companion to Charles Dickens*, 57–61.

Hancher, Michael. "Reading the Visual Text: *A Christmas Carol.*" *Yale Univ Lib Gazette* 74:1–2 (1999), 21–40.

Higbie, Robert. *Dickens and Imagination*, 69–72.

Jaffe, Audrey. *Scenes of Sympathy*, 27–46.

Loesberg, Jonathan. "Dickensian Deformed Children and the Hegelian Sublime." *Victorian Stud* 40:4 (1997), 637–38.

Newsom, Robert. *Charles Dickens Revisited*, 67–69.

Petroski, Karen. "'The Ghost of an Idea': Dickens' Uses of Phantasmagoria, 1842–44." *Dickens Q* 16:2 (1999), 71–93.

Slater, Michael. *An Intelligent Person's Guide*, 28–30.

Stone, Harry. "*A Christmas Carol*: Giving Nursery Tales a Higher Form," in Elton E. Smith and Robert Haas, eds., *The Haunted Mind*, 11–18.

Sutherland, John. *Who Betrays Elizabeth Bennet?*, 49–54.

Waters, Catherine. *Dickens and the Politics of the Family*, 71–82.

David Copperfield, 1850

Arnds, Peter O. *Wilhelm Raabe's "Der Hungerpastor" and Charles Dickens's "David Copperfield."*

Ayres, Brenda. *Dissenting Women in Dickens' Novels*, 13–32.

Baneth-Nouailhetas, Emilienne. "Textiles et texte: La Parole vestimentaire dans *David Copperfield*." *Q/W/E/R/T/Y* 6 (1996), 115–22.

Black, Barbara. "A Sisterhood of Rage and Beauty: Dickens' Rosa Dartle, Miss Wade, and Madame Defarge." *Dickens Stud Annual* 26 (1998), 93–104.

Brattin, Joel J. "'Let Me Pause Once More': Dickens' Manuscript Revisions in the Retrospective Chapters of *David Copperfield*." *Dickens Stud Annual* 26 (1998), 73–89.

Buckton, Oliver S. "'My Undisciplined Heart': Declassifying Homoerotic Secrets in *David Copperfield*." *ELH* 64 (1997), 189–217.

Bury, Laurent. "L'Ecriteau et l'ornement: La Prolifération des signes dans *David Copperfield*." *Q/W/E/R/T/Y* 6 (1996), 123–27.

Case, Alison A. *Plotting Women*, 109–12.

Chase, Karen, and Michael Levenson. *The Spectacle of Intimacy*, 115–19.

Clay, George R. "In Defense of Flat Characters: A Discussion of Their Value to Charles Dickens, Jane Austen, and Leo Tolstoy." *Intl Fiction R* 27:1–2 (2000), 20–24.

Cordery, Gareth. "Foucault, Dickens, and David Copperfield." *Victorian Lit and Culture* 26 (1998), 71–82.

Dames, Nicholas. *Amnesiac Selves*, 134–50.

Dutheil, Martine Hennard. "Rushdie's Affiliation with Dickens." *Dickens Stud Annual* 27 (1998), 213–17.

Dutheil de la Rochère, Martine Hennard. *Origin and Originality*, 64–73.

Faymonville, Carmen. "'Waste Not, Want Not': Even Redundant Women Have Their Uses," in Rita S. Kranidis, ed., *Imperial Objects*, 76–77.

Flint, Kate. "The Middle Novels: *Chuzzlewit*, *Dombey*, and *Copperfield*," in John O. Jordan, ed., *The Cambridge Companion*, 43–47.

Ford, Jane M. *Patriarchy and Incest*, 60–64.

Gager, Valerie L. *Shakespeare and Dickens*, 229–34.

Garnett, Robert R. "Why Not Sophy?: Desire and Agnes in *David Copperfield*." *Dickens Q* 14 (1997), 213–30.

Gaskell, Philip. *Landmarks in English Literature*, 52–57.

Glancy, Ruth. *Student Companion to Charles Dickens*, 73–89.

Goodlad, Lauren M. E. "'A Middle Class Cut into Two': Historiography and Victorian National Character." *ELH* 67 (2000), 157–61.

Hake, Steven. "Becoming Poor to Make Many Rich: The Resolution of Class Conflict in Dickens." *Dickens Stud Annual* 26 (1998), 109–18.

Harvey, John. *Men in Black*, 137–39.

Heinrich, Hans. *Zur Geschichte des 'Libertin,'* 185–91.

Hennelly, Mark M., Jr. "'Betwixt 'Em Somewheres': From Liminal to Liminoid in *David Copperfield, Bleak House,* and *Great Expectations*." *Dickens Q* 17 (2000), 199–212 and 18 (2001), 37–45.

Hennelly, Mark M., Jr. "The 'Mysterious Portal': Liminal Play in *David Copperfield, Bleak House* and *Great Expectations*." *Dickens Q* 15 (1998), 155–64 and 195–204.

Higbie, Robert. *Dickens and Imagination*, 97–111.

Hochman, Baruch, and Ilja Wachs. *Dickens: The Orphan Condition*, 55–85.

Hollington, Michael. "*David Copperfield* and *Wilhelm Meister*: A Preliminary *Rapprochement*." *Q/W/E/R/T/Y* 6 (1996), 129–38.

Hornback, Bert. "Dickens's Failure." *Dickens Q* 17 (2000), 140–47.

Houston, Gail Turley. *Royalties*, 101–14.

Joseph, Gerhard. "Prejudice in Jane Austen, Emma Tennant, Charles Dickens—and Us." *Stud in Engl Lit, 1500–1900* 40 (2000), 684–92.

Kincaid, James R. *Annoying the Victorians*, 53–60.

Kincaid, James R. "Dickens and the Construction of the Child," in Wendy S. Jacobson, ed., *Dickens and the Children of Empire*, 38–39.

Lanone, Catherine. "Ruptures mnémoniques et tissage narratif dans *David Copperfield*." *Q/W/E/R/T/Y* 6 (1996), 139–45.

Lepaludier, Laurent. "La description des rives de la Tamise dans *David Copperfield*: Logique descriptive, encodage idéologique et esthétique ambigue." *Cahiers Victoriens et Edouardiens* 49 (1999), 99–106.

Löschnigg, Martin. "'The prismatic hues of memory': Autobiographische Modellierung und die Rhetorik der Erinnerung in Dickens' *David Copperfield*." *Poetica* (Munich) 31 (1999), 175–200.

McCarthy, Patrick. "Making for Home: David Copperfield and His Fellow Travelers," in Murray Baumgarten and H. M. Daleski, eds., *Homes and Homelessness*, 21–32.

McGlamery, Gayla S., and Joseph J. Walsh. "Mr. (H)Omer and the Iliadic Heroes of *David Copperfield*." *Classical and Mod Lit* 20:2 (2000), 1–20.

Morgentaler, Goldie. *Dickens and Heredity*, 63–73, 101–4.

Natov, Roni, and Wendy W. Fairey. "Dickens's David and Carroll's

Alice: Representations of Victorian Liminality." *Australasian Victorian Stud J* 5 (1999), 143–49.

Newey, Vincent. "Dickensian Decadents," in Michael St. John, ed., *Romancing Decay*, 66–74.

Newsom, Robert. *Charles Dickens Revisited*, 109–13.

O'Farrell, Mary Ann. *Telling Complexions*, 86–110.

Palmer, William J. *Dickens and New Historicism*, 70–81, 131–34.

Peck, John. *Maritime Fiction*, 81–87.

Peltason, Timothy. "Life Writing," in Herbert F. Tucker, ed., *A Companion to Victorian Literature and Culture*, 362–63.

Plung, Daniel L. "Environed by Wild Beasts: Animal Imagery in Dickens's *David Copperfield*." *Dickens Q* 17 (2000), 216–23.

Polhemus, Robert M. "The Favorite Child: *David Copperfield* and the Scriptural Issue of Child-Wives," in Murray Baumgarten and H. M. Daleski, eds., *Homes and Homelessness*, 3–20.

Poussa, Patricia. "Dickens as Sociolinguist: Dialect in *David Copperfield*," in Irma Taavitsainen et al., eds., *Writing in Nonstandard English*, 27–42.

Preston, Shale. "True Romance? Dirty Davy and the Domestic Sublime: From the Alps to the Abject in *David Copperfield*." *Australasian Victorian Stud J* 3:2 (1998), 59–69.

Ramel, Annie. "'Brooks of Sheffield,' ou la question de la coupure dans *David Copperfield*." *Cahiers Victoriens et Edouardiens* 47 (1998), 339–48.

Russell, Shannon. "Recycling the Poor and Fallen: Emigration Politics and the Narrative Resolutions of *Mary Barton* and *David Copperfield*," in Rita S. Kranidis, ed., *Imperial Objects*, 43–57.

Ruth, Jennifer. "Mental Capital, Industrial Time, and the Professional in *David Copperfield*." *Novel* 32 (1999), 303–27.

Schor, Hilary M. *Dickens and the Daughter of the House*, 7–14, 70–72.

Sutherland, John. *Who Betrays Elizabeth Bennet?*, 90–101.

Thiele, David. "The 'transcendent and immortal . . . HEEP!': Class Consciousness, Narrative Authority, and the Gothic in *David Copperfield*." *Texas Stud in Lit and Lang* 42 (2000), 201–18.

Thornton, Sara. "The Vanity of Childhood: Constructing, Deconstructing, and Destroying the Child in the Novel of the 1840s," in Karín Lesnik-Oberstein, ed., *Children in Culture*, 134–37, 142–47.

Véga-Ritter, Max. "*David Copperfield* et autobiographie, la dimension autothanatographique." *Cahiers Victoriens et Edouardiens* 47 (1998), 351–62.

Welsh, Alexander. *Dickens Redressed*, 3–7, 9–12, 20–22, 83–85, 144–46, 157–60.

Wright, Terence. "Caresses that Comfort, Blows that Bind: Sex, Sentiment and the Sense of Touch in *David Copperfield*." *English* 48 (1999), 1–15.

Dombey and Son, 1848

Armstrong, Nancy. *Fiction in the Age of Photography*, 140–42.

Armstrong, Nancy. "Gender and the Victorian Novel," in Deirdre

David, ed., *The Cambridge Companion to the Victorian Novel*, 103–4.

Berry, Laura C. *The Child, the State, and the Victorian Novel*, 63–92.

Berry, Laura C. "In the Bosom of the Family: The Wet-Nurse, the Railroad, and *Dombey and Son*." *Dickens Stud Annual* 25 (1996), 1–22.

Bradbury, Nicola. "Dickens and the Form of the Novel," in John O. Jordan, ed., *The Cambridge Companion*, 157–60.

Colligan, Colette. "Raising the House Tops: Sexual Surveillance in Charles Dickens's *Dombey and Son* (1846–48)." *Dickens Stud Annual* 29 (2000), 99–118.

Flint, Kate. "The Middle Novels: *Chuzzlewit, Dombey*, and *Copperfield*," in John O. Jordan, ed., *The Cambridge Companion*, 40–43.

Gager, Valerie L. *Shakespeare and Dickens*, 201–7, 213–22.

Gane, Gillian. "The Hat, the Hook, the Eyes, the Teeth: Captain Cuttle, Mr. Carker, and Literacy." *Dickens Stud Annual* 25 (1996), 91–120.

Glancy, Ruth. *Student Companion to Charles Dickens*, 143–46.

Gohrisch, Jana. "Familiar Excess? Emotion and the Family in Victorian Literature." *REAL: Yrbk of Res in Engl and Am Lit* 16 (2000), 163–82.

Goodin, George. "Competitive Conversation in the Dialogue of Dickens." *Dickens Q* 18 (2001), 3–7.

Grove, Robin. "Dickens and Democracy." *Crit R* (Melbourne) 37 (1997), 3–16.

Harvey, John. *Men in Black*, 135–37.

Higbie, Robert. *Dickens and Imagination*, 74–96.

Houston, Gail Turley. *Royalties*, 99–101.

Levy, Anita. *Reproductive Urges*, 93–128.

Mancini, Michelle. "Demons on the Rooftops, Gypsies in the Street: The 'Secret Intelligence' of *Dombey and Son*." *Dickens Stud Annual* 30 (2001), 113–35.

May, Leila Silvana. *Disorderly Sisters*, 44–71.

Morgentaler, Goldie. *Dickens and Heredity*, 52–62, 122–32.

Newsom, Robert. *Charles Dickens Revisited*, 102–9.

Newsom, Robert. "Fictions of Childhood," in John O. Jordan, ed., *The Cambridge Companion*, 97–98.

Palmer, William J. *Dickens and New Historicism*, 134–39.

Peck, John. *Maritime Fiction*, 72–80.

Sanders, Andrew. "Dickens and the Millennium," in Juliet John and Alice Jenkins, eds., *Rethinking Victorian Culture*, 84–85.

Schor, Hilary M. *Dickens and the Daughter of the House*, 49–69.

Slater, Michael. *An Intelligent Person's Guide*, 17–19, 70–71.

Smith, Malvern van Wyk. "'What the waves were always saying': *Dombey and Son* and Textual Ripples on an African Shore," in Wendy S. Jacobson, ed., *Dickens and the Children of Empire*, 128–49.

Stewart, Garrett. "The Foreign Offices of British Fiction." *Mod Lang Q* 61 (2000), 184–206.

Surridge, Lisa. "Domestic Violence, Female Self-Mutilation, and the Healing of the Male in *Dombey and Son*." *Victorians Inst J* 25 (1997), 77–100.

Sutherland, John. *Who Betrays Elizabeth Bennet?*, 78–86.

Thornton, Sara. "The Vanity of Childhood: Constructing, Deconstructing, and Destroying the Child in the Novel of the 1840s," in Karín Lesnik-Oberstein, ed., *Children in Culture*, 129–31.

Toise, David W. "'As Good as Nowhere': Dickens's Dombey and Son, the Contingency of Value, and Theories of Domesticity." *Criticism* 41 (1999), 323–45.

Vrettos, Athena. "Defining Habits: Dickens and the Psychology of Repetition." *Victorian Stud* 42:3 (1999/2000), 412–21.

Waters, Catherine. *Dickens and the Politics of the Family*, 38–57.

West, Gilian. "Huffam and Son." *Dickensian* 95 (1999), 8–16.

Wolpers, Theodor. "Verlust und Wiedergewinn der Familie als Gefühlsgemeinschaft in Dickens' *Dombey and Son*: Figuren-relationen als Motiveinheiten," in Wolpers, ed., *Familienbildung als Schicksal*, 145–74.

Great Expectations, 1861

Afnan, Elham. "Imaginative Transformations: *Great Expectations* and *Sunset Boulevard*." *Dickensian* 94 (1998), 5–12.

Alsop, Derek, and Chris Walsh. *The Practice of Reading*, 76–95.

Ayres, Brenda. *Dissenting Women in Dickens' Novels*, 87–90.

Barzilai, Shuli. "Spiders, Spinners, and Spinsters: Dickens's *Great Expectations*," in Shlomith Rimmon-Kenan et al., eds., *Rereading Texts*, 85–97.

Baston, Jane. "Word and Image: The Articulation and Visualization of Power in *Great Expectations*." *Lit/Film Q* 24 (1996), 322–31.

Baumgarten, Murray. "Calligraphy and Code: Writing in *Great Expectations*." *Stanford Hum R* 8:1 (2000), 226–35.

Beatty, Bernard. "Two Kinds of Clothing: *Sartor Resartus* and *Great Expectations*," in Alice Jenkins and Juliet John, eds., *Rereading Victorian Fiction*, 44–56.

Benson, Sheila. "A Levinasian Reading of Miss Havisham: Learning to Accept Responsibility for the Other." *Q/W/E/R/T/Y* 9 (1999), 45–49.

Bradbury, Nicola. "Dickens and the Form of the Novel," in John O. Jordan, ed., *The Cambridge Companion*, 163–65.

Cheadle, Brian. "The Late Novels: *Great Expectations* and *Our Mutual Friend*," in John O. Jordan, ed., *The Cambridge Companion*, 78–84.

Cohen, Monica F. *Professional Domesticity*, 70–99.

Crago, Hugh. "Prior Expectations of *Great Expectations*: How One Child Learned to Read a Classic." *Coll Engl* 58 (1996), 676–92.

Darby, Margaret Flanders. "Listening to Estella." *Dickens Q* 16 (1999), 215–27.

Filmer, Kath. "The Specter of the Self in *Frankenstein* and *Great Expectations*," in Elton E. Smith and Robert Haas, eds., *The Haunted Mind*, 19–30.

Fischler, Alan. "Love in the Garden: *Maud, Great Expectations,* and W. S. Gilbert's *Sweethearts.*" *Stud in Engl Lit, 1500–1900* 37 (1997), 771–76.

Garnett, Robert R. "The Good and the Unruly in *Great Expectations*—and Estella." *Dickens Q* 16 (1999), 24–41.

Glancy, Ruth. *Student Companion to Charles Dickens,* 125–41.

Goodin, George. "Competitive Conversation in the Dialogue of Dickens." *Dickens Q* 18 (2001), 9–19.

Hennelly, Mark M., Jr. "'Betwixt 'Em Somewheres': From Liminal to Liminoid in *David Copperfield, Bleak House,* and *Great Expectations.*" *Dickens Q* 17 (2000), 199–212 and 18 (2001), 37–45.

Hennelly, Mark M., Jr. "The 'Mysterious Portal': Liminal Play in *David Copperfield, Bleak House* and *Great Expectations.*" *Dickens Q* 15 (1998), 155–64 and 195–204.

Higbie, Robert. *Dickens and Imagination,* 145–47.

Hochman, Baruch, and Ilja Wachs. *Dickens: The Orphan Condition,* 166–200.

Hollington, Michael. "'The Terror of Childhood': Gothic Realism in *Great Expectations.*" *Etudes Anglaises* 52 (1999), 422–34.

Hollington, Michael. "Wemmick's Pig: Notes on the Recycling Economies of *Great Expectations.*" *Q/W/E/R/T/Y* 9 (1999), 51–60.

Kincaid, James. "Pip and Jane and Recovered Memories." *Dickens Stud Annual* 25 (1996), 211–24.

Kincaid, James R. *Annoying the Victorians,* 50–53, 84–86.

Kincaid, James R. "Dickens and the Construction of the Child," in Wendy S. Jacobson, ed., *Dickens and the Children of Empire,* 39–41.

Krzemienski, Ed. "For Fun or Function?: Recreation and Class in *Great Expectations.*" *Aethlon* 16:2 (1999), 85–96.

Lindberg, Erik D. "Returning the Repressed: The Unconscious in Victorian and Modernist Narrative." *Narrative* 8 (2000), 71–77.

Litvack, Leon. "Dickens, Australia and Magwitch." *Dickensian* 95 (1999), 24–46 and 101–23.

Lloyd, Tom. *Crises of Realism,* 103–9.

Meckier, Jerome. "'Dashing in Now': *Great Expectations* and Charles Lever's *A Day's Ride.*" *Dickens Stud Annual* 26 (1998), 227–57.

Meckier, Jerome. "*Great Expectations*: Symmetry in (Com)motion." *Dickens Q* 15 (1998), 28–45.

Merchant, Peter. "From Eliot to Dickens: The Descent of the Stone Slab in *Great Expectations.*" *Dickensian* 95 (1999), 132–37.

Merchant, Peter. "*Great Expectations* and 'Elizabeth Villiers.'" *Dickens Q* 14 (1997), 243–46.

Morgentaler, Goldie. *Dickens and Heredity,* 72–84, 163–74.

Morgentaler, Goldie. "Meditating on the Low: A Darwinian Reading of *Great Expectations.*" *Stud in Engl Lit, 1500–1900* 38 (1998), 707–20.

Newlin, George. *Understanding "Great Expectations,"* 1–27.

Newsom, Robert. *Charles Dickens Revisited,* 146–53.

Palmer, William J. *Dickens and New Historicism,* 145–47.

Parker, David. "Wemmick's Cottage." *Dickensian* 95 (1999), 128–31.

Pettitt, Clare. "Monstrous Displacements: Anxieties of Exchange in *Great Expectations.*" *Dickens Stud Annual* 30 (2001), 243–58.

Rem, Tore. "Pip's Marshes and Wemmick's Castle: Nature in Dickens." *Q/W/E/R/T/Y* 9 (1999), 61–68.

Rosenberg, Edgar. "'Murder' 'Shot!' 'Drowned!': A Note on Dickens's Descriptive Headlines." *Q/W/E/R/T/Y* 9 (1999), 87–95.

Rosenberg, Edgar. "Towards *Great Expectations*: From Notebook to Novel." *Q/W/E/R/T/Y* 9 (1999), 69–85.

Rothfield, Lawrence. "Medical," in Herbert F. Tucker, ed., *A Companion to Victorian Literature and Culture*, 170–71.

Sadrin, Anny. "The Trappings of Romance in *Jane Eyre* and *Great Expectations*." *Dickens Q* 14 (1997), 69–89.

Schor, Hilary M. *Dickens and the Daughter of the House*, 153–77.

Sell, Kathleen. "The Narrator's Shame: Masculine Identity in *Great Expectations*." *Dickens Stud Annual* 26 (1998), 203–22.

Sheehan, Paul. "Marx, Money, and Monstrosity in *Great Expectations*." *Q/W/E/R/T/Y* 9 (1999), 97–104.

Simmons, James R., Jr. "'Every Discernible Thing in It Was Covered With Dust and Mould': Radcliffe's Château-le-Blanc and Dickens's Satis House." *Dickensian* 93 (1997), 11–12.

Smith, Grahame. *Charles Dickens*, 159–78.

Smith, Grahame. "Suppressing Narratives: Childhood and Empire in *The Uncommon Traveller* and *Great Expectations*," in Wendy S. Jacobson, ed., *Dickens and the Children of Empire*, 49–52.

Spurgin, Timothy A. "'It's Me Wot Has Done It!': Letters, Reviews, and *Great Expectations*." *Dickens Stud Annual* 27 (1998), 187–201.

Steward, Douglas. "Anti-Oedipalizing *Great Expectations*: Masochism, Subjectivity, Capitalism." *Lit and Psych* 45:3 (1999), 29–45.

Stewart, Garrett. "Dickens and Language," in John O. Jordan, ed., *The Cambridge Companion*, 149–51.

Stubblefield, Jay. "'What Shall I Say I Am—To-day?': Subjectivity and Accountability in *Frankenstein* and *Great Expectations*." *Dickens Q* 14 (1997), 232–42.

Sutherland, John. *Who Betrays Elizabeth Bennet?*, 168–74.

Thornton, Sara. "The Burning of Miss Havisham: Dickens, Fire and the 'Fire Baptism.'" *Q/W/E/R/T/Y* 9 (1999), 105–14.

Tredell, Nicolas, ed. *Charles Dickens: "Great Expectations,"* 11–167.

Tritter, Daniel F. "Mr. Jaggers at the Bar." *Dickens Q* 14 (1997), 92–105.

Vrettos, Athena. "Defining Habits: Dickens and the Psychology of Repetition." *Victorian Stud* 42:3 (1999/2000), 408–12.

Waters, Catherine. *Dickens and the Politics of the Family*, 84–88, 150–74.

Wiesenfarth, Joseph J. "Phillip Pirrip's Afterlife, or *Great Expectations* Again . . . and Again." *George Eliot-George Henry Lewes Stud* 36–37 (1999), 70–84.

Wirth-Nesher, Hana. "'I Must Be Put Somewheres, Dear Boy': Dickens, Twain, and National Geographies," in Shlomith Rimmon-Kenan et al., eds., *Rereading Texts*, 213–24.

Wynne, Deborah. "'We were unhealthy and unsafe': Dickens' *Great Expectations* and *All The Year Round*'s Anxiety Stories." *J of Victorian Culture* 5 (2000), 51–58.

Young, Arlene. *Culture, Class and Gender*, 97–100.

Young, Arlene. "Virtue Domesticated: Dickens and the Lower Middle Class." *Victorian Stud* 39:4 (1996), 496–98.

Hard Times, 1854

Childers, Joseph W. "Industrial Culture and the Victorian Novel," in Deirdre David, ed., *The Cambridge Companion to the Victorian Novel*, 86–89.

Cox, Carole. "Leavis and *Hard Times*." *The Use of Engl* 50 (1998), 55–61.

Edgecombe, Rodney Stenning. "Mrs. Sparsit, Sir Thomas Lawrence and *Coriolanus*." *Victorian Newsl* 97 (2000), 26–28.

Ewbank, Inga-Stina. "Dickens, Ibsen and Cross-Currents," in Ewbank et al., eds., *Anglo-Scandinavian Cross-Currents*, 302–8.

Ferns, John. *F. R. Leavis*, 66–71.

Garner, Joseph H. "Dickens's Dystopian Metacomedy: *Hard Times*, Morals, and Religion," in Jennifer A. Wagner-Lawlor, ed., *The Victorian Comic Spirit*, 141–51.

Glancy, Ruth. *Student Companion to Charles Dickens*, 91–107.

Harrison, John. "Dickens's Literary Architecture: Patterns of Ideas and Imagery in *Hard Times*." *Papers on Lang and Lit* 36 (2000), 115–36.

Heinrich, Hans. *Zur Geschichte des 'Libertin,'* 191–95.

Higbie, Robert. *Dickens and Imagination*, 122–31.

Humpherys, Anne. "Louisa Gradgrind's Secret: Marriage and Divorce in *Hard Times*." *Dickens Stud Annual* 25 (1996), 177–88.

Kearney, Anthony. "Leavis, *Hard Times* and English Teaching." *The Use of Engl* 49 (1997), 28–38.

Keen, Suzanne. *Victorian Renovations of the Novel*, 160–67.

Lampard, Ron. "The New Church in *Hard Times*." *Dickensian* 93 (1997), 109–15.

Law, Graham. "Industrial Designs: Form and Function in the 'Condition-of-England' Novel," in George Hughes, ed., *Corresponding Powers*, 136–37.

Lloyd, Tom. *Crises of Realism*, 93–95, 139–41.

Matsika, Greenwell. "Dickens in Africa: 'Africanizing' *Hard Times*," in Wendy S. Jacobson, ed., *Dickens and the Children of Empire*, 173–81.

Newey, Vincent. "Dickensian Decadents," in Michael St. John, ed., *Romancing Decay*, 64–66.

Newsom, Robert. *Charles Dickens Revisited*, 131–38.

Palmer, William J. *Dickens and New Historicism*, 81–86, 140–45.

Pennington, John. "From Fact to Fantasy in Victorian Fiction: Dickens's *Hard Times* and MacDonald's *Phantastes*." *Extrapolation* 38 (1997), 200–206.

Pittock, Malcolm. "Taking Dickens to Task: *Hard Times* Once More." *Cambridge Q* 27 (1998), 107–28.

Posner, Richard A. *Law and Literature*, 319–20.

Rogers, Philip. "Dystopian Intertexts: Dickens' *Hard Times* and Zamiatin's *We*." *Compar Lit Stud* 35 (1998), 393–408.

Sanders, Mike. "Manufacturing Accident: Industrialism and the Worker's Body in Early Victorian Fiction." *Victorian Lit and Culture* 28 (2000), 322–27.

Schor, Hilary. "Novels of the 1850s: *Hard Times, Little Dorrit*, and *A Tale of Two Cities*," in John O. Jordan, ed., *The Cambridge Companion*, 64–70.

Schor, Hilary M. *Dickens and the Daughter of the House*, 72–83.

Simpson, Margaret. *The Companion to "Hard Times,"* 17–234.

Slater, Michael. *An Intelligent Person's Guide*, 19–20, 26–27.

Stiltner, Barry. "*Hard Times*: The Disciplinary City." *Dickens Stud Annual* 30 (2001), 193–213.

Thomas, Deborah A. "*Hard Times,*" 3–133.

Vegh, Beatriz. "*Hard Times* Gone Modernist: The 1921 Rafael Barradas Illustrations for *Tiempos Difíciles*." *Dickens Q* 15 (1998), 3–25.

Wainwright, Valerie L. "On Goods, Virtues, and *Hard Times*." *Dickens Stud Annual* 26 (1998), 169–82.

Waters, Catherine. "Gender, Family, and Domestic Ideology," in John O. Jordan, ed., *The Cambridge Companion*, 131–33.

Welsh, Alexander. *Dickens Redressed*, 147–209.

Wenzel, Peter. "Structural Oppositions and Contradictions in Dickens's *Hard Times* and Mrs. Tonna's *Helen Fleetwood*." *Zeitschrift für Anglistik und Amerikanistik* 46 (1998), 316–24.

Wolf, Werner. "'I must go back a little to explain [her] motives [...]': Erklärung und Erklärbarkeit menschlichen Verhaltens, Handelns und Wesens in englischen Romanen des Realismus: *Hard Times* und *Adam Bede*." *Germanisch-Romanische Monatsschrift* 48 (1998), 442–53, 469–76.

Zlotnick, Susan. *Women, Writing, and the Industrial Revolution*, 33–44.

The Haunted Man, 1847

Daleski, H. M. "Seasonal Offerings: Some Recurrent Features in Dickens's Christmas Books." *Dickens Stud Annual* 27 (1998), 106–10.

Glancy, Ruth. *Student Companion to Charles Dickens*, 66–68.

Reed, James. "Dickens, Christmas, and the Baby in the Egg-Box." *Dickensian* 94 (1998), 165–71.

Shuttleworth, Sally. "'The Malady of Thought': Embodied Memory in Victorian Psychology and the Novel." *Australasian Victorian Stud J* 2 (1996), 1–4.

Little Dorrit, 1857

Ayres, Brenda. *Dissenting Women in Dickens' Novels*, 77–79, 90–92, 96–98, 101–3.

Black, Barbara. "A Sisterhood of Rage and Beauty: Dickens' Rosa Dartle, Miss Wade, and Madame Defarge." *Dickens Stud Annual* 26 (1998), 91–104.

Bradbury, Nicola. "Dickens and James: 'Watching with my eyes closed'—The Dream Abroad." *Dickens Q* 17 (2000), 82–86.

Bradbury, Nicola. "Dickens and the Form of the Novel," in John O. Jordan, ed., *The Cambridge Companion*, 162–63.

Case, Alison A. *Plotting Women*, 133–37.

Cohen, Monica F. *Professional Domesticity*, 101–24.

Dolezel, Lubomir. *Heterocosmica*, 81–88.

Edgecombe, Rodney Stenning. "The Displacemenrs of *Little Dorrit*." *JEGP* 96 (1997), 369–84.

Edgecombe, Rodney Stenning. "*Little Dorrit* and Canning's 'New Morality.'" *Mod Philology* 95 (1998), 484–89.

Edgecombe, Rodney Stenning. "Middle-Class Erasures: The Decreations of Mrs. General and Mr. Podsnap." *Stud in the Novel* 31 (1999), 279–93.

Edgecombe, Rodney Stenning. "Personification in the Late Novels of Dickens." *Dickensian* 95 (1999), 236–39.

Ferns, John. *F. R. Leavis*, 74–77.

Galletti, Chiara. "'Curiouser and Curiouser!': *The Old Curiosity Shop* and *Little Dorrit* — A Dickens Curiosity Story." *Acme* (Milano) 45:3 (1992), 43–60.

Glancy, Ruth. *Student Companion to Charles Dickens*, 148–51.

Glavin, John. *After Dickens*, 162–68.

Halevi-Wise, Yael. "Little Dorrit's Story: A Window into the Novel." *Dickensian* 94 (1998), 184–93.

Harris, Wendell V. "Contextualizing Coram's Foundling Hospital: Dickens's Use and Readers' Interests." *Reader* 43 (2000), 1–19.

Harrison, S. J. "Prunes and Prism: Wilde and Dickens." *Notes and Queries* 44 (1997), 351–52.

Higbie, Robert. *Dickens and Imagination*, 132–44.

Hochman, Baruch, and Ilja Wachs. *Dickens: The Orphan Condition*, 127–65.

Holway, Tatiana. "Imaginary Capital: The Shape of the Victorian Economy and the Shaping of Dickens's Career." *Dickens Stud Annual* 27 (1998), 34–40.

Justman, Stewart. *The Springs of Liberty*, 71–83.

Klaver, Claudia. "Natural Values and Unnatural Agents: *Little Dorrit* and the Mid-Victorian Crisis in Agency." *Dickens Stud Annual* 28 (1999), 13–35.

Lind, Nancy E. "The Acquisition of a Future: Arthur Clennam's Developmental Task in *Little Dorrit*." *Dickensian* 95 (1999), 138–43.

McKee, Patricia. *Public and Private*, 113–51.

Mighall, Robert. *A Geography of Victorian Gothic Fiction*, 106–10.

Myers, William. *The Presence of Persons*, 109–29.

Nelson, Harland S. "Dickens, Religion, and Nubile Girls." *Dickens Q* 14 (1997), 36–38.

Newsom, Robert. *Charles Dickens Revisited*, 138–45.

Novak, Daniel. "If Re-collecting Were Forgetting: Forged Bodies and Forgotten Labor in *Little Dorrit*." *Novel* 31 (1997), 21–42.

Palmer, William J. *Dickens and New Historicism*, 39–47.

Philpotts, Trey. "The 'Civil Service' and 'Administrative Reform': The Blame Game in *Little Dorrit*." *Dickens Q* 17 (2000), 14–21.

Retseck, Janet. "Sexing Miss Wade." *Dickens Q* 15 (1998), 217–24.

Runcie, C. A. "Recovering Meaning: *Little Dorrit* as Novel and Film." *Sydney Stud in Engl* 23 (1997–8), 58–78.

Sanders, Andrew. *Dickens and the Spirit of the Age*, 142–46.

Schor, Hilary. "Novels of the 1850s: *Hard Times, Little Dorrit*, and *A Tale of Two Cities*," in John O. Jordan, ed., *The Cambridge Companion*, 70–72.

Schor, Hilary M. *Dickens and the Daughter of the House*, 124–49.

Scoggin, Daniel P. "Speculative Plagues and the Ghosts of *Little Dorrit*." *Dickens Stud Annual* 29 (2000), 233–61.

Scribner, Margo. "The D.N.F. Watch in *Little Dorrit*: Making Time Tangible." *Willamette J of the Liberal Arts* 10 (1994), 17–29.

Sen, Sambudha. "*Bleak House* and *Little Dorrit*: The Radical Heritage." *ELH* 65 (1998), 945–59, 963–66.

Slater, Michael. *An Intelligent Person's Guide*, 30–32, 38–42, 108–9.

Smith, Jonathan. "Darwin's Barnacles, Dickens's Little Dorrit, and the Social Uses of Victorian Seaside Studies." *LIT* 10 (2000), 327–44.

Stewart, Garrett. "Dickens and Language," in John O. Jordan, ed., *The Cambridge Companion*, 143–48.

Storor, David. "Grotesque Storytelling: Dickens's Articulation of the 'Crisis of the Knowable Community' in *Bleak House* and *Little Dorrit*." *Dickensian* 94 (1998), 25–40.

Vlock, Deborah. *Dickens, Novel Reading*, 179–89.

Waters, Catherine. *Dickens and the Politics of the Family*, 89–121.

West, Gilian. "*Little Dorrit*: 'Thirty Years Ago. . . .'" *Dickensian* 95 (1999), 212–24.

West, Gilian. "Mrs Clennam's House: A Note." *Dickensian* 96 (2000), 243.

Wilson, Anna. "On History, Case History, and Deviance: Miss Wade's Symptoms and Their Interpretation." *Dickens Stud Annual* 26 (1998), 187–97.

Wolf, Sherri. "The Enormous Power of No Body: *Little Dorrit* and the Logic of Expansion." *Texas Stud in Lit and Lang* 42 (2000), 223–48.

Xu, Wenying. "The Opium Trade and *Little Dorrit*: A Case of Reading Silences." *Victorian Lit and Culture* 25 (1997), 53–65.

Young, Arlene. *Culture, Class and Gender*, 73–86.

Young, Arlene. "Virtue Domesticated: Dickens and the Lower Middle Class." *Victorian Stud* 39:4 (1996), 483–84, 499–508.

Martin Chuzzlewit, 1844

Ayres, Brenda. *Dissenting Women in Dickens' Novels*, 67–74.

Bowen, John. *Other Dickens*, 183–219.

Cavaliero, Glen. *The Alchemy of Laughter*, 132–36.

Chase, Karen, and Michael Levenson. *The Spectacle of Intimacy*, 92–94.

Dessner, Lawrence Jay. "'I Rise with Circumstances': Making It in Dickens's *Martin Chuzzlewit*." *Dickens Q* 14 (1997), 146–52.

Flint, Kate. "The Middle Novels: *Chuzzlewit, Dombey*, and *Copperfield*," in John O. Jordan, ed., *The Cambridge Companion*, 34–40.

Glancy, Ruth. *Student Companion to Charles Dickens*, 38–40.

Higbie, Robert. *Dickens and Imagination*, 62–67.

Kincaid, James. "Getting It Wrong Again and Again—Me and *Martin Chuzzlewit*," in Shlomith Rimmon-Kenan et al., eds., *Rereading Texts*, 335–45.

Kincaid, James R. *Annoying the Victorians*, 64–72, 78–83.

Lougy, Robert E. "Nationalism and Violence: America in Charles Dickens's *Martin Chuzzlewit*," in Wendy S. Jacobson, ed., *Dickens and the Children of Empire*, 105–13.

Malone, Cynthia Northcutt. "Near Confinement: Pregnant Women in the Nineteenth-Century British Novel." *Dickens Stud Annual* 29 (2000), 367–80.

Newsom, Robert. *Charles Dickens Revisited*, 97–100.

Petroski, Karen. "'The Ghost of an Idea': Dickens' Uses of Phantasmagoria, 1842–44." *Dickens Q* 16:2 (1999), 71–93.

Rem, Tore. "The Never-Ending Story? Two *Martin Chuzzlewits*." *Word and Image* 12 (1996), 280–90.

Sasaki, Toru. "Dickens in Confusion?: Discrepancies in the Dénouement of *Martin Chuzzlewit*." *Dickensian* 94 (1998), 21–24.

Slater, Michael. *An Intelligent Person's Guide*, 20–21.

Surgal, Jon. "The Parable of the Spoons and Ladles: Sibling and Crypto-Sibling Typology in *Martin Chuzzlewit*." *Dickens Stud Annual* 26 (1998), 51–67.

Tambling, Jeremy. "*Martin Chuzzlewit*: Dickens and Architecture." *English* 48 (1999), 147–66.

Toker, Leona. "Veblen, Dickens, and Martin Chuzzlewit's America." *Dickens Q* 15 (1998), 147–53.

Wolfreys, Julian. "Dickensian Architextures or, the City and the Ineffable," in Ruth Robbins and Julian Wolfreys, eds., *Victorian Identities*, 210–12.

The Mystery of Edwin Drood, 1870

Ayres, Brenda. *Dissenting Women in Dickens' Novels*, 108–10.

Buzard, James. "'Then on the Shore of the Wide World': The Victorian Nation and Its Others," in Herbert F. Tucker, ed., *A Companion to Victorian Literature and Culture*, 449–50.

Cox, Arthur J. "Magnetic Sympathy in *The Mystery of Edwin Drood*." *Dickensian* 96 (2000), 127–45 and 209–38.

Cox, Don Richard. "'Mr. Grewgious Experiences a New Sensation': How *Edwin Drood* Was Illustrated." *Dickensian* 93 (1997), 13–25.

Ford, Jane M. *Patriarchy and Incest*, 149–52.

Frank, Lawrence. "News from the Dead: Archaeology, Detection, and *The Mystery of Edwin Drood*." *Dickens Stud Annual* 28 (1999), 65–95.

Glancy, Ruth. *Student Companion to Charles Dickens*, 154–56.

Jacobson, Wendy S. "The Genesis of the Last Novel: *The Mystery of Edwin Drood*." *Dickens Stud Annual* 25 (1996), 197–207.

Marks, Patricia. "'With a Rush Retire': Robert Newell's *Edwin Drood* Adaptation." *Dickens Q* 17 (2000), 149–64.

Morgentaler, Goldie. *Dickens and Heredity*, 185–97.

Raven, Robert. "Some Observations on Charles Collins's Sketches for *Edwin Drood*." *Dickensian* 96 (2000), 118–26.

Reitz, Caroline. "Making an English Virtue of Necessity: Detective Fiction and Imperialism." *Genre* 31 (1998), 310–21.

Swain, Stella. "Narrative and Legality: Charles Dickens' *The Mystery of Edwin Drood*." *New Formations* 32 (1997), 77–90.

Tracy, Robert. "Disappearances: George Parkman and Edwin Drood." *Dickensian* 96 (2000), 101–17.

Nicholas Nickleby, 1839

Bowen, John. *Other Dickens*, 107–31.

Childers, Joseph W. "*Nicholas Nickleby*'s Problem of *Doux Commerce*." *Dickens Stud Annual* 25 (1996), 49–64.

Edgecombe, Rodney Stenning. "Anticlerical Gothic: The Tale of the Sisters in *Nicholas Nickleby*." *Mod Lang R* 94 (1999), 1–10.

Edgecombe, Rodney Stenning. "Marring Curious Tales: Code-Crossing Irony in *Nicholas Nickleby*." *Dickens Q* 18 (2001), 21–35.

Glancy, Ruth. *Student Companion to Charles Dickens*, 30–32.

Glavin, John. *After Dickens*, 70–78, 98–102, 121–31.

Goodin, George. "Competitive Conversation in the Dialogue of Dickens." *Dickens Q* 18 (2001), 7–9.

Heinrich, Hans. *Zur Geschichte des 'Libertin,'* 181–85.

Hennelly, Mark M., Jr. "Courtly Wild Men and Carnivalesque Pig Women in Dickens and Hardy." *Dickens Stud Annual* 26 (1998), 9–20.

Holway, Tatiana. "Imaginary Capital: The Shape of the Victorian Economy and the Shaping of Dickens's Career." *Dickens Stud Annual* 27 (1998), 27–31.

Newsom, Robert. *Charles Dickens Revisited*, 79–86.

Patten, Robert L. "From *Sketches* to *Nickleby*," in John O. Jordan, ed., *The Cambridge Companion*, 25–32.

Rem, Tore. "Playing Around with Melodrama: The Crummles Episodes in *Nicholas Nickleby*." *Dickens Stud Annual* 25 (1996), 267–81.

Schor, Hilary M. *Dickens and the Daughter of the House*, 44–46.

Vlock, Deborah. *Dickens, Novel Reading*, 48–54, 152–54.

Vlock, Deborah M. "Dickens, Theater, and the Making of a Victorian Reading Public." *Stud in the Novel* 29 (1997), 164–87.

The Old Curiosity Shop, 1841

Ayres, Brenda. *Dissenting Women in Dickens' Novels*, 74–77.

Bowen, John. *Other Dickens*, 132–56.

Bowen, John. "Spirit and the Allegorical Child: Little Nell's Mortal Aesthetic," in Wendy S. Jacobson, ed., *Dickens and the Children of Empire*, 13–24.

Galletti, Chiara. "'Curiouser and Curiouser!': *The Old Curiosity Shop* and *Little Dorrit*— A Dickens Curiosity Story." *Acme* (Milano) 45:3 (1992), 43–60.

Glancy, Ruth. *Student Companion to Charles Dickens*, 32–35.

Higbie, Robert. *Dickens and Imagination*, 58–64.

Kincaid, James R. *Annoying the Victorians*, 33–44.

McKee, Patricia. *Public and Private*, 77–112.

Morgentaler, Goldie. *Dickens and Heredity*, 46–52.

Newsom, Robert. *Charles Dickens Revisited*, 86–95.

Newsom, Robert. "Fictions of Childhood," in John O. Jordan, ed., *The Cambridge Companion*, 93–95.

Palmer, William J. *Dickens and New Historicism*, 35–39, 124–26.

Robson, Catherine. "Girls Underground, Boys Overseas: Some Graveyard Vignettes," in Wendy S. Jacobson, ed., *Dickens and the Children of Empire*, 119–22.

Robson, Catherine. *Men in Wonderland*, 75–93.

Schor, Hilary M. *Dickens and the Daughter of the House*, 19–22, 32–46.

Shelston, Alan. "Nell, Alice and Lizzie: Three Sisters amidst the Grotesque," in Richard Gravil, ed., *Master Narratives*, 101–9.

Slater, Michael. *An Intelligent Person's Guide*, 108–9.

Stoler, John A. "Affection and Lust in *The Old Curiosity Shop*: Dickens and Mary—Again." *McNeese R* 35 (1997), 90–102.

Thornton, Sara. "The Vanity of Childhood: Constructing, Deconstructing, and Destroying the Child in the Novel of the 1840s," in Karín Lesnik-Oberstein, ed., *Children in Culture*, 131–36, 143–47.

Tracy, Robert. "Clock Work: *The Old Curiosity Shop* and *Barnaby Rudge*." *Dickens Stud Annual* 30 (2001), 23–33.

Walsh, Richard. "Why We Wept for Little Nell: Character and Emotional Involvement." *Narrative* 5 (1997), 306–18.

Waters, Catherine. "Gender, Family, and Domestic Ideology," in John O. Jordan, ed., *The Cambridge Companion*, 124–27.

Oliver Twist, 1838

Ang, Susan. *The Widening World of Children's Literature*, 33–37.

Armstrong, Nancy. *Fiction in the Age of Photography*, 131–37, 141–44.

Ayres, Brenda. *Dissenting Women in Dickens' Novels*, 111–40.

Barloon, Jim. "The Black Hole of London: Rescuing Oliver Twist." *Dickens Stud Annual* 28 (1999), 1–9.

Berry, Laura C. *The Child, the State, and the Victorian Novel*, 28–62.

Bowen, John. *Other Dickens*, 16–18, 82–106.

Brantlinger, Patrick. *The Reading Lesson*, 69–83.

Dever, Carolyn. *Death and the Mother*, 26–29.

Glancy, Ruth. *Student Companion to Charles Dickens*, 41–55.

Harvey, Ronald C. "The Dialogue of Truth and Art in *Oliver Twist*." *Victorians Inst J* 26 (1998), 149–63.

Hennelly, Mark M., Jr. "'Deep Play' and 'Women's Ridicules' in *Oliver Twist*." *J of Evolutionary Psych* 19:1–2 (1998), 116–31; 19:3–4 (1998), 165–74; 20:1–2 (1999), 92–102.

Hochman, Baruch, and Ilja Wachs. *Dickens: The Orphan Condition*, 32–54.

Ireland, Ken. *The Sequential Dynamics of Narrative*, 199–200.

John, Juliet. "*Twist*ing the Newgate Tale: Dickens, Popular Culture and the Politics of Genre," in Juliet John and Alice Jenkins, eds., *Rethinking Victorian Culture*, 126–42.

Kincaid, James R. "Dickens and the Construction of the Child," in Wendy S. Jacobson, ed., *Dickens and the Children of Empire*, 36–38.

Lenard, Mary. "'Mr. Popular Sentiment': Dickens and the Gender

Politics of Sentimentalism and Social Reform Literature." *Dickens Stud Annual* 27 (1998), 46–53.

Lesnik-Oberstein, Karin. "*Oliver Twist*: The Narrator's Tale." *Textual Prectice* 15 (2001), 87–98.

Liggins, Emma. "'Such fine young chaps as them': Representations of the Male Criminal in the Newgate Novel," in Antony Rowland et al., eds., *Signs of Masculinity*, 79–86.

Litvak, Joseph. "Bad Scene: *Oliver Twist* and the Pathology of Entertainment." *Dickens Stud Annual* 26 (1998), 33–46.

Lloyd, Tom. *Crises of Realism*, 88–93, 96–98, 114–17.

Mighall, Robert. *A Geography of Victorian Gothic Fiction*, 39–45.

Morgentaler, Goldie. *Dickens and Heredity*, 37–46, 86–88, 99–101.

Morgentaler, Goldie. "The Long and the Short of Oliver and Alice: The Changing Size of the Victorian Child." *Dickens Stud Annual* 29 (2000), 83–94.

Myers, William. *The Presence of Persons*, 99–108.

Newsom, Robert. *Charles Dickens Revisited*, 73–79.

Newsom, Robert. "Fictions of Childhood," in John O. Jordan, ed., *The Cambridge Companion*, 95–96.

Palmer, William J. *Dickens and New Historicism*, 118–24.

Parker, David. "*Oliver Twist* and the Fugitive Family." *Dickens Stud Annual* 29 (2000), 41–56.

Robson, Catherine. "Down Ditches, on Doorsteps, in Rivers: *Oliver Twist*'s Journey to Respectability." *Dickens Stud Annual* 29 (2000), 61–77.

Schattschneider, Laura. "Mr Brownlow's Interest in Oliver Twist." *J of Victorian Culture* 6:1 (2001), 46–57.

Schor, Hilary M. *Dickens and the Daughter of the House*, 19–33.

Shaked, Gershon. "Dickens's *Oliver Twist* and Mendele's *The Book of Beggars*," in Murray Baumgarten and H. M. Daleski, eds., *Homes and Homelessness*, 297–305.

Slater, Michael. *An Intelligent Person's Guide*, 108–9.

Sullivan, Sheila. "Dickens's Newgate Vision: *Oliver Twist*, Moral Statistics, and the Construction of Progressive History." *Nineteenth Cent Stud* 14 (2000), 121–39.

Sutherland, John. *Who Betrays Elizabeth Bennet?*, 44–48.

Taylor, Jenny Bourne. "Representing Illegitimacy in Victorian Culture," in Ruth Robbins and Julian Wolfreys, eds., *Victorian Identities*, 134–36.

Tromp, Marlene. *The Private Rod*, 23–65.

Waters, Catherine. *Dickens and the Politics of the Family*, 29–38.

Wolfreys, Julian. "Dickensian Architextures or, the City and the Ineffable," in Ruth Robbins and Julian Wolfreys, eds., *Victorian Identities*, 204–8.

Our Mutual Friend, 1865

Ayres, Brenda. *Dissenting Women in Dickens' Novels*, 79–81.

Baumgarten, Murray. "The Imperial Child: Bella, *Our Mutual Friend*, and the Victorian Picturesque," in Wendy S. Jacobson, ed., *Dickens and the Children of Empire*, 54–65.

Brattin, Joel J. "'I will not have my word misconstrued': The Text of *Our Mutual Friend.*" *Dickens Q* 15 (1998), 167–72.

Cerny, Lothar. "'Life in Death': Art in Dickens's *Our Mutual Friend.*" *Dickens Q* 17 (2000), 22–33.

Chase, Karen, and Michael Levenson. "On the Parapets of Privacy," in Herbert F. Tucker, ed., *A Companion to Victorian Literature and Culture*, 425–26.

Chase, Karen, and Michael Levenson. *The Spectacle of Intimacy*, 143–46, 216–18.

Cheadle, Brian. "The Late Novels: *Great Expectations* and *Our Mutual Friend*," in John O. Jordan, ed., *The Cambridge Companion*, 84–90.

Cohen, Monica F. *Professional Domesticity*, 89–91.

Cottom, Daniel. *Ravishing Tradition*, 130–34, 136–39.

Crosby, Christina. "Financial," in Herbert F. Tucker, ed., *A Companion to Victorian Literature and Culture*, 236–38.

Dutheil, Martine Hennard. "Rushdie's Affiliation with Dickens." *Dickens Stud Annual* 27 (1998), 217–21.

Dutheil de la Rochère, Martine Hennard. *Origin and Originality*, 73–79.

Edgecombe, Rodney Stenning. "Middle-Class Erasures: The Decreations of Mrs. General and Mr. Podsnap." *Stud in the Novel* 31 (1999), 280–93.

Edgecombe, Rodney Stenning. "Personification in the Late Novels of Dickens." *Dickensian* 95 (1999), 230–32, 234–36.

Edgecombe, Rodney Stenning. "Prophetic Moments in Dickens and Carlyle." *Victorian Newsl* 95 (1999), 21–23.

Farrell, John P. "The Partners' Tale: Dickens and *Our Mutual Friend.*" *ELH* 66 (1999), 759–93.

Ford, Jane M. *Patriarchy and Incest*, 75–79.

Garnett, Robert R. "Dickens, The Virgin, and the Dredger's Daughter." *Dickens Stud Annual* 28 (1999), 45–63.

Gindele, Karen C. "Desire and Deconstruction: Reclaiming Centers." *Dickens Stud Annual* 29 (2000), 282–96.

Glancy, Ruth. *Student Companion to Charles Dickens*, 151–54.

Glavin, John. *After Dickens*, 48–70.

Hake, Steven. "Becoming Poor to Make Many Rich: The Resolution of Class Conflict in Dickens." *Dickens Stud Annual* 26 (1998), 114–15.

Hale, Keith. "Doing the Police in Different Voices: The Search for Identity in Dust Heaps and Waste Lands." *Dickens Stud Annual* 29 (2000), 303–18.

Heinrich, Hans. *Zur Geschichte des 'Libertin,'* 195–98.

Higbie, Robert. *Dickens and Imagination*, 147–58.

Ireland, Ken. *The Sequential Dynamics of Narrative*, 201–2.

Jackson-Houlston, C. M. *Ballads, Songs and Snatches*, 114–17.

McLaughlin, Joseph. *Writing the Urban Jungle*, 181–83.

Miller, Andrew H. *Novels behind Glass*, 119–58.

Morgentaler, Goldie. *Dickens and Heredity*, 175–85.

Morris, Pam. "A Taste for Change in *Our Mutual Friend*: Cultivation or Education?," in Juliet John and Alice Jenkins, eds., *Rethinking Victorian Culture*, 179–93.

Newey, Vincent. "Dickensian Decadents," in Michael St. John, ed., *Romancing Decay*, 74–82.

Newsom, Robert. *Charles Dickens Revisited*, 153–62.

Nunokawa, Jeff. "Sexuality in the Victorian Novel," in Deirdre David, ed., *The Cambridge Companion to the Victorian Novel*, 142–47.

Palmer, William J. *Dickens and New Historicism*, 92–99, 149–63.

Schor, Hilary M. *Dickens and the Daughter of the House*, 178–207.

Shelston, Alan. "Nell, Alice and Lizzie: Three Sisters amidst the Grotesque," in Richard Gravil, ed., *Master Narratives*, 115–21.

Shuman, Cathy. *Pedagogical Economies*, 123–69.

Surridge, Lisa. "'John Rokesmith's Secret': Sensation, Detection, and the Policing of the Feminine in *Our Mutual Friend*." *Dickens Stud Annual* 26 (1998), 265–79.

Sutherland, John. *Who Betrays Elizabeth Bennet?*, 185–90.

Taylor, Jonathan. "'Servants' Logic' and Analytical Chemistry: George Eliot, Charles Dickens, and Servants." *Dickens Stud Annual* 30 (2001), 272–79.

Thomas, Syd. "'Pretty Woman, Elegantly Framed': The Fate of Bella Wilfer in Dickens's *Our Mutual Friend*." *Dickens Q* 14 (1997), 3–21.

Waters, Catherine. *Dickens and the Politics of the Family*, 175–203.

Waters, Catherine. "Gender, Family, and Domestic Ideology," in John O. Jordan, ed., *The Cambridge Companion*, 123–24.

Young, Arlene. "Virtue Domesticated: Dickens and the Lower Middle Class." *Victorian Stud* 39:4 (1996), 494–96.

The Pickwick Papers, 1837

Bowen, John. *Other Dickens*, 44–81.

Bradbury, Nicola. "Dickens and the Form of the Novel," in John O. Jordan, ed., *The Cambridge Companion*, 153–55.

Cavaliero, Glen. *The Alchemy of Laughter*, 179–87.

Craig, Randall. *Promising Language*, 85–92, 94–104, 109–19.

Easson, Angus. "Don Pickwick: Dickens and the Transformations of Cervantes," in Alice Jenkins and Juliet John, eds., *Rereading Victorian Fiction*, 173–86.

Ford, Jane M. *Patriarchy and Incest*, 56–60.

Gager, Valerie L. *Shakespeare and Dickens*, 188–90.

Glancy, Ruth. *Student Companion to Charles Dickens*, 27–30.

Glavin, John. *After Dickens*, 83–97.

Grass, Sean C. "Pickwick, the Past, and the Prison." *Dickens Stud Annual* 29 (2000), 17–36.

Grossman, Jonathan H. "Representing Pickwick: The Novel and the Law Courts." *Nineteenth-Cent Lit* 52 (1997), 171–97.

Higbie, Robert. *Dickens and Imagination*, 50–56.

Kincaid, James R. *Annoying the Victorians*, 21–33, 48–50.

McCuskey, Brian W. "'Your Love-Sick Pickwick': The Erotics of Service." *Dickens Stud Annual* 25 (1996), 245–64.

Newsom, Robert. *Charles Dickens Revisited*, 61–73.

Orero, Pilar. "Spanish Wellerisms." *Proverbium* 15 (1998), 235–42.

Palmer, William J. *Dickens and New Historicism*, 24–35, 116–18.

Patten, Robert L. "From *Sketches* to *Nickleby*," in John O. Jordan, ed., *The Cambridge Companion*, 22–24.

Payne, David. "The Cockney and the Prostitute: Dickens and the Literary Market, 1836–37." *J of Victorian Culture* 4 (1999), 174–92.

Pool, Daniel. *Dickens' Fur Coat*, 16–25.

Posner, Richard A. *Law and Literature*, 140–42.

Preston, Shale. "Quantum Pickwick." *Yrbk of Engl Stud* 30 (2000), 82–95.

Schramm, Jan-Melissa. *Testimony and Advocacy*, 111–16.

A Tale of Two Cities, 1859

Black, Barbara. "A Sisterhood of Rage and Beauty: Dickens' Rosa Dartle, Miss Wade, and Madame Defarge." *Dickens Stud Annual* 26 (1998), 91–104.

Brett, R. L. *Faith and Doubt*, 121–24.

Glancy, Ruth. *Student Companion to Charles Dickens*, 109–24.

Glavin, John. *After Dickens*, 139–47.

Hennelly, Mark M., Jr. "'Like or No Like': Figuring the Scapegoat in *A Tale of Two Cities*." *Dickens Stud Annual* 30 (2001), 217–37.

Hollington, Michael. "The Losing Game: Exile and Threshold in *A Tale of Two Cities*." *Cahiers Victoriens et Edouardiens* 51 (2000), 189–203.

Ireland, Ken. *The Sequential Dynamics of Narrative*, 201.

Jacobson, Wendy S. "'The world within us': Jung and Dr Manette's Daughter." *Dickensian* 93 (1997), 95–107.

Kemper, Beth. "The 'Night Shadows' Passage in *A Tale of Two Cities*: Narrative Anxiety and Conscious Fiction-Building." *Kentucky Philol R* 10 (1995), 22–26.

Lamb, John B. "Domesticating History: Revolution and Moral Management in *A Tale of Two Cities*." *Dickens Stud Annual* 25 (1996), 227–41.

Mighall, Robert. *A Geography of Victorian Gothic Fiction*, 110–14.

Morgentaler, Goldie. *Dickens and Heredity*, 132–42.

Newlin, George. *Understanding "A Tale of Two Cities,"* 1–9.

Newsom, Robert. *Charles Dickens Revisited*, 145–46.

Ouellet, François. "De Bove à Dickens: une approche intertextuelle." *Dalhousie French Stud* 51 (2000), 70–83.

Palmer, William J. *Dickens and New Historicism*, 87–92.

Peyrache-Leborgne, Dominique. "Roman historique et roman-idylle chez Dickens et Hugo." *Rivista di Letterature Moderne e Comparate* 50 (1997), 163–81. (Also in *Dalhousie French Stud* 36 [1996], 51–66.)

Plotz, John. *The Crowd*, 39–40.

Rosen, David. "*A Tale of Two Cities*: Theology of Revolution." *Dickens Stud Annual* 27 (1998), 171–84.

Sanders, Andrew. "Dickens and the Millennium," in Juliet John and Alice Jenkins, eds., *Rethinking Victorian Culture*, 85–86.

Schor, Hilary. "Novels of the 1850s: *Hard Times, Little Dorrit*, and *A Tale of Two Cities*," in John O. Jordan, ed., *The Cambridge Companion*, 72–76.

Schor, Hilary M. *Dickens and the Daughter of the House*, 83–98.
Simmons, Clare A. *Eyes Across the Channel*, 135–62.
Sroka, Kenneth M. "A Tale of Two Gospels: Dickens and John."
Dickens Stud Annual 27 (1998), 145–66.
Sutherland, John. *Who Betrays Elizabeth Bennet?*, 149–60.
Tysdahl, Bjørn. "Europe Is Not the Other: *A Tale of Two Cities.*"
Dickens Q 15 (1998), 111–19.
Waters, Catherine. *Dickens and the Politics of the Family*, 122–49.

PETER DICKINSON

Eva, 1988

Graham, Kathryn V. "Exodus from the City: Peter Dickinson's *Eva.*"
Lion and the Unicorn 23 (1999), 79–85.

EILIS DILLON

The "Coriander," 1963

Rahn, Suzanne. "'Inishrone Is Our Island': Rediscovering the Irish
Novels of Eilís Dillon." *Lion and the Unicorn* 21 (1997), 354–60.

A Herd of Deer, 1969

Rahn, Suzanne. "'Inishrone Is Our Island': Rediscovering the Irish
Novels of Eilís Dillon." *Lion and the Unicorn* 21 (1997), 360–66.

The Island of Horses, 1956

Rahn, Suzanne. "'Inishrone Is Our Island': Rediscovering the Irish
Novels of Eilís Dillon." *Lion and the Unicorn* 21 (1997), 349–53.

JENNY DISKI

Rainforest, 1987

Bizzini, Silvia Caporale. "Language and Power in Jenny Diski's
Rainforest," in Richard Todd and Luisa Flora, eds., *Theme Parks*,
29–38.

BENJAMIN DISRAELI

Alroy, 1832

Dellamora, Richard. "Benjamin Disraeli, Judaism, and the Legacy of
William Beckford," in Jay Losey and William D. Brewer, eds.,
Mapping Male Sexuality, 145–72.

Coningsby, 1844

Deffenbacher, Kristina K. "Designing Progress: The Architecture of
Social Consciousness in Disraeli's 'Young England' Novels."
Victorian R 24 (1998), 2–4.
Keen, Suzanne. *Victorian Renovations of the Novel*, 146–59.
Kennedy, George A. "Reading Disraeli with Stendhal," in Raymond
A. Prier and Gerald Gillespie, eds., *Narrative Ironies*, 254–66.

Sybil, 1845

> Childers, Joseph W. "Industrial Culture and the Victorian Novel," in Deirdre David, ed., *The Cambridge Companion to the Victorian Novel*, 84–85.
>
> Deffenbacher, Kristina K. "Designing Progress: The Architecture of Social Consciousness in Disraeli's 'Young England' Novels." *Victorian R* 24 (1998), 1–2, 4–10.
>
> Gilmartin, Sophie. *Ancestry and Narrative*, 105–18.
>
> Houston, Gail Turley. *Royalties*, 24–26.
>
> Kane, Penny. *Victorian Families in Fact and Fiction*, 76–77.
>
> Law, Graham. "Industrial Designs: Form and Function in the 'Condition-of-England' Novel," in George Hughes, ed., *Corresponding Powers*, 134–36.
>
> Peck, John. *War, the Army and Victorian Literature*, 100–102.
>
> Pionke, Albert D. "Combining the Teo Nations: Trade Unions as Secret Societies, 1837–1845." *Victorian Newsl* 97 (2000), 10–13.
>
> Rowley, Kenneth. "Romancing the Writ: The Medieval 'Hocus-Pocus' of Benjamin Disraeli's *Sybil*." *Australasian Victorian Stud J* 3:2 (1998), 95–104.
>
> Sampson, Jennifer. "*Sybil*, or the Two Monarchs." *Stud in Philology* 95 (1998), 97–119.
>
> Zlotnick, Susan. *Women, Writing, and the Industrial Revolution*, 20–22, 53–56.

Tancred, 1847

> Gilmartin, Sophie. *Ancestry and Narrative*, 118–29.

Venetia, 1837

> Elfenbein, Andrew. *Byron and the Victorians*, 225–29.

Vivian Grey, 1826–1827

> Hibbard, Andrea. "*Vivian Grey* and the Silver-Fork Etiquette of Authorship." *Genre* 32 (1999), 249–65.
>
> Kennedy, George A. "Reading Disraeli with Stendhal," in Raymond A. Prier and Gerald Gillespie, eds., *Narrative Ironies*, 255–56.

The Young Duke, 1831

> Bachman, Maria K. "Benjamin Disraeli's *The Young Duke* and the Condition of England's Aristocrats." *Victorian Newsl* 98 (2000), 15–22.

MAUD DIVER

Candles in the Wind, 1909

> Druce, Robert. "National and Racial Stereotypes in the British Raj," in C. C. Barfoot, ed., *Beyond Pug's Tour*, 203, 210–11.

Lilamani: A Study of Possibilities, 1910

> Paxton, Nancy L. "Reconsidering Colonial Romance: Maud Diver and the 'Ethnographic Real,'" in Lynne Hapgood and Nancy L. Paxton, eds., *Outside Modernism*, 185–95.

The Singer Passes, 1934

> Paxton, Nancy L. "Reconsidering Colonial Romance: Maud Diver

and the 'Ethnographic Real,'" in Lynne Hapgood and Nancy L. Paxton, eds., *Outside Modernism*, 195–96.

GERTRUDE DIX

The Image Breakers, 1900

Heilmann, Ann. *New Woman Fiction*, 112–14, 171–74.
Ledger, Sally. *The New Woman*, 56–58.

FLORENCE DIXIE

Gloriana; or, The Revolution of 1900, 1890

Heilmann, Ann. "Masquerade, Sisterhood and the Dilemma of the Feminist as Artist and Woman in Late Nineteenth-Century British Women's Writing." *J of Gender Stud* 3 (1994), 161.
Heilmann, Ann. *New Woman Fiction*, 129–30, 137–40.
Heilmann, Ann. "(Un)Masking Desire: Cross-Dressing and the Crisis of Gender in New Woman Fiction." *J of Victorian Culture* 5 (2000), 95–107.

ELLA HEPWORTH DIXON

My Flirtations, 1892

Stetz, Margaret D. "Debating Aestheticism from a Feminist Perspective," in Talia Schaffer and Kathy Alexis Psomiades, eds., *Women and British Aestheticism*, 31–33.

The Story of a Modern Woman, 1894

Heilmann, Ann. "Masquerade, Sisterhood and the Dilemma of the Feminist as Artist and Woman in Late Nineteenth-Century British Women's Writing." *J of Gender Stud* 3 (1994), 157–58.
Heilmann, Ann. *New Woman Fiction*, 97–98, 169–70.
Ledger, Sally. *The New Woman*, 157–62.
Liggins, Emma. "Writing against the 'Husband-Fiend': Syphilis and Male Sexual Vice in the New Woman Novel." *Women's Writing* 7 (2000), 182–87.
Stetz, Margaret Diane. "The Bi-Social Oscar Wilde and 'Modern' Women." *Nineteenth-Cent Lit* 55 (2001), 515–37.

LEN DOHERTY

A Miner's Sons, 1955

Haywood, Ian. *Working-Class Fiction*, 120–22.

EMMA DONOGHUE

Hood, 1995

Quinn, Antoinette. "New Noises from the Woodshed: The Novels of

Emma Donoghue," in Liam Harte and Michael Parker, eds., *Contemporary Irish Fiction*, 154–65.

Smyth, Gerry. *The Novel and the Nation*, 163–65.

Wingfield, Rachel. "Lesbian Writers in the Mainstream: Sara Maitland, Jeanette Winterson and Emma Donoghue," in Elaine Hutton, ed., *Beyond Sex and Romance?*, 74–76.

Stir-fry, 1994

Quinn, Antoinette. "New Noises from the Woodshed: The Novels of Emma Donoghue," in Liam Harte and Michael Parker, eds., *Contemporary Irish Fiction*, 148–54.

Smyth, Gerry. *The Novel and the Nation*, 157–60.

Wingfield, Rachel. "Lesbian Writers in the Mainstream: Sara Maitland, Jeanette Winterson and Emma Donoghue," in Elaine Hutton, ed., *Beyond Sex and Romance?*, 69–71.

MENIE MURIEL DOWIE

Gallia, 1895

Cunningham, Gail. "'He-Notes': Reconstructing Masculinity," in Angelique Richardson and Chris Willis, eds., *The New Woman in Fiction and in Fact*, 96–101.

ARTHUR CONAN DOYLE

The Hound of the Baskervilles, 1902

Frank, Lawrence. "*The Hound of the Baskervilles*, the Man on the Tor, and a Metaphor for the Mind." *Nineteenth-Cent Lit* 54 (1999), 336–72.

Kestner, Joseph A. *The Edwardian Detective*, 34–45.

Mighall, Robert. *A Geography of Victorian Gothic Fiction*, 160–64.

Ostrowski, Witold. "The Composition of the Detective Novels of Arthur Conan Doyle." *Folia Litteraria Anglica* (Lodz) 1 (1997), 148–53.

Smith, Alan. "Mire, *Bog*, and Hell in *The Hound of the Baskervilles*." *Victorian Newsl* 94 (1998), 42–44.

Thoms, Peter. *Detection and Its Designs*, 121–44.

The Sign of the Four, 1890

Arata, Stephen. *Fictions of Loss*, 140–42.

Keep, Christopher, and Don Randall. "Addiction, Empire, and Narrative in Arthur Conan Doyle's *The Sign of the Four*." *Novel* 32 (1999), 207–19.

McDonald, Peter D. *British Literary Culture*, 135–40.

McLaughlin, Joseph. *Writing the Urban Jungle*, 53–74.

Ostrowski, Witold. "The Composition of the Detective Novels of Arthur Conan Doyle." *Folia Litteraria Anglica* (Lodz) 1 (1997), 144–47.

Otis, Laura. *Membranes*, 95–99.

Thomas, Ronald R. *Detective Fiction*, 220–39.

A Study in Scarlet, 1887

> McDonald, Peter D. *British Literary Culture,* 129–33.
> McLaughlin, Joseph. *Writing the Urban Jungle,* 27–46.
> Ostrowski, Witold. "The Composition of the Detective Novels of Arthur Conan Doyle." *Folia Litteraria Anglica* (Lodz) 1 (1997), 142–44.
> Otis, Laura. *Membranes,* 104–5.
> Sullivan, Sheila. "Hands across the Water, Crime across the Sea: Gender, Imperialist History, and Arthur Conan Doyle's America." *Victorians Inst J* 26 (1998), 100–112.
> Thomas, Ronald R. *Detective Fiction,* 220–39.

The Valley of Fear, 1914

> Kestner, Joseph A. *The Edwardian Detective,* 345–54.
> Ostrowski, Witold. "The Composition of the Detective Novels of Arthur Conan Doyle." *Folia Litteraria Anglica* (Lodz) 1 (1997), 153–59.

RODDY DOYLE

The Commitments, 1987

> Fairhall, James. "Northsiders," in Ellen Carol Jones, ed., *Joyce,* 70–79.
> Kunz, Don. "Alan Parker's Adaptation of Roddy Doyle's *The Commitments.*" *Lit/Film Q* 29 (2001), 53–57.
> Pirroux, Lorraine. "'I'm Black an' I'm Proud': Re-Inventing Irishness in Roddy Doyle's *The Commitments.*" *Coll Lit* 25:2 (1998), 45–57.
> Smyth, Gerry. *The Novel and the Nation,* 68–71.
> White, Caramine. *Reading Roddy Doyle,* 42–61.

Paddy Clarke Ha Ha Ha, 1993

> Cosgrove, Brian. "Roddy Doyle's Backward Look: Tradition and Modernity in *Paddy Clarke Ha Ha Ha.*" *Studies: An Irish Q R* 85 (1996), 231–42.
> Fairhall, James. "Northsiders," in Ellen Carol Jones, ed., *Joyce,* 55–58.
> Forrest-Hickman, Alan. "Growing Up Irish: An Update on Stephen Dedalus." *Publs of the Arkansas Philol Assoc* 22:1 (1996), 9–18.
> McGlynn, Mary. "'But I keep on thinking and I'll never come to a tidy ending': Roddy Doyle's Useful Nostalgia." *LIT* 10 (1999), 87–102.
> Smyth, Gerry. *The Novel and the Nation,* 79–81.
> White, Caramine. *Reading Roddy Doyle,* 98–115.

The Snapper, 1990

> Fairhall, James. "Northsiders," in Ellen Carol Jones, ed., *Joyce,* 58–63.
> Smyth, Gerry. *The Novel and the Nation,* 72–73.
> White, Caramine. *Reading Roddy Doyle,* 62–82.

The Van, 1991

> Fairhall, James. "Northsiders," in Ellen Carol Jones, ed., *Joyce,* 63–69.
> Smyth, Gerry. *The Novel and the Nation,* 73–76.
> Smyth, Gerry. "The Right to the City: Re-presentations of Dublin in Contemporary Irish Fiction," in Liam Harte and Michael Parker, eds., *Contemporary Irish Fiction,* 23–25.

White, Caramine. *Reading Roddy Doyle*, 83–97.

The Woman Who Walked Into Doors, 1996

Smyth, Gerry. *The Novel and the Nation*, 84–88.
White, Caramine. *Reading Roddy Doyle*, 116–41.

MARGARET DRABBLE

The Gates of Ivory, 1992

Bowen, Roger. "Investing in Conrad, Investing in the Orient: Margaret Drabble's *The Gates of Ivory*." *Twentieth Cent Lit* 45 (1999), 278–95.
Brownley, Martine Watson. *Deferrals of Domain*, 159–88.
Purdy, Dwight. "The Conrad Legacy: Margaret Drabble's *The Gates of Ivory*," in Laura L. Davis, ed., *Conrad's Century*, 259–66.
Sullivan, Mary Rose. "Margaret Drabble: Chronicler, Moralist, Artist," in Abby H. P. Werlock, ed., *British Women Writing Fiction*, 200–205.

The Middle Ground, 1980

Hanson, Clare. *Hysterical Fictions*, 112–16.
Sullivan, Mary Rose. "Margaret Drabble: Chronicler, Moralist, Artist," in Abby H. P. Werlock, ed., *British Women Writing Fiction*, 198–99.

The Millstone, 1965

Dervin, Dan. *Matricentric Narratives*, 35–37.
Enomoto, Yoshiko. "The Reality of Pregnancy and Motherhood for Women: Tsushima Yuko's *Choji* and Margaret Drabble's *The Millstone*." *Compar Lit Stud* 35 (1998), 116–24.
Zielinska, Alicja. "Between Acceptance and Rejection: Margaret Drabble's *The Millstone*." *Folia Litteraria Anglica* (Lodz) 1 (1997), 199–208.

The Radiant Way, 1987

Hanson, Clare. *Hysterical Fictions*, 116–20.
Sullivan, Mary Rose. "Margaret Drabble: Chronicler, Moralist, Artist," in Abby H. P. Werlock, ed., *British Women Writing Fiction*, 199–200.

Realms of Gold, 1975

Hanson, Clare. *Hysterical Fictions*, 109–12.

The Waterfall, 1969

Currier, Susan. "Liberation Fables 'in a Different Voice': Virginia Woolf's *To the Lighthouse* and Margaret Drabble's *The Waterfall*," in Jerilyn Fisher and Ellen S. Silber, eds., *Analyzing the Different Voice*, 175–89.
Dervin, Dan. *Matricentric Narratives*, 37–41.
Hanson, Clare. *Hysterical Fictions*, 101–4.
Nelson, Barbara. "The Exorcism of Madness." *B.A.S.: Brit and Am Stud* 1997: 89–97.
Nelson, Barbara A. "The Graying of *Jane Eyre*: Margaret Drabble's *The Waterfall* as Revision." *Michigan Academician* 29 (1997), 99–107.

The Witch of Exmoor, 1996

> Lorenz, Paul H. "The Interplay of Past and Present in Margaret Drabble's *The Witch of Exmoor*." *Publs of the Mississippi Philol Assoc* 1999: 57–64.

BRIEGE DUFFAUD

A Wreath Upon the Dead, 1993

> St. Peter, Christine. *Changing Ireland*, 88–93.

MAUREEN DUFFY

Illuminations, 1991

> Bode, Christoph. "Maureen Duffy: A Polyphonic Sub-Version of Realism." *Anglistik und Englischunterricht* 60 (1997), 41–54.
>
> Rowanchild, Anira. "The State of the Heart: Ideology and Narrative Structure in the Novels of Maureen Duffy and Caeia March," in Elaine Hutton, ed., *Beyond Sex and Romance?*, 40–42.

Love Child, 1971

> Fludernik, Monika. "The Genderization of Narrative." *GRAAT* 21 (1999), 153–75.

The Microcosm, 1966

> Bode, Christoph. "Maureen Duffy: A Polyphonic Sub-Version of Realism." *Anglistik und Englischunterricht* 60 (1997), 41–54.
>
> Rowanchild, Anira. "The State of the Heart: Ideology and Narrative Structure in the Novels of Maureen Duffy and Caeia March," in Elaine Hutton, ed., *Beyond Sex and Romance?*, 29–35.
>
> Smith, Patricia Juliana. *Lesbian Panic*, 144–52.

DAPHNE DU MAURIER

The Flight of the Falcon, 1965

> Auerbach, Nina. *Daphne du Maurier*, 92–96.

Frenchman's Creek, 1941

> Auerbach, Nina. *Daphne du Maurier*, 101–6.

The Glass-Blowers, 1963

> Auerbach, Nina. *Daphne du Maurier*, 56–61.

The House on the Strand, 1969

> Auerbach, Nina. *Daphne du Maurier*, 96–99.

Hungry Hill, 1943

> Auerbach, Nina. *Daphne du Maurier*, 2–10.

Jamaica Inn, 1936

> Auerbach, Nina. *Daphne du Maurier*, 101–10.
>
> Dodd, Philip. "Gender and Cornwall: Charles Kingsley and Daphne du Maurier," in K. D. M. Snell, ed., *The Regional Novel*, 128–29.

Mary Anne, 1954

    Auerbach, Nina. *Daphne du Maurier*, 60–63.

My Cousin Rachel, 1951

    Auerbach, Nina. *Daphne du Maurier*, 83–91, 129–32.

The Progress of Julius, 1933

    Auerbach, Nina. *Daphne du Maurier*, 79–86, 97–99.

Rebecca, 1938

    Armitt, Lucie. *Contemporary Women's Fiction*, 103–11.

    Auerbach, Nina. *Daphne du Maurier*, 15–17, 63–66, 101–5, 107–15, 117–23, 135–43, 145–47.

    Becker, Susanne. *Gothic Forms of Feminine Fictions*, 76–78.

    Butterly Nigro, Kathleen. "Rebecca as Desdemona: 'A Maid that Paragons Description and Wild Fame.'" *Coll Lit* 27…3 (2000), 144–57.

    Dickason, Robert. "Ambiguity and Uncertainty in *Rebecca*," in Sophie Marret, ed., *Féminin/Masculin*, 95–104.

    Dodd, Philip. "Gender and Cornwall: Charles Kingsley and Daphne du Maurier," in K. D. M. Snell, ed., *The Regional Novel*, 128–35.

    Fletcher, John. "Primal Scenes and the Female Gothic: *Rebecca* and *Gaslight*." *Screen* 36 (1995), 341–70.

    Harbord, Janet. "Between Identification and Desire: Rereading *Rebecca*." *Feminist R* 53 (1996), 95–107.

    Harpt, Scott. "Rebecca before Her Time." *J of Evolutionary Psych* 18 (1997), 186–90.

    Horner, Avril, and Sue Zlosnik. "'Extremely valuable property': The Marketing of *Rebecca*," in Judy Simons and Kate Fullbrook, eds., *Writing: A Woman's Business*, 48–63.

    Horner, Avril, and Sue Zlosnik. "'Those Curious, Sloping Letters': Reading the Writing of du Maurier's *Rebecca*." *BELLS: Barcelona Engl Lang and Lit Stud* 7 (1996), 105–15.

    McVea, Deborah J. "'She Ought to Have Been a Boy': Gender versus the Romance Narrative in Du Maurier's *Rebecca*." *Literatur in Wissenschaft und Unterricht* 31 (1998), 269–76.

    Trodd, Anthea. *Women's Writing in English*, 128–29.

    Wisker, Gina. "Don't Look Now!: The Compulsions and Revelations of Daphne du Maurier's Horror Writing." *J of Gender Stud* 8 (1999), 29–32.

The Scapegoat, 1957

    Auerbach, Nina. *Daphne du Maurier*, 9–15, 90–94, 127–29.

    Horneer, Avril, and Sue Zlosnik. "Daphne Du Maurier: The French Connection," in Richard Todd and Luisa Flora, eds., *Theme Parks*, 174–84.

GEORGE DU MAURIER

The Martian, 1897

    Auerbach, Nina. *Daphne du Maurier*, 26–29, 34–36.

    Denisoff, Dennis. *Aestheticism and Sexual Parody*, 93–96.

    Denisoff, Dennis. "'Men of My Own Sex': Genius, Sexuality, and

George Du Maurier's Artists," in Richard Dellamora, ed., *Victorian Sexual Dissidence*, 162–64.

Peter Ibbetson, 1891

Auerbach, Nina. *Daphne du Maurier*, 22–26, 31–34, 63–65.
Daly, Nicholas. *Modernism, Romance and the Fin de Siècle*, 158–61.

Trilby, 1894

Auerbach, Nina. *Daphne du Maurier*, 65–67, 82–84.
Campbell, Donna M. "Domesticating *Trilby*: Norris and the Naturalistic Art Novel." *Excavatio* 11 (1998), 129–36.
Denisoff, Dennis. *Aestheticism and Sexual Parody*, 83–93.
Denisoff, Dennis. "'Men of My Own Sex': Genius, Sexuality, and George Du Maurier's Artists," in Richard Dellamora, ed., *Victorian Sexual Dissidence*, 153–62.
Jenkins, Emily. "*Trilby*: Fads, Photographers, and 'Over-Perfect Feet.'" *Book Hist* 1 (1998), 221–67.
Peck, John. *War, the Army and Victorian Literature*, 142–43.
Pick, Daniel. "Powers of Suggestion: Svengali and the *Fin-de-Siècle*," in Bryan Cheyette and Laura Marcus, eds., *Modernity, Culture and 'the Jew,'* 105–20.
Posnar, Susan. "Alias Who?: Myth-Making in the Mesmeric/Hypnotic Dialogue (Nathaniel Hawthorne, George du Maurier, Margaret Atwood)." *New Comparison* 27/28 (1999), 289–95.

JANE DUNCAN

My Friend Flora, 1962

Hart, Lorena Laing, and Francis Russell Hart. "Jane Duncan: The Homecoming of Imagination," in Douglas Gifford and Dorothy McMillan, eds., *A History*, 470–71.

My Friend Sashie, 1972

Hart, Lorena Laing, and Francis Russell Hart. "Jane Duncan: The Homecoming of Imagination," in Douglas Gifford and Dorothy McMillan, eds., *A History*, 474–78.

My Friends the Hungry Generation, 1968

Hart, Lorena Laing, and Francis Russell Hart. "Jane Duncan: The Homecoming of Imagination," in Douglas Gifford and Dorothy McMillan, eds., *A History*, 472–74.

My Friends the Macleans, 1967

Hart, Lorena Laing, and Francis Russell Hart. "Jane Duncan: The Homecoming of Imagination," in Douglas Gifford and Dorothy McMillan, eds., *A History*, 471–72.

EDWARD LORD DUNSANY

The Curse of the Wise Woman, 1933

Joshi, S. T. "Lord Dunsany: The Career of a Fantaisiste," in Darrell Schweitzer, ed., *Discovering Classic Fantasy Fiction*, 19–23, 32–33.

Rory and Bran, 1936

> Joshi, S. T. "Lord Dunsany: The Career of a Fantaisiste," in Darrell Schweitzer, ed., *Discovering Classic Fantasy Fiction,* 24–25, 33–34.

The Story of Mona Sheehy, 1939

> Joshi, S. T. "Lord Dunsany: The Career of a Fantaisiste," in Darrell Schweitzer, ed., *Discovering Classic Fantasy Fiction,* 19–21, 33–34.

LAWRENCE DURRELL

The Alexandria Quartet, 1961

> Ashworth, Ann. "Alexandria and Her Goddesses: '. . . She Verges on the Goddess.'" *J of Evolutionary Psych* 18:1–2 (1997), 15–19.
>
> Gwynne, Rosalind. "Islam and Muslims in *The Alexandria Quartet.*" *Deus Loci* 5 (1997), 90–102.
>
> Hawthorne, Mark D. "*The Alexandria Quartet*: The Homosexual as Teacher/Guide." *Twentieth Cent Lit* 44 (1998), 328–46.
>
> Lacone-Labarthe, Judith. "'Not translate, but transplant': ambassades du récit (dans *Les Ambassadeurs* de Henry James, *Le Quatuor d'Alexandrie* de Lawrence Durrell et *Au-dessous du volcan* de Malcolm Lowry)." *Revue de Littérature Comparée* 74 (2000), 62–68.
>
> Lewis, Nancy. "Lawrence Durrell and Olivia Manning: Egypt, War, and Displacement." *Deus Loci* 4 (1995–1996), 97–104.
>
> Lorenz, Paul H. "*The Alexandria Quartet* in Family Therapy." *Deus Loci* 5 (1997), 210.
>
> Rose, John M. "Durrell and Plotinus: Mapping the City, Mapping Life." *Deus Loci* 5 (1997), 75–89.
>
> Sobhy, Soad. "The Fabulator's Perspective on Egypt in *The Alexandria Quartet.*" *Deus Loci* 4 (1995–1996), 85–96.
>
> Sobhy, Soad Hussein. "Lawrence Durrell's Heraldic Universe." *Gombak R* 3:1 (1998), 1–18.
>
> Swedan, Nahla. "Time and Structure in *The Alexandria Quartet*: Einstein and Narrative Perspective." *Deus Loci* 4 (1995–1996), 73–84.
>
> Truchlar, Leo. *Erinnerungslandschaften,* 23–30.
>
> Zahlan, Anne R. "Crossing the Border: Lawrence Durrell's Alexandrian Conversion to Postmodernism." *South Atlantic R* 64:4 (1999), 84–97.

The Avignon Quintet, 1974–85

> Alastrué, Ramón Plo. "Durrell Writing about Writers Writing: Towards a Spatial Definition of *The Avignon Quintet.*" *Miscelánea* 17 (1996), 207–25.
>
> Fietz, Lothar. "Geschichte und Entropie: Die Endzeit-Vision in Lawrence Durrells *Avignon-Quintett.*" *Literaturwissenschaftliches Jahrbuch im Auftrage der Görres-Gesellschaft* 32 (1991), 329–58.
>
> Lorenz, Paul H. "Quantum Mechanics and the Shape of Fiction: 'Non-Locality' in the *Avignon Quincunx.*" *Weber Stud* 14:1 (1997), 123–33.
>
> Michalczyk, Ewa. "Structure and Form in *The Avignon Quintet.*" *Anglica Wratislaviensia* 31 (1996), 35–41.
>
> Sobhy, Soad Hussein. "Lawrence Durrell's Heraldic Universe." *Gombak R* 3:1 (1998), 1–18.

Veldeman, Marie-Christine. "Love at Verfeuille: Duality of a Trinity." *Deus Loci* 5 (1997), 103–14.

Zahlan, Anne R. "Crossing the Border: Lawrence Durrell's Alexandrian Conversion to Postmodernism." *South Atlantic R* 64:4 (1999), 84–97.

Constance, 1982

Mathew, Mary. "'Our Many Larval Selves': Durrell's Livia and the Cross-Cultural Signal," in Marilyn Demarest Button and Toni Reed, eds., *The Foreign Woman in British Literature*, 159–66.

Justine, 1957

'Abdel-'Al, Nabîl. "Spirit of the Place in Lawrence Durrell's *Justine* vs. E. M. Forster's *Alexandria: A History and a Guide.*" *Gombak R* 4:1 (1999), 32–45.

Livia; or, Buried Alive, 1978

Mathew, Mary. "'Our Many Larval Selves': Durrell's Livia and the Cross-Cultural Signal," in Marilyn Demarest Button and Toni Reed, eds., *The Foreign Woman in British Literature*, 166–69.

Monsieur; or, The Prince of Darkness, 1974

Sobhy, Soad Hussein. "Lawrence Durrell's Heraldic Universe." *Gombak R* 3:1 (1998), 1–18.

Nunquam, 1970

Truchlar, Leo. *Erinnerungslandschaften*, 30–31.

Tunc, 1968

Mulvihill, James. "Conrad's Accountant and Durrell's *Tunc.*" *Notes on Contemp Lit* 30:3 (2000), 11–12.

Truchlar, Leo. *Erinnerungslandschaften*, 30–31.

ERIC RUCKER EDDISON

A Fish Dinner in Memison, 1941

D'Ammassa, Don. "Villains of Necessity: The Works of E. R. Eddison," in Darrell Schweitzer, ed., *Discovering Classic Fantasy Fiction*, 88–90.

The Mezentian Gate, 1958

D'Ammassa, Don. "Villains of Necessity: The Works of E. R. Eddison," in Darrell Schweitzer, ed., *Discovering Classic Fantasy Fiction*, 88–90.

Mistress of Mistresses, 1935

D'Ammassa, Don. "Villains of Necessity: The Works of E. R. Eddison," in Darrell Schweitzer, ed., *Discovering Classic Fantasy Fiction*, 88–90.

The Worm Ouroboros: A Romance, 1922

D'Ammassa, Don. "Villains of Necessity: The Works of E. R. Eddison," in Darrell Schweitzer, ed., *Discovering Classic Fantasy Fiction*, 91–93.

Oakes, David A. "The Eternal Circle: The Beginning and Ending of E.

R. Eddison's *The Worm Ouroboros.*" *Extrapolation* 40 (1999), 125–28.

Schuyler, William M., Jr. "E. R. Eddison's Metaphysics of the Hero." *New York R of Science Fiction* 31 (1991), 12–17.

EMILY EDEN

The Semi-detached House, 1859

Cohen, Monica F. *Professional Domesticity*, 37–43.

MARIA EDGEWORTH

The Absentee, 1812

Corbett, Mary Jean. *Allegories of Union*, 70–79.

Gilmartin, Sophie. *Ancestry and Narrative*, 30–53.

Johnston, Freya. "Public and Private Space in Jane Austen." *English* 46 (1997), 204–5.

Miller, Julia Anne. "Acts of Union: Family Violence and National Courtship in Maria Edgeworth's *The Absentee* and Sydney Owenson's *The Wild Irish Girl*," in Kathryn Kirkpatrick, ed., *Border Crossings*, 18–23, 29–31.

Plotz, John. *The Crowd*, 45–50.

Saito, Yasushi. "In the Shadow of Napoleon Bonaparte: *The Absentee* and Pax Britannica." *Shiron* 35 (1996), 35–52.

Tracy, Robert. *The Unappeasable Host*, 31–36.

Wohlgemut, Esther. "Maria Edgeworth and the Question of National Identity." *Stud in Engl Lit, 1500–1900* 39 (1999), 650–56.

Belinda, 1801

Bilger, Audrey. *Laughing Feminism*, 125–28, 157–61, 207–10.

Bilger, Audrey. "Mocking the 'Lords of Creation': Comic Male Characters in Frances Burney, Maria Edgeworth and Jane Austen." *Women's Writing* 1 (1994), 86–88.

Butler, Marilyn. "Edgeworth's Stern Father: Escaping Thomas Day, 1795–1801," in Alvaro Ribeiro and James G. Basker, eds., *Tradition in Transition*, 91–93.

Butler, Marilyn. "The Purple Turban and the Flowering Aloe Tree: Signs of Distinction in the Early-Nineteenth-Century Novel." *Mod Lang Q* 58 (1997), 488–95.

Cass, Jeffrey. "Fuseli's Milton Gallery: Satan's First Address to Eve as a Source for Maria Edgeworth's *Belinda.*" *ANQ* 14:2 (2001), 15–23.

Douthwaite, Julia. "Experimental Child-Rearing after Rousseau: Maria Edgeworth, *Practical Education* and *Belinda.*" *Irish J of Feminist Stud* 2:2 (1997), 35–56.

Ellison, Julie. *Cato's Tears*, 71–73.

Greenfield, Susan C. "'Abroad and at Home': Sexual Ambiguity, Miscegenation, and Colonial Boundaries in Edgeworth's *Belinda.*" *PMLA* 112 (1997), 214–24.

Kirkpatrick, Kathryn. "The Limits of Liberal Feminism in Maria

Edgeworth's *Belinda*," in Laura Dabundo, ed., *Jane Austen and Mary Shelley*, 73–80.

McCann, Andrew. *Cultural Politics in the 1790s*, 181–206.

Moore, Lisa L. *Dangerous Intimacies*, 76–78, 90–108.

Myers, Mitzi. "My Art Belongs to Daddy? Thomas Day, Maria Edgeworth, and the Pre-Texts of *Belinda*: Women Writers and Patriarchal Authority," in Paula R. Backscheider, ed., *Revising Women*, 104–46.

Castle Rackrent, 1800

Backus, Margot Gayle. *The Gothic Family Romance*, 98–106.

Bellamy, Liz. "Regionalism and Nationalism: Maria Edgeworth, Walter Scott and the Definition of Britishness," in K. D. M. Snell, ed., *The Regional Novel*, 58–63.

Burgess, Miranda J. "Violent Translations: Allegory, Gender, and Cultural Nationalism in Ireland, 1796–1806." *Mod Lang Q* 59 (1998), 64–70.

Constable, Kathleen. *A Stranger Within the Gates*, 111–20.

Corbett, Mary Jean. *Allegories of Union*, 39–50.

Diez Fabre, Silvia. "The After-Effects of Maria Edgeworth's *Castle Rackrent* on Some Twentieth Century Female Irish Novelists." *B.A.S.: Brit and Am Stud* 1998: 25–33.

Gilmartin, Sophie. *Ancestry and Narrative*, 44–46.

Graham, Colin. "History, Gender and the Colonial Moment: *Castle Rackrent*." *Irish Stud R* 14 (1996), 21–24.

Kreilkamp, Vera. *The Anglo-Irish Novel*, 26–55.

McLoughlin, T. O. *Contesting Ireland*, 189–210.

Neill, Michael. "Mantles, Quirks, and Irish Bulls: Ironic Guise and Colonial Subjectivity in Maria Edgeworth's *Castle Rackrent*." *R of Engl Stud* 52 (2001), 76–90.

Saguaro, Shelley. "Maria Edgeworth and the Politics of Commerce." *Moderna Sprak* 92 (1998), 147–59.

Tracy, Robert. "'The Cracked Lookingglass of a Servant': Inventing the Colonial Novel," in Shlomith Rimmon-Kenan et al., eds., *Rereading Texts*, 198–211.

Tracy, Robert. *The Unappeasable Host*, 9–24.

Trumpener, Katie. *Bardic Nationalism*, 60–62.

Ullrich, David W. "'Did the Warwickshire militia . . . teach the Irish to drink beer, or did they learn from the Irish to drink whiskey?': A Reading of Maria Edgeworth's *Castle Rackrent*," in Laura Dabundo, ed., *Jane Austen and Mary Shelley*, 83–92.

Ennui, 1809

Beesemyer, Irene A. "Romantic Masculinity in Edgeworth's *Ennui* and Scott's *Marmion*: In Itself a Border Story." *Papers on Lang and Lit* 35 (1999), 74–86.

Costello, Julie. "Maria Edgeworth and the Politics of Consumption: Eating, Breastfeeding, and the Irish Wet Nurse in *Ennui*," in Susan C. Greenfield and Carol Barash, eds., *Inventing Maternity*, 173–89.

Kreilkamp, Vera. *The Anglo-Irish Novel*, 32–34, 55–66.

Myers, Mitzi. "Canonical 'Orphans' and Critical *Ennui*: Rereading

Edgeworth's Cross-Writing." *Children's Lit* 25 (1997), 116–33.

Ó Gallchoir, Clíona. "Maria Edgeworth's Revolutionary Morality and the Limits of Realism." *Colby Q* 36 (2000), 93–97.

Tracy, Robert. *The Unappeasable Host*, 27–29.

Trumpener, Katie. *Bardic Nationalism*, 58–60, 214–16.

Waterman, David. "Masters and Pupils: Anglo-Irish Relations in Maria Edgeworth's *Ennui*." *Alizes* 16 (1998), 69–81.

Wohlgemut, Esther. "Maria Edgeworth and the Question of National Identity." *Stud in Engl Lit, 1500–1900* 39 (1999), 647–50.

Harrington, 1817

Page, Judith W. "Maria Edgeworth's *Harrington*: From Shylock to Shadowy Peddlers." *Wordsworth Circle* 32 (2001), 9–13.

Plotz, John. *The Crowd*, 43–75.

Helen, 1834

Bilger, Audrey. *Laughing Feminism*, 75–78, 210–12.

Bilger, Audrey. "Mocking the 'Lords of Creation': Comic Male Characters in Frances Burney, Maria Edgeworth and Jane Austen." *Women's Writing* 1 (1994), 93–94.

Pearson, Jacqueline. "'Arts of Appropriation': Language, Circulation, and Appropriation in the Work of Maria Edgeworth." *Yrbk of Engl Stud* 28 (1998), 226–34.

Leonora, 1806

Pearson, Jacqueline. "'Arts of Appropriation': Language, Circulation, and Appropriation in the Work of Maria Edgeworth." *Yrbk of Engl Stud* 28 (1998), 220–21.

Watson, Nicola J. *Revolution and the Form of the British Novel*, 78–82.

The Modern Griselda, 1805

Gillooly, Eileen. *Smile of Discontent*, 5–7.

Ormond, 1817

Kreilkamp, Vera. *The Anglo-Irish Novel*, 27–30, 66–69.

Trumpener, Katie. *Bardic Nationalism*, 62–66.

Watson, Nicola J. *Revolution and the Form of the British Novel*, 123–26.

Patronage, 1814

Bilger, Audrey. *Laughing Feminism*, 165–68.

Pearson, Jacqueline. "'Arts of Appropriation': Language, Circulation, and Appropriation in the Work of Maria Edgeworth." *Yrbk of Engl Stud* 28 (1998), 221–26.

Vivian, 1812

Etheridge, Kate. "Beyond the Didactic Theme: Public and Private Space in Maria Edgeworth's *Vivian*." *English* 46 (1997), 97–110.

GEORGE EGERTON

Keynotes, 1893

Dutta, Shanta. "Sue's 'Obscure' Sisters." *Thomas Hardy J* 12:2 (1996), 60–71.

Jusova, Iveta. "George Egerton and the Project of British Colonialism." *Tulsa Stud in Women's Lit* 19 (2000), 27–55.

Miles, Rosie. "George Egerton, Bitextuality and Cultural (Re)Production in the 1890s." *Women's Writing* 3 (1996), 243–54.

O'Toole, Tina. "*Keynotes* from Millstreet, Co. Cork: George Egerton's Transgressive Fictions." *Colby Q* 36 (2000), 145–55.

Stetz, Margaret D. "*Keynotes*: A New Woman, Her Publisher, and Her Material." *Stud in the Liter Imagination* 30:1 (1997), 89–102.

The Wheel of God, 1898

Heilmann, Ann. *New Woman Fiction*, 102–3.

GEORGE ELIOT

Adam Bede, 1859

Adams, Harriet F. "Rough Justice: Prematurity and Child-Murder in George Eliot's *Adam Bede*." *Engl Lang Notes* 37:4 (2000), 62–67.

Alley, Henry. *The Quest for Anonymity*, 40–53.

Argyros, Ellen. "*Without Any Check of Proud Reserve*," 150–65.

Ball, David. "The Idea of an English Gentleman: Mr Knightley and Arthur Donnithorne." *George Eliot R* 29 (1998), 46–50.

Berry, Laura C. *The Child, the State, and the Victorian Novel*, 127–57.

Bourke, Simon. "George Eliot: Community Ends." *Australasian Victorian Stud J* 4 (1998), 33–35.

Byerly, Alison. *Realism, Representation, and the Arts*, 111–13, 119–22, 134–36.

Chapman, Raymond. "The Larger Meaning of Your Voice: Varieties of Speech in George Eliot." *George Eliot R* 28 (1997), 25–29.

Clapp-Itnyre, Alisa M. "Dinah and the Secularization of Methodist Hymnody in Eliot's *Adam Bede*." *Victorians Inst J* 26 (1998), 41–61.

Cleere, Eileen. "Reproduction and Malthusian Economics: Fat, Fertility, and Family Planning in George Eliot's *Adam Bede*," in Ann Kibbey et al., eds., *On Your Left*, 150–79.

Coundouriotis, Eleni. "Hetty and History: The Political Consciousness of *Adam Bede*." *Dickens Stud Annual* 30 (2001), 285–303.

Craig, Randall. *Promising Language*, 153–83.

Davis, Philip. "Victorian Realist Prose and Sentimentality," in Alice Jenkins and Juliet John, eds., *Rereading Victorian Fiction*, 19–20.

De Sailly, Rosalind. "George Eliot, G. H. Lewes and the Victorian Science of Mind: Is Hetty the Missing Link in the Evolution of Feeling?" *Australasian Victorian Stud J* 2 (1996), 22–31.

De Sailly, Rosalind. "George Eliot, George Henry Lewes, and the Logic of Signs." *Lit and Aesthetics* 7 (1997), 116–23.

Gates, Sarah. "'The Sound of the Scythe Being Whetted': Gender, Genre, and Realism in *Adam Bede*." *Stud in the Novel* 30 (1998), 20–32.

Gould, Rosemary. "The History of an Unnatural Act: Infanticide and *Adam Bede*." *Victorian Lit and Culture* 25 (1997), 263–75.

Harris, Nicola. "Hardy and Eliot: The Eye of Narcissus' Looking-Glass." *George Eliot R* 28 (1997), 49–57.

Hochberg, Shifra. "*Adam Bede* and the Deconstruction of Dickensian Fancy." *Lamar J of the Hum* 25:1 (2000), 23–34.

Ireland, Ken. *The Sequential Dynamics of Narrative*, 228–29.

Korte, Barbara. *Body Language in Literature*, 164–67.

Kramer, David. "*Adam Bede* and the Development of Early Modernism." *George Eliot-George Henry Lewes Stud* 36–37 (1999), 58–69.

Krueger, Christine L. "Literary Defenses and Medical Prosecutions: Representing Infanticide in Nineteenth-Century Britain." *Victorian Stud* 40:2 (1997), 279–80.

Kushen, Betty. "Instinct and Heredity in Four Nineteenth-Century Novels: 'The Tangled Mystery of Mental Operations.'" *J of Evolutionary Psych* 18:3–4 (1997), 191–212.

Levine, Caroline. "Women or Boys? Gender, Realism, and the Gaze in *Adam Bede*." *Women's Writing* 3 (1996), 113–26.

Lewis, Robert P. "'Full Consciousness': Passion and Conversion in *Adam Bede*." *Rel and the Arts* 2 (1998), 423–42.

Li, Hao. *Memory and History in George Eliot*, 25–39.

Logan, Deborah Anna. *Fallenness in Victorian Women's Writing*, 92–125.

Loncar, Kathleen. *Legal Fiction*, 68–74.

McCaw, Neil. "Beyond 'A Water Toast Sympathy': George Eliot and the Silence of Ireland." *George Eliot-George Henry Lewes Stud* 38–39 (2000), 3–17.

McCaw, Neil. *George Eliot and Victorian Historiography*, 48–50.

McCormack, Kathleen. *George Eliot and Intoxication*, 72–77.

McDonagh, Josephine. "The Early Novels," in George Levine, ed., *The Cambridge Companion*, 40–47.

Marks, Clifford J. "George Eliot's Pictured Bible: *Adam Bede*'s Redeeming Methodism." *Christianity and Lit* 49 (2000), 311–27.

Martin, Carol A. "The Reader as Traveller, the Traveller as Reader in George Eliot." *George Eliot R* 29 (1998), 20–22.

Nunokawa, Jeff. "Sexuality in the Victorian Novel," in Deirdre David, ed., *The Cambridge Companion to the Victorian Novel*, 138–42.

Ogden, Daryl. "Double Visions: Sarah Stickney Ellis, George Eliot and the Politics of Domesticity." *Women's Stud* 25 (1996), 589–95.

Pletzen, Ermien van. "Eliot's *Adam Bede*." *Explicator* 56:1 (1997), 23–25.

Schor, Hilary M. "Show-Trials: Character, Conviction and the Law in Victorian Fiction." *Cardozo Stud in Law and Lit* 11 (1999), 179–95.

Seichepine, Marielle. "Souvenir et ressouvenir dans les romans de George Eliot." *Cahiers Victoriens et Edouardiens* 51 (2000), 121–24.

Shaw, Harry E. *Narrating Reality*, 219–22, 225–29.

Stern, Sheila. "Truth So Difficult: George Eliot and Georg Büchner, A Shared Theme." *Mod Lang R* 96 (2001), 1–13.

Stoddard, Eve W. "A Genealogy of Ruths: From Alien Harvester to Fallen Woman in Nineteenth-Century England," in Marilyn Demarest Button and Toni Reed, eds., *The Foreign Woman in British Literature*, 58–61.

Vigderman, Patricia. "The Traffic in Men: Female Kinship in Three Novels by George Eliot." *Style* 32 (1998), 18–35.

Wolf, Werner. "'I must go back a little to explain [her] motives [. . .]':
Erklärung und Erklärbarkeit menschlichen Verhaltens, Handelns
und Wesens in englischen Romanen des Realismus: *Hard Times*
und *Adam Bede*." *Germanisch-Romanische Monatsschrift* 48
(1998), 453–76.

Wolff, Michael. "Adam Bede's Families: At Home in Hayslope and
Nuneaton." *George Eliot-George Henry Lewes Stud* 32–33 (1997),
58–69.

Daniel Deronda, 1876

Alley, Henry. "Ego, Anonymity, and Healing in George Eliot." *George
Eliot R* 30 (1999), 30–33.

Alley, Henry. *The Quest for Anonymity*, 142–55.

Alsop, Derek, and Chris Walsh. *The Practice of Reading*, 96–118.

Anderson, Amanda. "George Eliot and the Jewish Question." *Yale J
of Criticism* 10 (1997), 39–58.

Andres, Sophia. "Fortune's Wheel in *Daniel Deronda*: Sociopolitical
Turns of the British Empire." *Victorians Inst J* 24 (1996), 87–105.

Andres, Sophia. "George Eliot's Challenge to Medusa's Gendered
Disparities." *Victorian Newsl* 95 (1999), 31–32.

Argyros, Ellen. *"Without Any Check of Proud Reserve,"* 181–88,
196–225.

Arkush, Allan. "Relativizing Nationalism: The Role of Klesmer in
George Eliot's *Daniel Deronda*." *Jewish Social Stud* 3:3 (1997),
61–73.

Beer, Gillian. *Darwin's Plots*, 169–95, 201–19.

Beer, John. *Providence and Love*, 203–11.

Brett, R. L. *Faith and Doubt*, 110–15.

Buckler, Julie A. "Novelistic Figuration, Narrative Metaphor: Western
and Russian Models of the Prima Donna." *Compar Lit* 50 (1998),
158–62.

Byerly, Alison. *Realism, Representation, and the Arts*, 127–33, 140–43.

Callahan, Laura. "The Seduction of Daniel Deronda." *Women's
Writing* 3 (1996), 177–88.

Campon, Maria. "Les corps déchirés de *Daniel Deronda*, corps
représentés, corps représentants." *Cahiers Victoriens et Edouardiens*
47 (1998), 37–48.

Carroll, Alicia. "'Arabian Nights': 'Make-Believe,' Exoticism, and
Desire in *Daniel Deronda*." *JEGP* 98 (1999), 219–38.

Chapman, Raymond. "The Larger Meaning of Your Voice: Varieties
of Speech in George Eliot." *George Eliot R* 28 (1997), 22–29.

Cheyette, Bryan. "White Skin, Black Masks: Jews and Jewishness in
the Writings of George Eliot and Frantz Fanon," in Keith Ansell-
Pearson et al., eds., *Cultural Readings of Imperialism*, 109–14.

Cohen, Monica. "From Home to Homeland: The Bohemian in *Daniel
Deronda*." *Stud in the Novel* 30 (1998), 324–50.

Cohen, Monica F. *Professional Domesticity*, 154–85.

Correa, Delia da Sousa. "'The Music Vibrating in Her Still': Music and
Memory in George Eliot's *The Mill on the Floss* and *Daniel
Deronda*." *Nineteenth-Cent Contexts* 21 (1999), 553–59.

Credland, Arthur G. "George Eliot and Archery." *George Eliot R* 31 (2000), 71–74.

Dever, Carolyn. *Death and the Mother*, 143–75.

Dramin, Edward. "'A New Unfolding of Life': Romanticism in the Late Novels of George Eliot." *Victorian Lit and Culture* 26 (1998), 283–93.

Drouet, Stéphanie. "'Princesses in exile' et 'Wandering Jews': quête et exil dans *Daniel Deronda* par George Eliot." *Cahiers Victoriens et Edouardiens* 51 (2000), 161–70.

Dupeyron-Lafay, Francoise. "Le corps dans *Daniel Deronda*." *Cahiers Victoriens et Edouardiens* 47 (1998), 51–65.

Farkas, Carol-Ann. "Beauty is as Beauty Does: Action and Appearance in Brontë and Eliot." *Dickens Stud Annual* 29 (2000), 323–46.

Flint, Kate. "George Eliot and Gender," in George Levine, ed., *The Cambridge Companion*, 173–79.

Franklin, J. Jeffrey. *Serious Play*, 108–11, 117–23.

Henry, Nancy. "George Eliot and Politics," in George Levine, ed., *The Cambridge Companion*, 152–57.

Hochberg, Shifra. "Animals in *Daniel Deronda*: Representation, Darwinian Discourse, and the Politics of Gender." *George Eliot-George Henry Lewes Stud* 30–31 (1996), 1–19.

Hutchinson, Stuart. "From *Daniel Deronda* to *The House of Mirth*." *Essays in Criticism* 47 (1997), 315–29.

Ireland, Ken. *The Sequential Dynamics of Narrative*, 231–32.

Jaffe, Audrey. *Scenes of Sympathy*, 20–22, 121–57.

Leicht, Kathleen. "The Voice of the Artist in *Daniel Deronda*." *Publs of the Missouri Philol Assoc* 22 (1997), 1–7.

Lesjak, Carolyn. "Labours of a Modern Storyteller: George Eliot and the Cultural Project of 'Nationhood' in *Daniel Deronda*," in Ruth Robbins and Julian Wolfreys, eds., *Victorian Identities*, 25–40.

Li, Hao. *Memory and History in George Eliot*, 150–86.

Loncar, Kathleen. *Legal Fiction*, 184–86.

Lovesey, Oliver. "The Other Woman in *Daniel Deronda*." *Stud in the Novel* 30 (1998), 505–20.

Lovesey, Oliver. "Tigresses, Tinsel Madonnas, and Citizens of the World: The 'Other' Woman in George Eliot's Fiction," in Marilyn Demarest Button and Toni Reed, eds., *The Foreign Woman in British Literature*, 117–18, 121–24.

McCaw, Neil. *George Eliot and Victorian Historiography*, 103–19, 126–38.

McCormack, Kathleen. *George Eliot and Intoxication*, 183–99.

McCormack, Kathleen. "George Eliot, Julia Cameron, and William Henry Fox Talbot: Photography and *Daniel Deronda*." *Word and Image* 12:2 (1996), 175–79.

Malcolm, David. "'Grand and Vague': Why Is *Daniel Deronda* about the Jews?" *George Eliot R* 29 (1998), 33–42.

Martin, Bruce K. "Music and Fiction: The Perils of Popularism." *Mosaic* 31:4 (1998), 21–39.

Menke, Richard. "Fiction as Vivisection: G. H. Lewes and George Eliot." *ELH* 67 (2000), 637–47.

Milbank, Alison. *Dante and the Victorians*, 90–96.

Miller, Derek. "A Note of Daniel Deronda's Circumcision." *George Eliot R* 29 (1998), 70.

Myers, William. *The Presence of Persons*, 197–206.

Newton, K. M. "George Eliot as Proto-Modernist." *Cambridge Q* 27 (1998), 275–78, 280–86.

Newton, K. M. "Sutherland's Puzzles: The Case of *Daniel Deronda*." *Essays in Criticism* 48 (1998), 1–11.

Noble, Michael J. "Presence of Mind: A. S. Byatt, George Eliot, and the Ontology of Ideas." *CEA Critic* 62:3 (2000), 48–56.

Peck, John. *Maritime Fiction*, 142–44.

Press, Jacob. "Same-Sex Unions in Modern Europe: *Daniel Deronda*, *Altneuland*, and the Homoerotics of Jewish Nationalism," in Eve Kosofsky Sedgwick, ed., *Novel Gazing*, 300–312.

Qualls, Barry. "George Eliot and Religion," in George Levine, ed., *The Cambridge Companion*, 130–36.

Redfield, Marc. *Phantom Formations*, 156–60.

Rignall, John. "George Eliot and the Furniture of the House of Fiction." *George Eliot R* 27 (1996), 23–30.

Roberts, Neil. *Meredith and the Novel*, 182–86.

Röder-Bolton, Gerlinde. "'A Binding History, Tragic and Yet Glorious': George Eliot and the Jewish Element in *Daniel Deronda*." *English* 49 (2000), 205–24.

Röder-Bolton, Gerlinde. *George Eliot and Goethe*, 99–274.

Rotenberg, Carl T. "George Eliot: Proto-Psychoanalyst." *Am J of Psychoanalysis* 59 (1999), 257–70.

Seichepine, Marielle. "Innovations anachroniques dans les romans de George Eliot." *Etudes Anglaises* 51 (1998), 158–66.

Seichepine, Marielle. "Souvenir et ressouvenir dans les romans de George Eliot." *Cahiers Victoriens et Edouardiens* 51 (2000), 119–24.

Shaw, Harry E. *Narrating Reality*, 246–52.

Shires, Linda M. "The Aesthetics of the Victorian Novel: Form, Subjectivity, Ideology," in Deirdre David, ed., *The Cambridge Companion to the Victorian Novel*, 72–74.

Shuttleworth, Sally. "'The Malady of Thought': Embodied Memory in Victorian Psychology and the Novel." *Australasian Victorian Stud J* 2 (1996), 6–8.

Silar, Theodore I. "Another Rabbinical Reference in *Daniel Deronda*." *George Eliot-George Henry Lewes Stud* 38–39 (2000), 80–84.

Stone, Wilfred. "The Play of Chance and Ego in *Daniel Deronda*." *Nineteenth-Cent Lit* 53 (1998), 25–55.

Szirotny, June Skye. "'The Terrible Possibilities of Crime': Gwendolen Harleth and Richard Singleton." *Engl Lang Notes* 38:4 (2001), 52–56.

Thompson, Andrew. *George Eliot and Italy*, 145–95.

Thompson, Andrew. "Giuseppe Mazzini and George Eliot's *Daniel Deronda*." *Quaderni del Dipartimento di Lingue e Letterature Straniere Moderne* (Genova) 6 (1993), 101–11.

Tridgell, Susan. "Doubtful Passions: *Love's Knowledge* and *Daniel Deronda*." *Crit R* (Melbourne) 38 (1998), 103–14.

Tromp, Marlene. "Gwendolen's Madness." *Victorian Lit and Culture* 28 (2000), 451–63.

Tromp, Marlene. *The Private Rod*, 199–239.

Tucker, Irene. *A Probable State*, 73–121.

Vigderman, Patricia. "The Traffic in Men: Female Kinship in Three Novels by George Eliot." *Style* 32 (1998), 18–35.

Vorachek, Laura. "'The Instrument of the Century': The Piano as an Icon of Female Sexuality in the Nineteenth Century." *George Eliot-George Henry Lewes Stud* 38–39 (2000), 26–43.

Welsh, Alexander. "The Later Novels," in George Levine, ed., *The Cambridge Companion*, 69–74.

Winkgens, Meinhard. "George Eliot und die Musik: Funktionsvarianten von Musik und Stimme in ihrem Romanwerk," in Stefan Horlacher and Marion Islinger, eds., *Expedition nach der Wahrheit*, 400–419.

Wintle, Sarah. "George Eliot's Peculiar Passion." *Essays in Criticism* 50 (2000), 33–41.

Wohlfarth, Marc E. "*Daniel Deronda* and the Politics of Nationalism." *Nineteenth-Cent Lit* 53 (1998), 188–210.

Yoon, Hae-ryung. "*Daniel Deronda*: A Goethean *Bildungsroman* Signifying George Eliot's Political Maturity." *J of Engl Lang and Lit* 43 (1997), 673–93.

Felix Holt, 1866

Alley, Henry. *The Quest for Anonymity*, 101–13.

Argyros, Ellen. *"Without Any Check of Proud Reserve,"* 196–225.

Brantlinger, Patrick. *The Reading Lesson*, 107–12.

Brock, A. G. van den. "The Politics of Religion in *Felix Holt*." *George Eliot R* 30 (1999), 38–46.

Carroll, Alicia. "The Giaour's Campaign: Desire and the Other in *Felix Holt, The Radical*." *Novel* 30 (1997), 237–56.

Childers, Joseph W. "Industrial Culture and the Victorian Novel," in Deirdre David, ed., *The Cambridge Companion to the Victorian Novel*, 91–93.

Cohen, Monica F. *Professional Domesticity*, 130–50.

Dramin, Edward. "'A New Unfolding of Life': Romanticism in the Late Novels of George Eliot." *Victorian Lit and Culture* 26 (1998), 276–79.

Franklin, J. Jeffrey. *Serious Play*, 96–103.

Franklin, J. Jeffrey. "The Victorian Novel's Performance of Interiority: *Felix Holt* on Trial." *Victorians Inst J* 26 (1998), 69–85.

Guth, Deborah. "George Eliot and Schiller: Narrative Ambivalence in *Middlemarch* and *Felix Holt*." *Mod Lang R* 94 (1999), 920–24.

Harris, Ruth. "*Silas Marner* and *Felix Holt*: Antitheses and Affinities." *George Eliot R* 31 (2000), 55–63.

Hobson, Christopher Z. "The Radicalism of *Felix Holt*: George Eliot and the Pioneers of Labor." *Victorian Lit and Culture* 26 (1998), 19–35.

Hollis, Hilda. "Felix Holt: Independent Spokesman or Eliot's Mouthpiece?" *ELH* 68 (2001), 155–74.

Li, Hao. *Memory and History in George Eliot*, 97–120.

Loncar, Kathleen. *Legal Fiction*, 50–54, 74–77, 126–33, 156–60.

Lovesey, Oliver. "Tigresses, Tinsel Madonnas, and Citizens of the World: The 'Other' Woman in George Eliot's Fiction," in Marilyn Demarest Button and Toni Reed, eds., *The Foreign Woman in British Literature*, 119–21.

McCormack, Kathleen. *George Eliot and Intoxication*, 135–57.

Milbank, Alison. *Dante and the Victorians*, 87–90.

Mossman, Mark. "*Felix Holt, the Radical*: Troubled Communities, Doubled Individualities." *George Eliot-George Henry Lewes Stud* 32–33 (1997), 50–58.

O'Toole, Tess. "Adoption and the 'Improvement of the Estate' in Trollope and Craik." *Nineteenth-Cent Lit* 52 (1997), 78–79.

Peck, John. *War, the Army and Victorian Literature*, 99–100.

Richards, Christine. "Towards a Critical Reputation: Henry James on *Felix Holt, the Radical*." *George Eliot R* 31 (2000), 47–52.

Schor, Hilary M. "Show-Trials: Character, Conviction and the Law in Victorian Fiction." *Cardozo Stud in Law and Lit* 11 (1999), 179–95.

Schramm, Jan-Melissa. *Testimony and Advocacy*, 130–34.

Shaw, Harry E. *Narrating Reality*, 222–25.

Thompson, Andrew. *George Eliot and Italy*, 98–119.

Thompson, Andrew. "Personal and Political: George Eliot's *Felix Holt* Reconsidered." *Quaderni del Dipartimento di Lingue e Letterature Straniere Moderne* (Genova) 5 (1992), 71–98.

Welsh, Alexander. "The Later Novels," in George Levine, ed., *The Cambridge Companion*, 60–61.

Zlotnick, Susan. *Women, Writing, and the Industrial Revolution*, 224–29.

Middlemarch, 1872

Alley, Henry. "Ego, Anonymity, and Healing in George Eliot." *George Eliot R* 30 (1999), 24–30.

Alley, Henry. *The Quest for Anonymity*, 114–45.

Andres, Sophia. "George Eliot's Challenge to Medusa's Gendered Disparities." *Victorian Newsl* 95 (1999), 30–31.

Argyros, Ellen. "*Without Any Check of Proud Reserve,*" 165–81.

Ashton, Rosemary. "The Figure of the German Professor in Nineteenth-Century English Fiction," in Susanne Stark, ed., *The Novel in Anglo-German Context*, 61–66.

Bachmann, Günter. *Philosophische Bewußtseinsformen in George Eliots "Middlemarch."*

Bailey, Suzanne. "Reading the 'Key': George Eliot and the Higher Criticism." *Women's Writing* 3 (1996), 129–39.

Baltazar, Lisa. "The Critique of Anglican Biblical Scholarship in George Eliot's *Middlemarch*." *Lit and Theology* 15 (2001), 40–58.

Beer, Gillian. *Darwin's Plots*, 139–68.

Billington, Josie. "'What Can I Do?': George Eliot, Her Reader and the Tasks of the Narrator in *Middlemarch*." *George Eliot R* 31 (2000), 13–25.

Bourke, Simon. "George Eliot: Community Ends." *Australasian Victorian Stud J* 4 (1998), 37–39.

Brett, R. L. *Faith and Doubt*, 105–10.

Brink, André. *The Novel*, 147–72.

Byatt, A. S. *On Histories and Stories*, 161–64.

Byerly, Alison. *Realism, Representation, and the Arts*, 113–17.

Cave, Terence. "A 'deep though broken wisdom': George Eliot, Pascal and *Middlemarch*." *Rivista di Letterature Moderne e Comparate* 51 (1998), 305–18.

Chapman, Raymond. "The Larger Meaning of Your Voice: Varieties of Speech in George Eliot." *George Eliot R* 28 (1997), 26–29.

Deresiewicz, William. "Heroism and Organicism in the Case of Lydgate." *Stud in Engl Lit, 1500–1900* 38 (1998), 723–37.

Doody, Terrence. *Among Other Things*, 112–15.

Dramin, Edward. "'A New Unfolding of Life': Romanticism in the Late Novels of George Eliot." *Victorian Lit and Culture* 26 (1998), 279–83.

Farkas, Carol-Ann. "Beauty is as Beauty Does: Action and Appearance in Brontë and Eliot." *Dickens Stud Annual* 29 (2000), 323–46.

Fontana, Ernest. "Middlemarch and Dante's 'Flakes of Fire.'" *Engl Lang Notes* 38:4 (2001), 49–52.

Franklin, J. Jeffrey. *Serious Play*, 34–79.

Gaskell, Philip. *Landmarks in English Literature*, 57–60.

Gates, Sarah. "'Dim Lights and Tangled Circumstance': Gender and Genre in George Eliot's Realism." *Genre* 31 (1998), 152–56.

Geppert, Hans Vilmar. "A Cluster of Signs: Semiotic Micrologies in Nineteenth-Century Realism—*Madame Bovary, Middlemarch, Effi Briest*." *Germanic R* 73 (1998), 239–50.

Gindele, Karen C. "The Web of Necessity: George Eliot's Theory of Ideology." *Texas Stud in Lit and Lang* 42 (2000), 255–86.

Gordon, Jan. "The 'Talking Cure' (Again): Gossip and the Paralyzed Patriarchy," in David T. Mitchell and Sharon L. Snyder, eds., *The Body and Physical Difference*, 216–18.

Guth, Deborah. "George Eliot and Schiller: Narrative Ambivalence in *Middlemarch* and *Felix Holt*." *Mod Lang R* 94 (1999), 917–20.

Harris, Nicola. "Hardy and Eliot: The Eye of Narcissus' Looking-Glass." *George Eliot R* 28 (1997), 49–57.

Harrison, James. "Eliot's *Middlemarch*." *Explicator* 57:2 (1999), 77–80.

Hauge, Hans. "The Ethical Demand: Responding to J. Hillis Miller's 'The Roar on the Other Side of Silence: Otherness in *Middlemarch*.'" *Edda* 3 (1995), 247–54.

Hirai, Masako. *Sisters in Literature*, 41–76.

Hoy, Thomas. "'The Message of a Magic Touch': *Middlemarch* and the Ether." *Australasian Victorian Stud J* 2 (1996), 13–20.

Ireland, Ken. *The Sequential Dynamics of Narrative*, 230–31.

Irvine, Mark. "Mrs. (Polly) Lewes's Comic *Middlemarch*." *George Eliot-George Henry Lewes Stud* 34–35 (1998), 28–47.

Jackson, R. L. P. "A History of the Lights and Shadows: The Secret Motion of *Middlemarch*." *Cambridge Q* 26 (1997), 1–18.

Judd, Catherine. *Bedside Seductions*, 123–51.

Karlin, Daniel. "Having the Whip-Hand in *Middlemarch.*" *George Eliot R* 28 (1997), 34–45. (Also in Alice Jenkins and Juliet John, eds., *Rereading Victorian Fiction*, 29–43.)

Katz, Leslie. "An End to Converting Patients' Stomachs into Drug-Shops: Lydgate's New Method of Charging His Patients in *Middlemarch.*" *George Eliot-George Henry Lewes Stud* 34–35 (1998), 48–59.

Kucich, John. "Intellectual Debate in the Victorian Novel: Religion, Science, and the Professional," in Deirdre David, ed., *The Cambridge Companion to the Victorian Novel*, 221–23.

Levin, Amy. "Silence, Gesture, and Meaning in *Middlemarch.*" *George Eliot-George Henry Lewes Stud* 30–31 (1996), 20–31.

Li, Hao. *Memory and History in George Eliot*, 121–49.

Lloyd, Tom. *Crises of Realism*, 128–40.

Loncar, Kathleen. *Legal Fiction*, 115–26, 150–55.

Lovesey, Oliver. "Tigresses, Tinsel Madonnas, and Citizens of the World: The 'Other' Woman in George Eliot's Fiction," in Marilyn Demarest Button and Toni Reed, eds., *The Foreign Woman in British Literature*, 118–20.

McCaw, Neil. *George Eliot and Victorian Historiography*, 76–81, 90–92, 123–26.

McCormack, Kathleen. *George Eliot and Intoxication*, 159–79.

Marks, Clifford J. "*Middlemarch*, Obligation, and Dorothea's Duplicity." *Rocky Mountain R of Lang and Lit* 54:2 (2000), 25–39.

Miller, Andrew H. *Novels behind Glass*, 189–218.

Miller, J. Hillis. "The Roar on the Other Side of Silence: Otherness in *Middlemarch*," in Shlomith Rimmon-Kenan et al., eds., *Rereading Texts*, 137–47. (Also in *Edda* 3 [1995], 237–44.)

Mitchell, Sherry L. "Saint Teresa and Dorothea Brooke: The Absent Road to Perfection in *Middlemarch.*" *Victorian Newsl* 92 (1997), 32–37.

Nurbhai, Saleel. "Idealisation and Irony in George Eliot's Middlemarch." *George Eliot-George Henry Lewes Stud* 38–39 (2000), 18–25.

O'Farrell, Mary Ann. *Telling Complexions*, 118–21.

Ogden, Daryl. "Double Visions: Sarah Stickney Ellis, George Eliot and the Politics of Domesticity." *Women's Stud* 25 (1996), 595–99.

Oh, Jung-Hwa. "Dorothea Brooke and the Story of *Bildung.*" *Feminist Stud in Engl Lit* 7 (2000), 159–86.

Paris, Bernard J. "*Middlemarch* Revisited: Changing Responses to George Eliot." *Am J of Psychoanalysis* 59 (1999), 237–55.

Payne, David. "The Serialist Vanishes: Producing Belief in George Eliot." *Novel* 33 (1999), 32–46.

Pool, Daniel. *Dickens' Fur Coat*, 200–203.

Postlethwaite, Diana. "George Eliot and Science," in George Levine, ed., *The Cambridge Companion*, 114–17.

Price, Leah. *The Anthology and the Rise of the Novel*, 122–24.

Redfield, Marc. *Phantom Formations*, 139–56.

Sampaio, Paula Sofia. "O Tratamento da Sexualidade em *Middlemarch*: Silêncios que Falam o Sexo." *Dedalus* 6 (1996), 51–62.

Seeber, Hans Ulrich, and Sabine Poeschel. "Dorothea Brooke und erotische Kunst in George Eliots *Middlemarch*." *Poetica* (Munich) 32 (2000), 443–73.

Seichepine, Marielle. "Innovations anachroniques dans les romans de George Eliot." *Etudes Anglaises* 51 (1998), 158–66.

Shaw, Harry E. *Narrating Reality*, 231–36, 254–62.

Shiller, Dana. "The Redemptive Past in the Neo-Victorian Novel." *Stud in the Novel* 29 (1997), 541–44.

Siegel, Carol. "'This Thing I Like My Sister May Not Do': Shakespearean Erotics and a Clash of Wills in *Middlemarch*." *Style* 32 (1998), 36–59.

Sodré, Ignês. "Maggie and Dorothea: Reparation and Working Through in George Eliot's Novels." *Am J of Psychoanalysis* 59 (1999), 195–208.

Staten, Henry. "Is *Middlemarch* Ahistorical." *PMLA* 115 (2000), 991–1003.

Sutherland, John. *Who Betrays Elizabeth Bennet?*, 197–201.

Szirotny, June Skye. "'No Sorrow I Have Thought More About': The Tragic Failure of George Eliot's St. Theresa." *Victorian Newsl* 93 (1998), 17–26.

Thompson, Andrew. *George Eliot and Italy*, 120–44.

Trott, Nicola. "*Middlemarch* and 'the Home Epic,'" in Richard Gravil, ed., *Master Narratives*, 139–57.

Vigderman, Patricia. "The Traffic in Men: Female Kinship in Three Novels by George Eliot." *Style* 32 (1998), 18–35.

Vorachek, Laura. "'The Instrument of the Century': The Piano as an Icon of Female Sexuality in the Nineteenth Century." *George Eliot-George Henry Lewes Stud* 38–39 (2000), 26–43.

Waddle, Keith A. "Mary Garth, The Wollstonecraftian Feminist in *Middlemarch*." *George Eliot-George Henry Lewes Stud* 28–29 (1995), 16–29.

Wainwright, Valerie. "Anatomizing Excellence: Middlemarch, Moral Saints and the Languages of Belief." *English* 49 (2000), 1–11.

Welsh, Alexander. "The Later Novels," in George Levine, ed., *The Cambridge Companion*, 61–69.

Winkgens, Meinhard. "George Eliot und die Musik: Funktionsvarianten von Musik und Stimme in ihrem Romanwerk," in Stefan Horlacher and Marion Islinger, eds., *Expedition nach der Wahrheit*, 401–24.

The Mill on the Floss, 1860

Alley, Henry. *The Quest for Anonymity*, 54–70.

Andres, Sophia. "George Eliot's Challenge to Medusa's Gendered Disparities." *Victorian Newsl* 95 (1999), 30.

Argyros, Ellen. *"Without Any Check of Proud Reserve,"* 97–135.

Barfoot, C. C. "Beyond *Pug's Tour*: Stereotyping Our 'Fellow-Creatures,'" in Barfoot, ed., *Beyond Pug's Tour*, 5–7.

Birden, Lorene. "Trois analyses du sel: le personnage du faux charitable dans les œuvres de George Eliot, Charles Dickens et Rebecca West." *Cahiers Victoriens et Edouardiens* 45 (1977), 61–67.

Bourke, Simon. "George Eliot: Community Ends." *Australasian Victorian Stud J* 4 (1998), 35–37.

Brett, R. L. *Faith and Doubt*, 99–101.

Chapman, Raymond. "The Larger Meaning of Your Voice: Varieties of Speech in George Eliot." *George Eliot R* 28 (1997), 22–29.

Chi, Hsin Ying. *Artist and Attic*, 43–63.

Correa, Delia da Sousa. "'The Music Vibrating in Her Still': Music and Memory in George Eliot's *The Mill on the Floss* and *Daniel Deronda*." *Nineteenth-Cent Contexts* 21 (1999), 541–53.

Craig, Randall. *Promising Language*, 43–46, 69–75.

Currie, Richard A. "Lewes's General Mind and the Judgment of St. Ogg's: *The Mill on the Floss* as Scientific Text." *Victorian Newsl* 92 (1997), 25–27.

Dee, Phyllis Susan. "Female Sexuality and Triangular Desire in *Vanity Fair* and *The Mill on the Floss*." *Papers on Lang and Lit* 35 (1999), 401–15.

Dessart, Jamie Thomas. "'Surrounded by a Gilt Frame': Mirrors and Reflection of Self in *Jane Eyre*, *Mill on the Floss*, and *Wide Saragasso Sea*." *Jean Rhys R* 8:1–2 (1997), 16–24.

Franken, Lynn. "The Wound of the Serpent: The Philoctetes Story in *The Mill on the Floss*." *Compar Lit Stud* 36 (1999), 24–42.

Gardner, Eric R. "Of Eyes and Musical Voices in 'The Great Temptation': Darwinian Sexual Selection in *The Mill on the Floss*." *Victorian Newsl* 93 (1998), 31–36.

Gillooly, Eileen. *Smile of Discontent*, 164–203.

Giobbi, Giuliana. "A Blurred Picture: Adolescent Girls Growing Up in Fanny Burney, George Eliot, Rosamond Lehmann, Elizabeth Bowen and Dacia Maraini." *J of European Stud* 25 (1995), 141–61.

Gruner, Elisabeth Rose. "Born and Made: Sisters, Brothers, and the Deceased Wife's Sister Bill." *Signs* 24 (1999), 427–29.

Guth, Deborah. "George Eliot and Schiller: The Case of *The Mill on the Floss*." *George Eliot-George Henry Lewes Stud* 34–35 (1998), 13–27.

Harper, Lila. "An Astonishing Change in Metaphor: Tom's Education and the Shrew-Mouse." *George Eliot-George Henry Lewes Stud* 38–39 (2000), 76–79.

Hayes, Mary Elizabeth. "Maggie's Education of 'Her Unknown Kindred' in George Eliot's *The Mill on the Floss*." *J of the Gypsy Lore Soc* 5:8 (1998), 117–31.

Klaver, J. M. I. "'I Will Ferry Thee Across': The Meaning of Fluvialism in George Eliot's *The Mill on the Floss*." *Rivista di Studi Vittoriani* 7:4 (1999), 71–88.

Lewis, Robert P. "The Pilgrim Maggie: Natural Glory, Natural History, and the Conversion of Tom Tulliver in *The Mill on the Floss*." *Lit and Theology* 12 (1998), 121–33.

Li, Hao. *Memory and History in George Eliot*, 49–59.

Loncar, Kathleen. *Legal Fiction*, 48–50, 164–66.

McCall, Ian. "The Portrayal of Childhood in Proust's *Jean Santeuil* and Eliot's *The Mill on the Floss*." *Compar Lit Stud* 36 (1999), 131–43.

McCaw, Neil. *George Eliot and Victorian Historiography*, 134–36.

McCormack, Kathleen. *George Eliot and Intoxication*, 77–85.

McDonagh, Josephine. "The Early Novels," in George Levine, ed., *The Cambridge Companion*, 47–48, 52–56.

Nord, Deborah Epstein. "'Marks of Race': Gypsy Figures and Eccentric Femininity in Nineteenth-Century Women's Writing." *Victorian Stud* 41:2 (1998), 199–202.

Rauch, Alan. *Useful Knowledge*, 190–204.

Röder-Bolton, Gerlinde. *George Eliot and Goethe*, 15–98.

Sadrin, Anny. "Time, Tense, Weather in Three 'Flood Novels': *Bleak House, The Mill on the Floss, To the Lighthouse*." *Yrbk of Engl Stud* 30 (2000), 102–5.

Seichepine, Marielle. "Souvenir et ressouvenir dans les romans de George Eliot." *Cahiers Victoriens et Edouardiens* 51 (2000), 116–25.

Shuttleworth, Sally. "'The Malady of Thought': Embodied Memory in Victorian Psychology and the Novel." *Australasian Victorian Stud J* 2 (1996), 4–6.

Sodré, Ignês. "Maggie and Dorothea: Reparation and Working Through in George Eliot's Novels." *Am J of Psychoanalysis* 59 (1999), 195–208.

Sutherland, John. *Who Betrays Elizabeth Bennet?*, 175–81.

Szirotny, June Skye. "Maggie Tulliver: November's Child." *George Eliot-George Henry Lewes Stud* 30–31 (1996), 59–62.

Winkgens, Meinhard. "George Eliot und die Musik: Funktionsvarianten von Musik und Stimme in ihrem Romanwerk," in Stefan Horlacher and Marion Islinger, eds., *Expedition nach der Wahrheit*, 407–9.

Wintle, Sarah. "George Eliot's Peculiar Passion." *Essays in Criticism* 50 (2000), 25–33.

Yoon, Hae-ryung. "*The Mill on the Floss*: Maggie Tulliver as the Heroine of Frustrated Vocational Energy." *J of Engl Lang and Lit* 44 (1998), 887–909.

Romola, 1863

Alley, Henry. *The Quest for Anonymity*, 82–95.

Bernardo, Susan M. "From Romola to *Romola*: The Complex Act of Naming," in Caroline Levine and Mark W. Turner, eds., *From Author to Text*, 89–101.

Brett, R. L. *Faith and Doubt*, 101–5.

Carroll, David. "George Eliot Martyrologist: The Case of Savonarola," in Caroline Levine and Mark W. Turner, eds., *From Author to Text*, 105–19.

Corner, Julian. "'Telling the Whole': Trauma, Drifting and Reconciliation in *Romola*," in Caroline Levine and Mark W. Turner, eds., *From Author to Text*, 67–86.

Dames, Nicholas. *Amnesiac Selves*, 206–34.

Gray, Beryl. "Power and Persuasion: Voices of Influence in *Romola*," in Caroline Levine and Mark W. Turner, eds., *From Author to Text*, 123–32.

Greenwood, Chris. "'An Imperceptible Start': The Sight of Humanity in *Romola*," in Caroline Levine and Mark W. Turner, eds., *From Author to Text*, 165–79.

Guth, Deborah. "George Eliot and Schiller: Rereading Savonarola." *Cahiers Victoriens et Edouardiens* 49 (1999), 71–81.

Ireland, Ken. *The Sequential Dynamics of Narrative*, 229–30.

Johnstone, Peggy Fitzhugh. "Conflicting Self-Perceptions in George Eliot's *Romola*." *Am J of Psychoanalysis* 59 (1999), 225–36.

Levine, Caroline. "The Prophetic Fallacy: Realism, Foreshadowing and Narrative Knowledge in *Romola*," in Caroline Levine and Mark W. Turner, eds., *From Author to Text*, 135–60.

Li, Hao. *Memory and History in George Eliot*, 76–96.

Liddle, Dallas. "Mentor and Sibyl: Journalism and the End(s) of Apprenticeship in George Eliot." *Victorians Inst J* 26 (1998), 30–34.

Loncar, Kathleen. *Legal Fiction*, 199–201.

McCaw, Neil. *George Eliot and Victorian Historiography*, 8–10.

McCormack, Kathleen. *George Eliot and Intoxication*, 111–30.

Milbank, Alison. *Dante and the Victorians*, 83–91.

Nardo, Anna K. "*Romola* and Milton: A Cultural History of Rewriting." *Nineteenth-Cent Lit* 53 (1998), 328–63.

Ormond, Leonee. "Angels and Archangels: *Romola* and the Paintings of Florence," in Caroline Levine and Mark W. Turner, eds., *From Author to Text*, 181–89.

Schramm, Jan-Melissa. *Testimony and Advocacy*, 162–64.

Sheets, Robin. "History and Romance: Harriet Beecher Stowe's *Agnes of Sorrento* and George Eliot's *Romola*." *Clio* 26 (1997), 323–46.

Simpson, Shona Elizabeth. "Mapping *Romola*: Physical Space, Women's Place," in Caroline Levine and Mark W. Turner, eds., *From Author to Text*, 53–65.

Thompson, Andrew. *George Eliot and Italy*, 68–97.

Welsh, Alexander. "The Later Novels," in George Levine, ed., *The Cambridge Companion*, 58–60.

Scenes of Clerical Life, 1858

Alley, Henry. *The Quest for Anonymity*, 27–39.

Barrat, Alain. "The Picture and the Message in George Eliot's *Scenes of Clerical Life*: The Thematic Function of the Rural Setting." *George Eliot-George Henry Lewes Stud* 30–31 (1996), 48–58.

Bidney, Martin. "*Scenes of Clerical Life* and Trifles of High-Order Clerical Life: Satirical and Empathetic Humor in George Eliot." *George Eliot-George Henry Lewes Stud* 36–37 (1999), 1–28.

Goetsch, Paul. "Das Verhältnis von Alltag und Religion in der neueren englischen Literatur." *Literaturwissenschaftliches Jahrbuch im Auftrage der Görres-Gesellschaft* 31 (1990), 211–32.

Li, Hao. *Memory and History in George Eliot*, 32–37.

Liddle, Dallas. "Mentor and Sibyl: Journalism and the End(s) of Apprenticeship in George Eliot." *Victorians Inst J* 26 (1998), 24–30.

Lynn, Andrew B. "Bondage, Acquiescence, and Blessedness: Spinoza's Three Kinds of Knowledge and *Scenes of Clerical Life*." *George Eliot-George Henry Lewes Stud* 30–31 (1996), 32–47.

McDonagh, Josephine. "The Early Novels," in George Levine, ed., *The Cambridge Companion*, 38–40, 48–52.

Seichepine, Marielle. "Souvenir et ressouvenir dans les romans de George Eliot." *Cahiers Victoriens et Edouardiens* 51 (2000), 117–20.

Shaw, Harry E. *Narrating Reality*, 240–46.

Thompson, Andrew. *George Eliot and Italy*, 50–67.

Silas Marner, 1861

Alley, Henry. *The Quest for Anonymity*, 71–81.

Breen, Margaret Soenser. "Silas Marner: George Eliot's Male Heroine." *George Eliot-George Henry Lewes Stud* 28–29 (1995), 1–15.

Brown, Kate E. "Loss, Revelry, and the Temporal Measures of *Silas Marner*: Performance, Regret, Recollection." *Novel* 32 (1999), 222–47.

Crehan, Stewart. "Scandalous Topicality: *Silas Marner* and the Political Unconscious." *Victorian Newsl* 92 (1997), 1–5.

Emery, Laura, and Margaret Keenan. "'I've Been Robbed!': Breaking the Silence in *Silas Marner*." *Am J of Psychoanalysis* 59 (1999), 209–23.

Fisch, Harold. *New Stories for Old*, 60–77.

Hall, Donald E. "The Private Pleasures of Silas Marner," in Jay Losey and William D. Brewer, eds., *Mapping Male Sexuality*, 181–95.

Harris, Ruth. "*Silas Marner* and *Felix Holt*: Antitheses and Affinities." *George Eliot R* 31 (2000), 55–63.

Jackson-Houlston, C. M. *Ballads, Songs and Snatches*, 65–67.

Li, Hao. *Memory and History in George Eliot*, 59–68.

Lloyd, Tom. *Crises of Realism*, 123–28.

Loncar, Kathleen. *Legal Fiction*, 148–50.

McCormack, Kathleen. *George Eliot and Intoxication*, 95–106.

Newton, K. M. "George Eliot as Proto-Modernist." *Cambridge Q* 27 (1998), 278–80.

Sicher, Efraim. "George Eliot's 'Glue Test': Language, Law, and Legitimacy in *Silas Marner*." *Mod Lang R* 94 (1999), 11–21.

Sicher, Efraim. "George Eliot's Rescripting of Scripture: The 'Ethics of Reading' in *Silas Marner*." *Simeia* 77 (1997), 243–70.

Sonstroem, David. "The Breaks in *Silas Marner*." *JEGP* 97 (1998), 545–67.

Stewart, Ralph. "Eliot's *Silas Marner*." *Explicator* 56:2 (1998), 76–78.

Taylor, Jenny Bourne. "Representing Illegitimacy in Victorian Culture," in Ruth Robbins and Julian Wolfreys, eds., *Victorian Identities*, 137–38.

ALICE THOMAS ELLIS

The Birds of the Air, 1980

Sceats, Sarah. *Food, Consumption and the Body*, 150–52.

Fairy Tale, 1996

Armitt, Lucie. *Contemporary Women's Fiction*, 134–46.

The Sin Eater, 1977

Sceats, Sarah. *Food, Consumption and the Body*, 143–46.

Unexplained Laughter, 1985

Sceats, Sarah. *Food, Consumption and the Body*, 152–54.

MARGARET ELPHINSTONE

A Sparrow's Flight, 1989

Gifford, Douglas. "Contemporary Fiction II: Seven Writers in Scotland," in Douglas Gifford and Dorothy McMillan, eds., *A History*, 604–6.

BUCHI EMECHETA

The Bride Price, 1982

Mezu, Rose Ure. "Buchi Emecheta's *The Bride Price* and *The Slave Girl*: A Schizoanalytic Perspective." *Ariel* 28:1 (1997), 131–40.

Destination Biafra, 1982

Uraizee, Joya. "Fragmented Borders and Female Boundary Markers in Buchi Emecheta's *Destination Biafra*." *J of the Midwest Mod Lang Assoc* 30:1–2 (1997), 16–28.

Uwakweh, Pauline Ada. "Female Choices: The Militant Option in Buchi Emecheta's *Destination Biafra* and Alice Walker's *Meridian*." *ALA Bull* 23:1 (1997), 47–59.

The Family, 1989

Abruña, Laura Niesen de. "Sea Changes: African-Caribbean and African Women Writers in England," in Abby H. P. Werlock, ed., *British Women Writing Fiction*, 279–80.

The Joys of Motherhood, 1979

Bazin, Nancy Topping. "Alcoholism in Third-World Literature: Buchi Emecheta, Athol Fugard and Anita Desai," in Jane Lilienfeld and Jeffrey Oxford, eds., *The Languages of Addiction*, 124–27.

Booker, M. Keith. *The African Novel in English*, 85–102.

Higonnet, Margaret. "Frames of Female Suicide." *Stud in the Novel* 32 (2000), 239–41.

Hogan, Patrick Colm. *Colonialism and Cultural Identity*, 173–212.

Skinner, John. *The Stepmother Tongue*, 96–98.

Kehinde, 1994

Abruña, Laura Niesen de. "Sea Changes: African-Caribbean and African Women Writers in England," in Abby H. P. Werlock, ed., *British Women Writing Fiction*, 278–79.

Gohrisch, Jana. "Crossing the Boundaries of Cultures: Buchi Emecheta's Novels." *Anglistik und Englischunterricht* 60 (1997), 129–42.

The Rape of Shavi, 1983

Mezu, Rose Ure. "The Perspective of the Other: Racism and Woman Power in Buchi Emecheta's *The Rape of Shavi*." *Bookbird* 36:1 (1998), 12–16.

The Slave Girl, 1977

Mezu, Rose Ure. "Buchi Emecheta's *The Bride Price* and *The Slave Girl*: A Schizoanalytic Perspective." *Ariel* 28:1 (1997), 140–45.

JOHN MEADE FALKNER

The Lost Stradivarius, 1895

Daly, Nicholas. "Somewhere there's Music: John Meade Falkner's *The Lost Stradivarius,*" in Michael St. John, ed., *Romancing Decay,* 97–106.

The Nebuly Coat, 1903

Wilson, Edward. "A Fictional Source for the Falling Tower in John Meade Falkner's *The Nebuly Coat.*" *Notes and Queries* 43 (1996), 439–41.

Wilson, Edward. "Literary Echoes and Sources in John Meade Falkner's *The Nebuly Coat.*" *R of Engl Stud* 189 (1997), 60–68.

FREDERICK WILLIAM FARRAR

Eric, Or Little by Little, 1858

Stoneley, Peter. "Family Values and the 'Republic of Boys': Tom Brown and Others." *J of Victorian Culture* 3 (1998), 81–88.

J. G. FARRELL

A Girl in the Head, 1967

Ackerley, Chris. "A Fox in the Dongeon: The Presence of Malcolm Lowry in the Early Fiction of J. G. Farrell," in Ralph J. Crane, ed., *J. G. Farrell,* 26–32.

Crane, Ralph J., and Jennifer Livett. *Troubled Pleasures,* 51–67.

Greacen, Lavinia. *J. G. Farrell,* 192–98.

Prusse, Michael C. *"Tomorrow is Another Day,"* 57–66.

The Hill Station, 1981

Crane, Ralph J., and Jennifer Livett. *Troubled Pleasures,* 122–36.

Greacen, Lavinia. *J. G. Farrell,* 365–69, 392–94.

Prusse, Michael C. *"Tomorrow is Another Day,"* 199–210.

The Lung, 1965

Ackerley, Chris. "A Fox in the Dongeon: The Presence of Malcolm Lowry in the Early Fiction of J. G. Farrell," in Ralph J. Crane, ed., *J. G. Farrell,* 20–26.

Crane, Ralph J., and Jennifer Livett. *Troubled Pleasures,* 43–50.

Greacen, Lavinia. *J. G. Farrell,* 81–97, 182–84.

Prusse, Michael C. *"Tomorrow is Another Day,"* 48–56.

A Man from Elsewhere, 1963

Crane, Ralph J., and Jennifer Livett. *Troubled Pleasures,* 37–43.

Prusse, Michael C. *"Tomorrow is Another Day,"* 39–47.

The Siege of Krishnapur, 1973

Caterson, Simon. "Literary Influence and the Superfluous Man: J. G. Farrell, Richard Hughes, Joseph Conrad," in Ralph J. Crane, ed., *J. G. Farrell,* 39–47.

Crane, Ralph J., and Jennifer Livett. *Troubled Pleasures,* 83–103.

Ellis, Juniper. "The Ends of Empire in J. G. Farrell's *The Siege of Krishnapur,*" in Ralph J. Crane, ed., *J. G. Farrell,* 96–110.

Greacen, Lavinia. *J. G. Farrell*, 271–78, 285–95, 297–305, 360–62.

Hartveit, Lars. "Moral Patterning and Re-Patterning in J. G. Farrell's Empire Trilogy," in Ralph J. Crane, ed., *J. G. Farrell*, 146–61.

Lea, Daniel. "Parodic Strategy and the Mutiny Romance in *The Siege of Krishnapur*," in Ralph J. Crane, ed., *J. G. Farrell*, 65–78.

Newman, Judie. "Rebounding Metaphors: Culture and Conquest in J. G. Farrell's *The Siege of Krishnapur*," in Ralph J. Crane, ed., *J. G. Farrell*, 80–94.

Prusse, Michael C. *"Tomorrow is Another Day,"* 130–55.

Williams, Patrick. "Men Performing Badly? Masculinity in J. G. Farrell's Empire Novels," in Ralph J. Crane, ed., *J. G. Farrell*, 163–77.

The Singapore Grip, 1978

Caterson, Simon. "Literary Influence and the Superfluous Man: J. G. Farrell, Richard Hughes, Joseph Conrad," in Ralph J. Crane, ed., *J. G. Farrell*, 37–47.

Crane, Ralph J. "'J. G. Farrell, an Australian': or, The Trope of Australia in the Fiction of J. G. Farrell." *J of Commonwealth Lit* 34:2 (1999), 51–57.

Crane, Ralph J., and Jennifer Livett. *Troubled Pleasures*, 104–21.

Ferns, Chris. "Walter Scott, J. G. Farrell, and the Dialogics of Historical Fiction," in Ralph J. Crane, ed., *J. G. Farrell*, 128–44.

Greacen, Lavinia. *J. G. Farrell*, 328–38, 343–53.

Hartveit, Lars. "Moral Patterning and Re-Patterning in J. G. Farrell's Empire Trilogy," in Ralph J. Crane, ed., *J. G. Farrell*, 146–61.

McLeod, John. "J. G. Farrell and Post-Imperial Fiction," in Ralph J. Crane, ed., *J. G. Farrell*, 190–93.

Prusse, Michael C. *"Tomorrow is Another Day,"* 156–82.

Smethurst, Paul. "Post-Imperial Topographies: The Undergrounding of History in J. G. Farrell's *The Singapore Grip*, Timothy Mo's *An Insular Possession*, and Graham Swift's *Waterland*," in Ralph J. Crane, ed., *J. G. Farrell*, 112–26.

Williams, Patrick. "Men Performing Badly? Masculinity in J. G. Farrell's Empire Novels," in Ralph J. Crane, ed., *J. G. Farrell*, 163–77.

Troubles, 1970

Caterson, Simon. "Literary Influence and the Superfluous Man: J. G. Farrell, Richard Hughes, Joseph Conrad," in Ralph J. Crane, ed., *J. G. Farrell*, 39–46.

Corcoran, Neil. *After Yeats and Joyce*, 49–52.

Crane, Ralph J., and Jennifer Livett. *Troubled Pleasures*, 68–82.

Delattre, Elisabeth. "Histoire et fiction dans *Troubles* de J. G. Farrell." *Etudes Irlandaises* 25:1 (2000), 65–79.

Greacen, Lavinia. *J. G. Farrell*, 60–63, 257–66.

Hartveit, Lars. "Moral Patterning and Re-Patterning in J. G. Farrell's Empire Trilogy," in Ralph J. Crane, ed., *J. G. Farrell*, 146–61.

Lea, Daniel. "*Troubles* and J. G. Farrell's Interiority Complex." *Etudes Irlandaises* 24:1 (1999), 79–88.

McLeod, John. "J. G. Farrell and Post-Imperial Fiction," in Ralph J. Crane, ed., *J. G. Farrell*, 187–90.

Prusse, Michael C. *"Tomorrow is Another Day,"* 103–29.

Tamplin, Ronald. "*Troubles* and the Irish Tradition," in Ralph J. Crane, ed., *J. G. Farrell*, 48–63.

Williams, Patrick. "Men Performing Badly? Masculinity in J. G. Farrell's Empire Novels," in Ralph J. Crane, ed., *J. G. Farrell*, 163–77.

SEBASTIAN FAULKS

Charlotte Gray, 1998

Middleton, Peter, and Tim Woods. *Literatures of Memory*, 19–22.

ELAINE FEINSTEIN

The Border, 1984

Lassner, Phyllis. "'Witness to Their Vanishing': Elaine Feinstein's Fictions of Jewish Continuity," in Abby H. P. Werlock, ed., *British Women Writing Fiction*, 117–18.

Children of the Rose, 1975

Lassner, Phyllis. "'Witness to Their Vanishing': Elaine Feinstein's Fictions of Jewish Continuity," in Abby H. P. Werlock, ed., *British Women Writing Fiction*, 113–14.

The Crystal Garden, 1974

Lassner, Phyllis. "'Witness to Their Vanishing': Elaine Feinstein's Fictions of Jewish Continuity," in Abby H. P. Werlock, ed., *British Women Writing Fiction*, 111–12.

The Ecstasy of Dr. Miriam Garner, 1976

Lassner, Phyllis. "'Witness to Their Vanishing': Elaine Feinstein's Fictions of Jewish Continuity," in Abby H. P. Werlock, ed., *British Women Writing Fiction*, 114–15.

Mother's Girl, 1988

Lassner, Phyllis. "'Witness to Their Vanishing': Elaine Feinstein's Fictions of Jewish Continuity," in Abby H. P. Werlock, ed., *British Women Writing Fiction*, 118–19.

The Shadow Master, 1978

Lassner, Phyllis. "'Witness to Their Vanishing': Elaine Feinstein's Fictions of Jewish Continuity," in Abby H. P. Werlock, ed., *British Women Writing Fiction*, 115–16.

The Survivors, 1982

Lassner, Phyllis. "'Witness to Their Vanishing': Elaine Feinstein's Fictions of Jewish Continuity," in Abby H. P. Werlock, ed., *British Women Writing Fiction*, 116–17.

GEOFFREY FENTON

Certain Tragicall Discourses of Bandello, 1567

Hadfield, Andrew. *Literature, Travel, and Colonial Writing*, 162–65.

ELIZA FENWICK

Secresy: or, The Ruin on the Rock, 1795

Bannet, Eve Tavor. *The Domestic Revolution*, 115–19.

Bunnell, Charlene E. "Breaking the Tie That Binds: Parents and Children in Romantic Fiction," in Andrea O'Reilly Herrera et al., eds., *Family Matters*, 34–41.

Emsley, Sarah. "Radical Marriage." *Eighteenth-Cent Fiction* 11 (1999), 477–98.

Watson, Nicola J. *Revolution and the Form of the British Novel*, 41–44.

KATHLEEN FERGUSON

The Maid's Tale, 1994

Smyth, Gerry. *The Novel and the Nation*, 88–91.

SUSAN FERRIER

Destiny, 1831

Price, Leah. "The Poetics of Pedantry from Thomas Bowdler to Susan Ferrier." *Women's Writing* 7 (2000), 77–85.

The Inheritance, 1824

Esterhammer, Angela. "Susan Ferrier's Allusions: Comedy, Morality, and the Presence of Milton," in Laura Dabundo, ed., *Jane Austen and Mary Shelley*, 66–71.

Price, Leah. "The Poetics of Pedantry from Thomas Bowdler to Susan Ferrier." *Women's Writing* 7 (2000), 76–85.

Marriage, 1818

Anderson, Carol, and Aileen M. Riddell. "The Other Great Unknowns: Women Fiction Writers of the Early Nineteenth Century," in Douglas Gifford and Dorothy McMillan, eds., *A History*, 189–92.

Price, Leah. "The Poetics of Pedantry from Thomas Bowdler to Susan Ferrier." *Women's Writing* 7 (2000), 75–85.

Walker, Marshall. *Scottish Literature since 1707*, 158–61.

HENRY FIELDING

Amelia, 1752

Battestin, Martin C. "Life-Writing without Letters: Fielding and the Problem of Evidence," in Warwick Gould and Thomas F. Staley, eds., *Writing the Lives of Writers*, 97–99.

Bender, John. "The Novel and the Rise of the Penitentiary: Narrative and Ideology in Defoe, Gay, Hogarth and Fielding," in Richard Kroll, ed., *The English Novel, Volume I*, 128–29.

Bertelsen, Lance. *Henry Fielding at Work*, 61–98.

Butler, Gerald J. "Making Fielding's Novels Speak for Law and Order," in David H. Richter, ed., *Ideology and Form*, 84–86.

Colburn, Glen. "'Struggling Manfully' through Henry Fielding's *Amelia*: Hysteria, Medicine, and the Novel in Eighteenth-Century England." *Stud in Eighteenth-Cent Culture* 26 (1998), 87–113.

Crump, Justine. "'*Il faut parier*': Pascal's Wager and Fielding's *Amelia*." *Mod Lang R* 95 (2000), 311–23.

Flynn, Carol Houlihan. "Closing Down the Theater, and Other Critical Abuses," in David H. Richter, ed., *Ideology and Form*, 94–102.

Gladfelder, Hal. "Criminal Trials and the Dilemmas of Narrative Realism, 1650–1750." *Prose Stud* 20:3 (1997), 38–42.

Gladfelder, Hal. *Criminality and Narrative*, 187–208.

Gores, Steven J. "The Miniature as Reduction and Talisman in Fielding's *Amelia*." *Stud in Engl Lit, 1500–1900* 37 (1997), 573–90.

Gores, Steven J. *Psychosocial Spaces*, 157–73.

Graeber, Wilhelm. *Der englische Roman in Frankreich*, 253–98.

Heinrich, Hans. *Zur Geschichte des 'Libertin,'* 141–46.

Ireland, Ken. *The Sequential Dynamics of Narrative*, 175–76.

Morse, David. *The Age of Virtue*, 142–44.

Pagliaro, Harold. *Henry Fielding*, 179–86.

Parker, Jo Alyson. *The Author's Inheritance*, 120–54.

Paulson, Ronald. *The Beautiful, Novel, and Strange*, 143–52.

Paulson, Ronald. *The Life of Henry Fielding*, 289–305.

Potter, Tiffany. *Honest Sins*, 145–68.

Rawson, Claude. "Henry Fielding," in John Richetti, ed., *The Cambridge Companion*, 125–27, 147–51.

Richetti, John. *The English Novel in History*, 150–59.

Rosengarten, Richard A. *Henry Fielding*, 91–115.

Skinner, Gillian. *Sensibility and Economics in the Novel*, 37–58.

Spacks, Patricia Meyer. "Ideology and Form: Novels at Work," in David H. Richter, ed., *Ideology and Form*, 17–29.

Swan, Beth. *Fictions of Law*, 128–30, 179–86.

Thompson, James. *Models of Value*, 143–45.

Thompson, Lynda M. *The 'Scandalous Memoirists,'* 55–57.

Wilputte, Earla A. "'Women Buried': Henry Fielding and Feminine Absence." *Mod Lang R* 95 (2000), 327–32.

Jonathan Wild, 1743

Bogel, Fredric V. *The Difference Satire Makes*, 150–88.

Cavaliero, Glen. *The Alchemy of Laughter*, 85–88.

Diyen, Hayat. "The Narrativity of Jonathan Wild in Defoe's *Account of Jonathan Wild* and Fielding's *The Life of Jonathan Wild the Great*." *Forum for Mod Lang Stud* 34 (1998), 16–27.

Graeber, Wilhelm. *Der englische Roman in Frankreich*, 299–307.

Jeffares, A. Norman. *Images of Invention*, 292–94.

McDowell, Paula. "Narrative Authority, Critical Complicity: The Case of *Jonathan Wild*." *Stud in the Novel* 30 (1998), 211–27.

Montandon, Alain. *Le roman au XVIIIe siècle*, 166–68.

Pagliaro, Harold. *Henry Fielding*, 155–63.

Paulson, Ronald. *The Life of Henry Fielding*, 124–33.

Potter, Tiffany. *Honest Sins*, 101–18.

Rawson, Claude. "Henry Fielding," in John Richetti, ed., *The Cambridge Companion*, 137–40.

Richter, David H. "Jonathan Wild and True Crime Fiction," in Richter, ed., *Ideology and Form*, 117–20.

Swan, Beth. *Fictions of Law*, 171–75.

Thompson, James. *Models of Value*, 140–42.

Joseph Andrews, 1742

Barney, Richard A. *Plots of Enlightenment*, 115–18.

Benton, Michael. *Studies in the Spectator Role*, 74–77.

Bony, Alain. "Affaires de famille: désaveu et reconnaissance dans *Joseph Andrews*." *Etudes Anglaises* 53 (2000), 29–35.

Campbell, Jill. "'The Exact Picture of His Mother': Recognizing Joseph Andrews," in Richard Kroll, ed., *The English Novel, Volume I*, 275–92.

Cavaliero, Glen. *The Alchemy of Laughter*, 174–79.

Cruise, James. *Governing Consumption*, 140–54.

Cruise, James. "Precept, Property, and 'Bourgeois' Practice in *Joseph Andrews*." *Stud in Engl Lit, 1500–1900* 37 (1997), 535–50.

DeRitter, Jones. "Blaming the Audience, Blaming the Gods: Unwitting Incest in Three Eighteenth-Century English Novels," in Thomas DiPiero and Pat Gill, eds., *Illicit Sex*, 221–38.

Derry, Stephen. "Mark Twain, Baker's *Chronicle*, and *Joseph Andrews*." *Notes and Queries* 44 (1997), 366–67.

Fisch, Harold. *New Stories for Old*, 41–57.

Frank, Judith. *Common Ground*, 31–46, 50–62.

Gautier, Gary. "Henry and Sarah Fielding on Romance and Sensibility." *Novel* 31 (1998), 198–204.

Graeber, Wilhelm. *Der englische Roman in Frankreich*, 71–110.

Keymer, Tom. "*Joseph Andrews*, Benjamin Martyn's *Timoleon*, and the Statue of Surprize." *Notes and Queries* 45 (1998), 460–61.

Montandon, Alain. *Le roman au XVIIIe siècle*, 168–72.

Morse, David. *The Age of Virtue*, 128–31.

Pagliaro, Harold. *Henry Fielding*, 136–51.

Parker, Jo Alyson. *The Author's Inheritance*, 23–38.

Parrinder, Patrick. "Highway Robbery and Property Circulation in Eighteenth-Century English Narratives." *Eighteenth-Cent Fiction* 13 (2001), 519–20.

Paulson, Ronald. *The Beautiful, Novel, and Strange*, 110–14.

Paulson, Ronald. *The Life of Henry Fielding*, 136–83.

Potter, Tiffany. *Honest Sins*, 83–100.

Rawson, Claude. "Henry Fielding," in John Richetti, ed., *The Cambridge Companion*, 130–37.

Richetti, John. *The English Novel in History*, 124–35.

Rivero, Albert J. "*Pamela/Shamela/Joseph Andrews*: Henry Fielding and the Duplicities of Representation," in Rivero, ed., *Augustan Subjects*, 216–22.

Rosengarten, Richard A. *Henry Fielding*, 51–89.

Rothman, Irving N. "Fielding's Comic Prose Epithalamium in *Joseph Andrews*: A Spenserian Imitation." *Mod Lang R* 93 (1998), 609–28.

Ruml, Treadwell, II. "Henry Fielding and Parson Adams: Whig Writer and Tory Priest." *JEGP* 97 (1998), 205–25.

Runge, Laura L. *Gender and Language*, 115–17.

Swan, Beth. *Fictions of Law*, 166–70.

Williams, Jeffrey. "The Narrative Circle: The Interpolated Tales in *Joseph Andrews*." *Stud in the Novel* 30 (1998), 473–88.

A Journey from this World to the Next, 1749

Baldwin, Barry. "A Latin Poem in Fielding." *Notes and Queries* 42:1 (1995), 63–66.

Pagliaro, Harold. *Henry Fielding*, 151–55.

Shamela, 1741

Frank, Judith. *Common Ground*, 46–57.

Mudge, Bradford K. *The Whore's Story*, 196–200.

Pagliaro, Harold. *Henry Fielding*, 128–35.

Paulson, Ronald. *The Life of Henry Fielding*, 140–44.

Potter, Tiffany. *Honest Sins*, 74–82.

Rawson, Claude. *Satire and Sentiment*, 279–81.

Rivero, Albert J. "*Pamela/Shamela/Joseph Andrews*: Henry Fielding and the Duplicities of Representation," in Rivero, ed., *Augustan Subjects*, 209–16.

Tom Jones, 1749

Alter, Robert. "Stendhal, Fielding, and the Fiction of Discrimination." *Providence* 3:1 (1995), 32–49.

Audigier, Jean-Pierre. "Le Roman de l'origine." *Corps Ecrit* 32 (1989), 125–33.

Barney, Richard A. *Plots of Enlightenment*, 115–18.

Battestin, Martin C. "*Tom Jones* on the Telly: Fielding, the BBC, and the Sister Arts." *Eighteenth-Cent Fiction* 10 (1998), 501–5.

Bellamy, Liz. *Commerce, Morality and the Eighteenth-Century Novel*, 82–98.

Bellman, Patrizia Nerozzi. "La conversazione nel romanzo inglese del Settecento." *Confronto Letterario* 12 (1995), 5–21.

Cavaliero, Glen. *The Alchemy of Laughter*, 104–10.

Cruise, James. *Governing Consumption*, 89–91.

Davis, Leith. *Acts of Union*, 56–63.

DeRitter, Jones. "Blaming the Audience, Blaming the Gods: Unwitting Incest in Three Eighteenth-Century English Novels," in Thomas DiPiero and Pat Gill, eds., *Illicit Sex*, 221–38.

Downie, J. A. *To Settle the Succession of the State*, 105–8, 152–55.

Drake, George. "*Tom Jones* and Alsatia." *Notes and Queries* 44 (1997), 200–201.

Drake, George A. "Historical Space in the 'History Of': Between Public and Private in *Tom Jones*." *ELH* 66 (1999), 707–32.

Gardiner, Ellen. *Regulating Readers*, 63–88.

Gladfelder, Hal. "Criminal Trials and the Dilemmas of Narrative Realism, 1650–1750." *Prose Stud* 20:3 (1997), 35–38.

Graeber, Wilhelm. *Der englische Roman in Frankreich*, 122–51.

Hundert, Edward. "Performing the Passions in Commercial Society: Bernard Mandeville and the Theatricality of Eighteenth-Century

Thought," in Kevin Sharpe and Steven N. Zwicker, eds., *Refiguring Revolutions*, 161–65.

Hutchings, W. B. "How pleasant to meet Mr. Fielding: The Narrator as Hero in *Tom Jones*," in Richard Gravil, ed., *Master Narratives*, 9–19.

Ireland, Ken. *The Sequential Dynamics of Narrative*, 174–75.

Loretelli, Rosamaria. "The Aesthetics of Empiricism and the Origin of the Novel." *Eighteenth Cent* 41 (2000), 98–102.

Lynch, Deidre Shauna. *The Economy of Character*, 96–101.

Michie, Allen. *Richardson and Fielding*, 76–81, 133–39.

Montandon, Alain. *Le roman au XVIIIe siècle*, 172–78.

Morse, David. *The Age of Virtue*, 135–43.

Pagliaro, Harold. *Henry Fielding*, 163–79.

Parker, Jo Alyson. *The Author's Inheritance*, 63–92.

Parrinder, Patrick. "Highway Robbery and Property Circulation in Eighteenth-Century English Narratives." *Eighteenth-Cent Fiction* 13 (2001), 520–23.

Paulson, Ronald. *The Beautiful, Novel, and Strange*, 116–26.

Paulson, Ronald. *The Life of Henry Fielding*, 184–260.

Potter, Tiffany. *Honest Sins*, 119–44.

Rader, Ralph. "*Tom Jones*: The Form in History," in David H. Richter, ed., *Ideology and Form*, 47–72.

Rawson, Claude. "Henry Fielding," in John Richetti, ed., *The Cambridge Companion*, 140–45.

Richetti, John. *The English Novel in History*, 135–50.

Richetti, John. "Ideology and Literary Form in Fielding's *Tom Jones*," in David H. Richter, ed., *Ideology and Form*, 31–43.

Rosengarten, Richard A. *Henry Fielding*, 51–89.

Schnackertz, Hermann Josef. "Hogarth und Fielding: Der Innovationsanspruch von Bilderzählung und Roman im 18. Jahrhundert." *Arbeiten aus Anglistik und Amerikanistik* 21:1 (1996), 68–83.

Schramm, Jan-Melissa. *Testimony and Advocacy*, 76–80.

Sherman, Sandra. "Reading at Arm's Length: Fielding's Contract with the Reader in *Tom Jones*." *Stud in the Novel* 30 (1998), 232–42.

Skinner, Gillian. *Sensibility and Economics in the Novel*, 15–31.

Stern, Simon. "*Tom Jones* and the Economies of Copyright." *Eighteenth-Cent Fiction* 9 (1997), 429–44.

Stevenson, John Allen. "Fielding's Mousetrap: Hamlet, Partridge, and the '45." *Stud in Engl Lit, 1500–1900* 37 (1997), 553–68.

Sutherland, John. *Who Betrays Elizabeth Bennet?*, 9–16.

Swan, Beth. *Fictions of Law*, 126–28, 175–79.

Thompson, James. *Models of Value*, 132–34, 136–40.

Toker, Leona. "The History of Jenny Jones: Fielding's 'Fine Old Moralism' Reconsidered," in Shlomith Rimmon-Kenan et al., eds., *Rereading Texts*, 149–59.

Varney, Andrew. *Eighteenth-Century Writers in their World*, 112–16.

Wilputte, Earla A. "'Women Buried': Henry Fielding and Feminine Absence." *Mod Lang R* 95 (2000), 327–32.

Zimmerman, Everett. *The Boundaries of Fiction*, 78–80, 137–62.

SARAH FIELDING

The Countess of Dellwyn, 1759

Child, Elizabeth. "'To Sing the Town': Women, Place, and Print Culture in Eighteenth-Century Bath." *Stud in Eighteenth-Cent Culture* 28 (1999), 163–67.

Skinner, Gillian. *Sensibility and Economics in the Novel*, 31–36.

David Simple, 1744–1753

Bellamy, Liz. *Commerce, Morality and the Eighteenth-Century Novel*, 131–38.

Gautier, Gary. "Henry and Sarah Fielding on Romance and Sensibility." *Novel* 31 (1998), 204–10.

Graeber, Wilhelm. *Der englische Roman in Frankreich*, 111–21.

Guest, Harriet. *Small Change*, 30–37.

Guest, Harriet. "'These Neuter Somethings': Gender Difference and Commercial Culture in Mid-Eighteenth-Century England," in Kevin Sharpe and Steven N. Zwicker, eds., *Refiguring Revolutions*, 180–85.

Haggerty, George E. *Unnatural Affections*, 23–36.

Nussbaum, Felicity. "Effeminacy and Femininity: Domestic Prose Satire and *David Simple.*" *Eighteenth-Cent Fiction* 11 (1999), 421–44.

Paulson, Ronald. *The Life of Henry Fielding*, 198–201.

Pettit, Alexander. "*David Simple* and the Attenuation of 'Phallic Power.'" *Eighteenth-Cent Fiction* 11 (1999), 169–84.

Richetti, John. *The English Novel in History*, 248–51.

Simms, Norman. "The Psychological Adventures of Sarah Fielding's *David Simple.*" *Etudes Anglaises* 49 (1996), 158–67.

Skinner, Gillian. *Sensibility and Economics in the Novel*, 15–31.

Stockstill, Ashley. "Better Homes and Gardens: The Fairy World(s) of Sarah Fielding and Sarah Scott." *Feminist Stud in Engl Lit* 6 (1998), 137–58.

Swan, Beth. *Fictions of Law*, 86–88.

The Governess; or, Little Female Academy, 1749

Suzuki, Mika. "*The Little Female Academy* and *The Governess.*" *Women's Writing* 1 (1994), 325–35.

The History of Ophelia, 1760

Skinner, Gillian. *Sensibility and Economics in the Novel*, 37–58.

SARAH FIELDING AND JANE COLLIER

The Cry: A New Dramatic Fable, 1754

Gardiner, Ellen. *Regulating Readers*, 110–33.

Lawlor, Clark. "The Grotesque, Reform and Sensibility in Dryden, Sarah Fielding and Jane Collier." *Brit J for Eighteenth-Cent Stud* 22 (1999), 196–204.

EVA FIGES

The Tree of Knowledge, 1990

> Stuby, Anna Maria. "'A Piece of Shrapnel Lodges in My Flesh, and When It Moves, I Write': The Fiction of Eva Figes." Anglistik und Englischunterricht 60 (1997), 113–27.

DARRELL FIGGIS

The Return of the Hero, 1923

> Quintelli-Neary, Marguerite. *Folklore and the Fantastic,* 108–13.

RONALD FIRBANK

The Artificial Princess, 1934

> Bristow, Joseph. *Effeminate England,* 108–13.

Concerning the Eccentricities of Cardinal Pirelli, 1926

> Hollinghurst, Alan. "'I Often Laugh When I'm Alone': The Novels of Ronald Firbank." *Yale R* 89:2 (2001), 14–18.

The Flower Beneath the Foot, 1923

> Hollinghurst, Alan. "'I Often Laugh When I'm Alone': The Novels of Ronald Firbank." *Yale R* 89:2 (2001), 8–11.

Sorrow in Sunlight, 1925

> Bristow, Joseph. *Effeminate England,* 121–23.
> Hollinghurst, Alan. "'I Often Laugh When I'm Alone': The Novels of Ronald Firbank." *Yale R* 89:2 (2001), 11–14.

Vainglory, 1915

> Hollinghurst, Alan. "'I Often Laugh When I'm Alone': The Novels of Ronald Firbank." *Yale R* 89:2 (2001), 2–8.

Valmouth, 1919

> Bristow, Joseph. *Effeminate England,* 119–21.
> Cavaliero, Glen. *The Alchemy of Laughter,* 73–75.
> Goldman, Jonathan. "The Parrotic Voice of the Frivolous: Fiction by Ronald Firbank, I. Compton-Burnett, and Max Beerbohm." *Narrative* 7 (1999), 289–96.
> Tuite, Clara. "Decadent Austen Entails: Forster, James, Firbank, and the 'Queer Taste' of *Sanditon* (comp. 1817, publ. 1925)," in Deidre Lynch, ed., *Janeites,* 130–35.

BARBARA FITZGERALD

Footprint upon Water, 1983

> Frehner, Ruth. *The Colonizers' Daughters,* 82–101.

PENELOPE FITZGERALD

At Freddie's, 1989

Gitzen, Julian. "Elements of Compression in the Novels of Penelope Fitzgerald." *Essays in Arts and Sciences* 26 (1997), 5–13.

The Beginning of Spring, 1988

Gitzen, Julian. "Elements of Compression in the Novels of Penelope Fitzgerald." *Essays in Arts and Sciences* 26 (1997), 1–13.

The Blue Flower, 1995

Byatt, A. S. *On Histories and Stories*, 59–63.

The Gate of Angels, 1990

Byatt, A. S. *On Histories and Stories*, 86–90.
Gitzen, Julian. "Elements of Compression in the Novels of Penelope Fitzgerald." *Essays in Arts and Sciences* 26 (1997), 3–13.

Innocence, 1987

Gitzen, Julian. "Elements of Compression in the Novels of Penelope Fitzgerald." *Essays in Arts and Sciences* 26 (1997), 1–13.

Offshore, 1979

Gitzen, Julian. "Elements of Compression in the Novels of Penelope Fitzgerald." *Essays in Arts and Sciences* 26 (1997), 1–13.

CAROLINE FORBES

The Needle on Full, 1985

Miller, Elaine. "Zero Tolerance in Wonderland: Some Political Uses of Imagination," in Elaine Hutton, ed., *Beyond Sex and Romance?*, 166–69.

FORD MADOX FORD

A Call, 1910

Leckie, Barbara. *Culture and Adultery*, 205–10.

The Good Soldier, 1915

Bender, Todd K. *Literary Impressionism*, 22–36, 147–50.
Bergonzi, Bernard. *War Poets*, 72–78.
Brooks, Neil. "Interred Textuality: *The Good Soldier* and *Flaubert's Parrot*." *Critique* (Washington, DC) 41 (1999), 45–51.
Foss, Chris. "Abjection and Appropriation: Male Subjectivity in *The Good Soldier*." *LIT* 9 (1998), 225–44.
Gasiorek, Andrzej. "Ford Madox Ford's Modernism and the Question of Tradition." *Engl Lit in Transition* 44 (2001), 14–20.
Katz, Tamar. *Impressionist Subjects*, 109–37.
Leckie, Barbara. *Culture and Adultery*, 210–43.
McCarthy, Jeffrey Mathes. "*The Good Soldier* and the War for British Modernism." *Mod Fiction Stud* 45 (1999), 303–39.
McCarthy, Patrick A. "In Search of Lost Time: Chronology and

Narration in *The Good Soldier.*" *Engl Lit in Transition* 40 (1997), 133–47.

Miller, R. H. "Graham Greene's 'Saddest Story.'" *Renascence* 51 (1999), 133–42.

Palmer, Marguerite. "Ford's *The Good Soldier.*" *Explicator* 56:2 (1998), 84–85.

Saunders, Max. "Ford, Eliot, Joyce, and the Problems of Literary Biography," in Warwick Gould and Thomas F. Staley, eds., *Writing the Lives of Writers*, 154–55.

Trotter, David. "The Modernist Novel," in Michael Levenson, ed., *The Cambridge Companion to Modernism*, 70–72.

Witkowsky, Peter. "Cranford Revisited: Ford's Debt to Mrs. Gaskell in *The Good Soldier.*" *Twentieth Cent Lit* 44 (1998), 291–303.

The Last Post, 1928

Trotter, David. "The Modernist Novel," in Michael Levenson, ed., *The Cambridge Companion to Modernism*, 95–98.

Parade's End, 1950

Ayers, David. *English Literature of the 1920s*, 10–19.

Bacigalupo, Massimo. "*Fine della parata*: La tetralogia bellica di Ford Madox Ford" *Quaderni del Dipartimento di Lingue e Letterature Straniere Moderne* (Genova) 9 (1997), 417–26.

Tate, Trudi. *Modernism, History and the First World War*, 50–62.

Tate, Trudi. "Rumour, Propaganda, and *Parade's End.*" *Essays in Criticism* 47 (1997), 332–50.

The Simple Life Limited, 1911

Schäffner, Raimund. *Anarchismus und Literatur in England*, 509–14.

When the Wicked Man, 1931

Lykiard, Alexis. *Jean Rhys Revisited*, 129–38.

ISABELLA FORD

On the Threshold, 1895

Heilmann, Ann. "Feminist Resitance, the Artist and 'A Room of One's Own' in New Woman Fiction." *Women's Writing* 2 (1995), 294–95.

Heilmann, Ann. *New Woman Fiction*, 60–64, 179–80.

Ledger, Sally. *The New Woman*, 53–56.

CECIL SCOTT FORESTER

The African Queen, 1935

Sternlicht, Sanford. *C. S. Forester and the Hornblower Saga*, 79–84.

Brown on Resolution, 1929

Sternlicht, Sanford. *C. S. Forester and the Hornblower Saga*, 56–59.

The Captain from Connecticut, 1941

Sternlicht, Sanford. *C. S. Forester and the Hornblower Saga*, 119–23.

Death to the French, 1932
> Sternlicht, Sanford. *C. S. Forester and the Hornblower Saga*, 74–76.

The Earthly Paradise, 1940
> Sternlicht, Sanford. *C. S. Forester and the Hornblower Saga*, 116–19.

The General, 1936
> Sternlicht, Sanford. *C. S. Forester and the Hornblower Saga*, 84–88.

The Good Shepherd, 1955
> Sternlicht, Sanford. *C. S. Forester and the Hornblower Saga*, 142–48.

Lord Hornblower, 1946
> Sternlicht, Sanford. *C. S. Forester and the Hornblower Saga*, 99–101.

The Paid Piper, 1924
> Sternlicht, Sanford. *C. S. Forester and the Hornblower Saga*, 41–44.

Payment Deferred, 1926
> Sternlicht, Sanford. *C. S. Forester and the Hornblower Saga*, 46–49.

Randall and the River of Time, 1950
> Sternlicht, Sanford. *C. S. Forester and the Hornblower Saga*, 133–41.

The Ship, 1943
> Sternlicht, Sanford. *C. S. Forester and the Hornblower Saga*, 123–26.

The Sky and the Forest, 1948
> Sternlicht, Sanford. *C. S. Forester and the Hornblower Saga*, 128–33.

Two and Twenty, 1931
> Sternlicht, Sanford. *C. S. Forester and the Hornblower Saga*, 59–61.

The Wonderful Week, 1927
> Sternlicht, Sanford. *C. S. Forester and the Hornblower Saga*, 49–51.

E. M. FORSTER

Howards End, 1910
> Armstrong, Paul B. "The Narrator in the Closet: The Ambiguous Narrative Voice in *Howards End*." *Mod Fiction Stud* 47 (2001), 306–28.
> Berg, James J. "The Industrialist and the Clerk in Merchant Ivory's *Howards End*." *West Virginia Univ Philol Papers* 44 (1998–1999), 131–37.
> Bristow, Joseph. *Effeminate England*, 74–80.
> Hill, Marylu. *Mothering Modernity*, 27–55.
> Hirai, Masako. *Sisters in Literature*, 77–120.
> Hoffman, Michael J., and Ann ter Haar. "'Whose Books Once Influenced Mine': The Relationship between E. M. Forster's *Howards End* and Virginia Woolf's *The Waves*." *Twentieth Cent Lit* 45 (1999), 46–60.
> Ito, Masanori. "Imperialism and the Restoration of Landownership in *Howards End*." *Shiron* 36 (1997), 49–65.
> Lloyd, Tom. *Crises of Realism*, 198–203.
> Martin, Robert K. "'It Must Have Been the Umbrella': Forster's

Queer Begetting," in Robert K. Martin and George Piggford, eds., *Queer Forster*, 266–73.

Mejia, Cristina. "Moral Capacities and Other Constraints," in Andrew Hadfield et al., eds., *The Ethics in Literature*, 218–28.

Murfin, Ross C. "Cultural Criticism and *Howards End*," in Alistair M. Duckworth, ed., *"Howards End,"* 345–63.

Murfin, Ross C. "Deconstruction and *Howards End*," in Alistair M. Duckworth, ed., *"Howards End,"* 447–67.

Murfin, Ross C. "Feminist and Gender Criticism and *Howards End*," in Alistair M. Duckworth, ed., *"Howards End,"* 379–400.

Murfin, Ross C. "Marxist Criticism and *Howards End*," in Alistair M. Duckworth, ed., *"Howards End,"* 416–31.

Murfin, Ross C. "Psychoanalytic Criticism and *Howards End*," in Alistair M. Duckworth, ed., *"Howards End,"* 313–29.

O'Dair, Sharon. "Beyond Necessity: The Consumption of Class, the Production of Status, and the Persistence of Inequality." *New Liter Hist* 31 (2000), 337–54.

Posner, Richard A. *Law and Literature*, 1–3.

Pykett, Lyn. *Engendering Fictions*, 117–23.

Quabeck, Katharina. "'Don't drag in the personal when it will not come': *Howards End* and Emotional Excess." *REAL: Yrbk of Res in Engl and Am Lit* 16 (2000), 199–210.

Sillars, Stuart. *Structure and Dissolution*, 31–61.

Stoddart, Scott F. "The 'Muddle' of Step-Parenting: Reconstructing Domestic Harmony in James and Forster," in Andrea O'Reilly Herrera et al., eds., *Family Matters*, 115–34, 139–44.

Thacker, Andrew. "E. M. Forster and the Motor Car." *Lit and Hist* 9:2 (2000), 37–50.

Turner, Henry S. "Empires of Objects: Accumulation and Entropy in E. M. Forster's *Howards End*." *Twentieth Cent Lit* 46 (2000), 328–41.

Womack, Kenneth. "'Only Connecting' with the Family: Class, Culture, and Narrative Therapy in E. M. Forster's *Howards End*." *Style* 31 (1997), 255–66.

The Longest Journey, 1907

Bristow, Joseph. *Effeminate England*, 61–63, 68–71.

Bristow, Joseph. "*Fratrum Societati*: Forster's Apostolic Dedications," in Robert K. Martin and George Piggford, eds., *Queer Forster*, 121–25.

Cucullu, Lois. "Shepherds in the Parlor: Forster's Apostles, Pagans, and Native Sons." *Novel* 32 (1998), 32–47.

Greenslade, William. "'Pan" and the Open Road: Critical Paganism in R. L. Stevenson, K. Grahame, E. Thomas and E. M. Forster," in Lynne Hapgood and Nancy L. Paxton, eds., *Outside Modernism*, 157–59.

Herz, Judith Scherer. "'This is the End of Parsival': The Orphic and the Operatic in *The Longest Journey*," in Robert K. Martin and George Piggford, eds., *Queer Forster*, 139–49.

Maurice, 1971

Bredbeck, Gregory W. "Missionary Positions: Reading the Bible in

Forster's 'The Life to Come,'" in Raymond-Jean Frontain, ed., *Reclaiming the Sacred*, 139–61.

Bredbeck, Gregory W. "'Queer Superstitions': Forster, Carpenter, and the Illusion of (Sexual) Identity," in Robert K. Martin and George Piggford, eds., *Queer Forster*, 32–34, 52–56.

Bristow, Joseph. *Effeminate England*, 80–82.

Bristow, Joseph. "*Fratrum Societati*: Forster's Apostolic Dedications," in Robert K. Martin and George Piggford, eds., *Queer Forster*, 126–28.

Buck, R. A. "Reading Forster's Style: Face Actions and Social Scripts in *Maurice*." *Style* 30 (1996), 69–91.

Curr, Matthew. "Recuperating E. M. Forster's *Maurice*." *Mod Lang Q* 62 (2001), 53–69.

Gilabert i Barberà, Pau. "Grècia i amor platònic en el *Maurice* d'E. M. Forster, o la grandesa i els límits de l'antinguitat com a inspiració." *BELLS: Barcelona Engl Lang and Lit Stud* 5 (1994), 39–56; 6 (1995), 71–88.

Labadie-Schwab, Elisabeth. "Onomastique et symbolique: *Maurice*, de E. M. Forster." *Etudes Anglaises* 53 (2000), 144–54.

Lane, Christopher. "Betrayal and Its Consolations in *Maurice*, 'Arthur Snatchfold,' and 'What Does It Matter? A Morality,'" in Robert K. Martin and George Piggford, eds., *Queer Forster*, 167–91.

Lane, Christopher. *The Burdens of Intimacy*, 197–99, 204–6, 208–11, 214–17.

Levine, June Perry. "The Functions of the Narrator's Voice in Literature and Film: Forster and Ivory's *Maurice*." *Lit/Film Q* 24 (1996), 309–21.

Martin, Robert K. "'It Must Have Been the Umbrella': Forster's Queer Begetting," in Robert K. Martin and George Piggford, eds., *Queer Forster*, 261–66.

Matz, Jesse. "*Maurice* in Time." *Style* 34 (2000), 188–207.

Pease, Allison. *Modernism, Mass Culture, and the Aesthetics of Obscenity*, 149–51.

Raschke, Debrah. "Breaking the Engagement with Philosophy: Re-envisioning Hetero/Homo Relations in *Maurice*," in Robert K. Martin and George Piggford, eds., *Queer Forster*, 151–63.

da Silva, Stephen. "Transvaluing Immaturity: Reverse Discourses of Male Homosexuality in E. M. Forster's Posthumously Published Fiction." *Criticism* 40 (1998), 245–66.

Valdeón García, Roberta A. "El tratamiento de la temática homosexual en cuatro novelistas ingleses: Lawrence, Forster, Waugh y Storey." *Cuadernos de Investigación Filológica* 23–24 (1997–1998), 139–62.

A Passage to India, 1924

Amirthanayagam, Guy. *The Marriage of Continents*, 30–31, 103–16.

Ayers, David. *English Literature of the 1920s*, 210–23.

Baucom, Ian. *Out of Place*, 101–3, 121–35.

Begum, Khani. "E. M. Forster's and David Lean's (Re)Presentations and (Re)Productions of Empire." *West Virginia Univ Philol Papers* 40 (1994–1995), 20–29.

Bivona, Daniel. *British Imperial Literature*, 159–65.

Blodgett, Harriet. "From *Jacob's Room* to *A Passage to India*: A Note." *ANQ* 12:4 (1999), 23.

Bredbeck, Gregory W. "Missionary Positions: Reading the Bible in Forster's 'The Life to Come,'" in Raymond-Jean Frontain, ed., *Reclaiming the Sacred*, 139–61.

Bristow, Joseph. *Effeminate England*, 83–91.

Coetzee, Jacques. "Beyond the Abyss: The Uses of Introspection in Three Modernist Texts." *Inter-Action* 4 (1996), 116–20.

Davidis, Maria M. "Forster's Imperial Romance: Chivalry, Motherhood, and Questing in *A Passage to India*." *J of Mod Lit* 23 (1999/2000), 259–76.

Delmas, Catherine. "La Métamorphose et le voyage en orient ou les avatars de la lecture: Conrad, Kipling, Forster." *Imaginaires* 4 (1999), 117–31.

Dolin, Kieran. *Fiction and the Law*, 177–92.

Doody, Terrence. *Among Other Things*, 247–49.

Franken, Lynn. "Poor Terrestrial Justice: Bakhtin and the Criminal Trial in the Novel." *Compar Lit* 49 (1997), 117–19.

Frenk, Joachim, and Christian Krug. "*A Passage to India*: The Deceptively Simple Present." *Zeitschrift für Anglistik und Amerikanistik* 46 (1998), 38–51.

Galin, Müge. *Between East and West*, 168–72.

Giffin, Michael. "Some Fusions and Diffusions of Horizon in a Gadamerian Reading of *A Passage to India*." *Lit and Theology* 12 (1998), 170–86.

Gordimer, Nadine. "Across Time and Two Hemispheres." *World Lit Today* 70:1 (1996), 111–14.

Gymnich, Marion. "Von *Greater Britain* zu *Little England*: Konstruktion und Dekonstruktion imperialistischer Denkweisen in Rudyard Kiplings *Kim*, E. M. Forsters *A Passage to India* und Joseph Conrads *Heart of Darkness*." *Anglistik und Englischunterricht* 58 (1996), 149–66.

Kischuck, John. "Forster's *A Passage to India*." *Explicator* 56:3 (1998), 142–44.

Lin, Lidan. "The Irony of Colonial Humanism: *A Passage to India* and the Politics of Posthumanism." *Ariel* 28:4 (1997), 133–50.

Lin, Wen-chi. "Law and (Anti-)Colonialism in *A Passage to India*." *Tamkang R* 25 (1995), 361–75.

Malik, Charu. "To Express the Subject of Friendship: Masculine Desire and Colonialism in *A Passage to India*," in Robert K. Martin and George Piggford, eds., *Queer Forster*, 221–34.

Marx, John. "Modernism and the Female Imperial Gaze." *Novel* 32:1 (1998), 51–75.

Messenger, Nigel. "Imperial Journeys, Bodily Landscapes and Sexual Anxiety: Adela's Visit to the Marabar in *A Passage to India*." *J of Commonwealth Lit* 33:1 (1998), 99–108.

Parry, Benita. "Materiality and Mystification in *A Passage to India*." *Novel* 31 (1998), 174–91.

Paxton, Nancy L. "Reconsidering Colonial Romance: Maud Diver and the 'Ethnographic Real,'" in Lynne Hapgood and Nancy L. Paxton, eds., *Outside Modernism*, 181–85.

Rajan, Balachandra. *Under Western Eyes*, 97–99.

Raschke, Debrah. "Forster's *A Passage to India*: Re-Envisioning Plato's Cave." *Comparatist* 21 (1997), 10–24.

Touval, Yonatan. "Colonial Queer Something," in Robert K. Martin and George Piggford, eds., *Queer Forster*, 237–52.

Walls, Elizabeth MacLeod. "An Aristotelian Reading of the Feminine Voice-as-Revolution in E. M. Forster's *A Passage to India*." *Papers on Lang and Lit* 35 (1999), 56–73.

Whitehead, John. *Eight Modern Masterpieces*, 19–37.

York, R. A. *The Rules of Time*, 67–81.

A Room with a View, 1908

Bristow, Joseph. *Effeminate England*, 72–74.

Cavaliero, Glen. *The Alchemy of Laughter*, 119–23.

Haralson, Eric. "'Thinking about Homosex' in Forster and James," in Robert K. Martin and George Piggford, eds., *Queer Forster*, 66–72.

Kullmann, Thomas. "Klassische Kunstwerke als Katalysatoren der emotionalen Emanzipation: Thomas Hardy, E. M. Forster," in Volker Kapp et al., eds., *Bilderwelten*, 47–74.

Lanone, Catherine. "'Moments of Being': la poétique du corps chez E. M. Forster." *Cahiers Victoriens et Edouardiens* 47 (1998), 93–100.

Lloyd, Tom. *Crises of Realism*, 188–98.

Rahaman, Tariq. "The Double-Plot in E. M. Forster's *A Room with a View*." *Liter Half-Yearly* 36:1 (1995), 94–116.

Where Angels Fear to Tread, 1905

Bristow, Joseph. *Effeminate England*, 65–68.

Martin, Robert K. "'It Must Have Been the Umbrella': Forster's Queer Begetting," in Robert K. Martin and George Piggford, eds., *Queer Forster*, 256–58.

Womack, Kenneth. "A Passage to Italy: Narrating the Family in Crisis in E. M. Forster's *Where Angels Fear to Tread*." *Mosaic* 33:3 (2000), 129–43.

AISLING FOSTER

Safe in the Kitchen, 1993

St. Peter, Christine. *Changing Ireland*, 80–82.

JOHN FOWLES

The Collector, 1963

Butler, Lance St. John. *Registering the Difference*, 103–7.

Caporaletti, Silvana. "Reading the End in the Beginning of John Fowles's *The Collector*." *Strumenti Critici* 15 (2000), 277–95.

Lanoix, Ann Caterine. "L'Enfermement dans *The Collector* de John Fowles." *La Licorne* 28 (1994), 93–100.

Daniel Martin, 1977

Barnum, Carol M. "The Nature of John Fowles," in James R. Aubrey, ed., *John Fowles and Nature*, 92–93.

Colletta, Lisa. "The Geography of Ruins: John Fowles's *Daniel Martin* and the Travel Narratives of D. H. Lawrence," in James R. Aubrey, ed., *John Fowles and Nature*, 212–27.

Olshen, Barry N. "The Archetype of the Green Man in the Writings of John Fowles," in James R. Aubrey, ed., *John Fowles and Nature*, 108–11.

Salami, Mahmoud. "The Archaeological Representation of the Orient in John Fowles's *Daniel Martin*." *Ariel* 29:3 (1998), 143–67.

Warburton, Eileen. "The Corpse in the Combe: The Vision of the Dead Woman in the Landscape of John Fowles," in James R. Aubrey, ed., *John Fowles and Nature*, 124–32.

The French Lieutenant's Woman, 1969

Bawden, Liz-Anne, Kevin Padian, and Hugh S. Torrens. "The Undercliff of John Fowles's *The French Lieutenant's Woman*: A Note on Geology and Geography," in James R. Aubrey, ed., *John Fowles and Nature*, 137–52.

Beatty, Patricia V. "The Undercliff as Inverted Pastoral: The Fowlesian *Felix Culpa* in *The French Lieutenant's Woman*," in James R. Aubrey, ed., *John Fowles and Nature*, 169–80.

Bényei, Tamás. *Acts of Attention*, 65–91.

Bényei, Tamás. "Seduction and the Politics of Reading in *The French Lieutenant's Woman*." *Hungarian J of Engl and Am Stud* 1:2 (1995), 121–39.

Butler, Lance St. John. *Registering the Difference*, 101–3.

Byatt, A. S. *On Histories and Stories*, 75–78.

Dodson, Mary Lynn. "*The French Lieutenant's Woman*: Pinter and Reisz's Adaptation of John Fowles's Adaptation." *Lit/Film Q* 26 (1998), 296–302.

Fawkner, H. W. "Landscape This Side of Landscape: Transcendence and Immanence in the Fiction of John Fowles," in James R. Aubrey, ed., *John Fowles and Nature*, 195–206.

Gilmour, Robin. "Using the Victorians: The Victorian Age in Contemporary Fiction," in Alice Jenkins and Juliet John, eds., *Rereading Victorian Fiction*, 191–93.

Girard, Gaïd. "Filmer la fascination: A propos d'une séquence de *The French Lieutenant's Woman*." *La Licorne* 37 (1996), 129–35.

Gutleben, Christian. "'Un mensonge qui dit toujours la vérité': le discours de la victime dans *The French Lieutenant's Woman* de John Fowles." *Recherches Anglaises et Nord-Américaines* 33 (2000), 45–53.

Gutleben, Christian. "La tradition victorienne à l'heure du postmodernisme: John Fowles, David Lodge, A. S. Byatt." *Etudes Anglaises* 51 (1998), 168–79.

Halliday, Iain. "Base and Basic Instincts: Italians in English Letters," in C. C. Barfoot, ed., *Beyond Pug's Tour*, 351–52, 361–62.

Horlacher, Stefan. "Zur Konzeption von Weiblichkeit: Das Bild der

Hexe in John Fowles' Roman *The French Lieutenant's Woman*," in Stefan Horlacher and Marion Islinger, eds., *Expedition nach der Wahrheit*, 585–616.

Jackson, Tony E. "Charles and the Hopeful Monster: Postmodern Evolutionary Theory in *The French Lieutenant's Woman.*" *Twentieth Cent Lit* 43 (1997), 221–41.

Jukic, Tatjana. "From Worlds to Worlds and the Other Way Around: The Victorian Inheritance in the Postmodern British Novel," in Richard Todd and Luisa Flora, eds., *Theme Parks*, 77–80.

Kadish, Doris Y. "Rewriting Women's Stories: *Ourika* and *The French Lieutenant's Woman.*" *South Atlantic R* 62:2 (1997), 74–86.

Landrum, David W. "Sarah and Sappho: Lesbian Reference in *The French Lieutenant's Woman.*" *Mosaic* 33:1 (2000), 59–75.

Lin, Rebecca. "Medusa, Siren or Sphinx: Retrieving the Female Gaze and Voice in *The French Lieutenant's Woman.*" *Stud in Lang and Lit* (Taipei) 8 (1998), 199–211.

Olson, Barbara K. *Authorial Divinity*, 31–33.

Padian, Kevin. "'Water out of a Woodland Spring': Sarah Woodruff and Nature in *The French Lieutenant's Woman*," in James R. Aubrey, ed., *John Fowles and Nature*, 181–92.

Punday, Daniel. "Meaning in Postmodern Worlds: The Case of *The French Lieutenant's Woman.*" *Semiotica* 115:3–4 (1997), 313–43.

Ross Suzanne. "Deep Time, Evolutionary Legacy, and the Darwinian Landscape in John Fowles's *The French Lieutenant's Woman*," in James R. Aubrey, ed., *John Fowles and Nature*, 154–67.

Shiller, Dana. "The Redemptive Past in the Neo-Victorian Novel." *Stud in the Novel* 29 (1997), 545–46.

Simonetti, Marie-Claire. "The Blurring of Time in *The French Lieutenant's Woman*: The Novel and the Film." *Lit/Film Q* 24 (1996), 301–8.

Smith, C. Jason. "Schrodinger's Cat and Sarah's Child: John Fowles's 'Quantum Narrative.'" *Mosaic* 32:2 (1999), 91–104.

Tucker, Stephanie. "Despair Not, Neither to Presume—*The French Lieutenant's Woman: A Screenplay.*" *Lit/Film Q* 24 (1996), 63–68.

Warburton, Eileen. "The Corpse in the Combe: The Vision of the Dead Woman in the Landscape of John Fowles," in James R. Aubrey, ed., *John Fowles and Nature*, 114–18.

Zare, Bonnie. "Reclaiming Masculinist Texts for Feminist Readers: Sarah Woodruff's *The French Lieutenant's Woman.*" *Mod Lang Stud* 27:3–4 (1997), 175–92.

A Maggot, 1985

Chivete de León, María José. "El desafío a la epistemología racionalista: *A Maggot* como novela detectivesca." *Cuadernos de Literatura Inglesa y Norteamericana* 2:2 (1997), 29–42.

Roessner, Jeffrey. "Unsolved Mysteries: Agents of Historical Change in John Fowles's *A Maggot.*" *Papers on Lang and Lit* 36 (2000), 302–22.

Thwaites, Tony. "The Abduction from the Imbroglio: Fowles's *A Maggot* and Some Aspects of the Story-Discourse Distinction." *LiNQ* 23:2 (1996), 57–67.

The Magus, 1966

>Auría, Carmen Pérez-Llantada. "From Metaphysics to Technique: The Blurring of Boundaries in John Fowles's *The Magus." Revista Canaria de Estudios Ingleses* 24 (1992), 119–29.

>Barnum, Carol M. "The Nature of John Fowles," in James R. Aubrey, ed., *John Fowles and Nature,* 89–93.

>Cichon, Anna, and Ewa Keblowska-Lawniczak. "Textualizing Subjectivity: The Use of Fictions and Theatricalities in *The Magus." Anglica Wratislaviensia* 31 (1996), 43–54.

>Fawkner, H. W. "Landscape This Side of Landscape: Transcendence and Immanence in the Fiction of John Fowles," in James R. Aubrey, ed., *John Fowles and Nature,* 207–11.

>Kefalea, Kirke. "Greek Myths and Greek Landscapes in John Fowles's *The Magus,"* in James R. Aubrey, ed., *John Fowles and Nature,* 230–37.

>Kuester, Martin. "Godgames in Paradise: Educational Strategies in Milton and Fowles." *Anglia* 115 (1997), 29–43.

>Robison, Jane E. "Echoes of the Masque in *The Magus." Publs of the Missouri Philol Assoc* 21 (1996), 77–82.

>Rommerskirchen, Barbara. *Constructing Reality: Constructivism and Narration in John Fowles's "The Magus."*

>Warburton, Eileen. "The Corpse in the Combe: The Vision of the Dead Woman in the Landscape of John Fowles," in James R. Aubrey, ed., *John Fowles and Nature,* 118–22.

M. E. FRANCIS

Miss Erin, 1898

>Murphy, James H. "'Things Which Seem to You Unfeminine': Gender and Nationalism in the Fiction of Some Upper Middle Class Catholic Women Novelists, 1880–1910," in Kathryn Kirkpatrick, ed., *Border Crossings,* 72–73.

R. AUSTIN FREEMAN

The D'Arblay Mystery, 1926

>Glover, David. "The Writers Who Knew Too Much: Populism and Paradox in Detective Fiction's Golden Age," in Warren Chernaik et al., eds., *The Art of Detective Fiction,* 41–44.

The Red Thumb Mark, 1907

>Kestner, Joseph A. *The Edwardian Detective,* 148–57.

JOHN FULLER

Flying to Nowhere, 1983

>Byatt, A. S. *On Histories and Stories,* 41–43.

>Gilmartin, Sophie. "Mapping the Margins: Translation, Invasion and Celtic Islands in Brian Moore and John Fuller," in Rod Mengham, ed., *An Introduction to Contemporary Fiction,* 176–80.

JANICE GALLOWAY

Foreign Parts, 1994

Gifford, Douglas. "Contemporary Fiction II: Seven Writers in Scotland," in Douglas Gifford and Dorothy McMillan, eds., *A History*, 610–11.

Reckwitz, Erhard. "Intertextuality: Between Continuity and Innovation," in Barbara Korte and Klaus Peter Müller, eds., *Unity in Diversity Revisited?*, 192–93.

The Trick Is to Keep Breathing, 1989

Gifford, Douglas. "Contemporary Fiction II: Seven Writers in Scotland," in Douglas Gifford and Dorothy McMillan, eds., *A History*, 607–9.

Oliver, Fiona. "The Self-Debasement of Scotland's Postcolonial Bodies." *SPAN* 42–43 (1996), 114–21.

Russell, Elizabeth. "Writing Abjection: Janice Galloway's *The Trick Is to Keep Breathing.*" *Dedalus* 6 (1996), 29–36.

JOHN GALSWORTHY

The Man of Property, 1906

Hapgood, Lynne. "The Unwritten Suburb: Defining Spaces in John Galsworthy's *The Man of Property*," in Lynne Hapgood and Nancy L. Paxton, eds., *Outside Modernism*, 162–77.

Hertel, Kirsten. *London zwischen Naturalismus und Moderne*, 221–301.

Langbauer, Laurie. *Novels of Everyday Life*, 222–25.

The White Monkey, 1924

Langbauer, Laurie. *Novels of Everyday Life*, 228–29.

JOHN GALT

Annals of the Parish, 1821

Walker, Marshall. *Scottish Literature since 1707*, 153–58.

Bogle Corbet, 1831

Bach, Susanne. "'A Nation of Emigrants': Eine historisch-soziologische Kontextualisierung der Auswanderungsthematik in John Galts *Bogle Corbet.*" *Zeitschrift für Kanada-Studien* 16:1 (1996), 58–79.

Trumpener, Katie. *Bardic Nationalism*, 277–88.

The Entail, 1822

Schoenfield, Mark. "The Family Plots: Land and Law in John Galt's *The Entail.*" *Scottish Liter J* 24:1 (1997), 60–64.

The Last of the Lairds, 1826

Simmons, Clare A. "Periodical Intrusions in Galt's *The Last of the Lairds.*" *Scottish Liter J* 24:1 (1997), 54–58.

The Member, 1832

Sassi, Carla. "Subverting Britannia's (Precarious) Balance: A Re-

Reading of John Galt's *The Member*—An Autobiography." *Rivista di Studi Vittoriani* 8:4 (1999), 25–45.

Snodgrass, Charles. "Dismembering *The Member*: Galt's 'Pawkie' Political Persona." *Scottish Liter J* 24:1 (1997), 66–70.

The Provost, 1822

Bardsley, Alyson. "Your Local Representative: John Galt's *The Provost*." *Scottish Liter J* 24:1 (1997), 72–76.

Trumpener, Katie. *Bardic Nationalism*, 153–56.

Walker, Marshall. *Scottish Literature since 1707*, 153–58.

JANE GARDAM

Bilgewater, 1976

Ang, Susan. *The Widening World of Children's Literature*, 153–55.

ALAN GARNER

The Owl Service, 1967

Ang, Susan. *The Widening World of Children's Literature*, 127–29.

Filmer-Davies, Cath. "Presence and Absence: God in Fantasy Literature." *Christianity and Lit* 47 (1997), 71–72.

Sullivan, C. W., III. "One More Time: The Conclusion of Alan Garner's *The Owl Service*." *J of the Fantastic in the Arts* 9:1 (1998), 46–54.

Red Shift, 1973

Ang, Susan. *The Widening World of Children's Literature*, 157–62.

The Stone Book Quartet, 1983

Thomson, Stephen. "Substitute Communities, Authentic Voices: The Organic Writing of the Child," in Karín Lesnik-Oberstein, ed., *Children in Culture*, 248–52.

GEORGE GASCOIGNE

The Adventures of Master F. J., 1573

Alwes, Derek B. "Elizabethan Dreaming: Fictional Dreams from Gascoigne to Lodge," in Constance C. Relihan, ed., *Framing Elizabethan Fictions*, 155, 162–67.

Austen, Gillian. "'Hir Acustomed Change': In Defence of Gascoigne's Elinor." *Imaginaires* 2 (1997), 9–30.

Cheney, Donald. "Narrative, Romance, and Epic," in Arthur F. Kinney, ed., *The Cambridge Companion*, 205–9.

Maslen, R. W. *Elizabethan Fictions*, 114–16, 132–57.

Staub, Susan C. "The Lady Francis Did Watch: Gascoigne's Voyeuristic Narrative," in Constance C. Relihan, ed., *Framing Elizabethan Fictions*, 41–54.

Taylor, Anthony Brian. "*The Adventures of Master F. J.* and *Twelfth Night*." *Notes and Queries* 45 (1998), 331–33.

ELIZABETH GASKELL

Cousin Phillis, 1865

Hughes, Linda K., and Michael Lund. *Victorian Publishing,* 161–64.

Milbank, Alison. *Dante and the Victorians,* 159–60.

Pettitt, Clare. "'Cousin Holman's Dresser': Science, Social Change, and the Pathologized Female in Gaskell's 'Cousin Phillis.'" *Nineteenth-Cent Lit* 52 (1998), 471–89.

Unsworth, Anna. "'A Purer Aether, a Diviner Air': Italian Influence on *Cousin Phillis.*" *Rivista di Studi Vittoriani* 1:1 (1996), 81–91.

Cranford, 1853

Cass, Jeffrey. "'The Scraps, Patches, and Rags of Daily Life': Gaskell's Oriental Other and the Conservation of Cranford." *Papers on Lang and Lit* 35 (1999), 417–32.

Croskery, Margaret Case. "Mothers without Children, Unity without Plot: *Cranford*'s Radical Charm." *Nineteenth-Cent Lit* 52 (1997), 198–220.

Davis, Philip. "Victorian Realist Prose and Sentimentality," in Alice Jenkins and Juliet John, eds., *Rereading Victorian Fiction,* 14–17.

Fenwick, Julie M. "Mothers of Empire in Elizabeth Gaskell's *Cranford.*" *Engl Stud in Canada* 23 (1997), 409–22.

Gillooly, Eileen. "Humor as Daughterly Defense in *Cranford,*" in Jennifer A. Wagner-Lawlor, ed., *The Victorian Comic Spirit,* 115–36.

Gillooly, Eileen. *Smile of Discontent,* 125–63.

Hughes, Linda K., and Michael Lund. *Victorian Publishing,* 84–95.

Knezevic, Borislav. "An Ethnography of the Provincial: The Social Geography of Gentility in Elizabeth Gaskell's *Cranford.*" *Victorian Stud* 41:3 (1998), 405–24.

Logan, Deborah Anna. *Fallenness in Victorian Women's Writing,* 193–98.

Miller, Andrew H. *Novels behind Glass,* 91–118.

Reeves, Margaret. "Textual, Contextual, and Ideological Contradictions in Elizabeth Gaskell's *Cranford.*" *Engl Stud in Canada* 23 (1997), 389–405.

Shelston, Alan. "*Cranford* and the Victorian Reader." *Rivista di Studi Vittoriani* 2:3 (1997), 19–32.

Singh, Veena. "The World of *Cranford*: A Structural Approach." *Rajasthan Univ Stud in Engl* 20 (1988), 33–39.

Mary Barton, 1848

Beck, Rudolf. "The Writing on the Cartridge: A Note on Elizabeth Gaskell's *Mary Barton* and Charles B. Tayler." *Notes and Queries* 45 (1998), 216–17.

Brantlinger, Patrick. *The Reading Lesson,* 94–96.

Brown, Pearl L. "From Elizabeth Gaskell's *Mary Barton* to Her *North and South*: Progress or Decline for Women?" *Victorian Lit and Culture* 28 (2000), 345–55.

Elliott, Dorice Williams. "Servants and Hands: Representing the Working Classes in Victorian Factory Novels." *Victorian Lit and Culture* 28 (2000), 379–83.

Gravil, Richard. "Negotiating *Mary Barton*," in Gravil, ed., *Master Narratives*, 87–100.

Graziano, Anne. "The Death of the Working-Class Hero in *Mary Barton* and *Alton Locke*." *J of Narrative Theory* 29 (1999), 135–51.

Guest, Harriet. "The Deep Romance of Manchester: Gaskell's *Mary Barton*," in K. D. M. Snell, ed., *The Regional Novel*, 78–98.

Hennelly, Mark M., Jr. "Letters 'All Bordered with Hearts and Darts': Sex, Lies, and Valentines in *Mary Barton*." *J of Evolutionary Psych* 20:3–4 (1999), 146–60; 21:1–2 (2000), 40–48.

Hughes, Linda K., and Michael Lund. *Victorian Publishing*, 35–48.

Ireland, Ken. *The Sequential Dynamics of Narrative*, 207–8.

Jackson-Houlston, C. M. *Ballads, Songs and Snatches*, 96–99, 101–8.

Johnson, Patricia E. "Art and Assassination in Elizabeth Gaskell's *Mary Barton*." *Victorians Inst J* 27 (1999), 149–62.

Law, Graham. "Industrial Designs: Form and Function in the 'Condition-of-England' Novel," in George Hughes, ed., *Corresponding Powers*, 136–37.

Lindner, Christoph. "Outside Looking In: Material Culture in Gaskell's Industrial Novels." *Orbis Litterarum* 55 (2000), 379–95.

Logan, Deborah Anna. *Fallenness in Victorian Women's Writing*, 83–89.

Loncar, Kathleen. *Legal Fiction*, 79–81.

Parker, Pamela Corpron. "Fictional Philanthropy in Elizabeth Gaskell's *Mary Barton* and *North and South*." *Victorian Lit and Culture* 25 (1997), 325–27.

Recchio, Thomas E. "A Monstrous Reading of *Mary Barton*: Fiction as 'Communitas.'" *Coll Lit* 23:3 (1996), 2–22.

Russell, Shannon. "Recycling the Poor and Fallen: Emigration Politics and the Narrative Resolutions of *Mary Barton* and *David Copperfield*," in Rita S. Kranidis, ed., *Imperial Objects*, 43–57.

Sabiston, Elizabeth Jean. "Anglo-American Connections: Elizabeth Gaskell, Harriet Beecher Stowe and the 'Iron of Slavery,'" in Carl Plasa and Betty J. Ring, eds., *The Discourse of Slavery*, 94–113.

Schor, Hilary M. "Show-Trials: Character, Conviction and the Law in Victorian Fiction." *Cardozo Stud in Law and Lit* 11 (1999), 179–95.

Smith, Valerie. "Fact or Fiction, the Acid Test: Gaskell, *Mary Barton* and Vitriol." *Gaskell Soc J* 12 (1998), 37–45.

Stitt, Megan Perigoe. *Metaphors of Change*, 66–69, 78–81, 97–101, 109–12, 120–23, 131–33, 142–45.

Surridge, Lisa. "Working-Class Masculinities in *Mary Barton*." *Victorian Lit and Culture* 28 (2000), 331–42.

Thaden, Barbara Z. *The Maternal Voice in Victorian Fiction*, 29–31.

Tyler, Shirley. "Women, Romantic Love and the Companionate Marriage in the Fiction of Mrs Gaskell and M. E. Braddon." *Australasian Victorian Stud J* 3:1 (1997), 109–11.

Wildt, Katherine Ann. *Elizabeth Gaskell's Use of Color*, 49–73.

Wyke, Terry. "The Culture of Self-Improvement: Real People in *Mary Barton*." *Gaskell Soc J* 13 (1999), 85–103.

Zlotnick, Susan. *Women, Writing, and the Industrial Revolution*, 68–71, 74–87.

Moorland Cottage, 1850

Camus, Marianne. "Degrés de l'absence: filles et mères chez Gaskell." *Cahiers Victoriens et Edouardiens* 47 (1998), 227–37.

Loncar, Kathleen. *Legal Fiction*, 56–59.

My Lady Ludlow, 1859

Hughes, Linda K., and Michael Lund. *Victorian Publishing*, 117–20.

Loncar, Kathleen. *Legal Fiction*, 35–39.

North and South, 1855

Brown, Pearl L. "From Elizabeth Gaskell's *Mary Barton* to Her *North and South*: Progress or Decline for Women?" *Victorian Lit and Culture* 28 (2000), 345–55.

Corbett, Mary Jean. *Allegories of Union*, 89–95.

Dainotto, Roberto M. *Place in Literature*, 75–102.

Gerard, Bonnie. "Victorian Things, Victorian Words: Representation and Redemption in Gaskell's *North and South*." *Victorian Newsl* 92 (1997), 21–24.

Guest, Harriet. "The Deep Romance of Manchester: Gaskell's *Mary Barton*," in K. D. M. Snell, ed., *The Regional Novel*, 87–89.

Hotz, Mary Elizabeth. "'Taught by Death What Life Should Be': Elizabeth Gaskell's Representation of Death in *North and South*." *Stud in the Novel* 32 (2000), 165–82.

Hughes, Linda K., and Michael Lund. *Victorian Publishing*, 110–18.

Ireland, Ken. *The Sequential Dynamics of Narrative*, 208–9.

Li, Fang. "*North and South*: East or West?" *Gaskell Soc J* 13 (1999), 104–5.

Lindner, Christoph. "Outside Looking In: Material Culture in Gaskell's Industrial Novels." *Orbis Litterarum* 55 (2000), 379–95.

Loncar, Kathleen. *Legal Fiction*, 50–52, 64–66, 99–104, 180–83.

O'Farrell, Mary Ann. *Telling Complexions*, 58–82.

Parker, Pamela Corpron. "Fictional Philanthropy in Elizabeth Gaskell's *Mary Barton* and *North and South*." *Victorian Lit and Culture* 25 (1997), 328–30.

Parker, Pamela Corpron. "From 'Ladies' Business' to 'Real Business': Elizabeth Gaskell's Capitalist Fantasy in *North and South*." *Victorian Newsl* 91 (1997), 1–3.

Peck, John. *War, the Army and Victorian Literature*, 96–99.

Pittock, Malcolm. "The Dove Ascending: The Case for Elizabeth Gaskell." *Engl Stud* (Amsterdam) 81 (2000), 538–47.

Rogers, Henry N., III. "'The Old Proud Attitude': The Power of Pride in Gaskell's *North and South*." *Publs of the Arkansas Philol Assoc* 24:1 (1998), 61–74.

Sanders, Mike. "Manufacturing Accident: Industrialism and the Worker's Body in Early Victorian Fiction." *Victorian Lit and Culture* 28 (2000), 322–27.

Stevenson, Catherine Barnes. "Romance and the Self-Made Man: Gaskell Rewrites Brontë." *Victorian Newsl* 91 (1997), 10–16.

Stitt, Megan Perigoe. *Metaphors of Change*, 21–23, 176–78.

Sutherland, John. *Who Betrays Elizabeth Bennet?*, 128–38.

Thaden, Barbara Z. *The Maternal Voice in Victorian Fiction*, 57–59.

Wildt, Katherine Ann. *Elizabeth Gaskell's Use of Color*, 75–100.

Young, Arlene. *Culture, Class and Gender*, 55–57, 84–86.

Zlotnick, Susan. *Women, Writing, and the Industrial Revolution*, 66–75, 99–122.

Ruth, 1853

Faymonville, Carmen. "'Waste Not, Want Not': Even Redundant Women Have Their Uses," in Rita S. Kranidis, ed., *Imperial Objects*, 78–81.

Gottlieb, Stacey. "'And God will teach her': Consciousness and Character in *Ruth* and *Aurora Leigh*." *Victorians Inst J* 24 (1996), 57–80.

Hatano, Yoko. "Evangelicalism in *Ruth*." *Mod Lang R* 95 (2000), 634–41.

Heinrich, Hans. *Zur Geschichte des 'Libertin,'* 215–19.

Hughes, Linda K., and Michael Lund. *Victorian Publishing*, 76–85.

Jaffe, Audrey. *Scenes of Sympathy*, 77–94.

Judd, Catherine. *Bedside Seductions*, 81–99.

Logan, Deborah Anna. *Fallenness in Victorian Women's Writing*, 38–48.

Loncar, Kathleen. *Legal Fiction*, 124–26, 223–25.

McGavran, Dorothy H. "Ruthless for Reform: Language, Lying, and Interpretation in Elizabeth Gaskell's *Ruth*." *Postscript* 12 (1995), 39–49.

Parker, Pam. "'The Power of Giving': Elizabeth Gaskell's *Ruth* and the Politics of Benevolence." *Gaskell Soc J* 13 (1999), 54–68.

Shumaker, Jeanette. "Gaskell's *Ruth* and Hardy's *Tess* as Novels of Free Union." *Dickens Stud Annual* 28 (1999), 151–68.

Stoddard, Eve W. "A Genealogy of Ruths: From Alien Harvester to Fallen Woman in Nineteenth-Century England," in Marilyn Demarest Button and Toni Reed, eds., *The Foreign Woman in British Literature*, 56–58.

Sutherland, John. *Who Betrays Elizabeth Bennet?*, 102–7.

Taylor, Jenny Bourne. "Representing Illegitimacy in Victorian Culture," in Ruth Robbins and Julian Wolfreys, eds., *Victorian Identities*, 136–37.

Thaden, Barbara Z. *The Maternal Voice in Victorian Fiction*, 35–39, 61–64, 67–69, 81–85.

Wildt, Katherine Ann. *Elizabeth Gaskell's Use of Color*, 103–31.

Sylvia's Lovers, 1863

Hughes, Linda K., and Michael Lund. *Victorian Publishing*, 47–67.

Lawson, Benjamin S. "From *Moby-Dick* to *Billy Budd*: Elizabeth Gaskell's *Sylvia's Lovers*." *South Atlantic R* 64:2 (1999), 37–55.

Loncar, Kathleen. *Legal Fiction*, 27–33.

Myer, Michael Grosvenor. "A Folksong Reference in Elizabeth Gaskell's *Sylvia's Lovers*." *Notes and Queries* 46 (1999), 44–45.

Peck, John. *Maritime Fiction*, 131–39.

Thaden, Barbara Z. *The Maternal Voice in Victorian Fiction*, 65–68, 82–92.

Twinn, Frances E. "Unpublished Letters and Geographical Errors in *Sylvia's Lovers*." *Notes and Queries* 48 (2001), 149–50.

Wives and Daughters, 1866

Billington, Josie. "Watching a Writer Write: Manuscript Revisions in Mrs Gaskell's *Wives and Daughters* and Why They Matter," in Philip Davis, ed., *Real Voices,* 224–34.

Camus, Marianne. "Degrés de l'absence: filles et mères chez Gaskell." *Cahiers Victoriens et Edouardiens* 47 (1998), 227–37.

Craig, Randall. *Promising Language,* 260–62.

Hughes, Linda K., and Michael Lund. *Victorian Publishing,* 12–34.

Stitt, Megan Perigoe. *Metaphors of Change,* 167–69, 179–81.

WILLIAM ALEXANDER GERHARDIE

The Polyglots, 1925

Cavaliero, Glen. *The Alchemy of Laughter,* 80–82.

PHEBE GIBBES

The Life and Adventures of Mr. Francis Clive, 1764

London, April. *Women and Property,* 125–27.

GEORGE GISSING

Born in Exile, 1892

Dale, Peter Allan. "Gissing and Bosanquet: Culture Unhoused." *Victorian Newsl* 95 (1999), 13–14.

Kramer, David. "George Gissing and Women's Work: Contextualizing the Female Professional." *Engl Lit in Transition* 43 (2000), 316–27.

Leavis, L. R. "Guilt, Love and Extinction: *Born in Exile* and *Under Western Eyes.*" *Neophilologus* 85 (2001), 154–60.

Neacey, Markus. "The Coming Man and the Will to Power in *Born in Exile.*" *Gissing J* 36:2 (2000), 20–30.

Pite, Ralph. "Place, Identity and *Born in Exile,*" in Alice Jenkins and Juliet John, eds., *Rereading Victorian Fiction,* 129–41.

Lott, Sydney. "Gissing and St. Sidwell." *Gissing J* 34:4 (1998), 23–26.

The Crown of Life, 1899

Coustillas, Pierre. "The Romantic Impulse in Gissing's Pacifist Novel *The Crown of Life.*" *Rivista di Studi Vittoriani* 1:2 (1996), 5–22.

Deary, Ian J. "Somatopsychic Distress in the Life and Novels of George Gissing." *Gissing J* 35:1 (1999), 4–13.

Demos, 1886

Connelly, Mark. *Orwell and Gissing,* 85–95.

Maltz, Diana. "Practical Aesthetics and Decadent Rationale in George Gissing." *Victorian Lit and Culture* 28 (2000), 60–63.

Schäffner, Raimund. *Anarchismus und Literatur in England,* 144–56.

Schäffner, Raimund. "Socialism and Conservatism in George Gissing's *Workers in the Dawn* and *Demos.*" *Gissing J* 34:2 (1998), 1–15.

Smith, Diane M. "The Evolution of the Working Class Novel in Europe: Darwinian Science and Literary Naturalism." *Excavatio* 8 (1996), 72–85.

Denzil Quarrier, 1892

Deledalle-Rhodes, Janice. "Eustace Glazzard: The Schopenhauerian Dilemma." *Gissing J* 36:4 (2000), 1–18.

Ettorre, Emanuela. "Sensational Gissing? Denzil Quarrier and the 'Politics' of Dissimulation." *Rivista di Studi Vittoriani* 8:4 (1999), 47–62.

In the Year of Jubilee, 1894

Kane, Penny. *Victorian Families in Fact and Fiction,* 30–31, 50–51.

Kramer, David. "George Gissing and Women's Work: Contextualizing the Female Professional." *Engl Lit in Transition* 43 (2000), 316–27.

Sjöholm, Christina. "The Darwinian Influence on Gissing's *In the Year of Jubilee.*" *Gissing J* 36:1 (2000), 1–10.

Isabel Clarendon, 1886

Cronin, Michael. "*Isabel Clarendon*: 'Hearts made sepulchres.'" *Gissing J* 33:3 (1997), 1–13.

The Nether World, 1889

DeVine, Christine. "'A Hell Constructed by Man': Depictions of the Poor in *The Nether World.*" *Gissing J* 37:1 (2001), 1–14.

Hertel, Kirsten. *London zwischen Naturalismus und Moderne,* 105–66.

Mbarek, Cherifa Krifa. "Compassion and Selfishness in Gissing's Slum Novels." *Gissing J* 36:3 (2000), 2–16.

Smith, Diane M. "The Evolution of the Working Class Novel in Europe: Darwinian Science and Literary Naturalism." *Excavatio* 8 (1996), 72–85.

Trotter, David. "Gissing's Fry-Ups: Food and the Definition of Working-Class Culture in Britain in the 1880s." *New Comparison* 24 (1997), 175–81.

New Grub Street, 1891

Brantlinger, Patrick. *The Reading Lesson,* 181–97.

Collins, Richard. "New Grub Street East." *Gissing J* 35:1 (1999), 17–24.

Connelly, Mark. *Orwell and Gissing,* 42–47.

Dale, Peter Allan. "Gissing and Bosanquet: Culture Unhoused." *Victorian Newsl* 95 (1999), 12–13.

Hedgecock, Liz. "'A Man of His Day': Literary Evolution and Masculinity in George Gissing's *New Grub Street,*" in Antony Rowland et al., eds., *Signs of Masculinity,* 117–35.

Kane, Penny. *Victorian Families in Fact and Fiction,* 34–36.

Kramer, David. "George Gissing and Women's Work: Contextualizing the Female Professional." *Engl Lit in Transition* 43 (2000), 316–27.

Neacey, Markus. "Lost Illusions and the Will to Die in *New Grub Street.*" *Gissing J* 34:4 (1998), 1–11.

Selig, Robert L. "Gissing's 'Spellbound' and *New Grub Street*." *Gissing J* 35:2 (1999), 27–31.

Stafford, Margot. "Keeping One's Own Counsel: Authorship, Literary Advice and *New Grub Street*." *Gissing J* 37:2 (2001), 1–18.

The Odd Women, 1893

Connelly, Mark. *Orwell and Gissing*, 75–82.

Keep, Christopher. "The Cultural Work of the Type-Writer Girl." *Victorian Stud* 40:3 (1997), 409–10, 413–15.

Kramer, David. "George Gissing and Women's Work: Contextualizing the Female Professional." *Engl Lit in Transition* 43 (2000), 316–27.

Ledger, Sally. *The New Woman*, 162–69.

Sanders, Lise Shapiro. "The Failures of the Romance: Boredom, Class, and Desire in George Gissing's *The Odd Women* and W. Somerset Maugham's *Of Human Bondage*." *Mod Fiction Stud* 47 (2000), 193–220.

Young, Arlene. *Culture, Class and Gender*, 146–53.

Our Friend the Charlatan, 1901

Deledalle-Rhodes, Janice. "*The Coming Man* and *La Cité Moderne*." *Gissing J* 35:2 (1999), 1–22.

The Private Papers of Henry Ryecroft, 1903

Brantlinger, Patrick. *The Reading Lesson*, 181–83.

Dale, Peter Allan. "Gissing and Bosanquet: Culture Unhoused." *Victorian Newsl* 95 (1999), 15.

Swann, Charles. "'Autobiografiction': Problems with Autobiographical Fictions and Fictional Autobiographies — Mark Rutherford's *Autobiography* and *Deliverance*, and Others." *Mod Lang R* 96 (2001), 32–36.

Thyrza, 1887

Dale, Peter Allan. "Gissing and Bosanquet: Culture Unhoused." *Victorian Newsl* 95 (1999), 12.

Deary, Ian J. "Somatopsychic Distress in the Life and Novels of George Gissing." *Gissing J* 35:1 (1999), 4–13.

Marroni, Francesco. "*Thyrza*: Gissing, Darwin and the Destinies of Innocence." *Gissing J* 34:3 (1998), 1–25.

Trotter, David. "Gissing's Fry-Ups: Food and the Definition of Working-Class Culture in Britain in the 1880s." *New Comparison* 24 (1997), 172–75.

The Unclassed, 1884

Maltz, Diana. "Practical Aesthetics and Decadent Rationale in George Gissing." *Victorian Lit and Culture* 28 (2000), 59–60.

Mbarek, Cherifa Krifa. "Compassion and Selfishness in Gissing's Slum Novels." *Gissing J* 36:3 (2000), 11–16.

Neacey, Markus. "The Hope of Pessimism and the Will to Live in *The Unclassed*." *Gissing J* 34:1 (1998), 8–17.

The Whirlpool, 1897

James, Simon. "Negotiating *The Whirlpool*." *Gissing J* 33:2 (1997), 15–24.

Maltz, Diana. "Practical Aesthetics and Decadent Rationale in George Gissing." *Victorian Lit and Culture* 28 (2000), 64–69.

Zimring, Rishona. "Gissing, Woolf, and the Drama of Home," in Laura Davis and Jeanette McVicker, eds., *Virginia Woolf and Her Influences*, 86–87.

Will Warburton, 1905

Villa, Luisa. "The Grocer's Romance: Economic Transactions and Radical Individualism in *Will Warburton*." *Gissing J* 36:2 (2000), 1–15.

Workers in the Dawn, 1880

Mbarek, Cherifa Krifa. "Compassion and Selfishness in Gissing's Slum Novels." *Gissing J* 36:3 (2000), 1–16.

Schäffner, Raimund. *Anarchismus und Literatur in England*, 144–56.

Schäffner, Raimund. "Socialism and Conservatism in George Gissing's *Workers in the Dawn* and *Demos*." *Gissing J* 34:2 (1998), 1–15.

Trotter, David. "Gissing's Fry-Ups: Food and the Definition of Working-Class Culture in Britain in the 1880s." *New Comparison* 24 (1997), 168–72.

RUMER GODDEN

The Dolls' House, 1957

Perrin, Noel. *A Child's Delight*, 16–20.

The Greengage Summer, 1958

Ang, Susan. *The Widening World of Children's Literature*, 130–34.

FRANCIS GODWIN

The Man in the Moon, 1638

Pioffet, Marie-Christine. "Godwin et Cyrano: Deux conceptions du voyage." *Dalhousie French Stud* 39–40 (1997), 45–57.

Trinkner, Diana. "Träume von Levania: Zur Rezeption neuer naturwissenschaftlicher Erkenntnisse am Beispiel von Galileis *Sidereus Nuncius* und Francis Godwins *The Man in the Moone*." *Morgen-Glantz* 8 (1998), 227–54.

Weber, Alan S. "Changes in Celestial Journey Literature, 1400–1650." *Culture and Cosmos* 1:1 (1997), 34–50.

WILLIAM GODWIN

Caleb Williams, 1794

Bellamy, Liz. *Commerce, Morality and the Eighteenth-Century Novel*, 166–70.

Benedict, Barbara M. *Curiosity*, 229–38.

Benedict, Barbara M. "Radcliffe, Godwin, and Self-Possession in the 1790s," in Linda Lang-Peralta, ed., *Women, Revolution, and the Novels of the 1790s*, 89–106.

Bour, Isabelle. "*Caleb Williams* et son double: *Adeline Mowbray* d'Amelia Opie." *Bull de la Société d'Etudes Anglo-Américaines des XVIIe et XVIIIe Siècles* 43 (1996), 93–101.

Brantlinger, Patrick. *The Reading Lesson*, 7–9, 46–48.

Brewer, William D. *The Mental Anatomies*, 40–44.

Cohen, Michael. "Godwin's *Caleb Williams*: Showing the Strains in Detective Fiction." *Eighteenth-Cent Fiction* 10 (1998), 203–19.

Cohen, Michael. *Murder Most Fair*, 40–50.

Dart, Gregory. *Rousseau, Robespierre and English Romanticism*, 76–98.

Edwards, Gavin. "William Godwin's Foreign Language: Stories and Families in *Caleb Williams* and *Political Justice*." *Stud in Romanticism* 39 (2000), 533–51.

Esterhammer, Angela. *The Romantic Performative*, 297–313.

Fisher, Carl. "The Crowd and the Public in Godwin's *Caleb Williams*," in Linda Lang-Peralta, ed., *Women, Revolution, and the Novels of the 1790s*, 47–65.

Gladfelder, Hal. *Criminality and Narrative*, 1–4, 209–11, 214–16, 219–24.

Haggerty, George E. "'The End of History': Identity and Dissolution in Apocalyptic Gothic." *Eighteenth Cent* 41 (2000), 228–33.

Jones, Chris. "Godwin and William James: The Psychology of Progress." *Prose Stud* 21:1 (1998), 39–40.

Kaufman, Robert. "The Sublime as Super-Genre of the Modern, or *Hamlet* in Revolution: Caleb Williams and His Problems." *Stud in Romanticism* 36 (1997), 541–74.

McCann, Andrew. *Cultural Politics in the 1790s*, 71–82.

Morse, David. *The Age of Virtue*, 247–48.

Parrinder, Patrick. "Highway Robbery and Property Circulation in Eighteenth-Century English Narratives." *Eighteenth-Cent Fiction* 13 (2001), 525–26.

Radcliffe, Evan. "Godwin from 'Metaphysician' to Novelist: *Political Justice, Caleb Williams*, and the Tension between Philosophical Argument and Narrative." *Mod Philology* 97 (2000), 540–53.

Reitz, Caroline. "Bad Cop/Good Cop: Godwin, Mill and the Imperial Origins of the English Detective." *Novel* 33 (2000), 175–93.

Ridley, Glynis. "Injustice in the Works of Godwin and Wollstonecraft," in Linda Lang-Peralta, ed., *Women, Revolution, and the Novels of the 1790s*, 72–82.

Schäffner, Raimund. *Anarchismus und Literatur in England*, 48–75.

Schramm, Jan-Melissa. *Testimony and Advocacy*, 89–94.

Stauffer, Andrew M. "Godwin, Provocation, and the Plot of Anger." *Stud in Romanticism* 39 (2000), 579–97.

Swan, Beth. *Fictions of Law*, 191–93.

Taylor, John A. *Popular Literature and . . . National Identity*, 80–91.

Thoms, Peter. *Detection and Its Designs*, 13–43.

Walsh, Cheryl. "Truth, Prejudice, and the Power of Narrative in *Caleb Williams*." *Engl Lang Notes* 35:4 (1998), 22–37.

Wehrs, Donald R. "Rhetoric, History, Rebellion: *Caleb Williams* and the Subversion of Eighteenth-Century Fiction," in Richard Kroll, ed., *The English Novel, Volume II*, 255–66.

Williams, Nicholas M. "'The Subject of Detection': Legal Rhetoric and Subjectivity in *Caleb Williams*." *Eighteenth-Cent Fiction* 9 (1997), 479–96.

Zimmerman, Everett. *The Boundaries of Fiction*, 163–77.

Cloudesly, 1830

Brewer, William D. "Male Rivalry and Friendship in the Novels of William Godwin," in Jay Losey and William D. Brewer, eds., *Mapping Male Sexuality*, 58–65.

Brewer, William D. *The Mental Anatomies*, 56–60, 62–64, 143–45.

Esterhammer, Angela. "Godwin's Suspicion of Speech Acts." *Stud in Romanticism* 39 (2000), 570–75.

Esterhammer, Angela. *The Romantic Performative*, 320–26.

Deloraine, 1833

Brewer, William D. "Male Rivalry and Friendship in the Novels of William Godwin," in Jay Losey and William D. Brewer, eds., *Mapping Male Sexuality*, 64–65.

Brewer, William D. *The Mental Anatomies*, 59–63, 106–10, 150–53, 190–92, 194–98.

Esterhammer, Angela. "Godwin's Suspicion of Speech Acts." *Stud in Romanticism* 39 (2000), 563–75.

Esterhammer, Angela. *The Romantic Performative*, 313–21.

Fleetwood, 1805

Brewer, William D. "Male Rivalry and Friendship in the Novels of William Godwin," in Jay Losey and William D. Brewer, eds., *Mapping Male Sexuality*, 51–65.

Esterhammer, Angela. "Godwin's Suspicion of Speech Acts." *Stud in Romanticism* 39 (2000), 563–66.

Esterhammer, Angela. *The Romantic Performative*, 310–16.

Jones, Chris. "Godwin and William James: The Psychology of Progress." *Prose Stud* 21:1 (1998), 46–48.

Mandeville, 1817

Brewer, William D. "Male Rivalry and Friendship in the Novels of William Godwin," in Jay Losey and William D. Brewer, eds., *Mapping Male Sexuality*, 50–65.

Brewer, William D. *The Mental Anatomies*, 16–18, 51–56, 92–94, 99–103, 161–66.

Trumpener, Katie. *Bardic Nationalism*, 225–30.

St. Leon, 1799

Brewer, William D. *The Mental Anatomies*, 44–48, 94–99, 134–36, 138–40, 190–93.

Esterhammer, Angela. "Godwin's Suspicion of Speech Acts." *Stud in Romanticism* 39 (2000), 566–69.

Esterhammer, Angela. *The Romantic Performative*, 318–20.

Jones, Chris. "Godwin and William James: The Psychology of Progress." *Prose Stud* 21:1 (1998), 40–45.

McCann, Andrew. *Cultural Politics in the 1790s*, 176–80.

Maertz, Gregory. "Generic Diversity and the Romantic Travel Novel: Godwin's *St. Leon: A Tale of the Sixteenth Century*," in Raymond A. Prier and Gerald Gillespie, eds., *Narrative Ironies*, 267–82.

Morse, David. *The Age of Virtue*, 249–51.

WILLIAM GOLDING

Close Quarters, 1987

Bényei, Tamás. *Acts of Attention*, 93–169.

Bényei, Tamás. "Tropics: Figure and Narrative in William Golding's Sea Trilogy." *AnaChronist* 1998: 193–232.

Jeng, Adela. "*To the Ends of the Earth* as Metafictional Parody." *Stud in Lang and Lit* (Taipei) 5 (1992), 77–94.

Pankhurst, Anne. "Interpreting Unknown Worlds: Functions of Metonymic Conceptualization in William Golding's *The Sea Trilogy.*" *Lang and Lit* (Harlow) 6 (1997), 121–30.

Darkness Visible, 1979

Carey, John. "H. G. Wells, T. S. Eliot and William Golding: Some Connections," in George Hughes, ed., *Corresponding Powers*, 228–31.

D'Amelio-Martiello, Nadia. "Dentelles étincelantes ajourant le tissu de la nuit cosmique: *Heart of Darkness* de Conrad et *Darkness Visible* de Golding," in Josiane Paccaud-Huguet, ed., *Joseph Conrad 1*, 21–41.

Fiddes, Paul S. *Freedom and Limit*, 228–30.

Jeng, Adela. "The Music That Frays and Breaks the String: Spiritual Language in *Darkness Visible.*" *Stud in Lang and Lit* (Taipei) 3 (1988), 121–32.

Mitchell, Michael. "Armed Angels: Visible Darkness in Malouf and Golding." *World Lit Today* 74 (2000), 770–77.

Reinfandt, Christoph. *Der Sinn der fiktionalen Wirklichkeiten*, 282–308.

Fire Down Below, 1989

Bényei, Tamás. *Acts of Attention*, 93–169.

Bényei, Tamás. "Tropics: Figure and Narrative in William Golding's Sea Trilogy." *AnaChronist* 1998: 193–232.

Jeng, Adela. "*To the Ends of the Earth* as Metafictional Parody." *Stud in Lang and Lit* (Taipei) 5 (1992), 77–94.

Pankhurst, Anne. "Interpreting Unknown Worlds: Functions of Metonymic Conceptualization in William Golding's *The Sea Trilogy.*" *Lang and Lit* (Harlow) 6 (1997), 121–30.

Free Fall, 1959

Fiddes, Paul S. *Freedom and Limit*, 217–20.

Hansen, Niels William. "Metaphysical Implications in William Golding's *Free Fall.*" *Angles on the Engl Speaking World* 11 (1999), 43–74.

The Inheritors, 1955

Carey, John. "H. G. Wells, T. S. Eliot and William Golding: Some Connections," in George Hughes, ed., *Corresponding Powers*, 227–28.

DePaolo, Charles. "Wells, Golding, and Auel: Representing the Neanderthal." *Science-Fiction Stud* 27 (2000), 426–31.

Elsbree, Langdon. "The Language of Extremity: The Four Elements in Golding's *The Inheritors*." *Extrapolation* 40 (1999), 233–42.

Fiddes, Paul S. *Freedom and Limit*, 220–23.

François, Pierre. *Inlets of the Soul*, 81–117.

Hoover, David L. *Language and Style in "The Inheritors,"* 1–168.

Lord of the Flies, 1954

Baker, James R. "Golding and Huxley: The Fables of Demonic Possession." *Twentieth Cent Lit* 46 (2000), 311–25.

Bay-Petersen, Ole. "Circular Imagery in *Lord of the Flies*." *Stud in Lang and Lit* (Taipei) 4 (1990), 103–19.

Engélibert, Jean-Paul. *La postérité de Robinson Crusoé*, 94–95, 174–204.

Epstein, E. L. "Significant Motifs in *Lord of the Flies*," in Clarice Swisher, ed., *Readings on "Lord of the Flies,"* 107–11.

Kruger, Arnold. "Golding's *Lord of the Flies*." *Explicator* 57:3 (1999), 167–69.

Morgado, Margarida. "The Season of Play: Constructions of the Child in the English Novel," in Karín Lesnik-Oberstein, ed., *Children in Culture*, 221–25.

Olsen, Kirstin. *Understanding "Lord of the Flies,"* 1–21.

Phillips, Richard. *Mapping Men and Empire*, 147–52.

Roncace, Mark. "The *Bacchae* and *Lord of the Flies*: A Few Observations with the Help of E. R. Dodds." *Classical and Mod Lit* 18 (1997), 37–51.

Singh, Minnie. "The Government of Boys: Golding's *Lord of the Flies* and Ballantyne's *Coral Island*." *Children's Lit* 25 (1997), 205–12.

York, R. A. *The Rules of Time*, 157–71.

The Paper Men, 1984

Chourova, Margarita. "'The Death of the Author' and the Tragicomic Allegory of William Golding's *The Paper Men*," in Richard Todd and Luisa Flora, eds., *Theme Parks*, 89–100.

Fiddes, Paul S. *Freedom and Limit*, 231–34.

Pincher Martin, 1956

Baker, James R. "Golding and Huxley: The Fables of Demonic Possession." *Twentieth Cent Lit* 46 (2000), 311–25.

Byatt, A. S. *On Histories and Stories*, 32–34.

Engélibert, Jean-Paul. *La postérité de Robinson Crusoé*, 95–96, 278–95.

McCarron, Kevin. "'In Contemplation of my Deliverance': *Robinson Crusoe* and *Pincher Martin*," in Lieve Spaas and Brian Stimpson, eds., *Robinson Crusoe*, 285–93.

Rites of Passage, 1980

Bényei, Tamás. *Acts of Attention*, 93–169.

Bényei, Tamás. "Tropics: Figure and Narrative in William Golding's Sea Trilogy." *AnaChronist* 1998: 193–232.

Bényei, Tamás. "'You Will Forgive the Figure?: Language, Metaphor and Translation in William Golding's *Rites of Passage*." *B.A.S.: Brit and Am Stud* 1998: 94–102.

Jeng, Adela. "*To the Ends of the Earth* as Metafictional Parody." *Stud in Lang and Lit* (Taipei) 5 (1992), 77–94.

Nadal, Marita. "William Golding's *Rites of Passage*: A Case of Transtextuality." *Miscelánea* 15 (1994), 405–20.

Pankhurst, Anne. "Interpreting Unknown Worlds: Functions of Metonymic Conceptualization in William Golding's *The Sea Trilogy*." *Lang and Lit* (Harlow) 6 (1997), 121–30.

Stephenson, William. "Sex, Drugs and the Economics of Masculinity in William Golding's *Rites of Passage*," in Antony Rowland et al., eds., *Signs of Masculinity*, 178–96.

The Spire, 1964

Fiddes, Paul S. *Freedom and Limit*, 211–14.

Fort, Camille. "*The Spire* de William Golding ou l'échec ambigu d'une sublimation." *Imaginaires* 4 (1999), 143–50.

Hallissy, Margaret. "'No Innocent Work': Theology and Psychology in William Golding's *The Spire*." *Christianity and Lit* 47 (1997), 37–55.

Hooker, Jeremy. *Writers in a Landscape*, 142–61.

Kendall, Tim. "'Joy, Fire, Joy': Blaise Pascal's 'Memorial' and the Visionary Explorations of T. S. Eliot, Aldous Huxley and William Golding." *Lit and Theology* 11 (1997), 309–11.

DOUGLAS GOLDRING

The Black Curtain, 1920

Ayers, David. *English Literature of the 1920s*, 156–58.

OLIVER GOLDSMITH

The Vicar of Wakefield, 1766

Bellamy, Liz. *Commerce, Morality and the Eighteenth-Century Novel*, 138–44.

Briggs, Peter M. "Oliver Goldsmith and the Muse of Disjunction." *Age of Johnson* 9 (1998), 237–42.

Brooks, Christopher K. "Goldsmith's Commercial Vicar: Spectacles and Speculation." *Coll Lang Assoc J* 41 (1998), 319–34.

Heinrich, Hans. *Zur Geschichte des 'Libertin,'* 146–48.

Jeffares, A. Norman. *Images of Invention*, 106–14.

Morse, David. *The Age of Virtue*, 219–22.

Paulson, Ronald. *The Beautiful, Novel, and Strange*, 202–23.

Preston, Thomas R. "Moral Spin Doctoring, Delusion, and Chance: Wakefield's Vicar Writes an Enlightenment Parable." *Age of Johnson* 11 (2000), 237–75.

Prier, Raymond Adolph. "Charlotte's *Vicar* and Goethe's Eighteenth-Century Tale about Werther," in Raymond A. Prier and Gerald Gillespie, eds., *Narrative Ironies*, 283–97.

Skinner, Gillian. *Sensibility and Economics in the Novel*, 61–81.

Swan, Beth. *Fictions of Law*, 186–89.

MARY GORDON

The Company of Women, 1980

Hallissy, Margaret. "'The Impulse of a Few Words': Authority, Divided Self, and Language in Mary Gordon's *Final Payments* and *The Company of Women.*" *Christianity and Lit* 50 (2001), 281–89.

Final Payments, 1978

Hallissy, Margaret. "'The Impulse of a Few Words': Authority, Divided Self, and Language in Mary Gordon's *Final Payments* and *The Company of Women.*" *Christianity and Lit* 50 (2001), 269–80.

Men and Angels, 1985

Kuebrich, David. "Apropos of a Modern Faith: Feminism, Class, and Motherhood in Mary Gordon's *Men and Angels.*" *Christianity and Lit* 46 (1997), 293–312.

CATHERINE GORE

The Hamiltons; or, Official Life in 1830, 1850

Hughes, Winifred. "Mindless Millinery: Catherine Gore and the Silver Fork Heroine." *Dickens Stud Annual* 25 (1996), 169–72.

Pin Money, 1834

Hughes, Winifred. "Mindless Millinery: Catherine Gore and the Silver Fork Heroine." *Dickens Stud Annual* 25 (1996), 162–68.

KENNETH GRAHAME

The Wind in the Willows, 1908

Fielitz, Sonja. "*Rewriting Children's Literature*: Kenneth Grahames *The Wind in the Willows* und seine Fort- und Umschreibungen." *Archiv für das Studium der neueren Sprachen und Literaturen* 237 (2000), 267–82.

Guroian, Vigen. *Tending the Heart of Virtue,* 88–97.

Hunt, Peter. *Children's Literature,* 244–48.

Rollin, Lucy, and Mark I. West. *Psychoanalytic Responses,* 45–50.

Sandner, David. *The Fantastic Sublime,* 43–45, 67–81, 83–86, 103–5, 140–46.

Sandner, David. "Mr. Bliss and Mr. Toad: Hazardous Driving in J. R. R. Tolkien's *Mr. Bliss* and Kenneth Grahame's *The Wind in the Willows.*" *Mythlore* 21:4 (1997), 36–38.

Schlobin, Roger C. "Danger and Compulsion in *The Wind in the Willows*: Or, Toad and Hyde Together At Last." *J of the Fantastic in the Arts* 8:1 (1997), 34–41. (Also in Elton E. Smith and Robert Haas, eds., *The Haunted Mind,* 31–38.)

Sutcliffe, Mary. "A Perilous Endeavor: The Riverbank and Beyond." *Children's Lit in Educ* 29:3 (1998), 143–51.

Wytenbroek, J. R. "Natural Mysticism in Kenneth Grahame's *The Wind in the Willows.*" *Mythlore* 21:2 (1996), 431–34.

SARAH GRAND

Adnam's Orchard, 1912

Mangum, Teresa. *Married, Middlebrow, and Militant,* 203–11.

The Beth Book, 1897

Heilmann, Ann. "Feminist Resitance, the Artist and 'A Room of One's Own' in New Woman Fiction." *Women's Writing* 2 (1995), 298–301.

Heilmann, Ann. *New Woman Fiction,* 184–89.

Jusova, Iveta. "Imperialist Feminism: Colonial Issues in Sarah Grand's *The Heavenly Twins* and *The Beth Book.*" *Engl Lit in Transition* 43 (2000), 309–13.

Mangum, Teresa. *Married, Middlebrow, and Militant,* 144–91.

Murphy, Patricia. "Reevaluating Female 'Inferiority': Sarah Grand versus Charles Darwin." *Victorian Lit and Culture* 26 (1998), 221–33.

Randolph, Lyssa. "The Child and the 'Genius': New Science in Sarah Grand's *The Beth Book.*" *Victorian R* 26:1 (2000), 64–77.

Richardson, Angelique. "Allopathic Pills?: Health, Fitness and New Woman Fictions." *Women: A Cultural R* 10:1 (1999), 1–21.

Richardson, Angelique. "The Eugenization of Love: Sarah Grand and the Morality of Genealogy." *Victorian Stud* 42:2 (1999/2000), 243–44.

A Domestic Experiment, 1891

Heilmann, Ann. *New Woman Fiction,* 122–24.

Mangum, Teresa. *Married, Middlebrow, and Militant,* 36–49.

The Heavenly Twins, 1893

Ardis, Ann. "Organizing Women: New Woman Writers, New Woman Readers, and Suffrage Feminism," in Nicola Diane Thompson, ed., *Victorian Women Writers,* 195–99.

Bogiatzis, Demetris. "Sexuality and Gender: 'The Interlude' of Sarah Grand's *The Heavenly Twins.*" *Engl Lit in Transition* 44 (2001), 46–60.

Hamilton, Lisa K. "New Women and 'Old' Men: Gendering Degeneration," in Talia Schaffer and Kathy Alexis Psomiades, eds., *Women and British Aestheticism,* 70–78.

Heilmann, Ann. "Masquerade, Sisterhood and the Dilemma of the Feminist as Artist and Woman in Late Nineteenth-Century British Women's Writing." *J of Gender Stud* 3 (1994), 157–60.

Heilmann, Ann. "Narrating the Hysteric: *Fin-de-Siècle* Medical Discourse and Sarah Grand's *The Heavenly Twins* (1893)," in Angelique Richardson and Chris Willis, eds., *The New Woman in Fiction and in Fact,* 123–34.

Heilmann, Ann. *New Woman Fiction,* 129–36.

Heilmann, Ann. "(Un)Masking Desire: Cross-Dressing and the Crisis of Gender in New Woman Fiction." *J of Victorian Culture* 5 (2000), 95–107.

Jusova, Iveta. "Imperialist Feminism: Colonial Issues in Sarah Grand's *The Heavenly Twins* and *The Beth Book.*" *Engl Lit in Transition* 43 (2000), 298–308.

Katz, Tamar. *Impressionist Subjects,* 57–62.

Larson, Jil. *Ethics and Narrative in the English Novel*, 57–63.

Larson, Jil. "Sexual Ethics in Fiction by Thomas Hardy and the New Woman Writers," in Alice Jenkins and Juliet John, eds., *Rereading Victorian Fiction*, 165–70.

Ledger, Sally. *The New Woman*, 113–18.

Liggins, Emma. "Writing against the 'Husband-Fiend': Syphilis and Male Sexual Vice in the New Woman Novel." *Women's Writing* 7 (2000), 180–82, 189–90.

Logan, Deborah Anna. *Fallenness in Victorian Women's Writing*, 201–17.

Mangum, Teresa. *Married, Middlebrow, and Militant*, 85–143.

Mouton, Michelle J. "Taking on Tennyson: Sarah Grand's *The Heavenly Twins* and the Ethics of Androgynous Reading." *Victorian R* 23 (1997), 184–207.

Richardson, Angelique. "Allopathic Pills?: Health, Fitness and New Woman Fictions." *Women: A Cultural R* 10:1 (1999), 1–21.

Richardson, Angelique. "The Eugenization of Love: Sarah Grand and the Morality of Genealogy." *Victorian Stud* 42:2 (1999/2000), 232–35, 238–43.

Ideala: A Study from Life, 1888

Mangum, Teresa. *Married, Middlebrow, and Militant*, 59–84.

Thompson, Nicola Diane. "Responding to the Woman Questions: Rereading Noncanonical Victorian Women Novelists," in Thompson, ed., *Victorian Women Writers*, 6–7.

Singularly Deluded, 1892

Mangum, Teresa. *Married, Middlebrow, and Militant*, 49–58.

The Winged Victory, 1916

Mangum, Teresa. *Married, Middlebrow, and Militant*, 211–18.

RICHARD GRAVES

The Spiritual Quixote, 1773

Bending, Stephen. "A Natural Revolution? Garden Politics in Eighteenth-Century England," in Kevin Sharpe and Steven N. Zwicker, eds., *Refiguring Revolutions*, 258–60.

ROBERT GRAVES

Claudius the God, 1934

Hopkins, Chris. "Robert Graves and the Historical Novel in the 1930s," in Patrick J. Quinn, ed., *New Perspectives*, 132–34.

Count Belisarius, 1938

Firla, Ian. "'Epics Are Out of Fashion': Graves's Short Story as a Model for His Longer Fiction's Narrative Techniques," in Patrick J. Quinn, ed., *New Perspectives*, 124–26.

I, Claudius, 1934

Hopkins, Chris. "Robert Graves and the Historical Novel in the 1930s," in Patrick J. Quinn, ed., *New Perspectives*, 128–35.

Presley, John Woodrow. "*Claudius*, The Scripts." *Lit/Film Q* 27 (1999), 167–72.

Seven Days in New Crete, 1949

Pordzik, Ralph. "*Mapping the Future(s)*: Formen und Funktionen der Metafiktionalität im englischen utopischen Roman." *Anglia* 118 (2000), 51–55.

Wife to Mr. Milton, 1943

McCormick, Ian. "Graves's Milton," in Patrick J. Quinn, ed., *New Perspectives*, 136–45.

ALASDAIR GRAY

The Fall of Kevin Walker, 1985

Bernstein, Stephen. *Alasdair Gray*, 82–96.

A History Maker, 1994

Bernstein, Stephen. *Alasdair Gray*, 134–52.

Lanark, 1981

Bernstein, Stephen. *Alasdair Gray*, 35–58.

Pordzik, Ralph. "*Mapping the Future(s)*: Formen und Funktionen der Metafiktionalität im englischen utopischen Roman." *Anglia* 118 (2000), 41–46, 58–60.

Stevenson, Randall. "Greenwich Meanings: Clocks and Things in Modernist and Postmodernist Fiction." *Yrbk of Engl Stud* 30 (2000), 132–33.

Walker, Marshall. *Scottish Literature since 1707*, 339–41.

McGrotty and Ludmilla, 1990

Bernstein, Stephen. *Alasdair Gray*, 82–96.

1982 Janine, 1984

Bernstein, Stephen. *Alasdair Gray*, 59–81.

Walker, Marshall. *Scottish Literature since 1707*, 338–41.

Whiteford, Eilidh. "Engendered Subjects: Subjectivity and National Identity in Alasdair Gray's *1982 Janine*." *Scotlands* 2 (1994), 66–82.

Poor Things, 1992

Bernstein, Stephen. *Alasdair Gray*, 109–33.

McMillan, Dorothy. "Constructed Out of Bewilderment: Stories of Scotland," in Ian A. Bell, ed., *Peripheral Visions*, 86–88.

Something Leather, 1991

Bernstein, Stephen. *Alasdair Gray*, 97–108.

HENRY GREEN

Back, 1946

Copeland, David. "Reading and Translating Romance in Henry Green's *Back*." *Stud in the Novel* 32 (2000), 49–67.

Rawlinson, Mark. *British Writing of the Second World War*, 199–204.

Treglown, Jeremy. *Romancing*, 161–63, 170–79.

Blindness, 1926

> Lucas, John. "From Realism to Radicalism: Sylvia Townsend Warner, Patrick Hamilton and Henry Green in the 1920s," in Lynne Hapgood and Nancy L. Paxton, eds., *Outside Modernism*, 214–17.
> Treglown, Jeremy. *Romancing*, 53–60.

Caught, 1943

> Rawlinson, Mark. *British Writing of the Second World War*, 103–7.
> Stonebridge, Lyndsey. "Bombs and Roses: The Writing of Anxiety in Henry Green's *Caught*." *Diacritics* 28:4 (1998), 25–43.
> Treglown, Jeremy. *Romancing*, 129–40.

Concluding, 1948

> Treglown, Jeremy. *Romancing*, 182–87, 192–95.

Doting, 1952

> Treglown, Jeremy. *Romancing*, 213–19.

Living, 1929

> Cavaliero, Glen. *The Alchemy of Laughter*, 225–27.
> Lucas, John. "From Realism to Radicalism: Sylvia Townsend Warner, Patrick Hamilton and Henry Green in the 1920s," in Lynne Hapgood and Nancy L. Paxton, eds., *Outside Modernism*, 214–21.
> Treglown, Jeremy. *Romancing*, 79–87.

Loving, 1945

> Treglown, Jeremy. *Romancing*, 152–58, 166–69.
> Whitehead, John. *Eight Modern Masterpieces*, 127–37.
> York, R. A. *The Rules of Time*, 110–25.

Nothing, 1950

> Treglown, Jeremy. *Romancing*, 195–201.

Party Going, 1939

> Dragomán, György. "'Everything Unexplained': The Structure of Secrecy and Secrecy as Structure in Henry Green's *Party Going*." *AnaChronist* 1996: 231–42.
> Treglown, Jeremy. *Romancing*, 104–11.

SARAH GREEN

The Fugitive, or Family Incidents, 1814

> Copeland, Edward. *Women Writing about Money*, 82–83, 172–74.

Scotch Novel Reading, 1824

> Pearson, Jacqueline. *Women's Reading in Britain*, 213–17.

GRAHAM GREENE

Brighton Rock, 1938

> Baldridge, Cates. *Graham Greene's Fictions*, 23–37, 129–38.
> Hoskins, Robert. *Graham Greene*, 79–99.
> Jacob, George C. "The Child/Woman as Femme Fatale in Graham Greene's Trilogy." *Notes on Contemp Lit* 29:1 (1999), 6–8.

Whitehouse, J. C. *Vertical Man*, 60–61, 73–75.

A Burnt-Out Case, 1961

Baldridge, Cates. *Graham Greene's Fictions*, 124–26.
Hill, Wm. Thomas. "*Manon Lescaut* and the Nature of Marie Rycker's Warning in Graham Greene's *A Burnt-Out Case*." *Tsukuba Stud in Lit* 15 (1998), 1–55.
Hoskins, Robert. *Graham Greene*, 164–76.
Pearce, Joseph. *Literary Converts*, 414–16.
Whitehouse, J. C. *Vertical Man*, 45, 49–52.

The Captain and the Enemy, 1988

Hoskins, Robert. *Graham Greene*, 283–304.

The Comedians, 1966

Baldridge, Cates. *Graham Greene's Fictions*, 140–65.
Hoskins, Robert. *Graham Greene*, 176–88.

The Confidential Agent, 1939

Baldridge, Cates. *Graham Greene's Fictions*, 37–40.
Buzard, James. "Mass-Observation, Modernism, and Auto-Ethnography." *Modernism/ Modernity* 4:3 (1997), 93–122.

Doctor Fisher of Geneva, 1980

Hoskins, Robert. *Graham Greene*, 243–56.

The End of the Affair, 1951

Baldridge, Cates. *Graham Greene's Fictions*, 77–83, 102–8.
Cash, William. *The Third Woman*, 1–318.
Hoskins, Robert. *Graham Greene*, 137–55.
Middleton, Darren J. N. "Graham Greene's *The End of the Affair*: Toward an Ironic God." *Notes on Contemp Lit* 29:3 (1999), 8–10.
Whitehouse, J. C. *Vertical Man*, 48–49, 52–53, 55–59, 70–72, 78–80.

England Made Me, 1935

Hoskins, Robert. *Graham Greene*, 48–50.

A Gun for Sale, 1936

Hoskins, Robert. *Graham Greene*, 53–77.

The Heart of the Matter, 1948

Baldridge, Cates. *Graham Greene's Fictions*, 70–77, 93–99.
Hoskins, Robert. *Graham Greene*, 113–15.
Jacob, George C. "The Child/Woman as Femme Fatale in Graham Greene's Trilogy." *Notes on Contemp Lit* 29:1 (1999), 6–8.
Miller, R. H. "Graham Greene's 'Saddest Story.'" *Renascence* 51 (1999), 133–42.
Pearce, Joseph. *Literary Converts*, 258–59, 412–14.
Scannell, James. "The Method is Unsound: The Aesthetic Dissonance of Colonial Justification in Kipling, Conrad, and Greene." *Style* 30 (1996), 414–26.
Whitehouse, J. C. *Vertical Man*, 46–49, 56–59, 63–65, 87–89.
Wilt, Judith. "The Cave of the Body: *The Heart of the Matter*." *Rel and the Arts* 1:3 (1997), 73–95.
York, R. A. *The Rules of Time*, 126–41.

The Honorary Consul, 1973

Baldridge, Cates. *Graham Greene's Fictions,* 84–87, 108–11.
Choi, Jae-suck. "A Trio of Hope: Graham Greene's *The Honorary Consul.*" *J of Engl Lang and Lit* 42 (1996), 839–53.
Dalm, Rudolf E. van. *A Structural Analysis of "The Honorary Consul,"* 51–222.
Hoskins, Robert. *Graham Greene,* 215–30.
Whitehouse, J. C. *Vertical Man,* 54–55, 60–62.

The Human Factor, 1978

Baldridge, Cates. *Graham Greene's Fictions,* 44–46.
Hoskins, Robert. *Graham Greene,* 231–42.

The Ministry of Fear, 1943

Baldridge, Cates. *Graham Greene's Fictions,* 90–92, 115–18.
DeCoste, Damon Marcel. "Modernism's Shell-Shocked History: Amnesia, Repetition, and the War in Graham Greene's *The Ministry of Fear.*" *Twentieth Cent Lit* 45 (1999), 428–45.
Hoskins, Robert. *Graham Greene,* 125–28.

Monsignor Quixote, 1982

Hoskins, Robert. *Graham Greene,* 257–82.
Whitehouse, J. C. *Vertical Man,* 55, 62–64, 81–82.

The Power and the Glory, 1940

Baldridge, Cates. *Graham Greene's Fictions,* 49–70.
Goetsch, Paul. "Das Verhältnis von Alltag und Religion in der neueren englischen Literatur." *Literaturwissenschaftliches Jahrbuch im Auftrage der Görres-Gesellschaft* 31 (1990), 211–32.
Hestenes, Mark. "To See the Kingdom: A Study of Graham Greene and Alan Paton." *Lit and Theology* 13 (1999), 311–20.
Hoskins, Robert. *Graham Greene,* 264–69.
Jacob, George C. "The Child/Woman as Femme Fatale in Graham Greene's Trilogy." *Notes on Contemp Lit* 29:1 (1999), 6–8.
Reeves, Troy. "Duty and Heroism in *The Power and the Glory.*" *Conf of Coll Teachers of Engl Stud* 63 (1998), 43–49.
Schweizer, Bernard. "Graham Greene and the Politics of Travel." *Prose Stud* 21:1 (1998), 114–20.
Whitehouse, J. C. *Vertical Man,* 53–54, 62–63, 67–70, 82–84, 87–89.

The Quiet American, 1955

Baldridge, Cates. *Graham Greene's Fictions,* 40–42, 122–24, 187–89.
Hoskins, Robert. *Graham Greene,* 155–64.
Olsen, Thomas G. "Unquiet Americans: Paul Theroux's *Saint Jack* and the Re-Vision of Graham Greene." *Symbiosis* 2:1 (1998), 75–90.
Whitehouse, J. C. *Vertical Man,* 52, 65–67.
Whitfield, Stephen J. "Limited Engagement: *The Quiet American* as History." *J of Am Stud* 30:1 (1996), 65–86.

The Third Man, 1950

Evans, Peter W. "*The Third Man* (1949): Constructions of the Self." *Forum for Mod Lang Stud* 31 (1995), 37–47.
Gribble, Jim. "*The Third Man*: Graham Greene and Carol Reed." *Lit/Film Q* 26 (1998), 235–39.

Hanley, Matthew M. "The Location of *The Third Man.*" *Josai Intl Univ Bull* 4:1 (1996), 135–53.

Schwab, Ulrike. "Authenticity and Ethics in the Film *The Third Man.*" *Lit/Film Q* 28 (2000), 2–6.

Travels with My Aunt, 1969

Hill, Wm. Thomas. "Journeying toward the Deep Incurable Egotism of Passion in Graham Greene's *Travels with My Aunt.*" *Stud in Lang and Lit* 32 (1997), 19–45.

Hoskins, Robert. *Graham Greene,* 189–213.

ROBERT GREENE

Gwydonius: The Carde of Fancie, 1584

Alwes, Derek B. "Elizabethan Dreaming: Fictional Dreams from Gascoigne to Lodge," in Constance C. Relihan, ed., *Framing Elizabethan Fictions,* 162–67.

Hadfield, Andrew. *Literature, Travel, and Colonial Writing,* 180–87.

Menaphon, 1589

Ackerley, Chris. "'Do Not Despair': Samuel Beckett and Robert Greene." *J of Beckett Stud* 6:1 (1996), 119–24.

Cantar, Brenda. "'Silenced But For The Word': The Discourse of Incest in Greene's *Pandosto* and *Menaphon.*" *Engl Stud in Canada* 23 (1997), 31–34.

Pandosto, 1588

Cantar, Brenda. "'Silenced But For The Word': The Discourse of Incest in Greene's *Pandosto* and *Menaphon.*" *Engl Stud in Canada* 23 (1997), 21–31.

Newcomb, Lori Humphrey. "The Romance of Service: The Simple History of *Pandosto*'s Servant Readers," in Constance C. Relihan, ed., *Framing Elizabethan Fictions,* 117–39.

WALTER GREENWOOD

Love on the Dole, 1933

Haywood, Ian. *Working-Class Fiction,* 49–57.

PHILIPPA GREGORY

Perfectly Correct, 1996

Mergenthal, Silvia. "Englishness/Englishnesses in Contemporary Fiction," in Barbara Korte and Klaus Peter Müller, eds., *Unity in Diversity Revisited?,* 54–59.

ELIZABETH GRIFFITH

The History of Lady Barton, 1771

Skinner, Gillian. *Sensibility and Economics in the Novel,* 92–111.

ROMESH GUNESEKERA

Reef, 1994

Amirthanayagam, Guy. *The Marriage of Continents*, 323–25.

NEIL GUNN

Butcher's Broom, 1934

Price, Richard. "Whose History, Which Novel?: Neil M. Gunn and the Gaelic Idea." *Scottish Liter J* 24:2 (1997), 88–100.

HENRY RIDER HAGGARD

Allan Quartermain, 1887

Demoor, Marysa. "The Black and White Minstrel Show: Rider Haggard's Exotic Romances," in C. C. Barfoot, ed., *Beyond Pug's Tour*, 177–81.

Dryden, Linda. "*Heart of Darkness* and *Allan Quatermain*: Apocalypse and Utopia." *Conradiana* 31 (1999), 173–78, 183–94.

Kästner, Jörg. "Alias Allan Quatermain: Sir Henry Rider Haggards phantastische Abenteuer." *Horen* 43:3 (1998), 79–91.

Pickrell, Alan. "Rider Haggard's Female Characters: From Goddess of the Cave to Goddess of the Screen." *Dime Novel Roundup* 67:1 (1998), 18–26.

Reitz, Bernhard. "Der Christian Gentleman als imperiales Konstrukt in den Afrika-Romanen Henry Rider Haggards." *Anglistik und Englischunterricht* 58 (1996), 73–90.

Ayesha, 1905

Kincaid, James R. *Annoying the Victorians*, 169–78.

Nicholson, Mervyn. "C. S. Lewis and the Scholarship of Imagination in E. Nesbit and Rider Haggard." *Renascence* 51 (1998), 50–60.

Reitz, Bernhard. "Der Christian Gentleman als imperiales Konstrukt in den Afrika-Romanen Henry Rider Haggards." *Anglistik und Englischunterricht* 58 (1996), 73–90.

Rodgers, Terence. "Restless Desire: Rider Haggard, Orientalism and the New Woman." *Women: A Cultural R* 10 (1999), 35–46.

Benita: An African Romance, 1906

Johnson, Heidi H. "Agricultural Anxiety, African Erasure: H. Rider Haggard's *Rural England* and *Benita: An African Romance*." *Victorians Inst J* 24 (1996), 113–33.

Eric Brighteyes, 1891

Wawn, Andrew. *The Vikings and the Victorians*, 332–35.

King Solomon's Mines, 1885

Arata, Stephen. *Fictions of Loss*, 95–104.

Armstrong, Nancy. *Fiction in the Age of Photography*, 235–42.

Chrisman, Laura. "Gendering Imperial Culture: *King Solomon's Mines* and Feminist Criticisms," in Keith Ansell-Pearson et al., eds., *Cultural Readings of Imperialism*, 290–303.

Daly, Nicholas. *Modernism, Romance and the Fin de Siècle*, 58–61.

Demoor, Marysa. "The Black and White Minstrel Show: Rider Haggard's Exotic Romances," in C. C. Barfoot, ed., *Beyond Pug's Tour*, 176–82.

Höglund, Johan A. *Mobilising the Novel*, 59–61.

Logan, Mawuena Kossi. *Narrating Africa*, 141–53.

Monsman, Gerald. "Of Diamonds and Deities: Social Anthropology in H. Rider Haggard's *King Solomon's Mines*." *Engl Lit in Transition* 43 (2000), 280–93.

Murphy, Patricia. "The Fissure *King*: Parody, Ideology, and the Imperialist Narrative," in Jennifer A. Wagner-Lawlor, ed., *The Victorian Comic Spirit*, 23–40.

Nicholson, Mervyn. "C. S. Lewis and the Scholarship of Imagination in E. Nesbit and Rider Haggard." *Renascence* 51 (1998), 49–50.

Pickrell, Alan. "Rider Haggard's Female Characters: From Goddess of the Cave to Goddess of the Screen." *Dime Novel Roundup* 67:1 (1998), 18–26.

Reitz, Bernhard. "Der Christian Gentleman als imperiales Konstrukt in den Afrika-Romanen Henry Rider Haggards." *Anglistik und Englischunterricht* 58 (1996), 73–90.

Rodgers, Terence. "Restless Desire: Rider Haggard, Orientalism and the New Woman." *Women: A Cultural R* 10 (1999), 35–46.

Stott, Rebecca. "'Scaping the Body: Of Cannibal Mothers and Colonial Landscapes," in Angelique Richardson and Chris Willis, eds., *The New Woman in Fiction and in Fact*, 153–55.

Vogel, Joseph O. "Merensky and Nachtigal in Southern Africa: A Contemporary Source for *King Solomon's Mines*." *J of African Travel Writing* 4 (1998), 20–30.

She, 1887

Arata, Stephen. *Fictions of Loss*, 95–104.

Daly, Nicholas. *Modernism, Romance and the Fin de Siècle*, 106–8.

Demoor, Marysa. "The Black and White Minstrel Show: Rider Haggard's Exotic Romances," in C. C. Barfoot, ed., *Beyond Pug's Tour*, 176–78.

Höglund, Johan A. *Mobilising the Novel*, 61–66.

Houston, Gail Turley. *Royalties*, 75–76.

Leerssen, Joep. "The Allochronic Periphery: Towards a Grammar of Cross-Cultural Representation," in C. C. Barfoot, ed., *Beyond Pug's Tour*, 291–93.

Malley, Shawn. "'Time Hath No Power Against Identity': Historical Continuity and Archaeological Adventure in H. Rider Haggard's *She*." *Engl Lit in Transition* 40 (1997), 275–93.

Michalski, Robert. "Divine Hunger: Culture and the Commodity in Rider Haggard's *She*." *J of Victorian Culture* 1 (1996), 76–94.

Murphy, Patricia. "The Gendering of History in *She*." *Stud in Engl Lit, 1500–1900* 39 (1999), 747–69.

Pickrell, Alan. "Rider Haggard's Female Characters: From Goddess of the Cave to Goddess of the Screen." *Dime Novel Roundup* 67:1 (1998), 18–26.

Reitz, Bernhard. "Der Christian Gentleman als imperiales Konstrukt in den Afrika-Romanen Henry Rider Haggards." *Anglistik und Englischunterricht* 58 (1996), 73–90.

Rodgers, Terence. "Restless Desire: Rider Haggard, Orientalism and the New Woman." *Women: A Cultural R* 10 (1999), 35–46.

MARGUERITE RADCLYFFE HALL

Adam's Breed, 1926

Buck, Claire. "'Still some obstinate emotion remains': Radclyffe Hall and the Meanings of Service," in Suzanne Raitt and Trudi Tate, eds., *Women's Fiction and the Great War,* 177–79.

The Unlit Lamp, 1924

Cline, Sally. *Radclyffe Hall,* 158–63, 174–77.

The Well of Loneliness, 1928

Ayers, David. *English Literature of the 1920s,* 140–45.

Breen, Margaret Soenser. "Narrative Inversion: The Biblical Heritage of *The Well of Loneliness* and *Desert of the Heart,*" in Raymond-Jean Frontain, ed., *Reclaiming the Sacred,* 187–206.

Buck, Claire. "'Still some obstinate emotion remains': Radclyffe Hall and the Meanings of Service," in Suzanne Raitt and Trudi Tate, eds., *Women's Fiction and the Great War,* 187–94.

Cline, Sally. *Radclyffe Hall,* 225–30.

Elfenbein, Andrew. *Romantic Genius,* 204–10.

Hill, Marylu. *Mothering Modernity,* 148–67.

Ledger, Sally. *The New Woman,* 142–45.

Lehnert, Gertrud. "Weiblichkeit als Maskerade: Zur Inszenierung der Geschlechterrollen bei Christoph Martin Wieland und Radclyffe Hall." *Forum Homosexualität und Literatur* 25 (1995), 7–28.

MacPike, Loralee. "Is Mary Llewellyn an Invert? The Modernist Supertext of *The Well of Loneliness,*" in Elizabeth Jane Harrison and Shirley Peterson, eds., *Unmanning Modernism,* 73–86.

Madden, Ed. "*The Well of Loneliness,* or the Gospel According to Radclyffe Hall," in Raymond-Jean Frontain, ed., *Reclaiming the Sacred,* 163–86.

Prince-Hughes, Tara. "'A Curious Double Insight': *The Well of Loneliness* and Native American Alternative Gender Traditions." *Rocky Mountain R of Lang and Lit* 53:2 (1999), 31–40.

Rosenbaum, S. P. *Aspects of Bloomsbury,* 116–18.

Taylor, Melanie A. "'The Masculine Soul Heaving in the Female Bosom': Theories of Inversion in *The Well of Loneliness.*" *J of Gender Stud* 7 (1998), 287–95.

Weatherhead, A. K. *Upstairs,* 113–17.

CICELY HAMILTON

William—An Englishman, 1919

Smith, Angela K. "'That silly suffrage . . .': The Paradox of World War I." *Nineteenth-Cent Feminisms* 3 (2000), 90–97.

ELIZABETH HAMILTON

The Cottagers of Glenburnie, 1808

> Anderson, Carol, and Aileen M. Riddell. "The Other Great Unknowns: Women Fiction Writers of the Early Nineteenth Century," in Douglas Gifford and Dorothy McMillan, eds., *A History*, 182–83.

Memoirs of Modern Philosophers, 1800

> Guest, Harriet. *Small Change*, 329–31.
> London, April. "Clock Time and Utopia's Time in Novels of the 1790s." *Stud in Engl Lit, 1500–1900* 40 (2000), 546–48.
> London, April. "Novel and History in Anti-Jacobin Satire." *Yrbk of Engl Stud* 30 (2000), 73–81.
> London, April. *Women and Property*, 179–84.
> Thaddeus, Janice. "Elizabeth Hamilton's *Modern Philosophers* and the Uncertainties of Satire," in James E. Gill, ed., *Cutting Edges*, 395–416.

MARY HAMILTON

Munster Village, 1778

> Bannet, Eve Tavor. *The Domestic Revolution*, 169–71.
> Swan, Beth. *Fictions of Law*, 47–51.

PATRICK HAMILTON

Craven House, 1926

> Lucas, John. "From Realism to Radicalism: Sylvia Townsend Warner, Patrick Hamilton and Henry Green in the 1920s," in Lynne Hapgood and Nancy L. Paxton, eds., *Outside Modernism*, 210–14.

JAMES HANLEY

Boy, 1931

> Armstrong, James. "The Publication, Prosecution, and Re-Publication of James Hanley's *Boy* (1931)." *Library* 19 (1997), 351–62.
> Haywood, Ian. *Working-Class Fiction*, 74–76.

THOMAS HARDY

Desperate Remedies, 1871

> Bulaila, A. Aziz M. "*Desperate Remedies*: Not Just a Minor Novel." *Thomas Hardy J* 14:1 (1998), 65–73.
> Garlock, David. "Entangled Genders: Plasticity, Indeterminacy, and Constructs of Sexuality in Darwin and Hardy." *Dickens Stud Annual* 27 (1998), 294–98.
> Hardy, Barbara. *Thomas Hardy*, 6–8.
> Harris, Nicola. "The Feminine Text: Reading and Knowing Hardy's Women." *Thomas Hardy Yrbk* 26 (1998), 31–32.

Irwin, Michael. "From Fascination to Listlessness: Hardy's Depiction of Love," in Charles P. C. Pettit, ed., *Reading Thomas Hardy*, 118–20, 122–24.

Irwin, Michael. *Reading Hardy's Landscapes*, 26–28, 74–77.

Irwin, Michael. "Readings of Realism," in Philip Davis, ed., *Real Voices*, 211–13.

Kurjiaka, Susan K. H. "Myths and Metaphors of Women's and Workers' Lives in Three Hardy Novels." *Mount Olive R* 7 (1993–1994), 86–91.

Millgate, Michael. "Obscure Rivalry: Thomas Hardy and Henry James in Early Career," in George Hughes, ed., *Corresponding Powers*, 175–76.

Radford, Andrew. "An Echo of Dickens in Hardy's *Desperate Remedies*." *Notes and Queries* 46 (1999), 481–82.

Sylvia, Richard. "Thomas Hardy's *Desperate Remedies*: 'All my sin has been because I love you so.'" *Colby Q* 35 (1999), 102–14.

Thomas, Jane. *Thomas Hardy, Femininity and Dissent*, 52–68.

Turner, Paul. *The Life of Thomas Hardy*, 18–26.

Far from the Madding Crowd, 1874

Ahmad, Suleiman M. "*Far from the Madding Crowd* in the British Provincial Theatre." *Thomas Hardy J* 16:1 (2000), 70–80.

Boumelha, Penny. "The Patriarchy of Class: *Under the Greenwood Tree*, *Far from the Madding Crowd*, *The Woodlanders*," in Dale Kramer, ed., *The Cambridge Companion to Thomas Hardy*, 130–34, 137–40.

Butler, Lance St. John. *Registering the Difference*, 185–87.

Craig, Randall. *Promising Language*, 12–17.

Daleski, H. M. *Thomas Hardy and Paradoxes of Love*, 56–82.

Dalziel, Pamela. "'She matched his violence with her own wild passion': Illustrating *Far from the Madding Crowd*," in Charles P. C. Pettit, ed., *Reading Thomas Hardy*, 1–28.

Gaye, Mamadou. "Rural Imagination and Intellectual Desires in Thomas Hardy's Wessex Novels." *Bridges* (Dakar) 8 (1997–1998), 121–24.

Gerard, Bonnie. "*Far from the Madding Crowd* and the Cultural Politics of Serialization." *Victorian Periodicals R* 30 (1997), 331–45.

Gossin, Pamela. "'All Danaë to the Stars': Nineteenth-Century Representations of Women in the Cosmos." *Victorian Stud* 40:1 (1996), 82–83.

Harris, Nicola. "The Feminine Text: Reading and Knowing Hardy's Women." *Thomas Hardy Yrbk* 26 (1998), 33–34.

Harris, Nicola. "Hardy and Eliot: The Eye of Narcissus' Looking-Glass." *George Eliot R* 28 (1997), 49–57.

Ireland, Ken. *The Sequential Dynamics of Narrative*, 235–36.

Irwin, Michael. "From Fascination to Listlessness: Hardy's Depiction of Love," in Charles P. C. Pettit, ed., *Reading Thomas Hardy*, 120–22, 128–29.

Irwin, Michael. *Reading Hardy's Landscapes*, 16–23, 47–49, 62–64, 78–81, 162–64.

Jackson-Houlston, C. M. *Ballads, Songs and Snatches*, 160–62.

Jann, Rosemary. "Hardy's Rustics and the Construction of Class." *Victorian Lit and Culture* 28 (2000), 419–20.

Johnson, Trevor. "A Possible Visual Source for Chapter One of *Far from the Madding Crowd*." *Thomas Hardy J* 14:2 (1998), 81–83.

Kurjiaka, Susan K. H. "Myths and Metaphors of Women's and Workers' Lives in Three Hardy Novels." *Mount Olive R* 7 (1993–1994), 86–91.

Law, Jules David. "Sleeping Figures: Hardy, History, and the Gendered Body." *ELH* 65 (1998), 224–32.

Millgate, Michael. "Obscure Rivalry: Thomas Hardy and Henry James in Early Career," in George Hughes, ed., *Corresponding Powers*, 180–84.

Peck, John. *War, the Army and Victorian Literature*, 111–13.

Schweik, Robert. "The Influence of Religion, Science, and Philosophy on Hardy's Writings," in Dale Kramer, ed., *The Cambridge Companion to Thomas Hardy*, 54–58.

Sprechman, Ellen Lew. *Seeing Women as Men*, 25–39.

Sumner, Rosemary. *A Route to Modernism*, 38–41.

Turner, Paul. *The Life of Thomas Hardy*, 41–48.

The Hand of Ethelberta, 1876

Dutta, Shanta. *Ambivalence in Hardy*, 23–36.

Ettorre, Emanuela. "*The Hand of Ethelberta*: Topologie e scritture dell'enigma femminile." *Rivista di Studi Vittoriani* 1:2 (1996), 143–72.

Hardy, Barbara. *Thomas Hardy*, 9–12.

Irwin, Michael. *Reading Hardy's Landscapes*, 65–68, 80–85.

Lennon, Peter. "*Ethelberta* in America: Past and Present." *Thomas Hardy J* 14:2 (1998), 45–51.

Lothe, Jakob. "Variants on Genre: *The Return of the Native, The Mayor of Casterbridge, The Hand of Ethelberta*," in Dale Kramer, ed., *The Cambridge Companion to Thomas Hardy*, 123–25.

O'Toole, Tess. *Genealogy and Fiction in Hardy*, 115–23.

Radford, Andrew. "Hardy's Subversion of Social Comedy in *The Hand of Ethelberta*." *Thomas Hardy J* 16:2 (2000), 63–69.

Thomas, Jane. *Thomas Hardy, Femininity and Dissent*, 85–95.

Turner, Paul. *The Life of Thomas Hardy*, 49–56.

Widdowson, Peter. *On Thomas Hardy*, 45–92.

Jude the Obscure, 1895

Andres, Sophia. "George Eliot's Challenge to Medusa's Gendered Disparities." *Victorian Newsl* 95 (1999), 28–29.

Brantlinger, Patrick. *The Reading Lesson*, 194–96.

Butler, Lance St. John. *Registering the Difference*, 177–80.

Codde, Philippe. "Jude the Obscure vs. Job the Assured: A Deconstructive Reading of Thomas Hardy's *Jude*." *Thomas Hardy Yrbk* 28 (2000), 5–16.

Cooper, Andrew. "Voicing the Language of Literature: Jude's Obscured Labor." *Victorian Lit and Culture* 28 (2000), 391–406.

Couture, Claude. "Fatalisme et individualisme: Analyse sociologique et comparative de *Jude l'Obscur* et *Tchipayuk*." *Francophonies d'Amérique* 6 (1996), 51–59.

Daleski, H. M. *Thomas Hardy and Paradoxes of Love*, 180–205.

Davis, William A., Jr. "Reading Failure in(to) Jude the Obscure: Hardy's Sue Bridehead and Lady Jeune's 'New Woman' Essays, 1885–1900." *Victorian Lit and Culture* 26 (1998), 53–68.

Doheny, John R. "Characterization in Hardy's *Jude the Obscure*: The Function of Arabella," in Charles P. C. Pettit, ed., *Reading Thomas Hardy*, 57–80.

Dougill, John. *Oxford in English Literature*, 186–96.

Dutta, Shanta. *Ambivalence in Hardy*, 111–30.

Efron, Arthur. "'A Bluer, Moister Atmosphere': Life-Energy in *Jude the Obscure*." *Paunch* 67–68 (1997), 55–64.

Gagnier, Regenia. "Further Reflections on Sympathetic Identification," in Shlomith Rimmon-Kenan et al., eds., *Rereading Texts*, 166–73.

Garlock, David. "Entangled Genders: Plasticity, Indeterminacy, and Constructs of Sexuality in Darwin and Hardy." *Dickens Stud Annual* 27 (1998), 302–3.

Gaye, Mamadou. "Rural Imagination and Intellectual Desires in Thomas Hardy's Wessex Novels." *Bridges* (Dakar) 8 (1997–1998), 130–32, 138–40.

Gibson, James. "*Jude the Obscure*: A Centennial Tribute." *Rivista di Studi Vittoriani* 2:4 (1997), 5–23.

Hardy, Barbara. "Good Times in *Jude the Obscure*, or, Rereading Hardy's Dogmatic Form," in Shlomith Rimmon-Kenan et al., eds., *Rereading Texts*, 21–35.

Hardy, Barbara. *Thomas Hardy*, 57–82.

Harris, Nicola. "Harmonious Inconsistency: The Formal Necessity of the Aged Child in *Jude the Obscure*." *Thomas Hardy Yrbk* 26 (1998), 45–50.

Hennelly, Mark M., Jr. "Courtly Wild Men and Carnivalesque Pig Women in Dickens and Hardy." *Dickens Stud Annual* 26 (1998), 20–27.

Ireland, Ken. *The Sequential Dynamics of Narrative*, 238–39.

Irwin, Michael. *Reading Hardy's Landscapes*, 45–46, 95–96, 130–31.

Jurta, Roxanne. "'Not-So-New' Sue: The Myth of *Jude the Obscure* as a New Woman Novel." *J of the Eighteen Nineties Soc* 26 (1999), 13–21.

Kearney, Anthony. "Edmund Gosse, Hardy's *Jude the Obscure*, and the Repercussions of 1886." *Notes and Queries* 47 (2000), 332–34.

Kearney, Anthony. "Hardy's *Jude the Obscure*." *Explicator* 57:3 (1999), 154–56.

Kincaid, James R. *Annoying the Victorians*, 233–47.

Kozubska, Ewa. "The Idea of the Eternal Return in Hardy's Novels." *Folia Litteraria Anglica* (Lodz) 1 (1997), 85–96.

Kramer, Dale. "Hardy and Readers: *Jude the Obscure*," in Kramer, ed., *The Cambridge Companion to Thomas Hardy*, 164–79.

Kullmann, Thomas. "Klassische Kunstwerke als Katalysatoren der emotionalen Emanzipation: Thomas Hardy, E. M. Forster," in Volker Kapp et al., eds., *Bilderwelten*, 47–74.

Lane, Christopher. *The Burdens of Intimacy*, 126–29.

Larson, Jil. *Ethics and Narrative in the English Novel*, 54–63.

Larson, Jil. "Sexual Ethics in Fiction by Thomas Hardy and the New Woman Writers," in Alice Jenkins and Juliet John, eds., *Rereading Victorian Fiction*, 159–70.

Ledger, Sally. *The New Woman*, 180–89.

Levine, George. "The Cartesian Hardy: I Think Therefore I'm Doomed." *Nineteenth Cent Stud* 11 (1997), 109–26.

Lock, Charles. "Hardy and the Railway." *Essays in Criticism* 50 (2000), 56–64.

McCormick, John. *Catastrophe and Imagination*, 33–35.

McDermott, Emily A. "An Ovidian Epigraph in *Jude the Obscure*." *Classical and Mod Lit* 19 (1999), 233–41.

Marsh, Joss. *Word Crimes*, 269–327.

Melfi, Mary Ann. "*Jude the Obscure*: Childhood Without Closure." *Durham Univ J* 87 (1995), 315–20.

Morrison, Ronald D. "Humanity towards Man, Woman, and the Lower Animals: Thomas Hardy's *Jude the Obscure* and the Victorian Humane Movement." *Nineteenth Cent Stud* 12 (1998), 65–77.

Neill, Edward. *Trial by Ordeal*, 89–106.

O'Malley, Patrick R. "Oxford's Ghosts: *Jude the Obscure* and the End of the Gothic." *Mod Fiction Stud* 46 (2000), 646–64.

O'Toole, Tess. *Genealogy and Fiction in Hardy*, 65–73.

Ray, Martin. "*Jude the Obscure* and Benjamin Jowett." *Thomas Hardy J* 14:2 (1998), 79–80.

Ren, Michele. "The Return of the Native: Hardy's Arabella, Agency, and Abjection," in Rita S. Kranidis, ed., *Imperial Objects*, 108–23.

Rivinus, Timothy M. "Tragedy of the Commonplace: The Impact of Addiction on Families in the Fiction of Thomas Hardy." *Lit and Medicine* 11 (1992), 237–65.

Rogers, Shannon L. "Medievalism in the Last Novels of Thomas Hardy: New Wine in Old Bottles." *Engl Lit in Transition* 42 (1999), 308–14.

Schaffer, Talia. *The Forgotten Female Aesthetes*, 216–41.

Schaffer, Talia. "Malet the Obscure: Thomas Hardy, 'Lucas Malet' and the Literary Politics of Early Modernism." *Women's Writing* 3 (1996), 261–80.

Sprechman, Ellen Lew. *Seeing Women as Men*, 101–20.

Sumner, Rosemary. *A Route to Modernism*, 68–79, 91–105.

Turner, Paul. *The Life of Thomas Hardy*, 141–51.

Widdowson, Peter. *On Thomas Hardy*, 168–95.

A Laodicean, 1881

Byerly, Alison. *Realism, Representation, and the Arts*, 176–78.

Durden, Mark. "Ritual and Deception: Photography and Thomas Hardy." *J of European Stud* 30 (2000), 62–68.

Garlock, David. "Entangled Genders: Plasticity, Indeterminacy, and Constructs of Sexuality in Darwin and Hardy." *Dickens Stud Annual* 27 (1998), 298–302.

Hardy, Barbara. *Thomas Hardy*, 12–15.

Irwin, Michael. *Reading Hardy's Landscapes*, 117–25.

Larson, Jil. *Ethics and Narrative in the English Novel*, 64–92.

Simons, Mark. "Hardy's Stereographic Technique." *Thomas Hardy J* 13:3 (1997), 88–89.

Thomas, Jane. *Thomas Hardy, Femininity and Dissent*, 96–112.

Turner, Paul. *The Life of Thomas Hardy*, 73–81.

Widdowson, Peter. *On Thomas Hardy*, 93–114.

The Mayor of Casterbridge, 1886

Blaisdell, Bob. "D. H. Lawrence and Thomas Hardy: 'All This about a Daughter who is no Daughter of Thine!'" *Thomas Hardy Yrbk* 28 (2000), 46–50.

Daleski, H. M. *Thomas Hardy and Paradoxes of Love*, 105–28.

Hardy, Barbara. *Thomas Hardy*, 29–42.

Harris, Nicola. "Hardy's *The Mayor of Casterbridge*, or, *totus mundus agit histrionem*." *Thomas Hardy Yrbk* 26 (1998), 36–42.

Hooker, Jeremy. *Writers in a Landscape*, 118–38.

Irwin, Michael. *Reading Hardy's Landscapes*, 13–16, 38–39, 74–77, 90–95, 158–63.

Jackson-Houlston, C. M. *Ballads, Songs and Snatches*, 152–54.

Jann, Rosemary. "Hardy's Rustics and the Construction of Class." *Victorian Lit and Culture* 28 (2000), 415–16.

Jays, David. "Cruel Intentions." *Sight and Sound* 11:2 (2001), 24–27.

Keen, Suzanne. *Victorian Renovations of the Novel*, 127–44.

Kozubska, Ewa. "The Idea of the Eternal Return in Hardy's Novels." *Folia Litteraria Anglica* (Lodz) 1 (1997), 85–97.

Lane, Christopher. *The Burdens of Intimacy*, 120–22, 124–27, 129–42.

Larson, Jil. *Ethics and Narrative in the English Novel*, 86–91.

Law, Jules David. "Sleeping Figures: Hardy, History, and the Gendered Body." *ELH* 65 (1998), 237–44.

Lilienfeld, Jane. "'I Could Drink a Quarter-Barrel to the Pitching': The Mayor of Casterbridge Viewed as an Alcoholic," in Jane Lilienfeld and Jeffrey Oxford, eds., *The Languages of Addiction*, 225–35.

Lilienfeld, Jane. *Reading Alcoholisms*, 13–83.

Lothe, Jakob. "Variants on Genre: *The Return of the Native, The Mayor of Casterbridge, The Hand of Ethelberta*," in Dale Kramer, ed., *The Cambridge Companion to Thomas Hardy*, 119–23.

Nigro, August. *The Net of Nemesis*, 101–10.

O'Toole, Tess. *Genealogy and Fiction in Hardy*, 19–23.

Radford, Andrew. "A Note on Hardy's *The Mayor of Casterbridge* and Brown's *The House with the Green Shutters*." *Thomas Hardy J* 15:3 (1999), 107–8.

Ramel, Annie. "The Crevice in the Canvas: A Study of *The Mayor of Casterbridge*." *Victorian Lit and Culture* 26 (1998), 259–70.

Reid, Fred. "Thomas Hardy, Humanism and History." *Thomas Hardy Yrbk* 27 (1998), 32–39.

Reid, Fred. "Wayfarers and Seafarers: Ideas of History in *The Mayor of Casterbridge*." *Thomas Hardy J* 13:3 (1997), 47–55.

Rivinus, Timothy M. "Tragedy of the Commonplace: The Impact of Addiction on Families in the Fiction of Thomas Hardy." *Lit and Medicine* 11 (1992), 237–65.

Saracino, Marilena. "*The Mayor of Casterbridge*: Thomas Hardy e l'estromissione del desiderio." *Rivista di Studi Vittoriani* 1:1 (1996), 139–58.

Sprechman, Ellen Lew. *Seeing Women as Men*, 59–76.

Sumner, Rosemary. *A Route to Modernism*, 55–63.

Sutherland, John. *Who Betrays Elizabeth Bennet?*, 224–31.

Thompson, J. B. "Hardy's *The Mayor of Casterbridge*." *Explicator* 59:2 (2001), 83–85.

Tobin, Thomas J. "Women as Others in *The Mayor of Casterbridge*." *McNeese R* 36 (1998), 19–26.

Turner, Paul. *The Life of Thomas Hardy*, 91–99.

Wolfreys, Julian. "Haunting Casterbridge, or 'the persistence of the unforeseen,'" in Wolfreys, ed., *"The Mayor of Casterbridge,"* 153–67.

A Pair of Blue Eyes, 1873

Armstrong, Tim. *Haunted Hardy*, 135–40.

Beer, Gillian. *Darwin's Plots*, 236–37.

Cronin, Meoghan Byrne. "'As a Diamond Kills an Opal': Charm and Countercharm in Thomas Hardy's *A Pair of Blue Eyes*." *Victorians Inst J* 26 (1998), 121–43.

Daleski, H. M. *Thomas Hardy and Paradoxes of Love*, 36–55.

Gilmartin, Sophie. *Ancestry and Narrative*, 215–25.

Gossin, Pamela. "'All Danaë to the Stars': Nineteenth-Century Representations of Women in the Cosmos." *Victorian Stud* 40:1 (1996), 83–86.

Hardy, Barbara. *Thomas Hardy*, 8–9.

Harris, Nicola. "The Feminine Text: Reading and Knowing Hardy's Women." *Thomas Hardy Yrbk* 26 (1998), 32–33.

Irwin, Michael. *Reading Hardy's Landscapes*, 71–77.

Jann, Rosemary. "Hardy's Rustics and the Construction of Class." *Victorian Lit and Culture* 28 (2000), 417–19.

Lock, Charles. "Hardy and the Railway." *Essays in Criticism* 50 (2000), 46–49.

Mallett, Phillip. "Hardy and Time," in Charles P. C. Pettit, ed., *Reading Thomas Hardy*, 156–58.

Millgate, Michael. "The 'Discarded' Preface to *A Pair of Blue Eyes*." *Thomas Hardy J* 13:3 (1997), 58–59.

O'Toole, Tess. *Genealogy and Fiction in Hardy*, 6–8, 58–64, 100–102.

Richardson, Angelique. "'Some Science underlies all Art': The Dramatization of Sexual Selection and Racial Biology in Thomas Hardy's *A Pair of Blue Eyes* and *The Well-Beloved*." *J of Victorian Culture* 3 (1998), 302–21.

Schweik, Robert. "'Life and Death are neighbours nigh': Hardy's *A Pair of Blue Eyes* and the Uses of Incongruity." *Philol Q* 76 (1997), 87–99.

Sumner, Rosemary. *A Route to Modernism*, 170–79.

Thomas, Jane. *Thomas Hardy, Femininity and Dissent*, 69–84.

Turner, Paul. *The Life of Thomas Hardy*, 34–40.

The Return of the Native, 1878

Awano, Shuji. "Irony and Heroism: Biblical and Classical Allusions in *The Return of the Native*." *Stud in Engl Lit* (Tokyo) 73 (1997), 17–33.

Barrell, John. "Geographies of Hardy's Wessex," in K. D. M. Snell, ed., *The Regional Novel*, 101–7.

Beer, Gillian. *Darwin's Plots*, 226–36.

Broderick, Catherine. "Semiotic Stylistics in Hardy's Discourse." *Kobe Coll Stud* 40:3 (1994), 39–49.

Chisholm, Richard. "The Attempted Resuscitation of Eustacia Vye." *Thomas Hardy J* 13:3 (1997), 83–85.

Cho, Ailee. "The Change of Rural Community and Women in *The Return of the Native*, *The Woodlanders*, and *Tess of the d'Urbervilles*." *J of Engl Lang and Lit* 43:1 (1997), 51–68.

Dainotto, Roberto M. *Place in Literature*, 40–74.

Daleski, H. M. *Thomas Hardy and Paradoxes of Love*, 83–104.

Dutta, Shanta. *Ambivalence in Hardy*, 37–55.

Elbarbary, Samir. "Mahfuz's *Midaq Alley* and Hardy's *The Return of the Native*: Some Parallels." *Al-'Arabiyya* 28 (1995), 81–94.

Gadouin, Isabelle. "Les jeux de l'amour et du hasard dans *The Return of the Native* de Thomas Hardy." *Cahiers Victoriens et Edouardiens* 49 (1999), 41–55.

Gadouin, Isabelle. "La scène tragique dans *The Return of the Native*, de Thomas Hardy." *Etudes Anglaises* 52 (1999), 5–16.

Gaye, Mamadou. "Rural Imagination and Intellectual Desires in Thomas Hardy's Wessex Novels." *Bridges* (Dakar) 8 (1997–1998), 124–25, 133–38.

Hardy, Barbara. *Thomas Hardy*, 22–29.

Harris, Nicola. "'The *Danse Macabre*': Hardy's *The Return of the Native*, Browning, Ruskin and the Grotesque." *Thomas Hardy Yrbk* 26 (1998), 24–29.

Harris, Nicola. "*The Return of the Native* and the Judgement of Paris: Power, Beauty or Knowledge." *Thomas Hardy Yrbk* 26 (1998), 22–23.

Hooker, Jeremy. *Writers in a Landscape*, 96–102.

Ireland, Ken. *The Sequential Dynamics of Narrative*, 236–37.

Irwin, Michael. "From Fascination to Listlessness: Hardy's Depiction of Love," in Charles P. C. Pettit, ed., *Reading Thomas Hardy*, 124–26.

Irwin, Michael. *Reading Hardy's Landscapes*, 28–30, 32–35, 44–50.

Jackson-Houlston, C. M. *Ballads, Songs and Snatches*, 155–57.

Jann, Rosemary. "Hardy's Rustics and the Construction of Class." *Victorian Lit and Culture* 28 (2000), 420–21.

Kozubska, Ewa. "The Idea of the Eternal Return in Hardy's Novels." *Folia Litteraria Anglica* (Lodz) 1 (1997), 88–92.

Lanning, George. "Thomas Hardy and the Bang-Up Locals." *Thomas Hardy J* 16:2 (2000), 54–58.

Law, Jules David. "Sleeping Figures: Hardy, History, and the Gendered Body." *ELH* 65 (1998), 232–37.

Lock, Charles. "Hardy and the Railway." *Essays in Criticism* 50 (2000), 54–56.

Lothe, Jakob. "Variants on Genre: *The Return of the Native, The Mayor of Casterbridge, The Hand of Ethelberta*," in Dale Kramer, ed., *The Cambridge Companion to Thomas Hardy*, 116–19.

McKee, Patricia. *Public and Private*, 186–218.

Malton, Sara. "'The Woman Shall Bear Her Iniquity': Death as Social Discipline in Thomas Hardy's *The Return of the Native*." *Stud in the Novel* 32 (2000), 147–63.

O'Hara, Patricia. "Narrating the Native: Victorian Anthropology and Hardy's *The Return of the Native*." *Nineteenth-Cent Contexts* 20 (1997), 147–63.

Paganelli, Eloisa. "The Promethean Rebellion in Thomas Hardy's *The Return of the Native*." *Res Publica Litterarum* 18 (1995), 195–200.

Schweik, Robert. "The Influence of Religion, Science, and Philosophy on Hardy's Writings," in Dale Kramer, ed., *The Cambridge Companion to Thomas Hardy*, 61–63.

Simons, Mark. "Hardy's Stereographic Technique." *Thomas Hardy J* 13:3 (1997), 91–93.

Sprechman, Ellen Lew. *Seeing Women as Men*, 41–57.

Swann, Charles. "A Hardy Debt to Hawthorne: *The Blithedale Romance* and *The Return of the Native*." *ANQ* 12:4 (1999), 13–17.

Tiefer, Hillary. "Clym Yeobright: Hardy's Comtean Hero." *Thomas Hardy J* 16:2 (2000), 43–51.

Turner, Paul. *The Life of Thomas Hardy*, 57–65.

Tess of the d'Urbervilles, 1891

Allingham, Philip V. "The Original Illustrations for Hardy's *Tess of the d'Urbervilles*: Drawn by Daniel A. Wehrschmidt, Ernest Borough-Johnson, and Joseph Syddall for the *Graphic* (1891)." *Thomas Hardy Yrbk* 24 (1998), 3–19.

Axelrod, Mark. *The Poetics of Novels*, 109–39.

Barrell, John. "Geographies of Hardy's Wessex," in K. D. M. Snell, ed., *The Regional Novel*, 107–18.

Beer, Gillian. *Darwin's Plots*, 199–200, 239–41.

Beliveau, Sara. "Rethinking English Naturalism: Feminine Decadence, Hardy's *Tess* and the French Context." *Excavatio* 11 (1998), 108–18.

Bloom, Harold, ed. *Thomas Hardy's Tess of the d'Urbervilles*, 10–75.

Butler, Lance St. John. *Registering the Difference*, 180–85.

Cho, Ailee. "The Change of Rural Community and Women in *The Return of the Native, The Woodlanders*, and *Tess of the d'Urbervilles*." *J of Engl Lang and Lit* 43:1 (1997), 51–68.

Craig, Randall. *Promising Language*, 105–7.

Daleski, H. M. *Thomas Hardy and Paradoxes of Love*, 151–79.

Daniel, Clay. "Orpheus, Eurydice and *Tess of the d'Urbervilles*." *Thomas Hardy J* 16:1 (2000), 63–68. (Also in *Thomas Hardy Yrbk* 27 [1998], 3–13.)

Davis, William A., Jr. "The Rape of Tess: Hardy, English Law, and the Case for Sexual Assault." *Nineteenth-Cent Lit* 52 (1997), 221–31.

Elbert, Monika. "Malinowski's Reading List: *Tess* as Field Guide to Woman." *Colby Q* 35 (1999), 49–65.

Ferguson, Susan L. "Drawing Fictional Lines: Dialect and Narrative in the Victorian Novel." *Style* 32:1 (1998), 1–17.

Fierz, Charles L. "Polanski Misses: A Critical Essay Concerning Polanski's Reading of Hardy's *Tess*." *Lit/Film Q* 27 (1999), 103–8.

Gallagher, Catherine. "*Tess of the d'Urbervilles*: Hardy's Anthropology of the Novel," in John Paul Riquelme, ed., *"Tess of the d'Urbervilles,"* 422–40.

Gaye, Mamadou. "Rural Imagination and Intellectual Desires in Thomas Hardy's Wessex Novels." *Bridges* (Dakar) 8 (1997–1998), 128–30.

Gaye, Mamadou. "Victime et coupable: *Tess of the d'Urbervilles*." *Recherches Anglaises et Nord-Américaines* 33 (2000), 55–70.

Gilchrist, Marianne McLeod. "Body and Soul, Love and Murder in *Tess of the d'Urbervilles*." *Thomas Hardy Yrbk* 28 (2000), 52–66.

Gossin, Pamela. "'All Danaë to the Stars': Nineteenth-Century Representations of Women in the Cosmos." *Victorian Stud* 40:1 (1996), 89–90.

Gribble, Jennifer. "Postmodern Tess: Recent Readings of *Tess of the d'Urbervilles*." *Sydney Stud in Engl* 25 (1999), 83–98.

Gussow, Adam. "Dreaming Holmberry-Lipped Tess: Aboriginal Reverie and Spectatorial Desire in *Tess of the d'Urbervilles*." *Stud in the Novel* 32 (2000), 442–61.

Hardy, Barbara. *Thomas Hardy*, 43–56.

Harris, Nicola. "Hardy's *Tess of the d'Urbervilles* and Turbervile's *Booke of Hunting*: A Case of Intertextuality?" *Thomas Hardy Yrbk* 26 (1998), 53–68.

Harris, Nicola. "An Impure Woman: The Tragic Paradox and Tess as Totem." *Thomas Hardy Yrbk* 26 (1998), 18–20.

Harris, Nicola. "Sleep Walking and Wish Fulfilment: Sadger and Hardy." *Thomas Hardy Yrbk* 29 (2000), 14–37.

Harvey, A. D. "Tess and Thomas Hardy." *Thomas Hardy Yrbk* 29 (2000), 41–46.

Heinrich, Hans. *Zur Geschichte des 'Libertin,'* 221–26.

Hennelly, Mark M., Jr. "The 'Original Tess': Pre-Texts—Tess, Fess, Tesserae, Carnivalesque." *Thomas Hardy Yrbk* 25 (1998), 26–59.

Ireland, Ken. *The Sequential Dynamics of Narrative*, 237–38.

Irwin, Michael. "From Fascination to Listlessness: Hardy's Depiction of Love," in Charles P. C. Pettit, ed., *Reading Thomas Hardy*, 130–32.

Irwin, Michael. *Reading Hardy's Landscapes*, 30–35, 45–50, 80–85, 125–33.

Jackson-Houlston, C. M. *Ballads, Songs and Snatches*, 164–66.

Kozubska, Ewa. "The Idea of the Eternal Return in Hardy's Novels." *Folia Litteraria Anglica* (Lodz) 1 (1997), 89–97.

Kurjiaka, Susan K. H. "Myths and Metaphors of Women's and Workers' Lives in Three Hardy Novels." *Mount Olive R* 7 (1993–1994), 86–91.

Larson, Jil. *Ethics and Narrative in the English Novel*, 82–86.

Law, Jules. "A 'Passing Corporeal Blight': Political Bodies in *Tess of the D'Urbervilles.*" *Victorian Stud* 40:2 (1997), 245–68.

Law, Jules David. "Sleeping Figures: Hardy, History, and the Gendered Body." *ELH* 65 (1998), 244–54.

Lloyd, Tom. *Crises of Realism*, 141–55.

Lock, Charles. "Hardy and the Railway." *Essays in Criticism* 50 (2000), 50–54.

Mallett, Phillip. "Hardy and Time," in Charles P. C. Pettit, ed., *Reading Thomas Hardy*, 163–69.

Mayer, Jed. "Germinating Memory: Hardy and Evolutionary Biology." *Victorian R* 26:1 (2000), 85–95.

Mitchell, Giles. "Narcissism and Death: A Study of Angel Clare in Hardy's *Tess of the d'Urbervilles.*" *Panjab Univ Res Bull* 20:2 (1989), 3–15.

Musselwhite, D. E. "Tess of the d'Urbervilles: 'A becoming woman' *or* Deleuze and Guattari Go to Wessex." *Textual Practice* 14 (2000), 499–516.

Nash, Tom. "*Tess of the d'Urbervilles*: The Symbolic Use of Folklore." *Engl Lang Notes* 35:4 (1998), 38–46.

Nelson, Ronald J. "Stirring Up Trouble: The Sign Painter in Hardy's *Tess of the d'Urbervilles.*" *Thomas Hardy J* 15:2 (1999), 60–69.

Nigro, August. *The Net of Nemesis*, 111–20.

O'Toole, Tess. *Genealogy and Fiction in Hardy*, 73–91, 107–9, 112–14.

Padian, Kevin. "'A Daughter of the Soil': Themes of Deep Time and Evolution in Thomas Hardy's *Tess of the d'Urbervilles.*" *Thomas Hardy J* 13:3 (1997), 65–77.

Radford, Andrew. "J. G. Frazer and a Strange Harvest Custom in Hardy's *Tess.*" *Notes and Queries* 48 (2001), 164–65.

Reid, Fred. "Thomas Hardy, Humanism and History." *Thomas Hardy Yrbk* 27 (1998), 32–39.

Riquelme, John Paul. "Echoic Language, Uncertainty, and Freedom in *Tess of the d'Urbervilles,*" in Riquelme, ed., *"Tess of the d'Urbervilles,"* 506–20.

Rivinus, Timothy M. "Tragedy of the Commonplace: The Impact of Addiction on Families in the Fiction of Thomas Hardy." *Lit and Medicine* 11 (1992), 237–65.

Roberts, Nancy. *Schools of Sympathy*, 89–106.

Rogers, Shannon L. "Medievalism in the Last Novels of Thomas Hardy: New Wine in Old Bottles." *Engl Lit in Transition* 42 (1999), 302–8.

Rooney, Ellen. "Tess and the Subject of Sexual Violence: Reading, Rape, Seduction," in John Paul Riquelme, ed., *"Tess of the d'Urbervilles,"* 462–83.

Schweik, Robert. "The Influence of Religion, Science, and Philosophy on Hardy's Writings," in Dale Kramer, ed., *The Cambridge Companion to Thomas Hardy*, 56–58.

Schweik, Robert. "Less than Faithfully Presented: Fictions in Modern Commentaries on Hardy's *Tess of the d'Urbervilles,*" in Charles P. C. Pettit, ed., *Reading Thomas Hardy*, 33–53.

Shires, Linda M. "The Radical Aesthetic of *Tess of the d'Urbervilles*," in Dale Kramer, ed., *The Cambridge Companion to Thomas Hardy*, 145–61.

Shumaker, Jeanette. "Gaskell's *Ruth* and Hardy's *Tess* as Novels of Free Union." *Dickens Stud Annual* 28 (1999), 151–68.

Shuttleworth, Sally. "'The Malady of Thought': Embodied Memory in Victorian Psychology and the Novel." *Australasian Victorian Stud J* 2 (1996), 9–11.

Sprechman, Ellen Lew. *Seeing Women as Men*, 77–100.

Sternlieb, Lisa. "'Three Leahs to Get One Rachel': Redundant Women in *Tess of the d'Urbervilles*." *Dickens Stud Annual* 29 (2000), 351–63.

Stewart, Garrett. "'Driven Well Home to the Reader's Heart': *Tess*'s Implicated Audience," in John Paul Riquelme, ed., *"Tess of the d'Urbervilles,"* 537–51.

Stoddard, Eve W. "A Genealogy of Ruths: From Alien Harvester to Fallen Woman in Nineteenth-Century England," in Marilyn Demarest Button and Toni Reed, eds., *The Foreign Woman in British Literature*, 61–64.

Tóth, Tibor. "'Did They Sacrifice to God Here?' 'No, I Believe to the Sun' (Thomas Hardy: *Tess of the d'Urbervilles*)." *B.A.S.: Brit and Am Stud* 4:1 (1999), 15–22.

Turner, Paul. *The Life of Thomas Hardy*, 123–33.

Wicke, Jennifer. "The Same and the Different: Standards and Standardization in Thomas Hardy's *Tess of the d'Urbervilles*," in John Paul Riquelme, ed., *"Tess of the d'Urbervilles,"* 571–89.

Widdowson, Peter. *On Thomas Hardy*, 115–33.

Williams, Melanie. "'Sensitive as Gossamer': Law and the Sexual Encounter in *Tess of the d'Urbervilles*." *Thomas Hardy J* 17:1 (2001), 54–60.

The Trumpet-Major, 1880

Irwin, Michael. *Reading Hardy's Landscapes*, 30–35, 50–52, 67–71.

Lanning, George. "Thomas Hardy and the Bang-Up Locals." *Thomas Hardy J* 16:2 (2000), 54–58.

Peck, John. *War, the Army and Victorian Literature*, 113–16.

Turner, Paul. *The Life of Thomas Hardy*, 66–72.

Two on a Tower, 1882

Barloon, Jim. "Star-Crossed Love: The Gravity of Science in Hardy's *Two on a Tower*." *Victorian Newsl* 94 (1998), 27–31.

Dutta, Shanta. *Ambivalence in Hardy*, 57–71.

Dutta, Shanta. "A Possible Shakespearean Allusion in *Two on a Tower*." *Thomas Hardy J* 13:2 (1997), 78–79.

Fjågesund, Peter. "Thomas Hardy's *Two on a Tower*: The Failure of a Symbol." *Thomas Hardy J* 14:1 (1998), 85–93.

Gossin, Pamela. "'All Danaë to the Stars': Nineteenth-Century Representations of Women in the Cosmos." *Victorian Stud* 40:1 (1996), 86–89.

Mallett, Phillip. "Hardy and Time," in Charles P. C. Pettit, ed., *Reading Thomas Hardy*, 158–60.

Sumner, Rosemary. *A Route to Modernism*, 21–33.

Thomas, Jane. *Thomas Hardy, Femininity and Dissent*, 113–30.

Turner, Paul. *The Life of Thomas Hardy*, 82–90.

Under the Greenwood Tree, 1872

Albertson, Kathy. "Duplicity in Hardy's Parson Maybold." *CEA Critic* 59:2 (1997), 33–40.

Assmann, Winnifred J. "A Pre-Raphaelite Beauty in 'A Rural Painting of the Dutch School': The Characterization of Fancy Day." *Thomas Hardy Yrbk* 25 (1998), 3–9.

Boumelha, Penny. "The Patriarchy of Class: *Under the Greenwood Tree, Far from the Madding Crowd, The Woodlanders*," in Dale Kramer, ed., *The Cambridge Companion to Thomas Hardy*, 130–37.

Bulaila, A. Aziz M. "Hardy's *Under the Greenwood Tree* and Lawrence's *The White Peacock*: Comparison and Influence." *Thomas Hardy Yrbk* 25 (1998), 11–18.

Byerly, Alison. *Realism, Representation, and the Arts*, 171–74.

Hardy, Barbara. *Thomas Hardy*, 17–21.

Irwin, Michael. *Reading Hardy's Landscapes*, 17–19.

Jann, Rosemary. "Hardy's Rustics and the Construction of Class." *Victorian Lit and Culture* 28 (2000), 416–17.

Mossman, Mark. "Unique Individualities, United Communities: *Under the Greenwood Tree* as Hardy's Workable World." *Thomas Hardy Yrbk* 25 (1998), 20–25.

Rogers, Shannon L. "Medievalism in the Last Novels of Thomas Hardy: New Wine in Old Bottles." *Engl Lit in Transition* 42 (1999), 299–300.

Turner, Paul. *The Life of Thomas Hardy*, 27–33.

The Well-Beloved, 1892

Claggett, Shalyn. "'One Shape of Many Names': A Note on Hardy's Epigraph to *The Well-Beloved*." *Thomas Hardy Yrbk* 29 (2000), 47–49.

Gilmartin, Sophie. *Ancestry and Narrative*, 200–202, 229–45.

Hardy, Barbara. *Thomas Hardy*, 15–17.

Harris, Nicola. "The Feminine Text: Reading and Knowing Hardy's Women." *Thomas Hardy Yrbk* 26 (1998), 33–34.

Irwin, Michael. *Reading Hardy's Landscapes*, 102–4, 107–10, 131–35.

Irwin, Michael. "Readings of Realism," in Philip Davis, ed., *Real Voices*, 220–23.

Marks, John. "The Pursuit of the Well-Beloved." *Thomas Hardy J* 13:2 (1997), 56–59.

O'Toole, Tess. *Genealogy and Fiction in Hardy*, 48–55, 132–39, 150–54.

Radford, Andrew. "A 'Survival' Explained in Hardy's *The Well-Beloved*." *Notes and Queries* 46 (1999), 480–81.

Richardson, Angelique. "'Some Science underlies all Art': The Dramatization of Sexual Selection and Racial Biology in Thomas Hardy's *A Pair of Blue Eyes* and *The Well-Beloved*." *J of Victorian Culture* 3 (1998), 321–30.

Sumner, Rosemary. *A Route to Modernism*, 72–79, 81–92.

Thomas, Jane. *Thomas Hardy, Femininity and Dissent*, 131–46.

Turner, Paul. *The Life of Thomas Hardy*, 152–58.

The Woodlanders, 1887

Bate, Jonathan. "Culture and Environment: From Austen to Hardy." *New Liter Hist* 30 (1999), 552–56.

Boumelha, Penny. "The Patriarchy of Class: *Under the Greenwood Tree, Far from the Madding Crowd, The Woodlanders,*" in Dale Kramer, ed., *The Cambridge Companion to Thomas Hardy,* 130–35, 140–42.

Cho, Ailee. "The Change of Rural Community and Women in *The Return of the Native, The Woodlanders,* and *Tess of the d'Urbervilles.*" *J of Engl Lang and Lit* 43:1 (1997), 51–68.

Daleski, H. M. *Thomas Hardy and Paradoxes of Love,* 129–50.

Dutta, Shanta. *Ambivalence in Hardy,* 73–91.

Gaye, Mamadou. "Rural Imagination and Intellectual Desires in Thomas Hardy's Wessex Novels." *Bridges* (Dakar) 8 (1997–1998), 125–28.

Harris, Nicola. "'A Pair of Jaundiced Eyes': *The Woodlanders* (1887) and the Blighted Tree of Knowledge." *Thomas Hardy Yrbk* 26 (1998), 5–14.

Irwin, Michael. *Reading Hardy's Landscapes,* 99–104.

Jann, Rosemary. "Hardy's Rustics and the Construction of Class." *Victorian Lit and Culture* 28 (2000), 421–23.

O'Toole, Tess. *Genealogy and Fiction in Hardy,* 97–100.

Radford, Andrew. "Hardy's *The Woodlanders.*" *Explicator* 58:3 (2000), 146–48.

Radford, Andrew. "The Unmanned Fertility Figure in Hardy's *The Woodlanders* (1887)." *Victorian Newsl* 99 (2001), 24–31.

Simons, Mark. "Hardy's Stereographic Technique." *Thomas Hardy J* 13:3 (1997), 89–91.

Sumner, Rosemary. *A Route to Modernism,* 40–43, 98–100.

Turner, Paul. *The Life of Thomas Hardy,* 100–108.

MARGARET HARKNESS

Captain Lobe, 1889

McLaughlin, Joseph. *Writing the Urban Jungle,* 4–14.

Schäffner, Raimund. *Anarchismus und Literatur in England,* 244–47.

A City Girl, 1887

Ledger, Sally. *The New Woman,* 43–50.

Out of Work, 1888

Schäffner, Raimund. *Anarchismus und Literatur in England,* 243–44.

BEATRICE HARRADEN

Ships that Pass in the Night, 1893

Willis, Chris. "'Heaven defend me from political or highly-educated women!': Packaging the New Woman for Mass Consumption," in Angelique Richardson and Chris Willis, eds., *The New Woman in Fiction and in Fact,* 55–57.

FRANK HARRIS

The Bomb, 1908
  Schäffner, Raimund. *Anarchismus und Literatur in England*, 473–85.

ROBERT HARRIS

Fatherland, 1992
  Fassbender, Bardo. "A Novel, Germany's Past, and the Dilemmas of Civilised Germans." *Contemp R* 265 (1994), 236–46.
  Parry, Ann. "Idioms for the Unrepresentable: Post-War Fiction and the Shoah." *J of European Stud* 27 (1997), 422–24.
  Rohmann, Gerd. "Images of Germany in Post-War English Fiction," in C. C. Barfoot, ed., *Beyond Pug's Tour*, 418–21.
  Schnöink-Juppe, Marion. "The Image of Nazi Germany in British Popular Literature," in C. C. Barfoot, ed., *Beyond Pug's Tour*, 405–11.

JOSEPHINE HART

Damage, 1991
  Mellard, James M. "Lacan and the New Lacanians: Josephine Hart's *Damage*, Lacanian Tragedy, and the Ethics of *Jouissance*." *PMLA* 113 (1998), 395–406.

L. P. HARTLEY

Facial Justice, 1960
  Ascari, Maurizio. "In Defence of Injustice: Dystopian Tensions in L. P. Hartley's *Facial Injustice*," in Vita Fortunati and Paola Spinozzi, eds., *Vite di utopia*, 267–76.
The Go-Between, 1953
  Craik, Roger. "Wanderers in the Zodiac: George Barker and L. P. Hartley." *Notes on Contemp Lit* 26:4 (1996), 8.
  Weatherhead, A. K. *Upstairs*, 134–36.
  York, R. A. *The Rules of Time*, 142–56.

JOHN MACDOUGALL HAY

Gillespie, 1914
  Smith, Iain Crichton. "Thoughts on J. MacDougall Hay's *Gillespie*." *Stud in Scottish Lit* 31 (1999), 1–13.
  Walker, Marshall. *Scottish Literature since 1707*, 220–23.

MARY HAYS

The Memoirs of Emma Courtney, 1796
  Bellamy, Liz. *Commerce, Morality and the Eighteenth-Century Novel*, 170–75.

Bour, Isabelle. "Sensibilité et répétition dans les romans révolution-
naires de Mary Hays." *Etudes Anglaises* 51 (1998), 143–54.
Guest, Harriet. *Small Change*, 297–304.
Jacobus, Mary. *Psychoanalysis and the Scene of Reading*, 203–34.
Skinner, Gillian. *Sensibility and Economics in the Novel*, 169–77.
Watson, Nicola J. *Revolution and the Form of the British Novel*, 44–49.
Wordsworth, Jonathan. *The Bright Work Grows*, 108–14.

The Victim of Prejudice, 1799

Bannet, Eve Tavor. *The Domestic Revolution*, 185–88.
Bour, Isabelle. "Sensibilité et répétition dans les romans révolution-
naires de Mary Hays." *Etudes Anglaises* 51 (1998), 143–54.
Hoagwood, Terence Allan. *Politics, Philosophy, and the Production*,
122–39.
Jones, Vivien. "Placing Jemima: Women Writers of the 1790s and the
Eighteenth-Century Prostitution Narrative." *Women's Writing* 4
(1997), 201–20.
Sherman, Sandra. "The Feminization of 'Reason' in Hays's *The Victim
of Prejudice*." *Centennial R* 41:1 (1997), 143–73.
Ty, Eleanor. "The Imprisoned Female Body in Mary Hays's *The
Victim of Prejudice*," in Linda Lang-Peralta, ed., *Women,
Revolution, and the Novels of the 1790s*, 133–50.
Watson, Nicola J. *Revolution and the Form of the British Novel*, 49–51.

SIAN HAYTON

Cells of Knowledge, 1989

Burgess, Moira. "The Modern Historical Tradition," in Douglas
Gifford and Dorothy McMillan, eds., *A History*, 464–65.
Gifford, Douglas. "Contemporary Fiction II: Seven Writers in
Scotland," in Douglas Gifford and Dorothy McMillan, eds., *A
History*, 612–15.

Hidden Daughters, 1992

Gifford, Douglas. "Contemporary Fiction II: Seven Writers in
Scotland," in Douglas Gifford and Dorothy McMillan, eds., *A
History*, 612–15.

The Last Flight, 1993

Gifford, Douglas. "Contemporary Fiction II: Seven Writers in Scotland,"
in Douglas Gifford and Dorothy McMillan, eds., *A History*, 615.

W. STEPHENS HAYWARD

The Experiences of a Lady Detective, 1864
Klein, Kathleen Gregory. *The Woman Detective*, 24–29.

ELIZA HAYWOOD

The Adventures of Eovaai, 1736
Ballaster, Ros. "A Gender of Opposition: Eliza Haywood's Scandal

Fiction," in Kirsten T. Saxton and Rebecca P. Bocchicchio, eds., *The Passionate Fictions*, 154–64.

Kubek, Elizabeth. "The Key to Stowe: Toward a Patriot Whig Reading of Eliza Haywood's *Eovaai*," in Chris Mounsey, ed., *Presenting Gender*, 225–51.

Bath-Intrigues, 1724

Hicks, Stephen J. "Eliza Haywood's Letter Technique in Three Early Novels (1721–27)." *Papers on Lang and Lit* 34 (1998), 420–36.

Betsy Thoughtless, 1751

Austin, Andrea. "Shooting Blanks: Potency, Parody, and Eliza Haywood's *The History of Miss Betsy Thoughtless*," in Kirsten T. Saxton and Rebecca P. Bocchicchio, eds., *The Passionate Fictions*, 259–80.

Ballaster, Ros. "Women and the Rise of the Novel: Sexual Prescripts," in Vivien Jones, ed., *Women and Literature in Britain*, 208–10.

Bannet, Eve Tavor. *The Domestic Revolution*, 89–91.

Barney, Richard A. *Plots of Enlightenment*, 283–90, 294–300.

Doody, Margaret Anne. "Deserts, Ruins and Troubled Waters: Female Dreams in Fiction and the Development of the Gothic Novel," in Richard Kroll, ed., *The English Novel, Volume II*, 61–62.

Ellis, Lorna. *Appearing to Diminish*, 71–87.

Flint, Christopher. *Family Fictions*, 207–48.

Hollis, Karen. "Eliza Haywood and the Gender of Print." *Eighteenth Cent* 38 (1997), 49–51, 60.

Ingrassia, Catherine. *Authorship, Commerce, and Gender*, 128–36.

Lynch, Deidre Shauna. *The Economy of Character*, 100–102.

Macey, J. David, Jr. "'Where the World May Ne'er Invade'?: Green Retreats and Garden Theatre in *La Princesse de Clèves*, *The History of Miss Betsy Thoughtless*, and *Cecilia*." *Eighteenth-Cent Fiction* 12 (1999), 81–87.

Oakleaf, David. "'Shady bowers! and purling streams!—Heavens, how insipid!': Eliza Haywood's Artful Pastoral," in Kirsten T. Saxton and Rebecca P. Bocchicchio, eds., *The Passionate Fictions*, 285–93.

Richetti, John. *The English Novel in History*, 200–205.

Richetti, John. "Histories by Eliza Haywood and Henry Fielding: Imitation and Adaptation," in Kirsten T. Saxton and Rebecca P. Bocchicchio, eds., *The Passionate Fictions*, 249–53.

Skinner, Gillian. "Women's Status as Legal and Civic Subjects: 'A Worse Condition Than Slavery Itself,'" in Vivien Jones, ed., *Women and Literature in Britain*, 96–101.

The British Recluse, 1722

Bocchicchio, Rebecca P. "'Blushing, Trembling, and Incapable of Defense': The Hysterics of *The British Recluse*," in Kirsten T. Saxton and Rebecca P. Bocchicchio, eds., *The Passionate Fictions*, 103–12.

The City Jilt, 1726

Backscheider, Paula R. "The Novel's Gendered Space," in Backscheider, ed., *Revising Women*, 25–27.

Ingrassia, Catherine. *Authorship, Commerce, and Gender*, 89–95.

Saxton, Kirsten T. "Telling Tales: Eliza Haywood and the Crimes of

Seduction in *The City Jilt, or, the Alderman turn'd Beau*," in Kirsten T. Saxton and Rebecca P. Bocchicchio, eds., *The Passionate Fictions*, 115–38.

Fantomina, 1724

Croskery, Margaret Case. "Masquing Desire: The Politics of Passion in Eliza Haywood's *Fantomina*," in Kirsten T. Saxton and Rebecca P. Bocchicchio, eds., *The Passionate Fictions*, 69–92.

Ellis, Lorna. *Appearing to Diminish*, 57–59.

Richetti, John. *The English Novel in History*, 84–87.

Tauchert, Ashley. "Woman in a Maze: *Fantomina*, Masquerade and Female Embodiment." *Women's Writing* 7 (2000), 469–83.

Warner, William B. "The Elevation of the Novel in England: Hegemony and Literary History," in Richard Kroll, ed., *The English Novel, Volume I*, 57–59.

The Fruitless Enquiry, 1727

Benedict, Barbara M. "The Curious Genre: Female Inquiry in Amatory Fiction." *Stud in the Novel* 30 (1998), 203–4.

Snader, Joe. *Caught Between Worlds*, 158–64.

Idalia, 1723

Hammond, Brean S. *Professional Imaginative Writing*, 225–27.

Richetti, John. *The English Novel in History*, 45–48.

Lasselia; or, The Self-Abandon'd, 1723

Oakleaf, David. "The Eloquence of Blood in Eliza Haywood's *Lasselia*." *Stud in Engl Lit, 1500–1900* 39 (1999), 483–95.

Letters from a Lady of Quality to a Chevalier, 1721

Hicks, Stephen J. "Eliza Haywood's Letter Technique in Three Early Novels (1721–27)." *Papers on Lang and Lit* 34 (1998), 420–36.

Love in Excess, 1719–1720

Benedict, Barbara M. *Curiosity*, 139–41.

Benedict, Barbara M. "The Curious Genre: Female Inquiry in Amatory Fiction." *Stud in the Novel* 30 (1998), 203–6.

Bowers, Toni. "Collusive Resistance: Sexual Agency and Partisan Politics in *Love in Excess*," in Kirsten T. Saxton and Rebecca P. Bocchicchio, eds., *The Passionate Fictions*, 48–64.

Fendler, Susanne. "Intertwining Literary Histories: Women's Contribution to the Rise of the Novel," in Fendler, ed., *Feminist Contributions*, 42–49.

King, Kathryn R. "Spying upon the Conjurer: Haywood, Curiosity, and 'The Novel' in the 1720s." *Stud in the Novel* 30 (1998), 178–90.

Prescott, Sarah. "The Debt to Pleasure: Eliza Haywood's *Love in Excess* and Women's Fiction of the 1720s." *Women's Writing* 7 (2000), 427–42.

Richetti, John. *The English Novel in History*, 38–45.

Richetti, John. "Popular Narrative in the Early Eighteenth Century: Formats and Formulas," in Richard Kroll, ed., *The English Novel, Volume I*, 83–85.

Starr, G. Gabrielle. "Rereading Prose Fiction: Lyric Convention in Aphra Behn and Eliza Haywood." *Eighteenth-Cent Fiction* 12 (1999), 13–18.

The Mercenary Lover: or, The Unfortunate Heiress, 1726

    Ingrassia, Catherine. *Authorship, Commerce, and Gender*, 95–102.

    Richetti, John. "Popular Narrative in the Early Eighteenth Century: Formats and Formulas," in Richard Kroll, ed., *The English Novel, Volume I*, 86–87.

Philadore and Placentia, 1727

    Ellis, Lorna. *Appearing to Diminish*, 53–56.

    Hicks, Stephen J. "Eliza Haywood's Letter Technique in Three Early Novels (1721–27)." *Papers on Lang and Lit* 34 (1998), 420–36.

    Parker, Todd C. *Sexing the Text*, 120–34.

    Snader, Joe. *Caught Between Worlds*, 158–61, 163–68.

    Thorn, Jennifer. "'A Race of Angels': Castration and Exoticism in Three Exotic Tales by Eliza Haywood," in Kirsten T. Saxton and Rebecca P. Bocchicchio, eds., *The Passionate Fictions*, 183–89.

The Rash Resolve, 1724

    Swan, Beth. *Fictions of Law*, 75–79.

A Spy upon the Conjuror, 1724

    Benedict, Barbara M. *Curiosity*, 146–49.

The Tea-Table, 1725

    Benedict, Barbara M. *Curiosity*, 144–46.

RICHARD HEAD

The English Rogue, 1665

    Wall, Cynthia. *The Literary and Cultural Spaces*, 134–37.

MARY HEARNE

The Female Deserters, 1719

    Turley, Hans. "The Anomalous Fiction of Mary Hearne." *Stud in the Novel* 30 (1998), 139–48.

The Lovers Week, 1718

    Turley, Hans. "The Anomalous Fiction of Mary Hearne." *Stud in the Novel* 30 (1998), 139–48.

ELIZABETH HELME

Louisa; or, the Cottage on the Moor, 1787

    Shaffer, Julie. "Familial Love, Incest, and Female Desire in Late Eighteenth- and Early Nineteenth-Century British Women's Novels." *Criticism* 41 (1999), 69–87.

GEORGE A. HENTY

Beric the Briton, 1892

    Hoberman, Ruth. *Gendering Classicism*, 104–11.

By Sheer Pluck, 1884
> Logan, Mawuena Kossi. *Narrating Africa*, 86–94.

The Dash for Khartoum, 1891
> Logan, Mawuena Kossi. *Narrating Africa*, 95–103.

With Buller in Natal, or a Born Leader, 1901
> Logan, Mawuena Kossi. *Narrating Africa*, 122–29.

With Kitchener in the Soudan, 1903
> Logan, Mawuena Kossi. *Narrating Africa*, 103–12.

With Roberts to Pretoria, 1902
> Logan, Mawuena Kossi. *Narrating Africa*, 129–37.

The Young Colonists, 1885
> Logan, Mawuena. "Pushing the Imperial/Colonial Agenda: George A. Henty's *The Young Colonists*." *J of African Children's and Youth Lit* 6 (1994–1995), 29–42.
> Logan, Mawuena Kossi. *Narrating Africa*, 115–22.

HAROLD HESLOP

The Gate of a Strange Field, 1933
> Haywood, Ian. *Working-Class Fiction*, 43–45.

Last Cage Down, 1935
> Haywood, Ian. *Working-Class Fiction*, 58–60.

ROBERT HICHENS

The Green Carnation, 1894
> Cavaliero, Glen. *The Alchemy of Laughter*, 23–25.

The Paradine Case, 1933
> Turnbull, Malcolm J. *Victims or Villains*, 74–76.

AIDAN HIGGINS

Balcony of Europe, 1972
> Alexander, George. "Pull the Mandrake, Never Mind the Shrieks: Reading Aidan Higgins." *HEAT* 11 (1999), 152–68.
> O'Brien, George. "The Aesthetics of Exile," in Liam Harte and Michael Parker, eds., *Contemporary Irish Fiction*, 50–52.

Langrishe, Go Down, 1966
> Frehner, Ruth. *The Colonizers' Daughters*, 106–31.
> Kreilkamp, Vera. *The Anglo-Irish Novel*, 234–47.

SUSAN HILL

I'm the King of the Castle, 1971
> Morgado, Margarida. "The Season of Play: Constructions of the Child

in the English Novel," in Karín Lesnik-Oberstein, ed., *Children in Culture*, 223–25.

The Mist in the Mirror, 1992

Théry, Michèle. "Fantômes du roman contemporain: *The Mist in the Mirror* de Susan Hill." *Etudes Anglaises* 50 (1997), 206–17.

The Woman in Black, 1983

Cox, Donna. "'I Have No Story to Tell!': Maternal Rage in Susan Hill's *The Woman in Black*." *Intertexts* 4:1 (2000), 74–88.

BARRY HINES

A Kestrel for a Knave, 1968

Haywood, Ian. *Working-Class Fiction*, 132–35.

JOSEPH HOCKING

The Madness of David Baring, 1900

Schäffner, Raimund. *Anarchismus und Literatur in England*, 495–504.

SALOME HOCKING

Belinda the Backward, 1905

Schäffner, Raimund. *Anarchismus und Literatur in England*, 504–9.

WILLIAM HOPE HODGSON

The Night Land, 1912

Hurley, Kelly. "The Modernist Abominations of William Hope Hodgson," in Andrew Smith and Jeff Wallace, eds., *Gothic Modernisms*, 136–47.

DESMOND HOGAN

A Curious Street, 1984

Deane, Paul. "The Great Chain of Irish Being Reconsidered: Desmond Hogan's *A Curious Street*." *Notes on Mod Irish Lit* 6 (1994), 39–48.

A Farewell to Prague, 1995

Smyth, Gerry. *The Novel and the Nation*, 153–57.

JAMES HOGG

The Brownie of Bodsbeck, 1818

de Groot, H. B. "The Historicity of *The Brownie of Bodsbeck*." *Stud in Hogg and His World* 6 (1995), 1–11.

Häcker, Martina. "Literary Dialects and Communication in *The Tale of Old Mortality* and *The Brownie of Bodsbeck.*" *Stud in Hogg and His World* 8 (1997), 1–11.

The Private Memoirs and Confessions of a Justified Sinner, 1824

Burwick, Frederick. "'Transcendental Buffoonery' and the Bifurcated Novel," in Raymond A. Prier and Gerald Gillespie, eds., *Narrative Ironies,* 66–71.

Heinritz, Reinhard, and Silvia Mergenthal. "Hogg, Hoffmann, and Their Diabolical Elixirs." *Stud in Hogg and His World* 7 (1996), 47–58.

McCulloch, Margery Palmer. "Hogg's *Justified Sinner* and Robin Jenkins's *Just Duffy.*" *Stud in Hogg and His World* 6 (1995), 12–21.

Mack, Douglas S. "The Body in the Opened Grave: Robert Burns and Robert Wringhim." *Stud in Hogg and His World* 7 (1996), 70–79.

Oost, Regina B. "'False Friends, Squeamish Readers, and Foolish Critics': The Subtext of Authorship in Hogg's *Justified Sinner.*" *Stud in Scottish Lit* 31 (1999), 86–106.

Walker, Marshall. *Scottish Literature since 1707,* 144–53.

Watson, Nicola J. *Revolution and the Form of the British Novel,* 170–76.

The Three Perils of Woman, 1823

Groves, David. "'One Touch of Nature': Allusions to *Troilus and Cressida* in James Hogg's *Three Perils of Woman.*" *Notes and Queries* 45 (1998), 203–5.

Mack, Douglas S. "Culloden and After: Scottish Jacobite Novels." *Eighteenth-Cent Life* 20:3 (1996), 92–106.

THOMAS HOLCROFT

The Adventures of Hugh Trevor, 1797

London, April. *Women and Property,* 165–67.

Schäffner, Raimund. *Anarchismus und Literatur in England,* 80–89.

Anna St. Ives, 1792

Binhammer, Katherine. "The Political Novel and the Seduction Plot: Thomas Holcroft's *Anna St. Ives.*" *Eighteenth-Cent Fiction* 11 (1999), 205–22.

London, April. *Women and Property,* 155–65.

Schäffner, Raimund. *Anarchismus und Literatur in England,* 80–89.

Young, Arlene. *Culture, Class and Gender,* 32–36.

The Memoirs of Bryan Perdue, 1805

Schäffner, Raimund. *Anarchismus und Literatur in England,* 80–89.

WINIFRED HOLTBY

The Crowded Street, 1924

Wallace, Diana. *Sisters and Rivals in British Women's Fiction,* 132–37.

South Riding, 1936

Shaw, Marion. "The Making of a Middle-Brow Success: Winifred Holtby's *South Riding,*" in Judy Simons and Kate Fullbrook, eds., *Writing: A Woman's Business,* 31–46.

Trodd, Anthea. *Women's Writing in English*, 100–102.
Wallace, Diana. *Sisters and Rivals in British Women's Fiction*, 144–50.

MARGARET JANE HOOPER

The House of Raby: Or, Our Lady of Darkness, 1854
Mighall, Robert. *A Geography of Victorian Gothic Fiction*, 92–98.

ANTHONY HOPE

Mrs. Maxon Protests, 1911
Harris, Janice Hubbard. *Edwardian Stories of Divorce*, 132–35.
The Prisoner of Zenda, 1894
Nyman, Jopi. *Under English Eyes*, 41–59.

CHRISTOPHER HOPE

Darkest England, 1996
Reckwitz, Erhard. "Intertextuality: Between Continuity and Innovation," in Barbara Korte and Klaus Peter Müller, eds., *Unity in Diversity Revisited?*, 194–95.

EMMA E. HORNIBROOK

Transito: A Story of Brazil, 1887
Forman, Ross G. "When Britons Brave Brazil: British Imperialism and the Adventure Tale in Latin America." *Victorian Stud* 42:3 (1999/2000), 470–77.

WILLIAM HENRY HUDSON

Green Mansions, 1904
Glendening, John. "Darwinian Entanglement in Hudson's *Green Mansions*." *Engl Lit in Transition* 43 (2000), 259–76.
Reeve, N. H. "Feathered Women: W. H. Hudson's *Green Mansions*," in Richard Kerridge and Neil Sammells, eds., *Writing the Environment*, 134–44.
The Purple Land, 1904
Hampsten, Elizabeth. "Revisiting a Land That England Lost." *North Dakota Q* 61:2 (1993), 92–107.
Rosman, Silvia. "Of Travelers, Foreigners and Nomads: The Nation in Translation." *Latin Am Liter R* 26 (1998), 17–29.

RICHARD HUGHES

The Fox in the Attic, 1961
Caterson, Simon. "Literary Influence and the Superfluous Man: J. G.

Farrell, Richard Hughes, Joseph Conrad," in Ralph J. Crane, ed., *J. G. Farrell*, 36–47.

A High Wind in Jamaica, 1929

Dellarosa, Franca. "Subversive Form and Meaning in *A High Wind in Jamaica*." *Welsh Writing in Engl* 2 (1996), 49–61.

Morgado, Margarida. "The Season of Play: Constructions of the Child in the English Novel," in Karín Lesnik-Oberstein, ed., *Children in Culture*, 218–21.

THOMAS HUGHES

Tom Brown at Oxford, 1861

Dougill, John. *Oxford in English Literature*, 95–96, 123–24.

Tom Brown's School Days, 1857

Ang, Susan. *The Widening World of Children's Literature*, 84–88.

Hunt, Peter. *Children's Literature*, 223–25.

Logan, Mawuena Kossi. *Narrating Africa*, 36–42.

Stoneley, Peter. "Family Values and the 'Republic of Boys': Tom Brown and Others." *J of Victorian Culture* 3 (1998), 74–81.

E. M. HULL

The Sheik, 1919

Ayers, David. *English Literature of the 1920s*, 193–98.

Wintle, Sarah. "*The Sheik*: What Can Be Made of a Daydream." *Women: A Cultural R* 7 (1996), 291–302.

FERGUS W. HUME

The Mystery of a Hansom Cab, 1886

MacDonald, Janice. "Parody and Detective Fiction," in Jerome H. Delamater and Ruth Prigozy, eds., *Theory and Practice*, 68–70.

EMYR HUMPHREYS

A Toy Epic, 1958

Thomas, M. Wynn. "Emyr Humphreys: Regional Novelist?," in K. D. M. Snell, ed., *The Regional Novel*, 204–11.

VIOLET HUNT

The Doll: A Happy Story, 1911

Harris, Janice Hubbard. *Edwardian Stories of Divorce*, 140–43.

The Last Ditch, 1918

Trotter, David. "The Modernist Novel," in Michael Levenson, ed., *The Cambridge Companion to Modernism*, 95–96.

RACHEL HUNTER

Lady Maclairn, or The Victim of Villainy, 1806
  Grundy, Isobel. "Rachel Hunter and the Victims of Slavery." *Women's Writing* 1 (1994), 25–33.

ALDOUS HUXLEY

Ape and Essence, 1949
  Baker, James R. "Golding and Huxley: The Fables of Demonic Possession." *Twentieth Cent Lit* 46 (2000), 311–25.

Brave New World, 1932
  Ferns, Chris. *Narrating Utopia*, 109–21, 124–30.
  McGiveron, Rafeeq O. "Huxley's *Brave New World.*" *Explicator* 57:1 (1998), 27–29.
  Sexton, James. "*Brave New World*, the Feelies, and Elinor Glyn." *Engl Lang Notes* 35:1 (1997), 35–37.
  Sisk, David W. *Transformations of Language*, 7–38.
  Turney, Jon. *Frankenstein's Footsteps*, 111–17.

Crome Yellow, 1921
  Rosenbaum, S. P. *Aspects of Bloomsbury*, 51–54.

The Genius and the Goddess, 1955
  Fairservice, David. "*The Genius and the Goddess*: Lampedusa's *La sirena.*" *Spunti e Ricerche* 10 (1994), 93–99.

Island, 1962
  Ferns, Chris. *Narrating Utopia*, 163–74.
  Pordzik, Ralph. "Gelebte Zukunft: Aldous Huxley, Marge Piercy und die Ambiguisierung der positiven Utopie, 1960–1980." *Anglistik* 11:2 (2000), 74–89.

Point Counter Point, 1928
  Ayers, David. *English Literature of the 1920s*, 163–66.
  Roston, Murray. *Modernist Patterns in Literature*, 86–117.

Time Must Have a Stop, 1944
  Goodrich, Janet L. "Bringing Order Out of Chaos: Huxley's *Time Must Have a Stop.*" *Extrapolation* 40 (1999), 145–52.

ELIZABETH INCHBALD

Nature and Art, 1796
  Bannet, Eve Tavor. *The Domestic Revolution*, 178–79, 188–89.
  Gladfelder, Hal. *Criminality and Narrative*, 212–15.
  Jones, Vivien. "Placing Jemima: Women Writers of the 1790s and the Eighteenth-Century Prostitution Narrative." *Women's Writing* 4 (1997), 201–20.
  Maurer, Shawn Lisa. "Masculinity and Morality in Elizabeth Inchbald's *Nature and Art*," in Linda Lang-Peralta, ed., *Women, Revolution, and the Novels of the 1790s*, 155–73.

Skinner, Gillian. *Sensibility and Economics in the Novel*, 162–64.
Swan, Beth. *Fictions of Law*, 140–46.
Wordsworth, Jonathan. *The Bright Work Grows*, 101–7.

A Simple Story, 1791

Ballaster, Ros. "Women and the Rise of the Novel: Sexual Prescripts," in Vivien Jones, ed., *Women and Literature in Britain*, 212–13.

Bannet, Eve Tavor. *The Domestic Revolution*, 79–80.

Boardman, Michael. "Inchbald's *A Simple Story*: An Anti-Ideological Reading," in David H. Richter, ed., *Ideology and Form*, 207–20. (Also in *Eighteenth Cent* 37 [1996], 271–84.)

Burgess, Miranda J. *British Fiction and the Production of Social Order*, 119–26.

Haggerty, George E. "Female Abjection in Inchbald's *A Simple Story*." *Stud in Engl Lit, 1500–1900* 36 (1996), 655–70.

Haggerty, George E. *Unnatural Affections*, 36–51.

Irwin, Michael. "Readings of Realism," in Philip Davis, ed., *Real Voices*, 217–20.

Nachumi, Nora. "'Those Simple Signs': The Performance of Emotion in Elizabeth Inchbald's *A Simple Story*." *Eighteenth-Cent Fiction* 11 (1999), 317–38.

Parker, Jo Alyson. "Complicating *A Simple Story*: Inchbald's Two Versions of Female Power." *Eighteenth-Cent Stud* 30 (1997), 255–67.

Ward, Candace. "Inordinate Desire: Schooling the Senses in Elizabeth Inchbald's *A Simple Story*." *Stud in the Novel* 31 (1999), 1–16.

CHRISTOPHER ISHERWOOD

Down There on a Visit, 1962

Faraone, Mario. "The Path That Leads to Safety: Spiritual Renewal and Autobiographical Narrative," in James J. Berg and Chris Freeman, eds., *The Isherwood Century*, 253–54.

McFarland, John. "'Always Dance': Sex and Salvation in Isherwood's Vedantism," in James J. Berg and Chris Freeman, eds., *The Isherwood Century*, 244–46.

da Silva, Stephen. "Strategically Minor: Isherwood's Revision of Forster's Mythology," in James J. Berg and Chris Freeman, eds., *The Isherwood Century*, 189–91.

Goodbye to Berlin, 1939

Edelson, Maria. "Photographs of the Unreal City: The Waste Land in *Goodbye to Berlin* by Christopher Isherwood." *Folia Litteraria Anglica* (Lodz) 2 (1998), 23–32. (In Polish.)

Holbeche, Yvonne. "Goodbye to Berlin: Erich Kästner and Christopher Isherwood." *AUMLA* 94 (2000), 35–51.

Shuttleworth, Antony. "In a Populous City: Isherwood in the Thirties," in James J. Berg and Chris Freeman, eds., *The Isherwood Century*, 156–61.

A Meeting by the River, 1967

> Faraone, Mario. "The Path That Leads to Safety: Spiritual Renewal and Autobiographical Narrative," in James J. Berg and Chris Freeman, eds., *The Isherwood Century,* 256–58.
>
> Kaplan, Carola M. "'The Wandering Stopped': An Interview with Christopher Isherwood," in James J. Berg and Chris Freeman, eds., *The Isherwood Century,* 261–65.
>
> McFarland, John. "'Always Dance': Sex and Salvation in Isherwood's Vedantism," in James J. Berg and Chris Freeman, eds., *The Isherwood Century,* 244–46.

The Memorial, 1932

> Kelley, James. "Aunt Mary, Uncle Henry, and Anti-Ancestral Impulses in *The Memorial,*" in James J. Berg and Chris Freeman, eds., *The Isherwood Century,* 141–49.

Mr. Norris Changes Trains, 1935

> Shuttleworth, Antony. "In a Populous City: Isherwood in the Thirties," in James J. Berg and Chris Freeman, eds., *The Isherwood Century,* 152–56.

Prater Violet, 1946

> Faraone, Mario. "The Path That Leads to Safety: Spiritual Renewal and Autobiographical Narrative," in James J. Berg and Chris Freeman, eds., *The Isherwood Century,* 248–49.

A Single Man, 1964

> Bergman, David. "Isherwood and the Violet Quill," in James J. Berg and Chris Freeman, eds., *The Isherwood Century,* 204–11.
>
> Bucknell, Katherine. "Who Is Christopher Isherwood?," in James J. Berg and Chris Freeman, eds., *The Isherwood Century,* 26–29.
>
> Faraone, Mario. "The Path That Leads to Safety: Spiritual Renewal and Autobiographical Narrative," in James J. Berg and Chris Freeman, eds., *The Isherwood Century,* 254–56.
>
> Garnes, David. "A Single Man, Then and Now," in James J. Berg and Chris Freeman, eds., *The Isherwood Century,* 196–202.
>
> Hawthorne, Mark D. "'The Sin for Which There Is No Forgiveness': Growing Old in Gay Men's Novels." *LIT* 7 (1997), 274–75.
>
> Kaplan, Carola M. "'The Wandering Stopped': An Interview with Christopher Isherwood," in James J. Berg and Chris Freeman, eds., *The Isherwood Century,* 270–72.
>
> McFarland, John. "'Always Dance': Sex and Salvation in Isherwood's Vedantism," in James J. Berg and Chris Freeman, eds., *The Isherwood Century,* 244–46.

The World in the Evening, 1954

> Faraone, Mario. "The Path That Leads to Safety: Spiritual Renewal and Autobiographical Narrative," in James J. Berg and Chris Freeman, eds., *The Isherwood Century,* 252–53.
>
> McFarland, John. "'Always Dance': Sex and Salvation in Isherwood's Vedantism," in James J. Berg and Chris Freeman, eds., *The Isherwood Century,* 240–43.

KAZUO ISHIGURO

An Artist of the Floating World, 1986

Davis, Rocío G. "Imaginary Homelands Revisited in the Novels of Kazuo Ishiguro." *Miscelánea* 15 (1994), 139–54.

Joyau, Isabelle. "Le discours du leurre dans les romans de Kazuo Ishiguro." *Etudes Anglaises* 50 (1997), 232–40.

Korte, Barbara. *Body Language in Literature,* 120–22.

Ma, Sheng-mei. "Kazuo Ishiguro's Persistent Dream for Postethnicity: Performance in Whiteface." *Post-Identity* 2:1 (1999), 71–88.

Mallett, Peter J. "The Revelation of Character in Kazuo Ishiguro's *The Remains of the Day* and *An Artist of the Floating World.*" *Shoin Liter R* 29 (1996), 1–20.

Sarvan, Charles. "Floating Signifiers and *An Artist of the Floating World.*" *J of Commonwealth Lit* 32:1 (1997), 93–100.

Shaffer, Brian W. *Understanding Kazuo Ishiguro,* 38–62.

A Pale View of Hills, 1982

Davis, Rocío G. "Imaginary Homelands Revisited in the Novels of Kazuo Ishiguro." *Miscelánea* 15 (1994), 139–54.

Gibson, Andrew. *Postmodernity, Ethics and the Novel,* 199–201.

Joyau, Isabelle. "Le discours du leurre dans les romans de Kazuo Ishiguro." *Etudes Anglaises* 50 (1997), 240–43.

Ma, Sheng-mei. "Kazuo Ishiguro's Persistent Dream for Postethnicity: Performance in Whiteface." *Post-Identity* 2:1 (1999), 71–88.

Shaffer, Brian W. *Understanding Kazuo Ishiguro,* 12–37.

Wood, Michael. *Children of Silence,* 176–81.

The Remains of the Day, 1989

Baneth-Nouailhetas, Emilienne. "'The Hazards of Uttering Witticisms . . .,' ou des dangers de l'humour dans *The Remains of the Day.*" *Q/W/E/R/T/Y* 9 (1999), 211–17.

Brînzeu, Pia. *Corridors of Mirrors,* 34–36.

Davis, Rocío G. "Imaginary Homelands Revisited in the Novels of Kazuo Ishiguro." *Miscelánea* 15 (1994), 139–54.

Davis, Rocío G. "*The Remains of the Day*: Kazuo Ishiguro's Sonnet on His Blindness." *Cuadernos de Investigación Filológica* 21–22 (1995–1996), 57–67.

Fendler, Susanne. "Immigrants in Britain: National Identities and Stereotypes," in Susanne Fendler and Ruth Wittlinger, eds., *The Idea of Europe in Literature,* 128–36.

González Bolía, Elsa C. "Una mirada sobre *The Remains of the Day.*" *Cuadernos de Literatura Inglesa y Norteamaricana* 1:1 (1996), 85–94.

Guth, Deborah. "Submerged Narratives in Kazuo Ishiguro's *The Remains of the Day.*" *Forum for Mod Lang Stud* 35 (1999), 126–37.

Jirgens, Karl E. "Narrator Resartus: Palimpsestic Revelations in Kazuo Ishiguro's *The Remains of the Day.*" *Q/W/E/R/T/Y* 9 (1999), 219–30.

Joyau, Isabelle. "Le discours du leurre dans les romans de Kazuo Ishiguro." *Etudes Anglaises* 50 (1997), 232–40.

Lang, James M. "Public Memory, Private History: Kazuo Ishiguro's *The Remains of the Day*." *Clio* 29 (2000), 143–65.

McDonough, Donald. "Off with Their Heads: The British Novel and the Rise of Fascism." *Tennessee Philol Bull* 33 (1996), 34–42.

Machu, Didier. "Stevens, comédien, officier et paladin." *Q/W/E/R/T/Y* 9 (1999), 231–39.

Mallett, Peter J. "The Revelation of Character in Kazuo Ishiguro's *The Remains of the Day* and *An Artist of the Floating World*." *Shoin Liter R* 29 (1996), 1–20.

Porée, Marc. "Retour à Darlington Hall: James Ivory traduit *The Remains of the Day*." *Etudes Anglaises* 52 (1999), 448–58.

Salecl, Renata. "Love: Providence or Despair." *New Formations* 23 (1994), 13–24.

Shaffer, Brian W. *Understanding Kazuo Ishiguro*, 63–89.

Slay, Jack, Jr. "Ishiguro's *The Remains of the Day*." *Explicator* 55:3 (1997), 180–82.

Suter, Rebecca. "'We're Like Butlers': Interculturality, Memory and Responsibility in Kazuo Ishiguro's *The Remains of the Day*." *Q/W/E/R/T/Y* 9 (1999), 241–50.

Teverson, Andrew. "Acts of Reading in Kazuo Ishiguro's *The Remains of the Day*." *Q/W/E/R/T/Y* 9 (1999), 251–58.

Winsworth, Ben. "Communicating and Not Communicating: The True and False Self in *The Remains of the Day*." *Q/W/E/R/T/Y* 9 (1999), 259–66.

The Unconsoled, 1994

Adelman, Gary. "Doubles on the Rocks: Ishiguro's *The Unconsoled*." *Critique* (Washington, DC) 42 (2001), 166–78.

Shaffer, Brian W. *Understanding Kazuo Ishiguro*, 90–122.

Wood, Michael. *Children of Silence*, 171–76.

ROSAMOND JACOB

The Troubled House, 1938

Backus, Margot Gayle. *The Gothic Family Romance*, 206–13.

VIOLET JACOB

Flemington, 1911

Anderson, Carol. "Tales of Her Own Countries: Violet Jacob," in Douglas Gifford and Dorothy McMillan, eds., *A History*, 355–57.

MURIEL JAEGER

The Question Mark, 1926

Stratton, Susan. "Muriel Jaeger's *The Question Mark*, a Response to Bellamy and Wells." *Foundation* 80 (2000), 62–68.

P. D. JAMES

A Certain Justice, 1997

  Rowland, Susan. *From Agatha Christie to Ruth Rendell,* 176–78.

The Children of Men, 1993

  Coale, Samuel. "Carnage and Conversion: The Art of P. D. James."
  Clues 20:1 (1999), 5–7.

Death of an Expert Witness, 1977

  Rowland, Susan. *From Agatha Christie to Ruth Rendell,* 57–59.

Devices and Desires, 1989

  Coale, Samuel. "Carnage and Conversion: The Art of P. D. James."
  Clues 20:1 (1999), 7–8.
  Cohen, Michael. *Murder Most Fair,* 117–18.
  Rowland, Susan. *From Agatha Christie to Ruth Rendell,* 81–83.
  Schmid, David. "The Locus of Disruption: Serial Murder and Generic
  Conventions in Detective Fiction," in Warren Chernaik et al., eds.,
  The Art of Detective Fiction, 83–88.

Innocent Blood, 1980

  Coale, Samuel. "Carnage and Conversion: The Art of P. D. James."
  Clues 20:1 (1999), 8–9.
  Marks, Pamela. "Mine Eyes Open: Anti-Romance in P. D. James's
  Innocent Blood." Clues 21:1 (2000), 73–85.

Original Sin, 1994

  Coale, Samuel. "Carnage and Conversion: The Art of P. D. James."
  Clues 20:1 (1999), 9–10.
  Rowland, Susan. *From Agatha Christie to Ruth Rendell,* 130–33.

Shroud for a Nightingale, 1971

  Rowland, Susan. *From Agatha Christie to Ruth Rendell,* 34–36.

The Skull Beneath the Skin, 1982

  Klein, Kathleen Gregory. *The Woman Detective,* 154–58.
  Nelson, Eric. "P. D. James and the Dissociation of Sensibility," in Abby
  H. P. Werlock, ed., *British Women Writing Fiction,* 56–66.
  Scott, Carolyn F. "'I am Duchess of Malfi still': The Identity-Death
  Nexus in *The Duchess of Malfi* and *The Skull beneath the Skin,*" in
  Jerome H. Delamater and Ruth Prigozy, eds., *Theory and Practice,*
  129–35.

A Taste for Death, 1986

  Coale, Samuel. "Carnage and Conversion: The Art of P. D. James."
  Clues 20:1 (1999), 10–12.
  Rowland, Susan. *From Agatha Christie to Ruth Rendell,* 152–54.

An Unsuitable Job for a Woman, 1973

  Klein, Kathleen Gregory. *The Woman Detective,* 153–58.
  Maassen, Irmgard. "An Unsuitable Job for a Woman? Gender, Genre
  and the New Detective Heroine," in H. Gustav Klaus and Stephen
  Knight, eds., *The Art of Murder,* 157–59.
  Rowland, Susan. *From Agatha Christie to Ruth Rendell,* 106–7.

STORM JAMESON

A Day Off, 1933

Vance, Sylvia. "Lorca's Mantle: The Rise of Fascism and the Work of Storm Jameson," in Maroula Joannou, ed., *Women Writers of the 1930s*, 126–30.

Europe to Let: The Memoirs of an Obscure Man, 1940

Labon, Joanna. "Come in from the Cold War: Rebecca West and Storm Jameson in 1930s Europe," in Maroula Joannou, ed., *Women Writers of the 1930s*, 208–12.

In the Second Year, 1936

Vance, Sylvia. "Lorca's Mantle: The Rise of Fascism and the Work of Storm Jameson," in Maroula Joannou, ed., *Women Writers of the 1930s*, 131–36.

RICHARD JEFFERIES

After London, or Wild England, 1885

Hooker, Jeremy. *Writers in a Landscape*, 38–55.

Bevis, the Story of a Boy, 1882

Hunt, Peter. *Children's Literature*, 144–46.

Green Ferne Farm, 1880

Jackson-Houlston, C. M. *Ballads, Songs and Snatches*, 132–38.

ROBIN JENKINS

Just Duffy, 1988

McCulloch, Margery Palmer. "Hogg's *Justified Sinner* and Robin Jenkins's *Just Duffy*." *Stud in Hogg and His World* 6 (1995), 12–21.

GERALDINE JEWSBURY

The Half-Sisters, 1848

Denisoff, Dennis. "Lady in Green with Novel: The Gendered Economics of the Visual Arts and Mid-Victorian Women's Writing," in Nicola Diane Thompson, ed., *Victorian Women Writers*, 156–60.

May, Leila Silvana. *Disorderly Sisters*, 108–22.

Surridge, Lisa. "Madame de Staël Meets Mrs. Ellis: Geraldine Jewsbury's *The Half Sisters*." *Carlyle Stud Annual* 1995: 81–95.

Zoe, 1845

Werner, Mary B., and Kenneth Womack. "Forbidden Love and Victorian Restraint in Geraldine Jewsbury's *Zoë*." *Cahiers Victoriens et Edouardiens* 45 (1977), 15–23.

B. S. JOHNSON

The Unfortunates, 1969

    Gibson, Andrew. *Postmodernity, Ethics and the Novel,* 94–96.

SAMUEL JOHNSON

Rasselas, 1759

    Ali, Muhsin Jassim. "*Rasselas* as a Colonial Discourse." *Central Inst of Engl and Foreign Languages Bull* 8:1 (1996), 47–60.

    Basker, James G. "Radical Affinities: Mary Wollstonecraft and Samuel Johnson," in Alvaro Ribeiro and James G. Basker, eds., *Tradition in Transition,* 43–47.

    Benedict, Barbara M. *Curiosity,* 186–87.

    Butler, Lance St. John. *Registering the Difference,* 53–56.

    Cass, Jeffrey. "'The Scraps, Patches, and Rags of Daily Life': Gaskell's Oriental Other and the Conservation of Cranford." *Papers on Lang and Lit* 35 (1999), 420–25.

    Kemmerer, Kathleen Nulton. *"A neutral being between sexes,"* 93–115.

    Krishnan, R. S. "'The Shortness of Our Present State': Locke's 'Time' and Johnson's 'Eternity' in *Rasselas*." *J of Evolutionary Psych* 19:1–2 (1998), 2–9.

    Lipking, Lawrence. *Samuel Johnson,* 186–97.

    Mayhew, Robert J. "Nature and the Choice of Life in *Rasselas*." *Stud in Engl Lit, 1500–1900* 39 (1999), 539–54.

    Montandon, Alain. *Le roman au XVIIIe siècle,* 85–90.

    Oueijan, Naji B. *The Progress of an Image,* 48–52.

    Piper, William Bowman. *Common Courtesy in Eighteenth-Century English Literature,* 124–26.

    Power, Stephen S. "Trough the Lens of *Orientalism*: Samuel Johnson's *Rasselas*." *West Virginia Univ Philol Papers* 40 (1994–1995), 6–10.

    Smith, Duane H. "Repetitive Patterns in Samuel Johnson's *Rasselas*." *Stud in Engl Lit, 1500–1900* 36 (1996), 623–37.

    Smith, M. van Wyk. "Father Lobo, Ethiopia, and the Transkei: Or, Why Rasselas Was Not a Mpondo Prince." *J of African Travel Writing* 4 (1998), 5–16.

    Snader, Joe. *Caught Between Worlds,* 270–75.

    Varney, Andrew. *Eighteenth-Century Writers in their World,* 215–20.

    Wechselblatt, Martin. *Bad Behavior,* 46–52.

JENNIFER JOHNSTON

The Captains and the Kings, 1972

    Donovan, Katie. "Secret Friendships, Forbidden Relations in the Novels of Jennifer Johnston." *Etudes Irlandaises* 23:1 (1998), 46–53.

    Kreilkamp, Vera. *The Anglo-Irish Novel,* 202–8.

The Christmas Tree, 1981

    Lynch, Rachael Sealy. "Public Spaces, Private Lives: Irish Identity and Female Selfhood in the Novels of Jennifer Johnston," in Kathryn Kirkpatrick, ed., *Border Crossings*, 250–52.

    St. Peter, Christine. *Changing Ireland*, 20–26.

    Winner, Anthony. "Disorders of Reading Short Novels." *Kenyon R* 18:1 (1996), 117–28.

Fool's Sanctuary, 1987

    Kreilkamp, Vera. *The Anglo-Irish Novel*, 213–15.

    Lynch, Rachael Sealy. "Public Spaces, Private Lives: Irish Identity and Female Selfhood in the Novels of Jennifer Johnston," in Kathryn Kirkpatrick, ed., *Border Crossings*, 258–60.

How Many Miles to Babylon?, 1974

    Backus, Margot Gayle. *The Gothic Family Romance*, 164–70.

    Kreilkamp, Vera. *The Anglo-Irish Novel*, 202–6.

The Illusionist, 1995

    Weekes, Ann Owens. "Figuring the Mother in Contemporary Irish Fiction," in Liam Harte and Michael Parker, eds., *Contemporary Irish Fiction*, 117–19.

The Invisible Worm, 1991

    Diez Fabre, Silvia. "Rewriting the Blakeian 'Invisible Worm' in the Work of Jennifer Johnston." *Cuadernos de Literatura Inglesa y Norteamericana* 2:1 (1997), 39–52.

    Frehner, Ruth. *The Colonizers' Daughters*, 205–26.

    Kreilkamp, Vera. *The Anglo-Irish Novel*, 214–20.

    Lynch, Rachael Sealy. "Public Spaces, Private Lives: Irish Identity and Female Selfhood in the Novels of Jennifer Johnston," in Kathryn Kirkpatrick, ed., *Border Crossings*, 260–67.

The Old Jest, 1979

    Donovan, Katie. "Secret Friendships, Forbidden Relations in the Novels of Jennifer Johnston." *Etudes Irlandaises* 23:1 (1998), 53–57.

    Lynch, Rachael Sealy. "Public Spaces, Private Lives: Irish Identity and Female Selfhood in the Novels of Jennifer Johnston," in Kathryn Kirkpatrick, ed., *Border Crossings*, 256–58.

The Railway Station Man, 1984

    Lynch, Rachael Sealy. "Public Spaces, Private Lives: Irish Identity and Female Selfhood in the Novels of Jennifer Johnston," in Kathryn Kirkpatrick, ed., *Border Crossings*, 254–56.

Shadows on Our Skin, 1977

    Cahalan, James M. *Double Visions*, 137–40.

    Donovan, Katie. "Secret Friendships, Forbidden Relations in the Novels of Jennifer Johnston." *Etudes Irlandaises* 23:1 (1998), 57–63.

    Lynch, Rachael Sealy. "Public Spaces, Private Lives: Irish Identity and Female Selfhood in the Novels of Jennifer Johnston," in Kathryn Kirkpatrick, ed., *Border Crossings*, 252–54.

CHRISTIAN ISOBEL JOHNSTONE

Clan-Albin, 1815

Trumpener, Katie. *Bardic Nationalism*, 217–18, 263–66.

LEWIS JONES

Cwmardy, 1937

Haywood, Ian. *Working-Class Fiction*, 60–63.

We Live, 1939

Haywood, Ian. *Working-Class Fiction*, 63–65.

JAMES JOYCE

Finnegans Wake, 1939

Adams, Hazard. "Blake and Joyce." *James Joyce Q* 35:4/36:1 (1998), 683–92.

Ady, Paul. "Joyce's *Finnegans Wake*." *Explicator* 59:2 (2001), 95–97.

Attridge, Derek. *Joyce Effects*, 86–92, 126–62.

Banham, Gary. "Water and Women in *Finnegans Wake*," in John Brannigan et al., eds., *Re: Joyce*, 182–93.

Beckman, Richard. "Jove's Word: *Finnegans Wake*, 80.20–81.13." *J of Mod Lit* 22 (1998–99), 373–84.

Bengal, Michael H. "'I Dig Joyce': Jack Kerouac and *Finnegans Wake*." *Philol Q* 77 (1998), 209–18.

Black, Martha Fodaski. "'The Last Word in Stolentelling': 'I had it from Lamppost Shawe,'" in Clive Hart et al., eds., *Images of Joyce*, vol. 1, 163–80.

Blumenbach, Ulrich. "A Bakhtinian Approach Towards Translating *Finnegans Wake*," in Clive Hart et al., eds., *Images of Joyce*, vol. 2, 645–48.

Boheemen-Saff, Christine van. "Epiphany and Postcolonial Affect," in Wim Tigges, ed., *Moments of Moment*, 203–5.

Boheemen-Saaf, Christine van. *Joyce, Derrida, Lacan, and the Trauma of History*, 158–210.

Boldrini, Lucia. *Joyce, Dante, and the Poetics of Literary Relations*, 26–189.

Boldrini, Lucia. "The Rule of Analogy and *Contrappasso*: Babel, Dante, Joyce and the Redemption of Language," in Clive Hart et al., eds., *Images of Joyce*, vol. 1, 183–87.

Bormanis, John. "Lilith on the Liffey: Gender, Rebellion, and Anticolonialism in *Finnegans Wake*." *James Joyce Q* 34:4 (1997), 489–500.

Bowen, Zack, and Alan Roughley. "Parsing Persse: The Codology of Hosty's Song," in Sebastian D. G. Knowles, ed., *Bronze By Gold*, 295–306.

Brivic, Sheldon. "Reality as Fetish: The Crime in *Finnegans Wake*." *James Joyce Q* 34:4 (1997), 449–59.

Brivic, Sheldon. "Toni Morrison's Funk at *Finnegans Wake.*" *Joyce Stud Annual* 9 (1998), 158–71.

Burgess, Anthony. "Joyce as Novelist," in Clive Hart et al., eds., *Images of Joyce*, vol. 2, 719–21.

Burns, Christy. "In the Original Sinse: The Gay Cliché and Verbal Transgression in *Finnegans Wake*," in Joseph Valente, ed., *Quare Joyce*, 201–19.

Burns, Christy L. *Gestural Politics*, 21–26, 29–33, 51–55, 76–85. 87–113, 141–68.

Burns, Christy L. "Parodic Irishness: Joyce's Reconfigurations of the Nation in *Finnegans Wake.*" *Novel* 31 (1998), 237–53.

Burrell, Harry. "Chemistry and Physics in *Finnegans Wake*, Part II." *Joyce Stud Annual* 8 (1997), 185–206.

Cadbury, Bill. "Sequence and Authority in Some *transition* Typescripts and Proofs," in Sam Slote and Wim van Mierlo, eds., *Genitricksling Joyce*, 159–84.

Cahalan, James M. *Double Visions*, 87–102.

Caserio, Robert L. "Casement, Joyce, and Pound: Some New Meanings of Treason," in Joseph Valente, ed., *Quare Joyce*, 139–53.

Cheng, Vincent J. "The General and the Sepoy: Imperialism and Power in the Museyroom," in Clive Hart et al., eds., *Images of Joyce*, vol. 2, 650–60.

Clark, Hilary. "'Legibly depressed': Shame, Mourning, and Melancholia in *Finnegans Wake.*" *James Joyce Q* 34:4 (1997), 461–70.

Connor, Steven. *James Joyce*, 73–98.

Dale, Scott. "Pluralities of Washerwomen's Working Talk in Joyce." *Studia Neophilologica* 71 (1999), 183–87.

Eco, Umberto. "A Portrait of the Artist as a Bachelor," in Liberato Santoro-Brienza, ed., *Talking of Joyce*, 24–26, 28–39.

Eide, Marian. "Beyond 'Syphilisation': *Finnegans Wake*, AIDS, and the Discourse of Contagion," in Joseph Valente, ed., *Quare Joyce*, 225–39.

Eide, Marian. "The Language of Flows: Fluidity, Virology, and *Finnegans Wake.*" *James Joyce Q* 34:4 (1997), 473–86.

Engelhart, Bernd. "'. . . or Ivan Slavansky Slavar' (*FW*: 355.11): The Integration of Slavonic Languages into *Finnegans Wake*," in Sam Slote and Wim van Mierlo, eds., *Genitricksling Joyce*, 135–44.

Ferrer, Daniel. "The Straat That Is Called Corkscrewed: Hypertext and the Devious Ways of *Wakean* Genetics," in Sam Slote and Wim van Mierlo, eds., *Genitricksling Joyce*, 185–88.

Ford, Jane M. *Patriarchy and Incest*, 137–45.

Fordham, Finn. "Mapping Echoland." *Joyce Stud Annual* 11 (2000), 167–200.

Fordham, Finn. "Sigla in Revision," in Sam Slote and Wim van Mierlo, eds., *Genitricksling Joyce*, 83–96.

Francis, Richard. "Ríos's *Larva: Midsummer Night's Babel* and *Finnegans Wake*: Just Desserts after Quashed Potatoes," in Clive Hart et al., eds., *Images of Joyce*, vol. 1, 229–36.

Franke, Damon. "In the 'nummifeed confusionary': Reading the

Negative Confession of *Finnegans Wake.*" *J of Narrative Theory* 30 (2000), 55–91.

Füger, Wilhelm. "SCRIPTSIGNS: Variants and Cultural Contexts of Iconicity in Joyce." *Joyce Stud Annual* 8 (1997), 60–79.

Gans, Bruce M. "The Imago." *North Dakota Q* 61:3 (1993), 38–48.

Gillespie, Michael Patrick. "Reading on the Edge of Chaos: *Finnegans Wake* and the Burden of Linearity." *J of Mod Lit* 22 (1998–99), 359–71.

Gold, Moshe. "A Proverbial Tale of Tree or Stone: Joyce's Rewriting of Plato's Reminders." *Joyce Stud Annual* 11 (2000), 66–98.

Gordon, John. "Joyce's Hitler," in Michael Patrick Gillespie, ed., *Joyce through the Ages*, 179–97.

Hagena, Katharina. "Stimme und Schrift in James Macphersons *The Poems of Ossian* und deren Echo in Joyces *Finnegans Wake.*" *Anglia* 118 (2000), 352–72.

Hayman, David. "Epiphanoiding," in Sam Slote and Wim van Mierlo, eds., *Genitricksling Joyce*, 27–41.

Hayman, David. "The Manystorytold of the *Wake*: How Narrative was Made to Inform the Non-Narrativity of the Night." *Joyce Stud Annual* 8 (1997), 81–114.

Herr, Cheryl. "Blue Notes: From Joyce to Jarman," in John Brannigan et al., eds., *Re: Joyce*, 211–23.

Herr, Cheryl Temple. "The Silence of the Hares: Peripherality in Ireland and in Joyce," in Vincent J. Cheng et al., eds., *Joycean Cultures*, 216–40.

Hitchcock, Peter. "Joyce's Subalternatives," in Ellen Carol Jones, ed., *Joyce*, 23–42.

Holloway, Julia Bolton. *Jerusalem*, 230–36.

Hulle, Dirk van. "Beckett—Mauthner—Zimmer—Joyce." *Joyce Stud Annual* 10 (1999), 143–61.

Hulle, Dirk van. "Reveiling the Ouragan of Spaces in Less than a Schoppinhour," in Sam Slote and Wim van Mierlo, eds., *Genitricksling Joyce*, 145–58.

Jaurretche, Colleen. "Waking to Obscurity: *Finnegans Wake* and John of the Cross's Dark Night." *Joyce Stud Annual* 8 (1997), 154–81.

Jenkins, William D. *The Adventure of the Detected Detective*, 1–139.

Katz, Daniel. *Saying I No More*, 134–39.

Knowlton, Eloise. *Joyce, Joyceans, and the Rhetoric of Citation*, 3–8, 75–78.

Landuyt, Inge, and Geert Lernout. "Joyce's Sources: *Les grands fleuves historiques.*" *Joyce Stud Annual* 6 (1995), 99–138.

Landuyt, Ingeborg. "Tale Told of Shem: Some Elements at the Inception of *FW* I.7," in Sam Slote and Wim van Mierlo, eds., *Genitricksling Joyce*, 115–25.

Lane, Jeremy. "Falling Asleep in the *Wake*: Reading as Hypnagogic Experience," in John Brannigan et al., eds., *Re: Joyce*, 163–78.

Lazzeri, Marinella. "*Museyroom*: Il gioco degli antagonismi familiari e cosmici." *Confronto Letterario* 13 (1996), 733–50.

Lewis, Ken. "Still Points within the *Wake*," in Clive Hart et al., eds., *Images of Joyce*, vol. 2, 662–71.

Lilly, Amy M. "Fascist Aesthetics and Formations of Collective Subjectivity in *Finnegans Wake.*" *James Joyce Q* 36:2 (1999), 107–23.

McCarthy, Patrick A. "Something out of the Common Groove: Joyce and Originality." *Philol Q* 77 (1998), 408–13.

McCarthy, Patrick A. "Totality and Fragmentation in Lowry and Joyce," in Frederick Asals and Paul Tiessen, eds., *A Darkness That Murmured*, 174–77.

McGee, Patrick. *Joyce Beyond Marx*, 11–14, 24–31, 75–80, 131–49, 161–68, 197–228, 230–39, 243–48, 250–68, 274–82, 286–89.

McGee, Patrick. "Masculine States and Feminine Republics: *Finnegans Wake* as Historical Document," in Ellen Carol Jones, ed., *Joyce*, 261–87.

McKenna, Bernard. "'This same prehistoric barrow 'tis, the orangery': Duelling and Dual Communities in *Finnegans Wake.*" *LIT* 10 (1999), 131–45.

McLuhan, Eric. *The Role of Thunder in "Finnegans Wake,"* 14–266.

MacMahon, Barbara. "The Effects of Word Substitution in Slips of the Tongue, *Finnegans Wake* and *The Third Policeman.*" *Engl Stud* (Amsterdam) 82 (2001), 231–45.

Maguire, Peter A. "*Finnegans Wake* and Irish Historical Memory." *J of Mod Lit* 22 (1998–99), 293–327.

Mahaffey, Vicki. *States of Desire*, 179–209.

Michels, James. "Local Colour and Personal Perfume: *Kells* . . . the *Wake* . . . the Letter," in Clive Hart et al., eds., *Images of Joyce*, vol. 2, 672–78.

Mierlo, Wim van. "*Finnegans Wake* and the Question of Histry!?," in Sam Slote and Wim van Mierlo, eds., *Genitricksling Joyce*, 43–64.

Mierlo, Wim van. "The Freudful Couchmare Revisited: Contextualizing Joyce and the New Psychology." *Joyce Stud Annual* 8 (1997), 115–53.

Murphy, Timothy S. "The Eternal Return of 'The seim anew': Joyce's Vico and Deleuze's Nietzsche." *James Joyce Q* 35:4/36:1 (1998), 715–31.

Norris, Andrew. "Subjectification: Character and the Mechanics of Reading in *Finnegans Wake*," in Clive Hart et al., eds., *Images of Joyce*, vol. 2, 680–86.

O'Brien, Edna. *James Joyce*, 139–48.

Quintelli-Neary, Marguerite. *Folklore and the Fantastic*, 59–79.

Panikkar, Chitra. "*Sânta* in Book IV of *Finnegans Wake.*" *James Joyce Q* 35:2–3 (1998), 461–65.

Pesch, Josef W. "Joyce and the Victorians," in Clive Hart et al., eds., *Images of Joyce*, vol. 1, 283–85.

Polhemus, Robert M. "The Lot Complex: Rereading the End of *Finnegans Wake* and Rewriting Incest," in Shlomith Rimmon-Kenan et al., eds., *Rereading Texts*, 119–31.

Polhemus, Robert M. "Pound's Instigation and Joyce's *Finnegans Wake*: A Lot in Common, a Lot Contested." *Stanford Hum R* 8:1 (2000), 252–60.

Powers, Michael J. "Issy's Mimetic Night Lessons: Interpellation and Resistance in *Finnegans Wake.*" *Joyce Stud Annual* 11 (2000), 102–22.

Presley, John Woodrow. *"Finnegans Wake, Lady Pokingham,* and Victorian Erotic Fantasy." *J of Popular Culture* 30:3 (1996), 67–80.

Presley, John Woodrow. "'Kakaopoetic Lippudenies of the Ungumptious': Imagery of Art and the Artist in *Finnegans Wake,*" in Alice Mills, ed., *Seriously Weird,* 119–34.

Purdy, Strother B. "Is There a Multiverse in *Finnegans Wake,* and Does That Make It a Religious Book?" *James Joyce Q* 36:3 (1999), 587–97.

Rabaté, Jean-Michel. "A Slice of Life for Mister Germ's Choice," in John Brannigan et al., eds., *Re: Joyce,* 135–44.

Rasula, Jed. *"Finnegans Wake* and the Character of the Letter." *James Joyce Q* 34:4 (1997), 517–26.

Rice, Thomas Jackson. "The Complexity of *Finnegans Wake." Joyce Stud Annual* 6 (1995), 79–98.

Roughley, Alan. *Reading Derrida Reading Joyce,* 22–31, 34–40, 44–57, 62–66, 84–89, 106–16, 120–26.

Santoro-Brienza, Liberato. "Joyce's Dialogue with Aquinas, Dante, Bruno, Vico, Svevo . . . ," in Santoro-Brienza, ed., *Talking of Joyce,* 56–58, 66–76, 81–83.

Schiff, Daniel J. "Synthesizing 'The Ballad of Persse O'Reilly,'" in Sebastian D. G. Knowles, ed., *Bronze By Gold,* 307–17.

Schork, R. J. "Significant Names in *Finnegans Wake* 46.20 and 371.22." *James Joyce Q* 34:4 (1997), 505–14.

Schork, R. J. "Some 'Scainted' Allusions in the *Wake,*" in Clive Hart et al., eds., *Images of Joyce,* vol. 2, 689–96.

Seidel, Michael. *"Finnegans Wake:* Joyce, Maria Edgeworth, George Orwell." *Joyce Stud Annual* 8 (1997), 183–85.

Shelton, Jen. "Issy's Footnote: Disruptive Narrative and the Discursive Structure of Incest in *Finnegans Wake." ELH* 66 (1999), 203–19.

Shloss, Carol Loeb. *"Finnegans Wake* and the Daughter's Fate," in Vincent J. Cheng et al., eds., *Joycean Cultures,* 95–109.

Slote, Sam. "Imposture Book through the Ages," in Sam Slote and Wim van Mierlo, eds., *Genitricksling Joyce,* 97–114.

Slote, Sam. "Nulled Nought: The Desistance of Ulyssean Narrative in *Finnegans Wake." James Joyce Q* 34:4 (1997), 531–38.

Slote, Sam. "The Prolific and the Devouring in 'The Ondt and the Gracehoper.'" *Joyce Stud Annual* 11 (2000), 49–65.

Soros, Erin. "Giving Death." *Differences* 10:1 (1998), 1–29.

Spurr, David. "Fatal Signatures: Forgery and Colonization in *Finnegans Wake,*" in Ellen Carol Jones, ed., *Joyce,* 245–60.

Stubbings, Diane. *Anglo-Irish Modernism,* 183–88.

Tindall, William York. *A Reader's Guide to "Finnegans Wake."*

Tracy, Robert. *The Unappeasable Host,* 180–82, 184–99.

Verene, Donald Phillip. "Vico's *Scienza nuova* and Joyce's *Finnegans Wake." Philos and Lit* 21 (1997), 392–403.

Versteegen, Heinrich. "Translating *Finnegans Wake:* Translatability and the Translator's Personality," in Clive Hart et al., eds., *Images of Joyce,* vol. 2, 698–706.

Weaver, Jack W. *Joyce's Music and Noise,* 96–118.

Whitley, Catherine. "Nations and the Night: Excremental History in James Joyce's *Finnegans Wake* and Djuna Barnes' *Nightwood*." *J of Mod Lit* 24:1 (2000), 81–98.

Whitley, Catherine. "The Politics of Representation in *Finnegans Wake*'s 'Ballad,'" in Vincent J. Cheng et al., eds., *Joycean Cultures*, 163–73.

Yared, Aida. "'In The Name of Annah': Islam and *Salam* in Joyce's *Finnegans Wake*." *James Joyce Q* 35:2–3 (1998), 401–25.

Yared, Aida. "Joyce's Sources: Sir Richard F. Burton's *Terminal Essay* in *Finnegans Wake*." *Joyce Stud Annual* 11 (2000), 124–66.

A Portrait of the Artist as a Young Man, 1917

Alsop, Derek, and Chris Walsh. *The Practice of Reading*, 119–39.

Attridge, Derek. *Joyce Effects*, 59–77.

Begnal, Michael H. "Stephen, Simon, and Eileen Vance: Autoeroticism in *A Portrait of the Artist as a Young Man*," in Michael Patrick Gillespie, ed., *Joyce through the Ages*, 107–16.

Begum, Khani. "Joyce and Stephen Dedalus: Male Artificers and Their Artifice," in Clive Hart et al., eds., *Images of Joyce*, vol. 2, 442–48.

Bentley, Louise. "Beyond the Liturgy: An Approach to Catholicism as Genre in the Work of James Joyce." *Lit and Theology* 12 (1998), 159–66.

Boheemen, Christine van. "Joyce's Sublime Body: Trauma, Textuality, and Subjectivity," in Vincent J. Cheng et al., eds., *Joycean Cultures*, 27–41.

Boheemen-Saff, Christine van. "Epiphany and Postcolonial Affect," in Wim Tigges, ed., *Moments of Moment*, 195–205.

Boheemen-Saaf, Christine van. *Joyce, Derrida, Lacan, and the Trauma of History*, 31–73.

Brown, Richard. "Dante as Refrigerator or Dante as an Ambiguous Sign in Joyce's Texts," in Clive Hart et al., eds., *Images of Joyce*, vol. 1, 188–94.

Brown, Richard. "James Joyce between Ibsen and Bjørnson: *A Portrait of the Artist* and *The Fisher Lass*," in Inga-Stina Ewbank et al., eds., *Anglo-Scandinavian Cross-Currents*, 280–93.

Brunel, Pierre. *Transparences du roman*, 111–45.

Burns, Christy L. *Gestural Politics*, 27–33, 55–63.

Cahalan, James M. *Double Visions*, 105–12.

Calderwood, James L. "Joyce's *Portrait*: Centered Mazes and Decentered Universes." *Joyce Stud Annual* 8 (1997), 4–36.

Castle, Gregory. "Confessing Oneself: Homoeros and Colonial *Bildung* in *A Portrait of the Artist as a Young Man*," in Joseph Valente, ed., *Quare Joyce*, 157–80.

Castle, Gregory. *Modernism and the Celtic Revival*, 188–207.

Clifford-Amos, Terence. "Space, Time and Form in *A Portrait of the Artist as a Young Man*." *Lang and Lit* (San Antonio) 23 (1998), 73–78.

Connor, Steven. *James Joyce*, 36–48.

Coyle, John, ed. *James Joyce*, 9–174.

Currier, Susan. "Portraits of Artists by Woolf and Joyce," in Beth Rigel Daugherty and Mary Beth Pringle, eds., *Approaches to Teaching*, 35–40.

Dwyer, June. "Feast and Famine: James Joyce and the Politics of Food." *Proteus* 17:1 (2000), 41–44.

Eckley, Grace. *The Steadfast James Joyce*, 119–27, 132–36, 147–52, 154–66, 170–73, 176–86.

Erzgräber, Willi. "Der moderne autobiographische Roman in England und Irland: D. H. Lawrence und James Joyce." *Literaturwissenschaftliches Jahrbuch im Auftrage der Görres-Gesellschaft* 34 (1993), 239–57.

Erzgräber, Willi. "James Joyce and Oscar Wilde," in Clive Hart et al., eds., *Images of Joyce*, vol. 1, 208–18.

Esty, Joshua D. "Excremental Postcolonialism." *Contemp Lit* 40 (1999), 51–53.

Fairhall, James. "Northsiders," in Ellen Carol Jones, ed., *Joyce*, 45–46.

Felton, Sharon. "Portraits of the Artists as Young Defiers: James Joyce and Muriel Spark." *Tennessee Philol Bull* 33 (1996), 24–33.

Forrest-Hickman, Alan. "Growing Up Irish: An Update on Stephen Dedalus." *Publs of the Arkansas Philol Assoc* 22:1 (1996), 9–18.

Fortuna, Diane. "The Art of the Labyrinth," in Philip Brady and James F. Carens, eds., *Critical Essays*, 187–208.

Gabler, Hans Walter. "The Genesis of *A Portrait of the Artist as a Young Man*," in Philip Brady and James F. Carens, eds., *Critical Essays*, 83–110.

Gleason, Paul. "Dante, Joyce, Beckett, and the Use of Memory in the Process of Literary Creation." *Joyce Stud Annual* 10 (1999), 104–40.

Goodheart, Eugene. "Joyce and the Common Life." *Rel and the Arts* 1:2 (1997), 57–72.

Gottfried, Roy. "Adolescence, Humor, and Adolescent Humor: One Way of Carving a Turkey," in Michael Patrick Gillespie, ed., *Joyce through the Ages*, 69–84.

Gottfried, Roy. *Joyce's Comic Portrait*, 113–16, 119–25, 132–37, 148–59.

Harder, Benjamin. "Stephen's Prop: Aspects of the Ashplant in *Portrait* and *Ulysses*," in Vincent J. Cheng et al., eds., *Joycean Cultures*, 241–51.

Hiraide, Shoji. "Joyce's Philosophy of Rhythm in *A Portrait of the Artist as a Young Man*." *Stud in Engl Lit* (Tokyo) 73 (1997), 51–64.

Holloway, Julia Bolton. *Jerusalem*, 217–20.

Howes, Marjorie. "'Goodbye Ireland I'm going to Gort': Geography, Scale, and Narrating the Nation," in Derek Attridge and Marjorie Howes, eds., *Semicolonial Joyce*, 70–75.

Jacobs, Joshua. "Joyce's Epiphanic Mode: Material Language and the Representation of Sexuality in *Stephen Hero* and *Portrait*." *Twentieth Cent Lit* 46 (2000), 20–32.

Kearney, Anthony. "Joyce's *A Portrait of the Artist as a Young Man*." *Explicator* 56:1 (1997), 33–35.

Kiberd, Declan. *Inventing Ireland*, 331–36.

Kiberd, Declan. "James Joyce and Mythic Realism," in K. D. M. Snell, ed., *The Regional Novel*, 142–46.

Kimball, Jean. *Odyssey of the Psyche*, 41–56.

Klein, Scott W. "National Histories, National Fictions: Joyce's *A Portrait of the Artist as a Young Man* and Scott's *The Bride of Lammermoor*." *ELH* 65 (1998), 1017–34.

Knowlton, Eloise. *Joyce, Joyceans, and the Rhetoric of Citation*, 43–46, 53–59.

Lane, Christopher. "Afterword: 'The Vehicle of Vague Speech,'" in Joseph Valente, ed., *Quare Joyce*, 274–82.

Leonard, Garry. *Advertising and Commodity Culture*, 175–207.

Leonard, Garry. "'The Nothing Place': Secrets and Sexual Orientation in Joyce," in Joseph Valente, ed., *Quare Joyce*, 89–96.

Lewis, Pericles. "The Conscience of the Race: The Nation as Church of the Modern Age," in Michael Patrick Gillespie, ed., *Joyce through the Ages*, 85–105.

Lilienfeld, Jane. *Reading Alcoholisms*, 85–157.

Lindberg, Erik D. "Returning the Repressed: The Unconscious in Victorian and Modernist Narrative." *Narrative* 8 (2000), 78–83.

Livingston, Rick. "Global Tropes/Worldly Readings: Narratives of Cosmopolitanism in Joyce, Rich, and Tagore." *Narrative* 5 (1997), 123–27.

McArthur, Murray. "The Origin of the Work of Art in *Portrait* V," in Clive Hart et al., eds., *Images of Joyce*, vol. 2, 450–62.

McGee, Patrick. *Joyce Beyond Marx*, 91–107.

Mahaffey, Vicki. "Framing, Being Framed, and the Janus Faces of Authority," in Philip Brady and James F. Carens, eds., *Critical Essays*, 290–313.

Mahaffey, Vicki. "Père-version and Im-mère-sion: Idealized Corruption in *A Portrait of the Artist as a Young Man* and *The Picture of Dorian Gray*," in Joseph Valente, ed., *Quare Joyce*, 121–27.

Mahaffey, Vicki. *States of Desire*, 75–81, 142–45.

Mezey, Jason Howard. "Ireland, Europe, The World, The Universe: Political Geography in *A Portrait of the Artist as a Young Man*." *J of Mod Lit* 22 (1998–99), 337–48.

Moliterno, Frank. *The Dialectics of Sense and Spirit*, 57–84.

Montanari, Anna. "'Lo mio primo amico': Influenze dantesche sull'evolversi del rapporto Stephen-Cranly da *Stephen Hero* a *A Portrait of the Artist as a Young Man*." *Confronto Letterario* 14 (1997), 271–81.

Mulrooney, Jonathan. "Stephen Dedalus and the Politics of Confession." *Stud in the Novel* 33 (2001), 165–75.

Nalbantian, Suzanne. *Aesthetic Autobiography*, 118–22.

Norris, David. "Purple Passages and Ellipsoidal Balls: Joycean (Con)Texts," in Clive Hart et al., eds., *Images of Joyce*, vol. 1, 65–75.

Parke, Nigel. "Stifled Cries and Whispering Shoes: Rites of Passage in the Modern Epiphany," in Wim Tigges, ed., *Moments of Moment*, 219–24.

Peters, Günter. "Epiphanien des Alltäglichen: Methoden literarischer Realisation bei Joyce, Ponge und Handke." *Poetica* (Munich) 30 (1998), 474–79.

Platt, Len. *Joyce and the Anglo-Irish*, 39–47.

Potts, Willard. *Joyce and the Two Irelands*, 109–23.

Prothero, James. "A Portrait of Sudden Joy: A Comparison of James Joyce's *A Portrait of the Artist as a Young Man* and C. S. Lewis's *Surprised by Joy.*" *Lamp-Post of the Southern California C. S. Lewis Soc* 11:3 (1987), 3–9.

Rabaté, Jean-Michel. "A Slice of Life for Mister Germ's Choice," in John Brannigan et al., eds., *Re: Joyce*, 128–35.

Rado, Lisa. *The Modern Androgyne Imagination*, 31–41.

Rantonen, Eila. "A Portrait of the Artist as a Sinning Young Man," in Clive Hart et al., eds., *Images of Joyce*, vol. 2, 465–71.

Rickard, John S. *Joyce's Book of Memory*, 18–22, 71–73, 162–64.

Sacchetto, Alberto. "*A Portrait of the Artist as a Young Man* di James Joyce: La formazione di Stephen Dedalus e il processo di individuazione junghiano." *Quaderni di Lingue e Letterature* 16 (1991), 211–25.

Santoro-Brienza, Liberato. "Joyce's Dialogue with Aquinas, Dante, Bruno, Vico, Svevo . . . ," in Santoro-Brienza, ed., *Talking of Joyce*, 46–47, 49–50, 56–62.

Schwall, Hedwig. "Forms of Hysteria in *A Portrait of the Artist as a Young Man* and *Stephen Hero.*" *Irish Univ R* 28 (1998), 281–93.

Schwarze, Tracey Teets. "Silencing Stephen: Colonial Pathologies in Victorian Dublin." *Twentieth Cent Lit* 43 (1997), 243–59.

Sheffield, Elisabeth. *Joyce's Abandoned Female Costumes*, 58–79.

Simmerman, Stephen K. "Joycean Liminality: Gabriel Conroy and Stephen Dedalus on the Verge of Becoming Artists." *Tennessee Philol Bull* 33 (1996), 43–52.

Stubbings, Diane. *Anglo-Irish Modernism*, 66–83.

Trotter, David. "The Modernist Novel," in Michael Levenson, ed., *The Cambridge Companion to Modernism*, 74–76.

Troy, Michele K. "Two Very Different Portraits: Anglo-American and German Reception of Joyce's *A Portrait of the Artist as a Young Man.*" *James Joyce Q* 35:1 (1997), 37–51.

Valente, Joseph. "Thrilled by His Touch: The Aestheticizing of Homosexual Panic in *A Portrait of the Artist as a Young Man*," in Valente, ed., *Quare Joyce*, 47–70.

Vanderham, Paul. *James Joyce and Censorship*, 65–67.

Ward, Geoff. "Throwaway: Joyce's Heroic Inutility," in John Brannigan et al., eds., *Re: Joyce*, 153–57.

Weaver, Jack W. *Joyce's Music and Noise*, 24–42.

Webb, Caroline. "'Bodily Weakness' and the 'Free Boy': Physicality as Subversive Agent in *A Portrait of the Artist as a Young Man*," in John Brannigan et al., eds., *Re: Joyce*, 87–102.

Yee, Cordell D. K. "The Aesthetics of Stephen's Aesthetic," in Philip Brady and James F. Carens, eds., *Critical Essays*, 68–80.

Stephen Hero, 1944

Begum, Khani. "Joyce and Stephen Dedalus: Male Artificers and Their Artifice," in Clive Hart et al., eds., *Images of Joyce*, vol. 2, 439–42.

Brown, Richard. "Dante as Refrigerator or Dante as an Ambiguous Sign in Joyce's Texts," in Clive Hart et al., eds., *Images of Joyce*, vol. 1, 191–94.

Burns, Christy L. *Gestural Politics*, 20–22, 25–29.

Castle, Gregory. *Modernism and the Celtic Revival*, 190–97.

Caufield, James Walter. "The Word as Will and Idea: Dedalean Aesthetics and the Influence of Schopenhauer." *James Joyce Q* 35:4/36:1 (1998), 695–711.

Connor, Steven. *James Joyce*, 28–36.

Gottfried, Roy. *Joyce's Comic Portrait*, 111–16, 117–47.

Haslett, Moyra. "'The Girl, or woman, or whatever she is . . .': Femininity and Nationalism in Joyce," in John Brannigan et al., eds., *Re: Joyce*, 52–57.

Jacobs, Joshua. "Joyce's Epiphanic Mode: Material Language and the Representation of Sexuality in *Stephen Hero* and *Portrait*." *Twentieth Cent Lit* 46 (2000), 20–32.

Knowlton, Eloise. *Joyce, Joyceans, and the Rhetoric of Citation*, 82–84.

Langbaum, Robert. "The Epiphanic Mode in Wordsworth and Modern Literature," in Wim Tigges, ed., *Moments of Moment*, 39–41.

Montanari, Anna. "'Lo mio primo amico': Influenze dantesche sull'evolversi del rapporto Stephen-Cranly da *Stephen Hero* a *A Portrait of the Artist as a Young Man*." *Confronto Letterario* 14 (1997), 271–81.

Nalbantian, Suzanne. *Aesthetic Autobiography*, 115–18.

Parke, Nigel. "Stifled Cries and Whispering Shoes: Rites of Passage in the Modern Epiphany," in Wim Tigges, ed., *Moments of Moment*, 220–23.

Platt, Len. *Joyce and the Anglo-Irish*, 39–42.

Potts, Willard. *Joyce and the Two Irelands*, 100–109.

Rabaté, Jean-Michel. "A Slice of Life for Mister Germ's Choice," in John Brannigan et al., eds., *Re: Joyce*, 124–26.

Rado, Lisa. *The Modern Androgyne Imagination*, 26–28.

Schwall, Hedwig. "Forms of Hysteria in *A Portrait of the Artist as a Young Man* and *Stephen Hero*." *Irish Univ R* 28 (1998), 281–93.

Stubbings, Diane. *Anglo-Irish Modernism*, 77–80.

Wolfreys, Julian. "*Stephen Hero*: Laughing in—and at—the Institution," in John Brannigan et al., eds., *Re: Joyce*, 63–76.

Ulysses, 1922

Allen, Judith. "The Shells of *Ulysses*: Paradigms of Inconclusiveness," in Clive Hart et al., eds., *Images of Joyce*, vol. 2, 472–77.

Alsop, Derek, and Chris Walsh. *The Practice of Reading*, 17–19.

Alter, Robert. *Canon and Creativity*, 151–83.

Alter, Robert. "Joyce's *Ulysses* and the Common Reader." *Modernism/Modernity* 3:3 (1998), 19–31.

Armstrong, Nancy. *Fiction in the Age of Photography*, 268–74.

Armstrong, Paul B. "James Joyce and the Politics of Reading: Power, Belief, and Justice in *Ulysses*." *B.A.S.: Brit and Am Stud* 1:1 (1996), 24–41.

Attridge, Derek. *Joyce Effects*, 93–125, 179–88.

Attridge, Derek. "The Postmodernity of Joyce: Chance, Coincidence, and the Reader." *Joyce Stud Annual* 6 (1995), 10–18.

Ballesteros González, Antonio. "Digression and Intertextual Parody in Thomas Nashe, Laurence Sterne and James Joyce," in David Pierce and Peter de Voogd, eds., *Laurence Sterne*, 58–64.

Balsamo, Gian. *Pruning the Genealogical Tree*, 53–138.

Balsamo, Gian. "The Reluctant Son: Satire of the Epics and Tragedies of Lineage in 'Scylla and Charybdis.'" *Lang and Lit* (San Antonio) 23 (1998), 81–93.

Basic, Sonja. "Faulkner and Joyce: A Joint Narrative/Stylistic Protocol." *Studia Romanica et Anglica Zagrabiensia* 42 (1997), 13–24.

Bazargan, Susan. "The Book of Punishment: Lists in the 'Cyclops' Episode." *James Joyce Q* 35:4/36:1 (1998), 747–59.

Beeretz, Sylvia. *"Tell us in plain words,"* 70–182.

Bentley, Louise. "Beyond the Liturgy: An Approach to Catholicism as Genre in the Work of James Joyce." *Lit and Theology* 12 (1998), 166–68.

Bishop, Edward L. "The 'Garbled History' of the First-edition *Ulysses*." *Joyce Stud Annual* 9 (1998), 3–36.

Bishop, John. "A Metaphysics of Coitus in 'Nausicaa,'" in Kimberly J. Devlin and Marilyn Reizbaum, eds., *"Ulysses" — En-Gendered Perspectives*, 185–209.

Black, Martha Fodaski. "S/He-Male Voices in *Ulysses*: Counterpointing the 'New Womanly Man,'" in Jolanta W. Wawrzycka and Marlena G. Corcoran, eds., *Gender in Joyce*, 62–80.

Boggs, John C. "'Wandering Rocks': Joyce's Adaptation of the Classical Myth," in Clive Hart et al., eds., *Images of Joyce*, vol. 2, 478–83.

Boheemen, Christine van. "Molly's Heavenly Body and the Economy of the Sign: The Invention of Gender in 'Penelope,'" in Kimberly J. Devlin and Marilyn Reizbaum, eds., *"Ulysses" — En-Gendered Perspectives*, 267–81.

Boheemen-Saaf, Christine van. *Joyce, Derrida, Lacan, and the Trauma of History*, 74–154.

Booker, M. Keith. *"Ulysses," Capitalism, and Colonialism*, 39–168.

Bornstein, George. *Material Modernism*, 118–39.

Bouazza, Abdellah. *"Ulysses* on the Tigris." *James Joyce Q* 35:2–3 (1998), 466–72.

Bowen, Zack. "All in a Night's Entertainment: The Codology of Haroun al Rashid, the *Thousand and One Nights*, Bloomusalem/Baghdad, the Uncreated Conscience of the Irish Race, and Joycean Self-Reflexivity." *James Joyce Q* 35:2–3 (1998), 297–306.

Bowen, Zack. "'Circe' as Pantomime," in Clive Hart et al., eds., *Images of Joyce*, vol. 2, 484–89.

Bowen, Zack. "Joyce's Endomorphic Encomia." *James Joyce Q* 34:3 (1997), 259–65.

Bramsbäck, Birgit. "A Banquet for Bloom: Images of Food and

Drink in *Ulysses*," in Clive Hart et al., eds., *Images of Joyce*, vol. 2, 490–97.

Brown, Richard. "The Absent-Minded War: The Boer War in James Joyce's *Ulysses*." *Kunapipi* 21:3 (1999), 81–89.

Brown, Richard. "Returning to the Economic in 'Ithaca,'" in Andrew Gibson, ed., *Joyce's "Ithaca,"* 177–98.

Brown, Susan Sutliff. "The Joyce Brothers in Drag: Fraternal Incest in *Ulysses*," in Jolanta W. Wawrzycka and Marlena G. Corcoran, eds., *Gender in Joyce*, 8–25.

Burgess, Anthony. "Joyce as Novelist," in Clive Hart et al., eds., *Images of Joyce*, vol. 2, 712–25.

Burns, Christy. "A Birth of Parody in 'Scylla and Charybdis,'" in Clive Hart et al., eds., *Images of Joyce*, vol. 2, 498–503.

Burns, Christy L. *Gestural Politics*, 36–51, 63–75, 121–30.

Byrnes, Robert. "Weiningerian Sex Comedy: Jewish Sexual Types Behind Molly and Leopold Bloom." *James Joyce Q* 34:3 (1997), 267–79.

Cahalan, James M. *Double Visions*, 94–96.

Callahan, Edward F. "*Ulysses* and the Audience of an Epic," in Clive Hart et al., eds., *Images of Joyce*, vol. 2, 505–11.

Castle, Gregory. "Colonial Discourse and the Subject of Empire in Joyce's 'Nausicaa,'" in Ellen Carol Jones, ed., *Joyce*, 115–44.

Castle, Gregory. *Modernism and the Celtic Revival*, 208–47.

Cavaliero, Glen. *The Alchemy of Laughter*, 231–35.

Cheng, Vincent J. "Authenticity and Identity: Catching the Irish Spirit," in Derek Attridge and Marjorie Howes, eds., *Semicolonial Joyce*, 240–59.

Cheu, Hoi Fung. "Translation, Transubstantiation, Joyce: Two Chinese Versions of *Ulysses*." *James Joyce Q* 35:1 (1997), 59–69.

Chin, Sheon Joo. "*Aristotle's Masterpiece*: Nora's Source Book," in Clive Hart et al., eds., *Images of Joyce*, vol. 1, 195–205.

Connor, Steven. "'From the House of Bondage to the Wilderness of Inhabitation': The Domestic Economies of 'Ithaca,'" in Andrew Gibson, ed., *Joyce's "Ithaca,"* 199–226.

Connor, Steven. *James Joyce*, 49–72.

Coyle, John, ed. *James Joyce*, 9–174.

Csaneda Caneda, Ma. Teresa. "'Who Was Gerty?': The Disruption of Voices in the 'Nausicaa' Episode of *Ulysses*." *BELLS: Barcelona Engl Land and Lit Stud* 6 (1995), 31–37.

Cussen, John. "Bloom's Drunk: A Rereading of the 'Eumaeus' Episode in James Joyce's *Ulysses*." *CEA Critic* 63:2 (2001), 56–74.

Daniel, Anne Margaret. "*Ulysses* Anglophone and a St. Louis Boy's Memory." *James Joyce Q* 35:1 (1997), 155–58.

Danius, Sara. "Orpheus and the Machine: Proust as Theorist of Technological Change, and the Case of Joyce." *Forum for Mod Lang Stud* 37 (2001), 135–39.

Davison, Neil R. "Joyce, Jewish Identity, and the Paris Bourse," in Clive Hart et al., eds., *Images of Joyce*, vol. 1, 23–44.

Dean, Tim. "Paring His Fingernails: Homosexuality and Joyce's Impersonalist Aesthetic," in Joseph Valente, ed., *Quare Joyce*, 241–63.

Derrida, Jacques. "Ulysses Gramophone: 'Hear say yes in Joyce,'" in Margot Norris, ed., *A Companion to James Joyce's "Ulysses,"* 69–90. (Translated by Tina Kendall.)

Devlin, Kimberly J. "'I saw that picture somewhere': Tracking the Symptom of the Sisters of Lazarus," in Margot Norris, ed., *A Companion to James Joyce's "Ulysses,"* 187–202.

Devlin, Kimberly J. "Visible Shades and Shades of Visibility: The En-Gendering of Death in 'Hades,'" in Kimberly J. Devlin and Marilyn Reizbaum, eds., *"Ulysses"—En-Gendered Perspectives*, 67–85.

Digou, Mike. "Joyce's *Ulysses.*" *Explicator* 58:4 (2000), 208–10.

Doherty, Gerald. "Imperialism and the Rhetoric of Sexuality in James Joyce's *Ulysses*," in Ellen Carol Jones, ed., *Joyce*, 207–29.

Donoghue, Denis. *The Practice of Reading*, 117–19, 223–25, 227–35.

Doody, Terrence. *Among Other Things*, 169–74, 182–86.

Downing, Gregory M. "Life Lessons from Untimely Death in James Joyce's *Ulysses.*" *Lit and Medicine* 19 (2000), 182–99.

Downing, Gregory M. "Richard Chevenix Trench and Joyce's Historical Study of Words." *Joyce Stud Annual* 9 (1998), 37–68.

Duffy, Enda. "Disappearing Dublin: *Ulysses*, Postcoloniality, and the Politics of Space," in Derek Attridge and Marjorie Howes, eds., *Semicolonial Joyce*, 37–56.

Duffy, Enda. "Interesting States: Birthing and the Nation in 'Oxen of the Sun,'" in Kimberly J. Devlin and Marilyn Reizbaum, eds., *"Ulysses"—En-Gendered Perspectives*, 210–28.

Duffy, Enda. "Molly's Throat," in Ellen Carol Jones, ed., *Joyce*, 241–44.

Eberl, Ulrich. "*Ulysses* as Transindividual Allegory," in Clive Hart et al., eds., *Images of Joyce*, vol. 2, 512–25.

Ellmann, Maud. "Skinscapes in 'Lotus-Eaters,'" in Kimberly J. Devlin and Marilyn Reizbaum, eds., *"Ulysses"—En-Gendered Perspectives*, 51–66.

Erzgräber, Willi. "James Joyce and Oscar Wilde," in Clive Hart et al., eds., *Images of Joyce*, vol. 1, 218–26.

Eyuboglu, Murat. "Davies, Beria, and *Ulysses*," in Sebastian D. G. Knowles, ed., *Bronze By Gold*, 171–85.

Fairhall, James. "Northsiders," in Ellen Carol Jones, ed., *Joyce*, 46–54.

Feuer, Lois. "Joyce the Postmodern: Shakespeare as Character in *Ulysses*," in Paul Franssen and Ton Hoenselaars, eds., *The Author as Character*, 167–78.

Fischer, Andreas. "Strange Words, Strange Music: The Verbal Music of 'Sirens,'" in Sebastian D. G. Knowles, ed., *Bronze By Gold*, 245–62.

Flesher, Erika Anne. "'I am getting on nicely in the dark': Picturing the Blind Spot in Illustrations for James Joyce's *Ulysses*," in Vincent J. Cheng et al., eds., *Joycean Cultures*, 177–200.

Fludernik, Monika. "The Rhetoric of Readerly Vraisemblance and the Strategies of Joyce's Rewritings," in Clive Hart et al., eds., *Images of Joyce*, vol. 1, 85–102.

Ford, Jane M. *Patriarchy and Incest*, 123–37.

Fracasso, Evelyn E. "Martin Cunningham: Saviour of Leopold Bloom in Joyce's *Ulysses.*" *Coll Lang Assoc J* 40 (1997), 497–507.

Fraser, Jennifer. "Intertextual Turnarounds: Joyce's Use of the Homeric 'Hymn to Hermes.'" *James Joyce Q* 36:3 (1999), 541–55.

Friedman, Susan Stanford. "Reading Joyce: Icon of Modernity? Champion of Alterity? Ventriloquist of Otherness?," in Vincent J. Cheng et al., eds., *Joycean Cultures*, 121–25.

Fritz, Antonia. "Oviditties in 'Ithaca,'" in Andrew Gibson, ed., *Joyce's "Ithaca,"* 77–101.

Gaskell, Philip. *Landmarks in English Literature*, 63–68.

Gibson, Andrew. "'An Aberration of the Light of Reason': Science and Cultural Politics in 'Ithaca,'" in Gibson, ed., *Joyce's "Ithaca,"* 133–74.

Gibson, Andrew. *Postmodernity, Ethics and the Novel*, 205–7.

Gillespie, Michael Patrick. "James Joyce and the Consumption of Irish History," in Gillespie, ed., *Joyce through the Ages*, 11–24.

Gillespie, Michael Patrick, and Paula F. Gillespie. *Recent Criticism of James Joyce's "Ulysses,"* 9–105.

Gooch, Michael. "Saintsbury's Anglo-Saxon in Joyce's 'Oxen of the Sun.'" *J of Mod Lit* 22 (1998–99), 401–4.

Goodwin, Willard. "'A Very Pretty Picture M. Matisse But You Must Not Call It Joyce': The Making of the Limited Editions Club *Ulysses*. With Lewis Daniel's Unpublished *Ulysses* Illustrations." *Joyce Stud Annual* 10 (1999), 85–102.

Gordon, John. "'Circe,' La Gioconda, and the Opera House of the Mind," in Sebastian D. G. Knowles, ed., *Bronze By Gold*, 277–93.

Gordon, John. "Tracking the Oxen." *J of Mod Lit* 22 (1998–99), 349–57.

Gottfried, Roy. *Joyce's Comic Portrait*, 148–59.

Grant, Alan. "Why Could Stephen Not Wear Gray Trousers?" *James Joyce Q* 36:3 (1999), 628–29.

Groce, Sara. "'Shes Restless Knowing Shes Pretty': Milly Bloom as Catalyst in *Ulysses*." *Conf of Coll Teachers of Engl Stud* 64 (1999), 23–29.

Gunn, Daniel P. "Beware of Imitations: Advertisement as Reflexive Commentary in *Ulysses*." *Twentieth Cent Lit* 42 (1996), 481–91.

Hamilton, Craig A. "Rhetoric and Homeric Paradigm in 'Scylla and Charybdis.'" *James Joyce Q* 35:4/36:1 (1998), 864–66.

Hampson, Robert. "'Allowing for Possible Error': Education and Catechism in 'Ithaca,'" in Andrew Gibson, ed., *Joyce's "Ithaca,"* 229–67.

Harder, Benjamin. "Stephen's Prop: Aspects of the Ashplant in *Portrait* and *Ulysses*," in Vincent J. Cheng et al., eds., *Joycean Cultures*, 241–51.

Harper, Margaret Mills. "Fabric and Fame in the *Odyssey* and 'Penelope,'" in Jolanta W. Wawrzycka and Marlena G. Corcoran, eds., *Gender in Joyce*, 170–83.

Harris, Susan Cannon. "Invasive Procedures: Imperial Medicine and Population Control in *Ulysses* and *The Satanic Verses*." *James Joyce Q* 35:2–3 (1998), 373–96.

Hart, Michael. "'Many Planes of Narrative': A Comparative Perspective on Sterne and Joyce," in David Pierce and Peter de Voogd, eds., *Laurence Sterne*, 65–80.

Haslett, Moyra. "'The Girl, or woman, or whatever she is . . .': Femininity and Nationalism in Joyce," in John Brannigan et al., eds., *Re: Joyce*, 45–51.

Henke, Suzette. "Joyce and Feminism *Encore*: Gazing at Gerty MacDowell," in Clive Hart et al., eds., *Images of Joyce*, vol. 1, 111–25.

Herr, Cheryl. "Old Wives' Tales as Portals of Discovery in 'Proteus,'" in Kimberly J. Devlin and Marilyn Reizbaum, eds., *"Ulysses"—En-Gendered Perspectives*, 30–41.

Higgins, Lesley. "'Lovely Seaside Girls' or 'Sweet Murderers of Men'? Fatal Women in *Ulysses*," in Jolanta W. Wawrzycka and Marlena G. Corcoran, eds., *Gender in Joyce*, 47–60.

Höfele, Andreas. "Wasteland Sprouting: Salman Rushdie's *The Satanic Verses* and the Cityscapes of Modernism," in Richard Todd and Luisa Flora, eds., *Theme Parks*, 42–48.

Hofheinz, Thomas. "Joyce's Northern Ireland," in John Brannigan et al., eds., *Re: Joyce*, 35–44.

Holloway, Julia Bolton. *Jerusalem*, 220–30.

Horujy, Sergey S. "*Ulysses* in a Russian Looking-Glass." *Joyce Stud Annual* 9 (1998), 69–157.

Iser, Wolfgang. "Patterns of Communication in Joyce's *Ulysses*," in Margot Norris, ed., *A Companion to James Joyce's "Ulysses,"* 108–27.

Ivory, James Maurice. *Identity and Narrative Metamorphoses*, 105–31.

Jacobus, Lee A. "Bring the Camera Whenever You Like: 'Wandering Rocks,' Cinema Ambulante, and Problems of Diegesis," in Clive Hart et al., eds., *Images of Joyce*, vol. 2, 526–35.

Jeffares, A. Norman. *Images of Invention*, 310–13.

Justman, Stewart. *The Springs of Liberty*, 93–107.

Kanthak, John F. "Judgement Approaches in *Ulysses*' 'Wandering Rocks.'" *Notes and Queries* 46 (1999), 484–87.

Katz, Daniel. *Saying I No More*, 39–42, 128–30.

Kelly, Dermot. "Joycean Parody: Irony and Transcendence," in Clive Hart et al., eds., *Images of Joyce*, vol. 2, 539–43.

Kelly, Joseph. *Our Joyce*, 85–89, 113–15, 128–31, 203–7.

Kershner, Brandon. "The World's Strongest Man: Joyce or Sandow?," in Clive Hart et al., eds., *Images of Joyce*, vol. 1, 243–50.

Kershner, R. B. "The Culture of *Ulysses*," in Vincent J. Cheng et al., eds., *Joycean Cultures*, 149–60.

Kershner, R. Brandon. "Framing Rudy and Photography." *J of Mod Lit* 22 (1998–99), 265–92.

Kershner, R. Brandon. "*Ulysses* and the Orient." *James Joyce Q* 35:2–3 (1998), 273–93.

Kiberd, Declan. *Inventing Ireland*, 327–55, 382–85.

Kiberd, Declan. "James Joyce and Mythic Realism," in K. D. M. Snell, ed., *The Regional Novel*, 136–63.

Kimball, Jean. "*Eros* and *Logos* in *Ulysses*: A Jungian Pattern," in Jolanta W. Wawrzycka and Marlena G. Corcoran, eds., *Gender in Joyce*, 112–28.

Kimball, Jean. "Growing Up Together: Joyce and Psychoanalysis," in Michael Patrick Gillespie, ed., *Joyce through the Ages*, 35–43.

Kimball, Jean. "The Japhet Connection: Roots and Branches in *Ulysses*." *James Joyce Q* 35:4/36:1 (1998), 855–58.

Kimball, Jean. *Odyssey of the Psyche*, 3–146.

King, John. "Trapping the Fox You Are(n't) with a Riddle: The Autobiographical Crisis of Stephen Dedalus in *Ulysses*." *Twentieth Cent Lit* 45 (1999), 299–312.

King, Mary C. "Hermeneutics of Suspicion: Nativism, Nationalism, and the Language Question in 'Oxen of the Sun.'" *James Joyce Q* 35:2–3 (1998), 349–68.

Klitgård, Ida. "Time, Narration, and Consciousness in the 'Proteus' Episode of James Joyce's *Ulysses*." *Angles on the Engl Speaking World* 9 (1996), 5–30.

Knapp, James A. "Joyce and Matisse Bound: Modernist Aesthetics in the Limited Editions Club *Ulysses*." *ELH* 67 (2000), 1055–78.

Knowles, Sebastian. "'O Lord I must stretch myself': Molly Bloom and *Frankenstein*," in Clive Hart et al., eds., *Images of Joyce*, vol. 1, 281–83. (Also in *James Joyce Q* 34:3 [1997], 303–12.)

Knowlton, Eloise. *Joyce, Joyceans, and the Rhetoric of Citation*, 90–100.

Kupinse, William. "Household Trash: Domesticity and National Identity in *The Lamplighter* and the 'Nausicaa' Episode of *Ulysses*." *South Carolina R* 32:1 (1999), 81–87.

Lamos, Colleen. "Anti-Oedipal Joyce," in Clive Hart et al., eds., *Images of Joyce*, vol. 2, 544–47.

Lamos, Colleen. "The Double Life of 'Eumaeus,'" in Kimberly J. Devlin and Marilyn Reizbaum, eds., *"Ulysses" — En-Gendered Perspectives*, 242–53.

Lamos, Colleen. "'A Faint Glimmer of Lesbianism' in Joyce," in Joseph Valente, ed., *Quare Joyce*, 185–97.

Lane, Christopher. "Afterword: 'The Vehicle of Vague Speech,'" in Joseph Valente, ed., *Quare Joyce*, 282–88.

Lanters, José. "Old Worlds, New Worlds, Alternative Worlds: *Ulysses*, *Metamorphoses* 13, and the Death of the Beloved Son." *James Joyce Q* 36:3 (1999), 525–38.

Law, Jules. "Political Sirens," in Kimberly J. Devlin and Marilyn Reizbaum, eds., *"Ulysses" — En-Gendered Perspectives*, 150–66.

Lawrence, Karen. "Legal Fiction or Pulp Fiction in 'Lestrygonians,'" in Kimberly J. Devlin and Marilyn Reizbaum, eds., *"Ulysses" — En-Gendered Perspectives*, 100–110.

Lawrence, Karen R. "'Beggaring Description': Economies of Language and the Language of Economy in 'Eumaeus,'" in Clive Hart et al., eds., *Images of Joyce*, vol. 2, 726–48.

Leckie, Barbara. "Reading Bodies, Reading Nerves: 'Nausicaa' and the Discourse of Censorship." *James Joyce Q* 34:1–2 (1996–1997), 65–81.

Ledden, Patrick J. "Bloom, Lawn Tennis, and the Gaelic Athletic Association." *James Joyce Q* 36:3 (1999), 630–33.

Ledden, Patrick J. "Education and Social Class in Joyce's Dublin." *J of Mod Lit* 22 (1998–99), 329–36.

Leonard, Garry. *Advertising and Commodity Culture*, 35–49, 142–74.

Leonard, Garry. "'A Little Trouble about Those White Corpuscles': Mockery, Heresy, and the Transubstantiation of Masculinity in 'Telemachus,'" in Kimberly J. Devlin and Marilyn Reizbaum, eds., *"Ulysses"—En-Gendered Perspectives*, 1–19.

Leonard, Garry. "'The Nothing Place': Secrets and Sexual Orientation in Joyce," in Joseph Valente, ed., *Quare Joyce*, 89–96.

Leonard, Garry M. "Authorizing the Reader: *Ulysses*, 'Freewriting,' and Artifacts of Popular Culture in the Underegraduate Classroom," in Clive Hart et al., eds., *Images of Joyce*, vol. 1, 56–63.

Leonard, Garry M. "'Life' in a World of Mass-Produced Objects: 'Kitsch' and Commodity Culture in Joyce," in Clive Hart et al., eds., *Images of Joyce*, vol. 2, 548–64.

Leonard, Philip. "Asymmetries and Obliterations: Derrida's Joyce's Judaism." *Renaissance and Mod Stud* 38 (1995), 88–95.

Levine, Jennifer. "James Joyce, Tattoo Artist: Tracing the Outlines of Homosocial Desire," in Joseph Valente, ed., *Quare Joyce*, 101–17.

Livorni, Ernesto. "'Ineluctable modality of the visible': Diaphane in the 'Proteus' Episode." *James Joyce Q* 36:2 (1999), 127–47.

Lohmann, Dieter. *KALYPSO bei Homer und James Joyce*.

Lowe-Evans, Mary. "Joyce and the Myth of the Mediatrix," in Jolanta W. Wawrzycka and Marlena G. Corcoran, eds., *Gender in Joyce*, 101–10.

McBride, Margaret. *"Ulysses" and the Metamorphosis of Stephen Dedalus*, 11–184.

McCarthy, Patrick A. "Something out of the Common Groove: Joyce and Originality." *Philol Q* 77 (1998), 402–8.

McCarthy, Patrick A. "Totality and Fragmentation in Lowry and Joyce," in Frederick Asals and Paul Tiessen, eds., *A Darkness That Murmured*, 173–80.

McCourt, John. *The Years of Bloom*, 42–48, 89–91.

McDowell, Lesley. "'Just you try it on': Style and Maternity in 'Oxen of the Sun,'" in John Brannigan et al., eds., *Re: Joyce*, 107–19.

McGarrity, Maria. "The 'Houses of decay' and Shakespeare's 'Sonnet 13': Another Nexus in 'Proteus.'" *James Joyce Q* 35:1 (1997), 153–55.

McGee, Patrick. "'Heavenly Bodies': *Ulysses* and the Ethics of Marxism," in Margot Norris, ed., *A Companion to James Joyce's "Ulysses,"* 220–37.

McGee, Patrick. *Joyce Beyond Marx*, 3–7, 18–25, 31–40, 43–63, 86–90, 113–16, 119–30, 175–91, 221–23.

McGee, Patrick. "Machines, Empire, and the Wise Virgins: Cultural Revolution in 'Aeolus,'" in Kimberly J. Devlin and Marilyn Reizbaum, eds., *"Ulysses"—En-Gendered Perspectives*, 86–99.

Mackey, Peter Francis. *Chaos Theory and James Joyce's Everyman*, 61–204.

Mackey, Peter Francis. "Chaos Theory and the Heroism of Leopold Bloom," in Michael Patrick Gillespie, ed., *Joyce through the Ages*, 46–62.

McLean, Clara D. "Wasted Words: The Body Language of Joyce's 'Nausicaa,'" in Vincent J. Cheng et al., eds., *Joycean Cultures*, 44–57.

Mahaffey, Vicki. "Sidereal Writing: Male Refractions and

Malefactions in 'Ithaca,'" in Kimberly J. Devlin and Marilyn Reizbaum, eds., *"Ulysses"—En-Gendered Perspectives*, 254–66.

Mahaffey, Vicki. "*Ulysses* and the End of Gender," in Margot Norris, ed., *A Companion to James Joyce's "Ulysses,"* 151–68.

Malamud, Randy. "Prostituting Language: 'Silent Means Consent,'" in Clive Hart et al., eds., *Images of Joyce*, vol. 2, 566–71.

Malamud, Randy. "'What the heart is': Interstices of Joyce's Poetry and Fiction." *South Atlantic R* 64:1 (1999), 91–100.

Maley, Willy. "'Kilt by kelt shell kithagain with kinagain': Joyce and Scotland," in Derek Attridge and Marjorie Howes, eds., *Semicolonial Joyce*, 211–16.

Malouf, Michael G. "Jules and Jim: Jules Romains and Joyce's 'Wandering Rocks.'" *James Joyce Q* 34:3 (1997), 341–44.

Manganaro, Marc. "Reading 'Culture' in Joyce's *Ulysses*." *James Joyce Q* 35:4/36:1 (1998), 765–78.

Martin, Bruce K. "Music and Fiction: The Perils of Popularism." *Mosaic* 31:4 (1998), 21–39.

Martin, Paul. "'Mr. Bloom and the Cyclops': Joyce and Antheil's Unfinished 'Opéra Mécanique,'" in Sebastian D. G. Knowles, ed., *Bronze By Gold*, 88–105.

Martyniuk, Irene A. "Illustrating *Ulysses*, Illustrating Joyce," in Vincent J. Cheng et al., eds., *Joycean Cultures*, 203–15.

Meaney, Gerardine. "Penelope, or, Myths Unravelling: Writing, Orality and Abjection in *Ulysses*." *Textual Prectice* 14 (2000), 519–28.

Meyers, Jeffrey. "Erotic Hangings in 'Cyclops.'" *James Joyce Q* 34:3 (1997), 345–48.

Mines, Ray, and Reed Way Dasenbrock. "'Nought nowhere was ever reached': Mathematics in *Ulysses*." *James Joyce Q* 35:1 (1997), 25–34.

Moliterno, Frank. *The Dialectics of Sense and Spirit*, 85–123, 130–39.

Moloney, Caitriona. "The Hags of *Ulysses*: The 'Poor Old Woman,' Cathleen Ni Houlihan, and the Phallic Mother." *James Joyce Q* 34:1–2 (1996–1997), 103–17.

Montesi, Albert. "Charlie Chaplin and Leopold Bloom," in Clive Hart et al., eds., *Images of Joyce*, vol. 1, 266–77.

Mooney, Susan. "Bronze by Gold by Bloom: Echo, the Invocatory Drive, and the 'Aurteur' in 'Sirens,'" in Sebastian D. G. Knowles, ed., *Bronze By Gold*, 229–44.

Murfin, Ross C. "Deconstruction and *Ulysses*," in Margot Norris, ed., *A Companion to James Joyce's "Ulysses,"* 47–64.

Murfin, Ross C. "Feminist and Gender Criticism and *Ulysses*," in Margot Norris, ed., *A Companion to James Joyce's "Ulysses,"* 129–43.

Murfin, Ross C. "Marxist Criticism and *Ulysses*," in Margot Norris, ed., *A Companion to James Joyce's "Ulysses,"* 203–17.

Murfin, Ross C. "Psychoanalytic Criticism and *Ulysses*," in Margot Norris, ed., *A Companion to James Joyce's "Ulysses,"* 169–81.

Murfin, Ross C. "Reader-Response Criticism and *Ulysses*," in Margot Norris, ed., *A Companion to James Joyce's "Ulysses,"* 91–103.

Murphy, Michael. "'Proteus' and Prose: Paternity or Workmanship?" *James Joyce Q* 35:1 (1997), 71–78.

Murphy, Sean P. "Interrogating the Powers of Agency, Resistance, and Subjectivity in the Composition Classroom: An Example from James Joyce's 'Nausicaa' Episode." *CEA Critic* 59:2 (1997), 42–51.

Murphy, Sean P. "The Reader, the Erotic, and James Joyce's 'Circe' Episode." *Readerly/Writerly Yexts* 4:2 (1997), 39–53.

Nalbantian, Suzanne. *Aesthetic Autobiography*, 123–33.

Nolan, Anne. "A Note on the Passionist Fathers of Mount Argus in *Ulysses*." *James Joyce Q* 36:3 (1999), 657–60.

Nolan, Emer. "State of the Art: Joyce and Postcolonialism," in Derek Attridge and Marjorie Howes, eds., *Semicolonial Joyce*, 86–93.

Norris, Margot. "A Critical History of *Ulysses*," in Norris, ed., *A Companion to James Joyce's "Ulysses,"* 21–39.

Norris, Margot. "Disenchanting Enchantment: The Theatrical Brothel of 'Circe,'" in Kimberly J. Devlin and Marilyn Reizbaum, eds., *"Ulysses"—En-Gendered Perspectives*, 229–41.

North, Michael. *Reading 1922*, 26–29.

Nunes, Mark. "Beyond the 'Holy See': Parody and Narrative Assemblage in 'Cyclops.'" *Twentieth Cent Lit* 45 (1999), 174–83.

O'Brien, Alyssa J. "The Molly Blooms of 'Penelope': Reading Joyce Archivally." *J of Mod Lit* 24:1 (2000), 7–24.

O'Brien, Edna. *James Joyce*, 93–107, 109–17.

Olaivar, Tamara. "'Your corporosity sagaciating O K?': *Ulysses* and Pauline Hopkins." *James Joyce Q* 34:1–2 (1996–1997), 173–74.

O'Neill, Christine. *Too Fine a Point: A Stylistic Analysis of the Eumaeus Episode in James Joyce's "Ulysses."*

Osteen, Mark. "Female Property: Women and Gift Exchange in *Ulysses*," in Jolanta W. Wawrzycka and Marlena G. Corcoran, eds., *Gender in Joyce*, 29–43.

Osteen, Mark. "A High Grade Ha: The 'Politicoecomedy' of Headwear in *Ulysses*," in Vincent J. Cheng et al., eds., *Joycean Cultures*, 253–80.

Osteen, Mark. "Meredith/Joyce: Bella Mount and Bella's Mount." *James Joyce Q* 35:4/36:1 (1998), 873–77.

Oxley, Robert. "Satiric Cataloguing of Names in the 'Cyclops' Episode of James Joyce's *Ulysses*," in Clive Hart et al., eds., *Images of Joyce*, vol. 2, 572–78.

Parkes, Adam. "'Literature and instruments for abortion': 'Nausicaa' and the *Little Review* Trial." *James Joyce Q* 34:3 (1997), 283–99.

Pearce, Sandra Manoogian. "Stephen's Ashplant as Bloom's Wonderbat in 'Circe''s Harlequinade." *James Joyce Q* 35:4/36:1 (1998), 866–71.

Pearce, Sandra Manoogian. "'Umbrellas Re-covered': A Note Uncovering Joyce's Sign of Sterility in *Dubliners*, *Exiles*, and *Ulysses*." *Colby Q* 33 (1997), 205–7.

Pease, Allison. *Modernism, Mass Culture, and the Aesthetics of Obscenity*, 107–15.

Peltonen, Kristiina. "Easter Symbolism in the Opening Scene of *Ulysses*," in Clive Hart et al., eds., *Images of Joyce*, vol. 2, 579–85.

Pesch, Josef W. "Joyce and the Victorians," in Clive Hart et al., eds., *Images of Joyce*, vol. 1, 281–83.

Pierce, David. "Close-Up: *The Countess Cathleen*," in Clive Hart et al., eds., *Images of Joyce*, vol. 2, 807–11.

Platt, L. H. "'If Brian Boru Could But Come Back And See Old Dublin Now': Materialism, the National Culture and *Ulysses* 17," in Andrew Gibson, ed., *Joyce's "Ithaca,"* 105–32.

Platt, Len. "Corresponding with the Greeks: An Overview of *Ulysses* as an Irish Epic." *James Joyce Q* 36:3 (1999), 507–21.

Platt, Len. *Joyce and the Anglo-Irish*, 48–233.

Platt, Len. "Pisgah Sights: The National Press and the Catholic Middle Class in 'Aeolus.'" *James Joyce Q* 35:4/36:1 (1998), 735–44.

Pollak, Paulina Salz. "Joyce's Use of the Structural Pattern from Mozart's *Don Giovanni* in the 'Circe' Chapter of *Ulysses*." *Engl Lang Notes* 36:1 (1998), 51–57.

Potts, Willard. *Joyce and the Two Irelands*, 144–97.

Quintelli-Neary, Marguerite. *Folklore and the Fantastic*, 25–55.

Rabaté, Jean-Michel. "On Joycean and Wildean Sodomy," in Joseph Valente, ed., *Quare Joyce*, 35–43.

Rademacher, Jörg W. "Totalized (Auto-)Biography as Fragmented Intertextuality: Shakespeare—Sterne—Joyce," in David Pierce and Peter de Voogd, eds., *Laurence Sterne*, 81–86.

Rado, Lisa. *The Modern Androgyne Imagination*, 39–56.

Ramsey, Harly. "Mourning, Melancholia, and the Maternal Body: Cultural Constructions of Bereavement in *Ulysses*," in Vincent J. Cheng et al., eds., *Joycean Cultures*, 59–74.

Randaccio, Monica. "Descent, Transition and Raising in James Joyce's *Ulysses* and Italo Svevo's *La coscienza di Zeno*." *Prospero* 6 (1999), 114–31.

Rangarajan, Sudarsan. "Joyce's *Ulysses*." *Explicator* 57:4 (1999), 223–24.

Reizbaum, Marilyn. *James Joyce's Judaic Other*, 35–132.

Reizbaum, Marilyn. "Joyce's Grand Nationals," in Ellen Carol Jones, ed., *Joyce*, 187–205.

Reizbaum, Marilyn. "When the Saints Come Marching In: Re-Deeming 'Cyclops,'" in Kimberly J. Devlin and Marilyn Reizbaum, eds., *"Ulysses"—En-Gendered Perspectives*, 167–84.

Richardson, Brian. "The Genealogies of *Ulysses*, the Invention of Postmodernism, and the Narratives of Literary History." *ELH* 67 (2000), 1035–51.

Richardson, Brian. "Make it Old: Lucian's *A True Story*, Joyce's *Ulysses*, and Homeric Patterns in Ancient Fiction." *Compar Lit Stud* 37 (2000), 371–81.

Rickard, John. "Stephen Dedalus among School Children: The Schoolroom and the Riddle of Authority in *Ulysses*." *Stud in the Liter Imagination* 30:2 (1997), 17–32.

Rickard, John S. *Joyce's Book of Memory*, 15–198.

Robaey, Jean. "Joyce, Flaubert e Vaes: Le strade di Dublin, Rouen e Londra—Note di lettura." *Lettore di Provincia* 27 (1996), 85–88.

Rodstein, Susan de Sola. "Back to 1904: Joyce, Ireland, and Nationalism," in Ellen Carol Jones, ed., *Joyce*, 145–85.

Rogers, Margaret. "Mining the Ore of 'Sirens': An Investigation of Structural Components," in Sebastian D. G. Knowles, ed., *Bronze By Gold*, 263–75.

Rogers, Margaret. "The Soggetto Cavato in 'Sirens,'" in Clive Hart et al., eds., *Images of Joyce*, vol. 2, 587–91.

Rohman, Todd, and Deborah H. Holdstein. "Ulysses Unbound: Examining the Digital (R)evolution of Narrative Context." *Works and Days* 17–18 (1999–2000), 249–62.

Roughley, Alan. *Reading Derrida Reading Joyce*, 66–75, 82–86, 98–100.

Ruprecht, Hans-George. "Intertextual Grounds for Construction and Deconstruction: Joyce's 'Cabman's Shelter' Revisited." *Versus* 77–78 (1997), 35–55.

Saenger, Michael Baird. "Will Stephen Wrest Vanity from Falstaff?" *James Joyce Q* 35:1 (1997), 152–53.

Santoro-Brienza, Liberato. "Joyce's Dialogue with Aquinas, Dante, Bruno, Vico, Svevo . . . ," in Santoro-Brienza, ed., *Talking of Joyce*, 53–54, 56–58, 63–66.

Sayers, William. "Molly's Monologue and the Old Woman's Complaint in James Stephens' *The Crock of Gold*." *James Joyce Q* 36:3 (1999), 640–47.

Schwaber, Paul. *The Cast of Characters*, 1–223.

Schwarze, Tracey Teets. "Voyeuristic Utopias and Lascivious Cities: Leopold Bloom, Urban Spectatorship and Social Reform." *Joyce Stud Annual* 8 (1997), 39–57.

Scott, Bonnie Kime. "Bloom's Transparent Vehicle of Desire," in Clive Hart et al., eds., *Images of Joyce*, vol. 2, 593–602.

Scott, Bonnie Kime. "Diversions from Mastery in 'Wandering Rocks,'" in Kimberly J. Devlin and Marilyn Reizbaum, eds., *"Ulysses"—En-Gendered Perspectives*, 136–49.

Scott, Bonnie Kime. "'The Young Girl,' Jane Heap, and Trials of Gender in *Ulysses*," in Vincent J. Cheng et al., eds., *Joycean Cultures*, 78–89.

Senn, Fritz. "'Ithaca': Portrait of the Chapter as a Long List," in Andrew Gibson, ed., *Joyce's "Ithaca,"* 31–76.

Senn, Fritz. "Kyklonomastics." *James Joyce Q* 36:3 (1999), 485–503.

Sepcic, Visnja. "A Biblical Intertext in Three Modernist Writers: Joyce, Lawrence, Krleza." *Studia Romanica et Anglica Zagrabiensia* 42 (1997), 351–52.

Sheffield, Elisabeth. *Joyce's Abandoned Female Costumes*, 8–10, 80–99.

Shelton, Jen. "Bad Girls: Gerty, Cissy, and the Erotics of Unruly Speech." *James Joyce Q* 34:1–2 (1996–1997), 87–100.

Shloss, Carol. "Behind the Veil: James Joyce and the Colonial Harem," in Ellen Carol Jones, ed., *Joyce*, 103–13.

Shloss, Carol. "Milly, Molly, and the Mullingar Photo Shop: Developing Negatives in 'Calypso,'" in Kimberly J. Devlin and Marilyn Reizbaum, eds., *"Ulysses"—En-Gendered Perspectives*, 42–50.

Shloss, Carol Loeb. "'Behind the Veil': James Joyce and the Colonial Harem." *James Joyce Q* 35:2–3 (1998), 333–42.

Sicari, Stephen. "Rereading *Ulysses*: 'Ithaca' and Modernist Allegory." *Twentieth Cent Lit* 43 (1997), 264–87.

Sicker, Philip. "Leopold's Travels: Swiftian Optics in Joyce's 'Cyclops.'" *Joyce Stud Annual* 6 (1995), 59–78.

Snyder, William, Jr. "Tap Tap. Jingle. Tap: Form is Content in 'The Sirens.'" *ANQ* 11:1 (1998), 24–27.

Soros, Erin. "Giving Death." *Differences* 10:1 (1998), 1–29.

Souris, Stephen. "Marcel and Molly as Modernist Bedfellows: An Analysis of Character and Consciousness in Proust's 'Combray' and Joyce's 'Penelope.'" *Conf of Coll Teachers of Engl Stud* 63 (1998), 59–68.

Spoo, Robert. "Copyright and the Ends of Ownership: The Case for a Public-domain *Ulysses* in America." *Joyce Stud Annual* 10 (1999), 5–62.

Spoo, Robert. "Genders of History in 'Nestor,'" in Kimberly J. Devlin and Marilyn Reizbaum, eds., *"Ulysses" — En-Gendered Perspectives*, 20–29.

Stanzel, Franz Karl. "Der weibliche Mann: Eine rückläufige Spurensuche von James Joyce zu Otto Weininger." *Poetica* (Munich) 29 (1997), 151–57.

Staten, Henry. "The Decomposing Form of Joyce's *Ulysses*." *PMLA* 112 (1997), 380–91.

Steinberg, Erwin R. "The Source(s) of Joyce's Anti-Semitism in *Ulysses*." *Joyce Stud Annual* 10 (1999), 63–84.

Steinberg, Erwin R., and Christian W. Hallstein. "*Ulysses*: An Anti-Bildungsroman." *Joyce Stud Annual* 11 (2000), 202–6.

Sternlieb, Lisa. "Molly Bloom: Acting Natural." *ELH* 65 (1998), 757–76.

Strobos, Semon. "Displacement of Affect in the Joycean Climax and Closure." *Colby Q* 33 (1997), 264–74.

Strobos, Semon. "Dreamwork in *Ulysses*: Displacement." *Arkansas R* 5:1–2 (1996), 10–38.

Strobos, Semon. "Freudian *Symbolisierung* and *Traumarbeit* in *Ulysses*' Construction and Stream of Consciousness." *Lang and Lit* (San Antonio) 20 (1995), 35–57.

Stubbings, Diane. *Anglo-Irish Modernism*, 163–79.

Sullivan, James P. "'All off for a buster': An Early Version." *Joyce Stud Annual* 10 (1999), 184–93.

Sutcliffe, Joe. "James Joyce: Not Making it New." *Cambridge Q* 27 (1998), 56–70.

Sword, Helen. "Modernist Hauntology: James Joyce, Hester Dowden, and Shakespeare's Ghost." *Texas Stud in Lit and Lang* 41 (1999), 180–98.

Thornton, Weldon. *Voices and Values in Joyce's "Ulysses,"* 35–170.

Topia, André. "La prolifération du potentiel: séries joyciennes, séries beckettiennes." *Etudes Anglaises* 53 (2000), 19–29.

Tracy, Robert. *The Unappeasable Host*, 159–62.

Tratner, Michael. "Cleaning Women and Prostitutes: Figures in the Dark in *To the Lighthouse* and *Ulysses*," in Clive Hart et al., eds., *Images of Joyce*, vol. 1, 299–308.

Trotter, David. "Gissing's Fry-Ups: Food and the Definition of Working-Class Culture in Britain in the 1880s." *New Comparison* 24 (1997), 162–64.

Trotter, David. "The Modernist Novel," in Michael Levenson, ed., *The Cambridge Companion to Modernism*, 83–86, 92–94.

Troy, Mark. "'Bbbbblllllblblblabschbl!,'" in Clive Hart et al., eds., *Images of Joyce*, vol. 1, 310–14.

Troy, Mark. "In/Out," in Clive Hart et al., eds., *Images of Joyce*, vol. 1, 157–62.

Turner, John Noel. "A Commentary on the Closing of 'Oxen of the Sun.'" *James Joyce Q* 35:1 (1997), 83–96.

Tysdahl, Björn. "Joyce and Protestant Sainthood," in Clive Hart et al., eds., *Images of Joyce*, vol. 1, 315–26.

Valente, Joseph. "A Child Is Being Eaten: Mourning, Transvestism, and the Incorporation of the Daughter in *Ulysses*." *James Joyce Q* 34:1–2 (1996–1997), 21–61.

Valente, Joseph. "'Neither fish nor flesh'; or How 'Cyclops' Stages the Double-Bind of Irish Manhood," in Derek Attridge and Marjorie Howes, eds., *Semicolonial Joyce*, 96–125.

Valente, Joseph. "The Perils of Masculinity in 'Scylla and Charybdis,'" in Kimberly J. Devlin and Marilyn Reizbaum, eds., *"Ulysses"—En-Gendered Perspectives*, 111–35.

Vanderham, Paul. *James Joyce and Censorship*, 16–168.

Vice, Sue. "Women's Voices: The Late Drafts of James Joyce and Malcolm Lowry." *BELLS: Barcelona Engl Lang and Lit Stud* 7 (1996), 171–81.

Vogler, Thomas. "The Whatness of Somehorse in *Ulysses*," in Clive Hart et al., eds., *Images of Joyce*, vol. 2, 614–29.

Ward, Geoff. "Throwaway: Joyce's Heroic Inutility," in John Brannigan et al., eds., *Re: Joyce*, 146–53, 157–60.

Warner, Deborah. "The Ballast-Office Time Ball and the Subjectivity of Time and Space." *James Joyce Q* 35:4/36:1 (1998), 861–63.

Weaver, Jack W. *Joyce's Music and Noise*, 47–95.

Weinstock, Jeffrey A. "The Disappointed Bridge: Textual Hauntings in Joyce's *Ulysses*." *J of the Fantastic in the Arts* 8 (1997), 347–69.

Wicht, Wolfgang. *Utopianism in James Joyce's "Ulysses,"* 39–238.

Williams, Tara. "A Polysymbolic Character: Irish and Jewish Folklore in the Apparition of Rudy," in Michael Patrick Gillespie, ed., *Joyce through the Ages*, 117–29.

Wood, Joley. "'Scylla and Charybdis' (and *Phaedrus*): The Influence of Plato and the Artistry of Joyce." *James Joyce Q* 36:3 (1999), 559–68.

Woodruff, Adam. "Nobody at Home: Bloom's Outlandish Retreat in the 'Cyclops' Chapter of *Ulysses*." *European J of Engl Stud* 3:3 (1999), 275–84.

Zhang, Aiping. "Faithfulness Through Alterations: The Chinese Translation of Molly's Soliloquy in James Joyce's *Ulysses*." *James Joyce Q* 36:3 (1999), 571–85.

Ziarek, Ewa. "Working the Limit: (M)other, Text, Abject in *Ulysses*," in Clive Hart et al., eds., *Images of Joyce*, vol. 2, 632–43.

Ziarek, Ewa Plonowska. "'Circe': Joyce's *Argumentum ad Feminam*," in Jolanta W. Wawrzycka and Marlena G. Corcoran, eds., *Gender in Joyce*, 150–65.

Ziaukas, Tim. "'Indispensable Wires': Joyce's *Ulysses* and the Origins of Public Relations." *Eire-Ireland* 31:3–4 (1996), 176–87.

Zida, Jean. "Theology and Art in the First Episode of James Joyce's *Ulysses*." *Bridges* (Dakar) 7 (1996), 77–91.

MOLLY KEANE

Devoted Ladies, 1934

Breen, Mary. "Piggies and Spoilers of Girls: The Representation of Sexuality in the Novels of Molly Keane," in Éibhear Walshe, ed., *Sex, Nation and Dissent*, 213–18.

Good Behaviour, 1981

Breen, Mary. "Piggies and Spoilers of Girls: The Representation of Sexuality in the Novels of Molly Keane," in Éibhear Walshe, ed., *Sex, Nation and Dissent*, 207–13.

Kreilkamp, Vera. *The Anglo-Irish Novel*, 181–83, 190–94.

O'Brien, Ellen L. "Anglo-Irish Abjection in the 'very nasty' Big House Novels of Molly Keane." *LIT* 10 (1999), 40–45.

Saville, Anthony. "Instrumentalism and the Interpretation of Narrative." *Mind* 105 (1996), 553–76.

Loving and Giving, 1988

Kreilkamp, Vera. *The Anglo-Irish Novel*, 181–83.

Taking Chances, 1929

Breen, Mary. "Piggies and Spoilers of Girls: The Representation of Sexuality in the Novels of Molly Keane," in Éibhear Walshe, ed., *Sex, Nation and Dissent*, 218–19.

Time After Time, 1983

Kreilkamp, Vera. *The Anglo-Irish Novel*, 181–83, 187–89.

O'Brien, Ellen L. "Anglo-Irish Abjection in the 'very nasty' Big House Novels of Molly Keane." *LIT* 10 (1999), 45–49.

Two Days in Aragon, 1941

Backus, Margot Gayle. *The Gothic Family Romance*, 194–205.

Frehner, Ruth. *The Colonizers' Daughters*, 181–98.

Kreilkamp, Vera. *The Anglo-Irish Novel*, 175–80.

Weatherhead, A. K. *Upstairs*, 103–4.

RICHARD KEARNEY

Sam's Fall, 1995

Smyth, Gerry. *The Novel and the Nation*, 168–71.

ANNIE KEARY

Castle Daly, 1875

Kelleher, Margaret. *The Feminization of Famine*, 67–69, 96–98.

HENRIETTA KEARY

St. Mungo's City, 1884

> Burgess, Moira. "Rediscovering Scottish Women's Fiction in the Nineteenth Century," in Douglas Gifford and Dorothy McMillan, eds., *A History*, 200–202.

ROBERT KEE

A Crowd is Not Company, 1947

> Rawlinson, Mark. *British Writing of the Second World War*, 184–87.

The Impossible Shore, 1949

> Rawlinson, Mark. *British Writing of the Second World War*, 190–93.

HUGH KELLY

Memoirs of a Magdalen; or, The History of Louisa Mildmay, 1766

> Ellis, Markman. *The Politics of Sensibility*, 186–89.

MAEVE KELLY

Florrie's Girls, 1989

> St. Peter, Christine. *Changing Ireland*, 32–39.

Necessary Treasons, 1985

> St. Peter, Christine. *Changing Ireland*, 163–69.

MAGGIE KELLY

Burning Issues, 1995

> Hutton, Elaine. "Good Lesbians, Bad Men and Happy Endings," in Hutton, ed., *Beyond Sex and Romance?*, 195–97.

JAMES KELMAN

How Late It Was, How Late, 1994

> Gilbert, Geoff. "Can Fiction Swear? James Kelman and the Booker Prize," in Rod Mengham, ed., *An Introduction to Contemporary Fiction*, 219–31.
>
> Kirk, John. "Figuring the Dispossessed: Images of the Urban Working Class in the Writing of James Kelman." *English: The J of the Engl Assoc* 48 (1999), 101–16.
>
> Pitchford, Nicola. "How Late It Was for England: James Kelman's Scottish Booker Prize." *Contemp Lit* 41 (2000), 693–725.

GENE KEMP

Gowie Corby Plays Chicken, 1979

> Watson, Victor. *Reading Series Fiction*, 193–97.

Juniper: A Mystery, 1986
  Watson, Victor. *Reading Series Fiction*, 198–200.
The Turbulent Term of Tyke Tiler, 1977
  Watson, Victor. *Reading Series Fiction*, 190–93.

MRS. EDWARD KENNARD

The Golf Lunatic and His Cycling Wife, 1902
  Wintle, Sarah. "Horses, Bikes and Automobiles: New Woman on the Move," in Angelique Richardson and Chris Willis, eds., *The New Woman in Fiction and in Fact*, 72–75.
The Motor Maniac, 1902
  Wintle, Sarah. "Horses, Bikes and Automobiles: New Woman on the Move," in Angelique Richardson and Chris Willis, eds., *The New Woman in Fiction and in Fact*, 75–78.

JAMES KENNAWAY

Tunes of Glory, 1956
  Walker, Marshall. *Scottish Literature since 1707*, 320–21.

ALISON KENNEDY

Looking for the Possible Dance, 1993
  Gifford, Douglas. "Contemporary Fiction II: Seven Writers in Scotland," in Douglas Gifford and Dorothy McMillan, eds., *A History*, 617–18.
  McMillan, Dorothy. "Constructed Out of Bewilderment: Stories of Scotland," in Ian A. Bell, ed., *Peripheral Visions*, 95–97.
  Oliver, Fiona. "The Self-Debasement of Scotland's Postcolonial Bodies." *SPAN* 42–43 (1996), 114–21.
So I Am Glad, 1995
  Gifford, Douglas. "Contemporary Fiction II: Seven Writers in Scotland," in Douglas Gifford and Dorothy McMillan, eds., *A History*, 619–21.

DAVID KER

Torn from Its Foundations, 1908
  Forman, Ross G. "When Britons Brave Brazil: British Imperialism and the Adventure Tale in Latin America." *Victorian Stud* 42:3 (1999/2000), 467–70.

PHILIP KERR

March Violets, 1989
  Schnöink-Juppe, Marion. "The Image of Nazi Germany in British Popular Literature," in C. C. Barfoot, ed., *Beyond Pug's Tour*, 407–10.

JESSIE KESSON

Another Time, Another Place, 1983

> Knudsen, Janice L. "Jessie Kesson's *Another Time, Another Place*: A Vision of Self." *Stud in Scottish Lit* 31 (1999), 203–9.
>
> Murray, Isobel. "Jessie Kesson," in Douglas Gifford and Dorothy McMillan, eds., *A History*, 491–92.

Glitter of Mica, 1963

> Murray, Isobel. "A Far Cry from the Kailyard: Jessie Kesson's *Glitter of Mica*," in Carol Anderson and Aileen Christianson, eds., *Scottish Women's Fiction*, 147–57.
>
> Murray, Isobel. "Jessie Kesson," in Douglas Gifford and Dorothy McMillan, eds., *A History*, 487–89.

The White Bird Passes, 1958

> Murray, Isobel. "Jessie Kesson," in Douglas Gifford and Dorothy McMillan, eds., *A History*, 481–87.
>
> Norquay, Glenda. "Borderlines: Jessie Kesson's *The White Bird Passes*," in Carol Anderson and Aileen Christianson, eds., *Scottish Women's Fiction*, 122–32.

JOHN KIDGELL

The Card, 1755

> Shevlin, Eleanor F. "The Plots of Early English Novels: Narrative Mappings Rooted in Land and Law." *Eighteenth-Cent Fiction* 11 (1999), 379–81.

CHARLES KINGSLEY

Alton Locke, 1850

> Alderson, David. "An Anatomy of the British Polity: *Alton Locke* and Christian Manliness," in Ruth Robbins and Julian Wolfreys, eds., *Victorian Identities*, 43–60.
>
> Brantlinger, Patrick. *The Reading Lesson*, 104–7.
>
> Childers, Joseph W. "Industrial Culture and the Victorian Novel," in Deirdre David, ed., *The Cambridge Companion to the Victorian Novel*, 82–83.
>
> Corbett, Mary Jean. *Allegories of Union*, 105–13.
>
> Franklin, J. Jeffrey. *Serious Play*, 182–95.
>
> Graziano, Anne. "The Death of the Working-Class Hero in *Mary Barton* and *Alton Locke*." *J of Narrative Theory* 29 (1999), 135–51.
>
> Law, Graham. "Industrial Designs: Form and Function in the 'Condition-of-England' Novel," in George Hughes, ed., *Corresponding Powers*, 137–39.
>
> Menke, Richard. "Cultural Capital and the Scene of Rioting: Male Working-Class Authorship in *Alton Locke*." *Victorian Lit and Culture* 28 (2000), 87–104.
>
> Noe, Mark D. "Kingsley's *Alton Locke*." *Explicator* 57:1 (1998), 24–26.
>
> Rauch, Alan. *Useful Knowledge*, 164–89.

Stitt, Megan Perigoe. *Metaphors of Change*, 72–79, 95–97, 100–104, 124–26, 134–37.

Hereward the Wake, 1866

Peck, John. *War, the Army and Victorian Literature*, 125–28.
Stitt, Megan Perigoe. *Metaphors of Change*, 28–36.
Wawn, Andrew. *The Vikings and the Victorians*, 318–19.

Hypatia, 1853

Prickett, Stephen. "Purging Christianity of its Semitic Origins: Kingsley, Arnold and the Bible," in Juliet John and Alice Jenkins, eds., *Rethinking Victorian Culture*, 66–70.

Two Years Ago, 1857

Kane, Penny. *Victorian Families in Fact and Fiction*, 24–26.
Stitt, Megan Perigoe. *Metaphors of Change*, 191–93.

The Water-Babies, 1863

Hunt, Peter. *Children's Literature*, 240–42.
Labbe, Jacqueline M. "The Godhead Regendered in Victorian Children's Literature," in Alice Jenkins and Juliet John, eds., *Rereading Victorian Fiction*, 102–4.
Melrose, Robin, and Diana Gardner. "The Language of Control in Victorian Children's Literature," in Ruth Robbins and Julian Wolfreys, eds., *Victorian Identities*, 146, 151–52, 157–58.
Milbank, Alison. *Dante and the Victorians*, 176–79.
Reynolds, Kimberley, and Paul Yates. "Too Soon: Representations of Childhood Death in Literature for Children," in Karín Lesnik-Oberstein, ed., *Children in Culture*, 164–66.
Scutter, Heather. "The Origins of *The Water-Babies*." *Australasian Victorian Stud J* 5 (1999), 79–86.

Westward Ho!, 1855

Altavista, Paola. "Charles Kingsley e il romanzo storico: *Westward Ho!*" *Quaderni del Dipartimento di Lingue e Letterature Straniere Moderne* (Genova) 10 (1998), 137–65.
Fasick, Laura. "The Seduction of Celibacy: Threats to Male Sexual Identity in Charles Kingsley's Writings," in Jay Losey and William D. Brewer, eds., *Mapping Male Sexuality*, 226–27.
Peck, John. *Maritime Fiction*, 151–53.
Peck, John. *War, the Army and Victorian Literature*, 41–47.
Schiefelbein, Michael. "'Blighted' by a 'Upas-Shadow': Catholicism's Function for Kingsley in *Westward Ho!*." *Victorian Newsl* 94 (1998), 10–16.
Stitt, Megan Perigoe. *Metaphors of Change*, 169–74, 181–83.
Trezise, Simon. *The West Country as a Literary Invention*, 96–101.

Yeast, 1848

Fasick, Laura. "The Seduction of Celibacy: Threats to Male Sexual Identity in Charles Kingsley's Writings," in Jay Losey and William D. Brewer, eds., *Mapping Male Sexuality*, 228–29.
Jackson-Houlston, C. M. *Ballads, Songs and Snatches*, 77–81.
Rauch, Alan. *Useful Knowledge*, 168–71.

W. H. G. KINGSTON

In the Wilds of Africa, 1871
  Logan, Mawuena Kossi. *Narrating Africa*, 49–53.

RUDYARD KIPLING

Captains Courageous, 1897
  Peck, John. *Maritime Fiction*, 159–62.
Kim, 1901
  Amirthanayagam, Guy. *The Marriage of Continents*, 69–89.
  Ang, Susan. *The Widening World of Children's Literature*, 94–97.
  Baucom, Ian. *Out of Place*, 86–101.
  Black, Barbara J. "An Empire's Great Expectations: Museums in
    Imperialist Boy Fiction." *Nineteenth-Cent Contexts* 21 (1999),
    240–46.
  Brody, Jennifer DeVere. *Impossible Purities*, 148–50.
  Bucher, Christine. "Envisioning the Imperial Nation in Kipling's
    Kim." *J of Commonwealth and Postcolonial Stud* 5:2 (1998), 7–17.
  Craft, Brigette Wilds. "Apprentice to Empire: or, 'What is Kim?'" *J of
    Commonwealth and Postcolonial Stud* 5:2 (1998), 18–35.
  Delmas, Catherine. "La Métamorphose et le voyage en orient ou les
    avatars de la lecture: Conrad, Kipling, Forster." *Imaginaires* 4
    (1999), 117–31.
  Didicher, Nicole E. "Adolescence, Imperialism, and Identity in *Kim*
    and *Pegasus in Flight*." *Mosaic* 34:2 (2001), 149–64.
  Eckford-Prossor, Melanie. "Colonizing Children: Dramas of
    Transformation." *J of Narrative Theory* 30 (2000), 237–62.
  Ellis, Juniper. "Writing Race: Education and Ethnography in
    Kipling's *Kim*." *Centennial R* 39 (1995), 315–29.
  Gymnich, Marion. "Von *Greater Britain* zu *Little England*: Konstruktion
    und Dekonstruktion imperialistischer Denkweisen in Rudyard
    Kiplings *Kim*, E. M. Forsters *A Passage to India* und Joseph Conrads
    Heart of Darkness." *Anglistik und Englischunterricht* 58 (1996), 149–66.
  Hervoche-Bertho, Brigitte. "The Wheel and the Way: Kipling's
    Symbolic Imagination in *Kim*." *Cahiers Victoriens et Edouardiens*
    47 (1998), 365–72.
  Höglund, Johan A. *Mobilising the Novel*, 66–71.
  Jussawalla, Feroza. "Kim, Huck and Naipaul: Using the Postcolonial
    Bildungsroman to (Re)Define Postcoloniality." *Links and Letters* 4
    (1997), 25–38.
  Jussawalla, Feroza. "(Re)Reading *Kim*: Defining Kipling's
    Masterpiece as Postcolonial." *J of Commonwealth and Postcolonial
    Stud* 5:2 (1998), 112–30.
  Khanna, Ranjana. "'Araby': Women's Time and the Time of the
    Nation," in Ellen Carol Jones, ed., *Joyce*, 92–94.
  Kutzer, M. Daphne. *Empire's Children*, 15–24.
  Lal, Malashri. "Questioning Otherness: Racial Indeterminacy in
    Kipling, Tagore and Paul Scott." *In-Between* 3:1 (1994), 3–13.

Lycett, Andrew. *Rudyard Kipling*, 331–33.

McBratney, John. "Passing and the Modern Persona in Kipling's Ethnographer Fiction." *Victorian Lit and Culture* 24 (1996), 39–45.

Matin, A. Michael. "'The Hun is at the gate!': Historicizing Kipling's Militaristic Rhetoric, From the Imperial Periphery to the National Center; Part One: The Russian Threat to British India." *Stud in the Novel* 31 (1999), 332–48.

Matteo, Chris Ann. "*Le grand jeu* and the Great Game: The Politics of Play in Walter Scott's *Waverley* and Rudyard Kipling's *Kim*." *J of Narrative Theory* 30 (2000), 163–80.

Morgado, Margarida. "The Season of Play: Constructions of the Child in the English Novel," in Karín Lesnik-Oberstein, ed., *Children in Culture*, 217–19.

Randall, Don. "The Kipling Given, Ondaatje's Take: Reading *Kim* through *The English Patient*." *J of Commonwealth and Postcolonial Stud* 5:2 (1998), 131–44.

Randall, Don. *Kipling's Imperial Boy*, 110–59.

Randall, Don. "Kipling's *Stalky & Co.*: Resituating the Empire and the 'Empire Boy.'" *Victorian R* 24 (1998), 163–74.

Ricketts, Harry. *The Unforgiving Minute*, 271–74.

Roy, Parama. *Indian Traffic*, 75–91.

Viola, Andre. "Empire of the Senses or a Sense of Empire? The Imaginary and the Symbolic in Kipling's *Kim*." *Ariel* 28:2 (1997), 159–69.

Wager, Timothy J. "Mapping the Ground, Grounding the Subject: Cartography and the Formation of Nation in Kipling's *Kim*." *Vanishing Point* 2 (1996), 135–50.

Watson, Tim. "Indian and Irish Unrest in Kipling's *Kim*," in Laura Chrisman and Benita Parry, eds., *Postcolonial Theory and Criticism*, 95–111.

The Light That Failed, 1890

Arata, Stephen. *Fictions of Loss*, 171–77.

Lycett, Andrew. *Rudyard Kipling*, 211–16.

Peck, John. *War, the Army and Victorian Literature*, 158–60.

Ricketts, Harry. *The Unforgiving Minute*, 166–75.

The Man Who Would Be King, 1888

Leerssen, Joep. "The Allochronic Periphery: Towards a Grammar of Cross-Cultural Representation," in C. C. Barfoot, ed., *Beyond Pug's Tour*, 291–93.

Marx, Edward. "How We Lost Kafiristan." *Representations* 67 (1999), 44–66.

Soubigou, Gilbert. "L'Aventurier-roi, personnage oublié de la littérature exotique." *Carnets de l'Exotisme* 12 (1993), 7–16.

Stalky & Co., 1899

Ang, Susan. *The Widening World of Children's Literature*, 92–94.

Bivona, Daniel. *British Imperial Literature*, 80–85.

Cavaliero, Glen. *The Alchemy of Laughter*, 135–40.

Kutzer, M. Daphne. *Empire's Children*, 40–44.

Lycett, Andrew. *Rudyard Kipling*, 60–62, 65–67, 300–302.

Randall, Don. *Kipling's Imperial Boy*, 89–109.
Randall, Don. "Kipling's *Stalky and Co.*: Resituating the Empire and the 'Empire Boy.'" *Victorian R* 24 (1998), 163–72.
Ricketts, Harry. *The Unforgiving Minute*, 241–43, 259–60.

ARTHUR KOESTLER

Darkness at Noon, 1940

George, Emery E. "*Hyperion* and *Darkness at Noon*: Resemblance with a Difference." *JEGP* 97 (1998), 51–68.
Posner, Richard A. *Law and Literature*, 137–38.

HANIF KUREISHI

The Black Album, 1995

Kaleta, Kenneth C. *Hanif Kureishi*, 125–34, 141–46.
Stein, Mark. "Posed Ethnicity and the Postethnic: Hanif Kureishi's Novels," in Heinz Antor and Klaus Stierstorfer, eds., *English Literatures in International Contexts*, 130–35.

The Buddha of Suburbia, 1988

Alliot, Bénédicte. "Misplacement in Hanif Kureishi's *The Buddha of Suburbia*." *Commonwealth Essays and Stud* 4 (1997), 95–100.
Baneth-Nouailhetas, Emilienne. "Karim/Kim: Mutations kiplingiennes dans *The Buddha of Suburbia*." *Q/W/E/R/T/Y* 7 (1997), 183–89.
Brînzeu, Pia. *Corridors of Mirrors*, 89–91, 119–21.
Brînzeu, Pia. "Imaginary Cities." *B.A.S.: Brit and Am Stud* 1:1 (1996), 56–62.
Carey, Cynthia. "Hanif Kureishi's *The Buddha of Suburbia* as a Post-Colonial Novel." *Commonwealth Essays and Stud* 4 (1997), 119–25.
Doyle, Waddick. "The Space between Identity and Otherness in Hanif Kureishi's *The Buddha of Suburbia*." *Commonwealth Essays and Stud* 4 (1997), 110–18.
Felski, Rita. "Nothing to Declare: Identity, Shame, and the Lower Middle Class." *PMLA* 115 (2000), 37–44.
Frank-Wilson, Marion. "World Fiction: The Transformation of the English/Western Literature Canon," in Susanne Fendler and Ruth Wittlinger, eds., *The Idea of Europe in Literature*, 89–94.
Huggan, Graham. *The Postcolonial Exotic*, 95–99.
Jena, Seema. "From Victims to Survivors." *Wasafiri* 17 (1993), 3–6.
Kaleta, Kenneth C. *Hanif Kureishi*, 62–84.
Mishrahi-Barak, Judith. "The Scope of Fiction in Hanif Kureishi's *The Buddha of Suburbia*: From Margin to Margin and Back to the Centre" *Etudes Britanniques Contemporaines* 13 (1998), 31–39.
Mishrahi-Barak, Judith. "Yoga and the *Bildungsroman* in Hanif Kureishi's *The Buddha of Suburbia*." *Commonwealth Essays and Stud* 4 (1997), 88–94.
Moore-Gilbert, Bart. "Hanif Kureishi's *The Buddha of Suburbia*: Hybridity in Contemporary Cultural Theory and Artistic Practice." *Q/W/E/R/T/Y* 7 (1997), 191–207.

Naranjo Acosta, Isaías. "Pilgrimage: On Hanif Kureishi's *The Buddha of Suburbia*." *Revista Canaria de Estudios Ingleses* 28 (1994), 53–63.

Needham, Anuradha Dingwaney. *Using The Master's Tools*, 111–15, 121–26.

Oubechou, Jamel. "'The Barbarians and the Philistines' in *The Buddha of Suburbia*: Dis/locating Culture." *Commonwealth Essays and Stud* 4 (1997), 101–9.

Sandhu, Sukhdev. "Pop Goes the Centre: Hanif Kureishi's London," in Laura Chrisman and Benita Parry, eds., *Postcolonial Theory and Criticism*, 133–53.

Schoene, Berthold. "Herald of Hybridity: The Emancipation of Difference in Hanif Kureishi's *The Buddha of Suburbia*." *Intl J of Cultural Stud* 1:1 (1998), 109–28.

Stein, Mark. "Posed Ethnicity and the Postethnic: Hanif Kureishi's Novels," in Heinz Antor and Klaus Stierstorfer, eds., *English Literatures in International Contexts*, 123–29.

Wallhead, Celia M. "Paradigms of Diversity in Hanif Kureishi's *The Buddha of Suburbia*." *Revista Canaria de Estudios Ingleses* 28 (1994), 65–79.

Weber, Jean Jacques. "The Absent Character of Gene in Hanif Kureishi's *The Buddha of Suburbia*." *Notes on Contemp Lit* 31:3 (2001), 8–10.

Yu-Cheng, Lee. "Expropriating the Authentic: Cultural Politics in Hanif Kureishi's *The Buddha of Suburbia*." *EurAmerica: A J of European and Am Stud* 26:3 (1996), 1–19.

Intimacy, 1998

Stein, Mark. "Posed Ethnicity and the Postethnic: Hanif Kureishi's Novels," in Heinz Antor and Klaus Stierstorfer, eds., *English Literatures in International Contexts*, 135–39.

LADY CAROLINE LAMB

Glenarvon, 1816

Douglass, Paul. "Playing Byron: Lady Caroline Lamb's *Glenarvon* and the Music of Isaac Nathan." *European Romantic R* 8:1 (1997), 1–24.

Judson, Barbara. "Roman à Clef and the Dynamics of Betrayal: The Case of *Glenarvon*." *Genre* 33 (2000), 151–69.

Watson, Nicola J. *Revolution and the Form of the British Novel*, 181–83.

Wordsworth, Jonathan. *The Bright Work Grows*, 209–14.

MARY ANN LAMB

Mrs. Leicester's School, 1807

Bottoms, Janet. "Every One Her Own Heroine: Conflicting Narrative Structures in *Mrs Leicester's School*." *Women's Writing* 7 (2000), 39–53.

Bottoms, Janet. "In the Absence of Mrs Leicester: Mary Lamb's Place in the Development of a Literature of Childhood," in Mary Hilton et al., eds., *Opening the Nursery Door*, 117–32.

Cracium, Adriana. "The Subject of Violence: Mary Lamb, Femme Fatale," in Harriet Kramer Linkin and Stephen C. Behrendt, eds., *Romanticism and Women Poets*, 49–55, 62–64.

Dobson, Meagan Hanrahan. "(Re)Considering Mary Lamb: Imagination and Memory in *Mrs. Leicester's School.*" *Charles Lamb Bull* 93 (1996), 12–21.

GEORGE LAMMING

The Emigrants, 1954

Procter, James. "Descending the Stairwell: Dwelling Places and Doorways in Early Post-War Black British Writing." *Kunapipi* 20:1 (1998), 24–30.

In the Castle of My Skin, 1953

James, Louis. *Caribbean Literature in English*, 34–36.

Kirpal, Viney. "George Lamming's *In the Castle of My Skin*: A Modern West Indian Novel." *Ariel* 28:2 (1997), 103–13.

Skinner, John. *The Stepmother Tongue*, 165–67.

Wilson-Tagoe, Nana. *Historical Thought and Literary Representation*, 80–82.

Natives of My Person, 1972

Wilson-Tagoe, Nana. *Historical Thought and Literary Representation*, 100–105.

Of Age and Innocence, 1958

Odhiambo, Christopher J. "Outside the Eyes of the Other: George Lamming and Definition in *Of Age and Innocence.*" *Res in African Literatures* 25:2 (1994), 121–30.

Wilson-Tagoe, Nana. *Historical Thought and Literary Representation*, 82–89.

Season of Adventure, 1958

Comfort, Susan. "Exile, Nationalism and Decolonizing History in George Lamming's *Season of Adventure.*" *World Lit Written in Engl* 34:2 (1995), 70–93.

James, Louis. *Caribbean Literature in English*, 141–42.

Wilson-Tagoe, Nana. *Historical Thought and Literary Representation*, 90–92.

Water with Berries, 1971

Wilson-Tagoe, Nana. *Historical Thought and Literary Representation*, 96–100.

JOHN LANCHESTER

The Debt to Pleasure, 1996

Reckwitz, Erhard. "Intertextuality: Between Continuity and

Innovation," in Barbara Korte and Klaus Peter Müller, eds., *Unity in Diversity Revisited?*, 193–94.

PHILIP LARKIN

A Girl in Winter, 1947

Hedgecock, Liz. "New Worlds for Old: Mythology and Exile in the Novels of Philip Larkin," in James Booth ed., *New Larkins for the Old*, 97–106.

Jill, 1946

Dougill, John. *Oxford in English Literature*, 222–24.

Hedgecock, Liz. "New Worlds for Old: Mythology and Exile in the Novels of Philip Larkin," in James Booth ed., *New Larkins for the Old*, 97–106.

MARY LAVIN

The House in Clewe Street, 1945

Lynch, Rachael Sealy. "'The Fabulous Female Form': The Deadly Erotics of the Male Gaze in Mary Lavin's *The House in Clewe Street*." *Twentieth Cent Lit* 43 (1997), 326–36.

EMILY LAWLESS

Grania, 1892

Cahalan, James M. *Double Visions*, 41–47.

Cahalan, James M. "Forging a Tradition: Emily Lawless and the Irish Literary Canon," in Kathryn Kirkpatrick, ed., *Border Crossings*, 44–53.

Matthews-Kane, Bridget. "Emily Lawless's *Grania*: Making for the Open." *Colby Q* 33 (1997), 223–35.

Meaney, Gerardine. "Decadence, Degeneration and Revolting Aesthetics: The Fiction of Emily Lawless and Katherine Cecil Thurston." *Colby Q* 36 (2000), 162–68.

Hurrish, 1886

Cahalan, James M. *Double Visions*, 32–37.

With Essex in Ireland, 1890

Mills, Lia. "Forging History: Emily Lawless's *With Essex in Ireland*." *Colby Q* 36 (2000), 132–43.

Patten, Eve. "With Essex in India? Emily Lawless's Colonial Consciousness." *European J of Engl Stud* 3 (1999), 285–97.

D. H. LAWRENCE

Aaron's Rod, 1922

Ayers, David. *English Literature of the 1920s*, 38–43.

Becket, Fiona. *D. H. Lawrence*, 100–104.

Doherty, Gerald. *Theorizing Lawrence*, 24–27.

Ellis, David. "Lawrence, Florence and Theft: *Petites misères* of Biographical Enquiry," in George Donaldson and Mara Kalnins, eds., *D. H. Lawrence in Italy and England*, 80–88.

Ferrall, Charles. *Modernist Writing and Reactionary Politics*, 124–26.

Gleason, Paul. "A Note on Plato and *Aaron's Rod.*" *D. H. Lawrence R* 27 (1998), 321–24.

Granofsky, Ronald. "'Jews of the Wrong Sort': D. H. Lawrence and Race." *J of Mod Lit* 23 (1999/2000), 221–23.

Granofsky, Ronald. "Modernism and D. H. Lawrence: Spatial Form and Selfhood in *Aaron's Rod.*" *Engl Stud in Canada* 26 (2000), 29–48.

Kalnins, Mara. "Play and Carnival in *Sea and Sardinia*," in George Donaldson and Mara Kalnins, eds., *D. H. Lawrence in Italy and England*, 100–103.

Mellown, Elgin W. "Music and Dance in D. H. Lawrence." *J of Mod Lit* 21 (1997), 58–60.

Wright, T. R. *D. H. Lawrence and the Bible*, 140–45.

The Boy in the Bush, 1990 (1924)

Wright, T. R. *D. H. Lawrence and the Bible*, 151–61.

Kangaroo, 1923

Ayers, David. *English Literature of the 1920s*, 129–33.

Brewster, Scott. "Jumping Continents: Abjection, *Kangaroo*, and the Celtic Uncanny." *D. H. Lawrence R* 27 (1998), 217–30.

Darroch, Robert. "Not the End of the Story: The Cambridge University Press *Kangaroo.*" *D. H. Lawrence R* 26 (1995–96), 327–52.

Doherty, Gerald. *Theorizing Lawrence*, 24–27.

Ferrall, Charles. *Modernist Writing and Reactionary Politics*, 124–25, 129–33.

Greiff, Louis K. *D. H. Lawrence*, 186–203.

Kaye, Peter. *Dostoevsky and English Modernism*, 59–62.

McCormick, John. *Catastrophe and Imagination*, 244–47.

Stewart, Jack. *The Vital Art of D. H. Lawrence*, 173–85.

Wright, T. R. *D. H. Lawrence and the Bible*, 145–51.

Lady Chatterley's Lover, 1928

Armstrong, Nancy. *Fiction in the Age of Photography*, 270–72.

Ayers, David. *English Literature of the 1920s*, 167–87.

Baldick, Chris. "Post-Mortem: Lawrence's Critical and Cultural Legacy," in Anne Fernihough, ed., *The Cambridge Companion to D. H. Lawrence*, 261–63.

Burack, Charles M. "Mortifying the Reader: The Assault on Verbal and Visual Consciousness in D. H. Lawrence's *Lady Chatterley's Lover.*" *Stud in the Novel* 29 (1997), 491–507.

Burack, Charles M. "Revitalizing the Reader: Literary Technique and the Language of Sacred Experience in D. H. Lawrence's *Lady Chatterley's Lover.*" *Style* 32:1 (1998), 102–26.

Clifford, Stephen P. *Beyond the Heroic "I,"* 271–322.

Disch, Thomas M. *The Dreams Our Stuff Is Made Of*, 116–17, 119–21.

Doherty, Gerald. "The Art of Appropriation: The Rhetoric of Sexuality in D. H. Lawrence." *Style* 30 (1996), 298–303.

Doherty, Gerald. "The Chatterley/Bolton Affair: The Freudian Path of Regression in *Lady Chatterley's Lover.*" *Papers on Lang and Lit* 34 (1998), 372–86.

Doherty, Gerald. "Metaphor and Mental Disturbance: The Case of *Lady Chatterley's Lover.*" *Style* 30 (1996), 113–26.

Doherty, Gerald. *Theorizing Lawrence*, 28–31, 46–49, 104–13.

Friedman, Alan W. "D. H. Lawrence: Pleasure and Death." *Stud in the Novel* 32 (2000), 220–25.

Gordon, Jan. "The 'Talking Cure' (Again): Gossip and the Paralyzed Patriarchy," in David T. Mitchell and Sharon L. Snyder, eds., *The Body and Physical Difference*, 202–10.

Greiff, Louis K. *D. H. Lawrence*, 147–85.

Holbrook, David. *"Wuthering Heights,"* 182–83.

Ingersoll, Earl G. *D. H. Lawrence, Desire, and Narrative*, 147–68.

Kellogg, David. "Reading Foucault Reading Lawrence: Body, Voice, and Sexuality in *Lady Chatterley's Lover.*" *D. H. Lawrence R* 28:3 (1999), 31–50.

Kojecky, Roger. "Knowing Good and Evil: T. S. Eliot and *Lady Chatterley's Lover.*" *ANQ* 11:3 (1998), 37–50.

Martz, Louis L. "Teaching *Lady Chatterley's Lover*," in M. Elizabeth Sargent and Garry Watson, eds., *Approaches to Teaching*, 226–27.

Mester, Terri A. *Movement and Modernism*, 120–22.

Milne, Drew. "Lawrence and the Politics of Sexual Politics," in Anne Fernihough, ed., *The Cambridge Companion to D. H. Lawrence*, 209–14.

Pease, Allison. *Modernism, Mass Culture, and the Aesthetics of Obscenity*, 136–64.

Pérez Hernández, Lorena. "A Linguistic Approach to the Erotism of *Lady Chatterley's Lover.*" *Cuadernos de Investigación Filológica* 23–24 (1997–1998), 213–31.

Salaün, Elise. "Erotisme littéraire et censure: La Révolution cachée." *Voix et Images* 23 (1998), 297–313.

Shiach, Morag. "Work and Selfhood in *Lady Chatterley's Lover*," in Anne Fernihough, ed., *The Cambridge Companion to D. H. Lawrence*, 87–101.

Tridgell, Susan. "Choosing Emotions: *Lady Chatterley's Lover.*" *Crit R* (Melbourne) 37 (1997), 119–30.

Valdeón García, Roberta A. "El tratamiento de la temática homosexual en cuatro novelistas ingleses: Lawrence, Forster, Waugh y Storey." *Cuadernos de Investigación Filológica* 23–24 (1997–1998), 139–62.

Wexler, Joyce. "D. H. Lawrence through a Postmodernist Lens." *D. H. Lawrence R* 27:1 (1997–1998), 47–64.

Wright, T. R. *D. H. Lawrence and the Bible*, 219–24.

Wright, Terry R. "Lawrence and Bataille: Recovering the Sacred, Remembering Jesus." *Lit and Theology* 13 (1999), 66–72.

Young, Jane Jaffe. *D. H. Lawrence on Screen*, 4–7.

The Lost Girl, 1920

Ardis, Ann. "Delimiting Modernism and the Literary Field: D. H.

Lawrence and *The Lost Girl*," in Lynne Hapgood and Nancy L. Paxton, eds., *Outside Modernism*, 123–39.

Cavaliero, Glen. *The Alchemy of Laughter*, 123–25.

Granofsky, Ronald. "'Jews of the Wrong Sort': D. H. Lawrence and Race." *J of Mod Lit* 23 (1999/2000), 220–21.

Sargent, M. Elizabeth. "*The Lost Girl*: Re-appraising the Post-War Lawrence on Women's Will and Ways of Knowing," in George Donaldson and Mara Kalnins, eds., *D. H. Lawrence in Italy and England*, 176–91.

Wexler, Joyce. "D. H. Lawrence through a Postmodernist Lens." *D. H. Lawrence R* 27:1 (1997–1998), 47–64.

Worthen, John. "Recovering *The Lost Girl*: Lost Heroines, Irrecoverable Texts, Irretrievable Landscapes," in George Donaldson and Mara Kalnins, eds., *D. H. Lawrence in Italy and England*, 211–27.

Mr. Noon, 1984

Ingersoll, Earl G. *D. H. Lawrence, Desire, and Narrative*, 129–46.

Wright, T. R. *D. H. Lawrence and the Bible*, 136–39.

The Plumed Serpent, 1926

Ayers, David. *English Literature of the 1920s*, 199–210.

Doherty, Gerald. *Theorizing Lawrence*, 24–27.

Ferrall, Charles. *Modernist Writing and Reactionary Politics*, 130–32.

Gilbert, Sandra M. "D. H. Lawrence's Mexican Hat Dance: Rereading *The Plumed Serpent*," in Shlomith Rimmon-Kenan et al., eds., *Rereading Texts*, 291–303.

Huerta, Teresa. "Modelos colectivos circulares en *Nostromo* de Conrad, *The Plumed Serpent* de Lawrence, y *Tirano Banderas* de Valle-Inclán." *RLA: Romance Languages Annual* 7 (1995), 509–14.

Hyde, Virginia. "Kate and the Goddess: Subtexts in *The Plumed Serpent*." *D. H. Lawrence R* 26 (1995–96), 249–66.

Hyde, Virginia Crosswhite. "Picking Up 'Life-Threads' in Lawrence's Mexico: Dialogism and Multiculturalism in *The Plumed Serpent*," in M. Elizabeth Sargent and Garry Watson, eds., *Approaches to Teaching*, 172–82.

Kinkead-Weekes, Mark. "Decolonising Imagination: Lawrence in the 1920s," in Anne Fernihough, ed., *The Cambridge Companion to D. H. Lawrence*, 71–73, 81–83.

Neilson, Brett. "D. H. Lawrence's 'Dark Page': Narrative Primitivism in *Women in Love* and *The Plumed Serpent*." *Twentieth Cent Lit* 43 (1997), 315–23.

Stevens, Hugh. "*The Plumed Serpent* and the Erotics of Primitive Masculinity," in M. Elizabeth Sargent and Garry Watson, eds., *Approaches to Teaching*, 219–38.

Stewart, Jack. *The Vital Art of D. H. Lawrence*, 185–92.

Thompson, Theresa Mae. "Postcolonial Questions for Teaching *The Plumed Serpent*," in M. Elizabeth Sargent and Garry Watson, eds., *Approaches to Teaching*, 221–25.

Wexler, Joyce. "D. H. Lawrence through a Postmodernist Lens." *D. H. Lawrence R* 27:1 (1997–1998), 47–64.

Wexler, Joyce. "Realism and Modernists' Bad Reputation." *Stud in the Novel* 31 (1999), 67–70.

Wright, T. R. *D. H. Lawrence and the Bible*, 193–207.

The Rainbow, 1915

Becket, Fiona. *D. H. Lawrence*, 22–24, 117–44.

Bell, Michael. "Lawrence and Modernism," in Anne Fernihough, ed., *The Cambridge Companion to D. H. Lawrence*, 188–90.

Burack, Charles M. "The Religious Initiation of the Reader in D. H. Lawrence's *The Rainbow*." *Mosaic* 33:3 (2000), 165–80.

Burden, Robert. "The Discursive Formations of History in D. H. Lawrence, *The Rainbow*." *Anglia* 115 (1997), 323–51.

Butler, Gerald J. "This Is Carbon: A Defense of D. H. Lawrence's *The Rainbow* Against His Admirers." *Recovering Lit* 25 (1999), 1–123.

Clifford, Stephen P. *Beyond the Heroic "I,"* 49–92.

Doherty, Gerald. "The Art of Appropriation: The Rhetoric of Sexuality in D. H. Lawrence." *Style* 30 (1996), 294–98.

Doherty, Gerald. *Theorizing Lawrence*, 38–40, 121–30.

Driskill, Richard T. *Madonnas and Maidens*, 179–81, 205–44.

Edwards, Justin D. "At the End of *The Rainbow*: Reading Lesbian Identities in D. H. Lawrence's Fiction." *Intl Fiction R* 27:1–2 (2000), 60–67.

Edwards, Justin D. "Historicizing the Homosocial: Shifting Lesbian Identities in *The Rainbow*." *Henry Street* 5:2 (1995), 33–48.

Eggert, Paul. "The Biographical Issue: Lives of Lawrence," in Anne Fernihough, ed., *The Cambridge Companion to D. H. Lawrence*, 164–67.

Ferrall, Charles. *Modernist Writing and Reactionary Politics*, 117–20.

Ferreira, Maria Aline Seabra. "The Foreigner Within: Teaching *The Rainbow* with the Help of Cixous, Kristeva, and Irigaray," in M. Elizabeth Sargent and Garry Watson, eds., *Approaches to Teaching*, 99–105.

Fox, Elizabeth M. "Closure and Foreclosure in *The Rainbow*." *D. H. Lawrence R* 27 (1998), 197–211.

Gawlik, Agnieszka. "Religious Approach to Duality of Human Existence in *The Rainbow*." *Acta Universitatis Nicolai Copernici: Engl Stud* 6 (1995), 51–65.

Greiff, Louis K. *D. H. Lawrence*, 109–40.

Hill, Marylu. *Mothering Modernity*, 107–35.

Hyde, Virginia Crosswhite. "Toasting and Caroling in *The Rainbow*: Dramatic Rituals in the Classroom," in M. Elizabeth Sargent and Garry Watson, eds., *Approaches to Teaching*, 213–14.

Ingersoll, Earl G. *D. H. Lawrence, Desire, and Narrative*, 50–90.

Liou, Liang-ya. "The Problematic of a Politics of Sexual Liberation: D. H. Lawrence's *The Rainbow* and *Women in Love*." *Stud in Lang and Lit* (Taipei) 7 (1996), 57–83.

Marsh, Nicholas. *D. H. Lawrence*, 12–19, 27–32, 43–50, 58–63, 78–86, 96–111, 123–30, 140–43, 152–63, 169–72, 176–82.

Mauzerall, Jorgette. "Strange Bedfellows: D. H. Lawrence and Feminist Psychoanalytic Theory in *The Rainbow*," in M. Elizabeth Sargent and Garry Watson, eds., *Approaches to Teaching*, 89–98.

Mester, Terri A. *Movement and Modernism*, 105–11.

Norris, Nanette. "Alchemy and *The Rainbow*." *D. H. Lawrence R* 26 (1995–96), 133–44.

Phillips, Gene, S.J. "Ken Russell's Two Lawrence Films: *The Rainbow* and *Women in Love*." *Lit/Film Q* 25 (1997), 68–72.

Pykett, Lyn. *Engendering Fictions*, 123–27.

Ross, Charles L., and Donald Buckley. "Lawrence in Hypertext: A Technology of Difference for Reading/Writing *The Rainbow* and 'Odour of Chrysanthemums,'" in M. Elizabeth Sargent and Garry Watson, eds., *Approaches to Teaching*, 70–78.

Schapiro, Barbara Ann. *D. H. Lawrence*, 79–101.

Sepcic, Visnja. "A Biblical Intertext in Three Modernist Writers: Joyce, Lawrence, Krleza." *Studia Romanica et Anglica Zagrabiensia* 42 (1997), 352–53.

Sillars, Stuart. *Structure and Dissolution*, 93–124.

Sillars, Stuart. "'Terrible and Dreadful': Lawrence, Gertler and the Visual Imagination," in George Donaldson and Mara Kalnins, eds., *D. H. Lawrence in Italy and England*, 193–200.

Slabyj, Luba. "Fathoming Flood and Father in *The Rainbow* and *The Virgin and the Gypsy*," in M. Elizabeth Sargent and Garry Watson, eds., *Approaches to Teaching*, 79–88.

Stewart, Jack. "Examining the Stylistic Diversity of *The Rainbow* and *Women in Love* in an Honors Seminar on Criticism and Research Methods," in M. Elizabeth Sargent and Garry Watson, eds., *Approaches to Teaching*, 215–16.

Stewart, Jack. *The Vital Art of D. H. Lawrence*, 51–72.

Sumner, Rosemary. *A Route to Modernism*, 93–96, 107–25.

Templeton, Wayne. "Teaching the Case of the Subversive Novel: The Role of Contemporary Reviews in *The Rainbow* Trial," in M. Elizabeth Sargent and Garry Watson, eds., *Approaches to Teaching*, 208–12.

Torgovnick, Marianna. "Narrating Sexuality: *The Rainbow*," in Anne Fernihough, ed., *The Cambridge Companion to D. H. Lawrence*, 33–47.

Wright, T. R. *D. H. Lawrence and the Bible*, 84–86, 92–110.

Wussow, Helen. *The Nightmare of History*, 145–48.

York, R. A. *The Rules of Time*, 36–51.

Sons and Lovers, 1913

Atkins, A. R. "*Sons and Lovers* and Book History," in M. Elizabeth Sargent and Garry Watson, eds., *Approaches to Teaching*, 202–3.

Baron, Helen. "Disseminated Consciousness in *Sons and Lovers*." *Essays in Criticism* 48 (1998), 357–77.

Ben-Ephraim, Gavriel. "The Disappearing Drive: Rereading Literature and Psychoanalysis —Lawrence and Freud," in Shlomith Rimmon-Kenan et al., eds., *Rereading Texts*, 110–14.

Blaisdell, Bob. "D. H. Lawrence and Thomas Hardy: 'All This about a Daughter who is no Daughter of Thine!'" *Thomas Hardy Yrbk* 28 (2000), 46–50.

Catovsky, Michael. "When Was Gertrude Morel Born? A Puzzle in *Sons and Lovers*." *Notes and Queries* 46 (1999), 67–68.

Doherty, Gerald. *Theorizing Lawrence*, 69–83.

Driskill, Richard T. *Madonnas and Maidens*, 1–33, 67–97, 107–37, 151–53, 205–26.

Eggert, Paul. "The Biographical Issue: Lives of Lawrence," in Anne Fernihough, ed., *The Cambridge Companion to D. H. Lawrence*, 160–63.

Erzgräber, Willi. "Der moderne autobiographische Roman in England und Irland: D. H. Lawrence und James Joyce." *Literaturwissenschaftliches Jahrbuch im Auftrage der Görres-Gesellschaft* 34 (1993), 239–57.

Ferrall, Charles. *Modernist Writing and Reactionary Politics*, 116–17.

Fiddes, Paul S. *Freedom and Limit*, 154–57, 164–66.

Greiff, Louis K. *D. H. Lawrence*, 28–46.

Harrison, John R. "The Flesh and the Word: The Evolution of a Metaphysic in the Early Work of D. H. Lawrence." *Stud in the Novel* 32:1 (2000), 29–48.

Ingersoll, Earl G. *D. H. Lawrence, Desire, and Narrative*, 26–49.

Ingersoll, Earl G. "Gender and Language in *Sons and Lovers*." *Midwest Q* 37 (1996), 434–47.

Jeffers, Thomas L. "'We children were the in-betweens': Character (De)Formation in *Sons and Lovers*." *Texas Stud in Lit and Lang* 42 (2000), 290–311.

Kato, Yosuke. "*Sons and Lovers* and Problems of Text-Editing." *Stud in Engl Lit* (Tokyo) 75 (1999), 19–26.

Kloss, Robert J. "The Symbolic Use of Flowers in Lawrence's *Sons and Lovers*." *J of Evolutionary Psych* 19 (1998), 31–40.

McVea, Deborah. "An Overlooked Irony in D. H. Lawrence's Use of Dialect in *Sons and Lovers*." *Notes and Queries* 44 (1997), 354–55.

Marsh, Nicholas. *D. H. Lawrence*, 4–12, 27–32, 36–43, 58–63, 69–77, 96–111, 116–23, 140–43, 145–51, 169–72, 176–82.

Mester, Terri A. *Movement and Modernism*, 100–102.

Phelps, James M. "Teaching *Sons and Lovers* in a Global Context in South Africa: Colonialism and Modernity," in M. Elizabeth Sargent and Garry Watson, eds., *Approaches to Teaching*, 204–7.

Rylance, Rick. "Ideas, Histories, Generations and Beliefs: The Early Novels to *Sons and Lovers*," in Anne Fernihough, ed., *The Cambridge Companion to D. H. Lawrence*, 26–29.

Schapiro, Barbara Ann. *D. H. Lawrence*, 21–53.

Smith, Andrew. "Vampirism, Masculinity and Degeneracy: D. H. Lawrence's Modernist Gothic," in Andrew Smith and Jeff Wallace, eds., *Gothic Modernisms*, 150–65.

Stewart, Jack. *The Vital Art of D. H. Lawrence*, 25–50.

Sumner, Rosemary. *A Route to Modernism*, 97–99.

Worthen, John. "Lawrence as Dramatist," in Anne Fernihough, ed., *The Cambridge Companion to D. H. Lawrence*, 150–52.

Wright, T. R. *D. H. Lawrence and the Bible*, 72–83.

Young, Jane Jaffe. *D. H. Lawrence on Screen*, 75–127, 176–81, 188–91.

The Trespasser, 1912

Rylance, Rick. "Ideas, Histories, Generations and Beliefs: The Early

Novels to *Sons and Lovers*," in Anne Fernihough, ed., *The Cambridge Companion to D. H. Lawrence*, 22–26.

Wright, T. R. *D. H. Lawrence and the Bible*, 70–72.

The White Peacock, 1911

Bulaila, A. Aziz M. "Hardy's *Under the Greenwood Tree* and Lawrence's *The White Peacock*: Comparison and Influence." *Thomas Hardy Yrbk* 25 (1998), 11–18.

Harrison, John R. "The Flesh and the Word: The Evolution of a Metaphysic in the Early Work of D. H. Lawrence." *Stud in the Novel* 32:1 (2000), 29–48.

Ingersoll, Earl G. *D. H. Lawrence, Desire, and Narrative*, 11–25.

Mester, Terri A. *Movement and Modernism*, 96–100.

Rylance, Rick. "Ideas, Histories, Generations and Beliefs: The Early Novels to *Sons and Lovers*," in Anne Fernihough, ed., *The Cambridge Companion to D. H. Lawrence*, 15–21.

Stewart, Jack. "Landscape Painting and Pre-Raphaelitism in *The White Peacock*." *D. H. Lawrence R* 27 (1998), 3–21.

Stewart, Jack. "The Title Image of Lawrence's *The White Peacock*." *Engl Lang Notes* 35:2 (1997), 69–72.

Stewart, Jack. *The Vital Art of D. H. Lawrence*, 9–24.

Sultan, Stanley. "Lawrence the Anti-Autobiographer." *J of Mod Lit* 23 (1999/2000), 225–48.

Wright, T. R. *D. H. Lawrence and the Bible*, 69–70.

Women in Love, 1920

Becket, Fiona. *D. H. Lawrence*, 145–89.

Bell, Michael. "Lawrence and Modernism," in Anne Fernihough, ed., *The Cambridge Companion to D. H. Lawrence*, 188–90.

Carpenter, Rebecca. "'More Likely to Be the End of Experience': *Women in Love*, Sati, and the Marriage-Plot Tradition," in M. Elizabeth Sargent and Garry Watson, eds., *Approaches to Teaching*, 217–20.

Clifford, Stephen P. *Beyond the Heroic "I,"* 49–52, 93–137.

Doherty, Gerald. "A Question of Gravity: The Erotics of Identification in *Women in Love*." *D. H. Lawrence R* 29:2 (2000), 25–37.

Doherty, Gerald. *Theorizing Lawrence*, 22–24, 51–66, 85–98, 157–60.

Donaldson, George. "Unestablished Balance in *Women in Love*," in George Donaldson and Mara Kalnins, eds., *D. H. Lawrence in Italy and England*, 52–75.

Driskill, Richard T. *Madonnas and Maidens*, 239–44.

Eggert, Paul. "The Biographical Issue: Lives of Lawrence," in Anne Fernihough, ed., *The Cambridge Companion to D. H. Lawrence*, 165–69.

Ferns, John. *F. R. Leavis*, 110–13.

Fiddes, Paul S. *Freedom and Limit*, 148–51.

Friedman, Alan W. "D. H. Lawrence: Pleasure and Death." *Stud in the Novel* 32 (2000), 207–14.

Greiff, Louis K. *D. H. Lawrence*, 73–108.

Harrison, Andrew. "Electricity and the Place of Futurism in *Women in Love*." *D. H. Lawrence R* 29:2 (2000), 7–20.

Hirai, Masako. *Sisters in Literature*, 121–210.

Ingersoll, Earl G. *D. H. Lawrence, Desire, and Narrative*, 91–128.

Jouve, Nicole Ward. *Female Genesis*, 103–17.

Kalnins, Mara. "Play and Carnival in *Sea and Sardinia*," in George Donaldson and Mara Kalnins, eds., *D. H. Lawrence in Italy and England*, 107–10.

Kane, Michael. *Modern Men*, 178–81.

Levy, Eric P. "The Paradoxes of Love in *Women in Love*." *Centennial R* 43 (1999), 575–84.

Liou, Liang-ya. "The Problematic of a Politics of Sexual Liberation: D. H. Lawrence's *The Rainbow* and *Women in Love*." *Stud in Lang and Lit* (Taipei) 7 (1996), 57–83.

Marsh, Nicholas. *D. H. Lawrence*, 19–32, 50–63, 86–111, 130–43, 163–72, 176–82.

Mellown, Elgin W. "Music and Dance in D. H. Lawrence." *J of Mod Lit* 21 (1997), 56–57.

Mester, Terri A. *Movement and Modernism*, 111–16.

Neilson, Brett. "D. H. Lawrence's 'Dark Page': Narrative Primitivism in *Women in Love* and *The Plumed Serpent*." *Twentieth Cent Lit* 43 (1997), 311–15.

O'Neill, Michael. "Liking or Disliking: Woolf, Conrad, Lawrence," in Richard Gravil, ed., *Master Narratives*, 176–79.

Peirce, Carol, and Lawrence W. Markert. "Team-Teaching Lawrence in a Culminating Senior Seminar," in M. Elizabeth Sargent and Garry Watson, eds., *Approaches to Teaching*, 228–29.

Phillips, Gene, S.J. "Ken Russell's Two Lawrence Films: *The Rainbow* and *Women in Love*." *Lit/Film Q* 25 (1997), 68–72.

Rosenbaum, S. P. *Aspects of Bloomsbury*, 45–47.

Schapiro, Barbara Ann. *D. H. Lawrence*, 103–29.

Sillars, Stuart. "'Terrible and Dreadful': Lawrence, Gertler and the Visual Imagination," in George Donaldson and Mara Kalnins, eds., *D. H. Lawrence in Italy and England*, 200–205.

Skukla, Narain Prasad. "Mystery and Individuality in *Women in Love*." *Panjab Univ Res Bull* 26 (1995), 101–7.

Stevens, Hugh. "Sex and the Nation: 'The Prussian Officer' and *Women in Love*," in Anne Fernihough, ed., *The Cambridge Companion to D. H. Lawrence*, 49–64.

Stewart, Jack. "Examining the Stylistic Diversity of *The Rainbow* and *Women in Love* in an Honors Seminar on Criticism and Research Methods," in M. Elizabeth Sargent and Garry Watson, eds., *Approaches to Teaching*, 215–16.

Stewart, Jack. "Linguistic Incantation and Parody in *Women in Love*." *Style* 30 (1996), 95–109.

Stewart, Jack. *The Vital Art of D. H. Lawrence*, 73–93, 117–30.

Sumner, Rosemary. *A Route to Modernism*, 89–93, 126–49.

Watson, G. "D. H. Lawrence (in *Women in Love*) on the Desire for Difference and 'the Fascism in Us All.'" *Cambridge Q* 26 (1997), 140–54.

Wexler, Joyce. "Realism and Modernists' Bad Reputation." *Stud in the Novel* 31 (1999), 63–67.

Worthen, John. "The First *Women in Love*." *D. H. Lawrence R* 28:1–2 (1999), 5–25.
Wright, T. R. *D. H. Lawrence and the Bible*, 129–34.
Wussow, Helen. *The Nightmare of History*, 90–99, 145–51.
Young, Jane Jaffe. *D. H. Lawrence on Screen*, 151–243.

JOHN LE CARRÉ

Call for the Dead, 1961

> Aronoff, Myron J. *The Spy Novels of John Le Carré*, 16–19, 40–42, 114–16.
> Cobbs, John L. *Understanding John le Carré*, 31–38.
> Shookman, Ellis. "Smiley 'lächelt': John le Carré and German Literature." *Oxford German Stud* 25 (1996), 135–64.

The Honourable Schoolboy, 1977

> Aronoff, Myron J. *The Spy Novels of John Le Carré*, 21–30, 47–49, 125–27, 145–48, 177–80.
> Cobbs, John L. *Understanding John le Carré*, 124–37.
> Everett, Glenn. "Smiley's Fallen Camelot: Allusions to Tennyson in John le Carre's Cambridge Circus Novels." *Papers on Lang and Lit* 27 (1991), 496–513.

The Little Drummer Girl, 1983

> Aronoff, Myron J. *The Spy Novels of John Le Carré*, 69–80, 181–82.
> Cobbs, John L. *Understanding John le Carré*, 151–66.

The Looking-Glass War, 1965

> Aronoff, Myron J. *The Spy Novels of John Le Carré*, 20–21, 42, 64–65, 141–43.
> Cobbs, John L. *Understanding John le Carré*, 65–74.

A Murder of Quality, 1962

> Cobbs, John L. *Understanding John le Carré*, 39–43.
> Pyrhönen, Heta. *Mayhem and Murder*, 129–32.

The Naive and Sentimental Lover, 1971

> Cobbs, John L. *Understanding John le Carré*, 83–90.

The Night Manager, 1993

> Aronoff, Myron J. *The Spy Novels of John Le Carré*, 99–102, 154–59.
> Cobbs, John L. *Understanding John le Carré*, 210–23.
> Schmid, Stefan. "Die Unsterblichkeit der Schattenmänner: John le Carré und der britische Spionageroman nach dem Kalten Krieg." *Literatur in Wissenschaft und Unterricht* 31 (1998), 346–63.

Our Game, 1995

> Aronoff, Myron J. *The Spy Novels of John Le Carré*, 102–3, 130–31.
> Cobbs, John L. *Understanding John le Carré*, 224–40.
> Schmid, Stefan. "Die Unsterblichkeit der Schattenmänner: John le Carré und der britische Spionageroman nach dem Kalten Krieg." *Literatur in Wissenschaft und Unterricht* 31 (1998), 346–63.

A Perfect Spy, 1986

Aronoff, Myron J. *The Spy Novels of John Le Carré*, 51–59, 149–50.
Cobbs, John L. *Understanding John le Carré*, 167–82.

The Russia House, 1989

Aronoff, Myron J. *The Spy Novels of John Le Carré*, 80–82, 97–98, 150–53, 182–84.
Cobbs, John L. *Understanding John le Carré*, 183–200.
Schmid, Stefan. "Die Unsterblichkeit der Schattenmänner: John le Carré und der britische Spionageroman nach dem Kalten Krieg." *Literatur in Wissenschaft und Unterricht* 31 (1998), 346–63.

The Secret Pilgrim, 1991

Aronoff, Myron J. *The Spy Novels of John Le Carré*, 30–38, 129–30, 153–54.
Cobbs, John L. *Understanding John le Carré*, 201–9.

A Small Town in Germany, 1968

Aronoff, Myron J. *The Spy Novels of John Le Carré*, 43, 65–68, 121–25.
Cobbs, John L. *Understanding John le Carré*, 74–82.

Smiley's People, 1980

Aronoff, Myron J. *The Spy Novels of John Le Carré*, 49–51, 148–49, 180–81.
Cobbs, John L. *Understanding John le Carré*, 138–50.
Everett, Glenn. "Smiley's Fallen Camelot: Allusions to Tennyson in John le Carre's Cambridge Circus Novels." *Papers on Lang and Lit* 27 (1991), 496–513.
Rippetoe, Rita. "Layered Genre Strategies in *Smiley's People*." *Clues* 20:1 (1999), 89–99.

The Spy Who Came in from the Cold, 1963

Aronoff, Myron J. *The Spy Novels of John Le Carré*, 19–20, 42.
Cobbs, John L. *Understanding John le Carré*, 44–63.
Hühn, Peter. "The Politics of Secrecy and Publicity: The Functions of Hidden Stories in Some Recent British Mystery Fiction," in Jerome H. Delamater and Ruth Prigozy, eds., *Theory and Practice*, 45–47.

The Tailor of Panama, 1996

Aronoff, Myron J. *The Spy Novels of John Le Carré*, 103–11, 131–32, 160–61.
Cobbs, John L. *Understanding John le Carré*, 241–55.
Schmid, Stefan. "Die Unsterblichkeit der Schattenmänner: John le Carré und der britische Spionageroman nach dem Kalten Krieg." *Literatur in Wissenschaft und Unterricht* 31 (1998), 346–63.

Tinker, Tailor, Soldier, Spy, 1974

Aronoff, Myron J. *The Spy Novels of John Le Carré*, 44–47, 68–69, 143–45.
Cobbs, John L. *Understanding John le Carré*, 91–123.
Everett, Glenn. "Smiley's Fallen Camelot: Allusions to Tennyson in John le Carre's Cambridge Circus Novels." *Papers on Lang and Lit* 27 (1991), 496–513.

SOPHIA LEE

The Recess, 1785

> Doody, Margaret Anne. "Deserts, Ruins and Troubled Waters: Female Dreams in Fiction and the Development of the Gothic Novel," in Richard Kroll, ed., *The English Novel, Volume II,* 75–80.
> Gores, Steven J. *Psychosocial Spaces,* 126–37.
> Haggerty, George E. *Unnatural Affections,* 66–70.

VERNON LEE

Miss Brown, 1884

> Agnew, Lois. "Vernon Lee and the Victorian Aesthetic Movement: 'Feminine Souls' and Shifting Sites of Contest." *Nineteenth-Cent Prose* 26:2 (1999), 136–40.
> Denisoff, Dennis. *Aestheticism and Sexual Parody,* 42–55.
> Fraser, Hilary. "Women and the Ends of Art History: Vision and Corporeality in Nineteenth-Century Critical Discourse." *Victorian Stud* 42:1 (1998/1999), 86–90.
> Psomiades, Kathy Alexis. "'Still Burning from This Strangling Embrace': Vernon Lee on Desire and Aesthetics," in Richard Dellamora, ed., *Victorian Sexual Dissidence,* 22–29.

JOSEPH SHERIDAN LEFANU

Carmilla, 1872

> Backus, Margot Gayle. *The Gothic Family Romance,* 127–34.
> Bozzetto, Roger. *Territoires des fantastiques,* 153–57.
> Brody, Jennifer DeVere. *Impossible Purities,* 166–67.
> Dupeyron-Lafay, Françoise. "La Paysage dans quelques œuvres de J. S. Le Fanu." *Imaginaires* 5 (2000), 67–78.
> Mighall, Robert. "'A pestilence which walketh in darkness': Diagnosing the Victorian Vampire," in Glennis Byron and David Punter, eds., *Spectral Readings,* 119–21.
> Thomas, Tammis Elise. "Masquerade Liberties and Female Power in Le Fanu's *Carm illa,*" in Elton E. Smith and Robert Haas, eds., *The Haunted Mind,* 39–65.
> Tracy, Robert. *The Unappeasable Host,* 66–72.
> Tracy, Robert. "Undead, Unburied: Anglo-Ireland and the Predatory Past." *LIT* 10 (1999), 19–24.

A Lost Name, 1868

> Mangum, Teresa. "Sheridan Le Fanu's Ungovernable Governess." *Stud in the Novel* 29 (1997), 214–33.

Uncle Silas, 1864

> González, Rosa M. "Sheridan Le Fanu's *Uncle Silas* (1864): An Irish Story Transposed to an English Setting." *Revista Canaria de Estudios Ingleses* 22–23 (1991), 101–10.
> Kreilkamp, Vera. *The Anglo-Irish Novel,* 96–98, 103–11.

Mangum, Teresa. "Sheridan Le Fanu's Ungovernable Governess." *Stud in the Novel* 29 (1997), 222–33.

ROSAMOND LEHMANN

The Ballad and the Source, 1944

Hanson, Clare. *Hysterical Fictions*, 34–38.

Simons, Judy. "Romance and the Feminine: Gender and Genre in the Novels of Rosamond Lehmann." *BELLS: Barcelona Engl Lang and Lit Stud* 7 (1996), 97–103.

Dusty Answer, 1927

Hanson, Clare. *Hysterical Fictions*, 26–31.

Lewis, Andrea. "'Glorious Pagan That I Adore': Resisting the National Reproductive Imperative in Rosamond Lehmann's *Dusty Answer*." *Stud in the Novel* 31 (1999), 357–69.

Wallace, Diana. *Sisters and Rivals in British Women's Fiction*, 166–72.

The Echoing Grove, 1953

Hanson, Clare. *Hysterical Fictions*, 38–42.

McCormick, John. *Catastrophe and Imagination*, 89–92.

Miller, Kristine A. "'We Don't See the Wood for the Trees': Gender and Class in Rosamond Lehmann's *The Echoing Grove*." *J of Mod Lit* 24:1 (2000), 99–112.

Wallace, Diana. *Sisters and Rivals in British Women's Fiction*, 181–88.

Invitation to the Waltz, 1932

Giobbi, Giuliana. "A Blurred Picture: Adolescent Girls Growing Up in Fanny Burney, George Eliot, Rosamond Lehmann, Elizabeth Bowen and Dacia Maraini." *J of European Stud* 25 (1995), 141–61.

A Note in Music, 1930

Pollard, Wendy. "Rosamond Lehmann's Political Philosophy: From *A Note in Music* (1930) to *No More Music* (1939)," in Maroula Joannou, ed., *Women Writers of the 1930s*, 87–92.

A Sea-Grape Tree, 1976

Hanson, Clare. *Hysterical Fictions*, 42–47.

The Weather in the Streets, 1936

Hanson, Clare. *Hysterical Fictions*, 31–34.

Pollard, Wendy. "Rosamond Lehmann's Political Philosophy: From *A Note in Music* (1930) to *No More Music* (1939)," in Maroula Joannou, ed., *Women Writers of the 1930s*, 93–94.

Simons, Judy. "Romance and the Feminine: Gender and Genre in the Novels of Rosamond Lehmann." *BELLS: Barcelona Engl Lang and Lit Stud* 7 (1996), 97–103.

Wallace, Diana. *Sisters and Rivals in British Women's Fiction*, 172–80.

MARY LELAND

The Killeen, 1985

St. Peter, Christine. *Changing Ireland*, 75–80.

TOM LENNON

When Love Comes to Town, 1993
  Smyth, Gerry. *The Novel and the Nation*, 160–63.

CHARLOTTE LENNOX

Euphemia, 1790
  Bannet, Eve Tavor. "The Theater of Politeness in Charlotte Lennox's
    British-American Novels." *Novel* 33 (1999), 73–90.
  Snader, Joe. *Caught Between Worlds*, 204–12.

The Female Quixote, 1752
  Ballaster, Ros. "Women and the Rise of the Novel: Sexual Prescripts,"
    in Vivien Jones, ed., *Women and Literature in Britain*, 207–8.
  Barney, Richard A. *Plots of Enlightenment*, 255–83, 290–300.
  Bellamy, Liz. *Commerce, Morality and the Eighteenth-Century Novel*,
    98–107.
  Cruise, James. *Governing Consumption*, 187–90.
  Doody, Margaret Anne. "Deserts, Ruins and Troubled Waters: Female
    Dreams in Fiction and the Development of the Gothic Novel," in
    Richard Kroll, ed., *The English Novel, Volume II*, 60–61.
  Ellis, Lorna. *Appearing to Diminish*, 63–71.
  Gardiner, Ellen. *Regulating Readers*, 89–109.
  Gordon, Scott Paul. "The Space of Romance in Lennox's *Female
    Quixote.*" *Stud in Engl Lit, 1500–1900* 38 (1998), 499–514.
  Haggerty, George E. *Unnatural Affections*, 11–13, 123–36.
  Hammond, Brean S. *Professional Imaginative Writing*, 232–35.
  Labbie, Erin F. "History as 'Retro': Veiling Inheritance in Lennox's
    The Female Quixote." *Bucknell R* 42:1 (1998), 79–95.
  Levin, Kate. "'The Cure of Arabella's Mind': Charlotte Lennox and
    the Disciplining of the Female Reader." *Women's Writing* 2 (1995),
    271–85.
  Levy, Anita. *Reproductive Urges*, 38–42.
  Levy, Anita. "Reproductive Urges: Literacy, Sexuality, and
    Eighteenth-Century Englishness," in Susan C. Greenfield and Carol
    Barash, eds., *Inventing Maternity*, 195–97.
  Mantegazza, Cinthia. "Su *The Female Quixote* di Charlotte Lennox e
    Don Quixote: Letture della realtà come affioramenti della dimen-
    sione del desiderio." *Cuadernos de Literatura Inglesa y
    Norteamericana* 3:1–2 (1998), 27–38.
  Martin, Mary Patricia. "'High and Noble Adventures': Reading the
    Novel *The Female Quixote.*" *Novel* 31 (1997), 45–60.
  Pearson, Jacqueline. *Women's Reading in Britain*, 201–6.
  Richetti, John. *The English Novel in History*, 205–11.
  Rothstein, Eric. "Woman, Women, and *The Female Quixote,*" in
    Albert J. Rivero, ed., *Augustan Subjects*, 249–69.
  Roulston, Christine. "Histories of Nothing: Romance and Femininity
    in Charlotte Lennox's *The Female Quixote.*" *Women's Writing* 2
    (1995), 25–41.

Schmid, Thomas H. "'My Authority': Hyper-Mimesis and the Discourse of Hysteria in *The Female Quixote*." *Rocky Mountain R of Lang and Lit* 51:1 (1997), 21–34.

Scrittori, Anna Rosa. "Riflessioni sul potere della finzione: *The Female Quixote* di Charlotte Lennox." *Annali di Ca' Foscari* 35:1–2 (1996), 287–301.

Zimmerman, Everett. "Personal Identity, Narrative, and History: *The Female Quixote* and *Redgauntlet*." *Eighteenth-Cent Fiction* 12 (2000), 372–81.

The Life of Harriot Stuart, 1751

Bannet, Eve Tavor. "The Theater of Politeness in Charlotte Lennox's British-American Novels." *Novel* 33 (1999), 73–90.

Sophia, 1762

Bannet, Eve Tavor. *The Domestic Revolution*, 85–86, 91–92.

DORIS LESSING

Ben, in the World, 2001

Hunter, Melanie R. Review of *Ben, in the World*. *Doris Lessing Newsl* 21:2 (2001), 6, 10.

Ingersoll, Earl G. Review of *Ben, in the World*. *Doris Lessing Newsl* 21:2 (2001), 1, 7.

Saxton, Ruth. "*Ben, in the World*, Sequel to *The Fifth Child*." *Doris Lessing Newsl* 21:2 (2001), 5, 8.

Sprague, Claire. "Where Are My People?" *Doris Lessing Newsl* 21:2 (2001), 1, 9–10.

Briefing for a Descent into Hell, 1971

Bazin, Nancy Topping. "Androgyny or Catastrophe: Doris Lessing's Vision in the Early 1970s," in Phyllis Sternberg Perrakis, ed., *Spiritual Exploration*, 33–36.

Hunter, Melanie, and Darby McIntosh. "'A Question of Wholes': Spiritual Intersection, Apocalyptic Vision in the Work of Doris Lessing." *Doris Lessing Newsl* 18:2 (1997), 9–10.

Canopus in Argos, 1979–1983

Galin, Müge. *Between East and West*, 82–97, 227–29.

Iyer, Nalini. "Intergalactic Empires, Benevolent Imperialism and the Quest for Form." *Doris Lessing Newsl* 20:1 (1999), 5–7.

Noble, Michael. "'This tale is our answer': Science and Narrative in Doris Lessing's *Canopus*." *Doris Lessing Newsl* 18:2 (1997), 4–5, 12, 15.

Rowland, Susan. "'Transformed and Translated': The Colonized Reader of Doris Lessing's *Canopus in Argos* Space Fiction," in Abby H. P. Werlock, ed., *British Women Writing Fiction*, 42–53.

Children of Violence, 1952–1969

Fand, Roxanne J. *The Dialogic Self*, 110–49.

Rubenstein, Roberta. "Mar(th)a Still Questing: Reading *Mara and Dann* through *Children of Violence*." *Doris Lessing Newsl* 21:1 (2000), 1, 10–13.

Yoon, Hyekyong. "Quest for Ideal City in Doris Lessing's *Children of Violence.*" *J of Engl Lang and Lit* 43 (1997), 589–608.

The Diaries of Jane Somers, 1984

Mepham, John. "Conversation and Friendship in Doris Lessing's Novels," in Richard Todd and Luisa Flora, eds., *Theme Parks,* 135–38.

Sceats, Sarah. "Flesh and Bones: Eating, Not Eating and the Social Vision of Doris Lessing," in Richard Todd and Luisa Flora, eds., *Theme Parks,* 148–49.

Sceats, Sarah. *Food, Consumption and the Body,* 85–90.

Tiger, Virginia. "Ages of Anxiety: *The Diaries of Jane Somers,*" in Phyllis Sternberg Perrakis, ed., *Spiritual Exploration,* 1–14.

The Diary of a Good Neighbor, 1983

Galin, Müge. *Between East and West,* 120–28.

Thomson, Rosemarie Garland. "Learning Something Else: Embracing the Dying Body in Doris Lessing's *The Diary of a Good Neighbor.*" *Iris* 38 (1999), 44–47.

The Fifth Child, 1988

Anievas Gamallo, Isabel C. "Motherhood and the Fear of the Other: Magic, Fable and the Gothic in Doris Lessing's *The Fifth Child,*" in Richard Todd and Luisa Flora, eds., *Theme Parks,* 113–23.

Rau, Albert. "'Living with the Alien': Approaching Doris Lessing, *The Fifth Child,* in Advanced EFL-Courses." *Neusprachliche Mitteilungen aus Wissenschaft und Praxis* 50:1 (1997), 28–33.

Sceats, Sarah. "Flesh and Bones: Eating, Not Eating and the Social Vision of Doris Lessing," in Richard Todd and Luisa Flora, eds., *Theme Parks,* 140–41, 143–44.

Sceats, Sarah. *Food, Consumption and the Body,* 172–74.

Sprague, Claire. "Where Are My People?" *Doris Lessing Newsl* 21:2 (2001), 1, 9–10.

The Four-Gated City, 1969

Brucker, Barbara S. *Das Ganze, dessen Teile wir sind,* 106–207.

Clayton, Cherry. "White Settlers in the Heart of Empire: Visionary Power in Lessing's *The Four-Gated City,*" in Phyllis Sternberg Perrakis, ed., *Spiritual Exploration,* 55–61.

Fand, Roxanne J. *The Dialogic Self,* 128–49.

Galin, Müge. *Between East and West,* 110–20, 183–85.

Hunter, Melanie, and Darby McIntosh. "'A Question of Wholes': Spiritual Intersection, Apocalyptic Vision in the Work of Doris Lessing." *Doris Lessing Newsl* 18:2 (1997), 8–10.

Kunkel, Deonne. "Patriarchy Revisited: Lessing's Reinvention of *Jane Eyre.*" *Doris Lessing Newsl* 21:1 (2000), 3–5, 14–15.

Mepham, John. "Conversation and Friendship in Doris Lessing's Novels," in Richard Todd and Luisa Flora, eds., *Theme Parks,* 130–35.

Munnick, Yvonne. "*The Four-Gated City*: Utopie et fin du monde chez Doris Lessing." *Anglophonia* 3 (1998), 135–45.

Sceats, Sarah. "Flesh and Bones: Eating, Not Eating and the Social

Vision of Doris Lessing," in Richard Todd and Luisa Flora, eds., *Theme Parks*, 146–47.

Sceats, Sarah. *Food, Consumption and the Body*, 81–85.

The Golden Notebook, 1962

Galin, Müge. *Between East and West*, 62–82.

Hunter, Melanie, and Darby McIntosh. "'A Question of Wholes': Spiritual Intersection, Apocalyptic Vision in the Work of Doris Lessing." *Doris Lessing Newsl* 18:2 (1997), 8–10.

Rudaityte, Regina. "Feminism Subverted: *Mrs. Dalloway* and *The Golden Notebook*." *Literatura* (Vilnius) 37:3 (1995), 89–96.

Sceats, Sarah. *Food, Consumption and the Body*, 78–81.

Smith, Patricia Juliana. *Lesbian Panic*, 92–101.

Watkins, Susan. *Twentieth-Century Women Novelists*, 63–75.

Yu, Je-boon. "Bakhtin's Dialogism and Feminism: The Dialogic Self in *Mrs. Dalloway* and the Heteroglossic Plot in *The Golden Notebook*." *J of Engl Lang and Lit* 43 (1997), 305–20.

The Good Terrorist, 1985

Scanlan, Margaret. *Plotting Terror*, 75–91.

Sceats, Sarah. *Food, Consumption and the Body*, 168–72.

Velcic, Vlatka. "Doris Lessing's Alice: Good House-Mother and Bad Terrorist." *Tennessee Philol Bull* 33 (1996), 63–72.

The Grass Is Singing, 1950

Bruner, Christopher. "Para-Images: The Shapes of Identity in *The Grass is Singing*." *Doris Lessing Newsl* 19:1 (1998), 8–11.

Buckton, Oliver S. "Race, Gender, and Anti-Pastoral Critique in Doris Lessing's *The Grass is Singing* and Olive Schreiner's *The Story of an African Farm*." *Doris Lessing Newsl* 20:2 (1999), 8–11.

Sceats, Sarah. *Food, Consumption and the Body*, 72–74.

If the Old Could . . ., 1984

Sceats, Sarah. *Food, Consumption and the Body*, 88–90.

Love, Again, 1995

Ingersoll, Earl G. "Still in Love with the Theater: Doris Lessing's *Love, Again*." *Doris Lessing Newsl* 19:2 (1998), 4–6.

Latz, Anna. "The Quest for Freedom in *Love, Again*." *Doris Lessing Newsl* 18:2 (1997), 3, 6–7, 13–14.

Perrakis, Phyllis Sternberg. "The Whirlpool and the Fountain: Inner Growth and *Love, Again*," in Perrakis, ed., *Spiritual Exploration*, 83–106.

The Making of the Representative for Planet 8, 1982

Galin, Müge. *Between East and West*, 82–97, 146–50.

Sceats, Sarah. *Food, Consumption and the Body*, 164–67.

Mara and Dann, 1999

Rubenstein, Roberta. "Mar(th)a Still Questing: Reading *Mara and Dann* through *Children of Violence*." *Doris Lessing Newsl* 21:1 (2000), 1, 10–13.

Tiger, Virginia. "'A Slog of Endurance': Lessing's *Mara and Dann*." *Doris Lessing Newsl* 20:2 (1999), 1, 19.

The Marriages between Zones Three, Four, and Five, 1980

Afnan, Elham. "Names in Doris Lessing's *The Marriages Between Zones Three, Four, and Five.*" *Doris Lessing Newsl* 19:1 (1998), 4.

Cohen-Safir, Claude. *Cartographie du féminin dans l'utopie*, 169–72.

Galin, Müge. *Between East and West*, 128–46.

Ingersoll, Earl G. "Pursuing Difference in *The Marriages Between Zones Three, Four, and Five*," in Phyllis Sternberg Perrakis, ed., *Spiritual Exploration*, 17–28.

Rowland, Susan. "'Transformed and Translated': The Colonized Reader of Doris Lessing's *Canopus in Argos* Space Fiction," in Abby H. P. Werlock, ed., *British Women Writing Fiction*, 49–53.

Martha Quest, 1952

Fand, Roxanne J. *The Dialogic Self*, 110–14, 117–20.

Galin, Müge. *Between East and West*, 117–20.

Mepham, John. "Conversation and Friendship in Doris Lessing's Novels," in Richard Todd and Luisa Flora, eds., *Theme Parks*, 125–30.

Sceats, Sarah. *Food, Consumption and the Body*, 74–76.

The Memoirs of a Survivor, 1974

Bazin, Nancy Topping. "Androgyny or Catastrophe: Doris Lessing's Vision in the Early 1970s," in Phyllis Sternberg Perrakis, ed., *Spiritual Exploration*, 38–42.

Brucker, Barbara S. *Das Ganze, dessen Teile wir sind*, 255–314.

Galin, Müge. *Between East and West*, 62–83.

Hunter, Melanie, and Darby McIntosh. "'A Question of Wholes': Spiritual Intersection, Apocalyptic Vision in the Work of Doris Lessing." *Doris Lessing Newsl* 18:2 (1997), 9–10.

Raschke, Debrah. "Cabalistic Gardens: Lessing's *Memoirs of a Survivor*," in Phyllis Sternberg Perrakis, ed., *Spiritual Exploration*, 43–53.

Sceats, Sarah. *Food, Consumption and the Body*, 15–18, 156–61.

Shikasta, 1979

Aguilar-Osuna, Juan Jesus. "Why Does George Sherban Cry?: A Note on Remembering and Forgetting." *Doris Lessing Newsl* 20:2 (1999), 16–17.

Galin, Müge. *Between East and West*, 82–97.

Webber, Jeannette. "Doris Lessing's Prophetic Voice in *Shikasta*: Cassandra or Sibyl?," in Phyllis Sternberg Perrakis, ed., *Spiritual Exploration*, 63–78.

The Summer Before the Dark, 1973

Bazin, Nancy Topping. "Androgyny or Catastrophe: Doris Lessing's Vision in the Early 1970s," in Phyllis Sternberg Perrakis, ed., *Spiritual Exploration*, 36–38.

Brucker, Barbara S. *Das Ganze, dessen Teile wir sind*, 208–54.

Hunter, Melanie, and Darby McIntosh. "'A Question of Wholes': Spiritual Intersecting, Universal Revisioning in the Work of Doris Lessing," in Phyllis Sternberg Perrakis, ed., *Spiritual Exploration*, 111–13.

CHARLES LEVER

The Bramleighs of Bishop's Folly, 1868
  Haddelsey, Stephen. *Charles Lever*, 123–35.
Charles O'Malley, 1841
  Haddelsey, Stephen. *Charles Lever*, 45–55.
  Jeffares, A. Norman. *Images of Invention*, 171–74.
A Day's Ride: A Life's Romance, 1860/61
  Meckier, Jerome. "'Dashing in Now': *Great Expectations* and Charles
    Lever's *A Day's Ride*." *Dickens Stud Annual* 26 (1998), 227–57.
The Dodd Family Abroad, 1854
  Haddelsey, Stephen. *Charles Lever*, 87–95.
Harry Lorrequer, 1839
  Haddelsey, Stephen. *Charles Lever*, 40–51.
Jack Hinton, 1843
  Jeffares, A. Norman. *Images of Invention*, 174–76.
The Knight of Gwynne, 1847
  Haddelsey, Stephen. *Charles Lever*, 75–85.
Lord Kilgobbin, 1872
  Haddelsey, Stephen. *Charles Lever*, 141–53.
  Jeffares, A. Norman. *Images of Invention*, 179–87.
  Kreilkamp, Vera. *The Anglo-Irish Novel*, 76–78.
The Martins of Cro' Martin, 1856
  Haddelsey, Stephen. *Charles Lever*, 95–103.
  Kreilkamp, Vera. *The Anglo-Irish Novel*, 78–95.
The O'Donoghue: A Tale of Ireland Fifty Years Ago, 1872
  Constable, Kathleen. *A Stranger Within the Gates*, 120–25.
  Haddelsey, Stephen. *Charles Lever*, 58–69.
  Jeffares, A. Norman. *Images of Invention*, 150–52, 155–57, 159–62.
  Kreilkamp, Vera. *The Anglo-Irish Novel*, 74–78.
St. Patrick's Eve, 1845
  Haddelsey, Stephen. *Charles Lever*, 69–71.
Sir Brook Fossbrooke, 1866
  Haddelsey, Stephen. *Charles Lever*, 118–23.
That Boy of Norcott's, 1869
  Haddelsey, Stephen. *Charles Lever*, 137–41.

AMY LEVY

Reuben Sachs, 1888
  Beckman, Linda Hunt. *Amy Levy*, 159–74.
  Hunt, Linda. "Amy Levy and the 'Jewish Novel': Representing
    Jewish Life in the Victorian Period." *Stud in the Novel* 26 (1994),
    235–53.
  Rochelson, Mari-Jane. "Jews, Gender, and Genre in Late-Victorian

England: Amy Levy's *Reuben Sachs*." *Women's Stud* 25 (1996), 311–25.

The Romance of a Shop, 1889

Beckman, Linda Hunt. *Amy Levy*, 153–59.

Young, Arlene. *Culture, Class and Gender*, 136–42.

C. S. LEWIS

The Chronicles of Narnia

Adey, Lionel. *C. S. Lewis*, 165–93.

Como, James. *Branches to Heaven*, 129–38.

Honda, Mineko. *The Imaginative World of C. S. Lewis*, 69–78.

Hunt, Peter. *Children's Literature*, 199–201.

Joeckel, Samuel T. "In Search of Narnia on a Platonic Map of Progressive Cognition." *Mythlore* 22:1 (1997), 8–11.

Khoddam, Salwa. "Balder the Beautiful: Aslan's Norse Ancestor in *The Chronicles of Narnia*." *Mythlore* 22:3 (1999), 66–76.

Miller, Laura. "*Sehnsucht* as Spiritual Exercise: C. S. Lewis and the Achievement of the Real in the *Chronicles of Narnia*." *Lamp-Post of the Southern California C. S. Lewis Soc* 22:3 (1998), 16–27.

Myers, Doris T. "Growing in Grace: The Anglican Spiritual Style in the *Chronicles of Narnia*," in David Mills, ed., *The Pilgrim's Guide*, 185–202.

Patterson, Nancy-Lou. "The 'Jasper-Lucent Landscapes' of C. S. Lewis." *Lamp-Post of the Southern California C. S. Lewis Soc* 22:4 (1998–1999), 6–24; 23:1 (1999), 16–32.

Rudd, David. "Is Man a Myth?: C. S. Lewis, Shadowlands, and Self-Destructive Fantasy." *New Comparison* 27/28 (1999), 228–38.

Sammons, Martha C. *"A Far-Off Country,"* 3–94.

Sayers, William. "C. S. Lewis and the Toponym Narnia." *Mythlore* 22:2 (1998), 54–55, 58.

Smith, Stephen M. "Awakening from the Enchantment of Worldliness: The *Chronicles of Narnia* as Pre-Apologetics," in David Mills, ed., *The Pilgrim's Guide*, 168–84.

Ward, Michael. "Through the Wardrobe: A Famous Image Explored." *Seven* 15 (1998), 55–70.

The Horse and His Boy, 1954

Adey, Lionel. *C. S. Lewis*, 167–70, 179–81.

Nicholson, Mervyn. "C. S. Lewis and the Scholarship of Imagination in E. Nesbit and Rider Haggard." *Renascence* 51 (1998), 49–51.

The Last Battle, 1956

Adey, Lionel. *C. S. Lewis*, 173–75, 180–83, 187–89.

Nicholson, Mervyn. "C. S. Lewis and the Scholarship of Imagination in E. Nesbit and Rider Haggard." *Renascence* 51 (1998), 51–52.

The Lion, the Witch, and the Wardrobe, 1950

Adey, Lionel. *C. S. Lewis*, 166–70.

Guroian, Vigen. *Tending the Heart of Virtue*, 127–39.

Lindskoog, Kathryn. *Surprised by C. S. Lewis*, 145–47.

Werner, Macy. "Forbidden Foods and Guilty Pleasures in Lewis' *The Lion, the Witch, and the Wardrobe* and Christina Rosetti's 'Goblin Market.'" *Mythlore* 22:2 (1998), 18–21.

The Magician's Nephew, 1955

Adey, Lionel. *C. S. Lewis*, 173–77.
Como, James. *Branches to Heaven*, 186–88.
Nicholson, Mervyn. "C. S. Lewis and the Scholarship of Imagination in E. Nesbit and Rider Haggard." *Renascence* 51 (1998), 52–60.

Out of the Silent Planet, 1938

Adey, Lionel. *C. S. Lewis*, 116–26.
Brew, Kelli. "*Metanoia*: The Hero's Change of Heart in C. S. Lewis's *Space Trilogy* and Charles Williams' *The Place of the Lion*." *Lamp-Post of the Southern California C. S. Lewis Soc* 21:1 (1997), 11–17.
Peters, Thomas C. "The War of the Worldviews: H. G. Wells and Scientism versus C. S. Lewis and Christianity," in David Mills, ed., *The Pilgrim's Guide*, 203–20.
Sammons, Martha C. *"A Far-Off Country,"* 97–184.
Smith, Lyle H. "Metaphors of Deep Heaven: The Platonic Context of C. S. Lewis's Interplanetary Trilogy." *Lamp-Post of the Southern California C. S. Lewis Soc* 21:4 (1997–1998), 4–17.

Perelandra, 1943

Adey, Lionel. *C. S. Lewis*, 117–20, 124–32.
Brew, Kelli. "*Metanoia*: The Hero's Change of Heart in C. S. Lewis's *Space Trilogy* and Charles Williams' *The Place of the Lion*." *Lamp-Post of the Southern California C. S. Lewis Soc* 21:1 (1997), 11–17.
Como, James. *Branches to Heaven*, 125–28, 153–56.
King, Don W. "The Poetry of Prose: C. S. Lewis, Ruth Ritter, and *Perelandra*." *Christianity and Lit* 49 (2000), 331–50.
Patterson, Nancy-Lou. "'This Equivocal Being': The Un-Man in C. S. Lewis's *Perelandra*." *Lamp-Post of the Southern California C. S. Lewis Soc* 19:3 (1995), 4–15; and 19:4 (1995-1996), 7–19.
Peters, Thomas C. "The War of the Worldviews: H. G. Wells and Scientism versus C. S. Lewis and Christianity," in David Mills, ed., *The Pilgrim's Guide*, 203–20.
Phemister, William. "Fantasy Set to Music: Donald Swann, C. S. Lewis and J. R. R. Tolkien." *Seven* 13 (1996), 67–69, 72–74.
Rogers, Katherin. "C. S. Lewis on Disobeying God, or, Peter Abelard Visits Perelandra." *Stud in Medievalism* 6:supplement (1996), 85–91.
Sammons, Martha C. *"A Far-Off Country,"* 97–184.
Smith, Lyle H. "Metaphors of Deep Heaven: The Platonic Context of C. S. Lewis's Interplanetary Trilogy." *Lamp-Post of the Southern California C. S. Lewis Soc* 21:4 (1997–1998), 4–17.
Tanner, John S. "The Psychology of Temptation in *Perelandra* and *Paradise Lost*: What Lewis Learned from Milton.'" *Renascence* 52 (2000), 131–40.

Prince Caspian, 1951

Guroian, Vigen. *Tending the Heart of Virtue*, 160–76.

The Silver Chair, 1953

Adey, Lionel. *C. S. Lewis,* 172–75.

That Hideous Strength, 1945

Adey, Lionel. *C. S. Lewis,* 132–41.

Brew, Kelli. "Facing the Truth on the Road to Salvation: An Analysis of *That Hideous Strength* and *Till We Have Faces." Lamp-Post of the Southern California C. S. Lewis Soc* 22:1 (1998), 10–12.

Brew, Kelli. "*Metanoia:* The Hero's Change of Heart in C. S. Lewis's *Space Trilogy* and Charles Williams' *The Place of the Lion." Lamp-Post of the Southern California C. S. Lewis Soc* 21:1 (1997), 11–17.

Dougill, John. *Oxford in English Literature,* 254–56.

Downing, David C. "The Discarded Image: Lewis the Scholar-Novelist on Merlin's Moral Taint." *Christian Scholar's R* 27 (1998), 406–15.

Fairfield, Leslie P. "Fragmentation and Hope: The Healing of the Modern Schisms in *That Hideous Strength,*" in David Mills, ed., *The Pilgrim's Guide,* 145–60.

Hill, Darci. "Mark Studdock's Heroism: Another Look at *That Hideous Strength." Mythlore* 22:2 (1998), 22–27.

Howard, Thomas. "The Triumphant Vindication of the Body: The End of Gnosticism in *That Hideous Strength,*" in David Mills, ed., *The Pilgrim's Guide,* 133–44.

Lindskoog, Kathryn. *Surprised by C. S. Lewis,* 58–62.

Peters, Thomas C. "The War of the Worldviews: H. G. Wells and Scientism versus C. S. Lewis and Christianity," in David Mills, ed., *The Pilgrim's Guide,* 203–20.

Reilly, John R. "The Torture Tutorial: Finding Out the Awful Truth in *That Hideous Strength* and *1984." Mythlore* 21:4 (1997), 39–41.

Sammons, Martha C. *"A Far-Off Country,"* 97–184.

Smith, Lyle H. "Metaphors of Deep Heaven: The Platonic Context of C. S. Lewis's Interplanetary Trilogy." *Lamp-Post of the Southern California C. S. Lewis Soc* 21:4 (1997–1998), 4–17.

Till We Have Faces, 1956

Adey, Lionel. *C. S. Lewis,* 151–64.

Brew, Kelli. "Facing the Truth on the Road to Salvation: An Analysis of *That Hideous Strength* and *Till We Have Faces." Lamp-Post of the Southern California C. S. Lewis Soc* 22:1 (1998), 10–12.

Como, James. *Branches to Heaven,* 183–85.

Donaldson, Mara E. "Baptizing the Imagination: The Fantastic as the Subversion of Fundamentalism." *J of the Fantastic in the Arts* 8 (1997), 185–97.

Honda, Mineko. *The Imaginative World of C. S. Lewis,* 107–43.

Landrum, David. "Three Bridge-Builders: Priest-Craft in *Till We Have Faces." Mythlore* 22:4 (2000), 59–67.

Lindskoog, Kathryn. *Surprised by C. S. Lewis,* 118–25.

Manganiello, Dominic. "*Till We Have Faces:* From Idolatry to Revelation." *Mythlore* 23:1 (2000), 31–46.

Patterson, Nancy-Lou. "The Holy House of Ungit." *Mythlore* 21:4 (1997), 4–15.

Sammons, Martha C. *"A Far-Off Country,"* 187–291.

Stephenson, Will, and Mimosa Stephenson. "Structure and Audience: C. S. Lewis's *Till We Have Faces.*" *Lamp-Post of the Southern California C. S. Lewis Soc* 21:1 (1997), 4–10.

The Voyage of the "Dawn Treader," 1952

Adey, Lionel. *C. S. Lewis*, 171–72, 174–75, 178–79.

Nicholson, Mervyn. "C. S. Lewis and the Scholarship of Imagination in E. Nesbit and Rider Haggard." *Renascence* 51 (1998), 41–48.

MATTHEW GREGORY LEWIS

The Monk, 1796

Blakemore, Steven. "Matthew Lewis's Black Mass: Sexual, Religious Inversion in *The Monk.*" *Stud in the Novel* 30 (1998), 521–39.

Brantlinger, Patrick. *The Reading Lesson*, 40–46.

Clemens, Valdine. *The Return of the Repressed*, 59–88.

Gamer, Michael. "Genres for the Prosecution: Pornography and the Gothic." *PMLA* 114 (1999), 1047–52.

Gamer, Michael. *Romanticism and the Gothic*, 76–89.

Heinrich, Hans. *Zur Geschichte des 'Libertin,'* 163–70.

Hendershot, Cyndy. *The Animal Within*, 12–20.

McCann, Andrew. *Cultural Politics in the 1790s*, 129–31, 135–44.

Macdonald, D. L. *Monk Lewis*, 76–80, 110–27, 129–36.

McLean, Clara D. "Lewis's *The Monk* and the Matter of Reading," in Linda Lang-Peralta, ed., *Women, Revolution, and the Novels of the 1790s*, 111–29.

Mudge, Bradford K. *The Whore's Story*, 219–22.

Mulman, Lisa Naomi. "Sexuality on the Surface: Catholicism and the Erotic Object in Lewis's *The Monk.*" *Bucknell R* 42:1 (1998), 98–109.

Tinkler-Villani, Valeria. "'I Saw, I Felt, But I Cannot Describe': Demonic Epiphany in Gothic Fiction," in Wim Tigges, ed., *Moments of Moment*, 105–13.

Watt, James. *Contesting the Gothic*, 84–95.

Whitlark, James. "A Developmental Approach to Religious Prejudices in *The Monk.*" *J of Compar Lit and Aesthetics* (Orissa, India) 22:1–2 (1999), 43–57.

WYNDHAM LEWIS

The Apes of God, 1930

Ayers, David. *English Literature of the 1920s*, 145–56.

Cavaliero, Glen. *The Alchemy of Laughter*, 221–23.

Miller, Tyrus. *Late Modernism*, 70–77, 93–110, 114–20.

Quéma, Anne. *The Agon of Modernism*, 64–65, 70–73, 76–78.

The Childermass, 1928

Miller, Tyrus. *Late Modernism*, 111–16.

Quéma, Anne. *The Agon of Modernism*, 94–98, 195–98.

Enemy of the Stars, 1932

Miller, Tyrus. *Late Modernism*, 88–93.

The Human Age, 1955

Quéma, Anne. *The Agon of Modernism*, 195–202.

Monstre Gai, 1955

Quéma, Anne. *The Agon of Modernism*, 49–51, 196–98.

The Revenge for Love, 1937

Neilson, Brett. "History's Stamp: Wyndham Lewis's *The Revenge for Love* and the Heidegger Controversy." *Compar Lit* 51 (1999), 24–39.

Quéma, Anne. *The Agon of Modernism*, 68–70.

Self Condemned, 1954

Orestano, Francesca. "Arctic Masks in a Castle of Ice: Gothic Vorticism and Wyndham Lewis's *Self Condemned*," in Andrew Smith and Jeff Wallace, eds., *Gothic Modernisms*, 167–84.

Quéma, Anne. *The Agon of Modernism*, 104–7.

Snooty Baronet, 1932

Lewis, Stephen E. "Love and Politics in Wyndham Lewis's *Snooty Baronet*." *Mod Lang Q* 61 (2000), 617–49.

Quéma, Anne. *The Agon of Modernism*, 46–49.

Tarr, 1918

Cavaliero, Glen. *The Alchemy of Laughter*, 218–21.

Ferrall, Charles. *Modernist Writing and Reactionary Politics*, 139–45.

Kramer, Andreas. "Nationality and Avant-Garde: Anglo-German Affairs in Wyndham Lewis's *Tarr*," in Susanne Stark, ed., *The Novel in Anglo-German Context*, 253–62.

Peppis, Paul. *Literature, Politics, and the English Avant-Garde*, 133–35, 140–61.

Quéma, Anne. *The Agon of Modernism*, 112–14.

Trotter, David. "The Modernist Novel," in Michael Levenson, ed., *The Cambridge Companion to Modernism*, 72–74.

DAVID LINDSAY

A Voyage to Arcturus, 1920

Elflandsson, Galad. "David Lindsay and the Quest for Muspel-Fire," in Darrell Schweitzer, ed., *Discovering Classic Fantasy Fiction*, 104–12.

Walker, Marshall. *Scottish Literature since 1707*, 224–25.

JOAN LINGARD

After Colette, 1993

Gifford, Douglas. "Contemporary Fiction II: Seven Writers in Scotland," in Douglas Gifford and Dorothy McMillan, eds., *A History*, 622–23.

Dreams of Love and Modest Glory, 1995

> Gifford, Douglas. "Contemporary Fiction II: Seven Writers in Scotland," in Douglas Gifford and Dorothy McMillan, eds., *A History*, 623–24.

Sisters by Rite, 1984

> St. Peter, Christine. *Changing Ireland*, 109–12.

The Women's House, 1989

> Gifford, Douglas. "Contemporary Fiction II: Seven Writers in Scotland," in Douglas Gifford and Dorothy McMillan, eds., *A History*, 621–22.

ELIZA LINTON

The One Too Many, 1894

> Sanders, Valerie. "Marriage and the Antifeminist Woman Novelist," in Nicola Diane Thompson, ed., *Victorian Women Writers*, 37–39.

The Rebel of the Family, 1880

> Heilmann, Ann. *New Woman Fiction*, 99–101.

> Thompson, Nicola Diane. "Responding to the Woman Questions: Rereading Noncanonical Victorian Women Novelists," in Thompson, ed., *Victorian Women Writers*, 5–6.

The True History of Joshua Davidson, Christian and Communist, 1872

> Schäffner, Raimund. *Anarchismus und Literatur in England*, 396–403.

PENELOPE LIVELY

City of the Mind, 1991

> Brînzeu, Pia. "Imaginary Cities." *B.A.S.: Brit and Am Stud* 1:1 (1996), 56–62.

> Moran, Mary Hurley. "The Novels of Penelope Lively: A Case for the Continuity of the Experimental Impulse in Postwar British Fiction." *South Atlantic R* 62:1 (1997), 112–15.

Cleopatra's Sister, 1993

> Brînzeu, Pia. *Corridors of Mirrors*, 157–61.

> Brînzeu, Pia. "A Prison of One's Own." *B.A.S.: Brit and Am Stud* 1998: 40–52.

> Jackson, Tony E. "The Desires of History, Old and New." *Clio* 28 (1999), 169–87.

> Moran, Mary Hurley. "The Novels of Penelope Lively: A Case for the Continuity of the Experimental Impulse in Postwar British Fiction." *South Atlantic R* 62:1 (1997), 115–17.

> Rich, Elizabeth. "Disciplined Identities: Western Author(ity) in Crisis in Penelope Lively's *Cleopatra's Sister*." *Post Identity* 1:2 (1998), 29–54.

Heat Wave, 1996

> Mergenthal, Silvia. "Englishness/Englishnesses in Contemporary

Fiction," in Barbara Korte and Klaus Peter Müller, eds., *Unity in Diversity Revisited?*, 54–59.

The Moon Tiger, 1987

Hearne, Betsy. "Across the Ages: Penelope Lively's Fiction for Children and Adults." *Horn Book Mag* 75 (1999), 166–68.

Jackson, Tony E. "The Desires of History, Old and New." *Clio* 28 (1999), 169–87.

- Moran, Mary Hurley. "The Novels of Penelope Lively: A Case for the Continuity of the Experimental Impulse in Postwar British Fiction." *South Atlantic R* 62:1 (1997), 108–12.

Reinfandt, Christoph. *Der Sinn der fiktionalen Wirklichkeiten,* 309–29.

CHARLES LLOYD

Edmund Oliver, 1798

Skinner, Gillian. *Sensibility and Economics in the Novel,* 174–77.

Stones, Graeme. "Charles Lloyd and *Edmund Oliver*: A Demonology." *Charles Lamb Bull* 95 (1996), 110–21.

DAVID LODGE

The British Museum Is Falling Down, 1965

Martin, Bruce K. *David Lodge,* 104–15.

Changing Places, 1975

Fernández Vázquez, José Santiago. "Apuntes para una lectura Bakhtiniana de *Changing Places* y *Small World*, de David Lodge." *Revista Canaria de Estudios Ingleses* 32–33 (1996), 131–40.

Martín, Bárbara Arizti. "Shortcircuiting Death: The Ending of *Changing Places* and the Death of the Novel." *Miscelánea* 17 (1996), 39–50.

Martin, Bruce K. *David Lodge,* 25–39.

Stanciu, Virgil. "Romancing the Campus (Random Thoughts on the Novels of David Lodge)." *B.A.S.: Brit and Am Stud* 1:1 (1996), 63–70.

Ginger, You're Barmy, 1962

Martin, Bruce K. *David Lodge,* 11–21.

Nice Work, 1988

Gutleben, Christian. "La tradition victorienne à l'heure du postmodernisme: John Fowles, David Lodge, A. S. Byatt." *Etudes Anglaises* 51 (1998), 168–72.

Koll-Stobbe, Amei. "Message Merchants: Cognitive Aspects of Advertising Cultural Discourse." *Folia Linguistica* 28 (1994), 385–98.

Martin, Bruce K. *David Lodge,* 57–69.

Martin, Bruce K. "Music and Fiction: The Perils of Popularism." *Mosaic* 31:4 (1998), 21–39.

Pascual Soler, Nieves, and José Luis Martínez-Dueñas Espejo.

"Innovación narrativa y retórica de la repetición en *Nice Work* de David Lodge." *Revista Canaria de Estudios Ingleses* 21 (1990), 265–75.

Rohmann, Gerd. "Images of Germany in Post-War English Fiction," in C. C. Barfoot, ed., *Beyond Pug's Tour*, 417–21.

Stanciu, Virgil. "Romancing the Campus (Random Thoughts on the Novels of David Lodge)." *B.A.S.: Brit and Am Stud* 1:1 (1996), 63–70.

Out of the Shelter, 1970

Martin, Bruce K. *David Lodge*, 2–11.

Mergenthal, Silvia. "'Nation and Narration': Continental Europe and the English Novel," in Susanne Fendler and Ruth Wittlinger, eds., *The Idea of Europe in Literature*, 35–37, 39–42.

Omasreiter-Blaicher, Ria. "Annäherung an Deutschland: Die Revision eines Feindbildes in David Lodges *Out of the Shelter.*" *Literatur in Wissenschaft und Unterricht* 31 (1998), 173–88.

Schwend, Joachim. "David Lodge, *Out of the Shelter*: Rites of Passage into Paradise?," in Susanne Stark, ed., *The Novel in Anglo-German Context*, 317–31.

Paradise News, 1991

Crowe, Marian E. "Intimations of Immortality: Catholicism in David Lodge's *Paradise News.*" *Renascence* 52:2 (2000), 143–61.

Martin, Bruce K. *David Lodge*, 141–51.

The Picturegoers, 1960

Martin, Bruce K. *David Lodge*, 94–104.

Small World, 1984

Carbone, Paola. "Qualche considerazione sul ruolo culturale del critico letterario attraverso la lettura di *Small World* di David Lodge." *Confronto Letterario* 13 (1996), 535–52.

Fernández Vázquez, José Santiago. "Apuntes para una lectura Bakhtiniana de *Changing Places* y *Small World*, de David Lodge." *Revista Canaria de Estudios Ingleses* 32–33 (1996), 131–40.

Friend, Joshua. "'Every Decoding Is Another Encoding': Morris Zapp's Poststructural Implications on Our Postmodern World." *Engl Lang Notes* 33:3 (1996), 61–67.

Gibert, Teresa. "La flor en el espejo y la luna sobre el agua, o las dificultades de traducir una novela inglesa al japonés." *BELLS: Barcelona Engl Lang and Lit Stud* 1 (1989), 93–98.

Godwin, Denise. "More Echoes from David Lodge's *Small World.*" *Literator* 14:1 (1993), 65–75.

Martin, Bruce K. *David Lodge*, 39–56.

Stanciu, Virgil. "Romancing the Campus (Random Thoughts on the Novels of David Lodge)." *B.A.S.: Brit and Am Stud* 1:1 (1996), 63–70.

Souls and Bodies, 1980

Martin, Bruce K. *David Lodge*, 115–27.

Therapy, 1995

Furst, Lilian R. *Just Talk*, 84–97.

Martin, Bruce K. *David Lodge*, 152–63.

THOMAS LODGE

A Margarite of America, 1596

> Alwes, Derek B. "Elizabethan Dreaming: Fictional Dreams from Gascoigne to Lodge," in Constance C. Relihan, ed., *Framing Elizabethan Fictions,* 155–56, 167.
>
> Davis, Walter R. "Silenced Women," in Constance C. Relihan, ed., *Framing Elizabethan Fictions,* 196–204.
>
> Wilson, Katharine. "From Arcadia to America: Thomas Lodge's Literary Landscapes." *Imaginaires* 5 (2000), 7–19.

Rosalynde, 1590

> Hadfield, Andrew. *Literature, Travel, and Colonial Writing,* 187–92.
>
> Kinney, Clare R. "Feigning Female Faining: Spenser, Lodge, Shakespeare, and Rosalind." *Mod Philology* 95 (1998), 293–98.
>
> Whitworth, Charles. "Wooing and Winning in Arden: *Rosalynde* and *As You Like It*." *Etudes Anglaises* 50 (1997), 387–99.
>
> Wilson, Katharine. "From Arcadia to America: Thomas Lodge's Literary Landscapes." *Imaginaires* 5 (2000), 7–19.

JANE LOUDON

The Mummy: A Tale of the Twenty-Second Century, 1827

> Alkon, Paul. "Bowdler Lives: Michigan's *Mummy*." *Science-Fiction Stud* 23:1 (1996), 123–30.
>
> Rauch, Alan. *Useful Knowledge,* 60–95.

MARIE BELLOC LOWNDES

The Lodger, 1913

> Kestner, Joseph A. *The Edwardian Detective,* 270–81.

MALCOLM LOWRY

Dark as the Grave Wherein My Friend Is Laid, 1968

> Bond, Greg. "Boundlessness beyond Boundlessness: The Sea, Drink, and Form in Malcolm Lowry's Fiction." *Mod Lang R* 94 (1999), 630–33.
>
> Bond, Greg. "Malcolm Lowry's 'History of Someone's Imagination': A Critical Reassessment of *Dark as the Grave wherein My Friend Is Laid*." *Malcolm Lowry R* 40 (1997), 76–110.
>
> Duplay, Mathieu. "The Operatic Paradigm: Voice, Sound, and Meaning in Lowry's Fiction," in Frederick Asals and Paul Tiessen, eds., *A Darkness That Murmured,* 166–67.

Lunar Caustic, 1968

> Bond, Greg. "Boundlessness beyond Boundlessness: The Sea, Drink, and Form in Malcolm Lowry's Fiction." *Mod Lang R* 94 (1999), 628.

October Ferry to Gabriola, 1970

> Bond, Greg. "Boundlessness beyond Boundlessness: The Sea, Drink,

and Form in Malcolm Lowry's Fiction." *Mod Lang R* 94 (1999), 633–34.

Filipczak, Dorota. "Dante 'Follows You Around, Sir!': The Deconstruction of *Inferno* in *October Ferry to Gabriola* by Malcolm Lowry." *Folia Litteraria Anglica* (Lodz) 1 (1997), 15–27.

Ultramarine, 1933

Bond, Greg. "Boundlessness beyond Boundlessness: The Sea, Drink, and Form in Malcolm Lowry's Fiction." *Mod Lang R* 94 (1999), 626–27.

Deane, Patrick. "*Ultramarine,* the Class War, and British Travel Writing in the 1930s," in Frederick Asals and Paul Tiessen, eds., *A Darkness That Murmured,* 119–27.

Under the Volcano, 1947

Ackerley, Chris. "A Fox in the Dongeon: The Presence of Malcolm Lowry in the Early Fiction of J. G. Farrell," in Ralph J. Crane, ed., *J. G. Farrell,* 19–28.

Ackerley, Chris. "Malcolm Lowry's Unimaginable Library of the Dead," in Frederick Asals and Paul Tiessen, eds., *A Darkness That Murmured,* 150–60.

Asals, Frederick. *The Making of Malcolm Lowry's "Under the Volcano."*

Bock, Martin. "Genius and Degeneration in *Under the Volcano,*" in Frederick Asals and Paul Tiessen, eds., *A Darkness That Murmured,* 107–14.

Bond, Greg. "Boundlessness beyond Boundlessness: The Sea, Drink, and Form in Malcolm Lowry's Fiction." *Mod Lang R* 94 (1999), 628–30.

Bowker, Gordon. "Constructing the Biographical Subject: The Case of Malcolm Lowry," in Warwick Gould and Thomas F. Staley, eds., *Writing the Lives of Writers,* 271–74.

DeCoste, Damon Marcel. "'Do you remember to-morrow?': Modernism and Its Second War in Malcolm Lowry's *Under the Volcano.*" *Mod Fiction Stud* 44 (1998), 767–84.

Duplay, Mathieu. "The Operatic Paradigm: Voice, Sound, and Meaning in Lowry's Fiction," in Frederick Asals and Paul Tiessen, eds., *A Darkness That Murmured,* 161–66.

Duplay, Mathieu. "Poétique de la dette: *Under the Volcano* et la tradition." *Recherches Anglaises et Nord-Américaines* 29 (1996), 145–64.

Henderson, Greig. "'Destroy the World!': Gnosis and Nihilism in *Under the Volcano,*" in Frederick Asals and Paul Tiessen, eds., *A Darkness That Murmured,* 69–82.

Lacone-Labarthe, Judith. "'Not translate, but transplant': ambassades du récit (dans *Les Ambassadeurs* de Henry James, *Le Quatuor d'Alexandrie* de Lawrence Durrell et *Au-dessous du volcan* de Malcolm Lowry)." *Revue de Littérature Comparée* 74 (2000), 68–74.

McCarthy, Patrick A. "Lowry and *The Lost Weekend.*" *Malcolm Lowry R* 33 (1993), 38–47.

McCarthy, Patrick A. "Totality and Fragmentation in Lowry and Joyce," in Frederick Asals and Paul Tiessen, eds., *A Darkness That Murmured,* 173–84.

McCormick, John. *Catastrophe and Imagination,* 85–89.

Ravvin, Norman. "Landscape's Narrative: Doing the Malcolm Lowry Walk." *Stud in Canadian Lit* 23:1 (1998), 228–37.

Schaffer, Pierre. "Achieving Intensity: Notes on the Dialogic Evolution of *Under the Volcano*," in Frederick Asals and Paul Tiessen, eds., *A Darkness That Murmured*, 83–103.

Soltan, Margaret. "From Black Magic to White Noise: Malcolm Lowry and Don DeLillo," in Frederick Asals and Paul Tiessen, eds., *A Darkness That Murmured*, 204–13.

Vice, Sue. "Women's Voices: The Late Drafts of James Joyce and Malcolm Lowry." *BELLS: Barcelona Engl Lang and Lit Stud* 7 (1996), 171–81.

JOHN LYLY

Euphues, 1578

Davis, Walter R. "Silenced Women," in Constance C. Relihan, ed., *Framing Elizabethan Fictions*, 187–90.

Hackett, Helen. *Women and Romance Fiction*, 76–85.

Hadfield, Andrew. *Literature, Travel, and Colonial Writing*, 166–80.

Linton, Joan Pong. "The Humanist in the Market: Gendering Exchange and Authorship in Lyly's *Euphues* Romances," in Constance C. Relihan, ed., *Framing Elizabethan Fictions*, 73–97.

Maslen, R. W. *Elizabethan Fictions*, 199–284.

Wilson, Katharine. "'An Ensample to All Women of Lightnesse': Lyly's Lucilla and Her Influence." *Imaginaires* 2 (1997), 31–46.

Wilson, Katharine. "Venus' Backside: The Real Ideal of Renaissance Prose Fiction." *Imaginaires* 3 (1998), 43–56.

PATRICIA LYNCH

The Bookshop on the Quay, 1956

Watson, Nancy. "A Revealing and Exciting Experience: Three of Patricia Lynch's Children's Novels." *Lion and the Unicorn* 21 (1997), 344–45.

Sally from Cork, 1960

Watson, Nancy. "A Revealing and Exciting Experience: Three of Patricia Lynch's Children's Novels." *Lion and the Unicorn* 21 (1997), 343–44.

The Turf-Cutter's Donkey, 1934

Watson, Nancy. "A Revealing and Exciting Experience: Three of Patricia Lynch's Children's Novels." *Lion and the Unicorn* 21 (1997), 342.

WESLEY GUARD LYTTLE

Betsy Gray, or the Hearts of Down, 1888

Reilly, Eileen. "Rebel, Muse, and Spouse: The Female in '98 Fiction." *Eire-Ireland* 34:2 (1999), 144–46.

ROSE MACAULAY

The World My Wilderness, 1950

Boxwell, D. A. "Recalling Forgotten, Neglected, Underrated, or Unjustly Out-of-Print Works." *War, Lit and the Arts* 11 (1999), 207–16.

EUGENE MCCABE

Death and Nightingales, 1992

Mikowski, Sylvie. "L'écriture de l'histoire dans *Death and Nightingales* de Eugène McCabe." *Etudes Irlandaises* 23:1 (1998), 91–100.

Smyth, Gerry. *The Novel and the Nation,* 138–40.

PATRICK MCCABE

The Butcher Boy, 1992

Emprin, Jacques. "Esquisse d'une typologie du prêtre dans le roman irlandais (1900–1970)." *Etudes Irlandaises* 25:1 (2000), 46–48.

Forrest-Hickman, Alan. "Growing Up Irish: An Update on Stephen Dedalus." *Publs of the Arkansas Philol Assoc* 22:1 (1996), 9–18.

Herron, Tom. "ContamiNation: Patrick McCabe and Colm Tóibín's Pathographies of the Republic," in Liam Harte and Michael Parker, eds., *Contemporary Irish Fiction,* 172–78.

McLoone, Martin. "The Abused Child of History: Neil Jordan's *The Butcher Boy.*" *Cineaste* 23:4 (1998), 32–36.

Potts, Donna. "From Tír na nÓg to Tír na Muck: Patrick McCabe's *The Butcher Boy.*" *New Hibernia R* 3:3 (1999), 83–95.

Smyth, Gerry. *The Novel and the Nation,* 81–84.

The Dead School, 1995

Herron, Tom. "ContamiNation: Patrick McCabe and Colm Tóibín's Pathographies of the Republic," in Liam Harte and Michael Parker, eds., *Contemporary Irish Fiction,* 178–83.

J. H. MCCARTHY

The Fair Irish Maid, 1911

Murphy, James H. "'Things Which Seem to You Unfeminine': Gender and Nationalism in the Fiction of Some Upper Middle Class Catholic Women Novelists, 1880–1910," in Kathryn Kirkpatrick, ed., *Border Crossings,* 73–74.

VAL MCDERMID

Blue Genes, 1996

Radford, Jill. "Lindsay Gordon Meets Kate Brannigan — Mainstreaming or Malestreaming: Representations of Women

Crime Fighters," in Elaine Hutton, ed., *Beyond Sex and Romance?*, 99–101.

Booked for Murder, 1996

Radford, Jill. "Lindsay Gordon Meets Kate Brannigan — Mainstreaming or Malestreaming: Representations of Women Crime Fighters," in Elaine Hutton, ed., *Beyond Sex and Romance?*, 91–92.

Common Murder, 1989

Radford, Jill. "Lindsay Gordon Meets Kate Brannigan — Mainstreaming or Malestreaming: Representations of Women Crime Fighters," in Elaine Hutton, ed., *Beyond Sex and Romance?*, 87–89.

Dead Beat, 1992

Radford, Jill. "Lindsay Gordon Meets Kate Brannigan — Mainstreaming or Malestreaming: Representations of Women Crime Fighters," in Elaine Hutton, ed., *Beyond Sex and Romance?*, 97–99.

Report for Murder, 1987

Radford, Jill. "Lindsay Gordon Meets Kate Brannigan — Mainstreaming or Malestreaming: Representations of Women Crime Fighters," in Elaine Hutton, ed., *Beyond Sex and Romance?*, 90–91.

GEORGE MACDONALD

Adela Cathcart, 1864

Ankeny, Rebecca Thomas. *The Story, the Teller, and the Audience*, 98–101.

Broome, F. Hal. "Dreams, Fairy Tales, and the Curing of Adela Cathcart." *North Wind* 13 (1994), 6–18.

Knoepflmacher, U. C. *Ventures into Childhood*, 142–45.

At the Back of the North Wind, 1871

Ankeny, Rebecca Thomas. *The Story, the Teller, and the Audience*, 41–45.

Holbrook, David. *A Study of George MacDonald*, 163–84.

Knoepflmacher, U. C. *Ventures into Childhood*, 229–67.

Lindskoog, Kathryn. *Surprised by C. S. Lewis*, 110–12.

Milbank, Alison. *Dante and the Victorians*, 179–80.

Reynolds, Kimberley, and Paul Yates. "Too Soon: Representations of Childhood Death in Literature for Children," in Karín Lesnik-Oberstein, ed., *Children in Culture*, 164–67.

Sandner, David. *The Fantastic Sublime*, 45–47, 83–100.

David Elginbrod, 1863

Ankeny, Rebecca Thomas. *The Story, the Teller, and the Audience*, 57–59.

Donal Grant, 1883

Ankeny, Rebecca Thomas. *The Story, the Teller, and the Audience*, 87–91.

The Golden Key, 1867

Holbrook, David. *A Study of George MacDonald,* 79–92.
Jeffrey, Kirstin. "The Progressive Key: A Study of Bunyan's Influence in MacDonald's *The Golden Key." North Wind* 16 (1997), 69–75.

Lilith, 1895

Hayward, Deirdre. "George MacDonald and Jacob Boehme: *Lilith* and the Seven-fold Pattern of Existence." *Seven* 16 (1999), 55–71.
Hein, Rolland. "Beyond Ideas: The Intrigue of the *Lilith* Manuscripts." *Seven* 14 (1997), 45–52.
Hein, Rolland. "The *Lilith* Manuscripts." *North Wind* 16 (1997), 15–17.
Holbrook, David. *A Study of George MacDonald,* 241–303.
Lykiard, Alexis. *Jean Rhys Revisited,* 48–50.
Milbank, Alison. *Dante and the Victorians,* 180–82.
Reis, Richard. "The Ignorant/Stupid Narrator in *Lilith." North Wind* 13 (1994), 24–28.
Spina, Giorgio. "*Lilith*: A Dark Labyrinth Towards the Light." *Seven* 12 (1995), 23–28.

Mary Marston, 1881

Ankeny, Rebecca Thomas. "Teacher and Pupil: Reading, Ethics, and Human Dignity in George MacDonald's *Mary Marston." Stud in Scottish Lit* 29 (1996), 227–37.

Phantastes, 1858

Ankeny, Rebecca Thomas. *The Story, the Teller, and the Audience,* 18–121.
Docherty, John. "A Note on the Structure and Conclusion of *Phantastes." North Wind* 7 (1988), 25–30.
Docherty, John. "The Sources of *Phantastes." North Wind* 9 (1990), 28–35; 10 (1991), 26–29.
Gaarden, Bonnie. "George MacDonald's *Phantastes*: The Spiral Journey to the Goddess." *Victorian Newsl* 96 (1999), 6–14.
Gray, William N. "George MacDonald, Julia Kristeva, and the Black Sun." *Stud in Engl Lit, 1500–1900* 36 (1996), 877–91.
Gunther, Adrian. "The Multiple Realms of George MacDonald's *Phantastes." Stud in Scottish Lit* 29 (1996), 174–90.
Gunther, Adrian. "The Structure of George MacDonald's *Phantastes." North Wind* 12 (1993), 43–59.
Holbrook, David. *A Study of George MacDonald,* 185–239.
Pennington, John. "From Fact to Fantasy in Victorian Fiction: Dickens's *Hard Times* and MacDonald's *Phantastes." Extrapolation* 38 (1997), 200–206.
Searsmith, Kelly. "The Angel in the Cosmos: *Phantastes*'s Recasting of the New Gentleman." *J of Pre-Raphaelite Stud* 8 (1999), 53–69.

The Princess and Curdie, 1883

Davies, Maria Gonzalez. "A Spiritual Presence in Fairyland: The Great-Great-Grandmother in the *Princess* Books." *North Wind* 12 (1993), 60–65.
Hayward, Deirdre. "The Mystical Sophia: More on the Great

Grandmother in the *Princess* Books." *North Wind* 13 (1994), 29–33.

Holbrook, David. *A Study of George MacDonald*, 113–45.

Labbe, Jacqueline M. "The Godhead Regendered in Victorian Children's Literature," in Alice Jenkins and Juliet John, eds., *Rereading Victorian Fiction*, 108–13.

The Princess and the Goblin, 1872

Davies, Maria Gonzalez. "A Spiritual Presence in Fairyland: The Great-Great-Grandmother in the *Princess* Books." *North Wind* 12 (1993), 60–65.

Guroian, Vigen. *Tending the Heart of Virtue*, 140–60.

Hayward, Deirdre. "The Mystical Sophia: More on the Great Grandmother in the *Princess* Books." *North Wind* 13 (1994), 29–33.

Holbrook, David. *A Study of George MacDonald*, 101–12.

Labbe, Jacqueline M. "The Godhead Regendered in Victorian Children's Literature," in Alice Jenkins and Juliet John, eds., *Rereading Victorian Fiction*, 108–13.

Melrose, Robin, and Diana Gardner. "The Language of Control in Victorian Children's Literature," in Ruth Robbins and Julian Wolfreys, eds., *Victorian Identities*, 147–48, 154–55.

Robert Falconer, 1868

Lindskoog, Kathryn. *Surprised by C. S. Lewis*, 104–6.

Sir Gibbie, 1879

Lindskoog, Kathryn. *Surprised by C. S. Lewis*, 112–17.

IAN MCDONALD

Hearts, Hands and Voices, 1992

Newsinger, John. "Myth, War, Contact: Ian McDonald's Irish Trilogy." *Foundation* 73 (1998), 51–55.

King of Morning, Queen of Day, 1991

Newsinger, John. "Myth, War, Contact: Ian McDonald's Irish Trilogy." *Foundation* 73 (1998), 48–51.

Sacrifice of Fools, 1996

Newsinger, John. "Myth, War, Contact: Ian McDonald's Irish Trilogy." *Foundation* 73 (1998), 55–58.

IAN MCEWAN

Black Dogs, 1992

Morrison, Jago. "Narration and Unease in Ian McEwan's Later Fiction." *Critique* (Washington, DC) 42 (2001), 261–68.

The Cement Garden, 1978

Antor, Heinz. "Sozialisation zwischen Norm und Tabubruch: Ian McEwans Roman *The Cement Garden* als Lektüre im Leistungskurs Englisch." *Literatur in Wissenschaft und Unterricht* 30 (1997), 267–85.

Pedot, Richard. "Le temps perverti: *The Cement Garden* de Ian McEwan." *Etudes Anglaises* 51 (1998), 284–96.

Roger, Angela. "Ian McEwan's Portrayal of Women." *Forum for Mod Lang Stud* 32 (1996), 14–16.

The Child in Time, 1987

McLeod, John. "Men Against Masculinity: The Fiction of Ian McEwan," in Antony Rowland et al., eds., *Signs of Masculinity,* 231–44.

Roger, Angela. "Ian McEwan's Portrayal of Women." *Forum for Mod Lang Stud* 32 (1996), 19–23.

Warner, Lionel. "Raising Paranoia: Child-Theft in Three 1980s Novels." *The Use of Engl* 52 (2000), 53–55.

The Comfort of Strangers, 1981

Lippe, George B. von der. "Death in Venice in Literature and Film: Six 20th-Century Versions." *Mosaic* 32:1 (1999), 35–54.

Richter, Virginia. "Tourists Lost in Venice: Daphne Du Maurier's *Don't Look Now* and Ian McEwan's *The Comfort of Strangers,*" in Manfred Pfister and Barbara Schaff, eds., *Venetian Views,* 181–94.

Roger, Angela. "Ian McEwan's Portrayal of Women." *Forum for Mod Lang Stud* 32 (1996), 16–19.

Seaboyer, Judith. "Sadism Demands a Story: Ian McEwan's *The Comfort of Strangers.*" *Mod Fiction Stud* 45 (1999), 957–81.

Enduring Love, 1997

Morrison, Jago. "Narration and Unease in Ian McEwan's Later Fiction." *Critique* (Washington, DC) 42 (2001), 255–62.

The Innocent, 1989

Bényei, Tamás. *Acts of Attention,* 187–223.

Bényei, Tamás. "Places in Between: The Subversion of Initiation in Ian McEwan's *The Innocent.*" *B.A.S.: Brit and Am Stud* 4:2 (1999), 66–73.

Mergenthal, Silvia. "'Nation and Narration': Continental Europe and the English Novel," in Susanne Fendler and Ruth Wittlinger, eds., *The Idea of Europe in Literature,* 37–42.

Roger, Angela. "Ian McEwan's Portrayal of Women." *Forum for Mod Lang Stud* 32 (1996), 23–25.

JOHN MCGAHERN

Amongst Women, 1990

Bonafous-Murat, Carole. "Le Rivage et la terre: L'Espace féminin dans *Amongst Women.*" *La Licorne* 32 (1995), 137–49.

Brihault, Jean. "L'Œuvre de John McGahern: De l'écriture du rituel au rituel de l'écriture." *La Licorne* 32 (1995), 107–17.

Corcoran, Neil. *After Yeats and Joyce,* 89–91.

Dukes, Gerry. "Les Transformations du récit dans *Entre toutes les femmes.*" *La Licorne* 32 (1995), 151–58.

Goarzin, Anne. "En quête du père: la difficile filiation dans les romans de John McGahern," in Sophie Marret, ed., *Féminin/Masculin,* 127–28.

Goarzin, Anne. "Figures de l'insularité dans *The Leavetaking* et *Amongst Women*." *La Licorne* 32 (1995), 119–35.

Holland, Siobhán. "Re-Citing the Rosary: Women, Catholicism and Agency in Brian Moore's *Cold Heaven* and John McGahern's *Amongst Women*," in Liam Harte and Michael Parker, eds., *Contemporary Irish Fiction*, 69–75.

Smyth, Gerry. *The Novel and the Nation*, 171–73.

The Barracks, 1963

Brihault, Jean. "L'Œuvre de John McGahern: De l'écriture du rituel au rituel de l'écriture." *La Licorne* 32 (1995), 107–17.

Cardin, Bertrand. "The Implicit in *The Barracks*." *Q/W/E/R/T/Y* 4 (1994), 275–78.

Corcoran, Neil. *After Yeats and Joyce*, 86–88.

Crowley, Cornelius. "Resentment, Repetition, Grace: Time in John McGahern's *The Barracks*." *Q/W/E/R/T/Y* 4 (1994), 279–89.

Kuch, Peter. "Elizabeth Reegan as a Subaltern Wife: Irish Writing as the 'Cracked Looking-Glass of a Servant.'" *Q/W/E/R/T/Y* 4 (1994), 291–97.

Louvel, Liliane. "John McGahern: *The Barracks*—Requiem un jour ordinaire." *La Licorne* 32 (1995), 87–105.

O'Brien, George. "The Aesthetics of Exile," in Liam Harte and Michael Parker, eds., *Contemporary Irish Fiction*, 37–39.

Ollier, Nicole. "Rétention, oppression et répression dans *The Barracks*, de John McGahern." *Q/W/E/R/T/Y* 4 (1994), 305–13.

Ollier, Nicole. "Step By Step Through *The Barracks* with John McGahern." *La Licorne* 32 (1995), 55–85.

Paccaud-Huguet, Josiane. "A Strangely Polished Looking-Glass: John McGahern's Peculiar Realism." *Q/W/E/R/T/Y* 4 (1994), 315–23.

Ross, Ciaran. "Containing and Being Contained: A Violent Sense of Otherness in *The Barracks*." *Q/W/E/R/T/Y* 4 (1994), 325–32.

Zeender, Marie-Noelle. "Michael Halliday: 'L'Insoutenable Absurdité de l'être.'" *Q/W/E/R/T/Y* 4 (1994), 333–37.

The Dark, 1965

Brihault, Jean. "L'Œuvre de John McGahern: De l'écriture du rituel au rituel de l'écriture." *La Licorne* 32 (1995), 107–17.

Cahalan, James M. *Double Visions*, 120–26.

Emprin, Jacques. "Esquisse d'une typologie du prêtre dans le roman irlandais (1900–1970)." *Etudes Irlandaises* 25:1 (2000), 42–44.

Goarzin, Anne. "En quête du père: la difficile filiation dans les romans de John McGahern," in Sophie Marret, ed., *Féminin/Masculin*, 124–32.

The Leavetaking, 1974

Goarzin, Anne. "En quête du père: la difficile filiation dans les romans de John McGahern," in Sophie Marret, ed., *Féminin/Masculin*, 123–24.

Goarzin, Anne. "Figures de l'insularité dans *The Leavetaking* et *Amongst Women*." *La Licorne* 32 (1995), 119–35.

PATRICK MACGILL

Fear!, 1921

Jeffery, Keith. "Irish Prose Writers of the First World War," in Kathleen Devine, ed., *Modern Irish Writers and the Wars*, 12–13.

The Red Horizon, 1916

Jeffery, Keith. "Irish Prose Writers of the First World War," in Kathleen Devine, ed., *Modern Irish Writers and the Wars*, 9–12.

PATRICK MCGINLEY

Bogmail, 1978

Brown, Richard E. "Patrick McGinley's Novels of Detection." *Colby Q* 33 (1997), 210–15.

Casey, Moira. "'the harmless deceptions of male companionship': Sexuality and Male Homosocial Desire in Patrick McGinley's *Bogmail*." *Colby Q* 35 (1999), 184–97.

The Devil's Diary, 1988

Brown, Richard E. "Patrick McGinley's Novels of Detection." *Colby Q* 33 (1997), 218–22.

Shea, Thomas F. "Patrick McGinley's Impressions of Flann O'Brien: *The Devil's Diary* and *At Swim-Two-Birds*." *Twentieth Cent Lit* 40 (1994), 272–80.

Foxprints, 1983

Brown, Richard E. "Patrick McGinley's Novels of Detection." *Colby Q* 33 (1997), 215–18.

Goosefoot, 1982

Brown, Richard E. "Patrick McGinley's Novels of Detection." *Colby Q* 33 (1997), 213–15.

ARTHUR MACHEN

The Great God Pan, 1894

Mighall, Robert. *A Geography of Victorian Gothic Fiction*, 199–203, 205–7.

Navarette, Susan J. *The Shape of Fear*, 188–93, 198–201.

The Three Imposters, 1895

Mighall, Robert. *A Geography of Victorian Gothic Fiction*, 155–57.

Navarette, Susan J. *The Shape of Fear*, 179–81.

WILLIAM MCILVANNEY

Laidlaw, 1977

Dickson, Beth. *William McIlvanney's "Laidlaw."*

Dickson, Beth. "William McIlvanney's Laidlaw Novels." *Laverock* 2 (1996), 27–28.

Klaus, H. Gustav. "The Existentialist Sleuth: William McIlvanney's

Detective Laidlaw," in H. Gustav Klaus and Stephen Knight, eds., *The Art of Murder*, 139–49.

The Papers of Tony Veitch, 1983

Dickson, Beth. "William McIlvanney's Laidlaw Novels." *Laverock* 2 (1996), 27–28.

Klaus, H. Gustav. "The Existentialist Sleuth: William McIlvanney's Detective Laidlaw," in H. Gustav Klaus and Stephen Knight, eds., *The Art of Murder*, 139–49.

Remedy is None, 1966

Walker, Marshall. *Scottish Literature since 1707*, 327–29.

Strange Loyalties, 1991

Dickson, Beth. "William McIlvanney's Laidlaw Novels." *Laverock* 2 (1996), 27–28.

Klaus, H. Gustav. "The Existentialist Sleuth: William McIlvanney's Detective Laidlaw," in H. Gustav Klaus and Stephen Knight, eds., *The Art of Murder*, 139–49.

JOHN MACKENNA

Clare: A Novel, 1993

Innes, Christopher. "Elemental, My Dear Clare: The Case of the Missing Poet," in Martin Middeke and Werner Huber, eds., *Biofictions*, 195–99.

COMPTON MACKENZIE

Sinister Street, 1913

Dougill, John. *Oxford in English Literature*, 136–39.

HENRY MACKENZIE

Julia de Roubigné, 1777

Ellis, Markman. *The Politics of Sensibility*, 114–24.

Manning, Susan L. "Enlightenment's Dark Dreams: Two Fictions of Henry Mackenzie and Charles Brockden Brown." *Eighteenth-Cent Life* 21:3 (1997), 46–53.

The Man of Feeling, 1771

Bellamy, Liz. *Commerce, Morality and the Eighteenth-Century Novel*, 150–56.

Duke, Paul, and Eric Sterling. "Mackenzie's *The Man of Feeling*." *Explicator* 55:2 (1997), 74–75.

Ellison, Julie. *Cato's Tears*, 12–15.

Fairer, David. "Sentimental Translation in Mackenzie and Sterne." *Essays in Criticism* 49 (1999), 132–51.

London, April. "Historiography, Pastoral, Novel: Genre in *The Man of Feeling*." *Eighteenth-Cent Fiction* 10 (1997), 43–62.

London, April. *Women and Property*, 67–80.

Haggerty, George E. *Men in Love*, 86–90.

Lynch, Deidre Shauna. *The Economy of Character*, 112–14.

Morse, David. *The Age of Virtue*, 210–14.

Skinner, Gillian. *Sensibility and Economics in the Novel*, 92–116.

Starr, George. "'Only a Boy': Notes on Sentimental Novels," in Richard Kroll, ed., *The English Novel, Volume I*, 39–43.

Walker, Marshall. *Scottish Literature since 1707*, 63–68.

Wildermuth, Mark E. "The Rhetoric of Common Sense and Uncommon Sensibility in Henry Mackenzie's *The Man of Feeling*." *Lamar J of the Hum* 23:2 (1997), 35–47.

Zimmerman, Everett. *The Boundaries of Fiction*, 206–13.

The Man of the World, 1773

Morse, David. *The Age of Virtue*, 210–14.

Snader, Joe. *Caught Between Worlds*, 198–204.

ELIZABETH MACKINTOSH

The Daughter of Time, 1951

Barnes, Geraldine. "Truth, Fiction, and *The Daughter of Time*." *Sydney Stud in Engl* 26 (2000), 55–67.

The Franchise Affair, 1948

Philips, Deborah, and Ian Haywood. *Brave New Causes*, 146–48.

BERNARD MACLAVERTY

Cal, 1983

Cahalan, James M. *Double Visions*, 140–46.

Haslam, Richard. "'The Pose Arranged and Lingered Over': Visualizing the 'Troubles,'" in Liam Harte and Michael Parker, eds., *Contemporary Irish Fiction*, 196–205.

Lamb, 1980

Haslam, Richard. "'The Pose Arranged and Lingered Over': Visualizing the 'Troubles,'" in Liam Harte and Michael Parker, eds., *Contemporary Irish Fiction*, 201–4.

EOIN MCNAMEE

Resurrection Man, 1994

Haslam, Richard. "'The Pose Arranged and Lingered Over': Visualizing the 'Troubles,'" in Liam Harte and Michael Parker, eds., *Contemporary Irish Fiction*, 205–8.

Hutchinson, Wesley. "*Resurrection Man* d'Eoin McNamee: décrire l'espace de Belfast." *Etudes Irlandaises* 23:1 (1998), 101–12.

Mikowski, Sylvie. "Contemporary War Fiction." *Etudes Irlandaises* 24:2 (1999), 67–80.

Ni-Riordain, Cliona. "Visions et révisions de Belfast dans le roman irlandais contemporain." *GRAAT* 19 (1998), 29–37.

Scanlan, Margaret. *Plotting Terror*, 37–56.
Smyth, Gerry. *The Novel and the Nation*, 120–23.

DEIRDRE MADDEN

Hidden Symptoms, 1986

Ni-Riordain, Cliona. "Visions et révisions de Belfast dans le roman irlandais contemporain." *GRAAT* 19 (1998), 29–37.
St. Peter, Christine. *Changing Ireland*, 117–19.
Smyth, Gerry. *The Novel and the Nation*, 117–20.

One by One in the Darkness, 1996

Mikowski, Sylvie. "Contemporary War Fiction." *Etudes Irlandaises* 24:2 (1999), 67–80.
St. Peter, Christine. *Changing Ireland*, 119–21.

SARA MAITLAND

Daughter of Jerusalem, 1978

Dervin, Dan. *Matricentric Narratives*, 76–81.
King, Jeannette. *Women and the Word*, 76–89.

Home Truths, 1993

Wingfield, Rachel. "Lesbian Writers in the Mainstream: Sara Maitland, Jeanette Winterson and Emma Donoghue," in Elaine Hutton, ed., *Beyond Sex and Romance?*, 68–69.

Three Times Table, 1991

Cosslett, Tess. "Feminism, Matrilinealism, and the 'House of Women' in Contemporary Women's Fiction." *J of Gender Stud* 5 (1996), 9–11.
Wingfield, Rachel. "Lesbian Writers in the Mainstream: Sara Maitland, Jeanette Winterson and Emma Donoghue," in Elaine Hutton, ed., *Beyond Sex and Romance?*, 67–68.

Virgin Territory, 1985

Alexander, Flora. "Contemporary Fiction III: The Anglo-Scots," in Douglas Gifford and Dorothy McMillan, eds., *A History*, 637–38.
Dervin, Dan. *Matricentric Narratives*, 81–83.
King, Jeannette. *Women and the Word*, 89–102.
Wingfield, Rachel. "Lesbian Writers in the Mainstream: Sara Maitland, Jeanette Winterson and Emma Donoghue," in Elaine Hutton, ed., *Beyond Sex and Romance?*, 60–65, 76–77.

LUCAS MALET

The Carissima: A Modern Grotesque, 1896

Lundberg, Patricia Lorimer. "Dialogic Fiction of the Supernatural: 'Lucas Malet.'" *Engl Lit in Transition* 41 (1998), 391–96.

The Gateless Barrier, 1901

Lundberg, Patricia Lorimer. "Dialogic Fiction of the Supernatural: 'Lucas Malet.'" *Engl Lit in Transition* 41 (1998), 396–400.

Schaffer, Talia. *The Forgotten Female Aesthetes*, 244–47.

The History of Sir Richard Calmady, 1901

Schaffer, Talia. "Connoisseurship and Concealment in *Sir Richard Calmady*: Lucas Malet's Strategic Aestheticism," in Talia Schaffer and Kathy Alexis Psomiades, eds., *Women and British Aestheticism*, 44–59.

Schaffer, Talia. *The Forgotten Female Aesthetes*, 200–216.

The Tall Villa, 1920

Lundberg, Patricia Lorimer. "Dialogic Fiction of the Supernatural: 'Lucas Malet.'" *Engl Lit in Transition* 41 (1998), 400–404.

The Wages of Sin, 1890

Schaffer, Talia. *The Forgotten Female Aesthetes*, 217–41.

Schaffer, Talia. "Malet the Obscure: Thomas Hardy, 'Lucas Malet' and the Literary Politics of Early Modernism." *Women's Writing* 3 (1996), 261–80.

WILLIAM H. MALLOCK

The Old Order Changes, 1886

Schäffner, Raimund. *Anarchismus und Literatur in England*, 156–63.

THOMAS MALORY

Le Morte Darthur, 1485

Ackerman, Felicia. "'Every man of worshyp': Emotion and Characterization in Malory's *Le Morte Darthur*." *Arthuriana* 11:2 (2001), 32–40.

Barczewski, Stephanie L. *Myth and National Identity*, 108–23.

Batt, Catherine. "Malory and Rape." *Arthuriana* 7:3 (1997), 78–94.

Bliss, Ann Elaine. "The Symbolic Importance of Processions in Malory's *Morte Darthur* and in Fifteenth-Century England," in D. Thomas Hanks Jr. and Jessica Gentry Brogdon, eds., *The Social and Literary Contexts*, 75–93.

Brönnimann, Werner. "Individuality and Community in Sir Thomas Malory's *Le Morte D'Arthur*: Narrative Models for National Identity," in Ulrich Müller and Kathleen Verduin, eds., *Mittelalter-Rezeption*, 62–72.

Cherewatuk, Karen. "Born-Again Virgins and Holy Bastards: Bors and Elyne and Lancelot and Galahad." *Arthuriana* 11:2 (2001), 52–61.

Cherewatuk, Karen. "The Saint's Life of Sir Launcelot: Hagiography and the Conclusion of Malory's *Morte Darthur*." *Arthuriana* 5:1 (1995), 62–73.

Cherewatuk, Karen. "Sir Thomas Malory's 'Grete Booke,'" in D. Thomas Hanks Jr. and Jessica Gentry Brogdon, eds., *The Social and Literary Contexts*, 42–67.

Cole, Harry E. "Forgiveness as Structure: 'The Book of Sir Launcelot and Queen Guinevere.'" *Chaucer R* 31:1 (1996), 36–44.

Cosslett, Tess. "Intertextuality in *Oranges Are Not The Only Fruit*: The Bible, Malory, and *Jane Eyre*," in Helena Grice and Tim Woods, eds., *"I'm telling you stories,"* 20–23.

Edwards, Elizabeth. *The Genesis of Narrative in Malory's "Morte Darthur."*

Falcetta, Jennie-Rebecca. "The Enduring Sacred Strain: The Place of *The Tale of the Sankgreal* within Sir Thomas Malory's *Morte Darthur*." *Christianity and Lit* 47 (1997), 21–33.

Field, P. J. C. "Malory and the Battle of Towton," in D. Thomas Hanks Jr. and Jessica Gentry Brogdon, eds., *The Social and Literary Contexts*, 68–74.

Field, P. J. C. *Malory: Texts and Sources*, 47–260.

Finke, Laurie A., and Martin B. Shichtman. "No Pain, No Gain: Violence as Symbolic Capital in Malory's *Morte d'Arthur*." *Arthuriana* 8:2 (1998), 115–31.

Gertz, SunHee Kim. *Chaucer to Shakespeare*, 151–62.

Göller, Karl Heinz. "Zur Aktualität des Artusstoffes heute," in Rüdiger Ahrens and Fritz-Wilhelm Neumann, eds., *Fiktion und Geschichte*, 1–5.

Grimm, Kevin T. "The Love and Envy of Sir Palomides." *Arthuriana* 11:2 (2001), 65–72.

Grimm, Kevin T. "Wynkyn de Worde and the Creation of Malory's *Morte Darthur*," in D. Thomas Hanks Jr. and Jessica Gentry Brogdon, eds., *The Social and Literary Contexts*, 134–53.

Haas, Kurtis B. "Ciceronian Rhetorical Principles in Malory's Last Book: *The Exoneration of Sir Lancelot*." *Studia Neophilologica* 71 (1999), 174–81.

Hanks, D. Thomas, Jr. "Malory's Anti-Knights: Balin and Breunys," in D. Thomas Hanks Jr. and Jessica Gentry Brogdon, eds., *The Social and Literary Contexts*, 94–110.

Hares-Stryker, Carolyn. "The Elaine of Astolat and Lancelot Dialogues: A Confusion of Intent." *Texas Stud in Lit and Lang* 39 (1997), 216–26.

Hess, Scott. "Jousting in the Classroom: On Teaching Malory." *Arthuriana* 9:1 (1999), 133–38.

Hoffman, Donald L. "Guenevere the Enchantress." *Arthuriana* 9:2 (1999), 30–35.

Hoffman, Donald L. "Perceval's Sister: Malory's Rejected Masculinities." *Arthuriana* 6:4 (1996), 72–80.

Ingham, Patricia Clare. *Sovereign Fantasies*, 68–70, 101–6, 192–226.

Kahan, Jeffrey. "Malory's *Le Morte D'Arthur*: A Possible Historical Source for *Cymbeline* 3.1." *Engl Lang Notes* 37:4 (2000), 19–20.

Kato, Takako. "Irregular Textual Divisions in Caxton's *Morte Darthur*: Paraphs and Chapter Divisions." *Poetica* (Tokyo) 53 (2000), 15–29.

Kelly, Kathleen Coyne. "Malory's Body Chivalric." *Arthuriana* 6:4 (1996), 52–65.

Kelly, Kathleen Coyne. "Malory's Multiple Virgins." *Arthuriana* 9:2 (1999), 21–27.

Kelly, Robert L. "Malory's Argument Against War with France: the

Political Geography of France and the Anglo-French Alliance in the *Morte Darthur*," in D. Thomas Hanks Jr. and Jessica Gentry Brogdon, eds., *The Social and Literary Contexts*, 111–33.

Kennedy, Beverly. "Adultery in Malory's *Le Morte d'Arthur*." *Arthuriana* 7:4 (1997), 63–84.

Kennedy, Beverly. "The Idea of Providence in Malory's *Le Morte Darthur*." *Arthuriana* 11:2 (2001), 5–17.

Kennedy, Edward Donald. "Malory's Guenevere: 'A Woman Who Had Grown a Soul.'" *Arthuriana* 9:2 (1999), 37–44.

Kim, Hyonjin. *The Knight without the Sword: A Social Landscape of Malorian Chivalry*.

Lewis, Celia M. "'Lawghyng and Smylyng Amonge Them': Humor in Malory's *Morte Darthur*." *Poetica* (Tokyo) 51 (1999), 11–26.

Lynch, Andrew. "*Malory Moralisé*: The Disarming of *Le Morte Darthur*, 1800–1918." *Arthuriana* 9:4 (1999), 81–90.

Lynch, Andrew. *Malory's Book of Arms*, 1–157.

Lynch, Andrew. "'Thou woll never have done': Ideology, Context, and Excess in Malory's War," in D. Thomas Hanks Jr. and Jessica Gentry Brogdon, eds., *The Social and Literary Contexts*, 24–41.

McBride, Christopher. "A Collocational Approach to Semantic Change: The Case of Worship and Honour in Malory and Spenser." *Lang and Lit* (Harlow) 7 (1998), 5–18.

McCarthy, Terence. "Old Worlds, New Worlds: King Arthur in England," in D. Thomas Hanks Jr. and Jessica Gentry Brogdon, eds., *The Social and Literary Contexts*, 5–23.

Mandel, Jerome. "'Polymorphous Sexualities' in Chrétien de Troyes and Sir Thomas Malory," in Piero Boitani and Anna Torti, eds., *The Body and the Soul*, 72–78.

Michelet, Fabienne L. "East and West in Malory's Roman War: The Implications of Arthur's Travels on the Continent." *Multilingua* 18:2–3 (1999), 209–25.

Mieszkowski, Gretchen. "The Prose *Lancelot*'s Galehot, Malory's Lavain, and the Queering of Late Medieval Literature." *Arthuriana* 5:1 (1995), 21–48.

Morse, Ruth. "Back To the Future: Malory's Genres." *Arthuriana* 7:3 (1997), 100–117.

Norris, Ralph. "The Tragedy of Balin: Malory's Use of the Balin Story in the *Morte Darthur*." *Arthuriana* 9:3 (1999), 52–65.

Parins, Marylyn J. "Two Early 'Expurgations' of the *Morte Darthur*." *Arthuriana* 7:3 (1997), 60–74.

Parry, Joseph D. "Following Malory Out of Arthur's World." *Mod Philology* 95 (1997), 147–69.

Perron, Paul. "On Re-Reading Malory's *Le Morte d'Arthur*: The Launcelot Episode." *Semiotica* 108:1–2 (1996), 65–82.

Radulescu, Raluca. "*John Vale's Book* and Sir Thomas Malory's *Le Morte Darthur*: A Political Agenda." *Arthuriana* 9:4 (1999), 69–78.

Ricciardi, Marc. "'Se what I shall do as for my trew parte': Fellowship and Fortitude in Malory's *Noble Tale of King Arthur and the Emperor Lucius*." *Arthuriana* 11:2 (2001), 20–30.

Sanders, Corinne. *Rape and Ravishment*, 234–64.

Saul, MaryLynn. "Courtly Love and Patriarchal Marriage Practice in Malory's *Le Morte Darthur.*" *Fifteenth-Cent Stud* 24 (1998), 50–62.

Schroeder, Peter R. "Saying but Little: Malory and the Suggestion of Emotion." *Arthuriana* 11:2 (2001), 43–51.

Shichtman, Martin B. "Percival's Sister: Genealogy, Virginity, and Blood." *Arthuriana* 9:2 (1999), 11–19.

Spivack, Charlotte, and Roberta Lynne Staples. *The Company of Camelot*, 129–35.

Stephenson, Will, and Mimosa Stephenson. "Launcelot and Lord Peter: A Medieval Murder Mystery and a Modern Analog." *Clues* 19:1 (1998), 17–23.

Sturges, Robert S. "Epistemology of the Bedchamber: Textuality, Knowledge, and the Representation of Adultery in Malory and the Prose *Lancelot.*" *Arthuriana* 7:4 (1997), 47–61.

Svogun, Margaret duMais. *Reading Romance*, 49–113.

Takamiya, Toshiyuki. "Chapter Divisions and Page Breaks in Caxton's *Morte Darthur.*" *Poetica* (Tokyo) 45 (1996), 63–78.

Wallace, Jean. "Exploring Arthur: Facilitating Student Growth While I Learn, Too." *Illinois Engl Bull* 84:3 (1997), 24–27.

Watson, Jessica Lewis. *Bastardy as a Gifted Status*, 33–69.

Weiss, Victoria L. "Grail Knight or Book Companion? The Inconsistent Sir Bors of Malory's *Morte Darthur.*" *Stud in Philology* 94 (1997), 417–27.

Wilkinson, Valerie Anne. "Malory's 'Tournament of Surluse.'" *Poetica* (Tokyo) 51 (1999), 31–45.

Wynne-Davies, Marion. *Women and Arthurian Literature*, 55–77.

MARY DELARIVIERE MANLEY

The Adventures of Rivella, 1714

Backscheider, Paula R. "The Novel's Gendered Space," in Backscheider, ed., *Revising Women*, 10–13.

Benedict, Barbara M. *Curiosity*, 141–42.

McDowell, Paula. *The Women of Grub Street*, 281–84.

Varney, Andrew. *Eighteenth-Century Writers in their World*, 133–37.

The New Atalantis, 1709

Benedict, Barbara M. *Curiosity*, 130–32.

Benedict, Barbara M. "The Curious Genre: Female Inquiry in Amatory Fiction." *Stud in the Novel* 30 (1998), 197–99.

Donovan, Josephine. "Women and the Framed-Novelle: A Tradition of Their Own." *Signs* 22 (1997), 970–72.

Herman, Ruth. "Enigmatic Gender in Delarivier Manley's *New Atalantis,*" in Chris Mounsey, ed., *Presenting Gender*, 202–20.

McDowell, Paula. *The Women of Grub Street*, 220–26, 232–42, 244–51, 253–59, 261–64, 267–72.

Mudge, Bradford K. *The Whore's Story*, 136–47.

Pollak, Ellen. "Guarding the Succession of the (E)State: Guardian-

Ward Incest and the Dangers of Representation in Delarivier Manley's *The New Atalantis.*" *Eighteenth Cent* 39 (1998), 220–36.

Richetti, John. *The English Novel in History*, 29–38.

Richetti, John. "Popular Narrative in the Early Eighteenth Century: Formats and Formulas," in Richard Kroll, ed., *The English Novel, Volume I*, 81–83.

Thompson, Lynda M. *The 'Scandalous Memoirists,'* 184–87.

Varney, Andrew. *Eighteenth-Century Writers in their World*, 131–33.

Wahl, Elizabeth Susan. *Invisible Relations*, 117–30.

The Power of Love, 1720

Rizzo, Betty. "Renegotiating the Gothic," in Paula R. Backscheider, ed., *Revising Women*, 65–67.

The Secret History of Queen Zarah and the Zarazians, 1705

Herman, Ruth. "Similarities Between Delarivier Manley's *Secret History of Queen Zarah* and the English Translation of *Hattigé.*" *Notes and Queries* 47 (2000), 193–96.

McDowell, Paula. *The Women of Grub Street*, 229–32, 266–69.

Richetti, John. "Popular Narrative in the Early Eighteenth Century: Formats and Formulas," in Richard Kroll, ed., *The English Novel, Volume I*, 79–81.

Varney, Andrew. *Eighteenth-Century Writers in their World*, 140–44.

FREDERIC MANNING

Her Privates We, 1930

Rignall, John. "Continuity and Rupture in English Novels of the First World War: Frederic Manning and R. H. Mottram," in Lynne Hapgood and Nancy L. Paxton, eds., *Outside Modernism*, 54–61.

Willis, J. H., Jr. "The Censored Language of War: Richard Aldington's *Death of a Hero* and Three Other War Novels of 1929." *Twentieth Cent Lit* 45 (1999), 472–73.

OLIVIA MANNING

The Battle Lost and Won, 1978

Abderrahim-Laib, Sakina. "Rapports féminin/masculin dans *The Levant Trilogy* d'Olivia Manning," in Sophie Marret, ed., *Féminin/Masculin*, 165–73.

Latham, Ernest H., Jr. "Watching from the Window: Olivia Manning in Romania, 1939–40." *J of the Am Romanian Acad of Arts and Sciences* 20 (1995), 92–112.

Lewis, Nancy. "Lawrence Durrell and Olivia Manning: Egypt, War, and Displacement." *Deus Loci* 4 (1995–1996), 97–104.

The Danger Tree, 1977

Abderrahim-Laib, Sakina. "Rapports féminin/masculin dans *The Levant Trilogy* d'Olivia Manning," in Sophie Marret, ed., *Féminin/Masculin*, 165–73.

Latham, Ernest H., Jr. "Watching from the Window: Olivia Manning in Romania, 1939–40." *J of the Am Romanian Acad of Arts and Sciences* 20 (1995), 92–112.

Lewis, Nancy. "Lawrence Durrell and Olivia Manning: Egypt, War, and Displacement." *Deus Loci* 4 (1995–1996), 97–104.

The Sum of Things, 1980

Abderrahim-Laib, Sakina. "Rapports féminin/masculin dans *The Levant Trilogy* d'Olivia Manning," in Sophie Marret, ed., *Féminin/Masculin*, 165–73.

Latham, Ernest H., Jr. "Watching from the Window: Olivia Manning in Romania, 1939–40." *J of the Am Romanian Acad of Arts and Sciences* 20 (1995), 92–112.

Lewis, Nancy. "Lawrence Durrell and Olivia Manning: Egypt, War, and Displacement." *Deus Loci* 4 (1995–1996), 97–104.

HILARY MANTEL

A Place of Greater Safety, 1992

Byatt, A. S. *On Histories and Stories*, 54–56.

CAEIA MARCH

Between the Worlds, 1996

Rowanchild, Anira. "The State of the Heart: Ideology and Narrative Structure in the Novels of Maureen Duffy and Caeia March," in Elaine Hutton, ed., *Beyond Sex and Romance?*, 42–44.

The Hide and Seek Files, 1988

Rowanchild, Anira. "The State of the Heart: Ideology and Narrative Structure in the Novels of Maureen Duffy and Caeia March," in Elaine Hutton, ed., *Beyond Sex and Romance?*, 38–40.

Three Ply Yarn, 1986

Rowanchild, Anira. "The State of the Heart: Ideology and Narrative Structure in the Novels of Maureen Duffy and Caeia March," in Elaine Hutton, ed., *Beyond Sex and Romance?*, 35–38.

BESSIE MARCHANT

Lois in Charge, or, A Girl of Grit, 1918

Forman, Ross G. "When Britons Brave Brazil: British Imperialism and the Adventure Tale in Latin America." *Victorian Stud* 42:3 (1999/2000), 477–81.

DEREK MARLOWE

A Single Summer with Lord B., 1969

Wilson, Frances. "'A Playful Desire of Imitation': The Ghost Stories at Diodati and *A Single Summer With L. B.*," in Martin Middeke and Werner Huber, eds., *Biofictions*, 162–73.

FLORENCE MARRYAT

The Blood of the Vampire, 1897

> Eldridge, Robert T. "The Other Vampire Novel of 1897: *The Blood of the Vampire* by Florence Marryat." *New York R of Science Fiction* 10:6 (1998), 10–12.

FREDERICK MARRYAT

Frank Mildmay, 1829

> Fulford, Tim. "Romanticizing the Empire: The Naval Heroes of Southey, Coleridge, Austen, and Marryat." *Mod Lang Q* 60 (1999), 161–96.
> Peck, John. *Maritime Fiction,* 53–59.

Masterman Ready, 1841–1842

> Logan, Mawuena Kossi. *Narrating Africa,* 42–48.

Mr. Midshipman Easy, 1836

> Peck, John. *Maritime Fiction,* 59–64.

Poor Jack, 1840

> Peck, John. *Maritime Fiction,* 64–66.

RICHARD MARSH

The Beetle, 1897

> Höglund, Johan A. *Mobilising the Novel,* 130–33.

HARRIET MARTINEAU

Deerbrook, 1842

> Easley, Alexis. "Gendered Observations: Harriet Martineau and the Woman Question," in Nicola Diane Thompson, ed., *Victorian Women Writers,* 87–95.
> Yates, Jennifer. "'Speaking of Romance . . .': The Power of the Female Voice in Harriet Martineau's *Deerbrook.*" *Australasian Victorian Stud J* 3:1 (1997), 99–105.

The Hour and the Man, 1841

> Belasco, Susan. "Harriet Martineau's Black Hero and the American Antislavery Movement." *Nineteenth-Cent Lit* 55 (2000), 157–94.

A. E. W. MASON

At the Villa Rose, 1910

> Kestner, Joseph A. *The Edwardian Detective,* 193–200.

ALLAN MASSIE

The Ragged Lion, 1994

> Rubenstein, Jill. "Auld Acquaintance: New Lives of Scott and

Hogg," in Martin Middeke and Werner Huber, eds., *Biofictions*, 64–69.

The Sins of the Father, 1991

Riordan, Colin. "The Sins of the Children: Peter Schneider, Allan Massie and the Legacy of Auschwitz." *J of European Stud* 27 (1997), 161–80.

CHARLES ROBERT MATURIN

Melmoth the Wanderer, 1820

Backus, Margot Gayle. *The Gothic Family Romance*, 113–26.

Dansky, Richard. "The Wanderer and the Scribbler: Maturin, Scott, and *Melmoth the Wanderer*." *Stud in Weird Fiction* 21 (1997), 2–10.

Ferrari, Roberta. "'From region to region': gli spazi del gotico in *Melmoth the Wanderer* di Charles R. Maturin." *Rivista di Letterature Moderne e Comparate* 52 (1999), 327–49.

Ireland, Ken. *The Sequential Dynamics of Narrative*, 186–87.

Kosok, Heinz. "The Colonial Experience in the Works of Charles Robert Maturin." *Anglia* 117 (1999), 356–57, 365–67.

Kreilkamp, Vera. *The Anglo-Irish Novel*, 96–104.

Sautel, Nadine. "Melmoth de Maturin: Le Diable errant." *Magazine Littéraire* 356 (1997), 58–61.

Tracy, Robert. "Undead, Unburied: Anglo-Ireland and the Predatory Past." *LIT* 10 (1999), 17–19.

Watson, Nicola J. *Revolution and the Form of the British Novel*, 157–64.

The Milesian Chief, 1812

Jeffares, A. Norman. *Images of Invention*, 141–45.

Kosok, Heinz. "The Colonial Experience in the Works of Charles Robert Maturin." *Anglia* 117 (1999), 357–65.

Trumpener, Katie. *Bardic Nationalism*, 146–48.

Zeender, Marie-Noelle. "Aspects du roman gothique irlandais avant et après l'Acte d'Union." *Etudes Irlandaises* 25:2 (2000), 90–92.

The Wild Irish Boy, 1808

Jeffares, A. Norman. *Images of Invention*, 135–41.

Kosok, Heinz. "The Colonial Experience in the Works of Charles Robert Maturin." *Anglia* 117 (1999), 359–65.

Pearson, Jacqueline. "Masculinizing the Novel: Women Writers and Intertextuality in Charles Robert Maturin's *The Wild Irish Boy*." *Stud in Romanticism* 36 (1997), 635–50.

WILLIAM SOMERSET MAUGHAM

Cakes and Ale, 1930

Connon, Bryan. *Somerset Maugham and the Maugham Dynasty*, 97–104.

Whitehead, John. *Eight Modern Masterpieces*, 63–77.

The Moon and Sixpence, 1919

Macey, J. David., Jr. "Fantasy as Necessity: The Role of the Biographer in *The Moon and Sixpence.*" *Stud in the Novel* 29 (1997), 61–72.

The Narrow Corner, 1932

Connon, Bryan. *Somerset Maugham and the Maugham Dynasty,* 104–5.

Of Human Bondage, 1915

Sanders, Lise Shapiro. "The Failures of the Romance: Boredom, Class, and Desire in George Gissing's *The Odd Women* and W. Somerset Maugham's *Of Human Bondage.*" *Mod Fiction Stud* 47 (2000), 201–20.

The Razor's Edge, 1944

Connon, Bryan. *Somerset Maugham and the Maugham Dynasty,* 177–80.

McIntire-Strasburg, Jeffrey O. "'India Changed Him': Modern Orientalism in the Film Adaptations of Somerset Maugham's *The Razor's Edge.*" *Popular Culture R* 10:1 (1999), 83–96.

Singh, Nikky-Guninder Kaur. "Crossing the Razor's Edge: Somerset Maugham and Hindu Philosophy." *Durham Univ J* 87 (1995), 329–41.

FLORA MACDONALD MAYOR

The Rector's Daughter, 1924

Trumpener, Katie. "The Virago Jane Austen," in Deidre Lynch, ed., *Janeites,* 159–60.

L. T. MEADE

The Cleverest Woman in England, 1898

Willis, Chris. "'Heaven defend me from political or highly-educated women!': Packaging the New Woman for Mass Consumption," in Angelique Richardson and Chris Willis, eds., *The New Woman in Fiction and in Fact,* 58–59.

GEORGE MEREDITH

The Adventures of Harry Richmond, 1871

Jones, Mervyn. *The Amazing Victorian,* 238–40.
Roberts, Neil. *Meredith and the Novel,* 89–110.

The Amazing Marriage, 1895

Craig, Randall. *Promising Language,* 51–54.
Jones, Mervyn. *The Amazing Victorian,* 169–72, 190–92.
Roberts, Neil. *Meredith and the Novel,* 243–53.

Beauchamp's Career, 1875

Jones, Mervyn. *The Amazing Victorian,* 189–95.
Roberts, Neil. *Meredith and the Novel,* 111–49.

Diana of the Crossways, 1885

    Craig, Randall. *Promising Language,* 186–88.

    Jones, Mervyn. *The Amazing Victorian,* 160–62, 216–18.

    Ledger, Sally. *The New Woman,* 133–38.

    Roberts, Neil. *Meredith and the Novel,* 205–29.

The Egoist, 1879

    Cavaliero, Glen. *The Alchemy of Laughter,* 164–66.

    Craig, Randall. *Promising Language,* 188–96.

    De Marco, Nick. "One Victorian's View of Marriage: George Meredith's *The Egoist.*" *Rivista di Studi Vittoriani* 1:2 (1996), 73–84.

    Gilmartin, Sophie. *Ancestry and Narrative,* 163–94.

    Gilmartin, Sophie. "The Sati, the Bride, and the Widow: Sacrificial Woman in the Nineteenth Century." *Victorian Lit and Culture* 25:1 (1997), 141–58.

    Green, Stephanie. "'Nature was strong in him': Spoiling the Empire Boy in George Meredith's *The Egoist.*" *Australasian Victorian Stud J* 5 (1999), 79–86.

    Ireland, Ken. *The Sequential Dynamics of Narrative,* 224–26.

    Jones, Mervyn. *The Amazing Victorian,* 164–68.

    Miller, Louise M. "Narcissism, 'Inner Genres,' and the Comic Spirit in *The Egoist.*" *Q/W/E/R/T/Y* 3 (1993), 123–32.

    Morrison, Mark. "Marketing British Modernism: *The Egoist* and Counter-Public Spheres." *Twentieth Cent Lit* 43 (1997), 439–61.

    Roberts, Neil. *Meredith and the Novel,* 150–86.

    Vlasopolos, Anca. "Focalization, the Cinematic Gaze, and Romance in Meredith and Woolf." *Woolf Stud Annual* 7 (2001), 3–21.

Evan Harrington, 1861

    Gilmartin, Sophie. *Ancestry and Narrative,* 130–62.

    Jones, Mervyn. *The Amazing Victorian,* 17–19.

    Kushen, Betty. "Instinct and Heredity in Four Nineteenth-Century Novels: 'The Tangled Mystery of Mental Operations.'" *J of Evolutionary Psych* 18:3–4 (1997), 191–212.

    Roberts, Neil. *Meredith and the Novel,* 47–61.

Lord Ormont and His Aminta, 1894

    Jones, Mervyn. *The Amazing Victorian,* 167–71.

    Roberts, Neil. *Meredith and the Novel,* 240–43.

One of Our Conquerors, 1891

    Roberts, Neil. *Meredith and the Novel,* 230–40.

    Soccio, Anna Enrichetta. "Male Insanity as Paradigm of Change in George Meredith's *One of Our Conquerors.*" *Rivista di Studi Vittoriani* 7:4 (1999), 127–40.

The Ordeal of Richard Feveral, 1859

    Ireland, Ken. *The Sequential Dynamics of Narrative,* 223–24.

    Jones, Mervyn. *The Amazing Victorian,* 33–35, 82–87.

    Kushen, Betty. "Instinct and Heredity in Four Nineteenth-Century Novels: 'The Tangled Mystery of Mental Operations.'" *J of Evolutionary Psych* 18:3–4 (1997), 191–212.

Osteen, Mark. "Meredith/Joyce: Bella Mount and Bella's Mount." *James Joyce Q* 35:4/36:1 (1998), 873–77.

Roberts, Neil. *Meredith and the Novel*, 13–46.

Sillars, Stuart. *Structure and Dissolution*, 34–37.

Soccio, Anna Enrichetta. "'What He Has Done Cannot Be Undone': Una lettura di *The Ordeal of Richard Feverel* di George Meredith." *Rivista di Studi Vittoriani* 2:3 (1997), 95–110.

Rhoda Fleming, 1865

Heinrich, Hans. *Zur Geschichte des 'Libertin,'* 219–21.

Jones, Mervyn. *The Amazing Victorian*, 179–81.

Roberts, Neil. *Meredith and the Novel*, 70–76.

Sandra Belloni, 1886

Cole, Natalie Bell. "The 'Foreign Eye' Outside and Within: Meredith's *Sandra Belloni*." *Victorians Inst J* 25 (1997), 133–53.

Roberts, Neil. *Meredith and the Novel*, 60–70.

The Shaving of Shagpat, 1856

Jones, Mervyn. *The Amazing Victorian*, 67–74.

The Tragic Comedians, 1880

Roberts, Neil. *Meredith and the Novel*, 187–204.

ISABEL MEREDITH

A Girl Among the Anarchists, 1903

Schäffner, Raimund. *Anarchismus und Literatur in England*, 456–71.

ELIZA METEYARD

Lucy Dean: The Noble Needlewoman, 1850

Faymonville, Carmen. "'Waste Not, Want Not': Even Redundant Women Have Their Uses," in Rita S. Kranidis, ed., *Imperial Objects*, 70–74.

LIA MILLS

Another Alice, 1996

Smyth, Gerry. *The Novel and the Nation*, 93–97.

A. A. MILNE

The Red House Mystery, 1922

Foxwell, Elizabeth. "Elementary My Dear Eeyore: A. A. Milne's Foray into Mystery." *Mystery Scene* 58 (1997), 37, 65.

Winnie–the–Pooh, 1926

Connolly, Paula T. "The Marketing of Romantic Childhood: Milne, Disney, and a Very Popular Stuffed Bear," in James Holt Gavran, ed., *Literature and the Child*, 188–207.

Kutzer, M. Daphne. *Empire's Children*, 96–103.
Lesnik-Oberstein, Karín. "Fantasy, Childhood and Literature: In Pursuit of Wonderlands," in Ceri Sullivan and Barbara White, eds., *Writing and Fantasy*, 200–205.

JAMES LESLIE MITCHELL

A Scots Quair, 1932–1934

Craig, Cairns. "Scotland and the Regional Novel," in K. D. M. Snell, ed., *The Regional Novel*, 237–38.
Haywood, Ian. *Working-Class Fiction*, 79–81.
Idle, Jeremy. "Lewis Grassic Gibbon and the Urgency of the Modern." *Stud in Scottish Lit* 31 (1999), 258–68.
Walker, Marshall. *Scottish Literature since 1707*, 235–39.

Spartacus, 1933

Malzahn, Manfred. "Masters and Slaves in Scottish Fiction and Ideology of the 1930s: James Leslie Mitchell's *Spartacus* and William Bell's *Rip van Scotland*." *Stud in Scottish Lit* 31 (1999), 225–31.

NAOMI MITCHISON

The Blood of the Martyrs, 1939

Hoberman, Ruth. *Gendering Classicism*, 130–36.
Maslen, Elizabeth. "Naomi Mitchison's Historical Fiction," in Maroula Joannou, ed., *Women Writers of the 1930s*, 146–50.

The Bull Calves, 1947

Calder, Jenni. "More Than Merely Ourselves: Naomi Mitchison," in Douglas Gifford and Dorothy McMillan, eds., *A History*, 448–50.
McCulloch, Margery Palmer. "Fictions of Development, 1920–1970," in Douglas Gifford and Dorothy McMillan, eds., *A History*, 369–70.

Cloud Cuckooland, 1925

Hoberman, Ruth. *Gendering Classicism*, 27–33.

The Conquered, 1923

Burgess, Moira. "The Modern Historical Tradition," in Douglas Gifford and Dorothy McMillan, eds., *A History*, 459–62.
Hoberman, Ruth. *Gendering Classicism*, 121–30.

The Corn King and the Spring Queen, 1931

Calder, Jenni. "More Than Merely Ourselves: Naomi Mitchison," in Douglas Gifford and Dorothy McMillan, eds., *A History*, 444–45.
Elphinstone, Margaret. "The Location of Magic in *The Corn King and the Spring Queen*," in Carol Anderson and Aileen Christianson, eds., *Scottish Women's Fiction*, 73–82.
Hoberman, Ruth. *Gendering Classicism*, 33–40.
Maslen, Elizabeth. "Naomi Mitchison's Historical Fiction," in Maroula Joannou, ed., *Women Writers of the 1930s*, 140–44.
Trodd, Anthea. *Women's Writing in English*, 115–16.

Lobsters on the Agenda, 1952

Calder, Jenni. "More Than Merely Ourselves: Naomi Mitchison," in Douglas Gifford and Dorothy McMillan, eds., *A History*, 450–51.

We Have Been Warned, 1935

Maslen, Elizabeth. "Naomi Mitchison's Historical Fiction," in Maroula Joannou, ed., *Women Writers of the 1930s*, 143–45.

When We Become Men, 1965

Calder, Jenni. "More Than Merely Ourselves: Naomi Mitchison," in Douglas Gifford and Dorothy McMillan, eds., *A History*, 452–53.

MARY RUSSELL MITFORD

Our Village, 1824

Lynch, Deidre. "Homes and Haunts: Austen's and Mitford's English Idylls." *PMLA* 115 (2000), 1103–7.

Wordsworth, Jonathan. *The Bright Work Grows*, 247–52.

NANCY MITFORD

Love in a Cold Climate, 1949

Hepburn, Allan. "The Fate of the Modern Mistress: Nancy Mitford and the Comedy of Marriage." *Mod Fiction Stud* 45 (1999), 356–65.

Pigeon Pie, 1940

McDonough, Donald. "Off with Their Heads: The British Novel and the Rise of Fascism." *Tennessee Philol Bull* 33 (1996), 34–42.

The Pursuit of Love, 1945

Hepburn, Allan. "The Fate of the Modern Mistress: Nancy Mitford and the Comedy of Marriage." *Mod Fiction Stud* 45 (1999), 340–56.

TIMOTHY MO

An Insular Possession, 1986

McLeod, John. "On the Chase for Gideon Nye: History and Representation in Timothy Mo's *An Insular Possession*." *J of Commonwealth Lit* 34:2 (1999), 61–72.

Smethurst, Paul. "Post-Imperial Topographies: The Undergrounding of History in J. G. Farrell's *The Singapore Grip*, Timothy Mo's *An Insular Possession*, and Graham Swift's *Waterland*," in Ralph J. Crane, ed., *J. G. Farrell*, 120–26.

The Monkey King, 1978

Lim, Shirley Geok-Lin. "Race, National Identity, and the Subject in the Novels of Timothy Mo," in Peter O. Stummer and Christopher Balme, eds., *Fusion of Cultures?*, 92–95.

The Redundancy of Courage, 1991

Davies, J. M. Q. "Refractions: Fiction, Historiography and Mo's *The Redundancy of Courage*." *Canadian R of Compar Lit* 23 (1996), 983–91.

Ho, Elaine Yee Lin. "Satire and the National Body: Timothy Mo's *The Redundancy of Courage.*" *SPAN* 42–43 (1996), 76–85.

Lim, Shirley Geok-Lin. "Race, National Identity, and the Subject in the Novels of Timothy Mo," in Peter O. Stummer and Christopher Balme, eds., *Fusion of Cultures?*, 98–100.

Sour Sweet, 1981

Gibson, Andrew. *Postmodernity, Ethics and the Novel,* 197–201.

Ho, Elaine Yee Lin. "Of Laundries and Restaurants: Fictions of Ethnic Space." *Wasafiri* 21 (1995), 16–19.

Lee, A. Robert. "Imagined Cities of China." *Wasafiri* 22 (1995), 25–30.

Lim, Shirley Geok-Lin. "Race, National Identity, and the Subject in the Novels of Timothy Mo," in Peter O. Stummer and Christopher Balme, eds., *Fusion of Cultures?*, 95–98.

McLeod, John. "Living In-Between: Interstitial Spaces of Possibility in Timothy Mo's *Sour Sweet,*" in Steven Earnshaw, ed., *Just Postmodernism,* 107–25.

Skinner, John. *The Stepmother Tongue,* 319–21.

Widmann, R. L. "Timothy Mo's *Sour Sweet*: A Novelist Reimagining the 'Colonial Mind.'" *J of Commonwealth and Postcolonial Stud* 2:1 (1994), 38–55.

MARY LOUISA MOLESWORTH

The Cuckoo Clock, 1877

Melrose, Robin, and Diana Gardner. "The Language of Control in Victorian Children's Literature," in Ruth Robbins and Julian Wolfreys, eds., *Victorian Identities,* 146–47, 153–54, 158.

Sircar, Sanjay. "Classic Fantasy Novel as Didactic Victorian Bildungsroman: *The Cuckoo Clock.*" *Lion and the Unicorn* 21 (1997), 163–92.

Sircar, Sanjay. "Locating a Classic: *The Cuckoo Clock* and Its Literary Context." *Children's Lit Assoc Q* 21:4 (1996–1997), 170–76.

The Palace in the Garden, 1887

Riga, Frank P. "(De)constructing the Patriarchal Family: Mary Louisa Molesworth and the Late Nineteenth-Century Children's Novel," in Andrea O'Reilly Herrera et al., eds., *Family Matters,* 99–113.

FRANCES MOLLOY

No Mate for the Magpie, 1985

Patten, Eve. "Fiction in Conflict: Northern Ireland's Prodigal Novelists," in Ian A. Bell, ed., *Peripheral Visions,* 133–35.

St. Peter, Christine. *Changing Ireland,* 50–53.

LADY BARBARA MONTAGU

The Histories of Some of the Penitents in the Magdalen-House, 1760

Ellis, Markman. *The Politics of Sensibility,* 178–84.

FLORENCE MONTGOMERY

Misunderstood, 1869

Reynolds, Kimberley, and Paul Yates. "Too Soon: Representations of Childhood Death in Literature for Children," in Karín Lesnik-Oberstein, ed., *Children in Culture,* 168–72.

MICHAEL MOORCOCK

The Eternal Champion, 1970

Hoey, Michael. "Disguising Doom: A Study of the Linguistic Features of Audience Manipulation in Michael Moorcock's *The Eternal Champion,*" in David Seed, ed., *Imagining Apocalypse,* 151–65.

GEORGE MOORE

The Brook Kerith, 1916

Jeffares, A. Norman. *Images of Invention,* 242–46.

A Drama in Muslin, 1886

Diez Fabre, Silvia. "George Moore's Critical Stance of the Irish Situation Looming in the Shadow of Colonial Discourse." *B.A.S.: Brit and Am Stud* 4:2 (1999), 113–19.

Frehner, Ruth. *The Colonizers' Daughters,* 19–39.

Ledger, Sally. *The New Woman,* 138–42.

Esther Waters, 1894

Berry, Betsy. "*Voyage in the Dark, Esther Waters,* and the Naturalistic Tradition." *Jean Rhys R* 7:1–2 (1996), 17–25.

Jeffares, A. Norman. *Images of Invention,* 228–30.

Lykiard, Alexis. *Jean Rhys Revisited,* 189–91.

O'Toole, Tess. "The Servant's Body: The Victorian Wet-Nurse and George Moore's *Esther Waters.*" *Women's Stud* 25 (1996), 329–46.

Stubbings, Diane. *Anglo-Irish Modernism,* 26–29.

Evelyn Innes, 1898

Devine, Paul. "Leitmotif and Epiphany: George Moore's *Evelyn Innes* and *The Lake,*" in Wim Tigges, ed., *Moments of Moment,* 160–67.

The Lake, 1905

Devine, Paul. "Leitmotif and Epiphany: George Moore's *Evelyn Innes* and *The Lake,*" in Wim Tigges, ed., *Moments of Moment,* 157–60, 168–75.

Emprin, Jacques. "Esquisse d'une typologie du prêtre dans le roman irlandais (1900–1970)." *Etudes Irlandaises* 25:1 (2000), 37–39.

Jeffares, A. Norman. *Images of Invention,* 235–37, 305–7.

Stubbings, Diane. *Anglo-Irish Modernism,* 41–44.

HANNAH MORE

Coelebs in Search of a Wife, 1809

Guest, Harriet. *Small Change,* 325–28.

Nardin, Jane. "Avoiding the Perils of the Muse: Hannah More, Didactic Literature, and Eighteenth-Century Criticism." *Papers on Lang and Lit* 36 (2000), 388–91.

Nardin, Jane. "Jane Austen, Hannah More, and the Novel of Education." *Persuasions* 20 (1998), 15–20.

Pearson, Jacqueline. *Women's Reading in Britain*, 88–92.

Snook, Edith. "Eve and More: The Citation of *Paradise Lost* in Hannah More's *Coelebs in Search of a Wife*." *Engl Stud in Canada* 26 (2000), 127–47.

Waldron, Mary. *Jane Austen and the Fiction of Her Time*, 89–95.

SYDNEY MORGAN

Florence Macarthy, 1818

Trumpener, Katie. *Bardic Nationalism*, 143–46.

The Missionary, 1811

Kelsall, Malcolm. "Reading Orientalism: *Woman or Ida of Athens*." *R of Natl Literatures and World Report* 1 (1998), 11–20.

Neff, D. S. "Hostages to Empire: The Anglo-Indian Problem in *Frankenstein*, *The Curse of Kehama*, and *The Missionary*." *European Romantic R* 8 (1997), 386–408.

Rajan, Balachandra. *Under Western Eyes*, 130–37.

The O'Briens and the O'Flaherties, 1827

Wright, Julia M. "'The Nation Begins to Form': Competing Nationalisms in Morgan's *The O'Briens and the O'Flaherties*." *ELH* 66 (1999), 939–58.

O'Donnel, 1814

Jeffares, A. Norman. *Images of Invention*, 123–30.

The Wild Irish Girl, 1806

Burgess, Miranda J. "Violent Translations: Allegory, Gender, and Cultural Nationalism in Ireland, 1796–1806." *Mod Lang Q* 59 (1998), 61–70.

Connolly, Claire. "'I accuse Miss Owenson': *The Wild Irish Girl* as Media Event." *Colby Q* 36 (2000), 98–113.

Corbett, Mary Jean. "Allegories of Prescription: Engendering Union in *The Wild Irish Girl*." *Eighteenth-Cent Life* 22:3 (1998), 92–101.

Corbett, Mary Jean. *Allegories of Union*, 54–70.

Dennis, Ian. *Nationalism and Desire*, 45–61.

Gilmartin, Sophie. *Ancestry and Narrative*, 34–39.

Jeffares, A. Norman. *Images of Invention*, 115–22.

Miller, Julia Anne. "Acts of Union: Family Violence and National Courtship in Maria Edgeworth's *The Absentee* and Sydney Owenson's *The Wild Irish Girl*," in Kathryn Kirkpatrick, ed., *Border Crossings*, 23–31.

Rajan, Balachandra. *Under Western Eyes*, 128–30.

Tracy, Robert. *The Unappeasable Host*, 29–30.

Watson, Nicola J. *Revolution and the Form of the British Novel*, 111–16.

Wordsworth, Jonathan. *The Bright Work Grows*, 154–59.

Zeender, Marie-Noelle. "Aspects du roman gothique irlandais avant et après l'Acte d'Union." *Etudes Irlandaises* 25:2 (2000), 86–90.

Woman: or, Ida of Athens, 1809

Kelsall, Malcolm. "Reading Orientalism: *Woman or Ida of Athens*." *R of Natl Literatures and World Report* 1 (1998), 11–20.

WILLIAM MORRIS

A Dream of John Ball, 1888

Salmon, Nicholas. "A Reassessment of *A Dream of John Ball*." *J of the William Morris Soc* 14:2 (2001), 29–36.

The House of the Wolfings, 1889

Salmon, Nicholas. "A Study in Victorian Historiography: William Morris's Germanic Romances." *J of the William Morris Soc* 14:2 (2001), 59–84.

Talbot, Norman. "William Morris and the Bear: Theme, Magic and Totem in the Romances," in Peter Faulkner and Peter Preston, eds., *William Morris*, 96–98, 100–102, 104–6.

News from Nowhere, 1890

Bartels, Dennis. "The Road to Nowhere: Morris, Utopia, and Global Climate Change." *J of the William Morris Soc* 12:3 (1997), 39–46.

Brantlinger, Patrick. *The Reading Lesson*, 196–203.

Buzard, James. "Ethnography as Interruption: *News from Nowhere*, Narrative, and the Modern Romance of Authority." *Victorian Stud* 40:3 (1997), 445–70.

Corrado, Adriana. "Beatrice and Ellen: Ideal Guides from Hell to Paradise," in Peter Faulkner and Peter Preston, eds., *William Morris*, 83–93.

Delveaux, Martin. "From Pastoral Arcadia to Stable-State Mini-Cities: Morris's *News from Nowhere* and Callenbach's *Ecotopia*." *J of the William Morris Soc* 14:1 (2000), 76–80.

Ferns, Chris. *Narrating Utopia*, 144–56.

Fitch, Eric L. "How Green was my *Utopia*?: A Reflection on William Morris's *News from Nowhere*, H. G. Wells's *Men Like Gods* and Ernest Callenbach's *Ecotopia*." *The Wellsian* 19 (1996), 30–35.

Highfill, Jannett. "International Trade in *News from Nowhere*." *J of the William Morris Soc* 12:2 (1997), 31–34.

Jacobs, Naomi. "Beauty and the Body in *News From Nowhere*." *J of the William Morris Soc* 12:2 (1997), 26–29.

Kelvin, Norman. "*News from Nowhere* and *The Spoils of Poynton*: Interiors and Exteriors," in Peter Faulkner and Peter Preston, eds., *William Morris*, 107–21.

Lawton, Lesley. "Lineaments of Ungratified Desire: William Morris's *News from Nowhere* as Utopian Romance." *Anglophonia* 3 (1998), 113–23.

Ledger, Sally. *The New Woman*, 50–52.

Mineo, Ady. "Beyond the Law of the Father: The 'New Woman' in

News from Nowhere," in Peter Faulkner and Peter Preston, eds., *William Morris*, 200–206.

Pinkney, Tony. "Cycling in Nowhere." *J of the William Morris Soc* 13:2 (1999), 28–32.

Schäffner, Raimund. *Anarchismus und Literatur in England*, 276–87.

The Roots of the Mountains, 1889

Salmon, Nicholas. "A Study in Victorian Historiography: William Morris's Germanic Romances." *J of the William Morris Soc* 14:2 (2001), 59–84.

Talbot, Norman. "William Morris and the Bear: Theme, Magic and Totem in the Romances," in Peter Faulkner and Peter Preston, eds., *William Morris*, 98–101.

The Story of the Glittering Plain, 1891

Dewan, Pauline. "Circular Designs in Morris's *The Story of the Glittering Plain.*" *J of the William Morris Soc* 12:4 (1998), 15–20.

Talbot, Norman. "The First Modern 'Secondary World' Fantasy: Morris's Craftsmanship in *The Story of the Glittering Plain.*" *J of the William Morris Soc* 13:2 (1999), 3–10.

Talbot, Norman. "'I Seek No Dream . . . but Rather the End of Dreams': The Deceptions of *The Story of the Glittering Plain.*" *Mythlore* 22:1 (1997), 26–31.

The Sundering Flood, 1897

Newman, Hilary. "Water in William Morris's Late Prose Romances." *J of the William Morris Soc* 13:4 (2000), 41–47.

The Water of the Wondrous Isles, 1897

Newman, Hilary. "Water in William Morris's Late Prose Romances." *J of the William Morris Soc* 13:4 (2000), 41–47.

The Well at the World's End, 1896

Newman, Hilary. "Water in William Morris's Late Prose Romances." *J of the William Morris Soc* 13:4 (2000), 41–47.

Talbot, Norman. "William Morris and the Bear: Theme, Magic and Totem in the Romances," in Peter Faulkner and Peter Preston, eds., *William Morris*, 102–6.

The Wood Beyond the World, 1894

Newman, Hilary. "The Influence of De La Motte Fouqué's *Sintram and His Companions* on William Morris's *The Wood Beyond the World.*" *J of the William Morris Soc* 14:2 (2001), 47–52.

ARTHUR MORRISON

A Child of the Jago, 1896

Hertel, Kirsten. *London zwischen Naturalismus und Moderne*, 167–219.

Joyce, Simon. "Castles in the Air: The People's Palace, Cultural Reformism, and the East End Working Class." *Victorian Stud* 39:4 (1996), 533–36.

Kane, Penny. *Victorian Families in Fact and Fiction*, 31–33.

NANCY BRYSSON MORRISON

The Gowk Storm, 1933

McCulloch, Margery Palmer. "Poetic Narrative in Nancy Brysson Morrison's *The Gowk Storm*," in Carol Anderson and Aileen Christianson, eds., *Scottish Women's Fiction*, 109–19.

MAVY MORRISSEY

Mother of Pearl, 1996

Smyth, Gerry. *The Novel and the Nation*, 91–93.

PENELOPE MORTIMER

The Pumpkin Eater, 1962

Dervin, Dan. *Matricentric Narratives*, 33–35.
Furst, Lilian R. *Just Talk*, 115–29.

RALPH HALE MOTTRAM

The Spanish Farm Trilogy, 1927

Rignall, John. "Continuity and Rupture in English Novels of the First World War: Frederic Manning and R. H. Mottram," in Lynne Hapgood and Nancy L. Paxton, eds., *Outside Modernism*, 46–54.

WILLA MUIR

Imagined Corners, 1931

Christianson, Aileen. "Dreaming Realities: Willa Muir's *Imagined Corners*," in Carol Anderson and Aileen Christianson, eds., *Scottish Women's Fiction*, 85–96.
Elphinstone, Margaret. "Willa Muir: Crossing the Genres," in Douglas Gifford and Dorothy McMillan, eds., *A History*, 406–8.

Mrs. Ritchie, 1933

Dickson, Beth. "'An ordinary little girl'?: Willa Muir's *Mrs Ritchie*," in Carol Anderson and Aileen Christianson, eds., *Scottish Women's Fiction*, 97–105.
Elphinstone, Margaret. "Willa Muir: Crossing the Genres," in Douglas Gifford and Dorothy McMillan, eds., *A History*, 408–10.

ROSA MULHOLLAND

Marcella Grace, 1886

Murphy, James H. "'Things Which Seem to You Unfeminine': Gender and Nationalism in the Fiction of Some Upper Middle Class Catholic Women Novelists, 1880–1910," in Kathryn Kirkpatrick, ed., *Border Crossings*, 61–67.

The Return of Mary O'Murrough, 1908

> Murphy, James H. "'Things Which Seem to You Unfeminine': Gender and Nationalism in the Fiction of Some Upper Middle Class Catholic Women Novelists, 1880–1910," in Kathryn Kirkpatrick, ed., *Border Crossings,* 74–77.

DINAH MARIA MULOCK

Hannah, 1871

> Gruner, Elisabeth Rose. "Born and Made: Sisters, Brothers, and the Deceased Wife's Sister Bill." *Signs* 24 (1999), 435–37, 440–45.

John Halifax, Gentleman, 1856

> Kushen, Betty. "Instinct and Heredity in Four Nineteenth-Century Novels: 'The Tangled Mystery of Mental Operations.'" *J of Evolutionary Psych* 18:3–4 (1997), 191–212.
>
> Young, Arlene. *Culture, Class and Gender,* 37–44.

King Arthur: Not a Love Story, 1886

> O'Toole, Tess. "Adoption and the 'Improvement of the Estate' in Trollope and Craik." *Nineteenth-Cent Lit* 52 (1997), 62–68.

The Little Lame Prince, 1875

> Labbe, Jacqueline M. "The Godhead Regendered in Victorian Children's Literature," in Alice Jenkins and Juliet John, eds., *Rereading Victorian Fiction,* 104–8.
>
> Philipose, Lily. "The Politics of the Hearth in Victorian Children's Fantasy: Dinah Mulock Craik's *The Little Lame Prince.*" *Children's Lit Assoc Q* 21:3 (1996), 133–39.

Olive, 1850

> Denisoff, Dennis. "Lady in Green with Novel: The Gendered Economics of the Visual Arts and Mid-Victorian Women's Writing," in Nicola Diane Thompson, ed., *Victorian Women Writers,* 164–67.

IRIS MURDOCH

An Accidental Man, 1971

> Richardson, Brian. *Unlikely Stories,* 161–64.

The Bell, 1958

> White, Roberta S. "Iris Murdoch: Mapping the Country of Desire," in Abby H. P. Werlock, ed., *British Women Writing Fiction,* 32–34.

The Black Prince, 1973

> Butler, Lance St. John. *Registering the Difference,* 15–22.
>
> Dente-Baschiera, Carla. "Re-Inventing Ambiguity for the 20th Century: *The Black Prince* by Iris Murdoch." *Textus* 11 (1998), 45–63.
>
> Tosi, Laura. "Metafiction in *The Black Prince* di Iris Murdoch." *Linguistica e Letteratura* 18:1–2 (1993), 181–215.
>
> White, Roberta S. "Iris Murdoch: Mapping the Country of Desire," in Abby H. P. Werlock, ed., *British Women Writing Fiction,* 26–28.

The Book and the Brotherhood, 1987

Fiddes, Paul S. *Freedom and Limit,* 189–91.
Vichy, Thérèse. "Iris Murdoch ou la tradition renouvelée." *Etudes Anglaises* 50 (1997), 157–68.

Bruno's Dream, 1969

Hussein Ali, Zahra A. "A Spectrum of Image-Making: Master Metaphors and Cognitive Acts in Murdoch's *Bruno's Dream.*" *Orbis Litterarum* 52 (1997), 379–95.
Sharrock, Graeme. "Patrick White and Iris Murdoch: Death as a Moral Summons in *The Eye of the Storm* and *Bruno's Dream.*" *Antipodes* 11:1 (1997), 41–44.

The Flight from the Enchanter, 1956

Philips, Deborah, and Ian Haywood. *Brave New Causes,* 16–17.

The Good Apprentice, 1985

Vichy, Thérèse. "Iris Murdoch ou la tradition renouvelée." *Etudes Anglaises* 50 (1997), 157–68.

The Green Knight, 1993

Arnell, Carla. "Romancing the Stone: Mysticism as a Guide to Moral Reflection in Iris Murdoch's *Green Knight.*" *Studia Mystica* 21 (2000), 126–49.
Purcell, Donald. "Iris Murdoch's *The Green Knight* and Simone Weil." *Cahiers Simone Weil* 19 (1996), 225–38.
Vichy, Thérèse. "Iris Murdoch ou la tradition renouvelée." *Etudes Anglaises* 50 (1997), 157–68.

The Message to the Planet, 1989

Vichy, Thérèse. "Iris Murdoch ou la tradition renouvelée." *Etudes Anglaises* 50 (1997), 157–68.

Nuns and Soldiers, 1980

Weatherhead, A. K. *Upstairs,* 149–51.
White, Roberta S. "Iris Murdoch: Mapping the Country of Desire," in Abby H. P. Werlock, ed., *British Women Writing Fiction,* 30–31.

The Philosopher's Pupil, 1983

Vichy, Thérèse. "Iris Murdoch ou la tradition renouvelée." *Etudes Anglaises* 50 (1997), 157–68.

The Red and the Green, 1965

Backus, Margot Gayle. *The Gothic Family Romance,* 179–94.

The Sea, the Sea, 1978

Chourova, Margarita. "*The Sea, the Sea*: Murdoch, Language and Magic." *Swiss Papers in Engl Lang and Lit* 13 (2000), 77–91.

Under the Net, 1954

Hooks, Susan Luck. "Development of Identity: Iris Murdoch's *Under the Net.*" *Mount Olive R* 8 (1995–1996), 72–79.
Spear, Hilda D. "Iris Murdoch for the Sixth Form." *The Use of Engl* 47 (1996), 227–35.

An Unofficial Rose, 1962

> White, Roberta S. "Iris Murdoch: Mapping the Country of Desire," in Abby H. P. Werlock, ed., *British Women Writing Fiction,* 28–30.

A Word Child, 1975

> Rogers, Rex and Wendy Stainton. "Word Children," in Karín Lesnik-Oberstein, ed., *Children in Culture,* 191–92.

LEOPOLD HAMILTON MYERS

The Near and the Far, 1929

> Amirthanayagam, Guy. *The Marriage of Continents,* 129–59.

V. S. NAIPAUL

A Bend in the River, 1979

> Gupta, Suman. *V. S. Naipaul,* 49–52.
> Kanneh, Kadiatu. "'Africa' and Cultural Translation: Reading Difference," in Keith Ansell-Pearson et al., eds., *Cultural Readings of Imperialism,* 267–72.
> Samantrai, Ranu. "Claiming the Burden: Naipaul's Africa." *Res in African Literatures* 31:1 (2000), 50–62.
> Seeber, Hans Ulrich. "Salim's Truth about the 'Mingling of Peoples' in Africa: A Comment on Naipaul's *A Bend in the River,*" in Heinz Antor and Klaus Stierstorfer, eds., *English Literatures in International Contexts,* 141–48.
> Wilson-Tagoe, Nana. *Historical Thought and Literary Representation,* 70–75.
> Wise, Christopher. "The Garden Trampled; or, The Liquidation of African Culture in V. S. Naipaul's *A Bend in the River.*" *Coll Lit* 23:3 (1996), 58–72.

The Enigma of Arrival, 1987

> Baucom, Ian. *Out of Place,* 176–84.
> Beecroft, Simon. "Sir Vidia's Shadow: V. S. Naipaul, the Writer and *The Enigma of Arrival.*" *J of Commonwealth Lit* 35:1 (2000), 71–85.
> Byatt, A. S. *On Histories and Stories,* 95–97.
> Casmier, Stephen. "Black Narcissus: Representation, Reproduction, Repetition and Seeing Yourself in V. S. Naipaul's *A House for Mr. Biswas* and *The Enigma of Arrival.*" *Commonwealth Essays and Stud* 18:1 (1995), 92–105.
> Crivelli, Renzo S. "The Paradox of Arrival: Naipaul and De Chirico." *Caribana* 3 (1992–1993), 79–95.
> Cundy, Catherine. *Salman Rushdie,* 68–75.
> Gupta, Suman. *V. S. Naipaul,* 54–59.
> Hayward, Helen. "Tradition, Innovation, and the Representation of England in V. S. Naipaul's *The Enigma of Arrival.*" *J of Commonwealth Lit* 32:2 (1997), 51–63.
> Hooker, Jeremy. *Writers in a Landscape,* 139–61.
> Huggan, Graham. *The Postcolonial Exotic,* 86–90.

James, Louis. *Caribbean Literature in English*, 167–68.

Labaune-Demeule, Florence. "De Chirico Revisited: The Enigma of Creation in V. S. Naipaul's *The Enigma of Arrival*." *Commonwealth Essays and Stud* 22:2 (2000), 107–18.

Mergenthal, Silvia. "Englishness/Englishnesses in Contemporary Fiction," in Barbara Korte and Klaus Peter Müller, eds., *Unity in Diversity Revisited?*, 59–60.

Tarantino, Elisabetta. "The House That Jack Did Not Build: Textual Strategies in V. S. Naipaul's *The Enigma of Arrival*." *Ariel* 29:4 (1998), 169–83.

Walker, W. John. "Unsettling the Sign: V. S. Naipaul's *The Enigma of Arrival*." *J of Commonwealth Lit* 32:2 (1997), 67–83.

Wittlinger, Ruth. "Englishness from the Outside," in Susanne Fendler and Ruth Wittlinger, eds., *The Idea of Europe in Literature*, 197–203.

Guerillas, 1975

Barnouw, Dagmar. "After the Culture Wars: V. S. Naipaul and Postcolonialism." *Arcadia* 34 (1999), 166–67.

Gupta, Suman. *V. S. Naipaul*, 46–49.

Perera, S. W. "In Defence of Naipaul's Attitude to the Other: A Comparative Study of Women in *The Mimic Men* and *Guerillas*." *Panjab Univ Res Bull* 26:1–2 (1995), 31–46.

Wilson-Tagoe, Nana. *Historical Thought and Literary Representation*, 68–70.

A House for Mr. Biswas, 1961

Amirthanayagam, Guy. *The Marriage of Continents*, 304–5.

Casmier, Stephen. "Black Narcissus: Representation, Reproduction, Repetition and Seeing Yourself in V. S. Naipaul's *A House for Mr. Biswas* and *The Enigma of Arrival*." *Commonwealth Essays and Stud* 18:1 (1995), 92–105.

Gupta, Suman. *V. S. Naipaul*, 14–17.

James, Louis. *Caribbean Literature in English*, 163–65.

Wilson-Tagoe, Nana. *Historical Thought and Literary Representation*, 58–60.

Miguel Street, 1959

Gupta, Suman. *V. S. Naipaul*, 4–7.

James, Louis. *Caribbean Literature in English*, 162–63.

The Mimic Men, 1967

Greenberg, Robert M. "Anger and the Alchemy of Literary Method in V. S. Naipaul's Political Fiction: The Case of *The Mimic Men*." *Twentieth Cent Lit* 46 (2000), 214–32.

Gupta, Suman. *V. S. Naipaul*, 29–32.

James, Louis. *Caribbean Literature in English*, 165–66.

Juneja, Om P. *Post Colonial Novel*, 34–36.

Perera, S. W. "In Defence of Naipaul's Attitude to the Other: A Comparative Study of Women in *The Mimic Men* and *Guerillas*." *Panjab Univ Res Bull* 26:1–2 (1995), 31–46.

Wilson-Tagoe, Nana. *Historical Thought and Literary Representation*, 60–67.

Mr. Stone and the Knights Companion, 1963

> Batt, Catherine. "Post-Colonial London, By Way of Medieval Romance: V. S. Naipaul's *Mr Stone and the Knights Companion.*" *Kunapipi* 21:2 (1999), 66–72.
>
> Gupta, Suman. *V. S. Naipaul,* 21–25.

The Mystic Masseur, 1957

> Gupta, Suman. *V. S. Naipaul,* 9–13.

The Suffrage of Elvira, 1958

> Gupta, Suman. *V. S. Naipaul,* 9–14.

A Way in the World, 1994

> Barnouw, Dagmar. "After the Culture Wars: V. S. Naipaul and Postcolonialism." *Arcadia* 34 (1999), 169–74.
>
> Jones, Stephanie. "The Politics and Poetics of Diaspora in V. S. Naipaul's *A Way in the World.*" *J of Commonwealth Lit* 35:1 (2000), 87–96.

THOMAS NASHE

The Unfortunate Traveller, 1594

> Alwes, Derek B. "Elizabethan Dreaming: Fictional Dreams from Gascoigne to Lodge," in Constance C. Relihan, ed., *Framing Elizabethan Fictions,* 155, 166–67.
>
> Ballesteros González, Antonio. "Digression and Intertextual Parody in Thomas Nashe, Laurence Sterne and James Joyce," in David Pierce and Peter de Voogd, eds., *Laurence Sterne,* 57–64.
>
> Cheney, Donald. "Narrative, Romance, and Epic," in Arthur F. Kinney, ed., *The Cambridge Companion,* 211–12.
>
> Gladfelder, Hal. *Criminality and Narrative,* 34–38.
>
> Hadfield, Andrew. *The English Renaissance,* 226–30.
>
> Hadfield, Andrew. *Literature, Travel, and Colonial Writing,* 192–96.
>
> Kirk, Andrew M. "'Travail' to 'Strange Nations': Recalling the Errant in *The Unfortunate Traveller.*" *JEGP* 97 (1998), 522–44.
>
> Relihan, Constance C. "Rhetoric, Gender, and Audience Construction in Thomas Nashe's *The Unfortunate Traveller,*" in Relihan, ed., *Framing Elizabethan Fictions,* 141–52.
>
> Totaro, Rebecca C. "Shakespeare's Fortunate Travellers: *As You Like It* and Nashe's *Unfortunate Traveller.*" *Q/W/E/R/T/Y* 7 (1997), 27–31.
>
> Wheeler, Laura Scavuzzo. "The Development of an Englishman: Thomas Nashe's *The Unfortunate Traveller,*" in John C. Hawley, ed., *Christian Encounters with the Other,* 56–70.

DOROTHY NELSON

In Night's City, 1982

> St. Peter, Christine. "Petrifying Time: Incest Narratives from Contemporary Ireland," in Liam Harte and Michael Parker, eds., *Contemporary Irish Fiction,* 133–37.

EDITH NESBIT

The Railway Children, 1906

Perrin, Noel. *A Child's Delight*, 101–7.

The Red House, 1902

Reimer, Mavis. "Treasure Seekers and Invaders: E. Nesbit's Cross-Writing of the Bastables." *Children's Lit* 25 (1997), 50–58.

Rothwell, Erika. "'You Catch It if You Try to Do Otherwise': The Limitations of E. Nesbit's Cross-Written Vision of the Child." *Children's Lit* 25 (1997), 66–69.

JOHN HENRY NEWMAN

Callista, 1856

Lankewish, Vincent A. "Love Among the Ruins: The Catacombs, the Closet, and the Victorian 'Early Christian' Novel." *Victorian Lit and Culture* 28 (2000), 247–65.

Schramm, Jan-Melissa. *Testimony and Advocacy*, 154–56.

Loss and Gain: The Story of a Convert, 1848

Fasick, Laura. "The Seduction of Celibacy: Threats to Male Sexual Identity in Charles Kingsley's Writings," in Jay Losey and William D. Brewer, eds., *Mapping Male Sexuality*, 222–23.

Viswanathan, Gauri. "Secular Criticism and the Politics of Religious Dissent," in Keith Ansell-Pearson et al., eds., *Cultural Readings of Imperialism*, 162–64.

EILÍS NÍ DHUIBHNE

The Bray House, 1990

Smyth, Gerry. *The Novel and the Nation*, 166–68.

JEFF NOON

Pollen, 1995

Jarrett, David. "Regions in Cyberspace: A Postmodern Reading of the Map of Manchester," in Wojciech H. Kalaga and Tadeusz Rachwal, eds., *Signs of Culture*, 118–22.

Vurt, 1993

Jarrett, David. "Regions in Cyberspace: A Postmodern Reading of the Map of Manchester," in Wojciech H. Kalaga and Tadeusz Rachwal, eds., *Signs of Culture*, 119–22.

LAWRENCE NORFOLK

The Pope's Rhinoceros, 1996

Byatt, A. S. *On Histories and Stories*, 67–69.

CAROLINE NORTON

Lost and Saved, 1863

> Gruner, Elisabeth Rose. "Plotting the Mother: Caroline Norton, Helen Huntingdon, and Isabel Vane." *Tulsa Stud in Women's Lit* 16 (1997), 303–19.
> Leckie, Barbara. *Culture and Adultery*, 122–39.
> Thaden, Barbara Z. *The Maternal Voice in Victorian Fiction*, 79–84.

MARY NORTON

The Borrowers, 1952

> Perrin, Noel. *A Child's Delight*, 29–33.
> Watson, Victor. *Reading Series Fiction*, 119–34.

The Borrowers Afield, 1955

> Watson, Victor. *Reading Series Fiction*, 119–34.

The Borrowers Afloat, 1959

> Watson, Victor. *Reading Series Fiction*, 119–34.

The Borrowers Aloft, 1961

> Watson, Victor. *Reading Series Fiction*, 119–34.

The Borrowers Avenged, 1982

> Watson, Victor. *Reading Series Fiction*, 119–34.

ALFRED NOYES

The Last Man, 1940

> Hooley, Tristram. "Blow It Up and Start All Over Again: Second World War Apocalypse Fiction and the Decadence of Modernity," in Michael St. John, ed., *Romancing Decay*, 192–93.
> Pittock, Malcolm. "*The Last Man* and *Nineteen Eighty-Four*." *Engl Lang Notes* 35:3 (1998), 67–72.

ROBERT NYE

The Memoirs of Lord Byron, 1989

> Maack, Annegret. "'The Life We Imagine': Byron's and Polidori's Memoirs as Character Construction," in Martin Middeke and Werner Huber, eds., *Biofictions*, 145–49.

ATTIE O'BRIEN

Priests and People: A No-Rent Romance, 1891

> Murphy, James H. "'Things Which Seem to You Unfeminine': Gender and Nationalism in the Fiction of Some Upper Middle Class Catholic Women Novelists, 1880–1910," in Kathryn Kirkpatrick, ed., *Border Crossings*, 69–70.

Through the Dark Night, 1897–1898

> Murphy, James H. "'Things Which Seem to You Unfeminine': Gender and Nationalism in the Fiction of Some Upper Middle Class Catholic Women Novelists, 1880–1910," in Kathryn Kirkpatrick, ed., *Border Crossings*, 67–69.

EDNA O'BRIEN

The Country Girls, 1960

> Cahalan, James M. *Double Visions*, 114–20.

Down by the River, 1996

> King, Sophia Hillan. "On the Side of Life: Edna O'Brien's Trilogy of Contemporary Ireland." *New Hibernia R* 4:2 (2000), 49–66.
>
> St. Peter, Christine. "Petrifying Time: Incest Narratives from Contemporary Ireland," in Liam Harte and Michael Parker, eds., *Contemporary Irish Fiction*, 137–42.

Girls in Their Married Bliss, 1964

> Cahalan, James M. *Double Visions*, 114–20.

House of Splendid Isolation, 1994

> Hatheway, William K. "Breaking the Tie That Binds: Feminine and National Representation in Edna O'Brien's *House of Splendid Isolation*." *North Dakota Q* 66:1 (1999), 122–33.
>
> King, Sophia Hillan. "On the Side of Life: Edna O'Brien's Trilogy of Contemporary Ireland." *New Hibernia R* 4:2 (2000), 49–66.

The Lonely Girl, 1962

> Cahalan, James M. *Double Visions*, 114–20.

Wild Decembers, 2000

> King, Sophia Hillan. "On the Side of Life: Edna O'Brien's Trilogy of Contemporary Ireland." *New Hibernia R* 4:2 (2000), 49–66.

FLANN O'BRIEN

At Swim-Two-Birds, 1939

> Corcoran, Neil. *After Yeats and Joyce*, 22–24.
>
> Lanters, José. *Unauthorized Versions*, 179–205.
>
> Merritt, Henry. "Games, Ending and Dying in Flann O'Brien's *At Swim-Two-Birds*." *Irish Univ R* 25 (1995), 308–17.
>
> Quintelli-Neary, Marguerite. *Folklore and the Fantastic*, 84–96.
>
> Weill-Mianowski, Marie. "Flann O'Brien: L'Exil intérieur ou l'errance du narrateur." *Cycnos* 15 (1998), 193–205.
>
> Zimmermann, Ralf. *Das Verschwinden der Wirklichkeit.*

The Hard Life, 1961

> Davison, Neil R. "'We are not a doctor for the body': Catholicism, the Female Grotesque, and Flann O'Brien's *The Hard Life*." *Lit and Psych* 45:4 (1999), 31–54.

The Third Policeman, 1967

> Gitzen, Julian. "The Wayward Theoreticians of Flann O'Brien." *Thalia* 15 (1995), 50–61.

Lanters, José. *Unauthorized Versions*, 206–34.

MacMahon, Barbara. "The Effects of Word Substitution in Slips of the Tongue, *Finnegans Wake* and *The Third Policeman*." *Engl Stud* (Amsterdam) 82 (2001), 231–45.

Mazzullo, Concetta. "Flann O'Brien's Hellish Otherworld: From *Baile Suibhne* to *The Third Policeman*." *Irish Univ R* 25 (1995), 318–27.

Quintelli-Neary, Marguerite. *Folklore and the Fantastic*, 83–96.

Weill-Mianowski, Marie. "Flann O'Brien: L'Exil intérieur ou l'errance du narrateur." *Cycnos* 15 (1998), 193–205.

Zimmermann, Ralf. *Das Verschwinden der Wirklichkeit*.

KATE O'BRIEN

As Music and Splendour, 1958

Fogarty, Anne. "The Ear of the Other: Dissident Voices in Kate O'Brien's *As Music and Splendour* and Mary Dorcey's *A Noise from the Woodshed*," in Éibhear Walshe, ed., *Sex, Nation and Dissent*, 175–90.

Weekes, Ann Owens. "A Trackless Road: Irish Nationalisms and Lesbian Writing," in Kathryn Kirkpatrick, ed., *Border Crossings*, 137–40.

Farewell Spain, 1937

Vásquez, Mary S. "The Loving Tourist in Kate O'Brien's *Farewell Spain*." *Monographic R/ Revista Monográfica* 12 (1996), 107–22.

The Land of Spices, 1941

Cahalan, James M. *Double Visions*, 106–8.

Mary Lavelle, 1936

Emprin, Jacques. "*Mary Lavelle* de Kate O'Brien ou l'exil et le désert de l'amour." *Cycnos* 15 (1998), 139–49.

Rueda Ramos, Carmen. "Bulls and Bullfighting in Literature in English from 1920–36: O'Brien's *Mary Lavelle* and Hemingway's *Fiesta*." *BELLS: Barcelona Engl Lang and Lit Stud* 6 (1995), 131–41.

Weekes, Ann Owens. "A Trackless Road: Irish Nationalisms and Lesbian Writing," in Kathryn Kirkpatrick, ed., *Border Crossings*, 132–37.

That Lady, 1946

Fogarty, Anne. "Other Spaces: Postcolonialism and the Politics of Truth in Kate O'Brien's *That Lady*." *European J of Engl Stud* 3:3 (1999), 342–53.

CLAIRR O'CONNOR

Belonging, 1991

St. Peter, Christine. *Changing Ireland*, 26–32.

JOSEPH O'CONNOR

Cowboys and Indians, 1991
  Smyth, Gerry. *The Novel and the Nation*, 150–53.

EIMAR O'DUFFY

Asses in Clover, 1933
  Lanters, José. *Unauthorized Versions*, 88–103.
  Quintelli-Neary, Marguerite. *Folklore and the Fantastic*, 129–34.
King Goshawk and the Birds, 1926
  Lanters, José. *Unauthorized Versions*, 51–68.
  Quintelli-Neary, Marguerite. *Folklore and the Fantastic*, 115–17.
The Spacious Adventures of the Man in the Street, 1928
  Lanters, José. *Unauthorized Versions*, 69–87.
  Quintelli-Neary, Marguerite. *Folklore and the Fantastic*, 117–29.

JULIA O'FAOLAIN

No Country for Young Men, 1980
  Cahalan, James M. *Double Visions*, 148–56.
  Maloy, Kelli. "Decolonizing the Mind: Memory (and) Loss in Julia
    O'Faolain's *No Country for Young Men.*" *Colby Q* 33 (1997),
    236–43.
  St. Peter, Christine. *Changing Ireland*, 82–88.

LIAM O'FLAHERTY

The Black Soul, 1924
  Cahalan, James M. *Double Visions*, 51–53.
Famine, 1937
  Kelleher, Margaret. *The Feminization of Famine*, 135–42.
Hollywood Cemetery, 1935
  Decker, James M., and Kenneth Womack. "Searching for Ethics in the
    Celluloid Graveyard: Waugh, O'Flaherty, and the Hollywood
    Novel." *Stud in the Hum* 25:1–2 (1998), 53–65.
Return of the Brute, 1929
  Jeffery, Keith. "Irish Prose Writers of the First World War," in
    Kathleen Devine, ed., *Modern Irish Writers and the Wars*, 13–15.

MARGARET OLIPHANT

A Beleaguered City, 1880
  Jay, Elisabeth. *Mrs Oliphant*, 161–65.
A Country Gentleman and His Family, 1886
  Jay, Elisabeth. *Mrs Oliphant*, 117–19.

Thaden, Barbara Z. *The Maternal Voice in Victorian Fiction*, 93–95.

Williams, Merryn. "Margaret Oliphant," in Douglas Gifford and Dorothy McMillan, eds., *A History*, 283–84.

Hester, 1883

Heilmann, Ann. "Mrs Grundy's Rebellion: Margaret Oliphant between Orthodoxy and the New Woman." *Women's Writing* 6 (1999), 223–26.

Sanders, Valerie. "Mrs Oliphant and Emotion." *Women's Writing* 6 (1999), 183–85.

Innocent, 1873

Thaden, Barbara Z. *The Maternal Voice in Victorian Fiction*, 40–46.

Janet, 1891

Sanders, Valerie. "Mrs Oliphant and Emotion." *Women's Writing* 6 (1999), 185.

John Drayton, 1851

Pettitt, Clare. "'Every man for himself, and God for us all!': Mrs Oliphant, Self-help, and Industrial Success Literature in *John Drayton* and *The Melvilles*." *Women's Writing* 6 (1999), 167–76.

Kirsteen, 1890

Hartman, Kabi. "'An Artist in Her Way': Representations of the Woman Artist in Margaret Oliphant's *Kirsteen*." *Schuylkill* 2:2 (1999), 74–84.

Heilmann, Ann. "Mrs Grundy's Rebellion: Margaret Oliphant between Orthodoxy and the New Woman." *Women's Writing* 6 (1999), 226–32.

Jay, Elisabeth. *Mrs Oliphant*, 196–98.

Sanders, Valerie. "Mrs Oliphant and Emotion." *Women's Writing* 6 (1999), 186–88.

Walker, Marshall. *Scottish Literature since 1707*, 182–83.

Williams, Merryn. "Margaret Oliphant," in Douglas Gifford and Dorothy McMillan, eds., *A History*, 284–86.

Young, Arlene. *Culture, Class and Gender*, 133–36.

The Ladies Lindores, 1883

Jay, Elisabeth. *Mrs Oliphant*, 134–36.

Thaden, Barbara Z. *The Maternal Voice in Victorian Fiction*, 91–93.

The Marriage of Elinor, 1892

Thaden, Barbara Z. *The Maternal Voice in Victorian Fiction*, 99–104.

The Melvilles, 1852

Pettitt, Clare. "'Every man for himself, and God for us all!': Mrs Oliphant, Self-help, and Industrial Success Literature in *John Drayton* and *The Melvilles*." *Women's Writing* 6 (1999), 167–76.

Miss Marjoribanks, 1866

Cavaliero, Glen. *The Alchemy of Laughter*, 28–30.

Chase, Karen, and Michael Levenson. *The Spectacle of Intimacy*, 216–19.

Houston, Gail Turley. *Royalties*, 154–57.

Jay, Elisabeth. *Mrs Oliphant*, 68–70.

Sanders, Valerie. "Marriage and the Antifeminist Woman Novelist," in Nicola Diane Thompson, ed., *Victorian Women Writers*, 33–34.

Sanders, Valerie. "Mrs Oliphant and Emotion." *Women's Writing* 6 (1999), 182–83.

Schaub, Melissa. "Queen of the Air or Constitutional Monarch?: Idealism, Irony, and Narrative Power in *Miss Marjoribanks*." *Nineteenth-Cent Lit* 55 (2000), 195–225.

Williams, Merryn. "Margaret Oliphant," in Douglas Gifford and Dorothy McMillan, eds., *A History*, 282–83.

The Perpetual Curate, 1864

Jay, Elisabeth. *Mrs Oliphant*, 84–86, 296–98.

Phoebe, Junior, 1876

Cohen, Monica. "Maximizing Oliphant: Begging the Question and the Politics of Satire," in Nicola Diane Thompson, ed., *Victorian Women Writers*, 99–103, 105–13.

Cohen, Monica F. *Professional Domesticity*, 4–6.

Jay, Elisabeth. *Mrs Oliphant*, 70–72.

O'Mealy, Joseph H. "Rewriting Trollope and Yonge: Mrs. Oliphant's *Phoebe Junior* and the Realism Wars." *Texas Stud in Lit and Lang* 39 (1997), 125–37.

Sanders, Valerie. "Marriage and the Antifeminist Woman Novelist," in Nicola Diane Thompson, ed., *Victorian Women Writers*, 34–35.

Young, Arlene. *Culture, Class and Gender*, 131–33.

Salem Chapel, 1863

Heller, Tamar. "'No Longer Innocent': Sensationalism, Sexuality, and the Allegory of the Woman Writer in Margaret Oliphant's *Salem Chapel*." *Nineteenth Cent Stud* 11 (1997), 95–105.

Jones, Shirley. "Motherhood and Melodrama: *Salem Chapel* and Sensation Fiction." *Women's Writing* 6 (1999), 239–49.

Tromp, Marlene. *The Private Rod*, 155–98.

Sir Tom, 1884

Thaden, Barbara Z. *The Maternal Voice in Victorian Fiction*, 130–34.

A Son of the Soil, 1866

Jay, Elisabeth. *Mrs Oliphant*, 86–88.

The Wizard's Son, 1884

Jay, Elisabeth. *Mrs Oliphant*, 168–70.

AMELIA OPIE

Adeline Mowbray; or, Mother and Daughter, 1801

Bannet, Eve Tavor. *The Domestic Revolution*, 119–24.

Bour, Isabelle. "*Caleb Williams* et son double: *Adeline Mowbray* d'Amelia Opie." *Bull de la Société d'Etudes Anglo-Américaines des XVIIe et XVIIIe Siècles* 43 (1996), 93–101.

Bunnell, Charlene E. "Breaking the Tie That Binds: Parents and Children in Romantic Fiction," in Andrea O'Reilly Herrera et al., eds., *Family Matters*, 41–45.

Howard, Carol. "'The Story of the Pineapple': Sentimental Abolitionism and Moral Motherhood in Amelia Opie's *Adeline Mowbray*." *Stud in the Novel* 30 (1998), 355–73.
Ty, Eleanor. *Empowering the Feminine*, 145–60.
Wordsworth, Jonathan. *The Bright Work Grows*, 147–53.

The Father and Daughter, 1812

Ty, Eleanor. *Empowering the Feminine*, 133–44.

Temper; or, Domestic Scenes, 1812

Ty, Eleanor. *Empowering the Feminine*, 161–77.

KATE O'RIORDAN

Involved, 1995

Ni-Riordain, Cliona. "Visions et révisions de Belfast dans le roman irlandais contemporain." *GRAAT* 19 (1998), 29–37.
Smyth, Gerry. *The Novel and the Nation*, 140–43.

GEORGE ORWELL

Burmese Days, 1934

Amirthanayagam, Guy. *The Marriage of Continents*, 117–28.
Brunsdale, Mitzi M. *Student Companion to George Orwell*, 53–58.
Kerr, Douglas. "Colonial Habitats: Orwell and Woolf in the Jungle." *Engl Stud* (Amsterdam) 78 (1997), 149–61.
Waterman, David. "Imperialism and Construction of Racial Superiority: George Orwell's *Burmese Days*." *In-Between* 6:1 (1997), 27–42.
Waterman, David F. *Disordered Bodies and Disrupted Borders*, 81–97.

A Clergyman's Daughter, 1935

Brunsdale, Mitzi M. *Student Companion to George Orwell*, 58–63.

Coming Up for Air, 1939

Brunsdale, Mitzi M. *Student Companion to George Orwell*, 106–14.
Connelly, Mark. *Orwell and Gissing*, 110–17.

Down and Out in Paris and London, 1933

Brunsdale, Mitzi M. *Student Companion to George Orwell*, 38–51.
Newsinger, John. *Orwell's Politics*, 24–31.

Homage to Catalonia, 1938

Brunsdale, Mitzi M. *Student Companion to George Orwell*, 87–103.
Connelly, Mark. *Orwell and Gissing*, 47–50.
Held, George. "In Defense of *Homage to Catalonia*." *Connecticut R* 17:2 (1995), 63–68.
Khan, Jalal Uddin. "The Spanish Civil War (1936–39): Its Treatment in André Malraux's *Man's Hope*, George Orwell's *Homage to Catalonia*, and Ernest Hemingway's *For Whom the Bell Tolls*." *Jadavpur J of Compar Lit* 33 (1995–96), 66–72.
Smith, Alan E. "Orwell's Writing Degree Zero: Language and Ideology in *Homage to Catalonia*." *Letras Peninsulares* 11:1 (1998), 295–307.

Keep the Aspidistra Flying, 1936

Brunsdale, Mitzi M. *Student Companion to George Orwell,* 63–70.

Nineteen Eighty–Four, 1948

Assmann, Aleida. "The Sun at Midnight: The Concept of Counter-Memory and Its Changes," in Leona Toker, ed., *Commitment in Reflection,* 224–30.

Bergonzi, Bernard. *War Poets,* 114–28.

Brunsdale, Mitzi M. *Student Companion to George Orwell,* 138–54.

Chesney, Thom D. "Looking Past James Nurnham: Machiavelli's *The Prince* in Orwell's *1984.*" *B.A.S.: Brit and Am Stud* 1998: 18–24.

Dadlez, E. M. *What's Hecuba to Him?,* 185–87.

Diamond, Cora. "Truth: Defenders, Debunkers, Despisers," in Leona Toker, ed., *Commitment in Reflection,* 201–10.

Ferns, Chris. *Narrating Utopia,* 112–32.

Goldstein, Philip. "Orwell as a (Neo)conservative: The Reception of *1984.*" *J of the Midwest Mod Lang Assoc* 33:1 (2000), 44–54.

Johnston, Laura. "'Orr' and 'Orwell': Le Guin's *The Lathe of Heaven* and Orwell's *Nineteen Eighty-Four.*" *Extrapolation* 40 (1999), 351–53.

Justman, Stewart. *The Springs of Liberty,* 109–15.

Lobdell, Jared C. "Stone Pastorals: Three Men on the Side of the Horses." *Extrapolation* 37 (1996), 346–51.

Newsinger, John. *Orwell's Politics,* 120–24, 128–32.

Olshanskaya, Natalia. "Anti-Utopian Carnival: Vladimir Voinovich Rewriting George Orwell." *Forum for Mod Lang Stud* 36 (2000), 426–35.

Pittock, Malcolm. "The Hell of *Nineteen Eighty-Four.*" *Essays in Criticism* 47 (1997), 143–61.

Pittock, Malcolm. "*The Last Man* and *Nineteen Eighty-Four.*" *Engl Lang Notes* 35:3 (1998), 67–72.

Rademacher, Michael. "George Orwell, Japan und die BBC: Die Rolle des totalitären Japan bei der Entstehung von *Nineteen Eighty-Four.*" *Archiv für das Studium der neueren Sprachen und Literaturen* 234 (1997), 33–54.

Rademacher, Michael. "Orwell and Hitler: *Mein Kampf* as a Source for *Nineteen Eighty-Four.*" *Zeitschrift für Anglistik und Amerikanistik* 47 (1999), 38–53.

Rae, Patricia. "'Just Junk': George Orwell's Real-Life Scavenging and *Nineteen Eighty-Four.*" *Engl Lang Notes* 38:1 (2000), 73–77.

Rae, Patricia. "Mr. Charrington's Junk Shop: T. S. Eliot and Modernist Poetics in *Nineteen Eighty-Four.*" *Twentieth Cent Lit* 43 (1997), 196–214.

Reilly, John R. "The Torture Tutorial: Finding Out the Awful Truth in *That Hideous Strength* and *1984.*" *Mythlore* 21:4 (1997), 39–41.

Resch, Robert Paul. "Utopia, Dystopia, and the Middle Class in George Orwell's *Nineteen Eighty-Four.*" *Boundary 2* 24:1 (1997), 137–76.

Sisk, David W. *Transformations of Language,* 37–56.

Templin, Charlotte. "The Old Prole Woman in Orwell's *1984.*" *Notes on Contemp Lit* 31:3 (2001), 6–7.

Tirohl, Blu. "'We are the dead . . . you are the dead': An Examination of Sexuality as a Weapon of Revolt in Orwell's *Nineteen Eighty-Four.*" *J of Gender Stud* 9 (2000), 55–61.

Wanner, Adrian. "The Underground Man as Big Brother: Dostoevsky's and Orwell's Anti-Utopia." *Utopian Stud* 8:1 (1997), 77–88.

Weisberg, David. *Chronicles of Disorder*, 153–60.

The Road to Wigan Pier, 1937

Bell, Ian A. "To See Ourselves: Travel Narratives and National Identity in Contemporary Britain," in Bell, ed., *Peripheral Visions*, 16–19.

Brunsdale, Mitzi M. *Student Companion to George Orwell*, 74–85.

Newsinger, John. *Orwell's Politics*, 33–41.

'OUIDA'

Folle-Farine, 1871

Gilbert, Pamela. "Ouida and the Other New Woman," in Nicola Diane Thompson, ed., *Victorian Women Writers*, 178–85.

Gilbert, Pamela K. *Disease, Desire, and the Body*, 159–81.

In Maremma, 1888

Russo, John Paul. "Ouida's Family Romance: *In Maremma.*" *Pop Culture R* 4:2 (1993), 37–49.

Moths, 1880

Schaffer, Talia. *The Forgotten Female Aesthetes*, 128–31.

Princess Napraxine, 1884

Schaffer, Talia. *The Forgotten Female Aesthetes*, 139–49.

Under Two Flags, 1867

Cole, David L. "'Child of the Tricolour': Ouida, Romance, and *Under Two Flags.*" *Illinois Engl Bull* 85:4 (1998), 74–80.

Gilbert, Pamela. "Ouida and the Other New Woman," in Nicola Diane Thompson, ed., *Victorian Women Writers*, 173–78.

Gilbert, Pamela K. *Disease, Desire, and the Body*, 141–59.

Peck, John. *War, the Army and Victorian Literature*, 119–22.

Schaffer, Talia. *The Forgotten Female Aesthetes*, 125–27.

JEAN LLEWELLYN OWENS

Margaret Becomes a Doctor, 1958

Philips, Deborah, and Ian Haywood. *Brave New Causes*, 63–65.

WILLIAM PAINTER

The Palace of Pleasure, 1566–1575

Hadfield, Andrew. *Literature, Travel, and Colonial Writing*, 147–60.

ROBERT PALTOCK

Peter Wilkins, 1750

Snader, Joe. *Caught Between Worlds*, 224–26, 232–44.

EDITH PARGETER

Hortensius Friend of Nero, 1936

Maslen, Elizabeth. "Naomi Mitchison's Historical Fiction," in Maroula Joannou, ed., *Women Writers of the 1930s,* 147–48.

WALTER HORATIO PATER

Gaston de Latour, 1896

Bidney, Martin. *Patterns of Epiphany,* 122–25.

Fontana, Ernest. "Dante, Pater's *Marius the Epicurean* and *Gaston de Latour.*" *Victorian Newsl* 92 (1997), 30–31.

Hennessey, Jan. "Une Tapisserie imaginaire." *Bull de la Société des Amis de Montaigne* 39–40 (1995), 67–71.

Moliterno, Frank. *The Dialectics of Sense and Spirit,* 99–101.

Monsman, Gerald. "Walter Pater, Circe, and the Paths of Darkness." *Nineteenth-Cent Prose* 24:2 (1997), 66–76.

Shuter, William F. *Rereading Walter Pater,* 71–72, 95–97.

Tucker, Paul. "The Use of the Definite Article in the Fiction of Walter Pater." *Rivista di Studi Vittoriani* 2:4 (1997), 105–24.

Marius the Epicurean, 1885

Bidney, Martin. *Patterns of Epiphany,* 116–22.

Coates, John. "Renan and Pater's *Marius the Epicurean.*" *Compar Lit Stud* 37 (2000), 402–22.

Fontana, Ernest. "Dante, Pater's *Marius the Epicurean* and *Gaston de Latour.*" *Victorian Newsl* 92 (1997), 28–30.

Lambert, Martine. "Entre la terre et l'idéal, être exilé de 'chez soi': Etude de trois 'portraits imaginaires' de Walter Pater: 'The Child in the House,' 'Emerald Uthwart' et *Marius the Epicurean.*" *Cahiers Victoriens et Edouardiens* 51 (2000), 213–15.

Lankewish, Vincent A. "Love Among the Ruins: The Catacombs, the Closet, and the Victorian 'Early Christian' Novel." *Victorian Lit and Culture* 28 (2000), 242–45, 252–65.

Losey, Jay. "Disguising the Self in Pater and Wilde," in Jay Losey and William D. Brewer, eds., *Mapping Male Sexuality,* 253–61.

Moliterno, Frank. *The Dialectics of Sense and Spirit,* 34–56, 97–99, 101–19.

Moran, Maureen F. "Walter Pater and the Esoteric Sensibility." *Cahiers Victoriens et Edouardiens* 49 (1999), 124–28.

Myers, William. *The Presence of Persons,* 67–69.

Potolsky, Matthew. "Fear of Falling: Walter Pater's *Marius the Epicurean* as a Dangerous Influence." *ELH* 65 (1998), 701–21.

Rama, R. P. "Walter Pater's *Marius the Epicurean*: A Point of View." *Rajasthan Univ Stud in Engl* 20 (1988), 70–76.

Shuter, William F. *Rereading Walter Pater,* 29–32, 47–51, 69–71, 103–8.

Toth, Sara. "'Doorways to Things Beyond': The Question of Religion in Walter Pater's Works, with a Special Focus on *Marius the Epicurean.*" *AnaChronist* 19–21 (2000), 167–85.

Tucker, Paul. "The Use of the Definite Article in the Fiction of Walter Pater." *Rivista di Studi Vittoriani* 2:4 (1997), 105–24.

F. C. PATRICK

The Irish Heiress, 1797

> London, April. "Clock Time and Utopia's Time in Novels of the 1790s." *Stud in Engl Lit, 1500–1900* 40 (2000), 548–50.

GLENN PATTERSON

Burning Your Own, 1988

> Patten, Eve. "Fiction in Conflict: Northern Ireland's Prodigal Novelists," in Ian A. Bell, ed., *Peripheral Visions,* 139–46.
> Smyth, Gerry. *The Novel and the Nation,* 126–29.

Fat Lad, 1992

> Kirkland, Richard. "Bourgeois Redemptions: The Fictions of Glenn Patterson and Robert McLiam Wilson," in Liam Harte and Michael Parker, eds., *Contemporary Irish Fiction,* 214–29.
> Smyth, Gerry. *The Novel and the Nation,* 129–32.

THOMAS LOVE PEACOCK

Crotchet Castle, 1831

> Cavaliero, Glen. *The Alchemy of Laughter,* 160–62.
> Mulvihill, James. "'A Species of Shop': Peacock and the World of Goods." *Keats-Shelley J* 49 (2000), 109–13.

Headlong Hall, 1816

> Dyer, Gary. *British Satire and the Politics of Style,* 115–20.
> Mulvihill, James. "A Periodical Source for Peacock's *Headlong Hall.*" *Notes and Queries* 44 (1997), 33435.
> Mulvihill, James. "'A Species of Shop': Peacock and the World of Goods." *Keats-Shelley J* 49 (2000), 102–9.
> Mulvihill, James "A Source for Peacock's *Headlong Hall.*" *Notes and Queries* 47 (2000), 327.

Melincourt, 1817

> McLane, Maureen N. *Romanticism and the Human Sciences,* 109–11.
> Mulvihill, James. "'A Species of Shop': Peacock and the World of Goods." *Keats-Shelley J* 49 (2000), 91–102.

Nightmare Abbey, 1818

> Ashton, Rosemary. "The Figure of the German Professor in Nineteenth-Century English Fiction," in Susanne Stark, ed., *The Novel in Anglo-German Context,* 68–69.
> Day, Aidan. *Romanticism,* 154–57.
> Dyer, Gary. *British Satire and the Politics of Style,* 108–13.
> Wordsworth, Jonathan. *Visionary Gleam,* 140–46.

MERVYN PEAKE

Gormenghast, 1950

Prungnaud, Joelle. *"Argol* et *Gormenghast,* ou la mise en ecriture du chateau." *Roman 20–50* 30 (2000), 141–52.

Titus Alone, 1959

Bratman, David. "Mervyn Peake, the Gormenghast Diptych, and *Titus Alone." New York R of Science Fiction* 8:9 (1996), 1, 4–6.

Tolley, Michael. "Grotesque Imaginings: Peaking through Keyholes," in Alice Mills, ed., *Seriously Weird,* 153–66.

Titus Groan, 1946

Kennedy, David. "'Beneath Umbrageous Ceilings': Postmodernism and the Psychology of Mervyn Peake's *Titus Groan." Bête Noire* 14–15 (1996), 349–57.

Mulvihill, James. "William Blake and Mervyn Peake's *Titus Groan." Notes on Contemp Lit* 29:2 (1999), 2–3.

Tolley, Michael. "Grotesque Imaginings: Peaking through Keyholes," in Alice Mills, ed., *Seriously Weird,* 153–66.

PHILIPPA PEARCE

Tom's Midnight Garden, 1958

Hunt, Peter. *Children's Literature,* 227–29.

MARGARET PENDER

The Green Cockade: A Tale of Ulster in 'Ninety-Eight, 1898

Reilly, Eileen. "Rebel, Muse, and Spouse: The Female in '98 Fiction." *Eire-Ireland* 34:2 (1999), 151–54.

MRS. FRANK PENNY

A Mixed Marriage, 1903

Bell, Srilekha. "Mrs. Frank Penny's *A Mixed Marriage:* 'A Tale Worth Reading.'" *Engl Lit in Transition* 44 (2001), 28–43.

WENDY PERRIAM

After Purple, 1982

Dervin, Dan. *Matricentric Narratives,* 96–106.

CARYL PHILLIPS

Cambridge, 1992

Birat, Kathie. "A Shameful Intercourse: Meaning and Signifying in Caryl Phillips's Novels of the Slave Trade." *GRAAT* 20 (1999), 33–47.

Chavanelle, Sylvie. "Caryl Phillips's *Cambridge*: Ironical (Dis)empowerment?" *Intl Fiction R* 25:1–2 (1998), 78–88.

Ledent, Bénédicte. "From a New-World Perspective to a New-World Vision: African America in the Works of Edouard Glissant and Caryl Phillips." *Commonwealth Essays and Stud* 21:2 (1999), 29–36.

Patteson, Richard F. *Caribbean Passages*, 130–39.

Schäffner, Raimund. "'Identity is not in the past to be found, but in the future to be constructed': History and Identity in Caryl Phillips's Novels," in Barbara Korte and Klaus Peter Müller, eds., *Unity in Diversity Revisited?*, 113–18.

Crossing the River, 1993

Birat, Kathie. "A Shameful Intercourse: Meaning and Signifying in Caryl Phillips's Novels of the Slave Trade." *GRAAT* 20 (1999), 33–47.

Ilona, Anthony. "*Crossing the River*: A Chronicle of the Black Diaspora." *Wasafiri* 22 (1995), 3–9.

Jaggi, Maya. "*Crossing the River*." *Wasafiri* 20 (1994), 25–29.

Ledent, Bénédicte. "From a New-World Perspective to a New-World Vision: African America in the Works of Edouard Glissant and Caryl Phillips." *Commonwealth Essays and Stud* 21:2 (1999), 29–36.

Ledent, Bénédicte. "'Overlapping Territories, Intertwined Histories': Cross-Culturality in Caryl Phillips's *Crossing the River*." *J of Commonwealth Lit* 30:1 (1995), 55–61.

Nowak, Helge. "Black British Literature: Unity or Diversity?," in Barbara Korte and Klaus Peter Müller, eds., *Unity in Diversity Revisited?*, 82–84.

Schäffner, Raimund. "'Identity is not in the past to be found, but in the future to be constructed': History and Identity in Caryl Phillips's Novels," in Barbara Korte and Klaus Peter Müller, eds., *Unity in Diversity Revisited?*, 118–23.

Skinner, John. *The Stepmother Tongue*, 180–82.

The Final Passage, 1985

Low, Gail. "Separate Spheres?: Representing London Through Women in Some Recent Black British Fiction." *Kunapipi* 21:2 (1999), 26–27.

Patteson, Richard F. *Caribbean Passages*, 116–24.

Higher Ground, 1989

Birat, Kathie. "A Shameful Intercourse: Meaning and Signifying in Caryl Phillips's Novels of the Slave Trade." *GRAAT* 20 (1999), 33–47.

Ledent, Bénédicte. "From a New-World Perspective to a New-World Vision: African America in the Works of Edouard Glissant and Caryl Phillips." *Commonwealth Essays and Stud* 21:2 (1999), 29–36.

Schäffner, Raimund. "'Identity is not in the past to be found, but in the future to be constructed': History and Identity in Caryl Phillips's Novels," in Barbara Korte and Klaus Peter Müller, eds., *Unity in Diversity Revisited?*, 110–13.

The Nature of Blood, 1997

> Ciocia, Stefania. "'The Extravagant and Wheeling Stranger': The Othello Figure in Caryl Phillips's *The Nature of Blood*." *Confronto Letterario* 16 (1999), 215–30.
>
> Flint, Kate. "Looking Backward? The Relevance of Britishness," in Barbara Korte and Klaus Peter Müller, eds., *Unity in Diversity Revisited?*, 46–48.
>
> Zorzi, Rosella Mamoli. "Intertextual Venice: Blood and Crime and Death Renewed in Two Contemporary Novels," in Manfred Pfister and Barbara Schaff, eds., *Venetian Views*, 225–36.

A State of Independence, 1986

> Patteson, Richard F. *Caribbean Passages*, 124–30.

TOM PHILLIPS

A Humument, 1981

> Wagner-Lawlor, Jennifer A. "A Portrait of the (Postmodern) Artist: Intertextual Subjectivity in Tom Phillips's *A Humument*." *Post Identity* 2:1 (1999), 89–103.

HAROLD PINTER

The Dwarfs, 1990

> Billington, Michael. *The Life and Work of Harold Pinter*, 58–65.
>
> Zinman, Toby Silverman. "Pinter as Novelist, or, Cobbler, Stick to Thy Last." *Cycnos* 14:1 (1997), 105–11.

JAMES PLUNKETT

Strumpet City, 1969

> Emprin, Jacques. "Esquisse d'une typologie du prêtre dans le roman irlandais (1900–1970)." *Etudes Irlandaises* 25:1 (2000), 39–41.

JANE PORTER

The Scottish Chiefs, 1808

> Dennis, Ian. *Nationalism and Desire*, 9–44.

Thaddeus of Warsaw, 1803

> Watson, Nicola J. *Revolution and the Form of the British Novel*, 118–23.

RAYMOND POSTGATE

Verdict of Twelve, 1940

> Turnbull, Malcolm J. *Victims or Villains*, 108–10.

DENNIS POTTER

Blackeyes, 1987

> Connelly, Gwendolyn. "Multiple Narratives in Dennis Potter's *Blackeyes*: Constructing Identity as Cultural Dialogue," in Vernon W. Gras and John R. Cook, eds., *The Passion of Dennis Potter*, 149–57.

Brimstone and Treacle, 1982

> Lippard, Chris. "Confined Bodies, Wandering Minds: Memory, Paralysis and the Self in Some Earlier Works of Dennis Potter," in Vernon W. Gras and John R. Cook, eds., *The Passion of Dennis Potter*, 118–21.

Hide and Seek, 1973

> Schwenger, Peter. *Fantasm and Fiction*, 57–59.

Pennies from Heaven, 1981

> Evans, Dave. "'Grasping the Constellation': Dennis Potter and the Mythologies of Popular Culture," in Vernon W. Gras and John R. Cook, eds., *The Passion of Dennis Potter*, 53–68.

ANTHONY POWELL

A Dance to the Music of Time, 1951–1975

> Hoffmann, Catherine. "Candaule et gyges: Anthony Powell invente un Tiepolo." *Imaginaires* 3 (1998), 113–22.
> Hoffmann, Catherine. "A Journey Through Narrative Valleys: The Writing and Rewriting of Heroic Myth in Anthony Powell's *Dance to the Music of Time*." *New Comparison* 27/28 (1999), 273–85.

The Valley of Bones, 1964

> Butler, Lance St. John. *Registering the Difference*, 174–76.

Venusberg, 1932

> Hopkins, Chris. "Chekhov and Gerhardi: The Russian Sources of Anthony Powell's *Venusberg* (1932)." *Engl Lang Notes* 37:3 (2000), 62–66.

RICHARD POWER

The Hungry Grass, 1969

> Emprin, Jacques. "Esquisse d'une typologie du prêtre dans le roman irlandais (1900–1970)." *Etudes Irlandaises* 25:1 (2000), 44–45.

JOHN COWPER POWYS

A Glastonbury Romance, 1932

> Nordius, Janina. *"I Am Myself Alone,"* 72–102.

Maiden Castle, 1936

> Hooker, Jeremy. *Writers in a Landscape*, 119–38.
> Nordius, Janina. *"I Am Myself Alone,"* 135–70.

Owen Glendower, 1940
 Nordius, Janina. *"I Am Myself Alone,"* 171–98.
Porius, 1951
 Nordius, Janina. *"I Am Myself Alone,"* 199–228.
Weymouth Sands, 1935
 Nordius, Janina. *"I Am Myself Alone,"* 103–34.
Wolf Solent, 1929
 Nordius, Janina. *"I Am Myself Alone,"* 44–71.

THEODORE FRANCIS POWYS

Mr. Weston's Good Wine, 1927
 Cavaliero, Glen. *The Alchemy of Laughter*, 201–4.

AMANDA PRANTERA

Conversations with Lord Byron on Perversion, 163 Years after his Lordship's Death, 1987
 Middeke, Martin. "The Triumph of Analogous Text over Digital Truth: Biography, *Différance*, and Deconstructive Play in Amanda Prantera's *Conversations with Lord Byron on Perversion, 163 Years after his Lordship's Death*," in Martin Middeke and Werner Huber, eds., *Biofictions*, 122–35.

SAMUEL JACKSON PRATT

Shenstone-Green; or, The New Paradise Lost, 1779
 London, April. *Women and Property*, 141–44.

EVADNE PRICE

Not So Quiet . . .: Stepdaughters of War, 1930
 Albrinck, Meg. "Borderline Women: Gender Confusion in Vera Brittain's and Evadne Price's War Narratives." *Narrative* 6 (1998), 271–88.

BARBARA PYM

An Academic Question, 1986
 Tsagaris, Ellen M. *The Subversion of Romance*, 127–31.
Crampton Hodnet, 1985
 McInnis, Judy B. "Communal Rites: Tea, Wine and Milton in Barbara Pym's Novels." *Renascence* 48 (1996), 282–84.
 Tsagaris, Ellen M. *The Subversion of Romance*, 48–55.
Excellent Women, 1952
 Fulton, Joe B. "Mildred's Mad Tea Party: Carnival in Barbara Pym's *Excellent Women*." *Dionysos* 6:2 (1996), 25–37.

Tsagaris, Ellen M. *The Subversion of Romance*, 57–75.

A Few Green Leaves, 1980

Little, Judy. *The Experimental Self*, 112–14.
McInnis, Judy B. "Communal Rites: Tea, Wine and Milton in Barbara Pym's Novels." *Renascence* 48 (1996), 290–93.
Tsagaris, Ellen M. *The Subversion of Romance*, 144–54.

A Glass of Blessings, 1958

Tsagaris, Ellen M. *The Subversion of Romance*, 97–103.

Jane and Prudence, 1953

Little, Judy. *The Experimental Self*, 101–3.
Tsagaris, Ellen M. *The Subversion of Romance*, 75–85.

Less Than Angels, 1955

Little, Judy. *The Experimental Self*, 105–12.
Tsagaris, Ellen M. *The Subversion of Romance*, 87–97.

No Fond Return of Love, 1961

Tsagaris, Ellen M. *The Subversion of Romance*, 105–18.

Quartet in Autumn, 1977

Little, Judy. *The Experimental Self*, 114–21.
Tosi, Laura. "Spazi di solitudine/solitudine degli spazi: L'emancipazione dell'anziano in *Quartet in Autumn* di Barbara Pym." *Annali di Ca' Foscari* 32:1–2 (1993), 359–76.
Tsagaris, Ellen M. *The Subversion of Romance*, 138–44.

Some Tame Gazelle, 1950

McInnis, Judy B. "Communal Rites: Tea, Wine and Milton in Barbara Pym's Novels." *Renascence* 48 (1996), 280–82.
Tsagaris, Ellen M. *The Subversion of Romance*, 31–48.

The Sweet Dove Died, 1978

Tsagaris, Ellen M. *The Subversion of Romance*, 133–38.

An Unsuitable Attachment, 1982

McInnis, Judy B. "Communal Rites: Tea, Wine and Milton in Barbara Pym's Novels." *Renascence* 48 (1996), 284–87.
Tsagaris, Ellen M. *The Subversion of Romance*, 118–27.

ANN RADCLIFFE

The Castles of Athlin and Dunbayne, 1789

Doody, Margaret Anne. "Deserts, Ruins and Troubled Waters: Female Dreams in Fiction and the Development of the Gothic Novel," in Richard Kroll, ed., *The English Novel, Volume II*, 83–86.

Gaston de Blondeville, 1826

Norton, Rictor. *Mistress of Udolpho*, 192–99.
Trumpener, Katie. *Bardic Nationalism*, 103–5.
Watt, James. *Contesting the Gothic*, 65–67.

The Italian, 1797

Burgess, Miranda J. *British Fiction and the Production of Social Order*, 163–72.

Carson, James P. "Enlightenment, Popular Culture, and Gothic Fiction," in John Richetti, ed., *The Cambridge Companion*, 269–72.

Choi. Julie. "Gothic Preoccupations: Penetrating Personal Boundaries in Radcliffe's *The Italian*." *Feminist Stud in Engl Lit* 7:2 (2000), 63–91.

Gautier, Gary. "Ann Radcliffe's *The Italian* in Context: Gothic Villains, Romantic Heroes, and a New Age of Power Relations." *Genre* 32 (1999), 201–22.

Heinrich, Hans. *Zur Geschichte des 'Libertin,'* 170–77.

Hendershot, Cyndy. *The Animal Within*, 45–50.

Hendershot, Cyndy. "The Possession of the Male Body: Masculinity in *The Italian, Psycho*, and *Dressed to Kill*." *Readerly/Writerly Texts* 2:2 (1995), 75–112.

Hoeveler, Diane Long. *Gothic Feminism*, 102–21.

Jacobs, Edward H. *Accidental Migrations*, 193–221.

Keane, Angela. *Women Writers and the English Nation*, 42–47.

Knox-Shaw, Peter. "'Strange Fits of Passion': Wordsworth and Mrs. Radcliffe." *Notes and Queries* 45 (1998), 188–89.

Mighall, Robert. *A Geography of Victorian Gothic Fiction*, 174–77.

Norton, Rictor. *Mistress of Udolpho*, 125–38, 146–51.

Schmitt, Cannon. *Alien Nation*, 21–25, 32–34, 36–47.

Swan, Beth. *Fictions of Law*, 193–204.

Temple, Kathryn. "Imagining Justice: Gender and Juridical Space in the Gothic Novel," in Thomas DiPiero and Pat Gill, eds., *Illicit Sex*, 68–85.

Tooley, Brenda. "Gothic Utopia: Heretical Sanctuary in Ann Radcliffe's *The Italian*." *Utopian Stud* 11:2 (2000), 42–56.

Watt, James. *Contesting the Gothic*, 117–19.

The Mysteries of Udolpho, 1794

Arnaud, Pierre. "Emily ou de l'éducation: *The Mysteries of Udolpho*, Bildungsroman feminin." *Bull de la Société d'Etudes Anglo-Américaines des XVIIe et XVIIIe Siècles* 43 (1996), 39–50.

Arnold, Ellen. "Deconstructing the Patriarchal Palace: Ann Radcliffe's Poetry in *The Mysteries of Udolpho*." *Women and Lang* 19:2 (1996), 21–29.

Becker, Susanne. *Gothic Forms of Feminine Fictions*, 27–33, 48–51.

Benedict, Barbara M. *Curiosity*, 229–38.

Benedict, Barbara M. "Radcliffe, Godwin, and Self-Possession in the 1790s," in Linda Lang-Peralta, ed., *Women, Revolution, and the Novels of the 1790s*, 89–106.

Bohls, Elizabeth A. *Women Travel Writers*, 209–29.

Botting, Fred. "*Dracula*, Romance and Radcliffean Gothic." *Women's Writing* 1 (1994), 195–98.

Dutoit, Thomas. "Epiphanic Reading in Ann Radcliffe's *The Mysteries of Udolpho*," in Wim Tigges, ed., *Moments of Moment*, 85–100.

Ellis, Kate Ferguson. "Ann Radcliffe and the Perils of Catholicism." *Women's Writing* 1 (1994), 165–68.

Gamer, Michael. *Romanticism and the Gothic*, 71–73.

Göbel, Walter. "Stimulating and Stifling the Emotions: An 18th-

Century Dilemma and a Gothic Example." *REAL: Yrbk of Res in Engl and Am Lit* 16 (2000), 136–42.

Hoeveler, Diane Long. *Gothic Feminism*, 85–102.

Ireland, Ken. *The Sequential Dynamics of Narrative*, 183.

Kozlowski, Lisa. "A Source for Ann Radcliffe's *The Mysteries of Udolpho*." *Notes and Queries* 44 (1997), 228–30.

MacKenzie, Scott. "Ann Radcliffe's Gothic Narrative and the Readers at Home." *Stud in the Novel* 31 (1999), 409–27.

Miall, David S. "The Preceptor as Fiend: Radcliffe's Psychology of the Gothic," in Laura Dabundo, ed., *Jane Austen and Mary Shelley*, 34–39.

Norton, Rictor. *Mistress of Udolpho*, 93–107, 140–45, 208–11.

Piper, William Bowman. *Reconcilable Differences*, 143–52, 153–71, 190–92.

Russett, Margaret. "Narrative as Enchantment in *The Mysteries of Udolpho*." *ELH* 65 (1998), 159–81.

Sage, Victor. "The Epistemology of Error: Reading and Isolation in *The Mysteries of Udolpho*." *Q/W/E/R/T/Y* 6 (1996), 107–13.

Schaff, Barbara. "Venetian Views and Voices in Radcliffe's *The Mysteries of Udolpho* and Braddon's *The Venetians*," in Manfred Pfister and Barbara Schaff, eds., *Venetian Views*, 89–98.

Simmons, James R., Jr. "'Every Discernible Thing in It Was Covered With Dust and Mould': Radcliffe's Château-le-Blanc and Dickens's Satis House." *Dickensian* 93 (1997), 11–12.

Soupel, Serge. "D'un archétype à l'autre: *The Mysteries of Udolpho* et *Robinson Crusoe*." *Bull de la Société d'Etudes Anglo-Américaines des XVIIe et XVIIIe Siècles* 43 (1996), 51–61.

Stoler, John. "Having Her Cake and Eating, Too: Ambivalence, Popularity, and the Psychosocial Implications of Ann Radcliffe's Fiction," in Laura Dabundo, ed., *Jane Austen and Mary Shelley*, 19–27.

Taylor, John A. *Popular Literature and . . . National Identity*, 69–80.

Townshend, Dale. "Constructions of Psychosis and Neurosis in Ann Radcliffe's *The Mysteries of Udolpho*." *Pretexts* 9 (2000), 175–206.

Watt, James. *Contesting the Gothic*, 109–15.

The Romance of the Forest, 1791

Botting, Fred. "*Dracula*, Romance and Radcliffean Gothic." *Women's Writing* 1 (1994), 188–94.

Bronfen, Elisabeth. "Hysteria, Phantasy and the Family Romance: Ann Radcliffe's *Romance of the Forest*." *Women's Writing* 1 (1994), 171–79.

Clery, E. J. "Ann Radcliffe and D. A. F. de Sade: Thoughts on Heroinism." *Women's Writing* 1 (1994), 203–12.

Gamer, Michael. *Romanticism and the Gothic*, 70–72.

Haggerty, George E. *Unnatural Affections*, 158–70.

Hoeveler, Diane Long. *Gothic Feminism*, 70–85.

Keane, Angela. *Women Writers and the English Nation*, 38–40.

Norton, Rictor. *Mistress of Udolpho*, 82–91.

Schaneman, Judith Clark. "Rewriting *Adèle et Théodore*: Intertextual Connections Between Madame de Genlis and Ann Radcliffe." *Compar Lit Stud* 38 (2001), 31–43.

Stoler, John. "Having Her Cake and Eating, Too: Ambivalence, Popularity, and the Psychosocial Implications of Ann Radcliffe's Fiction," in Laura Dabundo, ed., *Jane Austen and Mary Shelley*, 24–27.

Wein, Toni. "Legal Fictions, Legitimate Desires: The Law of Representation in *The Romance of the Forest*." *Genre* 30 (1997), 289–307.

A Sicilian Romance, 1790

Clemens, Valdine. *The Return of the Repressed*, 41–58.

Doody, Margaret Anne. "Deserts, Ruins and Troubled Waters: Female Dreams in Fiction and the Development of the Gothic Novel," in Richard Kroll, ed., *The English Novel, Volume II*, 86–89.

Hoeveler, Diane Long. *Gothic Feminism*, 58–70.

Mighall, Robert. *A Geography of Victorian Gothic Fiction*, 10–14.

Wordsworth, Jonathan. *The Bright Work Grows*, 75–81.

MARY-ANNE RADCLIFFE

Manfroné, or The One-Handed Monk, 1809

Haggerty, George E. *Unnatural Affections*, 171–73.

HUGH C. RAE

Night Pillow, 1967

Walker, Marshall. *Scottish Literature since 1707*, 326–27.

PIERS PAUL READ

A Married Man, 1979

Crowe, Marian E. "A Modern *Psychomachia*: The Catholic Fiction of Piers Paul Read." *Christianity and Lit* 47 (1998), 323–25.

Monk Dawson, 1970

Crowe, Marian E. "A Modern *Psychomachia*: The Catholic Fiction of Piers Paul Read." *Christianity and Lit* 47 (1998), 317–19.

On the Third Day, 1989

Crowe, Marian E. "A Modern *Psychomachia*: The Catholic Fiction of Piers Paul Read." *Christianity and Lit* 47 (1998), 319–22.

The Upstart, 1973

Crowe, Marian E. "A Modern *Psychomachia*: The Catholic Fiction of Piers Paul Read." *Christianity and Lit* 47 (1998), 311–12.

CHARLES READE

The Cloister and the Hearth, 1861

Thompson, Nicola Diane. *Reviewing Sex*, 33–36.

Hard Cash, 1863

Grigsby, Ann. "Charles Reade's *Hard Cash*: Lunacy Reform Through Sensationalism." *Dickens Stud Annual* 25 (1996), 141–57.

It Is Never Too Late to Mend, 1856
  Thompson, Nicola Diane. *Reviewing Sex,* 38–40, 68–70.
Peg Woffington, 1852
  Brody, Jennifer DeVere. *Impossible Purities,* 107–11.

PETER REDGROVE AND PENELOPE SHUTTLE

The Terrors of Dr Treviles, 1974
  Laird, Holly A. *Women Coauthors,* 162–81.

CLARA REEVE

The Old English Baron, 1778
  Andriopoulos, Stefan. "The Invisible Hand: Supernatural Agency in Political Economy and the Gothic Novel." *ELH* 66 (1999), 742–44.
  Fay, Elizabeth A. *A Feminist Introduction to Romanticism,* 117–20.
  Haggerty, George E. *Unnatural Affections,* 55–59.
  Perry, Ruth. "Women in Families: The Great Disinheritance," in Vivien Jones, ed., *Women and Literature in Britain,* 115–18.
  Watt, James. *Contesting the Gothic,* 47–49.
The School for Widows, 1791
  London, April. *Women and Property,* 121–23.

FORREST REID

The Garden God, 1905
  Cruise, Colin. "Error and Eros: The Fiction of Forrest Reid as a Defence of Homosexuality," in Éibhear Walshe, ed., *Sex, Nation and Dissent,* 65–67.
Pirates of the Spring, 1919
  Cruise, Colin. "Error and Eros: The Fiction of Forrest Reid as a Defence of Homosexuality," in Éibhear Walshe, ed., *Sex, Nation and Dissent,* 67–71.
The Retreat, 1936
  Cruise, Colin. "Error and Eros: The Fiction of Forrest Reid as a Defence of Homosexuality," in Éibhear Walshe, ed., *Sex, Nation and Dissent,* 81–84.
Uncle Stephen, 1931
  Cruise, Colin. "Error and Eros: The Fiction of Forrest Reid as a Defence of Homosexuality," in Éibhear Walshe, ed., *Sex, Nation and Dissent,* 75–81.
Young Tom, 1944
  Cruise, Colin. "Error and Eros: The Fiction of Forrest Reid as a Defence of Homosexuality," in Éibhear Walshe, ed., *Sex, Nation and Dissent,* 75–81.

MARY RENAULT

The Bull from the Sea, 1962

    Hoberman, Ruth. *Gendering Classicism,* 82–84.

    Zilboorg, Caroline. *The Masks of Mary Renault,* 157–59.

The Charioteer, 1953

    Zilboorg, Caroline. *The Masks of Mary Renault,* 84–87, 105–31.

The Friendly Young Ladies, 1944

    Zilboorg, Caroline. *The Masks of Mary Renault,* 87–96, 174–76.

Funeral Games, 1981

    Zilboorg, Caroline. *The Masks of Mary Renault,* 231–34.

The King Must Die, 1958

    Hoberman, Ruth. *Gendering Classicism,* 84–85.

    Zilboorg, Caroline. *The Masks of Mary Renault,* 156–58.

The Last of the Wine, 1956

    Zilboorg, Caroline. *The Masks of Mary Renault,* 142–49.

The Mask of Apollo, 1966

    Zilboorg, Caroline. *The Masks of Mary Renault,* 176–79, 202–4.

North Face, 1948

    Zilboorg, Caroline. *The Masks of Mary Renault,* 13–15, 40–42.

The Persian Boy, 1972

    Hoberman, Ruth. *Gendering Classicism,* 86–88.

    Zilboorg, Caroline. *The Masks of Mary Renault,* 225–26.

The Praise Singer, 1979

    Zilboorg, Caroline. *The Masks of Mary Renault,* 206–9, 238–42.

Purposes of Love, 1939

    Zilboorg, Caroline. *The Masks of Mary Renault,* 51–59, 76–78.

Return to Night, 1947

    Zilboorg, Caroline. *The Masks of Mary Renault,* 28–38.

RUTH RENDELL

A Dark-Adapted Eye, 1986

    Rowland, Susan. *From Agatha Christie to Ruth Rendell,* 59–61.

A Fatal Inversion, 1987

    Hühn, Peter. "The Crime Novels of Patricia Highsmith and Ruth Rendell: Reflections on a Genre." *Literatur in Wissenschaft und Unterricht* 33 (2000), 25–26.

The House of Stairs, 1988

    Rowland, Susan. *From Agatha Christie to Ruth Rendell,* 133–34.

A Judgement in Stone, 1977

    Hühn, Peter. "The Crime Novels of Patricia Highsmith and Ruth Rendell: Reflections on a Genre." *Literatur in Wissenschaft und Unterricht* 33 (2000), 21–22.

Hühn, Peter. "The Politics of Secrecy and Publicity: The Functions of Hidden Stories in Some Recent British Mystery Fiction," in Jerome H. Delamater and Ruth Prigozy, eds., *Theory and Practice*, 47–49.

Rowland, Susan. *From Agatha Christie to Ruth Rendell*, 154–56.

Kissing the Gunner's Daughter, 1991

Rowland, Susan. *From Agatha Christie to Ruth Rendell*, 36–38.

Master of the Moor, 1982

Leitch, Thomas M. "Not Just Another Whodunit: Disavowal as Evolution in Detective Fiction." *Clues* 20:1 (1999), 63–76.

Shake Hands Forever, 1975

Holmes, Martha Stoddard. "Between Men: How Ruth Rendell Reads for Gender," in Jerome H. Delamater and Ruth Prigozy, eds., *Theory and Practice*, 149–57.

Simisola, 1995

Rowland, Susan. *From Agatha Christie to Ruth Rendell*, 83–85.
York, R. A. *The Rules of Time*, 178–85.

Some Lie and Some Die, 1973

Leavy, Barbara Fass. "A Folklore Plot in Ruth Rendell's Wexford Series." *Clues* 20:2 (1999), 49–61.

An Unkindness of Ravens, 1985

Rowland, Susan. *From Agatha Christie to Ruth Rendell*, 178–80.

The Veiled One, 1988

Rowland, Susan. *From Agatha Christie to Ruth Rendell*, 107–9.

Wolf to the Slaughter, 1967

Pyrhönen, Heta. *Mayhem and Murder*, 166–77.

GEORGE W. M. REYNOLDS

The Mysteries of London, 1846

Rosenman, Ellen Bayak. "Spectacular Women: *The Mysteries of London* and the Female Body." *Victorian Stud* 40:1 (1996), 31–59.
Thomas, Trefor. "Rereading G. W. Reynolds's *The Mysteries of London*," in Alice Jenkins and Juliet John, eds., *Rereading Victorian Fiction*, 59–77.

JEAN RHYS

After Leaving Mr. Mackenzie, 1931

Emery, Mary Lou. "Refiguring the Postcolonial Imagination: Tropes of Visuality in Writing by Rhys, Kincaid, and Cliff." *Tulsa Stud in Women's Lit* 16 (1997), 264–67.
Gibson, Andrew. *Postmodernity, Ethics and the Novel*, 168–69, 171–73.
Gibson, Andrew. "Sensibility and Suffering in Rhys and Nin," in Andrew Hadfield et al., eds., *The Ethics in Literature*, 190–97.
Lewis, Andrea. "Immigrants, Prostitutes, and Chorus Girls: National

Identity in the Early Novels of Jean Rhys." *J of Commonwealth and Postcolonial Stud* 6:1 (1999), 82–95.

Lonsdale, Thorunn. "Literary Allusion in the Fiction of Jean Rhys," in Mary Condé and Thorunn Lansford, eds., *Caribbean Women Writers*, 54–56.

Lykiard, Alexis. *Jean Rhys Revisited*, 77–85.

Maurel, Sylvie. *Jean Rhys*, 27–50.

Savory, Elaine. *Jean Rhys*, 57–84.

Good Morning, Midnight, 1939

Butler, Lance St. John. *Registering the Difference*, 124–26.

Caples, Garrett. "White Noise: Vocal Frequencies in Jean Rhys's *Good Morning, Midnight." Jean Rhys R* 8:1–2 (1997), 5–11.

Gibson, Andrew. *Postmodernity, Ethics and the Novel*, 168–69, 172–73.

Gibson, Andrew. "Sensibility and Suffering in Rhys and Nin," in Andrew Hadfield et al., eds., *The Ethics in Literature*, 190–97.

Holden, Kate. "Formations of Discipline and Manliness: Culture, Politics and 1930's Women's Writing." *J of Gender Stud* 8:2 (1999), 141–57.

Lewis, Andrea. "Immigrants, Prostitutes, and Chorus Girls: National Identity in the Early Novels of Jean Rhys." *J of Commonwealth and Postcolonial Stud* 6:1 (1999), 82–95.

Lykiard, Alexis. *Jean Rhys Revisited*, 66–68.

Maurel, Sylvie. *Jean Rhys*, 102–27.

Radford, Jean. "Late Modernism and the Politics of History," in Maroula Joannou, ed., *Women Writers of the 1930s*, 37–40.

Savory, Elaine. *Jean Rhys*, 109–32.

Zimring, Rishona. "The Make-up of Jean Rhys's Fiction." *Novel* 33 (2000), 226–31.

Quartet, 1928

Lewis, Andrea. "Immigrants, Prostitutes, and Chorus Girls: National Identity in the Early Novels of Jean Rhys." *J of Commonwealth and Postcolonial Stud* 6:1 (1999), 82–95.

Lonsdale, Thorunn. "Literary Allusion in the Fiction of Jean Rhys," in Mary Condé and Thorunn Lansford, eds., *Caribbean Women Writers*, 47–50.

Maurel, Sylvie. *Jean Rhys*, 10–26.

Savory, Elaine. *Jean Rhys*, 38–40, 47–58.

Zimring, Rishona. "The Make-up of Jean Rhys's Fiction." *Novel* 33 (2000), 220–26.

Voyage in the Dark, 1934

Berry, Betsy. "*Voyage in the Dark, Esther Waters*, and the Naturalistic Tradition." *Jean Rhys R* 7:1–2 (1996), 17–25.

Dearlove, Judith E. "The Failure of the *Bildungsroman*: Jean Rhys and *Voyage in the Dark." Jean Rhys R* 8:1–2 (1997), 24–30.

Edelson, Maria. "International Consciousness and Alienation of Characters in *Voyage in the Dark* by Jean Rhys and *Isolation* by Jerzy Peterkiewicz." *Folia Litteraria Anglica* (Lodz) 1 (1997), 3–13.

Lewis, Andrea. "Immigrants, Prostitutes, and Chorus Girls: National

Identity in the Early Novels of Jean Rhys." *J of Commonwealth and Postcolonial Stud* 6:1 (1999), 82–95.

Maurel, Sylvie. *Jean Rhys*, 81–101.

Paschetto, Anna. "Anna Morgan, la straniera: Soggetto e silenzio in *Voyage in the Dark* di Jean Rhys." *Confronto Letterario* 12 (1995), 327–44.

Savory, Elaine. *Jean Rhys*, 85–108.

Stouck, Jordan. "Alternative Narratives of Race, Time, and Gender: Jean Rhys' *Voyage in the Dark*." *J of Commonwealth and Postcolonial Stud* 3:1 (1995), 53–59.

Wide Saragasso Sea, 1966

Becker, Susanne. *Gothic Forms of Feminine Fictions*, 73–75.

Bender, Todd K. *Literary Impressionism*, 85–96.

Chang, Kenny. "Feminist Revision and the Recentering of a Colonial Subject: Jean Rhys's *Wide Saragasso Sea*." *Stud in Lang and Lit* (Taipei) 8 (1998), 103–16.

Ciolkowski, Laura E. "Navigating the *Wide Saragasso Sea*: Colonial History, English Fiction, and British Empire." *Twentieth Cent Lit* 43 (1997), 339–54.

Davis, Todd F., and Kenneth Womack. "Reclaiming the Particular: The Ethics of Self and Sexuality in *Wide Saragasso Sea*." *Jean Rhys R* 11:1 (1999), 63–78.

Dessart, Jamie Thomas. "'Surrounded by a Gilt Frame': Mirrors and Reflection of Self in *Jane Eyre, Mill on the Floss*, and *Wide Saragasso Sea*." *Jean Rhys R* 8:1–2 (1997), 16–24.

Dolezel, Lubomir. *Heterocosmica*, 213–17.

Ferguson, Moira. "Sending the Younger Son Across the Wide Saragasso Sea: The New Colonizer Arrives." *Jean Rhys R* 6:1 (1993), 2–16.

Gering, August. "The Celtic Creole in Jean Rhys's *Wide Saragasso Sea*." *Jean Rhys R* 11:1 (1999), 35–61.

Hendershot, Cyndy. *The Animal Within*, 190–202.

Hogan, Patrick Colm. *Colonialism and Cultural Identity*, 83–102.

Hulme, Peter. "The Locked Heart: The Creole Family Romance of *Wide Saragasso Sea*—An Historical and Biographical Analysis." *Jean Rhys R* 6:1 (1993), 20–36.

Hulme, Peter. "The Place of *Wide Saragasso Sea*." *Wasafiri* 20 (1994), 5–11.

James, Louis. *Caribbean Literature in English*, 38–40.

Jouve, Nicole Ward. *Female Genesis*, 206–8.

Kineke, Sheila. "'Like a Hook Fits an Eye': Jean Rhys, Ford Madox Ford, and the Imperial Operations of Modernist Mentoring." *Tulsa Stud in Women's Lit* 16 (1997), 293–97.

Little, Judy. "Signifying Nothing: A Shakespearean Deconstruction of Rhys's Rochester." *Jean Rhys R* 7:1–2 (1996), 39–46.

Lock, Helen. "Rhys's Epistemological Battleground." *J of Commonwealth and Postcolonial Stud* 6:1 (1999), 96–103.

Lonsdale, Thorunn. "Literary Allusion in the Fiction of Jean Rhys," in Mary Condé and Thorunn Lansford, eds., *Caribbean Women Writers*, 59–65.

Louvel, Liliane. "*L'Etrange mer des Sargasses* de Jean Rhys." *GRAAT* 15 (1996), 49–61.

Mardorossian, Carine M. "Shutting Up the Subaltern: Silences, Stereotypes, and Double-Entendre in Jean Rhys's *Wide Saragossa Sea*." *Callaloo* 22 (1999), 1071–90.

Mardorossian, Carine Melkom. "Double (De)colonization and the Feminist Criticism of *Wide Saragossa Sea*." *Coll Lit* 26:2 (1999), 79–95.

Maurel, Sylvie. *Jean Rhys*, 128–66.

Narain, Denise deCaires. "English Gardens and West Indian Yards: The Politics of Location (One More Time)." *Wasafiri* 28 (1998), 37–38.

Neck-Yoder, Hilda van. "Colonial Desires, Silence, and Metonymy: 'All Things Considered' in *Wide Saragasso Sea*." *Texas Stud in Lit and Lang* 40 (1998), 184–203.

Plasa, Carl. *Textual Politics from Slavery to Postcolonialism*, 82–97.

Sarvan, Charles. "Flight, Entrapment, and Madness in Jean Rhys's *Wide Saragasso Sea*." *Intl Fiction R* 26 (1999), 58–65.

Savory, Elaine. *Jean Rhys*, 20–22, 33–36, 67–69, 97–99, 133–47, 203–8, 218–23.

Skinner, John. *The Stepmother Tongue*, 192–94.

Thum, Angela M. "*Wide Saragasso Sea*: A Rereading of Colonialism." *Michigan Academician* 30 (1998), 147–61.

Uraizee, Joya. "'She Walked Away Without Looking Back': Christophine and the Enigma of History in Jean Rhys's *Wide Saragasso Sea*." *Clio* 28 (1999), 261–77.

Walker, Joseph S. "When Texts Collide: The Re-Visioning Power of the Margin." *Colby Q* 35:1 (1999), 35–48.

Watson, Reginald. "Images of Blackness in the Works of Charlotte and Emily Brontë." *Coll Lang Assoc J* 44 (2001), 467–68.

Wickramagamage, Carmen. "An/other Side to Antoinette/Bertha: Reading 'Race' into *Wide Saragasso Sea*." *J of Commonwealth Lit* 35:1 (2000), 27–39.

DOROTHY RICHARDSON

Backwater, 1916

Bronfen, Elisabeth. *Dorothy Richardson's Art of Memory*, 13–16.

March Moonlight, 1967

Bronfen, Elisabeth. *Dorothy Richardson's Art of Memory*, 209–19.

Pilgrimage, 1915–1967

Bluemel, Kristin. *Experimenting on the Borders of Modernism*, 12–172.

Bronfen, Elisabeth. *Dorothy Richardson's Art of Memory*, 13–27, 117–67, 221–34.

Burford, Arianne. "Communities of Silence and Music in Virginia Woolf's *The Waves* and Dorothy Richardson's *Pilgrimage*," in Jeanette McVicker and Laura Davis, eds., *Virginia Woolf and Communities*, 269–74.

Gevirtz, Susan. "Into Ellipse: Geographic and Grammatic Disappearance in Dorothy Richardson's *Pilgrimage*." *Women's Stud* 26 (1997), 523–32.

Hill, Marylu. *Mothering Modernity*, 57–106.

Katz, Tamar. *Impressionist Subjects*, 138–68.

Kilian, Eveline. *Momente innerweltlicher Transzendenz*.

Langbauer, Laurie. *Novels of Everyday Life*, 40–42, 163–69.

Linett, Maren. "'The Wrong Material': Gender and Jewishness in Dorothy Richardson's *Pilgrimage*." *J of Mod Lit* 23 (1999/2000), 191–208.

McCracken, Scott. "Embodying the New Woman: Dorothy Richardson, Work and the London Cafe," in Avril Horner and Angela Keane, eds., *Body Matters*, 58–71.

Mepham, John. "Dorothy Richardson's 'Unreadability': Graphic Style and Narrative Strategy in a Modernist Novel." *Engl Lit in Transition* 43 (2000), 449–62.

Migliorini, Marta. "Il giardino: La realtà sommersa—Una lettura di *Pilgrimage* di Dorothy Richardson." *Confronto Letterario* 14 (1997), 723–45.

Pykett, Lyn. *Engendering Fictions*, 77–89.

Radford, Jean. "The Woman and the Jew: Sex and Modernity," in Bryan Cheyette and Laura Marcus, eds., *Modernity, Culture and 'the Jew,'* 91–103.

Rose, Jacqueline. *States of Fantasy*, 117–32.

Tötösy de Zepetnek, Steven. "Margit Kaffka and Dorothy Richardson: A Comparison." *Hungarian Stud* 11:1 (1996), 77–95.

Trodd, Anthea. *Women's Writing in English*, 57–66.

Winning, Joanne. ""The Past" is with me, seen anew': Biography's End in Dorothy Richardson's *Pilgrimage*," in Warwick Gould and Thomas F. Staley, eds., *Writing the Lives of Writers*, 212–22.

Winning, Joanna. *The Pilgrimage of Dorothy Richardson*, 14–175.

Pointed Roofs, 1915

Katz, Tamar. *Impressionist Subjects*, 144–47.

SAMUEL RICHARDSON

Clarissa, 1748

Ardholm, Helena M. *The Emblem and the Emblematic Habit*, 49–51.

Armstrong, Nancy. "Captivity and Cultural Capital in the English Novel." *Novel* 31 (1998), 374–79.

Armstrong, Nancy. "Writing Women and the Making of the Modern Middle Class," in Amanda Gilroy and W. M. Verhoeven, eds., *Epistolary Histories*, 29–34.

Audigier, Jean-Pierre. "Le Roman de l'origine." *Corps Ecrit* 32 (1989), 125–33.

Backscheider, Paula R. "The Rise of Gender as Political Category," in Backscheider, ed., *Revising Women*, 31–57.

Backus, Margot Gayle. *The Gothic Family Romance*, 48–74.

Barbé-Petit, Françoise. "Incertitude, fragmentation, discontinuité chez Hume et chez Richardson." *Bull de la Société d'Etudes Anglo-Américaines des XVIIe et XVIIIe Siècles* 43 (1996), 81–92.

Bellamy, Liz. *Commerce, Morality and the Eighteenth-Century Novel*, 73–82.

Bellman, Patrizia Nerozzi. "La conversazione nel romanzo inglese del Settecento." *Confronto Letterario* 12 (1995), 5–21.

Bowden, Martha. "Composing Herself: Music, Solitude, and St. Cecilia in *Clarissa*." *1650–1850: Ideas, Aesthetics, and Inquiries in the Early Mod Era* 2 (1996), 185–201.

Brown, Murray L. "Authorship and Generic Exploitation: Why Lovelace Must Fear *Clarissa*." *Stud in the Novel* 30 (1998), 246–58.

Burgess, Miranda J. *British Fiction and the Production of Social Order*, 55–68.

Carnell, Rachel K. "Clarissa's Treasonable Correspondence: Gender, Epistolary Politics, and the Public Sphere." *Eighteenth-Cent Fiction* 10 (1998), 269–86.

Case, Alison A. *Plotting Women*, 35–70.

Cavaliero, Glen. *The Alchemy of Laughter*, 7–9.

Chartier, Roger. "Richardson, Diderot et la lectrice impatiente." *Mod Lang Notes* 114 (1999), 647–66.

Chung, Ewha. "Samuel Richardson's *Clarissa*: Defining the 'Sacred' Community and Defencing Religious Education." *J of Engl Lang and Lit* 42 (1996), 813–26.

Dever, Carolyn. *Death and the Mother*, 20–22.

Doody, Margaret Anne. "The Gnostic *Clarissa*." *Eighteenth-Cent Fiction* 11 (1998), 49–78.

Doody, Margaret Anne. "Samuel Richardson: Fiction and Knowledge," in John Richetti, ed., *The Cambridge Companion*, 105–10.

Erickson, Robert A. *The Language of the Heart*, 185–238.

Frega, Donnalee. *Speaking in Hunger*, 1–129.

Fulton, Gordon D. *Styles of Meaning and Meanings of Style*, 3–174.

Fysh, Stephanie. *The Work(s) of Samuel Richardson*, 80–99.

Gardiner, Ellen. *Regulating Readers*, 38–62.

Gordon, Scott Paul. "Disinterested Selves: *Clarissa* and the Tactics of Sentiment." *ELH* 64 (1997), 473–96.

Graeber, Wilhelm. *Der englische Roman in Frankreich*, 152–82.

Gunn, Daniel P. "Is *Clarissa* Bourgeois Art?" *Eighteenth-Cent Fiction* 10 (1997), 1–14.

Heinrich, Hans. *Zur Geschichte des 'Libertin,'* 106–23.

Hinton, Laura. "The Heroine's Subjection: Clarissa, Sadomasochism, and Natural Law." *Eighteenth-Cent Stud* 32 (1999), 293–305.

Hinton, Laura. *The Perverse Gaze of Sympathy*, 35–74.

Irwin, Michael. "Readings of Realism," in Philip Davis, ed., *Real Voices*, 215–17.

Keymer, Thomas. "Dying by Numbers: *Tristram Shandy* and Serial Fiction (2)." *The Shandean* 9 (1997), 44–47.

Knights, Elspeth. "'Daring but to Touch the Hem of her Garment': Women Reading *Clarissa*." *Women's Writing* 7 (2000), 221–40.

Korba, Susan. "*Clarissa*'s 'Man of Violence' and *Grandison*'s 'Truly

Good Man': Masculine Homogeneity in Richardson," in Andrew P. Williams, ed., *The Image of Manhood*, 161–67.

Liebrand, Claudia. "Briefromane und ihre 'Lektüreanweisungen': Richardsons *Clarissa*, Goethes *Die Leiden des jungen Werthers*, Laclos' *Les Liaisons dangereuses*." *Arcadia* 32 (1997), 342–51.

London, April. *Women and Property*, 15–34, 42–53.

McIntosh, Carey. *The Evolution of English Prose*, 137–41.

Macpherson, Sandra. "Lovelace, Ltd." *ELH* 65 (1998), 99–117.

Martin, Mary Patricia. "Reading Reform in Richardson's *Clarissa*." *Stud in Engl Lit, 1500–1900* 37 (1997), 595–611.

Michie, Allen. *Richardson and Fielding*, 63–66, 136–41, 179–81.

Moglen, Helene. *The Trauma of Gender*, 57–85.

Monneyron, Frédéric. "L'Imaginaire du séducteur: Le Cas Lovelace." *Filigrana* 1995, 199–210.

Montandon, Alain. *Le roman au XVIIIe siècle*, 252–57.

Morse, David. *The Age of Virtue*, 120–28.

Ogden, Daryl S. "Richardson's Narrative Space-Off: Freud, Vision and the (Heterosexual) Problem of Reading *Clarissa*." *Lit and Psych* 42:4 (1996), 37–50.

Osland, Dianne. "Complaisance and Complacence, and the Perils of Pleasing in *Clarissa*." *Stud in Engl Lit, 1500–1900* 40 (2000), 491–505.

Paulson, Ronald. *The Beautiful, Novel, and Strange*, 132–35.

Pearson, Jacqueline. *Women's Reading in Britain*, 27–29.

Perry, Ruth. "Clarissa's Daughters, or The History of Innocence Betrayed: How Women Writers Rewrote Richardson." *Women's Writing* 1 (1994), 5–21.

Perry, Ruth. "Women in Families: The Great Disinheritance," in Vivien Jones, ed., *Women and Literature in Britain*, 122–29.

Potter, Tiffany. "'A Certain Sign that He Is One of Us': *Clarissa*'s Other Libertines." *Eighteenth-Cent Fiction* 11 (1999), 403–20.

Price, Leah. *The Anthology and the Rise of the Novel*, 25–42.

Rawson, Claude. *Satire and Sentiment*, 143–45.

Richetti, John. *The English Novel in History*, 99–117.

Roberts, Nancy. *Schools of Sympathy*, 27–45.

Runge, Laura L. *Gender and Language*, 147–55.

Schor, Hilary M. "Notes of a Libertine Daughter: *Clarissa*, Feminism, and *The Rise of the Novel*." *Stanford Hum R* 8:1 (2000), 94–114.

Schramm, Jan-Melissa. *Testimony and Advocacy*, 83–89.

Scofield, Martin. "Shakespeare and *Clarissa*: 'General Nature,' Genre and Sexuality." *Shakespeare Survey* 51 (1998), 27–43.

Smyth, Orla. "Books within Books: What Did Clarissa Harlowe Read? — A Note on the History of Reading Practices." *Bull de la Société d'Etudes Anglo-Américaines des XVIIe et XVIIIe Siècles* 48 (1999), 103–21.

Spencer, Jane. *Aphra Behn's Afterlife*, 138–41.

Swan, Beth. *Fictions of Law*, 38–42, 79–83, 108–24.

Taylor, Derek. "Clarissa Harlowe, Mary Astell, and Elizabeth Carter: John Norris of Bemerton's Female 'Descendants.'" *Eighteenth-Cent Fiction* 12 (1999), 19–38.

Thompson, Peggy. "Abuse and Atonement: The Passion of Clarissa Harlowe." *Eighteenth-Cent Fiction* 11 (1999), 255–70.

Tseng, Li-ling. "A Whore or a Whole: Conflict of Discourses in *Clarissa*." *Stud in Lang and Lit* (Taipei) 6 (1994), 127–39.

Tumbleson, Ray. "Potboiler Emancipation and the Prison of Pure Art: *Clarissa, The Wind,* and Surviving Rape." *Lit/Film Q* 25 (1997), 193–96.

Van Sant, Ann Jessie. "Revelation of the Heart through Entrapment and Trial," in Richard Kroll, ed., *The English Novel, Volume I,* 249–67.

Varney, Andrew. *Eighteenth-Century Writers in their World,* 48–61.

Vermillion, Mary. "*Clarissa* and the Marriage Act." *Eighteenth-Cent Fiction* 9 (1997), 395–412.

Zigarovich, Jolene. "Courting Death: Necrophilia in Samuel Richardson's *Clarissa*." *Stud in the Novel* 32 (2000), 112–27.

Zimmerman, Everett. *The Boundaries of Fiction,* 78–80, 118–34.

Pamela, 1740

Ardholm, Helena M. *The Emblem and the Emblematic Habit,* 47–49.

Armstrong, Nancy. "Captivity and Cultural Capital in the English Novel." *Novel* 31 (1998), 374–79.

Armstrong, Nancy. "Strategies of Self-Production: *Pamela,*" in Richard Kroll, ed., *The English Novel, Volume I,* 217–46.

Austin, Michael. "Lincolnshire Babylon: Competing Typologies in Pamela's 137th Psalm." *Eighteenth-Cent Fiction* 12 (2000), 501–14.

Bachman, Maria K. "The Confessions of *Pamela:* 'a strange medley of inconsistence.'" *Lit and Psych* 47:1–2 (2001), 12–28.

Barbé-Petit, Françoise. "Incertitude, fragmentation, discontinuité chez Hume et chez Richardson." *Bull de la Société d'Etudes Anglo-Américaines des XVIIe et XVIIIe Siècles* 43 (1996), 81–92.

Barchas, Janine. "Prefiguring Genre: Frontispiece Portraits from *Gulliver's Travels* to *Millenium Hall*." *Stud in the Novel* 30 (1998), 272–75.

Bony, Alain. "Ombres et lumières du sentiment: Retour à *Pamela*— Du Mythe goldonien au texte de Richardson." *Bull de la Société d'Etudes Anglo-Américaines des XVIIe et XVIIIe Siècles* 48 (1999), 181–201.

Bowen, Scarlett. "'A Sawce-box and Boldface Indeed': Refiguring the Female Servant in the Pamela-Antipamela Debate." *Stud in Eighteenth-Cent Culture* 28 (1999), 257–81.

Bowers, Toni. "'A Point of Conscience': Breastfeeding and Maternal Authority in *Pamela,* Part 2," in Susan C. Greenfield and Carol Barash, eds., *Inventing Maternity,* 138–52.

Burgess, Miranda J. *British Fiction and the Production of Social Order,* 35–45.

Cruise, James. *Governing Consumption,* 123–40.

Doody, Margaret Anne. "Samuel Richardson: Fiction and Knowledge," in John Richetti, ed., *The Cambridge Companion,* 100–105.

Durrenmatt, Jacques. "Diviser *Pamela*." *Q/W/E/R/T/Y* 4 (1994), 103–9.

Dussinger, John A. "'*Ciceronian* Eloquence': The Politics of Virtue in Richardson's *Pamela*." *Eighteenth-Cent Fiction* 12 (1999), 39–60.

Flint, Christopher. *Family Fictions*, 161–206.

Fysh, Stephanie. *The Work(s) of Samuel Richardson*, 57–79.

Gaskell, Philip. *Landmarks in English Literature*, 46–49.

Heinrich, Hans. *Zur Geschichte des 'Libertin,'* 80–85.

Höss, Tilman. "Pamela und der haarige Affe: Zur Soziologie des Frauenhasses in der modernen Literatur." *Anglia* 118 (2000), 67–71.

Ingrassia, Catherine. *Authorship, Commerce, and Gender*, 151–65.

Ingrassia, Catherine. "'I am become a Mere Usurer': *Pamela* and Domestic Stock-jobbing." *Stud in the Novel* 30 (1998), 303–19.

Keymer, Tom. "Getting Level: *Pamela*, Pope and J— W—." *Q/W/E/R/T/Y* 4 (1994), 111–19.

Littleton, Jacob. "'My Treacherous Heart': Non-Rhetorical Registers of Truth in Pamela's Ascent." *Eighteenth-Cent Fiction* 10 (1998), 287–301.

London, April. *Women and Property*, 34–38.

McIntosh, Carey. *The Evolution of English Prose*, 207–11.

Michie, Allen. *Richardson and Fielding*, 147–49.

Miller, Louise M. "Author, Artist, Reader: 'The Spirit of the Passages' and the Illustrations to *Pamela*." *Q/W/E/R/T/Y* 4 (1994), 121–30.

Montandon, Alain. "Pamela: Un Ange ordinaire?" *Q/W/E/R/T/Y* 4 (1994), 131–38.

Montandon, Alain. *Le roman au XVIIIe siècle*, 241–52.

Morère, Pierre. "L'Alchimie de l'écriture dans *Pamela* de Samuel Richardson." *Q/W/E/R/T/Y* 4 (1994), 139–44.

Morse, David. *The Age of Virtue*, 110–21.

Mudge, Bradford K. *The Whore's Story*, 185–99.

Paulson, Ronald. *The Beautiful, Novel, and Strange*, 128–32.

Price, Leah. *The Anthology and the Rise of the Novel*, 46–47, 56–57.

Raynie, Stephen. "Hayman and Gravelot's Anti-*Pamela* Designs for Richardson's Octavo Edition of *Pamela I* and *II*." *Eighteenth-Cent Life* 23:3 (1999), 77–91.

Richetti, John. *The English Novel in History*, 87–99.

Rivero, Albert J. "*Pamela/Shamela/Joseph Andrews*: Henry Fielding and the Duplicities of Representation," in Rivero, ed., *Augustan Subjects*, 209–15.

Schellenberg, Betty A. "'To Renew Their Former Acquaintance': Print, Gender, and Some Eighteenth-Century Sequels," in Paul Budra and Betty A. Schellenberg, eds., *Part Two*, 86–97.

Swan, Beth. *Fictions of Law*, 104–8.

Thompson, Lynda M. *The 'Scandalous Memoirists,'* 149–51.

Wilner, Arlene Fish. "'Thou Hast Made a Rake a Preacher': Beauty and the Beast in Richardson's *Pamela*." *Eighteenth-Cent Fiction* 13 (2001), 529–60.

Zschirnt, Christiane. "Fainting and Latency in the Eighteenth Century's Romantic Novel of Courtship." *Germanic R* 74:1 (1999), 48–66.

Sir Charles Grandison, 1754

Bellamy, Liz. *Commerce, Morality and the Eighteenth-Century Novel,* 107–18.

Bray, Joe. "The Source of 'Dramatized Consciousness': Richardson, Austen, and Stylistic Influence." *Style* 35:1 (2001), 18–28.

Doody, Margaret Anne. "Deserts, Ruins and Troubled Waters: Female Dreams in Fiction and the Development of the Gothic Novel," in Richard Kroll, ed., *The English Novel, Volume II,* 62–67.

Doody, Margaret Anne. "Samuel Richardson: Fiction and Knowledge," in John Richetti, ed., *The Cambridge Companion,* 110–14.

Ellis, Markman. *The Politics of Sensibility,* 166–68.

Fysh, Stephanie. *The Work(s) of Samuel Richardson,* 106–23.

Graeber, Wilhelm. *Der englische Roman in Frankreich,* 222–34.

Heinrich, Hans. *Zur Geschichte des 'Libertin,'* 123–26.

Keymer, Thomas. "Dying by Numbers: *Tristram Shandy* and Serial Fiction (2)." *The Shandean* 9 (1997), 44–47.

Korba, Susan. "*Clarissa*'s 'Man of Violence' and *Grandison*'s 'Truly Good Man': Masculine Homogeneity in Richardson," in Andrew P. Williams, ed., *The Image of Manhood,* 167–81.

Montandon, Alain. *Le roman au XVIIIe siècle,* 257–59.

Morse, David. *The Age of Virtue,* 141–46.

Price, Leah. *The Anthology and the Rise of the Novel,* 15–27, 32–34, 42–48.

Richetti, John. *The English Novel in History,* 251–59.

Swan, Beth. *Fictions of Law,* 83–86, 121–26.

Temple, Kathryn. "Printing like a Post-Colonialist: The Irish Piracy of *Sir Charles Grandison*." *Novel* 33 (2000), 157–71.

Young, Arlene. *Culture, Class and Gender,* 22–31.

CHARLOTTE RIDDELL

A Struggle for Fame, 1883

Kelleher, Margaret. "Charlotte Riddell's *A Struggle for Fame*: The Field of Women's Literary Production." *Colby Q* 36 (2000), 116–30.

JOAN RILEY

The Unbelonging, 1985

Abruña, Laura Niesen de. "Sea Changes: African-Caribbean and African Women Writers in England," in Abby H. P. Werlock, ed., *British Women Writing Fiction,* 282–87.

ANNE THACKERAY RITCHIE

Mrs. Dymond, 1885

Mourão, Manuela. "Interrogating the Female *Bildungsroman*: Anne Thackeray Ritchie's Marriage Fictions." *Nineteenth-Cent Feminisms* 3 (2000), 83–85.

Old Kensington, 1873

Mourão, Manuela. "Interrogating the Female *Bildungsroman*: Anne

Thackeray Ritchie's Marriage Fictions." *Nineteenth-Cent Feminisms* 3 (2000), 79–83.

The Story of Elizabeth, 1863

Mourão, Manuela. "Interrogating the Female *Bildungsroman*: Anne Thackeray Ritchie's Marriage Fictions." *Nineteenth-Cent Feminisms* 3 (2000), 76–79.

KEITH ROBERTS

Pavane, 1968

Dose, Gerd. "Alternate Worlds: Kingsley Amis' *The Alteration* and Keith Roberts' *Pavane*," in Rüdiger Ahrens and Fritz-Wilhelm Neumann, eds., *Fiktion und Geschichte*, 322–27, 330–36.

MICHELE ROBERTS

The Book of Mrs. Noah, 1987

King, Jeannette. *Women and the Word*, 41–54.

Sceats, Sarah. *Food, Consumption and the Body*, 128–32.

Daughters of the House, 1993

Hanson, Clare. "During Mother's Absence: The Fiction of Michèle Roberts," in Abby H. P. Werlock, ed., *British Women Writing Fiction*, 238–41.

Jouve, Nicole Ward. *Female Genesis*, 208–11.

King, Jeannette. *Women and the Word*, 64–76.

Parker, Emma. "From House to Home: A Kristevan Reading of Michèle Roberts's *Daughters of the House*." *Critique* (Washington, DC) 41 (2000), 153–71.

Sceats, Sarah. *Food, Consumption and the Body*, 133–35, 137–41.

Flesh and Blood, 1994

Hanson, Clare. "During Mother's Absence: The Fiction of Michèle Roberts," in Abby H. P. Werlock, ed., *British Women Writing Fiction*, 241–46.

In the Red Kitchen, 1990

Rowland, Susan. "Feminist Ethical Reading Strategies in Michèle Roberts's *In the Red Kitchen*: Hysterical Reading and Making Theory Hysterical," in Andrew Hadfield et al., eds., *The Ethics in Literature*, 169–82.

Rowland, Susan. "Women, Spiritualism and Depth Psychology in Michèle Roberts's Victorian Novel," in Alice Jenkins and Juliet John, eds., *Rereading Victorian Fiction*, 201–12.

A Piece of the Night, 1978

Dervin, Dan. *Matricentric Narratives*, 89–96.

Hanson, Clare. "During Mother's Absence: The Fiction of Michèle Roberts," in Abby H. P. Werlock, ed., *British Women Writing Fiction*, 232–35.

The Wild Girl, 1984

Hanson, Clare. "During Mother's Absence: The Fiction of Michèle Roberts," in Abby H. P. Werlock, ed., *British Women Writing Fiction,* 235–38.

King, Jeannette. *Women and the Word,* 104–17.

ELIZABETH ROBINS

George Mandeville's Husband, 1894

Heilmann, Ann. *New Woman Fiction,* 189–91.

EMMA ROBINSON

Mauleverer's Divorce: A Story of a Woman's Wrongs, 1858

Humpherys, Anne. "Breaking Apart: The Early Victorian Divorce Novel," in Nicola Diane Thompson, ed., *Victorian Women Writers,* 49–53.

MARY ROBINSON

The False Friend, 1799

Ty, Eleanor. *Empowering the Feminine,* 57–71.

The Natural Daughter, 1796

Setzer, Sharon M. "Romancing the Reign of Terror: Sexual Politics in Mary Robinson's *Natural Daughter.*" *Criticism* 39 (1997), 531–50.

Ty, Eleanor. *Empowering the Feminine,* 72–84.

Ty, Eleanor. "Feminine Power and Exquisite Sensibility: Mary Robinson's *The Natural Daughter.*" *Stud on Voltaire and the Eighteenth Cent* 348 (1996), 1414–17.

Walsingham; or, The Pupil of Nature, 1797

Arnold, Ellen. "Genre, Gender, and Cross-Dressing in Mary Robinson's *Walsingham.*" *Postscript* 16 (1999), 57–68.

Setzer, Sharon. "The Dying Game: Crossdressing in Mary Robinson's *Walsingham.*" *Nineteenth-Cent Contexts* 22 (2000), 305–24.

Shaffer, Julie. "Cross-Dressing and the Nature of Gender in Mary Robinson's *Walsingham,*" in Chris Mounsey, ed., *Presenting Gender,* 136–60.

Ty, Eleanor. *Empowering the Feminine,* 42–56.

REGINA MARIA ROCHE

The Children of the Abbey, 1796

Burgess, Miranda J. "Violent Translations: Allegory, Gender, and Cultural Nationalism in Ireland, 1796–1806." *Mod Lang Q* 59 (1998), 36–70.

Zeender, Marie-Noelle. "Aspects du roman gothique irlandais avant et après l'Acte d'Union." *Etudes Irlandaises* 25:2 (2000), 83–86.

Clermont, 1798

> Botting, Fred. "*Dracula,* Romance and Radcliffean Gothic." *Women's Writing* 1 (1994), 194–95.

ELIZABETH SINGER ROWE

Friendship in Death: In Twenty Letters from the Dead to the Living, 1728

> Prescott, Sarah. "The Debt to Pleasure: Eliza Haywood's *Love in Excess* and Women's Fiction of the 1720s." *Women's Writing* 7 (2000), 437–42.

SALMAN RUSHDIE

Grimus, 1975

> Cundy, Catherine. *Salman Rushdie,* 12–25.
> Hai, Ambreen. "'Marching In from the Peripheries': Rushdie's Feminized Artistry and Ambivalent Feminism," in M. Keith Booker, ed., *Critical Essays on Salman Rushdie,* 31–33.
> Israel, Nico. *Outlandish,* 130–37.
> Kuortti, Joel. *Fictions to Live In,* 34–51, 59–65.

The Ground Beneath Her Feet, 1999

> Pirbhai, Mariam. "The Paradox of Globalization as an 'Untotalizable Totality' in Salman Rushdie's *The Ground Beneath Her Feet." Intl Fiction R* 28:1–2 (2001), 54–66.

Haroun and the Sea of Stories, 1990

> Amirthanayagam, Guy. *The Marriage of Continents,* 294–96.
> Cundy, Catherine. *Salman Rushdie,* 85–93.
> Ellerby, Janet Mason. "Fiction under Siege: Rushdie's Quest for Narrative Emancipation in *Haroun and the Sea of Stories." Lion and the Unicorn* 22 (1998), 211–19.
> Goonetilleke, D. C. R. A. "*Haroun and the Sea of Stories* and Rushdie's Partial/Plural Identity." *World Lit Written in Engl* 35:2 (1996), 13–27.
> Kuortti, Joel. *Fictions to Live In,* 24–33.
> Lenz, Millicent. "The Magic of Story vs. the Panjandrums of Tyranny: Salman Rushdie's *Haroun and the Sea of Stories." Paradoxa* 2 (1996), 369–78.
> Merivale, Patricia. "The Telling of Lies and 'the Sea of Stories': *Haroun, Pinocchio* and the Postcolonial Artist Parable." *Ariel* 28:1 (1997), 193–206.
> Mukherjee, Meenakshi. *The Perishable Empire,* 149–63.
> Mukherjee, Meenakshi. "Politics and Children's Literature: A Reading of *Haroun and the Sea of Stories." Ariel* 29:1 (1998), 163–76.
> Petzold, Dieter. "Taking Games Seriously: Romantic Irony in Modern Fantasy for Children of All Ages," in James Holt McGavran, ed., *Literature and the Child,* 97–101.
> Plotz, Judith. "*Haroun* and the Politics of Children's Literature." *Children's Lit Assoc Q* 20:3 (1995), 100–104.

Reinfandt, Christoph. "'What's the Use of Stories that Aren't Even True?': Salman Rushdie as a Test Case for Literature and Literary Studies Today." *Literatur in Wissenschaft und Unterricht* 31 (1998), 85–89.

Schmidt-Haberkamp, Barbara. "Die Macht der Beschreibung: Salman Rushdies *Haroun and the Sea of Stories.*" *Poetica* (Munich) 32 (2000), 527–44.

Midnight's Children, 1981

Ball, John Clement. "Pessoptimism: Satire and the Menippean Grotesque in Rushdie's *Midnight's Children.*" *Engl Stud in Canada* 24 (1988), 61–78.

Bennett, Robert. "National Allegory or Carnivalesque Heteroglossia? *Midnight's Children*'s Narration of Indian National Identity." *Bucknell R* 43:2 (2000), 177–92.

Booker, M. Keith. "*Midnight's Children*, History, and Complexity: Reading Rushdie after the Cold War," in Booker, ed., *Critical Essays on Salman Rushdie*, 283–310.

Broich, Ulrich. "Memory and National Identity in Postcolonial Historical Fiction," in Heinz Antor and Kevin L. Cope, eds., *Intercultural Encounters*, 433–36.

Conner, Marc C. "*Midnight's Children* and the Apocalypse of Form." *Critique* (Washington, DC) 38 (1997), 289–98.

Cundy, Catherine. *Salman Rushdie*, 26–43.

Dutheil, Martine Hennard. "Rushdie's Affiliation with Dickens." *Dickens Stud Annual* 27 (1998), 209–21.

Dutheil de la Rochère, Martine Hennard. *Origin and Originality*, 1–34.

Fugmann, Nicole. "Situating Postmodern Aesthetics: Salman Rushdie's Spatial Historiography." *REAL: Yrbk of Res in Engl and Am Lit* 13 (1997), 336–38.

Ghosh, Bishnupriya. "An Invitation to Indian Postmodernity: Rushdie's English Vernacular as Situated Cultural Hybridity," in M. Keith Booker, ed., *Critical Essays on Salman Rushdie*, 147–50.

Göbel, Walter, and Damian Grant. "Salman Rushdie's Silver Medal," in David Pierce and Peter de Voogd, eds., *Laurence Sterne*, 88–98.

Green, David A. "Authoritarians and Chamchas: Social Milieux and Politics in Grass's *Die Blechtrommel* and Rushdie's *Midnight's Children*," in Susanne Stark, ed., *The Novel in Anglo-German Context*, 357–68.

Hai, Ambreen. "'Marching In from the Peripheries': Rushdie's Feminized Artistry and Ambivalent Feminism," in M. Keith Booker, ed., *Critical Essays on Salman Rushdie*, 27–29.

Heffernan, Teresa. "Apocalyptic Narratives: The Nation in Salman Rushdie's *Midnight's Children.*" *Twentieth Cent Lit* 46 (2000), 470–86.

Horrocks, David. "The Undisciplined Past: Novel Approaches to History in Grass and Rushdie," in Susanne Stark, ed., *The Novel in Anglo-German Context*, 347–55.

Huggan, Graham. *The Postcolonial Exotic*, 69–74.

Israel, Nico. *Outlandish*, 137–48.

Juneja, Om P. *Post Colonial Novel*, 98–101.

Juraga, Dubravka. "'The Mirror of Us All': *Midnight's Children* and the Twentieth-Century Bildungsroman," in M. Keith Booker, ed., *Critical Essays on Salman Rushdie*, 169–84.

Kortenaar, Neil ten. "Postcolonial Ekphrasis: Salman Rushdie Gives the Finger Back to the Empire." *Contemp Lit* 38 (1997), 232–58.

Kuchta, Todd M. "Allegorizing the Emergency: Rushdie's *Midnight's Children* and Benjamin's Theory of Allegory," in M. Keith Booker, ed., *Critical Essays on Salman Rushdie*, 205–21.

Kuortti, Joel. *Fictions to Live In*, 66–86.

Moss, Laura. "'Forget those damn fool realists!': Salman Rushdie's Self-Parody as the Magic Realist's *Last Sigh*." *Ariel* 29:4 (1998), 121–37.

Needham, Anuradha Dingwaney. *Using The Master's Tools*, 49–70.

Porée, Marc. "Les maisons aux esprits de Salman Rushdie." *Etudes Anglaises* 50 (1997), 169–81.

Ramsey-Kurz, Helga. "Does Saleem Really Miss the Spittoon?: Script and Scriptlessness in *Midnight's Children*." *J of Commonwealth Lit* 36:1 (2001), 127–42.

Reder, Michael. "Rewriting History and Identity: The Reinvention of Myth, Epic, and Allegory in Salman Rushdie's *Midnight's Children*," in M. Keith Booker, ed., *Critical Essays on Salman Rushdie*, 225–44.

Rege, Josna E. "Victim into Protagonist? *Midnight's Children* and the Post-Rushdie National Narratives of the Eighties." *Stud in the Novel* 29 (1997), 342–71.

Reinfandt, Christoph. *Der Sinn der fiktionalen Wirklichkeiten*, 330–53.

Reinfandt, Christoph. "'What's the Use of Stories that Aren't Even True?': Salman Rushdie as a Test Case for Literature and Literary Studies Today." *Literatur in Wissenschaft und Unterricht* 31 (1998), 77–80.

Skinner, John. *The Stepmother Tongue*, 329–30.

Thompson, Jon. "Superman and Salman Rushdie: *Midnight's Children* and the Disillusionment of History." *J of Commonwealth and Postcolonial Stud* 3:1 (1995), 1–23.

The Moor's Last Sigh, 1995

Baker, Stephen. "'You Must Remember This': Salman Rushdie's *The Moor's Last Sigh*." *J of Commonwealth Lit* 35:1 (2000), 43–54.

Ball, John Clement. "Acid in the Nation's Bloodstream: Satire, Violence, and the Indian Body Politic in Salman Rushdie's *The Moor's Last Sigh*." *Intl Fiction R* 27:1–2 (2000), 37–47.

Brînzeu, Pia. *Corridors of Mirrors*, 116–19.

Brînzeu, Pia. "A Palimpsest City: Bombay in Salman Rushdie's *The Moor's Last Sigh*." *B.A.S.: Brit and Am Stud* 1999: 9–14.

Cantor, Paul A. "Tales of the Alhambra: Rushdie's Use of Spanish History in *The Moor's Last Sigh*." *Stud in the Novel* 29 (1997), 323–37.

Chamlou, Laurence. "Paysages de l'entre-deux ou la langue en exil." *Imaginaires* 5 (2000), 135–46.

Cundy, Catherine. *Salman Rushdie*, 110–17.

Dutheil, Martine Hennard. "Rushdie's Affiliation with Dickens." *Dickens Stud Annual* 27 (1998), 209–21.

Dutheil de la Rochère, Martine Hennard. *Origin and Originality*, 20–23.

Ganapathy-Doré, Geetha. "A Counterpoint to History: The Feminine in Salman Rushdie's *The Moor's Last Sigh*," in Sophie Marret, ed., *Féminin/Masculin*, 175–83.

Ghosh, Bishnupriya. "An Invitation to Indian Postmodernity: Rushdie's English Vernacular as Situated Cultural Hybridity," in M. Keith Booker, ed., *Critical Essays on Salman Rushdie*, 135–47.

Greenberg, Jonathan. "'The Base Indian' or 'the Base Judean'?: *Othello* and the Metaphor of the Palimpsest in Salman Rushdie's *The Moor's Last Sigh*." *Mod Lang Stud* 29:2 (1999), 93–106.

Hai, Ambreen. "'Marching In from the Peripheries': Rushdie's Feminized Artistry and Ambivalent Feminism," in M. Keith Booker, ed., *Critical Essays on Salman Rushdie*, 41–47.

Henighan, Stephen. "Coming to Benengeli: The Genesis of Salman Rushdie's Rewriting of Juan Rulfo in *The Moor's Last Sigh*." *J of Commonwealth Lit* 33:2 (1998), 55–72.

Idris, Farhad B. "*The Moor's Last Sigh* and India's National Bourgeoisie: Reading Rushdie through Frantz Fanon," in M. Keith Booker, ed., *Critical Essays on Salman Rushdie*, 154–66.

Kuortti, Joel. *Fictions to Live In*, 183–218.

Lange, Bernd-Peter. "Dislocations: Migrancy in Nabokov and Rushdie." *Anglia* 117 (1999), 405–11.

Lange, Bernd-Peter. "Postcolonial Gothic: Salman Rushdie's *The Moor's Last Sigh*." *Literatur in Wissenschaft und Unterricht* 31 (1998), 365–75.

McNab, Chris. "Derrida, Rushdie and the Ethics of Mortality," in Andrew Hadfield et al., eds., *The Ethics in Literature*, 142–50.

Moss, Laura. "'Forget those damn fool realists!': Salman Rushdie's Self-Parody as the Magic Realist's *Last Sigh*." *Ariel* 29:4 (1998), 121–37.

Neumann, Fritz-Wilhelm. "*The Moor's Last Sigh*: Rushdie's Intercultural Family Saga," in Heinz Antor and Kevin L. Cope, eds., *Intercultural Encounters*, 467–78.

Porée, Marc. "Les maisons aux esprits de Salman Rushdie." *Etudes Anglaises* 50 (1997), 169–81.

Reinfandt, Christoph. "'What's the Use of Stories that Aren't Even True?': Salman Rushdie as a Test Case for Literature and Literary Studies Today." *Literatur in Wissenschaft und Unterricht* 31 (1998), 75–76, 80–81.

Rushdie, Salman. "*The Moor's Last Sight*" (interview with Charlie Rose, 1996), in Michael R. Reder. ed., *Conversations with Salman Rushdie*, 199–215.

Sood, Sujay. "The Politics of Escapism: Rushdie's *The Moor's Last Sigh*." *Commonwealth Essays and Studies* 19:1 (1996), 96–101.

Wallhead, Celia M. "The Subversive Sub-Text of Spices in Salman Rushdie's *The Moor's Last Sigh*." *Revista Canaria de Estudios Ingleses* 35 (1997), 61–76.

Weiss, Timothy. "Rushdie's Xanadu: Radical Typology in *The Moor's Last Sigh*." *New Comparison* 27/28 (1999), 314–24.

Wormald, Mark. "The Uses of Impurity: Fiction and Fundamentalism in Salman Rushdie and Jeanette Winterson," in Rod Mengham, ed., *An Introduction to Contemporary Fiction*, 200–201.

The Satanic Verses, 1988

Al-Raheb, Hani. "Religious Satire in Rushdie's *Satanic Verses*." *J of the Fantastic in the Arts* 6 (1995), 330–39.

Amirthanayagam, Guy. *The Marriage of Continents*, 296–321.

Baucom, Ian. *Out of Place*, 200–217.

Brennan, Timothy. "The Cultural Politics of Rushdie Criticism: All or Nothing," in M. Keith Booker, ed., *Critical Essays on Salman Rushdie*, 107–26.

Brînzeu, Pia. *Corridors of Mirrors*, 36–37, 87–89.

Cody, Michael. "Rushdie's *The Satanic Verses*." *Explicator* 56:4 (1998), 218–20.

Cundy, Catherine. *Salman Rushdie*, 65–84.

Davies, Mark. "Aspects of the Grotesque in Rushdie's *The Satanic Verses*," in Alice Mills, ed., *Seriously Weird*, 51–61.

Doody, Terrence. *Among Other Things*, 248–52.

Dutheil, Martine Hennard. "The Epigraph to *The Satanic Verses*: Defoe's Devil and Rushdie's Migrant." *Southern R* (Adelaide) 30 (1997), 51–67.

Dutheil, Martine Hennard. "From Orality to Literacy: The Case of *The Satanic Verses*." *Swiss Papers in Engl Lang and Lit* 11 (1998), 117–27.

Dutheil, Martine Hennard. "Rushdie's Affiliation with Dickens." *Dickens Stud Annual* 27 (1998), 209–21.

Dutheil de la Rochère, Martine Hennard. *Origin and Originality*, ix–xxxiv, 1–221.

Finney, Brian. "Demonizing Discourse in Salman Rushdie's *The Satanic Verses*." *Ariel* 29:3 (1998), 67–92.

Fort, Camille. "*The Satanic Verses*: portrait de Satan en bouc émissaire." *Recherches Anglaises et Nord-Américaines* 32 (1999), 29–41.

François, Pierre. *Inlets of the Soul*, 209–54.

Fugmann, Nicole. "Situating Postmodern Aesthetics: Salman Rushdie's Spatial Historiography." *REAL: Yrbk of Res in Engl and Am Lit* 13 (1997), 333–43.

Gibson, Andrew. *Postmodernity, Ethics and the Novel*, 207–9.

Gikandi, Simon. *Maps of Englishness*, 205–25.

Hai, Ambreen. "'Marching In from the Peripheries': Rushdie's Feminized Artistry and Ambivalent Feminism," in M. Keith Booker, ed., *Critical Essays on Salman Rushdie*, 20–25, 32–39.

Harris, Susan Cannon. "Invasive Procedures: Imperial Medicine and Population Control in *Ulysses* and *The Satanic Verses*." *James Joyce Q* 35:2–3 (1998), 373–96.

Höfele, Andreas. "Wasteland Sprouting: Salman Rushdie's *The Satanic Verses* and the Cityscapes of Modernism," in Richard Todd and Luisa Flora, eds., *Theme Parks*, 41–54.

Huggan, Graham. *The Postcolonial Exotic*, 90–95.

Israel, Nico. *Outlandish*, 157–74.

Ivory, James Maurice. *Identity and Narrative Metamorphoses*, 133–47.

Juneja, Om P. *Post Colonial Novel*, 104–6.

Kolodziejczyk, Dorota. "*The Satanic Verses* and the Rushdie Affair: Reading the Blasphemy." *Anglica Wratislaviensia* 33 (1998), 81–93.

Kuortti, Joel. *Fictions to Live In*, 125–71.

Kuortti, Joel. "'Nomsense': Salman Rushdie's *The Satanic Verses*." *Textual Practice* 13 (1999), 137–44.

Masse, Sophie. "Language versus Language in *The Satanic Verses*." *Commonwealth Essays and Studies* 20:1 (1997), 72–76.

May, Brian. "Memorials to Modernity: Postcolonial Pilgrimage in Naipaul and Rushdie." *ELH* 68 (2001), 241–62.

Phillips, Kathy J. "Salman Rushdie's *The Satanic Verses* as a Feminist Novel," in Cristina Bacchilega and Cornelia N. Moore, eds., *Constructions and Confrontations*, 103–7.

Porée, Marc. "Les maisons aux esprits de Salman Rushdie." *Etudes Anglaises* 50 (1997), 169–81.

Quayson, Ato. *Postcolonialism*, 79–84.

Reinfandt, Christoph. "'What's the Use of Stories that Aren't Even True?': Salman Rushdie as a Test Case for Literature and Literary Studies Today." *Literatur in Wissenschaft und Unterricht* 31 (1998), 82–85.

Rushdie, Salman. "*Satanic Verses*" (interview with W. L. Webb, 1988), in Michael R. Reder. ed., *Conversations with Salman Rushdie*, 87–100.

Sawhney, Simona. "Satanic Choices: Poetry and Prophecy in Rushdie's Novel." *Twentieth Cent Lit* 45 (1999), 253–74.

Scarpetta, Guy. *L'âge d'or du roman*, 27–61.

Schoene, Berthold. "Herald of Hybridity: The Emancipation of Difference in Hanif Kureishi's *The Buddha of Suburbia*." *Intl J of Cultural Stud* 1:1 (1998), 109–28.

Schulze-Engler, Frank. "Riding the Crisis: *The Satanic Verses* and the Silences of Literary Theory," in Peter O. Stummer and Christopher Balme, eds., *Fusion of Cultures?*, 193–203.

Su, Jung. "Crossing Frontiers: Diaspora Identity in *The Satanic Verses*." *EurAmerica* 29:1 (1999), 1–56.

Wormald, Mark. "The Uses of Impurity: Fiction and Fundamentalism in Salman Rushdie and Jeanette Winterson," in Rod Mengham, ed., *An Introduction to Contemporary Fiction*, 182–88, 194–96.

Shame, 1983

Coundouriotis, Eleni. "Materialism, the Uncanny, and History in Toni Morrison and Salman Rushdie." *LIT* 8 (1997), 207–22.

Cundy, Catherine. *Salman Rushdie*, 44–64.

Dayal, Samir. "The Liminalities of Nation and Gender: Salman Rushdie's *Shame*." *J of the Midwest Mod Lang Assoc* 31:2 (1998), 39–58.

Dutheil, Martine Hennard. "Rushdie's Affiliation with Dickens." *Dickens Stud Annual* 27 (1998), 209–21.

Dutheil de la Rochère, Martine Hennard. *Origin and Originality*, 1–5, 20–24, 27–34.

Fugmann, Nicole. "Situating Postmodern Aesthetics: Salman Rushdie's Spatial Historiography." *REAL: Yrbk of Res in Engl and Am Lit* 13 (1997), 336–41.

Hai, Ambreen. "'Marching In from the Peripheries': Rushdie's Feminized Artistry and Ambivalent Feminism," in M. Keith Booker, ed., *Critical Essays on Salman Rushdie*, 16–31.

Israel, Nico. *Outlandish*, 148–57.

Juneja, Om P. *Post Colonial Novel*, 102–4.

Kuortti, Joel. *Fictions to Live In*, 93–119.

Needham, Anuradha Dingwaney. *Using The Master's Tools*, 65–69.

O'Farrell, Mary Ann. *Telling Complexions*, 137–40.

Porée, Marc. "Les maisons aux esprits de Salman Rushdie." *Etudes Anglaises* 50 (1997), 169–81.

Reinfandt, Christoph. "'What's the Use of Stories that Aren't Even True?': Salman Rushdie as a Test Case for Literature and Literary Studies Today." *Literatur in Wissenschaft und Unterricht* 31 (1998), 81–82.

Su, Jung. "Articulating Silence: The Expropriation of the Periphery in *Shame*." *EurAmerica* 30:2 (2000), 71–109.

WILLIAM CLARK RUSSELL

The Deceased Wife's Sister, 1874

Gruner, Elisabeth Rose. "Born and Made: Sisters, Brothers, and the Deceased Wife's Sister Bill." *Signs* 24 (1999), 437–40.

JAMES RYAN

Home From England, 1995

Smyth, Gerry. *The Novel and the Nation*, 148–50.

VITA SACKVILLE-WEST

The Edwardians, 1930

Weatherhead, A. K. *Upstairs*, 74–80.

SIEGFRIED SASSOON

Memoirs of an Infantry Officer, 1937

Sillars, Stuart. *Structure and Dissolution*, 148–53.

DOROTHY L. SAYERS

Busman's Honeymoon, 1937

Brown, Janice. *The Seven Deadly Sins*, 173–213.

McGregor, Robert Kuhn. *Conundrums for the Long Week-End*, 85–87.

Owen, Kathleen Belin. "'The Game's Afoot': Predecessors and Pursuits of a Postmodern Detective Novel," in Jerome H. Delamater and Ruth Prigozy, eds., *Theory and Practice*, 76–78.

Rowland, Susan. *From Agatha Christie to Ruth Rendell*, 74–77.

Clouds of Witness, 1926

McGregor, Robert Kuhn. *Conundrums for the Long Week-End*, 55–57.

Rowland, Susan. *From Agatha Christie to Ruth Rendell*, 124–26.

The Five Red Herrings, 1931

McGregor, Robert Kuhn. *Conundrums for the Long Week-End*, 91–94, 131–34.

Gaudy Night, 1936

Brown, Janice. *The Seven Deadly Sins*, 147–72.

Dougill, John. *Oxford in English Literature*, 215–18.

Frank, Marion. "The Transformation of a Genre: The Feminist Mystery Novel," in Susanne Fendler, ed., *Feminist Contributions*, 85–92.

Glover, David. "The Writers Who Knew Too Much: Populism and Paradox in Detective Fiction's Golden Age," in Warren Chernaik et al., eds., *The Art of Detective Fiction*, 44–48.

Hall, Jasmine Y. "A Suitable Job for a Woman: Sexuality, Motherhood, and Professionalism in *Gaudy Night*," in Jerome H. Delamater and Ruth Prigozy, eds., *Theory and Practice*, 169–76.

Kline, Barbara. "Medieval Romance Cloaked in Detective Fiction: Sayers' *Gaudy Night*." *Stud in Medievalism* 6:suppl (1996), 92–101.

McFadden, Marya. "Queerness at Shrewsbury: Homoerotic Desire in *Gaudy Night*." *Mod Fiction Stud* 46 (2000), 355–76.

McGregor, Robert Kuhn. *Conundrums for the Long Week-End*, 162–64, 166–72.

Maassen, Irmgard. "An Unsuitable Job for a Woman? Gender, Genre and the New Detective Heroine," in H. Gustav Klaus and Stephen Knight, eds., *The Art of Murder*, 156–57.

Rowland, Susan. *From Agatha Christie to Ruth Rendell*, 171–73.

Have His Carcase, 1932

McGregor, Robert Kuhn. *Conundrums for the Long Week-End*, 134–40, 155–57, 173–75.

Murder Must Advertise, 1933

Brown, Janice. *The Seven Deadly Sins*, 115–31.

McGregor, Robert Kuhn. *Conundrums for the Long Week-End*, 143–45, 148–49.

Rowland, Susan. *From Agatha Christie to Ruth Rendell*, 51–54.

The Nine Tailors, 1934

Brown, Janice. *The Seven Deadly Sins*, 131–47.

McGregor, Robert Kuhn. *Conundrums for the Long Week-End*, 91–92, 106–9, 153–54.

Rowland, Susan. *From Agatha Christie to Ruth Rendell*, 146–48.

Strong Poison, 1930

Berglund, Birgitta. "Desires and Devices: On Women Detectives in

Fiction," in Warren Chernaik et al., eds., *The Art of Detective Fiction*, 140–42.

Brown, Janice. *The Seven Deadly Sins*, 80–82.

McGregor, Robert Kuhn. *Conundrums for the Long Week-End*, 82–83, 87–88, 91–92, 122–23.

Rowland, Susan. *From Agatha Christie to Ruth Rendell*, 29–30.

Stephenson, Will, and Mimosa Stephenson. "Launcelot and Lord Peter: A Medieval Murder Mystery and a Modern Analog." *Clues* 19:1 (1998), 19–23.

The Unpleasantness at the Bellona Club, 1928

McGregor, Robert Kuhn. *Conundrums for the Long Week-End*, 66–67, 70–73, 78–79.

Rowland, Susan. *From Agatha Christie to Ruth Rendell*, 100–102.

Whose Body?, 1923

McGregor, Robert Kuhn. *Conundrums for the Long Week-End*, 23–25, 30–35.

Turnbull, Malcolm J. *Victims or Villains*, 90–91.

OLIVE SCHREINER

From Man to Man, 1926

Burdett, Carolyn. "Capturing the Ideal: Olive Schreiner's *From Man to Man*," in Angelique Richardson and Chris Willis, eds., *The New Woman in Fiction and in Fact*, 167–80.

Burdett, Carolyn. *Olive Schreiner and the Progress of Feminism*, 88–108.

Clayton, Cherry. *Olive Schreiner*, 60–73.

Heilmann, Ann. "Feminist Resitance, the Artist and 'A Room of One's Own' in New Woman Fiction." *Women's Writing* 2 (1995), 301–3.

Lovell-Smith, Rose. "From Man to Man: Scientific and Religious Reference in a Feminist Novel." *Australasian Victorian Stud J* 2 (1996), 33–42.

McCracken, Scott. "Stages of Sand and Blood: The Performance of Gendered Subjectivity in Olive Schreiner's Colonial Allegories," in Alice Jenkins and Juliet John, eds., *Rereading Victorian Fiction*, 148–56.

The Story of an African Farm, 1883

Ardis, Ann. "Organizing Women: New Woman Writers, New Woman Readers, and Suffrage Feminism," in Nicola Diane Thompson, ed., *Victorian Women Writers*, 190–95.

Buckton, Oliver S. "Race, Gender, and Anti-Pastoral Critique in Doris Lessing's *The Grass is Singing* and Olive Schreiner's *The Story of an African Farm*." *Doris Lessing Newsl* 20:2 (1999), 8–11.

Burdett, Carolyn. *Olive Schreiner and the Progress of Feminism*, 17–45.

Clayton, Cherry. *Olive Schreiner*, 40–59.

Dyson, Mandy. "The Feminist as Romantic: Schreiner's Lyndall and the Romance Plot." *Australasian Victorian Stud J* 3:1 (1997), 90–97.

GoGwilt, Christopher. *The Fiction of Geopolitics*, 106–23.

Green, Louise. "The Unhealed Wound: Olive Schreiner's Expressive Art." *Pretexts* 6:1 (1997), 21–34.

Heilmann, Ann. "Masquerade, Sisterhood and the Dilemma of the Feminist as Artist and Woman in Late Nineteenth-Century British Women's Writing." *J of Gender Stud* 3 (1994), 160–61.

Knox-Shaw, Peter. "Unicorns on Rocks: The Expressionism of Olive Schreiner." *Engl Stud in Africa* 40:2 (1997), 13–29.

Krebs, Paula M. "Olive Schreiner's Racialization of South Africa." *Victorian Stud* 40:3 (1997), 440–43.

Lane, Christopher. *The Burdens of Intimacy*, 92–114.

Larson, Jil. *Ethics and Narrative in the English Novel*, 57–63.

Larson, Jil. "Sexual Ethics in Fiction by Thomas Hardy and the New Woman Writers," in Alice Jenkins and Juliet John, eds., *Rereading Victorian Fiction*, 161–63, 168–70.

Ledger, Sally. *The New Woman*, 77–83.

Lewis, Simon. "Graves with a View: Atavism and the European History of Africa." *Ariel* 27:1 (1996), 40–60.

McCracken, Scott. "Stages of Sand and Blood: The Performance of Gendered Subjectivity in Olive Schreiner's Colonial Allegories," in Alice Jenkins and Juliet John, eds., *Rereading Victorian Fiction*, 145–56.

Mohr, Hans Ulrich. "Drei Konstrukte weiblicher Verhaltensräume: Charlotte Smith, Olive Schreiner, Angela Carter." *Arbeiten aus Anglistik und Amerikanistik* 20 (1995), 317–33.

Murphy, Patricia. "Timely Interruptions: Unsettling Gender through Temporality in *The Story of an African Farm*." *Style* 32:1 (1998), 80–101.

Ogede, Ode. "An Early Image of Apartheid and Post-Apartheid Society: Olive Schreiner's *The Story of an African Farm*." *J of African Cultural Stud* 13 (2000), 251–56.

Partenza, Paola. "'Without Dreams and Phantoms Man Cannot Exist': La voce senza confini di Olive Schreiner." *Rivista di Studi Vittoriani* 2:3 (1997), 111–25.

Smith, Malvern van Wyk. "Napoleon and the Giant: Discursive Conflicts in Olive Schreiner's *Story of an African Farm*." *Ariel* 30:1 (1999), 151–63.

Späth, Eberhard. "Olive Schreiner, *The Story of an African Farm*: Zur Rezeption Afrikas in einem Roman und seiner Kritik," in Titus Heydenreich and Eberhard Späth, eds., *Afrika in den europäischen Literaturen*, 245–70.

Stott, Rebecca. "'Scaping the Body: Of Cannibal Mothers and Colonial Landscapes," in Angelique Richardson and Chris Willis, eds., *The New Woman in Fiction and in Fact*, 160–64.

Waterman, David. "Olive Schreiner's *The Story of an African Farm*: Power, Gender and Age." *Engl Stud in Africa* 40:1 (1997), 43–60.

Waterman, David F. *Disordered Bodies and Disrupted Borders*, 59–79.

Trooper Peter Halket, 1897

Burdett, Carolyn. "Love, Death and Money in Mashonaland: Olive Schreiner's *Trooper Peter Halket*." *Kunapipi* 21:3 (1999), 36–43.

Burdett, Carolyn. *Olive Schreiner and the Progress of Feminism*, 124–35.

Clayton, Cherry. *Olive Schreiner*, 95–101.

Ledger, Sally. *The New Woman*, 86–90.

Lewis, Simon. "Graves with a View: Atavism and the European History of Africa." *Ariel* 27:1 (1996), 40–60.

Stanley, Liz. "Encountering the Imperial and Colonial Past through Olive Schreiner's *Trooper Peter Halket of Mashonaland*." *Women's Writing* 7 (2000), 197–215.

Undine, 1929

Burdett, Carolyn. *Olive Schreiner and the Progress of Feminism*, 14–16.

Clayton, Cherry. *Olive Schreiner*, 29–39.

MANDA SCOTT

Hen's Teeth, 1996

Hutton, Elaine. "Good Lesbians, Bad Men and Happy Endings," in Hutton, ed., *Beyond Sex and Romance?*, 197–99.

PAUL SCOTT

The Jewel in the Crown, 1966

Bachmann, Holger. "Speaking of the Raj: Language in Paul Scott's *The Jewel in the Crown*." *English* 46 (1997), 227–47.

Dyer, Richard. "'There's Nothing I Can Do! Nothing!': Femininity, Seriality and Whiteness in *The Jewel in the Crown*." *Screen* 37 (1996), 225–39.

Lal, Malashri. "Questioning Otherness: Racial Indeterminacy in Kipling, Tagore and Paul Scott." *In-Between* 3:1 (1994), 3–13.

The Raj Quartet, 1976

Brann, Eva. "Tapestry with Images: Paul Scott's Raj Novels." *Philos and Lit* 23:1 (1999), 181–96.

Childs, Peter. *Paul Scott's "Raj Quartet": History and Division*.

Haswell, Janis. "Advancing the Dialogue: Reading Paul Scott's *Raj Quartet*." *Stud in the Novel* 32:1 (2000), 70–77.

Sharma, J. N. "The Bibighar Episode: Narration in *The Raj Quartet*." *In-Between* 5:1 (1995), 51–63.

Wijesinha, Rajiva. "Travesties: Romance and Reality in the *Raj Quartet*." *J of Compar Lit and Aesthetics* (Orissa, India) 21:1–2 (1998), 105–19.

Staying On, 1977

Amirthanayagam, Guy. *The Marriage of Continents*, 173–81.

Baneth-Nouailhetas, Emilienne. "Fatherland and Mother-Tongues in *Staying On*." *Commonwealth Essays and Stud* 4 (1997), 65–71.

Butler, Lance St. John. *Registering the Difference*, 84–88.

SARAH SCOTT

A Description of Millenium Hall, 1762

Bannet, Eve Tavor. *The Domestic Revolution,* 169–74.

Barchas, Janine. "Prefiguring Genre: Frontispiece Portraits from *Gulliver's Travels* to *Millenium Hall." Stud in the Novel* 30 (1998), 279–81.

Barney, Richard A. *Plots of Enlightenment,* 189–93.

Child, Elizabeth. "'To Sing the Town': Women, Place, and Print Culture in Eighteenth-Century Bath." *Stud in Eighteenth-Cent Culture* 28 (1999), 163–67.

Cruise, James. *Governing Consumption,* 190–91.

Guest, Harriet. *Small Change,* 43–45, 73–75, 95–98.

Haggerty, George E. *Unnatural Affections,* 88–102.

London, April. *Women and Property,* 110–21.

Moore, Lisa L. *Dangerous Intimacies,* 22–48, 71–78.

Morton, Nanette. "'A Most Sensible Oeconomy': From Spectacle to Surveillance in Sarah Scott's *Millenium Hall." Eighteenth-Cent Fiction* 11 (1999), 185–204.

Mudge, Bradford K. *The Whore's Story,* 214–18.

Nussbaum, Felicity A. "Feminotopias: The Pleasures of 'Deformity' in Mid-Eighteenth-Century England," in David T. Mitchell and Sharon L. Snyder, eds., *The Body and Physical Difference,* 161–70.

Pohl, Nicole. "'Sweet Place, Where Virtue Then Did Rest': The Appropriation of the Country-House Ethos in Sarah Scott's *Millenium Hall." Utopian Stud* 7:1 (1996), 49–59.

Stockstill, Ashley. "Better Homes and Gardens: The Fairy World(s) of Sarah Fielding and Sarah Scott." *Feminist Stud in Engl Lit* 6 (1998), 137–58.

The History of Sir George Ellison, 1766

Bannet, Eve Tavor. *The Domestic Revolution,* 167–69.

Ellis, Markman. *The Politics of Sensibility,* 87–114.

Guest, Harriet. *Small Change,* 44–47.

Guest, Harriet. "'These Neuter Somethings': Gender Difference and Commercial Culture in Mid-Eighteenth-Century England," in Kevin Sharpe and Steven N. Zwicker, eds., *Refiguring Revolutions,* 185–94.

Lutz, Alfred. "Commercial Capitalism, Classical Republicanism, and the Man of Sensibility in *The History of Sir George Ellison." Stud in Engl Lit, 1500–1900* 39 (1999), 557–69.

Moore, Lisa L. *Dangerous Intimacies,* 40–42.

Nussbaum, Felicity A. "Women and Race: 'A Difference of Complexion,'" in Vivien Jones, ed., *Women and Literature in Britain,* 77–84.

Wheeler, Roxann. "The Complexion of Desire: Racial Ideology and Mid-Eighteenth-Century British Novels." *Eighteenth-Cent Stud* 32 (1999), 315–16.

Woodard, Helena. *African-British Writings in the Eighteenth Century,* 76–78.

A Journey Through Every Stage of Life, 1754
    London, April. *Women and Property*, 110–14.

WALTER SCOTT

The Abbot, 1820
    Gilmartin, Sophie. *Ancestry and Narrative*, 68–83, 98–100.
The Antiquary, 1816
    Jackson-Houlston, C. M. *Ballads, Songs and Snatches*, 23–30.
    Lee, Yoon Sun. "A Divided Inheritance: Scott's Antiquarian Novel and the British Nation." *ELH* 64 (1997), 537–63.
    Ragaz, Sharon. "'The Truth in Masquerade': Byron's *Don Juan* and Walter Scott's *The Antiquary*." *Keats-Shelley J* 48 (1999), 30–34.
    Sutherland, Sheena. "'Antiquarian Old-Womanries'?: The Use of Quotation and the Subjectivisation of the Past in Scott's *The Antiquary*." *Scottish Liter J* 25:1 (1998), 37–44.
    Trumpener, Katie. *Bardic Nationalism*, 120–24.
    Watson, Nicola J. *Revolution and the Form of the British Novel*, 142–48.
The Betrothed, 1825
    Mitchell, Jerome. "Scott and Medieval Romance: Further Parallels," in Stefan Horlacher and Marion Islinger, eds., *Expedition nach der Wahrheit*, 546–49.
The Bride of Lammermoor, 1819
    Alexander, J. H. "'Das Goldene Schloss': A Likely Source for *The Bride of Lammermoor*." *Scott Newsl* 34 (1999), 2–6.
    Alexander, J. H. "Editing *The Bride of Lammermoor* and *A Legend of the Wars of Montrose*." *Scott Newsl* 32 (1998), 6–12.
    Bellamy, Liz. "Regionalism and Nationalism: Maria Edgeworth, Walter Scott and the Definition of Britishness," in K. D. M. Snell, ed., *The Regional Novel*, 71–72.
    Brookes, Gerry H. "Freedom and Responsibility in *The Bride of Lammermoor*." *Stud in Scottish Lit* 31 (1999), 131–50.
    Burgess, Miranda J. *British Fiction and the Production of Social Order*, 203–11.
    Chandler, James. *England in 1819*, 322–47.
    Fay, Elizabeth A. *A Feminist Introduction to Romanticism*, 139–43.
    Klein, Scott W. "National Histories, National Fictions: Joyce's *A Portrait of the Artist as a Young Man* and Scott's *The Bride of Lammermoor*." *ELH* 65 (1998), 1017–34.
    Mitchell, Jerome. "Scott and Medieval Romance: Further Parallels," in Stefan Horlacher and Marion Islinger, eds., *Expedition nach der Wahrheit*, 544–46.
    O'Neill, James N. "Scott's Bride and Tennyson's Maud." *Tennyson Res Bull* 7:1 (1997), 25–31.
    Simmons, Clare A. "Scottish Waste as Romantic Problem." *Wordsworth Circle* 31:2 (2000), 89–93.
    Sorensen, Janet. "Writing Historically, Speaking Nostalgically: The

Competing Languages of Nation in Scott's *The Bride of Lammermoor*," in Jean Pickering and Suzanne Kehde, eds., *Narratives of Nostalgia*, 30–49.

Ward, Ian. "Scott and the Waverley Constitution: A Study in Literary Constitutionalism." *Engl Stud* (Amsterdam) 79 (1998), 205–11.

Watt, James. *Contesting the Gothic*, 148–52.

Count Robert of Paris, 1831

Larrissy, Edward. "Yeats's 'Sailing to Byzantium' and Scott's *Count Robert of Paris*." *Notes and Queries* 42 (1995), 210–11.

Mitchell, Jerome. "Scott and Medieval Romance: Further Parallels," in Stefan Horlacher and Marion Islinger, eds., *Expedition nach der Wahrheit*, 549–52.

Stevenson, A. G. "A *Count Robert* Fragment (NLS MS 23140)." *Scott Newsl* 32 (1998), 16–19.

The Fortunes of Nigel, 1822

Burke, John J., Jr. "The Homoerotic Subtext in Scott's *The Fortunes of Nigel*: The Question of Evidence." *Clio* 29 (2000), 295–314.

Lackey, Lionel. "*Nigel* and *Peveril*: Scott and Gender Roles." *Engl Lang Notes* 37:3 (2000), 36–45.

Guy Mannering, 1815

Burgess, Miranda J. *British Fiction and the Production of Social Order*, 192–97.

Dekker, George G. "Border and Frontier: Tourism in Scott's *Guy Mannering* and Cooper's *The Pioneers*." *James Fenimore Cooper Soc Misc Papers* 9 (1997), 1–6.

Ferns, Chris. "Walter Scott, J. G. Farrell, and the Dialogics of Historical Fiction," in Ralph J. Crane, ed., *J. G. Farrell*, 137–41.

Ireland, Ken. *The Sequential Dynamics of Narrative*, 191–92.

Irvine, Robert P. "Enlightenment, Agency, and Romance: The Case of Scott's *Guy Mannering*." *J of Narrative Theory* 30 (2000), 29–50.

Lincoln, Andrew. "Scott's *Guy Mannering*: The Limits and Limitations of Anglo-British Identity." *Scottish Liter J* 26:1 (1999), 48–59.

Stitt, Megan Perigoe. *Metaphors of Change*, 61–65, 80–82, 92–95, 105–9, 116–20, 127–30.

Trumpener, Katie. *Bardic Nationalism*, 218–23, 236–38.

Watson, Nicola J. *Revolution and the Form of the British Novel*, 135–41.

The Heart of Midlothian, 1818

Austin, Carolyn F. "Home and Nation in *The Heart of Midlothian*." *Stud in Engl Lit, 1500–1900* 40 (2000), 621–33.

Chandler, James. *England in 1819*, 309–20.

Chun, Seung-hei. "Walter Scott's Historicism in *The Heart of Midlothian*." *J of Engl Lang and Lit* 41 (1995), 359–75.

Dolin, Kieran. *Fiction and the Law*, 51–70.

Hannaford, Richard. "Dumbiedikes, Ratcliffe, and a Surprising Jeanie Deans: Comic Alternatives in *The Heart of Mid-lothian*." *Stud in the Novel* 30 (1998), 1–15.

Ireland, Ken. *The Sequential Dynamics of Narrative*, 192.

Jackson-Houlston, C. M. *Ballads, Songs and Snatches*, 39–45.

Krueger, Christine L. "Literary Defenses and Medical Prosecutions: Representing Infanticide in Nineteenth-Century Britain." *Victorian Stud* 40:2 (1997), 279–80.

Lincoln, Andrew. "Conciliation, Resistance and the Unspeakable in *The Heart of Mid-Lothian*." *Philol Q* 79 (2000), 69–86.

Melrose, Andrew. "Writing 'The end of uncertainty': Imaginary Law, Imaginary Jacobites and Imaginary History in Walter Scott's *Heart of Midlothian* and *Redgauntlet*." *Scottish Liter J* 25:2 (1998), 34–42.

Schor, Hilary M. "Show-Trials: Character, Conviction and the Law in Victorian Fiction." *Cardozo Stud in Law and Lit* 11 (1999), 179–95.

Schramm, Jan-Melissa. *Testimony and Advocacy*, 95–98.

Shaw, Harry E. *Narrating Reality*, 213–17.

Stevenson, A. G. "'Indian Peter' and Scott's Interest in North American Natives." *Scott Newsl* 33 (1998), 13–16.

Stevenson, A. G. "Indian Peter and the Whistler: Kidnapping and North American Indians in *The Heart of Midlothian*." *Wordsworth Circle* 29 (1998), 162–64.

Stitt, Megan Perigoe. *Metaphors of Change*, 157–60, 162–66, 174–76.

Walker, Marshall. *Scottish Literature since 1707*, 132–36.

Ward, Ian. "The Jurisprudential Heart of Midlothian." *Scottish Liter J* 24:1 (1997), 25–36.

Ward, Ian. "Scott and the Waverley Constitution: A Study in Literary Constitutionalism." *Engl Stud* (Amsterdam) 79 (1998), 198–205.

Ivanhoe, 1819

Barczewski, Stephanie L. *Myth and National Identity*, 129–31.

Butler, Lance St. John. *Registering the Difference*, 129–31.

Dyer, Gary. "Irresolute Ravishers and the Sexual Economy of Chivalry in the Romantic Novel." *Nineteenth-Cent Lit* 55 (2000), 343–54, 366–68.

Dyer, Gary R. "*Ivanhoe*, Chivalry, and the Murder of Mary Ashford." *Criticism* 39 (1997), 383–402.

Ireland, Ken. *The Sequential Dynamics of Narrative*, 192–93.

Mitchell, Jerome. "Scott and Medieval Romance: Further Parallels," in Stefan Horlacher and Marion Islinger, eds., *Expedition nach der Wahrheit*, 546.

Morillo, John, and Wade Newhouse. "History, Romance, and the Sublime Sound of Truth in *Ivanhoe*." *Stud in the Novel* 32 (2000), 267–91.

Stitt, Megan Perigoe. *Metaphors of Change*, 23–27.

Tulloch, Graham. "A Note on *Ivanhoe*." *Scott Newsl* 32 (1998), 12–14.

Watt, James. *Contesting the Gothic*, 144–46.

Kenilworth, 1821

Garbin, Lydia. "Shakespeare at *Kenilworth*." *Scott Newsl* 35 (1999), 6–14.

Lackey, Lionel. "*Kenilworth*: Scott and Historical Honesty." *Scottish Liter J* 24:1 (1997), 40–51.

The Legend of Montrose, 1819

> Alexander, J. H. "Editing *The Bride of Lammermoor* and *A Legend of the Wars of Montrose.*" *Scott Newsl* 32 (1998), 6–12.

The Monastery, 1820

> Gilmartin, Sophie. *Ancestry and Narrative*, 71–74.

Old Mortality, 1816

> Chandler, James. *England in 1819*, 212–16.
> Dennis, Ian. *Nationalism and Desire*, 87–94.
> Häcker, Martina. "Literary Dialects and Communication in *The Tale of Old Mortality* and *The Brownie of Bodsbeck.*" *Stud in Hogg and His World* 8 (1997), 1–11.
> Rigney, Ann. *Imperfect Histories*, 20–31.
> Wedd, Mary. "*Old Mortality*: Editor and Narrator," in Richard Gravil, ed., *Master Narratives*, 37–46.
> Zimmerman, Everett. *The Boundaries of Fiction*, 217–20.

Peveril of the Peake, 1822

> Cousins, A. D., and Daniella E. Singer. "Scott's 'Character' of Buckingham in *Peveril of the Peak*, XXVIII: Dialogism, Speech/Writing, and Law." *Neophilologus* 81 (1997), 649–57.
> Lackey, Lionel. "*Nigel* and *Peveril*: Scott and Gender Roles." *Engl Lang Notes* 37:3 (2000), 36–45.
> Tait, Margaret. "*Peveril of the Peake.*" *Scott Newsl* 27 (1995), 13–14.

The Pirate, 1821

> Dennis, Ian. *Nationalism and Desire*, 106–15.
> Wawn, Andrew. *The Vikings and the Victorians*, 66–83.
> Weinstein, Mark. "Filthy Language in *The Pirate.*" *Scott Newsl* 32 (1998), 14–16.

Redgauntlet, 1824

> Allen, Emily. "Re-Marking Territory: *Redgauntlet* and the Restoration of Sir Walter Scott." *Stud in Romanticism* 37 (1998), 163–82.
> Case, Alison A. *Plotting Women*, 77–84.
> Chandler, James. *England in 1819*, 216–25.
> Dennis, Ian. *Nationalism and Desire*, 153–68.
> Evans, Deanna Delmar. "Scott's *Redgauntlet* and the Late Medieval Romance of Friendship, *Egar and Grime.*" *Stud in Scottish Lit* 31 (1999), 31–45.
> Jackson-Houlston, C. M. *Ballads, Songs and Snatches*, 35–39.
> Mack, Douglas S. "Culloden and After: Scottish Jacobite Novels." *Eighteenth-Cent Life* 20:3 (1996), 92–106.
> Melrose, Andrew. "Writing 'The end of uncertainty': Imaginary Law, Imaginary Jacobites and Imaginary History in Walter Scott's *Heart of Midlothian* and *Redgauntlet.*" *Scottish Liter J* 25:2 (1998), 34–42.
> Price, Leah. *The Anthology and the Rise of the Novel*, 54–59, 61–66.
> Shaw, Harry E. *Narrating Reality*, 1–3.
> Watson, Nicola J. *Revolution and the Form of the British Novel*, 149–53.

Welsh, Alexander. "History; or, The Difference between Scott's Hamlet and Goethe's." *Mod Lang Q* 59 (1998), 313–43.

Zimmerman, Everett. "Personal Identity, Narrative, and History: *The Female Quixote* and *Redgauntlet.*" *Eighteenth-Cent Fiction* 12 (2000), 381–90.

Rob Roy, 1817

Bellamy, Liz. "Regionalism and Nationalism: Maria Edgeworth, Walter Scott and the Definition of Britishness," in K. D. M. Snell, ed., *The Regional Novel,* 70–71.

Dennis, Ian. *Nationalism and Desire,* 94–106.

Dennis, Ian. "Rivalry and Desire in Scott's *Rob Roy.*" *Stud in Scottish Lit* 31 (1999), 245–57.

Sutherland, John. *Who Betrays Elizabeth Bennet?,* 34–38.

Wilson, Fiona. "Helen McGregor's Marked Body." *Scott Newsl* 36 (2000), 4–7.

Zimmerman, Everett. "Extreme Events: Scott's Novels and Traumatic History." *Eighteenth-Cent Fiction* 10 (1997), 66–78.

St. Ronan's Well, 1824

Burgess, Miranda J. *British Fiction and the Production of Social Order,* 219–34.

Jackson, Richard D. "George Crabbe and Scott's *Saint Ronan's Well.*" *Scott Newsl* 36 (2000), 7–21.

Jackson, Richard D. "Scott, Melrose and *Saint Ronan's Well.*" *Scott Newsl* 37 (2000), 8–23.

The Talisman, 1825

Bruzelius, Margaret. "'The King of England . . . Loved to Look upon A MAN': Melancholy and Masculinity in Scott's *Talisman.*" *Mod Lang Q* 62 (2001), 19–41.

Hopkins, Lisa. "Clothes and the Body of the Knight: The Making of Men in Sir Walter Scott's *The Talisman.*" *Wordsworth Circle* 27 (1996), 21–24.

Shaw, Harry E. *Narrating Reality,* 190–98.

The Two Drovers, 1827

Hussein Ali, Zahra A. "Adjusting the Borders of Self: Sir Walter Scott's *The Two Drovers.*" *Papers on Lang and Lit* 37 (2001), 65–84.

Johnson, Christopher. "Anti-Pugilism: Violence and Justice in Scott's *The Two Drovers.*" *Scottish Liter J* 22:1 (1995), 46–60.

Waverley, 1814

Bellamy, Liz. "Regionalism and Nationalism: Maria Edgeworth, Walter Scott and the Definition of Britishness," in K. D. M. Snell, ed., *The Regional Novel,* 66–70.

Day, Aidan. *Romanticism,* 141.

Dennis, Ian. *Nationalism and Desire,* 64–86.

Ercolani, Chiara. "De Walter Scott agli studi storici postmoderni: *Waverley*—Una finzione della storia?" *Lettore di Provincia* 29 (1998), 61–76.

Gordon, Jan. "The 'Talking Cure' (Again): Gossip and the Paralyzed

Patriarchy," in David T. Mitchell and Sharon L. Snyder, eds., *The Body and Physical Difference*, 213–15.

Lamont, Claire. "One Good Reason for Reading Scott: The Highland Works." *Scott Newsl* 23/24 (1993/1994), 2–8.

Lamont, Claire. "The Stereotype Scot and the Idea of Britain," in C. C. Barfoot, ed., *Beyond Pug's Tour*, 348–50.

Mack, Douglas S. "Culloden and After: Scottish Jacobite Novels." *Eighteenth-Cent Life* 20:3 (1996), 92–106.

Matteo, Chris Ann. "*Le grand jeu* and the Great Game: The Politics of Play in Walter Scott's *Waverley* and Rudyard Kipling's *Kim*." *J of Narrative Theory* 30 (2000), 163–80.

Morère, Pierre. "La nature dans *Waverley* de Walter Scott." *Etudes Anglaises* 51 (1998), 411–21.

Müllenbrock, Heinz-Joachim. "Scotts *Waverley* als 'Respons' auf Cervantes' *Don Quijote*." *Literaturwissenschaftliches Jahrbuch im Auftrage der Görres-Gesellschaft* 40 (1999), 139–54.

Müller, Wolfgang G. "Romantische und realistische Gestaltungselemente in Sir Walter Scotts *Waverley*," in Rüdiger Ahrens and Fritz-Wilhelm Neumann, eds., *Fiktion und Geschichte*, 201–16.

Murphy, Michael. "The Adventures of Waverley's Portmanteau." *Scott Newsl* 34 (1999), 7–11.

Robertson, Fiona. "Walter Scott, *Waverley*," in Duncan Wu, ed., *A Companion to Romanticism*, 211–17.

Schmidgen, Wolfram. "Picturing Property: *Waverley* and the Common Law." *Stud in the Novel* 29 (1997), 191–209.

Shaw, Harry E. *Narrating Reality*, 45–48, 104–7, 123–25, 186–88.

Suhamy, Henri. "*Waverley* ou le voyage dans le passé." *Bull de la Société d'Etudes Anglo-Américaines des XVIIe et XVIIIe Siècles* 42 (1996), 99–110.

Walker, Marshall. *Scottish Literature since 1707*, 121–30.

Ward, Ian. "Scott and the Waverley Constitution: A Study in Literary Constitutionalism." *Engl Stud* (Amsterdam) 79 (1998), 194–98.

Watson, Nicola J. *Revolution and the Form of the British Novel*, 127–35.

Zimmerman, Everett. "Extreme Events: Scott's Novels and Traumatic History." *Eighteenth-Cent Fiction* 10 (1997), 67–78.

Waverley Novels

Chandler, James. *England in 1819*, 131–35.

Lovell-Smith, Rose. "Qu'a donc pu lire Emily Brontë? Arrivals in the Waverley Novels and *Wuthering Heights*." *Brontë Soc Trans* 21:3 (1994), 79–85.

Mayer, Robert. "The Illogical Status of Novelistic Discourse: Scott's Footnotes for the Waverley Novels." *ELH* 66 (1999), 911–31.

Robertson, Fiona. "Scott's Halting Fellow: The Body of Shakespeare in the Waverley Novels." *Scott Newsl* 33 (1998), 2–10.

Smith, Edward C., III. "Honoré de Balzac and the 'Genius' of Walter Scott: Debt and Denial." *Compar Lit Stud* 36 (1999), 209–23.

Smith, Edward C., III. "Walter Scott, Literary History, and the 'Expressive' Tenets of Waverley Criticism." *Papers on Lang and Lit* 36 (2000), 357–74.

Stevenson, A. G. "Law Officers and Deforcement in the Waverley Novels." *Scott Newsl* 25/26 (1994/1995), 6–9.

Trumpener, Katie. *Bardic Nationalism,* 128–32, 139–41, 150–52.

Woodstock, 1826

Jackson-Houlston, C. M. *Ballads, Songs and Snatches,* 30–32.

Trela, D. J. "Sir Walter Scott on Oliver Cromwell: An Evenhanded Royalist Evaluates a Usurper." *Clio* 27 (1998), 204–20.

WILL SELF

My Idea of Fun: A Cautionary Tale, 1993

Hickman, Alan F. "Looking Before and After: The Search for the 'Inner Warrior' in Today's British Novel." *Publs of the Arkansas Philol Assoc* 25:1 (1999), 50–56.

ANNA SEWARD

Louisa: A Poetical Novel in Four Epistles, 1784

Robinson, Daniel. "Forging the Poetical Novel: The Elision of Form in Anna Seward's *Louisa.*" *Wordsworth Circle* 27 (1996), 25–29.

ANNA SEWELL

Black Beauty, 1877

Dingley, Robert. "A Horse of a Different Color: *Black Beauty* and the Pressures of Indebtedness." *Victorian Lit and Culture* 25 (1997), 241–50.

Dölvers, Horst. *Fables Less and Less Fabulous,* 146–61.

Ferguson, Moira. "Breaking in Englishness: *Black Beauty* and the Politics of Gender, Race and Class." *Women: A Cultural R* 5:1 (1994), 34–52.

Hollindale, Peter. "Plain Speaking: *Black Beauty* as a Quaker Text." *Children's Lit* 28 (2000), 96–111.

Hunt, Peter. *Children's Literature,* 147–49.

Morris, Tim. *You're Only Young Twice,* 15–31.

Stoneley, Peter. "Sentimental Emasculations: *Uncle Tom's Cabin* and *Black Beauty.*" *Nineteenth-Cent Lit* 54 (1999), 64–72.

EVELYN SHARP

The Making of a Prig, 1897

Heilmann, Ann. "Feminist Resistance, the Artist and 'A Room of One's Own' in New Woman Fiction." *Women's Writing* 2 (1995), 295–96.

GEORGE BERNARD SHAW

Cashel Byron's Profession, 1886

Peters, Sally. *Bernard Shaw,* 78–84.

JOHN SHEBBEARE

The Marriage Act: A Novel, 1754

>Shevlin, Eleanor F. "'Imaginary Productions' and 'Minute Contrivances': Law, Fiction, and Property in Eighteenth-Century England." *Stud in Eighteenth-Cent Culture* 28 (1999), 143–46.

MARY SHELLEY

Falkner, 1837

>Allen, Graham. "Public and Private Fidelity: Mary Shelley's 'Life of William Godwin' and *Falkner,*" in Michael Eberle-Sinatra, ed., *Mary Shelley's Fictions,* 224–41.

>Bennett, Betty T. *Mary Wollstonecraft Shelley,* 97–104.

>Bennett, Betty T. "'Not this time, Victor': Mary Shelley's Reversioning of Elizabeth, from *Frankenstein* to *Falkner,*" in Betty T. Bennett and Stuart Curran, eds., *Mary Shelley in Her Times,* 8–17.

>Brewer, William D. *The Mental Anatomies,* 78–82.

>Bunnell, Charlene E. "The Illusion of 'Great Expectations': Manners and Morals in Mary Shelley's *Lodore* and *Falkner,*" in Syndy M. Conger et al., eds., *Iconoclastic Departures,* 275–91.

>Jowell, Sharon L. "Mary Shelley's Mothers: The Weak, the Absent, and the Silent in *Lodore* and *Falkner.*" *European Romantic R* 8 (1997), 298–322.

>Saunders, Julia. "Rehabilitating the Family in Mary Shelley's *Falkner,*" in Michael Eberle-Sinatra, ed., *Mary Shelley's Fictions,* 211–22.

>Williams, John. *Mary Shelley,* 153–58.

Frankenstein, 1818

>Alwes, Karla. "The Alienation of Family in Mary Shelley's *Frankenstein,*" in Laura Dabundo, ed., *Jane Austen and Mary Shelley,* 109–17.

>Armitt, Lucie. *Contemporary Women's Fiction,* 58–62.

>Bartra, Roger. *The Artificial Savage,* 245–50.

>Bazin, Claire. "*Frankenstein*: Texte et monstre." *GRAAT* 15 (1996), 9–17.

>Beck, Rudolf. "'The Region of Beauty and Delight': Walton's Polar Fantasies in Mary Shelley's *Frankenstein.*" *Keats-Shelley J* 49 (2000), 24–29.

>Beer, John. "Mary Shelley, *Frankenstein,*" in Duncan Wu, ed., *A Companion to Romanticism,* 227–35.

>Benedict, Barbara M. *Curiosity,* 238–43.

>Bennett, Betty T. *Mary Wollstonecraft Shelley,* 30–42.

>Bennett, Betty T. "'Not this time, Victor': Mary Shelley's Reversioning of Elizabeth, from *Frankenstein* to *Falkner,*" in Betty T. Bennett and Stuart Curran, eds., *Mary Shelley in Her Times,* 1–8.

>Berry, Laura C. *The Child, the State, and the Victorian Novel,* 20–27.

>Best, Debra E. "The Monster in the Family: A Reconsideration of *Frankenstein*'s Domestic Relationships." *Women's Writing* 6 (1999), 365–81.

Bohls, Elizabeth A. *Women Travel Writers*, 230–45.

Borgmeier, Raimund. "Frankenstein in Texten und Medien." *Anglistik und Englischunterricht* 59 (1996), 33–53.

Bowen, Arlene. "Mary Shelley's Rose-Eating Cat, Lucian, and *Frankenstein*." *Keats-Shelley J* 45 (1996), 16–19.

Bozzetto, Roger. *Territoires des fantastiques*, 195–97.

Brantlinger, Patrick. *The Reading Lesson*, 59–65.

Brennan, Matthew C. *The Gothic Psyche*, 56–73.

Brennan, Matthew C. "Mary Shelley's Cautionary Narrative: *Frankenstein* as Therapy." *Lamar J of the Hum* 24:2 (1999), 5–11.

Brewer, William D. *The Mental Anatomies*, 24–26, 28–30, 62–66, 76–80, 183–88, 198–200, 206–9.

Caldwell, Janis McLarren. "Sympathy and Science in *Frankenstein*," in Andrew Hadfield et al., eds., *The Ethics in Literature*, 262–73.

Cass, Jeffrey. "The Contestatory Gothic in Mary Shelley's *Frankenstein* and J. W. Polidori's *Ernestus Berchtold*: The Spectre of a Colonialist Paradigm." *J of the Assoc for the Interdisciplinary Study of the Arts* 1:2 (1996), 33–41.

Chandler, Wayne A. "*Frankenstein*'s Many Readers." *Extrapolation* 37 (1996), 37–43.

Chantler, Ashley. "Echoes of Cowper in *Frankenstein*." *Notes and Queries* 46 (1999), 33–34.

Christie, William. "The Critical Metamorphoses of Mary Shelley's *Frankenstein*." *Sydney Stud in Engl* 25 (1999), 47–76.

Clemens, Valdine. *The Return of the Repressed*, 89–122.

Conger, Syndy M. "Prophecy and Sensibility: Mary Wollstonecraft in *Frankenstein*." *1650–1850: Ideas, Aesthetics, and Inquiries in the Early Mod Era* 3 (1997), 301–28.

Crisman, William. "'Now Misery Has Come Home': Sibling Rivalry in Mary Shelley's *Frankenstein*." *Stud in Romanticism* 36 (1997), 27–41.

Crook, Nora. "In Defence of the 1831 *Frankenstein*," in Michael Eberle-Sinatra, ed., *Mary Shelley's Fictions*, 3–18.

Daffron, Eric. "Male Bonding: Sympathy and Shelley's *Frankenstein*." *Nineteenth-Cent Contexts* 21 (1999), 415–31.

Day, Aidan. *Romanticism*, 193–94.

Dingley, Robert. "Shelley's *Frankenstein*." *Explicator* 57:4 (1999), 204–6.

Disch, Thomas M. *The Dreams Our Stuff Is Made Of*, 33–34.

Eberle-Sinatra, Michael. "Gender, Authorship and Male Domination: Mary Shelley's Limited Freedom in *Frankenstein* and *The Last Man*," in Eberle-Sinatra, ed., *Mary Shelley's Fictions*, 95–104.

Ellis, Markman. "Fictions of Science in Mary Shelley's *Frankenstein*." *Sydney Stud in Engl* 25 (1999), 27–44.

Engar, Ann. "Mary Shelley and the Romance of Science," in Laura Dabundo, ed., *Jane Austen and Mary Shelley*, 137–44.

Fay, Elizabeth A. *A Feminist Introduction to Romanticism*, 195–98.

Filmer, Kath. "The Specter of the Self in *Frankenstein* and *Great Expectations*," in Elton E. Smith and Robert Haas, eds., *The Haunted Mind*, 19–30.

Franco, Dean. "Mirror Images and Otherness in Mary Shelley's *Frankenstein*." *Lit and Psych* 44:1–2 (1998), 80–95.

Garrett, Erin Webster. "Recycling Zoraida: The Muslim Heroine in Mary Shelley's *Frankenstein*." *Cervantes* 20:1 (2000), 133–57.

Gigante, Denise. "Facing the Ugly: The Case of *Frankenstein*." *ELH* 67 (2000), 565–83.

Glance, Jonathan C. "'Beyond the Usual Bounds of Reverie?': Another Look at the Dreams in *Frankenstein*." *J of the Fantastic in the Arts* 7:4 (1996), 30–47.

Goodall, Jane. "Frankenstein and the Reprobate's Conscience." *Stud in the Novel* 31 (1999), 19–39.

Gores, Steven J. *Psychosocial Spaces*, 143–44.

Hansen, Mark. "'Not thus, after all, would life be given': *Technesis*, Technology and the Parody of Romantic Poetics in *Frankenstein*." *Stud in Romanticism* 36 (1997), 575–609.

Heffernan, James A. W. "Looking at the Monster: *Frankenstein* and Film." *Crit Inquiry* 24 (1997), 133–58.

Hendershot, Cyndy. *The Animal Within*, 73–86.

Hetherington, Naomi. "Creator and Created in Mary Shelley's *Frankenstein*." *Keats-Shelley R* 11 (1997), 1–39.

Hopkins, Lisa. "Engendering Frankenstein's Monster." *Women's Writing* 2 (1995), 77–84.

Kincaid, James R. *Annoying the Victorians*, 179–203.

Knowles, Sebastian. "'O Lord I must stretch myself': Molly Bloom and *Frankenstein*," in Clive Hart et al., eds., *Images of Joyce*, vol. 1, 281–83. (Also in *James Joyce Q* 34:3 [1997], 303–12.)

Komisaruk, Adam. "'So Guided by a Silken Cord': *Frankenstein*'s Family Values." *Stud in Romanticism* 38 (1999), 409–41.

Korg, Jacob. "*Frankenstein*: The Monster as a Work of Art." *Rivista di Studi Vittoriani* 6:3 (1998), 5–18.

Labbe, Jacqueline M. "A Monstrous Fiction: *Frankenstein* and the Wifely Ideal." *Women's Writing* 6 (1999), 345–60.

Lecercle, Jean-Jacques. "Alice and the Sphinx." *REAL: Yrbk of Res in Engl and Am Lit* 13 (1997), 25–27.

Liggins, Emma. "The Medical Gaze and the Female Corpse: Looking at Bodies in Mary Shelley's *Frankenstein*." *Stud in the Novel* 32 (2000), 129–42.

Lloyd, Tom. *Crises of Realism*, 56–71.

McBeth, Mark. "Shelley's *Frankenstein*." *Explicator* 57:3 (1999), 143–46.

McGavran, James Holt. "'Insurmountable Barriers to Our Union': Homosocial Male Bonding, Homosexual Panic, and Death on the Ice in *Frankenstein*." *European Romantic R* 11 (2000), 46–67.

McKee, Patricia. *Public and Private*, 67–76.

McLane, Maureen N. *Romanticism and the Human Sciences*, 84–108.

May, Leila Silvana. *Disorderly Sisters*, 163–75.

May, Stephen. *Stardust and Ashes*, 26–32.

Mulvey-Roberts, Marie. "The Corpse in the Corpus: *Frankenstein*, Rewriting Wollstonecraft and the Abject," in Michael Eberle-Sinatra, ed., *Mary Shelley's Fictions*, 197–206.

Nardin, Jane. "A Meeting on the Mer de Glace: *Frankenstein* and the History of Alpine Mountaineering." *Women's Writing* 6 (1999), 441–48.

Neff, D. S. "Hostages to Empire: The Anglo-Indian Problem in *Frankenstein, The Curse of Kehama*, and *The Missionary*." *European Romantic R* 8 (1997), 386–408.

Oost, Regina B. "Marketing *Frankenstein*: The Shelleys' Enigmatic Preface." *Engl Lang Notes* 35:1 (1997), 26–34.

O'Rourke, James. "The 1831 Introduction and Revisions to *Frankenstein*: Mary Shelley Dictates Her Legacy." *Stud in Romanticism* 38 (1999), 365–85.

Przybytek, Marius. "Re-Membering Frankenstein: Mapping the Myth of Shelley's Monster." *B.A.S.: Brit and Am Stud* 1998: 75–80.

Ralston, Ramona M., and Sid Sondergard. "Biodepictions of Mary Shelley: The Romantic Woman Artist as Mother of Monsters," in Martin Middeke and Werner Huber, eds., *Biofictions*, 201–10.

Rauch, Alan. *Useful Knowledge*, 96–128.

St. Clair, William. "The Impact of *Frankenstein*," in Betty T. Bennett and Stuart Curran, eds., *Mary Shelley in Her Times*, 38–63.

Samuels, Robert. *Writing Prejudices*, 73–86.

Schäffner, Raimund. *Anarchismus und Literatur in England*, 114–21.

Schoene-Harwood, Berthold, ed. *Mary Shelley: "Frankenstein,"* 7–177.

Seabury, Marcia Bundy. "The Monsters We Create: *Woman on the Edge of Time* and *Frankenstein*." *Critique* (Washington, DC) 42 (2001), 131–40.

Smith, Andrew. *Gothic Radicalism*, 26–28, 38–44, 46–58, 76–80, 84–86, 96–99.

Stubblefield, Jay. "'What Shall I Say I Am—To-day?': Subjectivity and Accountability in *Frankenstein* and *Great Expectations*." *Dickens Q* 14 (1997), 232–42.

Sutherland, John. *Who Betrays Elizabeth Bennet?*, 39–43.

Thompson, Terry W. "Shelley's *Frankenstein*." *Explicator* 58:1 (1999), 22–24.

Thompson, Terry W. "Shelley's *Frankenstein*." *Explicator* 58:4 (2000), 191–92.

Tomasi, Silvia. "Frankenst*ai*n or Frankenst*ii*n." *Confronto Letterario* 14 (1997), 231–38.

Tuite, Clara. "*Frankenstein*'s Monster and Malthus' 'Jaundiced Eye': Population, Body Politics, and the Monstrous Sublime." *Eighteenth-Cent Life* 22:1 (1998), 141–53.

Turney, Jon. *Frankenstein's Footsteps*, 13–42.

Vernon, Peter. "*Frankenstein*: Science and Electricity." *Etudes Anglaises* 50 (1997), 270–82.

Ward, Maryanne C. "A Painting of the Unspeakable: Henry Fuseli's *The Nightmare* and the Creation of Mary Shelley's *Frankenstein*." *J of the Midwest Mod Lang Assoc* 33:1 (2000), 20–30.

Williams, John. *Mary Shelley*, 41–70.

Wilson, Deborah S. "Technologies of Misogyny: The Transparent Maternal Body and Alternate Reproductions in Frankenstein,

Dracula, and Some Selected Media Discourses," in Deborah S. Wilson and Christine Moneera Laennec, eds., *Bodily Discursions*, 107–13.

Wilson, Frances. "'A Playful Desire of Imitation':The Ghost Stories at Diodati and *A Single Summer With L. B.*," in Martin Middeke and Werner Huber, eds., *Biofictions*, 162–73.

Wordsworth, Jonathan. *The Bright Work Grows*, 215–23.

Zimmerman, Phyllis. *Shelley's Fiction*, 101–240.

The Last Man, 1826

Ballesteros González, Antonio. "A Romantic Vision of Millenarian Disease: Placing and Displacing Death in Mary Shelley's *The Last Man*." *Miscelánea* 17 (1996), 51–61.

Bennett, Betty T. *Mary Wollstonecraft Shelley*, 76–86.

Brewer, William D. *The Mental Anatomies*, 74–78, 125–27, 134–36.

Cantor, Paul A. "The Apocalypse of Empire: Mary Shelley's *The Last Man*," in Syndy M. Conger et al., eds., *Iconoclastic Departures*, 193–208.

Canuel, Mark. "Acts, Rules, and *The Last Man*." *Nineteenth-Cent Lit* 53 (1998), 147–70.

Crossley, Robert. "Acts of God," in David Seed, ed., *Imagining Apocalypse*, 80–81.

Dadlez, E. M. *What's Hecuba to Him?*, 67–70.

Eberle-Sinatra, Michael. "Gender, Authorship and Male Domination: Mary Shelley's Limited Freedom in *Frankenstein* and *The Last Man*," in Eberle-Sinatra, ed., *Mary Shelley's Fictions*, 95–104.

Haggerty, George E. "'The End of History': Identity and Dissolution in Apocalyptic Gothic." *Eighteenth Cent* 41 (2000), 233–40.

Kostova, Ludmilla. *Tales of the Periphery*, 78–96.

Lew, Joseph W. "The Plague of Imperial Desire: Montesqieu, Gibbon, Brougham, and Mary Shelley's *The Last Man*," in Tim Fulford and Peter J. Kitson, eds., *Romanticism and Colonialism*, 261–78.

Schäffner, Raimund. *Anarchismus und Literatur in England*, 124–27.

Thomas, Sophie. "The Ends of the Fragment, the Problem of the Preface: Proliferation and Finality in *The Last Man*," in Michael Eberle-Sinatra, ed., *Mary Shelley's Fictions*, 22–37.

Walker, Constance. "Kindertotenlieder: Mary Shelley and the Art of Losing," in Betty T. Bennett and Stuart Curran, eds., *Mary Shelley in Her Times*, 139–46.

Webb, Samantha. "Reading the End of the World: The Last Man, History, and the Agency of Romantic Authorship," in Betty T. Bennett and Stuart Curran, eds., *Mary Shelley in Her Times*, 119–33.

Wells, Lynn. "The Triumph of Death: Reading and Narrative in Mary Shelley's *The Last Man*," in Syndy M. Conger et al., eds., *Iconoclastic Departures*, 212–31.

Williams, John. *Mary Shelley*, 103–15.

Wright, Julia M. "'Little England': Anxieties of Space in Mary Shelley's *The Last Man*," in Michael Eberle-Sinatra, ed., *Mary Shelley's Fictions*, 129–45.

Zimmerman, Phyllis. *Shelley's Fiction*, 248–54.

Lodore, 1835

Bennett, Betty T. *Mary Wollstonecraft Shelley,* 91–97.
Brewer, William D. "Mary Wollstonecraft and Mary Shelley: Ideological Affinities," in Laura Dabundo, ed., *Jane Austen and Mary Shelley,* 104–7.
Brewer, William D. *The Mental Anatomies,* 151–53, 179–81.
Bunnell, Charlene E. "Breaking the Tie That Binds: Parents and Children in Romantic Fiction," in Andrea O'Reilly Herrera et al., eds., *Family Matters,* 45–51.
Bunnell, Charlene E. "The Illusion of 'Great Expectations': Manners and Morals in Mary Shelley's *Lodore* and *Falkner,*" in Syndy M. Conger et al., eds., *Iconoclastic Departures,* 275–91.
Cronin, Richard. "Mary Shelley and Edward Bulwer: *Lodore* as Hybrid Fiction," in Michael Eberle-Sinatra, ed., *Mary Shelley's Fictions,* 39–52.
Gonda, Caroline. "*Lodore* and Fanny Derham's Story." *Women's Writing* 6 (1999), 329–41.
Jowell, Sharon L. "Mary Shelley's Mothers: The Weak, the Absent, and the Silent in *Lodore* and *Falkner.*" *European Romantic R* 8 (1997), 298–322.
Stafford, Fiona. "*Lodore*: A Tale of the Present Time?," in Michael Eberle-Sinatra, ed., *Mary Shelley's Fictions,* 181–92.
Vallins, David. "Mary Shelley and the Lake Poets: Negation and Transcendence in *Lodore,*" in Michael Eberle-Sinatra, ed., *Mary Shelley's Fictions,* 164–77.
Vargo, Lisa. "*Lodore* and the 'Novel of Society.'" *Women's Writing* 6 (1999), 425–38.
Williams, John. *Mary Shelley,* 143–53.

Mathilda, 1959

Barbour, Judith. "'The meaning of the tree': The Tale of Mirra in Mary Shelley's *Mathilda,*" in Syndy M. Conger et al., eds., *Iconoclastic Departures,* 98–112.
Bennett, Betty T. *Mary Wollstonecraft Shelley,* 48–54.
Brewer, William D. "Mary Wollstonecraft and Mary Shelley: Ideological Affinities," in Laura Dabundo, ed., *Jane Austen and Mary Shelley,* 100–103.
Brewer, William D. *The Mental Anatomies,* 66–78, 113–15, 171–76, 178–80, 200–202.
Bunnell, Charlene E. "*Mathilda*: Mary Shelley's Romantic Tragedy." *Keats-Shelley J* 46 (1997), 75–96.
Burwick, Frederick. "*Mathilda*—Who Knew Too Much," in Richard Gravil, ed., *Master Narratives,* 47–54.
Chatterjee, Ranita. "Mathilda: Mary Shelley, William Godwin, and the Ideologies of Incest," in Syndy M. Conger et al., eds., *Iconoclastic Departures,* 130–47.
Clemit, Pamela. "From *The Fields of Fancy* to *Mathilda,*" in Betty T. Bennett and Stuart Curran, eds., *Mary Shelley in Her Times,* 64–75.
François, Anne-Lise, and Daniel Mozes. "'Don't Say "I Love You"':

Agency, Gender and Romanticism in Mary Shelley's *Matilda*," in Michael Eberle-Sinatra, ed., *Mary Shelley's Fictions*, 57–72.

Garrett, Margaret Davenport. "Writing and Re-writing Incest in Mary Shelley's *Mathilda.*" *Keats-Shelley J* 45 (1996), 44–60.

Himes, Audra Dibert. "'Knewshame, and knewdesire': Ambivalence as Structure in Mary Shelley's *Mathilda*," in Syndy M. Conger et al., eds., *Iconoclastic Departures*, 115–26.

Hoeveler, Diane Long. *Gothic Feminism*, 158–83.

Jacobus, Mary. *Psychoanalysis and the Scene of Reading*, 166–201.

Keach, William. "The Shelleys and Dante's Matilda," in Nick Havely, ed., *Dante's Modern Afterlife*, 60–69.

Robinson, Charles E. "Mathilda as Dramatic Actress," in Betty T. Bennett and Stuart Curran, eds., *Mary Shelley in Her Times*, 76–87.

Vine, Steven. "The Father's Seduction in Mary Shelley's *Mathilda.*" *News from Nowhere* 2 (1997), 57–71. (Also in Tony Pinkney et al., eds., *Romantic Masculinities*, 57–71.)

Williams, John. *Mary Shelley*, 8–11, 66–70.

Zimmerman, Phyllis. *Shelley's Fiction*, 275–344.

Perkin Warbeck, 1830

Bennett, Betty T. *Mary Wollstonecraft Shelley*, 87–91.

Brewer, William D. *The Mental Anatomies*, 112–14, 123–26.

Brewer, William D. "William Godwin, Chivalry, and Mary Shelley's *The Fortunes of Perkin Warbeck.*" *Papers on Lang and Lit* 35 (1999), 187–203.

Garbin, Lidia. "Mary Shelley and Walter Scott: *The Fortunes of Perkin Warbeck* and the Historical Novel," in Michael Eberle-Sinatra, ed., *Mary Shelley's Fictions*, 150–59.

Hopkins, Lisa. "The Self and the Monstrous: *The Fortunes of Perkin Warbeck*," in Syndy M. Conger et al., eds., *Iconoclastic Departures*, 260–73.

Wake, Ann M. Frank. "Women in the Active Voice: Recovering Female History in Mary Shelley's *Valperga* and *Perkin Warbeck*," in Syndy M. Conger et al., eds., *Iconoclastic Departures*, 235–55.

Williams, John. *Mary Shelley*, 123–29.

Valperga, 1823

Bennett, Betty T. *Mary Wollstonecraft Shelley*, 54–61.

Brewer, William D. *The Mental Anatomies*, 71–74, 115–24, 150–52, 155–57, 175–79, 202–6, 209–11.

Carson, James P. "'A Sigh of Many Hearts': History, Humanity, and Popular Culture in *Valperga*," in Syndy M. Conger et al., eds., *Iconoclastic Departures*, 167–86.

Petronella, Vincent F. " Mary Shelley, Shakespeare, and the Romantic Theatre," in Laura Dabundo, ed., *Jane Austen and Mary Shelley*, 126–28.

Rajan, Tilottama. "Between Romance and History: Possibility and Contingency in Godwin, Leibniz, and Mary Shelley's *Valperga*," in Betty T. Bennett and Stuart Curran, eds., *Mary Shelley in Her Times*, 88–102.

Rossington, Michael. "Future Uncertain: The Republican Tradition and Its Destiny in *Valperga*," in Betty T. Bennett and Stuart Curran, eds., *Mary Shelley in Her Times*, 103–18.

Schäffner, Raimund. *Anarchismus und Literatur in England*, 121–24.

Schiefelbein, Michael. "'The Lessons of True Religion': Mary Shelley's Tribute to Catholicism in *Valperga*." *Rel and Lit* 30:2 (1998), 59–74.

Wake, Ann M. Frank. "Women in the Active Voice: Recovering Female History in Mary Shelley's *Valperga* and *Perkin Warbeck*," in Syndy M. Conger et al., eds., *Iconoclastic Departures*, 235–55.

White, Daniel E. "Mary Shelley's *Valperga*: Italy and the Revision of Romantic Aesthetics," in Michael Eberle-Sinatra, ed., *Mary Shelley's Fictions*, 75–92.

Williams, John. *Mary Shelley*, 77–89, 101–3.

Wordsworth, Jonathan. *The Bright Work Grows*, 239–46.

Zimmerman, Phyllis. *Shelley's Fiction*, 345–582.

PERCY BYSSHE SHELLEY

St. Irvyne, 1811

Finch, Peter. "Monstrous Inheritance: The Sexual Politics of Genre in Shelley's *St. Irvyne*." *Keats-Shelley J* 48 (1999), 35–68.

Zimmerman, Phyllis. *Shelley's Fiction*, 1–6, 158–60.

Zastrozzi, 1810

Zimmerman, Phyllis. *Shelley's Fiction*, 1–4, 94–97.

NAN SHEPHERD

A Pass in the Grampians, 1933

Watson, Roderick. "'To know Being': Substance and Spirit in the Work of Nan Shepherd," in Douglas Gifford and Dorothy McMillan, eds., *A History*, 420–21.

The Quarry Wood, 1928

Carter, Gillian. "Boundaries and Transgression in Nan Shepherd's *The Quarry Wood*," in Carol Anderson and Aileen Christianson, eds., *Scottish Women's Fiction*, 47–57.

Craig, Cairns. "Scotland and the Regional Novel," in K. D. M. Snell, ed., *The Regional Novel*, 234–36.

Watson, Roderick. "'To know Being': Substance and Spirit in the Work of Nan Shepherd," in Douglas Gifford and Dorothy McMillan, eds., *A History*, 416–20.

The Weatherhouse, 1930

Craig, Cairns. "Scotland and the Regional Novel," in K. D. M. Snell, ed., *The Regional Novel*, 234–36.

Lumsden, Alison. "Journey into Being: Nan Shepherd's *The Weatherhouse*," in Carol Anderson and Aileen Christianson, eds., *Scottish Women's Fiction*, 59–70.

Watson, Roderick. "'To know Being': Substance and Spirit in the Work of Nan Shepherd," in Douglas Gifford and Dorothy McMillan, eds., *A History*, 419–25.

FRANCES SHERIDAN

The Memoirs of Miss Sidney Bidulph, 1761–1767

Bannet, Eve Tavor. *The Domestic Revolution*, 112–15.

Burgess, Miranda J. *British Fiction and the Production of Social Order*, 77–84.

Richetti, John. *The English Novel in History*, 211–16.

Schellenberg, Betty A. "Frances Sheridan Reads John Home: Placing *Sidney Bidulph* in the Republic of Letters." *Eighteenth-Cent Fiction* 13 (2001), 561–77.

Spencer, Jane. "Women Writers and the Eighteenth-Century Novel," in John Richetti, ed., *The Cambridge Companion*, 223–26.

Swan, Beth. *Fictions of Law*, 43–46, 88–93.

SARAH SHERIFFE

Correlia; or, the Mystic Tomb, 1802

Shaffer, Julie. "Familial Love, Incest, and Female Desire in Late Eighteenth- and Early Nineteenth-Century British Women's Novels." *Criticism* 41 (1999), 87–93.

PHILIP SIDNEY

Arcadia, 1598

Alexander, Gavin. "Sidney's Interruptions." *Stud in Philology* 98 (2001), 184–204.

Alwes, Derek B. "Elizabethan Dreaming: Fictional Dreams from Gascoigne to Lodge," in Constance C. Relihan, ed., *Framing Elizabethan Fictions*, 156–67.

Bernard, John. "Metanarrative and Desire in the *New Arcadia*." *Sidney Newsl and J* 14:2 (1996/97), 33–42.

Berry, Edward. *The Making of Sir Philip Sidney*, 63–101, 163–91.

Borris, Kenneth. *Allegory and Epic*, 109–41.

Brumbaugh, Barbara. "Cecropia and the Church of Antichrist in Sir Philip Sidney's *New Arcadia*." *Stud in Engl Lit, 1500–1900* 38 (1998), 19–36.

Carver, Robert H. F. "'Transformed in Show': The Rhetoric of Transvestism in Sidney's *Arcadia*." *Engl Liter Renaissance* 28 (1998), 323–52.

Catty, Jocelyn. *Writing Rape, Writing Women*, 42–54.

Celovsky, Lisa. "Vanquished by Marriage: Tournaments in *The Faerie Queene* and the *New Arcadia* (1590)." *Sidney Newsl and J* 13:1 (1994/95), 20–34.

Cheney, Donald. "Narrative, Romance, and Epic," in Arthur F. Kinney, ed., *The Cambridge Companion*, 213–15.

Couton, Marie. "Métamorphose et métaphore dans l'*Arcadie* de Sir Philip Sidney." *Imaginaires* 4 (1999), 31–39.

DeZur, Kathryn. "Defending the Castle: The Political Problem of

Rhetorical Seduction and Good Huswifery in Sidney's *Old Arcadia.*" *Stud in Philology* 98 (2001), 93–113.

Dorangeon, Simone. "Sidney et son lecteur, ou l'éducation du regard dans *The Countess of Pembroke's Arcadia.*" *Imaginaires* 3 (1998), 9–24.

Dundas, Judith. "'A Light and Illuding Form': Sidney's Use of *Paronomasia.*" *Mod Lang R* 92 (1997), 273–81.

Everton, Michael. "Critical Thumbprints in Arcadia: Renaissance Pastoral and the Process of Critique." *Style* 35:1 (2001), 7–12.

Fox, Alistair. *The English Renaissance,* 115–34.

Hackett, Helen. *Women and Romance Fiction,* 101–29.

Hadfield, Andrew. *The English Renaissance,* 134–36.

Holmes, Marsha. "Betwixt a Lamb and a Monarch: Pamela's Rhetoric of Place in Sidney's *Old Arcadia.*" *Postscript* 12 (1995), 79–85.

Hopkins, Lisa. "Spartan Boys: John Ford and Philip Sidney." *Classical and Mod Lit* 17 (1997), 217–29.

Kinney, Clare R. "Endgames: Gender, Genre and Closure in Anna Weamys's *Continuation of Sir Philip Sidney's Arcadia.*" *Sidney Newsl and J* 15:1 (1997), 48–60.

Lei, Bi-qi Beatrice. "Relational Antifeminism in Sidney's *Arcadia.*" *Stud in Engl Lit, 1500–1900* 41 (2001), 25–41.

Levin, Richard A. "What? How? Female-Female Desire in Sidney's *New Arcadia.*" *Criticism* 39 (1997), 463–77.

Maslen, R. W. *Elizabethan Fictions,* 294–98.

Pask, Kevin. *The Emergence of the English Author,* 64–67, 73–81.

Platt, Peter G. "Admiration, Commiseration, and Gilden Roofs: Wonder and Uncertainty in Sidney's *Arcadia.*" *Sidney Newsl and J* 13:2 (1995), 13–22.

Prendergast, Maria Teresa Micaela. "Philoclea Parsed: Prose, Verse, and Femininity in Sidney's *Old Arcadia,*" in Constance C. Relihan, ed., *Framing Elizabethan Fictions,* 99–116.

Prendergast, Maria Teresa Micaela. *Renaissance Fantasies,* 86–116.

Preston, Claire. "Sidney's Arcadian Poetics: A Medicine of Cherries and the Philosophy of Cavaliers," in Neil Rhodes, ed., *English Renaissance Prose,* 91–108.

Richards, Jennifer. "The Art of Being Persuaded: Rhetoric and Effeminacy in Philip Sidney's *Old Arcadia.*" *Sidney Newsl and J* 13:2 (1995), 3–12.

Schwarz, Kathryn. *Tough Love,* 176–201.

Shuger, Debora. "Castigating Livy: The Rape of Lucretia and *The Old Arcadia.*" *Renaissance Q* 51:2 (1998), 526–48.

Spiller, Elizabeth A. "Speaking for the Dead: King Charles, Anna Weamys, and the Commemorations of Sir Philip Sidney's *Arcadia.*" *Criticism* 42 (2000), 229–47.

Starr, G. Gabrielle. "Rereading Prose Fiction: Lyric Convention in Aphra Behn and Eliza Haywood." *Eighteenth-Cent Fiction* 12 (1999), 1–4.

Thomas, Max W. "Urban Semiosis in Early Modern London." *Genre* 30 (1997), 16–18.

Worden, Blair. *The Sound of Virtue: Philip Sidney's Arcadia and Elizabethan Politics.*

ALAN SILLITOE

The Death of William Posters, 1965

Daniels, Stephen, and Simon Rycroft. "Mapping the Modern City: Alan Sillitoe's Nottingham Novels," in K. D. M. Snell, ed., *The Regional Novel,* 282–85.

Hanson, Gillian Mary. *Understanding Alan Sillitoe,* 44–45.

Down from the Hill, 1984

Hanson, Gillian Mary. *Understanding Alan Sillitoe,* 159–61.

Her Victory, 1982

Hanson, Gillian Mary. *Understanding Alan Sillitoe,* 146–53.

Key to the Door, 1961

Daniels, Stephen, and Simon Rycroft. "Mapping the Modern City: Alan Sillitoe's Nottingham Novels," in K. D. M. Snell, ed., *The Regional Novel,* 285–87.

Hanson, Gillian Mary. *Understanding Alan Sillitoe,* 37–38.

Last Loves, 1990

Hanson, Gillian Mary. *Understanding Alan Sillitoe,* 161–62.

Leonard's War, 1991

Hanson, Gillian Mary. *Understanding Alan Sillitoe,* 74–81.

Life Goes On, 1985

Hanson, Gillian Mary. *Understanding Alan Sillitoe,* 46–47.

The Open Door, 1989

Daniels, Stephen, and Simon Rycroft. "Mapping the Modern City: Alan Sillitoe's Nottingham Novels," in K. D. M. Snell, ed., *The Regional Novel,* 285–87.

Saturday Night and Sunday Morning, 1958

Daniels, Stephen, and Simon Rycroft. "Mapping the Modern City: Alan Sillitoe's Nottingham Novels," in K. D. M. Snell, ed., *The Regional Novel,* 274–82.

Hanson, Gillian Mary. *Understanding Alan Sillitoe,* 32–38.

Haywood, Ian. *Working-Class Fiction,* 100–105.

Varricchio, Mario. "Per una teoria del romanzo proletario: Il mito di *Saturday Night and Sunday Morning." Lettore di Provincia* 30 (1999), 83–109.

Snowstop, 1993

Hanson, Gillian Mary. *Understanding Alan Sillitoe,* 166–68.

A Start in Life, 1970

Hanson, Gillian Mary. *Understanding Alan Sillitoe,* 45–46.

The Storyteller, 1979

Hanson, Gillian Mary. *Understanding Alan Sillitoe,* 117–19.

MAY SINCLAIR

Audrey Craven, 1897

Raitt, Suzanne. *May Sinclair,* 68–73.

The Creators, 1910

> Pykett, Lyn. "Writing Around Modernism: May Sinclair and Rebecca West," in Lynne Hapgood and Nancy L. Paxton, eds., *Outside Modernism,* 112–13.
> Raitt, Suzanne. *May Sinclair,* 121–28.
> Trodd, Anthea. *Women's Writing in English,* 56–58.

The Divine Fire, 1904

> Raitt, Suzanne. *May Sinclair,* 86–96.
> Young, Arlene. *Culture, Class and Gender,* 160–88.

The Helpmate, 1907

> Raitt, Suzanne. *May Sinclair,* 99–103.

Kitty Tailleur, 1908

> Raitt, Suzanne. *May Sinclair,* 105–8.

Life and Death of Harriet Frean, 1922

> Raitt, Suzanne. *May Sinclair,* 241–67.
> Wallace, Diana. *Sisters and Rivals in British Women's Fiction,* 90–95.

Mary Olivier, 1919

> Hill, Marylu. *Mothering Modernity,* 137–48.
> Pykett, Lyn. "Writing Around Modernism: May Sinclair and Rebecca West," in Lynne Hapgood and Nancy L. Paxton, eds., *Outside Modernism,* 113–16.
> Raitt, Suzanne. *May Sinclair,* 213–40.
> Trodd, Anthea. *Women's Writing in English,* 57–59.

The Romantic, 1920

> Raitt, Suzanne. *May Sinclair,* 177–81.

The Three Sisters, 1914

> Raitt, Suzanne. *May Sinclair,* 140–44.
> Wallace, Diana. *Sisters and Rivals in British Women's Fiction,* 80–90.

The Tree of Heaven, 1917

> Raitt, Suzanne. *May Sinclair,* 166–71, 173–77.
> Smith, Angela K. "'That silly suffrage . . .': The Paradox of World War I." *Nineteenth-Cent Feminisms* 3 (2000), 90, 98–102.

FELICIA SKENE

The Inheritance of Evil, 1849

> Gruner, Elisabeth Rose. "Born and Made: Sisters, Brothers, and the Deceased Wife's Sister Bill." *Signs* 24 (1999), 430–33.

CHARLOTTE SMITH

The Banished Man, 1794

> Fletcher, Loraine. *Charlotte Smith,* 216–26.
> Keane, Angela. *Women Writers and the English Nation,* 90–96.

Celestina, 1791

Fletcher, Loraine. *Charlotte Smith,* 135–42.

Desmond, 1792

Binhammer, Katherine. "Revolutionary Domesticity in Charlotte Smith's *Desmond,*" in Linda Lang-Peralta, ed., *Women, Revolution, and the Novels of the 1790s,* 25–41.

Fletcher, Loraine. *Charlotte Smith,* 142–53.

Ford, Susan Allen. "Tales of the Times: Family and Nation in Charlotte Smith and Jane West," in Andrea O'Reilly Herrera et al., eds., *Family Matters,* 16–26.

Keane, Angela. *Women Writers and the English Nation,* 81–90.

Mellor, Anne K. *Mothers of the Nation,* 106–21.

Rosenblum, Joseph. "The Treatment of Women in the Novels of Charlotte Turner Smith," in Laura Dabundo, ed., *Jane Austen and Mary Shelley,* 45–51.

Watson, Nicola J. *Revolution and the Form of the British Novel,* 36–39.

Wikborg, Eleanor. "Political Discourse versus Sentimental Romance: Ideology and Genre in Charlotte Smith's *Desmond.*" *Engl Stud* (Amsterdam) 78 (1997), 522–31.

Emmeline, 1788

Bannet, Eve Tavor. *The Domestic Revolution,* 78–79, 80–81.

Doody, Margaret Anne. "Deserts, Ruins and Troubled Waters: Female Dreams in Fiction and the Development of the Gothic Novel," in Richard Kroll, ed., *The English Novel, Volume II,* 80–82.

Fletcher, Loraine. *Charlotte Smith,* 92–103.

Haggerty, George E. *Unnatural Affections,* 59–66.

Hoeveler, Diane Long. *Gothic Feminism,* 35–50.

Mohr, Hans Ulrich. "Drei Konstrukte weiblicher Verhaltensräume: Charlotte Smith, Olive Schreiner, Angela Carter." *Arbeiten aus Anglistik und Amerikanistik* 20 (1995), 317–33.

Piper, William Bowman. *Reconcilable Differences,* 172–75.

Rosenblum, Joseph. "The Treatment of Women in the Novels of Charlotte Turner Smith," in Laura Dabundo, ed., *Jane Austen and Mary Shelley,* 48–50.

Ethelinde, 1789

Copeland, Edward. *Women Writing about Money,* 52–54.

Fletcher, Loraine. *Charlotte Smith,* 107–21.

The Letters of a Solitary Wanderer, 1800–01

Fletcher, Loraine. *Charlotte Smith,* 292–96.

Wordsworth, Jonathan. *The Bright Work Grows,* 126–32.

Marchmont, 1796

Bannet, Eve Tavor. *The Domestic Revolution,* 189–93.

Fletcher, Loraine. *Charlotte Smith,* 250–55.

Rosenblum, Joseph. "The Treatment of Women in the Novels of Charlotte Turner Smith," in Laura Dabundo, ed., *Jane Austen and Mary Shelley,* 45–47.

Spencer, Jane. "Women Writers and the Eighteenth-Century Novel," in John Richetti, ed., *The Cambridge Companion,* 228–32.

Montalbert, 1795

> Bannet, Eve Tavor. *The Domestic Revolution,* 181–85.
> Fletcher, Loraine. *Charlotte Smith,* 241–47.

The Old Manor House, 1793

> Burgess, Miranda J. "Charlotte Smith, *The Old Manor House,*" in Duncan Wu, ed., *A Companion to Romanticism,* 122–29.
> Day, Aidan. *Romanticism,* 30–33.
> Fay, Elizabeth A. *A Feminist Introduction to Romanticism,* 130–32.
> Fletcher, Loraine. *Charlotte Smith,* 163–91.
> Keane, Angela. *Women Writers and the English Nation,* 96–102.
> King, Kathryn R. "Of Needles and Pens and Women's Work." *Tulsa Stud in Women's Lit* 14:1 (1995), 77–93.
> Rosenblum, Joseph. "The Treatment of Women in the Novels of Charlotte Turner Smith," in Laura Dabundo, ed., *Jane Austen and Mary Shelley,* 45–47.
> Snader, Joe. *Caught Between Worlds,* 211–17.

The Wanderings of Warwick, 1794

> Fletcher, Loraine. *Charlotte Smith,* 211–12.

The Young Philosopher, 1798

> Fletcher, Loraine. *Charlotte Smith,* 266–83.
> Keane, Angela. *Women Writers and the English Nation,* 102–7.
> Rosenblum, Joseph. "The Treatment of Women in the Novels of Charlotte Turner Smith," in Laura Dabundo, ed., *Jane Austen and Mary Shelley,* 45–51.

JOAN SMITH

A Masculine Ending, 1987

> Frank, Marion. "The Transformation of a Genre: The Feminist Mystery Novel," in Susanne Fendler, ed., *Feminist Contributions,* 92–100.

What Men Say, 1993

> Frank, Marion. "The Transformation of a Genre: The Feminist Mystery Novel," in Susanne Fendler, ed., *Feminist Contributions,* 100–107.

TOBIAS SMOLLETT

Ferdinand Count Fathom, 1753

> Beasley, Jerry C. *Tobias Smollett,* 120–50.
> Montandon, Alain. *Le roman au XVIIIe siècle,* 188–90.
> Richetti, John. *The English Novel in History,* 162–68.

Humphry Clinker, 1771

> Beasley, Jerry C. "Amiable Apparitions: Smollett's Fictional Heroines," in Albert J. Rivero, ed., *Augustan Subjects,* 243–45.
> Beasley, Jerry C. *Tobias Smollett,* 184–225.
> Beasley, Jerry C. "Tobias Smollett: The Scot in England." *Stud in Scottish Lit* 29 (1996), 26–28.

Case, Alison A. *Plotting Women*, 71–77.

Cavaliero, Glen. *The Alchemy of Laughter*, 128–31.

Folkenflik, Robert. "Self and Society: Comic Union in *Humphry Clinker*," in Richard Kroll, ed., *The English Novel, Volume II*, 128–36.

Frank, Judith. *Common Ground*, 90–126.

Gordon, Jan. "The 'Talking Cure' (Again): Gossip and the Paralyzed Patriarchy," in David T. Mitchell and Sharon L. Snyder, eds., *The Body and Physical Difference*, 210–13.

Gores, Steven J. *Psychosocial Spaces*, 67–70.

Lutz, Alfred. "Representing Scotland in *Roderick Random* and *Humphry Clinker*: Smollett's Development as a Novelist." *Stud in the Novel* 33:1 (2001), 1–12.

McKee, Patricia. *Public and Private*, 19–25, 28–37.

Miles, Peter. "*Humphry Clinker*: The Politics of Correspondence." *Brit J for Eighteenth-Cent Stud* 23 (2000), 167–81.

Montandon, Alain. *Le roman au XVIIIe siècle*, 286–90.

Morse, David. *The Age of Virtue*, 215–19.

Prior, Tim. "Lydia Melford and the Role of the Classical Body in Smollett's *Humphry Clinker*." *Stud in the Novel* 30 (1998), 489–504.

Richetti, John. *The English Novel in History*, 181–92.

Rosenblum, Michael. "Smollett's *Humphry Clinker*," in John Richetti, ed., *The Cambridge Companion*, 175–94.

Skinner, Gillian. *Sensibility and Economics in the Novel*, 81–90.

Sorensen, Janet. *The Grammar of Empire*, 104–37.

Walker, Marshall. *Scottish Literature since 1707*, 60–63.

Weed, David M. "Sentimental Misogyny and Medicine in *Humphry Clinker*." *Stud in Engl Lit, 1500–1900* 37 (1997), 615–34.

Peregrine Pickle, 1751

Beasley, Jerry C. "Amiable Apparitions: Smollett's Fictional Heroines," in Albert J. Rivero, ed., *Augustan Subjects*, 237–41.

Beasley, Jerry C. *Tobias Smollett*, 75–119.

Graeber, Wilhelm. *Der englische Roman in Frankreich*, 211–21.

Haggerty, George E. *Men in Love*, 74–78.

Ireland, Ken. *The Sequential Dynamics of Narrative*, 172–73.

McFarlane, Cameron. *The Sodomite in Fiction and Satire*, 122–33.

Montandon, Alain. *Le roman au XVIIIe siècle*, 182–88.

Richetti, John. *The English Novel in History*, 179–81.

Roderick Random, 1748

Barrell, John. "A Diffused Picture, an Uniform Plan: Roderick Random in the Labyrinth of Britain," in Richard Kroll, ed., *The English Novel, Volume II*, 97–103, 105–16.

Beasley, Jerry C. "Amiable Apparitions: Smollett's Fictional Heroines," in Albert J. Rivero, ed., *Augustan Subjects*, 232–41.

Beasley, Jerry C. *Tobias Smollett*, 35–74.

Beasley, Jerry C. "Tobias Smollett: The Scot in England." *Stud in Scottish Lit* 29 (1996), 24–26.

Davis, Leith. *Acts of Union*, 67–72.

Graeber, Wilhelm. *Der englische Roman in Frankreich*, 235–52.

Gwilliam, Tassie. "Female Fraud: Counterfeit Maidenheads in the Eighteenth Century." *J of the Hist of Sexuality* 6 (1996), 518–48.

Haggerty, George E. *Men in Love*, 74–78.

Lutz, Alfred. "Representing Scotland in *Roderick Random* and *Humphry Clinker*: Smollett's Development as a Novelist." *Stud in the Novel* 33:1 (2001), 1–12.

Lynch, Deidre Shauna. *The Economy of Character*, 83–85, 87–89, 102–12.

McFarlane, Cameron. *The Sodomite in Fiction and Satire*, 109–44.

Montandon, Alain. *Le roman au XVIIIe siècle*, 182–88.

Nelson, T. G. A. "Smollett's Representation and Critique of the Traffic in Women: A Narrative Strand in *Roderick Random*." *Philol Q* 78 (1999), 283–99.

Peck, John. *Maritime Fiction*, 22–27.

Richetti, John. *The English Novel in History*, 168–79.

Swan, Beth. *Fictions of Law*, 130–36.

Varney, Andrew. *Eighteenth-Century Writers in their World*, 106–13.

Sir Launcelot Greaves, 1762

Beasley, Jerry C. *Tobias Smollett*, 151–83.

Keymer, Thomas. "Dying by Numbers: *Tristram Shandy* and Serial Fiction (2)." *The Shandean* 9 (1997), 48–50.

SOMERVILLE AND ROSS

The Big House of Inver, 1925

Chen, Bi-ling. "De-Mystifying the Family Romance: A Feminist Reading of Somerville and Ross's *The Big House of Inver*." *Notes on Mod Irish Lit* 10 (1998), 17–25.

Frehner, Ruth. *The Colonizers' Daughters*, 162–76.

Kelleher, Margaret. *The Feminization of Famine*, 128–31.

Kreilkamp, Vera. *The Anglo-Irish Novel*, 123–25, 131–40, 175–77.

An Irish Cousin, 1889

Kreilkamp, Vera. *The Anglo-Irish Novel*, 115–23.

Laird, Holly A. *Women Coauthors*, 102–13.

Mount Music, 1919

Kreilkamp, Vera. *The Anglo-Irish Novel*, 123–31.

The Real Charlotte, 1894

Cahalan, James M. *Double Visions*, 75–77.

Greene, Nicole Pepinster. "Dialect and Social Identity in *The Real Charlotte*." *New Hibernia R* 4:1 (2000), 122–37.

Hall, Wayne E. "Landscape as Frame in *The Real Charlotte*." *New Hibernia R* 3:3 (1999), 96–115.

Kiberd, Declan. *Inventing Ireland*, 69–82.

Laird, Holly A. *Women Coauthors*, 113–26.

JOHN SOMMERFIELD

May Day, 1936

Haywood, Ian. *Working-Class Fiction*, 84–86.

MURIEL SPARK

The Ballad of Peckham Rye, 1960

Christianson, Aileen. "Certainty and Unease in Muriel Spark's *The Ballad of Peckham Rye*," in Carol Anderson and Aileen Christianson, eds., *Scottish Women's Fiction*, 135–45.

Sumera, Adam. "Muriel Spark's Novels in Poland and in German-Speaking Countries." *Folia Litteraria Anglica* (Lodz) 1 (1997), 185–95.

The Comforters, 1957

Carruthers, Gerard. "The Remarkable Fictions of Muriel Spark," in Douglas Gifford and Dorothy McMillan, eds., *A History*, 515–16.

The Driver's Seat, 1970

Carruthers, Gerard. "The Remarkable Fictions of Muriel Spark," in Douglas Gifford and Dorothy McMillan, eds., *A History*, 521–22.

A Far Cry from Kensington, 1988

Glavin, John. "Muriel Spark: Beginning Again," in Abby H. P. Werlock, ed., *British Women Writing Fiction*, 307–10.

The Girls of Slender Means, 1963

Glavin, John. "Muriel Spark: Beginning Again," in Abby H. P. Werlock, ed., *British Women Writing Fiction*, 299–304.

The Hothouse by the East River, 1973

Sumera, Adam. "Muriel Spark's Novels in Poland and in German-Speaking Countries." *Folia Litteraria Anglica* (Lodz) 1 (1997), 185–95.

The Mandelbaum Gate, 1965

Carruthers, Gerard. "The Remarkable Fictions of Muriel Spark," in Douglas Gifford and Dorothy McMillan, eds., *A History*, 520–21.

Memento Mori, 1959

Sumera, Adam. "Muriel Spark's Novels in Poland and in German-Speaking Countries." *Folia Litteraria Anglica* (Lodz) 1 (1997), 185–95.

The Prime of Miss Jean Brodie, 1961

Carruthers, Gerard. "The Remarkable Fictions of Muriel Spark," in Douglas Gifford and Dorothy McMillan, eds., *A History*, 518–19.

Felton, Sharon. "Portraits of the Artists as Young Defiers: James Joyce and Muriel Spark." *Tennessee Philol Bull* 33 (1996), 24–33.

Glavin, John. "Muriel Spark: Beginning Again," in Abby H. P. Werlock, ed., *British Women Writing Fiction*, 296–97.

Montgomery, Benilde. "Spark and Newman: Jean Brodie Reconsidered." *Twentieth Cent Lit* 43:1 (1997), 94–106.

Smith, Patricia Juliana. *Lesbian Panic*, 84–92.

Sumera, Adam. "Muriel Spark's Novels in Poland and in German-Speaking Countries." *Folia Litteraria Anglica* (Lodz) 1 (1997), 185–95.

The Public Image, 1968

Apostolou, Fotini. "Seduction, Simulacra and the Feminine: Spectacles and Images in Muriel Spark's *The Public Image*." *J of Gender Stud* 9 (2000), 281–95.

Sumera, Adam. "Muriel Spark's Novels in Poland and in German-Speaking Countries." *Folia Litteraria Anglica* (Lodz) 1 (1997), 185–95.

Robinson, 1958

Engélibert, Jean-Paul. *La postérité de Robinson Crusoé*, 97–98, 206–19, 299–306.

The Takeover, 1976

Mengham, Rod. "1973 The End of History: Cultural Change According to Muriel Spark," in Mengham, ed., *An Introduction to Contemporary Fiction*, 123–34.

STEPHEN SPENDER

The Backward Son, 1940

Leeming, David. *Stephen Spender*, 138–39.
Sternlicht, Sanford. *Stephen Spender*, 88–90.

The Temple, 1988

Leeming, David. *Stephen Spender*, 46–48, 252–53.
Sternlicht, Sanford. *Stephen Spender*, 90–92.

OLAF STAPLEDON

Last and First Men, 1930

Crossley, Robert. "Acts of God," in David Seed, ed., *Imagining Apocalypse*, 81–82.
Stone-Blackburn, Susan. "Science and Spirituality in *Back to Methuselah* and *Last and First Men*," in Milton T. Wolf, ed., *Shaw and Science Fiction*, 185–97.
Waugh, Robert H. "Spirals and Metaphors: The Shape of Divinity in Olaf Stapledon's Myth." *Extrapolation* 38 (1997), 207–14.

The Star Maker, 1937

Crossley, Robert. "Acts of God," in David Seed, ed., *Imagining Apocalypse*, 82–84.
May, Stephen. *Stardust and Ashes*, 78–81.
Waugh, Robert H. "Spirals and Metaphors: The Shape of Divinity in Olaf Stapledon's Myth." *Extrapolation* 38 (1997), 214–20.

JOHN GABRIEL STEDMAN

Narrative of a Five Years Expedition Against the Revolted Negroes of Surinam, 1796

Gwilliam, Tassie. "'Scenes of Horror,' Scenes of Sensibility: Sentimentality and Slavery in John Gabriel Stedman's *Narrative of a Five Years Expedition Against the Revolted Negroes of Surinam*." *ELH* 65 (1998), 653–69.

FLORA ANNIE STEEL

On the Face of the Waters, 1896

Johnson, Alan. "'Sanitary Duties' and Registered Women: A Reading of *On the Face of the Waters.*" *Yale J of Criticism* 11 (1998), 507–12.

Otsuki, Jennifer L. "The *Memsahib* and the Ends of Empire: Feminine Desire in Flora Annie Steel's *On the Face of the Waters.*" *Victorian Lit and Culture* 24 (1996), 5–27.

JAMES STEPHENS

The Crock of Gold, 1912

Quintelli-Neary, Marguerite. *Folklore and the Fantastic*, 138–48.

Sayers, William. "Molly's Monologue and the Old Woman's Complaint in James Stephens' *The Crock of Gold.*" *James Joyce Q* 36:3 (1999), 640–47.

The Demi-Gods, 1914

Quintelli-Neary, Marguerite. *Folklore and the Fantastic*, 139–48.

LAURENCE STERNE

A Sentimental Journey, 1768

Bandry, Anne. "Les Livres de Sterne: Suites et fins." *Bull de la Société d'Etudes Anglo-Américaines des XVIIe et XVIIIe Siècles* 50 (2000), 115–36.

Bandry, Anne. "Recréation du *Sentimental Journey* de Sterne: Une Suite récréative à but lucratif." *Bull de la Société d'Etudes Anglo-Américaines des XVIIe et XVIIIe Siècles* 49 (1999), 313–24.

Bell, Ian A. "To See Ourselves: Travel Narratives and National Identity in Contemporary Britain," in Bell, ed., *Peripheral Visions*, 6–8.

Bergner, Heinz. "Reisebericht und Roman: Laurence Sternes *Sentimental Journey Through France and Italy,*" in Xenja von Ertzdorff, ed., *Beschreibung der Welt*, 409–26.

Brown, Laura. "The Feminization of Ideology: Form and the Female in the Long Eighteenth Century," in David H. Richter, ed., *Ideology and Form*, 234–36.

Derry, Stephen. "*Mansfield Park*, Sterne's Starling, and Bunyan's Man of Despair." *Notes and Queries* 44 (1997), 322–23.

Ellis, Markman. *The Politics of Sensibility*, 71–79.

Frank, Judith. *Common Ground*, 63–89.

Gould, Rebecca. "Sterne's Sentimental Yorick as Male Hysteric." *Stud in Engl Lit, 1500–1900* 36 (1996), 641–51.

Hölter, Achim. "Johan Gottlieb Schummels *Empfindsame Reise durch Deutschland*: Ein scheiternder Dialog zwischen Autor und Leser in der deutschen Sterne-Rezeption." *Euphorion* 91:1 (1997), 23–63.

Ireland, Ken. *The Sequential Dynamics of Narrative*, 178–79.

Kay, Carol. "*A Sentimental Journey*: Purposeful Play," in Richard Kroll, ed., *The English Novel, Volume II*, 174–87.

Kraft, Elizabeth. "Laurence Sterne and the Chiasmus of Double Desire." *The Shandean* 11 (1999–2000), 55–62.

Lamb, Jonathan. "Sterne and Irregular Oratory," in John Richetti, ed., *The Cambridge Companion*, 153–70.

Lynch, Deidre Shauna. *The Economy of Character*, 112–18.

Montandon, Alain. *Le roman au XVIIIe siècle*, 439–50.

Mullan, John. "Sentimental Novels," in John Richetti, ed., *The Cambridge Companion*, 238–41.

New, Melvyn. "Sterne in the Future Tense." *The Shandean* 11 (1999–2000), 63–69.

New, Melvyn. "Three Sentimental Journeys: Sterne, Shklovsky, Svevo." *The Shandean* 11 (1999–2000), 126–32.

Paulson, Ronald. *The Beautiful, Novel, and Strange*, 153–58.

Polloczek, Dieter Paul. *Literature and Legal Discourse*, 27–36, 52–61.

Richetti, John. *The English Novel in History*, 265–69.

Ross, Ian Campbell. *Laurence Sterne*, 334–36, 392–94, 416–18.

Shankman, Steven. "Participation and Reflective Distance: The End of Laurence Sterne's *A Sentimental Journey* and the Resistance to Doctrine." *Rel and Lit* 29:3 (1997), 43–58.

Skinner, Gillian. *Sensibility and Economics in the Novel*, 112–16.

Starr, George. "'Only a Boy': Notes on Sentimental Novels," in Richard Kroll, ed., *The English Novel, Volume II*, 43–47.

Turner, Katherine S. H. "At the Boundaries of Fiction: Samuel Paterson's *Another Traveller!*," in Alvaro Ribeiro and James G. Basker, eds., *Tradition in Transition*, 144–56.

Werner, Florian. "Kindred Spirits? John Cleland's *Fanny Hill* and Laurence Sterne's *A Sentimental Journey*." *Zeitschrift für Anglistik und Amerikanistik* 48 (2000), 25–29.

Tristram Shandy, 1760–1767

Alsop, Derek, and Chris Walsh. *The Practice of Reading*, 28–50.

Bailey, Anne Hall. "When Worlds Collide: Tracing the Line of Descent in Laurence Sterne's *Tristram Shandy*." *Tennessee Philol Bull* 33 (1996), 53–62.

Ballesteros González, Antonio. "Digression and Intertextual Parody in Thomas Nashe, Laurence Sterne and James Joyce," in David Pierce and Peter de Voogd, eds., *Laurence Sterne*, 58–64.

Barney, Richard A. *Plots of Enlightenment*, 1–3.

Beidler, Paul G. "The Aesthetic of Scientific Discovery: Hume, Sterne, and the Literary Sketch." *Stud on Voltaire and the Eighteenth Cent* 378 (1999), 201–27.

Bell, Michael. "Laurence Sterne and the Twentieth Century," in David Pierce and Peter de Voogd, eds., *Laurence Sterne*, 39–54.

Blackwell, Bonnie. "*Tristram Shandy* and the Theater of the Mechanical Mother." *ELH* 68 (2001), 81–127.

Bonifazi, Barbara. "La retorica del silenzio in *Tristram Shandy* di Laurence Sterne." *Lettore di Provincia* 30 (1999), 41–56.

Braverman, Richard. "Satiric Embodiments: Butler, Swift, Sterne," in James E. Gill, ed., *Cutting Edges*, 80–82, 89–91.

Cavaliero, Glen. *The Alchemy of Laughter*, 61–70.

Cruise, James. *Governing Consumption*, 155–85.

Descargues, Madeleine. "Sterne, Nabokov and the Happy (Non)Ending of Biography," in David Pierce and Peter de Voogd, eds., *Laurence Sterne*, 167–78.

Dupas, Jean-Claude. "'A sun-dial in a grave: the founding gesture,'" in David Pierce and Peter de Voogd, eds., *Laurence Sterne*, 99–108.

Ellis, Markman. *The Politics of Sensibility*, 67–71.

Fairer, David. "Sentimental Translation in Mackenzie and Sterne." *Essays in Criticism* 49 (1999), 132–51.

Fanning, Christopher. "On Sterne's Page: Spatial Layout, Spatial Form, and Social Spaces in *Tristram Shandy*." *Eighteenth-Cent Fiction* 10 (1998), 429–50.

Fisher, Carl. "Madness to the Method: Sterne's *Tristram Shandy* as Mock-Educational Novel." *Tennessee Philol Bull* 35 (1998), 24–36.

Flint, Christopher. *Family Fictions*, 271–88.

Fourny, Corinne. "Dialogues in *Tristram Shandy*: Openness or Control?" *The Shandean* 9 (1997), 70–82.

Frank, Judith. *Common Ground*, 67–77.

Frischhertz, Eric J. "Laurence Sterne's Treatment of a New Mode of Discourse: Nonverbal Communication in *Tristram Shandy*." *Age of Johnson* 8 (1997), 255–76.

Gobel, Walter. "The Decentring of Man in *Tristram Shandy*." *The Shandean* 11 (1999–2000), 28–37.

Göbel, Walter, and Damian Grant. "Salman Rushdie's Silver Medal," in David Pierce and Peter de Voogd, eds., *Laurence Sterne*, 87–98.

Gourdon, Gisèle. "Confinements and Flights of the Characters in *Tristram Shandy*." *The Shandean* 10 (1998), 92–104.

Gow, James, and Mark Loveridge. "More on Walter's White Bear in *Tristram Shandy*." *Notes and Queries* 47 (2000), 201.

Gurr, Jens Martin. *"Tristram Shandy" and the Dialectic of Enlightenment*, 57–160.

Hardack, Richard. "Going Belly Up: Entries, Entrees, and the All-Consuming Encyclopedic Text." *LIT* 7 (1996), 140–48.

Hardin, Michael. "Is There A Straight Line in This Text?: The Homoerotics of *Tristram Shandy*." *Orbis Litterarum* 54 (1999), 185–200.

Harrison, Bernard. "Sterne and Sentimentalism," in Leona Toker, ed., *Commitment in Reflection*, 63–98.

Hart, Michael. "'Many Planes of Narrative': A Comparative Perspective on Sterne and Joyce," in David Pierce and Peter de Voogd, eds., *Laurence Sterne*, 65–80.

Hartvig, Gabriella. "The Rhetorical Sources of *Tristram Shandy*." *AnaChronist* 1997: 13–27.

Hilton, Michele. "*Tristram Shandy* and the Cant of French Criticism." *Henry Street* 7:1 (1998), 9–16.

Ireland, Ken. *The Sequential Dynamics of Narrative*, 177–78, 183–85.

Keymer, Thomas. "Dying by Numbers: *Tristram Shandy* and Serial Fiction." *The Shandean* 8 (1996), 41–63; 9 (1997), 34–62.

Keymer, Tom. "Horticulture Wars: *Tristram Shandy* and *Upon Appleton House.*" *The Shandean* 11 (1999–2000), 38–46.

Klein, Herbert. "Identity Reclaimed: The Art of Being Tristram," in David Pierce and Peter de Voogd, eds., *Laurence Sterne*, 123–32.

Lamb, Jonathan. "The Comic Sublime and Sterne's Fiction," in Richard Kroll, ed., *The English Novel, Volume II*, 163–69.

Laudando, Carla Maria. "Deluge of Fragments: Rabelais's 'Fourth Book,' Sterne's 'Fragment' and Beckett's 'Fizzles,'" in David Pierce and Peter de Voogd, eds., *Laurence Sterne*, 157–65.

Lawlor, Clark. "Consuming Time: Narrative and Disease in *Tristram Shandy.*" *Yrbk of Engl Stud* 30 (2000), 46–59.

Lawlor, Clark. "Sterne, Edward Baynard, and *The History of Cold Bathing*: Medical Shandeism." *Notes and Queries* 46 (1999), 22–25.

Lewis, Jayne. "'Where then lies the difference?': The (Ante)Postmodernity of *Tristram Shandy*," in Richard Gravil, ed., *Master Narratives*, 21–35.

London, April. *Women and Property*, 81–83.

Loveridge, Mark. "Walter's White Bear in *Tristram Shandy.*" *Notes and Queries* 46 (1999), 358–60.

Lynch, Deidre Shauna. *The Economy of Character*, 23–26.

Lynch, Jack. "The Relicks of Learning: Sterne among the Renaissance Encyclopedists." *Eighteenth-Cent Fiction* 13:1 (2000), 1–17.

Mazella, David. "'Be wary, Sir, when you imitate him': The Perils of Didacticism in *Tristram Shandy.*" *Stud in the Novel* 31 (1999), 152–74.

Milesi, Laurent. "'Have you not forgot to wind up the clock?': Tristram Shandy and Jacques le fataliste on the (Post?)Modern Psychoanalytic Couch," in David Pierce and Peter de Voogd, eds., *Laurence Sterne*, 179–95.

Moglen, Helene. *The Trauma of Gender*, 87–108.

Montandon, Alain. *Le roman au XVIIIe siècle*, 322–28, 507–15.

Morse, David. *The Age of Virtue*, 206–10.

Mullan, John. "Sentimental Novels," in John Richetti, ed., *The Cambridge Companion*, 238–43.

New, Melvyn. "Sterne and *The History of Cold-Bathing.*" *Notes and Queries* 44 (1997), 211–12.

Nockolds, Peter. "Conceived in Heaven: The Astronomy and Astrology of *Tristram Shandy.*" *The Shandean* 11 (1999–2000), 119–24.

Parnell, Tim. "Sterne and Kundera: The Novel of Variations and the 'noisy foolishness of human certainty,'" in David Pierce and Peter de Voogd, eds., *Laurence Sterne*, 147–55.

Parnell, Tim. "A Story Painted to the Heart? *Tristram Shandy* and Sentimentalism Reconsidered." *The Shandean* 9 (1997), 122–33.

Parnell, Tim. "*Tristram Shandy* and 'the gutter of Time.'" *The Shandean* 11 (1999–2000), 48–54.

Paulson, Ronald. *The Beautiful, Novel, and Strange*, 166–71.

Pegenaute, Louis. "Three Trapped Tigers in Shandy Hall," in David Pierce and Peter de Voogd, eds., *Laurence Sterne*, 133–45.

Piper, William Bowman. *Common Courtesy in Eighteenth-Century English Literature*, 85–110.

Polloczek, Dieter Paul. *Literature and Legal Discourse*, 39–52, 61–64.

Rademacher, Jörg W. "Totalized (Auto-)Biography as Fragmented Intertextuality: Shakespeare—Sterne—Joyce," in David Pierce and Peter de Voogd, eds., *Laurence Sterne*, 81–86.

Richetti, John. *The English Novel in History*, 269–77.

Richter, David H. "Narrativity and Stasis in Martin Rowson's *Tristram Shandy.*" *The Shandean* 11 (1999–2000), 70–88.

Ross, Ian Campbell. *Laurence Sterne*, 12–19, 215–23, 260–63.

Schonhorn, Manuel. "Tristram Shandy: Paradigm Change and the Heroisation of the Artist." *Stud on Voltaire and the Eighteenth Cent* 347 (1996), 667–69.

Shevlin, Eleanor F. "The Plots of Early English Novels: Narrative Mappings Rooted in Land and Law." *Eighteenth-Cent Fiction* 11 (1999), 399–402.

Sim, Stuart. "'All that exist are "islands of determinism"': Shandean Sentiment and the Dilemma of Postmodern Physics," in David Pierce and Peter de Voogd, eds., *Laurence Sterne*, 109–21.

Simms, Norman. "Stuffing Sausages as Satura and Foreplay: Apuleius's Lucius and Trim's Brother Tom." *The Shandean* 8 (1996), 113–18.

Swinden, Patrick. *Literature and the Philosophy of Intention*, 189–206.

Tadié, Alexis. "*Tristram Shandy* and Visual Perception." *Stud on Voltaire and the Eighteenth Cent* 347 (1996), 834–37.

Visser, Nicholas. "*Tristram Shandy* and the Straight Line of History." *Textual Practice* 12 (1998), 489–99.

Vlock, Deborah M. "Sterne, Descartes, and the Music in *Tristram Shandy.*" *Stud in Engl Lit, 1500–1900* 38 (1998), 517–33.

Wallace, Miriam L. "Gender Bending and Corporeal Limitations: The Modern Body in *Tristram Shandy.*" *Stud in Eighteenth-Cent Culture* 26 (1998), 175–91.

Washington, Gene. "Apropos Doors, Janus and Tristram." *The Shandean* 11 (1999–2000), 92–96.

Watts, Carol. "The Modernity of Sterne," in David Pierce and Peter de Voogd, eds., *Laurence Sterne*, 19–38.

Werner, Hans C. *Literary Texts as Nonlinear Patterns*, 131–68.

Woodard, Helena. *African-British Writings in the Eighteenth Century*, 78–82.

Yang, Wonkyung. "Childbirth and Female Midwifery in Laurence Sterne's *Tristram Shandy.*" *J of Engl Lang and Lit* 44 (1998), 789–806.

Zimmerman, Everett. *The Boundaries of Fiction*, 182–88, 191–203.

ROBERT LOUIS STEVENSON

Dr. Jekyll and Mr. Hyde, 1886

Arata, Stephen. *Fictions of Loss*, 33–45, 49–53.

Brantlinger, Patrick. *The Reading Lesson*, 166–81.

Brennan, Matthew C. *The Gothic Psyche*, 97–110.

Brody, Jennifer DeVere. *Impossible Purities*, 146–47.

Calanchi, Alessandra. "'Others Will Follow': Lo strano caso di Jekyll, Hyde e Sherlock Holmes." *Rivista di Studi Vittoriani* 3:5 (1998), 133–43.

Clemens, Valdine. *The Return of the Repressed*, 123–52.

Cookson, Gillian. "Engineering Influences on *Jekyll and Hyde*." *Notes and Queries* 46 (1999), 487–91.

Currie, Mark. *Postmodern Narrative Theory*, 117–34.

Forderer, Christof. *Ich-Eklipsen*, 129–33, 136–56.

Goh, Robbie B. H. "Textual Hyde and Seek: 'Gentility,' Narrative Play and Proscription in Stevenson's *Dr Jekyll and Mr Hyde*." *J of Narrative Theory* 29 (1999), 158–78.

Haggerty, George E. "'The End of History': Identity and Dissolution in Apocalyptic Gothic." *Eighteenth Cent* 41 (2000), 240–44.

Hampson, Robert. "*Chance* and the Secret Life: Conrad, Thackeray, Stevenson." *Conradian* 17:2 (1993), 105–22.

Hendershot, Cyndy. *The Animal Within*, 105–14.

Kane, Michael. *Modern Men*, 17–26.

Mighall, Robert. *A Geography of Victorian Gothic Fiction*, 145–53, 187–95.

Phelan, James E. "Freudian Commentary on the Parallels of the Male Homosexual Analysand to Robert Louis Stevenson's *The Strange Case of Dr. Jekyll and Mr. Hyde*." *J of Evolutionary Psych* 19 (1998), 215–22.

Pykett, Lyn. "Sensation and the Fantastic in the Victorian Novel," in Deirdre David, ed., *The Cambridge Companion to the Victorian Novel*, 206–8.

Robson, Catherine. *Men in Wonderland*, 154–57.

Rosner, Mary. "'A Total Subversion of Character': Dr. Jekyll's Moral Insanity." *Victorian Newsl* 93 (1998), 27–30.

Showalter, Elaine. "Dr. Jekyll's Closet," in Elton E. Smith and Robert Haas, eds., *The Haunted Mind*, 67–88.

Towheed, Shafquat. "R. L. Stevenson's Sense of the Uncanny: 'The Face in the Cheval-Glass.'" *Engl Lit in Transition* 42 (1999), 23–36.

Walker, Marshall. *Scottish Literature since 1707*, 206–14.

The Ebb–Tide, 1894

Buckton, Oliver S. "Reanimating Stevenson's Corpus." *Nineteenth-Cent Lit* 55 (2000), 53–58.

Ricks, Christopher. "A Note on 'The Hollow Men' and Stevenson's *The Ebb-Tide*." *Essays in Criticism* 51 (2001), 8–16.

Kidnapped, 1886

Buckton, Oliver S. "Reanimating Stevenson's Corpus." *Nineteenth-Cent Lit* 55 (2000), 46–47.

Sorensen, Janet. "'Belts of Gold' and 'Twenty-Pounders': Robert Louis Stevenson's Textualized Economies." *Criticism* 42 (2000), 280–92.

The Master of Ballantrae, 1889

Buckton, Oliver S. "Reanimating Stevenson's Corpus." *Nineteenth-Cent Lit* 55 (2000), 47–53.

Pearson, Nels C. "The Moment of Modernism: Schopenhauer's

'Unstable Phantom' in Conrad's *Heart of Darkness* and Stevenson's *The Master of Ballantrae.*" *Stud in Scottish Lit* 31 (1999), 182–202.

Treasure Island, 1883

Alexander, Doris. *Creating Literature Out of Life,* 23–43.

Buckton, Oliver S. "Reanimating Stevenson's Corpus." *Nineteenth-Cent Lit* 55 (2000), 45–46.

Davidson, Guy. "'Ancient Appetites': Romance and Desire in Robert Louis Stevenson." *Australasian Victorian Stud J* 3:1 (1997), 62–69.

Donald, Tania. "*Treasure Island*: A Book for Boys?" *Meridian* (La Trobe Univ.) 15 (1996), 173–84.

Hardesty, William H., III, and David D. Mann. "Odds on *Treasure Island.*" *Stud in Scottish Lit* 29 (1996), 29–36.

Hunt, Peter. *Children's Literature,* 234–36.

Melrose, Robin, and Diana Gardner. "The Language of Control in Victorian Children's Literature," in Ruth Robbins and Julian Wolfreys, eds., *Victorian Identities,* 148–49, 155–56, 158–62.

Möller, Joachim. "Lob der Subjektivität: Einige Illustrationen zu Stevensons *Treasure Island.*" *Literatur in Wissenschaft und Unterricht* 32 (1999), 127–36.

Peck, John. *Maritime Fiction,* 153–59.

Pierce, Jason A. "The Belle Lettrist and the People's Publisher; or, The Context of *Treasure Island*'s First-Form Publication." *Victorian Periodicals R* 31 (1998), 356–66.

Wood, Naomi J. "Gold Standards and Silver Subversions: *Treasure Island* and the Romance of Money." *Children's Lit* 26 (1998), 61–81.

J. I. M. STEWART

The Aylwins, 1966

Dougill, John. *Oxford in English Literature,* 209–11.

Death at the President's Lodging, 1936

Dougill, John. *Oxford in English Literature,* 199–201.

BRAM STOKER

Dracula, 1897

Alexander, Bryan. "*Dracula* and the Gothic Imagination of War." *J of Dracula Stud* 2 (2000), 15–23.

Arata, Stephen. *Fictions of Loss,* 111–32.

Armstrong, Nancy. "Gender and the Victorian Novel," in Deirdre David, ed., *The Cambridge Companion to the Victorian Novel,* 114–15, 119–20.

Backus, Margot Gayle. *The Gothic Family Romance,* 135–41.

Bierman, Joseph S. "A Crucial Stage in the Writing of *Dracula*," in William Hughes and Andrew Smith, eds., *Bram Stoker,* 151–71.

Botting, Fred. "*Dracula*, Romance and Radcliffean Gothic." *Women's Writing* 1 (1994), 181–87.

Bozzetto, Roger. *Territoires des fantastiques,* 153–57.

Brennan, Matthew C. *The Gothic Psyche*, 113–32.

Brennan, Matthew C. "The Novel as Nightmare: Decentering of the Self in Bram Stoker's *Dracula*." *J of the Fantastic in the Arts* 7:4 (1996), 48–59.

Breuer, Horst. "Atavismus bei Joseph Conrad, Bram Stoker und Eugene O'Neill." *Anglia* 117 (1999), 379–84.

Cain, Jimmie E., Jr. "'With the Unspeakables': *Dracula* and Russophobia—Tourism, Racism and Imperialism," in Elizabeth Miller, ed., *"Dracula,"* 104–15.

Case, Alison A. *Plotting Women*, 161–86.

Cerreta, Michele. "A Structural Analysis of *Dracula* by Bram Stoker." *Rivista di Studi Vittoriani* 1 (1996), 173–83.

Clemens, Valdine. "*Dracula*: The Reptilian Brain at the *fin de siècle*," in Elizabeth Miller, ed., *"Dracula,"* 205–18.

Clemens, Valdine. *The Return of the Repressed*, 153–83.

Clougherty, R. J., Jr. "Voiceless Outsiders: Count Dracula as Bram Stoker." *New Hibernia R* 4:1 (2000), 138–51.

Coad, David. "Other in *The Moonstone* and *Dracula*." *Annales du Monde Anglophone* 4 (1996), 33–53.

Cribb, Susan M. "'If I Had to Write with a Pen': Readership and Bram Stoker's Diary Narrative." *J of the Fantastic in the Arts* 10 (1999), 133–41.

Crossen, John F. "The Stake That Spoke: Vlad Dracula and a Medieval 'Gospel' of Violence," in Elizabeth Miller, ed., *"Dracula,"* 180–91.

Daly, Nicholas. "Incorporated Bodies: *Dracula* and the Rise of Professionalism." *Texas Stud in Lit and Lang* 39 (1997), 181–99.

Daly, Nicholas. *Modernism, Romance and the Fin de Siècle*, 30–52.

Davies, Bernard. "Inspirations, Imitations and In-Jokes in Stoker's *Dracula*," in Elizabeth Miller, ed., *"Dracula,"* 131–37.

Day, Gary. "The State of *Dracula*: Bureaucracy and the Vampire," in Alice Jenkins and Juliet John, eds., *Rereading Victorian Fiction*, 81–93.

Dickens, David B. "The German Matrix of Stoker's *Dracula*," in Elizabeth Miller, ed., *"Dracula,"* 31–40.

Edwards, Robert. "The Alien and the Familiar in *The Jewel of Seven Stars* and *Dracula*," in William Hughes and Andrew Smith, eds., *Bram Stoker*, 96–99, 112–14.

Fernbach, Amanda. "Dracula's Decadent Fetish," in Elizabeth Miller, ed., *"Dracula,"* 219–28.

Finn, Anne Marie. "Whose *Dracula* Is It Anyway? Dean, Balderston and the 'World Famous Vampire Play.'" *J of Dracula Stud* 1 (1999), 8–14.

Fleissner, Jennifer L. "Dictation Anxiety: The Stenographer's Stake in *Dracula*." *Nineteenth-Cent Contexts* 22 (2000), 417–48.

Gerke, Robert S. "The Structure of Horror in *Dracula*." *Bull of the West Virginia Assoc of Coll Engl Teachers* 15 (1993), 9–20.

Gold, Barri J. "Reproducing Empire: *Moreau* and Others." *Nineteenth Cent Stud* 14 (2000), 189–93.

Harse, Katie. "High Duty and Savage Delight: The Ambiguous

Nature of Violence in *Dracula*." *J of the Fantastic in the Arts* 10 (1999), 116–23.

Harse, Katie. "'Stalwart Manhood': Failed Masculinity in *Dracula*," in Elizabeth Miller, ed., *"Dracula,"* 229–38.

Hendershot, Cyndy. *The Animal Within*, 21–29.

Hensley, Wayne E. "Stoker's *Dracula*." *Explicator* 58:2 (2000), 89–90.

Hogle, Jerrold E. "Stoker's Counterfeit Gothic: *Dracula* and Theatricality at the Dawn of Simulation," in William Hughes and Andrew Smith, eds., *Bram Stoker*, 202–22.

Höglund, Johan A. *Mobilising the Novel*, 133–36.

Hopkins, Lisa. "Vampires and Snakes: Monstrosity and Motherhood in Bram Stoker." *Irish Stud R* 19 (1997), 5–8.

Hughes, William. "'Terrors That I Dare Not Think Of': Masculinity, Hysteria and Empiricism in Stoker's *Dracula*," in Elizabeth Miller, ed., *"Dracula,"* 93–103.

Hustis, Harriet. "Black and White and Read All Over: Performative Textuality in Bram Stoker's *Dracula*." *Stud in the Novel* 33:1 (2001), 18–31.

Jarrot, Sabine. *Le vampire dans la littérature*, 59–63, 99–107, 111–16, 156–57.

Kane, Michael. *Modern Men*, 125–38.

Kilgour, Maggie. "Vampiric Arts: Bram Stoker's Defence of Poetry," in William Hughes and Andrew Smith, eds., *Bram Stoker*, 52–59.

Kline, Michael. "The Vampire as Pathogen: Bram Stoker's *Dracula* and Francis Ford Coppola's *Bram Stoker's Dracula*." *West Virginia Univ Philol Papers* 42–43 (1997–1998), 36–44.

Kostova, Ludmilla. *Tales of the Periphery*, 145–58.

Leatherdale, Clive. "Stoker's Banana Skins: Errors, Illogicalities and Misconceptions in *Dracula*," in Elizabeth Miller, ed., *"Dracula,"* 138–54.

Ledger, Sally. *The New Woman*, 100–106.

Levy, Anita. *Reproductive Urges*, 129–45, 156–70.

Lewis, Pericles. "*Dracula* and the Epistemology of the Victorian Gothic Novel," in Elizabeth Miller, ed., *"Dracula,"* 71–81.

Lörinczi, Marinella. "The Technique of 'Reversal' in *Dracula* and *The Lady of the Shroud*," in Elizabeth Miller, ed., *"Dracula,"* 155–62.

McNally, Raymond. "Separation Granted; Divorce Denied; Annulment Unlikely." *J of Dracula Stud* 1 (1999), 25–27.

Marigny, Jean. "Secrecy as Strategy in *Dracula*." *J of Dracula Stud* 2 (2000), 3–7.

May, Leila S. "'Foul things of the night': Dread in the Victorian Body." *Mod Lang R* 93 (1998), 16–22.

Mighall, Robert. *A Geography of Victorian Gothic Fiction*, 225–35, 238–47, 267–85.

Mighall, Robert. "'A pestilence which walketh in darkness': Diagnosing the Victorian Vampire," in Glennis Byron and David Punter, eds., *Spectral Readings*, 108–16.

Mighall, Robert. "Sex, History and the Vampire," in William Hughes and Andrew Smith, eds., *Bram Stoker*, 62–75.

Milbank, Alison. "'Powers Old and New': Stoker's Alliances with

Anglo-Irish Gothic," in William Hughes and Andrew Smith, eds., *Bram Stoker*, 20–27.

Milburn, Diane. "'Denn die Toten reiten schnell': Anglo-German Cross-Currents in Bram Stoker's *Dracula*," in Susanne Stark, ed., *The Novel in Anglo-German Context*, 229–40.

Milburn, Diane. "'For the Dead Travel Fast': *Dracula* in Anglo-German Context," in Elizabeth Miller, ed., *"Dracula,"* 41–53.

Miller, Elizabeth. "Back to the Basics: Re-Examining Stoker's Sources for *Dracula*." *J of the Fantastic in the Arts* 10 (1999), 187–96.

Miller, Elizabeth. "Coffin Nails: Smokers and Non-Smokers in *Dracula*." *J of Dracula Stud* 1 (1999), 33–37.

Miller, Elizabeth. "Filing for Divorce: Count Dracula vs Vlad Tepes," in Miller, ed., *"Dracula,"* 165–79.

Mohr, Rowena. "The Vampire's Kiss: Gender, Desire and Power in *Dracula* and *The Penance of Portia James*." *Australasian Victorian Stud J* 4 (1998), 80–87.

Moss, Stephanie. "Bram Stoker and the London Stage." *J of the Fantastic in the Arts* 10 (1999), 124–32.

Muirhead, Marion. "Corruption Becomes Itself Corrupt: Entropy in *Dracula*," in Elizabeth Miller, ed., *"Dracula,"* 239–46.

Mulvey-Roberts, Marie. "*Dracula* and the Doctors: Bad Blood, Menstrual Taboo and the New Woman," in William Hughes and Andrew Smith, eds., *Bram Stoker*, 78–92.

Navarette, Susan J. *The Shape of Fear*, 126–29.

Nyberg, Suzanna. "Men in Love: The Fantasizing of Bram Stoker and Edvard Munch." *J of the Fantastic in the Arts* 8 (1997), 488–502.

Pedlar, Valerie. "*Dracula*: A Fin-de-Siècle Fantasy," in Dennis Walder, ed., *The Nineteenth-Century Novel*, 196–216.

Petersen, Per Serritslev. "Vampirizing the New Woman: Masculine Anxiety and Romance in Bram Stoker's *Dracula*." *B.A.S.: Brit and Am Stud* 6 (2000), 31–39.

Petit, Jean-Claude. "*Dracula*: une lecture au travers de la programmation neuro linguistique (P.N.L.)." *Etudes Irlandaises* 23:2 (1998), 39–52.

Rosenberg, Nancy F. "Desire and Loathing in Bram Stoker's *Dracula*." *J of Dracula Stud* 2 (2000), 8–14.

Ruthner, Clemens. "Bloodsuckers with Teutonic Tongues: The German-Speaking World and the Origins of *Dracula*," in Elizabeth Miller, ed., *"Dracula,"* 54–67.

Saldanha da Gama, Gilza. "Dracula's Heirs." *J of Dracula Stud* 2 (2000), 34–37.

Sandner, David. "Up-to-Date with a Vengeance: Modern Monsters in Bram Stoker's *Dracula* and Margaret Oliphant's 'The Secret Chamber.'" *J of the Fantastic in the Arts* 8 (1997), 294–309.

Scandura, Jani. "Deadly Professions: *Dracula*, Undertakers, and the Embalmed Corpse." *Victorian Stud* 40:1 (1996), 1–22.

Sceats, Sarah. "Oral Sex: Vampiric Transgression and the Writing of Angela Carter." *Tulsa Stud in Women's Lit* 20:1 (2001), 107–8.

Schmid, David. "Is the Pen Mightier than the Sword? The

Contradictory Function of Writing in *Dracula*," in Elizabeth Miller, ed., *"Dracula,"* 119–30.

Schmitt, Cannon. *Alien Nation*, 138–57.

Simmons, Clare A. "Fables of Continuity: Bram Stoker and Medievalism," in William Hughes and Andrew Smith, eds., *Bram Stoker*, 32–36.

Smith, Andrew. *Gothic Radicalism*, 129–47.

Soule, Arun. "*Dracula*: Of Shades and Shadows." *Rajasthan Univ Stud in Engl* 20 (1988), 77–83.

Stewart, Bruce. "Bram Stoker's *Dracula*: Possessed by the Spirit of the Nation?" *Irish Univ R* 29 (1999), 238–55.

Sutherland, John. *Who Betrays Elizabeth Bennet?*, 238–44.

Taylor, Susan B. "Stoker's *Dracula*." *Explicator* 55:1 (1996), 29–31.

Thomas, Ronald R. "Specters of the Novel: *Dracula* and the Cinematic Afterlife of the Victorian Novel," in John Kucich and Dianne F. Sadoff, eds., *Victorian Afterlife*, 288–95. (Also in *Nineteenth-Cent Contexts* 22 [2000], 77–98.)

Tracy, Robert. "Undead, Unburied: Anglo-Ireland and the Predatory Past." *LIT* 10 (1999), 14–16.

Valente, Joseph. "'Double Born': Bram Stoker and the Metrocolonial Gothic." *Mod Fiction Stud* 46 (2000), 632–43.

Wadge, Elisabeth. "The Scientific Spirit and the Spiritual Scientist: Moving in the Right Circles." *Victorian R* 26:1 (2000), 31–40.

Wilson, Deborah S. "Technologies of Misogyny: The Transparent Maternal Body and Alternate Reproductions in Frankenstein, Dracula, and Some Selected Media Discourses," in Deborah S. Wilson and Christine Moneera Laennec, eds., *Bodily Discursions*, 113–21.

Wixson, Kellie Donovan. "*Dracula*: An Anglo-Irish Gothic Novel," in Elizabeth Miller, ed., *"Dracula,"* 247–56.

Wynne, Catherine. "Mesmeric Exorcism, Idolatrous Beliefs, and Bloody Rituals: Mesmerism, Catholicism, and Second Sight in Bram Stoker's Fiction." *Victorian R* 26:1 (2000), 49–56.

The Jewel of Seven Stars, 1903

Edwards, Robert. "Crowning the King, Mourning his Mother: *The Jewel of Seven Stars* and *The Lady of the Shroud*," in William Hughes and Andrew Smith, eds., *Bram Stoker*, 134–41.

Hopkins, Lisa. "The Alien and the Familiar in *The Jewel of Seven Stars* and *Dracula*," in William Hughes and Andrew Smith, eds., *Bram Stoker*, 96–99, 112–14.

Seed, David. "Eruptions of the Primitive into the Present: *The Jewel of Seven Stars* and *The Lair of the White Worm*," in William Hughes and Andrew Smith, eds., *Bram Stoker*, 188–95.

The Lady of the Shroud, 1909

Edwards, Robert. "Crowning the King, Mourning his Mother: *The Jewel of Seven Stars* and *The Lady of the Shroud*," in William Hughes and Andrew Smith, eds., *Bram Stoker*, 140–48.

Kostova, Ludmilla. *Tales of the Periphery*, 185–92.

Lörinczi, Marinella. "The Technique of 'Reversal' in *Dracula* and *The Lady of the Shroud*," in Elizabeth Miller, ed., *"Dracula,"* 155–62.

Sage, Victor. "Exchanging Fantasies: Sex and the Serbian Crisis in *The Lady of the Shroud*," in William Hughes and Andrew Smith, eds., *Bram Stoker*, 116–32.

Simmons, Clare A. "Fables of Continuity: Bram Stoker and Medievalism," in William Hughes and Andrew Smith, eds., *Bram Stoker*, 35–39.

Wynne, Catherine. "Mesmeric Exorcism, Idolatrous Beliefs, and Bloody Rituals: Mesmerism, Catholicism, and Second Sight in Bram Stoker's Fiction." *Victorian R* 26:1 (2000), 56–61.

The Lair of the White Worm, 1911

Brody, Jennifer DeVere. *Impossible Purities*, 170–76.

Punter, David. "Echoes in the Animal House: *The Lair of the White Worm*," in William Hughes and Andrew Smith, eds., *Bram Stoker*, 173–87.

Seed, David. "Eruptions of the Primitive into the Present: *The Jewel of Seven Stars* and *The Lair of the White Worm*," in William Hughes and Andrew Smith, eds., *Bram Stoker*, 195–202.

The Snake's Pass, 1890

Bierman, Joseph S. "A Crucial Stage in the Writing of *Dracula*," in William Hughes and Andrew Smith, eds., *Bram Stoker*, 163–71.

Daly, Nicholas. *Modernism, Romance and the Fin de Siècle*, 54–85.

Hughes, William. "'For Ireland's Good': The Reconstruction of Rural Ireland in Bram Stoker's *The Snake's Pass*." *Irish Stud R* 12 (1995), 17–21.

ELIZABETH STONE

William Langshawe, 1842

Law, Graham. "Industrial Designs: Form and Function in the 'Condition-of-England' Novel," in George Hughes, ed., *Corresponding Powers*, 132–34.

DAVID STOREY

Radcliffe, 1963

Adelman, Gary. "Possession and Gothic Horror: David Storey's Use of *The Idiot* in *Radcliffe*." *J of Mod Lit* 24:1 (2000), 181–88.

Valdeón García, Roberta A. "El tratamiento de la temática homosexual en cuatro novelistas ingleses: Lawrence, Forster, Waugh y Storey." *Cuadernos de Investigación Filológica* 23–24 (1997–1998), 139–62.

Saville, 1976

Pittock, Malcolm. "David Storey and *Saville*: A Revaluation." *Forum for Mod Lang Stud* 32 (1996), 208–26.

NOEL STREATFEILD

Movie Shoes, 1949

Perrin, Noel. *A Child's Delight*, 75–78.

HESBA STRETTON

Enoch Roden's Training, 1865

Melrose, Robin, and Diana Gardner. "The Language of Control in Victorian Children's Literature," in Ruth Robbins and Julian Wolfreys, eds., *Victorian Identities,* 150–51, 157.

EITHNE STRONG

The Love Riddle, 1993

St. Peter, Christine. *Changing Ireland,* 56–59.

FRANCIS STUART

Black List, Section H, 1971

Caterson, S. J. "Joyce, the Künstlerroman and Minor Literature: Francis Stuart's *Black List, Section H.*" *Irish Univ R* 27:1 (1997), 87–97.

Corcoran, Neil. *After Yeats and Joyce,* 110–12.

GRAHAM SWIFT

Ever After, 1992

Byatt, A. S. *On Histories and Stories,* 73–74, 81–83.

Gilmour, Robin. "Using the Victorians: The Victorian Age in Contemporary Fiction," in Alice Jenkins and Juliet John, eds., *Rereading Victorian Fiction,* 195–98.

Malcolm, David. "Telling the Real in Contemporary British Fiction," in Wojciech H. Kalaga and Tadeusz Rachwal, eds., *Signs of Culture,* 102–13.

Mecklenburg, Susanne. *Martin Amis und Graham Swift,* 162–71.

Last Orders, 1996

Flint, Kate. "Looking Backward? The Relevance of Britishness," in Barbara Korte and Klaus Peter Müller, eds., *Unity in Diversity Revisited?,* 40–42.

Mecklenburg, Susanne. *Martin Amis und Graham Swift,* 171–80.

Poole, Adrian. "Graham Swift and the Mourning After," in Rod Mengham, ed., *An Introduction to Contemporary Fiction,* 162–66.

Out of This World, 1988

Mecklenburg, Susanne. *Martin Amis und Graham Swift,* 154–62.

Poole, Adrian. "Graham Swift and the Mourning After," in Rod Mengham, ed., *An Introduction to Contemporary Fiction,* 157–61.

Shuttlecock, 1981

Hickman, Alan Forrest. "It's a Wise Child: Teaching the Lessons of History in the Contemporary British Novel." *Publs of the Arkansas Philol Assoc* 24:1 (1998), 33–37.

Kaczvinsky, Donald P. "'For one thing, there are the gaps': History in Graham Swift's *Shuttlecock.*" *Critique* (Washington, DC) 40 (1998), 3–13.

Mecklenburg, Susanne. *Martin Amis und Graham Swift*, 137–43.

The Sweet-Shop Owner, 1980

Mecklenburg, Susanne. *Martin Amis und Graham Swift*, 129–37.

Waterland, 1983

Bényei, Tamás. "Narrative and Repetition in *Waterland*." *B.A.S.: Brit and Am Stud* 1:1 (1996), 109–16.

Barnard, Catherine. "*Waterland*, la lanterne magique du roman historique." *La Licorne* 22 (1992), 153–61.

Byatt, A. S. *On Histories and Stories*, 51–53, 69–71.

Gilmour, Robin. "Using the Victorians: The Victorian Age in Contemporary Fiction," in Alice Jenkins and Juliet John, eds., *Rereading Victorian Fiction*, 194–95.

Hickman, Alan F. "Looking Before and After: The Search for the 'Inner Warrior' in Today's British Novel." *Publs of the Arkansas Philol Assoc* 25:1 (1999), 56–59.

Ingelbien, Raphaël. "'England and Nowhere': Contestations of Englishness in Philip Larkin and Graham Swift." *English* 48 (1999), 38–47.

Ireland, Ken. *The Sequential Dynamics of Narrative*, 153–66.

Irish, Robert K. "'Let me Tell You': About Desire and Narrativity in Graham Swift's *Waterland*." *Mod Fiction Stud* 44 (1998), 917–32.

McKinney, Ronald H. "The Greening of Postmodernism: Graham Swift's *Waterland*." *New Liter Hist* 28 (1997), 821–32.

Mecklenburg, Susanne. *Martin Amis und Graham Swift*, 143–54.

Poole, Adrian. "Graham Swift and the Mourning After," in Rod Mengham, ed., *An Introduction to Contemporary Fiction*, 161–62.

Smethurst, Paul. "Post-Imperial Topographies: The Undergrounding of History in J. G. Farrell's *The Singapore Grip*, Timothy Mo's *An Insular Possession*, and Graham Swift's *Waterland*," in Ralph J. Crane, ed., *J. G. Farrell*, 113–25.

Uskalis, Eriks. "Making the 'Public' Male: Performing Masculinities, Power and Tradition in Graham Swift's *Waterland* and Peter Carey's *The Tax Inspector*," in Antony Rowland et al., eds., *Signs of Masculinity*, 246–54.

Warner, Lionel. "Raising Paranoia: Child-Theft in Three 1980s Novels." *The Use of Engl* 52 (2000), 49–50.

JONATHAN SWIFT

Gulliver's Travels, 1726

Barbé-Petit, Françoise. "La Violence et ses représentations dans *Gulliver's Travels* de Swift." *Bull de la Société d'Etudes Anglo-Américaines des XVIIe et XVIIIe Siècles* 44 (1997), 17–35.

Barchas, Janine. "Prefiguring Genre: Frontispiece Portraits from *Gulliver's Travels* to *Millenium Hall*." *Stud in the Novel* 30 (1998), 265–72.

Barnett, Louise K. "Deconstructing *Gulliver's Travels*: Modern Readers and the Problematic of Genre," in Nigel Wood, ed., *Jonathan Swift*, 255–66.

Bartra, Roger. *The Artificial Savage*, 175–200.

Benedict, Barbara M. *Curiosity*, 110–16.

Bennett, Sue. "The Act of Reading *Gulliver's Travels*." *Readerly/Writerly Texts* 2:1 (1994), 69–81.

Boucé, Paul-Gabriel. "Death in *Gulliver's Travels*: The Struldbruggs Revisited," in Rudolf Freiburg et al., eds., *Swift*, 1–13.

Boyle, Frank. *Swift as Nemesis*, 26–78.

Boyle, Frank T. "Chinese Utopianism and Gulliverian Narcissism in Swift's *Travels*," in Aileen Douglas et al., eds., *Locating Swift*, 117–28.

Braverman, Richard. "Satiric Embodiments: Butler, Swift, Sterne," in James E. Gill, ed., *Cutting Edges*, 86–89.

Castle, Terry J. "Why the Houyhnhnms Don't Write: Swift, Satire and the Fear of the Text," in Nigel Wood, ed., *Jonathan Swift*, 239–53.

Christie, William. "Intimations of Immortality in Swift and Keats: A Note." *R of Engl Stud* 48 (1997), 501–3.

Crook, Keith. *A Preface to Swift*, 157–61, 165–69, 172–77, 200–211.

DePorte, Michael. "Novelizing the *Travels*: Simon Moore's Gulliver." *Swift Stud* 12 (1997), 99–102.

Donoghue, Denis. "The Brainwashing of Lemuel Gulliver." *Southern R* (Baton Rouge) 32:1 (1996), 128–46.

Donoghue, Denis. *The Practice of Reading*, 165–86.

Doody, Margaret Anne. "Swift and the Mess of Narrative," in Aileen Douglas et al., eds., *Locating Swift*, 109–16.

Downie, J. A. *To Settle the Succession of the State*, 112–15.

Engell, James. *The Committed Word*, 52–62.

Esty, Joshua D. "Excremental Postcolonialism." *Contemp Lit* 40 (1999), 27–30.

Fausett, David. "'Another World, yet the Same': Ethnic Stereotyping in Early Travel Fiction," in C. C. Barfoot, ed., *Beyond Pug's Tour*, 137–40.

Forster, Jean-Paul. *Jonathan Swift*, 40–47, 81–84, 87–89, 115–17, 159–66, 177–82, 208–10.

Gardiner, Anne Barbeau. "'Be ye as the horse!': Swift, Spinoza, and the Society of Virtuous Atheists." *Stud in Philology* 97 (2000), 229–53.

Gill, James E. "Pharmakon, Pharmakos, and Aporetic Structure in Gulliver's 'Voyage to . . . the Houyhnhnms,'" in Gill, ed., *Cutting Edges*, 181–99.

Goldberg, Julia. "Houyhnhnm Subtext: Moral Conclusions and Linguistic Manipulation in *Gulliver's Travels*." *1650–1850: Ideas, Aesthetics, and Inquiries in the Early Mod Era* 4(1998), 269–84.

Hammond, Brean S. *Professional Imaginative Writing*, 271–75.

Hollindale, Peter. "Plain Speaking: *Black Beauty* as a Quaker Text." *Children's Lit* 28 (2000), 95–96.

Hudson, Nicholas. "*Gulliver's Travels* and Locke's Radical Nominalism." *1650–1850: Ideas, Aesthetics, and Inquiries in the Early Mod Era* 1(1994), 247–66.

Jestin, Loftus. "*Splendide Mendax*: Purposeful Misprision, Determinant Irony, in *Gulliver's Travels*." *Swift Stud* 14 (1999), 99–114.

Kelly, James William. "A Contemporary Source for the *Yahoos* in *Gulliver's Travels*." *Notes and Queries* 45 (1998), 68–70.

Klein, Jürgen, and Gerhild Riemann. "Enigmatic Folly or Foolish Enigma: Speculations on *Gulliver's Travels* Book III," in Rudolf Freiburg et al., eds., *Swift*, 91–98.

Knowles, Ronald. *"Gulliver's Travels": The Politics of Satire*, 3–148.

Lapraz-Severino, Françoise. "From 'Temple' to 'Temple,' or a Pun on One Avatar of Gulliver's Lodgings." *Cycnos* 10:2 (1993), 49–51.

Lengeler, Rainer. *"Gulliver's Travels*: Ein verkannter Klassiker?" *Literatur in Wissenschaft und Unterricht* 30 (1997), 105–18.

Loveridge, Mark. *A History of Augustan Fable*, 213–15.

McCrea, Brian. "Lemuel Gulliver's 'Treacherous' Religion: Swift's Redaction of Ecclesiastes." *Christianity and Lit* 49 (2000), 465–79.

McLeod, Bruce. *The Geography of Empire*, 181–86.

McLoughlin, T. O. *Contesting Ireland*, 77–85.

Mandell, Laura. *Misogynous Economies*, 90–93.

Matlak, Richard E. "Hindoo/Yahoo: Charles Grant and the Christianizing of India," in Rudolf Freiburg et al., eds., *Swift*, 113–25.

Montag, Warren. "Gulliver's Solitude: The Paradoxes of Swift's Anti-Individualism." *Eighteenth Cent* 42 (2001), 3–17.

Montandon, Alain. *Le roman au XVIIIe siècle*, 77–83.

Moore, Patrick J. "Ythaith Ogwir: A Study of *Gulliver's Travels* by Jonathan Swift, II." *J of Evolutionary Psych* 18:3–4 (1997), 213–24.

Morse, David. *The Age of Virtue*, 84–94.

Nash, Richard. "Of Sorrels, Bays, and Dapple Grays." *Swift Stud* 15 (2000), 110–13.

Nash, Walter. *Language and Creative Illusion*, 65–81.

Palmeri, Frank. "The Historian as Satirist and Satirized," in Aileen Douglas et al., eds., *Locating Swift*, 90–93.

Parker, Todd C. *Sexing the Text*, 54–56.

Perry, Susan. "Jonathan Swift's Skewed Ethos in Discussing the Grand Academy: Dr. Pangloss Meets Lemuel Gulliver." *Conf of Coll Teachers of Engl Stud* 62 (1997), 19–27.

Peterson, Leland D. "Gulliver's Secret Commission," in Rudolf Freiburg et al., eds., *Swift*, 201–11.

Phiddian, Robert. "A Hopeless Project: Gulliver Inside the Language of Science in Book III." *Eighteenth-Cent Life* 22:1 (1998), 50–61.

Pickering, Oliver. "Thomas Fitzgerald's Criticism of *Gulliver's Travels*," in Rudolf Freiburg et al., eds., *Swift*, 213–20.

Piper, William Bowman. *Reconcilable Differences*, 68–88.

Rawson, Claude. *Satire and Sentiment*, 29–34, 70–75.

Real, Hermann J. "The 'keen Appetite for Perpetuity of Life' Abated: The Struldbruggs, Again," in Rüdiger Ahrens and Fritz-Wilhelm Neumann, eds., *Fiktion und Geschichte*, 117–34.

Reymond, Jacqueline. "Le Merveilleux et l'Universel dans *Gulliver's Travels*." *La Licorne* 22 (1992), 207–27.

Richardson, John. "Christian and/or Ciceronian: Swift and Gulliver's Fourth Voyage." *Cambridge Q* 30:1 (2001), 37–49.

Richardson, John. "Still to Seek: Politics, Irony, Swift." *Essays in Criticism* 49 (1999), 300–316.

Rodino, Richard H. "'Splendide Mendax': Authors, Characters, and Readers in *Gulliver's Travels*," in Nigel Wood, ed., *Jonathan Swift*, 44–65.

Rosenblum, Joseph. "Gulliver's Dutch Uncle: Another Look at Swift and the Dutch." *Brit J for Eighteenth-Cent Stud* 24 (2001), 63–75.

Seidel, Michael. "*Gulliver's Travels* and the Contracts of Fiction," in John Richetti, ed., *The Cambridge Companion*, 72–87.

Shankar, S. *Textual Traffic*, 58–73.

Swan, Beth. *Fictions of Law*, 162–65.

Thickstun, Margaret Olofson. "The Puritan Origins of Gulliver's Conversion in Houyhnhnmland." *Stud in Engl Lit, 1500–1900* 37 (1997), 517–32.

Varney, Andrew. *Eighteenth-Century Writers in their World*, 23–32, 186–92.

Wagner, Peter. "Swift's Great Palimpsest: Intertextuality and Travel Literature in *Gulliver's Travels*." *Dispositio* 17 (1992), 107–32.

Woodard, Helena. *African-British Writings in the Eighteenth Century*, 110–15.

Zirker, Herbert. "Horse Sense and Sensibility: Some Issues Concerning Utopian Understanding in *Gulliver's Travels*." *Swift Stud* 12 (1997), 85–98.

ALGERNON CHARLES SWINBURNE

Lesbia Brandon, 1952

Alexander, Jonathan. "Sex, Violence and Identity: A. C. Swinburne and Uses of Sadomasochism." *Victorian Newsl* 90 (1996), 33–36.

Lane, Christopher. *The Burdens of Intimacy*, 74–92.

Vincent, John. "Flogging is Fundamental: Applications of Birch in Swinburne's *Lesbia Brandon*," in Eve Kosofsky Sedgwick, ed., *Novel Gazing*, 269–94.

Love's Cross Currents, 1901

Lane, Christopher. *The Burdens of Intimacy*, 81–84.

NETTA SYRETT

Anne Page, 1908

Ardis, Ann. "Netta Syrett's Aestheticization of Everyday Life: Countering the Counterdiscourse of Aestheticism," in Talia Schaffer and Kathy Alexis Psomiades, eds., *Women and British Aestheticism*, 235–36, 243–46.

Nobody's Fault, 1896

Heilmann, Ann. "Feminist Resitance, the Artist and 'A Room of One's Own' in New Woman Fiction." *Women's Writing* 2 (1995), 296–97.

Rose Cottingham Married, 1916

Heilmann, Ann. *New Woman Fiction*, 164–66.

Strange Marriage, 1930

> Ardis, Ann. "Netta Syrett's Aestheticization of Everyday Life: Countering the Counterdiscourse of Aestheticism," in Talia Schaffer and Kathy Alexis Psomiades, eds., *Women and British Aestheticism*, 236–39.

ELIZABETH TAYLOR

A Game of Hide and Seek, 1951

> Hanson, Clare. *Hysterical Fictions*, 85–89.

Palladian, 1946

> Hanson, Clare. *Hysterical Fictions*, 75–80.

The Sleeping Beauty, 1953

> Hanson, Clare. *Hysterical Fictions*, 89–93.

The Wedding Group, 1968

> Hanson, Clare. *Hysterical Fictions*, 93–96.

A Wreath of Roses, 1949

> Hanson, Clare. *Hysterical Fictions*, 80–85.
> Hanson, Clare. "Marketing the 'Woman Writer,'" in Judy Simons and Kate Fullbrook, eds., *Writing: A Woman's Business*, 71–75.

MEADOWS TAYLOR

Confessions of a Thug, 1839

> Kapila, Shuchi. "Educating Seeta: Philip Meadows Taylor's Romances of Empire." *Victorian Stud* 41:2 (1998), 215–16.

Seeta, 1872

> Kapila, Shuchi. "Educating Seeta: Philip Meadows Taylor's Romances of Empire." *Victorian Stud* 41:2 (1998), 223–35.
> Peck, John. *War, the Army and Victorian Literature*, 88–93.

UNA ASHWORTH TAYLOR

The City of Sarras, 1887

> Schaffer, Talia. *The Forgotten Female Aesthetes*, 52–54.

EMMA TENNANT

Alice Fell, 1980

> Wesley, Marilyn C. "Emma Tennant: The Secret Lives of Girls," in Abby H. P. Werlock, ed., *British Women Writing Fiction*, 185–86.

The Bad Sister, 1978

> Alexander, Flora. "Contemporary Fiction III: The Anglo-Scots," in Douglas Gifford and Dorothy McMillan, eds., *A History*, 631–32.
> Smith, Patricia Juliana. *Lesbian Panic*, 167–73.

The Half-Mother, 1983

 Wesley, Marilyn C. "Emma Tennant: The Secret Lives of Girls," in Abby H. P. Werlock, ed., *British Women Writing Fiction,* 178–82.

The House of Hospitalities, 1987

 Wesley, Marilyn C. "Emma Tennant: The Secret Lives of Girls," in Abby H. P. Werlock, ed., *British Women Writing Fiction,* 182–84.

The Queen of Stones, 1982

 Wesley, Marilyn C. "Emma Tennant: The Secret Lives of Girls," in Abby H. P. Werlock, ed., *British Women Writing Fiction,* 187–88.

Sisters and Strangers: A Moral Tale, 1991

 King, Jeannette. *Women and the Word,* 34–41.

Two Women of London, 1978

 Alexander, Flora. "Contemporary Fiction III: The Anglo-Scots," in Douglas Gifford and Dorothy McMillan, eds., *A History,* 632.
 Smith, Patricia Juliana. *Lesbian Panic,* 164–67.

Wild Nights, 1979

 Wesley, Marilyn C. "Emma Tennant: The Secret Lives of Girls," in Abby H. P. Werlock, ed., *British Women Writing Fiction,* 184–85.

WILLIAM MAKEPEACE THACKERAY

Catherine, 1840

 Harden, Edgar F. *Thackeray the Writer,* 59–87.
 Pearson, Richard. *W. M. Thackeray and the Mediated Text,* 77–86.
 Prawer, S. S. *Breeches and Metaphysics,* 90–93.

Denis Duval, 1864

 Prawer, S. S. *Breeches and Metaphysics,* 480–85.

Henry Esmond, 1852

 Dames, Nicholas. *Amnesiac Selves,* 125–34, 157–65.
 Fletcher, Robert P. "Visual Thinking and the Picture Story in *The History of Henry Esmond.*" *PMLA* 113 (1998), 379–92.
 Harrison, S. J. "Sons, Mothers, and Lovers in Thackeray and Virgil." *Notes and Queries* 47 (2000), 331–32.
 Peck, John. *War, the Army and Victorian Literature,* 58–64.
 Prawer, S. S. *Breeches and Metaphysics,* 358–63.
 Rogers, Henry N., III. "'How do I love Thee? Hummmm . . . ?': The Love Story in *Henry Esmond.*" *Publs of the Arkansas Philol Assoc* 25:1 (1999), 73–85.
 Sutherland, John. *Who Betrays Elizabeth Bennet?,* 108–14.

The History of Samuel Titmarsh and the Great Hoggarty Diamond, 1841

 Harden, Edgar F. *Thackeray the Writer,* 108–16.

Lovel the Widower, 1860

 Hampson, Robert. "*Chance* and the Secret Life: Conrad, Thackeray, Stevenson." *Conradian* 17:2 (1993), 105–22.
 Horn, Anne Layman. "Farcical Process, Fictional Product:

Thackeray's Theatrics in *Lovel the Widower.*" *Victorian Lit and Culture* 26 (1998), 135–51.

Pearson, Richard. *W. M. Thackeray and the Mediated Text,* 200–206.

Prawer, S. S. *Breeches and Metaphysics,* 454–56.

The Luck of Barry Lyndon, 1844

Cavaliero, Glen. *The Alchemy of Laughter,* 92–95.

Harden, Edgar F. *Thackeray the Writer,* 129–59.

Peck, John. *War, the Army and Victorian Literature,* 53–55.

Prawer, S. S. *Breeches and Metaphysics,* 195–209.

Rosdeitcher, Elizabeth. "Empires at Stake: Gambling and the Economic Unconscious in Thackeray." *Genre* 29 (1996), 411–17.

Watson, John. "Thackeray's Composite Characters: Autobiography and 'True History' in *Barry Lyndon.*" *AUMLA* 87 (1997), 25–38.

The Newcomes, 1854–1855

Byerly, Alison. *Realism, Representation, and the Arts,* 64–66.

Jackson-Houlston, C. M. *Ballads, Songs and Snatches,* 117–22.

McCormick, John. *Catastrophe and Imagination,* 25–26.

Prawer, S. S. *Breeches and Metaphysics,* 365–84.

Shillingsburg, Peter. *William Makepeace Thackeray,* 99–102.

Pendennis, 1849–1850

Butler, Lance St. John. *Registering the Difference,* 88–92.

Dames, Nicholas. *Amnesiac Selves,* 148–57, 162–66.

Franklin, J. Jeffrey. *Serious Play,* 169–82, 191–95.

Pearson, Richard. *W. M. Thackeray and the Mediated Text,* 177–94.

Prawer, S. S. *Breeches and Metaphysics,* 302–25.

Sen, Sambudha. "*Bleak House, Vanity Fair,* and the Making of an Urban Aesthetic." *Nineteenth-Cent Lit* 54 (2000), 482–84.

Shillingsburg, Peter. *William Makepeace Thackeray,* 107–15.

Watson, John L. "Pendennis's Loves: A Biographical Approach." *Cuadernos de Literatura Inglesa y Norteamericana* 1:2 (1996), 11–24.

Philip, 1862

Fisher, Judith L. "Thackeray as Editor and Author: *The Adventures of Philip* and the Inauguration of the *Cornhill Magazine.*" *Victorian Periodicals R* 33 (2000), 2–19.

Pearson, Richard. *W. M. Thackeray and the Mediated Text,* 60–73.

Prawer, S. S. *Breeches and Metaphysics,* 456–65.

The Ravenswing, 1869

Pearson, Richard. *W. M. Thackeray and the Mediated Text,* 86–95.

Rebecca and Rowena, 1850

Knoepflmacher, U. C. *Ventures into Childhood,* 79–81.

Prawer, S. S. *Breeches and Metaphysics,* 337–40.

The Rose and the Ring, 1854

Cavaliero, Glen. *The Alchemy of Laughter,* 136–38.

Vanity Fair, 1848

Brantlinger, Patrick. *The Reading Lesson,* 127–31.

Brody, Jennifer DeVere. *Impossible Purities,* 27–45.

Byerly, Alison. *Realism, Representation, and the Arts*, 66–69, 72–85.

Cavaliero, Glen. *The Alchemy of Laughter*, 110–13.

Dadlez, E. M. *What's Hecuba to Him?*, 93–95.

Dee, Phyllis Susan. "Female Sexuality and Triangular Desire in *Vanity Fair* and *The Mill on the Floss*." *Papers on Lang and Lit* 35 (1999), 391–400.

Frazee, John P. "The Creation of Becky Sharp in *Vanity Fair*." *Dickens Stud Annual* 27 (1998), 227–42.

Harden, Edgar F. *Thackeray the Writer*, 124–28, 170–93.

Harrison, S. J. "Sons, Mothers, and Lovers in Thackeray and Virgil." *Notes and Queries* 47 (2000), 329–32.

Heinrich, Hans. *Zur Geschichte des 'Libertin,'* 205–8.

Ireland, Ken. *The Sequential Dynamics of Narrative*, 206–7.

Kane, Penny. *Victorian Families in Fact and Fiction*, 59–61.

Litvak, Joseph. *Strange Gourmets*, 55–76.

McCuskey, Brian. "Fetishizing the Flunkey: Thackeray and the Uses of Deviance." *Novel* 32 (1999), 384–98.

Miller, Andrew H. *Novels behind Glass*, 14–49, 50–53, 64–68.

Nunokawa, Jeff. "Sexuality in the Victorian Novel," in Deirdre David, ed., *The Cambridge Companion to the Victorian Novel*, 131–33.

Peck, John. *War, the Army and Victorian Literature*, 55–58.

Perkin, J. Russell. "The Implied Theology of *Vanity Fair*." *Philol Q* 77 (1998), 79–101.

Pool, Daniel. *Dickens' Fur Coat*, 53–57, 63–65.

Prawer, S. S. *Breeches and Metaphysics*, 268–301.

Rosdeitcher, Elizabeth. "Empires at Stake: Gambling and the Economic Unconscious in Thackeray." *Genre* 29 (1996), 407–10, 418–26.

Schor, Hilary. "Fiction," in Herbert F. Tucker, ed., *A Companion to Victorian Literature and Culture*, 331–33.

Sen, Sambudha. "*Bleak House, Vanity Fair*, and the Making of an Urban Aesthetic." *Nineteenth-Cent Lit* 54 (2000), 480–502.

Shillingsburg, Peter. *William Makepeace Thackeray*, 63–79.

Simmons, Clare A. *Eyes Across the Channel*, 102–17.

Sutherland, John. *Who Betrays Elizabeth Bennet?*, 55–66.

Thornton, Sara. "The Vanity of Childhood: Constructing, Deconstructing, and Destroying the Child in the Novel of the 1840s," in Karín Lesnik-Oberstein, ed., *Children in Culture*, 131–47.

Watson, John. "Thackeray and Becky Sharp: Creating Women." *Dickens Stud Annual* 25 (1996), 305–21.

The Virginians, 1858–1859

Maszewska, Jadwiga. "Racism and Slavery in Thackeray's *The Virginians*." *Folia Litteraria Anglica* (Lodz) 2 (1998), 55–62.

Peck, John. *War, the Army and Victorian Literature*, 64–70.

Prawer, S. S. *Breeches and Metaphysics*, 416–35.

D. M. THOMAS

The White Hotel, 1981

Sauerberg, Lars Ole. "Fact-Flirting Fiction: Historiographical Potential or Involuntary Parody?" *European J of Engl Stud* 3 (1999), 190–205.

Stovel, Nora Foster. "Tatiana's Letter, A Literary Legacy: From Pushkin's *Eugene Onegin* to D. M. Thomas's *White Hotel.*" *Intl Fiction R* 25 (1998), 1–11.

Vice, Sue. *Holocaust Fiction*, 38–66.

Wallhead, Celia. "Eros and Thanatos in the Epiphany in D. M. Thomas's *The White Hotel*," in Wim Tigges, ed., *Moments of Moment*, 421–33.

KATHERINE CECIL THURSTON

The Fly on the Wheel, 1908

Meaney, Gerardine. "Decadence, Degeneration and Revolting Aesthetics: The Fiction of Emily Lawless and Katherine Cecil Thurston." *Colby Q* 36 (2000), 169–73.

WILLIAM TICKEN

Santos de Montenos, 1811

Saglia, Diego. "'O My Mother Spain!': The Peninsular War, Family Matters, and the Practice of Romantic Nation-Writing." *ELH* 65 (1998), 365–70.

COLM TÓIBÍN

The Heather Blazing, 1992

Herron, Tom. "ContamiNation: Patrick McCabe and Colm Tóibín's Pathographies of the Republic," in Liam Harte and Michael Parker, eds., *Contemporary Irish Fiction*, 183–89.

J. R. R. TOLKIEN

The Fellowship of the Ring, 1954

Lewis, Alex. "Thoughts on the Worth of a Warg." *Amon-Hen* 147 (1997), 11–15.

The Hobbit, 1937

Curry, Patrick. *Defending Middle-Earth*, 12–18.

Donaldson, Mara E. "Baptizing the Imagination: The Fantastic as the Subversion of Fundamentalism." *J of the Fantastic in the Arts* 8 (1997), 185–97.

Ferré, Vincent. "Tolkien et le Moyen Age, ou l'arbre et la feuille," in Michele Gally, ed., *La trace médiévale*, 121–40.

Green, William H. "King Thorin's Mines: *The Hobbit* as Victorian Adventure Novel." *Extrapolation* 42 (2001), 53–63.

Green, William H. "'Where's Mama?': The Construction of the Feminine in *The Hobbit.*" *Lion and the Unicorn* 22 (1998), 188–95.

Hunt, Peter. *Children's Literature*, 173–75.

Medcalf, Stephen. "'The Language Learned of Elves': Owen Barfield, *The Hobbit* and *The Lord of the Rings.*" *Seven* 16 (1999), 33–36.

Orr, Robert. "Some Slavic Echoes in J. R. R. Tolkien's Middle Earth." *Germano-Slavica* 8:2 (1994), 23–34.

Pearce, Joseph. *Tolkien: Man and Myth*, 153–57.

The Lord of the Rings, 1966

Aitken, Bill. *Literary Trails*, 187–97.

Armstrong, Helen. "An Have an Eye to That Dwarf. . . ." *Amon-Hen* 145 (1997), 13–14.

Armstrong, Helen. "There Are Two People in This Marriage." *Mallorn* 36 (1998), 5–12.

Betz, Charlie. "*The Lord of the Rings Tarot Deck*: Not Necessarily Middle-Earth." *Mallorn* 36 (1998), 13–15.

Bratman, David. "Top Ten Rejected Plot Twists from *The Lord of the Rings*: A Textual Excursion into the 'History of The Lord of the Rings.'" *Mythlore* 22:4 (2000), 13–38.

Burns, Marjorie. "Eating, Devouring, Sacrifice and Ultimate Just Desserts." *Mythlore* 21:2 (1996), 108–14.

Buttner, Anke. "Wagner and Rabbits: How a Nation's Press Goes Crazy. . . ." *Amon-Hen* 144 (1997), 13–15.

Carretero González, Margarita. "*The Lord of the Rings*: A Myth for Modern English*men*." *Mallorn* 36 (1998), 51–57.

Chance, Jane. "Power and Knowledge in Tolkien: The Problem of Difference in 'The Birthday Party.'" *Mythlore* 21:2 (1996), 115–20.

Christopher, Joe R. "The Moral Epiphanies in *The Lord of the Rings*." *Mythlore* 21:2 (1996), 121–25.

Clark, Craig. "Problems of Good and Evil in Tolkien's *The Lord of the Rings*." *Mallorn* 35 (1997), 15–19.

Critchett, David. "One Ring to Fool Them All, One Ring to Blind Them: The Propaganda of *The Lord of the Rings*." *Extrapolation* 38 (1997), 36–54.

Curry, Patrick. *Defending Middle-Earth*, 18–21, 31–33, 35–165.

Curry, Patrick. "'Less Noise and More Green': Tolkien's Ideology for England." *Mythlore* 21:2 (1996), 126–38.

Ellison, John. "Gandalf, Frodo, and Sherlock Holmes: Myth and Reality Compared in the Works of Tolkien and Conan Doyle." *Mallorn* 34 (1996), 25–32.

Ellison, John. "Tolkien's World and Wagner's: The Music of Language and the Language of Music." *Mallorn* 36 (1998), 35–42.

Fenwick, Mac. "Breastplates of Silk: Homeric Women in *The Lord of the Rings*." *Mythlore* 21:3 (1996), 17–23.

Ferré, Vincent. "Tolkien et le Moyen Age, ou l'arbre et la feuille," in Michele Gally, ed., *La trace médiévale*, 121–40.

Flieger, Verlyn. "Fantasy and Reality: J. R. R. Tolkien's World and the Fairy-Story Essay." *Mythlore* 22:3 (1999), 4–13.

Garbowski, Christopher. *Recovery and Transcendence*, 9–209.

Hawkins, Emma B. "Chalk Figures and Scouring in Tolkien-land." *Extrapolation* 41 (2000), 385–95.

Hood, Gwenyth. "The Earthly Paradise in Tolkien's *The Lord of the Rings*." *Mythlore* 21:2 (1996), 139–44.

Hopkins, Chris. "Tolkien and Englishness." *Mythlore* 21:2 (1996), 278–80.

Kutzer, M. Daphne. *Empire's Children*, 129–31.

Lacon, Ruth. "Of Cauldrons and Calderas: Some Thoughts on the Geology of Mordor." *Amon-Hen* 149 (1998), 15–16.

Medcalf, Stephen. "'The Language Learned of Elves': Owen Barfield, *The Hobbit* and *The Lord of the Rings*." *Seven* 16 (1999), 31–52.

Mellen, Philip. "Tolkien, Kafka, and the Germanic Model." *Germanic Notes and Reviews* 26:2 (1995), 112–14.

Milos, Karyn. "Too Deeply Hurt: Understanding Frodo's Decision to Depart." *Mallorn* 36 (1998), 17–23.

Niiler, Lucas P. "Green Reading: Tolkien, Leopold, and the Land Ethic." *J of the Fantastic in the Arts* 10 (1999), 276–85.

Orr, Robert. "Some Slavic Echoes in J. R. R. Tolkien's Middle Earth." *Germano-Slavica* 8:2 (1994), 23–34.

Pearce, Joseph. *Tolkien: Man and Myth*, 1–125.

Phemister, William. "Fantasy Set to Music: Donald Swann, C. S. Lewis and J. R. R. Tolkien." *Seven* 13 (1996), 70–72, 76–79.

Sanford, Len. "Fanfare for the Common Man." *Mallorn* 36 (1998), 43–50.

Scull, Christina. "Open Minds, Closed Minds in *The Lord of the Rings*." *Mythlore* 21:2 (1996), 151–56.

Shippey, Tom. "Tolkien as a Post-War Writer." *Mythlore* 21:2 (1996), 84–93.

Stanton, Michael N. "'Advise is a Dangerous Gift': (Pseudo)Proverbs in *The Lord of the Rings*." *Proverbium* 13 (1996), 331–46.

Stanton, Michael N. *Hobbits, Elves and Wizards*.

Sullivan, C. W., III. "J. R. R. Tolkien and the Telling of a Traditional Narrative." *J of the Fantastic in the Arts* 7:1 (1996), 75–82.

Whittingham, Elizabeth A. "The Mythology of the 'Ainulindale': Tolkien's Creation of Hope." *J of the Fantastic in the Arts* 9 (1998), 212–28.

Wicher, Andrzej. "J. R. R. Tolkien's Quarrel with Modernity: Some Reflections on Tolkien's Practical Philosophy," in Wojciech H. Kalaga and Tadeusz Rachwal, eds., *Signs of Culture*, 146–51.

Yandell, Stephen. "'A Pattern Which Our Nature Cries Out For': The Medieval Tradition of the Ordered Four in the Fiction of J. R. R. Tolkien." *Mythlore* 21:2 (1996), 375–92.

Yates, Jessica. "Tolkien as Anti-Totalitarian." *Mythlore* 21:2 (1996), 233–45.

Zimmer, Mary. "Creating and Re-creating Worlds with Words: The Religion and the Magic of Language in *The Lord of the Rings*." *Seven* 12 (1995), 65–77.

The Silmarillion, 1977

Bulles, Marcel. "Cirdan: One of Unknown Heroes?" *Amon-Hen* 138 (1996), 15–17.

Garbowski, Christopher. *Recovery and Transcendence*, 60–66, 137–47, 164–67.

Gough, John. "Tolkien's Creation Myth in *The Silmarillion*: Northern or Not?" *Children's Lit in Educ* 30:1 (1999), 1–8.

Himes, Jonathan. "What J. R. R. Tolkien Really Did with the Sampo." *Mythlore* 22:4 (2000), 69–85.

Lewis, Alex. "Historical Bias in the Making of *The Silmarillion*." *Mythlore* 21:2 (1996), 158–66.

Medcalf, Stephen. "'The Language Learned of Elves': Owen Barfield, *The Hobbit* and *The Lord of the Rings*." *Seven* 16 (1999), 39–42.

Schweicher, Eric. "Aspects of the Fall in *The Silmarillion*." *Mythlore* 21:2 (1996), 167–71.

Whittingham, Elizabeth A. "The Mythology of the 'Ainulindale': Tolkien's Creation of Hope." *J of the Fantastic in the Arts* 9 (1998), 212–28.

CHARLOTTE ELIZABETH TONNA

Helen Fleetwood, 1841

Elliott, Dorice Williams. "Servants and Hands: Representing the Working Classes in Victorian Factory Novels." *Victorian Lit and Culture* 28 (2000), 381–85.

Wenzel, Peter. "Structural Oppositions and Contradictions in Dickens's *Hard Times* and Mrs. Tonna's *Helen Fleetwood*." *Zeitschrift für Anglistik und Amerikanistik* 46 (1998), 316–24.

Zlotnick, Susan. *Women, Writing, and the Industrial Revolution*, 139–43, 150–52, 156–64.

JEFF TORRINGTON

Swing Hammer Swing, 1992

Reckwitz, Erhard. "Intertextuality: Between Continuity and Innovation," in Barbara Korte and Klaus Peter Müller, eds., *Unity in Diversity Revisited?*, 188–90.

ROSE TREMAIN

Restoration, 1989

Fendler, Susanne, and Ruth Wittlinger. "Rose Tremain's *Restoration* and Thatcherism." *Culture and Communication* 3:1 (2000), 29–50.

Sacred Country, 1992

Brînzeu, Pia. *Corridors of Mirrors*, 133–37.

ROBERT TRESSELL

The Ragged Trousered Philanthropists, 1914

Haywood, Ian. *Working-Class Fiction*, 22–34.

Wotton, George. "Writing from the Margins," in Ian A. Bell, ed., *Peripheral Visions*, 196–200.

WILLIAM TREVOR

The Boarding House, 1965

MacKenna, Dolores. *William Trevor*, 77–82.

The Children of Dymouth, 1976

    MacKenna, Dolores. *William Trevor*, 159–63.

Death in Summer, 1998

    MacKenna, Dolores. *William Trevor*, 187–94.

Elizabeth Alone, 1973

    MacKenna, Dolores. *William Trevor*, 101–6.

Felicia's Journey, 1994

    MacKenna, Dolores. *William Trevor*, 180–87.

Fools of Fortune, 1983

    Cahalan, James M. *Double Visions*, 156–63.
    Kreilkamp, Vera. *The Anglo-Irish Novel*, 221–30.
    MacKenna, Dolores. *William Trevor*, 121–26.
    Tracy, Robert. "Undead, Unburied: Anglo-Ireland and the Predatory
      Past." *LIT* 10 (1999), 30–31.

The Love Department, 1966

    MacKenna, Dolores. *William Trevor*, 82–87.

Miss Gomez and the Brethren, 1971

    MacKenna, Dolores. *William Trevor*, 97–101.

Mrs. Eckdorf in O'Neill's Hotel, 1969

    MacKenna, Dolores. *William Trevor*, 92–97.
    Mikowski, Sylvie. "*Mrs Eckdorf in O'Neill's Hotel* de William Trevor."
      GRAAT 19 (1998), 39–46.

My House in Umbria, 1991

    MacKenna, Dolores. *William Trevor*, 175–80.

The Old Boys, 1965

    MacKenna, Dolores. *William Trevor*, 70–76.

Other People's Worlds, 1980

    MacKenna, Dolores. *William Trevor*, 163–69.

The Silence in the Garden, 1988

    Kreilkamp, Vera. *The Anglo-Irish Novel*, 229–33.
    MacKenna, Dolores. *William Trevor*, 129–32.

A Standard of Behavior, 1958

    MacKenna, Dolores. *William Trevor*, 61–64.

ANTHONY TROLLOPE

The American Senator, 1877

    Markwick, Margaret. *Trollope and Women*, 118–26.

Ayala's Angel, 1881

    Markwick, Margaret. *Trollope and Women*, 27–29, 126–28.
    Miller, J. Hillis. *Black Holes*, 185–311 (rectos only).

Barchester Towers, 1857

    Andres, Sophia. "George Eliot's Challenge to Medusa's Gendered
      Disparities." *Victorian Newsl* 95 (1999), 29–30.

Cavaliero, Glen. *The Alchemy of Laughter*, 187–90.

Durey, Jill Felicity. "Petticoat Powers and Parsons: Anthony Trollope and the Influence of Women in the Church of England and Its Community." *Victorian R* 23 (1997), 18–24.

Ireland, Ken. *The Sequential Dynamics of Narrative*, 218–19.

Kincaid, James R. *Annoying the Victorians*, 224–32.

LaCom, Cindy. "'It Is More than Lame': Female Disability, Sexuality, and the Maternal in the Nineteenth-Century Novel," in David T. Mitchell and Sharon L. Snyder, eds., *The Body and Physical Difference*, 193–96.

McKee, Patricia. *Public and Private*, 113–33.

Markwick, Margaret. *Trollope and Women*, 132, 160, 164–65.

Thompson, Nicola Diane. *Reviewing Sex*, 66–70.

The Belton Estate, 1866

Markwick, Margaret. *Trollope and Women*, 172–81.

Turner, Mark W. *Trollope and the Magazines*, 92–134.

Can You Forgive Her?, 1864

Craig, Randall. *Promising Language*, 213–46.

Dames, Nicholas. *Amnesiac Selves*, 239–42.

Ireland, Ken. *The Sequential Dynamics of Narrative*, 219–20.

Markwick, Margaret. *Trollope and Women*, 85–92.

Moody, Ellen. *Trollope on the Net*, 201–19.

Castle Richmond, 1860

Corbett, Mary Jean. *Allegories of Union*, 136–45.

Keen, Suzanne. *Victorian Renovations of the Novel*, 44–61.

Kelleher, Margaret. "Anthony Trollope's *Castle Richmond*: Famine Narrative and 'Horrid Novel'?" *Irish Univ R* 25 (1995), 242–62.

Kelleher, Margaret. *The Feminization of Famine*, 39–57.

Markwick, Margaret. *Trollope and Women*, 157–61.

Moody, Ellen. *Trollope on the Net*, 36–41.

The Claverings, 1867

Markwick, Margaret. *Trollope and Women*, 65–70.

Moody, Ellen. *Trollope on the Net*, 99–126.

Doctor Thorne, 1858

Gillooly, Eileen. *Smile of Discontent*, 57–60.

Hatano, Yoko. "Trollope's Admirable Women and Their Literary Sisters: A Continuing Quest for the Bearer of the Country House Tradition." *Victorian Newsl* 91 (1997), 31–36.

Markwick, Margaret. *Trollope and Women*, 27–28, 112–14.

O'Toole, Tess. "Adoption and the 'Improvement of the Estate' in Trollope and Craik." *Nineteenth-Cent Lit* 52 (1997), 68–79.

Dr. Wortle's School, 1881

Markwick, Margaret. *Trollope and Women*, 70–73, 161–64.

The Duke's Children, 1880

Franklin, J. Jeffrey. *Serious Play*, 34–79.

Kincaid, James R. *Annoying the Victorians*, 217–24.

The Eustace Diamonds, 1872

Armstrong, Nancy. "Gender and the Victorian Novel," in Deirdre

David, ed., *The Cambridge Companion to the Victorian Novel,* 107–8.

Brantlinger, Patrick. *The Reading Lesson,* 133–41.

Craig, Randall. *Promising Language,* 240–44.

Markwick, Margaret. *Trollope and Women,* 60–65.

Miller, Andrew H. *Novels behind Glass,* 159–88.

O'Farrell, Mary Ann. *Telling Complexions,* 115–18.

Psomiades, Kathy Alexis. "Heterosexual Exchange and Other Victorian Fictions: *The Eustace Diamonds* and Victorian Anthropology." *Novel* 33 (1999), 93–117.

An Eye for an Eye, 1879

Corbett, Mary Jean. *Allegories of Union,* 183–85.

Moody, Ellen. *Trollope on the Net,* 36–38, 41–43.

The Fixed Period, 1882

Moody, Ellen. *Trollope on the Net,* 88–90, 96–98.

Framley Parsonage, 1861

Bury, Laurent. "Six dessins pour un roman: *Framley Parsonage* de Trollope et Millais." *Cahiers Victoriens et Edouardiens* 47 (1998), 157–71.

Gillooly, Eileen. *Smile of Discontent,* 55–60.

Hatano, Yoko. "Trollope's Admirable Women and Their Literary Sisters: A Continuing Quest for the Bearer of the Country House Tradition." *Victorian Newsl* 91 (1997), 31–36.

Langbauer, Laurie. *Novels of Everyday Life,* 107–10.

Maunder, Andrew. "'Monitoring the middle-classes': Intertextuality and Ideology in Trollope's *Framley Parsonage* and the *Cornhill Magazine*." *Victorian Periodicals R* 33 (2000), 44–60.

The Golden Lion of Granpère, 1872

Moody, Ellen. *Trollope on the Net,* 94–96, 148–52.

Harry Heathcote of Gangoil, 1873

Archibald, Diana C. "Angel in the Bush: Exporting Domesticity through Female Emigration," in Rita S. Kranidis, ed., *Imperial Objects,* 232–45.

He Knew He Was Right, 1869

Markwick, Margaret. *Trollope and Women,* 95–102, 183–202.

Moody, Ellen. *Trollope on the Net,* 47–80.

Wiesenthal, Chris. *Figuring Madness in Nineteenth-Century Fiction,* 63–96.

Is He Popenjoy?, 1878

Markwick, Margaret. *Trollope and Women,* 144–56.

John Caldigate, 1879

Markwick, Margaret. *Trollope and Women,* 163–72.

Peck, John. *Maritime Fiction,* 140–41.

The Kellys and the O'Kellys, 1848

Moody, Ellen. *Trollope on the Net,* 36–40.

Lady Anna, 1874

Markwick, Margaret. *Trollope and Women,* 129–31.

Moody, Ellen. *Trollope on the Net*, 155–80.

The Landleaguers, 1883

Moody, Ellen. *Trollope on the Net*, 36–38, 43–45.

The Last Chronicle of Barset, 1867

Markwick, Margaret. *Trollope and Women*, 24–28, 107–9.
Moody, Ellen. *Trollope on the Net*, 134–36.

The Macdermotts of Ballycloran, 1847

Corbett, Mary Jean. *Allegories of Union*, 117–28.
Moody, Ellen. *Trollope on the Net*, 1–29.

Marion Fay, 1882

Durey, Jill Felicity. "Petticoat Powers and Parsons: Anthony Trollope and the Influence of Women in the Church of England and Its Community." *Victorian R* 23 (1997), 25–39.

Miss Mackenzie, 1865

Maunder, Andrew. "'Alone into the wide, wide world': Trollope's *Miss Mackenzie* and the Mid-Victorian Etiquette Manual." *Victorian R* 26:2 (2000), 48–69.

Nina Balatka, 1867

Moody, Ellen. *Trollope on the Net*, 92–95.

An Old Man's Love, 1884

Craig, Randall. *Promising Language*, 79–82.

Orley Farm, 1862

Dolin, Kieran. *Fiction and the Law*, 97–120.
Leung, Yiu Nam. "The Problem of Law and Justice in Trollope's *Orley Farm*." *Tamkang R* 25 (1995), 331–40.
Markwick, Margaret. *Trollope and Women*, 52–60.
Moody, Ellen. *Trollope on the Net*, 127–29, 146–48.
Schramm, Jan-Melissa. *Testimony and Advocacy*, 127–30.

Phineas Finn, 1869

Corbett, Mary Jean. *Allegories of Union*, 148–50.
Craig, Randall. *Promising Language*, 220–22.
Felber, Lynette. "Trollope's Phineas Diptych as Sequel and Sequence Novel," in Paul Budra and Betty A. Schellenberg, eds., *Part Two*, 118–28.
Moody, Ellen. *Trollope on the Net*, 203–5.
Turner, Mark W. *Trollope and the Magazines*, 141–76.

Phineas Redux, 1874

Felber, Lynette. "Trollope's Phineas Diptych as Sequel and Sequence Novel," in Paul Budra and Betty A. Schellenberg, eds., *Part Two*, 118–28.
Moody, Ellen. *Trollope on the Net*, 134–36.

The Prime Minister, 1876

Craig, Randall. *Promising Language*, 239–41.
Markwick, Margaret. *Trollope and Women*, 134–38.

Rachel Ray, 1863

Markwick, Margaret. *Trollope and Women*, 29–38.

Turner, Mark W. *Trollope and the Magazines*, 48–87.

Ralph the Heir, 1871

  Hassler, Donald M. "Mixed Genres and True Heritages: From Trollope's *Ralph the Heir* to Delany's *Dhalgren*," in Elisabeth Anne Leonard, ed., *Into Darkness Peering*, 17–20.
  Turner, Mark W. *Trollope and the Magazines*, 172–76.

The Small House at Allington, 1864

  Gillooly, Eileen. *Smile of Discontent*, 60–63.
  Markwick, Margaret. *Trollope and Women*, 78–85, 103–7.
  Turner, Mark W. *Trollope and the Magazines*, 15–24.

The Three Clerks, 1858

  Markwick, Margaret. *Trollope and Women*, 102–3, 110–14.
  Shuman, Cathy. *Pedagogical Economies*, 78–105.

The Vicar of Bullhampton, 1870

  Markwick, Margaret. *Trollope and Women*, 38–49.

The Warden, 1855

  McDermott, Jim. "New Womanly Man: Feminized Heroism and the Politics of Compromise in *The Warden*." *Victorians Inst J* 27 (1999), 71–87.
  Markwick, Margaret. *Trollope and Women*, 26–28.
  Moody, Ellen. *Trollope on the Net*, 83–84, 90–92.
  York, R. A. *The Rules of Time*, 21–35.

The Way We Live Now, 1875

  Ireland, Ken. *The Sequential Dynamics of Narrative*, 220–21.
  Justman, Stewart. *The Springs of Liberty*, 84–92.
  Markwick, Margaret. *Trollope and Women*, 73–77.
  Moody, Ellen. *Trollope on the Net*, 48–49, 143–47, 174–77.
  Sutherland, John. *Who Betrays Elizabeth Bennet?*, 202–10.

FRANCES TROLLOPE

Charles Chesterfield, 1841

  Neville-Sington, Pamela. *Fanny Trollope*, 289–92.

Jessie Phillips, 1843

  Brandser, Kristin J. "In Defence of 'Murderous Mothers': Feminist Jurisprudence in Frances Trollope's *Jessie Phillips*." *J of Victorian Culture* 5 (2000), 179–204.
  Neville-Sington, Pamela. *Fanny Trollope*, 310–12.

Jonathan Jefferson Whitlaw, 1836

  Neville-Sington, Pamela. *Fanny Trollope*, 239–43.

Michael Armstrong, 1840

  Childers, Joseph W. "Industrial Culture and the Victorian Novel," in Deirdre David, ed., *The Cambridge Companion to the Victorian Novel*, 79–80.
  Elliott, Dorice Williams. "Servants and Hands: Representing the

Working Classes in Victorian Factory Novels." *Victorian Lit and Culture* 28 (2000), 377–79, 383–88.

Lenard, Mary. "'Mr. Popular Sentiment': Dickens and the Gender Politics of Sentimentalism and Social Reform Literature." *Dickens Stud Annual* 27 (1998), 53–58.

Neville-Sington, Pamela. *Fanny Trollope*, 272–78.

Zlotnick, Susan. *Women, Writing, and the Industrial Revolution*, 133–45, 150–53, 156–62, 164–66.

The Refugee in America, 1832

Neville-Sington, Pamela. *Fanny Trollope*, 131–33, 183–88.

The Vicar of Wrexhill, 1837

Neville-Sington, Pamela. *Fanny Trollope*, 236–37, 258–59.

JOANNA TROLLOPE

The Rector's Wife, 1992

Liladhar, Janine. "From the Soap Queen to the Aga-Saga: Different Discursive Frameworks of Familial Femininity in Contemporary 'Women's Genres.'" *J of Gender Stud* 9:1 (2000), 5–12.

York, R. A. *The Rules of Time*, 172–77.

JOHN TRUSLER

Life; Or, The Adventures of William Ramble, 1793

London, April. *Women and Property*, 133–35.

Modern Times; Or, The Adventures of Gabriel Outcast, 1785

London, April. *Women and Property*, 129–33.

KATHERINE TYNAN

A King's Woman, 1902

Reilly, Eileen. "Rebel, Muse, and Spouse: The Female in '98 Fiction." *Eire-Ireland* 34:2 (1999), 142–44.

EDWARD UPWARD

The Rotten Elements, 1969

Barley, Tony. "'A narrow strictness': Political Constraints in Edward Upward's *The Rotten Elements*." *Lit and Hist* 6:1 (1997), 63–77.

HELEN WADDELL

Peter Abelard, 1933

Fitzgerald, Jennifer. "'Truth's Martyr or Love's Martyr': Helen Waddell's *Peter Abelard*." *Colby Q* 36 (2000), 176–85.

LUCY WALFORD

Mr. Smith, 1874

Burgess, Moira. "Rediscovering Scottish Women's Fiction in the Nineteenth Century," in Douglas Gifford and Dorothy McMillan, eds., *A History,* 203–4.

GEORGE WALKER

The Vagabond, 1799

London, April. "Novel and History in Anti-Jacobin Satire." *Yrbk of Engl Stud* 30 (2000), 71–81.
London, April. *Women and Property,* 172–79.

ALAN WALL

Bless the Thief, 1997

Zwierlein, Anne-Julia. "'Bless the Thief for he Lightens your Burden': Fälschung und Subjektkonstitution in Peter Ackroyds *Chatterton* (1987) und Alan Walls *Bless the Thief* (1997)." *Poetica* (Munich) 32 (2000), 499–526.

MERVYN WALL

The Return of Fursey, 1948

Lanters, José. *Unauthorized Versions,* 258–71.
Quintelli-Neary, Marguerite. *Folklore and the Fantastic,* 99–108.
Schweitzer, Darrell. "Mervyn Wall and the Comedy of Despair," in Schweitzer, ed., *Discovering Classic Fantasy Fiction,* 57–62.

The Unfortunate Fursey, 1946

Lanters, José. *Unauthorized Versions,* 241–57.
Quintelli-Neary, Marguerite. *Folklore and the Fantastic,* 99–108.
Schweitzer, Darrell. "Mervyn Wall and the Comedy of Despair," in Schweitzer, ed., *Discovering Classic Fantasy Fiction,* 57–62.

EDGAR WALLACE

The Four Just Men, 1905

Kestner, Joseph A. *The Edwardian Detective,* 113–22.

HORACE WALPOLE

The Castle of Otranto, 1765

Andriopoulos, Stefan. "The Invisible Hand: Supernatural Agency in Political Economy and the Gothic Novel." *ELH* 66 (1999), 739–43.
Bozzetto, Roger. *Territoires des fantastiques,* 17–30.
Brantlinger, Patrick. *The Reading Lesson,* 35–39.

Campbell, Jill. "'I Am No Giant': Horace Walpole, Heterosexual Incest, and Love Among Men." *Eighteenth Cent* 39 (1998), 238–57.

Clemens, Valdine. *The Return of the Repressed*, 29–40.

Fay, Elizabeth A. *A Feminist Introduction to Romanticism*, 216–18.

Flint, Christopher. *Family Fictions*, 253–71.

Gamer, Michael. *Romanticism and the Gothic*, 167–72.

Haggerty, George E. *Men in Love*, 160–65.

Haggerty, George E. *Unnatural Affections*, 52–55.

Hall, Daniel. "The Gothic Tide: *Schauerroman* and Gothic Novel in the Late Eighteenth Century," in Susanne Stark, ed., *The Novel in Anglo-German Context*, 52–60.

Heinrich, Hans. *Zur Geschichte des 'Libertin,'* 155–58.

Hirai, Masako. "Burke's 'Sublime' and *The Castle of Otranto*: The Gothic Image and the Novel." *Kobe Coll Stud* 40:3 (1994), 1–12.

Ireland, Ken. *The Sequential Dynamics of Narrative*, 182–83.

Jacobs, Edward H. *Accidental Migrations*, 138–56.

Clingham, Greg. "'A by-stander often sees more of the game than those that play': Ann Yearsley Reads *The Castle of Otranto*." *Bucknell R* 42:1 (1998), 59–73.

McKee, Patricia. *Public and Private*, 22–25, 37–46.

Moglen, Helene. *The Trauma of Gender*, 112–37.

Montandon, Alain. *Le roman au XVIIIe siècle*, 455–56.

Morrissey, Lee. *From the Temple to the Castle*, 108–30.

Morrissey, Lee. "'To invent in art and folly': Postmodernism and Walpole's *Castle of Otranto*." *Bucknell R* 41:2 (1998), 86–97.

Porter, David. "From Chinese to Goth: Walpole and the Gothic Repudiation of Chinoiserie." *Eighteenth-Cent Life* 23:1 (1999), 46–58.

Watt, Ian P. "Time and Family in the Gothic Novel: *The Castle of Otranto*," in Richard Kroll, ed., *The English Novel, Volume II*, 191–203.

Watt, James. *Contesting the Gothic*, 25–41.

Wein, Toni. "Tangled Webs: Horace Walpole and the Practice of History in *The Castle of Otranto*." *Engl Lang Notes* 35:4 (1998), 12–20.

EDWARD WARD

The London Spy, 1698–1700

Wall, Cynthia. *The Literary and Cultural Spaces*, 137–41.

MARY AUGUSTA WARD

Daphne; or, Marriage a La Mode, 1909

Harris, Janice Hubbard. *Edwardian Stories of Divorce*, 127–32.

Delia Blanchflower, 1914

Sutton-Ramspeck, Beth. "Shot Out of the Canon: Mary Ward and the Claims of Conflicting Feminisms," in Nicola Diane Thompson, ed., *Victorian Women Writers*, 211–18.

Harvest, 1920

Small, Helen. "Mrs Humphry Ward and the First Casualty of War," in

Suzanne Raitt and Trudi Tate, eds., *Women's Fiction and the Great War*, 39–41.

Helbeck of Bannisdale, 1898

Barfoot, Gabrielle. "*Helbeck of Bannisdale*: A Study in Religious Conflict." *Prospero* 3 (1996), 145–52.

Marcella, 1894

Sutton-Ramspeck, Beth. "Shot Out of the Canon: Mary Ward and the Claims of Conflicting Feminisms," in Nicola Diane Thompson, ed., *Victorian Women Writers*, 206–7.

Missing, 1917

Small, Helen. "Mrs Humphry Ward and the First Casualty of War," in Suzanne Raitt and Trudi Tate, eds., *Women's Fiction and the Great War*, 35–38.

Robert Elsmere, 1888

Dougill, John. *Oxford in English Literature*, 125–27.
Israel, Kali. *Names and Stories*, 99–101.
Towheed, Shafquat. "W. E. Gladstone's Reception of *Robert Elsmere*: A Critical Re-evaluation." *Engl Lit in Transition* 40 (1997), 389–97.

MRS. WILFRID WARD

One Poor Scruple, 1899

Bergonzi, Bernard. *War Poets*, 159–65.

MARINA WARNER

Indigo, 1992

Cakebread, Caroline. "Sycorax Speaks: Marina Warner's *Indigo* and *The Tempest*," in Marianne Novy, ed., *Transforming Shakespeare*, 217–33.
López, Marta Sofía. "Historiographic Metafiction and Resistance Postmodernism," in Richard Todd and Luisa Flora, eds., *Theme Parks*, 216–20.

SYLVIA TOWNSEND WARNER

After the Death of Don Juan, 1938

Beer, Gillian. "Sylvia Townsend Warner: 'The Centrifugal Kick,'" in Maroula Joannou, ed., *Women Writers of the 1930s*, 84–86.

Lolly Willowes, 1926

Ayers, David. *English Literature of the 1920s*, 63–66.
Lucas, John. "From Realism to Radicalism: Sylvia Townsend Warner, Patrick Hamilton and Henry Green in the 1920s," in Lynne Hapgood and Nancy L. Paxton, eds., *Outside Modernism*, 204–9.

Summer Will Show, 1936

Beer, Gillian. "Sylvia Townsend Warner: 'The Centrifugal Kick,'" in Maroula Joannou, ed., *Women Writers of the 1930s*, 82–84.

ELIZABETH WATERHOUSE

The Island of Anarchy, 1887

Schäffner, Raimund. *Anarchismus und Literatur in England*, 491–94.

EVELYN WAUGH

Black Mischief, 1932

Meckier, Jerome. "Aldous Huxley, Evelyn Waugh, and Birth Control in *Black Mischief*." *J of Mod Lit* 23 (1999/2000), 277–90.

Patey, Douglas Lane. *The Life of Evelyn Waugh*, 96–104.

Wykes, David. *Evelyn Waugh*, 92–99.

Brideshead Revisited, 1945

Bényei, Tamás. *Acts of Attention*, 15–64.

Bényei, Tamás. "*Brideshead Revisited*: The Deferral of Paradise." *B.A.S.: Brit and Am Stud* 4:1 (1999), 47–53.

Bittner, David. "Sebastian's Silence: The Result of Viewpoint Limitations?" *Evelyn Waugh Newsl and Stud* 31:1 (1997), 2–3.

DeCoste, Damon Marcel. "Waugh's War and the Loop of History: From *Put Out More Flags* to *Brideshead Revisited* and Back Again." *Style* 34 (2000), 458–79.

Dougill, John. *Oxford in English Literature*, 172–75, 179–81.

Nagashima, Saeko. "Transition in the House-Imagery of Waugh's Novels." *Stud in Engl Lit* (Tokyo) 74 (1998), 62–66.

Osborne, John W. "The Character of Sebastian." *Evelyn Waugh Newsl and Stud* 31:3 (1997), 7–8.

Patey, Douglas Lane. *The Life of Evelyn Waugh*, 223–46.

Pearce, Joseph. *Literary Converts*, 235–37.

Pugh, Tison. "Romantic Friendship, Homosexuality, and Evelyn Waugh's *Brideshead Revisited*." *Engl Lang Notes* 38:4 (2001), 64–71.

Toynton, Evelyn. "Revisiting Brideshead." *Am Scholar* 67:4 (1998), 134–37.

Valdeón García, Roberta A. "El tratamiento de la temática homosexual en cuatro novelistas ingleses: Lawrence, Forster, Waugh y Storey." *Cuadernos de Investigación Filológica* 23–24 (1997–1998), 139–62.

Weatherhead, A. K. *Upstairs*, 93–98.

Wilson, John Howard. "Mishima's *Confessions of a Mask*: *Brideshead Revisited*?" *J of Evolutionary Psych* 20:1–2 (1999), 22–32.

Wilson, John Howard. "Wandering Jews in the Fiction of Evelyn Waugh, Part I." *Evelyn Waugh Newsl and Stud* 31:2 (1997), 3–4.

Wykes, David. *Evelyn Waugh*, 139–44.

Decline and Fall, 1928

Nagashima, Saeko. "Transition in the House-Imagery of Waugh's Novels." *Stud in Engl Lit* (Tokyo) 74 (1998), 54–57.

Patey, Douglas Lane. *The Life of Evelyn Waugh*, 60–73.

Wykes, David. *Evelyn Waugh*, 60–64.

A Handful of Dust, 1934

DeCoste, Damon Marcel. "Waugh's War and the Loop of History:

From *Put Out More Flags* to *Brideshead Revisited* and Back Again." *Style* 34 (2000), 463–65.

Gaye, Mamadou. "Evelyn Waugh's 'Heart of Darkness' in *A Handful of Dust.*" *Bridges* (Dakar) 7 (1996), 93–105.

Johnston, Georgia. "Evelyn Waugh's Narrative of History: Reading *A Handful of Dust.*" *Lamar J of the Hum* 23:1 (1997), 39–53.

Mathur, Piyush. "The Archigenderic Territories: *Mansfield Park* and *A Handful of Dust.*" *Women's Writing* 5 (1998), 71–79.

Nagashima, Saeko. "Transition in the House-Imagery of Waugh's Novels." *Stud in Engl Lit* (Tokyo) 74 (1998), 57–62.

Patey, Douglas Lane. *The Life of Evelyn Waugh*, 115–23.

Wilson, John Howard. "Wandering Jews in the Fiction of Evelyn Waugh, Part I." *Evelyn Waugh Newsl and Stud* 31:2 (1997), 2.

Wykes, David. *Evelyn Waugh*, 103–9.

Helena, 1950

Patey, Douglas Lane. *The Life of Evelyn Waugh*, 289–97.

Wilson, John Howard. "Wandering Jews in the Fiction of Evelyn Waugh, Part I." *Evelyn Waugh Newsl and Stud* 31:2 (1997), 1–2.

Wykes, David. *Evelyn Waugh*, 158–65.

Love Among the Ruins, 1953

Patey, Douglas Lane. *The Life of Evelyn Waugh*, 311–16.

The Loved One, 1948

Decker, James M., and Kenneth Womack. "Searching for Ethics in the Celluloid Graveyard: Waugh, O'Flaherty, and the Hollywood Novel." *Stud in the Hum* 25:1–2 (1998), 53–65.

Patey, Douglas Lane. *The Life of Evelyn Waugh*, 272–79.

Wilson, John Howard. "Wandering Jews in the Fiction of Evelyn Waugh, Part I." *Evelyn Waugh Newsl and Stud* 31:2 (1997), 4–5.

Wykes, David. *Evelyn Waugh*, 151–58.

Men at Arms, 1952

Doyle, Paul A. "Virginia's Rejection of Guy Crouchback." *Evelyn Waugh Newsl and Stud* 32:1 (1998), 6–7.

Patey, Douglas Lane. *The Life of Evelyn Waugh*, 303–9.

Wykes, David. *Evelyn Waugh*, 168–78.

Officers and Gentlemen, 1955

Wilson, John Howard. "Wandering Jews in the Fiction of Evelyn Waugh, Part II." *Evelyn Waugh Newsl and Stud* 31:3 (1997), 3–4.

Wykes, David. *Evelyn Waugh*, 180–88.

The Ordeal of Gilbert Pinfold, 1957

Patey, Douglas Lane. *The Life of Evelyn Waugh*, 338–41.

Wilson, John Howard. "Wandering Jews in the Fiction of Evelyn Waugh, Part II." *Evelyn Waugh Newsl and Stud* 31:3 (1997), 4.

Wykes, David. *Evelyn Waugh*, 190–93.

Put Out More Flags, 1942

Butler, Lance St. John. *Registering the Difference*, 56–58.

DeCoste, Damon Marcel. "Waugh's War and the Loop of History: From *Put Out More Flags* to *Brideshead Revisited* and Back Again." *Style* 34 (2000), 458–79.

Patey, Douglas Lane. *The Life of Evelyn Waugh*, 191–98.

Wilson, John Howard. "Wandering Jews in the Fiction of Evelyn Waugh, Part I." *Evelyn Waugh Newsl and Stud* 31:2 (1997), 3.

Wykes, David. *Evelyn Waugh*, 132–36.

Scoop, 1938

Patey, Douglas Lane. *The Life of Evelyn Waugh*, 156–64.

Wilson, John Howard. "Wandering Jews in the Fiction of Evelyn Waugh, Part I." *Evelyn Waugh Newsl and Stud* 31:2 (1997), 2–3.

Wykes, David. *Evelyn Waugh*, 81–83, 115–17.

Sword of Honour, 1965

Trout, Steven. "Miniaturization and Anticlimax in Evelyn Waugh's *Sword of Honour.*" *Twentieth Cent Lit* 43 (1997), 125–41.

Wilson, John Howard. "The Brothers Crouchback: History and Structure in *Sword of Honour.*" *J of Evolutionary Psych* 19:1–2 (1998), 79–87.

Wykes, David. *Evelyn Waugh*, 168–78, 182–88, 197–208.

Unconditional Surrender, 1961

Patey, Douglas Lane. *The Life of Evelyn Waugh*, 349–56.

Wilson, John Howard. "Wandering Jews in the Fiction of Evelyn Waugh, Part II." *Evelyn Waugh Newsl and Stud* 31:3 (1997), 4–5.

Wykes, David. *Evelyn Waugh*, 197–204.

Vile Bodies, 1930

DeCoste, Damon Marcel. "Waugh's War and the Loop of History: From *Put Out More Flags* to *Brideshead Revisited* and Back Again." *Style* 34 (2000), 465–68.

Nagashima, Saeko. "Transition in the House-Imagery of Waugh's Novels." *Stud in Engl Lit* (Tokyo) 74 (1998), 54–57.

Patey, Douglas Lane. *The Life of Evelyn Waugh*, 73–78.

Pearce, Joseph. *Literary Converts*, 159–61.

Thomas, Bronwen E. "'It's good to talk'?: An Analysis of a Telephone Conversation from Evelyn Waugh's *Vile Bodies.*" *Lang and Lit* (Harlow) 6 (1997), 105–17.

Wilson, John Howard. "John Wesley and *Vile Bodies.*" *Evelyn Waugh Newsl and Stud* 32:3 (1998), 1–3.

Wilson, John Howard. "Wandering Jews in the Fiction of Evelyn Waugh, Part I." *Evelyn Waugh Newsl and Stud* 31:2 (1997), 2.

Wykes, David. *Evelyn Waugh*, 67–71.

Work Suspended, 1943

Wykes, David. *Evelyn Waugh*, 119–22.

FAY WELDON

And the Wife Ran Away, 1967

Faulks, Lana. *Fay Weldon*, 11–15.

The Cloning of Joanna May, 1989

Armitt, Lucie. *Contemporary Women's Fiction*, 49–55, 146–51.

Caporale Bizzini, Silvia. "Identidad y diferencia en *The Cloning of Joanna May* de Fay Weldon." *Miscelánea* 16 (1995), 81–101.

Faulks, Lana. *Fay Weldon*, 59–63.

Darcy's Utopia, 1990

    Faulks, Lana. *Fay Weldon*, 63–67.

Down Among the Women, 1971

    Dowling, Finuala. *Fay Weldon's Fiction*, 45–51.

    Faulks, Lana. *Fay Weldon*, 15–21.

    Welnic, Ewa. "Humour in Fay Weldon's *Down Among the Women* and 'Weekend.'" *Acta Universitatis Nicolai Copernici: Engl Stud* 5 (1995), 31–35.

Female Friends, 1975

    Dowling, Finuala. *Fay Weldon's Fiction*, 51–54.

    Faulks, Lana. *Fay Weldon*, 21–24.

Growing Rich, 1992

    Faulks, Lana. *Fay Weldon*, 81–85.

The Heart of the Country, 1987

    Dowling, Finuala. *Fay Weldon's Fiction*, 128–36.

    Faulks, Lana. *Fay Weldon*, 67–70.

    Smith, Patricia Juliana. *Lesbian Panic*, 173–83.

The Hearts and Lives of Men, 1987

    Dowling, Finuala. *Fay Weldon's Fiction*, 136–41.

    Faulks, Lana. *Fay Weldon*, 74–77.

Leader of the Band, 1988

    Faulks, Lana. *Fay Weldon*, 52–56.

The Life and Loves of a She-Devil, 1983

    Cane, Aleta F. "Demythifying Motherhood in Three Novels by Fay Weldon," in Andrea O'Reilly Herrera et al., eds., *Family Matters*, 183–93.

    Dowling, Finuala. *Fay Weldon's Fiction*, 105–14.

    Faulks, Lana. *Fay Weldon*, 47–52.

    Martin, Sara. "The Power of Monstrous Women: Fay Weldon's *The Life and Loves of a She-Devil* (1983), Angela Carter's *Nights at the Circus* (1984) and Jeanette Winterson's *Sexing the Cherry* (1989)." *J of Gender Stud* 8 (1999), 193–209.

    Smith, Patricia Juliana. "'Women Like Us Must Learn to Stick Together': Lesbians in the Novels of Fay Weldon," in Abby H. P. Werlock, ed., *British Women Writing Fiction*, 135–41.

Life Force, 1992

    Cane, Aleta F. "Demythifying Motherhood in Three Novels by Fay Weldon," in Andrea O'Reilly Herrera et al., eds., *Family Matters*, 183–93.

    Faulks, Lana. *Fay Weldon*, 77–81.

Praxis, 1978

    Dervin, Dan. *Matricentric Narratives*, 66–72.

    Dowling, Finuala. *Fay Weldon's Fiction*, 58–60, 75–84.

    Faulks, Lana. *Fay Weldon*, 36–41.

The President's Child, 1982

    Dowling, Finuala. *Fay Weldon's Fiction*, 99–105.

Faulks, Lana. *Fay Weldon*, 45–47.

Puffball, 1980

Cane, Aleta F. "Demythifying Motherhood in Three Novels by Fay Weldon," in Andrea O'Reilly Herrera et al., eds., *Family Matters*, 183–93.

Dowling, Finuala. *Fay Weldon's Fiction*, 90–99.

Faulks, Lana. *Fay Weldon*, 41–44.

Remember Me, 1976

Dowling, Finuala. *Fay Weldon's Fiction*, 61–63, 66–74.

Faulks, Lana. *Fay Weldon*, 25–30.

Smith, Patricia Juliana. "'Women Like Us Must Learn to Stick Together': Lesbians in the Novels of Fay Weldon," in Abby H. P. Werlock, ed., *British Women Writing Fiction*, 126–31.

The Shrapnel Academy, 1986

Dowling, Finuala. *Fay Weldon's Fiction*, 120–28.

Faulks, Lana. *Fay Weldon*, 57–59.

Stanley, William Chad. "'Like a Nuclear Blast': Fay Weldon's Explosion of the Military Order in *The Shrapnel Academy*." *LIT* 11 (2001), 351–82.

Splitting, 1995

Dowling, Finuala. *Fay Weldon's Fiction*, 148–56.

Faulks, Lana. *Fay Weldon*, 86–88.

Trouble, 1993

Faulks, Lana. *Fay Weldon*, 88–89.

Words of Advice, 1977

Faulks, Lana. *Fay Weldon*, 30–35.

Smith, Patricia Juliana. "'Women Like Us Must Learn to Stick Together': Lesbians in the Novels of Fay Weldon," in Abby H. P. Werlock, ed., *British Women Writing Fiction*, 131–35.

Worst Fears, 1996

Faulks, Lana. *Fay Weldon*, 89–93.

H. G. WELLS

Ann Veronica, 1909

Hertel, Kirsten. *London zwischen Naturalismus und Moderne*, 349–86.

Christina Alberta's Father, 1925

Huguet, Christine. "Sargon le Magnifique Redivivus: la croix et le cercle chez H. G. Wells." *Etudes Anglaises* 53 (2000), 272–83.

The First Men in the Moon, 1901

Carey, John. "H. G. Wells, T. S. Eliot and William Golding: Some Connections," in George Hughes, ed., *Corresponding Powers*, 227–28.

Sandner, David. "Shooting for the Moon: Méliès, Verne, Wells, and the Imperial Satire." *Extrapolation* 39 (1998), 10–14.

The Food of the Gods, 1904

> DePaolo, Charles. "Herakleophorbia IV/Somatrem: H. G. Wells's Speculations upon Endocrinology." *The Wellsian* 23 (2000), 35–47.
>
> Parrinder, Patrick. "Edwardian Awakenings: H. G. Wells's Apocalyptic Romances (1898–1915)," in David Seed, ed., *Imagining Apocalypse,* 67.
>
> Parrinder, Patrick. "The View from Bun Hill: H. G. Wells, Kent and the Male Romance." *The Wellsian* 20 (1997), 45–48.
>
> Russell, W. M. S. "*The Food of the Gods* and *The Fatal Eggs*: Two Views of the Scientist." *Foundation* 80 (2000), 51–60.

The History of Mr. Polly, 1910

> Lessenich, Rolf. "The World of the Novels of H. G. Wells." *Anglia* 115 (1997), 304–8, 318–20.

In the Days of the Comet, 1906

> Ferns, Chris. *Narrating Utopia,* 88–100.
>
> Parrinder, Patrick. "Edwardian Awakenings: H. G. Wells's Apocalyptic Romances (1898–1915)," in David Seed, ed., *Imagining Apocalypse,* 68–70.

The Invisible Man, 1897

> Lake, David J. "Port Burdock in *The Invisible Man*: Where Does Griffin Die?" *The Wellsian* 23 (2000), 24–33.

The Island of Dr. Moreau, 1896

> Brody, Jennifer DeVere. *Impossible Purities,* 130–69.
>
> Disch, Thomas M. *The Dreams Our Stuff Is Made Of,* 62–64.
>
> Gold, Barri J. "Reproducing Empire: *Moreau* and Others." *Nineteenth Cent Stud* 14 (2000), 173–93.
>
> Gomel, Elana. "From Dr. Moreau to Dr. Mengele: The Biological Sublime." *Poetics Today* 21 (2000), 411–18.
>
> Hendershot, Cyndy. *The Animal Within,* 124–39.
>
> Hughes, David Y. "The Doctor Vivisected." *Science Fiction Stud* 24:1 (1997), 109–18.
>
> Krumm, Pascale. "*The Island of Doctor Moreau,* or the Case of Devolution." *Foundation* 75 (1999), 51–60.
>
> Lessenich, Rolf. "The World of the Novels of H. G. Wells." *Anglia* 115 (1997), 302–4.
>
> Roberts, Ian F. "Maupertius: Doppelgänger of Doctor Moreau." *Science-Fiction Stud* 28 (2001), 261–72.
>
> Schell, Heather. "Man-Eating Wives of the 1890s." *J of the Eighteen Nineties Soc* 26 (1999), 23–31.
>
> Turney, Jon. *Frankenstein's Footsteps,* 54–59.
>
> Vallorani, Nicoletta. "Hybridizing Science: The 'patchwork biology' of Dr. Moreau." *Cahiers Victoriens et Edouardiens* 46 (1997), 245–59.
>
> Youngs, Tim. "'The Plasticity of Living Forms': Beasts and Narrative in *The Octopus* and *The Island of Doctor Moreau.*" *Symbiosis* 1:1 (1997), 86–103.

Kipps, 1905

> Lessenich, Rolf. "The World of the Novels of H. G. Wells." *Anglia* 115 (1997), 308–13.

Partington, John S. "An Identification of and Suggested Reasons for the Differences between the 1905 H. G. Wells Novel, *Kipps: The Story of a Simple Soul*, and the 1941 Carol Reed Film, *Kipps*." *The Wellsian* 20 (1997), 32–37.

Men Like Gods, 1923

Ferns, Chris. *Narrating Utopia*, 88–101.

Fitch, Eric L. "How Green was my *Utopia*?: A Reflection on William Morris's *News from Nowhere*, H. G. Wells's *Men Like Gods* and Ernest Callenbach's *Ecotopia*." *The Wellsian* 19 (1996), 30–35.

A Modern Utopia, 1905

Cohen-Safir, Claude. *Cartographie du féminin dans l'utopie*, 81–83.

Ferns, Chris. *Narrating Utopia*, 88–92, 95–103.

Partington, John S. "The Death of the Static: H. G. Wells and the Kinetic Utopia." *Utopian Stud* 11:2 (2000), 96–111.

Pordzik, Ralph. "*Mapping the Future(s)*: Formen und Funktionen der Metafiktionalität im englischen utopischen Roman." *Anglia* 118 (2000), 46–50.

The New Machiavelli, 1910

Parrinder, Patrick. "The View from Bun Hill: H. G. Wells, Kent and the Male Romance." *The Wellsian* 20 (1997), 46–48.

The Sea Lady, 1902

Carey, John. "H. G. Wells, T. S. Eliot and William Golding: Some Connections," in George Hughes, ed., *Corresponding Powers*, 223–27.

The Shape of Things to Come, 1933

Farrell, Kirby. "H. G. Wells and Neoteny." *Cahiers Victoriens et Edouardiens* 46 (1997), 147–56.

Hardy, Sylvia. "H. G. Wells and British Cinema: The War of the Worlds." *Foundation* 28 (1999), 46–58.

The Time Machine, 1895

Batchelor, John. "Conrad and Wells at the End of the Century." *Crit R* (Melbourne) 38 (1998), 69–82.

Bignell, Jonathan. "Another Time, Another Space: Modernity, Subjectivity, and *The Time Machine*." *The Wellsian* 22 (1999), 34–47.

Brantlinger, Patrick. *The Reading Lesson*, 203–5.

Caldwell, Larry W. "'Time at the End of its Tether': H. G. Wells and the Subversion of Master Narrative." *Cahiers Victoriens et Edouardiens* 46 (1997), 127–38.

Debelius, Margaret. "H. G. Wells and the Riddle of the Sphinx." *J of the Eighteen Nineties Soc* 26 (1999), 3–11.

Disch, Thomas M. *The Dreams Our Stuff Is Made Of*, 61–63.

Farrell, Kirby. "H. G. Wells and Neoteny." *Cahiers Victoriens et Edouardiens* 46 (1997), 145–56.

Hollm, Jan. "*The Time Machine* and the Ecotopian Tradition." *The Wellsian* 22 (1999), 47–54.

Mayne, Alan. "The Virtual Time Machine: Part I." *The Wellsian* 19 (1996), 22–26.

Mayne, Alan. "The Virtual Time Machine: Part II—Some Physicists' Views of Time Travel." *The Wellsian* 20 (1997), 20–30.

Parrinder, Patrick. "Edwardian Awakenings: H. G. Wells's Apocalyptic Romances (1898–1915)," in David Seed, ed., *Imagining Apocalypse*, 62–66.

Partington, John. "*The Time Machine*: A Polemic on the Inevitability of Working Class Liberation and a Plea for a Socialist Solution to Late-Victorian Capitalist Exploitation." *The Wellsian* 19 (1996), 12–21.

Partington, John S. "*The Time Machine*: A Polemic on the Inevitability of Working-Class Liberation, and a Plea for a Socialist Solution to Late-Victorian Capitalist Exploitation." *Cahiers Victoriens et Edouardiens* 46 (1997), 167–78.

Philmus, Robert. "H. G. Wells's Revisi(tati)ons of *The Time Machine*." *Engl Lit in Transition* 41 (1998), 427–47.

Porta, Fernando. "One Text, Many Utopias: Some Examples of Intertextuality in *The Time Machine*." *The Wellsian* 20 (1997), 10–19.

Sargent, Lyman Tower. "*The Time Machine* in the Development of Wells's Social and Political Thought." *The Wellsian* 19 (1996), 3–10.

Scafella, Frank. "From Reason to Intelligence: Wells's White Sphinx as Chronotope of Nineteenth Century Science." *Cahiers Victoriens et Edouardiens* 46 (1997), 181–89.

Slusser, George. "Last Men and First Women: The Dynamics of Life Extension in Shaw and Heinlein," in Milton T. Wolf, ed., *Shaw and Science Fiction*, 142–44.

Slusser, George, and Danièle Chatelain. "Re-writing *The Time Machine* around Mrs. Watchett." *Cahiers Victoriens et Edouardiens* 46 (1997), 191–209.

Trout, Steven. "Narratives of Encounter: H. G. Wells's *The Time Machine* and the Literature of Imperialism." *J of Commonwealth and Postcolonial Stud* 5:1 (1997), 35–45.

Willis, Martin T. "Edison as Time Traveler: H. G. Wells's Inspiration for His First Scientific Character." *Science-Fiction Stud* 26 (1999), 284–92.

Tono-Bungay, 1909

Hammond, John. "Images of the Door in *Tono-Bungay*." *The Wellsian* 21 (1998), 18–21.

Keen, Suzanne. *Victorian Renovations of the Novel*, 167–77.

Kupinse, William. "Wasted Value: The Serial Logic of H. G. Wells's *Tono-Bungay*." *Novel* 33 (1999), 51–70.

Lessenich, Rolf. "The World of the Novels of H. G. Wells." *Anglia* 115 (1997), 313–20.

McCormick, John. *Catastrophe and Imagination*, 158–59.

The War in the Air, 1908

Gannon, Charles E. "'One Swift, Conclusive Smashing and an End': Wells, War, and the Collapse of Civilisation." *Foundation* 77 (1999), 35–37.

Miller, Tom. "*The War in the Air*: A Study in Plotting." *The Wellsian* 19 (1996), 27–29.

Miller, Tom. "*The War in the Air.* A Study in Plotting." *The Wellsian* 21 (1998), 22–24.

Parrinder, Patrick. "Edwardian Awakenings: H. G. Wells's Apocalyptic Romances (1898–1915)," in David Seed, ed., *Imagining Apocalypse*, 70–71.

Parrinder, Patrick. "The View from Bun Hill: H. G. Wells, Kent and the Male Romance." *The Wellsian* 20 (1997), 42–46.

The War of the Worlds, 1898

Aldiss, Brian. "The Referee of *The War of the Worlds.*" *Foundation* 77 (1999), 7–14.

Arata, Stephen. *Fictions of Loss*, 108–10.

Disch, Thomas M. *The Dreams Our Stuff Is Made Of*, 62–64.

Gailor, Denis. "Wells's *War of the Worlds,* the 'Invasion Story' and Victorian Moralism." *Crit Survey* 8:3 (1996), 270–76.

Gannon, Charles E. "'One Swift, Conclusive Smashing and an End': Wells, War, and the Collapse of Civilisation." *Foundation* 77 (1999), 40–45.

Huntington, John. "My Martians: Wells's Success." *Foundation* 77 (1999), 25–33.

Law, Richard. "The Narrator in Double Exposure in *The War of the Worlds.*" *The Wellsian* 23 (2000), 47–56.

May, Stephen. *Stardust and Ashes*, 36–39.

Parrinder, Patrick. "How Far Can We Trust the Narrator of *The War of the Worlds*?" *Foundation* 77 (1999), 15–24.

Renfroe, Craig S., Jr. "*The War of the Worlds*: Wells' Anti-Imperialist Support of Empire." *Postscript* 15 (1998), 43–51.

The Wheels of Chance, 1896

Young, Arlene. *Culture, Class and Gender*, 103–11.

The Wonderful Visit, 1895

Carey, John. "H. G. Wells, T. S. Eliot and William Golding: Some Connections," in George Hughes, ed., *Corresponding Powers*, 228–31.

The World Set Free, 1914

Gannon, Charles E. "'One Swift, Conclusive Smashing and an End': Wells, War, and the Collapse of Civilisation." *Foundation* 77 (1999), 37–40.

Parrinder, Patrick. "Edwardian Awakenings: H. G. Wells's Apocalyptic Romances (1898–1915)," in David Seed, ed., *Imagining Apocalypse*, 72–73.

IRVINE WELSH

Trainspotting, 1995

Gunn, Daniel. "Irvine Welsh: His Success, His Patois, His Translators and His 'Likesay.'" *Recherches Anglaises et Nord-Américaines* 30 (1997), 123–36.

McCarron, Kevin. "The Disenchanted Circle: Slave Narratives and Junk Narratives." *Dionysos* 8:1 (1998), 5–14.

Oliver, Fiona. "The Self-Debasement of Scotland's Postcolonial Bodies." *SPAN* 42–43 (1996), 114–21.

Skinner, John. *The Stepmother Tongue*, 290–92.

JANE WEST

The Advantages of Education; or, The History of Maria Williams, 1793

London, April. "Jane West and the Politics of Reading," in Alvaro Ribeiro and James G. Basker, eds., *Tradition in Transition*, 56–59.

Alicia de Lacy, 1814

Wood, Lisa. "'This Maze of History and Fiction': Conservatism, Genre, and the Problem of Domestic Freedom in Jane West's *Alicia de Lacy*." *Engl Stud in Canada* 23 (1997), 125–37.

A Gossip's Story, 1796

Bannet, Eve Tavor. *The Domestic Revolution*, 174–77.

London, April. "Jane West and the Politics of Reading," in Alvaro Ribeiro and James G. Basker, eds., *Tradition in Transition*, 59–62.

London, April. *Women and Property*, 188–90.

Skinner, Gillian. *Sensibility and Economics in the Novel*, 164–69.

Ty, Eleanor. *Empowering the Feminine*, 87–100.

Ty, Eleanor. "Jane West's Feminine Ideals of the 1790s." *1650–1850: Ideas, Aesthetics, and Inquiries in the Early Mod Era* 1(1994), 140–55.

Watson, Nicola J. *Revolution and the Form of the British Novel*, 75–77.

The Infidel Father, 1802

Ty, Eleanor. *Empowering the Feminine*, 116–30.

A Tale of the Times, 1799

Ford, Susan Allen. "Tales of the Times: Family and Nation in Charlotte Smith and Jane West," in Andrea O'Reilly Herrera et al., eds., *Family Matters*, 16–26.

London, April. "Jane West and the Politics of Reading," in Alvaro Ribeiro and James G. Basker, eds., *Tradition in Transition*, 62–67, 70–73.

London, April. *Women and Property*, 190–92, 197–200.

Ty, Eleanor. *Empowering the Feminine*, 100–115.

Watson, Nicola J. *Revolution and the Form of the British Novel*, 76–78.

REBECCA WEST

The Birds Fall Down, 1966

Norton, Ann V. *Paradoxical Feminism*, 82–92.

The Fountain Overflows, 1956

Norton, Ann V. *Paradoxical Feminism*, 32–36, 59–69, 100–103, 125–28, 141–45.

Harriet Hume, 1929

Norton, Ann V. *Paradoxical Feminism*, 51–56, 119–24.

Pykett, Lyn. "Writing Around Modernism: May Sinclair and Rebecca West," in Lynne Hapgood and Nancy L. Paxton, eds., *Outside Modernism*, 116–17.

The Harsh Voice, 1935
    Norton, Ann V. *Paradoxical Feminism*, 21–28.

The Judge, 1922
    Anderson, Carol. "Feminine Space, Feminine Sentence: Rebecca West's *The Judge*," in Carol Anderson and Aileen Christianson, eds., *Scottish Women's Fiction*, 33–42.
    Norton, Ann V. *Paradoxical Feminism*, 43–50, 94–97.
    Peterson, Shirley. "Modernism, Single Motherhood, and the Discourse of Women's Liberation in Rebecca West's *The Judge*," in Elizabeth Jane Harrison and Shirley Peterson, eds., *Unmanning Modernism*, 105–14.
    Pykett, Lyn. "Writing Around Modernism: May Sinclair and Rebecca West," in Lynne Hapgood and Nancy L. Paxton, eds., *Outside Modernism*, 117–21.
    Wallace, Diana. *Sisters and Rivals in British Women's Fiction*, 109–16.

The Return of the Soldier, 1918
    Ayers, David. *English Literature of the 1920s*, 58–63.
    Cowan, Laura. "The Fine Frenzy of Artistic Vision: Rebecca West's *The Return of the Soldier* as a Feminist Analysis of World War I." *Centennial R* 42 (1998), 285–308.
    Kavka, Misha. "Men in (Shell-)Shock: Masculinity, Trauma, and Psychoanalysis in Rebecca West's *The Return of the Soldier*." *Stud in Twentieth Cent Lit* 22 (1998), 151–68.
    Norton, Ann V. *Paradoxical Feminism*, 8–14.
    Wallace, Diana. *Sisters and Rivals in British Women's Fiction*, 102–9.

Sunflower, 1986
    Norton, Ann V. *Paradoxical Feminism*, 28–32, 113–18.
    Thomas, Sue. "Questioning Sexual Modernity: Rebecca West's *Sunflower*." *AUMLA* 89 (1998), 99–116.

The Thinking Reed, 1936
    Norton, Ann V. *Paradoxical Feminism*, 14–21, 56–58.
    Wallace, Diana. "Revising the Marriage Plot in Women's Fiction of the 1930s," in Maroula Joannou, ed., *Women Writers of the 1930s*, 71–73.

This Real Night, 1984
    Norton, Ann V. *Paradoxical Feminism*, 34–36, 63–67, 125–28.

THOMAS MARTIN WHEELER

Sunshine and Shadow, 1849–1850
    Haywood, Ian. *Working-Class Fiction*, 7–11.

T. H. WHITE

The Elephant and the Kangaroo, 1947
    Nelson, Marie. "T. H. White: Master of Transformation." *Neophilologus* 85 (2001), 315–20.

The Master, 1957

Nelson, Marie. "T. H. White: Master of Transformation." *Neophilologus* 85 (2001), 309–12.

Mistress Masham's Repose, 1946

Nelson, Marie. "T. H. White: Master of Transformation." *Neophilologus* 85 (2001), 312–15.

The Once and Future King, 1958

Berger, Christiane. "More than Just a Fashion: T. H. White's Use of Dress as a Means of Characterization." *Connotations* 7:1 (1997–1998), 135–40.

Brewer, Elizabeth. "Some Comments on 'T. H. White, Pacifism and Violence.'" *Connotations* 7:1 (1997–1998), 128–34.

Hadfield, Andrew. "T. H. White, Pacifism and Violence: The Once and Future Nation." *Connotations* 6 (1996–1997), 207–26.

Schmidt, Siegrid. "Innovative Artus-Rezeption: *Mummenschanz auf Tintagel, Der König auf Camelot*—Überlegungen zu Wilhelm Kubies Roman und T. H. White's Roman-Zyklus," in Ulrich Müller and Kathleen Verduin, eds., *Mittelalter-Rezeption*, 351–64.

Serrano, Amanda. "T. H. White's Defence of Guenever: Portrait of a 'Real' Person." *Mythlore* 21:1 (1995), 9–13.

Spivack, Charlotte, and Roberta Lynne Staples. *The Company of Camelot*, 62–66, 95–97, 100–104, 129–32.

Weller, Barry. "Wizards, Warriors, and the Beast Glatisant in Love," in Eve Kosofsky Sedgwick, ed., *Novel Gazing*, 227–48.

WILLIAM HALE WHITE

The Autobiography of Mark Rutherford, 1881

Swann, Charles. "'Autobiografiction': Problems with Autobiographical Fictions and Fictional Autobiographies—Mark Rutherford's *Autobiography* and *Deliverance*, and Others." *Mod Lang R* 96 (2001), 21–37.

Yvard, Jean-Michel. "Ecriture et spiritualité: La Question de la création littéraire chez William Hale White ('Mark Rutherford')." *Cahiers Victoriens et Edouardiens* 51 (2000), 251–62.

Clara Hopgood, 1896

Swann, Charles. "Clara Hopgood, Chess and Generalship." *ANQ* 12:2 (1999), 26–32.

Swann, Charles. "Dating the Action of *Clara Hopgood.*" *Notes and Queries* 46 (1999), 62–64.

Swann, Charles. "*Jane Eyre* and *Clara Hopgood.*" *Notes and Queries* 46 (1999), 64–65.

Mark Rutherford's Deliverance, 1885

Swann, Charles. "'Autobiografiction': Problems with Autobiographical Fictions and Fictional Autobiographies—Mark Rutherford's *Autobiography* and *Deliverance*, and Others." *Mod Lang R* 96 (2001), 21–37.

Swann, Charles. "Mark Rutherford's Ambiguous Deliverance:

Bunyan, Defoe, Spinoza, and Secular History." *R of Engl Stud* 49 (1998), 23–39.

Yvard, Jean-Michel. "Ecriture et spiritualité: La Question de la création littéraire chez William Hale White ('Mark Rutherford')." *Cahiers Victoriens et Edouardiens* 51 (2000), 251–62.

The Revolution in Tanner's Lane, 1887

Swann, Charles. "Facts in a Fiction; History in a Historical Novel: Mark Rutherford's *The Revolution in Tanner's Lane.*" *J of Victorian Culture* 1 (1996), 280–97.

Swann, Charles. "Mark Rutherford's *The Revolution in Tanner's Lane* and Carlyle's *French Revolution.*" *Notes and Queries* 43 (1996), 48–49.

Yvard, Jean-Michel. "Ecriture et spiritualité: La Question de la création littéraire chez William Hale White ('Mark Rutherford')." *Cahiers Victoriens et Edouardiens* 51 (2000), 251–62.

GEORGE WHYTE-MELVILLE

The Gladiators, 1863

Hoberman, Ruth. *Gendering Classicism,* 104–11.

OSCAR WILDE

The Picture of Dorian Gray, 1891

Aquien, Pascal. "La Première page de *The Picture of Dorian Gray* (Landscape, Inscape, Escape)." *Imaginaires* 5 (2000), 79–91.

Arata, Stephen. *Fictions of Loss,* 59–68.

Armstrong, Nancy. *Fiction in the Age of Photography,* 159–66.

Armstrong, Nancy. "Gender and the Victorian Novel," in Deirdre David, ed., *The Cambridge Companion to the Victorian Novel,* 117–18.

Backus, Margot Gayle. *The Gothic Family Romance,* 149–53.

Belford, Barbara. *Oscar Wilde,* 167–84.

Brantlinger, Patrick. *The Reading Lesson,* 9–11.

Brinkley, Edward S. "Homosexuality as (Anti)Illness: Oscar Wilde's *The Picture of Dorian Gray* and Gabriele D'Annunzio's *Il Piacere.*" *Stud in Twentieth Cent Lit* 22 (1998), 61–80.

Bristow, Joseph. *Effeminate England,* 36–38, 40–42.

Byerly, Alison. *Realism, Representation, and the Arts,* 186–89.

Cambray, Carole. "*The Picture of Dorian Gray* d'Oscar Wilde et les illustrations de Reynold Arnould: De la représentation en crise à la crise de la représentation." *Imaginaires* 3 (1998), 73–87.

Collins, Richard. "Reticence in the Decadence." *B.A.S.: Brit and Am Stud* 1997: 9–19.

Delogu, C. Jon. "'Making' et 'Marring' dans *Le Portrait de Dorian Gray.*" *Imaginaires* 1 (1996), 69–90.

Dewsnap, Desmond. "Oscar Wilde: Persona, Publicity, and the *Fin-de-Siècle* Author." *Postscript* 14 (1997), 105–23.

Eichner, Hans. "Against the Grain: Huysmans' *A Rebours,* Wilde's

Dorian Gray, and Hofmannsthal's *Der Tor und der Tod*," in Raymond A. Prier and Gerald Gillespie, eds., *Narrative Ironies*, 197–201.

Elfenbein, Andrew. *Byron and the Victorians*, 236–46.

Foldy, Michael S. *The Trials of Oscar Wilde*, 9–12, 114–16.

Forderer, Christof. *Ich-Eklipsen*, 156–61.

Frankel, Nicholas. *Oscar Wilde's Decorated Books*, 131–53.

Gagnier, Regenia. "Wilde and the Victorians," in Peter Raby, ed., *The Cambridge Companion to Oscar Wilde*, 18–33.

Gerigk, Horst-Jürgen. "Literarische Vergänglichkeit: Notizen zu Oscar Wildes *Bildnis des Dorian Gray* und Hugo von Hofmannsthals *Rosenkavalier* mit Rücksicht auf Johann Peter Hebels *Unverhofftes Wiedersehen*," in Volker Kapp et al., eds., *Bilderwelten*, 139–44.

Gold, Barri J. "The Domination of *Dorian Gray*." *Victorian Newsl* 91 (1997), 27–30.

Guy, Josephine M., and Ian Small. *Oscar Wilde's Profession*, 232–37, 265–66, 268–70.

Hamilton, Lisa K. "New Women and 'Old' Men: Gendering Degeneration," in Talia Schaffer and Kathy Alexis Psomiades, eds., *Women and British Aestheticism*, 67–70.

Heinrich, Hans. *Zur Geschichte des 'Libertin,'* 208–15.

Jaffe, Audrey. *Scenes of Sympathy*, 158–79.

Kalmár, György. "The Homograph of Dorian Gray." *B.A.S.: Brit and Am Stud* 1998: 88–93.

Kane, Michael. *Modern Men*, 42–52.

Lane, Christopher. *The Burdens of Intimacy*, 160–64.

Larson, Jil. *Ethics and Narrative in the English Novel*, 93–113.

Ledger, Sally. *The New Woman*, 108–11.

Lesjak, Carolyn. "Utopia, Use, and the Everyday: Oscar Wilde and a New Economy of Pleasure." *ELH* 67 (2000), 184–92.

Levy, Anita. *Reproductive Urges*, 129–55.

Liebman, Sheldon W. "Character Design in *The Picture of Dorian Gray*." *Stud in the Novel* 31 (1999), 296–313.

Liou, Liang-ya. "The Politics of a Transgressive Desire: Oscar Wilde's *The Picture of Dorian Gray*." *Stud in Lang and Lit* (Taipei) 6 (1994), 101–23.

Lloyd, Tom. *Crises of Realism*, 156–71.

Losey, Jay. "Disguising the Self in Pater and Wilde," in Jay Losey and William D. Brewer, eds., *Mapping Male Sexuality*, 261–66.

Louvel, Liliane. "*Curios & Mirabilis*: L'étrange cabinet de curiosités du château d'O," in Sophie Marret, ed., *Féminin/Masculin*, 77–82.

Mahaffey, Vicki. "Père-version and Im-mère-sion: Idealized Corruption in *A Portrait of the Artist as a Young Man* and *The Picture of Dorian Gray*," in Joseph Valente, ed., *Quare Joyce*, 121–22, 128–32.

Mahaffey, Vicki. *States of Desire*, 81–86.

Marez, Curtis. "The Other Addict: Reflections on Colonialism and Oscar Wilde's Opium Smoke Screen." *ELH* 64 (1997), 257–82.

Mighall, Robert. *A Geography of Victorian Gothic Fiction*, 195–99.

Monneyron, Frédéric. "Le Corps fantastique dans *The Picture of Dorian Gray* d'Oscar Wilde," in Jean Marigny, ed., *Images fantastiques du corps*, 91–98.

Nassaar, Christopher. "Wilde's *The Picture of Dorian Gray* and *Salome*." *Explicator* 57:1 (1998), 33–35.

Nassaar, Christopher S. "Wilde's *The Picture of Dorian Gray*." *Explicator* 57:4 (1999), 216–17.

Navarette, Susan J. *The Shape of Fear*, 45–58.

Nunokawa, Jeff. "The Importance of Being Bored: The Dividends of Ennui in *The Picture of Dorian Gray*," in Eve Kosofsky Sedgwick, ed., *Novel Gazing*, 151–65.

Pestka, Dariusz. "Analysis of Selected Elements Constituting *The Picture of Dorian Gray*." *Acta Universitatis Nicolai Copernici: Engl Stud* 6 (1995), 81–92.

Peters, John. "Style and Art in Wilde's *The Picture of Dorian Gray*: Form as Content." *Victorian R* 25:1 (1999), 1–10.

Pham-Thanh, Gilbert. "Création, re-création et récréation dans *The Picture of Dorian Gray*: Logique compensatrice ou stratégie d'évitement." *Cahiers Victoriens et Edouardiens* 51 (2000), 243–50.

Pireddu, Nicoletta. "'The Terrible Pleasure of a Double Life': Dorian Gray tra estetica ed etica." *Quaderni di Lingue e Letterature* 1997 (monographic number), 81–99.

Raeside, James. "The Spirit is Willing but the Flesh is Strong: Mishima Yukio's *Kinjiki* and Oscar Wilde." *Compar Lit Stud* 36 (1999), 6–12.

Rashkin, Esther. "Art as Symptom: A Portrait of Child Abuse in *The Picture of Dorian Gray*." *Mod Philology* 95 (1997), 68–80.

Richards, David. "Wilde's *The Picture of Dorian Gray*." *Notes and Queries* 48 (2001), 158.

Riquelme, John Paul. "Oscar Wilde's Aesthetic Gothic: Walter Pater, Dark Enlightenment, and *The Picture of Dorian Gray*." *Mod Fiction Stud* 46 (2000), 609–27.

Sammells, Neil. "Wilde Nature," in Richard Kerridge and Neil Sammells, eds., *Writing the Environment*, 128–30.

Sammells, Neil. *Wilde Style*, 53–62.

Seagroatt, Heather. "Hard Science, Soft Psychology, and Amorphous Art in *The Picture of Dorian Gray*." *Stud in Engl Lit, 1500–1900* 38 (1998), 741–57.

Silvestrini, Antonella. "Oscar Wilde: estetismo e malinconia in *The Picture of Dorian Gray*." *Quaderni di Lingue e Letterature* 21 (1996), 91–101.

Tyson, Nancy Jane. "Caliban in a Glass: Autoscopic Vision in *The Picture of Dorian Gray*," in Elton E. Smith and Robert Haas, eds., *The Haunted Mind*, 101–21.

Varty, Anne. *A Preface to Oscar Wilde*, 111–29.

Whyte, Peter. "Oscar Wilde et Théophile Gautier: Le Cas du *Portrait de Dorian Gray*." *Bull de la Société Théophile Gautier* 21 (1999), 279–94.

ELLEN WILKINSON

Clash, 1929

Ayers, David. *English Literature of the 1920s*, 123–28.
Haywood, Ian. "'Never Again?': Ellen Wilkinson's *Clash* and the Feminization of the General Strike." *Lit and Hist* 8:2 (1999), 34–42.

CHARLES WILLIAMS

Descent into Hell, 1937

Evans, Gwyneth. "'A Greater Universe': Landscape and the Intersection of Worlds in Novels by Charles Williams and John Cowper Powys." *New York R of Science Fiction* 8:11 (1996), 14–16.

The Place of the Lion, 1931

Brew, Kelli. "*Metanoia*: The Hero's Change of Heart in C. S. Lewis's *Space Trilogy* and Charles Williams' *The Place of the Lion*." *Lamp-Post of the Southern California C. S. Lewis Soc* 21:1 (1997), 11–17.

HELEN MARIA WILLIAMS

Julia, 1790

Ellis, Markman. *The Politics of Sensibility*, 214–21.
Kennedy, Deborah. "Responding to the French Revolution: Williams's *Julia* and Burney's *The Wanderer*," in Laura Dabundo, ed., *Jane Austen and Mary Shelley*, 5–9.
Watson, Nicola J. *Revolution and the Form of the British Novel*, 34–36.

NIGEL WILLIAMS

East of Wimbledon, 1993

Fendler, Susanne. "Immigrants in Britain: National Identities and Stereotypes," in Susanne Fendler and Ruth Wittlinger, eds., *The Idea of Europe in Literature*, 120–28.

ANGUS WILSON

The Middle Age of Mrs. Eliot, 1958

MacKay, Marina. "Mr. Wilson and Mrs. Woolf: A Camp Reconstruction of Bloomsbury." *J of Mod Lit* 23 (1999), 95–109.

No Laughing Matter, 1967

Cavaliero, Glen. *The Alchemy of Laughter*, 57–60.
Conradi, Peter. "Angus Wilson: Impersonations," in Richard Todd and Luisa Flora, eds., *Theme Parks*, 104–11.

Old Men at the Zoo, 1961

Spiering, Menno. "Englishness and Post-War Literature," in C. C. Barfoot, ed., *Beyond Pug's Tour*, 272–74.

ROBERT MCLIAM WILSON

Eureka Street, 1996

Kirkland, Richard. "Bourgeois Redemptions: The Fictions of Glenn Patterson and Robert McLiam Wilson," in Liam Harte and Michael Parker, eds., *Contemporary Irish Fiction*, 214–29.

Mikowski, Sylvie. "Contemporary War Fiction." *Etudes Irlandaises* 24:2 (1999), 67–80.

Ni-Riordain, Cliona. "Visions et révisions de Belfast dans le roman irlandais contemporain." *GRAAT* 19 (1998), 29–37.

Ripley Bogle, 1989

Patten, Eve. "Fiction in Conflict: Northern Ireland's Prodigal Novelists," in Ian A. Bell, ed., *Peripheral Visions*, 135–39.

Smyth, Gerry. *The Novel and the Nation*, 132–34.

JEANETTE WINTERSON

Art and Lies, 1994

Bom, Mette. "Language and Lies: Jeanette Winterson's Experimental Modes of Narration," in Helene Bengston et al., eds., *Sponsored by Demons*, 67–79.

Burns, Christy L. "Powerful Differences: Critique and *Eros* in Jeanette Winterson and Virginia Woolf." *Mod Fiction Stud* 44 (1998), 366–72, 376–89.

Maagaard, Cindie Aaen. "The Word Embodied in *Art & Lies*," in Helene Bengston et al., eds., *Sponsored by Demons*, 55–65.

Pressler, Christopher. *So Far So Linear*, 42–47.

Wood, Michael. *Children of Silence*, 183–86.

Boating for Beginners, 1985

Reynier, Christine. "L'art paradoxal de Jeanette Winterson." *Etudes Anglaises* 50 (1997), 183–93.

Wormald, Mark. "The Uses of Impurity: Fiction and Fundamentalism in Salman Rushdie and Jeanette Winterson," in Rod Mengham, ed., *An Introduction to Contemporary Fiction*, 189–94.

Gut Symmetries, 1997

Grice, Helena, and Tim Woods. "Grand (Dis)Unified Theories? Dislocated Discourses in *Gut Symmetries*," in Helena Grice and Tim Woods, eds., *"I'm telling you stories,"* 117–25.

Pressler, Christopher. *So Far So Linear*, 49–55.

Sinkinson, David Lloyd. "'Shadows, Signs, Wonders': Paracelsus, Synchronicity and the New Age of *Gut Symmetries*," in Helene Bengston et al., eds., *Sponsored by Demons*, 81–91.

Wood, Michael. *Children of Silence*, 189–91.

Oranges Are Not the Only Fruit, 1985

Armitt, Lucie. "The Grotesque Utopias of Jeanette Winterson and Monique Wittig," in Ceri Sullivan and Barbara White, eds., *Writing and Fantasy*, 186–88.

Brown, Amy Benson. "Inverted Conversions: Reading the Bible and

Writing the Lesbian Subject in *Oranges Are Not the Only Fruit*," in Raymond-Jean Frontain, ed., *Reclaiming the Sacred*, 233–52.

Carter, Keryn. "The Consuming Fruit: *Oranges*, Demons, and Daughters." *Critique* (Washington, DC) 40 (1998), 15–22.

Cosslett, Tess. "Intertextuality in *Oranges Are Not The Only Fruit*: The Bible, Malory, and *Jane Eyre*," in Helena Grice and Tim Woods, eds., *"I'm telling you stories,"* 15–27.

Duncker, Patricia. "Jeanette Winterson and the Aftermath of Feminism," in Helena Grice and Tim Woods, eds., *"I'm telling you stories,"* 77–88.

French, Jana L. "'I'm Telling You Stories . . . Trust Me': Gender, Desire, and Identity in Jeanette Winterson's Historical Fantasies." *J of the Fantastic in the Arts* 10 (1999), 231–52.

Hallam, Julia, and Margaret Marshment. "Framing Experience: Case Studies in the Reception of *Oranges Are Not the Only Fruit*." *Screen* 36 (1995), 1–15.

King, Jeannette. *Women and the Word*, 118–34.

Pressler, Christopher. *So Far So Linear*, 1–11.

Pykett, Lyn. "A New Way with Words? Jeanette Winterson's Post-Modernism," in Helena Grice and Tim Woods, eds., *"I'm telling you stories,"* 54–59.

Reynier, Christine. "L'art paradoxal de Jeanette Winterson." *Etudes Anglaises* 50 (1997), 183–93.

Rosemergy, Jan. "Navigating the Interior Journey: The Fiction of Jeanette Winterson," in Abby H. P. Werlock, ed., *British Women Writing Fiction*, 248–53.

Spelyte, Milda. "History as Narrative in J. Winterson's Fiction." *Literatura* (Vilnius) 41:3 (1999), 77–88.

Wingfield, Rachel. "Lesbian Writers in the Mainstream: Sara Maitland, Jeanette Winterson and Emma Donoghue," in Elaine Hutton, ed., *Beyond Sex and Romance?*, 66–67, 72–74.

Wormald, Mark. "The Uses of Impurity: Fiction and Fundamentalism in Salman Rushdie and Jeanette Winterson," in Rod Mengham, ed., *An Introduction to Contemporary Fiction*, 197–98.

The Passion, 1987

Bengston, Helene. "The Vast, Unmappable Cities of the Interior: Place and Passion in *The Passion*," in Bengston et al., eds., *Sponsored by Demons*, 17–26.

Bényei, Tamás. *Acts of Attention*, 171–85.

Bényei, Tamás. "Risking the Text: Stories of Love in Jeanette Winterson's *The Passion*." *Hungarian J of Engl and Am Stud* 3 (1997), 199–209.

Fahy, Thomas. "Fractured Bodies: Privileging the Incomplete in Jeanette Winterson's *The Passion*." *Mosaic* 33:3 (2000), 95–106.

French, Jana L. "'I'm Telling You Stories . . . Trust Me': Gender, Desire, and Identity in Jeanette Winterson's Historical Fantasies." *J of the Fantastic in the Arts* 10 (1999), 231–52.

Jukic, Tatjana. "Passions of a New Eve: A Contextual Reading of Jeanette Winterson's *The Passion*." *Studia Romanica et Anglica Zagrabiensia* 42 (1997), 201–9.

Palmer, Paulina. "Lesbian Fiction and the Postmodern: Genre, Narrativity, Sexual Politics," in Steven Earnshaw, ed., *Just Postmodernism*, 164–69.

Palmer, Paulina. "*The Passion*: Storytelling, Fantasy, Desire," in Helena Grice and Tim Woods, eds., *"I'm telling you stories,"* 103–15.

Pfister, Manfred. "*The Passion* from Winterson to Coryate," in Manfred Pfister and Barbara Schaff, eds., *Venetian Views*, 15–27.

Pressler, Christopher. *So Far So Linear*, 13–20.

Purinton, Marjean D. "Postmodern Romanticism: The Recuperation of Conceptual Romanticism in Jeanette Winterson's Postmodern Novel *The Passion*," in Larry H. Peer, ed., *Romanticism Across the Disciplines*, 67–89.

Pykett, Lyn. "A New Way with Words? Jeanette Winterson's Post-Modernism," in Helena Grice and Tim Woods, eds., *"I'm telling you stories,"* 54–59.

Reynier, Christine. "L'art paradoxal de Jeanette Winterson." *Etudes Anglaises* 50 (1997), 183–93.

Rosemergy, Jan. "Navigating the Interior Journey: The Fiction of Jeanette Winterson," in Abby H. P. Werlock, ed., *British Women Writing Fiction*, 253–55.

Seaboyer, Judith. "Second Death in Venice: Romanticism and the Compulsion to Repeat in Jeanette Winterson's *The Passion*." *Contemp Lit* 38 (1997), 483–508.

Spelyte, Milda. "History as Narrative in J. Winterson's Fiction." *Literatura* (Vilnius) 41:3 (1999), 77–88.

Wilson, Scott. "Passion at the End of History," in Helena Grice and Tim Woods, eds., *"I'm telling you stories,"* 61–74.

Sexing the Cherry, 1989

Armitt, Lucie. *Contemporary Women's Fiction*, 17–21, 35–37.

Armitt, Lucie. "The Grotesque Utopias of Jeanette Winterson and Monique Wittig," in Ceri Sullivan and Barbara White, eds., *Writing and Fantasy*, 188–89.

Clingham, Greg. "Winterson's Fiction and Enlightenment Historiography." *Bucknell R* 41:2 (1998), 59–79.

French, Jana L. "'I'm Telling You Stories . . . Trust Me': Gender, Desire, and Identity in Jeanette Winterson's Historical Fantasies." *J of the Fantastic in the Arts* 10 (1999), 231–52.

Gade, Bente. "Multiple Selves and Grafted Agents: A Postmodernist Reading of *Sexing the Cherry*," in Helene Bengston et al., eds., *Sponsored by Demons*, 27–39.

Martin, Sara. "The Power of Monstrous Women: Fay Weldon's *The Life and Loves of a She-Devil* (1983), Angela Carter's *Nights at the Circus* (1984) and Jeanette Winterson's *Sexing the Cherry* (1989)." *J of Gender Stud* 8 (1999), 193–209.

Onega, Susana. "Postmodernist Re-writings of the Puritan Commonwealth: Winterson, Ackroyd, Mukherjee," in Heinz Antor and Kevin L. Cope, eds., *Intercultural Encounters*, 443–52.

Pressler, Christopher. *So Far So Linear*, 22–31.

Pykett, Lyn. "A New Way with Words? Jeanette Winterson's Post-

Modernism," in Helena Grice and Tim Woods, eds., *"I'm telling you stories,"* 54–59.

Reynier, Christine. "L'art paradoxal de Jeanette Winterson." *Etudes Anglaises* 50 (1997), 183–93.

Rosemergy, Jan. "Navigating the Interior Journey: The Fiction of Jeanette Winterson," in Abby H. P. Werlock, ed., *British Women Writing Fiction*, 255–64.

Spelyte, Milda. "History as Narrative in J. Winterson's Fiction." *Literatura* (Vilnius) 41:3 (1999), 77–88.

Watkins, Susan. *Twentieth-Century Women Novelists*, 153–64.

Written on the Body, 1992

Armitt, Lucie. *Contemporary Women's Fiction*, 115–21.

Booth, Alison. "The Scent of a Narrative: Rank Discourse in *Flush* and *Written on the Body*." *Narrative* 8 (2000), 3–17.

Duncker, Patricia. "Jeanette Winterson and the Aftermath of Feminism," in Helena Grice and Tim Woods, eds., *"I'm telling you stories,"* 81–88.

Ender, Evelyne. "'Speculating Carnally'; or, Some Reflections on the Modernist Body." *Yale J of Criticism* 12:1 (1999), 113–30.

Fludernik, Monika. "The Genderization of Narrative." *GRAAT* 21 (1999), 153–75.

Gibson, Andrew. *Postmodernity, Ethics and the Novel*, 47–49.

Harris, Andrea L. *Other Sexes*, 129–47.

Kauer, Ute. "Narration and Gender: The Role of the First-Person Narrator in Jeanette Winterson's *Written on the Body*," in Helena Grice and Tim Woods, eds., *"I'm telling you stories,"* 41–50.

Nunn, Heather. "*Written on the Body*: An Anatomy of Horror, Melancholy and Love." *Women: A Cultural R* 7:1 (1996), 16–27.

Pearce, Lynne. "The Emotional Politics of Reading Winterson," in Helena Grice and Tim Woods, eds., *"I'm telling you stories,"* 30–38.

Pressler, Christopher. *So Far So Linear*, 33–40.

Reynier, Christine. "L'art paradoxal de Jeanette Winterson." *Etudes Anglaises* 50 (1997), 183–93.

Rubinson, Gregory J. "Body Languages: Scientific and Aesthetic Discourses in Jeanette Winterson's *Written on the Body*." *Critique* (Washington, DC) 42 (2001), 218–30.

Stowers, Cath. "The Erupting Lesbian Body: Reading *Written on the Body* as a Lesbian Text," in Helena Grice and Tim Woods, eds., *"I'm telling you stories,"* 89–99.

Wingfield, Rachel. "Lesbian Writers in the Mainstream: Sara Maitland, Jeanette Winterson and Emma Donoghue," in Elaine Hutton, ed., *Beyond Sex and Romance?*, 66.

Wood, Michael. *Children of Silence*, 188–89.

P. G. WODEHOUSE

Right Ho, Jeeves, 1934

Butler, Lance St. John. *Registering the Difference*, 35–38.

MARY WOLLSTONECRAFT

The Emigrants, 1793
    Snader, Joe. *Caught Between Worlds*, 217–21.
Maria, or The Wrongs of Woman, 1798
    Abbey, Ruth. "Back to the Future: Marriage as Friendship in the Thought of Mary Wollstonecraft." *Hypatia* 14:3 (1999), 89–90.
    Basker, James G. "Radical Affinities: Mary Wollstonecraft and Samuel Johnson," in Alvaro Ribeiro and James G. Basker, eds., *Tradition in Transition*, 54–55.
    Becker, Susanne. *Gothic Forms of Feminine Fictions*, 31–33.
    Bellamy, Liz. *Commerce, Morality and the Eighteenth-Century Novel*, 175–81.
    Burgess, Miranda J. *British Fiction and the Production of Social Order*, 144–49.
    Conger, Syndy McMillen. "Mary Shelley's Women in Prison," in Syndy M. Conger et al., eds., *Iconoclastic Departures*, 83–95.
    Fay, Elizabeth A. *A Feminist Introduction to Romanticism*, 145–47.
    Flint, Christopher. *Family Fictions*, 289–304.
    Gladfelder, Hal. *Criminality and Narrative*, 211–18.
    Guest, Harriet. *Small Change*, 296–97, 300–302.
    Haggerty, George E. *Unnatural Affections*, 103–19.
    Hoeveler, Diane Long. "Reading the Wound: Wollstonecraft's *Wrongs of Woman, or Maria* and Trauma Theory." *Stud in the Novel* 31 (1999), 387–406.
    Jacobs, Diane. *Her Own Woman*, 261–67.
    Johnson, Claudia L. "Mary Wollstonecraft: Styles of Radical Maternity," in Susan C. Greenfield and Carol Barash, eds., *Inventing Maternity*, 162–70.
    Jones, Vivien. "Placing Jemima: Women Writers of the 1790s and the Eighteenth-Century Prostitution Narrative." *Women's Writing* 4 (1997), 201–16.
    Jordan, Elaine. "Criminal Conversation: Mary Wollstonecraft's *The Wrongs of Woman*." *Women's Writing* 4 (1997), 221–32.
    Keane, Angela. *Women Writers and the English Nation*, 106–8.
    McCann, Andrew. *Cultural Politics in the 1790s*, 164–76.
    Moore, Jane. *Mary Wollstonecraft*, 43–47.
    Muller, Virginia L. "What Can Liberals Learn from Mary Wollstonecraft?" in Maria J. Falco, ed., *Feminist Interpretations*, 56–57.
    O'Quinn, Daniel. "Trembling: Wollstonecraft, Godwin and the Resistance to Literature." *ELH* 64 (1997), 767–82.
    Poovey, Mary. "Mary Wollstonecraft: The Gender of Genres in Late-Eighteenth-Century England," in Richard Kroll, ed., *The English Novel, Volume II*, 231–47.
    Poston, Carol H. "Mary Wollstonecraft and 'The Body Politic,'" in Maria J. Falco, ed., *Feminist Interpretations*, 89–90, 101–3.
    Ranger, C. M. "'Finely Fashioned Nerves' in Mary Wollstonecraft's *The Wrongs of Woman*." *Notes and Queries* 46 (1999), 27–28.

Ridley, Glynis. "Injustice in the Works of Godwin and Wollstonecraft," in Linda Lang-Peralta, ed., *Women, Revolution, and the Novels of the 1790s*, 82–88.

Sapiro, Virginia. "Wollstonecraft, Feminism, and Democracy: 'Being Bastilled,'" in Maria J. Falco, ed., *Feminist Interpretations*, 40–44.

Skinner, Gillian. *Sensibility and Economics in the Novel*, 177–84.

Swan, Beth. *Fictions of Law*, 54–66, 93–96, 137–40.

Temple, Kathryn. "Imagining Justice: Gender and Juridical Space in the Gothic Novel," in Thomas DiPiero and Pat Gill, eds., *Illicit Sex*, 68–85.

Todd, Janet. *Mary Wollstonecraft*, 427–34.

Watson, Nicola J. *Revolution and the Form of the British Novel*, 50–57.

Mary, A Fiction, 1787

Basker, James G. "Radical Affinities: Mary Wollstonecraft and Samuel Johnson," in Alvaro Ribeiro and James G. Basker, eds., *Tradition in Transition*, 44–45.

Haggerty, George E. *Unnatural Affections*, 103–12.

Jacobs, Diane. *Her Own Woman*, 50–53.

Moore, Jane. *Mary Wollstonecraft*, 16–24.

Todd, Janet. *Mary Wollstonecraft*, 111–15.

Zaw, Susan Khin. "The Reasonable Heart: Mary Wollstonecraft's View of the Relation Between Reason and Feeling in Morality, Moral Psychology, and Moral Development." *Hypatia* 13:1 (1998), 105–7.

EMMA CAROLINE WOOD

East Lynne, 1861

Gruner, Elisabeth Rose. "Plotting the Mother: Caroline Norton, Helen Huntingdon, and Isabel Vane." *Tulsa Stud in Women's Lit* 16 (1997), 303–19.

Humpherys, Anne. "Breaking Apart: The Early Victorian Divorce Novel," in Nicola Diane Thompson, ed., *Victorian Women Writers*, 53–56.

Jaffe, Audrey. *Scenes of Sympathy*, 95–118.

Loncar, Kathleen. *Legal Fiction*, 190–91.

McCuskey, Brian W. "The Kitchen Police: Servant Surveillance and Middle-Class Transgression." *Victorian Lit and Culture* 28 (2000), 367–74.

McKee, Patricia. *Public and Private*, 152–85.

Marcus, Laura. "Oedipus Express: Trains, Trauma and Detective Fiction," in Warren Chernaik et al., eds., *The Art of Detective Fiction*, 210.

Overton, Bill. "Children and Childlessness in the Novel of Female Adultery." *Mod Lang R* 94 (1999), 326–27.

Thaden, Barbara Z. *The Maternal Voice in Victorian Fiction*, 119–23.

The Orville College Boys, 1871

Gibbs, Christine. "Sensational Schoolboys: Mrs. Henry Wood's *The Orville College Boys*." *Lion and the Unicorn* 24 (2000), 45–59.

St. Martin's Eve, 1866

Stern, Rebecca. "'Personation' and 'Good Marking-Ink': Sanity, Performativity, and Biology in Victorian Sensation Fiction." *Nineteenth Cent Stud* 14 (2000), 49–55.

WALTER WOOD

The Enemy in Our Midst, 1906

Höglund, Johan A. *Mobilising the Novel*, 163–67.

LEONARD SIDNEY WOOLF

The Village in the Jungle, 1913

Amirthanayagam, Guy. *The Marriage of Continents*, 91–101.

Gooneratne, Yasmine. "Leonard Woolf's Novel of Sri Lanka: *The Village in the Jungle*," in Heinz Antor and Klaus Stierstorfer, eds., *English Literatures in International Contexts*, 397–402.

Ito, Yuko. "The Masked Reality in Leonard Woolf's Colonial Writings," in Jeanette McVicker and Laura Davis, eds., *Virginia Woolf and Communities*, 138–40.

Kerr, Douglas. "Colonial Habitats: Orwell and Woolf in the Jungle." *Engl Stud* (Amsterdam) 78 (1997), 149–61.

Kerr, Douglas. "Stories of the East: Leonard Woolf and the Genres of Colonial Discourse." *Engl Lit in Transition* 41 (1998), 270–74.

Rosenfeld, Natania. *Outsiders Together*, 42–44.

The Wise Virgins, 1914

Rosenfeld, Natania. *Outsiders Together*, 61–73.

VIRGINIA WOOLF

Between the Acts, 1941

Ames, Christopher. "Carnivalesque Comedy in *Between the Acts*." *Twentieth Cent Lit* 44 (1998), 394–407.

Banfield, Ann. *The Phantom Table*, 338–40.

Barber, Stephen. "Lip-Reading: Woolf's Secret Encounters," in Eve Kosofsky Sedgwick, ed., *Novel Gazing*, 421–37.

Barnaby, Edward. "Visualizing the Spectacle: Woolf's Metahistory Lesson in *Between the Acts*," in Ann Ardis and Bonnie Kime Scott, eds., *Virginia Woolf*, 311–17.

Beer, Gillian. *Virginia Woolf*, 18–27, 125–47, 169–76.

Bezrucka, Yvonne. "Assenza, violenza, proliferazione dei sensi in *Between the Acts* di Virginia Woolf." *Quaderni di Lingue e Letterature* 19 (1994), 97–107.

Blodgett, Harriet. "Food for Thought in Virginia Woolf's Novels." *Woolf Stud Annual* 3 (1997), 57–58.

Briggs, Julia. "The Novels of the 1930s and the Impact of History," in Sue Roe and Susan Sellers, eds., *The Cambridge Companion to Virginia Woolf*, 78–79, 84–88.

Busse, Kristina. "Reflecting the Subject in History: The Return of the Real in *Between the Acts.*" *Woolf Stud Annual* 7 (2001), 75–98.

Cuddy-Keane, Melba. "Virginia Woolf, Sound Technologies, and the New Aurality," in Pamela L. Caughie, ed., *Virginia Woolf . . . Reproduction*, 90–93.

DeKoven, Marianne. "The Community of Audience: Woolf's Drama of Public Woman," in Jeanette McVicker and Laura Davis, eds., *Virginia Woolf and Communities*, 245–47.

Detloff, Madelyn. "Thinking Peace Into Existence: The Spectacle of History in *Between the Acts.*" *Women's Stud* 28 (1999), 403–28.

Gilbert, Sandra. "What Is the Meaning of the Play?: Joyce, Woolf, and the History of the Future," in Clive Hart et al., eds., *Images of Joyce*, vol. 2, 761–62.

Glenny, Allie. *Ravenous Identity*, 203–27.

Gordon, Troy. "The Place of Cross-Sex Friendship in Woolf Studies," in Ann Ardis and Bonnie Kime Scott, eds., *Virginia Woolf*, 102–9.

Gough, Val. "'That Razor Edge of Balance': Virginia Woolf and Mysticism." *Woolf Stud Annual* 5 (1999), 71–76.

Greenberg, Judith. "'When Ears are Deaf and the Heart is Dry': Traumatic Reverberations in *Between the Acts.*" *Woolf Stud Annual* 7 (2001), 49–72.

Hawthorn, Jeremy. *Cunning Passages*, 190–200.

Johnston, Georgia. "Class Performance in *Between the Acts*: Audiences for Miss La Trobe and Mrs. Manresa." *Woolf Stud Annual* 3 (1997), 61–73.

Kennard, Jean E. "From Foe to Friend: Virginia Woolf's Changing View of the Male Homosexual." *Woolf Stud Annual* 4 (1998), 80–83.

Marcus, Laura. *Virginia Woolf*, 160–72.

Marder, Herbert. *The Measure of Life*, 253–57, 316–24.

Maze, John R. *Virginia Woolf*, 175–93.

Miller, Andrew John. "'Our Representative, Our Spokesman': Modernity, Professionalism, and Representation in Virginia Woolf's *Between the Acts.*" *Stud in the Novel* 33:1 (2001), 34–47.

Miller, Marlowe A. "Unveiling 'The Dialectic of Culture and Barbarism' in British Pageantry: Virginia Woolf's *Between the Acts.*" *Papers on Lang and Lit* 34 (1998), 134–60.

Mimlitsch, Michelle N. "Powers of Horror and Peace: Abjection and Community in Virginia Woolf's *Between the Acts*," in Jeanette McVicker and Laura Davis, eds., *Virginia Woolf and Communities*, 36–42.

Olson, Barbara K. *Authorial Divinity*, 96–99.

Oxindine, Annette. "Outing the Outsiders: Woolf's Exploration of Homophobia in *Between the Acts.*" *Woolf Stud Annual* 5 (1999), 115–29.

Peach, Linden. *Virginia Woolf*, 197–213.

Pridmore-Brown, Michele. "1939–40: Of Virginia Woolf, Gramophones, and Fascism." *PMLA* 113 (1998), 408–20.

Radford, Jean. "Late Modernism and the Politics of History," in Maroula Joannou, ed., *Women Writers of the 1930s*, 37.

Roe, Sue. "The Impact of Post-Impressionism," in Sue Roe and

Susan Sellers, eds., *The Cambridge Companion to Virginia Woolf*, 184–87.

Scott, Bonnie Kime. "The Subversive Mechanics of Woolf's Gramophone in *Between the Acts*," in Pamela L. Caughie, ed., *Virginia Woolf... Reproduction*, 97–111.

Sharon-Zisser, Shirley. "'Some Little Language Such as Lovers Use': Virginia Woolf's Elemental Erotics of Simile." *Am Imago* 58:2 (2001), 567–94.

Smith, Patricia Juliana. *Lesbian Panic*, 70–72.

Snaith, Anna. *Virginia Woolf*, 142–55.

Sumner, Rosemary. *A Route to Modernism*, 159–62, 166–68, 182–86.

Tratner, Michael. "Why Isn't *Between the Acts* a Movie?," in Pamela L. Caughie, ed., *Virginia Woolf... Reproduction*, 115–34.

Tremper, Ellen. "*Who Lived at Alfoxton?*," 81–84.

Troy, Mark. "'Bbbbbllllllblblblabschbl!,'" in Clive Hart et al., eds., *Images of Joyce*, vol. 1, 310–14.

Weihman, Lisa Golmitz. "The Problem of National Culture: Virginia Woolf's *Between the Acts* and Elizabeth Bowen's *The Last September*," in Ann Ardis and Bonnie Kime Scott, eds., *Virginia Woolf*, 69–77.

Weil, Lise. "Entering a Lesbian Field of Vision: *To the Lighthouse* and *Between the Acts*," in Eileen Barrett and Patricia Cramer, eds., *Virginia Woolf*, 241–57.

Westling, Louise. "Virginia Woolf and the Flesh of the World." *New Liter Hist* 30 (1999), 857–72.

Whittier-Ferguson, John. "The Burden of Drafts: Woolf's Revisions of *Between the Acts*." Text 10 (1997), 297–319.

Jacob's Room, 1922

Antor, Heinz. "(Post-)Moderne Historiographie und Biographie im englischen Roman des 20. Jahrhunderts: Virginia Woolf und Julian Barnes," in Rüdiger Ahrens and Fritz-Wilhelm Neumann, eds., *Fiktion und Geschichte*, 417–19.

Ayers, David. *English Literature of the 1920s*, 66–78.

Banfield, Ann. *The Phantom Table*, 330–32.

Blodgett, Harriet. "Food for Thought in Virginia Woolf's Novels." *Woolf Stud Annual* 3 (1997), 48–49.

Blodgett, Harriet. "From *Jacob's Room* to *A Passage to India*: A Note." *ANQ* 12:4 (1999), 23.

Bradshaw, David. "The Socio-Political Vision of the Novels," in Sue Roe and Susan Sellers, eds., *The Cambridge Companion to Virginia Woolf*, 196–99.

Dalgarno, Emily. *Virginia Woolf and the Visible World*, 55–60.

Glenny, Allie. *Ravenous Identity*, 99–115.

Gough, Val. "'That Razor Edge of Balance': Virginia Woolf and Mysticism." *Woolf Stud Annual* 5 (1999), 63–66.

Harris, Susan C. "The Ethics of Indecency: Censorship, Sexuality, and the Voice of the Academy in the Narration of *Jacob's Room*." *Twentieth Cent Lit* 43 (1997), 420–37.

Kaye, Peter. *Dostoevsky and English Modernism*, 74–76.

Kennard, Jean E. "From Foe to Friend: Virginia Woolf's Changing View of the Male Homosexual." *Woolf Stud Annual* 4 (1998), 71–72.

Knowles, Sebastian D. G. "Narrative, Death, and Desire: The Three Senses of Humor in *Jacob's Room*." *Woolf Stud Annual* 5 (1999), 97–112.

Levenback, Karen L. *Virginia Woolf and the Great War*, 40–47.

Little, Judy. *The Experimental Self*, 38–47.

Marcus, Laura. *Virginia Woolf*, 32–35, 81–91.

Marshik, Celia. "Publication and 'Public Women': Prostitution and Censorship in Three Novels by Virginia Woolf." *Mod Fiction Stud* 45 (1999), 865–73.

Maze, John R. *Virginia Woolf*, 51–60.

Nelson-McDermott, Catherine. "Disorderly Conduct: Parody and Coded Humor in *Jacob's Room* and *The Years*." *Woolf Stud Annual* 5 (1999), 81–88.

Neverow, Vera. "Thinking Back Through Our Mothers, Thinking in Common: Virginia Woolf's Photographic Imagination and the Community of Narrators in *Jacob's Room, A Room of One's Own*, and *Three Guineas*," in Jeanette McVicker and Laura Davis, eds., *Virginia Woolf and Communities*, 65–85.

Peach, Linden. *Virginia Woolf*, 67–87.

Raitt, Suzanne. "Finding a Voice: Virginia Woolf's Early Novels," in Sue Roe and Susan Sellers, eds., *The Cambridge Companion to Virginia Woolf*, 42–46.

Rosenbaum, S. P. *Aspects of Bloomsbury*, 9–14.

Salomon, Alyza Lee. "Naming Defoe's Influence in *Jacob's Room*." *Virginia Woolf Misc* 55 (2000), 3–4.

Snaith, Anna. *Virginia Woolf*, 79–82.

Tremper, Ellen. *"Who Lived at Alfoxton?,"* 191–92.

Wussow, Helen. *The Nightmare of History*, 116–22, 126–28.

Mrs. Dalloway, 1925

Allan, Tuzyline Jita. "The Death of Sex and the Soul in *Mrs. Dalloway* and Nella Larsen's *Passing*," in Eileen Barrett and Patricia Cramer, eds., *Virginia Woolf*, 95–112.

Anderson, Idris Baker. "The Greel Optative in the Narrative Style of *To the Lighthouse*," in Laura Davis and Jeanette McVicker, eds., *Virginia Woolf and Her Influences*, 195–201.

Ayers, David. *English Literature of the 1920s*, 78–88.

Banfield, Ann. *The Phantom Table*, 204–6, 220–22.

Barrett, Eileen. "Unmasking Lesbian Passion: The Inverted World of *Mrs. Dalloway*," in Eileen Barrett and Patricia Cramer, eds., *Virginia Woolf*, 146–62.

Beer, Gillian. *Virginia Woolf*, 52–56, 159–62.

Blake, Amy. "Woolf's *Mrs Dalloway*." *Explicator* 56:4 (1998), 209–10.

Blodgett, Harriet. "Food for Thought in Virginia Woolf's Novels." *Woolf Stud Annual* 3 (1997), 49–51.

Briggs, Marlene A. "Veterans and Civilians: The Mediation of Traumatic Knowledge in *Mrs. Dalloway*," in Jeanette McVicker and Laura Davis, eds., *Virginia Woolf and Communities*, 43–48.

Burns, Christy L. "Powerful Differences: Critique and *Eros* in Jeanette Winterson and Virginia Woolf." *Mod Fiction Stud* 44 (1998), 372–75.

Caughie, Pamela L. "How Do We Keep Desire from Passing with Beauty?" *Tulsa Stud in Women's Lit* 19 (2000), 269–84.

Childs, Donald J. "Mrs. Dalloway's Unexpected Guests: Virginia Woolf, T. S. Eliot, and Matthew Arnold." *Mod Lang Q* 58 (1997), 63–82.

Dalgarno, Emily. *Virginia Woolf and the Visible World*, 69–84.

DeKoven, Marianne. "The Community of Audience: Woolf's Drama of Public Woman," in Jeanette McVicker and Laura Davis, eds., *Virginia Woolf and Communities*, 238–39.

DeMeester, Karen. "Trauma and Recovery in Virginia Woolf's *Mrs. Dalloway*." *Mod Fiction Stud* 44 (1998), 649–68.

Dick, Susan. "Literary Realism in *Mrs Dalloway, To the Lighthouse, Orlando* and *The Waves*," in Sue Roe and Susan Sellers, eds., *The Cambridge Companion to Virginia Woolf*, 51–57.

Dunn, June Elizabeth. "'Beauty Shines on Two Dogs Doing What Two Women Must Not Do': Puppy Love, Same-Sex Desire and Homosexual Coding in *Mrs. Dalloway*," in Ann Ardis and Bonnie Kime Scott, eds., *Virginia Woolf*, 176–81.

Fayad, Mona. "The Process of Becoming: Engendering the Subject in Mercè Rodoreda." *Catalan R* 2:2 (1987), 119–29.

Flynn, Deirdre. "Virginia Woolf's Women and the Fashionable Elite: On Noy Fitting In," in Jeanette McVicker and Laura Davis, eds., *Virginia Woolf and Communities*, 167–72.

Frome, Susan. "Vanessa Redgrave's Mrs. Dalloway: Revolutionary or Recluse?" *Lit/Film Q* 28 (2000), 227–29.

Gilbert, Sandra. "What Is the Meaning of the Play?: Joyce, Woolf, and the History of the Future," in Clive Hart et al., eds., *Images of Joyce*, vol. 2, 766–68.

Gillespie, Diane F. "'Human nature is on you': Septimus Smith, the Camera Eye, and the Classroom," in Laura Davis and Jeanette McVicker, eds., *Virginia Woolf and Her Influences*, 162–66.

Glenny, Allie. *Ravenous Identity*, 117–32.

Greenberg, Judith. "Woolf's Ancient Song: Traces of the Dead Echoing into the Future," in Ann Ardis and Bonnie Kime Scott, eds., *Virginia Woolf*, 140–46.

Gualtieri-Reed, Elizabeth J. "*Mrs. Dalloway*: Revising Religion." *Centennial R* 43 (1999), 205–25.

Haefele, Lisa. "Violent Conversions, Rhetorical Weapons: *Mrs. Dalloway* and the Influence of a Nationalist Literary History," in Laura Davis and Jeanette McVicker, eds., *Virginia Woolf and Her Influences*, 209–13.

Hankins, Leslie. "'To kindle and illuminate': Woolf's Hot Flashes Against Ageism—Challenges for Cinema," in Laura Davis and Jeanette McVicker, eds., *Virginia Woolf and Her Influences*, 26–34.

Hankins, Leslie Kathleen. "'Colour Burning on a Framework of Steel': Virginia Woolf, Marleen Gorris, Eileen Atkins, and *Mrs. Dalloway*(s)." *Women's Stud* 28 (1999), 367–73.

Harper, Howard. "*Mrs. Dalloway*, The Film," in Laura Davis and Jeanette McVicker, eds., *Virginia Woolf and Her Influences*, 167–71.

Harrington, Gary. "Woolf's *Mrs. Dalloway*." *Explicator* 56:3 (1998), 144–45.

Henke, Suzette. "Virginia Woolf and Post-Traumatic Subjectivity," in Ann Ardis and Bonnie Kime Scott, eds., *Virginia Woolf*, 147–52.

Higgins, Lesley, and Marie-Christine Leps. "From Contingency to Essence: Fictions of Identity in Novels and Films," in Ann Ardis and Bonnie Kime Scott, eds., *Virginia Woolf*, 276–82.

Hoff, Molly. "Coming of Age in *Mrs. Dalloway*." *Woolf Stud Annual* 3 (1997), 95–117.

Hoff, Molly. "The Pseudo-Homeric World of *Mrs. Dalloway*." *Twentieth Cent Lit* 45 (1999), 186–202.

Hoff, Molly. "Woolf's *Mrs. Dalloway*." *Explicator* 55:4 (1997), 215–18.

Hoff, Molly. "Woolf's *Mrs Dalloway*." *Explicator* 57:2 (1999), 95–97.

Hoff, Molly. "Woolf's *Mrs Dalloway*." *Explicator* 58:3 (2000), 148–50.

Hoff, Molly. "Woolf's *Mrs Dalloway*." *Explicator* 59:1 (2000), 32–33.

Hoff, Molly. "Woolf's *Mrs Dalloway*." *Explicator* 59:2 (2001), 95–97.

Holmesland, Oddvar. *Form as Compensation for Life*, 26–80.

Howard, Douglas L. "*Mrs Dalloway*: Virginia Woolf's Redemptive Cycle." *Lit and Theology* 12 (1998), 149–57.

Hurtley, J. A. "On the Arrival of *Mrs. Dalloway*: Badalona 1930." *Catalan R* 5:1 (1991), 121–32.

Jones, Gloria G. "Free Indirect Style in *Mrs. Dalloway*." *Postscript* 14 (1997), 69–80.

Kaivola, Karen. "Revisiting Woolf's Representations of Androgyny: Gender, Race, Sexuality, and Nation." *Tulsa Stud in Women's Lit* 18 (1999), 248–51.

Katz, Tamar. *Impressionist Subjects*, 175–80.

Kennard, Jean E. "From Foe to Friend: Virginia Woolf's Changing View of the Male Homosexual." *Woolf Stud Annual* 4 (1998), 72–73.

Knox-Shaw, Peter. "The Otherness of Septimus Warren Smith." *Durham Univ J* 87 (1995), 99–108.

Korte, Barbara. *Body Language in Literature*, 112–14.

Lackey, Michael. "Woolf's *Mrs Dalloway*." *Explicator* 57:4 (1999), 225–27.

Langbauer, Laurie. *Novels of Everyday Life*, 184–98.

Levenback, Karen L. *Virginia Woolf and the Great War*, 44–82.

Levy, Heather. "'The Cruel Yet Delicate Foot of a Chinese Murderess': The Impact of Woolf's Images of Asia in the Postcolonial Korean Classroom," in Laura Davis and Jeanette McVicker, eds., *Virginia Woolf and Her Influences*, 147–52.

Lilienfeld, Jane. "Accident, Incident, and Meaning: Traces of Trauma in Virginia Woolf's Narrativity," in Ann Ardis and Bonnie Kime Scott, eds., *Virginia Woolf*, 154–56.

Little, Judy. *The Experimental Self*, 47–49.

Lord, Catherine M. "The Frames of Septimus Smith: Through Twenty Four Hours in the City of *Mrs. Dalloway*, 1923, and of Millennial London—Art Is a Shocking Experience." *Parallax* 5:3 (1999), 36–46.

Marcus, Laura. *Virginia Woolf*, 68–81.

Marder, Herbert. *The Measure of Life*, 344–46.

Maze, John R. *Virginia Woolf*, 61–84.

Mimlitsch, Michelle N. "Envisioning/Revisioning Woolf in Film at the End of the Twentieth Century," in Ann Ardis and Bonnie Kime Scott, eds., *Virginia Woolf*, 283–89.

Monte, Steven. "Ancients and Moderns in *Mrs. Dalloway*." *Mod Lang Q* 61 (2000), 587–616.

Montes, Catalina. "Una réplica a *The Waste Land*: *Mrs. Dalloway*." *BELLS: Barcelona Engl Lang and Lit Stud* 1 (1989), 125–37.

Nalbantian, Suzanne. *Aesthetic Autobiography*, 158–65.

North, Michael. *Reading 1922*, 81–86.

O'Dair, Sharon. "Beyond Necessity: The Consumption of Class, the Production of Status, and the Persistence of Inequality." *New Liter Hist* 31 (2000), 337–54.

Olson, Barbara K. *Authorial Divinity*, 84–88.

Peach, Linden. *Virginia Woolf*, 88–112.

Primamore, Elizabeth. "A Don, Virginia Woolf, the Masses, and the Case of Miss Kilman." *LIT* 9 (1998), 121–37.

Quinn, Laurie. "A Woolf with Political Teeth: Classing Virginia Woolf Now and in the Twenty-First Century," in Ann Ardis and Bonnie Kime Scott, eds., *Virginia Woolf*, 328–29.

Rhee, Suk-koo. "Hegemonic Discourse and Counter-Discourse in *Mrs. Dalloway*." *J of Engl Lang and Lit* 43 (1997), 69–84.

Richardson, Brian. *Unlikely Stories*, 96–100.

Roe, Sue. "The Impact of Post-Impressionism," in Sue Roe and Susan Sellers, eds., *The Cambridge Companion to Virginia Woolf*, 180–84.

Roof, Judith. "Hocus Crocus," in Ann Ardis and Bonnie Kime Scott, eds., *Virginia Woolf*, 97–100.

Rosenbaum, S. P. *Aspects of Bloomsbury*, 14–20.

Rosenfeld, Natania. "Links Into Fences: The Subtext of Class Division in *Mrs. Dalloway*." *LIT* 9 (1998), 139–56.

Rosenfeld, Natania. *Outsiders Together*, 96–105, 107–12.

Rudaityte, Regina. "Feminism Subverted: *Mrs. Dalloway* and *The Golden Notebook*." *Literatura* (Vilnius) 37:3 (1995), 84–89.

Santone, Laura. "Sotto il segno di Virginia Woolf: *Il Tempo innamorato* di Gianna Manzini." *Confronto Letterario* 12 (1995), 687–702.

Searls, Damion. "'Against such moments there contrasted Baron Marbot': Reading 'Being' and 'Non-Being' in *Mrs. Dalloway* and Traditional Memoirs," in Laura Davis and Jeanette McVicker, eds., *Virginia Woolf and Her Influences*, 262–68.

Searls, Damion. "Marbot's *Memoirs* and *Mrs. Dalloway*." *Virginia Woolf Misc* 50 (1997), 4.

Searls, Damion. "The Timing of *Mrs. Dalloway*." *Women's Stud* 28 (1999), 361–65.

Smith, Marilyn Schwinn. "Narration, Memory, and Identity: *Mrs. Dalloway* at the End of the Century," in Ann Ardis and Bonnie Kime Scott, eds., *Virginia Woolf*, 158–63.

Smith, Patricia Juliana. *Lesbian Panic*, 41–64.

Snaith, Anna. *Virginia Woolf*, 71–76.

Sypher, Eileen. "Shifting Boundaries: 'New' and Traditional Women in Virginia Woolf." *Women's Writing* 3 (1996), 299–303.

Tate, Trudi. *Modernism, History and the First World War*, 151–70.

Tremper, Ellen. *"Who Lived at Alfoxton?,"* 155–61.

Warner, Lawrence. "The Gaze of Medusa in *Mrs. Dalloway* and *Three Guineas.*" *Lectura Dantis* 12 (1993), 93–101.

Waterman, David F. *Disordered Bodies and Disrupted Borders*, 21–33.

Whitebrook, Maureen. *Identity, Narrative and Politics*, 74–82.

Whitworth, Michael. "'The Indian and His Cross' in *Mrs Dalloway.*" *Virginia Woolf Misc* 49 (1997), 4.

Wilt, Judith. "The Cave of the Body: *The Heart of the Matter.*" *Rel and the Arts* 1:3 (1997), 73–95.

Wilt, Judith. "The Ghost and the Omnibus: The Gothic Virginia Woolf," in Andrew Smith and Jeff Wallace, eds., *Gothic Modernisms*, 65–73.

York, R. A. *The Rules of Time*, 52–66.

Young, John. "Woolf's *Mrs Dalloway.*" *Explicator* 58:2 (2000), 99–100.

Yu, Je-boon. "Bakhtin's Dialogism and Feminism: The Dialogic Self in *Mrs. Dalloway* and the Heteroglossic Plot in *The Golden Notebook.*" *J of Engl Lang and Lit* 43 (1997), 305–20.

Night and Day, 1919

Goldman, Jane. *The Feminist Aesthetics of Virginia Woolf*, 92–93.

Marcus, Laura. *Virginia Woolf*, 61–63.

Maze, John R. *Virginia Woolf*, 35–49.

Olson, Barbara K. *Authorial Divinity*, 66–67.

Peach, Linden. *Virginia Woolf*, 56–64.

Raitt, Suzanne. "Finding a Voice: Virginia Woolf's Early Novels," in Sue Roe and Susan Sellers, eds., *The Cambridge Companion to Virginia Woolf*, 39–42.

Rosenfeld, Natania. *Outsiders Together*, 59–61, 74–80.

Smith, Patricia Juliana. *Lesbian Panic*, 37–40.

Snaith, Anna. *Virginia Woolf*, 31–34.

Tremper, Ellen. *"Who Lived at Alfoxton?,"* 85–95.

Whitworth, Michael. "'The Lighted Strip of History': Virginia Woolf and Einsteinian Simultaneity," in Ann Ardis and Bonnie Kime Scott, eds., *Virginia Woolf*, 307–8.

Wussow, Helen. *The Nightmare of History*, 99–108.

Zemgulys, Andrea P. "'*Night and Day* Is Dead': Virginia Woolf in London 'Literary and Historic.'" *Twentieth Cent Lit* 46 (2000), 56–74.

Zimring, Rishona. "Gissing, Woolf, and the Drama of Home," in Laura Davis and Jeanette McVicker, eds., *Virginia Woolf and Her Influences*, 87–89.

Orlando, 1928

Aiazzi, Anna Maria. "Dalla sinusoide al vortice: *Orlando* di Virginia Woolf." *Rivista di Letterature Moderne e Comparate* 53 (2000), 409–27.

Aleksiuk, Natasha. "'A Thousand Angles': Photographic Irony in the

Work of Julia Margaret Cameron and Virginia Woolf." *Mosaic* 33:2 (2000), 136–41.

Antor, Heinz. "(Post-)Moderne Historiographie und Biographie im englischen Roman des 20. Jahrhunderts: Virginia Woolf und Julian Barnes," in Rüdiger Ahrens and Fritz-Wilhelm Neumann, eds., *Fiktion und Geschichte*, 416–17.

Banfield, Ann. *The Phantom Table*, 202–3.

Bazargan, Susan. "The Uses of the Land: Vita Sackville-West's Pastoral Writings and Virginia Woolf's *Orlando*." *Woolf Stud Annual* 5 (1999), 25–52.

Beer, Gillian. *Virginia Woolf*, 56–64, 98–101.

Boxwell, D. A. "(Dis)orienting Spectacle: The Politics of *Orlando*'s Sapphic Camp." *Twentieth Cent Lit* 44 (1998), 306–24.

Craft-Fairchild, Catherine. "'Same Person . . . Just a Different Sex': Sally Potter's Construction of Gender in *Orlando*." *Woolf Stud Annual* 7 (2001), 23–44.

Cummins, June. "What are They Really Afraid Of?: Repression, Anxiety, and Lesbian Subtext in the Cultural Reception of Sally Potter's *Orlando*," in Laura Davis and Jeanette McVicker, eds., *Virginia Woolf and Her Influences*, 20–25.

Denisoff, Dennis. "The Forest beyond the Frame: Picturing Women's Desires in Vernon Lee and Virginia Woolf," in Talia Schaffer and Kathy Alexis Psomiades, eds., *Women and British Aestheticism*, 257–67.

Dick, Susan. "Literary Realism in *Mrs Dalloway, To the Lighthouse, Orlando* and *The Waves*," in Sue Roe and Susan Sellers, eds., *The Cambridge Companion to Virginia Woolf*, 62–65.

Duncker, Patricia. "The Impossibility of Making Writing: Mrs Arbuthnot, Mrs Lewes and Mrs Woolf." *Women: A Cultural R* 9 (1998), 312–23.

Ferriss, Suzanne, and Kathleen Waites. "Unclothing Gender: The Postmodern Sensibility in Sally Potter's *Orlando*." *Lit/Film Q* 27 (1999), 110–14.

Goldman, Jane. *The Feminist Aesthetics of Virginia Woolf*, 110–11.

Gualtieri, Elena. *Virginia Woolf's Essays*, 104–15.

Hankins, Leslie Kathleen. "*Orlando*: 'A Precipice Marked V': Between 'A Miracle of Discretion' and 'Lovemaking Unbelievable: Indiscretions Incredible,'" in Eileen Barrett and Patricia Cramer, eds., *Virginia Woolf*, 180–99.

Herrmann, Anne. *Queering the Moderns*, 65–85.

Higgins, Lesley, and Marie-Christine Leps. "From Contingency to Essence: Fictions of Identity in Novels and Films," in Ann Ardis and Bonnie Kime Scott, eds., *Virginia Woolf*, 276–82.

Hill, Marylu. *Mothering Modernity*, 189–208.

Hovey, Jaime. "'Kissing a Negress in the Dark': Englishness as a Masquerade in Woolf's *Orlando*." *PMLA* 112 (1997), 393–403.

Humm, Maggie. "The Business of a 'New Art': Woolf, Potter and Postmodernism," in Judy Simons and Kate Fullbrook, eds., *Writing: A Woman's Business*, 112–24.

Ivory, James Maurice. *Identity and Narrative Metamorphoses*, 43–74.

Jondot, Jacqueline. "La Maman et la putain." *Imaginaires* 2 (1997), 139–49.

Jouve, Nicole Ward. "Virginia Woolf and Psychoanalysis," in Sue Roe and Susan Sellers, eds., *The Cambridge Companion to Virginia Woolf*, 267–69.

Kaivola, Karen. "Revisiting Woolf's Representations of Androgyny: Gender, Race, Sexuality, and Nation." *Tulsa Stud in Women's Lit* 18 (1999), 251–57.

Kaivola, Karen. "Virginia Woolf, Vita Sackville-West, and the Question of Sexual Identity." *Woolf Stud Annual* 4 (1998), 36–38.

Kellermann, Ralf. "Luhmanns Systemtheorie und die sozialhistorischen Bedeutungen von Virginia Woolfs *Orlando*: Ein Beitrag zur funktionalen Hermeneutik des Narrativen," in Thomas Bleitner et al., eds., *Praxisorientierte Literaturtheorie*, 157–89.

Lackey, Michael. "Woolf and the Necessity of Atheism." *Virginia Woolf Misc* 53 (1999), 3–4.

Macedo, Ana Gabriela. "From the Amazon to the *Flâneuse*: Women at the Turn of the Century." *BELLS: Barcelona Engl Lang and Lit Stud* 7 (1996), 63–71.

Marchi, Dudley M. "Virginia Woolf Crossing the Borders of History, Culture, and Gender: The Case of Montaigne, Pater, and Gournay." *Compar Lit Stud* 34 (1997), 15–27.

Marcus, Laura. *Virginia Woolf*, 114–33.

Marshik, Celia. "Publication and 'Public Women': Prostitution and Censorship in Three Novels by Virginia Woolf." *Mod Fiction Stud* 45 (1999), 873–80.

Miles, Kathryn. "'That perpetual marriage of granite and rainbow': Searching for 'The New Biography' in Virginia Woolf's *Orlando*," in Jeanette McVicker and Laura Davis, eds., *Virginia Woolf and Communities*, 212–17.

Minow-Pinkney, Makiko. "Virginia Woolf and the Age of Motor Cars," in Pamela L. Caughie, ed., *Virginia Woolf . . . Reproduction*, 160–65.

Nalbantian, Suzanne. *Aesthetic Autobiography*, 165–68.

Olson, Barbara K. *Authorial Divinity*, 67–69.

Peach, Linden. *Virginia Woolf*, 137–55.

Pidduck, Julianne. "Travels with Sally Potter's *Orlando*: Gender, Narrative, Movement." *Screen* 38 (1997), 172–89.

Piggford, George. "'Who's That Girl?': Annie Lennox, Woolf's *Orlando*, and Female Camp Androgyny." *Mosaic* 30:3 (1997), 47–57.

Porter, David. "*Orlando* on Her Mind? An Unpublished Letter from Virginia Woolf to Lady Sackville." *Woolf Stud Annual* 7 (2001), 103–13.

Rabinowitz, Paula. "Crossings: Reading *Orlando*." *North Dakota Q* 56:3 (1988), 87–94.

Rado, Lisa. *The Modern Androgyne Imagination*, 160–71.

Ramsey, Tamara Ann. "Producing Queer Affiliations: Feminist, Lesbian, Aesthetic, and Queer Reading Practices," in Laura Davis and Jeanette McVicker, eds., *Virginia Woolf and Her Influences*, 275–81.

Rosenfeld, Natania. *Outsiders Together*, 134–45.

Saupe, Anja. "'Ich bestand aus nichts anderem': Zum Verhältnis von Konstruktion, Destruktion und Rekonstruktion von Geschlechtsidentität in Erzählungen der Moderne." *Literatur für Leser* 22:3 (1999), 144–61.

Stape, J. H. "'The Man at Worthing' and the Author of 'The Most Insipid Verse She Had Ever Read': Two Allusions in *Orlando*." *Virginia Woolf Misc* 50 (1997), 5–6.

Trodd, Anthea. *Women's Writing in English*, 186–88.

Waller, L. Elizabeth. "Writing the Real: Virginia Woolf and an Ecology of Language." *Bucknell R* 44:1 (2000), 142–46.

Watkins, Susan. "Sex Change and Media Change: From Woolf's to Potter's *Orlando*." *Mosaic* 31:3 (1998), 41–57.

Watkins, Susan. *Twentieth-Century Women Novelists*, 108–21.

Whitworth, Michael. "'The Lighted Strip of History': Virginia Woolf and Einsteinian Simultaneity," in Ann Ardis and Bonnie Kime Scott, eds., *Virginia Woolf*, 309.

Young, Suzanne. "The Unnatural Object of Modernist Aesthetics: Artifice in Woolf's *Orlando*," in Elizabeth Jane Harrison and Shirley Peterson, eds., *Unmanning Modernism*, 168–83.

To the Lighthouse, 1927

Ayers, David. *English Literature of the 1920s*, 88–95.

Banfield, Ann. *The Phantom Table*, 176–81, 285–89.

Banfield, Ann. "Tragic Time: The Problem of the Future in Cambridge Philosophy and *To the Lighthouse*." *Modernism/Modernity* 7:1 (2000), 43–75.

Baróthy, Judit. "The Androgynous Mind: A Contrastive Analysis of Virginia Woolf's *To the Lighthouse* and Boris Pasternak's *Zhenya Luvers' Childhood*." *AnaChronist* 1996: 79–97.

Barrett, Eileen. "The Language of Fabric in *To the Lighthouse*," in Beth Rigel Daugherty and Mary Beth Pringle, eds., *Approaches to Teaching*, 54–59.

Bazin, Nancy Topping. "Articulating the Questions, Searching for Answers: How *To the Lighthouse* Can Help," in Beth Rigel Daugherty and Mary Beth Pringle, eds., *Approaches to Teaching*, 107–13.

Beer, Gillian. *Virginia Woolf*, 29–47, 157–59.

Bellamy, Suzanne. "'Painting the Words': A Version of Lily Briscoe's Paintings from *To the Lighthouse*," in Ann Ardis and Bonnie Kime Scott, eds., *Virginia Woolf*, 244–50.

Bezrucka, Yvonne. "L'estetica di *To the Lighthouse*: La tentazione della bellezza astratta e il rifiuto delle 'strane indicazioni.'" *Quaderni del Dipartimento di Lingue e Letterature Straniere Moderne* (Genova) 7 (1995), 291–315.

Blodgett, Harriet. "Food for Thought in Virginia Woolf's Novels." *Woolf Stud Annual* 3 (1997), 45–47, 52–54.

Bradshaw, David. "The Socio-Political Vision of the Novels," in Sue Roe and Susan Sellers, eds., *The Cambridge Companion to Virginia Woolf*, 199–204.

Braendlin, Bonnie. "'I Have Had My Vision': Teaching *To the Lighthouse* as Künstlerroman," in Beth Rigel Daugherty and Mary Beth Pringle, eds., *Approaches to Teaching*, 148–53.

Carubia, Josephine M. "'The Blessed Island of Good Boots': Virginia Woolf's Deployment of Fetishism in *To the Lighthouse*," in Laura Davis and Jeanette McVicker, eds., *Virginia Woolf and Her Influences*, 282–87.

Caughie, Pamela L. "How Do We Keep Desire from Passing with Beauty?" *Tulsa Stud in Women's Lit* 19 (2000), 269–84.

Caughie, Pamela L. "Returning to the Lighthouse: A Postmodern Approach," in Beth Rigel Daugherty and Mary Beth Pringle, eds., *Approaches to Teaching*, 47–53.

Cobb, Gerald T. "From the Dark House to the Lighthouse: The Ramsays as Dysfunctional Family," in Beth Rigel Daugherty and Mary Beth Pringle, eds., *Approaches to Teaching*, 114–18.

Cousineau, Diane. *Letters and Labyrinths*, 57–80.

Crater, Theresa L. "Lily Briscoe's Vision: The Articulation of Silence." *Rocky Mountain R of Lang and Lit* 50:2 (1996), 121–35.

Cuddy-Keane, Melba. "Virginia Woolf, Sound Technologies, and the New Aurality," in Pamela L. Caughie, ed., *Virginia Woolf . . . Reproduction*, 85–87.

Currier, Susan. "Liberation Fables 'in a Different Voice': Virginia Woolf's *To the Lighthouse* and Margaret Drabble's *The Waterfall*," in Jerilyn Fisher and Ellen S. Silber, eds., *Analyzing the Different Voice*, 175–89.

Currier, Susan. "Portraits of Artists by Woolf and Joyce," in Beth Rigel Daugherty and Mary Beth Pringle, eds., *Approaches to Teaching*, 35–40.

Dalgarno, Emily. *Virginia Woolf and the Visible World*, 22–27, 84–96.

Davis, Laura. "Reading and Writing: Helping Students Discover Meaning in *To the Lighthouse*," in Beth Rigel Daugherty and Mary Beth Pringle, eds., *Approaches to Teaching*, 35–40.

DeSalvo, Louise. "What Teaching *To the Lighthouse* Taught Me about Reading Virginia Woolf," in Beth Rigel Daugherty and Mary Beth Pringle, eds., *Approaches to Teaching*, 91–96.

Dever, Carolyn. *Death and the Mother*, 203–12.

Di Blasio, Francesca. "La scrittura isotopica e l'explicit indefinito di *To the Lighthouse*." *Confronto Letterario* 14 (1997), 665–75.

Dick, Susan. "Literary Realism in *Mrs Dalloway, To the Lighthouse, Orlando* and *The Waves*," in Sue Roe and Susan Sellers, eds., *The Cambridge Companion to Virginia Woolf*, 57–62.

Doody, Terrence. *Among Other Things*, 98–99, 102–4.

Duncker, Patricia. "The Impossibility of Making Writing: Mrs Arbuthnot, Mrs Lewes and Mrs Woolf." *Women: A Cultural R* 9 (1998), 312–23.

Epes, Isota Tucker. "The Liberation of Lily Briscoe," in Ann Ardis and Bonnie Kime Scott, eds., *Virginia Woolf*, 252–56.

Folsom, Marcia McClintock. "Transformations: Teaching *To the Lighthouse* with Autobiographies and Family Chronicles," in Beth Rigel Daugherty and Mary Beth Pringle, eds., *Approaches to Teaching*, 119–25.

Forbes, Shannon. "'When Sometimes she Imagined Herself like her Mother': The Contrasting Responses of Cam and Mrs. Ramsay to the Role of the Engel in the House." *Stud in the Novel* 32 (2000), 464–83.

Foy, Roslyn Reso. "Sanity and Madness; Art and Life: A Study of Community in Virginia Woolf's *To the Lighthouse* and Mary Butts's *Armed with Madness*." *Atenea* 20:2 (2000), 95–102.

Gay, Jane de. "Behind the Purple Triangle: Art and Iconography in *To the Lighthouse*." *Woolf Stud Annual* 5 (1999), 1–21.

Gilbert, Sandra. "What Is the Meaning of the Play?: Joyce, Woolf, and the History of the Future," in Clive Hart et al., eds., *Images of Joyce*, vol. 2, 768–78.

Glenny, Allie. *Ravenous Identity*, 133–54.

Goldman, Jane. "Artist and Feminist Communities of 1910: Post-Impressionsim, Suffrage Aesthetics, and Intersubjectivity in *To the Lighthouse*," in Jeanette McVicker and Laura Davis, eds., *Virginia Woolf and Communities*, 259–67.

Goldman, Jane. *The Feminist Aesthetics of Virginia Woolf*, 166–85.

Goldman, Jane, ed. *Virginia Woolf: "To the Lighthouse," "The Waves,"* 29–167.

Goring, Paul. "The Shape of *To the Lighthouse*: Lily Briscoe's Painting and the Reader's Vision." *Word and Image* 10:3 (1994), 222–29.

Gough, Val. "'That Razor Edge of Balance': Virginia Woolf and Mysticism." *Woolf Stud Annual* 5 (1999), 66–71.

Hargreaves, Tracy. "The Grotesque and the Great War in *To the Lighthouse*," in Suzanne Raitt and Trudi Tate, eds., *Women's Fiction and the Great War*, 132–48.

Henke, Suzette. "Virginia Woolf's *To the Lighthouse*: (En)Gendering Epiphany," in Wim Tigges, ed., *Moments of Moment*, 261–78.

Herman, David. "Dialogue in a Discourse Context: Discourse-Analytic Models and Woolf's *To the Lighthouse*." *Virginia Woolf Misc* 52 (1998), 3–4.

Hermetet, Anne-Rachel. "Adieux au référent: Le Peintre dans *To the Lighthouse* de Virginia Woolf et *La Vie mode d'emploi* de Georges Perec." *Roman 20–50* 28 (1999), 103–14.

Hill, Marylu. *Mothering Modernity*, 181–88.

Holmesland, Oddvar. *Form as Compensation for Life*, 86–146.

Hussey, Mark. "'For Nothing Is Simply One Thing': Knowing the World in *To the Lighthouse*," in Beth Rigel Daugherty and Mary Beth Pringle, eds., *Approaches to Teaching*, 41–46.

Ingram, Penelope. "'One drifts apart': *To the Lighthouse* as Art of Response." *Philos and Lit* 23 (1999), 78–94.

Jondot, Jacqueline. "A Green Shawl over the Edge of a Picture Frame." *Imaginaires* 3 (1998), 89–103.

Jouve, Nicole Ward. *Female Genesis*, 119–25.

Jouve, Nicole Ward. "Virginia Woolf and Psychoanalysis," in Sue Roe and Susan Sellers, eds., *The Cambridge Companion to Virginia Woolf*, 260–62, 265–67.

Kaivola, Karen. "Revisiting Woolf's Representations of Androgyny:

Gender, Race, Sexuality, and Nation." *Tulsa Stud in Women's Lit* 18 (1999), 249–51.

Kato, Megumi. "The Milk Problem in *To the Lighthouse*." *Virginia Woolf Misc* 50 (1997), 5.

Kato, Megumi. "The Politics/Poetics of Motherhood in *To the Lighthouse*," in Jeanette McVicker and Laura Davis, eds., *Virginia Woolf and Communities*, 102–7.

Krouse, Tonya. "'I would rather be a cyborg than a goddess': Lily Briscoe, Mrs. Ramsay, and the Postmodern Sublime," in Laura Davis and Jeanette McVicker, eds., *Virginia Woolf and Her Influences*, 294–99.

Laurence, Patricia. "'Some Rope to Throw to the Reader': Teaching the Diverse Rhythms of *To the Lighthouse*," in Beth Rigel Daugherty and Mary Beth Pringle, eds., *Approaches to Teaching*, 66–71.

Lee, Hermione. "Am I Afraid of Virginia Woolf?," in Warwick Gould and Thomas F. Staley, eds., *Writing the Lives of Writers*, 231–32.

Levenback, Karen L. "Teaching *To the Lighthouse* as a Civilian War Novel," in Beth Rigel Daugherty and Mary Beth Pringle, eds., *Approaches to Teaching*, 142–47.

Levenback, Karen L. *Virginia Woolf and the Great War*, 83–113.

Levy, Heather. "'The Cruel Yet Delicate Foot of a Chinese Murderess': The Impact of Woolf's Images of Asia in the Postcolonial Korean Classroom," in Laura Davis and Jeanette McVicker, eds., *Virginia Woolf and Her Influences*, 147–52.

Lilienfeld, Jane. "'A Lunch a few drops of something': The Opium Narrative in *To the Lighthouse*," in Laura Davis and Jeanette McVicker, eds., *Virginia Woolf and Her Influences*, 38–42.

Lilienfeld, Jane. *Reading Alcoholisms*, 159–231.

Lindhoff, Lena. "Das weibliche Androgyne: Kunst als andere Praxis des Wissens in Virginia Woolfs *To the Lighthouse*," in Christa Bürger, ed., *Literatur und Leben*, 41–61.

Little, Judy. *The Experimental Self*, 49–53.

Lumsden, Robert. "Virginia Woolf's 'As If' in *To the Lighthouse*: The Modernist Philosophy of Meaning in Absentia," in Robert J. C. Young et al., eds., *The Silent Word*, 119–31.

McNaron, Toni A. H. "Look Again: Reading *To the Lighthouse* from an Aesthetic of Likeness," in Beth Rigel Daugherty and Mary Beth Pringle, eds., *Approaches to Teaching*, 85–90.

McVicker, Jeanette. "Reading *To the Lighthouse* as a Critique of the Imperial," in Beth Rigel Daugherty and Mary Beth Pringle, eds., *Approaches to Teaching*, 97–104.

Marcus, Laura. *Virginia Woolf*, 90–96, 103–14.

Marotte, Mary Ruth. "Re-constructing Femininity in Woolf and Cixous: Awakening the Need to Create." *Publs of the Arkansas Philol Assoc* 25:1 (1999), 61–71.

Maze, John R. *Virginia Woolf*, 85–118.

Minogue, Sally. "Was it a Vision? Structuring Emptiness in *To the Lighthouse*." *J of Mod Lit* 21 (1997), 281–94.

Nalbantian, Suzanne. *Aesthetic Autobiography*, 140–58.

Nantet, Marie-Victoire. "Peindre la vie." *Imaginaires* 3 (1998), 105–11.

Neverow, Vara. "Compulsory Heterosexuality and the Lesbian Continuum in *To the Lighthouse*: A Woman's Studies Approach," in Beth Rigel Daugherty and Mary Beth Pringle, eds., *Approaches to Teaching*, 169–75.

Olson, Barbara K. *Authorial Divinity*, 88–91.

O'Neill, Michael. "Liking or Disliking: Woolf, Conrad, Lawrence," in Richard Gravil, ed., *Master Narratives*, 169–75.

Oxindine, Annette. "Pear Trees beyond Eden: Women's Knowing Reconfigured in Woolf's *To the Lighthouse* and Hurston's *Their Eyes Were Watching God*," in Beth Rigel Daugherty and Mary Beth Pringle, eds., *Approaches to Teaching*, 163–68.

Paul, Janis M. "Teaching *To the Lighthouse* as a Traditional Novel," in Beth Rigel Daugherty and Mary Beth Pringle, eds., *Approaches to Teaching*, 35–40.

Peach, Linden. *Virginia Woolf*, 113–36.

Perkins, Wendy. "Virginia Woolf's Dialogues with the 'New Woman,'" in Andrea O'Reilly Herrera et al., eds., *Family Matters*, 150–65.

Petric-Bajlo, Estella. "Playing Roles: A Reading of Virginia Woolf's Novel *To the Lighthouse*." *Studia Romanica et Anglica Zagrabiensia* 42 (1997), 299–312.

Pinkerton, Mary. "Reading Provisionally: Narrative Theory and *To the Lighthouse*," in Beth Rigel Daugherty and Mary Beth Pringle, eds., *Approaches to Teaching*, 60–65.

Poster, Jem. "A Combination of Interest: Virginia Woolf's *To the Lighthouse*." *Crit Survey* 8 (1996), 210–15.

Pratt, Annis. "Twenty Years to the Lighthouse: A Teaching Voyage," in Beth Rigel Daugherty and Mary Beth Pringle, eds., *Approaches to Teaching*, 72–78.

Rado, Lisa. *The Modern Androgyne Imagination*, 152–60.

Raschke, Debrah. "*To the Lighthouse* 'Through the Looking Glass': Woolf's and Irigaray's Metaphysics," in Laura Davis and Jeanette McVicker, eds., *Virginia Woolf and Her Influences*, 288–93.

Rosenbaum, S. P. *Aspects of Bloomsbury*, 20–28.

Rosenfeld, Natania. *Outsiders Together*, 124–34.

Sadrin, Anny. "Time, Tense, Weather in Three 'Flood Novels': *Bleak House, The Mill on the Floss, To the Lighthouse*." *Yrbk of Engl Stud* 30 (2000), 96–100.

Schwenger, Peter. *Fantasm and Fiction*, 69–72.

Silbergleid, Robin Paula. "'We perished, each alone': Loss and Lyricism in Woolf, Maso, and Young," in Jeanette McVicker and Laura Davis, eds., *Virginia Woolf and Communities*, 57–63.

Smith, Angela. "Thresholds in 'Prelude' and *To the Lighthouse*." *Commonwealth Essays and Stud* 4 (1997), 39–49.

Smith, Patricia Juliana. *Lesbian Panic*, 64–70.

Snaith, Anna. *Virginia Woolf*, 65–67, 76–79.

Stewart, Jack. "A 'Need of Distance and Blue': Space, Color, and Creativity in *To the Lighthouse*." *Twentieth Cent Lit* 46 (2000), 78–95.

Stockton, Sharon. "Public Space and Private Time: Perspective in *To the Lighthouse* and in Einstein's Special Theory." *Essays in Arts and Sciences* 27 (1998), 95–113.

Sumner, Rosemary. *A Route to Modernism*, 150–54, 170–79.

Sypher, Eileen. "Shifting Boundaries: 'New' and Traditional Women in Virginia Woolf." *Women's Writing* 3 (1996), 303–6.

Torsello, Carol Taylor. "How Woolf Creates Point of View in *To the Lighthouse*: An Application of Systemic-Functional Grammar to a Literary Text." *Occasional Papers in Systemic Ling* 5 (1991), 159–74.

Tratner, Michael. "Cleaning Women and Prostitutes: Figures in the Dark in *To the Lighthouse* and *Ulysses*," in Clive Hart et al., eds., *Images of Joyce*, vol. 1, 299–308.

Tremper, Ellen. *"Who Lived at Alfoxton?,"* 161–90.

Trezise, Simon. *The West Country as a Literary Invention*, 223–28.

Trotter, David. "The Modernist Novel," in Michael Levenson, ed., *The Cambridge Companion to Modernism*, 80–83.

Tsagaris, Ellen. "Every Picture Tells a Story: Woolf and the Artist's Vision." *Virginia Woolf Misc* 55 (2000), 2–3.

Vanita, Ruth. "Brining Buried Things to Light: Homoerotic Alliances in *To the Lighthouse*," in Eileen Barrett and Patricia Cramer, eds., *Virginia Woolf*, 165–78.

Vlasopolos, Anca. "Focalization, the Cinematic Gaze, and Romance in Meredith and Woolf." *Woolf Stud Annual* 7 (2001), 3–21.

Volk-Birke, Sabine. "'Nothing Is Simply One Thing': Das Problem der Wahrnehmung in Virginia Woolfs Roman *To the Lighthouse*." *Literaturwissenschaftliches Jahrbuch im Auftrage der Görres-Gesellschaft* 34 (1993), 115–30.

Weatherhead, A. K. *Upstairs*, 65–70.

Weil, Lise. "Entering a Lesbian Field of Vision: *To the Lighthouse* and *Between the Acts*," in Eileen Barrett and Patricia Cramer, eds., *Virginia Woolf*, 241–57.

Yunis, Susan. "*To the Lighthouse* and Painting," in Beth Rigel Daugherty and Mary Beth Pringle, eds., *Approaches to Teaching*, 129–35.

The Voyage Out, 1915

Banfield, Ann. *The Phantom Table*, 24–25.

Beer, Gillian. *Virginia Woolf*, 13–16.

Bradshaw, David. "The Socio-Political Vision of the Novels," in Sue Roe and Susan Sellers, eds., *The Cambridge Companion to Virginia Woolf*, 192–96.

Dalgarno, Emily. *Virginia Woolf and the Visible World*, 50–53.

Glenny, Allie. *Ravenous Identity*, 77–98.

Hill, Marylu. *Mothering Modernity*, 170–80.

Johnson, Erica L. "Contours of Travel and Exile in *The Voyage Out*." *J of Narrative Theory* 31 (2001), 65–83.

Landon, Lana Hartman, and Laurel Smith. "A Community of Correspondences: Two Women, Letters, and *The Voyage Out*," in Jeanette McVicker and Laura Davis, eds., *Virginia Woolf and Communities*, 17–22.

Low, Lisa. "Woolf's Allusions to *Hedda Gabler* in *The Voyage Out*." *Virginia Woolf Misc* 50 (1997), 3–4.

McCombe, John P. "*The Voyage Out*: No *Tempest* in a Teapot— Woolf's Revision of Shakespeare and Critique of Female Education." *Ariel* 31:1–2 (2000), 275–304.

Marcus, Laura. *Virginia Woolf*, 10–18.

Marshik, Celia. "Publication and 'Public Women': Prostitution and Censorship in Three Novels by Virginia Woolf." *Mod Fiction Stud* 45 (1999), 856–65.

Maze, John R. *Virginia Woolf*, 11–34.

Montgomery, Nick. "Colonial Rhetoric and the Maternal Voice: Deconstruction and Disengagement in Virginia Woolf's *The Voyage Out*." *Twentieth Cent Lit* 46 (2000), 34–53.

Myers, Elyse. "Virginia Woolf and the 'Voyage Out' from Victorian Science," in Ann Ardis and Bonnie Kime Scott, eds., *Virginia Woolf*, 298–304.

Olson, Barbara K. *Authorial Divinity*, 64–66.

Pardee, Shiela. "Assuming Psyche's Task: Virginia Woolf Responds to James Frazer," in Ann Ardis and Bonnie Kime Scott, eds., *Virginia Woolf*, 291–96.

Peach, Linden. *Virginia Woolf*, 41–56.

Rado, Lisa. *The Modern Androgyne Imagination*, 149–52.

Raitt, Suzanne. "Finding a Voice: Virginia Woolf's Early Novels," in Sue Roe and Susan Sellers, eds., *The Cambridge Companion to Virginia Woolf*, 34–39.

Rosenfeld, Natania. *Outsiders Together*, 26–37.

Selboe, Tone. "'A novel about silence'?: Virginia Woolfs debutroman *The Voyage Out*." *Edda* 4 (1996), 317–26. (In Norwegian.)

Sillars, Stuart. *Structure and Dissolution*, 26–30.

Smith, Patricia Juliana. *Lesbian Panic*, 18–37.

Smith, Patricia Juliana. "'The Things People Don't Say': Lesbian Panic in *The Voyage Out*," in Eileen Barrett and Patricia Cramer, eds., *Virginia Woolf*, 128–44.

Toby, Michelle Bollard. "From Bridal Bier to Death Bed: Woolf's Rejection of the Beautiful Death," in Laura Davis and Jeanette McVicker, eds., *Virginia Woolf and Her Influences*, 105–10.

Trodd, Anthea. *Women's Writing in English*, 179–82.

Urstad, Tone Sundt. "'Real Things Under the Show': Imagery Patterns in Virginia Woolf's *The Voyage Out*." *LIT* 9 (1998), 161–93.

Wussow, Helen. *The Nightmare of History*, 52–59, 75–77.

The Waves, 1931

Banfield, Ann. *The Phantom Table*, 270–71, 289–90, 308–9.

Beer, Gillian. *Virginia Woolf*, 62–72, 74–90.

Blodgett, Harriet. "Food for Thought in Virginia Woolf's Novels." *Woolf Stud Annual* 3 (1997), 54–55.

Briggs, Julia. "The Novels of the 1930s and the Impact of History," in Sue Roe and Susan Sellers, eds., *The Cambridge Companion to Virginia Woolf*, 75–78.

Burford, Arianne. "Communities of Silence and Music in Virginia Woolf's *The Waves* and Dorothy Richardson's *Pilgrimage*," in Jeanette McVicker and Laura Davis, eds., *Virginia Woolf and Communities*, 269–74.

Cuddy-Keane, Melba. "Virginia Woolf, Sound Technologies, and the New Aurality," in Pamela L. Caughie, ed., *Virginia Woolf . . . Reproduction*, 87–90.

Cusin, Michel. "On Translating *The Waves* into French." *Virginia Woolf Misc* 54 (1999), 3–4.

Dalgarno, Emily. *Virginia Woolf and the Visible World*, 101–28.

DeKoven, Marianne. "The Community of Audience: Woolf's Drama of Public Woman," in Jeanette McVicker and Laura Davis, eds., *Virginia Woolf and Communities*, 240–41.

Dick, Susan. "Literary Realism in *Mrs Dalloway, To the Lighthouse, Orlando* and *The Waves*," in Sue Roe and Susan Sellers, eds., *The Cambridge Companion to Virginia Woolf*, 66–71.

Doody, Terrence. *Among Other Things*, 134–37.

Duncker, Patricia. "The Impossibility of Making Writing: Mrs Arbuthnot, Mrs Lewes and Mrs Woolf." *Women: A Cultural R* 9 (1998), 312–23.

Eykmann, Christoph. *Ästhetische Erfahrung in der Lebenswelt*, 165–76.

Fand, Roxanne J. *The Dialogic Self*, 52–91.

Glenny, Allie. *Ravenous Identity*, 155–73.

Goldman, Jane. *The Feminist Aesthetics of Virginia Woolf*, 186–206.

Goldman, Jane, ed. *Virginia Woolf: "To the Lighthouse," "The Waves,"* 29–167.

Gordon, Craig. "Breaking Habits, Building Communities: Virginia Woolf and the Neuroscientific Body." *Modernism/Modernity* 7:1 (2000), 25–41.

Hackett, Robin. "Sapphism and Degeneracy in *The Waves*," in Laura Davis and Jeanette McVicker, eds., *Virginia Woolf and Her Influences*, 44–48.

Hackett, Robin. "Supplanting Shakespeare's Rising Sons: A Perverse Reading through Woolf's *The Waves*." *Tulsa Stud in Women's Lit* 18 (1999), 263–78.

Harris, Andrea L. "'Bare Things': Returning to the Senses in Virginia Woolf's *The Waves*." *LIT* 7 (1997), 339–48.

Harris, Andrea L. *Other Sexes*, 25–62.

Hoffman, Michael J., and Ann ter Haar. "'Whose Books Once Influenced Mine': The Relationship between E. M. Forster's *Howards End* and Virginia Woolf's *The Waves*." *Twentieth Cent Lit* 45 (1999), 46–60.

Holmesland, Oddvar. *Form as Compensation for Life*, 151–84.

Jouve, Nicole Ward. "Virginia Woolf and Psychoanalysis," in Sue Roe and Susan Sellers, eds., *The Cambridge Companion to Virginia Woolf*, 256–59.

Katz, Tamar. *Impressionist Subjects*, 180–97.

Kennard, Jean E. "From Foe to Friend: Virginia Woolf's Changing View of the Male Homosexual." *Woolf Stud Annual* 4 (1998), 73–75.

Kramp, Michael. "The Resistant Social/Sexual Subjectivity of Hall's Ogilvy and Woolf's Rhoda." *Rocky Mountain R of Lang and Lit* 52:2 (1998), 29–46.

Little, Judy. *The Experimental Self*, 53–75.

Lucenti, Lisa Marie. "Virginia Woolf's *The Waves*: To Defer that 'appalling moment.'" *Criticism* 40 (1998), 75–93.

McCormick, John. *Catastrophe and Imagination*, 49–50.

Marcus, Laura. *Virginia Woolf*, 132–36.

Marder, Herbert. *The Measure of Life*, 45–52.

Maze, John R. *Virginia Woolf*, 119–51.

Medd, Jodie. "Re-Inverting Stephen Gordon: Rhoda Talks Back to Radclyffe Hall," in Laura Davis and Jeanette McVicker, eds., *Virginia Woolf and Her Influences*, 117–23.

Miltner, Robert. "*The Waves*: A Weave." *Pleiades* 15:2 (1995), 83–100.

Minow-Pinkney, Makiko. "Virginia Woolf and the Age of Motor Cars," in Pamela L. Caughie, ed., *Virginia Woolf . . . Reproduction*, 178–79.

Olson, Barbara K. *Authorial Divinity*, 82–84, 91–96.

Oxindine, Annette. "Rhoda Submerged: Lesbian Suicide in *The Waves*," in Eileen Barrett and Patricia Cramer, eds., *Virginia Woolf*, 203–20.

Peach, Linden. "No Longer a View: Virginia Woolf in the 1930s and the 1930s in Virginia Woolf," in Maroula Joannou, ed., *Women Writers of the 1930s*, 195–200.

Peach, Linden. *Virginia Woolf*, 158–67.

Rado, Lisa. *The Modern Androgyne Imagination*, 171–77.

Rich, Susanna. "*De Undarum Natura*: Lucretius and Woolf in *The Waves*." *J of Mod Lit* 23 (1999/2000), 249–57.

Rosenbaum, S. P. *Aspects of Bloomsbury*, 28–36.

Rosenfeld, Natania. *Outsiders Together*, 149–52.

Sherard, Tracey. "'Parcival in the Forest of Gender': Wagner, Homosexuality, and *The Waves*," in Ann Ardis and Bonnie Kime Scott, eds., *Virginia Woolf*, 62–67.

Snaith, Anna. *Virginia Woolf*, 82–86.

Sumner, Rosemary. *A Route to Modernism*, 179–83.

Terentowicz, Urszula. "The World and the Word in *The Waves* by Virginia Woolf." *Lubelskie Materialy Neofilologiczne* 19 (1995), 49–64.

Tremper, Ellen. *"Who Lived at Alfoxton?,"* 191–227.

Trotter, David. "The Modernist Novel," in Michael Levenson, ed., *The Cambridge Companion to Modernism*, 94–95.

Wallace, Miriam L. "Theorizing Relational Subjects: Metonymic Narrative in *The Waves*." *Narrative* 8 (2000), 294–317.

Waller, L. Elizabeth. "Writing the Real: Virginia Woolf and an Ecology of Language." *Bucknell R* 44:1 (2000), 146–54.

Whitworth, Michael. "'The Lighted Strip of History': Virginia Woolf and Einsteinian Simultaneity," in Ann Ardis and Bonnie Kime Scott, eds., *Virginia Woolf*, 308–9.

The Years, 1937

Barber, Stephen. "Lip-Reading: Woolf's Secret Encounters," in Eve Kosofsky Sedgwick, ed., *Novel Gazing*, 406–14, 434–37.

Blodgett, Harriet. "Food for Thought in Virginia Woolf's Novels." *Woolf Stud Annual* 3 (1997), 56–57.

Bradshaw, David. "Hyams Place: *The Years*, the Jews and the British Union of Fascists," in Maroula Joannou, ed., *Women Writers of the 1930s*, 179–89.

Bradshaw, David. "The Socio-Political Vision of the Novels," in Sue Roe and Susan Sellers, eds., *The Cambridge Companion to Virginia Woolf*, 204–7.

Briggs, Julia. "The Novels of the 1930s and the Impact of History," in Sue Roe and Susan Sellers, eds., *The Cambridge Companion to Virginia Woolf*, 79–84.

Cramer, Patricia. "'Pearls and the Porpoise': *The Years*—A Lesbian Memoir," in Eileen Barrett and Patricia Cramer, eds., *Virginia Woolf*, 222–38.

Dalgarno, Emily. *Virginia Woolf and the Visible World*, 96–100.

DeHay, Terry. "Gathering Around the Punch Bowl: Woolf's Alternative Narrative Communities," in Jeanette McVicker and Laura Davis, eds., *Virginia Woolf and Communities*, 182–86.

Glenny, Allie. *Ravenous Identity*, 175–202.

Hanson, Clare. "Virginia Woolf in the House of Love: Compulsory Heterosexuality in *The Years*." *J of Gender Stud* 6 (1997), 55–62.

Kennard, Jean E. "From Foe to Friend: Virginia Woolf's Changing View of the Male Homosexual." *Woolf Stud Annual* 4 (1998), 75–80.

Lee, Hermione. "Am I Afraid of Virginia Woolf?," in Warwick Gould and Thomas F. Staley, eds., *Writing the Lives of Writers*, 232–33.

Levenback, Karen L. *Virginia Woolf and the Great War*, 114–53.

Marcus, Laura. *Virginia Woolf*, 136–52.

Marder, Herbert. *The Measure of Life*, 117–21, 166–69, 190–93, 214–30.

Maze, John R. *Virginia Woolf*, 153–73.

Naccarato, Peter. "Re-Defining Feminist Fiction in *The Years*," in Ann Ardis and Bonnie Kime Scott, eds., *Virginia Woolf*, 199–206.

Nelson-McDermott, Catherine. "Disorderly Conduct: Parody and Coded Humor in *Jacob's Room* and *The Years*." *Woolf Stud Annual* 5 (1999), 88–93.

Peach, Linden. "No Longer a View: Virginia Woolf in the 1930s and the 1930s in Virginia Woolf," in Maroula Joannou, ed., *Women Writers of the 1930s*, 201–3.

Peach, Linden. *Virginia Woolf*, 168–94.

Saariluoma, Liisa. "Virginia Woolf's *The Years*: Identity and Time in an Anti-Family Novel." *Orbis Litterarum* 54 (1999), 276–97.

Snaith, Anna. *Virginia Woolf*, 90–112.

Swanson, Diana L. "An Antigone Complex? The Political Psychology of *The Years* and *Three Guineas*." *Woolf Stud Annual* 3 (1997), 28–42.

Sypher, Eileen. "Shifting Boundaries: 'New' and Traditional Women in Virginia Woolf." *Women's Writing* 3 (1996), 306–8.

Wussow, Helen. *The Nightmare of History*, 169–72.

LADY MARY WROTH

Urania, 1621

Beilin, Elaine. "Winning 'The Harts of the People': The Role of the

Political Subject in the *Urania*," in Sigrid King, ed., *Pilgrimage for Love*, 1–17.

Breitenberg, Mark. *Anxious Masculinity*, 198–200.

Catty, Jocelyn. *Writing Rape, Writing Women*, 182–226.

Cavanagh, Sheila T. *Cherished Torment*, 19–218.

Farabaugh, Robin. "Ariadne, Venus, and Labyrinth: Classical Sources and the Thread of Instruction in Mary Wroth's Works." *JEGP* 96 (1997), 204–21.

Gil, Daniel Juan. "The Currency of the Beloved and the Authority of Lady Mary Wroth." *Mod Lang Stud* 29:2 (1999), 73–91.

Hackett, Helen. *Women and Romance Fiction*, 159–82.

Kennedy, Gwynne. *Just Anger*, 115–42.

Kinney, Clare R. "Mary Wroth's Guilty 'secret art': The Poetics of Jealousy in *Pamphilia to Amphilanthus*," in Barbara Smith and Ursula Appelt, eds., *Write or Be Written*, 69–81.

Laroche, Rebecca. "Pamphilia Across a Crowded Room: Mary Wroth's Entry into Literary History." *Genre* 30 (1997), 267–86.

Payne, Paula Harms. "Finding a Poetic Voice of Her Own: Lady Mary Wroth's *Urania* and *Pamphilia to Amphilanthus*," in Sigrid King, ed., *Pilgrimage for Love*, 209–20.

Roberts, Josephine A. "Deciphering Women's Pastoral: Coded Language in Wroth's *Love's Victory*," in Claude J. Summers and Ted-Larry Pebworth, eds., *Representing Women*, 165–68.

Shaver, Anne. "Agency and Marriage in the Fictions of Lady Mary Wroth and Margaret Cavendish, Duchess of Newcastle," in Sigrid King, ed., *Pilgrimage for Love*, 177–90.

Thomas, Max W. "Urban Semiosis in Early Modern London." *Genre* 30 (1997), 19–23.

JOHN WYNDHAM

Chocky, 1968

Ketterer, David. "John Wyndham and 'the Searing Anguishes of Childhood': From 'Fairy Story' to *Chocky*." *Extrapolation* 41 (2000), 94–101.

The Chrysalids, 1955

Philips, Deborah, and Ian Haywood. *Brave New Causes*, 32–33.

CHARLOTTE YONGE

The Armourer's 'Prentices, 1864

Johnson, Maria Poggi. "The King, the Priest and the Armorer: A Victorian Historical Fantasy of the *Via Media*." *Clio* 28 (1999), 399–413.

The Clever Woman of the Family, 1865

Fiamengo, Janice. "Forms of Suffering in Charlotte Yonge's *The Clever Woman of the Family*." *Victorian R* 25:2 (2000), 80–101.

LaCom, Cindy. "'It Is More than Lame': Female Disability, Sexuality, and the Maternal in the Nineteenth-Century Novel," in David T. Mitchell and Sharon L. Snyder, eds., *The Body and Physical Difference*, 196–99.

Sanders, Valerie. "Marriage and the Antifeminist Woman Novelist," in Nicola Diane Thompson, ed., *Victorian Women Writers*, 29–30.

Thompson, Nicola Diane. "Responding to the Woman Questions: Rereading Noncanonical Victorian Women Novelists," in Thompson, ed., *Victorian Women Writers*, 4–5.

Wheatley, Kim. "Death and Domestication in Charlotte M. Yonge's *The Clever Woman of the Family.*" *Stud in Engl Lit, 1500–1900* 36 (1996), 895–913.

The Daisy Chain, 1856

Ang, Susan. *The Widening World of Children's Literature*, 66–69.

Sanders, Valerie. "Marriage and the Antifeminist Woman Novelist," in Nicola Diane Thompson, ed., *Victorian Women Writers*, 27–28.

Sturrock, June. "Sequels, Series, and Sensation Novels: Charlotte Yonge and the Popular-Fiction Market of the 1850s and 1860s," in Paul Budra and Betty A. Schellenberg, eds., *Part Two*, 103–13.

Vaughan-Pow, Catharine J. "A One-Way Ticket? Emigration and the Colonies in the Works of Charlotte M. Yonge," in Rita S. Kranidis, ed., *Imperial Objects*, 253–62.

Dynevor Terrace, 1857

Sturrock, Jane. "Literary Women of the 1850s and Charlotte Mary Yonge's *Dynevor Terrace*," in Nicola Diane Thompson, ed., *Victorian Women Writers*, 117–30.

Heartsease, 1854

Sanders, Mike. "Manufacturing Accident: Industrialism and the Worker's Body in Early Victorian Fiction." *Victorian Lit and Culture* 28 (2000), 322–27.

Thompson, Nicola Diane. *Reviewing Sex*, 91–94.

The Heir of Redclyffe, 1853

Thompson, Nicola Diane. *Reviewing Sex*, 87–92, 99–101.

The Long Vacation, 1895

Vaughan-Pow, Catharine J. "A One-Way Ticket? Emigration and the Colonies in the Works of Charlotte M. Yonge," in Rita S. Kranidis, ed., *Imperial Objects*, 253–62.

Magnum Bonum; or, Mother Carey's Brood, 1879

Schaffer, Talia. "The Mysterious Magnum Bonum: Fighting to Read Charlotte Yonge." *Nineteenth-Cent Lit* 55 (2000), 247–75.

Modern Broods, 1900

Vaughan-Pow, Catharine J. "A One-Way Ticket? Emigration and the Colonies in the Works of Charlotte M. Yonge," in Rita S. Kranidis, ed., *Imperial Objects*, 253–62.

My Young Alcides, 1874

Vaughan-Pow, Catharine J. "A One-Way Ticket? Emigration and the Colonies in the Works of Charlotte M. Yonge," in Rita S. Kranidis, ed., *Imperial Objects*, 253–62.

The Pillars of the House, 1873

Vaughan-Pow, Catharine J. "A One-Way Ticket? Emigration and the Colonies in the Works of Charlotte M. Yonge," in Rita S. Kranidis, ed., *Imperial Objects,* 253–62.

The Trial, 1864

Sturrock, June. "Sequels, Series, and Sensation Novels: Charlotte Yonge and the Popular-Fiction Market of the 1850s and 1860s," in Paul Budra and Betty A. Schellenberg, eds., *Part Two,* 103–13.

Unknown to History, 1882

Gilmartin, Sophie. *Ancestry and Narrative,* 86–101.

ISRAEL ZANGWILL

The Big Bow Mystery, 1891

Scheick, William J. "'Murder in My Soul': Genre and Ethos in Zangwill's *The Big Bow Mystery." Engl Lit in Transition* 40 (1997), 23–32.

Children of the Ghetto, 1892

Childers, Joseph. "At Home in the Empire," in Murray Baumgarten and H. M. Daleski, eds., *Homes and Homelessness,* 215–26.

Rochelson, Meri-Jane. "Israel Zangwill and *Children of the Ghetto." Judaism* 48:1 (1999), 84–101.

Berkeley Hall; or, The Pupil of Experience, 1796

London, April. "Clock Time and Utopia's Time in Novels of the 1790s." *Stud in Engl Lit, 1500–1900* 40 (2000), 550–55.

Dorothea, or, a Ray of the New Light, 1801

London, April. "Clock Time and Utopia's Time in Novels of the 1790s." *Stud in Engl Lit, 1500–1900* 40 (2000), 548–49.

Emily Herbert; or, Perfidy Punished, 1787

Nelson, Bonnie. "*Emily Herbert*: Forerunner of Jane Austen's *Lady Susan*." *Women's Writing* 1 (1994), 317–22.

The Female American, or, the Extraordinary Adventures of Unca Eliza Winkfield, 1767

Joseph, Betty. "Re(playing) Crusoe/Pocahontas: Circum-Atlantic Stagings in *The Female American*." *Criticism* 42 (2000), 317–33.

Wheeler, Roxann. "The Complexion of Desire: Racial Ideology and Mid-Eighteenth-Century British Novels." *Eighteenth-Cent Stud* 32 (1999), 323–28.

Henry Willoughby: A Novel, 1798

London, April. "Clock Time and Utopia's Time in Novels of the 1790s." *Stud in Engl Lit, 1500–1900* 40 (2000), 545–46.

The History of Charlotte Summers, the Fortunate Parish Girl, 1750

Graeber, Wilhelm. *Der englische Roman in Frankreich*, 183–97.

Love Letters Between a Certain Late Nobleman and the famous Mr. Wilson, 1723

McFarlane, Cameron. *The Sodomite in Fiction and Satire*, 99–104.

My Secret Life, c. 1888

Pease, Allison. *Modernism, Mass Culture, and the Aesthetics of Obscenity*, 58–60, 62–64.

Rhoda: A Novel, 1816

Gilson, David. "Jane Austen and *Rhoda*." *Persuasions* 20 (1998), 21–29.

LIST OF BOOKS INDEXED

Adey, Lionel. *C. S. Lewis: Writer, Dreamer, and Mentor.* Grand Rapids (MI) and Cambridge (UK): William B. Eerdmans, 1998.

Ahrens, Rüdiger, and Fritz-Wilhelm Neumann, eds. *Fiktion und Geschichte in der anglo-amerikanischen Literatur: Festschrift für Heinz-Joachim Müllenbrock zum 60. Geburtstag.* Heidelberg: Universitätsverlag C. Winter, 1998.

Aitken, Bill. *Literary Trails.* New Delhi: HarperCollins, 1996.

Alexander, Doris. *Creating Literature Out of Life: The Making of Four Masterpieces.* University Park: Pennsylvania State University Press, 1996.

Alley, Henry. *The Quest for Anonymity: The Novels of George Eliot.* Newark: University of Delaware Press; London: Associated University Presses, 1997.

Alsop, Derek, and Chris Walsh. *The Practice of Reading: Interpreting the Novel.* New York: St. Martin's, 1999.

Altaba-Artal, Dolors. *Aphra Behn's English Feminism: Wit and Satire.* Selinsgrove, PA: Susquehanna University Press; London: Associated University Presses, 1999.

Alter, Robert. *Canon and Creativity: Modern Writing and the Authority of Scripture.* New Haven (CT) and London: Yale University Press, 2000.

Amirthanayagam, Guy. *The Marriage of Continents: Multiculturalism in Modern Literature.* Lanham, MD: University Press of America, 2000.

Anderson, Carol, and Aileen Christianson, eds. *Scottish Women's Fiction, 1920s to 1960s: Journeys into Being.* East Linton (UK): Tuckwell Press, 2000.

Ang, Susan. *The Widening World of Children's Literature.* London: Macmillan; New York: St. Martin's, 2000.

Ankeny, Rebecca Thomas. *The Story, the Teller, and the Audience in George MacDonald's Fiction.* Lewiston, NY: Edwin Mellen Press, 2000.

Ansell-Pearson, Keith, Benita Parry, and Judith Squires, eds. *Cultural Readings of Imperialism: Edward Said and the Gravity of History.* New York: St. Martin's, 1997.

Antor, Heinz, and Kevin L. Cope, eds. *Intercultural Encounters—Studies in English Literatures: Essays Presented to Rüdiger Ahrens on the Occasion of His Sixtieth Birthday.* Heidelberg: Universitätsverlag C. Winter, 1999.

Antor, Heinz, and Klaus Stierstorfer, eds. *English Literatures in International Contexts.* Heidelberg: Universitätsverlag C. Winter, 2000.

Arata, Stephen. *Fictions of Loss in the Victorian Fin de Siècle.* Cambridge: Cambridge University Press, 1996.

Ardholm, Helena M. *The Emblem and the Emblematic Habit of Mind in "Jane Eyre" and "Wuthering Heights."* Göteborg: Acta Universitatis Gothoburgensis, 1999.

Ardis, Ann, and Bonnie Kime Scott, eds. *Virginia Woolf: Turning the Centuries—Selected Papers from the Ninth Annual Conference on Virginia Woolf (University of Delaware: June 10–13, 1999).* New York: Pace University Press, 2000.

Argyros, Ellen. *"Without Any Check of Proud Reserve": Sympathy and Its Limits in George Eliot's Novels.* New York: Peter Lang, 1999.

Armitt, Lucie. *Contemporary Women's Fiction and the Fantastic.* London: Macmillan; New York: St. Martin's, 2000.

Armstrong, Katherine A. *Defoe: Writer as Agent.* Victoria, BC: University of Victoria English Literary Studies, 1996.

Armstrong, Nancy. *Fiction in the Age of Photography: The Legacy of British Realism.* Cambridge (MA) and London: Harvard University Press, 1999.

Armstrong, Tim. *Haunted Hardy: Poetry, History, Memory.* New York: Palgrave, 2000.

Arnds, Peter O. *Wilhelm Raabe's "Der Hungerpastor" and Charles Dickens's "David Copperfield": Intertextuality of Two Bildungsromane.* New York: Peter Lang, 1997.

Aronoff, Myron J. *The Spy Novels of John Le Carré: Balancing Ethics and Politics.* New York: St. Martin's, 1999.

Asals, Frederick. *The Making of Malcolm Lowry's "Under the Volcano."* Athens: University of Georgia Press, 1997.

Asals, Frederick, and Paul Tiessen, eds. *A Darkness That Murmured: Essays on Malcolm Lowry and the Twentieth Century.* Toronto: University of Toronto Press, 2000.

Ash, Beth Sharon. *Writing In Between: Modernity and Psychosocial Dilemma in the Novels of Joseph Conrad.* New York: St. Martin's, 1999.

Attridge, Derek. *Joyce Effects: On Language, Theory, and History.* Cambridge: Cambridge University Press, 2000.

Attridge, Derek, and Marjorie Howes, eds. *Semicolonial Joyce.* Cambridge: Cambridge University Press, 2000.

Aubrey, James R., ed. *John Fowles and Nature: Fourteen Perspectives on Landscape.* Madison and Teaneck, NJ: Fairleigh Dickinson University Press; London: Associated University Presses, 1999.

Auerbach, Nina. *Daphne du Maurier, Haunted Heiress.* Philadelphia: University of Pennsylvania Press, 2000.

Axelrod, Mark. *The Poetics of Novels: Fiction and Its Execution.* London: Macmillan; New York: St. Martin's, 1999.

Ayers, David. *English Literature of the 1920s.* Edinburgh: Edinburgh University Press, 1999.

Ayres, Brenda. *Dissenting Women in Dickens' Novels.* Westport (CT) and London: Greenwood Press, 1998.

Bacchilega, Cristina, and Cornelia N. Moore, eds. *Constructions and*

Confrontations: Changing Representations of Women and Feminisms, East and West—Selected Essays. Honolulu: College of Languages, Linguistics and Literature, University of Hawai'i, 1996.

Bachmann, Günter. *Philosophische Bewußtseinsformen in George Eliots "Middlemarch."* Frankfurt: Peter Lang, 2000.

Backscheider, Paula R., ed. *Revising Women: Eighteenth-Century "Women's Fiction" and Social Engagement.* Baltimore (MD) and London: Johns Hopkins University Press, 2000.

Backus, Margot Gayle. *The Gothic Family Romance: Heterosexuality, Child Sacrifice, and the Anglo-Irish Colonial Order.* Durham (NC) and London: Duke University Press, 1999.

Baker, Phil. *Beckett and the Mythology of Psychoanalysis.* London: Macmillan; New York: St. Martin's, 1997.

Baldridge, Cates. *Graham Greene's Fictions: The Virtues of Extremity.* Columbia and London: University of Missouri Press, 2000.

Balsamo, Gian. *Pruning the Genealogical Tree: Procreation and Lineage in Literature, Law, and Religion.* Lewisburg, PA: Bucknell University Press; London: Associated University Presses, 1999.

Banfield, Ann. *The Phantom Table: Woolf, Fry, Russell and the Epistemology of Modernism.* Cambridge: Cambridge University Press, 2000.

Bannet, Eve Tavor. *The Domestic Revolution: Enlightenment Feminisms and the Novel.* Baltimore (MD) and London: Johns Hopkins University Press, 2000.

Barczewski, Stephanie L. *Myth and National Identity in Nineteenth-Century Britain: The Legends of King Arthur and Robin Hood.* Oxford and New York: Oxford University Press, 2000.

Barfoot, C. C., ed. *Beyond Pug's Tour: National and Ethnic Stereotyping in Theory and Literary Practice.* Amsterdam and Atlanta (GA): Rodopi, 1997.

Barney, Richard A. *Plots of Enlightenment: Education and the Novel in Eighteenth-Century England.* Stanford, CA: Stanford University Press, 1999.

Barrett, Eileen, and Patricia Cramer, eds. *Virginia Woolf: Lesbian Readings.* New York and London: New York University Press, 1997.

Bartra, Roger. *The Artificial Savage: Modern Myths of the Wild Man.* Translated by Christopher Follett. Ann Arbor: University of Michigan Press, 1997.

Battigelli, Anna. *Margaret Cavendish and the Exiles of the Mind.* Lexington: University Press of Kentucky, 1998.

Baucom, Ian. *Out of Place: Englishness, Empire, and the Locations of Identity.* Princeton, NJ: Princeton University Press, 1999.

Baumgarten, Murray, and H. M. Daleski, eds. *Homes and Homelessness in the Victorian Imagination.* New York: AMS Press, 1998.

Bayard, Pierre. *Who Killed Roger Ackroyd? The Mystery Behind the Agatha Christie Mystery.* Translated by Carol Cosman. New York: New Press, 2000.

Beasley, Jerry C. *Tobias Smollett: Novelist.* Athens (GA) and London: University of Georgia Press, 1998.

Becker, Susanne. *Gothic Forms of Feminine Fictions.* Manchester and New York: Manchester University Press, 1999.

Becket, Fiona. *D. H. Lawrence: The Thinker as Poet*. London: Macmillan; New York: St. Martin's, 1997.

Beckman, Linda Hunt. *Amy Levy: Her Life and Letters*. Athens: Ohio University Press, 2000.

Beer, Gillian. *Darwin's Plots: Evolutionary Narrative in Darwin, George Eliot and Nineteenth-Century Fiction*. 2nd ed. Cambridge: Cambridge University Press, 2000.

Beer, Gillian. *Virginia Woolf: The Common Ground—Essays by Gillian Beer*. Ann Arbor: University of Michigan Press, 1996.

Beer, John. *Providence and Love: Studies in Wordsworth, Channing, Myers, George Eliot, and Ruskin*. Oxford: Clarendon, 1998.

Beeretz, Sylvia. *"Tell us in plain words": Narrative Strategies in James Joyce's "Ulysses."* Frankfurt: Peter Lang, 1998.

Begam, Richard. *Samuel Beckett and the End of Modernity*. Stanford, CA: Stanford University Press, 1996.

Belford, Barbara. *Oscar Wilde: A Certain Genius*. New York: Random House, 2000.

Bell, Ian A., ed. *Peripheral Visions: Images of Nationhood in Contemporary British Fiction*. Cardiff: University of Wales Press, 1995.

Bell, Robert H., ed. *Critical Essays on Kingsley Amis*. New York: G. K. Hall; London: Prentice Hall International, 1998.

Bellamy, Liz. *Commerce, Morality and the Eighteenth-Century Novel*. Cambridge: Cambridge University Press, 1998.

Bender, Todd K. *Literary Impressionism in Jean Rhys, Ford Madox Ford, Joseph Conrad, and Charlotte Brontë*. New York and London: Garland Publishing, 1997.

Benedict, Barbara M. *Curiosity: A Cultural History of Early Modern Inquiry*. Chicago and London: University of Chicago Press, 2001.

Bengston, Helene, Marianne Børch, and Cindie Maagaard, eds. *Sponsored by Demons: The Art of Jeanette Winterson*. Agedrup (Denmark): Scholars Press, 1999.

Bennett, Betty T. *Mary Wollstonecraft Shelley: An Introduction*. Baltimore (MD) and London: Johns Hopkins University Press, 1998.

Bennett, Betty T., and Stuart Curran, eds. *Mary Shelley in Her Times*. Baltimore (MD) and London: Johns Hopkins University Press, 2000.

Benton, Michael. *Studies in the Spectator Role: Literature, Painting and Pedagogy*. London and New York: Routledge, 2000.

Bényei, Tamás. *Acts of Attention: Figure and Narrative in Postwar British Novels*. Frankfurt: Peter Lang, 1999.

Berg, James J., and Chris Freeman, eds. *The Isherwood Century: Essays on the Life and Work of Christopher Isherwood*. Madison and London: University of Wisconsin Press, 2000.

Bergonzi, Bernard. *War Poets and Other Subjects*. Aldershot (UK): Ashgate, 1999.

Bernstein, Stephen. *Alasdair Gray*. Lewisburg, PA: Bucknell University Press; London: Associated University Presses, 1999.

Berry, Edward. *The Making of Sir Philip Sidney*. Toronto: University of Toronto Press, 1998.

Berry, Laura C. *The Child, the State, and the Victorian Novel*. Charlottesville and London: University Press of Virginia, 1999.

Bertelsen, Lance. *Henry Fielding at Work: Magistrate, Businessman, Writer.* New York: Palgrave, 2000.

Bidney, Martin. *Patterns of Epiphany: From Wordsworth to Tolstoy, Pater, and Barrett Browning.* Carbondale and Edwardsville: Southern Illinois University Press, 1997.

Bilger, Audrey. *Laughing Feminism: Subversive Comedy in Frances Burney, Maria Edgeworth, and Jane Austen.* Detroit, MI: Wayne State University Press, 1998.

Billington, Michael. *The Life and Work of Harold Pinter.* London: Faber and Faber, 1996.

Birkett, Jennifer, and Kate Ince, eds. *Samuel Beckett.* London and New York: Longman, 2000.

Bivona, Daniel. *British Imperial Literature, 1870–1940: Writing and the Administration of Empire.* Cambridge: Cambridge University Press, 1998.

Blanton, Casey. *Travel Writing: The Self and the World.* New York: Twayne, 1997.

Blau, Herbert. *Sails of the Herring Fleet: Essays on Beckett.* Ann Arbor: University of Michigan Press, 2000.

Bleitner, Thomas, Joachim Gerdes, and Nicole Selmer, eds. *Praxisorientierte Literaturtheorie: Annäherungen an Texte der Moderne.* Bielefeld: Aisthesis Verlag, 1999.

Bloom, Harold, ed. *Thomas Hardy's "Tess of the d'Urbervilles": Bloom's Notes.* Broomall, PA: Chelsea House Publishers, 1996.

Bluemel, Kristin. *Experimenting on the Borders of Modernism: Dorothy Richardson's "Pilgrimage."* Athens (GA) and London: University of Georgia Press, 1997.

Bogel, Fredric V. *The Difference Satire Makes: Rhetoric and Reading from Jonson to Byron.* Ithaca (NY) and London: Cornell University Press, 2001.

Boheemen-Saaf, Christine van. *Joyce, Derrida, Lacan, and the Trauma of History: Reading, Narrative and Postcolonialism.* Cambridge: Cambridge University Press, 1999.

Bohls, Elizabeth A. *Women Travel Writers and the Language of Aesthetics, 1716–1818.* Cambridge: Cambridge University Press, 1995.

Böhn, Andreas, ed. *Formzitate, Gattungsparodien, ironische Formverwendung: Gattungsformen jenseits von Gattungsgrenzen.* St. Ingbert (Germany): Röhrig Universitätsverlag, 1999.

Boitani, Piero, and Anna Torti, eds. *The Body and the Soul in Medieval Literature.* Cambridge: D. S. Brewer, 1999.

Boldrini, Lucia. *Joyce, Dante, and the Poetics of Literary Relations: Language and Meaning in "Finnegans Wake."* Cambridge: Cambridge University Press, 2001.

Booker, M. Keith. *The African Novel in English: An Introduction.* Portsmouth, NH: Heinemann; Oxford: James Currey, 1998.

Booker, M. Keith. *"Ulysses," Capitalism, and Colonialism: Reading Joyce after the Cold War.* Westport (CT) and London: Greenwood Press, 2000.

Booker, M. Keith, ed. *Critical Essays on Salman Rushdie.* New York: G. K. Hall, 1999.

Booth, James, ed. *New Larkins for the Old: Critical Essays.* London: Macmillan; New York: St. Martin's, 2000.

Bornstein, George. *Material Modernism: The Politics of the Page.* Cambridge: Cambridge University Press, 2001.

Borris, Kenneth. *Allegory and Epic in English Renaissance Literature: Heroic Form in Sidney, Spenser, and Milton.* Cambridge: Cambridge University Press, 2000.

Bowen, John. *Other Dickens: Pickwick to Chuzzlewit.* Oxford and New York: Oxford University Press, 2000.

Boyle, Frank. *Swift as Nemesis: Modernity and Its Satirist.* Stanford, CA: Stanford University Press, 2000.

Bozzetto, Roger. *Territoires des fantastiques: Des romans gothiques aux récits d'horreur moderne.* Aix-en-Provence: Publications de l'Université de Provence, 1998.

Brady, Philip, and James F. Carens, eds. *Critical Essays on James Joyce's "A Portrait of the Artist as a Young Man."* New York: G. K. Hall; London: Prentice Hall International, 1998.

Brannigan, John, Geoff Ward, and Julian Wolfreys, eds. *Re: Joyce—Text, Culture, Politics.* London: Macmillan; New York: St. Martin's, 1998.

Brantlinger, Patrick. *The Reading Lesson: The Threat of Mass Literacy in Nineteenth-Century British Fiction.* Bloomington and Indianapolis: Indiana University Press, 1998.

Breitenberg, Mark. *Anxious Masculinity in Early Modern England.* Cambridge: Cambridge University Press, 1996.

Brennan, Matthew C. *The Gothic Psyche: Disintegration and Growth in Nineteenth-Century English Literature.* Columbia, SC: Camden House, 1997.

Brett, R. L. *Faith and Doubt: Religion and Secularization in Literature from Wordsworth to Larkin.* Macon, GA: Mercer University Press, 1997.

Brewer, William D. *The Mental Anatomies of William Godwin and Mary Shelley.* Madison and Teaneck, NJ: Fairleigh Dickinson University Press; London: Associated University Presses, 2001.

Brink, André. *The Novel: Language and Narrative from Cervantes to Calvino.* Washington Square: New York University Press, 1998.

Brînzeu, Pia. *Corridors of Mirrors: The Spirit of Europe in Contemporary British and Romanian Fiction.* Lanham, MD: University Press of America, 2000.

Bristow, Joseph. *Effeminate England: Homoerotic Writing after 1885.* New York: Columbia University Press, 1995.

Bristow, Joseph, and Trev Lynn Broughton, eds. *The Infernal Desires of Angela Carter: Fiction, Femininity, Feminism.* London and New York: Longman, 1997.

Brockmeier, Peter, and Carola Veit, eds. *Komik und Solipsismus im Werk Samuel Becketts.* Stuttgart: Metzler, 1997.

Brody, Jennifer DeVere. *Impossible Purities: Blackness, Femininity, and Victorian Culture.* Durham (NC) and London: Duke University Press, 1998.

Bronfen, Elisabeth. *Dorothy Richardson's Art of Memory: Space, Identity, Text.* Translated by Victoria Appelbe. Manchester and New York: Manchester University Press, 1999.

Brooke, Christopher. *Jane Austen: Illusion and Reality.* Cambridge: D. S. Brewer, 1999.

Brown, Janice. *The Seven Deadly Sins in the Work of Dorothy L. Sayers.* Kent (OH) and London: Kent State University Press, 1998.

Brownley, Martine Watson. *Deferrals of Domain: Contemporary Women Novelists and the State.* New York: St. Martin's, 2000.

Brucker, Barbara S. *Das Ganze, dessen Teile wir sind: Zu Tradition und Erfahrung des inneren Raumes bei Doris Lessing.* Würzburg: Königshausen & Neumann, 1999.

Brunel, Pierre. *Transparences du roman: Le romancier et ses doubles au XXe siècle (Calvino, Cendrars, Cortázar, Echenoz, Joyce, Kundera, Thomas Mann, Proust, Torga, Yourcenar).* Paris: Librairie José Corti, 1997.

Brunsdale, Mitzi M. *Student Companion to George Orwell.* Westport (CT) and London: Greenwood Press, 2000.

Bryden, Mary. *Samuel Beckett and the Idea of God.* London: Macmillan; New York: St. Martin's, 1998.

Budra, Paul, and Betty A. Schellenberg, eds. *Part Two: Reflections on the Sequel.* Toronto: University of Toronto Press, 1998.

Buning, Marius, Danielle De Ruyter, Matthijs Engelberts, and Sjef Houppermans, eds. *Beckett versus Beckett.* Amsterdam and Atlanta (GA): Rodopi, 1998.

Burdett, Carolyn. *Olive Schreiner and the Progress of Feminism: Evolution, Gender, Empire.* New York: Palgrave, 2001.

Bürger, Christa, ed. (with Lena Lindhoff). *Literatur und Leben: Stationen weiblichen Schreibens im 20. Jahrhundert.* Stuttgart: M & P, Verlag für Wissenschaft und Forschung, 1996.

Burgess, Miranda J. *British Fiction and the Production of Social Order, 1740–1830.* Cambridge: Cambridge University Press, 2000.

Burns, Christy L. *Gestural Politics: Stereotype and Parody in Joyce.* Albany: State University of New York Press, 2000.

Butler, Lance St. John. *Registering the Difference: Reading Literature through Register.* Manchester and New York: Manchester University Press, 1999.

Button, Marilyn Demarest, and Toni Reed, eds. *The Foreign Woman in British Literature: Exotics, Aliens, and Outsiders.* Westport (CT) and London: Greenwood Press, 1999.

Byatt, A. S. *On Histories and Stories: Selected Essays.* Cambridge: Harvard University Press, 2001 (c. 2000).

Byerly, Alison. *Realism, Representation, and the Arts in Nineteenth-Century Literature.* Cambridge: Cambridge University Press, 1997.

Byron, Glennis, and David Punter, eds. *Spectral Readings: Towards a Gothic Geography.* London: Macmillan; New York: St. Martin's, 1999.

Cahalan, James M. *Double Visions: Women and Men in Modern and Contemporary Irish Fiction.* Syracuse, NY: Syracuse University Press, 1999.

Carabine, Keith. *The Life and the Art: A Study of Conrad's "Under Western Eyes."* Amsterdam and Atlanta (GA): Rodopi, 1996.

Carabine, Keith, and Owen Knowles (with Paul Armstrong), eds. *Conrad, James and Other Relations.* Boulder, CO: Social Science Monographs; Lublin: Maria Curie-Sklodowska University, 1998.

Carnell, Jennifer. *The Literary Lives of Mary Elizabeth Braddon.* Hastings (UK): Sensation Press, 2000.

Casanova, Pascal. *Beckett l'abstracteur: Anatomie d'une révolution littéraire.* Paris: Seuil, 1997.

Case, Alison A. *Plotting Women: Gender and Narration in the Eighteenth- and Nineteenth-Century British Novel.* Charlottesville and London: University Press of Virginia, 1999.

Cash, William. *The Third Woman: The Secret Passion that Inspired "The End of the Affair."* London: Little, Brown, 2000.

Castle, Gregory. *Modernism and the Celtic Revival.* Cambridge: Cambridge University Press, 2001.

Catty, Jocelyn. *Writing Rape, Writing Women in Early Modern England.* London: Macmillan; New York: St. Martin's, 1999.

Caughie, Pamela L., ed. *Virginia Woolf in the Age of Mechanical Reproduction.* New York and London: Garland Publishing, 2000.

Cavaliero, Glen. *The Alchemy of Laughter: Comedy in English Fiction.* London: Macmillan; New York: St. Martin's, 2000.

Cavanagh, Sheila T. *Cherished Torment: The Emotional Geography of Lady Mary Wroth's "Urania."* Pittsburgh, PA: Duquesne University Press, 2001.

Chandler, James. *England in 1819: The Politics of Literary Culture and the Case of Romantic Historicism.* Chicago and London: University of Chicago Press, 1998.

Chase, Karen, and Michael Levenson. *The Spectacle of Intimacy: A Public Life for the Victorian Family.* Princeton (NJ) and Oxford: Princeton University Press, 2000.

Cheng, Vincent J., Kimberly J. Devlin, and Margot Norris, eds., *Joycean Cultures / Culturing Joyces.* Newark: University of Delaware Press; London: Associated University Presses, 1998.

Chernaik, Warren, Martin Swales, and Robert Vilain, eds. *The Art of Detective Fiction.* London: Macmillan; New York: St. Martin's, 2000.

Cheyette, Bryan, and Laura Marcus, eds. *Modernity, Culture and 'the Jew.'* Stanford, CA: Stanford University Press, 1998.

Chi, Hsin Ying. *Artist and Attic: A Study of Poetic Space in Nineteenth-Century Women's Writing.* Lanham, MD: University Press of America, 1999.

Childs, Peter. *Paul Scott's "Raj Quartet": History and Division.* Victoria (BC): University of Victoria, 1998.

Chisholm, Kate. *Fanny Burney: Her Life, 1752–1840.* London: Chatto & Windus, 1998.

Chrisman, Laura, and Benita Parry, eds. *Postcolonial Theory and Criticism.* Cambridge: D. S. Brewer, 2000. (Essays and Studies 1999, volume 52.)

Clayton, Cherry. *Olive Schreiner.* New York: Twayne; London: Prentice Hall International, 1997.

Clemens, Valdine. *The Return of the Repressed: Gothic Horror from "The Castle of Otranto" to "Alien."* Albany: State University of New York Press, 1999.

Clifford, Stephen P. *Beyond the Heroic "I": Reading Lawrence, Hemingway, and "Masculinity."* Lewisburg, PA: Bucknell University Press; London: Associated University Presses, 1998.

Cline, Sally. *Radclyffe Hall: A Woman Called John*. London: John Murray, 1997.

Coates, John. *Social Discontinuity in the Novels of Elizabeth Bowen*. Lewiston, NY: Edwin Mellen Press, 1998.

Cobbs, John L. *Understanding John le Carré*. Columbia: University of South Carolina Press, 1998.

Cohen, Michael. *Murder Most Fair: The Appeal of Mystery Fiction*. Madison and Teaneck, NJ: Fairleigh Dickinson University Press; London: Associated University Presses, 2000.

Cohen, Monica F. *Professional Domesticity in the Victorian Novel: Women, Work and Home*. Cambridge: Cambridge University Press, 1998.

Cohen-Safir, Claude. *Cartographie du féminin dans l'utopie: De l'Europe à l'Amérique*. Paris and Montréal: L'Harmattan, 2000.

Cohn, Ruby. *A Beckett Canon*. Ann Arbor: University of Michigan Press, 2001.

Collinge, Linda. *Beckett traduit Beckett: De "Malone meurt" à "Malone Dies"—l'imaginaire en traduction*. Geneva: Librairie Droz, 2000.

Como, James. *Branches to Heaven: The Geniuses of C. S. Lewis*. Dallas, TX: Spence Publishing Co., 1998.

Condé, Mary, and Thorunn Lonsdale, eds. *Caribbean Women Writers: Fiction in English*. New York: St. Martin's, 1999.

Conger, Syndy M., Frederick S. Frank, and Gregory O'Dea, eds. (Jennifer Yocum, asst. ed.). *Iconoclastic Departures: Mary Shelley after "Frankenstein"—Essays in Honor of the Bicentenary of Mary Shelley's Birth*. Madison and Teaneck, NJ: Fairleigh Dickinson University Press; London: Associated University Presses, 1997.

Connelly, Mark. *Orwell and Gissing*. New York: Peter Lang, 1997.

Connon, Bryan. *Somerset Maugham and the Maugham Dynasty*. London: Sinclair-Stevenson, 1997.

Connor, Steven. *James Joyce*. Plymouth (UK): Northcote House, 1996.

Constable, Kathleen. *A Stranger Within the Gates: Charlotte Brontë and Victorian Irishness*. Lanham, MD: University Press of America, 2000.

Cooke, Brett, George E. Slusser, and Haume Marti-Olivella, eds. *The Fantastic Other: An Interface of Perspectives*. Amsterdam and Atlanta (GA): Rodopi, 1998.

Copeland, Edward. *Women Writing about Money: Women's Fiction in England, 1790–1820*. Cambridge: Cambridge University Press, 1995.

Copeland, Edward, and Juliet McMaster, eds. *The Cambridge Companion to Jane Austen*. Cambridge: Cambridge University Press, 1997.

Corbett, Mary Jean. *Allegories of Union in Irish and English Writing, 1790–1870: Politics, History, and the Family from Edgeworth to Arnold*. Cambridge: Cambridge University Press, 2000.

Corcoran, Neil. *After Yeats and Joyce: Reading Modern Irish Literature*. Oxford and New York: Oxford University Press, 1997.

Cottom, Daniel. *Ravishing Tradition: Cultural Forces and Literary History*. Ithaca (NY) and London: Cornell University Press, 1996.

Cousineau, Diane. *Letters and Labyrinths: Women Writing/Cultural Codes*. Newark: University of Delaware Press; London: Associated University Presses, 1997.

Coyle, John, ed. *James Joyce: "Ulysses," "A Portrait of the Artist as a Young Man."* New York: Columbia University Press, 1998.

Craig, Randall. *Promising Language: Betrothal in Victorian Law and Fiction.* Albany: State University of New York Press, 2000.

Crane, Ralph J., ed. *J. G. Farrell: The Critical Grip.* Dublin: Four Courts Press, 1999.

Crane, Ralph J., and Jennifer Livett. *Troubled Pleasures: The Fiction of J. G. Farrell.* Portland, OR: Four Courts Press, 1997.

Crook, Keith. *A Preface to Swift.* London and New York: Longman, 1998.

Cruise, James. *Governing Consumption: Needs and Wants, Suspended Characters, and the 'Origins' of Eighteenth-Century English Novels.* Lewisburg, PA: Bucknell University Press; London: Associated University Presses, 1999.

Cundy, Catherine. *Salman Rushdie.* Manchester and New York: Manchester University Press, 1996.

Currie, Mark. *Postmodern Narrative Theory.* New York: St. Martin's, 1998.

Curry, Patrick. *Defending Middle-Earth: Tolkien, Myth and Modernity.* New York: St. Martin's, 1997.

Dabundo, Laura, ed. *Jane Austen and Mary Shelley, and Their Sisters.* Lanham, MD: University Press of America, 2000.

Dadlez, E. M. *What's Hecuba to Him? Fictional Events and Actual Emotions.* University Park: Pennsylvania State University Press, 1997.

Dainotto, Roberto M. *Place in Literature: Regions, Cultures, Communities.* Ithaca (NY) and London: Cornell University Press, 2000.

Daleski, H. M. *Thomas Hardy and Paradoxes of Love.* Columbia and London: University of Missouri Press, 1997.

Dalgarno, Emily. *Virginia Woolf and the Visible World.* Cambridge: Cambridge University Press, 2001.

Dalm, Rudolf E. van. *A Structural Analysis of "The Honorary Consul" by Graham Greene.* Amsterdam and Atlanta (GA): Rodopi, 1999.

Daly, Nicholas. *Modernism, Romance and the Fin de Siècle: Popular Fiction and British Culture, 1880–1914.* Cambridge: Cambridge University Press, 1999.

Dames, Nicholas. *Amnesiac Selves: Nostalgia, Forgetting, and British Fiction, 1810–1870.* Oxford and New York: Oxford University Press, 2001.

Dart, Gregory. *Rousseau, Robespierre and English Romanticism.* Cambridge: Cambridge University Press, 1999.

Daugherty, Beth Rigel, and Mary Beth Pringle, eds. *Approaches to Teaching Woolf's "To the Lighthouse."* New York: Modern Language Association of America, 2001.

David, Deirdre, ed. *The Cambridge Companion to the Victorian Novel.* Cambridge: Cambridge University Press, 2001.

Davies, Paul. *Beckett and Eros: Death of Humanism.* London: Macmillan; New York: St. Martin's, 2000.

Davis, Laura, and Jeanette McVicker, eds. *Virginia Woolf and Her Influences: Selected Papers from the Seventh Annual Conference on Virginia Woolf (Plymouth State College, Plymouth, New Hampshire, June 12–15, 1997).* New York: Pace University Press, 1998.

Davis, Laura L., ed. *Conrad's Century: The Past and Future Splendour.*

Boulder, CO: Social Science Monographs; Lublin: Maria Curie-Sklodowska University, 1998.

Davis, Leith. *Acts of Union: Scotland and the Literary Negotiation of the British Nation, 1707–1830*. Stanford, CA: Stanford University Press, 1998.

Davis, Philip, ed. *Real Voices: On Reading*. New York: St. Martin's, 1997.

Day, Aidan. *Angela Carter: The Rational Glass*. Manchester and New York: Manchester University Press, 1998.

Day, Aidan. *Romanticism*. London and New York: Routledge, 1996.

Delamater, Jerome H., and Ruth Prigozy, eds. *Theory and Practice of Classic Detective Fiction*. Westport (CT) and London: Greenwood Press, 1997.

Dellamora, Richard, ed. *Victorian Sexual Dissidence*. Chicago and London: University of Chicago Press, 1999.

Denisoff, Dennis. *Aestheticism and Sexual Parody, 1840–1940*. Cambridge: Cambridge University Press, 2001.

Dennis, Ian. *Nationalism and Desire in Early Historical Fiction*. London: Macmillan; New York: St. Martin's, 1997.

Dervin, Dan. *Matricentric Narratives: Recent British Women's Fiction in a Postmodern Mode*. Lewiston, NY: Edwin Mellen Press, 1997.

Detis, Elisabeth. *Daniel Defoe démasqué: Lecture de l'œuvre romanesque*. Paris and Montreal: L'Harmattan, 1999.

Dever, Carolyn. *Death and the Mother from Dickens to Freud: Victorian Fiction and the Anxiety of Origins*. Cambridge: Cambridge University Press, 1998.

Devine, Kathleen, ed. *Modern Irish Writers and the Wars*. Gerrards Cross (UK): Colin Smythe, 1999.

Devlin, Kimberly J., and Marilyn Reizbaum, eds. *"Ulysses"–En-Gendered Perspectives: Eighteen New Essays on the Episodes*. Columbia: University of South Carolina Press, 1999.

Dickson, Beth. *William McIlvanney's "Laidlaw."* Glasgow: Association for Scottish Literary Studies, 1998.

DiPiero, Thomas, and Pat Gill, eds. *Illicit Sex: Identity Politics in Early Modern Culture*. Athens: University of Georgia Press, 1997.

Disch, Thomas M. *The Dreams Our Stuff Is Made Of: How Science Fiction Conquered the World*. New York: Free Press, 1998.

Doherty, Gerald. *Theorizing Lawrence: Nine Meditations on Tropological Themes*. New York: Peter Lang, 1999.

Dolezel, Lubomir. *Heterocosmica: Fiction and Possible Worlds*. Baltimore (MD) and London: Johns Hopkins University Press, 1998.

Dolin, Kieran. *Fiction and the Law: Legal Discourse in Victorian and Modernist Literature*. Cambridge: Cambridge University Press, 1999.

Dölvers, Horst. *Fables Less and Less Fabulous: English Fables and Parables of the Nineteenth Century and Their Illustrations*. Newark: University of Delaware Press; London: Associated University Presses, 1997.

Donaldson, George, and Mara Kalnins, eds. *D. H. Lawrence in Italy and England*. London: Macmillan; New York: St. Martin's, 1999.

Donoghue, Denis. *The Practice of Reading*. New Haven (CT) and London: Yale University Press, 1998.

Doody, Terrence. *Among Other Things: A Description of the Novel.* Baton Rouge: Louisiana State University Press, 1998.

Dougill, John. *Oxford in English Literature: The Making, and Undoing, of 'The English Athens.'* Ann Arbor: University of Michigan Press, 1998.

Douglas, Aileen, Patrick Kelly, and Ian Campbell Ross, eds. *Locating Swift: Essays from Dublin on the 250th Anniversary of the Death of Jonathan Swift, 1667–1745.* Dublin and Portland (OR): Four Courts Press, 1998.

Dowling, Finuala. *Fay Weldon's Fictions.* Madison and Teaneck, NJ: Fairleigh Dickinson University Press; London: Associated University Presses, 1998.

Downie, J. A. *To Settle the Succession of the State: Literature and Politics, 1678–1750.* New York: St. Martin's, 1994.

Driskill, Richard T. *Madonnas and Maidens: Sexual Confusion in Lawrence and Gide.* New York: Peter Lang, 1999.

Dryden, Linda. *Joseph Conrad and the Imperial Romance.* London: Macmillan; New York: St. Martin's, 2000.

Duckworth, Alistair M., ed. *"Howards End": Complete, Authoritative Text with Biographical and Historical Contexts, Critical History, and Essays from Five Contemporary Critical Perspectives.* Boston: Bedford Books, 1997.

Dutheil de la Rochère, Martine Hennard. *Origin and Originality in Rushdie's Fiction.* Bern: Peter Lang, 1999.

Dutta, Shanta. *Ambivalence in Hardy: A Study of his Attitude to Women.* London: Macmillan; New York: St. Martin's, 2000.

Dyer, Gary. *British Satire and the Politics of Style, 1789–1832.* Cambridge: Cambridge University Press, 1997.

Earnshaw, Steven, ed. *Just Postmodernism.* Amsterdam and Atlanta (GA): Rodopi, 1997.

Easton, Alison, ed. *Angela Carter.* New York: St. Martin's, 2000.

Eberle-Sinatra, Michael, ed. *Mary Shelley's Fictions: From "Frankenstein" to "Falkner."* London: Macmillan; New York: St. Martin's, 2000.

Eckley, Grace. *The Steadfast James Joyce: A Social Context for the Early Joyce.* San Bernardino, CA: Borgo Press, 1997.

Edwards, Elizabeth. *The Genesis of Narrative in Malory's "Morte Darthur."* Cambridge (UK) and Rochester (NY): D. S. Brewer, 2001.

Elfenbein, Andrew. *Byron and the Victorians.* Cambridge: Cambridge University Press, 1995.

Elfenbein, Andrew. *Romantic Genius: The Prehistory of a Homosexual Role.* New York: Columbia University Press, 1999.

Ellis, Lorna. *Appearing to Diminish: Female Development and the British Bildungsroman, 1750–1850.* Lewisburg, PA: Bucknell University Press; London: Associated University Presses, 1999.

Ellis, Markman. *The Politics of Sensibility: Race, Gender and Commerce in the Sentimental Novel.* Cambridge: Cambridge University Press, 1996.

Ellison, Julie. *Cato's Tears and the Making of Anglo-American Emotion.* Chicago and London: University of Chicago Press, 1999.

Engélibert, Jean-Paul. *La postérité de Robinson Crusoé: Un mythe littéraire de la modernité, 1954–1986.* Geneva: Librairie Droz, 1997.

Engell, James. *The Committed Word: Literature and Public Values.* University Park: Pennsylvania State University Press, 1999.

Engler, Bernd, and Kurt Müller, eds. *Exempla: Studien zur Bedeutung und Funktion exemplarischen Erzählens.* Berlin: Duncker and Humblot, 1995.

Erickson, Robert A. *The Language of the Heart, 1600–1750.* Philadelphia: University of Pennsylvania Press, 1997.

Ertzdorff, Xenja von, ed. (with Rudolf Scholz). *Beschreibung der Welt: Zur Poetik der Reise- und Länderberichte — Vorträge eines interdisziplinären Symposiums vom 8. bis 13. Juni 1998 an der Justus-Liebig-Universität Gießen.* Amsterdam and Atlanta (GA): Rodopi, 2000.

Esterhammer, Angela. *The Romantic Performative: Language and Action in British and German Romanticism.* Stanford, CA: Stanford University Press, 2000.

Ewbank, Inga-Stina, Olav Lausund, and Bjørn Tysdahl, eds. *Anglo-Scandinavian Cross-Currents.* Oslo: Norvik Press, 1999.

Eykman, Christoph. *Ästhetische Erfahrung in der Lebenswelt des westeuropäischen und amerikanischen Romans: Von der Romantik bis zur Gegenwart.* Tübingen and Basel: Francke Verlag, 1997.

Falco, Maria J., ed. *Feminist Interpretations of Mary Wollstonecraft.* University Park: Pennsylvania State University Press, 1996.

Fand, Roxanne J. *The Dialogic Self: Reconstructing Subjectivity in Woolf, Lessing, and Atwood.* Selinsgrove, PA: Susquehanna University Press; London: Associated University Presses, 1999.

Faulkner, Peter, and Peter Preston, eds. *William Morris: Centenary Essays — Papers from the Morris Centenary Conference organized by the William Morris Society at Exeter College Oxford, 30 June – 3 July 1996.* Exeter (UK): University of Exeter Press, 1999.

Faulks, Lana. *Fay Weldon.* New York: Twayne; London: Prentice Hall International, 1998.

Fay, Elizabeth A. *A Feminist Introduction to Romanticism.* Malden (MA) and Oxford: Blackwell, 1998.

Federico, Annette R. *Idol of Suburbia: Marie Corelli and Late-Victorian Literary Culture.* Charlottesville and London: University Press of Virginia, 2000.

Fendler, Susanne, ed. *Feminist Contributions to the Literary Canon: Setting Standards of Taste.* Lewiston, NY: Edwin Mellen Press, 1997.

Fendler, Susanne, and Ruth Wittlinger, eds. *The Idea of Europe in Literature.* London: Macmillan; New York: St. Martin's, 1999.

Fernihough, Anne, ed. *The Cambridge Companion to D. H. Lawrence.* Cambridge: Cambridge University Press, 2001.

Ferns, Chris. *Narrating Utopia: Ideology, Gender, Form in Utopian Literature.* Liverpool (UK): Liverpool University Press, 1999.

Ferns, John. *F. R. Leavis.* New York: Twayne, 2000.

Ferrall, Charles. *Modernist Writing and Reactionary Politics.* Cambridge: Cambridge University Press, 2001.

Ferreira, Fernanda Durão. *As fontes portuguesas de Robinson Crusoe.* Lisbon: Fim de Século, 1996.

Fiddes, Paul S. *Freedom and Limit: A Dialogue between Literature and Christian Doctrine.* Macon, GA: Mercer University Press, 1999.

Field, P. J. C. *Malory: Texts and Sources.* Cambridge: D. S. Brewer, 1998.

Fisch, Harold. *New Stories for Old: Biblical Patterns in the Novel*. London: Macmillan; New York: St. Martin's, 1998.

Fisher, Jerilyn, and Ellen S. Silber, eds. *Analyzing the Different Voice: Feminist Psychological Theory and Literary Texts*. Lanham, MD: Rowman and Littlefield, 1998.

Fletcher, Loraine. *Charlotte Smith: A Critical Biography*. London: Macmillan; New York: St. Martin's, 1998.

Flint, Christopher. *Family Fictions: Narrative and Domestic Relations in Britain, 1688–1798*. Stanford, CA: Stanford University Press, 1998.

Foldy, Michael S. *The Trials of Oscar Wilde: Deviance, Morality, and Late-Victorian Society*. New Haven (CT) and London: Yale University Press, 1997.

Ford, Jane M. *Patriarchy and Incest from Shakespeare to Joyce*. Gainesville: University Press of Florida, 1998.

Forderer, Christof. *Ich-Eklipsen: Doppelgänger in der Literatur seit 1800*. Stuttgart and Weimar: J. B. Metzler, 1999.

Forster, Jean-Paul. *Jonathan Swift: The Fictions of the Satirist—From Parody to Vision*. Bern: Peter Lang, 1998.

Fox, Alistair. *The English Renaissance: Identity and Representation in Elizabethan England*. Oxford and Malden (MA): Blackwell, 1997.

Foy, Roslyn Reso. *Ritual, Myth, and Mysticism in the Work of Mary Butts: Between Feminism and Modernism*. Fayetteville: University of Arkansas Press, 2000.

François, Pierre. *Inlets of the Soul: Contemporary Fiction in English and the Myth of the Fall*. Amsterdam and Atlanta (GA): Rodopi, 1999.

Frank, Judith. *Common Ground: Eighteenth-Century English Satiric Fiction and the Poor*. Stanford, CA: Stanford University Press, 1997.

Frankel, Nicholas. *Oscar Wilde's Decorated Books*. Ann Arbor: University of Michigan Press, 2000.

Franklin, J. Jeffrey. *Serious Play: The Cultural Form of the Nineteenth-Century Realist Novel*. Philadelphia: University of Pennsylvania Press, 1999.

Franssen, Paul, and Ton Hoenselaars, eds. *The Author as Character: Representing Historical Writers in Western Literature*. Madison and Teaneck, NJ: Fairleigh Dickinson University Press; London: Associated University Presses, 1999.

Frega, Donnalee. *Speaking in Hunger: Gender, Discourse, and Consumption in "Clarissa."* Columbia: University of South Carolina Press, 1998.

Frehner, Ruth. *The Colonizers' Daughters: Gender in the Anglo-Irish Big House Novel*. Tübingen and Basel: Francke Verlag, 1999.

Freiburg, Rudolf, Arno Loffler, and Wolfgang Zach, eds. *Swift: The Enigmatic Dean*. Tübingen: Stauffenburg Verlag, 1998.

Frontain, Raymond-Jean, ed. *Reclaiming the Sacred: The Bible in Gay and Lesbian Culture*. New York: Haworth, 1997.

Fulford, Tim, and Peter J. Kitson, eds. *Romanticism and Colonialism: Writing and Empire, 1780–1830*. Cambridge: Cambridge University Press, 1998.

Fulton, Gordon D. *Styles of Meaning and Meanings of Style in Richardson's "Clarissa."* Montreal and Kingston: McGill-Queen's University Press, 1999.

Furst, Lilian R. *Just Talk: Narratives of Psychotherapy*. Lexington: University Press of Kentucky, 1999.

Fysh, Stephanie. *The Work(s) of Samuel Richardson*. Newark: University of Delaware Press; London: Associated University Presses, 1997.

Gager, Valerie L. *Shakespeare and Dickens: The Dynamics of Influence*. Cambridge: Cambridge University Press, 1996.

Galin, Müge. *Between East and West: Sufism in the Novels of Doris Lessing*. Albany: State University of New York Press, 1997.

Galle, Roland, and Rudolf Behrens, eds. *Konfigurationen der Macht in der Frühen Neuzeit*. Heidelberg: Universitätsverlag C. Winter, 2000.

Gally, Michèle, ed. *La trace médiévale et les écrivains d'aujourd'hui*. Paris: Presses Universitaires de France, 2000.

Gamble, Sarah. *Angela Carter: Writing from the Front Line*. Edinburgh: Edinburgh University Press, 1997.

Gamer, Michael. *Romanticism and the Gothic: Genre, Reception, and Canon Formation*. Cambridge: Cambridge University Press, 2000.

Garbowski, Christopher. *Recovery and Transcendence for the Contemporary Mythmaker: The Spiritual Dimension in the Works of J. R. R. Tolkien*. Lublin (Poland): Maria Curie-Sklodowska University Press, 2000.

Gardiner, Ellen. *Regulating Readers: Gender and Literary Criticism in the Eighteenth-Century Novel*. Newark: University of Delaware Press; London: Associated University Presses, 1999.

Gaskell, Philip. *Landmarks in English Literature*. Edinburgh: Edinburgh University Press, 1998.

Gay, David, James G. Randall, and Arlette Zinck, eds. *Awakening Words: John Bunyan and the Language of Community*. Newark: University of Delaware Press; London: Associated University Presses, 2000.

Gertz, SunHee Kim. *Chaucer to Shakespeare, 1337–1580*. New York: Palgrave, 2001.

Gibson, Andrew. *Postmodernity, Ethics and the Novel: From Leavis to Levinas*. London and New York: Routledge, 1999.

Gibson, Andrew, ed. *Joyce's "Ithaca."* Amsterdam and Atlanta (GA): Rodopi, 1996. (European Joyce Studies 6.)

Gibson, Andrew, and Robert Hampson, eds. *Conrad and Theory*. Amsterdam and Atlanta (GA): Rodopi, 1998.

Gifford, Douglas, and Dorothy McMillan, eds. *A History of Scottish Women's Writing*. Edinburgh: Edinburgh University Press, 1997.

Gikandi, Simon. *Maps of Englishness: Writing Identity in the Culture of Colonialism*. New York: Columbia University Press, 1996.

Gilbert, Pamela K. *Disease, Desire, and the Body in Victorian Women's Popular Novels*. Cambridge and New York: Cambridge University Press, 1997.

Gill, James E., ed. *Cutting Edges: Postmodern Critical Essays on Eighteenth-Century Satire*. Knoxville: University of Tennessee Press, 1995.

Gillespie, Michael Patrick, ed. *Joyce through the Ages: A Nonlinear View*. Gainesville: University Press of Florida, 1999.

Gillespie, Michael Patrick, and Paula F. Gillespie. *Recent Criticism of James Joyce's "Ulysses": An Analytical Review*. Rochester (NY) and Woodbridge (UK): Camden House, 2000.

Gillooly, Eileen. *Smile of Discontent: Humor, Gender, and Nineteenth-Century British Fiction.* Chicago and London: University of Chicago Press, 1999.

Gilmartin, Sophie. *Ancestry and Narrative in Nineteenth-Century British Literature: Blood Relations from Edgeworth to Hardy.* Cambridge: Cambridge University Press, 1998.

Gilroy, Amanda, and W. M. Verhoeven, eds. *Epistolary Histories: Letters, Fiction, Culture.* Charlottesville and London: University Press of Virginia, 2000.

Gladfelder, Hal. *Criminality and Narrative in Eighteenth-Century England: Beyond the Law.* Baltimore (MD) and London: Johns Hopkins University Press, 2001.

Glancy, Ruth. *Student Companion to Charles Dickens.* Westport (CT) and London: Greenwood Press, 1999.

Glavin, John. *After Dickens: Reading, Adaptation and Performance.* Cambridge: Cambridge University Press, 1999.

Glenny, Allie. *Ravenous Identity: Eating and Eating Distress in the Life and Work of Virginia Woolf.* New York: St. Martin's, 1999.

GoGwilt, Christopher. *The Fiction of Geopolitics: Afterimages of Culture, from Wilkie Collins to Alfred Hitchcock.* Stanford, CA: Stanford University Press, 2000.

Goldberg, Jonathan. *Desiring Women Writing: English Renaissance Examples.* Stanford, CA: Stanford University Press, 1997.

Goldman, Jane. *The Feminist Aesthetics of Virginia Woolf: Modernism, Post-Impressionism and the Politics of the Visual.* Cambridge: Cambridge University Press, 1998.

Goldman, Jane, ed. *Virginia Woolf: "To the Lighthouse," "The Waves."* New York: Columbia University Press, 1998.

Gores, Steven J. *Psychosocial Spaces: Verbal and Visual Readings of British Culture, 1750–1820.* Detroit, MI: Wayne State University Press, 2000.

Gottfried, Roy. *Joyce's Comic Portrait.* Gainesville: University Press of Florida, 2000.

Gould, Warwick, and Thomas F. Staley, eds. *Writing the Lives of Writers.* London: Macmillan; New York: St. Martin's, 1998.

Graeber, Wilhelm. *Der englische Roman in Frankreich, 1741–1763: Über-setzungsgeschichte als Beitrag zur französischen Literaturgeschichte.* Heidelberg: Universitätsverlag C. Winter, 1995.

Gras, Vernon W., and John R. Cook, eds. *The Passion of Dennis Potter: International Collected Essays.* New York: St. Martin's, 2000.

Gravil, Richard, ed. *Master Narratives: Tellers and Telling in the English Novel.* Aldershot (UK): Ashgate, 2001.

Greacen, Lavinia. *J. G. Farrell: The Making of a Writer.* London: Bloomsbury Publishing, 1999.

Greenfield, Susan C., and Carol Barash, eds. *Inventing Maternity: Politics, Science, and Literature, 1650–1865.* Lexington: University Press of Kentucky, 1999.

Greiff, Louis K. *D. H. Lawrence: Fifty Years on Film.* Carbondale and Edwardsville: Southern Illinois University Press, 2001.

Grice, Helena, and Tim Woods, eds. *"I'm telling you stories": Jeanette Winterson and the Politics of Reading.* Amsterdam and Atlanta (GA): Rodopi, 1998.

Grossman, Evelyne. *L'Esthétique de Beckett*. Liège (Belgium): Editions SEDES, 1998.

Gualtieri, Elena. *Virginia Woolf's Essays: Sketching the Past*. London: Macmillan; New York: St. Martin's, 2000.

Guest, Harriet. *Small Change: Women, Learning, Patriotism, 1750–1810*. Chicago and London: University of Chicago Press, 2000.

Gupta, Suman. *V. S. Naipaul*. Plymouth (UK): Northcote House, 1999.

Guroian, Vigen. *Tending the Heart of Virtue: How Classic Stories Awaken a Child's Moral Imagination*. New York and Oxford: Oxford University Press, 1998.

Gurr, Jens Martin. *"Tristram Shandy" and the Dialectic of Enlightenment*. Heidelberg: Universitätsverlag C. Winter, 1999.

Guy, Josephine M., and Ian Small. *Oscar Wilde's Profession: Writing and the Culture Industry in the Late Nineteenth Century*. Oxford and New York: Oxford University Press, 2000.

Hackett, Helen. *Women and Romance Fiction in the English Renaissance*. Cambridge: Cambridge University Press, 2000.

Haddelsey, Stephen. *Charles Lever: The Lost Victorian*. Gerrards Cross (UK): Colin Smythe, 2000.

Hadfield, Andrew. *The English Renaissance, 1500–1620*. Oxford and Malden (MA): Blackwell, 2001.

Hadfield, Andrew. *Literature, Travel, and Colonial Writing in the English Renaissance, 1545–1625*. Oxford: Clarendon, 1998.

Hadfield, Andrew, Dominic Rainsford, and Tim Woods, eds. *The Ethics in Literature*. London: Macmillan; New York: St. Martin's, 1999.

Haggerty, George E. *Men in Love: Masculinity and Sexuality in the Eighteenth Century*. New York: Columbia University Press, 1999.

Haggerty, George E. *Unnatural Affections: Women and Fiction in the Later 18th Century*. Bloomington and Indianapolis: Indiana University Press, 1998.

Hammond, Brean S. *Professional Imaginative Writing in England, 1670–1740: "Hackney for Bread."* Oxford: Clarendon, 1997.

Hampson, Robert. *Cross-Cultural Encounters in Joseph Conrad's Malay Fiction*. New York: Palgrave, 2000.

Hanks, D. Thomas, Jr., and Jessica Gentry Brogdon, eds. *The Social and Literary Contexts of Malory's "Morte Darthur."* Cambridge: D. S. Brewer, 2000.

Hanson, Clare. *Hysterical Fictions: The 'Woman's Novel' in the Twentieth Century*. London: Macmillan; New York: St. Martin's, 2000.

Hanson, Gillian Mary. *Understanding Alan Sillitoe*. Columbia: University of South Carolina Press, 1999.

Hapgood, Lynne, and Nancy L. Paxton, eds. *Outside Modernism: In Pursuit of the English Novel, 1900–30*. London: Macmillan; New York: St. Martin's, 2000.

Harden, Edgar F. *Thackeray the Writer: From Journalism to "Vanity Fair."* London: Macmillan; New York: St. Martin's, 1998.

Harding, D. W. *Regulated Hatred and Other Essays on Jane Austen*. Edited by Monica Lawlor. London and Atlantic Highlands (NJ): Athlone Press, 1998.

Hardy, Barbara. *Thomas Hardy: Imagining Imagination in Hardy's*

Poetry and Fiction. London and New Brunswick (NJ): Athlone Press, 2000.

Harris, Andrea L. *Other Sexes: Rewriting Difference from Woolf to Winterson*. Albany: State University of New York Press, 2000.

Harris, Janice Hubbard. *Edwardian Stories of Divorce*. New Brunswick, NJ: Rutgers University Press, 1996.

Harrison, Elizabeth Jane, and Shirley Peterson, eds. *Unmanning Modernism: Gendered Re-Readings*. Knoxville: University of Tennessee Press, 1997.

Hart, Clive, C. George Sandulescu, Bonnie K. Scott, and Fritz Senn, eds. *Images of Joyce*. 2 vols. Gerrards Cross (UK): Colin Smythe, 1998.

Harte, Liam, and Michael Parker, eds. *Contemporary Irish Fiction: Themes, Tropes, Theories*. London: Macmillan; New York: St. Martin's, 2000.

Harvey, John. *Men in Black*. Chicago and London: University of Chicago Press, 1995.

Havely, Nick, ed. *Dante's Modern Afterlife: Reception and Response from Blake to Heaney*. London: Macmillan; New York: St. Martin's, 1998.

Hawkridge, Audrey. *Jane and Her Gentlemen: Jane Austen and the Men in Her Life and Novels*. London and Chester Springs (PA): Peter Owen, 2000.

Hawley, John C., ed. *Christian Encounters with the Other*. Washington Square: New York University Press, 1998.

Hawthorn, Jeremy. *Cunning Passages: New Historicism, Cultural Materialism and Marxism in the Contemporary Literary Debate*. London: Arnold, 1996.

Haywood, Ian. *Working-class Fiction: From Chartism to "Trainspotting."* Plymouth (UK): Northcote House, 1997.

Heilmann, Ann. *New Woman Fiction: Women Writing First-Wave Feminism*. London: Macmillan; New York: St. Martin's, 2000.

Heinrich, Hans. *Zur Geschichte des 'Libertin' in der englischen Literatur: Verführer auf der Insel*. Heidelberg: Universitätsverlag C. Winter, 1999.

Heise, Ursula K. *Chronoschisms: Time, Narrative, and Postmodernism*. Cambridge: Cambridge University Press, 1997.

Hendershot, Cyndy. *The Animal Within: Masculinity and the Gothic*. Ann Arbor: University of Michigan Press, 1998.

Henighan, Tom. *Brian W. Aldiss*. New York: Twayne, 1999.

Herrera, Andrea O'Reilly, Elizabeth Mahn Nollen, and Sheila Reitzel Foor, eds. *Family Matters in the British and American Novel*. Bowling Green, OH: Bowling Green State University Popular Press, 1997.

Herrmann, Anne. *Queering the Moderns: Poses/Portraits/Performances*. New York: Palgrave, 2000.

Hertel, Kirsten. *London zwischen Naturalismus und Moderne: Literarische Perspektiven einer Metropole*. Heidelberg: Universitätsverlag C. Winter, 1997.

Heydenreich, Titus, and Eberhard Späth, eds. *Afrika in den europäischen Literaturen zwischen 1860 und 1930*. Erlangen (Germany): Universitätsbund Erlangen-Nürnberg, 2000.

Higbie, Robert. *Dickens and Imagination*. Gainesville: University Press of Florida, 1998.

Hill, Marylu. *Mothering Modernity: Feminism, Modernism, and the Maternal Muse*. New York and London: Garland Publishing, 1999.

Hilton, Mary, Morag Styles, and Victor Watson, eds. *Opening the Nursery Door: Reading, Writing and Childhood, 1600–1900*. London and New York: Routledge, 1997.

Hinton, Laura. *The Perverse Gaze of Sympathy: Sadomasochistic Sentiments from "Clarissa" to "Rescue 911."* Albany: State University of New York Press, 1999.

Hirai, Masako. *Sisters in Literature: Female Sexuality in "Antigone," "Middlemarch," "Howards End" and "Women in Love."* London: Macmillan; New York: St. Martin's, 1998.

Hoagwood, Terence Allan. *Politics, Philosophy, and the Production of Romantic Texts*. DeKalb: Northern Illinois University Press, 1996.

Hoberman, Ruth. *Gendering Classicism: The Ancient World in Twentieth-Century Women's Historical Fiction*. Albany: State University of New York Press, 1997.

Hochman, Baruch, and Ilja Wachs. *Dickens: The Orphan Condition*. Madison and Teaneck, NJ: Fairleigh Dickinson University Press; London: Associated University Presses, 1999.

Höglund, Johan A. *Mobilising the Novel: The Literature of Imperialism and The First World War*. Uppsala: Uppsala University, 1997.

Hoeveler, Diane Long. *Gothic Feminism: The Professionalization of Gender from Charlotte Smith to the Brontës*. University Park: Pennsylvania State University Press, 1998.

Hoeveler, Diane Long, and Lisa Jadwin. *Charlotte Brontë*. New York: Twayne; London: Prentice Hall International, 1997.

Hogan, Patrick Colm. *Colonialism and Cultural Identity: Crises of Tradition in the Anglophone Literatures of India, Africa, and the Caribbean*. Albany: State University of New York Press, 2000.

Holbrook, David. *A Study of George MacDonald and the Image of Woman*. Lewiston, NY: Edwin Mellen Press, 2000.

Holbrook, David. *"Wuthering Heights": A Drama of Being*. Sheffield (UK): Academic Press, 1997.

Holloway, Julia Bolton. *Jerusalem: Essays on Pilgrimage and Literature*. New York: AMS Press, 1998.

Holmesland, Oddvar. *Form as Compensation for Life: Fictive Patterns in Virginia Woolf's Novels*. Columbia, SC: Camden House, 1998.

Honda, Mineko. *The Imaginative World of C. S. Lewis: A Way to Participate in Reality*. Lanham, MD: University Press of America, 2000.

Hooker, Jeremy. *Writers in a Landscape*. Cardiff: University of Wales Press, 1996.

Hoover, David L. *Language and Style in "The Inheritors."* Lanham, MD: University Press of America, 1999.

Horlacher, Stefan, and Marion Islinger, eds. *Expedition nach der Wahrheit—Poems, Essays, and Papers in Honour of Theo Stemmler: Festschrift zum 60. Geburtstag von Theo Stemmler*. Heidelberg: Universitätsverlag C. Winter, 1996.

Hoskins, Robert. *Graham Greene: An Approach to the Novels*. New York and London: Garland Publishing, 1999.

Houppermans, Sjef, ed. *Beckett & La Psychanalyse & Psychoanalysis*. Amsterdam and Atlanta (GA): Rodopi, 1996.

Houston, Gail Turley. *Royalties: The Queen and Victorian Writers.* Charlottesville and London: University Press of Virginia, 1999.

Huggan, Graham. *The Postcolonial Exotic: Marketing the Margins.* London and New York: Routledge, 2001.

Hughes, George, ed. *Corresponding Powers: Studies in Honour of Professor Hisaaki Yamanouchi.* Cambridge: D. S. Brewer, 1997.

Hughes, Linda K., and Michael Lund. *Victorian Publishing and Mrs. Gaskell's Work.* Charlottesville and London: University Press of Virginia, 1999.

Hughes, William, and Andrew Smith, eds. *Bram Stoker: History, Psychoanalysis and the Gothic.* London: Macmillan; New York: St. Martin's, 1998.

Hunt, Peter. *Children's Literature.* Oxford and Malden (MA): Blackwell, 2001.

Hutton, Elaine, ed. *Beyond Sex and Romance? The Politics of Contemporary Lesbian Fiction.* London: Women's Press, 1998.

Ingersoll, Earl G. *D. H. Lawrence, Desire, and Narrative.* Gainesville: University Press of Florida, 2001.

Ingham, Patricia Clare. *Sovereign Fantasies: Arthurian Romance and the Making of Britain.* Philadelphia: University of Pennsylvania Press, 2001.

Ingrassia, Catherine. *Authorship, Commerce, and Gender in Early Eighteenth-Century England: A Culture of Paper Credit.* Cambridge: Cambridge University Press, 1998.

Ireland, Ken. *The Sequential Dynamics of Narrative: Energies at the Margins of Fiction.* Madison and Teaneck, NJ: Fairleigh Dickinson University Press; London: Associated University Presses, 2001.

Irwin, Michael. *Reading Hardy's Landscapes.* London: Macmillan; New York: St. Martin's, 2000.

Israel, Kali. *Names and Stories: Emilia Dilke and Victorian Culture.* New York and Oxford: Oxford University Press, 1999.

Israel, Nico. *Outlandish: Writing Between Exile and Diaspora.* Stanford, CA: Stanford University Press, 2000.

Ivory, James Maurice. *Identity and Narrative Metamorphoses in Twentieth-Century British Literature.* Lewiston, NY: Edwin Mellen Press, 2000.

Izarra, Laura P. Zuntini de. *Mirrors and Holographic Labyrinths: The Process of a 'New' Aesthetic Synthesis in the Novels of John Banville.* San Francisco, CA: International Scholars Publications, 1999.

Jackson-Houlston, C. M. *Ballads, Songs and Snatches: The Appropriation of Folk Song and Popular Culture in British Nineteenth-Century Realist Prose.* Aldershot (UK): Ashgate, 1999.

Jacobs, Diane. *Her Own Woman: The Life of Mary Wollstonecraft.* New York: Simon and Schuster, 2001.

Jacobs, Edward H. *Accidental Migrations: An Archaeology of Gothic Discourse.* Lewisburg, PA: Bucknell University Press; London: Associated University Presses, 2000.

Jacobson, Wendy S., ed. *Dickens and the Children of Empire.* New York: Palgrave, 2000.

Jacobus, Mary. *Psychoanalysis and the Scene of Reading.* Oxford and New York: Oxford University Press, 1999.

Jaffe, Audrey. *Scenes of Sympathy: Identity and Representation in Victorian Fiction*. Ithaca (NY) and London: Cornell University Press, 2000.

James, Louis. *Caribbean Literature in English*. London and New York: Longman, 1999.

Jarrot, Sabine. *Le vampire dans la littérature du XIXe au XXe siècle: De l'Autre à un autre soi-même*. Paris and Montreal: L'Harmattan, 1999.

Jay, Elisabeth. *Mrs Oliphant: "A Fiction to Herself"—A Literary Life*. Oxford: Clarendon, 1995.

Jeffares, A. Norman. *Images of Invention: Essays on Irish Writing*. Gerrards Cross (UK): Colin Smythe, 1996.

Jenkins, Alice, and Juliet John, eds. *Rereading Victorian Fiction*. London: Macmillan; New York: St. Martin's, 2000.

Jenkins, William D. *The Adventure of the Detected Detective: Sherlock Holmes in James Joyce's "Finnegans Wake."* Westport (CT) and London: Greenwood Press, 1998.

Joannou, Maroula, ed. *Women Writers of the 1930s: Gender, Politics and History*. Edinburgh: Edinburgh University Press, 1999.

John, Juliet, and Alice Jenkins, eds. *Rethinking Victorian Culture*. London: Macmillan; New York: St. Martin's, 2000.

Johnson, George M. *J. D. Beresford*. New York: Twayne; London: Prentice Hall International, 1998.

Jones, Ellen Carol, ed. *Joyce: Feminism / Post / Colonialism*. Amsterdam and Atlanta (GA): Rodopi, 1998. (European Joyce Studies 8.)

Jones, Jo Elwyn, and J. Francis Gladstone. *The "Alice" Companion*. Washington Square: New York University Press, 1998.

Jones, Mervyn. *The Amazing Victorian: A Life of George Meredith*. London: Constable, 1999.

Jones, Susan. *Conrad and Women*. Oxford: Clarendon, 1999.

Jones, Vivien, ed. *Women and Literature in Britain, 1700–1800*. Cambridge: Cambridge University Press, 2000.

Jordan, John O., ed. *The Cambridge Companion to Charles Dickens*. Cambridge: Cambridge University Press, 2001.

Josipovici, Gabriel. *On Trust: Art and the Temptations of Suspicion*. New Haven (CT) and London: Yale University Press, 1999.

Jouve, Nicole Ward. *Female Genesis: Creativity, Self and Gender*. New York: St. Martin's, 1998.

Judd, Catherine. *Bedside Seductions: Nursing and the Victorian Imagination, 1830–1880*. New York: St. Martin's, 1998.

Juneja, Om P. *Post Colonial Novel: Narratives of Colonial Consciousness*. New Delhi: Creative Books, 1995.

Justman, Stewart. *The Springs of Liberty: The Satiric Tradition and Freedom of Speech*. Evanston, IL: Northwestern University Press, 1999.

Kalaga, Wojciech H., and Tadeusz Rachwal, eds. *Signs of Culture: Simulacra and the Real*. Frankfurt: Peter Lang, 2000.

Kaleta, Kenneth C. *Hanif Kureishi: Postcolonial Storyteller*. Austin: University of Texas Press, 1998.

Kane, Michael. *Modern Men: Mapping Masculinity in English and German Literature, 1880–1930*. London and New York: Cassell, 1999.

Kane, Penny. *Victorian Families in Fact and Fiction*. New York: St. Martin's, 1995.

Kapp, Volker, Helmuth Kiesel, and Klaus Lubbers, eds. *Bilderwelten als Vergegenwärtigung und Verrätselung der Welt: Literatur und Kunst um die Jahrhundertwende*. Berlin: Duncker and Humblot, 1997.

Katz, Daniel. *Saying I No More: Subjectivity and Consciousness in the Prose of Samuel Beckett*. Evanston, IL: Northwestern University Press, 1999.

Katz, Tamar. *Impressionist Subjects: Gender, Interiority, and Modernist Fiction in England*. Urbana and Chicago: University of Illinois Press, 2000.

Kaye, Peter. *Dostoevsky and English Modernism, 1900–1930*. Cambridge: Cambridge University Press, 1999.

Keane, Angela. *Women Writers and the English Nation in the 1790s: Romantic Belongings*. Cambridge: Cambridge University Press, 2000.

Keen, Suzanne. *Victorian Renovations of the Novel: Narrative Annexes and the Boundaries of Representation*. Cambridge: Cambridge University Press, 1998.

Kelleher, Margaret. *The Feminization of Famine: Expressions of the Inexpressible*. Durham, NC: Duke University Press, 1997.

Kelly, Joseph. *Our Joyce: From Outcast to Icon*. Austin: University of Texas Press, 1998.

Kemmerer, Kathleen Nulton. *"A neutral being between the sexes": Samuel Johnson's Sexual Politics*. Lewisburg, PA: Bucknell University Press; London: Associated University Presses, 1998.

Kennedy, Gwynne. *Just Anger: Representing Women's Anger in Early Modern England*. Carbondale and Edwardsville: Southern Illinois University Press, 2000.

Kerridge, Richard, and Neil Sammells, eds. *Writing the Environment: Ecocriticism and Literature*. London and New York: Zed Books, 1998.

Kestner, Joseph A. *The Edwardian Detective, 1901–1915*. Aldershot (UK): Ashgate, 2000.

Kibbey, Ann, Thomas Foster, Carol Siegel, and Ellen Berry, eds. *On Your Left: Historical Materialism in the 1990s*. New York and London: New York University Press, 1996.

Kiberd, Declan. *Inventing Ireland*. Cambridge: Harvard University Press, 1995.

Kilian, Eveline. *Momente innerweltlicher Transzendenz: Die Augenblickserfahrung in Dorothy Richardsons Romanzyklus "Pilgrimage" und ihr ideengeschichtlicher Kontext*. Tübingen: Max Niemeyer Verlag, 1997.

Kim, Hyonjin. *The Knight without the Sword: A Social Landscape of Malorian Chivalry*. Rochester, NY: D. S. Brewer, 2000.

Kimball, Jean. *Odyssey of the Psyche: Jungian Patterns in Joyce's "Ulysses."* Carbondale and Edwardsville: Southern Illinois University Press, 1997.

Kincaid, James R. *Annoying the Victorians*. New York and London: Routledge, 1995.

King, Jeannette. *Women and the Word: Contemporary Women Novelists and the Bible*. London: Macmillan; New York: St. Martin's, 2000.

King, Kathryn R. *Jane Barker, Exile: A Literary Career, 1675–1725*. Oxford: Clarendon, 2000.

King, Sigrid, ed. *Pilgrimage for Love: Essays in Early Modern Literature in Honor of Josephine A. Roberts*. Tempe: Arizona Center for Medieval and Renaissance Studies, 1999.

Kinney, Arthur F., ed. *The Cambridge Companion to English Literature, 1500–1600*. Cambridge: Cambridge University Press, 2000.

Kirkpatrick, Kathryn, ed. *Border Crossings: Irish Women Writers and National Identities*. Tuscaloosa and London: University of Alabama Press, 2000.

Klaus, H. Gustav, and Stephen Knight, eds. *The Art of Murder: New Essays on Detective Fiction*. Tübingen: Stauffenburg Verlag, 1998.

Klein, Kathleen Gregory. *The Woman Detective: Gender & Genre*. 2nd ed. Urbana and Chicago: University of Illinois Press, 1995.

Knoepflmacher, U. C. *Ventures into Childhood: Victorians, Fairy Tales, and Femininity*. Chicago and London: University of Chicago Press, 1998.

Knowles, Ronald. *"Gulliver's Travels": The Politics of Satire*. New York: Twayne, 1996.

Knowles, Sebastian D. G., ed. *Bronze By Gold: The Music of Joyce*. New York: Garland Publishing, 1999.

Knowlton, Eloise. *Joyce, Joyceans, and the Rhetoric of Citation*. Gainesville: University Press of Florida, 1998.

Korte, Barbara. *Body Language in Literature*. Toronto: University of Toronto Press, 1997.

Korte, Barbara, and Klaus Peter Müller, eds. *Unity in Diversity Revisited? British Literature and Culture in the 1990s*. Tübingen: Gunter Narr Verlag, 1998.

Kostova, Ludmilla. *Tales of the Periphery: The Balkans in Nineteenth-Century British Writing*. Veliko Turnovo (Bulgaria): PIK University Press, 1997.

Krajka, Wieslaw, ed. *Joseph Conrad: East European, Polish and Worldwide*. Boulder, CO: East European Monographs; Lublin: Marie Curie-Sklodowska University, 1999.

Kramer, Dale, ed. *The Cambridge Companion to Thomas Hardy*. Cambridge: Cambridge University Press, 1999.

Kranidis, Rita S., ed. *Imperial Objects: Essays on Victorian Women's Emigration and the Unauthorized Imperial Experience*. New York: Twayne, 1998.

Kreilkamp, Vera. *The Anglo-Irish Novel and the Big House*. Syracuse, NY: Syracuse University Press, 1998.

Kroll, Richard, ed. *The English Novel, Volume 1: 1700 to Fielding*. London and New York: Longman, 1998.

Kroll, Richard, ed. *The English Novel, Volume 2: Smollett to Austen*. London and New York: Longman, 1998.

Kucich, John, and Dianne F. Sadoff, eds. *Victorian Afterlife: Postmodern Culture Rewrites the Nineteenth Century*. Minneapolis and London: University of Minnesota Press, 2000.

Kuortti, Joel. *Fictions to Live In: Narration as an Argument for Fiction in Salman Rushdie's Novels*. Frankfurt: Peter Lang, 1998.

Kutzer, M. Daphne. *Empire's Children: Empire and Imperialism in Classic British Children's Books*. New York and London: Garland Publishing, 2000.

Laird, Holly A. *Women Coauthors*. Urbana and Chicago: University of Illinois Press, 2000.

Lamb, Jonathan. *Preserving the Self in the South Seas, 1680–1840*. Chicago and London: University of Chicago Press, 2001.

Lambdin, Laura Cooner, and Robert Thomas Lambdin, eds. *A Companion to Jane Austen Studies*. Westport (CT) and London: Greenwood Press, 2000.

Lane, Christopher. *The Burdens of Intimacy: Psychoanalysis and Victorian Masculinity*. Chicago and London: University of Chicago Press, 1999.

Langbauer, Laurie. *Novels of Everyday Life: The Series in English Fiction, 1850–1930*. Ithaca (NY) and London: Cornell University Press, 1999.

Lang-Peralta, Linda, ed. *Women, Revolution, and the Novels of the 1790s*. East Lansing: Michigan State University Press, 1999.

Lanters, José. *Unauthorized Versions: Irish Menippean Satire, 1919–1952*. Washington, DC: Catholic University of America Press, 2000.

Larson, Jil. *Ethics and Narrative in the English Novel, 1880–1914*. Cambridge: Cambridge University Press, 2001.

Laskowski, William. *Kingsley Amis*. New York: Twayne; London: Prentice Hall International, 1998.

Leach, Karoline. *In the Shadow of the Dreamchild: A New Understanding of Lewis Carroll*. London and Chester Springs (PA): Peter Owen, 1999.

Leckie, Barbara. *Culture and Adultery: The Novel, the Newspaper, and the Law, 1857–1914*. Philadelphia: University of Pennsylvania Press, 1999.

Ledger, Sally. *The New Woman: Fiction and Feminism at the Fin de Siècle*. Manchester and New York: Manchester University Press, 1997.

Lee, Alison. *Angela Carter*. New York: Twayne, 1997.

Leeming, David. *Stephen Spender: A Life in Modernism*. New York: Henry Holt, 1999.

Leonard, Elisabeth Anne, ed. *Into Darkness Peering: Race and Color in the Fantastic*. Westport (CT) and London: Greenwood Press, 1997.

Leonard, Garry. *Advertising and Commodity Culture in Joyce*. Gainesville: University Press of Florida, 1998.

Lernout, Geert, and Marc Maufort, eds. *Interpreting Minority: A Comparative Approach*. Antwerp: Vlaamse Vereniging voor Algemene en Vergelijkende Literatuurwetenschap, 1998.

Lesnik-Oberstein, Karín, ed. *Children in Culture: Approaches to Childhood*. London: Macmillan; New York: St. Martin's, 1998.

Levenback, Karen L. *Virginia Woolf and the Great War*. Syracuse, NY: Syracuse University Press, 1999.

Levenson, Michael, ed. *The Cambridge Companion to Modernism*. Cambridge: Cambridge University Press, 1999.

Levine, Caroline, and Mark W. Turner, eds. *From Author to Text: Re-reading George Eliot's "Romola."* Aldershot (UK): Ashgate, 1998.

Levine, George, ed. *The Cambridge Companion to George Eliot*. Cambridge: Cambridge University Press, 2001.

Levy, Anita. *Reproductive Urges: Popular Novel-Reading, Sexuality, and the English Nation*. Philadelphia: University of Pennsylvania Press, 1999.

Li, Hao. *Memory and History in George Eliot: Transfiguring the Past*. London: Macmillan; New York: St. Martin's, 2000.

Lie, Nadia, and Theo D'haen, eds. *Constellation Caliban: Figurations of a Character*. Amsterdam and Atlanta (GA): Rodopi, 1997.

Lilienfeld, Jane. *Reading Alcoholisms: Theorizing Character and Narrative in Selected Novels of Thomas Hardy, James Joyce, and Virginia Woolf*. New York: St. Martin's, 1999.

Lilienfeld, Jane, and Jeffrey Oxford, eds. *The Languages of Addiction*. New York: St. Martin's, 1999.

Lindskoog, Kathryn. *Surprised by C. S. Lewis, George MacDonald, and Dante: An Array of Original Discoveries*. Macon, GA: Mercer University Press, 2001.

Linkin, Harriet Kramer, and Stephen C. Behrendt, eds. *Romanticism and Women Poets: Opening the Doors of Reception*. Lexington: University Press of Kentucky, 1999.

Lipking, Lawrence. *Samuel Johnson: The Life of an Author*. Cambridge (MA) and London: Harvard University Press, 1998.

Little, Judy. *The Experimental Self: Dialogic Subjectivity in Woolf, Pym, and Brooke-Rose*. Carbondale and Edwardsville: Southern Illinois University Press, 1996.

Litvak, Joseph. *Strange Gourmets: Sophistication, Theory, and the Novel*. Durham (NC) and London: Duke University Press, 1997.

Lloyd, Tom. *Crises of Realism: Representing Experience in the British Novel, 1816–1910*. Lewisburg, PA: Bucknell University Press; London: Associated University Presses, 1997.

Logan, Deborah Anna. *Fallenness in Victorian Women's Writing: Marry, Stitch, Die, or Do Worse*. Columbia and London: University of Missouri Press, 1998.

Logan, Mawuena Kossi. *Narrating Africa: George Henty and the Fiction of Empire*. New York and London: Garland Publishing, 1999.

Lohmann, Dieter. *KALYPSO bei Homer und James Joyce: Eine vergleichende Untersuchung des 1. und 5. Buches der "Odyssee" und der 4. Episode ('Calypso') im "Ulysses" von J. Joyce*. Tübingen: Stauffenburg Verlag, 1998.

Loncar, Kathleen. *Legal Fiction: Law in the Novels of Nineteenth Century Women Novelists*. London: Minerva Press, 1995.

London, April. *Women and Property in the Eighteenth-Century English Novel*. Cambridge: Cambridge University Press, 1999.

Losey, Jay, and William D. Brewer, eds. *Mapping Male Sexuality: Nineteenth-Century England*. Madison and Teaneck, NJ: Fairleigh Dickinson University Press; London: Associated University Presses, 2000.

Loveridge, Mark. *A History of Augustan Fable*. Cambridge: Cambridge University Press, 1998.

Luckhurst, Roger. *"The Angle Between Two Walls": The Fiction of J. G. Ballard*. New York: St. Martin's, 1997.

Lycett, Andrew. *Rudyard Kipling*. London: Weidenfeld and Nicolson, 1999.

Lykiard, Alexis. *Jean Rhys Revisited*. Exeter (UK): Stride, 2000.

Lynch, Andrew. *Malory's Book of Arms: The Narrative of Combat in "Le Morte Darthur."* Cambridge: D. S. Brewer, 1997.

Lynch, Deidre, ed. *Janeites: Austen's Disciples and Devotees*. Princeton (NJ) and Oxford: Princeton University Press, 2000.

Lynch, Deidre Shauna. *The Economy of Character: Novels, Market Culture, and the Business of Inner Meaning.* Chicago and London: University of Chicago Press, 1998.

McBride, Margaret. *"Ulysses" and the Metamorphosis of Stephen Dedalus.* Lewisburg, PA: Bucknell University Press; London: Associated University Presses, 2001.

McCann, Andrew. *Cultural Politics in the 1790s: Literature, Radicalism and the Public Sphere.* London: Macmillan; New York: St. Martin's, 1999.

McCaw, Neil. *George Eliot and Victorian Historiography: Imagining the National Past.* London: Macmillan; New York: St. Martin's, 2000.

McCormack, Kathleen. *George Eliot and Intoxication: Dangerous Drugs for the Condition of England.* London: Macmillan; New York: St. Martin's, 2000.

McCormick, John. *Catastrophe and Imagination: English and American Writings from 1870 to 1950.* New ed. New Brunswick (NJ) and London: Transaction Publishers, 1998.

McCourt, John. *The Years of Bloom: James Joyce in Trieste, 1904–1920.* Madison: University of Wisconsin Press, 2000.

Macdonald, D. L. *Monk Lewis: A Critical Biography.* Toronto: University of Toronto Press, 2000.

McDonald, Peter D. *British Literary Culture and Publishing Practice, 1884–1914.* Cambridge: Cambridge University Press, 1997.

McDowell, Paula. *The Women of Grub Street: Press, Politics, and Gender in the London Literary Marketplace, 1678–1730.* Oxford: Clarendon, 1998.

McFarlane, Cameron. *The Sodomite in Fiction and Satire, 1660–1750.* New York: Columbia University Press, 1997.

McGavran, James Holt, ed. *Literature and the Child: Romantic Continuations, Postmodern Contestations.* Iowa City: University of Iowa Press, 1999.

McGee, Patrick. *Joyce Beyond Marx: History and Desire in "Ulysses" and "Finnegans Wake."* Gainesville: University Press of Florida, 2001.

McGregor, Robert Kuhn (with Ethan Lewis). *Conundrums for the Long Week-End: England, Dorothy L. Sayers, and Lord Peter Wimsey.* Kent (OH) and London: Kent State University Press, 2000.

McIntosh, Carey. *The Evolution of English Prose, 1700–1800: Style, Politeness, and Print Culture.* Cambridge: Cambridge University Press, 1998.

Mackey, Peter Francis. *Chaos Theory and James Joyce's Everyman.* Gainesville: University Press of Florida, 1999.

McKee, Patricia. *Public and Private: Gender, Class, and the British Novel, 1764–1878.* Minneapolis and London: University of Minnesota Press, 1997.

MacKenna, Dolores. *William Trevor: The Writer and His Work.* Dublin: New Island Books, 1999.

McLane, Maureen N. *Romanticism and the Human Sciences: Poetry, Population, and the Discourse of the Species.* Cambridge: Cambridge University Press, 2000.

McLaughlin, Joseph. *Writing the Urban Jungle: Reading Empire in London from Doyle to Eliot.* Charlottesville and London: University Press of Virginia, 2000.

MacLean, Gerald, Donna Landry, and Joseph P. Ward, eds. *The Country and the City Revisited: England and the Politics of Culture, 1550–1850*. Cambridge: Cambridge University Press, 1999.

McLeod, Bruce. *The Geography of Empire in English Literature, 1580–1745*. Cambridge: Cambridge University Press, 1999.

McLoughlin, T. O. *Contesting Ireland: Irish Voices against England in the Eighteenth Century*. Dublin and Portland (OR): Four Courts Press, 1999.

McLuhan, Eric. *The Role of Thunder in "Finnegans Wake."* Toronto: University of Toronto Press, 1997.

McMinn, Joseph. *The Supreme Fictions of John Banville*. Manchester and New York: Manchester University Press, 1999.

McVicker, Jeanette, and Laura Davis, eds. *Virginia Woolf and Communities: Selected Papers from the Eighth Annual Conference on Virginia Woolf (Saint Louis University, Saint Louis, Missouri, June 4–7, 1998)*. New York: Pace University Press, 1999.

Mahaffey, Vicki. *States of Desire: Wilde, Yeats, Joyce, and the Irish Experiment*. New York and Oxford: Oxford University Press, 1998.

Mandell, Laura. *Misogynous Economies: The Business of Literature in Eighteenth-Century Britain*. Lexington: University Press of Kentucky, 1999.

Mangum, Teresa. *Married, Middlebrow, and Militant: Sarah Grand and the New Woman Novel*. Ann Arbor: University of Michigan Press, 1998.

Marcus, Laura. *Virginia Woolf*. Plymouth (UK): Northcote House, 1997.

Marder, Herbert. *The Measure of Life: Virginia Woolf's Last Years*. Ithaca (NY) and London: Cornell University Press, 2000.

Marigny, Jean, ed. *Images fantastiques du corps*. Grenoble: Université Stendhal-Grenoble, 1998.

Markwick, Margaret. *Trollope and Women*. London and Rio Grande (OH): Hambledon Press, 1997.

Marret, Sophie, ed. *Féminin/Masculin: Littératures et cultures anglo-saxonnes—Actes du 38e congrès de la Société des Anglicistes de l'Enseignement Supérieur (SAES), Rennes, mai 1998*. Rennes: Presses Universitaires, 1999.

Marsh, Joss. *Word Crimes: Blasphemy, Culture, and Literature in Nineteenth-Century England*. Chicago and London: University of Chicago Press, 1998.

Marsh, Nicholas. *D. H. Lawrence: The Novels*. New York: St. Martin's, 2000.

Marsh, Nicholas. *Emily Brontë: "Wuthering Heights."* New York: St. Martin's, 1999.

Marsh, Nicholas. *Jane Austen: The Novels*. New York: St. Martin's, 1998.

Marshall, W. Gerald, ed. *The Restoration Mind*. Newark: University of Delaware Press; London: Associated University Presses, 1997.

Martin, Bruce K. *David Lodge*. New York: Twayne, 1999.

Martin, Robert K., and George Piggford, eds. *Queer Forster*. Chicago and London: University of Chicago Press, 1997.

Maslen, R. W. *Elizabethan Fictions: Espionage, Counter-Espionage, and the Duplicity of Fiction in Early Elizabethan Prose Narratives*. Oxford: Clarendon, 1997.

Maurel, Sylvie. *Jean Rhys*. New York: St. Martin's, 1998.

May, Leila Silvana. *Disorderly Sisters: Sibling Relations and Sororal Resistance in Nineteenth-Century British Literature*. Lewisburg, PA: Bucknell University Press; London: Associated University Presses, 2001.

May, Stephen. *Stardust and Ashes: Science Fiction in Christian Perspective*. London: Society for Promoting Christian Knowledge, 1998.

Mayer, Robert. *History and the Early English Novel: Matters of Fact from Bacon to Defoe*. Cambridge: Cambridge University Press, 1997.

Maze, John R. *Virginia Woolf: Feminism, Creativity, and the Unconscious*. Westport (CT) and London: Greenwood Press, 1997.

Meanor, Patrick. *Bruce Chatwin*. New York: Twayne; London: Prentice Hall International, 1997.

Mecklenburg, Susanne. *Martin Amis und Graham Swift: Erfolg durch bodenlosen Moralismus im zeitgenössischen britischen Roman*. Heidelberg: Universitätsverlag C. Winter, 2000.

Mellor, Anne K. *Mothers of the Nation: Women's Political Writing in England, 1780–1830*. Bloomington and Indianapolis: Indiana University Press, 2000.

Mengham, Rod, ed. *An Introduction to Contemporary Fiction: International Writing in English since 1970*. Cambridge: Polity Press, 1999.

Mester, Terri A. *Movement and Modernism: Yeats, Eliot, Lawrence, Williams, and Early Twentieth-Century Dance*. Fayetteville: University of Arkansas Press, 1997.

Michie, Allen. *Richardson and Fielding: The Dynamics of a Critical Rivalry*. Lewisburg, PA: Bucknell University Press; London: Associated University Presses, 1999.

Middeke, Martin, and Werner Huber, eds. *Biofictions: The Rewriting of Romantic Lives in Contemporary Fiction and Drama*. Rochester, NY: Camden House, 1999.

Middleton, Peter, and Tim Woods. *Literatures of Memory: History, Time and Space in Postwar Writing*. Manchester and New York: Manchester University Press, 2000.

Mighall, Robert. *A Geography of Victorian Gothic Fiction: Mapping History's Nightmares*. Oxford and New York: Oxford University Press, 1999.

Milbank, Alison. *Dante and the Victorians*. Manchester and New York: Manchester University Press, 1998.

Miller, Andrew H. *Novels Behind Glass: Commodity Culture and Victorian Narrative*. Cambridge: Cambridge University Press, 1995.

Miller, Elizabeth, ed. *"Dracula": The Shade and the Shadow—A Critical Anthology. (Papers Presented at 'Dracula 97,' A Centenary Celebration, Los Angeles, August 1997.)* Westcliff-on-Sea (UK): Desert Island, 1998.

Miller, J. Hillis. *Black Holes*. Stanford, CA: Stanford University Press, 1999.

Miller, Tyrus. *Late Modernism: Politics, Fiction, and the Arts Between the World Wars*. Berkeley: University of California Press, 1999.

Mills, Alice, ed. *Seriously Weird: Papers on the Grotesque*. New York: Peter Lang, 1999.

Mills, David, ed. *The Pilgrim's Guide: C. S. Lewis and the Art of Witness.* Grand Rapids, MI: Eerdmans, 1998.

Mitchell, David T., and Sharon L. Snyder, eds. *The Body and Physical Difference: Discourses of Disability.* Ann Arbor: University of Michigan Press, 1997.

Moglen, Helene. *The Trauma of Gender: A Feminist Theory of the English Novel.* Berkeley: University of California Press, 2001.

Moliterno, Frank. *The Dialectics of Sense and Spirit in Pater and Joyce.* Greensboro, NC: ELT Press, 1998.

Montandon, Alain. *Le roman au XVIIIe siècle en Europe.* Paris: Presses Universitaires de France, 1999.

Moody, Ellen. *Trollope on the Net.* London and Rio Grande (OH): Hambledon Press, 1999.

Moore, Gene M., Owen Knowles, and J. H. Stape, eds. *Conrad: Intertexts and Appropriations—Essays in Memory of Yves Hervouet.* Amsterdam and Atlanta (GA): Rodopi, 1997.

Moore, Jane. *Mary Wollstonecraft.* Plymouth (UK): Northcote House, 1999.

Moore, Lisa L. *Dangerous Intimacies: Toward a Sapphic History of the British Novel.* Durham (NC) and London: Duke University Press, 1997.

Morgentaler, Goldie. *Dickens and Heredity: When Like Begets Like.* London: Macmillan; New York: St. Martin's, 2000.

Morris, Ivor. *Jane Austen and the Interplay of Character.* London and New Brunswick (NJ): Athlone Press, 1999.

Morris, Tim. *You're Only Young Twice: Children's Literature and Film.* Urbana and Chicago: University of Illinois Press, 2000.

Morrissey, Lee. *From the Temple to the Castle: An Architectural History of British Literature, 1660–1760.* Charlottesville and London: University Press of Virginia, 1999.

Morse, David. *The Age of Virtue: British Culture from the Restoration to Romanticism.* London: Macmillan; New York: St. Martin's, 2000.

Moseley, Merritt. *Understanding Julian Barnes.* Columbia: University of South Carolina Press, 1997.

Mroczkowski, Przemyslaw. *Chaucer to Chesterton: English Classics from Polish Perspective.* Lublin: Towarzystwo Naukowe, 1996.

Mudge, Bradford K. *The Whore's Story: Women, Pornography, and the British Novel, 1684–1830.* Oxford and New York: Oxford University Press, 2000.

Mukherjee, Meenakshi. *The Perishable Empire: Essays on Indian Writing in English.* New Delhi: Oxford University Press, 2000.

Müller, Ulrich, and Kathleen Verduin, eds. *Mittelalter-Rezeption, V.* Göppingen: Kümmerle, 1996.

Mullett, Michael. *John Bunyan in Context.* Pittsburgh, PA: Duquesne University Press, 1997.

Myers, William. *The Presence of Persons: Essays on Literature, Science and Philosophy in the Nineteenth Century.* Aldershot (UK): Ashgate, 1998.

Najder, Zdzislaw. *Conrad in Perspective: Essays on Art and Fidelity.* Cambridge: Cambridge University Press, 1997.

Nalbantian, Suzanne. *Aesthetic Autobiography: From Life to Art in Marcel*

Proust, James Joyce, Virginia Woolf and Anaïs Nin. New York: St. Martin's, 1997.

Nash, Walter. *Language and Creative Illusion.* London and New York: Longman, 1998.

Navarette, Susan J. *The Shape of Fear: Horror and the Fin de Siècle Culture of Decadence.* Lexington: University Press of Kentucky, 1998.

Nayder, Lillian. *Wilkie Collins.* New York: Twayne; London: Prentice Hall International, 1997.

Needham, Anuradha Dingwaney. *Using the Master's Tools: Resistance and the Literature of the African and South-Asian Diasporas.* New York: St. Martin's, 2000.

Neill, Edward. *The Politics of Jane Austen.* London: Macmillan; New York: St. Martin's, 1999.

Neill, Edward. *Trial by Ordeal: Thomas Hardy and the Critics.* Columbia, SC: Camden House, 1999.

Neville-Sington, Pamela. *Fanny Trollope: The Life and Adventures of a Clever Woman.* London and New York: Viking, 1997.

Newlin, George. *Understanding "A Tale of Two Cities": A Student Casebook to Issues, Sources, and Historical Documents.* Westport (CT) and London: Greenwood Press, 1998.

Newlin, George. *Understanding "Great Expectations": A Student Casebook to Issues, Sources, and Historical Documents.* Westport (CT) and London: Greenwood Press, 1997.

Newsinger, John. *Orwell's Politics.* London: Macmillan; New York: St. Martin's, 1999.

Newsom, Robert. *Charles Dickens Revisited.* New York: Twayne, 2000.

Nigro, August. *The Net of Nemesis: Studies in Tragic Bond/age.* Selinsgrove, PA: Susquehanna University Press; London: Associated University Presses, 2000.

Nokes, David. *Jane Austen: A Life.* New York: Farrar, Straus and Giroux, 1997.

Nordius, Janina. *"I Am Myself Alone": Solitude and Transcendence in John Cowper Powys.* Göteborg: Acta Universitatis Gothoburgensis, 1997.

Norris, Margot, ed. *A Companion to James Joyce's "Ulysses": Biographical and Historical Contexts, Critical History, and Essays from Five Contemporary Critical Perspectives.* Boston and New York: Bedford Books, 1998.

North, Michael. *Reading 1922: A Return to the Scene of the Modern.* New York and Oxford: Oxford University Press, 1999.

Norton, Ann V. *Paradoxical Feminism: The Novels of Rebecca West.* Lanham, MD: International Scholars Publications, 2000.

Norton, Rictor. *Mistress of Udolpho: The Life of Ann Radcliffe.* London and New York: Leicester University Press, 1999.

Novy, Marianne, ed. *Transforming Shakespeare: Contemporary Women's Re-Visions in Literature and Performance.* New York: St. Martin's, 1999.

Nyman, Jopi. *Under English Eyes: Constructions of Europe in Early Twentieth-Century British Fiction.* Amsterdam and Atlanta (GA): Rodopi, 2000.

Nyman, Jopi, and John A. Stotesbury, eds. *Postcolonialism and Cultural*

Resistance. Joensuu (Finland): Faculty of Humanities, University of Joensuu, 1999.

O'Brien, Edna. *James Joyce: A Penguin Life.* New York: Viking, 1999.

O'Donnell, Mary Ann, Bernard Dhuicq, and Guyonne Leduc, eds. *Aphra Behn (1640–1689): Identity, Alterity, Ambiguity.* Paris: L'Harmattan, 2000.

O'Farrell, Mary Ann. *Telling Complexions: The Nineteenth-Century English Novel and the Blush.* Durham (NC) and London: Duke University Press, 1997.

Olsen, Kirstin. *Understanding "Lord of the Flies": A Student Casebook to Issues, Sources, and Historical Documents.* Westport (CT) and London: Greenwood Press, 2000.

Olson, Barbara K. *Authorial Divinity in the Twentieth Century: Omniscient Narration in Woolf, Hemingway, and Others.* Lewisburg, PA: Bucknell University Press; London: Associated University Presses, 1997.

Onega, Susana. *Metafiction and Myth in the Novels of Peter Ackroyd.* Columbia, SC: Camden House, 1999.

O'Neill, Christine. *Too Fine a Point: A Stylistic Analysis of the Eumaeus Episode in James Joyce's "Ulysses."* Trier (Germany): Wissenschaftlicher Verlag, 1996.

Oppenheim, Lois. *The Painted Word: Samuel Beckett's Dialogue with Art.* Ann Arbor: University of Michigan Press, 2000.

Otis, Laura. *Membranes: Metaphors of Invasion in Nineteenth-Century Literature, Science, and Politics.* Baltimore (MD) and London: Johns Hopkins University Press, 1999.

O'Toole, Tess. *Genealogy and Fiction in Hardy: Family Lineage and Narrative Lines.* London: Macmillan; New York: St. Martin's, 1997.

Oueijan, Naji B. *The Progress of an Image: The East in English Literature.* New York: Peter Lang, 1996.

Paccaud-Huguet, Josiane, ed. *Joseph Conrad 1: la fiction et l'Autre.* Paris and Caen: Lettres Modernes Minard, 1998.

Pacheco, Anita, ed. *Early Women Writers: 1600–1720.* London and New York: Longman, 1998.

Pagliaro, Harold. *Henry Fielding: A Literary Life.* New York: St. Martin's, 1998.

Palmer, William J. *Dickens and New Historicism.* New York: St. Martin's, 1997.

Panagopoulos, Nic. *The Fiction of Joseph Conrad: The Influence of Schopenhauer and Nietzsche.* Frankfurt: Peter Lang, 1998.

Parker, Jo Alyson. *The Author's Inheritance: Henry Fielding, Jane Austen, and the Establishment of the Novel.* DeKalb: Northern Illinois University Press, 1998.

Parker, Todd C. *Sexing the Text: The Rhetoric of Sexual Difference in British Literature, 1700–1750.* Albany: State University of New York Press, 2000.

Pask, Kevin. *The Emergence of the English Author: Scripting the Life of the Poet in Early Modern England.* Cambridge: Cambridge University Press, 1996.

Patey, Douglas Lane. *The Life of Evelyn Waugh: A Critical Biography.* Oxford (UK) and Cambridge (MA): Blackwell, 1998.

Patteson, Richard F. *Caribbean Passages: A Critical Perspective on New Fiction from the West Indies.* Boulder (CO) and London: Lynne Rienner Publishers, 1998.

Paulson, Ronald. *The Life of Henry Fielding: A Critical Biography.* Oxford and Malden (MA): Blackwell, 2000.

Paulson, Ronald. *The Beautiful, Novel, and Strange: Aesthetics and Heterodoxy.* Baltimore (MD) and London: Johns Hopkins University Press, 1996.

Peach, Linden. *Virginia Woolf.* New York: St. Martin's, 2000.

Pearce, Joseph. *Literary Converts: Spiritual Inspiration in an Age of Unbelief.* London: HarperCollins, 1999.

Pearce, Joseph. *Tolkien: Man and Myth.* London: HarperCollins, 1998.

Pearson, Jacqueline. *Women's Reading in Britain, 1750–1835: A Dangerous Recreation.* Cambridge: Cambridge University Press, 1999.

Pearson, Richard. *W. M. Thackeray and the Mediated Text: Writing for Periodicals in the Mid-Nineteenth Century.* Aldershot (UK): Ashgate, 2000.

Pease, Allison. *Modernism, Mass Culture, and the Aesthetics of Obscenity.* Cambridge: Cambridge University Press, 2000.

Peck, John. *Maritime Fiction: Sailors and the Sea in British and American Novels, 1719–1917.* New York: Palgrave, 2001.

Peck, John. *War, the Army and Victorian Literature.* London: Macmillan; New York: St. Martin's, 1998.

Peer, Larry H., ed. *Romanticism Across the Disciplines.* Lanham, MD: University Press of America, 1998.

Peppis, Paul. *Literature, Politics, and the English Avant-Garde: Nation and Empire, 1901–1918.* Cambridge: Cambridge University Press, 2000.

Perkins, Moreland. *Reshaping the Sexes in "Sense and Sensibility."* Charlottesville: University Press of Virginia, 1998.

Perrakis, Phyllis Sternberg, ed. *Spiritual Exploration in the Works of Doris Lessing.* Westport (CT) and London: Greenwood Press, 1999.

Perrin, Noel. *A Child's Delight.* Hanover (NH) and London: University Press of New England, 1997.

Peters, John G. *Conrad and Impressionism.* Cambridge: Cambridge University Press, 2001.

Peters, Sally. *Bernard Shaw: The Ascent of the Superman.* New Haven (CT) and London: Yale University Press, 1996.

Pettit, Charles P. C. *Reading Thomas Hardy.* London: Macmillan; New York: St. Martin's, 1998.

Pfister, Manfred, and Barbara Schaff, eds. *Venetian Views, Venetian Blinds: English Fantasies of Venice.* Amsterdam: Rodopi, 1999.

Philips, Deborah, and Ian Haywood. *Brave New Causes: Women in British Postwar Fictions.* London and Washington (DC): Leicester University Press, 1998.

Phillips, Richard. *Mapping Men and Empire: A Geography of Adventure.* London and New York: Routledge, 1997.

Pickering, Jean, and Suzanne Kehde, eds. *Narratives of Nostalgia, Gender, and Nationalism.* Washington Square: New York University Press, 1997.

Pierce, David, and Peter de Voogd, eds. *Laurence Sterne in Modernism and Postmodernism.* Amsterdam and Atlanta (GA): Rodopi, 1996.

Pilling, John. *Beckett before Godot.* Cambridge: Cambridge University Press, 1997.

Pinkney, Tony, Keith Hanley, and Fred Botting, eds. *Romantic Masculinities.* Keele (UK): Keele University Press, 1997.

Piper, William Bowman. *Common Courtesy in Eighteenth-Century English Literature.* Newark: University of Delaware Press; London: Associated University Presses, 1997.

Piper, William Bowman. *Reconcilable Differences in Eighteenth-Century English Literature.* Newark: University of Delaware Press; London: Associated University Presses, 1999.

Plasa, Carl. *Textual Politics from Slavery to Postcolonialism: Race and Identification.* London: Macmillan; New York: St. Martin's, 2000.

Plasa, Carl, and Betty J. Ring, eds. *The Discourse of Slavery: Aphra Behn to Toni Morrison.* London and New York: Routledge, 1994.

Platt, Len. *Joyce and the Anglo-Irish: A Study of Joyce and the Literary Revival.* Amsterdam and Atlanta (GA): Rodopi, 1998.

Plotz, John. *The Crowd: British Literature and Public Politics.* Berkeley: University of California Press, 2000.

Polloczek, Dieter Paul. *Literature and Legal Discourse: Equity and Ethics from Sterne to Conrad.* Cambridge: Cambridge University Press, 1999.

Pool, Daniel. *Dickens' Fur Coat and Charlotte's Unanswered Letters: The Rows and Romances of England's Great Victorian Novelists.* New York: HarperCollins, 1997.

Posner, Richard A. *Law and Literature.* Rev. and enl. ed. Cambridge (MA) and London: Harvard University Press, 1998.

Potter, Tiffany. *Honest Sins: Georgian Libertinism and the Plays and Novels of Henry Fielding.* Montreal and Kingston: McGill-Queen's University Press, 1999.

Potts, Willard. *Joyce and the Two Irelands.* Austin: University of Texas Press, 2000.

Prawer, S. S. *Breeches and Metaphysics: Thackeray's German Discourse.* Oxford: Legenda, 1997.

Prendergast, Maria Teresa Micaela. *Renaissance Fantasies: The Gendering of Aesthetics in Early Modern Fiction.* Kent (OH) and London: Kent State University Press, 1999.

Pressler, Christopher. *So Far So Linear: Responses to the Work of Jeanette Winterson.* 2nd ed. Nottingham (UK): Paupers' Press, 2000.

Price, Leah. *The Anthology and the Rise of the Novel: From Richardson to George Eliot.* Cambridge: Cambridge University Press, 2000.

Prier, Raymond A., and Gerald Gillespie, eds. *Narrative Ironies.* Amsterdam and Atlanta (GA): Rodopi, 1997.

Prusse, Michael C. *"Tomorrow is Another Day": The Fictions of James Gordon Farrell.* Tübingen: Francke Verlag, 1997.

Pultar, Gönül. *Technique and Tradition in Beckett's Trilogy of Novels.* Lanham, MD: University Press of America, 1996.

Pykett, Lyn. *Engendering Fictions: The English Novel in the Early Twentieth Century.* London: Edward Arnold, 1995.

Pykett, Lyn, ed. *Wilkie Collins.* New York: St. Martin's, 1998.

Pyrhönen, Heta. *Mayhem and Murder: Narrative and Moral Problems in the Detective Story.* Toronto: University of Toronto Press, 1999.

Quayson, Ato. *Postcolonialism: Theory, Practice or Process?* Cambridge: Polity Press, 2000.

Quéma, Anne. *The Agon of Modernism: Wyndham Lewis's Allegories, Aesthetics, and Politics.* Lewisburg, PA: Bucknell University Press; London: Associated University Presses, 1999.

Quinn, Patrick J., ed. *New Perspectives on Robert Graves.* Selinsgrove, PA: Susquehanna University Press; London: Associated University Presses, 1999.

Quintelli-Neary, Marguerite. *Folklore and the Fantastic in Twelve Modern Irish Novels.* Westport (CT) and London: Greenwood Press, 1997.

Raby, Peter, ed. *The Cambridge Companion to Oscar Wilde.* Cambridge: Cambridge University Press, 1997.

Rado, Lisa. *The Modern Androgyne Imagination: A Failed Sublime.* Charlottesville and London: University Press of Virginia, 2000.

Raitt, Suzanne. *May Sinclair: A Modern Victorian.* Oxford: Clarendon, 2000.

Raitt, Suzanne, and Trudi Tate, eds. *Women's Fiction and the Great War.* Oxford: Clarendon, 1997.

Rajan, Balachandra. *Under Western Eyes: India from Milton to Macaulay.* Durham (NC) and London: Duke University Press, 1999.

Randall, Don. *Kipling's Imperial Boy: Adolescence and Cultural Hybridity.* New York: Palgrave, 2000.

Rauch, Alan. *Useful Knowledge: The Victorians, Morality, and the March of Intellect.* Durham (NC) and London: Duke University Press, 2001.

Rawlinson, Mark. *British Writing of the Second World War.* Oxford: Clarendon, 2000.

Rawson, Claude. *Satire and Sentiment, 1660–1830.* Cambridge: Cambridge University Press, 1994.

Reder, Michael R., ed. *Conversations with Salman Rushdie.* Jackson: University Press of Mississippi, 2000.

Redfield, Marc. *Phantom Formations: Aesthetic Ideology and the "Bildungsroman."* Ithaca (NY) and London: Cornell University Press, 1996.

Reichertz, Ronald. *The Making of the Alice Books: Lewis Carroll's Uses of Earlier Children's Literature.* Montreal and Kingston: McGill-Queen's University Press, 1997.

Reid, Robin Anne. *Arthur C. Clarke: A Critical Companion.* Westport (CT) and London: Greenwood Press, 1997.

Reif-Hulser, Monika, ed. *Borderlands: Negotiating Boundaries in Post-Colonial Writing.* Amsterdam: Rodopi, 1999.

Reinfandt, Christoph. *Der Sinn der fiktionalen Wirklichkeiten: Ein systemtheoretischer Entwurf zur Ausdifferenzierung des englischen Romans vom 18. Jahrhundert bis zur Gegenwart.* Heidelberg: Universitätsverlag C. Winter, 1997.

Reizbaum, Mailyn. *James Joyce's Judaic Other.* Stanford, CA: Stanford University Press, 1999.

Relihan, Constance C. *Framing Elizabethan Fictions: Contemporary Approaches to Early Modern Narrative Prose.* Kent (OH) and London: Kent State University Press, 1996.

Rhodes, Neil, ed. *English Renaissance Prose: History, Language, and*

Politics. Tempe, AZ: Medieval & Renaissance Texts & Studies (Arizona State University), 1997.

Ribeiro, Alvaro, and James G. Basker, eds. *Tradition in Transition: Women Writers, Marginal Texts, and the Eighteenth-Century Canon*. Oxford: Clarendon, 1996.

Richardson, Angelique, and Chris Willis, eds. *The New Woman in Fiction and in Fact: Fin-de-Siècle Feminisms*. New York: Palgrave, 2001.

Richardson, Brian. *Unlikely Stories: Causality and the Nature of Modern Narrative*. Newark: University of Delaware Press; London: Associated University Presses, 1997.

Richetti, John, ed. *The Cambridge Companion to the Eighteenth-Century Novel*. Cambridge: Cambridge University Press, 1996.

Richetti, John. *The English Novel in History, 1700–1780*. London and New York: Routledge, 1999.

Richter, David H., ed. *Ideology and Form in Eighteenth-Century Literature*. Lubbock: Texas Tech University Press, 1999.

Rickard, John S. *Joyce's Book of Memory: The Mnemotechnic of "Ulysses."* Durham (NC) and London: Duke University Press, 1999.

Ricketts, Harry. *The Unforgiving Minute: A Life of Rudyard Kipling*. London: Chatto and Windus, 1999.

Rigney, Ann. *Imperfect Histories: The Elusive Past and the Legacy of Romantic Historicism*. Ithaca (NY) and London: Cornell University Press, 2001.

Rimmon-Kenan, Shlomith, Leone Toker, and Shuli Barzilai, eds. *Rereading Texts / Rethinking Critical Presuppositions: Essays in Honour of H. M. Daleski*. Frankfurt: Peter Lang, 1997.

Riquelme, John Paul, ed. *"Tess of the d'Urbervilles": Complete, Authoritative Text with Biographical and Historical Contexts, Critical History, and Essays from Five Contemporary Critical Perspectives*. Boston: Bedford Books, 1998.

Rivero, Albert J., ed. *Augustan Subjects: Essays in Honor of Martin C. Battestin*. Newark: University of Delaware Press; London: Associated University Presses, 1997.

Robbins, Ruth, and Julian Wolfreys, eds. *Victorian Identities: Social and Cultural Formations in Nineteeenth-Century Literature*. London: Macmillan; New York: St. Martin's, 1996.

Roberts, Andrew Michael. *Conrad and Masculinity*. London: Macmillan; New York: St. Martin's, 2000.

Roberts, Nancy. *Schools of Sympathy: Gender and Identification through the Novel*. Montreal and Kingston: McGill-Queen's University Press, 1997.

Roberts, Neil. *Meredith and the Novel*. London: Macmillan; New York: St. Martin's, 1997.

Robson, Catherine. *Men in Wonderland: The Lost Girlhood of the Victorian Gentleman*. Princeton (NJ) and Oxford: Princeton University Press, 2001.

Röder-Bolton, Gerlinde. *George Eliot and Goethe: An Elective Affinity*. Amsterdam and Atlanta (GA): Rodopi, 1998.

Roe, Sue, and Susan Sellers, eds. *The Cambridge Companion to Virginia Woolf*. Cambridge: Cambridge University Press, 2000.

Rollin, Lucy, and Mark I. West. *Psychoanalytic Responses to Children's Literature*. Jefferson (NC) and London: McFarland and Co., 1999.

Rommerskirchen, Barbara. *Constructing Reality: Constructivism and Narration in John Fowles's "The Magus."* Frankfurt: Peter Lang, 1999.

Rose, Jacqueline. *States of Fantasy*. Oxford: Clarendon, 1996.

Rosenbaum, S. P. *Aspects of Bloomsbury: Studies in Modern English Literary and Intellectual History*. London: Macmillan; New York: St. Martin's, 1998.

Rosenfeld, Natania. *Outsiders Together: Virginia and Leonard Woolf*. Princeton, NJ: Princeton University Press, 2000.

Rosengarten, Richard A. *Henry Fielding and the Narration of Providence: Divine Design and the Incursions of Evil*. New York: Palgrave, 2000.

Ross, Ian Campbell. *Laurence Sterne: A Life*. Oxford and New York: Oxford University Press, 2001.

Roston, Murray. *Modernist Patterns in Literature and the Visual Arts*. Washington Square: New York University Press, 2000.

Roughley, Alan. *Reading Derrida Reading Joyce*. Gainesville: University Press of Florida, 1999.

Rowland, Antony, Emma Liggins, and Eriks Uskalis, eds. *Signs of Masculinity: Men in Literature 1700 to the Present*. Amsterdam and Atlanta (GA): Rodopi, 1998.

Rowland, Susan. *From Agatha Christie to Ruth Rendell: British Women Writers in Detective and Crime Fiction*. New York: Palgrave, 2001.

Roy, Parama. *Indian Traffic: Identities in Question in Colonial and Postcolonial India*. Berkeley: University of California Press, 1998.

Rudd, David. *Enid Blyton and the Mystery of Children's Literature*. London: Macmillan; New York: St. Martin's, 2000.

Ruderman, Anne Crippen. *The Pleasures of Virtue: Political Thought in the Novels of Jane Austen*. Lanham (MD) and London: Rowman and Littlefield, 1995.

Runge, Laura L. *Gender and Language in British Literary Criticism, 1660–1790*. Cambridge: Cambridge University Press, 1997.

St. John, Michael, ed. *Romancing Decay: Ideas of Decadence in European Culture*. Aldershot (UK): Ashgate, 1999.

St. Peter, Christine. *Changing Ireland: Strategies in Contemporary Women's Fiction*. London: Macmillan; New York: St. Martin's, 2000.

Sammells, Neil. *Wilde Style: The Plays and Prose of Oscar Wilde*. Harlow (UK): Pearson Education/Longman, 2000.

Sammons, Martha C. *"A Far-Off Country": A Guide to C. S. Lewis's Fantasy Fiction*. Lanham, MD: University Press of America, 2000.

Samuels, Robert. *Writing Prejudices: The Psychoanalysis and Pedagogy of Discrimination from Shakespeare to Toni Morrison*. Albany: State University of New York Press, 2001.

Sanders, Andrew. *Dickens and the Spirit of the Age*. Oxford: Clarendon, 1999.

Sandner, David. *The Fantastic Sublime: Romanticism and Transcendence in Nineteenth-Century Children's Fantasy Literature*. Westport (CT) and London: Greenwood Press, 1996.

Santoro-Brienza, Liberato, ed. *Talking of Joyce*. Dublin: University College Dublin Press, 1998.

Sargent, M. Elizabeth, and Garry Watson, eds. *Approaches to Teaching the Works of D. H. Lawrence*. New York: Modern Language Association of America, 2001.

Saunders, Corinne. *Rape and Ravishment in the Literature of Medieval England*. Cambridge: D. S. Brewer, 2001.

Savory, Elaine. *Jean Rhys*. Cambridge: Cambridge University Press, 1998.

Saxton, Kirsten T., and Rebecca P. Bocchicchio, eds. *The Passionate Fictions of Eliza Haywood: Essays on Her Life and Work*. Lexington: University Press of Kentucky, 2000.

Scanlan, Margaret. *Plotting Terror: Novelists and Terrorists in Contemporary Fiction*. Charlottesville and London: University Press of Virginia, 2001.

Scarpetta, Guy. *L'âge d'or du roman*. Paris: Bernard Grasset, 1996.

Sceats, Sarah. *Food, Consumption and the Body in Contemporary Women's Fiction*. Cambridge: Cambridge University Press, 2000.

Schaffer, Talia. *The Forgotten Female Aesthetes: Literary Culture in Late-Victorian England*. Charlottesville and London: University Press of Virginia, 2000.

Schaffer, Talia, and Kathy Alexis Psomiades, eds. *Women and British Aestheticism*. Charlottesville and London: University Press of Virginia, 1999.

Schäffner, Raimund. *Anarchismus und Literatur in England: Von der Französischen Revolution bis zum Ersten Weltkrieg*. Heidelberg: Universitätsverlag C. Winter, 1997.

Schapiro, Barbara Ann. *D. H. Lawrence and the Paradoxes of Psychic Life*. Albany: State University of New York Press, 1999.

Schmitt, Cannon. *Alien Nation: Nineteenth-Century Gothic Fictions and English Nationality*. Philadelphia: University of Pennsylvania Press, 1997.

Schoene-Harwood, Berthold, ed. *Mary Shelley: "Frankenstein."* New York: Columbia University Press, 2000.

Schor, Hilary M. *Dickens and the Daughter of the House*. Cambridge: Cambridge University Press, 1999.

Schramm, Jan-Melissa. *Testimony and Advocacy in Victorian Law, Literature, and Theology*. Cambridge: Cambridge University Press, 2000.

Schwaber, Paul. *The Cast of Characters: A Reading of "Ulysses."* New Haven (CT) and London: Yale University Press, 1999.

Schwarz, Daniel R. *Rereading Conrad*. Columbia and London: University of Missouri Press, 2001.

Schwarz, Kathryn. *Tough Love: Amazon Encounters in the English Renaissance*. Durham (NC) and London: Duke University Press, 2000.

Schweitzer, Darrell, ed. *Discovering Classic Fantasy Fiction: Essays on the Antecedents of Fantastic Literature*. San Bernardino, CA: Borgo Press, 1996.

Schwenger, Peter. *Fantasm and Fiction: On Textual Envisioning*. Stanford, CA: Stanford University Press, 1999.

Sedgwick, Eve Kosofsky, ed. *Novel Gazing: Queer Readings in Fiction*. Durham (NC) and London: Duke University Press, 1997.

Seeber, Barbara K. *General Consent in Jane Austen: A Study of Dialogism*. Montreal and Kingston: McGill-Queen's University Press, 2000.

Seed, David, ed. *Imagining Apocalypse: Studies in Cultural Crisis.* London: Macmillan; New York: St. Martin's, 2000.

Shaffer, Brian W. *Understanding Kazuo Ishiguro.* Columbia: University of South Carolina Press, 1998.

Shankar, S. *Textual Traffic: Colonialism, Modernity, and the Economy of the Text.* Albany: State University of New York Press, 2001.

Sharpe, Kevin, and Steven N. Zwicker, eds. *Refiguring Revolutions: Aesthetics and Politics from the English Revolution to the Romantic Revolution.* Berkeley: University of California Press, 1998.

Shaw, Debra Benita. *Women, Science and Fiction: The "Frankenstein" Inheritance.* New York: Palgrave, 2000.

Shaw, Harry E. *Narrating Reality: Austen, Scott, Eliot.* Ithaca (NY) and London: Cornell University Press, 1999.

Sheffield, Elisabeth. *Joyce's Abandoned Female Costumes, Gratefully Received.* Madison and Teaneck, NJ: Fairleigh Dickinson University Press; London: Associated University Presses, 1998.

Sherman, Sandra. *Finance and Fictionality in the Early Eighteenth Century: Accounting for Defoe.* Cambridge: Cambridge University Press, 1996.

Shillingsburg, Peter. *William Makepeace Thackeray: A Literary Life.* New York: Palgrave, 2001.

Shuman, Cathy. *Pedagogical Economies: The Examination and the Victorian Literary Man.* Stanford, CA: Stanford University Press, 2000.

Shuter, William F. *Rereading Walter Pater.* Cambridge: Cambridge University Press, 1997.

Sillars, Stuart. *Structure and Dissolution in English Writing, 1910–1920.* London: Macmillan; New York: St. Martin's, 1999.

Sim, Stuart, and David Walker. *Bunyan and Authority: The Rhetoric of Dissent and the Legitimation Crisis in Seventeenth-Century England.* Bern: Peter Lang, 2000.

Simmons, Clare A. *Eyes Across the Channel: French Revolutions, Party History and British Writing, 1830–1882.* Amsterdam: Harwood Academic Publishers, 2000.

Simons, Judy, and Kate Fullbrook, eds. *Writing: A Woman's Business— Women, Writing and the Marketplace.* Manchester and New York: Manchester University Press, 1998.

Simpson, Margaret. *The Companion to "Hard Times."* Westport, CT: Greenwood Press, 1997.

Sisk, David W. *Transformations of Language in Modern Dystopias.* Westport (CT) and London: Greenwood Press, 1997.

Skinner, Gillian. *Sensibility and Economics in the Novel, 1740–1800: The Price of a Tear.* London: Macmillan; New York: St. Martin's, 1999.

Skinner, John. *The Stepmother Tongue: An Introduction to New Anglophone Fiction.* New York: St. Martin's, 1998.

Slater, Michael. *An Intelligent Person's Guide to Dickens.* London: Duckworth, 1999.

Slote, Sam, and Wim van Mierlo, eds. *Genitricksling Joyce.* Amsterdam and Atlanta (GA): Rodopi, 1999. (European Joyce Studies 9.)

Smith, Andrew. *Gothic Radicalism: Literature, Philosophy and Psychoanalysis in the Nineteenth Century.* London: Macmillan; New York: St. Martin's, 2000.

Smith, Andrew, and Jeff Wallace, eds. *Gothic Modernisms*. New York: Palgrave, 2001.

Smith, Barbara, and Ursula Appelt, eds. *Write or Be Written: Early Modern Women Poets and Cultural Constraints*. Aldershot (UK) and Burlington (VT): Ashgate, 2001.

Smith, Elton E., and Robert Haas, eds. *The Haunted Mind: The Supernatural in Victorian Literature*. Lanham, MD: Scarecrow Press, 1999.

Smith, Grahame. *Charles Dickens: A Literary Life*. New York: St. Martin's, 1996.

Smith, Patricia Juliana. *Lesbian Panic: Homoeroticism in Modern British Women's Fiction*. New York: Columbia University Press, 1997.

Smyth, Gerry. *The Novel and the Nation: Studies in the New Irish Fiction*. London and Chicago: Pluto Press, 1997.

Snader, Joe. *Caught Between Worlds: British Captivity Narratives in Fact and Fiction*. Lexington: University Press of Kentucky, 2000.

Snaith, Anna. *Virginia Woolf: Public and Private Negotiations*. London: Macmillan; New York: St. Martin's, 2000.

Snell, K. D. M., ed. *The Regional Novel in Britain and Ireland, 1800–1990*. Cambridge: Cambridge University Press, 1998.

Sorensen, Janet. *The Grammar of Empire in Eighteenth-Century British Writing*. Cambridge: Cambridge University Press, 2000.

Spaas, Lieve, and Brian Stimpson, eds. *Robinson Crusoe: Myths and Metamorphoses*. London: Macmillan; New York: St. Martin's, 1996.

Spargo, Tamsin. *The Writing of John Bunyan*. Aldershot (UK): Ashgate, 1997.

Spear, Hilda D., ed. *George Mackay Brown: A Survey of His Work and a Full Bibliography*. Lewiston, NY: Edwin Mellen Press, 2000.

Spencer, Jane. *Aphra Behn's Afterlife*. Oxford and New York: Oxford University Press, 2000.

Spinks, C. W., and John Deely, eds. *Semiotics 1998*. New York: Peter Lang, 1999.

Spinks, C. W., and John Deely, eds. *Semiotics 1997*. New York: Peter Lang, 1998.

Spinks, C. W., and John Deely, eds. *Semiotics 1996*. New York: Peter Lang, 1996.

Spivack, Charlotte, and Roberta Lynne Staples. *The Company of Camelot: Arthurian Characters in Romance and Fantasy*. Westport (CT) and London: Greenwood Press, 1994.

Sprechman, Ellen Lew. *Seeing Women as Men: Role Reversal in the Novels of Thomas Hardy*. Lanham, MD: University Press of America, 1995.

Squillace, Robert. *Modernism, Modernity, and Arnold Bennett*. Lewisburg, PA: Bucknell University Press; London: Associated University Presses, 1997.

Stanton, Michael N. *Hobbits, Elves and Wizards: The Wonders and Worlds of J. R. R. Tolkien's "Lord of the Rings."* New York: Palgrave, 2001.

Stark, Susanne, ed. *The Novel in Anglo-German Context: Cultural Cross-Currents and Affinities — Papers from the Conference held at the University of Leeds from 15 to 17 September 1997*. Amsterdam and Atlanta (GA): Rodopi, 2000.

Sternlicht, Sanford. *C. S. Forester and the Hornblower Saga*. Rev. ed. Syracuse, NY: Syracuse University Press, 1999.

Sternlicht, Sanford. *Stephen Spender*. New York: Twayne, 1992.

Stewart, Bruce, ed. *Beckett and Beyond*. Gerrards Cross (UK): Colin Smythe, 1999.

Stewart, Jack. *The Vital Art of D. H. Lawrence: Vision and Expression*. Carbondale and Edwardsville: Southern Illinois University Press, 1999.

Stitt, Megan Perigoe. *Metaphors of Change in the Language of Nineteenth-Century Fiction: Scott, Gaskell, and Kingsley*. Oxford: Clarendon, 1998.

Stoneman, Patsy. *Emily Brontë: "Wuthering Heights."* New York: Columbia University Press, 1998.

Stubbings, Diane. *Anglo-Irish Modernism and the Maternal*. New York: Palgrave, 2000.

Stummer, Peter O., and Christopher Balme, eds. *Fusion of Cultures?* Amsterdam and Atlanta (GA): Rodopi, 1996.

Sullivan, Ceri, and Barbara White, eds. *Writing and Fantasy*. London and New York: Longman, 1999.

Sullivan, Megan. *Women in Northern Ireland: Cultural Studies and Material Conditions*. Gainesville: University Press of Florida, 1999.

Summers, Claude J., and Ted-Larry Pebworth, eds. *Representing Women in Renaissance England*. Columbia and London: University of Missouri Press, 1997.

Sumner, Rosemary. *A Route to Modernism: Hardy, Lawrence, Woolf*. London: Macmillan; New York: St. Martin's, 2000.

Sundmark, Björn. *Alice's Adventures in the Oral-Literary Continuum*. Lund (Sweden): Lund University Press, 1999.

Sussman, Henry, and Christopher Devenney, eds. *Engagement and Indifference: Beckett and the Political*. Albany: State University of New York Press, 2001.

Sutherland, John. *Who Betrays Elizabeth Bennet? Further Puzzles in Classic Fiction*. Oxford and New York: Oxford University Press, 1999.

Svogun, Margaret duMais. *Reading Romance: Literacy, Psychology, and Malory's "Le Morte D'Arthur."* New York: Peter Lang, 2000.

Swan, Beth. *Fictions of Law: Investigation of the Law in Eighteenth-Century English Fiction*. Frankfurt: Peter Lang, 1997.

Swinden, Patrick. *Literature and the Philosophy of Intention*. London: Macmillan; New York: St. Martin's, 1999.

Swisher, Clarice, ed. *Readings on "Lord of the Flies."* San Diego, CA: Greenhaven, 1997.

Taavitsainen, Irma, Gunnel Melchers, and Päivi Pahta, eds. *Writing in Nonstandard English*. Amsterdam and Philadelphia (PA): John Benjamins, 1999.

Tate, Trudi. *Modernism, History and the First World War*. Manchester and New York: Manchester University Press, 1998.

Taylor, John A. *Popular Literature and the Construction of British National Identity, 1707–1850*. San Francisco: International Scholars Publications, 1997.

Teachman, Debra. *Student Companion to Jane Austen*. Westport (CT) and London: Greenwood Press, 2000.

Teachman, Debra. *Understanding "Pride and Prejudice": A Student Casebook to Issues, Sources, and Historical Documents.* Westport (CT) and London: Greenwood Press, 1997.

Thaddeus, Janice Farrar. *Frances Burney: A Literary Life.* London: Macmillan; New York: St. Martin's, 2000.

Thaden, Barbara Z. *The Maternal Voice in Victorian Fiction: Rewriting the Patriarchal Family.* New York and London: Garland Publishing, 1997.

Thomas, Deborah A. *"Hard Times": A Fable of Fragmentation and Wholeness.* New York: Twayne; London: Prentice Hall International, 1997.

Thomas, Jane. *Thomas Hardy, Femininity and Dissent: Reassessing the 'Minor' Novels.* London: Macmillan; New York: St. Martin's, 1999.

Thomas, Ronald R. *Detective Fiction and the Rise of Forensic Science.* Cambridge: Cambridge University Press, 1999.

Thompson, Andrew. *George Eliot and Italy: Literary, Cultural and Political Influences from Dante to the "Risorgimento."* London: Macmillan; New York: St. Martin's, 1998.

Thompson, James. *Models of Value: Eighteenth-Century Political Economy and the Novel.* Durham (NC) and London: Duke University Press, 1996.

Thompson, Lynda M. *The 'Scandalous Memoirists': Constantia Phillips, Laetitia Pilkington and the Shame of 'Publick Fame.'* Manchester and New York: Manchester University Press, 2000.

Thompson, Nicola Diane. *Reviewing Sex: Gender and the Reception of Victorian Novels.* Washington Square: New York University Press, 1996.

Thompson, Nicola Diane, ed. *Victorian Women Writers and the Woman Question.* Cambridge: Cambridge University Press, 1999.

Thoms, Peter. *Detection and Its Designs: Narrative and Power in 19th-Century Detective Fiction.* Athens: Ohio University Press, 1998.

Thormählen, Marianne. *The Brontës and Religion.* Cambridge: Cambridge University Press, 1999.

Thornton, Weldon. *Voices and Values in Joyce's "Ulysses."* Gainesville: University Press of Florida, 2000.

Tigges, Wim, ed. *Moments of Moment: Aspects of the Literary Epiphany.* Amsterdam and Atlanta (GA): Rodopi, 1999.

Tindall, William York. *A Reader's Guide to "Finnegans Wake."* Syracuse, NY: Syracuse University Press, 1996.

Todd, Janet, ed. *Aphra Behn Studies.* Cambridge: Cambridge University Press, 1996.

Todd, Janet. *The Critical Fortunes of Aphra Behn.* Columbia, SC: Camden House, 1998.

Todd, Janet. *Mary Wollstonecraft: A Revolutionary Life.* New York: Columbia University Press, 2000.

Todd, Richard, and Luisa Flora, eds. *Theme Parks, Rainforests and Sprouting Wastelands: European Essays on Theory and Performance in Contemporary British Fiction.* Amsterdam and Atlanta (GA): Rodopi, 2000.

Toker, Leona, ed. *Commitment in Reflection: Essays in Literature and Moral Philosophy.* New York and London: Garland Publishing, 1994.

Tomalin, Claire. *Jane Austen: A Life*. New York: Knopf, 1997.

Touret, Michèle, ed. *Lectures de Beckett*. Rennes (France): Presses Universitaires de Rennes, 1998.

Tracy, Robert. *The Unappeasable Host: Studies in Irish Identities*. Dublin: University College Dublin Press, 1998.

Traub, Valerie, M. Lindsay Kaplan, and Dympna Callaghan, eds. *Feminist Readings of Early Modern Culture: Emerging Subjects*. Cambridge: Cambridge University Press, 1996.

Tredell, Nicolas, ed. *Charles Dickens: "Great Expectations."* New York: Columbia University Press, 2000.

Treglown, Jeremy. *Romancing: The Life and Work of Henry Green*. New York: Random House, 2000.

Treichler, Paula A., Lisa Cartwright, and Constance Penley, eds. *The Visible Woman: Imaging Technologies, Gender, and Science*. New York and London: New York University Press, 1998.

Tremper, Ellen. *"Who Lived at Alfoxton?" Virginia Woolf and English Romanticism*. Lewisburg, PA: Bucknell University Press; London: Associated University Presses, 1998.

Trezise, Simon. *The West Country as a Literary Invention: Putting Fiction In Its Place*. Exeter (UK): University of Exeter Press, 2000.

Trodd, Anthea. *Women's Writing in English: Britain, 1900–1945*. London and New York: Longman, 1998.

Tromp, Marlene. *The Private Rod: Marital Violence, Sensation, and the Law in Victorian Britain*. Charlottesville and London: University Press of Virginia, 2000.

Tromp, Marlene, Pamela K. Gilbert, and Aeron Haynie, eds. *Beyond Sensation: Mary Elizabeth Braddon in Context*. Albany: State University of New York Press, 2000.

Troost, Linda, and Sayre Greenfield, eds. *Jane Austen in Hollywood*. Lexington: University Press of Kentucky, 1998.

Truchlar, Leo. *Erinnerungslandschaften: Essays zur anglo-amerikanischen Literatur und andere Prosa*. Vienna: Böhlau Verlag, 1995.

Trumpener, Katie. *Bardic Nationalism: The Romantic Novel and the British Empire*. Princeton, NJ: Princeton University Press, 1997.

Tsagaris, Ellen M. *The Subversion of Romance in the Novels of Barbara Pym*. Bowling Green, OH: Bowling Green State University Popular Press, 1998.

Tsuchiya, Kiyoshi, ed. *Dissent and Marginality: Essays on the Borders of Literature and Religion*. London: Macmillan; New York: St. Martin's, 1997.

Tucker, Herbert F., ed. *A Companion to Victorian Literature and Culture*. Malden (MA) and Oxford: Blackwell, 1999.

Tucker, Irene. *A Probable State: The Novel, the Contract, and the Jews*. Chicago and London: University of Chicago Press, 2000.

Turnbull, Malcolm J. *Elusion Aforethought: The Life and Writing of Anthony Berkeley Cox*. Bowling Green, OH: Bowling Green State University Popular Press, 1996.

Turnbull, Malcolm J. *Victims or Villains: Jewish Images in Classic English Detective Fiction*. Bowling Green, OH: Bowling Green State University Popular Press, 1998.

Turner, Mark W. *Trollope and the Magazines: Gendered Issues in Mid-Victorian Britain*. London: Mcmillan; New York: St. Martin's, 2000.

Turner, Paul. *The Life of Thomas Hardy: A Critical Biography*. Oxford and Malden (MA): Blackwell, 1998.

Turney, Jon. *Frankenstein's Footsteps: Science, Genetics and Popular Culture*. New Haven (CT) and London: Yale University Press, 1998.

Ty, Eleanor. *Empowering the Feminine: The Narratives of Mary Robinson, Jane West, and Amelia Opie, 1796–1812*. Toronto: University of Toronto Press, 1998.

Uhlmann, Anthony. *Beckett and Poststructuralism*. Cambridge: Cambridge University Press, 1999.

Valente, Joseph, ed. *Quare Joyce*. Ann Arbor: University of Michigan Press, 1998.

Vanderham, Paul. *James Joyce and Censorship: The Trials of "Ulysses."* Washington Square: New York University Press, 1998.

Varney, Andrew. *Eighteenth-Century Writers in Their World: A Mighty Maze*. London: Macmillan; New York: St. Martin's, 1999.

Varty, Anne. *A Preface to Oscar Wilde*. London and New York: Longman, 1998.

Vice, Sue. *Holocaust Fiction*. London and New York: Routledge, 2000.

Vine, Steve. *Emily Brontë*. New York: Twayne; London: Prentice Hall International, 1998.

Vlock, Deborah. *Dickens, Novel Reading, and the Victorian Popular Theatre*. Cambridge: Cambridge University Press, 1998.

Wagenbaur, Thomas, ed. *The Poetics of Memory*. Tübingen: Stauffenburg Verlag, 1998.

Wagner-Lawlor, Jennifer A., ed. *The Victorian Comic Spirit: New Perspectives*. Aldershot (UK): Ashgate, 2000.

Wagstaff, Christopher, ed. *A Sacred Quest: The Life and Writings of Mary Butts*. Kingston, NY: McPherson & Co., 1995.

Wahl, Elizabeth Susan. *Invisible Relations: Representations of Female Intimacy in the Age of Enlightenment*. Stanford, CA: Stanford University Press, 1999.

Walder, Dennis, ed. *The Nineteenth-Century Novel: Identities*. London: Open University Press/Routledge, 2001.

Waldron, Mary. *Jane Austen and the Fiction of Her Time*. Cambridge: Cambridge University Press, 1999.

Walker, Marshall. *Scottish Literature since 1707*. London and New York: Longman, 1996.

Wall, Cynthia. *The Literary and Cultural Spaces of Restoration London*. Cambridge: Cambridge University Press, 1998.

Wallace, Diana. *Sisters and Rivals in British Women's Fiction, 1914–39*. London: Macmillan; New York: St. Martin's, 2000.

Walshe, Éibhear, ed. *Elizabeth Bowen Remembered: The Farahy Addresses*. Dublin and Portland (OR): Four Courts Press, 1998.

Walshe, Éibhear, ed. *Sex, Nation and Dissent in Irish Writing*. Cork (Ireland): Cork University Press, 1997.

Warren, Austin. *In Continuity: The Last Essays of Austin Warren*. Edited by George A. Panichas. Macon, GA: Mercer University Press, 1996.

Waterman, David F. *Disordered Bodies and Disrupted Borders:*

Representations of Resistance in Modern British Literature. Lanham, MD: University Press of America, 1999.

Waters, Catherine. *Dickens and the Politics of the Fa*mily. Cambridge: Cambridge University Press, 1997.

Watkins, Susan. *Twentieth-Century Women Novelists: Feminist Theory into Practice.* New York: Palgrave, 2001.

Watson, Jessica Lewis. *Bastardy as a Gifted Status in Chaucer and Malory.* Lewiston, NY: Edwin Mellen Press, 1996.

Watson, Nicola J. *Revolution and the Form of the British Novel, 1790–1825: Intercepted Letters, Interrupted Seductions.* Oxford: Clarendon, 1994.

Watson, Victor. *Reading Series Fiction: From Arthur Ransome to Gene Kemp.* London and New York: RoutledgeFalmer, 2000.

Watt, James. *Contesting the Gothic: Fiction, Genre and Cultural Conflict, 1764–1832.* Cambridge: Cambridge University Press, 1999.

Wawn, Andrew. *The Vikings and the Victorians: Inventing the Old North in Nineteenth-Century Britain.* Cambridge: D. S. Brewer, 2000.

Wawrzycka, Jolanta W., and Marlena G. Corcoran, eds. *Gender in Joyce.* Gainesville: University Press of Florida, 1997.

Weatherhead, A. K. *Upstairs: Writers and Residences.* Madison and Teaneck, NJ: Fairleigh Dickinson University Press; London: Associated University Presses, 2000.

Weaver, Jack W. *Joyce's Music and Noise: Theme and Variation in His Writings.* Gainesville: University Press of Florida, 1998.

Wechselblatt, Martin. *Bad Behavior: Samuel Johnson and Modern Cultural Authority.* Lewisburg, PA: Bucknell University Press; London: Associated University Presses, 1998.

Weisberg, David. *Chronicles of Disorder: Samuel Beckett and the Cultural Politics of the Modern Novel.* Albany: State University of New York Press, 2000.

Welsh, Alexander. *Dickens Redressed: The Art of "Bleak House" and "Hard Times."* New Haven (CT) and London: Yale University Press, 2000.

Werlock, Abby H. P., ed. *British Women Writing Fiction.* Tuscaloosa and London: University of Alabama Press, 2000.

Werner, Hans C. *Literary Texts as Nonlinear Patterns: A Chaotics Reading of "Rainforest," "Transparent Things," "Travesty," and "Tristram Shandy."* Göteborg: Acta Universitatis Gothoburgensis, 1999.

Wertheimer, Molly Meijer, ed. *Listening to Their Voices: The Rhetorical Activities of Historical Women.* Columbia: University of South Carolina Press, 1995.

White, Caramine. *Reading Roddy Doyle.* Syracuse, NY: Syracuse University Press, 2001.

Whitebrook, Maureen. *Identity, Narrative and Politics.* London and New York: Routledge, 2001.

Whitehead, John. *Eight Modern Masterpieces: Critical Essays.* Munslow (UK): Hearthstone, 1994.

Whitehouse, J. C. *Vertical Man: The Human Being in the Catholic Novels of Graham Greene, Sigrid Undset, and Georges Bernanos.* London: Saint Austin Press, 1999.

Wicht, Wolfgang. *Utopianism in James Joyce's "Ulysses."* Heidelberg: Universitätsverlag C. Winter, 2000.

Widdowson, Peter. *On Thomas Hardy: Late Essays and Earlier*. London: Macmillan; New York: St. Martin's, 1998.

Wiesenthal, Chris. *Figuring Madness in Nineteenth-Century Fiction*. London: Macmillan; New York: St. Martin's, 1997.

Wildt, Katherine Ann. *Elizabeth Gaskell's Use of Color in Her Industrial Novels and Short Stories*. Lanham, MD: University Press of America, 1999.

Williams, Andrew P., ed. *The Image of Manhood in Early Modern Literature*. Westport (CT) and London: Greenwood Press, 1999.

Williams, John. *Mary Shelley: A Literary Life*. London: Macmillan; New York: St. Martin's, 2000.

Williams, Keith, and Steven Matthews, eds. *Rewriting the Thirties: After Modernism*. London: Longman, 1997.

Wilson, Deborah S., and Christine Moneera Laennec, eds. *Bodily Discursions: Genders, Representations, Technologies*. Albany: State University of New York Press, 1997.

Wilson-Tagoe, Nana. *Historical Thought and Literary Representation in West Indian Literature*. Gainesville: University Press of Florida, 1998.

Winning, Joanne. *The Pilgrimage of Dorothy Richardson*. Madison: University of Wisconsin Press, 2000.

Wolf, Milton T., ed. *Shaw and Science Fiction*. University Park: Pennsylvania State University Press, 1997. (Vol. 17 of *SHAW: The Annual of Bernard Shaw Studies*.)

Wolfreys, Julian, ed. *"The Mayor of Casterbridge": Thomas Hardy*. London: Macmillan; New York: St. Martin's, 2000.

Wolpers, Theodor, ed. *Familienbildung als Schicksal: Wandlungen eines Motivbereichs in der neueren Literatur—Bericht über Kolloquien der Kommission für literaturwissenschaftliche Motiv- und Themenforschung, 1991–1994*. Göttingen: Vandenhoeck and Ruprecht, 1996.

Wood, Michael. *Children of Silence: On Contemporary Fiction*. New York: Columbia University Press, 1998.

Wood, Nigel, ed. *Jonathan Swift*. London and New York: Longman, 1999.

Woodard, Helena. *African-British Writings in the Eighteenth Century: The Politics of Race and Reason*. Westport (CT) and London: Greenwood Press, 1999.

Wordsworth, Jonathan. *The Bright Work Grows: Women Writers of the Romantic Age*. Poole (UK) and Washington (DC): Woodstock Books, 1997.

Wordsworth, Jonathan. *Visionary Gleam: Forty Books from the Romantic Period*. Poole (UK) and New York: Woodstock Books, 1996.

Wright, T. R. *D. H. Lawrence and the Bible*. Cambridge: Cambridge University Press, 2000.

Wu, Duncan, ed. *A Companion to Romanticism*. Oxford and Malden (MA): Blackwell, 1998.

Wulf, Catharina. *The Imperative of Narration: Beckett, Bernhard, Schopenhauer, Lacan*. Brighton (UK): Sussex Academic Press, 1997.

Wussow, Helen. *The Nightmare of History: The Fictions of Virginia Woolf and D. H. Lawrence*. Bethlehem, PA: Lehigh University Press; London: Associated University Presses, 1998.

Wykes, David. *Evelyn Waugh: A Literary Life*. London: Macmillan; New York: St. Martin's, 1999.

Wynne-Davies, Marion. *Women and Arthurian Literature: Seizing the Sword*. London: Macmillan; New York: St. Martin's, 1996.

York, R. A. *The Rules of Time: Time and Rhythm in the Twentieth-Century Novel*. Madison and Teaneck, NJ: Fairleigh Dickinson University Press; London: Associated University Presses, 1999.

Young, Arlene. *Culture, Class and Gender in the Victorian Novel: Gentlemen, Gents and Working Women*. London: Macmillan; New York: St. Martin's, 1999.

Young, Jane Jaffe. *D. H. Lawrence on Screen: Re-Visioning Prose Style in the Films of 'The Rocking Horse Winner,' "Sons and Lovers," and "Women in Love."* New York: Peter Lang, 1999.

Young, Robert J. C., Ban Kah Choon, and Robbie B. H. Goh, eds. *The Silent Word: Textual Meaning and the Unwritten*. Singapore: Singapore University Press and World Scientific Publishing, 1998.

Zilboorg, Caroline. *The Masks of Mary Renault: A Literary Biography*. Columbia and London: University of Missouri Press, 2001.

Zimmerman, Everett. *The Boundaries of Fiction: History and the Eighteenth-Century British Novel*. Ithaca (NY) and London: Cornell University Press, 1996.

Zimmerman, Phyllis. *Shelley's Fiction*. Los Angeles: Darami Press, 1998.

Zimmermann, Ralf. *Das Verschwinden der Wirklichkeit: Über Möglichkeiten und Grenzen der Kreativität in Flann O'Briens "At Swim-Two-Birds" und "The Third Policeman."* Frankfurt: Peter Lang, 1999.

Zlotnick, Susan. *Women, Writing, and the Industrial Revolution*. Baltimore (MD) and London: Johns Hopkins University Press, 1998.

Zonitch, Barbara. *Familiar Violence: Gender and Social Upheaval in the Novels of Frances Burney*. Newark: University of Delaware Press; London: Associated University Presses, 1997.

INDEX

Aaron's Rod, 295–96
The Abbot, 406
ABBOTT, EDWIN (1838–1926), 1
The ABC Murders, 101
The Absentee, 165
An Academic Question, 375
An Accidental Man, 354
ACKROYD, PETER (1949–),
   1–2
Adam Bede, 168–70
Adam's Breed, 228
ADAMS, DOUGLAS
   (1952–2001), 2
ADAMS, RICHARD (1920–), 2
Adela Cathcart, 326
*Adeline Mowbray; or, Mother and
   Daughter*, 365–66
Adnam's Orchard, 219
*The Advantages of Education; or,
   The History of Maria Williams*,
   474
The Adventures of Eovaai, 244–45
*The Adventures of Harry
   Richmond*, 343
The Adventures of Hugh Trevor,
   250
The Adventures of Master F. J.,
   204
*The Adventures of Mr. Verdant
   Green, an Oxford
   Undergraduate*, 62
The Adventures of Rivella, 338
Adventures of the Lady Lucy, 9
Affliction, see *Trouble*
The African Queen, 194
After Colette, 318

After Leaving Mr. Mackenzie,
   382–83
After London, or Wild England,
   259
After Purple, 371
After the Death of Don Juan, 464
Against a Dark Background, 29
An Age, see *Cryptozoic*
Agnes Grey, 63
AINSWORTH, WILLIAM HAR-
   RISON (1805–1882), 2
ALDINGTON, RICHARD
   (1892–1962), 3
ALDISS, BRIAN (1925–), 3–4
ALEXANDER, RUPERT
   (fl. 1890s), 4
The Alexandria Quartet, 163
Alice Fell, 448
Alice's Adventures in Wonderland,
   90–91
Alicia de Lacy, 474
All Sorts and Conditions of Man,
   54
ALLAN, DOT (1892–1964), 4
Allan Quartermain, 226
ALLEN, GRANT (1848–1899), 4
ALLINGHAM, MARGERY
   (1904–1966), 5
Almayer's Folly, 108–9
Alroy, 154
The Alteration, 5
Alton Locke, 288–89
Amalgamemnon, 75
The Amazing Marriage, 343
AMBLER, ERIC (1909–1998), 5
Amelia, 186–87

The American Senator, 456
AMIS, KINGSLEY (1922–1995),
    5–7
AMIS, KINGSLEY, and
    ROBERT CONQUEST
    (1917–), 7
AMIS, MARTIN (1949–), 7–8
Amongst Women, 329–30
AMORY, THOMAS
    (1691?–1788?), 8
The Ampersand, 108
Ancestral, see *Home Truths*
And the Wife Ran Away, 467
ANDERSON, LINDA (1949–),
    8
Ann Veronica, 469
Anna of the Five Towns, 50
*Anna: or Memoirs of a Welch
    Heiress*, 50
Anna St. Ives, 250
Annals of the Parish, 203
Anne Page, 447
ANNESLEY, JAMES
    (1715–1760), 8
Another Alice, 345
Another Time, Another Place, 288
The Anti-Death League, 5
The Antiquary, 406
Antonina, 104
Ape and Essence, 253
The Apes of God, 317
Appointment with Death, 101
Arcadia, 421–22
ARCHER, JEFFREY (1940–),
    8
ARLEN, MICHAEL
    (1895–1956), 9
Armadale, 104–5
Armed with Madness, 86
The Armourer's 'Prentices, 507
ARNIM, ELIZABETH VON
    (1866–1941), 9
ARNOLD, W. D. (1828–1859), 9
The Arrow of Gold, 109
Art and Lies, 481
The Artificial Princess, 192
An Artist of the Floating World,
    256
As for the Woman, 122
As Music and Splendour, 362

Ashe of Rings, 86–87
ASHTON, HELEN (1891–1958),
    9
Asses in Clover, 363
At Freddie's, 193
At Swim-Two-Birds, 361
At the Back of the North Wind,
    326
At the Villa Rose, 341
Athena, 30
ATKINSON, KATE
    (dates unavailable), 9
The Atrocity Exhibition, 27
AUBIN, PENELOPE
    (1685–1731?), 9–10
Audrey Craven, 423
Aurora Floyd, 59
AUSTEN, JANE (1775–1817),
    10–25
*The Autobiography of Mark
    Rutherford*, 476
The Avignon Quintet, 163–64
Awakening, see *Lilamani*
The Awkward Girl, 90
Ayala's Angel, 456
Ayesha, 226
The Aylwins, 437

Babel Tower, 87
Back, 221
The Backward Son, 430
Backwater, 385
The Bad Sister, 448
BAGE, ROBERT (1728–1801),
    25–26
BAGNOLD, ENID (1889–1981),
    26
BAILEY, PAUL (1937–), 26
BAINBRIDGE, BERYL
    (1933–), 26
BAINES, ELIZABETH
    (dates unavailable), 26
Balcony of Europe, 248
BALDWIN, WILLIAM
    (ca. 1515–1563), 26–27
The Ball and the Cross, 99
The Ballad and the Source, 307
The Ballad of Peckham Rye, 429
BALLANTYNE, ROBERT
    MICHAEL (1825–1894), 27

BALLARD, J. G. (1930–), 27–29
BALMFORTH, RAMSDEN
(1861–1941), 29
BANCROFT, EDWARD
(1744–1821), 29
The Banished Man, 424
BANKS, IAIN (1954–), 29–30
BANKS, LYNN REID (1929–),
30
BANVILLE, JOHN (1946–),
30–32
Barchester Towers, 456–57
BARDWELL, LELAND
(1928–), 32
*Barefoot in the Head: A European
Fantasia*, 3
Barham Downs, 25
BARING-GOULD, SABINE
(1834–1924), 32
BARKE, JAMES (1905–1953),
32–33
BARKER, ELSPETH (1940–),
33
BARKER, JANE (ca. 1675–1743),
33–34
BARKER, PAT (1943–), 34–35
Barnaby Rudge, 132
BARNES, JULIAN (1946–),
35–37
The Barracks, 330
BARRETT, EATON STAN-
NARD (1786–1820), 37
BARRIE, JAMES MATTHEW
(1860–1937), 37
BARSTOW, STAN (1928–), 37
Basil, 105
BATEMAN, COLIN (1962–), 38
Bath-Intrigues, 245
The Battle Lost and Won, 339
The Battle of Dorking, 99
BEARDSLEY, AUBREY
(1872–1898), 38
Beauchamp's Career, 343
BECKETT, MARY (1926–), 38
BECKETT, SAMUEL
(1906–1989), 38–46
BECKFORD, WILLIAM
(1760–1844), 46–47
BEDE, CUTHBERT, see
EDWARD BRADLEY

BEERBOHM, MAX
(1872–1956), 47
The Beetle, 341
Before She Met Me, 35
Before the Fact, 122
A Beginner, 77
The Beginning of Spring, 193
BEHAN, BRENDAN
(1923–1964), 47
Behind the Scenes at the Museum,
9
BEHN, APHRA (1640–1689),
47–50
A Beleaguered City, 363
Belinda, 165–66
Belinda the Backward, 249
The Bell, 354
BELLENDEN, FRANCES, see
SARAH GRAND
Belonging, 362
The Belton Estate, 457
Ben, in the World, 309
A Bend in the River, 356
Benita: An African Romance, 226
BENNETT, ANNA MARIA
(ca. 1750–1808), 50
BENNETT, ARNOLD
(1867–1931), 50–51
BENNETT, RONAN (1956–),
51
BENSON, E. F. (1867–1940), 51
BENSON, GODFREY R.
(1864–1945), 51
BENTLEY, E. C. (1875–1956), 52
BENTLEY, JOHN (1908–), 52
BENTLEY, PHYLLIS
(1894–1977), 52
BERESFORD, J. D. (1873–1947),
52–53
BERGER, JOHN (1926–),
53–54
Beric the Briton, 247
BERKELEY, ANTHONY, see
ANTHONY BERKELEY
COX
*Berkeley Hall; or, The Pupil of
Experience*, 511
BESANT, WALTER (1836–1901),
54
Beside the Ocean of Time, 77

BEST, HERBERT (1894–1980),
54
The Beth Book, 219
The Betrothed, 406
*Betsy Gray, or the Hearts of
Down*, 324
Betsy Thoughtless, 245
Between, 75
Between the Acts, 487–89
Between the Worlds, 340
Bevis, the Story of a Boy, 259
Beware the Cat, 26–27
*The Bewitchments of Love and
Hate*, 120
The Big Bow Mystery, 509
The Big House of Inver, 428
Bilgewater, 204
BILLANY, DAN (fl. 1940–1950),
54
The Biographer's Moustache, 5
Birchwood, 30–31
The Birds Fall Down, 474
The Birds of the Air, 181
The Birth Machine, 26
The Black Album, 292
The Black Band, 59
Black Beauty, 412
The Black Curtain, 217
Black Dogs, 328
Black Ivory, 27
Black List, Section H, 443
Black Mischief, 465
The Black Prince, 354
The Black Prophet, 90
The Black Soul, 363
Blackeyes, 374
BLACKLIN, MALCOLM, see
AIDAN CHAMBERS
BLACKMORE, RICHARD D.
(1825–1900), 54
BLATCHFORD, ROBERT
(1851–1943), 54
Bleak House, 132–35
Bless the Thief, 462
Blindness, 222
The Blood of the Martyrs, 346
The Blood of the Vampire, 341
Blow Your House Down, 34
The Blue Afternoon, 58
The Blue Flower, 193

Blue Genes, 325–26
BLYTON, ENID (1897–1968), 55
The Boarding House, 455
Boating for Beginners, 481
BODKIN, M. MCDONNELL
(1850–1933), 55
The Body in the Library, 101
Bogle Corbet, 203
Bogmail, 331
BOLGER, DERMOT (1959–   ),
55
The Bomb, 243
The Book and the Brotherhood,
355
The Book of Evidence, 31
The Book of Mrs. Noah, 392
Booked for Murder, 326
The Bookshop on the Quay, 324
The Border, 185
Born in Exile, 209
BORROW, GEORGE
(1803–1881), 55
The Borrowers, 360
The Borrowers Afield, 360
The Borrowers Afloat, 360
The Borrowers Aloft, 360
The Borrowers Avenged, 360
Borstal Boy, 47
BOSTON, LUCY (1892–1990),
55–56
BOWEN, ELIZABETH
(1899–1973), 56–58
Boy, 229
The Boy in the Bush, 296
BOYD, ELIZABETH (fl. 1739),
58
BOYD, WILLIAM (1952–   ), 58
BRADBURY, MALCOLM
(1932–2000), 58–59
BRADDON, MARY ELIZA-
BETH (1837–1915), 59–62
BRADLEY, EDWARD
(1827–1889), 62
BRADY, ANN, see FRANCES
MOLLOY
BRAINE, JOHN (1922–1986), 62
The Bramleighs of Bishop's Folly,
313
Brave New World, 253
The Bray House, 359

BRETON, NICHOLAS
(1545?–1626), 62
BREW, MARGARET (fl. 1885),
62
The Bride of Lammermoor, 406–7
The Bride Price, 182
Brideshead Revisited, 465
Brief Lives, 76
Briefing for a Descent into Hell,
309
BRIERLY, WALTER
(1900–1972), 62
BRIGHT, MARY CHAVELITA,
see GEORGE EGERTON
The Bright Temptation, 103
The Brightfount Diaries, 3
Brighton Rock, 222–23
Brimstone and Treacle, 374
*The British Museum Is Falling
Down*, 320
The British Recluse, 245
BRITTAIN, VERA (1893?–1970),
62–63
BRODERICK, JOHN
(1927–1989), 63
BRONTË, ANNE (1820–1849),
63–64
BRONTË, CHARLOTTE
(1816–1855), 64–71
BRONTË, EMILY (1818–1848),
71–74
The Brook Kerith, 349
BROOKE, EMMA (d. 1926), 74
BROOKE, FRANCES
(1724–1789), 75
BROOKE, HENRY (1703–1783),
75
BROOKE-ROSE, CHRISTINE
(1926–), 75
BROOKNER, ANITA (1928–),
76
BROPHY, BRIGID (1929–1995),
77
BROUGHTON, RHODA
(1840–1920), 77
BROWN, GEORGE DOUGLAS
(1869–1902), 77
BROWN, GEORGE MACKAY
(1921–1996), 77
Brown on Resolution, 194

The Brownie of Bodsbeck, 249–50
BROWNJOHN, ALAN (1931–),
77
BRUNNER, JOHN (1934–1995),
78
Bruno's Dream, 355
BRUNTON, MARY (1778–1818),
78
BRYHER, WINIFRED
(1884–1983), 78
BUCHAN, JOHN (1875–1940),
78–79
The Buddha of Suburbia, 292–93
The Bull Calves, 346
The Bull from the Sea, 381
BULWER-LYTTON, EDWARD
(1803–1873), 79–80
BUNYAN, JOHN (1628–1688),
80–81
BURDEKIN, KATHARINE
(1896–1963), 81–82
BURGESS, ANTHONY
(1917–1993), 82
Burmese Days, 366
BURNETT, FRANCES HODG-
SON (1849–1924), 82–83
BURNEY, FANNY (1752–1840),
83–86
Burning Issues, 286
Burning Your Own, 370
A Burnt-Out Case, 223
BURY, LADY CHARLOTTE
(1775–1861), 86
Busman's Honeymoon, 400–401
The Butcher Boy, 325
Butcher's Broom, 226
BUTLER, SAMUEL
(1835–1902), 86
BUTTS, MARY (1890–1937),
86–87
By Sheer Pluck, 248
BYATT, A. S. (1936–), 87–89

CAINE, HALL (1853–1931), 89
CAIRD, MONA (1854–1932),
89–90
Cakes and Ale, 342
Cal, 333
Caleb Williams, 212–14
A Call, 193

Call for the Dead, 304
CALLAGHAN, MARY ROSE
    (1944–), 90
Callista, 359
The Camberwell Miracle, 52
Cambridge, 371–72
CAMERON, ELIZABETH
    JANE, see JANE DUNCAN
Camilla, 83–84
CAMPBELL, CHARLOTTE S.
    M., see LADY CHARLOTTE
    BURY
CAMPBELL, HAZEL (fl. 1930),
    90
Can You Forgive Her?, 457
Candles in the Wind, 155
Canopus in Argos, 309
The Captain and the Enemy, 223
The Captain from Connecticut,
    194
Captain Lobe, 242
Captain Singleton, 123–24
The Captains and the Kings, 260
Captains Courageous, 290
The Capture of Paul Beck, 55
The Card (Bennett), 50
The Card (Kidgell), 288
*The Carissima: A Modern
    Grotesque*, 334
CARLETON, WILLIAM
    (1794–1869), 90
Carmilla, 306
CARROLL, LEWIS (1832–1898),
    90–92
CARSWELL, CATHERINE
    (1879–1946), 92–93
CARTER, ANGELA
    (1940–1992), 93–96
CARY, JOYCE (1888–1957),
    96–97
Cashel Byron's Profession, 412
Castle Daly, 285
The Castle of Otranto, 462–63
Castle Rackrent, 166
Castle Richmond, 457
*The Castles of Athlin and
    Dunbayne*, 376
Catherine, 449
Caught, 222
Cause for Alarm, 5

CAUTE, DAVID (1936–), 97
CAVENDISH, MARGARET
    (1624?–1674), 97–98
The Caxtons, 79
Cecilia, 84
Celestina, 425
Cells of Knowledge, 244
The Cement Garden, 328–29
The Century's Daughter, 34
A Certain Justice, 258
*Certain Tragicall Discourses of
    Bandello*, 185
CHALLANS, EILEEN MARY,
    see MARY RENAULT
CHAMBERS, AIDAN (1934–),
    98
The Champion of Virtue, see *The
    Old English Baron*
Chance, 109–10
Changing Places, 320
CHAPLIN, SID (1916–1986), 98
The Charioteer, 381
Charles Chesterfield, 460
CHARLES, MOIE (fl. 1950s), 98
Charles O'Malley, 313
Charlotte Gray, 185
Chatterton, 1
CHATWIN, BRUCE
    (CHARLES B.) (1940–1989),
    98–99
CHAUCER, DANIEL, see
    FORD MADOX FORD
CHESNEY, GEORGE
    (1830–1895), 99
CHESTERTON, G. K.
    (1874–1936), 99–100
CHETTLE, HENRY (d. 1607),
    100
CHETWOOD, WILLIAM
    RUFUS (d. 1766), 100
The Child in Time, 329
A Child of the Jago, 352
The Childermass, 317
CHILDERS, ERSKINE
    (1870–1922), 100
Childhood's End, 102
The Children of Dymouth, 456
The Children of Green Knowe, 55
The Children of Men, 258
The Children of the Abbey, 393

Children of the Ghetto, 509
Children of the Rose, 185
Children of Violence, 309–10
The Chimes, 135
Chocky, 507
CHOLMONDELEY, MARY
(1859–1925), 100–101
CHRISTIE, AGATHA
(1890–1976), 101–2
Christina Alberta's Father, 469
A Christmas Carol, 135–36
The Christmas Tree, 261
The Chronicles of Cloyne, 62
The Chronicles of Narnia, 314
The Chrysalids, 507
The Chymical Wedding, 103
A City Girl, 242
The City Jilt, 245–46
The City of Sarras, 448
City of the Mind, 319
Clan-Albin, 262
Clara Hopgood, 476
Clare: A Novel, 332
Clarissa, 386–89
CLARKE, ARTHUR C.
(1917–), 102
CLARKE, AUSTIN (1896–1974),
103
CLARKE, FRANCES E. B., see
SARAH GRAND
CLARKE, LINDSAY (1939–),
103
Clash, 480
Claudius the God, 220
The Claverings, 457
Clayhanger, 50–51
CLELAND, JOHN (1708–1789),
103–4
CLELAND, MARY (fl. 1920s), 104
Cleo, 52
Cleopatra's Sister, 319
A Clergyman's Daughter, 366
Clermont, 394
The Clever Woman of the Family,
507–8
The Cleverest Woman in England,
343
CLIFFORD, LUCY (1853–1929),
104
A Clockwork Orange, 82

The Cloister and the Hearth, 379
The Cloning of Joanna May, 467
Close Quarters, 215
A Closed Eye, 76
Cloud Cuckooland, 346
Cloudesly, 214
Clouds of Witness, 401
CODY, LIZA (1944–), 104
Coelebs in Search of a Wife,
349–50
The Coin of Carthage, 78
The Collector, 199
COLLIER, JANE, see SARAH
FIELDING AND JANE COL-
LIER
COLLIER, JOHN (1901–1980),
104
COLLINS, WILKIE (1824–1889),
104–8
Colonel Jacque, 124
Colonel Sun, 5
The Comedians, 223
The Comfort of Strangers, 329
The Comforters, 429
The Coming Race, 79
Coming Up for Air, 366
The Commitments, 158
A Common Enemy, 52
COMMON, JACK (fl. 1950s), 108
Common Murder, 326
Company, 38–39
The Company of Women, 218
Complicity, 29
COMPTON-BURNETT, IVY
(1892–1969), 108
*Concerning the Eccentricities of
Cardinal Pirelli*, 192
Concluding, 222
Concrete Island, 27
Confessions of a Thug, 448
*Confessions of the Nun of St.
Omer*, 122
The Confidential Agent, 223
Coningsby, 154
The Conquered, 346
CONQUEST, ROBERT, see
KINGSLEY AMIS AND
ROBERT CONQUEST
CONRAD, JOSEPH (1857–1924),
108–19

CONRAD, JOSEPH, and FORD MADOX FORD, 120
Consider Phlebas, 29
Constance, 164
CONSTANTINE, MURRAY, see KATHARINE BURDEKIN
CONSTANTINE, STORM (1956–), 120
Conversations with Lord Byron on Perversion, 163 Years after his Lordship's Death, 375
COOKSON, CATHERINE (1906–1998), 120
COOPER, SUSAN MARY (1935–), 120
The Coral Island, 27
CORBETT, ELIZABETH BUR-GOYNE (b. 1846), 121
CORELLI, MARIE (1864–1924), 121
The "Coriander," 154
The Corn King and the Spring Queen, 346
CORNWELL, DAVID, see JOHN LE CARRÉ
Correlia; or, the Mystic Tomb, 421
COSTELLO, MARY (dates unavailable), 121
The Cottagers of Glenburnie, 229
Count Belisarius, 220
Count de Vinevil, 9
Count Robert of Paris, 407
The Countess of Dellwyn, 191
A Country Gentleman and His Family, 363–64
The Country Girls, 361
Cousin Phillis, 205
COVENTRY, FRANCIS (1725–1754), 121–22
Cowboys and Indians, 363
COX, ANTHONY BERKELEY (1893–1971), 122
CRAIK, MRS., see DINAH MARIA MULOCK
Crampton Hodnet, 375
Cranford, 205
Crash, 27–28
Craven House, 229
The Creators, 424
The Crime of the Century, 5

The Crock of Gold, 431
Crome Yellow, 253
Crooked House, 101
Cross Channel, 35
Crossing the River, 372
Crotchet Castle, 370
The Crow Road, 29
A Crowd is Not Company, 286
The Crowded Street, 250
The Crown of Life, 209
The Crucible of Time, 78
The Cry: A New Dramatic Fable, 191
Cryptozoic, 3
The Crystal Garden, 185
The Crystal World, 28
The Cuckoo Clock, 348
A Curious Street, 249
The Curse of the Wise Woman, 162
Curtain: Poirot's Last Case, 101
Cwmardy, 262

DACRE, CHARLOTTE (1782–1841), 122
The Daisy Chain, 508
Damage, 243
DAMANT, MARY (fl. 1887), 123
Dan Leno and the Limehouse Golem, 1
A Dance to the Music of Time, 374
The Danger Tree, 339–40
DANGERFIELD, THOMAS (1650–1685), 123
Daniel Deronda, 170–73
Daniel Martin, 200
Daphne; or, Marriage a La Mode, 463
The D'Arblay Mystery, 202
Darcy's Utopia, 468
The Dark, 330
Dark as the Grave Wherein My Friend Is Laid, 322
The Dark Is Rising, 120
The Dark Light Years, 3
The Dark Tide, 62
A Dark-Adapted Eye, 381
Darkest England, 251
Darkness at Noon, 292
Darkness Visible, 215
The Dash for Khartoum, 248

Daughter of Jerusalem, 334
The Daughter of Time, 333
The Daughters of Danaus, 89
Daughters of the House, 392
David Copperfield, 136–38
David Elginbrod, 326
David Simple, 191
DAVIOT, GORDON, see ELIZ-
    ABETH MACKINTOSH
DAVYS, MARY (1674–1732), 123
The Day of the Sardine, 98
A Day Off, 259
A Day's Ride: A Life's Romance,
    313
Dead Babies, 7
Dead Beat, 326
Dead Lagoon, 131
The Dead School, 325
The Dead Secret, 105
DEANE, SEAMUS (1940–   ),
    123
Dear Faustina, 77
Death and Nightingales, 325
Death at the President's Lodging,
    437
Death in Summer, 456
Death in the House, 122
Death of a Ghost, 5
Death of a Hero, 3
Death of an Expert Witness, 258
Death of Felicity Taverner, 87
The Death of the Heart, 56
The Death of William Posters, 423
Death on the Nile, 101
Death to the French, 195
The Debt to Pleasure, 294–95
The Debut, 76
The Deceased Wife's Sister, 400
Decline and Fall, 465
The Decline of the West, 97
DEENEY, EILÍS, see EILÍS NÍ
    DHUIBHNE
Deerbrook, 341
DEFOE, DANIEL (1660–1731),
    123–31
DELAFIELD, E. M. (1890–1943),
    131
DE LA RAMÉE, MARIE
    LOUISE, see 'OUIDA'
Delia Blanchflower, 463

DELONEY, THOMAS
    (1543?–1600), 131
Deloraine, 214
The Demi-Gods, 431
Demos, 209–10
Denis Duval, 449
Denzil Quarrier, 210
DE QUINCEY, THOMAS
    (1785–1859), 131
Descent into Hell, 480
*The Description of a New Blazing-
    World*, 97–98
A Description of Millenium Hall,
    405
Desmond, 425
Desperate Remedies, 229–30
Destination Biafra, 182
Destiny, 186
Devices and Desires, 258
The Devil's Diary, 331
Devoted Ladies, 285
Diana of the Crossways, 344
The Diaries of Jane Somers, 310
The Diary of a Good Neighbor,
    310
DIBDIN, MICHAEL (1947–   ),
    131
DICKENS, CHARLES
    (1812–1870), 132–54
DICKINSON, PETER (1927–   ),
    154
Difficulties With Girls, 5
DILLON, EILIS (1920–1994), 154
*Dirk Gently's Holistic Detective
    Agency*, 2
Discipline, 78
DISKI, JENNY (1947–   ), 154
DISRAELI, BENJAMIN
    (1804–1881), 154–55
DIVER, MAUD (1867–1945),
    155–56
The Divine Fire, 424
The Divorced, 86
Divorcing Jack, 38
DIX, GERTRUDE
    (fl. 1895–1900), 156
DIXIE, FLORENCE
    (1857–1905), 156
DIXON, ELLA HEPWORTH
    (1855?–1932), 156

Doctor Copernicus, 31
Doctor Criminale, 58
Doctor Fisher of Geneva, 223
Dr. Jekyll and Mr. Hyde, 435–36
Doctor Thorne, 457
Dr. Wortle's School, 457
The Doctor's Wife, 59
The Dodd Family Abroad, 313
DODGSON, CHARLES
    LUTWIDGE, see LEWIS
    CARROLL
Dodo, 51
DOHERTY, LEN (1930–), 156
The Doll: A Happy Story, 252
The Dolls' House, 212
Dombey and Son, 138–40
A Domestic Experiment, 219
*Don Tomazo, or The Juvenile
    Rambles of Thomas
    Dangerfield*, 123
Donal Grant, 326
DONOGHUE, EMMA (1969–),
    156–57
Dora Myrl, the Lady Detective, 55
*Dorothea, or, a Ray of the New
    Light*, 511
Doting, 222
DOWIE, MENIE MURIEL
    (1867–1945), 157
Down Among the Women, 468
*Down and Out in Paris and
    London*, 366
Down by the River, 361
Down from the Hill, 423
Down There on a Visit, 254
DOYLE, ARTHUR CONAN
    (1859–1930), 157–58
DOYLE, RODDY (1958–),
    158–59
DRABBLE, MARGARET
    (1939–), 159–60
Dracula, 437–41
Dracula Unbound, 3
A Drama in Muslin, 349
A Dream of John Ball, 351
*Dreams of Love and Modest
    Glory*, 319
The Driver's Seat, 429
The Drought, 28
The Drowned World, 28

DUFFAUD, BRIEGE
    (dates unavailable), 160
Duffy, 35
DUFFY, MAUREEN (1933–),
    160
The Duke's Children, 457
DU MAURIER, DAPHNE
    (1907–1989), 160–61
DU MAURIER, GEORGE
    (1834–1896), 161–62
*The Dumb Virgin; or, The Force of
    Imagination*, 47
DUNCAN, JANE (1910–1976),
    162
DUNN, MARY CHAVELITA,
    see GEORGE EGERTON
DUNSANY, EDWARD LORD
    (1878–1957), 162–63
DURRELL, LAWRENCE
    (1912–1990), 163–64
Dusty Answer, 307
The Dwarfs, 373
Dynevor Terrace, 508

The Early History of Jacob Stahl, 52
The Earthly Paradise, 195
Earthly Powers, 82
East Lynne, 486
East of Wimbledon, 480
The Ebb–Tide, 436
The Echoing Grove, 307
*The Ecstasy of Dr. Miriam
    Garner*, 185
EDDISON, ERIC RUCKER
    (1882–1945), 164–65
EDEN, EMILY (1797–1869), 165
EDGEWORTH, MARIA
    (1767–1849), 165–67
Edmund Oliver, 320
The Edwardians, 400
EGERTON, GEORGE
    (1859–1945), 167–68
The Egoist, 344
The Egyptologists, 7
The Eighty-Minute Hour, 3
Eleanor's Victory, 59
The Elephant and the Kangaroo,
    475
ELIOT, GEORGE (1819–1880),
    168–81

Elizabeth Alone, 456
Ellen, Countess of Castle Howel, 50
ELLERMAN, ANNIE WINIFRED, see WINIFRED BRYHER
ELLIS, ALICE THOMAS (1932–), 181
ELPHINSTONE, MARGARET (1947–), 182
EMECHETA, BUCHI (1944–), 182
The Emigrants (Lamming), 294
The Emigrants (Wollstonecraft), 485
Emily Herbert; or, Perfidy Punished, 511
Emma, 10–13
Emmeline (Brunton), 78
Emmeline (Smith), 425
Empire of the Sun, 28
The Enchantments of Flesh and Spirit, 120
The End of the Affair, 223
The End of the Battle, see *Unconditional Surrender*
The End of the High Bridge, 32
Ending Up, 5
Enduring Love, 329
Enemies of the System: A Tale of Homo Uniformis, 3
The Enemy in Our Midst, 487
Enemy of the Stars, 318
England Made Me, 223
English Music, 1
The English Rogue, 247
The Enigma of Arrival, 356–57
Ennui, 166–67
Enoch Roden's Training, 443
The Entail, 203
Erewhon, 86
Eric Brighteyes, 226
Eric, Or Little by Little, 183
Esther Waters, 349
The Eternal Champion, 349
Ethelinde, 425
Eugene Aram, 79
Euphemia, 308
Euphues, 324
Eureka Street, 481

Europe to Let: The Memoirs of an Obscure Man, 259
The Eustace Diamonds, 457–58
Eva, 154
Eva Trout, 56
Evan Harrington, 344
Eve at the Driving Wheel, 98
Evelina, 84–85
Evelyn Innes, 349
Ever After, 443
Evil under the Sun, 101
Excellent Women, 375–76
Excession, 29–30
Exilius, or, The Banished Roman, 33
The Experiences of a Lady Detective, 244
An Eye for an Eye, 458
The Eye in the Door, 34

Facial Justice, 243
The Fair Irish Maid, 325
The Fair Jilt, 47
FAIRFIELD, CICELY ISABEL, see REBECCA WEST
Fairy Tale, 181
The Faithful Lovers, 52
Falkner, 413
FALKNER, JOHN MEADE (1858–1932), 183
The Fall of Kevin Walker, 221
The False Friend, 393
Familiar Letters Betwixt a Gentleman and a Lady, 123
The Family, 182
Family and Friends, 76
A Family Romance, 76
Famine, 363
The *Famous Five* Series, 55
Fanny Hill, 103–4
Fantomina, 246
A Far Cry from Kensington, 429
Far from the Madding Crowd, 230–31
Farewell Spain, 362
A Farewell to Prague, 249
FARRAR, FREDERICK WILLIAM (1831–1903), 183
FARRELL, J. G. (1935–1979), 183–85

FARRELL, M. J., see MOLLY
KEANE
The Fashion in Shrouds, 5
Fat Lad, 370
The Fat Woman's Joke, see *And
the Wife Ran Away*
A Fatal Inversion, 381
Father, 9
The Father and Daughter, 366
Fatherland, 243
FAULKS, SEBASTIAN
(1953–), 185
Fear!, 331
A Fearful Joy, 96
FEINSTEIN, ELAINE (1930–),
185
Felicia's Journey, 456
Felix Holt, 173–74
The Fellowship of the Ring, 452
*The Female American, or, the
Extraordinary Adventures of
Unca Eliza Winkfield*, 511
The Female Deserters, 247
Female Friends, 468
The Female Quixote, 308–9
FENTON, GEOFFREY
(1539–1608), 185
Fenton's Quest, 60
FENWICK, ELIZA
(fl. 1795–1810), 186
Ferdinand Count Fathom, 426
FERGUSON, KATHLEEN
(dates unavailable), 186
FERRIER, SUSAN (1782–1854),
186
A Few Green Leaves, 376
Fiddle City, 35
FIELDING, HENRY
(1707–1754), 186–91
FIELDING, SARAH
(1710–1763), 191
FIELDING, SARAH, AND
JANE COLLIER (fl. 1753), 191
The Fifth Child, 310
FIGES, EVA (1932–), 192
FIGGIS, DARRELL (1882–1925),
192
The Final Passage, 372
Final Payments, 218
Finnegans Wake, 262–67

FIRBANK, RONALD
(1886–1926), 192
Fire Down Below, 215
First Among Equals, 8
First Light, 1
The First Men in the Moon, 469
A Fish Dinner in Memison, 164
FITZGERALD, BARBARA
(1911–1982), 192
FITZGERALD, PENELOPE
(1916–2000), 193
The Five Red Herrings, 401
The Fixed Period, 458
Flatland, 1
Flaubert's Parrot, 35–36
Fleetwood, 214
Flemington, 257
Flesh and Blood, 392
The Flight from the Enchanter, 355
The Flight of the Falcon, 160
Florence Macarthy, 350
Florrie's Girls, 286
The Flower Beneath the Foot, 192
Flowers for the Judge, 5
The Fly on the Wheel, 452
The Flying Inn, 99
Flying to Nowhere, 202
The Folks That Live on the Hill, 5
Folle-Farine, 368
The Food of the Gods, 470
The Fool of Quality, 75
Fools of Fortune, 456
Fool's Sanctuary, 261
Footprint upon Water, 192
FORBES, CAROLINE
(dates unavailable), 193
FORD, FORD MADOX
(1873–1939), 120, 193–94
FORD, ISABELLA (1855–1924),
194
Foreign Parts, 203
FORESTER, CECIL SCOTT
(1899–1966), 194–95
Forgotten Life, 3
FORSTER, E. M. (1879–1970),
195–99
The Fortunes of Nigel, 407
FOSTER, AISLING
(dates unavailable), 199
The Fountain Overflows, 474

The Fountains of Paradise, 102
The Four Just Men, 462
The Four-Gated City, 310–11
FOWLES, JOHN (1926–),
199–202
The Fox in the Attic, 251–52
Foxprints, 331
Framley Parsonage, 458
The Franchise Affair, 333
FRANCIS, M. E. (1859–1930), 202
Frank Mildmay, 341
Frankenstein, 413–17
Frankenstein Unbound, 3
Fraud, 76
Free Fall, 215
Freedom, Farewell!, 52
FREEMAN, R. AUSTIN
(1862–1943), 202
The French Lieutenant's Woman,
200–201
Frenchman's Creek, 160
The Friendly Young Ladies, 381
Friends and Relations, 56
*Friendship in Death: In Twenty
Letters from the Dead to the
Living,* 394
From Man to Man, 402
The Fruitless Enquiry, 246
The Fugitive, or Family Incidents,
222
*The Fulfilments of Fate and
Desire,* 120
FULLER, JOHN (1937–), 202
Funeral Games, 381

Gallia, 157
GALLOWAY, JANICE (1956–),
203
GALSWORTHY, JOHN
(1867–1933), 203
GALT, JOHN (1779–1839), 203–4
The Game, 87
A Game of Hide and Seek, 448
GARDAM, JANE (1928–), 204
The Garden God, 380
GARNER, ALAN (1934–), 204
GASCOIGNE, GEORGE
(1542?–1577), 204
GASKELL, ELIZABETH
(1810–1865), 205–9

Gaston de Blondeville, 376
Gaston de Latour, 369
The Gate of a Strange Field, 248
The Gate of Angels, 193
Gate to the Sea, 78
The Gateless Barrier, 334–35
The Gates of Ivory, 159
Gaudy Night, 401
The General, 195
The Genius and the Goddess, 253
George Mandeville's Husband, 393
GERHARDIE, WILLIAM
ALEXANDER (1895–1977),
209
The Ghost from the Grand Banks,
102
The Ghost Road, 34
Ghosts, 31
GIBBES, PHEBE (fl. 1764–1788),
209
GIBBON, LEWIS GRASSIC, see
JAMES LESLIE MITCHELL
Gillespie, 243
Ginger, You're Barmy, 320
A Girl Among the Anarchists, 345
A Girl in the Head, 183
A Girl in Winter, 295
Girl on a Bicycle, 32
Girl, 20, 6
Girls in Their Married Bliss, 361
The Girls of Slender Means, 429
GISSING, GEORGE
(1857–1903), 209–12
Give Them Stones, 38
The Gladiators, 477
A Glass of Blessings, 376
The Glass-Blowers, 160
A Glastonbury Romance, 374
Glenarvon, 293
Glitter of Mica, 288
*Gloriana; or, The Revolution of
1900,* 156
The Go-Between, 243
GODDEN, RUMER (1907–1998),
212
God's Counterpoint, 52
GODWIN, FRANCIS
(1562–1633), 212
GODWIN, WILLIAM
(1756–1836), 212–15

Going to the Dogs, 36
The Golden Key, 327
The Golden Lion of Granpère, 458
The Golden Notebook, 311
GOLDING, WILLIAM (1911–1993), 215–17
GOLDRING, DOUGLAS (1887–1960), 217
GOLDSMITH, OLIVER (1730?–1774), 217
The Golf Lunatic and His Cycling Wife, 287
The Good Apprentice, 355
Good Behaviour, 285
A Good Man in Africa, 58
Good Morning, Midnight, 383
The Good Shepherd, 195
The Good Soldier, 193–94
The Good Terrorist, 311
Goodbye to Berlin, 254
Goosefoot, 331
GORDON, MARY (1949–), 218
GORE, CATHERINE (1799–1861), 218
The Gorilla Hunters, 27
Gormenghast, 371
The Goslings, see A World of Women
A Gossip's Story, 474
The Governess; or, Little Female Academy, 191
Gowie Corby Plays Chicken, 286
The Gowk Storm, 353
GRAHAME, KENNETH (1859–1932), 218
GRAND, SARAH (1854–1943), 219–20
Grania, 295
The Grass Is Singing, 311
GRAVES, RICHARD (1715–1804), 220
GRAVES, ROBERT (1895–1985), 220–21
GRAY, ALASDAIR (1934–), 221
Great Expectations, 140–43
The Great Fire of London, 1
The Great God Pan, 331
A Great Man, 51

The Great Wave, 89–90
The Green Carnation, 248
The Green Cockade: A Tale of Ulster in 'Ninety-Eight, 371
Green Ferne Farm, 259
The Green Hat, 9
GREEN, HENRY (1905–1973), 221–22
The Green Knight, 355
The Green Man, 6
Green Mansions, 251
GREEN, SARAH (fl. 1808–1824), 222
GREENE, GRAHAM (1904–1991), 222–25
GREENE, ROBERT (1558–1592), 225
The Greengage Summer, 212
Greenmantle, 78
Greenvoe, 77
GREENWOOD, WALTER (1903–1974), 225
GREGORY, PHILIPPA (1954–), 225
Grettir the Outlaw, 32
Greybeard, 3
GRIFFITH, ELIZABETH (1727?–1793), 225
Grimus, 394
The Ground Beneath Her Feet, 394
Growing Rich, 468
Guerillas, 357
Gulliver's Travels, 444–47
A Gun for Sale, 223
GUNESEKERA, ROMESH (1954–), 226
GUNN, NEIL (1891–1973), 226
Gut Symmetries, 481
Guy Mannering, 407
Gwendolen, see The Family
Gwydonius: The Carde of Fancie, 225

HAGGARD, HENRY RIDER (1856–1925), 226–28
The Half-Crown House, 9
The Half-Mother, 449
The Half-Sisters, 259

HALL, MARGUERITE RAD-
CLYFFE (1883–1943), 228
HAMILTON, CICELY
(1872–1952), 228
HAMILTON, ELIZABETH
(1758–1816), 229
HAMILTON, MARY
(1756–1816), 229
HAMILTON, PATRICK
(1904–1962), 229
*The Hamiltons; or, Official Life in
1830*, 218
The Hammer of God, 102
The Hampdenshire Wonder, see
The Wonder
The Hand of Ethelberta, 231
A Handful of Dust, 465–66
The Hand-Reared Boy, 3
HANLEY, JAMES (1901–1985),
229
Hannah, 354
The Happy Foreigner, 26
*The Happy Unfortunate; or, The
Female Page*, 58
Hard Cash, 379
The Hard Life, 361
Hard Times, 143–44
HARDY, THOMAS (1840–1928),
229–42
HARKNESS, MARGARET
(1854–1923), 242
Harold, Last of the Saxon Kings,
79
Haroun and the Sea of Stories,
394–95
HARRADEN, BEATRICE
(1864–1936), 242
Harriet Hume, 474
Harriet Said . . ., 26
Harrington, 167
HARRIS, FRANK (1856–1931),
243
HARRIS, JOHN BEYNON, see
JOHN WYNDHAM
HARRIS, ROBERT (1957–), 243
HARRISON, MARY ST. LEGER
KINGSLEY, see LUCAS
MALET
Harry Heathcote of Gangoil, 458
Harry Lorrequer, 313

The Harsh Voice, 475
HART, JOSEPHINE (1942–),
243
HARTLEY, L. P. (1895–1972), 243
Harvest, 463–64
The Haunted Man, 144
Have His Carcase, 401
Hawksmoor, 2
HAY, JOHN MACDOUGALL
(1881–1919), 243
HAYCRAFT, ANNA, see ALICE
THOMAS ELLIS
HAYS, MARY (1760–1843),
243–44
HAYTON, SIAN (1944–), 244
HAYWARD, W. STEPHENS
(fl. 1860s–1880s), 244
HAYWOOD, ELIZA
(1693?–1756), 244–47
He Knew He Was Right, 458
HEAD, RICHARD
(1637?–1686), 247
Headlong Hall, 370
HEARNE, MARY
(fl. 1718–1720), 247
Heart and Science, 105
The Heart of Midlothian, 407–8
The Heart of the Country, 468
The Heart of the Matter, 223
The Hearts and Lives of Men, 468
Hearts, Hands and Voices, 328
Heartsease, 508
The Heat of the Day, 56–57
Heat Wave, 319–20
The Heather Blazing, 452
The Heavenly Twins, 219–20
The Heir of Redclyffe, 508
Helbeck of Bannisdale, 464
HELDMANN, RICHARD
BERNARD, see RICHARD
MARSH
Helen, 167
Helen Fleetwood, 455
Helena, 466
Hello America, 28
Hellonica Spring, 3
Hellonica Summer, 3
Hellonica Winter, 3
HELME, ELIZABETH
(1787–1816), 247

The Helpmate, 424
Henry Dunbar, 60
Henry Esmond, 449
Henry Willoughby: A Novel, 511
Hen's Teeth, 404
HENTY, GEORGE A.
    (1832–1902), 247–48
Her Privates We, 339
Her Victory, 423
A Herd of Deer, 154
Hereward the Wake, 289
Hermsprong, or Man as He Is Not,
    25
Heroes and Villains, 93
*The Heroine; or Adventures of a
    Fair Romance Reader*, 37
HESLOP, HAROLD
    (1898–1983), 248
Hester, 364
HICHENS, ROBERT
    (1864–1950), 248
Hidden Daughters, 244
Hidden Symptoms, 334
Hide and Seek (Collins), 105
Hide and Seek (Potter), 374
The Hide and Seek Files, 340
HIGGINS, AIDAN (1927–), 248
A High Wind in Jamaica, 252
Higher Ground, 372
High-Rise, 28
Hilda Lessways, 51
The Hill Station, 183
HILL, SUSAN (1942–), 248–49
HINES, BARRY (1939–), 249
HINKSON, KATHARINE, see
    KATHARINE TYNAN
His Monkey Wife, 104
*The Histories of Some of the
    Penitents in the Magdalen-
    House*, 348
A History Maker, 221
The History of Charles Wentworth,
    29
*The History of Charlotte
    Summers, the Fortunate Parish
    Girl*, 511
The History of Emily Montague,
    75
The History of Lady Barton, 225
The History of Mr. Polly, 470

The History of Ophelia, 191
*The History of Pompey the Little;
    or, The Life and Adventures of a
    Lap-Dog*, 121–22
*The History of Samuel Titmarsh
    and the Great Hoggarty
    Diamond*, 449
The History of Sir George Ellison,
    405
*The History of Sir Richard
    Calmady*, 335
*The History of the Nun; or, The
    Fair Vow-Breaker*, 47
*A History of the World in 10 1/2
    Chapters*, 36
The Hobbit, 452–53
HOCKING, JOSEPH
    (1860–1937), 249
HOCKING, SALOME (fl. 1905),
    249
HODGSON, WILLIAM HOPE
    (1877–1918), 249
HOGAN, DESMOND (1950–),
    249
HOGG, JAMES (1770–1835),
    249–50
HOLCROFT, THOMAS
    (1745–1809), 250
The Hollow, 101
Hollywood Cemetery, 363
HOLTBY, WINIFRED
    (1898–1935), 250–51
Homage to Catalonia, 366
Home From England, 400
Home Truths, 334
HOMESPUN, PRUDENTIA, see
    JANE WEST
The Honorary Consul, 224
Honourable Estate, 62–63
The Honourable Schoolboy,
    304
Hood, 156–57
HOOPER, MARGARET JANE
    (fl. 1850s), 251
HOPE, ANTHONY (1863–1933),
    251
HOPE, CHRISTOPHER
    (1944–), 251
HOPE, JOSEPHINE, see MRS.
    WILFRID WARD

HORNIBROOK, EMMA E. (fl.
    1880s), 251
The Horse and His Boy, 314
The Horse's Mouth, 96
Hortensius Friend of Nero, 369
The Hotel, 57
Hotel du Lac, 76
Hothouse, see *The Long
    Afternoon of Earth*
The Hothouse by the East River,
    429
The Hound of the Baskervilles,
    157
The Hour and the Man, 341
A House for Mr. Biswas, 357
The House in Clewe Street, 295
The House in Demetrius Road, 52
The House in Paris, 57
The House of Doctor Dee, 2
The House of Hospitalities, 449
*The House of Raby: Or, Our Lady
    of Darkness*, 251
House of Splendid Isolation, 361
The House of Stairs, 381
The House of the Wolfings, 351
The House of Women, 120
The House on the Strand, 160
*The House with the Green
    Shutters*, 77
Housemates, 52
How Far Can You Go?, see *Souls
    and Bodies*
How It Is, 39–40
How Late It Was, How Late, 286
How Many Miles to Babylon?, 261
Howards End, 195–96
HUDSON, WILLIAM HENRY
    (1841–1922), 251
HUGHES, RICHARD
    (1900–1976), 251–52
HUGHES, THOMAS
    (1822–1896), 252
HULL, E. M. (fl. 1920s–1930s), 252
The Human Age, 318
The Human Factor, 224
HUME, FERGUS W.
    (1859–1932), 252
HUMPHREYS, EMYR
    (1919–), 252
Humphry Clinker, 426–27

A Humument, 373
The Hungry Grass, 374
Hungry Hill, 160
HUNT, VIOLET (1866–1942), 252
HUNTER, RACHEL
    (1754–1813), 253
Hurrish, 295
HUXLEY, ALDOUS
    (1894–1963), 253
Hypatia, 289

I, Claudius, 220–21
I Like It Here, 6
I Want It Now, 6
Idalia, 246
Ideala: A Study from Life, 220
If the Old Could . . ., 311
ILES, FRANCIS, see ANTHONY
    BERKELEY COX
Ill Seen Ill Said, 40
Illuminations, 160
The Illusionist, 261
I'm the King of the Castle, 248–49
The Image Breakers, 156
Imaginary Letters, 87
Imagined Corners, 353
IMLAY, GILBERT, see MARY
    WOLLSTONECRAFT
An Imperfect Mother, 52
Imperial Earth, 102
The Impossible Shore, 286
In Maremma, 368
In Night's City, 358
In the Castle of My Skin, 294
In the Days of the Comet, 470
In the Red Kitchen, 392
In the Second Year, 259
In the Wilds of Africa, 290
In the Year of Jubilee, 210
INCHBALD, ELIZABETH
    (1753–1821), 253–54
Indigo, 464
*The Infernal Desire Machines of
    Doctor Hoffmann*, 93
The Infidel Father, 474
The Information, 7
The Inheritance, 186
The Inheritance of Evil, 424
The Inheritors (Conrad and Ford),
    120

The Inheritors (Golding), 215–16
The Inner House, 54
INNES, MICHAEL, see J. I. M.
  STEWART
Innocence, 193
Innocent, 364
The Innocent, 329
Innocent Blood, 258
An Insular Possession, 347
Intimacy, 293
Inversions, 30
The Invisible Man, 470
The Invisible Worm, 261
Invitation to the Waltz, 307
Involved, 366
IRELAND, MICHAEL, see
  DARRELL FIGGIS
An Irish Cousin, 428
The Irish Heiress, 370
Is He Popenjoy?, 458
Isabel Clarendon, 210
ISHERWOOD, CHRISTOPHER
  (1904–1986), 254–55
ISHIGURO, KAZUO (1954–),
  256–57
Island, 253
An Island Called Moreau, 3
The Island of Anarchy, 465
The Island of Dr. Moreau, 470
The Island of Horses, 154
The Island of Sheep, 79
It Is Never Too Late to Mend, 380
The Italian, 376–77
Ivanhoe, 408

Jack Hinton, 313
Jack of Newbury, 131
Jack Sheppard, 2
JACOB, ROSAMOND (fl. 1930s),
  257
JACOB, VIOLET (1863–1946),
  257
Jacob's Room, 489–90
JAEGER, MURIEL
  (fl. 1926–1943), 257
Jake's Thing, 6
Jamaica Inn, 160
JAMES, P. D. (1920–), 258
JAMESON, STORM (1891–1986),
  259

Jane and Prudence, 376
Jane Eyre, 64–67
Janet, 364
The Jasmine Farm, 9
JEFFERIES, RICHARD
  (1848–1887), 259
JENKINS, ROBIN (1912–), 259
Jessie Phillips, 460
The Jewel in the Crown, 404
The Jewel of Seven Stars, 441
JEWSBURY, GERALDINE
  (1812–1880), 259
Jill, 295
John Caldigate, 458
John Drayton, 364
John Halifax, Gentleman, 354
John Marchmont's Legacy, 60
JOHNSON, B. S. (1933–1973), 260
JOHNSON, SAMUEL
  (1709–1784), 260
JOHNSTON, JENNIFER
  (1930–), 260–61
JOHNSTONE, CHRISTIAN
  ISOBEL (1781–1857), 262
Jonathan Jefferson Whitlaw, 460
Jonathan Wild, 187–88
JONES, LEWIS (1897–1939), 262
Joseph Andrews, 188–89
Joshua Haggard's Daughter, 60
A Journal of the Plague Year,
  124–25
*A Journey from this World to the
  Next*, 189
The Journey Home, 55
*A Journey Through Every Stage of
  Life*, 406
JOYCE, JAMES (1882–1941),
  262–85
The Joys of Motherhood, 182
Jude the Obscure, 231–33
The Judge, 475
A Judgement in Stone, 381–82
Julia, 480
Julia de Roubigné, 332
Juniper: A Mystery, 287
Just Duffy, 259
Justine, 164

Kangaroo, 296
Kate Hannigan, 120

KAVANAGH, DAN, see JULIAN
    BARNES
KEANE, MOLLY (1904–1996),
    285
KEARNEY, RICHARD
    (1954–), 285
KEARY, ANNIE (1825–1879),
    285
KEDDIE, HENRIETTA
    (1827–1914), 286
KEE, ROBERT (1919–), 286
Keep the Aspidistra Flying, 367
Kehinde, 182
KELLY, HUGH (1739–1777), 286
KELLY, MAEVE (1930–), 286
KELLY, MAGGIE (1969–), 286
The Kellys and the O'Kellys, 458
KELMAN, JAMES (1946–), 286
KEMP, GENE (1926–), 286–87
Kenilworth, 409
KENNARD, MRS. EDWARD
    (MARY E.) (fl. 1883–1902), 287
KENNAWAY, JAMES
    (1928–1968), 287
KENNEDY, ALISON (1965–),
    287
Kepler, 31–32
KER, DAVID (1842–1914), 287
KERR, PHILIP (1956–), 287
KESSON, JESSIE (1916–1994),
    288
A Kestrel for a Knave, 249
Key to the Door, 423
Keynotes, 167–68
Kiddar's Luck, 108
KIDGELL, JOHN (fl. 1766), 288
Kidnapped, 436
The Killeen, 307
Kim, 290–91
A Kind of Loving, 37
The Kindness of Women, 29
King Arthur: Not a Love Story,
    354
King Goshawk and the Birds, 363
The King Must Die, 381
The King of a Rainy Country, 77
King of Morning, Queen of Day,
    328
King Solomon's Mines, 226–27
A King's Woman, 461

KINGSLEY, CHARLES
    (1819–1875), 288–89
KINGSTON, W. H. G.
    (1814–1880), 290
KIPLING, RUDYARD
    (1865–1936), 290–92
Kipps, 470–71
Kirsteen, 364
Kissing the Gunner's Daughter,
    382
Kitty and Virgil, 26
Kitty Tailleur, 424
Klosterheim, 131
The Knight of Gwynne, 313
KOESTLER, ARTHUR
    (1905–1983), 292
KOUYOUMDJIAN, DIKRAN,
    see MICHAEL ARLEN
KUREISHI, HANIF (1956–),
    292–93

The Ladies Lindores, 364
Lady Anna, 458–59
Lady Audley's Secret, 60–61
Lady Chatterley's Lover, 296–97
Lady Julia Mandeville, 75
*Lady Maclairn, or The Victim of
    Villainy*, 253
The Lady of the Shroud, 441–42
Lady Susan, 13
The Lady's Drawing Room, 8
The Lady's Mile, 61
Laidlaw, 331–32
The Lair of the White Worm, 442
The Lake, 349
Lamb, 333
LAMB, LADY CAROLINE
    (1785–1828), 293
LAMB, MARY ANN
    (1764–1847), 293–94
LAMMING, GEORGE
    (1927–), 294
Lanark, 221
LANCHESTER, JOHN
    (1962–), 294–95
The Land of Spices, 362
The Land of the Leal, 33
The Landleaguers, 459
Landon Deecroft, 29
Langrishe, Go Down, 248

A Laodicean, 233–34
LARKIN, PHILIP (1922–1985), 295
LASCELLES, LADY CAROLINE, see MARY ELIZABETH BRADDON
Lasselia; or, The Self-Abandon'd, 246
Last and First Men, 430
The Last Battle, 314
Last Cage Down, 248
The Last Chronicle of Barset, 459
The Last Ditch, 252
The Last Flight, 244
Last Loves, 423
The Last Man (Noyes), 360
The Last Man (Shelley), 417
The Last of the Lairds, 203
The Last of the Wine, 381
Last Orders, 443
The Last Post, 194
The Last September, 57–58
The Last Testament of Oscar Wilde, 2
Lavengro, 55
LAVIN, MARY (1912–1996), 295
The Law and the Lady, 105
LAW, JOHN, see MARGARET HARKNESS
LAWLESS, EMILY (1845–1913), 295
LAWRENCE, D. H. (1885–1930), 295–304
Leader of the Band, 468
The Leavetaking, 330
LE CARRÉ, JOHN (1931–   ), 304–5
LEE, SOPHIA (1750–1824), 306
LEE, VERNON (1856–1935), 306
LEFANU, JOSEPH SHERIDAN (1814–1873), 306–7
The Legend of Montrose, 409
LEHMANN, ROSAMOND (1903–1990), 307
LELAND, MARY (dates unavailable), 307
LENNON, TOM (dates unavailable), 308
LENNOX, CHARLOTTE (1729–1804), 308–9

Leonard's War, 423
Leonora, 167
Lesbia Brandon, 447
Less Than Angels, 376
LESSING, DORIS (1919–   ), 309–12
Letters from a Lady of Quality to a Chevalier, 246
The Letters of a Solitary Wanderer, 425
LEVER, CHARLES (1806–1872), 313
LEVY, AMY (1861–1889), 313–14
LEWIS, C. S. (1898–1963), 314–17
LEWIS, MATTHEW GREGORY (1775–1818), 317
LEWIS, WYNDHAM (1882–1957), 317–18
The Libertine, 122
The Life and Adventures of Mr. Francis Clive, 209
The Life and Amorous Adventures of Lucinda, 10
Life and Death of Harriet Frean, 424
The Life and Death of Mr. Badman, 80
The Life and Loves of a She-Devil, 468
Life Force, 468
Life Goes On, 423
Life in the West, 4
The Life of Charlotta du Pont, 10
The Life of Harriot Stuart, 309
The Life of John Buncle, Esq., 8
The Life of Madam de Beaumont, 10
Life; Or, The Adventures of William Ramble, 461
The Light That Failed, 291
Lilac and Flag: An Old Wives' Tale of a City, 53
Lilamani: A Study of Possibilities, 155
Lilith, 327
LINDSAY, DAVID (1878–1945), 318
LINGARD, JOAN (1932–   ), 318–19
The Lining of the Patch-Work Screen, 33

LINTON, ELIZA (1822–1898),
  319
The Lion, the Witch, and the
  Wardrobe, 314–15
Little Dorrit, 144–46
The Little Drummer Girl, 304
The Little Girls, 58
The Little Lame Prince, 354
Little Lord Fauntleroy, 82
The Little Minister, 37
A Little Princess, 82
LIVELY, PENELOPE (1933–),
  319–20
Livia; or, Buried Alive, 164
Living, 222
LLOYD, CHARLES (1775–1839),
  320
Lobsters on the Agenda, 347
LODGE, DAVID (1935–),
  320–21
LODGE, THOMAS (1558–1625),
  322
The Lodger, 322
Lodore, 418
Lois in Charge, or, A Girl of Grit,
  340
Lolly Willowes, 464
London Fields, 7
The London Spy, 463
The Lonely Girl, 361
The Long Afternoon of Earth, 4
The Long Day Wanes, 82
The Long Shadows, 77
The Long Vacation, 508
The Long View, 52
The Longest Journey, 196
Look to the Lady, 5
Looking for the Possible Dance,
  287
The Looking-Glass War, 304
Lord Hornblower, 195
Lord Jim, 110–12
Lord Kilgobbin, 313
Lord of the Flies, 216
The Lord of the Rings, 453–54
Lord Ormont and His Aminta, 344
Lord Raingo, 51
Lorna Doone, 54
Loss and Gain: The Story of a
  Convert, 359

Lost and Saved, 360
The Lost Girl, 297–98
A Lost Name, 306
The Lost Ones, 40–41
The Lost Stradivarius, 183
LOUDON, JANE (1807–1858),
  322
Louisa: A Poetical Novel in Four
  Epistles, 412
Louisa; or, the Cottage on the
  Moor, 247
Love, 93
Love, Again, 311
Love Among the Ruins, 466
Love and Freindship, 13–14
Love Child, 160
The Love Department, 456
Love in a Cold Climate, 347
Love in Excess, 246
Love Letters Between a Certain
  Late Nobleman and the famous
  Mr. Wilson, 511
Love Letters Between a Nobleman
  and His Sister, 48
Love on the Dole, 225
The Love Riddle, 443
The Loved One, 466
Lovel the Widower, 449–50
The Lovers Week, 247
Love's Cross Currents, 447
Love's Intrigues, 33
Love's Pilgrim, 52
Loving, 222
Loving and Giving, 285
LOWNDES, MARIE BELLOC
  (1868–1947), 322
LOWRY, MALCOLM
  (1909–1957), 322–24
The L-Shaped Room, 30
LUCAS, MARGARET, see
  MARGARET CAVENDISH
The Luck of Barry Lyndon, 450
Lucky Jim, 6
The Lucky Mistake: A New Novel,
  48
Lucretia; or, The Children of the
  Night, 79
Lucy Dean: The Noble
  Needlewoman, 345
Lunar Caustic, 322

The Lung, 183
LYLY, JOHN (1554–1606),
324
LYNCH, PATRICIA (1898–1972),
324
LYTTLE, WESLEY GUARD
(1844–1896), 324

MACAULAY, ROSE
(1881–1958), 325
MCCABE, EUGENE (1930–),
325
MCCABE, PATRICK (1955–),
325
MCCARTHY, J. H. (1861–1936),
325
MCDERMID, VAL (1955–),
325–26
The Macdermotts of Ballycloran,
459
MACDONALD, GEORGE
(1824–1905), 326–28
MCDONALD, IAN (1960–),
328
The Macedonian, 87
MCEWAN, IAN (1948–),
328–29
MCFALL, FRANCES, see
SARAH GRAND
MCGAHERN, JOHN (1934–),
329–30
MACGILL, PATRICK
(1890–1963), 331
MCGINLEY, PATRICK
(1937–), 331
McGrotty and Ludmilla, 221
MACHEN, ARTHUR
(1863–1947), 331
MCILVANNEY, WILLIAM
(1936–), 331–32
MACKAY, MARY, see MARIE
CORELLI
MACKENNA, JOHN (1952–),
332
MACKENZIE, COMPTON
(1883–1974), 332
MACKENZIE, HENRY
(1745–1831), 332–33
MACKINTOSH, ELIZABETH
(1897–1952), 333

MACLAVERTY, BERNARD
(1945–), 333
MCNAMEE, EOIN (1961–),
333–34
MACPHERSON, WINIFRED,
see WINIFRED BRYHER
MADDEN, DEIRDRE (1960–),
334
The Madness of David Baring, 249
A Maggot, 201
The Magic Toyshop, 94
The Magician's Nephew, 315
*Magnum Bonum; or, Mother
Carey's Brood,* 508
Magnus, 77
The Magus, 202
Maiden Castle, 374
The Maid's Tale, 186
MAITLAND, SARA (1950–),
334
Major Operation, 33
Makeshift, 4
The Making of a Prig, 412
*The Making of the Representative
for Planet 8,* 311
The Malacia Tapestry, 4
MALET, LUCAS (1852–1931),
334–35
Malice Aforethought, 122
MALLOCK, WILLIAM H.
(1849–1923), 335
Malone Dies, 41–42
MALORY, THOMAS
(1410?–1471?), 335–38
The *Malory Towers* Series, 55
Man and Wife, 105
Man As He Is, 26
A Man from Elsewhere, 183
A Man from the North, 51
The Man in the Moon, 212
The Man of Feeling, 332–33
The Man of Property, 203
The Man of the World, 333
The Man Who Knew Too Much,
99
The Man Who Was Thursday,
99–100
The Man Who Wasn't There, 34
The Man Who Would Be King,
291

Manalive, 100
The Mandelbaum Gate, 429
Mandeville, 214
Manfroné, or The One-Handed Monk, 379
MANLEY, MARY DELARIV-IERE (1663–1724), 338–39
MANNING, FREDERIC (1882–1935), 339
MANNING, OLIVIA (1915–1980), 339–40
Mansfield Park, 14–16
MANTEL, HILARY (1952–), 340
Mara and Dann, 311
Marcella, 464
Marcella Grace, 353
MARCH, CAEIA (dates unavailable), 340
March Moonlight, 385
March Violets, 287
MARCHANT, BESSIE (1862–1941), 340
Marchmont, 425
Margaret Becomes a Doctor, 368
A Margarite of America, 322
Maria, or The Wrongs of Woman, 485–86
Marion Fay, 459
Marius the Epicurean, 369
Mark Rutherford's Deliverance, 476–77
MARKHAM, ROBERT, see KINGSLEY AMIS
MARLOWE, DEREK (1938–1996), 340
Marriage, 186
The Marriage Act: A Novel, 413
The Marriage of Elinor, 364
The Marriages between Zones Three, Four, and Five, 312
A Married Man, 379
MARRYAT, FLORENCE (1837–1899), 341
MARRYAT, FREDERICK (1792–1848), 341
MARSH, RICHARD (1867–1915), 341
Martha Quest, 312
The Martian, 161–62

Martin Chuzzlewit, 146–47
Martin Rattler, 27
MARTINEAU, HARRIET (1802–1876), 341
The Martins of Cro' Martin, 313
Mary, A Fiction, 486
Mary Anne, 161
Mary Barton, 205–6
Mary Lavelle, 362
Mary Marston, 327
Mary Olivier, 424
A Masculine Ending, 426
The Mask of Apollo, 381
MASON, A. E. W. (1865–1948), 341
MASSIE, ALLAN (1938–), 341–42
The Master, 476
The Master of Ballantrae, 436–37
Master of the Moor, 382
Masterman Ready, 341
Mathilda, 418–19
MATILDA, ROSA, see CHARLOTTE DACRE
MATURIN, CHARLES ROBERT (1782–1824), 342
MAUGHAM, WILLIAM SOMERSET (1874–1965), 342–43
Mauleverer's Divorce: A Story of a Woman's Wrongs, 393
Maureen Moore: A Romance of '98, 4
Maurice, 196–97
May Day, 428
MAYOR, FLORA MACDONALD (1872–1932), 343
The Mayor of Casterbridge, 234–35
MEADE, L. T. (ELIZABETH THOMASINA) (1854–1914), 343
Means-Test Man, 62
A Meeting by the River, 255
Mefisto, 32
Melincourt, 370
MELMOTH, COURTNEY, see SAMUEL JACKSON PRATT
Melmoth the Wanderer, 342
The Melvilles, 364
The Member, 203–4

Memento Mori, 429
Memoirs: containing the Lives of Several Ladies of Great Britain, 8
The Memoirs of a Cavalier, 125
Memoirs of a Coxcomb, 104
Memoirs of a Magdalen; or, The History of Louisa Mildmay, 286
The Memoirs of a Survivor, 312
Memoirs of an Infantry Officer, 400
The Memoirs of Bryan Perdue, 250
The Memoirs of Emma Courtney, 243–44
The Memoirs of Lord Byron, 360
The Memoirs of Miss Sidney Bidulph, 421
Memoirs of Modern Philosophers, 229
The Memorial, 255
Men and Angels, 218
Men at Arms, 466
Men Like Gods, 471
Menaphon, 225
The Mercenary Lover: or, The Unfortunate Heiress, 247
Mercier and Camier, 42
MEREDITH, GEORGE (1828–1909), 343–45
MEREDITH, ISABEL (fl. 1900–1940), 345
The Message to the Planet, 355
METEYARD, ELIZA (1816–1879), 345
Metroland, 36
The Mezentian Gate, 164
Michael Armstrong, 460–61
The Microcosm, 160
The Middle Age of Mrs. Eliot, 480
The Middle Ground, 159
Middlemarch, 174–77
Midnight's Children, 395–96
Miguel Street, 357
The Milesian Chief, 342
The Mill on the Floss, 177–79
MILLS, LIA (dates unavailable), 345
The Millstone, 159
MILNE, A. A. (1882–1956), 345–46

Milton in America, 2
The Mimic Men, 357
A Miner's Sons, 156
The Ministry of Fear, 224
The Miseries of Mavillia, 62
Miss Brown, 306
Miss Erin, 202
Miss Gomez and the Brethren, 456
Miss Mackenzie, 459
Miss Marjoribanks, 364–65
Missing, 464
The Missionary, 350
The Mist in the Mirror, 249
Mister Johnson, 96–97
Mr. Midshipman Easy, 341
Mr. Noon, 298
Mr. Norris Changes Trains, 255
Mr. Skeffington, 9
Mr. Smith, 462
Mr. Standfast, 79
Mr. Stone and the Knights Companion, 358
Mr. Weston's Good Wine, 375
Mrs. Dalloway, 490–94
Mrs. Dymond, 391
Mrs. Eckdorf in O'Neill's Hotel, 456
Mrs Keith's Crime, 104
Mrs. Leicester's School, 293–94
Mistress Masham's Repose, 476
Mrs. Maxon Protests, 251
Mistress of Mistresses, 164
Mrs. Ritchie, 353
Misunderstood, 349
MITCHELL, JAMES LESLIE (1901–1935), 346
MITCHISON, NAOMI (1897–1999), 346–47
MITFORD, MARY RUSSELL (1787–1855), 347
MITFORD, NANCY (1904–1973), 347
A Mixed Marriage, 371
MO, TIMOTHY (1950–), 347–48
Modern Broods, 508
The Modern Griselda, 167
Modern Times; Or, The Adventures of Gabriel Outcast, 461
A Modern Utopia, 471

MOLESWORTH, MARY
LOUISA (1839–1921), 348
Moll Flanders, 125–27
Molloy, 42–43
MOLLOY, FRANCES
(1947–1991), 348
The Monastery, 409
Money: A Suicide Note, 7
The Monk, 317
Monk Dawson, 379
The Monkey King, 347
The Monkey Puzzle, 53
Monkey Wrench, 104
*Monsieur; or, The Prince of
Darkness*, 164
Monsignor Quixote, 224
Monstre Gai, 318
MONTAGU, LADY BARBARA
(d. 1765), 348
Montalbert, 426
MONTGOMERY, FLORENCE
(1843–1923), 349
The Moon and Sixpence, 342–43
The Moon Tiger, 320
The Moonstone, 105–6
MOORCOCK, MICHAEL
(1939–   ), 349
MOORE, GEORGE
(1852–1933), 349
Moorland Cottage, 207
The Moor's Last Sigh, 396–98
MORE, HANNAH (1745–1833),
349–50
Moreau's Other Island, see *An
Island Called Moreau*
MORGAN, SYDNEY
(1783?–1859), 350–51
MORRIS, WILLIAM
(1834–1896), 351–52
MORRISON, ARTHUR
(1863–1945), 352
MORRISON, NANCY BRYS-
SON (1903–1986), 353
MORRISSEY, MAVY
(dates unavailable), 353
Le Morte Darthur, 335–38
MORTIMER, PENELOPE
(1918–1999), 353
Mother of Pearl, 353
Mother's Girl, 185

Moths, 368
The Motor Maniac, 287
MOTTRAM, RALPH HALE
(1883–1971), 353
Mt. Henneth, 26
Mount Music, 428
The Mountain of Adventure, 55
Movie Shoes, 442
MUIR, WILLA (1890–1970), 353
MULHOLLAND, ROSA
(1841–1921), 353–54
MULOCK, DINAH MARIA
(1826–1887), 354
*The Mummy: A Tale of the
Twenty-Second Century*, 322
Munster Village, 229
The Murder at the Vicarage, 101
Murder Must Advertise, 401
The Murder of Delicia, 121
A Murder of Quality, 304
The Murder of Roger Ackroyd,
101
Murder on the Orient Express,
101–2
MURDOCH, IRIS (1919–1999),
354–56
Murphy, 43–44
My Cousin Rachel, 161
My Flirtations, 156
My Friend Flora, 162
My Friend Sashie, 162
*My Friends the Hungry
Generation*, 162
My Friends the Macleans, 162
My House in Umbria, 456
*My Idea of Fun: A Cautionary
Tale*, 412
My Lady Ludlow, 207
My Novel, 80
My Secret Life, 511
My Young Alcides, 508
MYERS, LEOPOLD HAMIL-
TON (1881–1944), 356
The Mysteries of London, 382
The Mysteries of Udolpho,
377–78
The Mysterious Affair at Styles,
102
The Mystery of a Hansom Cab,
252

The Mystery of Edwin Drood,
147–48
The Mystic Masseur, 358

NAIPAUL, V. S. (1932–), 356–58
The Naive and Sentimental Lover,
304
The Napoleon of Notting Hill, 100
Narrative of a Five Years
Expedition Against the Revolted
Negroes of Surinam, 430
The Narrow Corner, 343
NASHE, THOMAS (1567–1601),
358
National Velvet, 26
Natives of My Person, 294
The Natural Daughter, 393
Nature and Art, 253–54
The Nature of Blood, 373
The Near and the Far, 356
The Nebuly Coat, 183
Necessary Treasons, 286
The Needle on Full, 193
NELSON, DOROTHY
(dates unavailable), 358
NESBIT, EDITH (1858–1924),
359
The Nether World, 210
New Amazonia: A Foretaste of the
Future, 121
The New Atalantis, 338–39
New Grub Street, 210–11
The New Machiavelli, 471
The New Magdalen, 106
A New Voyage Round the World,
127
The Newcomes, 450
NEWMAN, JOHN HENRY
(1801–1890), 359
News from Nowhere, 351–52
The Newton Letter, 32
NÍ DHUIBHNE, EILÍS
(1954–), 359
Nice Work, 320–21
Nicholas Nickleby, 148
The Nigger of the "Narcissus,"
112–13
Night and Day, 494
Night and Morning, 80
The Night Land, 249

The Night Manager, 304
Night Pillow, 379
Nightmare Abbey, 370
Nights at the Circus, 94–95
Nightspawn, 32
Nina Balatka, 459
The Nine Tailors, 401
Nineteen Eighty-Four, 367–68
1982 Janine, 221
No Country for Young Men, 363
No Fond Return of Love, 376
No Laughing Matter, 460
No Mate for the Magpie, 348
No Name, 106
No Other Man, see *The Last Man*
(Noyes)
The Noble Slaves, 10
Nobody's Fault, 447
The *Noddy* Series, 55
Non-Stop, see *Starship*
NOON, JEFF (1957–), 359
NOONAN, ROBERT, see
ROBERT TRESSELL
NORDEN, CHARLES, see
LAWRENCE DURRELL
NORFOLK, LAWRENCE
(1963–), 359
North and South, 207–8
North Face, 381
Northanger Abbey, 16–18
NORTON, CAROLINE
(1808–1877), 360
NORTON, MARY (1903–1992),
360
Nostromo, 113–14
Not So Quiet . . .: Stepdaughters of
War, 375
Not Wisely But Too Well, 77
A Note in Music, 307
Nothing, 222
Nothing Like the Sun, 82
NOYES, ALFRED (1880–1958),
360
The Nun; or, The Perjur'd Beauty:
A True Novel, 48
Nunquam, 164
Nuns and Soldiers, 355
NYE, ROBERT (1939–), 360

O Caledonia, 33

Oakfield, or Fellowship in the East, 9
O'BRIEN, ATTIE (1840–1883), 360–61
O'BRIEN, EDNA (1932–   ), 361
O'BRIEN, FLANN (1911–1966), 361–62
O'BRIEN, KATE (1897–1974), 362
The O'Briens and the O'Flaherties, 350
O'CONNOR, CLAIRR (dates unavailable), 362
O'CONNOR, JOSEPH (1963–   ), 363
October Ferry to Gabriola, 322–23
The Odd Women, 211
O'Donnel, 350
The O'Donoghue: A Tale of Ireland Fifty Years Ago, 313
O'DUFFY, EIMAR (1893–1935), 363
Of Age and Innocence, 294
Of Human Bondage, 343
O'FAOLAIN, JULIA (1932–   ), 363
Officers and Gentlemen, 466
Offshore, 193
O'FLAHERTY, LIAM (1896–1984), 363
O'HARA, ELIZABETH, see EILÍS NÍ DHUIBHNE
The Old Boys, 456
The Old Curiosity Shop, 148–49
The Old Devils, 6
The Old English Baron, 380
The Old Jest, 261
Old Kensington, 391–92
The Old Manor House, 426
An Old Man's Love, 459
Old Men at the Zoo, 480
Old Mortality, 409
The Old Order Changes, 335
The Old Wives' Tale, 51
Olga Knaresbrook, Detective, 90
OLIPHANT, MARGARET (1828–1897), 363–65
Olive, 354
Oliver Twist, 149–50
On a Huge Hill, 53

On the Black Hill, 98
On the Face of the Waters, 431
On the Third Day, 379
On the Threshold, 194
The Once and Future King, 476
Once in Europa, 54
One by One in the Darkness, 334
One Fat Englishman, 6
One of Our Conquerors, 344
One Poor Scruple, 464
The One Too Many, 319
One Wonderful Week, see *The Wonderful Week*
O'NOLAN, BRIAN, see FLANN O'BRIEN
The Open Door, 423
Open the Door!, 92–93
OPIE, AMELIA (1769–1853), 365–66
The Optimist, 131
Oranges Are Not the Only Fruit, 481–82
The Ordeal of Gilbert Pinfold, 466
The Ordeal of Richard Feveral, 344–45
Original Sin, 258
O'RIORDAN, KATE (dates unavailable), 366
Orlando, 494–97
Orley Farm, 459
Ormond, 167
Oroonoko, 48–50
The Orville College Boys, 486
ORWELL, GEORGE (1903–1950), 366–68
Other People: A Mystery Story, 7
Other People's Worlds, 456
'OUIDA' (1839–1908), 368
Our Friend the Charlatan, 211
Our Game, 304
Our Mutual Friend, 150–52
Our Village, 347
Out, 75
Out of the Shelter, 321
Out of the Silent Planet, 315
Out of This World, 443
Out of Work, 242
Owen Glendower, 375
OWENS, JEAN LLEWELLYN (dates unavailable), 368

OWENSON, SYDNEY, see SYD-
NEY MORGAN
The Owl Service, 204

Paddy Clarke Ha Ha Ha, 158
PAGET, VIOLET, see VERNON
LEE
The Paid Piper, 195
PAINTER, WILLIAM (b. 1540),
368
A Pair of Blue Eyes, 235–36
The Palace in the Garden, 348
The Palace of Pleasure, 368
A Pale View of Hills, 256
Palladian, 448
PALTOCK, ROBERT
(1697–1767), 368
Pamela, 389–90
Pandosto, 225
The Paper Men, 216
The Papers of Tony Veitch, 332
Parade's End, 194
The Paradine Case, 248
Paradise News, 321
PARGETER, EDITH
(1913–1995), 369
Party Going, 222
A Pass in the Grampians, 420
A Passage to India, 197–99
The Passion, 482–83
The Passion of New Eve,
95–96
The Passions, 122
Pastors and Masters, 108
*A Patch-Work Screen for the
Ladies*, 33–34
PATER, WALTER HORATIO
(1839–1894), 369
Pathway of the Gods, 90
PATRICK, MRS. F. C. (fl. 1890s),
370
Patronage, 167
Pattern for Perfidy, 52
PATTERSON, GLENN
(1961–), 370
Paul Clifford, 80
Pavane, 392
Payment Deferred, 195
PEACOCK, THOMAS LOVE
(1785–1866), 370

PEAKE, MERVYN (1911–1968),
371
PEARCE, PHILIPPA (1920–),
371
Peckover, 53
PEESLAKE, GAFFER, see
LAWRENCE DURRELL
Peg Woffington, 380
*Peggy: A Tale of the Irish
Rebellion*, 123
Pelham, 80
Pendennis, 450
PENDER, MARGARET
(1850?–1920), 371
Pennies from Heaven, 374
PENNY, MRS. FRANK (d. 1939),
371
Peregrine Pickle, 427
Perelandra, 315
A Perfect Spy, 305
Perfectly Correct, 225
Perkin Warbeck, 419
The Perpetual Curate, 365
PERRIAM, WENDY (1940–),
371
The Persian Boy, 381
Persuasion, 18–20
Peter Abelard, 461
Peter Ibbetson, 162
Peter Pan in Kensington Gardens,
37
Peter Wilkins, 368
Peveril of the Peake, 409
Phantastes, 327
Philadore and Placentia, 247
Philip, 450
PHILLIPS, CARYL (1958–),
371–73
PHILLIPS, TOM (1927–), 373
The Philosopher's Pupil, 355
Phineas Finn, 459
Phineas Redux, 459
Phoebe, Junior, 365
The Piccadilly Murder, 122
The Pickwick Papers, 152–53
The Picture of Dorian Gray, 477–79
The Picturegoers, 321
A Piece of the Night, 392
*Piers Plainness: Seven Years'
Prenticeship*, 100

Pig Earth, 54
Pigeon Pie, 347
Pilgrimage, 385–86
The Pilgrim's Progress, 80–81
The Pillars of the House, 509
Pin Money, 218
Pincher Martin, 216
PINTER, HAROLD (1930–), 373
The Pirate, 409
Pirates of the Spring, 380
A Place of Greater Safety, 340
The Place of the Lion, 480
The Player of Games, 30
The Plumed Serpent, 298–99
PLUNKETT, JAMES (1920–), 373
Point Counter Point, 253
Pointed Roofs, 386
The Poisoned Chocolates Case, 122
Police at the Funeral, 5
Pollen, 359
The Polyglots, 209
Poor Jack, 341
Poor Things, 221
The Pope's Rhinoceros, 359
The Porcupine, 36–37
Porius, 375
PORTER, JANE (1776–1850), 373
A Portrait of the Artist as a Young Man, 267–70
Possession, 87–89
POSTGATE, RAYMOND (1896–1971), 373
POTTER, DENNIS (1935–1994), 374
POWELL, ANTHONY (1905–2000), 374
The Power and the Glory, 224
The Power House, 79
The Power of Love, 339
POWER, RICHARD (1928–1970), 374
POWYS, JOHN COWPER (1872–1963), 374–75
POWYS, THEODORE FRANCIS (1875–1953), 375
The Praise Singer, 381

Prancing Nigger, see *Sorrow in Sunlight*
PRANTERA, AMANDA (1942–), 375
Prater Violet, 255
PRATT, SAMUEL JACKSON (1749–1814), 375
Praxis, 468
The Present and the Past, 108
The President's Child, 468–69
Prester John, 79
The Pretty Lady, 51
PRICE, EVADNE (1896–1985), 375
Pride and Prejudice, 20–22
Priests and People: A No-Rent Romance, 360
The Prime Minister, 459
The Prime of Miss Jean Brodie, 429
Prince Caspian, 315
The Princess and Curdie, 327–28
The Princess and the Goblin, 328
Princess Napraxine, 368
The Prisoner, 53
The Prisoner of Zenda, 251
The Prisoners of Hartling, 53
The Private Memoirs and Confessions of a Justified Sinner, 250
The Private Papers of Henry Ryecroft, 211
A Private View, 76
The Professor, 68
The Progress of Julius, 161
Proud Man, 81
Providence, 76
The Provost, 204
The Public Image, 429–30
Puffball, 469
The Pumpkin Eater, 353
The Purple Land, 251
Purposes of Love, 381
The Pursuit of Love, 347
Put Out More Flags, 466–67
Putting the Boot In, 37
PYM, BARBARA (1913–1980), 375–76

The Quarry Wood, 420

Quartet, 383
Quartet in Autumn, 376
The Queen of Stones, 449
The Question Mark, 257
The Quiet American, 224
Quiet Corner, 53

The Rachel Papers, 7
Rachel Ray, 459–60
Radcliffe, 442
RADCLIFFE, ANN (1764–1823), 376–79
RADCLIFFE, MARY-ANNE (fl. 1810), 379
The Radiant Way, 159
RAE, HUGH C. (1935–   ), 379
The Ragged Lion, 341–42
The Ragged Trousered Philanthropists, 455
The Railway Children, 359
The Railway Station Man, 261
The Rainbow, 299–300
Rainforest, 154
The Raj Quartet, 404
Ralph the Heir, 460
Randall and the River of Time, 195
The Rape of Shavi, 182
The Rash Resolve, 247
Rasselas, 260
Rates of Exchange, 59
The Ravenswing, 450
RAYNER, OLIVE PRATT, see GRANT ALLEN
The Razor's Edge, 343
READ, PIERS PAUL (1941–   ), 379
READE, CHARLES (1814–1884), 379–80
Reading in the Dark, 123
The Real Charlotte, 428
Realms of Gold, 159
Rebecca, 161
Rebecca and Rowena, 450
The Rebel of the Family, 319
The Recess, 306
The Rector's Daughter, 343
The Rector's Wife, 461
The Red and the Green, 355
The Red Horizon, 331
The Red House, 359

The Red House Mystery, 345
Red Pottage, 100–101
Red Shift, 204
The Red Thumb Mark, 202
Redgauntlet, 409–10
REDGROVE, PETER (1932–   ), and PENELOPE SHUTTLE (1947–   ), 380
The Redundancy of Courage, 347–48
Reef, 226
REEVE, CLARA (1729–1807), 380
The Reform'd Coquet, 123
The Refugee in America, 461
Regeneration, 34–35
REID, FORREST (1875?–1947), 380
The Remains of the Day, 256–57
Remedy is None, 332
Remember Me, 469
Remembrance Day, 4
RENAULT, MARY (1905–1983), 381
RENDELL, RUTH (1930–   ), 381–82
Rendezvous with Rama, 102
Report for Murder, 326
Report on Probability A, 4
The Rescue, 114
Restoration, 455
Resurrection Man, 333–34
The Retreat, 380
The Return of Fursey, 462
The Return of Mary O'Murrough, 354
Return of the Brute, 363
The Return of the Hero, 192
The Return of the Native, 236–37
The Return of the Soldier, 475
Return to Night, 381
Reuben Sachs, 313–14
The Revenge for Love, 318
Revolution: A Story of the Near Future in England, 53
The Revolution in Tanner's Lane, 477
REYNOLDS, GEORGE W. M. (1814–1879), 382
Rhoda: A Novel, 511

Rhoda Fleming, 345
RHYS, JEAN (1894–1979),
  382–85
Riceyman Steps, 51
RICHARDSON, DOROTHY
  (1873–1957), 385–86
RICHARDSON, SAMUEL
  (1689–1761), 386–91
RIDDELL, CHARLOTTE
  (1832–1906), 391
The Riddle of the Sands, 100
The Riddle of the Tower, 53
Rifleman Dodd, see *Death to the
  French*
Right Ho, Jeeves, 484
RILEY, JOAN (1958–   ), 391
Ripley Bogle, 481
RITCHIE, ANNE THACKERAY
  (1837–1919), 391–92
Rites of Passage, 216–17
The River at Green Knowe, 56
The Riverside Villas Murder, 6
The Road to Wigan Pier, 368
Rob Roy, 410
Robert Elsmere, 464
Robert Falconer, 328
ROBERTS, KEITH (1935–2000),
  392
ROBERTS, MICHELE (1949–   ),
  392–93
ROBINS, ELIZABETH
  (1862–1952), 393
Robinson, 430
Robinson Crusoe, 127–30
ROBINSON, EMMA
  (1814–1890), 393
ROBINSON, MARY
  (1758–1800), 393
ROCHE, REGINA MARIA
  (1764?–1845), 393–94
Roderick Random, 427–28
Roman Wall, 78
Romance, 120
The Romance of a Shop, 314
The Romance of the Forest,
  378–79
The Romantic, 424
The Romany Rye, 55
Romola, 179–80
Room at the Top, 62

A Room with a View, 199
The Roots of the Mountains, 352
Rory and Bran, 163
Rosalynde, 322
The Rose and the Ring, 450
Rose Cottingham Married, 447
ROSSETTI, OLIVIA, see
  ISABEL MEREDITH
The Rotten Elements, 461
The Rover, 115
ROWE, ELIZABETH SINGER
  (1674–1737), 394
Roxana, 130–31
A Rude Awakening, 4
Running Wild, 29
RUSHDIE, SALMAN (1947–   ),
  394–400
RUSSELL, MARY ANNETTE
  BEAUCHAMP, see ELIZA-
  BETH VON ARNIM
RUSSELL, WILLIAM CLARK
  (1844–1911), 400
The Russia House, 305
The Russian Girl, 6
Russian Hide-and-Seek, 6
Ruth, 208
RUTHERFORD, MARK, see
  WILLIAM HALE WHITE
RYAN, JAMES
  (dates unavailable), 400

SACKVILLE-WEST, VITA
  (1892–1962), 400
Sacred Country, 455
Sacrifice of Fools, 328
Safe in the Kitchen, 199
St. Irvyne, 420
St. Leon, 214–15
St. Martin's Eve, 487
St. Mungo's City, 286
St. Patrick's Eve, 313
St. Ronan's Well, 410
Salem Chapel, 365
*The Saliva Tree and Other Strange
  Growths,* 4
Sally from Cork, 324
Sam's Fall, 285
Sanditon, 22–23
Sandra Belloni, 345
Sandwichman, 62

Santos de Montenos, 452
SASSOON, SIEGFRIED
   (1886–1967), 400
The Satanic Verses, 398–99
*Saturday Night and Sunday
   Morning,* 423
Saville, 442
SAYERS, DOROTHY L.
   (1893–1957), 400–402
The Scapegoat, 161
Scenes from the Life of Cleopatra,
   87
Scenes of Clerical Life, 180–81
The School for Widows, 380
SCHREINER, OLIVE
   (1855–1920), 402–4
Scoop, 467
Scotch Novel Reading, 222
A Scots Quair, 346
SCOTT, MANDA
   (dates unavailable), 404
SCOTT, PAUL (1920–1978), 404
SCOTT, SARAH (1723–1795),
   405–6
SCOTT, WALTER (1771–1832),
   406–12
The Scottish Chiefs, 373
The Sea Lady, 471
The Sea, the Sea, 355
A Sea-Grape Tree, 307
Season of Adventure, 294
The Second Prison, 51
Secresy: or, The Ruin on the Rock,
   186
The Secret Agent, 115–17
The Secret Garden, 82–83
*The Secret History of Queen
   Zarah and the Zarazians,* 339
The Secret Pilgrim, 305
Seeta, 448
Self Condemned, 318
SELF, WILL (1961–   ), 412
Self-Control, 78
The Semi-detached House, 165
Sense and Sensibility, 23–25
A Sentimental Journey, 431–32
Sentimental Tommy, 37
Seven, Bobsworth, 53
Seven Days in New Crete, 221
Several Perceptions, 96

SEWARD, ANNA (1742–1809),
   412
SEWELL, ANNA (1820–1878),
   412
Sexing the Cherry, 483–84
Shadow Dance, 96
The Shadow Master, 185
Shadow of a Sun, 89
Shadows on Our Skin, 261
Shake Hands Forever, 382
Shame, 399–400
Shamela, 189
The Shape of Things to Come, 471
SHARP, EVELYN (1869–1955),
   412
The Shaving of Shagpat, 345
SHAW, GEORGE BERNARD
   (1856–1950), 412
She, 227–28
SHEBBEARE, JOHN
   (1709–1788), 413
The Sheik, 252
SHELLEY, MARY (1797–1851),
   413–20
SHELLEY, PERCY BYSSHE
   (1792–1822), 420
*Shenstone-Green; or, The New
   Paradise Lost,* 375
SHEPHERD, NAN (1893–1981),
   420
SHERIDAN, FRANCES
   (1724–1766), 421
SHERIFFE, SARAH
   (fl. 1802–1823), 421
Shikasta, 312
The Ship, 195
Ships that Pass in the Night, 242
Shirley, 68–69
The Shrapnel Academy, 469
Shroud for a Nightingale, 258
SHUTTLE, PENELOPE, see
   PETER REDGROVE AND
   PENELOPE SHUTTLE
Shuttlecock, 443–44
A Sicilian Romance, 379
SIDNEY, PHILIP (1554–1586),
   421–22
The Siege of Krishnapur, 183–84
The Sign of the Four, 157
Silas Marner, 181

The Silence in the Garden, 456
The Silk Stocking Murders, 122
SILLITOE, ALAN (1928–), 423
The Silmarillion, 454–55
The Silver Chair, 316
Simisola, 382
The Simple Life Limited, 194
A Simple Story, 254
The Sin Eater, 181
SINCLAIR, MAY (1870–1942),
  423–24
The Singapore Grip, 184
The Singer Passes, 155–56
The Singing-Men at Cashel, 103
A Single Man, 255
A Single Summer with Lord B.,
  340
Singlehanded, see *Brown on
  Resolution*
Singularly Deluded, 220
Sinister Street, 332
The Sins of the Father, 342
Sir Brook Fossbrooke, 313
Sir Charles Grandison, 390–91
Sir Gibbie, 328
Sir Launcelot Greaves, 428
Sir Tom, 365
*Sisters and Strangers: A Moral
  Tale*, 449
Sisters by Rite, 319
SKENE, FELICIA (1821–1899),
  424
The Skull Beneath the Skin, 258
The Sky and the Forest, 195
The Slave Girl, 182
Sleep in Peace, 52
The Sleeping Beauty, 448
Sleeping Murder, 102
The Small House at Allington, 460
A Small Town in Germany, 305
Small World, 321
Smiley's People, 305
SMITH, CECIL LEWIS
  TROUGHTON, see CECIL
  SCOTT FORESTER
SMITH, CHARLOTTE
  (1749–1806), 424–26
SMITH, HELEN ZENNA, see
  EVADNE PRICE
SMITH, JOAN (1953–), 426

SMITH, SARAH, see HESBA
  STRETTON
SMOLLETT, TOBIAS
  (1721–1771), 426–28
The Snake's Pass, 442
The Snapper, 158
Snell's Folly, 53
Snooty Baronet, 318
Snowstop, 423
So I Am Glad, 287
Sociable Letters, 98
*A Soldier Erect; or, Further
  Adventures of the Hand-Reared
  Boy*, 4
Some Lie and Some Die, 382
Some Tame Gazelle, 376
SOMERVILLE AND ROSS
  (1858–1949 and 1862–1915), 428
Something Leather, 221
Somewhere East of Life, 4
SOMMERFIELD, JOHN
  (fl. 1930s–1940s), 428
A Son of the Soil, 365
The Songlines, 98–99
The Songs of Distant Earth, 102
Sons and Lovers, 300–301
Sophia, 309
The Sorcery Shop, 54
Sorrow in Sunlight, 192
The Sorrows of Satan, 121
The Soul of Lilith, 121
Souls and Bodies, 321
Sour Sweet, 348
South Riding, 250–51
*The Spacious Adventures of the
  Man in the Street*, 363
The Spanish Farm Trilogy, 353
The Spanish Maiden, see *Transito*
SPARK, MURIEL (1918–),
  429–30
A Sparrow's Flight, 182
Spartacus, 346
SPENDER, STEPHEN
  (1909–1995), 430
The Spire, 217
The Spiritual Quixote, 220
Splitting, 469
A Spy upon the Conjuror, 247
*The Spy Who Came in from the
  Cold*, 305

Stalky & Co., 291–92
A Standard of Behavior, 456
Stanley and the Women, 6
STAPLEDON, OLAF
  (1886–1950), 430
The Star Maker, 430
Staring at the Sun, 37
Starship, 4
A Start in Life (Brookner), 76
A Start in Life (Sillitoe), 423
A State of Independence, 373
Staying On, 404
STEDMAN, JOHN GABRIEL
  (1744–1797), 430
STEEL, FLORA ANNIE
  (1847–1929), 431
Stephen Hero, 270–71
STEPHENS, JAMES
  (1882–1950), 431
STERNE, LAURENCE
  (1713–1768), 431–35
STEVENSON, ROBERT LOUIS
  (1850–1894), 435–37
STEWART, J. I. M. (1906–1994),
  437
Still Life, 89
Stir-fry, 157
STOKER, BRAM (1847–1912),
  437–42
The Stone Book Quartet, 204
STONE, ELIZABETH (fl. 1842),
  442
The Stones of Green Knowe, 56
STOREY, DAVID (1933–), 442
The Story of a Modern Woman,
  156
The Story of an African Farm,
  402–3
The Story of Barbara, 61
The Story of Elizabeth, 392
The Story of Mona Sheehy, 163
The Story of the Glittering Plain,
  352
The Storyteller, 423
Strange Loyalties, 332
Strange Marriage, 448
A Strange Story, 80
A Stranger at Green Knowe, 56
STREATFEILD, NOEL
  (1895–1986), 442

STRETTON, HESBA
  (1832–1911), 443
STRONG, EITHNE (1921–),
  443
Strong Poison, 401–2
A Struggle for Fame, 391
Strumpet City, 373
STUART, FRANCIS
  (1902–2000), 443
A Study in Scarlet, 158
Success, 7
The Suffrage of Elvira, 358
The Sum of Things, 340
The Summer Before the Dark, 312
Summer Will Show, 464
The Sun Dances at Easter, 103
The Sundering Flood, 352
Sunflower, 475
Sunshine and Shadow, 475
A Superfluous Woman, 74
The Sure Traveller, 104
The Survivors, 185
Suspense, 117
Swastika Night, 82
Sweet Danger, 5
The Sweet Dove Died, 376
SWEETMAN, MARY E., see M.
  E. FRANCIS
The Sweet-Shop Owner, 444
SWIFT, GRAHAM (1949–),
  443–44
SWIFT, JONATHAN
  (1667–1745), 444–47
SWINBURNE, ALGERNON
  CHARLES (1837–1909), 447
Swing Hammer Swing, 455
Sword of Honour, 467
Sybil, 155
Sylvia's Lovers, 208
Sylvie and Bruno, 92
SYRETT, NETTA (1865–1943),
  447–48

The Tailor of Panama, 305
Take A Girl Like You, 6
The Takeover, 430
Taking Chances, 285
A Tale of the Times, 474
A Tale of Two Cities, 153–54
The Talisman, 410

Talking It Over, 37
The Tall Villa, 335
Tancred, 155
The Tapestry, 53
Tarr, 318
A Taste for Death, 258
TAYLOR, ELIZABETH
    (1912–1975), 448
TAYLOR, (PHILIP) MEAD-
    OWS (1808–1876), 448
TAYLOR, UNA ASHWORTH
    (fl. 1886–1924), 448
The Tea-Table, 247
Temper; or, Domestic Scenes, 366
The Temple, 430
The Tenant of Wildfell Hall, 63–64
TENNANT, EMMA (1937–),
    448–49
The Terrors of Dr Treviles, 380
Tess of the d'Urbervilles, 237–40
Testament of Friendship, 63
Testament of Youth, 63
Textermination, 75
TEY, JOSEPHINE, see ELIZA-
    BETH MACKINTOSH
THACKERAY, WILLIAM
    MAKEPEACE (1811–1863),
    449–451
Thaddeus of Warsaw, 373
That Boy of Norcott's, 313
That Hideous Strength, 316
That Lady, 362
That Uncertain Feeling, 6
Therapy, 321
These Lynnekers, 53
They Do It with Mirrors, 102
The Thin Seam, 98
The Thinking Reed, 475
The Third Man, 224–25
The Third Policeman, 361–62
The Thirty-Nine Steps, 79
This Real Night, 475
THOMAS, D. M. (1935–),
    451–52
Thou Art the Man, 61
The Three Clerks, 460
The Three Hostages, 79
The Three Imposters, 331
The Three Perils of Woman, 250
Three Ply Yarn, 340

The Three Sisters, 424
3001: The Final Odyssey, 102
Three Times Dead, see *The Trail
    of the Serpent*
Three Times Table, 334
Through the Dark Night, 361
Through the Looking-Glass, 92
Thru, 75
THURSTON, KATHERINE
    CECIL (d. 1911), 452
Thyrza, 211
TICKEN, WILLIAM
    (fl. 1806–1811), 452
Till We Have Faces, 316–17
Time After Time, 285
Time in a Red Coat, 77
The Time Machine, 471–72
Time Must Have a Stop, 253
Time's Arrow, 8
Tinker, Tailor, Soldier, Spy, 305
Titanic Town, 121
Titus Alone, 371
Titus Groan, 371
To Stay Alive, 8
To the Indies, see *The Earthly
    Paradise*
To the Lighthouse, 497–502
To the North, 58
TÓIBÍN, COLM (1955–), 452
TOLKIEN, J. R. R. (1892–1974),
    452–55
The Toll Bridge, 98
Tom Brown at Oxford, 252
Tom Brown's School Days, 252
Tom Jones, 189–91
Tommy and Grizel, 37
Tom's Midnight Garden, 371
TONNA, CHARLOTTE ELIZA-
    BETH (1790–1846), 455
Tono-Bungay, 472
Torn from Its Foundations, 287
TORRINGTON, JEFF
    (dates unavailable), 455
A Toy Epic, 252
Tracks in the Snow, 51
The Tragic Comedians, 345
The Trail of the Serpent, 61
Trainspotting, 473–74
Traitor's Purse, 5
Transition, 74

Transito: A Story of Brazil, 251
The Trap, 54
Travels with My Aunt, 225
Treasure Island, 437
The Tree of Heaven, 424
The Tree of Knowledge, 192
TREMAIN, ROSE (1943–), 455
Trent's Last Case, 52
The Trespasser, 301–2
TRESSELL, ROBERT
    (1870–1911), 455
TREVOR, WILLIAM (1928–),
    455–56
The Trial, 509
Trial and Error, 122
The Trick Is to Keep Breathing,
    203
Trilby, 162
Tristram Shandy, 432–35
TROLLOPE, ANTHONY
    (1815–1882), 456–60
TROLLOPE, FRANCES
    (1780–1863), 460–61
TROLLOPE, JOANNA
    (1943–), 461
Trooper Peter Halket, 403–4
Trouble, 469
The Troubled House, 257
Troubles, 184–85
*The True History of Joshua
    Davidson, Christian and
    Communist*, 319
The Trumpet-Major, 240
TRUSLER, JOHN (1735–1820),
    461
Tunc, 164
Tunes of Glory, 287
The Turbulent Term of Tyke Tiler,
    287
The Turf-Cutter's Donkey, 324
The Twenty-Fifth Hour, 54
Two and Twenty, 195
Two Days in Aragon, 285
The Two Drovers, 410
Two on a Tower, 240–41
2001: A Space Odyssey, 102
2061: Odyssey Three, 102
2010: Odyssey Two, 102
Two Women of London, 449
Two Years Ago, 289

TYNAN, KATHARINE
    (1861–1931), 461
The Type-writer Girl, 4
TYTLER, SARAH, see HENRI-
    ETTA KEDDIE

Ultramarine, 323
Ulysses, 271–85
The Unbelonging, 391
The Unclassed, 211
Uncle Silas, 306–7
Uncle Stephen, 380
Unconditional Surrender, 467
The Unconsoled, 257
Under the Greenwood Tree, 241
Under the Net, 355
Under the Volcano, 323–24
Under Two Flags, 368
Under Western Eyes, 117–19
Undine, 404
Unexplained Laughter, 181
The Unfinished Road, 53
*The Unfortunate Bride; or, The
    Blind Lady a Beauty*, 50
The Unfortunate Fursey, 462
*The Unfortunate Happy Lady: A
    True History*, 50
The Unfortunate Traveller, 358
The Unfortunates, 260
*The Unhappy Mistake; or, The
    Impious Vow Punish'd*, 50
Union Street, 35
Unity, 53
An Unkindness of Ravens, 382
Unknown to History, 509
The Unlit Lamp, 228
The Unnamable, 44–45
An Unofficial Rose, 356
*The Unpleasantness at the Bellona
    Club*, 402
An Unsuitable Attachment, 376
An Unsuitable Job for a Woman,
    258
The Untouchable, 32
The Upstart, 379
UPWARD, EDWARD (1903–),
    461
Urania, 506–7
Use of Weapons, 30
Utz, 99

The Vagabond, 462
Vainglory, 192
The Valley of Bones, 374
The Valley of Fear, 158
Valmouth, 192
Valperga, 419
The Van, 158–59
Vanity Fair, 450–51
Vathek, 46–47
The Veiled One, 382
Venetia, 155
The Venetians, 62
Venus and Tannhäuser, 38
Venusberg, 374
Verbivore, 75
Verdict of Twelve, 373
Vermilion Sands, 29
The Vicar of Bullhampton, 460
The Vicar of Wakefield, 217
The Vicar of Wrexhill, 461
The Viceroy of Ouidah, 99
The Victim of Prejudice, 244
Victory, 119
Vile Bodies, 467
The Village in the Jungle, 487
Villette, 69–71
VINE, BARBARA, see RUTH RENDELL
Vinland, 77
The Virgin in the Garden, 89
Virgin Territory, 334
The Virginians, 451
Vivian, 167
Vivian Grey, 155
Voyage in the Dark, 383–84
The Voyage of the "Dawn Treader," 317
The Voyage Out, 502–3
A Voyage to Arcturus, 318
The Voyages and Adventures of Captain Robert Boyle, 100
The Voyages, Dangerous Adventures, and Imminent Escapes of Captain Richard Falconer, 100
The Voyages, Travels, and Adventures of William Owen Gwin Vaughan, 100
Vurt, 359

WADDELL, HELEN (1889–1965), 461
The Wages of Sin, 335
The Waking of Willie Ryan, 63
WALFORD, LUCY (1845–1915), 462
WALKER, GEORGE (1772–1847), 462
Walking on Glass, 30
WALL, ALAN (dates unavailable), 462
WALL, MERVYN (1908–1997), 462
WALLACE, EDGAR (1875–1932), 462
WALPOLE, HORACE (1717–1797), 462–63
Walsingham; or, The Pupil of Nature, 393
The Wanderer, 85–86
The Wanderings of Warwick, 426
The Wanting Seed, 82
The War in the Air, 472–73
The War of the Worlds, 473
WARD, EDWARD (1667–1731), 463
WARD, MARY AUGUSTA (MRS. HUMPHRY) (1851–1920), 463–64
WARD, MRS. WILFRID (1864–1932), 464
The Warden, 460
WARNER, MARINA (1946–   ), 464
WARNER, SYLVIA TOWNSEND (1893–1978), 464
The Wasp Factory, 30
The Watchers and the Watched, 98
The Water of the Wondrous Isles, 352
Water with Berries, 294
The Water-Babies, 289
The Waterfall, 159
WATERHOUSE, ELIZABETH (fl. 1884–1912), 465
Waterland, 444
Watership Down, 2
The Watsons, 25
Watt, 45–46
Waverley, 410–11

Waverley Novels, 411–12
The Waves, 503–5
WAUGH, EVELYN (1903–1966), 465–67
A Way in the World, 358
The Way of All Flesh, 86
The Way We Live Now, 460
We Can't All be Heroes, You Know, see *To Stay Alive*
We Have Been Warned, 347
We Live, 262
The Weather in the Streets, 307
The Weatherhouse, 420
The Wedding Group, 448
WELDON, FAY (1933–   ), 467–69
The Well at the World's End, 352
The Well of Loneliness, 228
The Well-Beloved, 241–42
WELLS, H. G. (1866–1946), 469–73
WELSH, IRVINE (1958–   ), 473–74
WEST, JANE (1758–1852), 474
WEST, REBECCA (1892–1983), 474–75
Westward Ho!, 289
Weymouth Sands, 375
What Dreams May Come, 53
What Men Say, 426
What Will He Do with It?, 80
The Wheel of God, 168
WHEELER, THOMAS MARTIN (fl. 1850s–1860s), 475
The Wheels of Chance, 473
When Love Comes to Town, 308
When the Wicked Man, 194
When We Become Men, 347
Where Angels Fear to Tread, 199
The Whirlpool, 211–12
The White Bird Passes, 288
The White Hotel, 451–52
The White Monkey, 203
The White Peacock, 302
WHITE, PHYLLIS DOROTHY JAMES, see P. D. JAMES
WHITE, T. H. (1906–1964), 475–76
WHITE, WILLIAM HALE (1831–1913), 476–77

Whom God Hath Joined, 51
Whose Body?, 402
WHYTE-MELVILLE, GEORGE (1821–1878), 477
Wide Saragasso Sea, 384–85
Wife to Mr. Milton, 221
Wild Decembers, 361
The Wild Girl, 393
The Wild Irish Boy, 342
The Wild Irish Girl, 350–51
The Wild MacRaes, 33
Wild Nights, 449
WILDE, OSCAR (1854–1900), 477–79
WILKINSON, ELLEN (1891–1947), 480
Will Warburton, 212
William—An Englishman, 228
William Langshawe, 442
WILLIAMS, CHARLES (1886–1945), 480
WILLIAMS, HELEN MARIA (1761–1827), 480
WILLIAMS, NIGEL (1948–   ), 480
WILLOUGHBY, THOMAS, see THOMAS DANGERFIELD
WILSON, ANGUS (1913–1991), 480
WILSON, ROBERT MCLIAM (1964–   ), 480
The Wind in the Willows, 218
Winefred: A Story of the Chalk Cliffs, 32
The Wing of Azrael, 90
The Winged Victory, 220
Winnie-the-Pooh, 345–46
WINSTANLEY, EDITH MAUD, see E. M. HULL
WINTERSON, JEANETTE (1959–   ), 481–84
Wise Children, 96
The Wise Virgins, 487
The Witch of Exmoor, 160
Witch Wood, 79
With Buller in Natal, or a Born Leader, 248
With Essex in Ireland, 295
With Kitchener in the Soudan, 248
With Roberts to Pretoria, 248

Wives and Daughters, 209
The Wizard's Son, 365
WODEHOUSE, P. G.
  (1881–1975), 484
Wolf Solent, 375
Wolf to the Slaughter, 382
WOLLSTONECRAFT, MARY
  (1759–1797), 485–86
The Woman in Black, 249
The Woman in White, 106–8
The Woman of Knockaloe, 89
Woman: or, Ida of Athens, 351
The Woman Who Did, 4
*The Woman Who Walked Into
  Doors*, 159
The Woman's Daughter, 55
Women in Love, 302–4
The Women's House, 319
The Wonder, 53
The Wonderful Visit, 473
The Wonderful Week, 195
The Wood Beyond the World, 352
WOOD, EMMA CAROLINE
  (MRS. HENRY) (1814–1887),
  486–87
WOOD, WALTER (b. 1866), 487
The Woodlanders, 242
Woodstock, 412
WOOLF, LEONARD SIDNEY
  (1880–1969), 487
WOOLF, VIRGINIA
  (1882–1941), 487–506
A Word Child, 356
Words of Advice, 469
Work Suspended, 467
Workers in the Dawn, 212
The World His Pillow, 33
The World in the Evening, 255
The World My Wilderness, 325

A World of Love, 58
A World of Women, 53
The World Set Free, 473
*The Worm Ouroboros: A
  Romance*, 164–65
Wormwood: A Drama of Paris,
  121
Worst Fears, 469
A Wreath of Roses, 448
A Wreath Upon the Dead, 160
Written on the Body, 484
WROTH, LADY MARY
  (1587?–1651?), 506–7
Wuthering Heights, 71–74
WYNDHAM, JOHN
  (1903–1969), 507

The Years, 505–6
Yeast, 289
YONGE, CHARLOTTE
  (1823–1901), 507–9
YORKE, HENRY, see HENRY
  GREEN
You Can't Do Both, 6–7
The Young Colonists, 248
*The Young Diana: An Experiment
  of the Future*, 121
The Young Duke, 155
The Young Fur Traders, 27
The Young Philosopher, 426
Young Tom, 380

ZANGWILL, ISRAEL
  (1864–1926), 509
Zanoni, 80
Zastrozzi, 420
Zoe, 259
Zofloya, 122
Zuleika Dobson, 47